MW01074420

THE PRENTICE HALL

ANTHOLOGY
OF SCIENCE FICTION
AND FANTASY

GARYN G. ROBERTS

Northwestern Michigan College

Prentice
Hall

Upper Saddle River, New Jersey 07458

Library of Congress Cataloging-in-Publication Data

The Prentice Hall anthology of science fiction and fantasy/[edited by] Garyn G. Roberts.
    p. cm.
   Includes bibliographical references and index.
   ISBN 0-13-021280-6
    1. Science fiction, American. 2. Fantasy fiction, American. 3. Science fiction, English.
  4. Fantasy fiction, English. I. Roberts, Garyn G. II. Prentice-Hall, Inc.

PS374.S35 P69 2001
813'.087608—dc21   00-026411

VP, Editorial Director: Charlyce Jones-Owen
Editor in Chief: Leah Jewell
Sr. Acquisitions Editor: Carrie Brandon
Editorial Assistants: Sandy Hrasdzira and Thomas DeMarco
AVP, Director of Manufacturing
  and Production: Barbara Kittle
Managing Editor: Mary Rottino
Production Liaison: Fran Russello
Project Manager: Linda B. Pawelchak
Manufacturing Manager: Nick Sklitsis
Prepress and Manufacturing Buyer: Marianne Gloriande
Cover Design: Robert Farrar-Wagner
Cover Art: Robert A. Madle and agent for the Estate of Forrest J Ackerman.
  Original painting by Frank R. Paul first appeared on the cover of the
  November 1934 issue of *Wonder Stories*.
Marketing Manager: Brandy Dawson
Author Photo: Virginia Woods Roberts

Acknowledgments begin on page 1163, which constitutes
a continuation of this copyright page.

This book was set in 10/11 Janson by Progressive Information Technologies
and was printed and bound by RR Donnelley and Sons Company.
The cover was printed by The Lehigh Press, Inc.

©2003 by Prentice-Hall, Inc.
A Division of Pearson Education
Upper Saddle River, New Jersey 07458

All rights reserved. No part of this book may be reproduced,
in any form or by any means, without permission
in writing from the publisher.

Printed in the United States of America
10 9 8 7 6

ISBN 0-13-021280-6

Prentice-Hall International (UK) Limited, *London*
Prentice-Hall of Australia Pty. Limited, *Sydney*
Prentice-Hall Canada Inc., *Toronto*
Prentice-Hall Hispanoamericana, S.A., *Mexico*
Prentice-Hall of India Private Limited, *New Delhi*
Prentice-Hall of Japan, Inc., *Tokyo*
Pearson Education Asia Pte. Ltd., *Singapore*
Editora Prentice-Hall do Brasil, Ltda., *Rio de Janeiro*

Dedication

This book is dedicated to

Tom
(best younger brother imaginable, one rare kind of hero)

and to

Robert Bloch, Ray Bradbury, Chester Gould, and Jack Williamson
(favorite storytellers and dear friends)

and

Forrest J Ackerman, E. F. Bleiler, August W. Derleth, James Gunn,
Peter Haining, and Sam Moskowitz
(premiere scholars and preservers of the art)

Acknowledgments

Glyn Alyn Roberts and Cleo Ann Gilbert Roberts,
Virginia M. Woods Roberts, David Glyn Roberts,
Lauryn Leighann Roberts and Karyn Morgan Glenys Roberts

Gary Hoppenstand, Ph.D.

Ray Walsh, Curious Books, East Lansing

Bruce Ayres, Capital City Comics, Madison and Milwaukee

Greg Ketter, Dreamhaven, Minneapolis

Friends and Colleagues at
University of Wisconsin — Whitewater
Bowling Green State University
Mankato State University
Michigan State University
Northwestern Michigan College

Team Members, Consummate Professionals, and Newly Found Friends who saw this book
from idea to print: Carrie Brandon, Literature Editor; Sandy Hrasdzira, Assistant to the
Literature Editor; Frederick T. Courtright, Permissions Specialist; Linda B. Pawelchak,
Production Editor; Robert Farrar-Wagner, Art Director; Karen Pugliano, Image Specialist;
Beth Boyd, Image Specialist; Brandy Dawson, Marketing Specialist; Rachel Falk, Marketing
Specialist; Christine R. Moodie, Marketing Specialist; Lynn Pearlman, Mary Rottino, and
Frances Russello; Gianna Carradona (who was there in the formative days); and Allison
Pojanowski (who believed in the project from the start and helped get it the attention
it needed).

Reviewers: Virginia Allen, Iowa State University; Allan L. Eller, Binghamton University;
Rafeeq O. McGiveron, Lansing Community College; and Carolyn Wendell, Monroe
Community College.

Visionaries and Legends of Science Fiction and Fantasy who have helped mightily as facilita-
tors, art providers, and agents: Forrest J Ackerman, Edd and Dean Cartier, Lail Finlay,
Robert A. Madle, Barry N. Malzberg, George R. R. Martin, Charles F. Miller,
Burton R. Pollin, and Robert Weinberg.

Friends and Family not mentioned by name here, but close to my heart.

Special Thanks to:

Virginia, for constant love and understanding, for invaluable ideas, essential reference work, proofreading, and for a range of sacrifices and expertises needed to complete this book.

Dave and Lauryn, for their understanding of, patience with, and unending love and support for their dad.

Dad, Mom, and Tom for incomparable inspiration, eternal faith, and love supplied their son and brother.

Doug Campbell and Rochelle Hammontree, two tremendous colleagues and consummate professionals, for excellent, invaluable reference work.

And,

Rex Antinozzi, M.D.; Thomas R. Bannow, D.O.; Kurt and Laura Froese, D.C.s; Bruce Lee, D.D.S.; Robert P. Niedbalski, D.O.; and Dale Carpenter of Ultimate Fitness—Friends, Professionals, and Scientists who practice proactive, as well as reactive, health care. The 1920s scientists and founders of *Amazing Stories* would have approved.

In a book full of hopes, fantasies, dreams, and sciences, I harbor one fear above all others—I fear I will never be able to tell each of you how much I love you who have comprised my life.

CONTENTS

High Fantasy   207

Ancestors and Disciples of Robert E. Howard and J. R. R. Tolkien   207

SECTION THREE
SCIENCE FICTION

Jules Verne, Herbert George Wells, Hugo Gernsback, and the Early Days of Modern Scientifiction   343

viii   Contents

SECTION FOUR
AN HISTORICAL PERSPECTIVE

SECTION FIVE
LISTS AND BIBLIOGRAPHIES

FOREWORD

This may be the best one-volume library of science fiction that I have seen. Such judgments depend on taste and the mood of the moment, but any science fiction collection that neglects these stories would be weaker for it. Comprehensive, it runs all the way from Mary Shelley, Nathaniel Hawthorne, and Edgar Allan Poe, back in the 1830s, down to today. The essays and the wide-ranging selections make it an illustrated history of the genre. I know nothing like it.

The history of science fiction can begin anywhere. Once, on the theory that it explores the zone of possibility just beyond the proven, we began our own science fiction course with Homer's *Odyssey*. The Greeks had arrived in the Mediterranean world as bold sea-roamers, pushing into unknown lands, almost as modern cosmologists are doing today. Homer's myths must reflect rumors the Greeks had heard and their own speculations about what might lie beyond the world they knew.

A milestone in the history of science itself occurred in 1660, the year the British Royal Society was formed by the "natural philosophers," busy displacing the lore of alchemy with experimental evidence. I used to include the third book of *Gulliver's Travels* (1726) in the reading list. A defender of tradition and the status quo, Swift was satirizing science. His flying island is Laputa, Spanish for "the whore." By the irony of accident, one of his fools has discovered the two moons in orbit around Mars.

Brian Aldiss selects Mary Shelley's *Frankenstein* (1818) as the first work of real science fiction. Ben Franklin had risked his life to prove that lightning was electricity. Electric current from Volta's new batteries had made the legs of a dead frog twitch. Mary used lightning to animate dead human organs. That is extrapolation, the basic process of speculative fiction.

Jules Verne, the first successful science fiction author, was generally careful to base his extrapolation on the science of his time. His spacecraft in *From the Earth to the Moon* (1865) is fired from a great cannon, which he happened to locate near the future *Apollo* launch site. The actual *Nautilus*, the first nuclear submarine, was named for Captain Nemo's undersea craft in *Twenty Thousand Leagues Under the Sea* (1870).

H. G. Wells looked so far ahead that Verne became a critic of his vision. The year he spent as a student of Thomas Henry Huxley, the great defender of Darwin's theory of evolution, had given Wells the grasp of change, social and technological as well as biological, that made him the chief creator of modern science fiction. Beginning with *The Time Machine* (1895), he not only pioneered such concepts as time travel, interplanetary war, and genetic engineering, but also stated the significant theme that progress limits itself, that high technology carries its own death warrant.

The genre still lacked a common name. Verne's novels had been *Voyages Extraordinaires*. Wells's were "scientific romances." The stories of Hawthorne and Poe were known simply as "tales." When science fiction did begin to find a habitation in the pulp magazines, the romances of Edgar Rice Burroughs and A. Merritt were "different" or "unusual" stories. The science fiction in *Weird Tales* was "weird-scientific." Hugo Gernsback published my own first story as "scientifiction."

Weird Tales, founded in 1923 and edited from 1924 until 1939 by Farnsworth Wright, was perhaps the first publication to offer a regular haven for science fiction, along with the mix of fantasy and horror that made it "the unique magazine." Wright was a man I loved for his generosities to me and for the noble battle that kept the magazine afloat through his long battle with Parkinson's disease. Fondly remembered and several times revived, it is alive today.

I am happy to see so many of its veterans here—H. P. Lovecraft, Robert Bloch, Clark Ashton Smith, Robert E. Howard, C. L. Moore, Ray Bradbury, Frank Belknap Long, Edmond Hamilton. (Tennessee Williams is missing.) Lovecraft was a plausible heir to Edgar Allan Poe. Howard created Conan the Barbarian. Hamilton, with his tales of the Interstellar Patrol, was inventing space opera.

The annual Hugo Awards were named in Gernsback's honor. Born in Luxembourg in 1884, he arrived in America in 1904 with a battery invention that failed, became a promoter of technology, and then a magazine publisher. *Amazing Stories*, which began with the issue for May 1926, was the first magazine devoted to science fiction, though he coined the name only in 1929, when he had lost *Amazing* and founded *Science Wonder Stories*.

Amazing was an instant success, half of that due to the Austrian-born artist Frank R. Paul. He produced something over 150 covers for Gernsback magazines, one of them reproduced on the cover of this book. Trained as an architect before he turned to art, he displayed a fine imagination for fantastic future worlds and alien landscapes, his alien beings often more lifelike than his humans. He set the pattern for early science fiction art, and his influence is still visible in its splendid flowering today.

My own experience in science fiction began with *Amazing*. Growing up on an isolated hardscrabble ranch in eastern New Mexico, I had seen only a few fascinating bits of it: Poe's tales, two or three stray novels whose titles I don't recall, and Mark Twain's *Connecticut Yankee*. Gernsback's early issues opened a wonder world of reprinted classics that enchanted me. I began trying to do my own, and still I haven't stopped.

Editors and magazines have played a major role in shaping science fiction. Gernsback wanted basic science, spectacular prediction, and educational value. Harry Bates, in *Astounding Stories of Super-Science* (1930), replaced the scientific lectures with pulp fiction patterns: strong heroes, positive themes, dramatic action. John W. Campbell, of *Astounding* from 1938 until he died in 1971, had a respect for science, a creative imagination, and an idealistic vision of the human future that inspired a whole school of new writers: Robert Heinlein, Isaac Asimov, Lester Del Rey, Theodore Sturgeon, Sprague De Camp, and A. E. van Vogt. They made the next dozen years "the golden age of science fiction."

The Magazine of Fantasy and Science Fiction, founded in 1949 and edited at first by Tony Boucher and J. Francis McComas, was a far different dog. Boucher, something of an aesthete, was an accomplished writer and reviewer and a fan of Gregorian chant. He and McComas, with their concerns for character, style, and literary quality, carried the field a long step forward from its pulp ancestry.

With *Galaxy*, begun in 1950, Horace Gold added psychology and sociology to the editorial mix. Gold was an odd agoraphobe, who edited the magazine from his own apartment and worked with his writers by telephone, often calling long after midnight. With none of Campbell's faith in splendid things to come, he was driven by a sardonic pessimism, perhaps born of his own experience in World War II as much as from the Holocaust and the mushroom cloud of Hiroshima. He recruited writers who shared his dark outlook and paid well for stories. Campbell had been diverted into dianetics. *Galaxy* soon led the field.

For many years, science fiction lived and in fact flourished in what we used to call the "pulp ghetto." Literary critics despised it. There was no book market for it until after the war, when a few fans began reprinting the magazine serials they had loved. They discovered such success that major publishers took over the field. Writers unhappy in the ghetto had always longed to escape the science fiction label and emerge in the literary mainstream. Some of them succeeded with best-selling books.

Myself, I've always been content in the science fiction world. It began as a small community where we had to circle our wagons against indifference or scorn. We were able to read everything and know each other. I found many of the others richly worth knowing. Though old friendships endure, science fiction has grown and diversified far beyond the reach of any valid general statement about it, including this one. The Science Fiction Writers of America now has upwards of a thousand members. Many fans, devoted to the endless trilogies of some favorite writer, know nobody else.

Science fiction began creeping into the classroom forty years ago. Since the formation of the Science Fiction Research Association in 1970, the genre has been granted a degree of academic respectability. Such scholarly journals as *Extrapolation, Science Fiction Studies,* and the British *Foundation* are now dedicated to it. Library shelves have filled with classic reprints, critical studies, and anthologies. Skeptics are asking if science fiction is dead. I don't think so. So long as we live under the hammer of technology, we will be wondering about the next impact. Will it shatter us? Or forge us into something new?

Most of the recent collections have a rather limited focus. I love this book for its extraordinay compass, spanning the whole history of the genre, and for all the great stories that gave it exciting new directions when they first appeared, stories I am excited to read again. It is an unexpected honor to find one of my own among them.

Jack Williamson

ABOUT JACK WILLIAMSON

Jack Williamson, born John Stewart Williamson, April 29, 1908, is Science Fiction and Fantasy's most important practitioner and scholar today. He has been awarded and cited many times over for his stories and related contributions to Science Fiction and Fantasy, which began with the publication of his short story "The Metal Man" in the pages of Hugo Gernsback's December 1928 issue of *Amazing Stories*. Williamson continues to be a successful novelist, with books such as *The Silicon Dagger* (1999) and *Terra Forming Earth* (completed and forthcoming), is a regular contributor to the field's most important publications (*Science Fiction Age* and *Analog Science Fiction and Fact*), and is a lecturer at Eastern New Mexico University (Portales, New Mexico), where he retired in 1977.

Among Jack Williamson's classic works are *Golden Blood* (*Weird Tales*, 1933), *The Legion of Space* series (begun in 1934 in the pages of *Astounding Stories* with the title novel and followed by *The Cometeers*, 1936; *One Against the Legion*, 1939; and *Queen of the Legion*, 1983), *Darker Than You Think* (*Unknown*, 1940), and *The Humanoids* series (begun in 1947 with "With Folded Hands" and continued in several stories through *The Humanoid Touch*, 1980). Williamson has contributed to many magazines besides *Amazing Stories*, *Weird Tales*, *Astounding*, *Unknown*, *Science Fiction Age*, and *Analog*. These include *Science Wonder Stories*, *Air Wonder Stories*, *Wonder Stories*, *Argosy*, *Startling Stories*, *Marvel Science Stories*, *Thrilling Wonder Stories*, *Thrilling Mystery*, *Galaxy*, and *The Magazine of Fantasy and Science Fiction*. His stories and novels have appeared in hundreds of printings of hardcover and paperback books and have been translated into a variety of languages.

A versatile author whose themes and story lines include space opera, technology, cybernetics, alternate universes, artificial intelligence, genetic engineering, and more, Jack Williamson has always been a first-rate storyteller and social critic. He earned his Ph.D. in 1964 from the University of Colorado at Boulder and has long been considered one of the top experts on the life and career of H. G. Wells. As a scholar and Science Fiction historian, Jack Williamson has done perhaps more than anyone else to legitimize and advocate Science Fiction and Fantasy as an academic, intellectual pursuit. With his colleagues and friends, he continues to build one of the world's most significant Science Fiction and Fantasy archives at Eastern New Mexico University.

One of the single best volumes of Science Fiction and Fantasy history is Jack Williamson's enthralling 1985 Hugo Award–winning autobiography—*Wonder's Child: My Life in Science Fiction* (1984). Richard A. Hauptmann's *The Work of Jack Williamson: An Annotated Bibliography and Guide* (1998) is also worthy of note. Some of Williamson's classic Science Fiction and Fantasy has recently been re-released in a beautiful series of limited edition books published by Haffner Press. These volumes include *The Metal Man and Others* (1999), *Wolves of Darkness* (1999), *Wizard's Isle* (2000), *Spider Island* (2001), and a fifth volume forthcoming.

The term "Grand Master," conferred upon him many times and in many places, does not do the quietly brilliant, unassuming, and dearly loved and respected Jack Williamson justice. He is currently writing a new Legion of Space short story.

PREFACE

Parameters, or, *Amazing Stories* versus *Weird Tales*, *Astounding Stories* versus *Unknown Worlds*

The stories showcased and analyzed here are "Fantasy" and/or "Science Fiction" written and published in English, or Fantasy and/or Science Fiction translated into and published in English. This book's contents, discussions, and organization are designed to explore the distinctions and similarities between two broadly yet specifically defined genres of fiction—Fantasy and Science Fiction. "Genres," for the purpose of this book, are generally and simply defined as artistic and story categories. Definitions and differences between stories and story genres are important starting points for analysis and appreciation; however, from a larger cultural, anthropological, and sociological perspective, similarities between stories and story forms may be more telling and significant. For the purpose of this book, "society" and "culture" are essentially interchangeable terms, referencing a group of interrelated people tied together by common mythology. A mythology is an all-encompassing narrative/story or a complex of interrelated component stories that serves as cultural definition, religion, reality, and explanation and justification of action. Crossovers between Fantasy and Science Fiction, as well as crossovers between Fantasy, Science Fiction, and other genres, such as Mysteries, Detective Fiction, Westerns, Adventure stories, and more, are explored.

Herein, the reader will find a range of ethnicities, mythologies, religions, and perspectives represented. Women writers, women's writing, and female story characters are found throughout this book, since women writers were and are integral parts of Fantasy and Science Fiction (F&SF) history. (An investigation of authors' pseudonyms from the first half of the twentieth century, for example, shows that women were much more a part of F&SF history than previously thought by students of these genres.) It is important to remember that modern F&SF was first articulated, if not begun, by a young woman named Mary Shelley and her archetypal novel, *Frankenstein, or the Modern Prometheus* (1818, rev. 1831).

With the exception of J. R. R. Tolkien's "Chapter Five: Riddles in the Dark" (1937), all stories reprinted here are complete; even the famed Tolkien sequence, which features Bilbo Baggins and Gollum, stands by itself, outside the larger context of Tolkien's novel, as a complete tale.

Many of the authors included in this book have created series F&SF story characters of various sorts and degrees of popular and critical success. At first, the temptation was to feature the best series characters and their best stories, regardless of other considerations, such as story themes. But, if this was to be done, then as good and important as Fritz Leiber's Fahfrd and the Grey Mouser story, "The Bazaar of the Bizarre" (*Fantastic*, August 1963), is, what may be an even more representative landmark story of Leiber's life achievements and contributions to the genre— "Smoke Ghost" (*Unknown Worlds*, October 1941)—would have to be excluded. Further, much of the popular success of Leiber's swashbuckling duo is an extension of that enjoyed by Robert E. Howard's more archetypal stories of Conan the Barbarian, such as "The Tower of the Elephant" (*Weird Tales*, March 1933). With this in mind, the temptation then became to ignore all series characters categorically. This plan would not have been prudent either. "The Tower of the Elephant" is one of Howard's most important contributions to Heroic Fantasy, and to ignore it because it is a Conan story would be as short-sighted as including all series characters and stories without abandon.

Other difficult choices needed to be made. The list of great Ray Bradbury stories is extensive, but only one could be chosen. In this case, after much thought, one of Bradbury's short stories featured in *The Martian Chronicles* (1950)— "There Will Come Soft Rains"—was chosen because Bradbury has cited it as a personal favorite, and because the profound message of the story about humans comes from a setting uniquely devoid of humans. Other authors presented similar difficulties—but what problems to have! Some of these authors included Catherine Moore, Edmond Hamilton, Leigh Brackett, Robert Bloch, George R. R. Martin, William Gibson (it was difficult to pass on both "Johnny Neumonic" and "The Gernsback Continuum"), Edgar Allan Poe, and Nathaniel Hawthorne. In a few cases, such as with Judith Merril, Philip José Farmer, and Orson Scott Card, the stories presented here were the authors' first professional sales—this was interesting, but not really a consideration.

So, then, the single most difficult aspect of assembling this tribute to stories of imagination and science was narrowing the list of stories to be included. There was a wealth of tremendous tales composed by tremendous, visioned authors from which to choose. Factors for story inclusion were

1. The readability and fun of each story
2. Expert opinion of professional authors of F&SF
3. Hardcore fan enthusiasm for each story
4. Authors' favorites of their own stories
5. Story length
6. Story completeness (as single-standing works)
7. Unique and important contribution of each story to larger topic(s)
8. Each story's ability to represent the larger body of work by the author

Such parameters, though barriers of sorts, helped keep the project focused. In short, this book is as limited and defined, yet comprehensive, as possible.

In addition, one primary goal of the total story and content selection is to provide an effective mix of both "popular" and "canonical" stories, familiar/traditional tales, and once-popular but now "lost classics." Any story worth anything as an intellectual construct, as a credible and representative piece of cultural anthropology, as an enthralling narrative work, is or once was popular—of the people. There is no other way. Fantasy and Science Fiction are highly democratic types of literature. Everyone is eligible to participate, and there are really no sacred cows in terms of story content.

For example, just as there were well-documented conflicts between Howard Phillips Lovecraft and Hugo Gernsback, Groff Conklin and E. E. "Doc" Smith, and Sam Moskowitz and Donald A. Wollheim, there has been an ongoing philosophical battle between fans (often, but not always, proponents of the popular) and scholars (often, but not always, proponents of the canonical) of F&SF for years. The truly seasoned expert of F&SF knows that both Lovecraft and

Gernsback were giants, and that both fanaticism and scholarship are integral parts of the F&SF mix.

There is another matter. Many authors of Fantasy and Science Fiction resist (in some cases vehemently) the notion that they are genre specific, or easily and narrowly categorized in terms of the stories they write. Ray Bradbury, Harlan Ellison, Dean R. Koontz, and Clive Barker are four such authors. These wordsmiths quite appropriately deem themselves "magicians of words," "imaginative thinkers," "proponents of the fantastic," and so on.

The organization of stories in this book was consciously constructed, but there exists extensive overlapping of themes, settings, character types, and so on between the stories categorized here as Fantasy and Science Fiction. In addition to being organized by genre, the stories are set up chronologically (historically—by date of first appearance) and thematically. Some of the stories, such as Robert Louis Stevenson's "The Body Snatchers" (*Pall Mall Gazette*, Extra Christmas Issue, 1884), Fredric Brown's "Arena" (*Astounding Science-Fiction*, July 1944), and Arthur C. Clarke's "The Sentinel" (*10 Story Fantasy*, Spring 1951), are included not only because they stand alone as important literary contributions to Fantasy and Science Fiction, but also because they were successfully adapted into motion pictures and/or television episodes.

Please note the essay included near the end of the book. It is great fun to read and provides important contextual information for the stories and discussions included in this volume, and for the larger topics of Fantasy and Science Fiction.

Ever since the early days of the twentieth century, when pulp magazine Science Fiction saw its genesis in the United States at the hands of Hugo Gernsback, definitions of Science Fiction and Fantasy have been passionately debated. Gernsback set forth his definitions of Science Fiction in the editorials in the pages of *Amazing Stories*. Meanwhile, the faltering *Weird Tales*, later to be deemed the "greatest Fantasy magazine of all time," published the Fantasy and Science Fiction alike of H. P. Lovecraft, Edmond Hamilton, Catherine Moore, Clark Ashton Smith, and others. Ironically, *Weird Tales* had published Science Fiction in its coarse wood pulp pages for three years before *Amazing Stories* arrived. By the 1930s, former *Amazing Stories* author John W. Campbell edited the most revered Science Fiction pulp magazine ever—*Astounding Stories*—and its Fantasy counterpart, *Unknown Worlds*. Even the hard scientist Gernsback would let elements of wonder and fantasy creep into *Amazing Stories* and his other publications. The distinctions are important and unimportant.

The essays and headnotes in this book are intended as general overviews, places to begin and continue intellectual inquiry. More about these authors and stories may be found in a variety of multimedia sources. Some of these are listed at the back of this volume. Know that the best scholars of Fantasy and Science Fiction of all time include Everett F. Bleiler, August Derleth, and Sam Moskowitz. The work of these three gentlemen is first rate. There have been and are others.

Remember that all stories are fiction, autobiography, and metaphor. They are also all true. Read and understand the works of Ray Bradbury and this becomes obvious. Remember, too, as Clive Barker and others before him have reminded us: there are no new stories, just retellings of the old. The old myths and legends are still powerful and viable today. Consider the current mastery of Steven Spielberg and George Lucas. Read Jack Williamson's Legion of Space series (begun in the 1930s), add some of Alex Raymond's classic newspaper comic strip, *Flash Gordon* (also from the 1930s), and some of James Fenimore Cooper's Leatherstocking series (begun in the 1820s), and the result is the *Star Wars* saga. Indiana Jones has ancestors in the nineteenth-century works of H. Rider Haggard (1856–1925) and Talbot Mundy (1879–1940), and in the pages of turn-of-the-century *Argosy* magazine. Stephen King astutely acknowledges and details his cultural and literary heritage in one of the single best studies of the Dark Fantasy genre in his book *Danse Macabre* (1981).

As the author/editor/compiler of *The Prentice Hall Anthology of Science Fiction and Fantasy*, my intent is to provide a fair and realistic representation and discussion of Fantasy and Science Fiction of the nineteenth and twentieth centuries. A primary goal of this book is to provide bases for further investigation. My sincere hope is that this book be considered a tribute to a group of people and a tradition of storytelling and imagining that are unmatched in excellence. We owe these thinkers, these visionaries and humanitarians, a great deal. For me, they number among my most important treasures—my family and friends. Many good and tremendous authors and stories are not presented here. Go find them, and enjoy the quest.

Garyn G. Roberts, Ph.D.

INTRODUCTION

STORIES FOR THE MILLENNIUM: SCIENCE FICTION AND FANTASY AS CONTEMPORARY MYTHOLOGY

Science Fiction and Fantasy stories have been part of the human experience since the first person contemplated the stars in the sky and wondered about the nature of life. In fact, Science Fiction and Fantasy today are the products of ancient folklore and profound, enduring ancient stories or myths.

Before the days of print media, speculations about and tales of the universe in which we live were disseminated by word of mouth and were patterned in structure so as to allow for easy retelling. They were bound by tradition and reflected both the cultural heritage and the personal experiences and beliefs of the storyteller. These stories existed in various versions because there was no fixed way to record them. The ownership of the tales was collective; in other words, these speculations were jointly created, embellished, and owned. They were and are products of societies and cultures.

When the first print media arrived and were then distributed to large portions of societies, stories of Fantasy and Science Fiction were some of the first printed. By the 1700s, newspapers and similar publications carried not only news of the day, but fictions and speculations about that news and the world of that time. In the United States, Benjamin Day's *New York Sun* was one of the first newspapers to feature such stories. By the 1800s, newspapers across the country printed Science Fiction and Fantasy as well.

Sometime before the beginning of the Civil War (generally considered to be about 1860), dime novels also carried tales of Fantasy and Science Fiction. As a print medium, dime novels were a variation of newspapers. In format, they were designed to look like newspapers of the day. Dime novels were published two or three columns to a page, featured sensational story titles (or headlines), included formula-(pattern)-based stories, and were targeted at a popular audience at an affordable price. These publications were produced weekly, sold in serial installments (which featured cliffhangers that helped guarantee the market for the next issue), were distributed largely by the postal service, had weekly press runs in the hundreds of thousands, measured their profits in the fraction of a penny per issue, and thrived on popular genre fiction such as Westerns, Mysteries, Adventures, Fantasy, and especially toward the end of the nineteenth century, Science Fiction. A rough British equivalent to the American dime novel at this time was called the "Penny Dreadful."

At the turn of the century, dime novels flourished, and traditional newspapers carried the Science Fiction and Fantasy of popular authors of the day. At this time also, a variation of the dime novel first appeared. Called "pulp" magazines because of the highly coarse, acid-laden pulpwood paper on which these supposedly ephemeral publications were printed, pulps were able to capitalize and improve upon the strengths of the dime novel medium.

Just prior to World War I, events conspired to bring the era of the dime novel to a close. For one thing, the postal service decided to increase postage rates for novels being shipped through the mails. Though the increase was seemingly modest, only a penny or two, this increase more than eliminated the small profit per issue dime novels had enjoyed. The medium that, along with newspapers, had helped to form a popular experience or popular culture in the United States, and had been instrumental in making print and literacy available to those who previously had access to neither, went under. From a business standpoint, dime novel publishers made profits by selling many copies at low profit margins per issue. But when even that low profit margin was erased, all income was erased for the publishers.

Pulp magazine publishers did some things differently and were able to maintain an extensive popular entertainment market until the arrival of the paperback book and network television. First, pulps varied their formats. In other words, they published a range of novels, short stories, features, and so on in each issue. This helped these magazines get around the postal increases prescribed for novels sent through the mail. Second, and more importantly, pulps did not rely exclusively on the postal service for their distribution. In fact, the postal service and subscription services were far less important to the success and viability of pulps as a marketable product than they were to dime novels. Pulps utilized newsstand and related retail sales techniques for the majority of their distribution. In addition, in the 1890s, the four-color printing process became financially viable (it is no accident that this is when color comic strips became popular in newspapers such as those owned by William Randolph Hearst, The Chicago Tribune-New York News Syndicate, and others), and pulp magazines began featuring garish, beautiful, exotic, alluring, and striking cover paintings that attracted and created sales. Ironically, and only partially accurately, the term "pulp fiction," which indicates a secondary, lesser kind of story comes from the mass medium that was named for its paper material. "Pulp" has come to mean not only inferior-grade paper, but inferior-grade fiction. Those who truly have read pulp magazine fiction know that some of the most important writing of the first half of the twentieth century appeared in the pages of the pulpwood magazine.

In the 1890s as well, motion pictures were in their infant stages as an internationally popular entertainment medium. Ten years later, Fantasy and Science Fiction movies were made. By the 1920s, filmmakers produced enduring Fantasies, Dark Fantasies, and Science Fiction. By the 1930s, motion pictures had attained sound, and Fantasy and Science Fiction stories were not only the subjects of feature-length films, they were the subjects of a range of twelve- and fifteen-chapter movie serials. Heroes and heroines from the pulp magazines, newspaper comic strips, and radio, as well as newly created heroes and heroines, fought epic battles to do what was right and save their universes from impending peril and ultimate apocalyptic destruction.

By the time of the Great Depression (approximately 1929 to World War II), a whole array of popular print and nonprint media featured stories of Fantasy and

Science Fiction. There were juvenile serial novels, newspaper comic strips, Big Little Books, and comic books in print that featured great adventures in lost worlds and distant galaxies. (Big Little Books were highly popular pulp paper books that told stories from the movies and radio, but primarily served as a bridge between newspaper comic strips and comic books.) At this time also, network radio featured serial dramas and special presentations of Science Fiction and Fantasy. "The Theater of the Mind," radio was especially fit for stories of imagination, speculation, terror, and optimism. Tom Swift, Buck Rogers, and Flash Gordon were popular Science Fiction heroes.

By the time the Great Depression was followed by World War II in the United States, the pulp magazine was past its prime. A great vehicle for popular mythology, entertainment, and escapism, the pulp magazine was supplanted by the paperback book (which was smaller in size and saved paper for the war effort, and which was more easily transported to military personnel at the various fronts and theaters of the world apocalypse) and network television. When the first paperbacks appeared in 1938, they primarily reprinted pulp magazine stories. (In turn, the first pulp magazines had reprinted dime novel stories.) Television dramas similarly reproduced and imitated radio dramas.

Today, Science Fiction and Fantasy flourish in print media such as hard cover and paperback books, digest and slick paper magazines, and comic books. Science Fiction and Fantasy are also staples of the nonprint media of motion pictures, television, and animation. In addition, the myths and stories of Fantasy and Science Fiction are further developed and made available to people via computer technologies such as the World Wide Web. There are literally hundreds of thousands of Internet sites dedicated to Science Fiction and Fantasy topics.

Fantasy and Science Fiction provide the fictional and factual stories of our times. These stories define us. As human beings, our frontiers have shifted continuously, and so have our mindsets regarding who and what we are in the greater scheme of the universe. In the early years of the new millennium, Fantasy and Science Fiction are our most important fictions. These narratives define and reflect who we are and what we aspire to be. While partially designed as entertainment, these stories also predict what we can achieve and what we should avoid. They are applications of religious and moral truths, and they remind us of the great potentialities of life.

SECTION ONE

TWO ARCHETYPAL STORIES

Charles A. Platt's rendering (as it appeared in *The Complete Works of Edgar Allan Poe,* 1884) of the Gothic structure in Poe's "The Fall of the House of Usher" (1839) is, in its own way, an atmospheric excursion into terror and the unknown.

ENDURING TRADITIONS OF MARY SHELLEY AND EDGAR ALLAN POE

MARY SHELLEY (1797–1851) AND EDGAR ALLAN POE (1809–1849) defined much of what we today call "Fantasy" and "Science Fiction." Mary Shelley not only produced the Dark Fantasy of Frankenstein's monster in her novel *Frankenstein, or, The Modern Prometheus* (1818, rev. 1831), she created the Science Fiction of the monster as well. Although Boris Karloff's portrayal of the tragic mutation in the movie *Frankenstein* is the image that has remained ever since 1931, Shelley's original tale is much richer and more detailed than the fun, even admirable, portrayal by Karloff. In her novel, and in some of her other writings, Mary Shelley addressed, in a very progressive and open fashion, the moral and social dilemmas and issues of her day. These dilemmas and issues, which are still relevant today, include reanimation of human flesh, genetic engineering, cloning, the nature and quality of life, love, compassion, and mortality.

Edgar Allan Poe made similar contributions to traditions of Fantasy and Science Fiction. Like England's Mary Shelley, America's Poe was a master of a range of writing and storytelling styles and techniques. And, as was the case with Shelley, Poe was by no means the first person to tell tales of Fantasy and Science Fiction. Yet, both Mary Shelley and Edgar Allan Poe solidified traditions of these existing story forms and created master patterns or models, called archetypes, that stand tall in contemporary fiction.

Edgar Allan Poe wrote an array of stories that were based in Fantasy (specifically Dark Fantasy or Horror) and Science Fiction. Unlike Shelley, Poe did not produce one single novel-length masterpiece that defines him to this day. Instead, he wrote and published a number of very pointed stories about the horrors and uncertainties of life, and about the possibilities of science. Poe's "The Fall of the House of Usher" (1839) is landmark fare, and with all its trappings stands as the ultimate haunted house or Gothic story.

As masters of Gothic storytelling, Mary Shelley and Edgar Allan Poe had predecessors. For example, there were Gothic epics such as Horace Walpole's *The Castle of Otranto* (1764), Ann Radcliffe's *The Mysteries of Udolpho* (1794), and Matthew Gregory Lewis's *The Monk* (1796). In short, Gothic stories are defined by a central symbol, an icon, that is an architectural structure or building such as a haunted house, decaying castle, or moldering old estate. Within the confines of this mysterious building are found long, decadent family histories and atrocities augmented by elements of the supernatural. This setting provides the vehicle for fictions that examine the inner workings of the individual and society alike.

Mary Shelley and Edgar Allan Poe wrote Fantasy, Horror stories, and works of Science Fiction. They studied existing traditions in these fields and made them their own. Shelley's and Poe's respective influences on subsequent storytellers and writers have been profound. In truth, all Science Fiction and Fantasy that follow the work of these two masters owe direct tribute to them.

🏵 MARY (WOLLSTONECRAFT) SHELLEY (1797–1851)

When recounting the history of nineteenth- and twentieth-century Fantasy and Science Fiction, celebrants and critics have almost invariably turned to the work of Mary Shelley as a starting point. There is sound logic in this approach in that Shelley's Frankenstein, or, The Modern Prometheus *(1818, rev. 1831) is an (if not "the") archetypal narrative of modern-day Science Fiction and Fantasy.*

Mary Wollstonecraft (later Mary Shelley) was born and raised in late-eighteenth- and early-nineteenth-century English literary aristocracy. As is the case with all popular and socially significant authors, Mary was well aware of her cultural and literary heritage. And she drew heavily upon the same, coordinating and expanding that heritage. A leading thinker, humanitarian, and feminist of her day, Mary Shelley was foremost a great storyteller of the human condition.

"The Mortal Immortal: A Tale," as is the case with Shelley's "Roger Dodsworth: The Re-Animated Englishman" (written 1826, published 1863) and "The Transformation" (1830), is not nearly as complex and socially critical as Frankenstein, *but it is nonetheless a poignant fantasy with elements that are still highly relevant today. For the nearly two centuries that have followed her creative life, storytellers have tried to emulate, imitate, and pay tribute to Mary Shelley and her works. Themes of immortality and reanimation and the consequences and implications of both have found their way into the works of Arthur Conan Doyle, H. P. Lovecraft, Robert Bloch, C. L. Moore, Ray Bradbury, and others.*

The Mortal Immortal: A Tale
(Keepsake for MDCCCXXXIV, *1833*)

July 16, 1833—This is a memorable anniversary for me; on it I complete my three hundred and twenty-third year!

The Wandering Jew?—certainly not. More than eighteen centuries have passed over his head. In comparison with him, I am a very young Immortal.

Am I, then, immortal? This is a question which I have asked myself, by day and night, for now three hundred and three years, and yet cannot answer it. I detected a gray hair amidst my brown locks this very day—that surely signifies decay. Yet it may have remained concealed there for three hundred years—for some persons have become entirely white-headed before twenty years of age.

I will tell my story, and my reader shall judge for me. I will tell my story, and so contrive to pass some few hours of a long eternity, become so wearisome to me. For ever! Can it be? to live for ever! I have heard of enchantments, in which the victims were plunged into a deep sleep, to wake after a hundred years, as fresh as ever: I have heard of the Seven Sleepers—thus to be immortal would not be so burdensome: but, oh! the weight of never-ending time—the tedious passage of the still-succeeding hours! How happy was the fabled Nourjahad!—but to my task.

All the world has heard of Cornelius Agrippa. His memory is as immortal as his arts have made me. All the world has also heard of his scholar, who, unawares, raised the foul fiend during his master's absence, and was destroyed by him. The report, true or false, of this accident was attended with many inconveniences to the renowned philosopher. All his scholars at once deserted him—his servants disappeared. He had no one near him to put coals on his ever-burning fires while he slept, or to attend to the changeful colours of his medicines while he studied. Experiment after experiment failed, because one pair of hands was insufficient to complete them: the dark spirits laughed at him for not being able to retain a single mortal in his service.

I was then very young—very poor—and very much in love. I had been for about a year the pupil of Cornelius, though I was absent when this accident took place. On my return, my friends implored me not to return to the alchemist's abode. I trembled as I listened to the dire tale they told; I required no second warning; and when Cornelius came and offered me a purse of gold if I would remain under his roof, I felt as if Satan himself tempted me. My teeth chattered—my hair stood on end:—I ran off as fast as my trembling knees would permit.

My failing steps were directed whither for two years they had every evening been attracted,—a gently bubbling spring of pure living waters, beside which lingered a dark-haired girl, whose beaming eyes were fixed on the path I was accustomed each night to tread. I cannot remember the hour when I did not love Bertha; we had been neighbours and playmates from infancy—her parents, like mine, were of humble life, yet respectable—our attachment had been a source of pleasure to them. In an evil hour a malignant fever carried off both her father and mother, and Bertha became an orphan. She would have found a home beneath my paternal roof, but unfortunately, the old lady of the near castle, rich, childless, and solitary, declared her intention to adopt her. Henceforth Bertha was clad in silk—inhabited a marble palace—and was looked on as being highly favoured by fortune. But in her new situation among her new associates, Bertha remained true to the friend of her humbler days; she often visited the cottage of my father, and when forbidden to go thither, she would stray towards the neighbouring wood, and meet me beside its shady fountain.

She often declared that she owed no duty to her new protectress equal in sanctity to that which bound us. Yet still I was too poor to marry, and she grew weary of being tormented on my account. She had a haughty but an impatient spirit, and grew angry at the obstacles that prevented our union. We met now after an absence, and she had been sorely beset while I was away; she complained bitterly, and almost reproached me for being poor. I replied hastily,—

"I am honest, if I am poor—were I not, I might soon become rich!"

This explanation produced a thousand questions. I feared to shock her by owning the truth, but she drew it from me: and then, casting a look of disdain on me: she said

"You pretend to love, and you fear to face the Devil for my sake!"

I protested that I had only dreaded to offend her;—while she dwelt on the magnitude of the reward that I should receive. Thus encouraged—shamed by her—led on by love and hope, laughing at my late fears, with quick steps and a light heart I returned to accept the offers of the alchemist, and was instantly installed in my office.

A year passed away. I became possessed of no insignificant sum of money. Custom had banished my fears. In spite of the most painful vigilance, I had never detected the trace of a cloven foot; nor was the studious silence of our abode ever disturbed by demoniac howls. I still continued my stolen interviews with Bertha, and hope dawned on me—hope—but not perfect joy; for Bertha fancied that love and securities were enemies, and her pleasure was to divide them in my bosom. Though true of heart, she was somewhat of a coquette in manner; and I was jealous as a Turk. She slighted me in a thousand ways, yet would never acknowledge herself to be in the wrong. She would drive me mad with anger, and then force me to beg her pardon. Sometimes she fancied that I was not sufficiently submissive, and then she had some story of a rival, favoured by her protectress. She was surrounded by silk-clad youths—the rich and gay—What chance had the sad-robed scholar of Cornelius compared with these?

On one occasion the philosopher made such large demands upon my time that I was unable to meet her as I was wont. He was engaged in some mighty work, and I was forced to remain, day and night, feeding his furnaces and watching his chemical preparations. Bertha waited for me in vain at the fountain. Her haughty spirit fired at this neglect; and when at last I stole out during the few short minutes allotted to me for slumber, and hoped to be consoled by her, she received me with disdain, dismissed me in scorn, and vowed that any man should possess her hand rather than he who could not be in two places at once for her sake. She would be revenged!—And truly she was. In my dingy retreat I heard that she had been hunting, attended by Albert Hoffer. Albert Hoffer was favoured by her protectress, and the three passed in cavalcade before my smoky window. Methought that they mentioned my name—it was followed by a laugh of derision, as her dark eyes glanced contemptuously towards my abode.

Jealousy, with all its venom and all its misery, entered my breast. Now I shed a torrent of tears, to think that I should never call her mine; and, anon, I imprecated a thousand curses on her inconstancy. Yet still I must stir the fires of the alchemist, still attend on the changes of his unintelligible medicines.

Cornelius had watched for three days and nights, nor closed his eyes. The progress of his alembics was slower than he expected: in spite of his anxiety, sleep weighed upon his eyelids. Again and again he threw off drowsiness with more than human energy; again and again it stole away his senses. He eyes his crucibles wistfully. "Not ready yet," he murmured; will another night pass before the work is accomplished? Winzy, you are vigilant—you are faithful—you have slept, my boy—you slept last night. Look at that glass vessel. The liquid it contains is of a soft rose colour: the moment it begins to change its hue, awaken me—till then I may close my eyes. First, it will turn white, and then emit golden flashes: but wait not till then; when the rose-colour fades, rouse me." I scarcely heard the last words muttered as they were in sleep. Even then he did not quite yield to nature. "Winzy, my boy," he again said, "do not touch the vessel—do not put it to your lips; it's a philter—a philter to cure love; you would not cease to love your Bertha—beware to drink!"

And he slept. His venerable head sunk on his breast, and I scarce heard his regular breathing. For a few minutes I watched the vessel—the rosy hue of the liquid remained unchanged. Then my thoughts wandered—they visited the fountain, and dwelt on a thousand charming scenes never to be renewed—never! Serpents and adders were in my heart as the word "Never!" half formed itself on my lips. False girl!—false and cruel! Never more would she smile on me as that evening she smiled on Albert. Worthless, detested woman! I would not remain unrevenged—she should see Albert expire at her feet—she should die beneath my vengeance. She had smiled in disdain and triumph—she knew my wretchedness and her power. Yet what power had she?—the power of exciting my hate—my utter scorn—my—oh, all but indifference. Could I attain that—could I regard her with careless eyes, transferring my *rejected* love to one fairer and more true, that were indeed a victory!

A bright flash darted before my eyes. I had forgotten the medicine of the adept; I gazed on it with wonder: flashes of admirable beauty, more bright than those which the diamond emits when the sun's rays are on it, glanced from the surface of the liquid; an odour the most fragrant and grateful stole over my sense; the vessel seemed one globe of living radiance, lovely to the eye, and most inviting to the taste. The first thought, instinctively inspired by the grosser sense, was, I will—I must drink, I raised the vessel to my lips. "It will cure me of love—of torture!" Already I had quaffed half of the most delicious liquor ever tasted by the palate of man, when the philosopher stirred. I started—I dropped the glass—the fluid flamed and glanced along the floor, while I felt Cornelius's grip at my throat, as he shrieked aloud, "Wretch! you have destroyed the labour of my life!"

The philosopher was totally unaware that I had drunk any portion of his drug. His idea was, and I gave a tacit assent to it, that I had raised the vessel from curiosity, and that, frighted at its brightness, and the flashes of intense light it gave forth, I had let it fall. I never undeceived him. The fire of the medicine was quenched—the fragrance died away—he grew calm, as a philosopher should under the heaviest trials, and dismissed me to rest.

I will not attempt to describe the sleep of glory and bliss which bathed my soul in paradise during the remaining hours of that memorable night. Words would be faint and shallow types of my enjoyment, or of the gladness that possessed my bosom when I woke. I trod air—my thoughts were in heaven. Earth appeared heaven, and my inheritance upon it was to be one trance of delight. "This it is to be cured of love," I thought; "I will see Bertha this day, and she will find her lover cold and regardless; too happy to be disdainful, yet how utterly indifferent to her!"

The hours danced away. The philosopher secure that he had once succeeded, and believing that he might again, began to concoct the same medicine once more. He was shut up with his books and drugs, and I had a holiday. I dressed myself with care; I looked in an old but polished shield, which served me for a mirror; methought my good looks had wonderfully improved. I hurried beyond the precincts of the town, joy in my soul, the beauty of heaven and earth around me. I turned my steps toward the castle—I could look on its lofty turrets with lightness of heart, for I was cured of love. My Bertha saw me afar off, as I came up the avenue. I know not what sudden impulse animated her bosom, but at the sight she sprung with a light fawn-like bound down the marble steps, and was hastening towards me. But I had been perceived by another person. The old high-born hag, who called herself her protectress, and was her tyrant, had seen me also; she hobbled, panting, up the terrace; a page, as ugly as herself, held up her train, and fanned her as she hurried along, and stopped my fair girl with a "How, now, my bold mistress? whither so fast? Back to your cage—hawks are abroad!"

Bertha clasped her hands—her eyes were still bent on my approaching figure. I saw the contest. How I abhorred the old crone who checked the kind impulses of my Bertha's softening heart. Hitherto, respect for her rank had caused me to avoid the lady of the castle; now I disdained such trivial considerations. I was cured of love and lifted above all human fears; I hastened forwards, and soon reached the terrace. How lovely Bertha looked! her eyes flashing fire, her cheeks glowing with impatience and anger, she was a thousand times more graceful and charming than ever—I no longer loved—Oh! no, I adored—worshipped—idolized her!

She had that morning been persecuted, with more than usual vehemence, to consent to an immediate marriage with my rival. She was reproached with the encouragement that she had shown him—she was threatened with being turned out of doors with disgrace and shame. Her proud spirit rose in arms at the threat; but when she remembered the scorn that she had heaped upon me, and how, perhaps, she had thus lost one whom she now regarded as her only friend, she wept with remorse and rage. At that moment I appeared, "O, Winzy!" she exclaimed, "take me to your mother's cot; swiftly let me leave the detested luxuries and wretchedness of this noble dwelling—take me to poverty and happiness."

I clasped her in my arms with transport. The old lady was speechless with fury, and broke forth into invective only when we were fax on our road to my natal cottage. My mother received the fair fugitive, escaped from a gilt cage to nature and liberty, with tenderness and joy; my father, who loved her, welcomed her heartily; it was a day of rejoicing, which did not need the addition of the celestial potion of the alchemist to steep me in delight.

Soon after this eventful day I became the husband of Bertha. I ceased to be the scholar of Cornelius, but I continued his friend. I always felt grateful to him for having, unawares, procured me that delicious draught of a divine elixir, which instead of curing me of love (sad cure! solitary and joyless remedy for evils which seem blessings to the memory), had inspired me with courage and resolution, thus winning for me an inestimable treasure in my Bertha.

I often called to mind that period of trance-like inebriation with wonder. The drink of Cornelius had not fulfilled the task for which he affirmed that it had been prepared, but its effects were more potent and blissful than words can express. They had faded by degrees, yet they lingered long—and painted life in hues of splendour. Bertha often wondered at my lightness of heart and unaccustomed gaiety; for, before, I had been rather serious, or even sad, in my disposition. She loved me the better for my cheerful temper, and our days were winged by joy.

Five years afterwards I was suddenly summoned to the bedside of the dying Cornelius. He had sent for me in haste, conjuring my instant presence. I found him stretched on his pallet, enfeebled even to death; all of life that yet remained animated his piercing eyes, and they were fixed on a glass vessel, full of a roseate liquid.

"Behold," he said, in a broken and inward voice, "the vanity of human wishes! A second time my hopes are about to be crowned, a second time they are destroyed. Look at that liquor—you remember five years ago I had prepared the same, with the same success;—then, as now, my thirsting lips expected to taste the immortal elixir—you dashed it from me! and at present it is too late."

He spoke with difficulty, and fell back on his pillow. I could not help saying—

"How, revered master, can a cure for love restore you to life?"

A faint smile gleamed across his face as I listened earnestly to his scarcely intelligible answer.

"A cure for love and for all things—the Elixir of Immortality. Ah! if now I might drink, I should live for ever!"

As he spoke, a golden flash gleamed from the fluid; a well-remembered fragrance stole over the air; he raised himself, all weak as he was—strength seemed miraculously to re-enter his frame—he stretched forth his hand—a loud explosion startled me—a ray of fire shot up from the elixir, and the glass vessel which contained it was shivered to atoms! I turned my eyes towards the philosopher; he had fallen back—his eyes were glassy—his features rigid—he was dead!

But I lived, and was to live for ever! So said the unfortunate alchemist, and for a few days I believed his words. I remembered the glorious drunkenness that had followed my stolen draught. I reflected on the change I had felt in my frame—in my soul. The bounding elasticity of the one—the buoyant lightness of the other. I surveyed myself in a mirror, and could perceive no change in my features during the space of the five years which had elapsed. I remembered the radiant hues and grateful scent of that delicious beverage—worthy the gift it was capable of bestowing—I was, then, *Immortal!*

A few days after I laughed at my credulity. The old proverb, that "a prophet is least regarded in his own country," was true with respect to me and my defunct master. I loved him as a man—I respected him as a sage—but I derided the notion that he could command the powers of darkness, and laughed at the superstitious fears with which he was regarded by the vulgar. He was a wise philosopher, but had no acquaintance with any spirits but those clad in flesh and blood. His science was simply human; and human science, I persuaded myself, could never conquer nature's laws so far as to imprison the soul for ever within its carnal habitation. Cornelius had brewed a soul-refreshing drink—more inebriating than wine—sweeter and more fragrant than any fruit: it possessed probably strong medicinal powers, imparting gladness to the heart and vigour to the limbs; but its effects would wear out; already were they diminished in my frame. I was a lucky fellow to have quaffed health and joyous spirits, and perhaps long life, at my master's hands; but my good fortune ended there: longevity was far different from immortality.

I continued to entertain this belief for many years. Sometimes a thought stole across me—Was the alchemist indeed deceived? But my habitual credence was, that I should meet the fate of all the children of Adam at my appointed time—a little late, but still at a natural age. Yet it was certain that I retained a wonderfully youthful look. I was laughed at for my vanity in consulting the mirror so often, but I consulted it in vain—my brow was untrenched—my cheeks—my eyes— my whole person continued as untarnished as in my twentieth year.

I was troubled. I looked at the faded beauty of Bertha—I seemed more like her son. By degrees our neighbors began to make similar observations, and I found at last that I went by the name of the scholar bewitched. Bertha herself grew uneasy. She became jealous and peevish, and at length she began to question me. We had no children; we were all in all to each other; and though, as she grew older, her vivacious spirit became a little allied to ill-temper, and her beauty sadly diminished, I cherished her in my heart as the mistress I had idolized, the wife I had sought and won with such perfect love.

At last our situation became intolerable: Bertha was fifty—I twenty years of age. I had in very shame, in some measure adopted the habits of a more advanced age; I no longer mingled in the dance among the young and gay, but my heart bounded along with them while I restrained my feet; and a sorry figure I cut among the Nestors of our village. But before the time I mention things were altered—we were universally shunned; we were—at least, I was—reported to have kept up an iniquitous acquaintance with some of my former master's supposed friends. Poor Bertha was pitied, but deserted. I was regarded with horror and detestation.

What was to be done? We sat by our winter fire—poverty had made itself felt, for none would buy the produce of my farm; and often I had been forced to journey twenty miles, to some place where I was not known, to dispose of our property. It was true we had saved something for an evil day—that day was come.

We sat by our lone fireside—the old-hearted youth and his antiquated wife. Again Bertha insisted on knowing the truth; she recapitulated all she had ever heard said about me, and added her own observations. She conjured me to cast off the spell; she described how much more comely gray hairs were than my chestnut locks; she descanted on the reverence and respect due to age — how preferable to the slight regard paid to mere children: could I imagine that the despicable gifts of youth and good looks outweighed disgrace, hatred, and scorn? Nay, in the end I should be burned as a dealer in the black art, while she, to whom I had not deigned to communicate any portion of my good fortune, might be stoned as my accomplice. At length she insinuated that I must share my secret with her, and bestow on her like benefits to those I myself enjoyed, or she would denounce me — and then she burst into tears.

Thus beset, methought it was the best way to tell the truth I revealed it as tenderly as I could, and spoke only of a *very long life*, not of immortality — which representation, indeed, coincided best with my own ideas. When I ended, I rose and said,

"And now, my Bertha, will you denounce the lover of your youth? — You will not, I know. But it is too hard, my poor wife, that you should suffer from my ill-luck and the accursed arts of Cornelius. I will leave you — you have wealth enough, and friends will return in my absence. I will go; young as I seem, and strong as I am, I can work and gain my bread among strangers, unsuspected and unknown. I loved you in youth; God is my witness that I would not desert you in age, but that your safety and happiness require it."

I took my cap and moved towards the door; in a moment Bertha's arms were round my neck, and her lips were pressed to mine. "No, my husband, my Winzy," she said, "you shall not go alone — take me with you; we will remove from this place, and, as you say, among strangers we shall be unsuspected and safe. I am not so very old as quite to shame you, my Winzy; and I dare say the charm will soon wear off, and, with the blessing of God, you will become more elderly-looking, as is fitting; you shall not leave me."

I returned the good soul's embrace heartily. "I will not, my Bertha, but for your sake, I had not thought of such a thing. I will be your true, faithful husband while you are spared to me, and do my duty by you to the last."

The next day we prepared secretly for our emigration. We were obliged to make great pecuniary sacrifices — it could not be helped. We realized a sum sufficient, at least, to maintain us while Bertha lived; and without saying adieu to any one, quitted our native country to take refuge in a remote part of western France.

It was a cruel thing to transport poor Bertha from her native village, and the friends of her youth, to a new country, new language, new customs. The strange secret of my destiny rendered this removal immaterial to me; but I compassionated her deeply, and was glad to perceive that she found compensation for her misfortunes in a variety of little ridiculous circumstances. Away from all tell-tale chroniclers, she sought to decrease the apparent disparity of our ages by a thousand feminine arts — rouge, youthful dress, and assumed juvenility of manner. I could not be angry — Did not I myself wear a mask? Why quarrel with hers, because it was less successful? I grieved deeply when I remembered that this was my Bertha, whom I had loved so fondly, and won with such transport — the dark-eyed, dark-haired girl, with smiles of enchanting archness and a step like a fawn — this mincing, simpering, jealous old woman. I should have revered her gray locks and withered cheeks; but thus? — It was my work, I knew; but I did not the less deplore this type of human weakness.

Her jealousy never slept. Her chief occupation was to discover that, in spite of outward appearances, I was myself growing old. I verily believed that the poor soul loved me truly in her heart, but never had a woman so tormenting a mode of displaying fondness. She would discern wrinkles in my face and decrepitude in my walk, while I bounded along in youthful vigour, the youngest looking of twenty youths. I never dared address another woman: on one occasion, fancying that the belle of the village regarded me with favouring eyes, she brought me a gray wig. Her constant discourse among her acquaintances was, that though I looked so young, there was ruin at work within my frame; and she affirmed that the worst symptom about me was my apparent health. My youth was a disease, she said, and I ought at all times to prepare for a sudden and awful death, at least to awake some morning white-headed, and bowed down with all the marks of advanced years. I let her talk—I often joined in her conjectures. Her warnings chimed in with my never-ceasing speculations concerning my state, and I took an earnest, though painful, interest in listening to all that her quick wit and excited imagination could say on the subject.

Why dwell on these minute circumstances? We lived on for many long years. Bertha became bed-ridden and paralytic; I nursed her as a mother might a child. She grew peevish, and still harped upon one string—of how long I should survive her. It has ever been a source of consolation to me, that I performed my duty scrupulously towards her. She had been mine in youth, she was mine in age, and at last, when I heaped the sod over her corpse, I wept to feel that I had lost all that really bound me to humanity.

Since then how many have been my cares and woes, how few and empty my enjoyments! I pause here in my history—I will pursue it no further. A sailor without rudder or compass, tossed on a stormy sea— a traveller lost on a wide-spread heath, without land mark or stone to guide him—such have I been: more lost, more hopeless than either. A nearing ship, a gleam from some far cot, may save them; but I have no beacon except the hope of death.

Death! mysterious, ill-visaged friend of weak humanity! Why alone of all mortals have you cast me from your sheltering fold? O, for the peace of the grave! the deep silence of the iron-bound tomb! that thought would cease to work in my brain, and my heart beat no more with emotions varied only by new forms of sadness!

Am I immortal? I return to my first question. In the first place, is it not more probable that the beverage of the alchemist was fraught rather with longevity than eternal life? Such is my hope. And then be it remembered, that I only drank *half* of the potion prepared by him. Was not the whole necessary to complete the charm? To have drained half the Elixir of Immortality is but to be half immortal—my For-ever is thus truncated and null.

But again, who shall number the years of the half of eternity? I often try to imagine by what rule the infinite may be divided. Sometimes I fancy age advancing upon me. One gray hair I have found. Fool! do I lament? Yes, the fear of age and death often creeps coldly into my heart; and the more I live, the more I dread death, even while I abhor life. Such an enigma is man—born to perish—when he wars, as I do, against the established laws of his nature.

But for this anomaly of feeling surely I might die: the medicine of the alchemist would not be proof against fire—sword—and the strangling waters. I have gazed upon the blue depths of many a placid lake, and the tumultuous rushing of many a mighty river, and have said, Peace inhabits those waters; yet I have turned my steps away, to live yet another day. I have asked myself, whether suicide would be a crime in one to whom thus only the portals of the other world could be open. I have done all, except presenting myself as a soldier or duellist, an object of destruction to my—no, *not* my fellow-mortals, and therefore I have shrunk away. They are not my fellows. The inextinguishable power of life in my frame, and their ephemeral existence, places us wide as the poles asunder. I could not raise a hand against the meanest or the most powerful among them.

Thus I have lived on for many a year—alone and weary of myself—desirous of death, yet never dying—a mortal immortal. Neither ambition nor avarice can enter my mind, and the ardent love that gnaws at my heart, never to be returned—never to find an equal on which to expend itself—lives there only to torment me.

This very day I conceived a design by which I may end all—without self-slaughter, without making another man a Cain—an expedition, which mortal frame can never survive, even endued with the youth and strength that inhabits mine. Thus I shall put my immortality to the test, and rest forever—or return, the wonder and benefactor of the human species.

Before I go, a miserable vanity has caused me to pen these pages. I would not die, and leave no name behind. Three centuries have passed since I quaffed the fatal beverage; another year shall not elapse before, encountering gigantic dangers—warring with the powers of frost in their home—beset by famine, toil, and tempest—I yield this body, too tenacious a cage for a soul which thirsts for freedom to the destructive elements of air and water—or, if I survive, my name shall be recorded as one of the most famous among the sons of men; and, my task achieved, I shall adopt more resolute means, and, by scattering and annihilating the atoms that compose my frame set at liberty the life imprisoned within, and so cruelly prevented from soaring from this dim earth to a sphere more congenial to its immortal essence.

 # EDGAR ALLAN POE (1809–1849)

Because of the depth and breadth of his contributions to literary and cultural forms (such as criticism, poetry, and prose) and story genres (such as Dark Fantasy/Horror, Crime/Detective/Mystery Fiction, and Science Fiction), Edgar Allan Poe is probably the most important American author of all time. Though heavily influenced by the existing European tradition of his day (specifically that from England, Germany, and France), Poe served as an important bridge between what had been the world literary canon and what it would be in the new United States republic. Fans and scholars alike have long been able to delineate the archetypal significance and the metaphors of "The Fall of the House of Usher," a narrative that expanded on similar works, such as Horace Walpole's The Castle of Otranto *(1764) and Ann Radcliffe's* The Mysteries of Udolpho *(1794).*

Few stories have been as imitated and have had as much tribute paid to them as has "Usher." Two of the most revered such tributes are Ray Bradbury's "Usher II" from The Martian Chronicles *(1950) (originally published as "Carnival of Madness" in* Thrilling Wonder Stories, *April 1950) and Robert R. McCammon's* Usher's Passing *(1984).*

Haunted houses and related and sundry Gothic structures had served as story conventions long before Poe's day, but never before had these conventions taken on the kind of significance and achieved the literary credibility (in regard to the individual and society, the psyche and larger public mental health) that they did in this Poe tale of people and the dark side.

The Fall of the House of Usher
(Burton's Gentleman's Magazine, *September 1839*)

> Son cœur est un luth suspendu;
> Sitôt qu'on le touche il résonne.
> DE BÉRANGER

During the whole of a dull, dark, and soundless day in the autumn of the year, when the clouds hung oppressively low in the heavens, I had been passing alone, on horseback, through a singularly dreary tract of country; and at length found myself, as the shades of the evening drew on, within view of the melancholy House of Usher. I know not how it was—but, with the first glimpse of the building, a sense of insufferable gloom pervaded my spirit. I say insufferable; for the feeling was unrelieved by any of that half-pleasurable, because poetic, sentiment, with which the mind usually receives even the sternest natural images of the desolate or terrible. I looked upon the scene before me—upon the mere house, and the simple landscape features of the domain—upon the bleak walls—upon the vacant eye-like windows—upon a few rank sedges—and upon a few white trunks of decayed trees—with an utter depression of soul which I can compare to no earthly sensation more properly than to the after-dream of the reveller upon opium—the bitter lapse into everyday life—the hideous dropping off of the veil. There was an iciness, a sinking, a sickening of the heart—an unredeemed dreariness of thought which no goading of the imagination could torture into aught of the sublime. What was it—I paused to think—what was it that so unnerved me in the contemplation of the House of Usher? It was a mystery all insoluble; nor could I grapple with the shadowy fancies that crowded upon me as I pondered. I was forced to fall back upon the unsatisfactory conclusion, that while, beyond doubt, there *are* combinations of very simple natural objects which have the power of thus affecting us, still the analysis of this power lies among considerations beyond our depth. It was possible, I reflected, that a mere different arrangement of the particulars of the scene, of the details of the picture, would be sufficient to modify, or perhaps to annihilate its capacity for sorrowful impression; and, acting upon this idea, I reined my horse to the precipitous brink of a black and lurid tarn that lay in unruffled lustre by the dwelling, and gazed down—but with a shudder even more thrilling than before—upon the remodelled and inverted images of the grey sedge, and the ghastly tree-stems, and the vacant and eye-like windows.

Nevertheless, in this mansion of gloom I now proposed to myself a sojourn of some weeks. Its proprietor, Roderick Usher, had been one of my boon companions in boyhood; but many years had elapsed since our last meeting. A letter, however, had lately reached me in a distant part of the country—a letter from him—which, in its wildly importunate nature, had admitted of no other than a personal reply. The MS. gave evidence of nervous agitation. The writer spoke of acute bodily illness—of a mental disorder which oppressed him—and of an earnest desire to see me, as his best, and indeed his only personal friend, with a view of attempting, by the cheerfulness of my society, some alleviation of his malady. It was the manner in which all this, and much more, was said—it was the apparent *heart* that went with his request—which allowed me no room for hesitation; and I accordingly obeyed forthwith what I still considered a very singular summons.

Although, as boys, we had been even intimate associates, yet I really knew little of my friend. His reserve had been always excessive and habitual. I was aware, however, that his very ancient family had been noted, time out of mind, for a peculiar sensibility of temperament, displaying itself, through long ages, in many works of exalted art, and manifested, of late, in repeated deeds of munificent yet unobtrusive charity, as well as in a passionate devotion to the intricacies, perhaps even more than to the orthodox and easily recognizable beauties, of musical science. I had learned, too, the very remarkable fact, that the stem of the Usher race, all time-honoured as it was, had put forth, at no period, any enduring branch; in other words, that the entire family lay in the direct line of descent, and had always, with very trifling and very temporary variation, so lain. It was this deficiency, I considered, while running over in thought the perfect keeping of the character of the premises with the accredited character of the people, and while speculating upon the possible influence which the one, in the long lapse of centuries, might have exercised upon the other—it was this deficiency, perhaps, of collateral issue, and the consequent undeviating transmission, from sire to son, of the patrimony with the name, which had, at length, so identified the two as to merge the original title of the estate in the quaint and equivocal appellation of the "House of Usher"—an appellation which seemed to include, in the minds of the peasantry who used it, both the family and the family mansion.

I have said that the sole effect of my somewhat childish experiment—that of looking down within the tarn—had been to deepen the first singular impression. There can be no doubt that the consciousness of the rapid increase of my superstition—for why should I not so term it?—served mainly to accelerate the increase itself. Such, I have long known, is the paradoxical law of all sentiments having terror as a basis. And it might have been for this reason only, that, when I again uplifted my eyes to the house itself, from its image in the pool, there grew in my mind a strange fancy—a fancy so ridiculous, indeed, that I but mention it to show the vivid force of the sensations which oppressed me. I had so worked upon my imagination as really to believe that about the whole mansion and domain there hung an atmosphere peculiar to themselves and their immediate vicinity—an atmosphere which had no affinity with the air of heaven, but which had reeked up from the decayed trees, and the grey wall, and the silent tarn—a pestilent and mystic vapour, dull, sluggish, faintly discernible, and leaden-hued.

Shaking off from my spirit what *must* have been a dream, I scanned more narrowly the real aspect of the building. Its principal feature seemed to be that of an excessive antiquity. The discoloration of ages had been great. Minute *fungi* overspread the whole exterior, hanging in a fine tangled web-work from the eaves. Yet all this was apart from any extraordinary dilapidation. No portion of the masonry had fallen; and there appeared to be a wild inconsistency between its still perfect adaptation of parts, and the crumbling condition of the individual stones. In this there was much that reminded me of the specious totality of old woodwork which has rotted for long years in some neglected vault, with no disturbance from the breath of the external air. Beyond this indication of extensive decay, however, the fabric gave little token of instability. Perhaps the eye of a scrutinizing observer might have discovered a barely perceptible fissure, which, extending from the roof of the building in front, made its way down the wall in a zigzag direction, until it became lost in the sullen waters of the tarn.

Noticing these things, I rode over a short causeway to the house. A servant in waiting took my horse, and I entered the Gothic archway of the hall. A valet, of stealthy step, thence conducted me, in silence, through many dark and intricate passages in my progress to the *studio* of his master. Much that I encountered on the way contributed, I know not how, to heighten the vague sentiments of which I have already spoken. While the objects around me—while the carvings of the ceilings, the sombre tapestries of the walls, the ebon blackness of the floors, and the phantasmagoric armorial trophies which rattled as I strode, were but matters to which, or to such as which, I had been accustomed from my infancy—while I hesitated not to acknowledge how familiar was all this—I still wondered to find how unfamiliar were the fancies which ordinary images were stirring up. On one of the staircases, I met the physician of the family. His countenance, I thought, wore a mingled expression of low cunning and perplexity. He accosted me with trepidation and passed on. The valet now threw open a door and ushered me into the presence of his master.

The room in which I found myself was very large and lofty. The windows were long, narrow, and pointed, and at so vast a distance from the black oaken floor as to be altogether inaccessible from within. Feeble gleams of encrimsoned light made their way through the trellised panes, and served to render sufficiently distinct the more prominent objects around; the eye, however, struggled in vain to reach the remoter angles of the chamber, or the recesses of the vaulted and fretted ceiling. Dark draperies hung upon the walls. The general furniture was profuse, comfortless, antique, and tattered. Many books and musical instruments lay scattered about, but failed to give any vitality to the scene. I felt that I breathed an atmosphere of sorrow. An air of stern, deep, and irredeemable gloom hung over and pervaded all.

Upon my entrance, Usher arose from a sofa on which he had been lying at full length, and greeted me with a vivacious warmth which had much in it, I at first thought, of an overdone cordiality—of the constrained effort of the *ennuyé* man of the world. A glance, however, at his countenance, convinced me of his perfect sincerity. We sat down; and for some moments, while he spoke not, I gazed upon him with a feeling half of pity, half of awe. Surely, man had never before so terribly altered, in so brief a period, as had Roderick Usher! It was with difficulty that I could bring myself to admit the identity of the wan being before me with the companion of my early boyhood. Yet the character of his face had been at all times remarkable. A cadaverousness of complexion; an eye large, liquid, and luminous beyond comparison; lips somewhat thin and very pallid, but of a surpassingly beautiful curve; a nose of a delicate Hebrew model, but with a breadth of nostril unusual in similar formations; a finely-moulded chin, speaking, in its want of prominence, of a want of moral energy; hair of a more than web-like softness and tenuity; these features, with an inordinate expansion above the regions of the temple, made up altogether a countenance not easily to be forgotten. And now in the mere exaggeration of the prevailing character of these features, and of the expression they were wont to convey, lay so much of change that I doubted to whom I spoke. The now ghastly pallor of the skin, and the now miraculous lustre of the eye, above all things startled and even awed me. The silken hair, too, had been suffered to grow all unheeded, and as, in its wild gossamer texture, it floated rather than fell about the face, I could not, even with effort, connect its arabesque expression with any idea of simple humanity.

In the manner of my friend I was at once struck with an incoherence—an inconsistency; and I soon found this to arise from a series of feeble and futile struggles to overcome an habitual trepidancy—an excessive nervous agitation. For something of this nature I had indeed been prepared, no less by his letter, than by reminiscences of certain boyish traits, and by conclusions deduced from his peculiar physical conformation and temperament. His action was alternately vivacious and sullen. His voice varied rapidly from a tremulous indecision (when the animal spirits seemed utterly in abeyance) to that species of energetic concision—that abrupt, weighty, unhurried, and hollow-sounding enunciation—that leaden, self-balanced and perfectly modulated guttural utterance, which may be observed in the lost drunkard, or the irreclaimable eater of opium, during the periods of his most intense excitement.

It was thus that he spoke of the object of my visit, of his earnest desire to see me, and of the solace he expected me to afford him. He entered, at some length, into what he conceived to be the nature of his malady. It was, he said, a constitutional and a family evil, and one for which he despaired to find a remedy—a mere nervous affection, he immediately added, which would undoubtedly soon pass off. It displayed itself in a host of unnatural sensations. Some of these, as he detailed them, interested and bewildered me; although, perhaps, the terms, and the general manner of the narration had their weight. He suffered much from a morbid acuteness of the senses; the most insipid food was alone endurable; he could wear only garments of certain texture; the odours of all flowers were oppressive; his eyes were tortured by even a faint light; and there were but peculiar sounds, and these from stringed instruments, which did not inspire him with horror.

To an anomalous species of terror I found him a bounden slave. "I shall perish," said he, "I *must* perish in this deplorable folly. Thus, thus, and not otherwise, shall I be lost. I dread the events of the future, not in themselves, but in their results. I shudder at the thought of any, even the most trivial, incident, which may operate upon this intolerable agitation of soul. I have, indeed, no abhorrence of danger, except in its absolute effect—in terror. In this unnerved—in this pitiable condition—I feel that the period will sooner or later arrive when I must abandon life and reason together, in some struggle with the grim phantasm, FEAR."

I learned, moreover, at intervals, and through broken and equivocal hints, another singular feature of his mental condition. He was enchained by certain superstitious impressions in regard to the dwelling which he tenanted, and whence, for many years, he had never ventured forth—in regard to an influence whose supposititious force was conveyed in terms too shadowy here to be re-stated—an influence which some peculiarities in the mere form and substance of his family mansion, had, by dint of long sufferance, he said, obtained over his spirit—an effect which the *physique* of the grey walls and turrets, and of the dim tarn into which they all looked down, had, at length, brought about upon the *morale* of his existence.

He admitted, however, although with hesitation, that much of the peculiar gloom which thus afflicted him could be traced to a more natural and far more palpable origin—to the severe and long-continued illness—indeed to the evidently approaching dissolution—of a tenderly beloved sister—his sole companion for long years—his last and only relative on earth. "Her decease," he said, with a bitterness which I can never forget "would leave him (him the hopeless and the frail) the last of the ancient race of the Ushers." While he spoke, the Lady Madeline (for so was she called) passed slowly through a remote portion of the apartment, and, without having noticed my presence, disappeared. I regarded her with an utter astonishment not unmingled with dread—and yet I found it impossible to account for such feelings. A sensation of stupor oppressed me, as my eyes followed her retreating steps. When a door, at length, closed upon her, my glance sought instinctively and eagerly the countenance of the brother—but he had buried his face in his hands, and I could only perceive that a far more than ordinary wanness had overspread the emaciated fingers through which trickled many passionate tears.

The disease of the Lady Madeline had long baffled the skill of her physicians. A settled apathy, a gradual wasting away of the person, and frequent although transient affections of a partially cataleptical character, were the unusual diagnosis. Hitherto she had steadily borne up against the pressure of her malady, and had not betaken herself finally to bed; but, on the closing in of the evening of my arrival at the house, she succumbed (as her brother told me at night with inexpressible agitation) to the prostrating power of the destroyer; and I learned that the glimpse I had obtained of her person would thus probably be the last I should obtain—that the lady, at least while living, would be seen by me no more.

For several days ensuing, her name was unmentioned by either Usher or myself: and during this period I was busied in earnest endeavours to alleviate the melancholy of my friend. We painted and read together; or I listened, as if in a dream, to the wild improvisations of his speaking guitar. And thus, as a closer and still closer intimacy admitted me more unreservedly into the recesses of his spirit, the more bitterly did I perceive the futility of all attempt at cheering a mind from which darkness, as if an inherent positive quality, poured forth upon all objects of the moral and physical universe, in one unceasing radiation of gloom.

I shall ever bear about me a memory of the many solemn hours I thus spent alone with the master of the House of Usher. Yet I should fail in any attempt to convey an idea of the exact character of the studies, or of the occupations, in which he involved me, or led me the way. An excited and highly distempered ideality threw a sulphureous lustre over all. His long improvised dirges will ring for ever in my ears. Among other things, I hold painfully in mind a certain singular perversion and amplification of the wild air of the last waltz of Von Weber. From the paintings over which his elaborate fancy brooded, and which grew, touch by touch, into vagueness at which I shuddered the more thrillingly, because I shuddered knowing not why;—from these paintings (vivid as their images now are before me) I would in vain endeavour to educe more than a small portion which should lie within the compass of merely written words. By the utter simplicity, by the nakedness of his designs, he arrested and overawed attention. If ever mortal painted an idea, that mortal was Roderick Usher. For me at least—in the circumstances then surrounding me—there arose out of the pure abstractions which the hypochondriac contrived to throw upon his canvas, an intensity of intolerable awe, no shadow of which felt I ever yet in the contemplation of the certainly glowing yet too concrete reveries of Fuseli.

One of the phantasmagoric conceptions of my friend, partaking not so rigidly of the spirit of abstraction, may be shadowed forth, although feebly, in words. A small picture presented the interior of an immensely long and rectangular vault or tunnel, with low walls, smooth, white, and without interruption or device. Certain accessory points of the design served well to convey the idea that this excavation lay at an exceeding depth below the surface of the earth. No outlet was observed in any portion of its vast extent, and no torch, or other artificial source of light was discernible; yet a flood of intense rays rolled throughout, and bathed the whole in a ghastly and inappropriate splendour.

I have just spoken of that morbid condition of the auditory nerve which rendered all music intolerable to the sufferer, with the exception of certain effects of stringed instruments. It was, perhaps, the narrow limits to which he thus confined himself upon the guitar, which gave birth, in great measure, to the fantastic character of his performances. But the fervid *facility* of his *impromptus* could not be so accounted for. They must have been, and were, in the notes, as well as in the words of his wild fantasias (for he not unfrequently accompanied himself with rhymed verbal improvisation), the result of that intense mental collectedness and concentration to which I have previously alluded as observable only in particular moments of the highest artificial excitement. The words of one of these rhapsodies I have easily remembered. I was, perhaps, the more forcibly impressed with it, as he gave it, because, in the under or mystic current of its meaning, I fancied that I perceived, and for the first time, a full consciousness on the part of Usher, of the tottering of his lofty reason upon her throne. The verses, which were entitled "The Haunted Palace," ran very nearly, if not accurately, thus:

I

In the greenest of our valleys,
   By good angels tenanted,
Once a fair and stately palace—
   Radiant palace—reared its head.
In the monarch Thought's dominion—
   It stood there!
Never seraph spread a pinion
   Over fabric half so fair.

II

Banners yellow, glorious, golden,
   On its roof did float and flow;
(This—all this—was in the olden
   Time long ago)
And every gentle air that dallied,
   In that sweet day,
Along the ramparts plumed and pallid,
   A wingèd odour went away.

III

Wanderers in that happy valley
   Through two luminous windows saw
Spirits moving musically
   To a lute's well tunèd law,
Round about a throne, where sitting
   (Porphyrogene!)

In state his glory well befitting,
    The ruler of the realm was seen.

IV

And all with pearl and ruby glowing
    Was the fair palace door,
Through which came flowing, flowing, flowing
    And sparkling evermore,
A troop of echoes whose sweet duty
    Was but to sing,
In voices of surpassing beauty,
    The wit and wisdom of their king.

V

But evil things, in robes of sorrow,
    Assailed the monarch's high estate;
(Ah, let us mourn, for never morrow
    Shall dawn upon him, desolate!)
And, round about his home, the glory
    That blushed and bloomed
Is but a dim-remembered story
    Of the old time entombed.

VI

And travellers now within that valley,
    Through the red-litten windows, see
Vast forms that move fantastically
    To a discordant melody;
While, like a rapid ghastly river,
    Through the pale door,
A hideous throng rush out forever,
    And laugh—but smile no more.

I well remember that suggestions arising from this ballad led us into a train of thought wherein there became manifest an opinion of Usher's which I mention not so much on account of its novelty (for other men[1] have thought thus), as on account of the pertinacity with which he maintained it. This opinion, in its general form, was that of the sentience of all vegetable things. But, in his disordered fancy, the idea had assumed a more daring character, and trespassed, under certain conditions, upon the kingdom of inorganization. I lack words to express the full extent, or the earnest *abandon* of his persuasion. The belief, however, was connected (as I have previously hinted) with the grey stones of the home of his forefathers. The conditions of the sentience had been here, he imagined, fulfilled in the method of collocation of these stones—in the order of their arrangement, as well as in that of the many *fungi* which overspread them, and of the decayed trees which stood around—above all, in the long undisturbed endurance of this arrangement, and in its reduplication in the still waters of the tarn. Its evidence—

---

[1] Watson, Dr Percival, Spallanzani, and especially the Bishop of Landaff.

the evidence of the sentience—was to be seen, he said (and I here started as he spoke) in the gradual yet certain condensation of an atmosphere of their own about the waters and the walls. The result was discoverable, he added, in that silent, yet importunate and terrible influence which for centuries had moulded the destinies of his family, and which made *him* what I now saw him—what he was. Such opinions need no comment, and I will make none.

Our books—the books which, for years, had formed no small portion of the mental existence of the invalid—were, as might be supposed, in strict keeping with this character of phantasm. We pored together over such works as the *Ververt et Chartreuse* of Gresset; the *Belphegor* of Machiavelli; the *Heaven and Hell* of Swedenborg; the *Subterranean Voyage of Nicholas Klimm* by Holberg; the *Chiromancy* of Robert Flud, of Jean D'Indaginé, and of De la Chambre; the *Journey into the Blue Distance* of Tieck; and the *City of the Sun* of Campanella. One favourite volume was a small octavo edition of the *Directorium Inquisitorum*, by the Dominican Eymeric de Gironne; and there were passages in Pomponius Mela, about the old African Satyrs and Ægipans, over which Usher would sit dreaming for hours. His chief delight, however, was found in the perusal of an exceedingly rare and curious book in quarto Gothic—the manual of a forgotten church—the *Vigilæ Mortuorum secundum Chorum Ecclesiæ Maguntinæ*.

I could not help thinking of the wild ritual of this work, and of its probable influence upon the hypochondriac, when, one evening, having informed me abruptly that the Lady Madeline was no more, he stated his intention of preserving her corpse for a fortnight (previously to its final interment), in one of the numerous vaults within the main walls of the building. The worldly reason, however, assigned for this singular proceeding, was one which I did not feel at liberty to dispute. The brother had been led to his resolution (so he told me) by consideration of the unusual character of the malady of the deceased, of certain obtrusive and eager inquiries on the part of her medical men, and of the remote and exposed situation of the burial ground of the family. I will not deny that when I called to mind the sinister countenance of the person whom I met upon the staircase, on the day of my arrival at the house, I had no desire to oppose what I regarded as at best but a harmless, and by no means an unnatural, precaution.

At the request of Usher, I personally aided him in the arrangements for the temporary entombment. The body having been encoffined, we two alone bore it to its rest. The vault in which we placed it (and which had been so long unopened that our torches, half-smothered in its oppressive atmosphere, gave us little opportunity for investigation) was small, damp, and entirely without means of admission for light; lying, at great depth, immediately beneath that portion of the building in which was my own sleeping apartment. It had been used, apparently, in remote feudal times, for the worst purpose of a donjon-keep, and, in later days, as a place of deposit for powder, or some other highly combustible substance, as a portion of its floor, and the whole interior of a long archway through which we reached it, were carefully sheathed with copper. The door, of massive iron, had been, also, similarly protected. Its immense weight caused an unusually sharp grating sound, as it moved upon its hinges.

Having deposited our mournful burden upon trestles within this region of horror, we partially turned aside the yet unscrewed lid of the coffin, and looked upon the face of the tenant. A striking similitude between the brother and sister now first arrested my attention; and Usher, divining, perhaps, my thoughts, murmured out some few words from which I learned that the deceased and himself had been twins, and that sympathies of a scarcely intelligible nature had always existed between them. Our glances, however, rested not long upon the dead—for we could not regard her unawed. The disease which had thus entombed the lady in the maturity of youth, had left, as usual in all maladies of a strictly cataleptical character, the mockery of a faint blush upon the bosom and the face, and that suspiciously lingering smile upon the lip which is so terrible in death. We replaced and screwed down the lid, and, having secured the door of iron, made our way, with toil, into the scarcely less gloomy apartments of the upper portion of the house.

And now, some days of bitter grief having elapsed, an observable change came over the features of the mental disorder of my friend. His ordinary manner had vanished. His ordinary occupations were neglected or forgotten. He roamed from chamber to chamber with hurried, unequal, and objectless step. The pallor of his countenance had assumed, if possible, a more ghastly hue—but the luminousness of his eye had utterly gone out. The once occasional huskiness of his tone was heard no more; and a tremulous quaver, as if of extreme terror, habitually characterized his utterance. There were times, indeed, when I thought his unceasingly agitated mind was labouring with some oppressive secret, to divulge which he struggled for the necessary courage. At times, again, I was obliged to resolve all into the mere inexplicable vagaries of madness, for I beheld him gazing upon vacancy for long hours, in an attitude of the profoundest attention, as if listening to some imaginary sound. It was no wonder that his condition terrified—that it infected me. I felt creeping upon me, by slow yet certain degrees, the wild influences of his own fantastic yet impressive superstitions.

It was, especially, upon retiring to bed late in the night of the seventh or eighth day after the placing of the Lady Madeline within the donjon, that I experienced the full power of such feelings. Sleep came not near my couch—while the hours waned and waned away. I struggled to reason off the nervousness which had dominion over me. I endeavoured to believe that much, if not all of what I felt, was due to the bewildering influence of the gloomy furniture of the room—of the dark and tattered draperies, which, tortured into motion by the breath of a rising tempest, swayed fitfully to and fro upon the walls, and rustled uneasily about the decorations of the bed. But my efforts were fruitless. An irrepressible tremor gradually pervaded my frame; and, at length, there sat upon my very heart an incubus of utterly causeless alarm. Shaking this off with a gasp and a struggle, I uplifted myself upon the pillows, and, peering earnestly within the intense darkness of the chamber, hearkened—I know not why, except that an instinctive spirit prompted me—to certain low and indefinite sounds which came, through the pauses of the storm, at long intervals, I knew not whence. Overpowered by an intense sentiment of horror, unaccountable yet unendurable, I threw on my clothes with haste (for I felt that I should sleep no more during the night), and endeavoured to arouse myself from the pitiable condition into which I had fallen, by pacing rapidly to and fro through the apartment.

I had taken but few turns in this manner, when a light step on an adjoining staircase arrested my attention. I presently recognized it as that of Usher. In an instant afterward he rapped, with a gentle touch, at my door, and entered, bearing a lamp. His countenance was, as usual, cadaverously wan—but, moreover, there was a species of mad hilarity in his eyes—an evident restrained *hysteria* in his whole demeanour. His air appalled me—but anything was preferable to the solitude which I had so long endured, and I even welcomed his presence as a relief.

"And you have not seen it?" he said abruptly, after having stared about him for some moments in silence — "you have not then seen it? — but, stay! you shall." Thus speaking, and having carefully shaded his lamp, he hurried to one of the casements, and threw it freely open to the storm.

The impetuous fury of the entering gust nearly lifted us from our feet. It was, indeed, a tempestuous yet sternly beautiful night, and one wildly singular in its terror and its beauty. A whirlwind had apparently collected its force in our vicinity; for there were frequent and violent alterations in the direction of the wind; and the exceeding density of the clouds (which hung so low as to press upon the turrets of the house) did not prevent our perceiving the lifelike velocity with which they flew careering from all points against each other, without passing away into the distance. I say that even their exceeding density did not prevent our perceiving this — yet we had no glimpse of the moon or stars — nor was there any flashing forth of the lightning. But the under surfaces of the huge masses of agitated vapour, as well as all terrestrial objects immediately around us, were glowing in the unnatural light of a faintly luminous and distinctly visible gaseous exhalation which hung about and enshrouded the mansion.

"You must not — you shall not behold this!" said I, shudderingly, to Usher, as I led him, with a gentle violence, from the window to a seat. "These appearances, which bewilder you, are merely electrical phenomena not uncommon — or it may be that they have their ghastly origin in the rank miasma of the tarn. Let us close this casement; — the air is chilling and dangerous to your frame. Here is one of your favourite romances. I will read, and you shall listen; — and so we will pass away this terrible night together."

The antique volume which I had taken up was the *Mad Trist* of Sir Launcelot Canning; but I had called it a favourite of Usher's more in sad jest than in earnest; for, in truth, there is little in its uncouth and unimaginative prolixity which could have had interest for the lofty and spiritual ideality of my friend. It was, however, the only book immediately at hand; and I indulged a vague hope that the excitement which now agitated the hypochondriac might find relief (for the history of mental disorder is full of similar anomalies) even in the extremeness of the folly which I should read. Could I have judged, indeed, by the wild overstrained air of vivacity with which he hearkened, or apparently hearkened, to the words of the tale, I might well have congratulated myself upon the success of my design.

I had arrived at that well-known portion of the story where Ethelred, the hero of the Trist, having sought in vain for peaceable admission into the dwelling of the hermit, proceeds to make good an entrance by force. Here, it will be remembered, the words of the narrative run thus:

"And Ethelred, who was by nature of a doughty heart, and who was now mighty withal, on account of the powerfulness of the wine which he had drunken, waited no longer to hold parley with the hermit, who, in sooth, was of an obstinate and maliceful turn, but, feeling the rain upon his shoulders, and fearing the rising of the tempest, uplifted his mace outright, and, with blows, made quickly room in the plankings of the door for his gauntleted hand; and now pulling therewith sturdily, he so cracked, and ripped, and tore all asunder, that the noise of the dry and hollow-sounding wood alarmed and reverberated throughout the forest."

At the termination of this sentence I started, and for a moment, paused; for it appeared to me (although I at once concluded that my excited fancy had deceived me) — it appeared to me that, from some very remote portion of the mansion, there came, indistinctly, to my ears, what might have been, in its exact similarity of character, the echo (but a stifled and dull one certainly) of the very cracking and ripping sound which Sir Launcelot had so particularly described. It was, beyond doubt, the coincidence alone which had arrested my attention; for, amid the rattling of the sashes of the casements, and the ordinary commingled noises of the still increasing storm, the sound, in itself, had nothing, surely, which should have interested or disturbed me. I continued the story:

"But the good champion Ethelred, now entering within the door, was sore enraged and amazed to perceive no signal of the maliceful hermit; but, in the stead thereof, a dragon of a scaly and prodigious demeanour, and of a fiery tongue, which sate in guard before a palace of gold, with a floor of silver; and upon the wall there hung a shield of shining brass with this legend enwritten—

Who entereth herein, a conqueror hath bin;
Who slayeth the dragon, the shield he shall win;

and Ethelred uplifted his mace, and struck upon the head of the dragon, which fell before him, and gave up his pesty breath, with a shriek so horrid and harsh, and withal so piercing, that Ethelred had fain to close his ears with his hands against the dreadful noise of it, the like whereof was never before heard."

Here again I paused abruptly, and now a feeling of wild amazement—for there could be no doubt whatever that, in this instance, I did actually hear (although from what direction it proceeded I found it impossible to say) a low and apparently distant, but harsh, protracted, and most unusual screaming or grating sound—the exact counterpart of what my fancy had already conjured up for the dragon's unnatural shriek as described by the romancer.

Oppressed, as I certainly was, upon the occurrence of the second and most extraordinary coincidence, by a thousand conflicting sensations, in which wonder and extreme terror were predominant, I still retained sufficient presence of mind to avoid exciting, by any observation, the sensitive nervousness of my companion. I was by no means certain that he had noticed the sounds in question; although, assuredly, a strange alteration had, during the last few minutes, taken place in his demeanour. From a position fronting my own, he had gradually brought round his chair, so as to sit with his face to the door of the chamber; and thus I could but partially perceive his features, although I saw that his lips trembled as if he were murmuring inaudibly. His head had dropped upon his breast—yet I knew that he was not asleep, from the wide and rigid opening of the eye as I caught a glance of it in profile. The motion of his body, too, was at variance with this idea—for he rocked from side to side with a gentle yet constant and uniform sway. Having rapidly taken notice of all this, I resumed the narrative of Sir Launcelot, which thus proceeded:

"And now, the champion, having escaped from the terrible fury of the dragon, bethinking himself of the brazen shield, and of the breaking up of the enchantment which was upon it, removed the carcass from out of the way before him, and approached valorously over the silver pavement of the castle to where the shield was upon the wall; which in sooth tarried not for his full coming, but fell down at his feet upon the silver floor, with a mighty great and terrible ringing sound."

No sooner had these syllables passed my lips, than—as if a shield of brass had indeed, at the moment, fallen heavily upon a floor of silver—I became aware of a distinct, hollow, metallic, and clangorous, yet apparently muffled reverberation. Completely unnerved, I leaped to my feet; but the measured rocking movement of Usher was undisturbed. I rushed to the chair in which he sat. His eyes were bent fixedly before him, and throughout his whole countenance there reigned a stony rigidity. But, as I placed my hand upon his shoulder, there came a strong shudder over his whole person; a sickly smile quivered about his lips; and I saw that he spoke in a low, hurried, and gibbering murmur, as if unconscious of my presence. Bending closely over him, I at length drank in the hideous import of his words.

"Not hear it? — yes, I hear it, and *have* heard it. Long — long — long — many minutes, many hours, many days, have I heard it — yet I dared not — oh, pity me, miserable wretch that I am! — I dared not — I *dared* not speak! *We have put her living in the tomb!* Said I not that my senses were acute? I *now* tell you that I heard her first feeble movements in the hollow coffin. I heard them — many, many days ago — yet I dared not — *I dared not speak!* And now — to-night — Ethelred — ha! ha! — the breaking of the hermit's door, and the death-cry of the dragon, and the clangour of the shield! — say, rather, the rending of her coffin, and the grating of the iron hinges of her prison, and her struggles within the coppered archway of the vault! Oh whither shall I fly? Will she not be here anon? Is she not hurrying to upbraid me for my haste? Have I not heard her footstep on the stair? Do I not distinguish that heavy and horrible beating of her heart? MADMAN!" here he sprang furiously to his feet, and shrieked out his syllables, as if in the effort he were giving up his soul — "MADMAN! I TELL YOU THAT SHE NOW STANDS WITHOUT THE DOOR!"

As if in the superhuman energy of his utterance there had been found the potency of a spell — the huge antique panels to which the speaker pointed, threw slowly back, upon the instant, their ponderous and ebony jaws. It was the work of the rushing gust — but then without those doors there DID stand the lofty and enshrouded figure of the Lady Madeline of Usher. There was blood upon her white robes, and the evidence of some bitter struggle upon every portion of her emaciated frame. For a moment she remained trembling and reeling to and fro upon the threshold, then, with a low moaning cry, fell heavily inward upon the person of her brother, and in her violent and now final death-agonies, bore him to the floor a corpse, and a victim to the terrors he had anticipated.

From that chamber, and from that mansion, I fled aghast. The storm was still abroad in all its wrath as I found myself crossing the old causeway. Suddenly there shot along the path a wild light, and I turned to see whence a gleam so unusual could have issued; for the vast house and its shadows were alone behind me. The radiance was that of the full, setting, and blood-red moon which now shone vividly through that once barely discernible fissure of which I have before spoken as extending from the roof of the building, in a zigzag direction, to the base. While I gazed, this fissure rapidly widened — there came a fierce breath of the whirlwind — the entire orb of the satellite burst at once upon my sight — my brain reeled as I saw the mighty walls rushing asunder — there was a long tumultuous shouting sound like the voice of a thousand waters — and the deep and dank tarn at my feet closed sullenly and silently over the fragments of the "HOUSE OF USHER."

SECTION TWO

FANTASY

Virgil Finlay (1914–1971) was a very popular interior and cover illustrator for Fantasy and Science Fiction pulp magazines. Though he did some exquisite paintings, his specialty was black and white line drawings. This Finlay drawing accompanied Abraham Merritt's *The Face in the Abyss* (1923), when the story was reprinted in the pages of the October 1940 issue of *Famous Fantastic Mysteries*.

STORIES OF THE FANTASTIQUE, TALES OF THE QUEST

S TRICTLY SPEAKING, ALL FICTION IS A FORM OF FANTASY. ALSO, with rare exception, themes of fear and impending death and of a quest pervade both Fantasy and Science Fiction. Dark Fantasy emphasizes the themes of horror, fear, and impending death. Often times, the quest in Dark Fantasy is to survive the horror and looming death. High Fantasy emphasizes a moral quest in which "Good" forces are in direct conflict with "Evil" forces. The ultimate goal for Good is to complete the quest and achieve a victory that preserves the state of the known and existing world of the story. Horror and impending death themes are integral in the High Fantasy story, but the moral quest takes center stage.

DARK FANTASY

Edgar Allan Poe, Howard Phillips Lovecraft, and Stephen King—and Traditions Before, Between, and Since

Stories of horror, fear, the unknown, the supernatural, and death assuredly date back as far as does humanity. Sociologists and psychologists tell us that no single human issue—not even sex—dominates our conscious being more than that of mortality and immortality. Dark Fantasy has been perpetuated in the folklore and mass media of the last two centuries.

In terms of straight-out horror stories still read today, the work of Edgar Allan Poe is unparalleled. The ghost stories of Charles Dickens, Elizabeth Gaskell, Joseph Sheridan LeFanu, and others mark the Dark Fantasy of the second half of the nineteenth century. Tales of horror and the supernatural from this period also feature monsters, such as Ambrose Bierce's Damned Thing and Bram Stoker's Dracula. At the turn of the century, William Hope Hodgson reinvigorated and popularized stories of sea monsters.

By the 1920s, pulp magazines specialized in Dark Fantasy stories. Such was the case of the most famous Fantasy magazine of all time—*Weird Tales*. In its pages, Fantasy, Dark Fantasy, and Science Fiction combined, and Howard Phillips Lovecraft quietly became the most important writer of Dark Fantasy since Edgar Allan Poe. Lovecraft was well versed in literary history, and his stories of Fantasy, Dark Fantasy, and Science Fiction inspired his fellow authors and readers alike. Today, Lovecraft is remembered as a master of Supernatural fiction, Dark Fantasy that is more atmospheric than it is gory. Only moderately acclaimed and recognized critically at his death, and almost exclusively an author of ephemeral magazine fiction, H. P. Lovecraft enjoys a substantial legacy and following today. Certainly part of the author's enduring nature is attributable to August Derleth and Donald Wandrei's preservation of his work in the pages of hardcover books published under their Arkham House imprint.

From Howard Phillips Lovecraft's day forward, a range of specialists in Dark Fantasy fiction have emerged. Chief among these are Robert Bloch, Ray Bradbury, Shirley Jackson, and Stephen King. Since Lovecraft's day, as well, popular print and nonprint media, such as motion pictures, radio drama, television, and paperback novels, have carried forth and expanded on the traditions of Dark Fantasy.

During the last three decades of the twentieth century, Stephen King has been recognized as the master teller of Dark Fantasies. King himself, like master writers before him, is a hybrid of traditions and heritages. His strength as a writer is found in his ability to re-present past tales of darkness and dread to unsuspecting contemporary audiences. Make no mistake, however: time will prove Stephen King as significant an author (perhaps in different ways) to the twentieth century as Edgar Allan Poe was to the nineteenth.

NATHANIEL HAWTHORNE (1804–1864)

Considered one of the most important allegorists of the first half of the nineteenth century, Nathaniel Hawthorne incorporated much of his Puritan heritage and fascination with the supernatural into his prose. As was the case with Mary Shelley and Edgar Allan Poe, Hawthorne utilized enthralling storytelling as a vehicle to investigate and comment on the human condition—and some of its baser elements.

Both Puritan heritage and supernatural thematic elements mark "Young Goodman Brown." The story is appropriately deemed Dark Fantasy as it traces the quest of its puritanical title character to that place deep in the metaphoric woods where the revelation of inner self is surprising, ironic, and even logical. Gothic conventions that include dark atmosphere and setting, rigid and frightening character types and stereotypes, and blind religious fervor highlight the narrative.

Part of the romance of Hawthorne's tale is its reflection of early colonial American history; part of its horror is the story's applicability to people and society today. Authors since Nathaniel Hawthorne who have carried forth the story of the quest to a dark inner self include Herman Melville, Charles Dickens, Harriet Beecher Stowe, Louisa May Alcott, Joseph Conrad, Stephen King, and Clive Barker.

Young Goodman Brown
(New England Magazine, *April 1835*)

Young Goodman Brown came forth at sunset into the street of Salem village; but put his head back, after crossing the threshold, to exchange a parting kiss with his young wife. And Faith, as the wife was aptly named, thrust her own pretty head into the street, letting the wind play with the pink ribbons of her cap while she called to Goodman Brown.

"Dearest heart," whispered she, softly and rather sadly, when her lips were close to his ear, "prithee put off your journey until sunrise and sleep in your own bed to-night. A lone woman is troubled with such dreams and such thoughts that she's afeard of herself sometimes. Pray tarry with me this night, dear husband, of all nights in the year."

"My love and my Faith," replied young Goodman Brown, "of all nights in the year, this one night must I tarry away from thee. My journey, as thou callest it, forth and back again, must needs be done 'twixt now and sunrise. What, my sweet, pretty wife, dost thou doubt me already, and we but three months married?"

"Then God bless you!" said Faith, with the pink ribbons; "and may you find all well when you come back."

"Amen!" cried Goodman Brown. "Say thy prayers, dear Faith, and go to bed at dusk, and no harm will come to thee."

So they parted; and the young man pursued his way until, being about to turn the corner by the meeting house, he looked back and saw the head of Faith still peeping after him with a melancholy air, in spite of her pink ribbons.

"Poor little Faith!" thought he, for his heart smote him. "What a wretch am I to leave her on such an errand! She talks of dreams, too. Methought as she spoke there was trouble in her face, as if a dream had warned her what work is to be done to-night. But no, no; 'twould kill her to think it. Well, she's a blessed angel on earth; and after this one night I'll cling to her skirts and follow her to heaven."

With this excellent resolve for the future, Goodman Brown felt himself justified in making more haste on his present evil purpose. He had taken a dreary road, darkened by all the gloomiest trees of the forest, which barely stood aside to let the narrow path creep through, and closed immediately behind. It was all as lonely as could be; and there is this peculiarity in such a solitude, that the traveller knows not who may be concealed by the innumerable trunks and the thick boughs overhead; so that with lonely footsteps he may yet be passing through an unseen multitude.

"There may be a devilish Indian behind every tree," said Goodman Brown to himself; and he glanced fearfully behind him as he added, "What if the devil himself should be at my very elbow!"

His head being turned back, he passed a crook of the road, and, looking forward again, beheld the figure of a man, in grave and decent attire, seated at the foot of an old tree. He arose at Goodman Brown's approach and walked onward side by side with him.

"You are late, Goodman Brown," said he. "The clock of the Old South was striking as I came through Boston; and that is full fifteen minutes agone."

"Faith kept me back a while," replied the young man, with a tremor in his voice, caused by the sudden appearance of his companion, though not wholly unexpected.

It was now deep dusk in the forest, and deepest in that part of it where these two were journeying. As nearly as could be discerned, the second traveller was about fifty years old, apparently in the same rank of life as Goodman Brown, and bearing a considerable resemblance to him, though perhaps more in expression than features. Still they might have been taken for father and son. And yet, though the elder person was as simply clad as the younger and as simple in manner too, he had an indescribable air of one who knew the world, and who would not have felt abashed at the governor's dinner table or in King William's court, were it possible that his affairs should call him thither. But the only thing about him that could be fixed upon as remarkable was his staff, which bore the likeness of a great black snake, so curiously wrought that it might almost be seen to twist and wriggle itself like a living serpent. This, of course, must have been an ocular deception, assisted by the uncertain light.

"Come, Goodman Brown," cried his fellow-traveller, "this is a dull pace for the beginning of a journey. Take my staff, if you are so soon weary."

"Friend," said the other, exchanging his slow pace for a full stop, "having kept covenant by meeting thee here, it is my purpose now to return whence I came. I have scruples touching the matter thou wot'st of."

"Sayest thou so?" replied he of the serpent, smiling apart. "Let us walk on, nevertheless, reasoning as we go; and if I convince thee not thou shalt turn back. We are but a little way in the forest yet."

"Too far! too far!" exclaimed the goodman, unconsciously resuming his walk. "My father never went into the woods on such an errand, nor his father before him. We have been a race of honest men and good Christians since the days of the martyrs; and shall I be the first of the name of Brown that ever took this path and kept—"

"Such company, thou wouldst say," observed the elder person, interpreting his pause. "Well said, Goodman Brown! I have been as well acquainted with your family as with ever a one among the Puritans; and that's no trifle to say. I helped your grandfather, the constable, when he lashed the Quaker woman so smartly through the streets of Salem; and it was I that brought your father a pitch-pine knot, kindled at my own hearth, to set fire to an Indian village, in King Philip's war. They were my good friends, both; and many a pleasant walk have we had along this path, and returned merrily after midnight. I would fain be friends with you for their sake."

"If it be as thou sayest," replied Goodman Brown, "I marvel they never spoke of these matters; or, verily, I marvel not, seeing that the least rumor of the sort would have driven them from New England. We are a people of prayer, and good works to boot, and abide no such wickedness."

"Wickedness or not," said the traveller with the twisted staff, "I have a very general acquaintance here in New England. The deacons of many a church have drunk the communion wine with me; the selectmen of divers towns make me their chairman; and a majority of the Great and General Court are firm supporters of my interest. The governor and I, too—But these are state secrets."

"Can this be so?" cried Goodman Brown, with a stare of amazement at his undisturbed companion. "Howbeit, I have nothing to do with the governor and council; they have their own ways, and are no rule for a simple husbandman like me. But, were I to go on with thee, how should I meet the eye of that good old man, our minister, at Salem village? O, his voice would make me tremble both Sabbath day and lecture day."

Thus far the elder traveller had listened with due gravity; but now burst into a fit of irrepressible mirth, shaking himself so violently that his snakelike staff actually seemed to wriggle in sympathy.

"Ha! ha! ha!" shouted he again and again; then composing himself. "Well, go on, Goodman Brown, go on; but, prithee, don't kill me with laughing."

"Well, then, to end the matter at once," said Goodman Brown, considerably nettled, "there is my wife, Faith. It would break her dear little heart; and I'd rather break my own."

"Nay, if that be the case," answered the other, "e'en go thy ways, Goodman Brown. I would not for twenty old women like the one hobbling before us that Faith should come to any harm."

As he spoke, he pointed his staff at a female figure on the path, in whom Goodman Brown recognized a very pious and exemplary dame, who had taught him his catechism in youth, and was still his moral and spiritual adviser, jointly with the minister and Deacon Gookin.

"A marvel, truly, that Goody Cloyse should be so far in the wilderness at night-fall," said he. "But, with your leave, friend, I shall take a cut through the woods until we have left this Christian woman behind. Being a stranger to you, she might ask whom I was consorting with and whither I was going."

"Be it so," said his fellow-traveller. "Betake you to the woods, and let me keep the path."

Accordingly the young man turned aside, but took care to watch his companion, who advanced softly along the road until he had come within a staff's length of the old dame. She, meanwhile, was making the best of her way, with singular speed for so aged a woman, and mumbling some indistinct words—a prayer, doubtless—as she went. The traveller put forth his staff and touched her withered neck with what seemed the serpent's tail.

"The devil!" screamed the pious old lady.

"Then Goody Cloyse knows her old friend?" observed the traveller, confronting her and leaning on his writhing stick.

"Ah, forsooth, and is it your worship indeed?" cried the good dame. "Yea, truly is it, and in the very image of my old gossip. Goodman Brown, the grandfather of the silly fellow that now is. But—would your worship believe it?—my broomstick hath strangely disappeared, stolen, as I suspect, by that unhanged witch, Goody Cory, and that, too, when I was all anointed with the juice of smallage, and cinquefoil, and wolf's bane—"

"Mingled with fine wheat and the fat of a new-born babe," said the shape of old Goodman Brown.

"Ah, your worship knows the recipe," cried the old lady, cackling aloud. "So, as I was saying, being all ready for the meeting, and no horse to ride on, I made up my mind to foot it; for they tell me there is a nice young man to be taken into communion to-night. But now your good worship will lend me your arm, and we shall be there in a twinkling."

"That can hardly be," answered her friend. "I may not spare you my arm, Goody Cloyse; but here is my staff, if you will."

So saying, he threw it down at her feet, where, perhaps, it assumed life, being one of the rods which its owner had formerly lent to the Egyptian magi. Of this fact, however, Goodman Brown could not take cognizance. He had cast up his eyes in astonishment, and, looking down again, beheld neither Goody Cloyse nor the serpentine staff, but his fellow-traveller alone, who waited for him as calmly as if nothing had happened.

"That old woman taught me my catechism," said the young man; and there was a world of meaning in this simple comment.

They continued to walk onward, while the elder traveller exhorted his companion to make good speed and persevere in the path, discoursing so aptly that his arguments seemed rather to spring up in the bosom of his auditor than to be suggested by himself. As they went, he plucked a branch of maple to serve for a walking stick, and began to strip it of the twigs and little boughs, which were wet with evening dew. The moment his fingers touched them they became strangely withered and dried up as with a week's sunshine. Thus the pair proceeded, at a good free pace, until suddenly, in a gloomy hollow of the road, Goodman Brown sat himself down on the stump of a tree and refused to go any farther.

"Friend," said he, stubbornly, "my mind is made up. Not another step will I budge on this errand. What if a wretched old woman do choose to go to the devil when I thought she was going to heaven: is that any reason why I should quit my dear Faith and go after her?"

"You will think better of this by and by," said his acquaintance, composedly. "Sit here and rest yourself a while; and when you feel like moving again, there is my staff to help you along."

Without more words, he threw his companion the maple stick, and was as speedily out of sight as if he had vanished into the deepening gloom. The young man sat a few moments by the roadside, applauding himself greatly, and thinking with how clear a conscience he should meet the minister in his morning walk, nor shrink from the eye of good old Deacon Gookin. And what calm sleep would be his that very night, which was to have been spent so wickedly, but so purely and sweetly now, in the arms of Faith! Amidst these pleasant and praiseworthy meditations, Goodman Brown heard the tramp of horses along the road, and deemed it advisable to conceal himself within the verge of the forest, conscious of the guilty purpose that had brought him thither, though now so happily turned from it.

On came the hoof tramps and the voices of the riders, two grave old voices, conversing soberly as they drew near. These mingled sounds appeared to pass along the road, within a few yards of the young man's hiding-place; but, owing doubtless to the depth of the gloom at that particular spot, neither the travellers nor their steeds were visible. Though their figures brushed the small boughs by the wayside, it could not be seen that they intercepted, even for a moment, the faint gleam from the strip of bright sky athwart which they must have passed. Goodman Brown alternately crouched and stood on tiptoe, pulling aside the branches and thrusting forth his head as far as he durst without discerning so much as a shadow. It vexed him the more, because he could have sworn, were such a thing possible, that he recognized the voices of the minister and Deacon Gookin, jogging along quietly, as they were wont to do, when bound to some ordination or ecclesiastical council. While yet within hearing, one of the riders stopped to pluck a switch.

"Of the two, reverend sir," said the voice like the deacon's, "I had rather miss an ordination dinner than to-night's meeting. They tell me that some of our community are to be here from Falmouth and beyond, and others from Connecticut and Rhode Island, besides several of the Indian powwows, who, after their fashion, know almost as much deviltry as the best of us. Moreover, there is a goodly young woman to be taken into communion."

"Mighty well, Deacon Gookin!" replied the solemn old tones of the minister. "Spur up, or we shall be late. Nothing can be done, you know, until I get on the ground."

The hoofs clattered again; and the voices, talking so strangely in the empty air, passed on through the forest, where no church had ever been gathered or solitary Christian prayed. Whither, then, could these holy men be journeying so deep into the heathen wilderness? Young Goodman Brown caught hold of a tree for support, being ready to sink down on the ground, faint and overburdened with the heavy sickness of his heart. He looked up to the sky, doubting whether there really was a heaven above him. Yet there was the blue arch, and the stars brightening in it.

"With heaven above and Faith below, I will yet stand firm against the devil!" cried Goodman Brown.

While he still gazed upward into the deep arch of the firmament and had lifted his hands to pray, a cloud, though no wind was stirring, hurried across the zenith and hid the brightening stars. The blue sky was still visible except directly overhead, where this black mass of cloud was sweeping swiftly northward. Aloft in the air, as if from the depths of the cloud, came a confused and doubtful sound of voices. Once the listener fancied that he could distinguish the accents of townspeople of his own, men and women, both pious and ungodly, many of whom he had met at the communion table, and had seen others rioting at the tavern. The next moment, so indistinct were the sounds, he doubted whether he had heard aught but the murmur of the old forest, whispering without a wind. Then came a stronger swell of those familiar tones, heard daily in the sunshine at Salem village, but never until now from a cloud of night. There was one voice, of a young woman, uttering lamentations, yet with an uncertain sorrow, and entreating for some favor, which, perhaps, it would grieve her to obtain; and all the unseen multitude, both saints and sinners, seemed to encourage her onward.

"Faith!" shouted Goodman Brown, in a voice of agony and desperation; and the echoes of the forest mocked him, crying, "Faith! Faith!" as if bewildered wretches were seeking her all through the wilderness.

The cry of grief, rage, and terror was yet piercing the night, when the unhappy husband held his breath for a response. There was a scream, drowned immediately in a louder murmur of voices, fading into far-off laughter, as the dark cloud swept away, leaving the clear and silent sky above Goodman Brown. But something fluttered lightly down through the air and caught on the branch of a tree. The young man seized it, and beheld a pink ribbon.

"My Faith is gone!" cried he, after one stupefied moment. "There is no good on earth; and sin is but a name. Come, devil; for to thee is this world given."

And, maddened with despair, so that he laughed loud and long, did Goodman Brown grasp his staff and set forth again, at such a rate that he seemed to fly along the forest path rather than to walk or run. The road grew wilder and drearier and more faintly traced, and vanished at length, leaving him in the heart of the dark wilderness, still rushing onward with the instinct that guides mortal man to evil. The whole forest was peopled with frightful sounds—the creaking of the trees, the howling of wild beasts, and the yell of Indians; while sometimes the wind tolled like a distant church bell, and sometimes gave a broad roar around the traveller, as if all Nature were laughing him to scorn. But he was himself the chief horror of the scene, and shrank not from its other horrors.

"Ha! ha! ha!" roared Goodman Brown when the wind laughed at him. "Let us hear which will laugh loudest. Think not to frighten me with your deviltry. Come witch, come wizard, come Indian powwow, come devil himself, and here comes Goodman Brown. You may as well fear him as he fear you."

In truth, all through the haunted forest there could be nothing more frightful than the figure of Goodman Brown. On he flew among the black pines, brandishing his staff with frenzied gestures, now giving vent to an inspiration of horrid blasphemy, and now shouting forth such laughter as set all the echoes of the forest laughing like demons around him. The fiend in his own shape is less hideous than when he rages in the breast of man. Thus sped the demoniac on his course, until, quivering among the trees, he saw a red light before him, as when the felled trunks and branches of a clearing have been set on fire, and throw up their lurid blaze against the sky, at the hour of midnight. He paused, in a lull of the tempest that had driven him onward, and heard the swell of what seemed a hymn, rolling solemnly from a distance with the weight of many voices. He knew the tune; it was a familiar one in the choir of the village meeting house. The verse died heavily away, and was lengthened by a chorus, not of human voices, but of all the sounds of the benighted wilderness pealing in awful harmony together. Goodman Brown cried out; and his cry was lost to his own ear by its unison with the cry of the desert.

In the interval of silence he stole forward until the light glared full upon his eyes. At one extremity of an open space, hemmed in by the dark wall of the forest, arose a rock, bearing some rude, natural resemblance either to an altar or a pulpit, and surrounded by four blazing pines, their tops aflame, their stems untouched, like candles at an evening meeting. The mass of foliage that had overgrown the summit of the rock was all on fire, blazing high into the night and fitfully illuminating the whole field. Each pendent twig and leafy festoon was in a blaze. As the red light arose and fell, a numerous congregation alternately shone forth, then disappeared in shadow, and again grew, as it were, out of the darkness, peopling the heart of the solitary woods at once.

"A grave and dark-clad company," quoth Goodman Brown.

In truth they were such. Among them, quivering to and fro between gloom and splendor, appeared faces that would be seen next day at the council board of the province, and others which, Sabbath after Sabbath, looked devoutly heavenward, and benignantly over the crowded pews, from the holiest pulpits in the land. Some affirm that the lady of the governor was there. At least there were high dames well known to her, and wives of honored husbands, and widows, a great multitude, and ancient maidens, all of excellent repute, and fair young girls, who trembled lest their mothers should espy them. Either the sudden gleams of light flashing over the obscure field bedazzled Goodman Brown, or he recognized a score of the church members of Salem village famous for their especial sanctity. Good old Deacon Gookin had arrived, and waited at the skirts of that venerable saint, his revered pastor. But, irreverently consorting with these grave, reputable, and pious people, these elders of the church, these chaste dames and dewy virgins, there were men of dissolute lives and women of spotted fame, wretches given over to all mean and filthy vice, and suspected even of horrid crimes. It was strange to see that the good shrank not from the wicked, nor were the sinners abashed by the saints. Scattered also among their pale-faced enemies were the Indian priests, or powwows, who had often scared their native forest with more hideous incantations than any known to English witchcraft.

"But where is Faith?" thought Goodman Brown, and, as hope came into his heart, he trembled.

Another verse of the hymn arose, a slow and mournful strain, such as the pious love, but joined to words which expressed all that our nature can conceive of sin, and darkly hinted at far more. Unfathomable to mere mortals is the lore of fiends. Verse after verse was sung; and still the chorus of the desert swelled between like the deepest tone of a mighty organ; and with the final peal of that dreadful anthem there came a sound, as if the roaring wind, the rushing streams, the howling beasts, and every other voice of the unconverted wilderness was mingling and according with the voice of guilty man in homage to the prince of all. The four blazing pines threw up a loftier flame, and obscurely discovered shapes and visages of horror on the smoke wreaths above the impious assembly. At the same moment the fire on the rock shot redly forth and formed a glowing arch above its base, where now appeared a figure. With reverence be it spoken, the figure bore no slight similitude, both in garb and manner, to some grave divine of the New England churches.

"Bring forth the converts!" cried a voice that echoed through the field and rolled into the forest.

At the word, Goodman Brown stepped forth from the shadow of the trees and approached the congregation, with whom he felt a loathful brotherhood by the sympathy of all that was wicked in his heart. He could have well nigh sworn that the shape of his own dead father beckoned him to advance, looking downward from a smoke wreath, while a woman, with dim features of despair, threw out her hand to warn him back. Was it his mother? But he had no power to retreat one step, nor to resist, even in thought, when the minister and good old Deacon Gookin seized his arms and led him to the blazing rock. Thither came also the slender form of a veiled female, led between Goody Cloyse, that pious teacher of the catechism, and Martha Carrier, who had received the devil's promise to be queen of hell. A rampant hag was she. And there stood the proselytes beneath the canopy of fire.

"Welcome, my children," said the dark figure, "to the communion of your race. Ye have found thus young your nature and your destiny. My children, look behind you!"

They turned; and flashing forth, as it were, in a sheet of flame, the fiend worshippers were seen; the smile of welcome gleamed darkly on every visage.

"There," resumed the sable form, "are all whom ye have reverenced from youth. Ye deemed them holier than yourselves, and shrank from your own sin, contrasting it with their lives of righteousness and prayerful aspirations heavenward. Yet here are they all in my worshipping assembly. This night it shall be granted you to know their secret deeds; how hoary-bearded elders of the church have whispered wanton words to the young maids of their households; how many a woman, eager for widow's weeds, has given her husband a drink at bedtime and let him sleep his last sleep in her bosom; how beardless youths have made haste to inherit their fathers' wealth; and how fair damsels—blush not, sweet ones—have dug little graves in the garden, and bidden me, the sole guest, to an infant's funeral. By the sympathy of your human hearts for sin ye shall scent out all the places—whether in church, bed chamber, street, field, or forest—where crime has been committed, and shall exult to behold the whole earth one stain of guilt, one mighty blood spot. Far more than this. It shall be yours to penetrate, in every bosom, the deep mystery of sin, the fountain of all wicked arts, and which inexhaustibly supplies more evil impulses than human power—than my power at its utmost—can make manifest in deeds. And now, my children, look upon each other."

They did so; and, by the blaze of the hell-kindled torches, the wretched man beheld his Faith, and the wife her husband, trembling before that unhallowed altar.

"Lo, there ye stand, my children," said the figure, in a deep and solemn tone, almost sad with its despairing awfulness, as if his once angelic nature could yet mourn for our miserable race. "Depending upon one another's hearts, ye had still hoped that virtue were not all a dream. Now are ye undeceived. Evil is the nature of mankind. Evil must be your only happiness. Welcome again, my children, to the communion of your race."

"Welcome," repeated the fiend worshippers, in one cry of despair and triumph.

And there they stood, the only pair, as it seemed, who were yet hesitating on the verge of wickedness in this dark world. A basin was hollowed, naturally, in the rock. Did it contain water, reddened by the lurid light? or was it blood? or, perchance, a liquid flame? Herein did the shape of evil dip his hand and prepare to lay the mark of baptism upon their foreheads, that they might be partakers of the mystery of sin, more conscious of the secret guilt of others, both in deed and thought, than they could now be of their own. The husband cast one look at his pale wife, and Faith at him. What polluted wretches would the next glance show them to each other, shuddering alike at what they disclosed and what they saw!

"Faith! Faith!" cried the husband, "look up to heaven, and resist the wicked one."

Whether Faith obeyed, he knew not. Hardly had he spoken when he found himself amid calm night and solitude, listening to a roar of the wind which died heavily away through the forest. He staggered against the rock, and felt it chill and damp; while a hanging twig, that had been all on fire, besprinkled his cheek with the coldest dew.

The next morning young Goodman Brown came slowly into the street of Salem village, staring around him like a bewildered man. The good old minister was taking a walk along the graveyard to get an appetite for breakfast and meditate his sermon, and bestowed a blessing, as he passed, on Goodman Brown. He shrank from the venerable saint as if to avoid an anathema. Old Deacon Gookin was at domestic worship, and the holy words of his prayer were heard through the open window. "What God doth the wizard pray to?" quoth Goodman Brown. Goody Cloyse, that excellent old Christian, stood in the early sunshine at her own lattice, catechizing a little girl who had brought her a pint of morning's milk. Goodman Brown snatched away the child as from the grasp of the fiend himself. Turning the corner by the meeting house, he spied the head of Faith, with the pink ribbons, gazing anxiously forth, and bursting into such joy at sight of him that she skipped along the street and almost kissed her husband before the whole village. But Goodman Brown looked sternly and sadly into her face, and passed on without a greeting.

Had Goodman Brown fallen asleep in the forest and only dreamed a wild dream of a witch meeting?

Be it so, if you will; but, alas! it was a dream of evil omen for young Goodman Brown. A stern, a sad, a darkly meditative, a distrustful, if not a desperate, man did he become from the night of that fearful dream. On the Sabbath day, when the congregation were singing a holy psalm, he could not listen, because an anthem of sin rushed loudly upon his ear and drowned all the blessed strain. When the minister spoke from the pulpit, with power and fervid eloquence and with his hand on the open Bible, of the sacred truths of our religion, and of saintlike lives and triumphant deaths, and of future bliss or misery unutterable, then did Goodman Brown turn pale, dreading lest the roof should thunder down upon the gray blasphemer and his hearers. Often, awaking suddenly at midnight, he shrank from the bosom of Faith; and at morning or eventide, when the family knelt down at prayer, he scowled, and muttered to himself, and gazed sternly at his wife, and turned away. And when he had lived long, and was borne to his grave, a hoary corpse, followed by Faith, an aged woman, and children and grandchildren, a goodly procession, besides neighbors not a few, they carved no hopeful verse upon his tombstone; for his dying hour was gloom.

 ELIZABETH (CLEGHORN) GASKELL (1810–1865)

An important social historian of Victorian times, England's Elizabeth Gaskell is still revered today for her portrayals of industrial city life and rural life of the period, her true-to-life stories of the emotional and social troubles of nineteenth-century women, and her biography of her friend and contemporary Charlotte Brontë. Though her writing was often compared to that of Jane Austen, Gaskell's writing shared more than passing similarity to that of her American counterpart Nathaniel Hawthorne. Similar cultures and shared personal experiences often lead to similar cultural products—music, art, and writing included.

It is also perhaps more than coincidence that Gaskell flourished in the time of Dickens, the great social critic and founder of Household Words. *However, it is important to note that Gaskell provided us with some uniquely female perspectives on the same general topics found in Dickens's writing. She was a counterpart to, not a shadow of, the great man.*

"The Old Nurse's Story" is a classic Victorian ghost story that is told in the form of reminiscence by the tale's main character. Though clearly a period piece, the story maintains its veracity and reader interest to this day. In terms of literary history, it set the stage for some of the later writing of Dickens, Louisa May Alcott, Henry James, M. R. James, Algernon Blackwood, and others.

The Old Nurse's Story
(Household Words, *Christmas Number, 1852*)

You know, my dears, that your mother was an orphan, and an only child; and I dare say you have heard that your grandfather was a clergyman up in Westmoreland, where I come from. I was just a girl in the village school, when, one day, your grandmother came in to ask the mistress if there was any scholar there who would do for a nurse-maid; and mighty proud I was, I can tell ye, when the mistress called me up, and spoke to my being a good girl at my needle, and a steady honest girl, and one whose parents were very respectable, though they might be poor. I thought I should like nothing better than to serve the pretty young lady, who was blushing as deep as I was, as she spoke of the coming baby, and what I should have to do with it. However, I see you don't care so much for this part of my story, as for what you think is to come, so I'll tell you at once. I was engaged and settled at the parsonage before Miss Rosamond (that was the baby, who is now your mother) was born. To be sure, I had little enough to do with her when she came, for she was never out of her mother's arms, and slept by her all night long; and proud enough was I sometimes when missis trusted her to me. There never was such a baby before or since, though you've all of you been fine enough in your turns; but for sweet, winning ways, you've none of you come up to your mother. She took after her mother, who was a real lady born; a Miss Furnivall, a granddaughter of Lord Furnivall's, in Northumberland. I believe she had neither brother nor sister, and had been brought up in my lord's family till she had married your grandfather, who was just a curate, son to a shopkeeper in Carlisle—but a clever, fine gentleman as ever was—and one who was as a right-down hard worker in his parish, which was very wide, and scattered all abroad over the Westmoreland Fells. When your mother, little Miss Rosamond, was about four or five years old, both her parents died in a fortnight—one after the other. Ah! that was a sad time. My pretty young mistress and me was looking for another baby, when my master came home from one of his long rides, wet, and tired, and took the fever he died of; and then she never held up her head again, but just lived to see her dead baby, and have it laid on her breast before she sighed away her life. My mistress had asked me, on her death-bed, never to leave Miss Rosamond; but if she had never spoken a word, I would have gone with the little child to the end of the the world.

The next thing, and before we had well stilled our sobs, the executors and guardians came to settle the affairs. They were my poor young mistress's own cousin, Lord Furnivall, and Mr. Esthwaite, my master's brother, a shopkeeper in Manchester; not so well-to-do then as he was afterwards, and with a large family rising about him. Well! I don't know if it were their settling, or because of a letter my mistress wrote on her death-bed to her cousin, my lord; but somehow it was settled that Miss Rosamond and me were to go to Furnivall Manor House, in Northumberland, and my lord spoke as if it had been her mother's wish that she should live with his family, and as if he had no objections, for that one or two more or less could make no difference in so grand a household. So, though that was not the way in which I should have wished the coming of my bright and pretty pet to have been looked at—who was like a sunbeam in any family, be it never so grand—I was well pleased that all the folks in the Dale should stare and admire, when they heard I was as going to be young lady's maid at my Lord Furnivall's at Furnivall Manor.

But I made a mistake in thinking we were to go and live where my lord did. It turned out that the family had left Furnivall Manor House fifty years or more. I could not hear that my poor young mistress had ever been there, though she had been brought up in the family; and I was sorry for that, for I should have liked Miss Rosamond's youth to have passed where her mother's had been.

My lord's gentleman, from whom I asked as many questions as I durst, said that the Manor House was at the foot of the Cumberland Fells, and a very grand place; that an old Miss Furnivall, a great-aunt of my lord's, lived there, with only a few servants; but that it was a very healthy place, and my lord had thought that it would suit Miss Rosamond very well for a few years, and that her being there might perhaps amuse his old aunt.

I was bidden by my lord to have Miss Rosamond's things ready by a certain day. He was a stern proud man, as they say all the Lords Furnivall were; and he never spoke a word more than was necessary. Folk did say he had loved my young mistress; but that, because she knew that his father would object, she would never listen to him, and married Mr. Esthwaite; but I don't know. He never married at any rate. But he never took much notice of Miss Rosamond; which I thought he might have done if he had cared for her dead mother. He sent his gentleman with us to the

Manor House, telling him to join him at Newcastle that same evening; so there was no great length of time for him to make us known to all the strangers before he, too, shook us off; and we were left, two lonely young things (I was not eighteen), in the great old Manor House. It seems like yesterday that we drove there. We had left our own dear parsonage very early, and we had both cried as if our hearts would break, though we were travelling in my lord's carriage, which I thought so much of once. And now it was long past noon on a September day, and we stopped to change horses for the last time at a little smoky town, all full of colliers and miners. Miss Rosamond had fallen asleep, but Mr. Henry told me to waken her, that she might see the park and the Manor House as we drove up. I thought it rather a pity; but I did what he bade me, for fear he should complain of me to my lord. We had left all signs of a town, or even a village, and were then inside the gates of a large wild park—not like the parks here in the south, but with rocks, and the noise of running water, and gnarled thorn-trees, and old oaks, all white and peeled with age.

The road went up about two miles, and then we saw a great and stately house, with many trees close around it, so close that in some places their branches dragged against the walls when the wind blew; and some hung broken down; for no one seemed to take much charge of the place;—to lop the wood, or to keep the moss-covered carriage-way in order. Only in front of the house all was clear. The great oval drive was without a weed; and neither tree nor creeper was allowed to grow over the long, many-windowed front; at both sides of which a wing projected, which were each the ends of other side fronts; for the house, although it was so desolate, was even grander than I expected. Behind it rose the Fells, which seemed unenclosed and bare enough; and on the left hand of the house, as you stood facing it, was a little, old-fashioned flower-garden, as I found out afterwards. A door opened out upon it from the west front; it had been scooped out of the thick dark wood for some old Lady Furnivall; but the branches of the great forest trees had grown and overshadowed it again, and there were very few flowers that would live there at that time.

When we drove up to the great front entrance, and went into the hall I thought we should be lost—it was so large, and vast, and grand. There was a chandelier all of bronze, hung down from the middle of the ceiling; and I had never seen one before, and looked at it all in amaze. Then, at one end of the hall, was a great fire-place, as large as the sides of the houses in my country, with massy andirons and dogs to hold the wood; and by it were heavy old-fashioned sofas. At the opposite end of the hall, to the left as you went in—on the western side—was an organ built into the wall, and so large that it filled up the best part of that end. Beyond it, on the same side, was a door; and opposite, on each side of the fire-place, were also doors leading to the east front; but those I never went through as long as I stayed in the house, so I can't tell you what lay beyond.

The afternoon was closing in, and the hall, which had no fire lighted in it, looked dark and gloomy, but we did not stay there a moment. The old servant, who had opened the door for us, bowed to Mr. Henry, and took us in through the door at the further side of the great organ, and led us through several smaller halls and passages into the west drawing-room, where he said that Miss Furnivall was sitting. Poor little Miss Rosamond held very tight to me, as if she were scared and lost in that great place, and as for myself, I was not much better. The west drawing-room was very cheerful-looking, with a warm fire in it, and plenty of good, comfortable furniture about. Miss Furnivall was an old lady not far from eighty, I should think, but I do not know. She was thin and tall, and had a face as full of fine wrinkles as if they had been drawn all over it with a needle's point. Her eyes were very watchful, to make up, I suppose, for her being so deaf as to be obliged to use a trumpet. Sitting with her, working at the same great piece of tapestry, was Mrs. Stark, her maid and companion, and almost as old as she was. She had lived with Miss Furnivall ever since they both were young, and now she seemed more like a friend than a servant; she looked so cold and grey, and stony, as if she had never loved or cared for any one; and I don't suppose she did care for any one, except her mistress; and, owing to the great deafness of the latter, Mrs. Stark treated her very much as if she were a child. Mr. Henry gave some message from my lord, and then he bowed good-bye to us all,—taking no notice of my sweet little Miss Rosamond's outstretched hand—and left us standing there, being looked at by the two old ladies through their spectacles.

I was right glad when they rung for the old footman who had shown us in at first, and told him to take us to our rooms. So we went out of that great drawing-room, and into another sitting-room, and out of that, and then up a great flight of stairs, and along a broad gallery—which was something like a library, having books all down one side, and windows and writing-tables all down the other—till we came to our rooms, which I was not sorry to hear were just over the kitchens; for I began to think I should be lost in that wilderness of a house. There was an old nursery, that had been used for all the little lords and ladies long ago, with a pleasant fire burning in the grate, and the kettle boiling on the hob, and tea-things spread out on the table; and out of that room was the night-nursery, with a little crib for Miss Rosamond close to my bed. And old James called up Dorothy, his wife, to bid us welcome; and both he and she were so hospitable and kind, that by and by Miss Rosamond and me felt quite at home; and by the time tea was over, she was sitting on Dorothy's knee, and chattering away as fast as her little tongue could go. I soon found out that Dorothy was from Westmoreland, and that bound her and me together, as it were; and I would never wish to meet with kinder people than were old James and his wife. James had lived pretty nearly all his life in my lord's family, and thought there was no one so grand as they. He even looked down a little on his wife; because, till he had married her, she had never lived in any but a farmer's household. But he was very fond of her, as well he might be. They had one servant under them, to do all the rough work. Agnes they called her; and she and me, and James and Dorothy, with Miss Furnivall and Mrs. Stark, made up the family; always remembering my sweet little Miss Rosamond! I used to wonder what they had done before she came, they thought so much of her now. Kitchen and drawing-room, it was all the same. The hard, sad Miss Furnivall, and the cold Mrs. Stark, looked pleased when she came fluttering in like a bird, playing and pranking hither and thither, with a continual murmur, and pretty prattle of gladness. I am sure, they were sorry many a time when she flitted away into the kitchen, though they were too proud to ask her to stay with them, and were a little surprised at her taste; though to be sure, as Mrs. Stark said, it was not to be wondered at, remembering what stock her father had come of. The great, old rambling house was a famous place for little Miss Rosamond. She made expeditions all over it, with me at her heels; all, except the east wing, which was never opened, and whither we never thought of going. But in the western and northern part was many a pleasant room; full of things that were curiosities to us, though they might not have been to people who had seen more. The windows were darkened by the sweeping boughs of the trees, and the ivy which had overgrown them: but, in the green gloom, we could manage to see old China jars and carved ivory boxes, and great heavy books, and, above all, the old pictures!

Once, I remember, my darling would have Dorothy go with us to tell us who they all were; for they were all portraits of some of my lord's family, though Dorothy could not tell us the names of every one. We had gone through most of the rooms, when we came to the old state drawing-room over the hall, and there was a picture of Miss Furnivall; or, as she was called in those days, Miss Grace, for she was the younger sister. Such a beauty she must have been! but with such a set, proud look, and such scorn looking out of her handsome eyes, with her eyebrows just a little raised, as if she wondered how any one could have the impertinence to look at her; and her lip curled at us, as we stood there gazing. She had a dress on, the like of which I had never seen before, but it was all the fashion when she was young: a hat of some soft white stuff like beaver, pulled a little over her brows, and a beautiful plume of feathers sweeping round it on one side; and her gown of blue satin was open in front to a quilted white stomacher.

"Well, to be sure!" said I, when I had gazed my fill. "Flesh is grass, they do say; but who would have thought that Miss Furnivall had been such an out-and-out beauty, to see her now?"

"Yes," said Dorothy. "Folks change sadly. But if what my master's father used to say was true, Miss Furnivall, the elder sister, was handsomer than Miss Grace. Her picture is here somewhere; but, if I show it you, you must never let on, even to James, that you have seen it. Can the little lady hold her tongue, think you?" asked she.

I was not so sure, for she was such a little sweet, bold, open-spoken child, so I set her to hide herself; and then I helped Dorothy to turn a great picture, that leaned with its face towards the wall, and was not hung up as the others were. To be sure, it beat Miss Grace for beauty; and, I think, for scornful pride, too, though in that matter it might be hard to choose. I could have looked at it an hour, but Dorothy seemed half frightened at having shown it to me, and hurried it back again, and bade me run and find Miss Rosamond, for that there were some ugly places about the house, where she should like ill for the child to go. I was a brave, high-spirited girl, and thought little of what the old woman said, for I liked hide-and-seek as well as any child in the parish; so off I ran to find my little one.

As winter drew on, and the days grew shorter, I was sometimes almost certain that I heard a noise as if some one was playing on the great organ in the hall. I did not hear it every evening; but, certainly, I did very often; usually when I was sitting with Miss Rosamond, after I had put her to bed, and keeping quite still and silent in the bedroom. Then I used to hear it booming and swelling away in the distance. The first night, when I went down to my supper, I asked Dorothy who had been playing music, and James said very shortly that I was a gowk to take the wind sough-ing among the trees for music: but I saw Dorothy look at him very fearfully, and Bessy, the kitchen-maid, said something beneath her breath, and went quite white. I saw they did not like my question, so I held my peace till I was with Dorothy alone, when I knew I could get a good deal out of her. So, the next day, I watched my time, and I coaxed and asked her who it was that played the organ; for I knew that it was the organ and not the wind well enough, for all I had kept silence before James. But Dorothy had had her lesson, I'll warrant, and never a word could I get from her. So then I tried Bessy, though I had always held my head rather above her, as I was evened to James and Dorothy, and she was little better than their servant. So she said I must never, never tell; and if I ever told, I was never to say *she* had told me; but it was a very strange noise, and she had heard it many a time, but most of all on win-ter nights, and before storms; and folks did say, it was the old lord playing on the great organ in the hall, just as he used to do when he was alive; but who the old lord was, or why he played, and why he played on stormy winter evenings in particular, she either could not or would not tell me. Well! I told you I had a brave heart; and I thought it was rather pleasant to have that grand music rolling about the house, let who would be the player; for now it rose above the great gusts of wind, and wailed and triumphed just like a living creature, and then it fell to a softness most complete; only it was always music, and tunes, so it was nonsense to call it the wind. I thought at first that it might be Miss Furnivall who played, unknown to Bessy; but, one day when I was in the hall by myself, I opened the organ and peeped all about it and around it, as I had done to the organ in Crosthwaite Church once before, and I saw it was all broken and destroyed inside, though it looked so brave and fine; and then, though it was noonday, my flesh began to creep a little, and I shut it up, and run away pretty quickly to my own bright nursery; and I did not like hearing the music for some time after that, any more than James and Dorothy did. All this time Miss Rosamond was making herself more and more beloved. The old ladies liked her to dine with them at their early dinner; James stood behind Miss Furnivall's chair, and I behind Miss Rosamond's all in state; and, after dinner, she would play about in a corner of the great drawing-room, as still as any mouse, while Miss Furnivall slept, and I had my dinner in the kitchen. But she was glad enough to come to me in the nursery afterwards; for, as she said, Miss Furnivall was so sad, and Mrs. Stark so dull; but she and I were merry enough; and, by-and-by, I got not to care for that weird rolling music, which did one no harm, if we did not know where it came from.

That winter was very cold. In the middle of October the frosts began, and lasted many, many weeks. I remember, one day at dinner, Miss Furnivall lifted up her sad, heavy eyes, and said to Mrs. Stark, "I am afraid we shall have a terrible winter," in a strange kind of meaning way. But Mrs. Stark pretended not to hear, and talked very loud of something else. My little lady and I did not care for the frost; not we! As long as it was dry we climbed up the steep brows, behind the house, and went up on the Fells, which were bleak, and bare enough, and there we ran races in the fresh, sharp air; and once we came down by a new path that took us past the two old gnarled holly-trees, which grew about halfway down by the east side of the house. But the days grew shorter and shorter; and the old lord, if it was he, played away more and more stormily and sadly on the great organ. One Sunday afternoon,—it must have been towards the end of November—I asked Dorothy to take charge of little Missey when she came out of the drawing-room, after Miss Furnivall had had her nap; for it was too cold to take her with me to church, and yet I wanted to go. And Dorothy was glad enough to promise, and was so fond of the child that all seemed well; and Bessy and I set off very briskly, though the sky hung heavy and black over the white earth, as if the night had never fully gone away; and the air, though still, was very biting and keen.

"We shall have a fall of snow," said Bessy to me. And sure enough, even while we were in church, it came down thick, in great large flakes, so thick it almost darkened the windows. It had stopped snowing before we came out, but it lay soft, thick and deep beneath our feet, as we tramped home. Before we got to the hall the moon rose, and I think it was lighter then,—what with the moon, and what with the white dazzling snow—than it had been when we went to church, between two and three o'clock. I have not told you that Miss Furnivall and Mrs. Stark never went to church: they used to read the prayers together, in their quiet gloomy way; they seemed to feel the Sunday very long without their tapestry-work to be busy at. So when I went to Dorothy in the kitchen, to fetch Miss Rosamond and take her up-stairs with me, I did not much wonder when the old woman told me that the ladies had kept the child with them, and that she had never come to the kitchen, as I had bidden her, when she was tired of behaving pretty in the drawing-room. So I took off my things and went to find her, and bring her to her supper in the nursery. But when I went into the best drawing-room, there sat the two old ladies, very still and quiet, dropping out a word now and then, but looking as if nothing so bright and merry as Miss Rosamond had ever been near them. Still I thought she might be hiding from me; it was one of her pretty ways; and that she had persuaded them to look as if they knew nothing about her; so I went softly peeping under this sofa, and behind that chair, making believe I was sadly frightened at not finding her.

"What's the matter, Hester?" said Mrs. Stark, sharply. I don't know if Miss Furnivall had seen me, for, as I told you, she was very deaf, and she sat quite still, idly staring into the fire, with her hopeless face. "I'm only looking for my little Rosy-Posy," replied I, still thinking that the child was there, and near me, though I could not see her.

"Miss Rosamond is not here," said Mrs. Stark. "She went away more than an hour ago to find Dorothy." And she too turned and went on looking into the fire.

My heart sank at this, and I began to wish I had never left my darling. I went back to Dorothy and told her. James was gone out for the day, but she and me and Bessy took lights and went up into the nursery first, and then we roamed over the great large house, calling and entreating Miss Rosamond to come out of her hiding-place, and not frighten us to death in that way. But there was no answer; no sound.

"Oh!" said I at last, "Can she have got into the east wing and hidden there?"

But Dorothy said it was not possible, for that she herself had never been in there; that the doors were always locked, and my lord's steward had the keys, she believed; at any rate, neither she nor James had ever seen them: so I said I would go back, and see if, after all, she was not hidden in the drawing-room, unknown to the old ladies; and if I found her there, I said, I would whip her well for the fright she had given me; but I never meant to do it. Well, I went back to the west drawing-room, and I told Mrs. Stark we could not find her anywhere, and asked for leave to look all about the furniture there, for I thought now, that she might have fallen asleep in some warm hidden corner; but no! we looked, Miss Furnivall got up and looked, trembling all over, and she was nowhere there; then we set off again, every one in the house, and looked in all the places we had searched before, but we could not find her. Miss Furnivall shivered and shook so much, that Mrs. Stark took her back into the warm drawing-room; but not before they had made me promise to bring her to them when she was found. Well-a-day! I began to think she never would be found, when I bethought me to look out into the great front court, all covered with snow. I was upstairs when I looked out; but, it was such clear moonlight, I could see, quite plain, two little footprints, which might be traced from the hall door, and round the corner of the east wing. I don't know how I got down, but I tugged open the great, stiff hall door; and, throwing the skirt of my gown over my head for a cloak, I ran out. I turned the east corner, and there a black shadow fell on the snow; but when I came again into the moonlight, there were the little footmarks going up—up to the Fells. It was bitter cold; so cold that the air almost took the skin off my face as I ran, but I ran on, crying to think how my poor little darling must be perished, and frightened. I was within sight of the holly-trees when I saw a shepherd coming down the hill, bearing something in his arms wrapped in his maud. He shouted to me, and asked me if I had lost a bairn; and, when I could not speak for crying, he bore towards me, and I saw my wee bairnie lying still, and white, and stiff, in his arms, as if she had been dead. He told me he had been up the Fells to gather in his sheep, before the deep cold of night came on, and that under the holly-trees (black marks on the hillside, where no other bush was for miles around) he had found my little lady—my lamb—my queen—my darling—stiff and cold, in the terrible sleep which is frost-begotten. Oh! the joy, and the tears of having her in my arms once again! for I would not let him carry her; but took her, maud and all, into my own arms, and held her near my own warm neck and heart, and felt the life stealing slowly back again into her little gentle limbs. But she was still insensible when we reached the hall, and I had no breath for speech. We went in by the kitchen door.

"Bring the warming-pan," said I; and I carried her upstairs and began undressing her by the nursery fire, which Bessy had kept up. I called my little lammie all the sweet and playful names I could think of,—even while my eyes were blinded by my tears; and at last, oh! at length she opened her large blue eyes. Then I put her into her warm bed, and sent Dorothy down to tell Miss Furnivall that all was well; and I made up my mind to sit by my darling's bedside the live-long night. She fell away into a soft sleep as soon as her pretty head had touched the pillow, and I watched by her till morning light; when she wakened up bright and clear—or so I thought at first—and, my dears, so I think now.

She said that she had fancied that she should like to go to Dorothy, for that both the old ladies were asleep, and it was very dull in the drawing-room; and that, as she was going through the west lobby, she saw the snow through the high window falling—falling—soft and steady, but she wanted to see it lying pretty and white on the ground; so she made her way into the great hall; and then, going to the window, she saw it bright and soft upon the drive; but while she stood there, she saw a little girl, not so old as she was, "but so pretty," said my darling, "and this little girl beckoned to me to come out; and oh, she was so pretty and so sweet, I could not choose but go." And then this other little girl had taken her by the hand, and side by side the two had gone round the east corner.

"Now you are a naughty little girl, and telling stories," said I. "What would your good mamma, that is in heaven, and never told a story in her life, say to her little Rosamond, if she heard her—and I dare say she does—telling stories!"

"Indeed, Hester," sobbed out my child, "I'm telling you true. Indeed I am."

"Don't tell me!" said I, very stern. "I tracked you by your footmarks through the snow; there were only yours to be seen: and if you had had a little girl to go hand-in-hand with you up the hill, don't you think the footprints would have gone along with yours?"

"I can't help it, dear, dear Hester," said she, crying, "if they did not; I never looked at her feet, but she held my hand fast and tight in her little one, and it was very, very cold. She took me up the Fell-path, up to the holly trees; and there I saw a lady weeping and crying; but when she saw me, she hushed her weeping, and smiled very proud and grand, and took me on her knee, and began to lull me to sleep; and that's all, Hester—but that is true; and my dear mamma knows it is," said she, crying. So I thought the child was in a fever, and pretended to believe her, as she went over her story—over and over again, and always the same. At last Dorothy knocked at the door with Miss Rosamond's breakfast; and she told me the old ladies were down in the eating parlour, and that they wanted to speak to me. They had both been into the night-nursery the evening before, but it was after Miss Rosamond was asleep; so they had only looked at her—not asked me any questions.

"I shall catch it," thought I to myself, as I went along the north gallery. "And yet," I thought, taking courage, "it was in their charge I left her; and it's they that's to blame for letting her steal away unknown and unwatched." So I went in boldly, and told my story. I told it all to Miss Furnivall, shouting it close to her ear; but when I came to the mention of the other little girl out in the snow, coaxing and tempting her out, and wiling her up to the grand and beautiful lady by the holly-tree, she threw her arms up—her old and withered arms—and cried aloud, "Oh! Heaven, forgive! Have mercy!"

Mrs. Stark took hold of her; roughly enough, I thought; but she was past Mrs. Stark's management, and spoke to me, in a kind of wild warning and authority.

"Hester! keep her from that child! It will lure her to her death! That evil child! Tell her it is a wicked, naughty child." Then Mrs. Stark hurried me out of the room; where, indeed, I was glad enough to go; but Miss Furnivall kept shrieking out, "Oh! have mercy! Wilt Thou never forgive! It is many a long year ago"——

I was very uneasy in my mind after that. I durst never leave Miss Rosamond, night or day, for fear lest she might slip off again, after some fancy or other; and all the more, because I thought I could make out that Miss Furnivall was crazy, from the odd ways about her; and I was afraid lest something of the same kind (which might be in the family, you know) hung over my darling. And the great frost never ceased all this time; and, whenever it was a more stormy night than usual, between the gusts, and through the wind, we heard the old lord playing on the great organ. But, old lord, or not, wherever Miss Rosamond went, there I followed; for my love for her, pretty helpless orphan, was stronger than my fear for the grand and terrible sound. Besides, it rested with me to keep her cheerful and merry, as beseemed her age. So we played together, and wandered together, here and there, and everywhere; for I never dared to lose sight of her again in that large and rambling house. And so it happened, that one afternoon, not long before Christmas Day, we were playing together on the billiard-table in the great hall (not that we knew the right way of playing, but she liked to roll the smooth ivory balls with her pretty hands, and I liked to do whatever she did); and, by-and-by, without our noticing it, it grew dusk indoors, though it was still light in the open air, and I was thinking of taking her back into the nursery, when, all of a sudden, she cried out:

"Look, Hester! look! there is my poor little girl out in the snow!"

I turned towards the long narrow windows, and there, sure enough, I saw a little girl, less than my Miss Rosamond—dressed all unfit to be out-of-doors such a bitter night—crying, and beating against the window-panes, as if she wanted to be let in. She seemed to sob and wail, till Miss Rosamond could bear it no longer, and was flying to the door to open it, when, all of a sudden, and close upon us, the great organ pealed out so loud and thundering, it fairly made me tremble; and all the more, when I remembered me that, even in the stillness of that dead-cold weather, I had heard no sound of little battering hands upon the window-glass, although the Phantom Child had seemed to put forth all its force; and, although I had seen it wail and cry, no faintest touch of sound had fallen upon my ears. Whether I remembered all this at the very moment, I do not know; the great organ sound had so stunned me into terror; but this I know, I caught up Miss Rosamond before she got the hall-door opened, and clutched her, and carried her away, kicking and screaming, into the large bright kitchen, where Dorothy and Agnes were busy with their mince-pies.

"What is the matter with my sweet one?" cried Dorothy, as I bore in Miss Rosamond, who was sobbing as if her heart would break.

"She won't let me open the door for my little girl to come in; and she'll die if she is out on the Fells all night. Cruel, naughty Hester," she said, slapping me; but she might have struck harder, for I had seen a look of ghastly terror on Dorothy's face, which made my very blood run cold.

"Shut the back-kitchen door fast, and bolt it well," said she to Agnes. She said no more; she gave me raisins and almonds to quiet Miss Rosamond: but she sobbed about the little girl in the snow, and would not touch any of the good things. I was thankful when she cried herself to sleep in bed. Then I stole down to the kitchen, and told Dorothy I had made up my mind. I would carry my darling back to my father's house in Applethwaite; where, if we lived humbly, we lived at peace. I said I had been frightened enough with the old lord's organ-playing; but now, that I had seen for myself this little moaning child, all decked out as no child in the neighbourhood could be, beating and battering to get in, yet always without any sound or noise—with the dark wound on its right shoulder; and that Miss Rosamond had known it again for the phantom that had nearly lured her to her death (which Dorothy knew was true); I would stand it no longer.

I saw Dorothy change colour once or twice. When I had done, she told me she did not think I could take Miss Rosamond with me, for that she was my lord's ward, and I had no right over her; and she asked me, would I leave the child that I was so fond of, just for sounds and sights that could do me no harm; and that they had all had to get used to in their turns? I was all in a hot, trembling passion; and I said it was very well for her to talk, that knew what these sights and noises betokened, and that had, perhaps, had something to do with the Spectre-Child while it was alive. And I taunted her so, that she told me all she knew, at last; and then I wished I had never been told, for it only made me more afraid than ever.

She said she had heard the tale from old neighbours, that were alive when she was first married; when folks used to come to the hall sometimes, before it had got such a bad name on the country side: it might not be true, or it might, what she had been told.

The old lord was Miss Furnivall's father—Miss Grace, as Dorothy called her, for Miss Maude was the elder, and Miss Furnivall by rights. The old lord was eaten up with pride. Such a proud man was never seen or heard of; and his daughters were like him. No one was good enough to wed them, although they had choice enough; for they were the great beauties of their day, as I had seen by their portraits, where they hung in the state drawing-room. But, as the old saying is, "Pride will have a fall;" and these two haughty beauties fell in love with the same man, and he no better than a foreign musician, whom their father had down from London to play music with him at the Manor House. For, above all things, next to his pride, the old lord loved music. He could play on nearly every instrument that ever was heard of: and it was a strange thing it did not soften him; but he was a fierce dour old man, and had broken his poor wife's heart with his cruelty, they said. He was mad after music, and would pay any money for it. So he got this foreigner to come; who made such beautiful music, that they said the very birds on the trees stopped their singing to listen. And, by degrees, this foreign gentleman got such a hold over the old lord, that nothing would serve him but that he must come every year; and it was he that had the great organ brought from Holland, and built up in the hall, where it stood now. He taught the old lord to play on it; but many and many a time, when Lord Furnivall was thinking of nothing but his fine organ, and his finer music, the dark foreigner was walking abroad in the woods with one of the young ladies; now Miss Maude, and then Miss Grace.

Miss Maude won the day and carried off the prize, such as it was; and he and she were married, all unknown to any one; and before he made his next yearly visit, she had been confined of a little girl at a farm-house on the Moors, while her father and Miss Grace thought she was away at Doncaster Races. But though she was a wife and a mother, she was not a bit softened, but as haughty and as passionate as ever; and perhaps more so, for she was jealous of Miss Grace, to whom her foreign husband paid a deal of court—by way of blinding her—as he told his wife. But Miss Grace triumphed over Miss Maude, and Miss Maude grew fiercer and fiercer, both with her husband and with her sister; and the former—who could easily shake off what was disagreeable, and hide himself in foreign countries—went away a month before his usual time that summer, and half-threatened that he would never come back again. Meanwhile, the little girl was left at the farm-house, and her mother used to have her horse saddled and gallop wildly over the hills to see her once every week, at the very least—for where she loved, she loved; and where she hated, she hated. And the old lord went on playing—playing on his organ; and the servants thought the sweet music he made had soothed down his awful temper, of which (Dorothy said) some terrible tales could be told. He grew infirm too, and had to walk with a crutch; and his son—that was the present Lord Furnivall's father—was with the army in America, and the other son at sea; so Miss Maude had it pretty much her own way, and she and Miss Grace grew colder and bitterer to each other every day; till at last they hardly ever spoke, except when the old lord was by. The foreign musician came again the next summer, but it was for the last time; for they led him such a life with their jealousy and their passions, that he grew weary, and went away, and never was heard of again. And Miss Maude, who had always meant to have her marriage acknowledged when her father should be dead, was left now a deserted wife—whom nobody knew to have been married—with a child that she dared not own, although she loved it to distraction; living with a father whom she feared, and a sister whom she hated. When the next summer passed over and the dark foreigner never came, both Miss Maude and Miss Grace grew gloomy and sad; they had a haggard look about them, though they looked handsome as ever. But by-and-by Miss Maude brightened; for her father grew more and more infirm, and more than ever carried away by his music; and she and Miss Grace lived almost entirely apart, having separate rooms, the one on the west side, Miss Maude on the east—those very rooms which were now shut up. So she thought she might have her little girl with her, and no one need ever know except those who dared not speak about it, and were bound to believe that it was, as she said, a cottager's child she had taken a fancy to. All this, Dorothy said, was pretty well known; but what came afterwards no one knew, except Miss Grace, and Mrs. Stark, who was even then her maid, and much more of a friend to her than ever her sister had been. But the servants supposed, from words that were dropped, that Miss Maude had triumphed over Miss Grace, and told her that all the time the dark foreigner had been mocking her with pretended love—he was her own husband; the colour left Miss Grace's cheek and lips that very day for ever, and she was heard to say many a time that sooner or later she would have her revenge; and Mrs. Stark was for ever spying about the east rooms.

One fearful night, just after the New Year had come in, when the snow was lying thick and deep, and the flakes were still falling—fast enough to blind any one who might be out and abroad—there was a great and violent noise heard, and the old lord's voice above all, cursing and swearing awfully,—and the cries of a little child,—and the proud defiance of a fierce woman,—and the sound of a blow,—and a dead stillness,—and moans and wailings dying away on the hill-side! Then the old lord summoned all his servants, and told them, with terrible oaths, and words more terrible, that his daughter had disgraced herself, and that he had turned her out of doors,—her, and her child,—and that if ever they gave her help,—or food,—or shelter,—he prayed that they might never enter Heaven. And, all the while, Miss Grace stood by him, white and still as any stone; and when he had ended she heaved a great sigh, as much as to say her work was done, and her end was accomplished. But the old lord never touched his organ again, and died within the year; and no wonder! for, on the morrow of that wild and fearful night, the shepherds, coming down the Fell side, found Miss Maude sitting, all crazy and smiling, under the holly-trees, nursing a dead child,—with a terrible mark on its right shoulder. "But that was not what killed it," said

Dorothy;, "it was the frost and the cold; — every wild creature was in its hole, and every beast in its fold, — while the child and its mother were turned out to wander on the Fells! And now you know all! and I wonder if you are less frightened now?"

I was more frightened than ever; but I said I was not. I wished Miss Rosamond and myself well out of that dreadful house for ever; but I would not leave her, and I dared not take her away. But oh! how I watched her, and guarded her! We bolted the doors, and shut the window-shutters fast, an hour or more before dark, rather than leave them open five minutes too late. But my little lady still heard the weird child crying and mourning; and not all we could do or say could keep her from wanting to go to her, and let her in from the cruel wind and the snow. All this time, I kept away from Miss Furnivall and Mrs. Stark, as much as ever I could; for I feared them — I knew no good could be about them, with their grey hard faces, and their dreamy eyes, looking back into the ghastly years that were gone. But, even in my fear, I had a kind of pity — for Miss Furnivall, at least. Those gone down to the pit can hardly have a more hopeless look than that which was ever on her face. At last I even got so sorry for her — who never said a word but what was quite forced from her — that I prayed for her; and I taught Miss Rosamond to pray for one who had done a deadly sin; but often when she came to those words, she would listen, and start up from her knees, and say, "I hear my little girl plaining and crying very sad — Oh! let her in, or she will die!"

One night — just after New Year's Day had come at last, and the long winter had taken a turn, as I hoped — I heard the west drawing-room bell ring three times, which was the signal for me. I would not leave Miss Rosamond alone, for all she was asleep — for the old lord had been playing wilder than ever — and I feared lest my darling should waken to hear the spectre child; see her I knew she could not. I had fastened the windows too well for that. So I took her out of her bed and wrapped her up in such outer clothes as were most handy, and carried her down to the drawing-room, where the old ladies sat at their tapestry work as usual. They looked up when I came in, and Mrs. Stark asked, quite astounded, "Why did I bring Miss Rosamond there, out of her warm bed?" I had begun to whisper, "Because I was afraid of her being tempted out while I was away, by the wild child in the snow," when she stopped me short (with a glance at Miss Furnivall), and said Miss Furnivall wanted me to undo some work she had done wrong, and which neither of them could see to unpick. So I laid my pretty dear on the sofa, and sat down on a stool by them, and hardened my heart against them, as I heard the wind rising and howling.

Miss Rosamond slept on sound, for all the wind blew so; and Miss Furnivall said never a word, nor looked round when the gusts shook the windows. All at once she started up to her full height, and put up one hand, as if to bid us listen.

"I hear voices!" said she. "I hear terrible screams — I hear my father's voice!"

Just at that moment my darling wakened with a sudden start: "My little girl is crying, oh, how she is crying!" and she tried to get up and go to her, but she got her feet entangled in the blanket, and I caught her up; for my flesh had begun to creep at these noises, which they heard while we could catch no sound. In a minute or two the noises came, and gathered fast, and filled our ears; we, too, heard voices and screams, and no longer heard the winter's wind that raged abroad. Mrs. Stark looked at me, and I at her, but we dared not speak. Suddenly Miss Furnivall went towards the door, out into the ante-room, through the west lobby, and opened the door into the great hall. Mrs. Stark followed, and I durst not be left, though my heart almost stopped beating for fear. I wrapped my darling tight in my arms, and went out with them. In the hall the screams were louder than ever; they sounded to come from the east wing—nearer and nearer—close on the other side of the locked-up doors—close behind them. Then I noticed that the great bronze chandelier seemed all alight, though the hall was dim, and that a fire was blazing in the vast hearth-place, though it gave no heat; and I shuddered up with terror, and folded my darling closer to me. But as I did so, the east door shook, and she, suddenly struggling to get free from me, cried, "Hester! I must go! My little girl is there; I hear her; she is coming! Hester, I must go!"

I held her tight with all my strength; with a set will, I held her. If I had died, my hands would have grasped her still, I was so resolved in my mind. Miss Furnivall stood listening, and paid no regard to my darling, who had got down to the ground, and whom I, upon my knees now, was holding with both my arms clasped round her neck; she still striving and crying to get free.

All at once the east door gave way with a thundering crash, as if torn open in a violent passion, and there came into that broad and mysterious light, the figure of a tall old man, with grey hair and gleaming eyes. He drove before him, with many a relentless gesture of abhorrence, a stern and beautiful woman, with a little child clinging to her dress.

"O Hester! Hester!" cried Miss Rosamond. "It's the lady! the lady below the holly-trees; and my little girl is with her. Hester! Hester! let me go to her; they are drawing me to them. I feel them—I feel them. I must go!"

Again she was almost convulsed by her efforts to get away; but I held her tighter and tighter, till I feared I should do her a hurt; but rather that than let her go towards those terrible phantoms. They passed along towards the great hall-door, where the winds howled and ravened for their prey; but before they reached that, the lady turned; and I could see that she defied the old man with a fierce and proud defiance; but then she quailed—and then she threw up her arms wildly and piteously to save her child—her little child—from a blow from his uplifted crutch.

And Miss Rosamond was torn as by a power stronger than mine, and writhed in my arms, and sobbed (for by this time the poor darling was growing faint).

"They want me to go with them on to the Fells—they are drawing me to them. Oh, my little girl! I would come, but cruel, wicked Hester holds me very tight." But when she saw the uplifted crutch she swooned away, and I thanked God for it. Just at this moment—when the tall old man, his hair streaming as in the blast of a furnace, was going to strike the little shrinking child—Miss Furnivall, the old woman by my side, cried out, "Oh, father! father! spare the little innocent child!" But just then I saw—we all saw—another phantom shape itself, and grow clear out of the blue and misty light that filled the hall; we had not seen her till now, for it was another lady who stood by the old man, with a look of relentless hate and triumphant scorn. That figure was very beautiful to look upon, with a soft white hat drawn down over the proud brows, and a red and curling lip. It was dressed in an open robe of blue satin. I had seen that figure before. It was the likeness of Miss Furnivall in her youth; and the terrible phantoms moved on, regardless of old Miss Furnivall's wild entreaty,—and the uplifted crutch fell on the right shoulder of the little child, and the younger sister looked on, stony and deadly serene. But at that moment, the dim lights, and the fire that gave no heat, went out of themselves, and Miss Furnivall lay at our feet stricken down by the palsy—death-stricken.

Yes! she was carried to her bed that night never to rise again. She lay with her face to the wall, muttering low but muttering alway: "Alas! alas! what is done in youth can never be undone in age! What is done in youth can never be undone in age!"

✸ CHARLES (JOHN HUFFAM) DICKENS (1812–1870)

Internationally renowned social critic of his day, prolific magazine wordsmith, expert at maximizing monies made from sales of writing, and pioneer of copyright law, Charles Dickens is also remembered for his popular Gothic/Victorian ghost stories.

"No. 1 Branch Line: The Signalman," like the most successful ghost stories (ghost stories being some of the hardest prose to write convincingly and credibly), provides rich atmosphere and creates genuine suspense. The romance of the railroad holds to this day.

An extensive number of noteworthy authors have been influenced by Charles Dickens, but those who worked in the Dickensian ghost story tradition include Joseph Sheridan LeFanu, Robert Louis Stevenson, M. R. James, H. G. Wells, and more recently, James P. Blaylock and Tim Powers. Two famous twentieth-century railroad ghost stories that pay homage to "No. 1 Branch Line: The Signalman" are Carl Jacobi's "Phantom Brass" (Railroad Stories, August 1934) and Robert Bloch's "That Hell-Bound Train" (The Magazine of Fantasy and Science Fiction, September 1958).

No. 1 Branch Line: The Signalman
(Mugby Junction: The Extra Christmas Number of All the Year Round, *1866*)

'Halloa! Below there!'

When he heard a voice thus calling to him, he was standing at the door of his box, with a flag in his hand, furled round its short pole. One would have thought, considering the nature of the ground, that he could not have doubted from what quarter the voice came; but, instead of looking up to where I stood on the top of the steep cutting nearly over his head, he turned himself about and looked down the Line. There was something remarkable in his manner of doing so, though I could not have said, for my life, what. But, I know it was remarkable enough to attract my notice, even though his figure was foreshortened and shadowed, down in the deep trench, and mine was high above him, so steeped in the glow of an angry sunset that I had shaded my eyes with my hand before I saw him at all.

'Halloa! Below!'

From looking down the Line, he turned himself about again, and, raising his eyes, saw my figure high above him.

'Is there any path by which I can come down and speak to you?'

He looked up at me without replying, and I looked down at him without pressing him too soon with a repetition of my idle question. Just then, there came a vague vibration in the earth and air, quickly changing into a violent pulsation, and an oncoming rush that caused me to start back, as though it had force to draw me down. When such vapour as rose to my height from this rapid train had passed me and was skimming away over the landscape, I looked down again, and saw him refurling the flag he had shown while the train went by.

I repeated my enquiry. After a pause, during which he seemed to regard me with fixed attention, he motioned with his rolled-up flag towards a point on my level, some two or three hundred yards distant. I called down to him, 'All right!' and made for that point. There, by dint of looking closely about me, I found a rough zigzag descending path notched out: which I followed.

The cutting was extremely deep, and unusually precipitate. It was made through a clammy stone that became oozier and wetter as I went down. For these reasons, I found the way long enough to give me time to recall a singular air of reluctance or compulsion with which he had pointed out the path.

When I came down low enough upon the zigzag descent, to see him again, I saw that he was standing between the rails on the way by which the train had lately passed, in an attitude as if he were waiting for me to appear. He had his left hand at his chin, and that left elbow rested on his right hand crossed over his breast. His attitude was one of such expectation and watchfulness, that I stopped a moment, wondering at it.

I resumed my downward way, and, stepping out upon the level of the railroad and drawing nearer to him, saw that he was a dark sallow man, with a dark beard and rather heavy eyebrows. His post was in as solitary and dismal a place as ever I saw. On either side, a dripping wet wall of jagged stone, excluding all view but a strip of sky; the perspective one way, only a crooked prolongation of this great dungeon; the shorter perspective in the other direction, terminating in a gloomy red light, and the gloomier entrance to a black tunnel, in whose massive architecture there was a barbarous, depressing and forbidding air. So little sunlight ever found its way to this spot, that it had an earthy, deadly smell; and so much cold wind rushed through it, that it struck chill to me, as if I had left the natural world.

Before he stirred, I was near enough to him to have touched him. Not even then removing his eyes from mine, he stepped back one step, and lifted his hand.

This was a lonesome post to occupy (I said), and it had riveted my attention when I looked down from up yonder. A visitor was a rarity, I should suppose; not an unwelcome rarity, I hoped? In me, he merely saw a man who had been shut up within narrow limits all his life, and who, being at last set free, had a newly awakened interest in these great works. To such purpose I spoke to him; but I am far from sure of the terms I used, for, besides that I am not happy in opening any conversation, there was something in the man that daunted me.

He directed a most curious look towards the red light near the tunnel's mouth, and looked all about it, as if something were missing from it, and then looked at me.

That light was part of his charge? Was it not?

He answered in a low voice: 'Don't you know it is?'

The monstrous thought came into my mind as I perused the fixed eyes and the saturnine face, that this was a spirit, not a man. I have speculated since, whether there may have been infection in his mind.

In my turn, I stepped back. But in making the action, I detected in his eyes some latent fear of me. This put the monstrous thought to flight.

'You look at me,' I said, forcing a smile, 'as if you had a dread of me.'

'I was doubtful,' he returned, 'whether I had seen you before.'

'Where?'

He pointed to the red light he had looked at.

'There?' I said.

Intently watchful of me, he replied (but without sound), 'Yes.'

'My good fellow, what should I do there? However, be that as it may, I never was there, you may swear.'

'I think I may,' he rejoined. 'Yes. I am sure I may.'

His manner cleared, like my own. He replied to my remarks with readiness, and in well chosen words. Had he much to do there? Yes; that was to say, he had enough responsibility to bear; but exactness and watchfulness were what was required of him, and of actual work—manual labour he had next to none. To change that signal, to trim those lights, and to turn this iron handle now and then, was all he had to do under that head. Regarding those many long and lonely hours of which I seemed to make so much, he could only say that the routine of his life had shaped itself into that form, and he had grown used to it. He had taught himself a language down here—if only to know it by sight, and to have formed his own crude ideas of its pronunciation, could be called learning it. He had also worked at fractions and decimals, and tried a little algebra; but he was, and had been as a boy, a poor hand at figures. Was it necessary for him when on duty, always to remain in that channel of damp air, and could he never rise into the sunshine from between those high stone walls? Why, that depended upon times and circumstances. Under some conditions there would be less upon the Line than under others, and the same held good as to certain hours of the day and night. In bright weather, he did choose occasions for getting a little above these lower shadows; but, being at all times liable to be called by his electric bell, and at such times listening for it with redoubled anxiety, the relief was less than I would suppose.

He took me into his box, where there was a fire, a desk for an official book in which he had to make certain entries, a telegraphic instrument with its dial face and needles, and the little bell of which he had spoken. On my trusting that he would excuse the remark that he had been well educated, and (I hoped I might say without offence), perhaps educated above that station, he observed that instances of slight incongruity in such-wise would rarely be found wanting among large bodies of men; that he had heard it was so in workhouses, in the police force, even in that last desperate resource, the army; and that he knew it was so, more or less, in any great railway staff. He had been, when young (if I could believe it, sitting in that hut; he scarcely could), a student of natural philosophy, and had attended lectures; but he had run wild, misused his opportunities, gone down, and never risen again. He had no complaint to offer about that. He had made his bed, and he lay upon it. It was far too late to make another.

All that I have here condensed, he said in a quiet manner, with his grave dark regards divided between me and the fire. He threw in the word 'Sir' from time to time, and especially when he referred to his youth: as though to request me to understand that he claimed to be nothing but what I found him. He was several times interrupted by the little bell, and had to read off messages, and send replies. Once, he had to stand without the door, and display a flag as a train passed, and make some verbal communication to the driver. In the discharge of his duties I observed him to be remarkably exact and vigilant, breaking off his discourse at a syllable, and remaining silent until what he had to do was done.

In a word, I should have set this man down as one of the safest of men to be employed in that capacity, but for the circumstance that while he was speaking to me twice broke off with a fallen colour, turned his face towards the little bell when it did *not* ring, opened the door of the hut (which was kept shut to exclude the unhealthy damp), and looked out towards the red light near the mouth of the tunnel. On both those occasions, he came back to the fire with the inexplicable air upon him which I had remarked, without being able to define, when we were so far asunder.

Said I when I rose to leave him: 'You almost make me think that I have met with a contented man.'

(I am afraid I must acknowledge that I said it to lead him on.)

'I believe I used to be so,' he rejoined, in the low voice in which he had first spoken; 'but I am troubled, sir, I am troubled.'

He would have recalled the words if he could. He had said them, however, and I took them up quickly.

'With what? What is your trouble?'

'It is very difficult to impart, sir. It is very, very difficult to speak of. If ever you make me another visit, I will try to tell you.'

'But I expressly intend to make you another visit. Say, when shall it be?'

'I go off early in the morning, and I shall be on again at ten tomorrow night, sir.'

'I will come at eleven.'

He thanked me, and went out at the door with me. 'I'll show my white light, sir,' he said, in his peculiar low voice, 'till you have found the way up. When you have found it, don't call out! And when you are at the top, don't call out!'

His manner seemed to make the place strike colder to me, but I said no more than 'Very well.'

'And when you come down tomorrow night, don't call out! Let me ask you a parting question. What made you cry "Halloa! Below there!" tonight?'

'Heaven knows,' said I. 'I cried something to that effect—'

'Not to that effect, sir. Those were the very words. I know them well.'

'Admit those were the very words. I said them, no doubt, because I saw you below.'

'For no other reason?'

'What other reason could I possibly have?'

'You had no feeling that they were conveyed to you in any supernatural way?'

'No.'

He wished me goodnight, and held up his light. I walked by the side of the down Line of rails (with a very disagreeable sensation of a train coming behind me), until I found the path. It was easier to mount than to descend, and I got back to my inn without any adventure.

Punctual to my appointment, I placed my foot on the first notch of the zigzag next night, as the distant clocks were striking eleven. He was waiting for me at the bottom, with his white light on. 'I have not called out,' I said, when we came close together; 'may I speak now?' 'By all means, sir.' 'Goodnight then, and here's my hand.' 'Goodnight, sir, and here's mine.' With that, we walked side by side to his box, entered it, closed the door, and sat down by the fire.

'I have made up my mind, sir,' he began, bending forward as soon as we were seated, and speaking in a tone but a little above a whisper, 'that you shall not have to ask me twice what troubles me. I took you for someone else yesterday evening. That troubles me.'

'That mistake?'

'No. That someone else.'

'Who is it?'

'I don't know.'

'Like me?'

'I don't know. I never saw the face. The left arm is across the face, and the right arm is waved. Violently waved. This way.'

I followed his action with my eyes, and it was the action of an arm gesticulating with the utmost passion and vehemence: 'For God's sake clear the way!'

'One moonlit night,' said the man, 'I was sitting here, when I heard a voice cry "Halloa! Below there!" I stared up, looked from that door, and saw this someone else standing by the red light near the tunnel, waving as I just now showed you.

The voice seemed hoarse with shouting, and it cried, "Look out! Look out!" And then again "Halloa! Below there! Look out!" I caught up my lamp, turned it on red, and ran towards the figure, calling, "What's wrong? What has happened? Where?" It stood just outside the blackness of the tunnel. I advanced so close upon it that I wondered at its keeping the sleeve across its eyes. I ran right up at it, and had my hand stretched out to pull the sleeve away, when it was gone.'

'Into the tunnel,' said I.

'No. I ran on into the tunnel, five hundred yards. I stopped and held my lamp above my head, and saw the figures of the measured distance, and saw the wet stains stealing down the walls and trickling through the arch. I ran out again, faster than I had run in (for I had a mortal abhorrence of the place upon me), and I looked all round the red light with my own red light, and I went up the iron ladder to the gallery atop of it, and I came down again, and ran back here. I telegraphed both ways, "An alarm has been given. Is anything wrong?" The answer came back, both ways: "All well." '

Resisting the slow touch of a frozen finger tracing out my spine, I showed him how that this figure must be a deception of his sense of sight, and how that figures, originating in disease of the delicate nerves that minister to the functions of the eye, were known to have often troubled patients, some of whom had become conscious of the nature of their affliction, and had even proved it by experiments upon themselves. 'As to an imaginary cry,' said I, 'do but listen for a moment to the wind in this unnatural valley while we speak so low, and to the wild harp it makes of the telegraph wires!'

That was all very well, he returned, after we had sat listening for a while, and he ought to know something of the wind and the wires, he who so often passed long winter nights there, alone and watching. But he would beg to remark that he had not finished.

I asked his pardon, and he slowly added these words, touching my arm:

'Within six hours after the appearance, the memorable accident on this Line happened, and within ten hours the dead and wounded were brought along through the tunnel over the spot where the figure had stood.'

A disagreeable shudder crept over me, but I did my best against it. It was not to be denied, I rejoined, that this was a remarkable coincidence, calculated deeply to impress his mind. But it was unquestionable that remarkable coincidences did continually occur, and they must be taken into account in dealing with such a subject. Though to be sure I must admit, I added (for I thought I saw that he was going to bring the objection to bear upon me), men of common sense did not allow much for coincidences in making the ordinary calculations of life.

He again begged to remark that he had not finished.

I again begged his pardon for being betrayed into interruptions.

'This,' he said, again laying his hand upon my arm, and glancing over his shoulder with hollow eyes, 'was just a year ago. Six or seven months passed, and I had recovered from the surprise and shock, when one morning, as the day was breaking, I, standing at that door, looked towards the red light, and saw the spectre again.' He stopped, with a fixed look at me.

'Did it cry out?'

'No. It was silent.'

'Did it wave its arm?'

'No. It leaned against the shaft of the light, with both hands before the face. Like this.'

Once more, I followed his action with my eyes. It was an action of mourning. I have seen such an attitude in stone figures on tombs.

'Did you go up to it?'

'I came in and sat down, partly to collect my thoughts, partly because it had turned me faint. When I went to the door again, daylight was above me, and the ghost was gone.'

'But nothing followed? Nothing came of this?'

He touched me on the arm with his forefinger twice or thrice, giving a ghastly nod each time:

'That very day, as a train came out of the tunnel, I noticed, at a carriage window on my side, what looked like a confusion of hands and heads, and something waved. I saw it, just in time to signal the driver, Stop! He shut off, and put his brake on, but the train drifted past here a hundred and fifty yards or more. I ran after it, and, as I went along, heard terrible screams and cries. A beautiful young lady had died instantaneously in one of the compartments, and was brought in here, and laid down on this floor between us.'

Involuntarily, I pushed my chair back, as I looked from the boards at which he pointed, to himself.

'True, sir. True. Precisely as it happened, so I tell it you.'

I could think of nothing to say, to any purpose, and my mouth was very dry. The wind and the wires took up the story with a long lamenting wail.

He resumed. 'Now, sir, mark this, and judge how my mind is troubled. The spectre came back, a week ago. Ever since, it has been there, now and again, by fits and starts.'

'At the light?'

'At the Danger-light.'

'What does it seem to do?'

He repeated, if possible with increased passion and vehemence, that former gesticulation of 'For God's sake clear the way!'

Then, he went on. 'I have no peace or rest for it. It calls to me for many minutes together, in an agonized manner, "Below there! Look out! Look out!" It stands waving to me. It rings my little bell—'

I caught at that. 'Did it ring your bell yesterday evening when I was here, and you went to the door?'

'Twice.'

'Why, see,' said I, 'how your imagination misleads you. My eyes were on the bell, and my ears were open to the bell, and if I am a living man, it did *not* ring at those times. No, nor at any other time, except when it was rung in the natural course of physical things by the station communicating with you.'

He shook his head. 'I have never made a mistake as to that, yet, sir. I have never confused the spectre's ring with the man's. The ghost's ring is a strange vibration in the bell that it derives from nothing else, and I have not asserted that the bell stirs to the eye. I don't wonder that you failed to hear it. But *I* heard it.'

'And did the spectre seem to be there, when you looked out?'

'It *was* there.'

'Both times?'

He repeated firmly: 'Both times.'

'Will you come to the door with me, and look for it now?'

He bit his underlip as though he were somewhat unwilling, but arose. I opened the door, and stood on the step, while he stood in the doorway. There, was the

Danger-light. There, was the dismal mouth of the tunnel. There, were the high wet stone walls of the cutting. There, were the stars above them.

'Do you see it?' I asked him, taking particular note of his face. His eyes were prominent and strained; but not very much more so, perhaps, than my own had been when I had directed them earnestly towards the same spot.

'No,' he answered. 'It is not there.'

'Agreed,' said I.

We went in again, shut the door, and resumed our seats. I was thinking how best to improve this advantage, if it might be called one, when he took up the conversation in such a matter of course way, so assuming that there could be no serious question of fact between us, that I felt myself placed in the weakest of positions.

'By this time you will fully understand, sir,' he said, 'that what troubles me so dreadfully, is the question, What does the spectre mean?'

I was not sure, I told him, that I did fully understand.

'What is its warning against?' he said, ruminating, with his eyes on the fire, and only by times turning them on me. 'What is the danger? Where is the danger? There is danger overhanging, somewhere on the Line. Some dreadful calamity will happen. It is not to be doubted this third time, after what has gone before. But surely this is a cruel haunting of *me*. What can I do?'

He pulled out his handkerchief, and wiped the drops from his heated forehead.

'If I telegraph Danger, on either side of me, or on both, I can give no reason for it,' he went on, wiping the palms of his hands. 'I should get into trouble, and do no good. They would think I was mad. This is the way it would work: Message: "Danger! Take care!" Answer: "What danger? Where?" Message: "Don't know. But for God's sake take care!" They would displace me. What else could they do?'

His pain of mind was most pitiable to see. It was the mental torture of a conscientious man, oppressed beyond endurance by an unintelligible responsibility involving life.

'When it first stood under the Danger-light,' he went on, putting his dark hair back from his head, and drawing his hands outwards across and across his temples in an extremity of feverish distress, 'why not tell me where that accident was to happen—if it must happen? Why not tell me how it could be averted—if it could have been averted? When on its second coming it hid its face, why not tell me instead: "She is going to die. Let them keep her at home"? If it came, on those two occasions, only to show me that its warnings were true, and so to prepare me for the third, why not warn me plainly now? And I, Lord help me! A mere poor signalman on this solitary station! Why not go to somebody with credit to be believed, and power to act!'

When I saw him in this state, I saw that for the poor man's sake, as well as for the public safety, what I had to do for the time was, to compose his mind. Therefore, setting aside all question of reality or unreality between us, I represented to him that whoever thoroughly discharged his duty, must do well, and that at least it was his comfort that he understood his duty, though he did not understand these confounding appearances. In this effort I succeeded far better than in the attempt to reason him out of his conviction. He became calm; the occupations incidental to his post as the night advanced, began to make larger demands on his attention; and I left him at two in the morning. I had offered to stay through the night, but he would not hear of it.

That I more than once looked back at the red light as I ascended the pathway, that I did not like the red light, and that I should have slept but poorly if my bed had been under it, I see no reason to conceal. Nor did I like the two sequences of the accident and the dead girl. I see no reason to conceal that, either.

But, what ran most in my thoughts was the consideration how ought I to act, having become the recipient of this disclosure? I had proved the man to be intelligent, vigilant, painstaking and exact; but how long might he remain so, in his state of mind? Though in a subordinate position, still he held a most important trust, and would I (for instance) like to stake my own life on the chances of his continuing to execute it with precision?

Unable to overcome a feeling that there would be something treacherous in my communicating what he had told me to his superiors in the company, without first being plain with himself and proposing a middle course to him, I ultimately resolved to offer to accompany him (otherwise keeping his secret for the present) to the wisest medical practitioner we could hear of in those parts, and to take his opinion. A change in his time of duty would come round next night, he had apprised me, and he would be off an hour or two after sunrise, and on again soon after sunset. I had appointed to return accordingly.

Next evening was a lovely evening, and I walked out early to enjoy it. The sun was not yet quite down when I traversed the field-path near the top of the deep cutting. I would extend my walk for an hour, I said to myself, half an hour on and half an hour back, and it would then be time to go to my signalman's box.

Before pursuing my stroll, I stepped to the brink, and mechanically looked down, from the point from which I had first seen him. I cannot describe the thrill that seized upon me, when, close at the mouth of the tunnel, I saw the appearance of a man, with his left sleeve across his eyes, passionately waving his right arm.

The nameless horror that oppressed me, passed in a moment, for in a moment I saw that this appearance of a man was a man indeed, and that there was a little group of other men standing at a short distance, to whom he seemed to be rehearsing the gesture he made. The Danger-light was not yet lighted. Against its shaft, a little low hut, entirely new to me, had been made of some wooden supports and tarpaulin. It looked no bigger than a bed.

With an irresistible sense that something was wrong—with a flashing self-reproachful fear that fatal mischief had come of my leaving the man there, and causing no one to be sent to overlook or correct what he did—I descended the notched path with all the speed I could make.

'What is the matter?' I asked the men.

'Signalman killed this morning, sir.'

'Not the man belonging to that box?'

'Yes, sir.'

'Not the man I know?'

'You will recognize him, sir, if you knew him,' said the man who spoke for the others, solemnly uncovering his own head and raising an end of the tarpaulin, 'for his face is quite composed.'

'O! how did this happen, how did this happen?' I asked, turning from one to another as the hut closed in again.

'He was cut down by an engine, sir. No man in England knew his work better. But somehow he was not clear of the outer rail. It was just at broad day. He had struck the light, and had the lamp in his hand. As the engine came out of the tunnel, his back was towards her, and she cut him down. That man drove her, and was showing how it happened. Show the gentleman, Tom.'

The man who wore a rough dark dress, stepped back to his former place at the mouth of the tunnel!

'Coming round the curve in the tunnel, sir,' he said, 'I saw him at the end, like as if I saw him down a perspective-glass. There was no time to check speed, and I knew him to be very careful. As he didn't seem to take heed of the whistle, I shut it off when we were running down upon him, and called to him as loud as I could call.'

'What did you say?'

'I said, Below there! Look out! Look out! For God's sake clear the way!'

I started.

'Ah! it was a dreadful time, sir. I never left off calling to him. I put this arm before my eyes, not to see, and I waved this arm to the last; but it was no use.'

Without prolonging the narrative to dwell on any one of its curious circumstances more than on any other, I may, in closing it, point out the coincidence that the warning of the engine-driver included, not only the words which the unfortunate signalman had repeated to me as haunting him, but also the words which I my-self—not he—had attached, and that only in my own mind, to the gesticulation he had imitated.

 # HARRIET BEECHER STOWE (1811–1896)

It is said that Queen Victoria wept when she read Harriet Beecher Stowe's Uncle Tom's Cabin *(1852), the internationally best-selling nineteenth-century book. While Stowe created this landmark abolitionist and humanist allegory and political tract, and while literary history has cast her as a sentimentalist whose two main writing themes were evangelical Christianity and female domesticity, in reality, there was much more to her life of letters. Like Nathaniel Hawthorne, Stowe had a deep-rooted Puritan heritage; quite unlike Hawthorne, she despised slavery.*

Harriet Beecher Stowe wrote at least ten adult novels and produced a range of shorter fiction. "The Ghost in the Cap'n Brown House" is one such shorter work. The story is significant not only because it is the work of Stowe, but also because it is a classic nineteenth-century ghost story, complete with Gothic trimmings (including a haunted house), folkloric themes, and gossip. The author's cultural heritage and personal beliefs flavor the story and help to make it a unique and distinctly American variant of the traditional ghost story of Charles Dickens, Elizabeth Gaskell, and other contemporary practitioners of supernatural fiction.

The Ghost in the Cap'n Brown House

(Atlantic, *vol. 26, no. 158, December 1870*)

Now, Sam, tell us certain true, is there any such things as ghosts?'

'Be there ghosts?' said Sam, immediately translating into his vernacular grammar: 'wal, now that are's jest the question, ye see.'

'Well, grandma thinks there are, and Aunt Lois thinks it's all nonsense. Why, Aunt Lois don't even believe the stories in Cotton Mather's "Magnalia." '

'Wanter know?' said Sam, with a tone of slow, languid meditation.

We were sitting on a bank of the Charles River, fishing. The soft melancholy red of evening was fading off in streaks on the glassy water, and the houses of Oldtown were beginning to loom through the gloom, solemn and ghostly. There are times and tones and moods of nature that make all the vulgar, daily real seem shadowy, vague, and supernatural, as if the outlines of this hard material present were fading into the invisible and unknown. So Oldtown, with its elm-trees, its great square white houses, its meeting-house and tavern and blacksmith's shop and mill, which at high noon seem as real and as commonplace as possible, at this hour of the evening were dreamy and solemn. They rose up blurred, indistinct, dark; here and there winking candles sent long lines of light through the shadows, and little drops of unforeseen rain rippled the sheeny darkness of the water.

'Wal, you see, boys, in them things it's jest as well to mind your granny. There's a consid'able sight o' gumption in grandmas. You look at the folks that's allus tellin' you what they don't believe,—they don't believe this, and they don't believe that,—and what sort o' folks is they? Why, like yer Aunt Lois, sort o' stringy and dry. There ain't no 'sorption got out o' not believin' nothin'.

'Lord a massy! we don't know nothin' 'bout them things. We hain't ben there, and can't say that there ain't no ghosts and sich; can we, now?'

We agreed to that fact, and sat a little closer to Sam in the gathering gloom.

'Tell us about the Cap'n Brown house, Sam.'

'Ye didn't never go over the Cap'n Brown house?'

No, we had not that advantage.

'Wal, yer see, Cap'n Brown he made all his money to sea, in furrin parts, and then come here to Oldtown to settle down.

'Now, there ain't now knowin' 'bout these 'ere old shipmasters, where they's ben, or what they's ben a doin', or how they got their money. Ask me no questions, and I'll tell ye no lies, is 'bout the best philosophy for them. Wal, it didn't do no good to ask Cap'n Brown questions too close, 'cause you didn't git no satisfaction. Nobody rightly knew 'bout who his folks was, or where they come from, and, ef a body asked him, he used to say that the very fust he know'd 'bout himself he was a young man walkin' the streets in London.

'But, yer see, boys, he hed money, and that is about all folks wanter know when a man comes to settle down. And he bought that 'are place, and built that 'are house. He built it all sea-cap'n fashion, so's to feel as much at home as he could. The parlor was like a ship's cabin. The table and chairs was fastened down to the floor, and the closets was made with holes to set the casters and the decanters and bottles in, jest's they be at sea; and there was stanchions to hold on by; and they say that blowy nights the cap'n used to fire up pretty well with his grog, till he hed about all he could carry, and then he'd set and hold on, and hear the wind blow, and kind o' feel out to sea right there to hum. There wasn't no Mis' Cap'n Brown, and there didn't seem likely to be none. And whether there ever hed been one, nobody know'd. He hed an old black Guinea nigger-woman, named Quassia, that did his work. She was shaped pretty much like one o' these 'ere great crooknecked-squashes. She wa'n't no gret beauty, I can tell you; and she used to wear a gret red turban and a yaller short gown and red petticoat, and a gret string o' gold beads round her neck, and gret big gold hoops in her ears, made right in the middle o' Africa among the heathen there. For all she was black, she thought a heap o' herself, and was consid'able sort o' predominative over the cap'n. Lord massy! boys, it's allus so. Get a man and a woman together,—any sort o' woman you're a mind to, don't care who 'tis,—and one way or another she gets the rule over him, and he jest has to train to her fife. Some does it one way, and some does it another; some does it by jawin', and some does it by kissin', and some does it by faculty and contrivance; but one way or another they allers does it. Old Cap'n Brown was a good stout, stocky kind o' John Bull sort o' fellow, and a good judge o' sperits, and allers kep' the best in them are cupboards o' his'n; but, fust and last, things in his house went pretty much as old Quassia said.

'Folks got to kind o' respectin' Quassia. She come to meetin' Sunday regular, and sot all fixed up in red and yaller and green, with glass beads and what not, lookin' for all the world like one o' them ugly Indian idols; but she was well-behaved as any Christian. She was a master hand at cookin'. Her bread and biscuits couldn't be beat, and no couldn't her pies, and there wa'n't no such pound-cake as she made nowhere. Wal, this 'ere story I'm a goin' to tell you was told me by Cinthy Pendleton. There ain't a more respectable gal, old or young, than Cinthy nowheres. She lives over to Sherburne now, and I hear tell she's sot up a manty-makin' business; but then she used to do tailorin' in Oldtown. She was a member o' the church, and a good Christian as ever was. Wal, ye see, Quassia she got Cinthy to come up and spend a week to the Cap'n Brown house, a doin' tailorin' and a fixin' over his close: 'twas along toward the fust o' March. Cinthy she sot by the fire in the front parlor with her goose and her press-board and her work: for there wa'n't no company callin', and the snow was drifted four feet deep right across the front door; so there wa'n't much danger o' any body comin' in. And the cap'n he was a perlite man to wimmen; and Cinthy she liked it jest as well not to have company, 'cause the cap'n he'd make himself entertainin' tellin' on her sea-stories, and all about this adventures among the Ammonites, and Perresites, and Jebusites, and all sorts o' heathen people he'd been among.

'Wal, that 'are week there come on the master snow-storm. Of all the snow-storms that hed ben, that 'are was the beater; and I tell you the wind blew as if 'twas the last chance it was ever goin' to hev. Wal, it's kind o' scary like to be shet up in a lone house with all natur' a kind o' breakin' out, and goin' on so, and the snow a comin' down so thick ye can't see 'cross the street, and the wind a pipin' and a squeelin' and a rumblin' and a tumblin' fust down this chimney and then down that. I tell you, it sort o' sets a feller thinkin' o' the three great things,—death, judgment, and etarnaty; and I don't care who the folks is, nor how good they be, there's times when they must be feelin' putty consid'able solemn.

'Wal, Cinthy she said she kind o' felt so along, and she hed a sort o' queer feelin' come over her as if there was somebody or somethin' round the house more'n appeared. She said she sort o' felt it in the air; but it seemed to her silly, and she tried to get over it. But two or three times, she said, when it got to be dusk, she felt somebody go by her up the stairs. The front entry wa'n't very light in the day time, and in the storm, come five o'clock, it was so dark that all you could see was jest a gleam o' somethin', and two or three times when she started to go up stairs she see a soft white suthin' that seemed goin' up before her, and she stopped with her heart a beatin' like a trip-hammer, and she sort o' saw it go up and along the entry to the cap'n's door, and then it seemed to go right through, 'cause the door didn't open.

'Wal, Cinthy says she to old Quassia, says she, "Is there anybody lives in this house but us?"

'"Anybody lives here?" says Quassia: "What you mean?" says she.

'Says Cinthy, "I thought somebody went past me on the stairs last night and to-night."

'Lord massy! how old Quassia did screech and laugh. "Good Lord!" says she, "how foolish white folks is! Somebody went past you? Was't the capt'in?"

'"No, it wa'n't the cap'n," says she: "it was somethin' soft and white, and moved very still; it was like somethin' in the air," says she.

'Then Quassia she haw-hawed louder. Says she, "It's hysterikes, Miss Cinthy; that's all it is."

'Wal, Cinthy she was kind o' 'shamed, but for all that she couldn't help herself. Sometimes evenin's she'd be a settin' with the cap'n, and she'd think she'd hear somebody a movin' in his room overhead; and she knowed it wa'n't Quassia, 'cause Quassia was ironin' in the kitchen. She took pains once or twice to find out that 'are.

'Wal, ye see, the cap'n's room was the gret front upper chamber over the parlor, and then right opposite to it was the gret spare chamber where Cinthy slept. It was jest as grand as could be, with a gret four-post mahogany bedstead and damask curtains brought over from England; but it was cold enough to freeze a white bear solid,—the way spare chambers allers is. Then there was the entry between, run straight through the house: one side was old Quassia's room, and the other was a sort o' storeroom, where the old cap'n kep' all sorts o' traps.

'Wal, Cinthy she kep' a hevin' things happen and a seein' thins, till she didn't railly know what was in it. Once when she come into the parlor jest at sundown, she was sure she see a white figure a vanishin' out o' the door that went towards the side entry. She said it was so dusk, that all she could see was jest this white figure, and it jest went out still as a cat as she come in.

'Wal, Cinthy didn't like to speak to the cap'n about it. She was a close woman, putty prudent, Cinthy was.

'But one night, 'bout the middle o' the week, this 'ere thing kind o' come to a crisis.

'Cinthy said she'd ben up putty late a sewin' and a finishin' off down in the parlor; and the cap'n he sot up with her, and was consid'able cheerful and entertainin', tellin' her all about things over the Bermudys, and off to Chiny and Japan, and round the world ginerally. The storm that hed been a blowin' all the week was about as furious as ever; and the cap'n he stirred up a mess o' flip, and hed it for her hot to go to bed on. He was a good-natured critter, and allers had feelin's for lone women; and I s'pose he knew 'twas sort o' desolate for Cinthy.

'Wal, takin' the flip so right the last think afore goin' to bed, she went right off to sleep as sound as a nut, and slep' on till somewhere about mornin', when she said somethin' waked her broad awake in a minute. Her eyes flew wide open like a spring, and the storm hed gone down and the moon come out: and there, standin' right in the moonlight by her bed, was a woman jest as white as a sheet, with black hair hangin' down to her waist, and the brightest, mourn-fullest black eyes you ever see. She stood there lookin' right at Cinthy; and Cinthy thinks that was what waked her up; 'cause, you know, ef anybody stands and looks steady at folks asleep it's apt to wake 'em.

'Any way, Cinthy said she felt jest as ef she was turnin' to stone. She couldn't move nor speak. She lay a minute, and then she shut her eyes, and begun to say her prayers; and a minute after she opened 'em, and it was gone.

'Cinthy was a sensible gal, and one that allers hed her thoughts about her; and she jest got up and put a shawl round her shoulders, and went first and looked at the doors, and they was both on 'em locked jest as she left 'em when she went to bed. Then she looked under the bed and in the closet, and felt all round the room; where she couldn't see she felt her way, and there wa'n't nothin' there.

'Wal, next mornin' Cinthy got up and went home, and she kep' it to herself a good while. Finally, one day when she was workin' to our house she told Hepsy about it, and Hepsy she told me.'

'Well, Sam,' we said, after a pause, in which we heard only the rustle of leaves and the ticking of branches against each other, 'what do you suppose it was?'

'Wal, there 'tis: you know jest as much about it as I do. Hepsy told Cinthy it might 'a' ben a dream; so it might, but Cinthy she was sure it wa'n't a dream, 'cause she remembers plain hearin' the old clock on the stairs strike four while she had her eyes open lookin' at the woman; and then she only shet 'em a minute, jest to say 'Now I lay me,' and opened 'em and she was gone.

'Wal, Cinthy told Hepsy, and Hepsy she kep' it putty close. She didn't tell it to nobody except Aunt Sally Dickerson and the Widder Bije Smith and your Grandma Badger and the minister's wife and they every one o' 'em 'greed it ought to be kep close, 'cause it would make talk. Wal, come spring somehow or other it seemed to 'a' got all over Oldtown. I heard on 't to the store and up to the tavern; and Jake Marshall he says to me one day, "What's this 'ere about the cap'n's house?" And the Widder Loker she says to me, "There's ben a ghost seen in the cap'n's house;" and I heard on 't clear over to Needham and Sherburne.

'Some o' the women they drew themselves up putty stiff and proper. Your Aunt Lois was one on 'em.

'"Ghost," says she; "don't tell me! Perhaps it would be best ef 'twas a ghost," says she. She didn't think there ought to be no sich doin's in nobody's house; and your grandma she shet her up, and told her she didn't oughter talk so.'

'Talk how?' said I, interrupting Sam with wonder. 'What did Aunt Lois mean?'

'Why, you see,' said Sam mysteriously, 'there allers is folks in every town that's jest like the Sadducees in old times: they won't believe in angel nor sperit, no way you can fix it; and ef things is seen and done in a house, why, they say, it's 'cause there's somebody there; there's some sort o' deviltry or trick about it.

'So the story got round that there was a woman kep' private in Cap'n Brown's house, and that he brought her from furrin parts; and it growed and growed, till there was all sorts o' ways o' tellin on 't.

'Some said they'd seen her a settin at an open winder. Some said that moonlight nights they'd seen her a walkin' out in the back garden kind o' in and out 'mong the bean-poles and squash-vines.

'You see, it come on spring and summer; and the winders o' the Cap'n Brown house stood open, and folks was all a watchin' on 'em day and night. Aunt Sally Dickerson told the minister's wife that she'd seen a plain daylight a woman a settin' at the chamber winder atween four and five o'clock in the mornin',—jist a settin' a lookin' out and a doin' nothin', like anybody else. She was very white and pale, and had black eyes.

'Some said that it was a nun the cap'n had brought away from a Roman Catholic convent in Spain, and some said he'd got her out o' the Inquisition.

'Aunt Sally said she thought the minister ought to call and inquire why she didn't come to meetin', and who she was, and all about her: 'cause, you see, she said it might be all right enough ef folks only know'd jest how things was; but ef they didn't, why, folks will talk.'

'Well, did the minister do it?'

'What, Parson Lothrop? Wal, no, he didn't. He made a call on the cap'n in a regular way, and asked arter his health and all his family. But the cap'n he seemed jest as jolly and chipper as a spring robin, and he gin the minister some o' his old Jamaiky; and the minister he come away and said he didn't see nothin'; and no he didn't. Folks never does see nothin' when they aint' lookin' where 'tis. Fact is, Parson Lothrop wa'n't fond o' interferin'; he was a master hand to slick things over. Your grandma she used to mourn about it, 'cause she said he never gin no p'int to the doctrines; but 'twas all of a piece, he kind o' took every thing the smooth way.

'But your grandma she believed in the ghost, and so did Lady Lothrop. I was up to her house t'other day fixin' a door-knob, and says she, "Sam your wife told me a strange story about the Cap'n Brown house."

'"Yes, ma'am, she did," says I.

'"Well, what do you think of it?" says she.

'"Wal, sometimes I think, and then agin I don't know," says I. "There's Cinthy she's a member o' the church and a good pious gal," says I.

'"Yes, Sam," says Lady Lothrop, says she; "and Sam," says she, "it is jest like something that happened once to my grandmother when she was livin' in the old Province House in Bostin." Says she, "These 'ere things is the mysteries of Providence, and it's jest as well not to have 'em too much talked about."

'"Jest so," says I, — "jest so." That 'are's what every woman I've talked with says; and I guess, fust and last, I've talked with twenty, — good, safe church-members, — and they's every one o' opinion that this 'ere oughtn't to be talked about. Why, over to the deakin's t'other night we went it all over as much as two or three hours, and we concluded that the best way was to keep quite still about it; and that's jest what they say over to Needham and Sherburne. I've been all round a hushin' this 'ere up, and I hain't found but a few people that hedn't the particulars one way or another." There 'ere what I says to Lady Lothrop. The fact was, I never did see no report so, nor make sich sort o' sarchin's o' heart, as this 'ere. It railly did beat all; 'cause, ef 'twas a ghost, why there was the p'int proved, ye see. Cinthy's a church-member, and she *see* it, and got right up and sarched the room: but then agin, ef 'twas a woman, why that 'are was kind o' awful; it gives cause, ye see, for thinkin' all sorts o' things. There was Cap'n Brown, to be sure, he wa'n't a church-member; but yet he was as honest and regular a man as any goin', as fur as any on us could see. To be sure, nobody know'd where he come from but that wa'n't no reason agin' him: this 'ere might a ben a crazy sister, or some poor critter that he took out o' the best o' motives; and the Scriptur' says, "Charity hopeth all things." But then, ye see, folks will talk, — that 'are's the pester o' all these things, — and they did some on 'em talk consid'able strong about the cap'n; but somehow or other, there didn't nobody come to the p'int o' facin' on him down, and sayin' square out, "Cap'n Brown, have you got a woman in your house, or hain't you? or is it a ghost, or what is it?" Folks somehow never does come to that. Ye see, there was the cap'n so respectable, a settin' up every Sunday there in his pew, with his ruffles round his hands and his red broadcloth cloak and his cocked hat. Why, folks' hearts sort o' failed 'em when it come to sayin' any thing right to him. They thought and kind o' whispered round that the minister or the deakins oughter do it: but Lord massy! ministers, I s'pose, has feelin's like the rest on us; they don't want to eat all the hard cheeses that nobody else won't eat. Anyhow, there wasn't nothin' said direct to the cap'n; and jest for want o' that all the folks in Oldtown kep' a bilin' and a bilin' like a kettle o' soap, till it seemed all the time as if they'd bile over.

'Some o' the wimmen tried to get somethin' out o' Quassy. Lord massy! you might as well 'a' tried to get it out an old tom-turkey, that'll strut and gobble and quitter, and drag his wings on the ground, and fly at you, but won't say nothin'. Quassy she screeched her queer sort o' laugh; and she told 'em that they was a makin' fools o' themselves, and that the cap'n's matters wa'n't none o' their bisness; and that was true enough. As to goin' into Quassia's room, or into any o' the store-rooms or closets she kep' the keys of, you might as well hev gone into a lion's den. She kep' all her places locked up tight; and there was no gettin' at nothin' in the Cap'n Brown house, else I believe some o' the wimmen would 'a' sent a sarch-warrant.'

'Well,' said I, 'what came of it? Didn't anybody ever find out?'

'Wal,' said Sam, 'it come to an end sort o', and didn't come to an end. It was jest this 'ere way. You see, along in October, jest in the cider-makin' time, Abel Flint he was took down with dysentery and died. You 'member the Flint house: it stood on a little rise o' ground jest lookin' over towards the Brown house. Wal, there was Aunt Sally Dickerson and the Widder Bije Smith, they set up with the corpse. He was laid out in the back chamber, you see, over the milk-room and kitchen; but there was cold victuals and sich in the front chamber where the watchers sot. Wal, now, Aunt Sally she told me that between three and four o'clock she heard wheels a rumblin', and she went to the winder, and it was clear starlight; and she see a coach come up to the Cap'n Brown house; and she see the cap'n come out bringin' a woman all wrapped in a cloak, and old Quassy came arter with her arms full o' bundles; and he put her into the kerridge, and shet her in, and it driv off; and she see old Quassy stand lookin' over the fence arter it. She tried to wake up the widder, but 'twas towards mornin', and the widder allers was a hard sleeper; so there wa'n't no witness but her.'

'Well, then, it wasn't a ghost,' said I, 'after all, and it *was* a woman.'

'Wal, there 'tis, you see. Folks don't know that 'are yit, 'cause there it's jest as broad as 'tis long. Now, look at it. There's Cinthy, she's a good, pious gal: she locks her chamber doors, both on 'em, and goes to bed, and wakes up in the night, and there's a woman there. She jest shets her eyes, and the woman's gone. She gits up and looks, and both doors is locked jest as she left 'em. That 'ere woman wa'n't flesh and blood now, now way,—not such flesh and blood as we knows on; but then they say Cinthy might hev dreamed it!

'Wal, now, look at it t'other way. There's Aunt Sally Dickerson; she's a good woman and a church-member: wal, she sees a woman in a cloak with all her bundles brought out o' Cap'n Brown's house, and put into a kerridge, and driv off, atween three and four o'clock in the mornin'. Wal, that 'ere shows there must 'a' ben a real live woman kep' there privately, and so what Cinthy saw wasn't a ghost.

'Wal, now, Cinthy says Aunt Sally might 'a' dreamed it,—that she got her head so full o' stories about the Cap'n Brown house, and watched it till she got asleep, and hed this 'ere dream; and, as there didn't nobody else see it, it might 'a' ben, you know. Aunt Sally's clear she didn't dream, and then agin Cinthy's clear *she* didn't dream; but which on 'em was awake, or which on 'em was asleep, is what ain't settled on Oldtown yet.'

ROBERT LOUIS STEVENSON (1850–1894)

Robert Louis Stevenson is Clive Barker's single favorite author, although Barker is not unique in his admiration for Stevenson and his writing. Stevenson was an extremely intelligent, well-read thinker who in his day and still today was and is considered both intellectual and popular. He is best remembered as the author of several enduring swashbuckling adventures set on land and at sea. Among the more famous of these are Treasure Island *(1881–82)*, Kidnapped *(1886)*, The Black Arrow: A Tale of the Two Roses *(1888)*, The Master of Ballantrae *(1889)*, and* David Balfour *(1893). Stevenson was also a poet, a playwright, an essayist, and a travel log writer.*

In story theme, Robert Louis Stevenson sometimes reflected Dickensian and Victorian traditions and often foreshadowed the works of Rafael Sabatini and William Hope Hodgson. He was also a master storyteller of macabre, psychological, and supernatural Dark Fantasy. Of these works, The Strange Case of Dr. Jekyll and Mr. Hyde *(1886) is the most famous. Most of Stevenson's major works of adventure and horror have been adapted into plays, movies, radio dramas, and television movies several times each. Such was the case with "The Body Snatcher," a motion picture vehicle for Boris Karloff in 1945 that portrayed, in Dark Fantasy form, the real-life nineteenth-century problem of grave robbing.*

The Body Snatcher

(originally published as "The Body-Snatchers" in Pall Mall Gazette, *Extra Christmas Issue, 1884)*

Every night in the year, four of us sat in the small parlour of the *George* at Debenham—the undertaker, and the landlord, and Fettes, and myself. Sometimes there would be more; but blow high, blow low, come rain or snow or frost, we four would be each planted in his own particular arm-chair. Fettes was an old drunken Scotsman, a man of education obviously, and a man of some property, since he lived in idleness. He had come to Debenham years ago, while still young, and by a mere continuance of living and grown to be an adopted townsman. His blue camlet cloak was a local antiquity, like the church-spire. His place in the parlour at the *George*, his absence from church, his old, crapulous, disreputable vices, were all things of course in Debenham. He had some vague Radical opinions and some fleeting infidelities, which he would now and again set forth and emphasize with tottering slaps upon the table. He drank rum—five glasses regularly every evening; and for the greater portion of his nightly visit to the *George* sat, with his glass in his right hand, in a state of melancholy alcoholic saturation. We called him the Doctor, for he was supposed to have some special knowledge of medicine and had been known, upon a pinch, to set a fracture or reduce a dislocation; but beyond these slight particulars, we had no knowledge of his character and antecedents.

One dark winter night—it had struck nine some time before the landlord joined us—there was a sick man in the *George*, a great neighbouring proprietor suddenly struck down with apoplexy on his way to Parliament; and the great man's still greater London doctor had been telegraphed to his bedside. It was the first time that such a thing had happened in Debenham, for the railway was but newly open, and we were all proportionately moved by the occurrence.

"He's come," said the landlord, after he had filled and lighted his pipe.

"He?" said I. "Who?—not the doctor?"

"Himself," replied our host.

"What is his name?"

"Dr. Macfarlane," said the landlord.

Fettes was far through his third tumbler, stupidly fuddled, now nodding over, now staring mazily around him; but at the last word he seemed to awaken and repeated the name "Macfarlane" twice, quietly enough the first time, but with sudden emotion at the second.

"Yes," said the landlord, "that's his name, Doctor Wolfe Macfarlane."

Fettes became instantly sober; his eyes awoke, his voice became clear, loud and steady, his language forcible and earnest. We were all startled by the transformation, as if a man had risen from the dead.

"I beg your pardon," he said, "I am afraid I have not been paying much attention to your talk. Who is this Wolfe Macfarlane?" And then, when he had heard the landlord out, "It cannot be, it cannot be," he added; "and yet I would like well to see him face to face."

"Do you know him, Doctor?" asked the undertaker, with a gasp.

"God forbid!" was the reply. "And yet the name is a strange one; it were too much to fancy two. Tell me, landlord, is he old?"

"Well," said the host, "he's not a young man, to be sure, and his hair is white; but he looks younger than you."

"He is older, though; years older. But," with a slap upon the table, "it's the rum you see in my face—rum and sin. This man, perhaps, may have an easy conscience and a good digestion. Conscience! Hear me speak. You would think I was some good, old, decent Christian, would you not? But no, not I; I never canted. Voltaire might have canted if he'd stood in my shoes; but the brains"—with a rattling fillip on his bald head—"the brains were clear and active and I saw and made no deductions."

"If you know this doctor," I ventured to remark, after a somewhat awful pause, "I should gather that you do not share the landlord's good opinion."

Fettes paid no regard to me.

"Yes," he said, with sudden decision, "I must see him face to face."

There was another pause and then a door was closed rather sharply on the first floor and a step was heard upon the stair.

"That's the doctor," cried the landlord. "Look sharp and you can catch him."

It was but two steps from the small parlour to the door of the old *George* inn; the wide oak staircase landed almost in the street; there was room for a Turkey rug and nothing more between the threshold and the last round of the descent; but this little space was every evening brilliantly lit up, not only by the light upon the stair and the great signal-lamp below the sign, but by the warm radiance of the bar-room window. The *George* thus brightly advertised itself to passers-by in the cold street. Fettes walked steadily to the spot and we, who were hanging behind, beheld the two men meet, as one of them had phrased it, face to face. Dr. Macfarlane was alert and vigorous. His white hair set off his pale and placid, although energetic, countenance. He was richly dressed in the finest of broadcloth and the whitest of linen, with a great gold watch-chain, and studs and spectacles of the same precious material. He wore a broad-folded tie, white and speckled with lilac, and he carried on his arm a comfortable driving-coat of fur. There was no doubt but he became his years, breathing, as he did, of wealth and consideration;

and it was a surprising contrast to see our parlour sot—bald, dirty, pimpled and robed in his old camlet cloak—confront him at the bottom of the stairs.

"Macfarlane!" he said somewhat loudly, more like a herald than a friend.

The great doctor pulled up short on the fourth step, as though the familiarity of the address surprised and somewhat shocked his dignity.

"Toddy Macfarlane!" repeated Fettes.

The London man almost staggered. He stared for the swiftest of seconds at the man before him, glanced behind him with a sort of scare, and then in a startled whisper, "Fettes!" he said, "you!"

"Ay," said the other, "me! Did you think I was dead too? We are not so easy shut of our acquaintance."

"Hush, hush!" exclaimed the doctor. "Hush, hush! this meeting is so unexpected—I can see you are unmanned. I hardly knew you, I confess, at first, but I am overjoyed—overjoyed to have this opportunity. For the present it must be how-d'ye-do and goodbye in one, for my fly is waiting and I must not fail the train; but you shall—let me see—yes—you shall give me your address and you can count on early news of me. We must do something for you, Fettes. I fear you are out at elbows; but we must see to that for auld lang syne, as once we sang at suppers."

"Money!" cried Fettes; "money from you! The money that I had from you is lying where I cast it in the rain."

Dr. Macfarlane had talked himself into some measure of superiority and confidence, but the uncommon energy of this refusal cast him back into his first confusion.

A horrible, ugly look came and went across his almost venerable countenance. "My dear fellow," he said, "be it as you please; my last thought is to offend you. I would intrude on none. I will leave you my address, however—"

"I do not wish it—I do not wish to know the roof that shelters you," interrupted the other. "I heard your name; I feared it might be you; I wished to know if, after all, there were a God; I know now that there is none. Begone!"

He still stood in the middle of the rug, between the stair and the doorway; and the great London physician, in order to escape, would be forced to step to one side. It was plain that he hesitated before the thought of this humiliation. White as he was, there was a dangerous glitter in his spectacles; but while he still paused uncertain, he became aware that the driver of his fly was peering in from the street at this unusual scene and caught a glimpse at the same time of our little body from the parlour, huddled by the corner of the bar. The presence of so many witnesses decided him at once to flee. He crouched together, brushing on the wainscot, and made a dart like a serpent, striking for the door. But his tribulation was not yet entirely at an end, for even as he was passing Fettes clutched him by the arm and these words came in a whisper, and yet painfully distinct, "Have you seen it again?"

The great rich London doctor cried out aloud with a sharp, throttling cry; he dashed his questioner across the open space, and, with his hands over his head, fled out of the door like a detected thief. Before it had occurred to one of us to make a movement, the fly was already rattling towards the station. The scene was over like a dream, but the dream had left proofs and traces of its passage. Next day the servant found the fine gold spectacles broken on the threshold, and that very night we were all standing breathless by the bar-room window, and Fettes at our side, sober, pale, and resolute in look.

"God protect us, Mr. Fettes!" said the landlord, coming first into possession of his customary senses. "What in the universe is all this? These are strange things you have been saying."

Fettes turned towards us; he looked us each in succession in the face. "See if you can hold your tongues," said he. "That man Macfarlane is not safe to cross; those that have done so already have repented it too late."

And then, without so much as finishing his third glass, far less waiting for the other two, he bade us goodbye and went forth, under the lamp of the hotel, into the black night.

We three turned to our places in the parlour, with the big red fire and four clear candles; and as we recapitulated what had passed the first chill of our surprise soon changed into a glow of curiosity. We sat late; it was the latest session I have known in the old *George*. Each man, before we parted, had his theory that he was bound to prove; and none of us had any nearer business in this world than to track out the past of our condemned companion, and surprise the secret that he shared with the great London doctor. It was no great boast, but I believe I was a better hand at worming out a story than either of my fellows at the *George*; and perhaps there is now no other man alive who could narrate to you the following foul and unnatural events.

In his young days Fettes studied medicine in the schools of Edinburgh. He had talent of a kind, the talent that picks up swiftly what it hears and readily retails it for its own. He worked little at home; but he was civil, attentive, and intelligent in the presence of his masters. They soon picked him out as a lad who listened closely and remembered well; nay, strange as it seemed to me when I first heard it, he was in those days well favoured, and pleased by his exterior. There was, at that period, a certain extramural teacher of anatomy, whom I shall here designate by the letter K. His name was subsequently too well known. The man who bore it skulked through the streets of Edinburgh in disguise, while the mob that applauded at the execution of Burke called loudly for the blood of his employer. But Mr. K——was then at the top of his vogue; he enjoyed a popularity due partly to his own talent and address, partly to the incapacity of his rival, the university professor. The students, at least, swore by his name, and Fettes believed himself, and was believed by others, to have laid the foundations of success when he had acquired the favour of this meteorically famous man. Mr. K——was a *bon vivant* as well as an accomplished teacher; he liked a sly allusion no less than a careful preparation. In both capacities Fettes enjoyed and deserved his notice, and by the second year of his attendance he held the half-regular position of second demonstrator or sub-assistant in his class.

In this capacity, the charge of the theatre and lecture-room devolved in particular upon his shoulders. He had to answer for the cleanliness of the premises and the conduct of the other students, and it was a part of his duty to supply, receive, and divide the various subjects. It was with a view to this last—at that time very delicate—affair that he was lodged by Mr. K——in the same wynd, and at last in the same building, with the dissecting-rooms. Here, after a night of turbulent pleasures, his hand still tottering, his sight still misty and confused, he would be called out of bed in the black hours before the winter dawn by the unclean and desperate interlopers who supplied the table. He would open the door to these men, since infamous throughout the land. He would help them with their tragic burthen, pay them their sordid price, and remain alone, when they were gone, with the unfriendly relics of humanity. From such a scene he would return to snatch another hour or two of slumber, to repair the abuses of the night, and refresh himself for the labours of the day.

Few lads could have been more insensible to the impressions of a life thus passed among the ensigns of mortality. His mind was closed against all general considerations. He was incapable of interest in the fate and fortunes of another, the slave of his own desires and low ambitions. Cold, light, and selfish in the last resort, he had that modicum of prudence, miscalled morality, which keeps a man from inconvenient drunkenness or punishable theft. He coveted, besides, a measure of consideration from his masters and his fellow-pupils, and he had no desire to fail conspicuously in the external parts of life. Thus he made it his pleasure to gain some distinction in his studies, and day after day rendered unimpeachable eye-service to his employer, Mr. K——. For his day of work he indemnified himself by nights of roaring, blackguardly enjoyment; and when that balance had been struck, the organ that he called his conscience declared itself content.

The supply of subjects was a continual trouble to him as well as to his master. In that large and busy class, the raw material of the anatomists kept perpetually running out; and the business thus rendered necessary was not only unpleasant in itself, but threatened dangerous consequences to all who were concerned. It was the policy of Mr. K—— to ask no questions in his dealings with the trade. "They bring the body, and we pay the price," he used to say, dwelling on the alliteration—"*quid pro quo*." And again, and somewhat profanely, "Ask no questions," he would tell his assistants, "for conscience' sake." There was no understanding that the subjects were provided by the crime of murder. Had that idea been broached to him in words, he would have recoiled in horror; but the lightness of his speech upon so grave a matter was, in itself, an offence against good manners, and a temptation to the men with whom he dealt. Fettes, for instance, had often remarked to himself upon the singular freshness of the bodies. He had been struck again and again by the hang-dog, abominable looks of the ruffians who came to him before the dawn; and, putting things together clearly in his private thoughts, he perhaps attributed a meaning too immoral and too categorical to the unguarded counsels of his master. He understood his duty, in short, to have three branches: to take what was brought, to pay the price, and to avert the eye from any evidence of crime.

One November morning this policy of silence was put sharply to the test. He had been awake all night with a racking toothache—pacing his room like a caged beast or throwing himself in fury on his bed—and had fallen at last into that profound, uneasy slumber that so often follows on a night of pain, when he was awakened by the third or fourth angry repetition of the concerted signal. There was a thin, bright moonshine: it was bitter cold, windy, and frosty; the town had not yet awakened, but an indefinable stir already preluded the noise and business of the day. The ghouls had come later than usual, and they seemed more than usually eager to be gone. Fettes, sick with sleep, lighted them upstairs. He heard their grumbling Irish voices through a dream; and as they stripped the sack from their sad merchandise he leaned dozing with his shoulder propped against the wall; he had to shake himself to find the men their money. As he did so his eyes lighted on the dead face. He started; he took two steps nearer, with the candle raised.

"God Almighty!" he cried. "That is Jane Galbraith!"

The men answered nothing, but they shuffled nearer the door.

"I know her, I tell you," he continued. "She was alive and hearty yesterday. It's impossible she can be dead; it's impossible you should have got this body fairly."

"Sure, sir, you're mistaken entirely," asserted one of the men.

But the other looked Fettes darkly in the eyes, and demanded the money on the spot.

It was impossible to misconceive the threat or to exaggerate the danger. The lad's heart failed him. He stammered some excuses, counted out the sum, and saw his hateful visitors depart. No sooner were they gone than he hastened to confirm his doubts. By a dozen unquestionable marks he identified the girl he had jested with the day before. He saw, with horror, marks upon her body that might well betoken violence. A panic seized him, and he took refuge in his room. There he reflected at length over the discovery that he had made; considered soberly the bearing of Mr. K——'s instructions and the danger to himself of interference in so serious a business, and at last, in sore perplexity, determined to wait for the advice of his immediate superior, the class assistant.

This was a young doctor, Wolfe Macfarlane, a high favourite among all the restless students, clever, dissipated, and unscrupulous to the last degree. He had travelled and studied abroad. His manners were agreeable and a little forward. He was an authority on the stage, skilful on the ice or the links with skate or golf-club; he dressed with nice audacity, and, to put the finishing touch upon his glory, he kept a gig and a strong trotting-horse. With Fettes he was on terms of intimacy; indeed their relative positions called for some community of life; and when subjects were scarce the pair would drive far into the country in Macfarlane's gig, visit and desecrate some lonely graveyard, and return before dawn with their booty to the door of the dissecting-room.

On that particular morning Macfarlane arrived somewhat earlier than his wont. Fettes heard him, and met him on the stairs, told him his story, and showed him the cause of his alarm. Macfarlane examined the marks on her body.

"Yes," he said with a nod, "it looks fishy."

"Well, what should I do?" asked Fettes.

"Do?" repeated the other. "Do you want to do anything? Least said soonest mended, I should say."

"Someone else might recognize her," objected Fettes. "She was as well known as the Castle Rock."

"We'll hope not," said Macfarlane, "and if anybody does—well you didn't, don't you see, and there's an end. The fact is, this has been going on too long. Stir up the mud, and you'll get K——into the most unholy trouble; you'll be in a shocking box yourself. So will I, if you come to that. I should like to know how any one of us would look, or what the devil we should have to say for ourselves, in any Christian witness-box. For me, you know there's one thing certain—that, practically speaking, all our subjects have been murdered."

"Macfarlane!" cried Fettes.

"Come now!" sneered the other. "As if you hadn't suspected it yourself!"

"Suspecting is one thing—"

"And proof another. Yes, I know; and I'm as sorry as you are this should have come here," tapping the body with his cane. "The next best thing for me is not to recognize it; and," he added coolly, "I don't. You may, if you please. I don't dictate, but I think a man of the world would do as I do; and I may add, I fancy that is what K——would look for at our hands. The question is, why did he choose us two for his assistants? And I answer, because he didn't want old wives."

This was the tone of all others to affect the mind of a lad like Fettes. He agreed to imitate Macfarlane. The body of the unfortunate girl was duly dissected, and no one remarked or appeared to recognize her.

One afternoon, when his day's work was over, Fettes dropped into a popular tavern and found Macfarlane sitting with a stranger. This was a small man, very pale and dark, with coal-black eyes. The cut of his features gave a promise of intellect and refinement which was but feebly realized in his manners, for he proved, upon a nearer acquaintance, coarse, vulgar, and stupid. He exercised, however, a very remarkable control over Macfarlane; issued orders like the Great Bashaw; became inflamed at the least discussion or delay, and commented rudely on the servility with which he was obeyed. This most offensive person took a fancy to Fettes on the spot, plied him with drinks, and honoured him with unusual confidences on his past career. If a tenth part of what he confessed were true, he was a very loathsome rogue; and the lad's vanity was tickled by the attention of so experienced a man.

"I'm a pretty bad fellow myself," the stranger remarked, "but Macfarlane is the boy—Toddy Macfarlane I call him. Toddy, order your friend another glass." Or it might be, "Toddy, you jump up and shut the door." "Toddy hates me," he said again. "Oh, yes, Toddy, you do!"

"Don't call me that confounded name," growled Macfarlane.

"Hear him! Did you ever see the lads play knife? He would like to do that all over my body," remarked the stranger.

"We medicals have a better way than that," said Fettes. "When we dislike a dead friend of ours, we dissect him."

Macfarlane looked up sharply, as though this jest was scarcely to his mind.

The afternoon passed. Gray, for that was the stranger's name, invited Fettes to join them at dinner, ordered a feast so sumptuous that the tavern was thrown in commotion, and when all was done commanded Macfarlane to settle the bill. It was late before they separated; the man Gray was incapably drunk. Macfarlane, sobered by his fury, chewed the cud of the money he had been forced to squander and the slights he had been obliged to swallow. Fettes, with various liquors singing in his head, returned home with devious footsteps and a mind entirely in abeyance. Next day Macfarlane was absent from the class, and Fettes smiled to himself as he imagined him still squiring the intolerable Gray from tavern to tavern. As soon as the hour of liberty had struck he posted from place to place in quest of his last night's companions. He could find them, however, nowhere; so returned early to his rooms, went early to bed, and slept the sleep of the just.

At four in the morning he was awakened by the well-known signal. Descending to the door, he was filled with astonishment to find Macfarlane with his gig, and in the gig one of those long and ghastly packages with which he was so well acquainted.

"What?" he cried. "Have you been out alone? How did you manage?"

But Macfarlane silenced him roughly, bidding him turn to business. When they had got the body upstairs and laid it on the table, Macfarlane made at first as if he were going away. Then he paused and seemed to hesitate; and then, "You had better look at the face," said he, in tones of some constraint. "You had better," he repeated, as Fettes only stared at him in wonder.

"But where, and how, and when did you come by it?" cried the other. "Look at the face," was the only answer.

Fettes was staggered; strange doubts assailed him. He looked from the young doctor to the body, and then back again. At last, with a start, he did as he was bidden. He had almost expected the sight that met his eyes, and yet the shock was cruel. To see, fixed in the rigidity of death and naked on that coarse layer of sackcloth, the man whom he had left well-clad and full of meat and sin upon the threshold of a tavern, awoke, even in the thoughtless Fettes, some of the terrors of the conscience. It was a *cras tibi* which re-echoed in his soul, that two whom he had known should have come to lie upon these icy tables. Yet these were only secondary thoughts. His first concern regarded Wolfe. Unprepared for a challenge so momentous, he knew not how to look his comrade in the face. He durst not meet his eye, and he had neither words nor voice at his command.

It was Macfarlane himself who made the first advance. He came up quietly behind and laid his hand gently but firmly on the other's shoulder.

"Richardson," said he, "may have the head."

Now Richardson was a student who had long been anxious for that portion of the human subject to dissect. There was no answer, and the murderer resumed: "Talking of business, you must pay me; your accounts, you see, must tally."

Fettes found a voice, the ghost of his own: "Pay you!" he cried. "Pay you for that?"

"Why, yes, of course you must. By all means and on every possible account, you must," returned the other. "I dare not give it for nothing, you dare not take it for nothing; it would compromise us both. This is another case like Jane Galbraith's. The more things are wrong the more we must act as if all were right. Where does old K——keep his money—"

"There," answered Fettes hoarsely, pointing to a cupboard in the corner.

"Give me the key, then," said the other, calmly, holding out his hand.

There was an instant's hesitation, and the die was cast. Macfarlane could not suppress a nervous twitch, the infinitesimal mark of an immense relief, as he felt the key turn between his fingers. He opened the cupboard, brought out pen and ink and a paper-book that stood in one compartment, and separated from the funds in a drawer a sum suitable to the occasion.

"Now, look here," he said, "there is the payment made—first proof of your good faith: first step to your security. You have now to clinch it by a second. Enter the payment in your book, and then you for your part may defy the devil."

The next few seconds were for Fettes an agony of thought; but in balancing his terrors it was the most immediate that triumphed. Any future difficulty seemed almost welcome if he could avoid a present quarrel with Macfarlane. He set down the candle which he had been carrying all the time, and with a steady hand entered the date, the nature, and the amount of the transaction.

"And now," said Macfarlane, "it's only fair that you should pocket the lucre. I've had my share already. By-the-by, when a man of the world falls into a bit of luck, has a few shillings extra in his pocket—I'm ashamed to speak of it, but there's a rule of conduct in the case. No treating, no purchase of expensive classbooks, no squaring of old debts; borrow, don't lend."

"Macfarlane," began Fettes, still somewhat hoarsely. "I have put my neck in a halter to oblige you."

"To oblige me?" cried Wolfe. "Oh, come! You did, as near as I can see the matter, what you downright had to do in self defence. Suppose I got into trouble, where would you be? This second little matter flows clearly from the first. Mr. Gray is the continuation of Miss Galbraith. You can't begin and then stop. If you begin, you must keep on beginning; that's the truth. No rest for the wicked."

A horrible sense of blackness and the treachery of fate seized hold upon the soul of the unhappy student.

"My God" he cried, "but what have I done? and when did I begin? To be made a class assistant—in the name of reason, where's the harm in that? Service wanted the position; Service might have got it. Would *he* have been where *I* am now?"

"My dear fellow," said Macfarlane, "what a boy you are! What harm *has* come to you? What harm *can* come to you if you hold your tongue? Why, man, do you know what this life is? There are two squads of us—the lions and the lambs. If you're a lamb, you'll come to lie upon these tables like Gray or Jane Galbraith; if you're a lion, you'll live and drive a horse like me, like K——, like all the world with any wit or courage. You're staggered at the first. But look at K——! My dear fellow, you're clever, you have pluck. I like you, and K—— likes you. You were born to lead the hunt; and I tell you, on my honour and my experience of life, three days from now you'll laugh at all these scarecrows like a high-school boy at a farce."

And with that Macfarlane took his departure and drove off up the wynd in his gig to get under cover before daylight. Fettes was thus left alone with his regrets. He saw the miserable peril in which he stood involved. He saw, with inexpressible dismay, that there was no limit to his weakness, and that, from concession to concession, he had fallen from the arbiter of Macfarlane's destiny to his paid and helpless accomplice. He would have given the world to have been a little braver at the time, but it did not occur to him that he might still be brave. The secret of Jane Galbraith and the cursed entry in the daybook closed his mouth.

Hours passed; the class began to arrive; the members of the unhappy Gray were dealt out to one and to another, and received without remark. Richardson was made happy with the head; and before the hour of freedom rang Fettes trembled with exultation to perceive how far they had already gone towards safety.

For two days he continued to watch, with increasing joy, the dreadful process of disguise.

On the third day Macfarlane made his appearance. He had been ill, he said; but he made up for lost time by the energy with which he directed the students. To Richardson in particular he extended the most valuable assistance and advice, and that student, encouraged by the praise of the demonstrator, burned high with ambitious hopes, and saw the medal already in his grasp.

Before the week was out Macfarlane's prophecy had been fulfilled. Fettes had outlived his terrors and had forgotten his baseness. He began to plume himself upon his courage, and had so arranged the story in his mind that he could look back on these events with an unhealthy pride. Of his accomplice he saw but little. They met, of course, in the business of the class; they received their orders together from Mr. K——. At times they had a word or two in private, and Macfarlane was from first to last particularly kind and jovial. But it was plain that he avoided any reference to their common secret; and even when Fettes whispered to him that he had cast in his lot with the lions and forsworn the lambs, he only signed to him smilingly to hold his peace.

At length an occasion arose which threw the pair once more into a closer union. Mr. K—— was again short of subjects; pupils were eager, and it was a part of this teacher's pretensions to be always well supplied. At the same time there came the news of a burial in the rustic graveyard of Glencorse. Time has little changed the place in question. It stood then, as now, upon the crossroad, out of call of human habitations, and buried fathom deep in the foliage of six cedar trees. The cries of the sheep upon the neighbouring hills, the streamlets upon either hand, one loudly singing among pebbles, the other dripping furtively from pond to pond, the stir of the wind in mountainous old flowering chestnuts, and once in seven days the voice of the bell and the old tunes of the precentor, were the only sounds that disturbed the silence around the rural church. The Resurrection

Man—to use a by-name of the period—was not to be deterred by any of the sanctities of customary piety. It was part of his trade to despise and desecrate the scrolls and trumpets of old tombs, the paths worn by the feet of worshippers and mourners, and the offerings and the inscriptions of bereaved affection. To rustic neighbourhoods, where love is more than commonly tenacious, and where some bonds of blood or fellowship unite the entire society of a parish, the body-snatcher, far from being repelled by natural respect, was attracted by the ease and safety of the task. To bodies that had been laid in earth, in joyful expectation of a far different awakening, there came that hasty, lamp-lit, terror-haunted resurrection of the spade and mattock. The coffin was forced, the cerements torn, and the melancholy relics, clad in sackcloth, after being rattled for hours on moonless by-ways, were at length exposed to uttermost indignities before a class of gaping boys.

Somewhat as two vultures may swoop upon a dying lamb, Fettes and Macfarlane were to be let loose upon a grave in that green and quiet resting-place. The wife of a farmer, a woman who had lived for sixty years, and been known for nothing but good butter and a godly conversation, was to be rooted from her grave at midnight and carried, dead and naked, to that far-away city that she had always honoured with her Sunday best; the place beside her family was to be empty till the crack of doom; her innocent and almost venerable members to be exposed to that last curiosity of the anatomist.

Late one afternoon the pair set forth, well wrapped in cloaks and furnished with a formidable bottle. It rained without remission—a cold, dense, lashing rain. Now and again there blew a puff of wind, but these sheets of falling water kept it down. Bottle and all, it was a sad and silent drive as far as Penicuik, where they were to spend the evening. They stopped once, to hide their implements in a thick bush not far from the churchyard, and once again at the Fisher's Tryst, to have a toast before the kitchen fire and vary their nips of whisky with a glass of ale. When they reached their journey's end the gig was housed, the horse was fed and comforted, and the two young doctors in a private room sat down to the best dinner and the best wine the house afforded. The lights, the fire, the beating rain upon the window, the cold, incongruous work that lay before them, added zest to their enjoyment of the meal. With every glass their cordiality increased. Soon Macfarlane handed a little pile of gold to his companion.

"A compliment," he said. "Between friends these little damned accommodations ought to fly like pipe-lights."

Fettes pocketed the money, and applauded the sentiment to the echo. "You are a philosopher," he cried. "I was an ass till I knew you. You and K——between you, by the Lord Harry! but you'll make a man of me."

"Of course we shall," applauded Macfarlane. "A man? I tell you, it required a man to back me up the other morning. There are some big, brawling, forty-year-old cowards who would have turned sick at the look of the damned thing; but not you—you kept your head. I watched you."

"Well, and why not?" Fettes thus vaunted himself. "It was no affair of mine. There was nothing to gain on the one side but disturbance, and on the other I could count on your gratitude, don't you see?" And he slapped his pocket till the gold pieces rang.

Macfarlane somehow felt a certain touch of alarm at these unpleasant words. He may have regretted that he had taught his young companion so successfully, but he had no time to interfere, for the other noisily continued in this boastful strain:

"The great thing is not to be afraid. Now, between you and me, I don't want to hang—that's practical; but for all cant, Macfarlane, I was born with a contempt. Hell, God, Devil, right, wrong, sin, crime, and all the old gallery of curiosities—they may frighten boys, but men of the world, like you and me, despise them. Here's to the memory of Gray!"

It was by this time growing somewhat late. The gig, according to order, was brought round to the door with both lamps brightly shining, and the young men had to pay their bill and take the road. They announced that they were bound for Peebles, and drove in that direction till they were clear of the last houses of the town; then, extinguishing the lamps, returned upon their course, and followed a by-road towards Glencorse. There was no sound but that of their own passage, and the incessant, strident pouring of the rain. It was pitch dark; here and there a white gate or a white stone in the wall guided them for a short space across the night; but for the most part it was at a foot pace, and almost groping, that they picked their way through that resonant blackness to their solemn and isolated destination. In the sunken woods that traverse the neighbourhood of the burying-ground the last glimmer failed them, and it became necessary to kindle a match and re-illumine one of the lanterns of the gig. Thus, under the dripping trees, and environed by huge and moving shadows, they reached the scene of their unhallowed labours.

They were both experienced in such affairs, and powerful with the spade; and they had scarce been twenty minutes at their task before they were rewarded by a dull rattle on the coffin lid. At the same moment Macfarlane, having hurt his hand upon a stone, flung it carelessly above his head. The grave, in which they now stood almost to the shoulders, was close to the edge of the plateau of the graveyard; and the gig lamp had been propped, the better to illuminate their labours, against a tree, and on the immediate verge of the steep bank descending to the stream. Chance had taken a sure aim with the stone. Then came a clang of broken glass; night fell upon them; sounds alternately dull and ringing announced the bounding of the lantern down the bank, and its occasional collision with the trees. A stone or two, which it had dislodged in its descent rattled behind it into the profundities of the glen; and then silence, like night, resumed its sway; and they might bend their hearing to its utmost pitch, but naught was to be heard except the rain, now marching to the wind, now steadily falling over miles of open country.

They were so nearly at an end of their abhorred task that they judged it wisest to complete it in the dark. The coffin was exhumed and broken open; the body inserted in the dripping sack and carried between them to the gig; one mounted to keep it in its place, and the other, taking the horse by the mouth, groped along by the wall and bush until they reached the wider road by the Fisher's Tryst. Here was a faint disused radiancy, which they hailed like daylight; by that they pushed the horse to a good pace and began to rattle along merrily in the direction of the town.

They had both been wetted to the skin during their operations, and now, as the gig jumped among the deep ruts, the thing that stood propped between them fell now upon one and now upon the other. At every repetition of the horrid contact each instinctively repelled it with greater haste; and the process, natural although it was, began to tell upon the nerves of the companions. Macfarlane made some ill-favoured jest about the farmer's wife, but it came hollowly from his lips, and was allowed to drop in silence. Still their unnatural burthen bumped from side to side; and now the head would be laid, as if in confidence, upon their shoulders, and now the drenching sackcloth would flap idly about their faces. A creeping chill began to possess the soul of Fettes. He peered at the bundle, and it seemed somehow larger than at first. All over the countryside, and from every degree of distance, the farm dogs accompanied their passage with tragic ululations; and it grew and grew upon his mind that some unnatural miracle had been achieved, that some nameless change had befallen the dead body, and that it was in fear of their unholy burthen that the dogs were howling.

"For God's sake," said he, making a great effort to arrive at speech, "for God's sake, let's have a light!"

Seemingly Macfarlane was affected in the same direction; for though he made no reply, he stopped the horse, passed the reins to his companion, got down, and proceeded to kindle the remaining lamp. They had by that time got no farther than the crossroad down to Auchendinny. The rain still poured as though the deluge were returning, and it was no easy matter to make a light in such a world of wet and darkness. When at last the flickering blue flame had been transferred to the wick and began to expand and clarify, and shed a wide circle of misty brightness round the gig, it became possible for the two young men to see each other and the thing they had along with them. The rain had moulded the rough sacking to the outlines of the body underneath; the head was distinct from the trunk, the shoulders plainly modelled; something at once spectral and human riveted their eyes upon the ghastly comrade of their drive.

For some time Macfarlane stood motionless, holding up the lamp. A nameless dread was swathed, like a wet sheet, about the body, and tightened the white skin upon the face of Fettes; a fear that was meaningless, a horror of what could not be, kept mounting to his brain. Another beat of the watch, and he had spoken. But his comrade forestalled him.

"That is not a woman," said Macfarlane, in a hushed voice.

"It was a woman when we put her in," whispered Fettes.

"Hold that lamp," said the other. "I must see her face."

And as Fettes took the lamp his companion untied the fastenings of the sack and drew down the cover from the head. The light fell very clear upon the dark, well-moulded features and smooth-shaven cheeks of a too familiar countenance, often beheld in dreams of both of these young men. A wild yell rang up into the night; each leaped from his own side into the roadway; the lamp fell, broke, and was extinguished; and the horse, terrified by this unusual commotion, bounded and went off towards Edinburgh at a gallop, bearing along with it, sole occupant of the gig, the body of the dead and long-dissected Gray.

AMBROSE (GWINETT) BIERCE (1842–1914?)

Ambrose Bierce's life was as exciting and adventurous as his fiction. A veteran of both the Civil War and William Randolph Hearst's newspaper empire, Bierce was well traveled. Like Harriet Beecher Stowe, he was originally a product of Ohio and attained national stature in his lifetime. In his newspaper writing, Bierce wrote pointed social and political commentary and could often be at least as cynical as Mark Twain—hence, the nickname "Bitter Bierce." Bierce was a talented, versatile, and prolific author; he was a short story writer, novelist, poet, essayist, and critic. He disappeared in Mexico sometime after 1914, when he was reporting on that country's civil war. Some believe he fell victim to Pancho Villa.

The author's contributions to Dark Fantasy can generally be divided into two categories — horror stories based on the atrocities of war Bierce witnessed firsthand and stories of the supernatural. Perhaps his most famous story from the first group is "An Occurrence at Owl Creek Bridge," collected in Tales of Soldiers and Civilians *in 1891 and presented as a* Twilight Zone *television episode by Rod Serling on February 28, 1964. Bierce's "The Damned Thing" falls into the second category and evokes memories of stories of the supernatural and madness by Joseph Sheridan LeFanu, Guy de Maupassant, and Charlotte Gilman Perkins.*

The Damned Thing

(Tales From New York Town Topics, *vol. 30, no. 23, December 7, 1893*)

I

One Does Not Always Eat What Is on the Table

By the light of a tallow candle which had been placed on one end of a rough table a man was reading something written in a book. It was an old account book, greatly worn; and the writing was not, apparently, very legible, for the man sometimes held the page close to the flame of the candle to get a stronger light on it. The shadow of the book would then throw into obscurity a half of the room, darkening a number of faces and figures; for besides the reader, eight other men were present. Seven of them sat against the rough log walls, silent, motionless, and the room being small, not very far from the table. By extending an arm any one of them could have touched the eighth man, who lay on the table, face upward, partly covered by a sheet, his arms at his sides. He was dead.

The man with the book was not reading aloud; and no one spoke; all seemed to be waiting for something to occur; the dead man only was without expectation. From the blank darkness outside came in, through the aperture that served for a window, all the ever unfamiliar noises of night in the wilderness — the long nameless note of a distant coyote; the stilly pulsing thrill of tireless insects in trees; strange cries of night birds so different from those of the birds of day; the drone of great blundering beetles, and all that mysterious chorus of small sounds that seem always to have been but heard when they have suddenly ceased, as if conscious of an indiscretion. But nothing of all this was noted in that company; its members were not overmuch addicted to idle interest in matters of no practical importance; that was obvious in every line of their rugged faces — obvious even in the dim light of the single candle. They were evidently men of the vicinity — farmers and woodsmen.

The person reading was a trifle different; one would have said of him that he was of the world, worldly, albeit there was that in his attire which attested a certain fellowship with the organisms of his environment. His coat would hardly have passed in San Francisco; his foot-gear was not of urban origin, and the hat that lay by him on the floor (he was the only one uncovered) was such that if one had considered it as an article of mere personal adornment he would have missed its meaning. In countenance the man was rather prepossessing, with just a hint of sternness; though that he may have assumed or cultivated, as appropriate to one in authority. For he was a coroner. It was by virtue of his office that he had possession of the book in which he was reading; it had been found among the dead man's effects — in his cabin, where the inquest was now taking place.

When the coroner had finished reading he put the book into his breast pocket. At that moment the door was pushed open and a young man entered. He, clearly, was not of mountain birth and breeding: he was clad as those who dwell in cities. His clothing was dusty, however, as from travel. He had, in fact, been riding hard to attend the inquest.

The coroner nodded; no one else greeted him.

'We have waited for you,' said the coroner. 'It is necessary to have done with this business to-night.'

The young man smiled. 'I am sorry to have kept you,' he said. 'I went away, not to evade your summons, but to post to my newspaper an account of what I suppose I am called back to relate.'

The coroner smiled.

'The account that you posted to your newspaper,' he said, 'differs, probably, from that which you will give here under oath.'

'But you say it is incredible.'

'That is nothing to you, sir, if I also swear that it is true.'

The coroner was silent for a time, his eyes upon the floor. The men about the sides of the cabin talked in whispers, but seldom withdrew their gaze from the face of the corpse. Presently the coroner lifted his eyes and said: 'We will resume the inquest.'

The men removed their hats. The witness was sworn.

'What is your name?' the coroner asked.

'William Harker.'

'Age?'

'Twenty-seven.'

'You knew the deceased, Hugh Morgan?'

'Yes.'

'You were with him when he died?'

'Near him.'

'How did that happen—your presence, I mean?'

'I was visiting at this place to shoot and fish. A part of my purpose, however, was to study him and his odd, solitary way of life. He seemed a good model for a character in fiction. I sometimes write stories.'

'I sometimes read them.'

'Thank you.'

'Stories in general—not yours.'

Some of the jurors laughed. Against a sombre background humor shows high lights. Soldiers in the intervals of battle laugh easily, and a jest in the death chambers conquers by surprise.

'Relate the circumstances of this man's death,' said the coroner. 'You may use any notes or memoranda that you please.'

The witness understood. Pulling a manuscript from his breast pocket he held it near the candle and turning the leaves until he found the passage that he wanted began to read.

II

What May Happen in a Field of Wild Oats

'. . . The sun had hardly risen when we left the house. We were looking for quail, each with a shotgun, but we had only one dog. Morgan said that our best ground was beyond a certain ridge that he pointed out, and we crossed it by a trail through the *chaparral*. On the other side was comparatively level ground, thickly covered with wild oats. As we emerged from the *chaparral* Morgan was but a few yards in advance. Suddenly we heard, at a little distance to our right and partly in front, a noise as of some animal thrashing about in the bushes which we could see were violently agitated.

'"We've started a deer," I said. "I wish we had brought a rifle."

'Morgan, who had stopped and was intently watching the agitated *chaparral*, said nothing, but had cocked both barrels of his gun and was holding it in readiness to aim. I thought him a trifle excited, which surprised me, for he had a reputation for exceptional coolness, even in moments of sudden and imminent peril.

'"O, come," I said. "You are not going to fill up a deer with quail-shot, are you?"

'Still he did not reply; but catching a sight of his face as he turned it slightly toward me I was struck by the intensity of his look. Then I understood that we had serious business in hand and my first conjecture was that we had "jumped" a grizzly. I advanced to Morgan's side, cocking my piece as I moved.

'The bushes were now quiet and the sounds had ceased, but Morgan was as attentive to the place as before.

'"What is it? What the devil is it?" I asked.

'"That Damned Thing!" he replied, without turning his head. His voice was husky and unnatural. He trembled visibly.

'I was about to speak further, when I observed the wild oats near the place of the disturbance moving in the most inexplicable way. I can hardly describe it. It seemed as if stirred by a streak of wind, which not only bent it, but pressed it down—crushed it so that it did not rise; and this movement was slowly prolonging itself directly toward us.

'Nothing that I had ever seen affected me so strangely as this unfamiliar and unaccountable phenomenon, yet I am unable to recall any sense of fear. I remember—and tell it here because, singularly enough, I recollected it then—that once in looking carelessly out of an open window I momentarily mistook a small tree close at hand for one of a group of larger trees at a little distance away. It looked the same size as the others, but being more distinctly and sharply defined in mass and detail seemed out of harmony with them. It was a mere falsification of the law of aërial perspective, but it startled, almost terrified me. We so rely upon the orderly operation of familiar natural laws that any seeming suspension of them is noted as a menace to our safety, a warning of unthinkable calamity. So now the apparently causeless movement of the herbage and the slow, undeviating approach of the line of disturbance were distinctly disquieting. My companion appeared actually frightened, and I could hardly credit my senses when I saw him suddenly throw his gun to his shoulder and fire both barrels at the agitated grain! Before the smoke of the discharge had cleared away I heard a loud savage cry—a scream like that of a wild animal—and flinging his gun upon the ground Morgan sprang away and ran swiftly from the spot. At the same instant I was thrown violently to the ground by the impact of something unseen in the smoke—some soft, heavy substance that seemed thrown against me with great force.

'Before I could get upon my feet and recover my gun, which seemed to have been struck from my hands, I heard Morgan crying out as if in mortal agony, and mingling with his cries were such hoarse, savage sounds as one hears from fighting dogs. Inexpressibly terrified, I struggled to my feet and looked in the direction of

Morgan's retreat; and may Heaven in mercy spare me from another sight like that! At a distance of less than thirty yards was my friend, down upon one knee, his head thrown back at a frightful angle, hatless, his long hair in disorder and his whole body in violent movement from side to side, backward and forward. His right arm was lifted and seemed to lack the hand—at least, I could see none. The other arm was invisible. At times, as my memory now reports this extraordinary scene, I could discern but a part of his body; it was as if he had been partly blotted out—I cannot otherwise express it—then a shifting of his position would bring it all into view again.

'All this must have occurred within a few seconds, yet in that time Morgan assumed all the postures of a determined wrestler vanquished by superior weight and strength. I saw nothing but him, and him not always distinctly. During the entire incident his shouts and curses were heard, as if through an enveloping uproar of such sounds of rage and fury as I had never heard from the throat of man or brute!

'For a moment only I stood irresolute, then throwing down my gun I ran forward to my friend's assistance. I had a vague belief that he was suffering from a fit, or some form of convulsion. Before I could reach his side he was down and quiet. All sounds had ceased, but with a feeling of such terror as even these awful events had not inspired I now saw again the mysterious movements of the wild oats, prolonging itself from the trampled area about the prostrate man towards the edge of a wood. It was only when it had reached the wood that I was able to withdraw my eyes and look at my companion. He was dead.'

III

A Man Though Naked May Be in Rags

The coroner rose from his seat and stood beside the dead man. Lifting an edge of the sheet he pulled it away, exposing the entire body, althogether naked and showing in the candle-light a claylike yellow. It had, however, broad maculations of bluish black, obviously caused by extravasated blood from contusions. The chest and sides looked as if they had been beaten with a bludgeon. There were dreadful lacerations; the skin was torn in strips and shreds.

The coroner moved round to the end of the table and undid a silk handkerchief which had been passed under the chin and knotted on the top of the head. When the handkerchief was drawn away it exposed what had been the throat. Some of the jurors who had risen to get a better view repented their curiosity and turned away their faces. Witness Harker went to the open window and leaned out across the sill, faint and sick. Dropping the handkerchief upon the dead man's neck the coroner stepped to an angle of the room and from a pile of clothing produced one garment after another, each of which he held up a moment for inspection. All were torn, and stiff with blood. The jurors did not make a closer inspection. They seemed rather uninterested. They had, in truth, seen all this before; the only thing that was new to them being Harker's testimony.

'Gentlemen,' the coroner said, 'we have no more evidence, I think. Your duty has been already explained to you; if there is nothing you wish to ask you may go outside and consider your verdict.'

The foreman rose—a tall, bearded man of sixty, coarsely clad.

'I should like to ask one question, Mr. Coroner,' he said. 'What asylum did this yer last witness escape from?'

'Mr. Harker,' said the coroner, gravely and tranquilly, 'from what asylum did you last escape?'

Harker flushed crimson again, but said nothing, and the seven jurors rose and solemnly filed out of the cabin.

'If you have done insulting me, sir,' said Harker, as soon as he and the officer were left alone with the dead man, 'I suppose I am at liberty to go?'

'Yes.'

Harker started to leave, but paused, with his hand on the door latch. The habit of his profession was strong in him—stronger than his sense of personal dignity. He turned about and said:

'The book that you have there—I recognize it as Morgan's diary. You seemed greatly interested in it; you read in it while I was testifying. May I see it? The public would like—'

'The book will cut no figure in this matter,' replied the official; slipping it into his coat pocket; 'and the entries in it were made before the writer's death.'

As Harker passed out of the house the jury reëntered and stood about the table, on which the now covered corpse showed under the sheet with sharp definition. The foreman seated himself near the candle, produced from his breast pocket a pencil and scrap of paper and wrote rather laboriously the following verdict, which with various degrees of effort all signed:

'We, the jury, do find that the remains come to their death at the hands of a mountain lion, but some of us thinks, all the same, they had fits.'

IV

An Explanation from the Tomb

In the diary of the late Hugh Morgan are certain interesting entries having, possibly, a scientific value as suggestions. At the inquest upon his body the book was not put in evidence; possibly the coroner thought it not worth while to confuse the jury. The date of the first of the entries mentioned cannot be ascertained; the upper part of the leaf is torn away; the part of the entry remaining follows:

'. . . would run in a half-circle, keeping his head turned always toward the centre, and again he would stand still, barking furiously. At last he ran away into the brush as fast as he could go. I thought at first that he had gone mad, but on returning to the house found no other alteration in his manner than what was obviously due to fear of punishment.

'Can a dog see with his nose? Do odors impress some cerebral centre with images of the thing that emitted them? . . .

'*Sept. 2.*—Looking at the stars last night as they rose above the crest of the ridge east of the house, I observed them successively disappear—from left to right. Each was eclipsed but an instant, and only a few at the same time, but along the entire length of the ridge all that were within a degree or two of the crest were blotted out. It was as if something had passed along between me and them; but I could not see it, and the stars were not thick enough to define its outline. Ugh! I don't like this.'

Several weeks' entries are missing, three leaves being torn from the book.

'*Sept. 27.*—It has been about here again—I find evidences of its presence every day. I watched again all last night in the same cover, gun in hand, double-charged with buckshot. In the morning the fresh footprints were there, as before. Yet I would have sworn that I did not sleep—indeed, I hardly sleep at all. It is terrible, insupportable! If these amazing experiences are real I shall go mad; if they are fanciful I am mad already.

'*Oct. 3.*—I shall not go—it shall not drive me away. No, this is *my* house, *my* land. God hates a coward . . .

'*Oct. 5.*—I can stand it no longer; I have invited Harker to pass a few weeks with me—he has a level head. I can judge from his manner if he thinks me mad.

'*Oct. 7.*—I have the solution of the mystery; it came to me last night—suddenly, as by revelation. How simple—how terribly simple!

'There are sounds that we cannot hear. At either end of the scale are notes that stir no chord of that imperfect instrument, the human ear. They are too high or too grave. I have observed a flock of blackbirds occupying an entire tree-top—the tops of several trees—and all in full song. Suddenly—in a moment—at absolutely the same instant—all spring into the air and fly away. How? They could not all see one another—whole tree-tops intervened. At no point could a leader have been visible to all. There must have been a signal of warning or command, high and shrill above the din, but by me unheard. I have observed, too, the same simultaneous flight when all were silent, among not only blackbirds, but other birds—quail, for example, widely separated by bushes—even on opposite sides of a hill.

'It is known to seamen that a school of whales basking or sporting on the surface of the ocean, miles apart, with the convexity of the earth between, will sometimes dive at the same instant—all gone out of sight in a moment. The signal has been sounded—too grave for the ear of the sailor at the masthead and his comrades on the deck—who nevertheless feel its vibrations in the ship as the stones of a cathedral are stirred by the bass of the organ.

'As with sounds, so with colors. At each end of the solar spectrum the chemist can detect the presence of what are known as 'actinic' rays. They represent colors—integral colors in the composition of light—which we are unable to discern. The human eye is an imperfect instrument; its range is but a few octaves of the real 'chromatic scale.' I am not mad; there are colors that we cannot see.

'And, God help me! the Damned Thing is of such a color!'

✣ ABRAHAM ("BRAM") STOKER (1847–1912)

Bram Stoker was an Irishman who loved storytelling, myth and legend, and the theater. He was the author of short stories and novels that covered a range of topics that include, but are not limited to, Dark Fantasy and supernatural fiction. Today, of course, Stoker is best remembered for his 1897 novel, Dracula. *Ironically,* Dracula *was not the first vampire story by any stretch of the imagination—in fact or fiction. John Polidori had published* The Vampyre *in 1819, James Malcolm Rymer began his Penny Dreadful installments of* Varney the Vampyre *(a roguish highwayman) in 1847, and Joseph Sheridan LeFanu had published "Carmilla" in 1872. All are replete with myth and legend.*

Among his other novels, The Jewel of the Seven Stars *(1903) and* The Lair of the White Worm *(1911) are Stoker's most recognized Gothic outings. Interestingly, his best writing may be found in his shorter works. And appropriately, Stoker's* Dracula *was a popular theater production before it was transferred to celluloid in* Nosferatu *(1922) and the archetypal vampire vehicle for Bela Lugosi,* Dracula, *in 1931.*

"Dracula's Guest" was part of Bram Stoker's original manuscript for his 1897 novel. However, it was excised before publication. This short work stands by itself as a complete

work of atmospheric supernatural fiction. It also serves as an effective introduction and even prequel to Stoker's novel. Today, vampire stories are alive and well, and their practitioners have maintained and expanded the related mythology.

Dracula's Guest

(from the original manuscript, Dracula, *1897)*

When we started for our drive the sun was shining brightly on Munich, and the air was full of the joyousness of early summer. Just as we were about to depart, Herr Delbrück (the maître d'hôtel of the Quatre Saisons, where I was staying) came down, bareheaded, to the carriage and, after wishing me a pleasant drive, said to the coachman, still holding his hand on the handle of the carriage door:

"Remember you are back by nightfall. The sky looks bright but there is a shiver in the north wind that says there may be a sudden storm. But I am sure you will not be late." Here he smiled, and added, "for you know what night it is."

Johann answered with an emphatic, "Ja, mein Herr," and, touching his hat, drove off quickly. When we had cleared the town, I said, after signalling to him to stop:

"Tell me, Johann, what is to-night?"

He crossed himself, as he answered laconically: "Walpurgisnacht." Then he took out his watch, a great, old-fashioned German silver thing as big as a turnip, and looked at it, with his eyebrows gathered together and a little impatient shrug of his shoulders. I realised that this was his way of respectfully protesting against the unnecessary delay, and sank back in the carriage, merely motioning him to proceed. He started off rapidly, as if to make up for lost time. Every now and then the horses seemed to throw up their heads and sniffed the air suspiciously. On such occasions I often looked round in alarm. The road was pretty bleak, for we were traversing a sort of high, wind-swept plateau. As we drove, I saw a road that looked but little used, and which seemed to dip through a little, winding valley. It looked so inviting that, even at the risk of offending him, I called Johann to stop—and when he had pulled up, I told him I would like to drive down that road. He made all sorts of excuses, and frequently crossed himself as he spoke. This somewhat piqued my curiosity, so I asked him various questions. He answered fencingly, and repeatedly looked at his watch in protest. Finally I said:

"Well, Johann, I want to go down this road. I shall not ask you to come unless you like; but tell me why you do not like to go, that is all I ask." For answer he seemed to throw himself off the box, so quickly did he reach the ground. Then he stretched out his hands appealingly to me, and implored me not to go. There was just enough of English mixed with the German for me to understand the drift of his talk. He seemed always just about to tell me something—the very idea of which evidently frightened him; but each time he pulled himself up, saying, as he crossed himself: "Walpurgisnacht!"

I tried to argue with him, but it was difficult to argue with a man when I did not know his language. The advantage certainly rested with him, for although he began to speak in English, of a very crude and broken kind, he always got excited and broke into his native tongue—and every time he did so, he looked at his watch. Then the horses became restless and sniffed the air. At this he grew very pale, and, looking around in a frightened way, he suddenly jumped forward, took them by the bridles and led them on some twenty feet. I followed, and asked why he had done this. For answer he crossed himself, pointed to the spot we had left and drew his carriage in the direction of the other road, indicating a cross, and said, first in German, then in English: "Buried him—him what killed themselves."

I remembered the old custom of burying suicides at crossroads: "Ah! I see, a suicide. How interesting!" But for the life of me I could not make out why the horses were frightened.

Whilst we were talking, we heard a sort of sound between a yelp and a bark. It was far away; but the horses got very restless, and it took Johann all his time to quiet them. He was pale, and said: "It sounds like a wolf—but yet there are no wolves here now."

"No?" I said, questioning him; "isn't it long since the wolves were so near the city?"

"Long, long," he answered, "in the spring and summer; but with the snow the wolves have been here not so long."

Whilst he was petting the horses and trying to quiet them, dark clouds drifted rapidly across the sky. The sunshine passed away, and a breath of cold wind seemed to drift past us. It was only a breath, however, and more in the nature of a warning than a fact, for the sun came out brightly again. Johann looked under his lifted hand at the horizon and said:

"The storm of snow, he comes before long time." Then he looked at his watch again, and, straightway holding his reins firmly—for the horses were still pawing the ground restlessly and shaking their heads—he climbed to his box as though the time had come for proceeding on our journey.

I felt a little obstinate and did not at once get into the carriage.

"Tell me," I said, "about this place where the road leads," and I pointed down.

Again he crossed himself and mumbled a prayer, before he answered: "It is unholy."

"What is unholy?" I enquired.

"The village."

"Then there is a village?"

"No, no. No one lives there hundreds of years." My curiosity was piqued: "But you said there was a village."

"There was."

"Where is it now?"

Whereupon he burst out into a long story in German and English, so mixed up that I could not quite understand exactly what he said, but roughly I gathered that long ago, hundreds of years, men had died there and been buried in their graves; and sounds were heard under the clay, and when the graves were opened, men and women were found rosy with life, and their mouths red with blood. And so, in haste to save their lives (aye, and their souls!—and here he crossed himself) those who were left fled away to other places, where the living lived, and the dead were dead and not—not something. He was evidently afraid to speak the last words. As he proceeded with his narration, he grew more and more excited. It seemed as if his imagination had got hold of him, and he ended in a perfect paroxysm of fear—white-faced, perspiring, trembling and looking round him, as if expecting that some dreadful presence would manifest itself there in the bright sunshine on the open plain. Finally, in an agony of desperation, he cried:

"Walpurgisnacht!" and pointed to the carriage for me to get in. All my English blood rose at this, and, standing back, I said:

"You are afraid, Johann—you are afraid. Go home; I shall return alone; the walk will do me good." The carriage door was open. I took from the seat my oak walking-stick—which I always carry on my holiday excursions—and closed the door, pointing back to Munich, and said, "Go home, Johann—Walpurgisnacht doesn't concern Englishmen."

The horses were now more restive than ever, and Johann was trying to hold them in, while excitedly imploring me not to do anything so foolish. I pitied the poor fellow, he was so deeply in earnest; but all the same I could not help laughing. His English was quite gone now. In his anxiety he had forgotten that his only means of making me understand was to talk my language, so he jabbered away in his native German. It began to be a little tedious. After giving the direction, "Home!" I turned to go down the cross-road into the valley.

With a despairing gesture, Johann turned his horses towards Munich. I leaned on my stick and looked after him. He went slowly along the road for a while: then there came over the crest of the hill a man tall and thin. I could see so much in the distance. When he drew near the horses, they began to jump and kick about, then to scream with terror. Johann could not hold them in; they bolted down the road, running away madly. I watched them out of sight, then looked for the stranger, but I found that he, too, was gone.

With a light heart I turned down the side road through the deepening valley to which Johann had objected. There was not the slightest reason, that I could see, for his objection; and I daresay I tramped for a couple of hours without thinking of time or distance, and certainly without seeing a person or a house. So far as the place was concerned, it was desolation itself. But I did not notice this particularly till, on turning a bend in the road, I came upon a scattered fringe of wood; then I recognised that I had been impressed unconsciously by the desolation of the region through which I had passed.

I sat down to rest myself, and began to look around. It struck me that it was considerably colder than it had been at the commencement of my walk—a sort of sighing sound seemed to be around me, with, now and then, high overhead, a sort of muffled roar. Looking upwards I noticed that great thick clouds were drifting rapidly across the sky from North to South at a great height. There were signs of coming storm in some lofty stratum of the air. I was a little chilly, and, thinking that it was the sitting still after the exercise of walking, I resumed my journey.

The ground I passed over was now much more picturesque. There were no striking objects that the eye might single out; but in all there was a charm of beauty. I took little heed of time and it was only when the deepening twilight forced itself upon me that I began to think of how I should find my way home. The brightness of the day had gone. The air was cold, and the drifting of clouds high overhead was more marked. They were accompanied by a sort of far-away rushing sound, through which seemed to come at intervals that mysterious cry which the driver had said came from a wolf. For a while I hesitated. I had said I would see the deserted village, so on I went, and presently came on a wide stretch of open country, shut in by hills all around. Their sides were covered with trees which spread down to the plain, dotting, in clumps, the gentler slopes and hollows which showed here and there. I followed with my eye the winding of the road, and saw that it curved close to one of the densest of these clumps and was lost behind it.

As I looked there came a cold shiver in the air, and the snow began to fall. I thought of the miles and miles of bleak country I had passed, and then hurried on to seek the shelter of the wood in front. Darker and darker grew the sky, and faster and heavier fell the snow, till the earth before and around me was a glistening white carpet the further edge of which was lost in misty vagueness. The road was here but crude, and when on the level its boundaries were not so marked, as when it passed through the cuttings; and in a little while I found that I must have strayed from it, for I missed underfoot the hard surface, and my feet sank deeper in the grass and moss. Then the wind grew stronger and blew with ever increasing force, till I was fain to run before it. The air became icy-cold, and in spite of my exercise I began to suffer. The snow was now falling so thickly and whirling around me in such rapid eddies that I could hardly keep my eyes open. Every now and then the heavens were torn asunder by vivid lightning, and in the flashes I could see ahead of me a great mass of trees, chiefly yew and cypress all heavily coated with snow.

I was soon amongst the shelter of the trees, and there, in comparative silence, I could hear the rush of the wind high overhead. Presently the blackness of the storm had become merged in the darkness of the night. By-and-by the storm seemed to be passing away: it now only came in fierce puffs or blasts. At such moments the weird sound of the wolf appeared to be echoed by many similar sounds around me.

Now and again, through the black mass of drifting cloud, came a straggling ray of moonlight, which lit up the expanse, and showed me that I was at the edge of a dense mass of cypress and yew trees. As the snow had ceased to fall, I walked out from the shelter and began to investigate more closely. It appeared to me that, amongst so many old foundations as I had passed, there might be still standing a house in which, though in ruins, I could find some sort of shelter for a while. As I skirted the edge of the copse, I found that a low wall encircled it, and following this I presently found an opening. Here the cypresses formed an alley leading up to a square mass of some kind of building. Just as I caught sight of this, however, the drifting clouds obscured the moon, and I passed up the path in darkness. The wind must have grown colder, for I felt myself shiver as I walked; but there was hope of shelter, and I groped my way blindly on.

I stopped, for there was a sudden stillness. The storm had passed; and, perhaps in sympathy with nature's silence, my heart seemed to cease to beat. But this was only momentarily; for suddenly the moonlight broke through the clouds, showing me that I was in a graveyard, and that the square object before me was a great massive tomb of marble, as white as the snow that lay on and all around it. With the moonlight there came a fierce sigh of the storm, which appeared to resume its course with a long, low howl, as of many dogs or wolves. I was awed and shocked, and felt the cold perceptibly grow upon me till it seemed to grip me by the heart. Then while the flood of moonlight still fell on the marble tomb, the storm gave further evidence of renewing, as though it was returning on its track. Impelled by some sort of fascination, I approached the sepulchre to see what it was, and why such a thing stood alone in such a place. I walked around it, and read, over the Doric door, in German—

COUNTESS DOLINGEN OF GRATZ
IN STYRIA
SOUGHT AND FOUND DEATH
1801.

On the top of the tomb seemingly driven through the solid marble—for the structure was composed of a few vast blocks of stone—was a great iron spike or stake. On going to the back I saw, graven in great Russian letters:

"The dead travel fast."

There was something so weird and uncanny about the whole thing that it gave me a turn and made me feel quite faint. I began to wish, for the first time, that I had taken Johann's advice. Here a thought struck me, which came under almost mysterious circumstances and with a terrible shock. This was Walpurgis Night!

Walpurgis Night, when according to the belief of millions of people, the devil was abroad—when the graves were opened and the dead came forth and walked. When all evil things of earth and air and water held revel. This very place the driver had specially shunned. This was the depopulated village of centuries ago. This was where the suicide lay; and this was the place where I was alone—unmanned, shivering with cold in a shroud of snow with a wild storm gathering again upon me! It took all my philosophy, all the religion I had been taught, all my courage, not to collapse in a paroxysm of fright.

And now a perfect tornado burst upon me. The ground shook as though thousands of horses thundered across it; and this time the storm bore on its icy wings, not snow, but great hailstones which drove with such violence that they might have come from the thongs of Balearic slingers—hailstones that beat down leaf and branch and made the shelter of the cypresses of no more avail than though their stems were standing-corn. At the first I had rushed to the nearest tree; but I was soon fain to leave it and seek the only spot that seemed to afford refuge, the deep Doric doorway of the marble tomb. There, crouching against the massive bronze-door, I gained a certain amount of protection from the beating of the hailstones, for now they only drove against me as they ricochetted from the ground and the side of the marble.

As I leaned against the door, it moved slightly and opened inwards. The shelter of even a tomb was welcome in that pitiless tempest, and I was about to enter it when there came a flash of forked-lightning that lit up the whole expanse of the heavens. In the instant, as I am a living man, I saw, as my eyes were turned into the darkness of the tomb, a beautiful woman, with rounded cheeks and red lips, seemingly sleeping on a bier. As the thunder broke overhead, I was grasped as by the hand of a giant and hurled out into the storm. The whole thing was so sudden that, before I could realize the shock, moral as well as physical, I found the hailstones beating me down. At the same time I had a strange, dominating feeling that I was not alone. I looked towards the tomb. Just then there came another blinding flash, which seemed to strike the iron stake that surmounted the tomb and to pour through to the earth, blasting and crumbling the marble, as in a burst of flame. The dead woman rose for a moment of agony, while she was lapped in the flame, and her bitter scream of pain was drowned in the thundercrash. The last thing I heard was this mingling of dreadful sound, as again I was seized in the giant-grasp and dragged away, while the hailstones beat on me, and the air around seemed reverberant with the howling of wolves. The last sight that I remembered was a vague, white, moving mass, as if all the graves around me had sent out the phantoms of their sheeted-dead, and that they were closing in on me through the white cloudiness of the driving hail.

* * *

Gradually there came a sort of vague beginning of consciousness; then a sense of weariness that was dreadful. For a time I remembered nothing; but slowly my senses returned. My feet seemed positively racked with pain, yet I could not move them. They seemed to be numbed. There was an icy feeling at the back of my neck and all down my spine, and my ears, like my feet, were dead, yet in torment; but there was in my breast a sense of warmth which was, by comparison, delicious. It was as a nightmare—a physical nightmare, if one may use such an expression; for some heavy weight on my chest made it difficult for me to breathe.

This period of semi-lethargy seemed to remain a long time, and as it faded away I must have slept or swooned. Then came a sort of loathing, like the first stage of sea-sickness, and a wild desire to be free from something—I knew not what. A vast stillness enveloped me, as though all the world were asleep or dead— only broken by the low panting as of some animal close to me. I felt a warm rasping at my throat, then came a consciousness of the awful truth, which chilled me to the heart and sent the blood surging up through my brain. Some great animal was lying on me and now licking my throat. I feared to stir, for some instinct of prudence bade me lie still; but the brute seemed to realize that there was now some change in me, for it raised its head. Through my eyelashes I saw above me the two great flaming eyes of a gigantic wolf. Its sharp white teeth gleamed in the gaping red mouth, and I could feel its hot breath fierce and acrid upon me.

For another spell of time I remembered no more. Then I became conscious of a low growl, followed by a yelp, renewed again and again. Then, seemingly very far away, I heard a "Holloa! holloa!" as of many voices calling in unison. Cautiously I raised my head and looked in the direction whence the sound came; but the cemetery blocked my view. The wolf still continued to yelp in a strange way, and a red glare began to move round the grove of cypresses, as though following the sound. As the voices drew closer, the wolf yelped faster and louder. I feared to make either sound or motion. Nearer came the red glow, over the white pall which stretched into the darkness around me. Then all at once from beyond the trees there came at a trot a troop of horsemen bearing torches. The wolf rose from my breast and made for the cemetery. I saw one of the horsemen (soldiers by their caps and their long military cloaks) raise his carbine and take aim. A companion knocked up his arm, and I heard the ball whizz over my head. He had evidently taken my body for that of the wolf. Another sighted the animal as it slunk away, and a shot followed. Then, at a gallop, the troop rode forward—some towards me, others following the wolf as it disappeared amongst the snow-clad cypresses.

As they drew nearer I tried to move, but was powerless, although I could see and hear all that went on around me. Two or three of the soldiers jumped from their horses and knelt beside me. One of them raised my head, and placed his hand over my heart.

"Good news, comrades!" he cried. "His heart still beats!"

Then some brandy was poured down my throat; it put vigour into me, and I was able to open my eyes fully and look around. Lights and shadows were moving among the trees, and I heard men call to one another. They drew together, uttering frightened exclamations; and the lights flashed as the others came pouring out of the cemetery pell-mell, like men possessed. When the further ones came close to us, those who were around me asked them eagerly:

"Well, have you found him?"

The reply rang out hurriedly:

"No! no! Come away quick—quick! This is no place to stay, and on this of all nights!"

"What was it?" was the question, asked in all manner of keys. The answer came variously and all indefinitely as though the men were moved by some common impulse to speak, yet were restrained by some common fear from giving their thoughts.

"It—it—indeed!" gibbered one, whose wits had plainly given out for the moment.

"A wolf—and yet not a wolf!" another put in shudderingly.

"No use trying for him without the sacred bullet," a third remarked in a more ordinary manner.

"Serve us right for coming out on this night! Truly we have earned our thousand marks!" were the ejaculations of a fourth.

"There was blood on the broken marble," another said after a pause—"the lightning never brought that there. And for him—is he safe? Look at his throat! See, comrades, the wolf has been lying on him and keeping his blood warm."

The officer looked at my throat and replied:

"He is all right; the skin is not pierced. What does it all mean? We should never have found him but for the yelping of the wolf."

"What became of it?" asked the man who was holding up my head, and who seemed the least panic-stricken of the party, for his hands were steady and without tremor. On his sleeve was the chevron of a petty officer.

"It went to its home," answered the man, whose long face was pallid, and who actually shook with terror as he glanced around him fearfully. "There are graves enough there in which it may lie. Come, comrades—come quickly! Let us leave this cursed spot."

The officer raised me to a sitting posture, as he uttered a word of command; then several men placed me upon a horse. He sprang to the saddle behind me, took me in his arms, gave the word to advance; and, turning our faces away from the cypresses, we rode away in swift, military order.

As yet my tongue refused its office, and I was perforce silent. I must have fallen asleep; for the next thing I remembered was finding myself standing up, supported by a soldier on each side of me. It was almost broad daylight, and to the north a red streak of sunlight was reflected, like a path of blood, over the waste of snow. The officer was telling the men to say nothing of what they had seen, except that they found an English stranger, guarded by a large dog.

"Dog! that was no dog," cut in the man who had exhibited such fear. "I think I know a wolf when I see one."

The young officer answered calmly: "I said a dog."

"Dog!" reiterated the other ironically. It was evident that his courage was rising with the sun; and, pointing to me, he said, "Look at his throat. Is that the work of a dog, master?"

Instinctively I raised my hand to my throat, and as I touched it I cried out in pain. The men crowded round to look, some stooping down from their saddles; and again there came the calm voice of the young officer:

"A dog, as I said. If aught else were said we should only be laughed at."

I was then mounted behind a trooper, and we rode on into the suburbs of Munich. Here we came across a stray carriage, into which I was lifted, and it was driven off to the Quatre Saisons—the young officer accompanying me, whilst a trooper followed with his horse, and the others rode off to their barracks.

When we arrived, Herr Delbrück rushed so quickly down the steps to meet me, that it was apparent he had been watching within. Taking me by both hands he solicitously led me in. The officer saluted me and was turning to withdraw, when I recognized his purpose, and insisted that he should come to my rooms. Over a glass of wine I warmly thanked him and his brave comrades for saving me. He replied simply that he was more than glad, and that Herr Delbrück had at the first taken steps to make all the searching party pleased; at which ambiguous utterance the maître d'hôtel smiled, while the officer pleaded duty and withdrew.

"But Herr Delbrück," I enquired, "how and why was it that the soldiers searched for me?"

He shrugged his shoulders, as if in depreciation of his own deed, as he replied:

"I was so fortunate as to obtain leave from the commander of the regiment in which I served, to ask for volunteers."

"But how did you know I was lost?" I asked.

"The driver came hither with the remains of his carriage, which had been upset when the horses ran away."

"But surely you would not send a search-party of soldiers merely on this account?"

"Oh, no!" he answered; "but even before the coachman arrived, I had this telegram from the Boyar whose guest you are," and he took from his pocket a telegram which he handed to me, and I read:

> BISTRITZ.
>
> Be careful of my guest—his safety is most precious to me. Should aught happen to him, or if he be missed, spare nothing to find him and ensure his safety. He is English and therefore adventurous. There are often dangers from snow and wolves and night. Lose not a moment if you suspect harm to him. I answer your zeal with my fortune.—Dracula.

As I held the telegram in my hand, the room seemed to whirl around me; and, if the attentive maître d'hôtel had not caught me, I think I should have fallen. There was something so strange in all this, something so weird and impossible to imagine, that there grew on me a sense of my being in some way the sport of opposite forces—the mere vague idea of which seemed in a way to paralyse me. I was certainly under some form of mysterious protection. From a distant country had come, in the very nick of time, a message that took me out of the danger of the snow-sleep and the jaws of the wolf.

❧ W(ILLIAM) W(YMARK) JACOBS (1863–1943)

W. W. Jacobs was a prolific English author of wide-ranging plays, novels, and short stories. A contemporary of Arthur Conan Doyle, William Hope Hodgson, and others from the late Victorian and early Edwardian periods, Jacobs was primarily a writer of adventure stories and tales of the high seas. Gary Hoppenstand has recently resurrected some of the best of Jacobs's short fiction in a collection entitled "The Monkey's Paw" and Other Tales of Mystery and the Macabre. Ironically, as Hoppenstand points out, Jacobs is remembered today for really only one story—that archetypal masterpiece of totemism and the macabre—"The Monkey's Paw."

In terms of subject matter, atmosphere, and thematic development, this W. W. Jacobs classic hearkens back to Robert Chambers's "The King in Yellow" of seven years earlier. Like Bram Stoker, Jacobs was enamored with stage and theater, and he spent the last years of his life writing for this entertainment form. H. P. Lovecraft, Mary Elizabeth Counselman, and Robert Bloch were among those later inspired by the writing of W. W. Jacobs.

The Monkey's Paw

(Harper's Magazine, *vol. 105, September 1902*)

Without, the night was cold and wet, but in the small parlor of Lakesnam Villa the blinds were drawn and the fire burned brightly. Father and son were at chess, the former, who possessed ideas about the game involving radical changes, putting his king into such sharp and unnecessary perils that it even provoked comment from the white-haired old lady knitting placidly by the fire.

"Hark at the wind," said Mr. White, who, having seen a fatal mistake after it was too late, was amiably desirous of preventing his son from seeing it.

"I'm listening," said the latter, grimly surveying the board as he stretched out his hand. "Check."

"I should hardly think that he'd come tonight," said his father, with his hand poised over the board.

"Mate," replied the son.

"That's the worst of living so far out," bawled Mr. White, with sudden and un-looked-for violence; "of all the beastly, slushy, out-of-the-way places to live in, this is the worst. Pathway's a bog, and the road's a torrent. I don't know what people are thinking about. I suppose because only two houses on the road are let, they think it doesn't matter."

"Never mind, dear," said his wife soothingly; "perhaps you'll win the next one."

Mr. White looked up sharply, just in time to intercept a knowing glance between mother and son. The words died away on his lips, and he hid a guilty grin in his thin gray beard.

"There he is," said Herbert White, as the gate banged to loudly and heavy footsteps came toward the door.

The old man rose with hospitable haste, and opening the door, was heard condoling with the new arrival. The new arrival also condoled with himself, so that Mrs. White said, "Tut, tut!" and coughed gently as her husband entered the room, followed by a tall burly man, beady of eye and rubicund of visage.

"Sergeant Major Morris," he said, introducing him.

The sergeant major shook hands, and taking the proffered seat by the fire, watched contentedly while his host got out whisky and tumblers and stood a small copper kettle on the fire.

At the third glass his eyes got brighter, and he began to talk, the little family circle regarding with eager interest this visitor from distant parts, as he squared his broad shoulders in the chair and spoke of strange scenes and doughty deeds, of wars and plagues and strange peoples.

"Twenty-one years of it," said Mr. White, nodding at his wife and son. "When he went away he was a slip of a youth in the warehouse. Now look at him."

"He don't look to have taken much harm," said Mrs. White politely.

"I'd like to go to India myself," said the old man, "just to look round a bit, you know."

"Better where you are," said the sergeant major, shaking his head. He put down the empty glass and, sighing softly, shook it again.

"I should like to see those old temples and fakirs and jugglers," said the old man. "What was that you started telling me the other day about a monkey's paw or something, Morris?"

"Nothing," said the soldier hastily. "Leastways, nothing worth hearing."

"Monkey's paw?" said Mrs. White curiously.

"Well, it's just a bit of what you might call magic, perhaps," said the sergeant major offhandedly.

His three listeners leaned forward eagerly. The visitor absentmindedly put his empty glass to his lips and then set it down again. His host filled it for him.

"To look at," said the sergeant major, fumbling in his pocket, "it's just an ordinary little paw, dried to a mummy."

He took something out of his pocket and proffered it. Mrs. White drew back with a grimace, but her son, taking it, examined it curiously.

"And what is there special about it?" inquired Mr. White, as he took it from his son and, having examined it, placed it upon the table.

"It had a spell put on it by an old fakir," said the sergeant major, "a very holy man. He wanted to show that fate ruled people's lives, and that those who interfered with it did so to their sorrow. He put a spell on it so that three separate men could have three wishes from it."

His manner was so impressive that his hearers were conscious that their light laughter jarred somewhat.

"Well, why don't you have three, sir?" said Herbert White cleverly.

The soldier regarded him in the way that middle age is wont to regard presumptuous youth. "I have," he said quietly, and his blotchy face whitened.

"And did you really have the three wishes granted?" asked Mrs. White.

"I did," said the sergeant major, and his glass tapped against his strong teeth.

"And has anybody else wished?" inquired the old lady.

"The first man had his three wishes, yes," was the reply. "I don't know what the first two were, but the third was for death. That's how I got the paw."

His tones were so grave that a hush fell upon the group.

"If you've had your three wishes, it's no good to you now, then, Morris," said the old man at last. "What do you keep it for?"

The soldier shook his head. "Fancy, I suppose," he said slowly. "I did have some idea of selling it, but I don't think I will. It has caused enough mischief already. Besides, people won't buy. They think it's a fairy tale, some of them, and those who do think anything of it want to try it first and pay me afterward."

"If you could have another three wishes," said the old man, eyeing him keenly, "would you have them?"

"I don't know," said the other. "I don't know."

He took the paw, and dangling it between his front finger and thumb, suddenly threw it upon the fire. White, with a slight cry, stooped down and snatched it off.

"Better let it burn," said the soldier solemnly.

"If you don't want it, Morris," said the old man, "give it to me."

"I won't," said his friend doggedly. "I threw it on the fire. If you keep it, don't blame me for what happens. Pitch it on the fire again, like a sensible man."

The other shook his head and examined his new possession closely. "How do you do it?" he inquired.

"Hold it up in your right hand and wish aloud," said the sergeant major, "but I warn you of the consequences."

"Sounds like the *Arabian Nights*," said Mrs. White, as she rose and began to set the supper. "Don't you think you might wish for four pairs of hands for me?"

Her husband drew the talisman from his pocket and then all three burst into laughter as the sergeant major, with a look of alarm on his face, caught him by the arm.

"If you must wish," he said gruffly, "wish for something sensible."

Mr. White dropped it back into his pocket, and placing chairs, motioned his friend to the table. In the business of supper the talisman was partly forgotten, and afterward the three sat listening in an enthralled fashion to a second installment of the soldier's adventures in India.

"If the tale about the monkey's paw is not more truthful than those he has been telling us," said Herbert, as the door closed behind their guest, just in time for him to catch the last train, "we shan't make much out of it."

"Did you give him anything for it, father?" inquired Mrs. White, regarding her husband closely.

"A trifle," said he, coloring slightly. "He didn't want it, but I made him take it. And he pressed me again to throw it away."

"Likely," said Herbert, with pretended horror. "Why, we're going to be rich, and famous, and happy. Wish to be an emperor, father, to begin with; then you can't be henpecked."

He darted round the table, pursued by the maligned Mrs. White armed with an antimacassar.

Mr. White took the paw from his pocket and eyed it dubiously. "I don't know what to wish for, and that's a fact," he said slowly. "It seems to me I've got all I want."

"If you only cleared the house, you'd be quite happy, wouldn't you?" said Herbert, with his hand on his shoulder. "Well, wish for two hundred pounds, then; that'll just do it."

His father, smiling shamefacedly at his own credulity, held up the talisman, as his son, with a solemn face somewhat marred by a wink at his mother, sat down at the piano and struck a few impressive chords.

"I wish for two hundred pounds," said the old man distinctly.

A fine crash from the piano greeted the words, interrupted by a shuddering cry from the old man. His wife and son ran toward him.

"It moved," he cried, with a glance of disgust at the object as it lay on the floor. "As I wished it twisted in my hands like a snake."

"Well, I don't see the money," said his son, as he picked it up and placed it on the table, "and I bet I never shall."

"It must have been your fancy, father," said his wife, regarding him anxiously.

He shook his head. "Never mind, though; there's no harm done, but it gave me a shock all the same."

They sat down by the fire again while the two men finished their pipes. Outside, the wind was higher than ever, and the old man started nervously at the sound of a door banging upstairs. A silence unusual and depressing settled upon all three, which lasted until the old couple rose to retire for the night.

"I expect you'll find the cash tied up in a big bag in the middle of your bed," said Herbert, as he bade them good night, "and something horrible squatting up on top of the wardrobe watching you as you pocket your ill-gotten gains."

II

In the brightness of the wintry sun next morning as it streamed over the breakfast table, Herbert laughed at his fears. There was an air of prosaic wholesomeness about the room which it had lacked on the previous night, and the dirty, shriveled little paw was pitched on the sideboard with a carelessness which betokened no great belief in its virtues.

"I suppose all old soldiers are the same," said Mrs. White. "The idea of our listening to such nonsense! How could wishes be granted in these days? And if they could, how could two hundred pounds hurt you, father?"

"Might drop on his head from the sky," said the frivolous Herbert.

"Morris said the things happened so naturally," said his father, "that you might if you so wished attribute it to coincidence."

"Well, don't break into the money before I come back," said Herbert, as he rose from the table. "I'm afraid it'll turn you into a mean, avaricious man, and we shall have to disown you."

His mother laughed, and following him to the door, watched him down the road, and returning to the breakfast table, was very happy at the expense of her husband's credulity. All of which did not prevent her from scurrying to the door at the postman's knock, nor prevent her from referring somewhat shortly to retired sergeant majors of bibulous habits when she found that the post brought a tailor's bill.

"Herbert will have some more of his funny remarks, I expect, when he comes home," she said, as they sat at dinner.

"I dare say," said Mr. White, pouring himself out some beer; "but for all that, the thing moved in my hand; that I'll swear to."

"You thought it did," said the old lady soothingly.

"I say it did," replied the other. "There was no thought about it; I had just— What's the matter?"

His wife made no reply. She was watching the mysterious movements of a man outside, who, peering in an undecided fashion at the house, appeared to be trying to make up his mind to enter. In mental connection with the two hundred pounds, she noticed that the stranger was well-dressed and wore a silk hat of glossy newness. Three times he paused at the gate, and then walked on again. The fourth time he stood with his hand upon it, and then with sudden resolution flung it open and walked up the path. Mrs. White at the same moment placed her hands behind her, and hurriedly unfastening the strings of her apron, put that useful article of apparel beneath the cushion of her chair.

She brought the stranger, who seemed ill at ease, into the room. He gazed furtively at Mrs. White, and listened in a preoccupied fashion as the old lady apologized for the appearance of the room, and her husband's coat, a garment which he usually reserved for the garden. She then waited as patiently as her sex would permit for him to broach his business, but he was at first strangely silent.

"I—was asked to call," he said at last, and stooped and picked a piece of cotton from his trousers. "I come from Maw and Meggins."

The old lady started. "Is anything the matter?" she asked breathlessly. "Has anything happened to Herbert? What is it? What is it?"

Her husband interposed. "There, there, mother," he said hastily. "Sit down, and don't jump to conclusions. You've not brought bad news, I'm sure, sir," and he eyed the other wistfully.

"I'm sorry—" began the visitor.

"Is he hurt?" demanded the mother.

The visitor bowed in assent. "Badly hurt," he said quietly, "but he is not in any pain."

"Oh, thank God!" said the old woman, clasping her hands. "Thank God for that! Thank—"

She broke off suddenly as the sinister meaning of the assurance dawned upon her and she saw the awful confirmation of her fears in the other's averted face. She caught her breath, and turning to her slower-witted husband, laid her trembling old hand upon his. There was a long silence.

"He was caught in the machinery," said the visitor at length, in a low voice.

"Caught in the machinery," repeated Mr. White, in a dazed fashion, "yes."

He sat staring blankly out at the window, and taking his wife's hand between his own, pressed it as he had been wont to do in their old courting days nearly forty years before.

"He was the only one left us," he said, turning gently to the visitor. "It is hard."

The other coughed, and rising, walked slowly to the window. "The firm wished me to convey their sincere sympathy with you in your great loss," he said, without looking round. "I beg that you will understand I am only their servant and merely obeying orders."

There was no reply; the old woman's face was white, her eyes staring, and her breath inaudible; on the husband's face was a look such as his friend the sergeant might have carried into his first action.

"I was to say that Maw and Meggins disclaim all responsibility," continued the other. "They admit no liability at all, but in consideration of your son's services they wish to present you with a certain sum as compensation."

Mr. White dropped his wife's hand, and rising to his feet, gazed with a look of horror at his visitor. His dry lips shaped the words, "How much?"

"Two hundred pounds," was the answer.

Unconscious of his wife's shriek, the old man smiled faintly, put out his hands like a sightless man, and dropped, a senseless heap, to the floor.

III

In the huge new cemetery, some two miles distant, the old people buried their dead, and came back to a house steeped in shadow and silence. It was all over so quickly that at first they could hardly realize it, and remained in a state of expectation as though of something else to happen—something else which was to lighten this load, too heavy for old hearts to bear. But the days passed, and expectation gave place to resignation—the hopeless resignation of the old, sometimes miscalled apathy. Sometimes they hardly exchanged a word, for now they had nothing to talk about, and their days were long to weariness.

It was about a week after that that the old man, waking suddenly in the night, stretched out his hand and found himself alone. The room was in darkness, and the sound of subdued weeping came from the window. He raised himself in bed and listened.

"Come back," he said tenderly. "You will be cold."

"It is colder for my son," said the old woman, and wept afresh.

The sound of her sobs died away on his ears. The bed was warm, and his eyes heavy with sleep. He dozed fitfully, and then slept until a sudden wild cry from his wife awoke him with a start.

"The monkey's paw!" she cried wildly. "The monkey's paw!"

He started up in alarm. "Where? Where is it? What's the matter?"

She came stumbling across the room toward him. "I want it," she said quietly. "You've not destroyed it?"

"It's in the parlor, on the bracket," he replied, marveling. "Why?"

She cried and laughed together, and bending over, kissed his cheek.

"I only just thought of it," she said hysterically. "Why didn't I think of it before? Why didn't you think of it?"

"Think of what?" he questioned.

"The other two wishes," she replied rapidly. "We've only had one."

"Was not that enough?" he demanded fiercely.

"No," she cried triumphantly; "we'll have one more. Go down and get it quickly, and wish our boy alive again."

The man sat up in bed and flung the bedclothes from his quaking limbs. "Good God, you are mad!" he cried, aghast.

"Get it," she panted; "get it quickly, and wish—Oh, my boy, my boy!"

Her husband struck a match and lit the candle. "Get back to bed," he said unsteadily. "You don't know what you are saying."

"We had the first wish granted," said the old woman feverishly; "why not the second?"

"A coincidence," stammered the old man.

"Go and get it and wish," cried the old woman, and dragged him toward the door.

He went down in the darkness, and felt his way to the parlor, and then to the mantelpiece. The talisman was in its place, and a horrible fear that the unspoken wish might bring his mutilated son before him ere he could escape from the room seized upon him, and he caught his breath as he found that he had lost the direction of the door. His brow cold with sweat, he felt his way round the table, and groped along the wall until he found himself in the small passage with the unwholesome thing in his hand.

Even his wife's face seemed changed as he entered the room. It was white and expectant, and to his fears seemed to have an unusual look upon it. He was afraid of her.

"Wish!" she cried, in a strong voice.

"It is foolish and wicked," he faltered.

"Wish!" repeated his wife.

He raised his hand. "I wish my son alive again."

The talisman fell to the floor, and he regarded it shudderingly. Then he sank trembling into a chair as the old woman, with burning eyes, walked to the window and raised the blind.

He sat until he was chilled with the cold, glancing occasionally at the figure of the old woman peering through the window. The candle end, which had burnt below the rim of the china candlestick, was throwing pulsating shadows on the ceiling and walls, until, with a flicker larger than the rest, it expired. The old man, with an unspeakable sense of relief at the failure of the talisman, crept back to his bed, and a minute or two afterward the old woman came silently and apathetically beside him.

Neither spoke, but both lay silently listening to the ticking of the clock. A stair creaked, and a squeaky mouse scurried noisily through the wall. The darkness was oppressive, and after lying for some time screwing up his courage, the husband took the box of matches, and striking one, went downstairs for a candle.

At the foot of the stairs the match went out, and he paused to strike another, and at the same moment a knock, so quiet and stealthy as to be scarcely audible, sounded on the front door.

The matches fell from his hand. He stood motionless, his breath suspended until the knock was repeated. Then he turned and fled swiftly back to his room, and closed the door behind him. A third knock sounded through the house.

"*What's that?*" cried the old woman, starting up.

"A rat," said the old man, in shaking tones—"a rat. It passed me on the stairs."

His wife sat up in bed, listening. A loud knock resounded through the house.

"It's Herbert!" she screamed. "It's Herbert!"

She ran to the door, but her husband was before her, and catching her by the arm, held her tightly.

"What are you going to do?" he whispered hoarsely.

"It's my boy; it's Herbert!" she cried, struggling mechanically. "I forgot it was two miles away. What are you holding me for? Let go. I must open the door."

"For God's sake don't let it in," cried the old man, trembling.

"You're afraid of your own son," she cried, struggling. "Let me go. I'm coming, Herbert; I'm coming."

There was another knock, and another. The old woman with a sudden wrench broke free and ran from the room. Her husband followed to the landing, and called after her appealingly as she hurried downstairs. He heard the chain rattle back and the bottom bolt drawn slowly and stiffly from the socket. Then the old woman's voice, strained and panting.

"The bolt," she cried loudly. "Come down. I can't reach it."

But her husband was on his hands and knees groping wildly on the floor in search of the paw. If he could only find it before the thing outside got in. A perfect fusillade of knocks reverberated through the house, and he heard the scraping of a chair as his wife put it down in the passage against the door. He heard the creaking of the bolt as it came slowly back, and at the same moment, he found the monkey's paw, and frantically breathed his third and last wish.

The knocking ceased suddenly, although the echoes of it were still in the house. He heard the chair drawn back and the door opened. A cold wind rushed up the staircase, and a long loud wail of disappointment and misery from his wife gave him courage to run down to her side, and then to the gate beyond. The street lamp flickering opposite shone on a quiet and deserted road.

⁂ H(OWARD) P(HILLIPS) LOVECRAFT (1890–1937)

Of Howard Phillips Lovecraft, much is known and written, and much remains mystery. This, combined with the body of work that Lovecraft produced, has led to the popular following of (and speculation about) the author for more than seventy years. The author's Cthulu Mythos stories (beginning with "The Call of Cthulu," Weird Tales, February 1928) have been in print since their first publication and have been imitated by admirers since Lovecraft's day.

Although much of H. P. Lovecraft's writing appeared in Weird Tales between 1923 and 1938, Lovecraft wrote for a range of semiprofessional, professional, and highly popular publications during his lifetime. A Dark Fantasy master with a significance to the genre on the order of Poe and King, Lovecraft was also a master of Science Fiction. In fact, Weird Tales in the 1920s was, along with Argosy, the primary venue for Science Fiction prior to the arrival of Hugo Gernsback's Amazing Stories in 1926. Weird Tales was where Edmond Hamilton got his start in the 1920s.

Lovecraft's most famous understudy was probably the young Robert Bloch, with whom he had a mutual admiration. Others influenced by the author include August Derleth,

Frank Belknap Long, Clark Ashton Smith, Robert E. Howard, Ramsey Campbell, and Brian Lumley.

"The Colour Out of Space" is a landmark blend of Dark Fantasy and Science Fiction and has spawned many imitations. Certainly, 1950s Science Fiction invasion movies took some of their lead from traditions established by this Lovecraft story and similar work by H. G. Wells.

The Colour Out of Space
(Amazing Stories, *September 1927)*

West of Arkham the hills rise wild, and there are valleys with deep woods that no axe has ever cut. There are dark narrow glens where the trees slope fantastically, and where thin brooklets trickle without ever having caught the glint of sunlight. On the gentler slopes there are farms, ancient and rocky, with squat, moss-coated cottages brooding eternally over old New England secrets in the lee of great ledges; but these are all vacant now, the wide chimneys crumbling and the shingled sides bulging perilously beneath low gambrel roofs.

The old folk have gone away, and foreigners do not like to live there. French-Canadians have tried it, Italians have tried it, and the Poles have come and departed. It is not because of anything that can be seen or heard or handled, but because of something that is imagined. The place is not good for imagination, and does not bring restful dreams at night. It must be this which keeps the foreigners away, for old Ammi Pierce has never told them of anything he recalls from the strange days. Ammi, whose head has been a little queer for years, is the only one who still remains, or who ever talks of the strange days; and he dares to do this because his house is so near the open fields and the travelled roads around Arkham.

There was once a road over the hills and through the valleys, that ran straight where the blasted heath is now; but people ceased to use it and a new road was laid curving far toward the south. Traces of the old one can still be found amidst the weeds of a returning wilderness, and some of them will doubtless linger even when half the hollows are flooded for the new reservoir. Then the dark woods will be cut down and the blasted heath will slumber far below blue waters whose surface will mirror the sky and ripple in the sun. And the secrets of the strange days will be one with the deep's secrets; one with the hidden lore of old ocean, and all the mystery of primal earth.

When I went into the hills and vales to survey for the new reservoir they told me the place was evil. They told me this in Arkham, and because that is a very old town full of witch legends I thought the evil must be something which grandams had whispered to children through centuries. The name "blasted heath" seemed to me very odd and theatrical, and I wondered how it had come into the folklore of a Puritan people. Then I saw that dark westward tangle of glens and slopes for myself, and ceased to wonder at anything beside its own elder mystery. It was morning when I saw it, but shadow lurked always there. The trees grew too thickly, and their trunks were too big for any healthy New England wood. There was too much silence in the dim alleys between them, and the floor was too soft with the dank moss and mattings of infinite years of decay.

In the open spaces, mostly along the line of the old road, there were little hillside farms; sometimes with all the buildings standing, sometimes with only one or two, and sometimes with only a lone chimney or fast-filling cellar. Weeds and briers reigned, and furtive wild things rustled in the undergrowth. Upon everything was a haze of restlessness and oppression; a touch of the unreal and the grotesque, as if some vital element of perspective or chiaroscuro were awry. I did not wonder that the foreigners would not stay, for this was no region to sleep in. It was too much like a landscape of Salvator Rosa; too much like some forbidding woodcut in a tale of terror.

But even all this was not so bad as the blasted heath. I knew it the moment I came upon it at the bottom of a spacious valley; for no other name could fit such a thing, or any other thing fit such a name. It was as if the poet had coined the phrase from having seen this one particular region. It must, I thought as I viewed it, be the outcome of a fire; but why had nothing new ever grown over those five acres of grey desolation that sprawled open to the sky like a great spot eaten by acid in the woods and fields? It lay largely to the north of the ancient road line, but encroached a little on the other side. I felt an odd reluctance about approaching, and did so at last only because my business took me through and past it. There was no vegetation of any kind on that broad expanse, but only a fine grey dust or ash which no wind seemed ever to blow about. The trees near it were sickly and stunted, and many dead trunks stood or lay rotting at the rim. As I walked hurriedly by I saw the tumbled bricks and stones of an old chimney and cellar on my right, and the yawning black maw of an abandoned well whose stagnant vapours played strange tricks with the hues of the sunlight. Even the long, dark woodland climb beyond seemed welcome in contrast, and I marvelled no more at the frightened whispers of Arkham people. There had been no house or ruin near; even in the old days the place must have been lonely and remote. And at twilight, dreading to repass that ominous spot, I walked circuitously back to the town by the curving road on the south. I vaguely wished some clouds would gather, for an odd timidity about the deep skyey voids above had crept into my soul.

In the evening I asked old people in Arkham about the blasted heath, and what was meant by that phrase "strange days" which so many evasively muttered. I could not, however, get any good answers, except that all the mystery was much more recent than I had dreamed. It was not a matter of old legendry at all, but something within the lifetime of those who spoke. It had happened in the 'eighties, and a family had disappeared or was killed. Speakers would not be exact; and because they all told me to pay no attention to old Ammi Pierce's crazy tales, I sought him out the next morning, having heard that he lived alone in the ancient tottering cottage where the trees first begin to get very thick. It was a fearsomely ancient place, and had begun to exude the faint miasmal odour which clings about houses that have stood too long. Only with persistent knocking could I rouse the aged man, and when he shuffled timidly to the door I could tell he was not glad to see me. He was not so feeble as I had expected; but his eyes drooped in a curious way, and his unkempt clothing and white beard made him seem very worn and dismal.

Not knowing just how he could best be launched on his tales, I feigned a matter of business; told him of my surveying, and asked vague questions about the district. He was far brighter and more educated than I had been led to think, and before I knew it had grasped quite as much of the subject as any man I had talked with in Arkham. He was not like other rustics I had known in the sections where reservoirs were to be. From him there were no protests at the miles of old wood and farmland to be blotted out, though perhaps there would have been had not his home lain outside the bounds of the future lake. Relief was all that he showed; relief at the doom of the dark ancient valleys through which he had roamed all his life. They were better under water now—better under water since the strange days. And with this opening his husky voice sank low, while his body leaned forward and his right forefinger began to point shakily and impressively.

It was then that I heard the story, and as the rambling voice scraped and whispered on I shivered again and again despite the summer day. Often I had to recall the speaker from ramblings, piece out scientific points which he knew only by a fading parrot memory of professors' talk, or bridge over gaps, where his sense of logic and continuity broke down. When he was done I did not wonder that his mind had snapped a trifle, or that the folk of Arkham would not speak much of the blasted heath. I hurried back before sunset to my hotel, unwilling to have the stars come out above me in the open; and the next day returned to Boston to give up my position. I could not go into that dim chaos of old forest and slope again, or face another time that grey blasted heath where the black well yawned deep beside the tumbled bricks and stones. The reservoir will soon be built now, and all those elder secrets will be safe forever under watery fathoms. But even then I do not believe I would like to visit that country by night—at least not when the sinister stars are out; and nothing could bribe me to drink the new city water of Arkham.

It all began, old Ammi said, with the meteorite. Before that time there had been no wild legends at all since the witch trials, and even then these western woods were not feared half so much as the small island in the Miskatonic where the devil held court beside a curious stone altar older than the Indians. These were not haunted woods, and their fantastic dusk was never terrible till the strange days. Then there had come that white noontide cloud, that string of explosions in the air, and that pillar of smoke from the valley far in the wood. And by night all Arkham had heard of the great rock that fell out of the sky and bedded itself in the ground beside the well at the Nahum Gardner place. That was the house which had stood where the blasted heath was to come—the trim white Nahum Gardner house amidst its fertile gardens and orchards.

Nahum had come to town to tell people about the stone, and dropped in at Ammi Pierce's on the way. Ammi was forty then, and all the queer things were fixed very strongly in his mind. He and his wife had gone with the three professors from Miskatonic University who hastened out the next morning to see the weird visitor from unknown stellar space, and had wondered why Nahum had called it so large the clay before. It had shrunk, Nahum said as he pointed out the big brownish mound above the ripped earth and charred grass near the archaic well-sweep in his front yard; but the wise men answered that stones do not shrink. Its heat lingered persistently, and Nahum declared it had glowed faintly in the night. The professors tried it with a geologist's hammer and found it was oddly soft. It was, in truth, so soft as to be almost plastic; and they gouged rather than chipped a specimen to take back to the college for testing. They took it in an old pail borrowed from Nahum's kitchen, for even the small piece refused to grow cool. On the trip back they stopped at Ammi's to rest, and seemed thoughtful when Mrs. Pierce remarked that the fragment was growing smaller and burning the bottom of the pail. Truly, it was not large, but perhaps they had taken less than they thought.

The day after that—all this was in June of '82—the professors had trooped out again in a great excitement. As they passed Ammi's they told him what queer things the specimen had done, and how it had faded wholly away when they put it in a glass beaker. The beaker had gone, too, and the wise men talked of the strange stone's affinity for silicon. It had acted quite unbelievably in that well-ordered laboratory; doing nothing at all and showing no occluded gases when heated on charcoal, being wholly negative in the borax bead, and soon proving itself absolutely non-volatile at any producible temperature, including that of the oxyhydrogen blowpipe. On an anvil it appeared highly malleable, and in the dark its luminosity was very marked. Stubbornly refusing to grow cool, it soon had the college in a state of real excitement; and when upon heating before the spectroscope it displayed shining bands unlike any known colours of the normal spectrum there was much breathless talk of new elements, bizzare optical properties, and other things which puzzled men of science are wont to say when faced by the unknown.

Hot as it was, they tested it in a crucible with all the proper reagents. Water did nothing. Hydrochloric acid was the same. Nitric acid and even aqua regia merely hissed and spattered against its torrid invulnerability. Ammi had difficulty in recalling all these things, but recognized some solvents as I mentioned them in the usual order of use. There were ammonia and caustic soda, alcohol and ether, nauseous carbon disulphide and a dozen others; but although the weight grew steadily less as time passed, and the fragment seemed to be slightly cooling, there was no change in the solvents to show that they had attacked the substance at all. It was a metal, though, beyond a doubt. It was magnetic, for one thing; and after its immersion in the acid solvents there seemed to be faint traces of the Widmänstätten figures found on meteoric iron. When the cooling had grown very considerable, the testing was carried on in glass; and it was in a glass beaker that they left all the chips made of the original fragment during the work. The next morning both chips and beaker were gone without trace, and only a charred spot marked the place on the wooden shelf where they had been.

All this the professors told Ammi as they paused at his door, and once more he went with them to see the stony messenger from the stars, though this time his wife did not accompany him. It had now most certainly shrunk, and even the sober professors could not doubt the truth of what they saw. All around the dwindling brown lump near the well was a vacant space, except where the earth had caved in; and whereas it had been a good seven feet across the day before, it was now scarcely five. It was still hot, and the sages studied its surface curiously as they detached another and larger piece with hammer and chisel. They gouged deeply this time, and as they pried away the smaller mass they saw that the core of the thing was not quite homogeneous.

They had uncovered what seemed to be the side of a large coloured globule embedded in the substance. The colour, which resembled some of the bands in the meteor's strange spectrum, was almost impossible to describe; and it was only by analogy that they called it colour at all. Its texture was glossy, and upon tapping it appeared to promise both brittleness and hollowness. One of the professors gave it a smart blow with a hammer, and it burst with a nervous little pop. Nothing emitted, and all trace of the thing vanished with the puncturing. It left behind a hollow spherical space about three inches across, and all thought it probable that others would be discovered as the enclosing substance wasted away.

Conjecture was vain; so after a futile attempt to find additional globules by drilling, the seekers left again with their new specimen — which proved, however, as baffling in the laboratory as its predecessor. Aside from being almost plastic, having heat, magnetism, and slight luminosity, cooling slightly in powerful acids, possessing an unknown spectrum, wasting away in air, and attacking silicon compounds with mutual destruction as a result, it presented no identifying features whatsoever; and at the end of the tests the college scientists were forced to own that they could not place it. It was nothing of this earth, but a piece of the great outside; and as such dowered with outside properties and obedient to outside laws.

That night there was a thunderstorm, and when the professors went out to Nahum's the next day they met with a bitter disappointment. The stone, magnetic as it had been, must have had some peculiar electrical property; for it had "drawn lightning," as Nahum said, with a singular persistence. Six times within an hour the farmer saw the lightning strike the furrow in the front yard, and when the storm was over nothing remained but a ragged pit by the ancient well-sweep, half-choked with a caved-in earth. Digging had borne no fruit, and the scientists verified the fact of the utter vanishment. The failure was total; so that nothing was left to do but go back to the laboratory and test again the disappearing fragment left carefully cased in lead. That fragment lasted a week, at the end of which nothing of value had been learned of it. When it had gone, no residue was left behind, and in time the professors felt scarcely sure they had indeed seen with waking eyes that cryptic vestige of the fathomless gulfs outside; that lone, weird message from other universes and other realms of matter, force, and entity.

As was natural, the Arkham papers made much of the incident with its collegiate sponsoring, and sent reporters to talk with Nahum Gardner and his family. At least one Boston daily also sent a scribe, and Nahum quickly became a kind of local celebrity. He was a lean, genial person of about fifty, living with his wife and three sons on the pleasant farmstead in the valley. He and Ammi exchanged visits frequently, as did their wives; and Ammi had nothing but praise for him after all these years. He seemed slightly proud of the notice his place had attracted, and talked often of the meteorite in the succeeding weeks. That July and August were hot; and Nahum worked hard at his haying in the ten-acre pasture across Chapman's Brook; his rattling wain wearing deep ruts in the shadowy lanes between. The labour tired him more than it had in other years, and he felt that age was beginning to tell on him.

Then fell the time of fruit and harvest. The pears and apples slowly ripened, and Nahum vowed that his orchards were prospering as never before. The fruit was growing to phenomenal size and unwonted gloss, and in such abundance that extra barrels were ordered to handle the future crop. But with the ripening came sore disappointment, for of all that gorgeous array of specious lusciousness not one single jot was fit to eat. Into the fine flavour of the pears and apples had crept a stealthy bitterness and sickishness, so that even the smallest bites induced a lasting disgust. It was the same with the melons and tomatoes, and Nahum sadly saw that his entire crop was lost. Quick to connect events, he declared that the meteorite had poisoned the soil, and thanked Heaven that most of the other crops were in the upland lot along the road.

Winter came early, and was very cold. Ammi saw Nahum less often than usual, and observed that he had begun to look worried. The rest of his family too, seemed to have grown taciturn; and were far from steady in their churchgoing or their attendance at the various social events of the countryside. For this reserve or melancholy no cause could be found, though all the household confessed now and then to poorer health and a feeling of vague disquiet. Nahum himself gave the most definite statement of anyone when he said he was disturbed about certain footprints in the snow. They were the usual winter prints of red squirrels, white rabbits, and foxes, but the brooding farmer professed to see something not quite right about their nature and arrangement. He was never specific, but appeared to think that they were not as characteristic of the anatomy and habits of squirrels and rabbits and foxes as they ought to be. Ammi listened without interest to this talk until one night when he drove past Nahum's house in his sleigh on the way back from Clark's Corners. There had been a moon, and a rabbit had run across the road, and the leaps of that rabbit were longer than either Ammi or his horse liked. The latter, indeed, had almost run away when brought up by a firm rein. Thereafter Ammi gave Nahum's tales more respect, and wondered why the Gardner dogs seemed so cowed and quivering every morning. They had, it developed, nearly lost the spirit to bark.

In February the McGregor boys from Meadow Hill were out shooting woodchucks, and not far from the Gardner place bagged a very peculiar specimen. The proportions of its body seemed slightly altered in a queer way impossible to describe, while its face had taken on an expression which no one ever saw in a woodchuck before. The boys were genuinely frightened, and threw the thing away at once, so that only their grotesque tales of it ever reached the people of the countryside. But the shying of horses near Nahum's house had now become an acknowledged thing, and all the basis for a cycle of whispered legend was fast taking form.

People vowed that the snow melted faster around Nahum's than it did anywhere else, and early in March there was an awed discussion in Potter's general store at Clark's Corners. Stephen Rice had driven past Gardner's in the morning, and had noticed the skunk-cabbages coming up through the mud by the woods across the road. Never were things of such size seen before, and they held strange colours that could not be put into any words. Their shapes were monstrous, and the horse had snorted at an odour which struck Stephen as wholly unprecedented. That afternoon several persons drove past to see the abnormal growth, and all agreed that plants of that kind ought never to sprout in a healthy world. The bad fruit of the fall before was freely mentioned, and it went from mouth to mouth that there was poison in Nahum's ground. Of course it was the meteorite; and remembering how strange the men from the college had found that stone to be, several farmers spoke about the matter to them.

One day they paid Nahum a visit; but having no love of wild tales and folklore were very conservative in what they inferred. The plants were certainly odd, but all skunk-cabbages are more or less odd in shape and hue. Perhaps some mineral element from the stone had entered the soil, but it would soon be washed away. And as for the footprints and frightened horses—of course this was mere country talk which such a phenomenon as the aerolite would be certain to start. There was really nothing for serious men to do in cases of wild gossip, for superstitious rustics will say and believe anything. And so all through the strange days the professors stayed away in contempt. Only one of them, when given two phials of dust for analysis in a police job over a year and a half later, recalled that the queer colour of that skunk-cabbage had been very like one of the anomalous bands of light shown by the meteor fragment in the college spectroscope, and like the brittle globule found imbedded in the stone from the abyss. The samples in this analysis case gave the same odd bands at first, though later they lost the property.

The trees budded prematurely around Nahum's, and at night they swayed ominously in the wind. Nahum's second son Thaddeus, a lad of fifteen, swore that they swayed also when there was no wind; but even the gossips would not credit this. Certainly, however, restlessness was in the air. The entire Gardner family developed the habit of stealthy listening, though not for any sound which they could consciously name. The listening was, indeed, rather a product of moments when consciousness seemed half to slip away. Unfortunately such moments increased week by week, till it became common speech that "something was wrong with all Nahum's folks." When the early saxifrage came out it had another strange colour; not quite like that of the skunk-cabbage, but plainly related and equally unknown to anyone who saw it. Nahum took some blossoms to Arkham and showed them to the editor of the *Gazette,* but that dignitary did no more than write a humorous article about them, in which the dark fears of rustics were held up to polite ridicule. It was a mistake of Nahum's to tell a stolid city man about the way the great, overgrown mourning-cloak butterflies behaved in connection with these saxifrages.

April brought a kind of madness to the country folk, and began that disuse of the road past Nahum's which led to its ultimate abandonment. It was the vegetation. All the orchard trees blossomed forth in strange colours, and through the stony soil of the yard and adjacent pasturage there sprang up a bizarre growth which only a botanist could connect with the proper flora of the region. No sane wholesome colours were anywhere to be seen except in the green grass and leafage; but everywhere were those hectic and prismatic variants of some diseased, underlying primary tone without a place among the known tints of earth. The "Dutchman's breeches" became a thing of sinister menace, and the bloodroots grew insolent in their chromatic perversion. Ammi and the Gardners thought that most of the colours had a sort of haunting familiarity, and decided that they reminded one of the brittle globule in the meteor. Nahum ploughed and sowed the ten-acre pasture and the upland lot, but did nothing with the land around the house. He knew it would be of no use, and hoped that the summer's strange growths would draw all the poison from the soil. He was prepared for almost anything now, and had grown used to the sense of something near him waiting to be heard. The shunning of his house by neighbors told on him, of course; but it told on his wife more. The boys were better off, being at school each day; but they could not help being frightened by the gossip. Thaddeus, an especially sensitive youth, suffered the most.

In May the insects came, and Nahum's place became a nightmare of buzzing and crawling. Most of the creatures seemed not quite usual in their aspects and motions, and their nocturnal habits contradicted all former experience. The Gardners took to watching at night—watching in all directions at random for something—they could not tell what. It was then that they all owned that Thaddeus had been right about the trees. Mrs. Gardner was the next to see it from the window as she watched the swollen boughs of a maple against a moonlit sky. The boughs surely moved, and there was no wind. It must be the sap. Strangeness had come into everything growing now. Yet it was none of Nahum's family at all who made the next discovery. Familiarity had dulled them, and what they could not see was glimpsed by a timid windmill salesman from Bolton who drove by one night in ignorance of the country legends. What he told in Arkham was given a short paragraph in the *Gazette;* and it was there that all the farmers, Nahum included, saw it first. The night had been dark and the buggy-lamps faint, but around a farm in the valley which everyone knew from the account must be Nahum's, the darkness had been less thick. A dim though distinct luminosity seemed to inhere in all the vegetation, grass, leaves, and blossoms alike, while at one moment a detached piece of the phosphorescence appeared to stir furtively in the yard near the barn.

The grass had so far seemed untouched, and the cows were freely pastured in the lot near the house, but toward the end of May the milk began to be bad. Then Nahum had the cows driven to the uplands, after which this trouble ceased. Not long after this the change in grass and leaves became apparent to the eye. All the verdure was going grey, and was developing a highly singular quality of brittleness. Ammi was now the only person who ever visited the place, and his visits were becoming fewer and fewer. When school closed the Gardners were virtually cut off from the world, and sometimes let Ammi do their errands in town. They were failing curiously both physically and mentally, and no one was surprised when the news of Mrs. Gardner's madness stole around.

It happened in June, about the anniversary of the meteor's fall, and the poor woman screamed about things in the air which she could not describe. In her raving there was not a single specific noun, but only verbs and pronouns. Things moved and changed and fluttered, and ears tingled to impulses which were not wholly sounds. Something was taken away—she was being drained of something—something was fastening itself on her that ought not to be—someone must make it keep off—nothing was ever still in the night—the walls and windows shifted. Nahum did not send her to the county asylum, but let her wander about the house as long as she was harmless to herself and others. Even when her expression changed he did nothing. But when the boys grew afraid of her, and Thaddeus nearly fainted at the way she made faces at him, he decided to keep her locked in the attic. By July she had ceased to speak and crawled on all fours, and before that month was over Nahum got the mad notion that she was slightly luminous in the dark, as he now clearly saw was the case with the nearby vegetation.

It was a little before this that the horses had stampeded. Something had aroused them in the night, and their neighing and kicking in their stalls had been terrible. There seemed virtually nothing to do to calm them, and when Nahum opened the stable door they all bolted out like frightened woodland deer. It took a week to track all four, and when found they were seen to be quite useless and unmanageable. Something had snapped in their brains, and each one had to be shot for its own good. Nahum borrowed a horse from Ammi for his haying, but found it would not approach the barn. It shied, balked, and whinnied, and in the end he could do nothing but drive it into the yard while the men used their own strength to get the heavy wagon near enough the hayloft for convenient pitching. And all the while the vegetation was turning grey and brittle. Even the flowers whose hues had been so strange were greying now, and the fruit was coming out grey and dwarfed and tasteless. The asters and golden-rod bloomed grey and distorted, and the roses and zinnias and hollyhocks in the front yard were such blasphemous-looking things that Nahum's oldest boy Zenas cut them down. The strangely puffed insects died about that time, even the bees that had left their hives and taken to the woods.

By September all the vegetation was fast crumbling to a greyish powder, and Nahum feared that the trees would die before the poison was out of the soil. His wife now had spells of terrific screaming, and he and the boys were in a constant state of nervous tension. They shunned people now, and when school opened the boys did not go. But it was Ammi, on one of his rare visits, who first realised that the well water was no longer good. It had a evil taste that was not exactly fetid nor exactly salty, and Ammi advised his friend to dig another well on higher ground to use till the soil was good again. Nahum, however, ignored the warning, for he had by that time become calloused to strange and unpleasant things. He and the boys continued to use the tainted supply, drinking it as listlessly and mechanically as they ate their meagre and ill-cooked meals and did their thankless and monotonous chores through the aimless days. There was something of stolid resignation about them all, as if they walked half in another world between lines of nameless guards to a certain and familiar doom.

Thaddeus went mad in September after a visit to the well. He had gone with a pail and had come back empty-handed, shrieking and waving his arms, and sometimes lapsing into an inane titter or a whisper about "the moving colours down there." Two in one family was pretty bad, but Nahum was very brave about it. He let the boy run about for a week until he began stumbling and hurting himself, and then he shut him in an attic room across the hall from his mother's. The way they screamed at each other from behind their locked doors was very terrible, especially to little Merwin, who fancied they talked in some terrible language that was not of earth. Merwin was getting frightfully imaginative, and his restlessness was worse after the shutting away of the brother who had been his greatest playmate.

Almost at the same time the mortality among the live-stock commenced. Poultry turned greyish and died very quickly, their meat being found dry and noisome upon cutting. Hogs grew inordinately fat, then suddenly began to undergo loathsome changes which no one could explain. Their meat was of course useless, and Nahum was at his wit's end. No rural veterinary would approach his place, and the city veterinary from Arkham was openly baffled. The swine began growing grey and brittle and falling to pieces before they died, and their eyes and muzzles developed singular alterations. It was very inexplicable, for they had never been fed from the tainted vegetation. Then something struck the cows. Certain areas or sometimes the whole body would be uncannily shrivelled or compressed, and atrocious collapses or disintegrations were common. In the last stages—and death was always the result—there would be a greying and turning brittle like that which beset the hogs. There could be no question of poison, for all the cases occurred in a locked and undisturbed barn. No bites of prowling things could have brought the virus, for what live beast of earth can pass through solid obstacles? It must be only natural disease—yet what disease could wreak such results was beyond any mind's guessing. When the harvest came there was not an animal surviving on the place, for the stock and poultry were dead and the dogs had run away. These dogs, three in number, had all vanished one night and were never heard of again. The five cats had left some time before, but their going was scarcely noticed since there now seemed to be no mice, and only Mrs. Gardner had made pets of the graceful felines.

On the nineteenth of October Nahum staggered into Ammi's house with hideous news. The death had come to poor Thaddeus in his attic room, and it had come in a way which could not be told. Nahum had dug a grave in the railed family plot behind the farm, and had put therein what he found. There could have been nothing from outside, for the small barred window and locked door were intact; but it was much as it had been in the barn. Ammi and his wife consoled the stricken man as best they could, but shuddered as they did so. Stark terror seemed to cling round the Gardners and all they touched, and the very presence of one in the house was a breath from regions unnamed and unnamable. Ammi accompanied Nahum home with the greatest reluctance, and did what he might to calm the hysterical sobbing of little Merwin. Zenas needed no calming. He had come of late to do nothing but stare into space and obey what his father told him; and Ammi thought that his fate was very merciful. Now and then Merwin's screams were answered faintly from the attic, and in response to an inquiring look Nahum said that his wife was getting very feeble. When night approached, Ammi managed to get away; for not even friendship could make him stay in that spot when the faint glow of the vegetation began and the trees may or may not have swayed without wind. It was really lucky for Ammi that he was not more imaginative. Even as things were, his mind was bent ever so slightly; but had he been able to connect and reflect upon all the portents around him he must inevitably have turned a total maniac. In the twilight he hastened home, the screams of the mad woman and the nervous child ringing horribly in his ears.

Three days later Nahum burst into Ammi's kitchen in the early morning, and in the absence of his host stammered out a desperate tale once more, while Mrs. Pierce listened in a clutching fright. It was little Merwin this time. He was gone. He had gone out late at night with a lantern and pail for water, and had never come back. He'd been going to pieces for days, and hardly knew what he was about. Screamed at everything. There had been a frantic shriek from the yard then, but before the father could get to the door the boy was gone. There was no glow from the lantern he had taken, and of the child himself no trace. At the time Nahum thought the lantern and pail were gone too; but when dawn came, and the man had plodded back from his all-night search of the woods and fields, he had found some very curious things near the well. There was a crushed and apparently somewhat melted mass of iron which had certainly been the lantern; while a bent handle and twisted iron hoops beside it, both half-fused, seemed to hint at the remnants of the pail. That was all. Nahum was past imagining, Mrs. Pierce was blank, and Ammi, when he had reached home and heard the tale, could give no guess. Merwin was gone, and there would be no use in telling the people around, who shunned all Gardners now. No use, either, in telling the city people at Arkham who laughed at everything. Thad was gone, and now Merwin was gone. Something was creeping and creeping and waiting to be seen and heard. Nahum would go soon, and he wanted Ammi to look after his wife and Zenas if they survived him. It must all be a judgment of some sort; though he could not fancy what for, since he had always walked uprightly in the Lord's ways so far as he knew.

For over two weeks Ammi saw nothing of Nahum; and then, worried about what might have happened, he overcame his fears and paid the Gardner place a visit. There was no smoke from the great chimney, and for a moment the visitor was apprehensive of the worst. The aspect of the whole farm was shocking— greyish withered grass and leaves on the ground, vines falling in brittle wreckage from archaic walls and gables, and great bare trees clawing up at the grey November sky with a studied malevolence which Ammi could not but feel had come from some subtle change in the tilt of the branches. But Nahum was alive, after all. He was weak, and lying on a couch in the low-ceiled kitchen, but perfectly conscious and able to give simple orders to Zenas. The room was deadly cold; and as Ammi visibly shivered, the host shouted huskily to Zenas for more wood. Wood, indeed, was sorely needed; since the cavernous fireplace was unlit and empty, with a cloud of soot blowing about in the chill wind that came down the chimney. Presently Nahum asked him if the extra wood had made him any more comfortable, and then Ammi saw what had happened. The stoutest cord had broken at last, and the hapless farmer's mind was proof against more sorrow.

Questioning tactfully, Ammi could get no clear data at all about the missing Zenas. "In the well—he lives in the well—" was all that the clouded father would say. Then there flashed across the visitor's mind a sudden thought of the mad wife, and he changed his line of inquiry. "Nabby? Why, here she is!" was the surprised response of poor Nahum, and Ammi soon saw that he must search for himself. Leaving the harmless babbler on the couch, he took the keys from their nail beside the door and climbed the creaking stairs to the attic. It was very close and noisome up there, and no sound could be heard from any direction. Of the four doors in sight, only one was locked, and on this he tried various keys of the ring he had taken. The third key proved the right one, and after some fumbling Ammi threw open the low white door.

It was quite dark inside, for the window was small and half-obscured by the crude wooden bars; and Ammi could see nothing at all on the wide-planked floor. The stench was beyond enduring, and before proceeding further he had to retreat to another room and return with his lungs filled with breathable air. When he did enter he saw something dark in the corner, and upon seeing it more clearly he screamed outright. While he screamed he thought a momentary cloud eclipsed the window, and a second later he felt himself brushed as if by some hateful current of vapour. Strange colours danced before his eyes; and had not a present horror numbed him he would have thought of the globule in the meteor that the geologist's hammer had shattered, and of the morbid vegetation that had sprouted in the spring. As it was he thought only of the blasphemous monstrosity which confronted him, and which all too clearly had shared the nameless fate of young Thaddeus and the live-stock. But the terrible thing about the horror was that it very slowly and perceptibly moved as it continued to crumble.

Ammi would give me no added particulars of this scene, but the shape in the corner does not reappear in his tale as a moving object. There are things which cannot be mentioned, and what is done in common humanity is sometimes cruelly judged by the law. I gathered that no moving thing was left in that attic room, and that to leave anything capable of motion there would have been a deed so monstrous as to damn any accountable being to eternal torment. Anyone but a stolid farmer would have fainted or gone mad, but Ammi walked conscious through that low doorway and locked the accursed secret behind him. There would be Nahum to deal with now; he must be fed and tended, and removed to some place where he could be cared for.

Commencing his descent of the dark stairs, Ammi heard a thud below him. He even thought a scream had been suddenly choked off, and recalled nervously the clammy vapour which had brushed by him in that frightful room above. What presence had his cry and entry started up? Halted by some vague fear, he heard still further sounds below. Indubitably there was a sort of heavy dragging, and a most detestably sticky noise as of some fiendish and unclean species of suction. With an associative sense goaded to feverish heights, he thought unaccountably of what he had seen upstairs. Good God! What eldritch dream-world was this into which he had blundered? He dared move neither backward nor forward, but stood there trembling at the black curve of the boxed-in staircase. Every trifle of the scene burned itself into his brain. The sounds, the sense of dread expectancy, the darkness, the steepness of the narrow steps—and merciful Heaven!—the faint but unmistakable luminosity of all the woodwork in sight; steps, sides, exposed laths, and beams alike.

Then there burst forth a frantic whinny from Ammi's horse outside, followed at once by a clatter which told of a frenzied runaway. In another moment horse and buggy had gone beyond earshot, leaving the frightened man on the dark stairs to guess what had sent them. But that was not all. There had been another sound out there. A sort of liquid splash—water—it must have been the well. He had left Hero untied near it, and a buggywheel must have brushed the coping and knocked in a stone. And still the pale phosphorescence glowed in that detestably ancient woodwork. God! how old the house was! Most of it built before 1670, and the gambrel roof no later than 1730.

A feeble scratching on the floor downstairs now sounded distinctly, and Ammi's grip tightened on a heavy stick he had picked up in the attic for some purpose. Slowly nerving himself, he finished his descent and walked boldly toward the kitchen. But he did not complete the walk, because what he sought was no longer there. It had come to meet him, and it was still alive after a fashion. Whether it had crawled or whether it had been dragged by any external forces, Ammi could not say; but the death had been at it. Everything had happened in the last half-hour, but collapse, greying, and disintegration were already far advanced. There was a horrible brittleness, and dry fragments were scaling off. Ammi could not touch it, but looked horrifiedly into the distorted parody that had been a face. "What was it, Nahum—what was it?" He whispered, and the cleft, bulging lips were just able to crackle out a final answer.

"Nothin' . . . nothin' . . . the colour . . . it burns . . . cold an' wet, but it burns . . . it lived in the well. . . . I seen it . . . a kind of smoke . . . jest like the flowers last spring . . . the well shone at night . . . Thad an' Merwin an' Zenas . . . everything alive . . . suckin' the life out of everything . . . in that stone . . . it must a' come in that stone . . . pizened the whole place . . . dun't know what it wants . . . that round thing them men from the college dug outen the stone . . . they smashed it . . . it was that same colour . . . jest the same, like the flowers an' plants . . . must a' ben more of 'em . . . seeds . . . seeds . . . they growed . . . I seen it the fust time this week . . . must a' got strong on Zenas . . . he was a big boy, full o' life . . . it beats down your mind an' then gets ye . . . burns ye up . . . in the well water . . . you was right about that . . . evil water . . . Zenas never come back from the well . . . can't git away . . . draws ye . . . ye know summ'at's comin' but tain't no use . . . I seen it time an' agin senct Zenas was took . . . whar's Nabby, Ammi? . . . my head's no good . . . dun't know how long sense I fed her . . . it'll git her ef we ain't keerful . . . jest a colour . . . her face gittin' to hev that colour sometimes towards night . . . an' it burns an' sucks . . . it come from some place whar things ain't as they is here . . . one of them professors said so . . . he was right . . . look out, Ammi, it'll do suthin' more . . . sucks the life out . . ."

But that was all. That which spoke could speak no more because it had completely caved in. Ammi laid a red checked tablecloth over what was left and reeled out the back door into the fields. He climbed the slope to the ten-acre pasture and stumbled home by the north road and the woods. He could not pass that well from which his horses had run away. He had looked at it through the window, and had seen that no stone was missing from the rim. Then the lurching buggy had not dislodged anything after all—the splash had been something else—something which went into the well after it had done with poor Nahum. . . .

When Ammi reached his house the horses and buggy had arrived before him and thrown his wife into fits of anxiety. Reassuring her without explanations, he set out at once for Arkham and notified the authorities that the Gardner family was no more. He indulged in no details, but merely told of the deaths of Nahum and Nabby, that of Thaddeus being already known, and mentioned that the cause seemed to be the same strange ailment which had killed the live-stock. He also stated that Merwin and Zenas had disappeared. There was considerable questioning at the police station, and in the end Ammi was compelled to take three officers to the Gardner farm, together with the coroner, the medical examiner, and the veterinary who had treated the diseased animals. He went much against his will, for the afternoon was advancing and he feared the fall of night over that accursed place, but it was some comfort to have so many people with him.

The six men drove out in a democrat-wagon, following Ammi's buggy, and arrived at the pest-ridden farmhouse about four o'clock. Used as the officers were to gruesome experiences, not one remained unmoved at what was found in the attic and under the red checked tablecloth on the floor below. The whole aspect of the farm with its grey desolation was terrible enough, but those two crumbling objects were beyond all bounds. No one could look long at them, and even the medical examiner admitted that there was very little to examine. Specimens could be analysed, of course, so he busied himself in obtaining them—and here it develops that a very puzzling aftermath occurred at the college laboratory where the two phials of dust were finally taken. Under the spectroscope both samples gave off an unknown spectrum, in which many of the baffling bands were precisely like those which the strange meteor had yielded in the previous year. The property of emitting this spectrum vanished in a month, the dust thereafter consisting mainly of alkaline phosphates and carbonates.

Ammi would not have told the men about the well if he had thought they meant to do anything then and there. It was getting toward sunset, and he was anxious to be away. But he could not help glancing nervously at the stony curb by the great sweep, and when a detective questioned him he admitted that Nahum had feared something down there—so much so that he had never even thought of searching it for Merwin or Zenas. After that nothing would do but that they empty and explore the well immediately, so Ammi had to wait trembling while pail after pail of rank water was hauled up and splashed on the soaking ground outside. The men sniffed in disgust at the fluid, and toward the last held their noses against the foetor they were uncovering. It was not so long a job as they had feared it would be, since the water was phenomenally low. There is no need to speak too exactly of what they found. Merwin and Zenas were both there, in part, though the vestiges were mainly skeletal. There were also a small deer and a large dog in about the same state, and a number of bones of small animals. The ooze and slime at the bottom seemed inexplicably porous and bubbling, and a man who descended on hand-holds with a long pole found that he could sink the wooden shaft to any depth in the mud of the floor without meeting any solid obstruction.

Twilight had now fallen, and lanterns were brought from the house. Then, when it was seen that nothing further could be gained from the well, everyone went indoors and conferred in the ancient sitting-room while the intermittent light of a spectral half-moon played wanly on the grey desolation outside. The men were frankly nonplussed by the entire case, and could find no convincing common element to link the strange vegetable conditions, the unknown disease of live-stock and humans, and the unaccountable deaths of Merwin and Zenas in the tainted well. They had heard the common country talk, it is true; but could not believe that anything contrary to natural law had occurred. No doubt the meteor had poisoned the soil, but the illness of persons and animals who had eaten nothing grown in that soil was another matter. Was it the well water? Very possibly. It might be a good idea to analyse it. But what peculiar madness could have made both boys jump into the well? Their deeds were so similar—and the fragments showed that they had both suffered from the grey brittle death. Why was everything so grey and brittle?

It was the coroner, seated near a window overlooking the yard, who first noticed the glow about the well. Night had fully set in, and all the abhorrent grounds seemed faintly luminous with more than the fitful moonbeams; but this new glow was something definite and distinct, and appeared to shoot up from the black pit like a softened ray from a searchlight, giving dull reflections in the little ground pools where the water had been emptied. It had a very queer colour, and as all the men clustered round the window Ammi gave a violent start. For this strange beam of ghastly miasma was to him of no unfamiliar hue. He had seen that colour before, and feared to think what it might mean. He had seen it in the nasty brittle globule in that aerolite two summers ago, had seen it in the crazy vegetation of the springtime, and had thought he had seen it for an instant that very morning against the small barred window of that terrible attic room where nameless things had happened. It had flashed there a second, and a clammy and hateful current of vapour had brushed past him—and then poor Nahum had been taken by something of that colour. He had said so at the last—said it was like the globule and the plants. After that had come the runaway in the yard and the splash in the well—and now that well was belching forth to the night a pale insidious beam of the same demoniac tint.

It does credit to the alertness of Ammi's mind that he puzzled even at that tense moment over a point which was essentially scientific. He could not but wonder at his gleaning of the same impression from a vapour glimpsed in the daytime, against a window opening on the morning sky, and from a nocturnal exhalation seen as a phosphorescent mist against the black and blasted landscape. It wasn't right—it was against Nature—and he thought of those terrible last words of his stricken friend, "It come from some place whar things ain't as they is here . . . one o' them professors said so. . . ."

All three horses outside, tied to a pair of shrivelled saplings by the road, were now neighing and pawing frantically. The wagon driver started for the door to do something, but Ammi laid a shaky hand on his shoulder. "Dun't go out thar," he whispered. "They's more to this nor what we know. Nahum said somethin' lived in the well that sucks your life out. He said it must be some'at growed from a round ball like one we all seen in the meteor stone that fell a year ago June. Sucks an' burns, he said, an' is jest a cloud of colour like that light out thar now, that ye can hardly see an' can't tell what it is. Naham thought it feeds on everything livin' an' gits stronger all the time. He said he seen it this last week. It must be somethin' from away off in the sky like the men from the college last year says the meteor stone was. The way it's made an' the way it works ain't like no way o' God's world. It's some'at from beyond."

So the men paused indecisively as the light from the well grew stronger and the hitched horses pawed and whinnied in increasing frenzy. It was truly an awful moment; with terror in that ancient and accursed house itself, four monstrous sets of fragments—two from the house and two from the well—in the woodshed behind, and that shaft of unknown and unholy iridescence from the slimy depths in front. Ammi had restrained the driver on impulse, forgetting how uninjured he himself was after the clammy brushing of that coloured vapour in the attic room, but perhaps it is just as well that he acted as he did. No one will ever know what was abroad that night; and though the blasphemy from beyond had not so far hurt any human of unweakened mind, there is no telling what it might not have done at that last moment, and with its seemingly increased strength and the special signs of purpose it was soon to display beneath the half-clouded moonlit sky.

All at once one of the detectives at the window gave a short, sharp gasp. The others looked at him, and then quickly followed his own gaze upward to the point at which its idle straying had been suddenly arrested. There was no need for words. What had been disputed in country gossip was disputable no longer, and it is because of the thing which every man of that party agreed in whispering later on, that the strange days are never talked about in Arkham. It is necessary to premise that there was no wind at that hour of the evening. One did arise not long afterward, but there was absolutely none then. Even the dry tips of the lingering hedge-mustard, grey and blighted, and the fringe on the roof of the standing democrat-wagon were unstirred. And yet amid that tense, godless calm the high bare boughs of all the trees in the yard were moving. They were twitching morbidly and spasmodically, clawing in convulsive and epileptic madness at the moonlit clouds; scratching impotently in the noxious air as if jerked by some allied and bodiless line of linkage with subterrene horrors writhing and struggling below the black roots.

Not a man breathed for several seconds. Then a cloud of darker depth passed over the moon, and the silhouette of clutching branches faded out momentarily. At this there was a general cry; muffled with awe, but husky and almost identical from every throat. For the terror had not faded with the silhouette, and in a fearsome instant of deeper darkness the watchers saw wriggling at that tree top height a thousand tiny points of faint and unhallowed radiance, tipping each bough like the fire of St. Elmo or the flames that come down on the apostles' heads at Pentecost. It was a monstrous constellation of unnatural light, like a glutted swarm of corpse-fed fireflies dancing hellish sarabands over an accursed marsh; and its colour was that same nameless intrusion which Ammi had come to recognize and dread. All the while the shaft of phosphorescence from the well was getting brighter and brighter, bringing to the minds of the huddled men, a sense of doom and abnormality which far outraced any image their conscious minds could form. It was no longer *shining* out; it was *pouring* out; and as the shapeless stream of unplaceable colour left the well it seemed to flow directly into the sky.

The veterinary shivered, and walked to the front door to drop the heavy extra bar across it. Ammi shook no less, and had to tug and point for lack of controllable voice when he wished to draw notice to the growing luminosity of the trees. The neighing and stamping of the horses had become utterly frightful, but not a soul of that group in the old house would have ventured forth for any earthly reward. With the moments the shining of the trees increased, while their restless branches seemed to strain more and more toward verticality. The wood of the well-sweep was shining now, and presently a policeman dumbly pointed to some wooden sheds and bee-hives near the stone wall on the west. They were commencing to shine, too, though the tethered vehicles of the visitors seemed so far unaffected. Then there was a wild commotion and clopping in the road, and as Ammi quenched the lamp for better seeing they realized that the span of frantic greys had broken their sapling and run off with the democrat-wagon.

The shock served to loosen several tongues, and embarrassed whispers were exchanged. "It spreads on everything organic that's been around here," muttered the medical examiner. No one replied, but the man who had been in the well gave a hint that his long pole must have stirred up something intangible. "It was awful," he added. "There was no bottom at all. Just ooze and bubbles and the feeling of something lurking under there." Ammi's horse still pawed and screamed deafeningly in the road outside, and nearly drowned its owner's faint quaver as he mumbled his formless reflections. "It come from that stone—it growed down thar—it got everything livin'—it fed itself on 'em, mind and body—Thad an' Merwin, Zenas an' Nabby—Nahum was the last—they all drunk the water—it got strong on 'em—it come from beyond, whar things ain't like they be here—now it's goin' home—"

At this point, as the column of unknown colour flared suddenly stronger and began to weave itself into fantastic suggestions of shape which each spectator later described differently, there came from poor tethered Hero such a sound as no man before or since ever heard from a horse. Every person in that low-pitched sitting-room stopped his ears, and Ammi turned away from the window in horror and nausea. Words could not convey it—when Ammi looked out again the hapless beast lay huddled inert on the moonlit ground between the splintered shafts of the buggy. That was the last of Hero till they buried him next day. But the present was no time to mourn, for almost at this instant a detective silently called attention to something terrible in the very room with them. In the absence of the lamplight it was clear that a faint phosphorescence had begun to pervade the entire apartment. It glowed on the broad-planked floor and the fragment of rag carpet, and shimmered over the sashes of the small-paned windows. It ran up and down the exposed corner-posts, coruscated about the shelf and mantel, and infected the very doors and furniture. Each minute saw it strengthen, and at last it was very plain that healthy living things must leave that house.

Ammi showed them the back door and the path up through the fields to the ten-acre pasture. They walked and stumbled as in a dream, and did not dare look back till they were far away on the high ground. They were glad of the path, for they could not have gone the front way, by that well. It was bad enough passing the glowing barn and sheds, and those shining orchard trees with their gnarled, fiendish contours; but thank Heaven the branches did their worst twisting high up. The moon went under some very black clouds as they crossed the rustic bridge over Chapman's Brook, and it was blind groping from there to the open meadows.

When they looked back toward the valley and the distant Gardner place at the bottom they saw a fearsome sight. All the farm was shining with the hideous unknown blend of colour; trees, buildings, and even such grass and herbage as had not been wholly changed to lethal grey brittleness. The boughs were all straining skyward, tipped with tongues of foul flame, and lambent tricklings of the same monstrous fire were creeping about the ridgepoles of the house, barn and sheds. It was a scene from a vision of Fuseli, and over all the rest reigned that riot of luminous amorphousness, that alien and undimensioned rainbow of cryptic poison from the well—seething, feeling, lapping, reaching, scintillating, straining, and malignly bubbling in its cosmic and unrecognizable chromaticism.

Then without warning the hideous thing shot vertically up toward the sky like a rocket or meteor, leaving behind no trail and disappearing through a round and curiously regular hole in the clouds before any man could gasp or cry out. No watcher can ever forget that sight, and Ammi stared blankly at the stars of Cygnus, Deneb twinkling above the others, where the unknown colour had melted into the Milky Way. But his gaze was the next moment called swiftly to earth by the crackling in the valley. It was just that. Only a wooden ripping and crackling, and not an explosion, as so many others of the party vowed. Yet the outcome was the same, for in one feverish kaleidoscopic instant there burst up from that doomed and accursed farm a gleamingly eruptive cataclysm of unnatural sparks and substance; blurring the glance of the few who saw it, and sending forth to the zenith a bombarding cloudburst of such coloured and fantastic fragments as our universe must needs disown. Through quickly re-closing vapours they followed the great morbidity that had vanished, and in another second they had vanished too. Behind and below was only a darkness to which the men dared not return, and all about was a mounting wind which seemed to sweep down in black, frore gusts from interstellar space. It shrieked and howled, and lashed the fields and distorted woods in a mad cosmic frenzy, till soon the trembling party realized it would be no use waiting for the moon to show what was left down there at Nahum's.

Too awed even to hint theories, the seven shaking men trudged back toward Arkham by the north road. Ammi was worse than his fellows, and begged them to see him inside his own kitchen, instead of keeping straight on to town. He did not wish to cross the blighted, wind-whipped woods alone to his home on the main road. For he had had an added shock that the others were spared, and was crushed forever with a brooding fear he dared not even mention for many years to come. As the rest of the watchers on that tempestuous hill had stolidly set their faces toward the road, Ammi had looked back an instant at the shadowed valley of desolation so lately sheltering his ill-starred friend. And from that stricken, far-away spot he had seen something feebly rise, only to sink down again upon the place from which the great shapeless horror had shot into the sky. It was just a colour—but not any colour of our earth or heavens. And because Ammi recognized that colour, and knew that this last faint remnant must still lurk down there in the well, he has never been quite right since.

Ammi would never go near the place again, It is forty-four years now since the horror happened, but he has never been there, and will be glad when the new reservoir blots it out. I shall be glad, too, for I do not like the way the sunlight changed colour around the mouth of that abandoned well I passed. I hope the water will always be very deep—but even so, I shall never drink it. I do not think I shall visit the Arkham country hereafter. Three of the men who had been with Ammi returned the next morning to see the ruins by daylight, but there were not any real ruins. Only the bricks of the chimney, the stones of the cellar, some mineral and metallic litter here and there, and the rim of that nefandous well. Save for Ammi's dead horse, which they towed away and buried, and the buggy which they shortly returned to him, everything that had ever been living had gone. Five eldritch acres of dusty grey desert remained, nor has anything ever grown there since. To this day it sprawls open to the sky like a great spot eaten by acid in the woods and fields, and the few who have ever dared glimpse it in spite of the rural tales have named it "the blasted heath."

The rural tales are queer. They might be even queerer if city men and college chemists could be interested enough to analyse the water from that disused well, or the grey dust that no wind seems to disperse. Botanists, too, ought to study the stunted flora on the borders of that spot, for they might shed light on the country notion that the blight is spreading—little by little, perhaps an inch a year. People say the colour of the neighboring herbage is not quite right in the spring, and that wild things leave queer prints in the light winter snow. Snow never seems quite so heavy on the blasted heath as it is elsewhere. Horses—the few that are left in this motor age—grow skittish in the silent valley; and hunters cannot depend on their dogs too near the splotch of greyish dust.

They say the mental influences are very bad, too; numbers went queer in the years after Nahum's taking, and always they lacked the power to get away. Then the stronger-minded folk all left the region, and only the foreigners tried to live in the crumbling old homesteads. They could not stay, though; and one sometimes wonders what insight beyond ours their wild, weird stories of whispered magic have given them. Their dreams at night, they protest, are very horrible in that grotesque country; and surely the very look of the dark realm is enough to stir a morbid fancy. No traveler has ever escaped a sense of strangeness in those deep ravines, and artists shiver as they paint thick woods whose mystery is as much of the spirits as of the eye. I myself am curious about the sensation I derived from my one lone walk before Ammi told me his tale. When twilight came I had vaguely wished some clouds would gather, for an odd timidity about the deep skyey voids above had crept into my soul.

Do not ask me for my opinion. I do not know—that is all. There was no one but Ammi to question; for Arkham people will not talk about the strange days, and all three professors who saw the aerolite and its coloured globule are dead. There were other globules—depend upon that. One must have fed itself and escaped, and probably there was another which was too late. No doubt it is still down the well—I know there was something wrong with the sunlight I saw above the miasmal brink. The rustics say the blight creeps an inch a year, so perhaps there is a kind of growth or nourishment even now. But whatever demon hatching is there, it must be tethered to something or else it would quickly spread. Is it fastened to the roots of those trees that claw the air? One of the current Arkham tales is about fat oaks that shine and move as they ought not to do at night.

What it is, only God knows. In terms of matter I suppose the thing Ammi described would be called a gas, but this gas obeyed the laws that are not of our cosmos. This was no fruit of such worlds and suns as shine on the telescopes and photographic plates of our observatories. This was no breath from the skies whose motions and dimensions our astronomers measure or deem too vast to measure. It was just a colour out of space—a frightful messenger from unformed realms of infinity beyond all Nature as we know it; from realms whose mere existence stuns the brain and numbs us with the black extra-cosmic gulfs it throws open before our frenzied eyes.

I doubt very much if Ammi consciously lied to me, and I do not think his tale was all a freak of madness as the townsfolk had forewarned. Something terrible came to the hills and valleys on that meteor, and something terrible—though I know not in what proportion—still remains. I shall be glad to see the water come. Meanwhile I hope nothing will happen to Ammi. He saw so much of the thing— and its influence was so insidious. Why has he never been able to move away? How clearly he recalled those dying words of Nahum's—"can't git away—draws ye—ye know summ'at's comin' but tain't no use—" Ammi is such a good old man—when the reservoir gang gets to work I must write the chief engineer to keep a sharp watch on him. I would hate to think of him as the grey, twisted, brittle monstrosity which persists more and more in troubling my sleep.

﷼ M(ARY) E(LIZABETH) COUNSELMAN
(1911–1995)

The works of Washington Irving, Edgar Allan Poe, and Bram Stoker were some of the influences on the writing of Mary Elizabeth Counselman. Counselman was a newspaper writer, as were Abraham Merritt, Walter B. Gibson, Fredric Brown, and other crafters of Fantasy and Science Fiction. Like William Faulkner and Robert R. McCammon, she was a product of the deep South—in her case, Alabama—and her stories are often set in the rural South.

Counselman incorporated nostalgia, folklore, myth, legend, old tradition, and supernatural elements in her storytelling. Like Fantasy writer Clark Ashton Smith, she was also an accomplished poet and author of adventure stories. As did her contemporary Catherine Moore, Mary Counselman and her publishers used her initials in her bylines to hide her gender. In the twenty-fifth anniversary issue of Weird Tales (1948), the same reader poll that voted Seabury Quinn the then-favorite author selected M. E. Counselman's "The Three Marked Pennies"—originally unillustrated, last-minute backup material—as the readers' single favorite Weird Tales story. "The Three Marked Pennies," as is the case with some of Counselman's other tales, features a puzzle or mystery. Its rural setting and theme of perverse ritual can be favorably compared to some of Robert Bloch's stories and predates and foreshadows Shirley Jackson's "The Lottery."

The Three Marked Pennies
(Weird Tales, *August* 1934)

Every one agreed, after it was over, that the whole thing was the conception of a twisted brain, a game of chess played by a madman—in which the pieces, instead of carved bits of ivory or ebony, were human beings.

It was odd that no one doubted the authenticity of the "contest." The public seems never for a moment to have considered it the prank of a practical joker, or even a publicity stunt. Jeff Haverty, editor of the *News*, advanced a theory that the affair was meant to be a clever, if rather elaborate, psychological experiment—which would end in the revealing of the originator's identity and a big laugh for every one.

Perhaps it was the glamorous manner of announcement that gave the thing such wide-spread interest. Branton, the southern town of about 30,000 people in which the affair occurred, awoke one April morning to find all its trees, telephone poles, house-sides and store-fronts plastered with a strange sign. There were scores of them, written on yellow copy-paper on an ordinary typewriter. The sign read:

"*During this day of April 15, three pennies will find their way into the pockets of this city. On each penny there will be a well-defined mark. One is a square; one is a circle; and one is a cross. These three pennies will change hands often, as do all coins, and on the seventh day after this announcement (April 21) the possessor of each marked penny will receive a gift.*

"*To the first: $100,000 in cash.*

"*To the second: A trip around the world.*

"*To the third: Death.*

"The answer to this riddle lies in the marks on the three coins: circle, square, and cross. Which of these symbolizes wealth? Which, travel? Which, death? The answer is not an obvious one.

"To him who finds it and obtains the first penny, $100,000 will be sent without delay. To him who has the second penny, a first-class ticket for the earliest world-touring steamer to sail will be presented. But to the possessor of the third marked coin will be given — death. If you are afraid your penny is the third, give it away — but it may be the first or the second!

"Show your marked penny to the editor of the 'News' on April 21, giving your name and address. He will know nothing of this contest until he reads one of these signs. He is requested to publish the names of the three possessors of the coins April 21, with the mark on the penny each holds.

"It will do no good to mark a coin of your own, as the dates of the true coins will be sent to Editor Haverty."

By noon every one had read the notice, and the city was buzzing with excitement. Clerks began to examine the contents of cash register drawers. Hands rummaged in pockets and purses. Stores and banks were flooded with customers wanting silver changed to coppers.

Jeff Haverty was the target for a barrage of queries, and his evening edition came with a lengthy editorial embodying all he knew about the mystery, which was exactly nothing. A note had come that morning with the rest of his mail — a note unsigned, and typewritten on the same yellow paper in a plain stamped envelope with the postmark of that city. It said merely: *"Circle — 1920. Square — 1909. Cross — 1928. Please do not reveal these dates until after April 21."*

Haverty complied with the request, and played up the story for all it was worth.

The first penny was found in the street by a small boy, who promptly took it to his father. His father, in turn, palmed it off hurriedly on his barber, who gave it in change to a patron before he noted the deep cross cut in the coin's surface.

The patron took it to his wife, who immediately paid it to the grocer. "It's too long a chance, honey!" she silenced her mate's protests. "I don't like the idea of that death-threat in the notice . . . and this certainly must be the third penny. What else could that little cross stand for? Crosses over graves — don't you see the significance?"

And when that explanation was wafted abroad, the cross-marked penny began to change hands with increasing rapidity.

The other two pennies bobbed up before dusk — one marked with a small perfect square, the other with a neat circle.

The square-marked penny was discovered in a slot-machine by the proprietor of the Busy Bee Café. There was no way it could have got there, he reported, mystified and a little frightened. Only four people, all of them old patrons, had been in the café that day. And not one of them had been near the slot-machine — located at the back of the place as it was, and filled with stale chewing-gum which, at a glance, was worth nobody's penny. Furthermore, the proprietor had examined the thing for a chance coin the night before and had left it empty when he locked up; yet there was the square-marked penny nestling alone in the slot-machine at closing time April 15.

He had stared at the coin a long time before passing it in change to an elderly spinster.

"It ain't worth it," he muttered to himself. "I got a restaurant that's makin' me a thin livin', and I ain't in no hurry to get myself bumped off, on the long chance I might get that hundred thousand or that trip instead. No-sirree!"

The spinster took one look at the marked penny, gave a short mouse-like squeak, and flung it into the gutter as though it were a tarantula.

"My land!" she quavered. "I don't want that thing in my pocket-book!"

But she dreamed that night of foreign ports, or coolies jabbering in brittle tongue, of barracuda fins cutting the surface of deep blue water, and the ruins of ancient cities.

A negro workman picked up the penny next morning and clung to it all day, dreaming of Harlem, before he succumbed at last to gnawing fear. And the square-marked penny changed hands once more.

The circle-marked penny was first noted in a stack of coins by a teller of the Farmer's Trust.

"We get marked coins every now and then," he said. "I didn't notice this one especially—it may have been here for days."

He pocketed it gleefully, but discovered with a twinge of dismay next morning that he had passed it out to someone without noticing it.

"I wanted to keep it!" he sighed. "For better or for worse!"

He glowered at the stacks of some one else's money before him, and wondered furtively how many tellers ever really escaped with stolen goods.

A fruit-seller had received the penny. He eyed it dubiously. "Mebbe you bring-a me those mon, heh?" He showed it to his fat, greasy wife, who made the sign of horns against the "evil eye."

"T'row away!" she commanded shrilly. "She iss bad lock!"

Her spouse shrugged and sailed the circle-marked coin across the street. A ragged child pounced on it and scuttered away to buy a twist of licorice. And the circle-marked penny changed hands once more—clutched at by avaricious fingers, stared at by eyes grown sick of familiar scenes, relinquished again by the power of fear.

Those who came into brief possession of the three coins were fretted by the drag and shove of conflicting advice.

"Keep it!" some urged. "Think! It may mean a trip around the world! Paris! China! London! Oh, why couldn't I have got the thing?"

"Give it away," others admonished. "Maybe it's the third penny—you can't tell. Maybe the symbols don't mean what they seem to, and the square one is the death-penny! I'd throw it away, if I were you."

"No! No!" still others cried. "Hang on to it! It may bring you $100,000. *A hundred thousand dollars!* In these times! Why, fellow, you'd be the same as a millionaire!"

The meaning of the three symbols was on every one's tongue, and no one agreed with his neighbor's solution to the riddle.

"It's as plain as the nose on my face," one man would declare. "The circle represents the globe—the travel-penny, see?"

"No, no. The cross means that. 'Cross' the seas, don't you get it? Sort of a pun effect. The circle means money—shape of a coin, understand?"

"And the square one—?"

"A grave. A square hole for a coffin, see? Death. It's quite simple. I wish I could get hold of that circle one!"

"You're crazy! The cross one is for death—everybody says so. And believe me, everybody's getting rid of it as soon as they get it! It may be a joke of some kind . . . no danger at all . . . but I wouldn't like to be the holder of that cross-marked penny when April twenty-first rolls around!"

"I'd keep it and wait till the other two had got what was due them. Then, if mine turned out to be the wrong one, I'd throw it away!" one man said importantly.

"But he won't pay up till all three pennies are accounted for, I shouldn't think," another answered him. "And maybe the offer doesn't hold good after April twenty-first—and you'd be losing one hundred thousand dollars or a world tour just because you're scared to find out!"

"That's a big stake, man," another murmured. "But frankly, I wouldn't like to take the chance. He might give me his third gift!"

"He" was how every one designated the unknown originator of the contest; though, of course, there was no more clue to his sex than to his identity.

"He must be rich," some said, "to offer such expensive prizes."

"And crazy!" others exploded, "threatening to kill the third one. He'll never get away with it!"

"But clever," still others admitted, "to think up the whole business. He knows human nature, whoever he is. I'm inclined to agree with Haverty—it's all a sort of psychological experiment. He's trying to see whether desire for travel or greed for money is stronger than fear of death."

"Does he mean to pay up, do you think?"

"That remains to be seen!"

On the sixth day, Branton had reached a pitch of excitement amounting almost to hysteria. No one could work for wondering about the outcome of the bizarre test on the morrow.

It was known that a grocer's delivery boy held the square-marked coin, for he had been boasting of his indifference as to whether or not the square did represent a yawning grave. He exhibited the penny freely, making jokes about what he intended to do with his hundred thousand dollars—but on the morning of the last day he lost his nerve. Seeing a blind beggar woman huddled in her favorite corner between two shops, he passed close to her and surreptitiously dropped the cent piece into her box of pencils.

"I had it!" he wailed to a friend after he had reached his grocery. "I had it right here in my pocket last night, and now it's gone! See, I've got a hole in the darn' thing—the penny must have dropped out!"

It was also known who held the circle-marked penny. A young soda clerk, with the sort of ready smile that customers like to see across a marble counter, had discovered the coin and fished it from the cash drawer, exulting over his good fortune.

"Bud Skinner's got the circle penny," people told one another, wavering between anxiety and gladness. "I hope the kid *does* get that world tour—it'd tickle him so! He seems to get such a kick out of life; it's a sin he has to be stuck in this slow burg!"

Finally it was found who held the cross-marked cent piece. "Carlton . . . poor devil!" people murmured in subdued tones. "Death would be a godsend to him. Wonder he hasn't shot himself before this. Guess he just hasn't the nerve."

The man with the cross-marked penny smiled bitterly. "I hope this blasted little symbol means what they all think it means!" he confided to a friend.

At last the eagerly awaited day came. A crowd formed in the street outside the newspaper office to see the three possessors of the three marked coins show Haverty their pennies and give him their names to publish. For their benefit the editor met the trio on the sidewalk outside the building, so that all might see them.

The evening edition ran the three people's photographs, with the name, address, and the mark on each one's penny under each picture. Branton read . . . and held its breath.

On the morning of April twenty-second, the old blind beggar woman sat in her accustomed place, musing on the excitement of the previous day, when several people had led her—she knew by the odor of fish from the market across the street—to the newspaper office. There some one had asked her name and many other puzzling things which had bewildered her until she had almost burst into tears.

"Let me alone!" she had whispered. "I ask only enough food to keep from starving, and a place to sleep. Why are you pushing me around like this and yelling at me? Let me go back to my corner! I don't like all this confusion and strangeness that I can't see—it frightens me!"

Then they had told her something about a marked penny they had found in her alms-box, and other things about a large sum of money and some impending danger that threatened her. She was glad when they led her back to her cranny between the shops.

Now as she sat in her accustomed spot, nodding comfortably and humming a little under her breath, a paper fluttered down into her lap. She felt the stiff oblong, knew it was an envelope, and called a bystander to her side.

"Open this for me, will you?" she requested. "Is it a letter? Read it to me."

The bystander tore open the envelope and frowned. "It's a note," he told her. "Typewritten, and it's not signed. It just says—what the devil?—just says: '*The four corners of the earth are exactly the same.*' And . . . hey! look at this! . . . oh, I'm sorry; I forgot you're . . . it's a steamship ticket for a world tour! Look, didn't you have one of the marked pennies?"

The blind woman nodded drowsily. "Yes, the one with the square, they said." She sighed faintly. "I had hoped I would get the money, or . . . the other, so I would never have to beg again."

"Well, here's your ticket." The bystander held it out to her uncertainly. "Don't you want it?" as the beggar made no move to take it.

"No," snapped the blind woman. "What good would it be to me?" She seized the ticket in sudden rage, and tore it into bits.

At nearly the same hour, Kenneth Carlton was receiving a fat manila envelope from the postman. He frowned as he squinted at the local postmark over the stamp. His friend Evans stood beside him, paler than Carlton.

"Open it, open it!" he urged. "Read it—no, don't open it, Ken. I'm scared! After all . . . it's a terrible way to go. Not knowing where the blow's coming from, and—"

Carlton emitted a macabre chuckle, ripping open the heavy envelope. "It's the best break I've had in years, Jim. I'm glad! Glad, Jim, do you hear? It will be quick, I hope . . . and painless. What's this, I wonder. A treatise on how to blow off the top of your head?" He shook the contents of the letter onto a table, and then, after a moment, he began to laugh . . . mirthlessly . . . hideously.

His friend stared at the little heap of crisp bills, all of a larger denomination than he had ever seen before. "The money! You get the hundred thousand, Ken! I can't believe. . . . " He broke off to snatch up a slip of yellow paper among the bills. "*Wealth is the greatest cross a man can bear,*" he read aloud the typewritten words. "It doesn't make sense . . . wealth? Then . . . the cross-mark stood for wealth? I don't understand."

Carlton's laughter cracked. "He has depth, that bird—whoever he is! Nice irony there, Jim—wealth being a burden instead of the blessing most people consider it. I suppose he's right, at that. But I wonder if he knows the really ironic part of this act of his little play? A hundred thousand dollars to a man with—cancer. Well, Jim, I have a month or less to spend it in . . . one more damnable month to suffer through before it's all over!"

His terrible laughter rose again, until his friend had to clap hands to ears, shutting out the sound.

But the strangest part of the whole affair was Bud Skinner's death. Just after the rush hour at noon, he had found a small package, addressed to him, on a back counter in the drug store. Eagerly he tore off the brown paper wrappings, a dozen or so friends crowding about him.

A curiously wrought silver box was what he found. He pressed the catch with trembling fingers and snapped back the lid. An instant later his face took on a queer expression—and he slid noiselessly to the tile floor of the drug store.

The ensuing police investigation unearthed nothing at all, except that young Skinner had been poisoned with *crotalin*—snake venom—administered through a pin-prick on his thumb when he pressed the trick catch on the little silver box. This, and the typewritten note in the otherwise empty box: "*Life ends where it began— nowhere,*" were all they found as an explanation of the clerk's death. Nor was anything else ever brought to light about the mysterious contest of the three marked pennies—which are probably still in circulation somewhere in the United States.

ROBERT BLOCH (1917–1994)

Best remembered as the author of Psycho *(1959), the novel that Alfred Hitchcock made into the famous film with the same title in 1960, Robert Bloch was more importantly the author of hundreds of short stories, novels, radio plays, movie screenplays, television dramas, and other popular stories and social criticisms. He made significant contributions to the popular genres of Dark Fantasy/Horror, Mystery and Detective Fiction, Science Fiction, and more. Many of Bloch's stories incorporate elements of comedy; many showcase the author's vast knowledge of world and literary history. A trademark of Bloch's tales is the twist ending, and because of this, many consider him the twentieth century's O. Henry.*

Between 1935 and 1952, Bloch had sixty-seven stories, novellas, and novelettes appear in Weird Tales *alone. Between 1935 and his death in 1994, Bloch published many hundreds of stories of various types and lengths in a range of other magazines including, but not limited to,* Amazing Stories, Fantastic Adventures, Imaginative Tales, Unknown Worlds, *and* Unusual Stories. *In the 1940s, 1950s, and 1960s, Robert Bloch's stories were the basis for several motion pictures; Bloch himself wrote screenplays that were made into movies. Of his many written and produced television plays, his three episodes for the original* Star Trek *series, entitled "What Are Little Girls Made Of?" (10/22/66)—a cloning story; "Catspaw" (10/27/67)—a rare fantasy for* Star Trek; *and "Wolf in the Fold" (12/22/67)—a clever "Jack the Ripper" in outer space story, are perhaps most famous.*

Ray Bradbury and Stephen King have acknowledged the profound influence of Robert Bloch on their writing. Often imitated, yet never matched in literary style, Bloch was also a gentleman of exceptional quality.

"Catnip" features a rural setting similar to that of Mary Elizabeth Counselman's "The Three Marked Pennies" and Shirley Jackson's "The Lottery"; it contains the famous Bloch twist ending and tells the story of a child gone horribly wrong.

Catnip

(Weird Tales, *March 1948*)

Ronnie Shires stood before the mirror and slicked back his hair. He straightened his new sweater and stuck out his chest. Sharp! Had to watch the way he looked, with graduation only a few weeks away and that election for class president coming up. If he could get to be president then, next year in high school he'd be a real wheel. Go out for second team or something. But he had to watch the angles—

"Ronnie! Better hurry or you'll be late!"

Ma came out of the kitchen, carrying his lunch. Ronnie wiped the grin off his face. She walked up behind him and put her arms around his waist.

"Hon, I only wish your father were here to see you—"

Ronnie wriggled free. "Yeah, sure. Say, Ma."

"Yes?"

"How's about some loot, huh? I got to get some things today."

"Well, I suppose. But try to make it last, son. This graduation costs a lot of money, seems to me."

"I'll pay you back some day." He watched her as she fumbled in her apron pocket and produced a wadded-up dollar bill.

"Thanks. See you." He picked up his lunch and ran outside. He walked along, smiling and whistling, knowing Ma was watching him from the window. She was always watching him, and it was a real drag.

Then he turned the corner, halted under a tree, and fished out a cigarette. He lit it and sauntered slowly across the street, puffing deeply. Out of the corner of his eye he watched the Ogden house just ahead.

Sure enough, the front screen door banged and Marvin Ogden came down the steps. Marvin was fifteen, one year older than Ronnie, but smaller and skinnier. He wore glasses and stuttered when he got excited, but he was valedictorian of the graduating class.

Ronnie came up behind him, walking fast.

"Hello, Snot-face!"

Marvin wheeled. He avoided Ronnie's glare, but smiled weakly at the pavement.

"I said hello, Snot-face! What's the matter, don't you know your own name, jerk?"

"Hello—Ronnie."

"How's old Snot-face today?"

"Aw, gee, Ronnie. Why do you have to talk like that? I never did anything to you, did I?"

Ronnie spit in the direction of Marvin's shoes. "I'd like to see you just try doing something to me, you four-eyed little—"

Marvin began to walk away, but Ronnie kept pace.

"Slow down, jag. I wanna talk to you."

"Wh-what is it, Ronnie? I don't want to be late."

"Shut your yap."

"But—"

"Listen, you. What was the big idea in History exam yesterday when you pulled your paper away?"

"You know, Ronnie. You aren't supposed to copy somebody else's answers."

"You trying to tell me what to do, square?"

"N-no. I mean, I only want to keep you out of trouble. What if Miss Sanders found out, and you want to be elected class president? Why, if anybody knew—"

Ronnie put his hand on Marvin's shoulder. He smiled. "You wouldn't ever tell her about it, would you, Snot-face?" he murmured.

"Of course not! Cross my heart!"

Ronnie continued to smile. He dug his fingers into Marvin's shoulder. With his other hand he swept Marvin's books to the ground. As Marvin bent forward to pick them up, he kicked Marvin as hard as he could, bringing his knee up fast. Marvin sprawled on the sidewalk. He began to cry. Ronnie watched him as he attempted to rise.

"This is just a sample of what you got coming if you squeal," he said. He stepped on the fingers of Marvin's left hand. "Creep!"

Marvin's snivelling faded from his ears as he turned the corner at the end of the block. Mary June was waiting for him under the trees. He came up behind her and slapped her, hard.

"Hello, you!" he said.

Mary June jumped about a foot, her curls bouncing on her shoulders. Then she turned and saw who it was.

"Oh, Ronnie! You oughtn't to—"

"Shut up. I'm in a hurry. Can't be late the day before election. You lining up the chicks?"

"Sure, Ronnie. You know, I promised. I had Ellen and Vicky over at the house last night and they said they'd vote for you for sure. All the girls are gonna vote for you."

"Well, they better." Ronnie threw his cigarette butt against a rosebush in the Elsner's yard.

"Ronnie—you be careful—want to start a fire?"

"Quit bossing me." He scowled.

"I'm not trying to boss you, Ronnie. Only—"

"Aw, you make me sick!" He quickened his pace, and the girl bit her lip as she endeavored to keep step with him. Ronnie, wait for me!"

"Wait for me!" he mocked her. "What's the matter, you afraid you'll get lost or something?"

"No. *You* know. I don't like to pass that old Mrs. Mingle's place. She always stares at me and makes faces."

"She's nuts!"

"I'm scared of her, Ronnie. Aren't you?"

"Me scared of that old bat? She can go take a flying leap!"

"Don't talk so loud, she'll hear you."

"Who cares?"

Ronnie marched boldly past the tree-shadowed cottage behind the rusted iron fence. He stared insolently at the girl, who made herself small against his shoulder, eyes averted from the ramshackle edifice. He deliberately slackened his pace as they passed the cottage, with its boarded-up windows, screened-in porch and general air of withdrawal from the world.

Mrs. Mingle herself was not in evidence today. Usually she could be seen in the weed-infested garden at the side of the cottage; a tiny, dried-up old woman, bending over her vines and plants, mumbling incessantly to herself or to the raddled black tomcat which served as her constant companion.

"Old prune-face ain't around!" Ronnie observed, loudly. "Must be off someplace on her broomstick."

"Ronnie—please!"

"Who cares?" Ronnie pulled Mary June's curls. "You dames are scared of everything, ain't you?"

"*Aren't*, Ronnie."

"Don't tell *me* how to talk!" Ronnie's gaze shifted again to the silent house, huddled in the shadows. A segment of shadow at the side of the cottage seemed to be moving. A black blur detached itself from the end of the porch. Ronnie recognized Mrs. Mingle's cat. It minced down the path towards the gate.

Quickly, Ronnie stooped and found a rock. He grasped it, rose, aimed, and hurled the missile in one continuous movement.

The cat hissed, then squawled in pain as the rock grazed its ribs.

"Oh, Ronnie!"

"Come on, let's run before she see us!"

They flew down the street. The school bell drowned out the cat-yowl.

"Here we go," said Ronnie. "You do my homework for me? Good. Give it here at once."

He snatched the papers from Mary June's hand and sprinted ahead. The girl stood watching him, smiling her admiration. From behind the fence the cat watched, too, and licked its jaws.

2.

It happened that afternoon, after school. Ronnie and Joe Gordan and Seymour Higgins were futzing around with a baseball and he was talking about the outfit Ma promised to buy him this summer if the dressmaking business picked up. Only he made it sound as if he was getting the outfit for sure, and that they could all use the mask and mitt. It didn't hurt to build it up a little, with the election tomorrow. He had to stand in good with the whole gang.

He knew if he hung around the school yard much longer, Mary June would come out and want him to walk her home. He was sick of her. Oh, she was all right for homework and such stuff, but these guys would just laugh at him if he went off with a dame.

So he said how about going down the street in front of the pool hall and maybe hang around to see if somebody would shoot a game? He'd pay. Besides, they could smoke.

Ronnie knew that these guys didn't smoke, but it sounded cool and that's what he wanted. They all followed him down the street, pounding their cleats on the sidewalk. It made a lot of noise, because everything was so quiet.

All Ronnie could hear was the cat. They were passing Mrs. Mingle's and there was this cat, rolling around in the garden on its back and on its stomach, playing with some kind of ball. It purred and meowed and whined.

"Look!" yelled Joe Gordan. "Dizzy cat's havin' a fit 'r something, huh?"

"Lice," said Ronnie. "Damned mangy old thing's fulla lice and fleas and stuff. I socked it a good one this morning."

"Ya did?"

"Sure. With a rock. This big, too." He made a watermelon with his hands.

"Weren't you afraid of old lady Mingle?"

"Afraid? Why, that dried-up old—"

"Catnip," said Seymour Higgins. "That's what he's got. Ball of catnip. Old Mingle buys it for him. My old man says she buys everything for that cat; special food and sardines. Treats it like a baby. Ever see them walk down the street together?"

"Catnip, huh?" Joe peered through the fence. "Wonder why they like it so much. Gets 'em wild, doesn't it? Cat's'll do anything for catnip."

The cat squealed, sniffing and clawing at the ball. Ronnie scowled at it. "I hate cats. Somebody oughta drowned that damn thing."

"Better not let Mrs. Mingle hear you talk like that," Seymour cautioned. "She'll put the evil eye on you."

"Bull!"

"Well, she grows them herbs and stuff and my old lady says—"

"Bull!"

"All right. But I wouldn't go monkeying around her or her old cat, either."

"I'll show you."

Before he knew it, Ronnie was opening the gate. He advanced towards the black tomcat as the boys gaped.

The cat crouched over the catnip, eyes flattened against a velveteen skull. Ronnie hesitated a moment, gauging the glitter of claws, the glare of agate eyes. But the gang was watching—

"Scat!" he shouted. He advanced, waving his arms. The cat sidled backwards. Ronnie feinted with his hand and scooped up the catnip ball.

"See? I got it, you guys. I got—"

"Put that down!"

He didn't see the door open. He didn't see her walk down the steps. But suddenly she was there. Leaning on her cane, wearing a black dress that fitted tightly over her tiny frame, she seemed hardly any bigger than the cat which crouched at her side. Her hair was grey and wrinkled and dead, her face was grey and wrinkled and dead, but her eyes—

They were agate eyes, like the cat's. They glowed. And when she talked, she spit the way the cat did.

"Put that down young man!"

Ronnie began to shake. It was only a chill, everybody gets chills now and then, and could he help it if he shook so hard the catnip just fell out of his hand?

He wasn't scared. He had to show the gang he wasn't scared of this skinny little dried-up old woman. It was hard to breathe, he was shaking so, but he managed. He filled his lungs and opened his mouth.

"You—you old witch!" he yelled.

The agate eyes widened. They were bigger than she was. All he could see were the eyes. Witch eyes. Now that he said it, he knew it was true. Witch. She was a witch.

"You insolent puppy. I've a good mind to cut out your lying tongue!"

Geez, she wasn't kidding!

Now she was coming closer, and the cat was inching up on him, and then she raised the cane in the air, she was going to hit him, the witch was after him, oh Ma, no, don't, oh—

Ronnie ran.

3.

Could he help it? Geez, the guys ran too. They'd run before he did, even. He had to run, the old bat was crazy, anybody could see that. Besides, if he'd stayed she'd of tried to hit him and maybe he'd let her have it. He was only trying to keep out of trouble. That was all.

Ronnie told it to himself over and over at supper time. But that didn't do any good, telling it to himself. It was the guys he had to tell it to, and fast. He had to explain it before election tomorrow—

"Ronnie. What's the matter? You sick?"

"No, Ma."

"Then why don't you answer a person? I declare, you haven't said ten words since you came in the house. And you aren't eating your supper."

"Not hungry."

"Something bothering you, son?"

"No. Leave me alone."

"It's that election tomorrow, isn't it?"

"Leave me alone." Ronnie rose. "I'm goin' out."

"Ronnie!"

"I got to see Joe. Important."

"Back by nine, remember."

"Yeah. Sure."

He went outside. The night was cool. Windy for this time of year. Ronnie shivered a little as he turned the corner. Maybe a cigarette—

He lit a match and a shower of sparks spiralled to the sky. Ronnie began to walk, puffing nervously. He had to see Joe and the others and explain. Yeah, right now, too. If they told anybody else—

It was dark. The light on the corner was out, and the Ogdens weren't home. That made it darker, because Mrs. Mingle never showed a light in her cottage.

Mrs. Mingle. Her cottage was up ahead. He'd better cross the street.

What was the matter with him? Was he getting chicken-guts? Afraid of that damned old woman, that old witch! He puffed, gulped, expanded his chest. Just let her try anything. Just let her be hiding under the trees waiting to grab out at him with her big claws and hiss—what was he talking about, anyway? That was the cat. Nuts to her cat, and her too. He'd show them!

Ronnie walked past the dark shadow where Mrs. Mingle dwelt. He whistled defiance, and emphasized it by shooting his cigarette butt across the fence. Sparks flew and were swallowed by the mouth of the night.

Ronnie paused and peered over the fence. Everything was black and still. There was nothing to be afraid of. Everything was black—

Everything except that flicker. It came from up the path, under the porch. He could see the porch now because there was a light. Not a steady light; a wavering light. Like a fire. A fire—where his cigarette had landed! The cottage was beginning to burn!

Ronnie gulped and clung to the fence. Yes, it was on fire all right. Mrs. Mingle would come out and the firemen would come and they'd find the butt and see him and then—

He fled down the street. The wind cat howled behind him, the wind that fanned the flames that burned the cottage—

Ma was in bed. He managed to slow down and walk softly as he slipped into the house, up the stairs. He undressed in the dark and sought the white womb between the bedsheets. When he got the covers over his head he had another chill. Lying there, trembling, not daring to look out of the window and see the glare from the other side of the block, Ronnie's teeth chattered. He knew he was going to pass out in a minute.

Then he heard the screaming from far away. Fire-engines. Somebody had called them. He needn't worry now. Why should the sound frighten him? It was only a siren, it wasn't Mrs. Mingle screaming, it couldn't be. She was all right. He was all right. Nobody knew . . .

Ronnie fell asleep with the wind and the siren wailing in his ears.

His slumber was deep and only once was there an interruption. That was along towards morning, when he thought he heard a noise at the window. It was a scraping sound. The wind, of course. And it must have been the wind, too, that sobbed and whined and whimpered beneath the windowsill at dawn. It was only Ronnie's imagination, Ronnie's conscience, that transformed the sound into the wailing of a cat . . .

4.

"Ronnie!"

It wasn't the wind, it wasn't a cat. Ma was calling him.

"Ronnie! Oh, Ronnie!"

He opened his eyes, shielding them from the sunshafts.

"I declare, you might answer a person." He heard her grumbling to herself downstairs. Then she called again.

"Ronnie!"

"I'm coming, Ma."

He got out of bed, went to the bathroom, and dressed. She was waiting for him in the kitchen.

"Land sakes, you sure slept sound last night. Didn't you hear the fire-engines?"

Ronnie dropped a slice of toast. "What engines?"

Ma's voice rose. "Don't you know? Why boy, it was just awful—Mrs. Mingle's cottage burned down."

"Yeah?" He had trouble picking up the toast again.

"The poor old lady—just think of it—trapped in there—"

He had to shut her up. He couldn't stand what was coming next. But what could he say, how could he stop her?

"Burned alive. The whole place was on fire when they got there. The Ogdens saw it when they came home and Mr. Ogden called the firemen, but it was too late. When I think of that old lady it just makes me—"

Without a word, Ronnie rose from the table and left the room. He didn't wait for his lunch. He didn't bother to examine himself in the mirror. He went outside, before he cried, or screamed, or hauled off and hit Ma in the puss.

The puss—

It was waiting for him on the front walk. The black bundle with the agate eyes. The cat.

Mrs. Mingle's cat, waiting for him to come out.

Ronnie took a deep breath before he opened the gate. The cat didn't make a sound, didn't stir. It just hunched up on the sidewalk and stared at him.

He watched it for a moment, then cast about for a stick. There was a hunk of lath near the porch. He picked it up and swung it. Then he opened the gate.

"Scat!" he said.

The cat retreated. Ronnie walked away. The cat moved after him. Ronnie wheeled, brandishing the stick.

"Scram before I let you have it!"

The cat stood still.

Ronnie stared at it. Why hadn't the damn thing burned up in the fire? And what was it doing here?

He gripped the lath. It felt good between his fingers, splinters and all. Just let that mangy tom start anything—

He walked along, not looking back. What was the matter with him? Suppose the cat did follow him. It couldn't hurt him any. Neither could old Mingle. She was dead. The dirty witch. Talking about cutting his tongue out. Well, she got what was coming to her, all right. Too bad her scroungy cat was still around. If it didn't watch out, he'd fix it, too. He should worry now.

Nobody was going to find out about that cigarette. Mrs. Mingle was dead. He ought to be glad, everything was all right, sure, he felt great.

The shadow followed him down the street.

"Get out of here!"

Ronnie turned and heaved the lath at the cat. It hissed. Ronnie heard the wind hiss, heard his cigarette butt hiss, heard Mrs. Mingle hiss.

He began to run. The cat ran after him.

"Hey, Ronnie!"

Marvin Ogden was calling him. He couldn't stop now, not even to hit the punk. He ran on. The cat kept pace.

Then he was winded and he slowed down. It was just in time, too. Up ahead was a crowd of kids, standing on the sidewalk in front of a heap of charred, smoking boards.

They were looking at Mingle's cottage—

Ronnie closed his eyes and darted back up the street. The cat followed.

He had to get rid of it before he went to school. What if people saw him with her cat? Maybe they'd start to talk. He had to get rid of it—

Ronnie ran clear down to Sinclair Street. The cat was right behind him. On the corner he picked up a stone and let fly. The cat dodged. Then it sat down on the sidewalk and looked at him. Just looked.

Ronnie couldn't take his eyes off the cat. It stared so. Mrs. Mingle had stared, too. But she was dead. And this was only a cat. A cat he had to get away from, fast.

The streetcar came down Sinclair Street. Ronnie found a dime in his pocket and boarded the car. The cat didn't move. He stood on the platform as the car pulled away and looked back at the cat. It just sat there.

Ronnie rode around the loop, then transferred to the Hollis Avenue bus. It brought him over to the school, ten minutes late. He got off and started to hurry across the street.

A shadow crossed the entrance to the building.

Ronnie saw the cat. It squatted there, waiting.

He ran.

That's all Ronnie remembered of the rest of the morning. He ran. He ran, and the cat followed. He couldn't go to school, he couldn't be there for the election, he couldn't get rid of the cat. He ran.

Up and down the streets, back and forth, all over the whole neighborhood; stopping and dodging and throwing stones and swearing and panting and sweating. But always the running, and always the cat right behind him. Once it started to chase him and before he knew it he was heading straight for the place where the burned smell filled the air, straight for the ruins of Mrs. Mingle's cottage. The cat wanted him to go there, wanted him to see—

Ronnie began to cry. He sobbed and panted all the way home. The cat didn't make a sound. It followed him. All right, let it. He'd fix it. He'd tell Ma. Ma would get rid of it for him. Ma.

"Ma!"

He yelled as he ran up the steps.

No answer. She was out. Marketing.

And the cat crept up the steps behind him.

Ronnie slammed the door, locked it. Ma had her key. He was safe now. Safe at home. Safe in bed—he wanted to go to bed and pull the covers over his head, wait for Ma to come and make everything all right.

There was a scratching at the door.

"Ma!" His scream echoed through the empty house.

He ran upstairs. The scratching died away.

And then he heard the footsteps on the porch, the slow footsteps; he heard the rattling and turning of the doorknob. It was old lady Mingle, coming from the grave. It was the witch, coming to get him. It was—

"Ma!"

"Ronnie, what's the matter? What you doing home from school?"

He heard her. It was all right. Just in time, Ronnie closed his mouth. He couldn't tell her about the cat. He mustn't ever tell her. Then everything would come out. He had to be careful what he said.

"I got sick to my stomach," he said. "Miss Sanders said I should come home and lay down."

Then Ma was up the stairs, helping him undress, asking should she get the doctor, fussing over him and putting him to bed. And he could cry and she didn't know it wasn't from a gut-ache. What she didn't know wouldn't hurt her. It was all right.

Yes, it was all right now, and he was in bed. Ma brought him some soup for lunch. He wanted to ask her about the cat, but he didn't dare. Besides, he couldn't hear it scratching. Must have run away when Ma came home.

Ronnie lay in bed and dozed as the afternoon shadows ran in long black ribbons across the bedroom floor. He smiled to himself. What a sucker he was! Afraid of a cat. Maybe there wasn't even a cat—all in his mind. Dope!

"Ronnie—you all right?" Ma called up from the foot of the stairs. "Yes, Ma. I feel lots better."

Sure, he felt better. He could get up now and eat supper if he wanted. In just a minute he'd put his clothes on and go downstairs. He started to push the sheets off. It was dark in the room, now. Just about supper-time—

Then Ronnie heard it. A scratching. A scurrying. From the hall? No. It couldn't be in the hall. Then where?

The window. It was open. And the scratching came from the ledge outside. He had to close it, fast. Ronnie jumped out of bed, barking his shin against a chair as he groped through the dusk. Then he was at the window, slamming it down, tight.

He heard the scratching.

And it came from *inside the room!*

Ronnie hurled himself upon the bed, clawing the covers up to his chin. His eyes bulged against the darkness.

Where was it?

He saw nothing but shadows. Which shadow moved?

Where was it?

Why didn't it yowl so he could locate it? Why didn't it make a noise? Yes, and why was it here? Why did it follow him? What was it trying to do to him?

Ronnie didn't know. All he knew was that he lay in bed, waiting, thinking of Mrs. Mingle and her cat and how she was a witch and died because he'd killed her. Or had he killed her? He was all mixed up, he couldn't remember, he didn't even know what was real and what wasn't real any more. He couldn't tell which shadow would move next.

And then he could.

The round shadow was moving. The round black ball was inching across the floor from beneath the window. It was the cat, all right, because shadows don't have claws that scrape. Shadows don't leap through the air and perch on the bedpost, grinning at you with yellow eyes and yellow teeth—grinning the way Mrs. Mingle grinned.

The cat was big. Its eyes were big. Its teeth were big, too.

Ronnie opened his mouth to scream.

Then the shadow was sailing through the air, springing at his face, at his open mouth. The claws fastened in his cheeks, forcing his jaws apart, and the head dipped down—

Far away, under the pain, someone was calling.

"Ronnie! Oh, Ronnie! What's the matter with you?"

Everything was fire and he lashed out and suddenly the shadow went away and he was sitting bolt upright in bed. His mouth worked but no sound came out. Nothing came out except that gushing red wetness.

"Ronnie! Why don't you answer me?"

A guttural sound came from deep within Ronnie's throat, but no words. There would never be any words.

"Ronnie—what's the matter? Has the cat got your tongue—?"

✠ SHIRLEY JACKSON (1919–1965)

Psychological horror, folk tradition, a small rural community, and a harvest ritual taken to the extreme are the basis for Shirley Jackson's "The Lottery," one of the most popular, controversial, and critically acclaimed short stories of the last one hundred years.

A versatile author who appeared in both "slick" magazines such as The New Yorker *and "pulp" magazine digests such as* The Magazine of Fantasy and Science Fiction, *Shirley Jackson specialized in stories of gothicism, horror, the supernatural, and weird fiction. Influenced by the writing of Henry James, Walter de la Mare, and Elizabeth Bowen, Jackson used her writing to explore people and their characters and provided vivid description in a popular, easily readable way. Her stories often study the ironies and cruelties of life.*

Stephen King's The Long Walk *(1979) is highly derivative of Shirley Jackson's "The Lottery," as its central organizing device is a study of unexamined ritual. The realism that Jackson employs in "The Lottery" is unsettling and is the realism of Stephen Crane, Jack London, and Ambrose Bierce; it thematically predicts some of the work of Clive Barker.*

The Lottery
(The New Yorker, *June 26, 1948*)

The morning of June 27th was clear and sunny, with the fresh warmth of a full-summer day; the flowers were blossoming profusely and the grass was richly green. The people of the village began to gather in the square, between the post office and the bank, around ten o'clock; in some towns there were so many people that the lottery took two days and had to be started on June 26th, but in this village, where there were only about three hundred people, the whole lottery took less than two hours, so it could begin at ten o'clock in the morning and still be through in time to allow the villagers to get home for noon dinner.

The children assembled first, of course. School was recently over for the summer, and the feeling of liberty sat uneasily on most of them; they tended to gather together quietly for a while before they broke into boisterous play, and their talk was still of the classroom and the teacher, of books and reprimands. Bobby Martin had already stuffed his pockets full of stones, and the other boys soon followed his example, selecting the smoothest and roundest stones; Bobby and Harry Jones and Dickie Delacroix—the villagers pronounced this name "Dellacroy"—eventually made a great pile of stones in one corner of the square and guarded it against the raids of the other boys. The girls stood aside, talking among themselves, looking over their shoulders at the boys, and the very small children rolled in the dust or clung to the hands of their older brothers or sisters.

Soon the men began to gather, surveying their own children, speaking of planting and rain, tractors and taxes. They stood together, away from the pile of stones in the corner, and their jokes were quiet and they smiled rather than laughed. The women, wearing faded house dresses and sweaters, came shortly after their menfolk. They greeted one another and exchanged bits of gossip as they went to join their husbands. Soon the women, standing by their husbands, began to call to their children, and the children came reluctantly, having to be called four or five times. Bobby Martin ducked under his mother's grasping hand and ran, laughing, back to the pile of stones. His father spoke up sharply, and Bobby came quickly and took his place between his father and his oldest brother.

The lottery was conducted—as were the square dances, the teen-age club, the Halloween program—by Mr. Summers, who had time and energy to devote to civic activities. He was a round-faced, jovial man and he ran the coal business, and people were sorry for him, because he had no children and his wife was a scold. When he arrived in the square, carrying the black wooden box, there was a murmur of conversation among the villagers, and he waved and called, "Little late today, folks." The postmaster, Mr. Graves, followed him, carrying a three-legged stool, and the stool was put in the center of the square and Mr. Summers set the black box down on it. The villagers kept their distance, leaving a space between themselves and the stool, and when Mr. Summers said, "Some of you fellows want to give me a hand?" there was a hesitation before two men, Mr. Martin and his oldest son, Baxter, came forward to hold the box steady on the stool while Mr. Summers stirred up the papers inside it.

The original paraphernalia for the lottery had been lost long ago, and the black box now resting on the stool had been put into use even before Old Man Warner, the oldest man in town, was born. Mr. Summers spoke frequently to the villagers about making a new box, but no one liked to upset even as much tradition as was represented by the black box. There was a story that the present box had been made with some pieces of the box that had preceded it, the one that had been constructed when the first people settled down to make a village here. Every year, after the lottery, Mr. Summers began talking again about a new box, but every year the subject was allowed to fade off without anything's being done. The black box grew shabbier each year; by now it was no longer completely black but splintered badly along one side to show the original wood color, and in some places faded or stained.

Mr. Martin and his oldest son, Baxter, held the black box securely on the stool until Mr. Summers had stirred the papers thoroughly with his hand. Because so much of the ritual had been forgotten or discarded, Mr. Summers had been successful in having slips of paper substituted for the chips of wood that had been used for generations. Chips of wood, Mr. Summers had argued, had been all very well when the village was tiny, but now that the population was more than three hundred and likely to keep on growing, it was necessary to use something that would fit more easily into the black box. The night before the lottery, Mr. Summers and Mr. Graves made up the slips of paper and put them in the box, and it was then taken to the safe of Mr. Summers' coal company and locked up until Mr. Summers was ready to take it to the square next morning. The rest of the year, the box was put away, sometimes one place, sometimes another; it had spent one year in Mr. Graves's barn and another year underfoot in the post office, and sometimes it was set on a shelf in the Martin grocery and left there.

There was a great deal of fussing to be done before Mr. Summers declared the lottery open. There were the lists to make up—of heads of families, heads of households in each family, members of each household in each family. There was the proper swearing-in of Mr. Summers by the postmaster, as the official of the lottery; at one time, some people remembered, there had been a recital of some sort, performed by the official of the lottery, a perfunctory, tuneless chant that had been rattled off duly each year; some people believed that the official of the lottery used to stand just so when he said or sang it, others believed that he was supposed to walk among the people, but years and years ago this part of the ritual had been allowed to lapse. There had been, also, a ritual salute, which the official of the lottery had had to use in addressing each person who came up to draw from the box, but this also had changed with time, until now it was felt necessary only for the official to speak to each person approaching. Mr. Summers was very good at all this; in his clean white shirt and blue jeans, with one hand resting carelessly on the black box, he seemed very proper and important as he talked interminably to Mr. Graves and the Martins.

Just as Mr. Summers finally left off talking and turned to the assembled villagers, Mrs. Hutchinson came hurriedly along the path to the square, her sweater thrown over her shoulders, and slid into place in the back of the crowd. "Clean forgot what day it was," she said to Mrs. Delacroix, who stood next to her, and they both laughed softly. "Thought my old man was out back stacking wood," Mrs. Hutchinson went on, "and then I looked out the window and the kids was gone, and then I remembered it was the twenty-seventh and came a-running." She dried her hands on her apron, and Mrs. Delacroix said, "You're in time, though. They're still talking away up there."

Mrs. Hutchinson craned her neck to see through the crowd and found her husband and children standing near the front. She tapped Mrs. Delacroix on the arm as a farewell and began to make her way through the crowd. The people separated good-humoredly to let her through; two or three people said, in voices just loud enough to be heard across the crowd, "Here comes your Missus Hutchinson," and "Bill, she made it after all." Mrs. Hutchinson reached her husband, and Mr. Summers, who had been waiting, said cheerfully, "Thought we were going to have to get on without you, Tessie." Mrs. Hutchinson said, grinning, "Wouldn't have me leave m'dishes in the sink, now, would you, Joe?," and soft laughter ran through the crowd as the people stirred back into position after Mrs. Hutchinson's arrival.

"Well, now," Mr. Summers said soberly, "guess we better get started, get this over with, so's we can go back to work. Anybody ain't here?"

"Dunbar," several people said. "Dunbar, Dunbar."

Mr. Summers consulted his list. "Clyde Dunbar," he said. "That's right. He's broke his leg, hasn't he? Who's drawing for him?"

"Me, I guess," a woman said, and Mr. Summers turned to look at her. "Wife draws for her husband," Mr. Summers said. "Don't you have a grown boy to do it for you, Janey?" Although Mr. Summers and everyone else in the village knew the answer perfectly well, it was the business of the official of the lottery to ask such questions formally. Mr. Summers waited with an expression of polite interest while Mrs. Dunbar answered.

"Horace's not but sixteen yet," Mrs. Dunbar said regretfully. "Guess I gotta fill in for the old man this year."

"Right," Mr. Summers said. He made a note on the list he was holding. Then he asked, "Watson boy drawing this year?"

A tall boy in the crowd raised his hand. "Here," he said. "I'm drawing for m'mother and me." He blinked his eyes nervously and ducked his head as several voices in the crowd said things like "Good fellow, Jack," and "Glad to see your mother's got a man to do it."

"Well," Mr. Summers said, "guess that's everyone. Old Man Warner make it?"

"Here," a voice said, and Mr. Summers nodded.

A sudden hush fell on the crowd as Mr. Summers cleared his throat and looked at the list. "All ready?" he called. "Now, I'll read the names—heads of families first—and the men come up and take a paper out of the box. Keep the paper folded in your hand without looking at it until everyone has had a turn. Everything clear?"

The people had done it so many times that they only half listened to the directions; most of them were quiet, wetting their lips, not looking around. Then Mr. Summers raised one hand high and said, "Adams." A man disengaged himself from the crowd and came forward. "Hi, Steve," Mr. Summers said, and Mr. Adams said, "Hi, Joe." They grinned at one another humorlessly and nervously. Then Mr. Adams reached into the black box and took out a folded paper. He held it firmly by one corner as he turned and went hastily back to his place in the crowd, where he stood a little apart from his family, not looking down at his hand.

"Allen," Mr. Summers said. "Anderson. . . . Bentham."

"Seems like there's no time at all between lotteries any more," Mrs. Delacroix said to Mrs. Graves in the back row. "Seems like we got through with the last one only last week."

"Time sure goes fast," Mrs. Graves said.

"Clark. . . . Delacroix."

"There goes my old man," Mrs. Delacroix said. She held her breath while her husband went forward.

"Dunbar," Mr. Summers said, and Mrs. Dunbar went steadily to the box while one of the women said, "Go on, Janey," and another said, "There she goes."

"We're next," Mrs. Graves said. She watched while Mr. Graves came around from the side of the box, greeted Mr. Summers gravely, and selected a slip of paper from the box. By now, all through the crowd there were men holding the small folded papers in their large hands, turning them over and over nervously. Mrs. Dunbar and her two sons stood together, Mrs. Dunbar holding the slip of paper.

"Harburt. . . . Hutchinson."

"Get up there, Bill," Mrs. Hutchinson said, and the people near her laughed.

"Jones."

"They do say," Mr. Adams said to Old Man Warner, who stood next to him, "that over in the north village they're talking of giving up the lottery."

Old Man Warner snorted. "Pack of crazy fools," he said. "Listening to the young folks, nothing's good enough for *them*. Next thing you know, they'll be wanting to go back to living in caves, nobody work any more, live *that* way for a while. Used to be a saying about 'Lottery in June, corn be heavy soon.' First thing you know, we'd all be eating stewed chickweed and acorns. There's *always* been a lottery," he added petulantly. "Bad enough to see young Joe Summers up there joking with everybody."

"Some places have already quit lotteries," Mrs. Adams said.

"Nothing but trouble in *that*," Old Man Warner said stoutly. "Pack of young fools."

"Martin." And Bobby Martin watched his father go forward. "Overdyke. . . . Percy."

"I wish they'd hurry," Mrs. Dunbar said to her older son. "I wish they'd hurry."

"They're almost through," her son said.

"You get ready to run tell Dad," Mrs. Dunbar said.

Mr. Summers called his own name and then stepped forward precisely and selected a slip from the box. Then he called, "Warner."

"Seventy-seventh year I been in the lottery," Old Man Warner said as he went through the crowd. "Seventy-seventh time."

"Watson." The tall boy came awkwardly through the crowd. Someone said, "Don't be nervous, Jack," and Mr. Summers said, "Take your time, son."

"Zanini."

After that, there was a long pause, a breathless pause, until Mr. Summers, holding his slip of paper in the air, said, "All right, fellows." For a minute, no one moved, and then all the slips of paper were opened. Suddenly, all the women began to speak at once, saying, "Who is it?," "Who's got it?," "Is it the Dunbars?," "Is it the Watsons?" Then the voices began to say, "It's Hutchinson. It's Bill," "Bill Hutchinson's got it."

"Go tell your father," Mrs. Dunbar said to her older son.

People began to look around to see the Hutchinsons. Bill Hutchinson was standing quiet, staring down at the paper in his hand. Suddenly, Tessie Hutchinson shouted to Mr. Summers, "You didn't give him time enough to take any paper he wanted. I saw you. It wasn't fair!"

"Be a good sport, Tessie," Mrs. Delacroix called, and Mrs. Graves said, "All of us took the same chance."

"Shut up, Tessie," Bill Hutchinson said.

"Well, everyone," Mr. Summers said, "that was done pretty fast, and now we've got to be hurrying a little more to get done in time." He consulted his next list. "Bill," he said, "you draw for the Hutchinson family. You got any other households in the Hutchinsons?"

"There's Don and Eva," Mrs. Hutchinson yelled. "Make *them* take their chance!"

"Daughters draw with their husbands' families, Tessie," Mr. Summers said gently. "You know that as well as anyone else."

"It wasn't *fair*," Tessie said.

"I guess not, Joe," Bill Hutchinson said regretfully. "My daughter draws with her husband's family, that's only fair. And I've got no other family except the kids."

"Then, as far as drawing for families is concerned, it's you," Mr. Summers said in explanation, "and as far as drawing for households is concerned, that's you, too. Right?"

"Right," Bill Hutchinson said.

"How many kids, Bill?" Mr. Summers asked formally.

"Three," Bill Hutchinson said. "There's Bill, Jr., and Nancy, and little Dave. And Tessie and me."

"All right, then," Mr. Summers said. "Harry, you got their tickets back?"

Mr. Graves nodded and held up the slips of paper. "Put them in the box, then," Mr. Summers directed. "Take Bill's and put it in."

"I think we ought to start over," Mrs. Hutchinson said, as quietly as she could. "I tell you it wasn't *fair.* You didn't give him time enough to choose. *Every*body saw that."

Mr. Graves had selected the five slips and put them in the box, and he dropped all the papers but those onto the ground, where the breeze caught them and lifted them off.

"Listen, everybody," Mrs. Hutchinson was saying to the people around her.

"Ready, Bill?" Mr. Summers asked, and Bill Hutchinson, with one quick glance around at his wife and children, nodded.

"Remember," Mr. Summers said, "take the slips and keep them folded until each person has taken one. Harry, you help little Dave." Mr. Graves took the hand of the little boy, who came willingly with him up to the box. "Take a paper out of the box, Davy," Mr. Summers said. Davy put his hand into the box and laughed. "Take just *one* paper," Mr. Summers said. "Harry, you hold it for him." Mr. Graves took the child's hand and removed the folded paper from the tight fist and held it while little Dave stood next to him and looked up at him wonderingly.

"Nancy next," Mr. Summers said. Nancy was twelve, and her school friends breathed heavily as she went forward, switching her skirt, and took a slip daintily from the box. "Bill, Jr.," Mr. Summers said, and Billy, his face red and his feet overlarge, nearly knocked the box over as he got a paper out. "Tessie," Mr. Summers said. She hesitated for a minute, looking around defiantly, and then set her lips and went up to the box. She snatched a paper out and held it behind her.

"Bill," Mr. Summers said, and Bill Hutchinson reached into the box and felt around, bringing his hand out at last with the slip of paper in it.

The crowd was quiet. A girl whispered, "I hope it's not Nancy," and the sound of the whisper reached the edges of the crowd.

"It's not the way it used to be," Old Man Warner said clearly. "People ain't the way they used to be."

"All right," Mr. Summers said. "Open the papers. Harry, you open little Dave's."

Mr. Graves opened the slip of paper and there was a general sigh through the crowd as he held it up and everyone could see that it was blank. Nancy and Bill, Jr., opened theirs at the same time, and both beamed and laughed, turning around to the crowd and holding their slips of paper above their heads.

"Tessie," Mr. Summers said. There was a pause, and then Mr. Summers looked at Bill Hutchinson, and Bill unfolded his paper and showed it. It was blank.

"It's Tessie," Mr. Summers said, and his voice was hushed. "Show us her paper, Bill."

Bill Hutchinson went over to his wife and forced the slip of paper out of her hand. It had a black spot on it, the black spot Mr. Summers had made the night before with the heavy pencil in the coal-company office. Bill Hutchinson held it up, and there was a stir in the crowd.

"All right, folks," Mr. Summers said. "Let's finish quickly."

Although the villagers had forgotten the ritual and lost the original black box, they still remembered to use stones. The pile of stones the boys had made earlier was ready; there were stones on the ground with the blowing scraps of paper that had come out of the box. Mrs. Delacroix selected a stone so large she had to pick it up with both hands and turned to Mrs. Dunbar. "Come on," she said. "Hurry up."

Mrs. Dunbar had small stones in both hands, and she said, gasping for breath, "I can't run at all. You'll have to go ahead and I'll catch up with you."

The children had stones already, and someone gave little Davy Hutchinson a few pebbles.

Tessie Hutchinson was in the center of a cleared space by now, and she held her hands out desperately as the villagers moved in on her. "It isn't fair," she said. A stone hit her on the side of the head.

Old Man Warner was saying, "Come on, come on, everyone." Steve Adams was in the front of the crowd of villagers, with Mrs. Graves beside him.

"It isn't fair, it isn't right," Mrs. Hutchinson screamed, and then they were upon her.

DAMON (FRANCIS) KNIGHT (1922-   )

Damon Knight's contributions to the genres of Fantasy and Science Fiction are many and varied. Knight has long been a successful, critically acclaimed, and awarded author and editor. In 1941, he became a member of the famous Science Fiction group of fans and writers called The Futurians. Knight was an early Science Fiction genre critic and prolifically published Science Fiction and Fantasy book reviews.

In more recent years, Knight has been (along with his famous author wife, Kate Wilhelm) instrumental in organizing and teaching the Clarion Workshops for aspiring Fantasy and Science Fiction writers. His credentials also include stints as a Fantasy and Science Fiction magazine editor and a range of edited anthologies and collections of genre fiction. Like Hugo Gernsback, John W. Campbell, and Frederik Pohl, Damon Knight has been involved in most aspects of Fantasy and Science Fiction writing and publishing.

"To Serve Man" is undoubtedly one of the most imitated and parodied works of Fantasy and Science Fiction ever written. This Damon Knight story became one of the most famous Twilight Zone *episodes of all time. As is the case with works by Robert Bloch, "To Serve Man" rests its success as a story on the turn of a phrase, on misunderstanding and misdirection. Dark Fantasy, Science Fiction, and Black Humor combine in this landmark story of imaginative fiction.*

To Serve Man
(Galaxy, *November 1950*)

The Kanamit were not very pretty, it's true. They looked something like pigs and something like people, and that is not an attractive combination. Seeing them for the first time shocked you; that was their handicap. When a thing with the countenance of a fiend comes from the stars and offers a gift, you are disinclined to accept.

I don't know what we expected interstellar visitors to look like—those who thought about it at all, that is. Angels, perhaps, or something too alien to be really awful. Maybe that's why we were all so horrified and repelled when they landed in their great ships and we saw what they really were like.

The Kanamit were short and very hairy—thick, bristly brown-gray hair all over their abominably plump bodies. Their noses were snoutlike and their eyes small, and they had thick hands of three fingers each. They wore green leather harness and green shorts, but I think the shorts were a concession to our notions of public decency. The garments were quite modishly cut, with slash pockets and half-belts in the back. The Kanamit had a sense of humor, anyhow.

There were three of them at this session of the U.N., and, Lord, I can't tell you how queer it looked to see them there in the middle of a solemn plenary session— three fat piglike creatures in green harness and shorts, sitting at the long table below the podium, surrounded by the packed arcs of delegates from every nation. They sat correctly upright, politely watching each speaker. Their flat ears drooped over the earphones. Later on, I believe, they learned every human language, but at this time they knew only French and English.

They seemed perfectly at ease—and that, along with their humor, was a thing that tended to make me like them. I was in the minority; I didn't think they were trying to put anything over.

The delegate from Argentina got up and said that his government was interested in the demonstration of a new cheap power source, which the Kanamit had made at the previous session, but that the Argentine government could not commit itself as to its future policy without a much more thorough examination.

It was what all the delegates were saying, but I had to pay particular attention to Señor Valdes, because he tended to sputter and his diction was bad. I got through the translation all right, with only one or two momentary hesitations, and then switched to the Polish-English line to hear how Gregori was doing with Janciewicz. Janciewicz was the cross Gregori had to bear, just as Valdes was mine.

Janciewiez repeated the previous remarks with a few ideological variations, and then the Secretary-General recognized the delegate from France, who introduced Dr. Denis Lévèque, the criminologist, and a great deal of complicated equipment was wheeled in.

Dr. Lévèque remarked that the question in many people's minds had been aptly expressed by the delegate from the U.S.S.R. at the preceding session, when he demanded, "What is the motive of the Kanamit? What is their purpose in offering us these unprecedented gifts, while asking nothing in return?"

The doctor then said, "At the request of several delegates and with the full consent of our guests, the Kanamit, my associates and I have made a series of tests upon the Kanamit with the equipment which you see before you. These tests will now be repeated."

A murmur ran through the chamber. There was a fusillade of flashbulbs, and one of the TV cameras moved up to focus on the instrument board of the doctor's equipment. At the same time, the huge television screen behind the podium lighted up, and we saw the blank faces of two dials, each with its pointer resting at zero, and a strip of paper tape with a stylus point resting against it.

The doctor's assistants were fastening wires to the temples of one of the Kanamit, wrapping a canvas-covered rubber tube around his forearm, and taping something to the palm of his right hand.

In the screen, we saw the paper tape begin to move while the stylus traced a slow zigzag pattern along it. One of the needles began to jump rhythmically; the other flipped over and stayed there, wavering slightly.

"These are the standard instruments for testing the truth of a statement," said Dr. Lévèque. "Our first object, since the physiology of the Kanamit is unknown to us, was to determine whether or not they react to these tests as human beings do. We will now repeat one of the many experiments which were made in the endeavor to discover this."

He pointed to the first dial. "This instrument registers the subject's heartbeat. This shows the electrical conductivity of the skin in the palm of his hand, a measure of perspiration, which increases under stress. And this—" pointing to the tape-and-stylus device — "shows the pattern and intensity of the electrical waves emanating from his brain. It has been shown, with human subjects, that all these readings vary markedly depending upon whether the subject is speaking the truth."

He picked up two large pieces of cardboard, one red and one black. The red one was a square about three feet on a side; the black was a rectangle three and a half feet long. He addressed himself to the Kanama.

"Which of these is longer than the other?"

"The red," said the Kanama.

Both needles leaped wildly, and so did the line on the unrolling tape.

"I shall repeat the question," said the doctor. "Which of these is longer than the other?"

"The black," said the creature.

This time the instruments continued in their normal rhythm.

"How did you come to this planet?" asked the doctor.

"Walked," replied the Kanama.

Again the instruments responded, and there was a subdued ripple of laughter in the chamber.

"Once more," said the doctor. "How did you come to this planet?"

"In a spaceship," said the Kanama, and the instruments did not jump.

The doctor again faced the delegates. "Many such experiments were made," he said, "and my colleagues and myself are satisfied that the mechanisms are effective. Now — " he turned to the Kanama — "I shall ask our distinguished guest to reply to the question put at the last session by the delegate of the U.S.S.R. — namely, what is the motive of the Kanamit people in offering these great gifts to the people of Earth?"

The Kanama rose. Speaking this time in English, he said, "On my planet there is a saying, 'There are more riddles in a stone than in a philosopher's head.' The motives of intelligent beings, though they may at times appear obscure, are simple things compared to the complex workings of the natural universe. Therefore I hope that the people of Earth will understand, and believe, when I tell you that our mission upon your planet is simply this — to bring to you the peace and plenty which we ourselves enjoy, and which we have in the past brought to other races throughout the galaxy. When your world has no more hunger, no more war, no more needless suffering, that will be our reward."

And the needles had not jumped once.

The delegate from the Ukraine jumped to his feet, asking to be recognized, but the time was up and the Secretary-General closed the session.

I met Gregori as we were leaving the chamber. His face was red with excitement. "Who promoted that circus?" he demanded.

"The tests looked genuine to me," I told him.

"A circus!" he said vehemently. "A second-rate farce! If they were genuine, Peter, why was debate stifled?"

"There'll be time for debate tomorrow, surely."

"Tomorrow the doctor and his instruments will be back in Paris. Plenty of things can happen before tomorrow. In the name of sanity, man, how can anybody trust a thing that looks as if it ate the baby?"

I was a little annoyed. I said, "Are you sure you're not more worried about their politics than their appearance?"

He said, "Bah," and went away.

The next day reports began to come in from government laboratories all over the world where the Kanamit's power source was being tested. They were wildly enthusiastic. I don't understand such things myself, but it seemed that those little metal boxes would give more electrical power than an atomic pile, for next to nothing and nearly forever. And it was said that they were so cheap to manufacture that everybody in the world could have one of his own. In the early afternoon there were reports that seventeen countries had already begun to set up factories to turn them out.

The next day the Kanamit turned up with plans and specimens of a gadget that would increase the fertility of any arable land by 60 to 100 per cent. It speeded the formation of nitrates in the soil, or something. There was nothing in the newscasts any more but stories about the Kanamit. The day after that, they dropped their bombshell.

"You now have potentially unlimited power and increased food supply," said one of them. He pointed with his three-fingered hand to an instrument that stood on the table before him. It was a box on a tripod, with a parabolic reflector on the front of it. "We offer you today a third gift which is at least as important as the first two."

He beckoned to the TV men to roll their cameras into closeup position. Then he picked up a large sheet of cardboard covered with drawings and English lettering. We saw it on the large screen above the podium; it was all clearly legible.

"We are informed that this broadcast is being relayed throughout your world," said the Kanama. "I wish that everyone who has equipment for taking photographs from television screens would use it now."

The Secretary-General leaned forward and asked a question sharply, but the Kanama ignored him.

"This device," he said, "generates a field in which no explosive, of whatever nature, can detonate."

There was an uncomprehending silence.

The Kanama said, "It cannot now be suppressed. If one nation has it, all must have it." When nobody seemed to understand, he explained bluntly, "There will be no more war."

That was the biggest news of the millennium, and it was perfectly true. It turned out that the explosions the Kanama was talking about included gasoline and Diesel explosions. They had simply made it impossible for anybody to mount or equip a modern army.

We could have gone back to bows and arrows, of course, but that wouldn't have satisfied the military. Besides, there wouldn't be any reason to make war. Every nation would soon have everything.

Nobody ever gave another thought to those lie-detector experiments, or asked the Kanamit what their politics were. Gregori was put out; he had nothing to prove his suspicions.

I quit my job with the U.N. a few months later, because I foresaw that it was going to die under me anyhow. U.N. business was booming at the time, but after a year or so there was going to be nothing for it to do. Every nation on Earth was well on the way to being completely self-supporting; they weren't going to need much arbitration.

I accepted a position as translator with the Kanamit Embassy, and it was there that I ran into Gregori again. I was glad to see him, but I couldn't imagine what he was doing there.

"I thought you were on the opposition," I said. "Don't tell me you're convinced the Kanamit are all right."

He looked rather shamefaced. "They're not what they look, anyhow," he said.

It was as much of a concession as he could decently make, and I invited him down to the embassy lounge for a drink. It was an intimate kind of place, and he grew confidential over the second daiquiri.

"They fascinate me," he said. "I hate them instinctively still—that hasn't changed—but I can evaluate it. You were right, obviously; they mean us nothing but good. But do you know—" he leaned across the table—"the question of the Soviet delegate was never answered."

I am afraid I snorted.

"No, really," he said. "They told us what they wanted to do—'to bring to you the peace and plenty which we ourselves enjoy.' But they didn't say *why*."

"Why do missionaries—"

"Missionaries be damned!" he said angrily. "Missionaries have a religious motive. If these creatures have a religion, they haven't once mentioned it. What's more, they didn't send a missionary group; they sent a diplomatic delegation—a group representing the will and policy of their whole people. Now just what have the Kanamit, as a people or a nation, got to gain from our welfare?"

I said, "Cultural—"

"Cultural cabbage soup! No, it's something less obvious than that, something obscure that belongs to their psychology and not to ours. But trust me, Peter, there is no such thing as a completely disinterested altruism. In one way or another, they have something to gain."

"And that's why you're here," I said. "To try to find out what it is."

"Correct. I wanted to get on one of the ten-year exchange groups to their home planet, but I couldn't; the quota was filled a week after they made the announcement. This is the next best thing. I'm studying their language, and you know that language reflects the basic assumptions of the people who use it. I've got a fair command of the spoken lingo already. It's not hard, really, and there are hints in it. Some of the idioms are quite similar to English. I'm sure I'll get the answer eventually."

"More power," I said, and we went back to work.

I saw Gregori frequently from then on, and he kept me posted about his progress. He was highly excited about a month after that first meeting; said he'd got hold of a book of the Kanamit's and was trying to puzzle it out. They wrote in ideographs, worse than Chinese, but he was determined to fathom it if it took him years. He wanted my help.

Well, I was interested in spite of myself, for I knew it would be a long job. We spent some evenings together, working with material from Kanamit bulletin boards and so forth, and with the extremely limited English-Kanamit dictionary they issued to the staff. My conscience bothered me about the stolen book, but gradually I became absorbed by the problem. Languages are my field, after all. I couldn't help being fascinated.

We got the title worked out in a few weeks. It was *How to Serve Man*, evidently a handbook they were giving out to new Kanamit members of the embassy staff. They had new ones in, all the time now, a shipload about once a month; they were opening all kinds of research laboratories, clinics and so on. If there was anybody on Earth besides Gregori who still distrusted those people, he must have been somewhere in the middle of Tibet.

It was astonishing to see the changes that had been wrought in less than a year. There were no more standing armies, no more shortages, no unemployment. When you picked up a newspaper you didn't see H-BOMB or SATELLITE leaping out at you; the news was always good. It was a hard thing to get used to. The Kanamit were working on human biochemistry, and it was known around the embassy that they were nearly ready to announce methods of making our race taller and stronger and healthier—practically a race of supermen—and they had a potential cure for heart disease and cancer.

I didn't see Gregori for a fortnight after we finished working out the title of the book; I was on a long-overdue vacation in Canada. When I got back, I was shocked by the change in his appearance.

"What on earth is wrong, Gregori?" I asked. "You look like the very devil."

"Come down to the lounge."

I went with him, and he gulped a stiff Scotch as if he needed it.

"Come on, man, what's the matter?" I urged.

"The Kanamit have put me on the passenger list for the next exchange ship," he said. "You, too, otherwise I wouldn't be talking to you."

"Well," I said, "but—"

"They're not altruists."

I tried to reason with him. I pointed out they'd made Earth a paradise compared to what it was before. He only shook his head.

Then I said, "Well, what about those lie-detector tests?"

"A farce," he replied, without heat. "I said so at the time, you fool. They told the truth, though, as far as it went."

"And the book?" I demanded, annoyed. "What about that—*How to Serve Man*? That wasn't put there for you to read. They *mean* it. How do you explain that?"

"I've read the first paragraph of that book," he said. "Why do you suppose I haven't slept for a week?"

I said, "Well?" and he smiled a curious, twisted smile.

"It's a cookbook," he said.

JACK FINNEY (PSD. FOR WALTER BRANDEN FINNEY) (1911–1995)

If Robert Bloch is best remembered as the author of the 1959 novel that became Alfred Hitchcock's 1960 movie Psycho, *then, perhaps, Jack Finney is best remembered for his 1955 serial novel* The Body Snatchers, *that became Don Siegel's 1956 movie* The Invasion of the Body Snatchers. *Even though both novels and movie adaptations are landmark works, the generalization is unfair and far from complete.*

Jack Finney was the author of a range of Fantasy and Science Fiction stories, and he wrote for magazines such as Collier's *(in which* The Body Snatchers *first appeared),* The Saturday Evening Post, *and* McCall's. *Some of his most memorable stories fell into two groups: 1950s Dark Fantasies that foreshadowed the type of story later showcased on Rod Serling's* The Twilight Zone, *and Time-Travel stories, such as his famous novel* Time and Again *(1970) and its sequel,* From Time to Time *(1995).*

"The Third Level" is both a Dark Fantasy and Time-Travel story, and it was the first such story by an author who epitomized 1950s popular fiction. Both Edward Page Mitchell and H. G. Wells dealt with similar themes in their stories years earlier. Jack Finney's contemporaries who wrote similar stories include Ray Bradbury, Charles Beaumont, Richard Matheson, and Shirley Jackson.

The Third Level

*(*The Magazine of Fantasy and Science Fiction, *October 1952)*

The presidents of the New York Central and the New York, New Haven and Hartford railroads will swear on a stack of timetables that there are only two. But

I say there are three, because I've *been* on the third level at Grand Central Station. Yes, I've taken the obvious step: I talked to a psychiatrist friend of mine, among others. I told him about the third level at Grand Central Station, and he said it was a waking-dream wish fulfillment. He said I was unhappy. That made my wife kind of mad, but he explained that he meant the modern world is full of insecurity, fear, war, worry and all the rest of it, and that I just want to escape. Well, hell, who doesn't? Everybody I know wants to escape, but they don't wander down into any third level at Grand Central Station.

But that's the reason, he said, and my friends all agreed. Everything points to it, they claimed. My stamp collecting, for example; that's a "temporary refuge from reality." Well, maybe, but my grandfather didn't need any refuge from reality; things were pretty nice and peaceful in his day, from all I hear, and he started my collection. It's a nice collection, too, blocks of four of practically every U.S. issue, first-day covers, and so on. President Roosevelt collected stamps, too, you know.

Anyway, here's what happened at Grand Central. One night last summer I worked late at the office. I was in a hurry to get uptown to my apartment so I decided to take the subway from Grand Central because it's faster than the bus.

Now, I don't know why this should have happened to me. I'm just an ordinary guy named Charley, thirty-one years old, and I was wearing a tan gabardine suit and a straw hat with a fancy band; I passed a dozen men who looked just like me. And I wasn't trying to escape from anything; I just wanted to get home to Louisa, my wife.

I turned into Grand Central from Vanderbilt Avenue, and went down the steps to the first level, where you take trains like the Twentieth Century. Then I walked down another flight to the second level, where the suburban trains leave from, ducked into an arched doorway heading for the subway—and got lost. That's easy to do. I've been in and out of Grand Central hundreds of times, but I'm always bumping into new doorways and stairs and corridors. Once I got into a tunnel about a mile long and came out in the lobby of the Roosevelt Hotel. Another time I came up in an office building on Forty-sixth Street, three blocks away.

Sometimes I think Grand Central is growing like a tree, pushing out new corridors and staircases like roots. There's probably a long tunnel that nobody knows about feeling its way under the city right now, on its way to Times Square, and maybe another to Central Park. And maybe—because for so many people through the years Grand Central *has* been an exit, a way of escape—maybe that's how the tunnel I got into . . . But I never told my psychiatrist friend about that idea.

The corridor I was in began angling left and slanting downward and I thought that was wrong, but I kept on walking. All I could hear was the empty sound of my own footsteps and I didn't pass a soul. Then I heard that sort of hollow roar ahead that means open space and people talking. The tunnel turned sharp left; I went down a short flight of stairs and came out on the third level at Grand Central Station. For just a moment I thought I was back on the second level, but I saw the room was smaller, there were fewer ticket windows and train gates, and the information booth in the center was wood and old-looking. And the man in the booth wore a green eyeshade and long black sleeve protectors. The lights were dim and sort of flickering. Then I saw why; they were open-flame gaslights.

There were brass spittoons on the floor, and across the station a glint of light caught my eye; a man was pulling a gold watch from his vest pocket. He snapped open the cover, glanced at his watch, and frowned. He wore a derby hat, a black four-button suit with tiny lapels, and he had a big, black, handle-bar mustache. Then I looked around and saw that everyone in the station was dressed like eighteen-ninety-something; I never saw so many beards, sideburns and fancy mustaches in my life. A woman walked in through the train gate; she wore a dress with leg-of-mutton sleeves and skirts to the top of her high-buttoned shoes. Back of her, out on the tracks, I caught a glimpse of a locomotive, a very small Currier & Ives locomotive with a funnel-shaped stack. And then I knew.

To make sure, I walked over to a newsboy and glanced at the stack of papers at his feet. It was The *World*; and The *World* hasn't been published for years. The lead story said something about President Cleveland. I've found that front page since, in the Public Library files, and it was printed June 11, 1894.

I turned toward the ticket windows knowing that here—on the third level at Grand Central—I could buy tickets that would take Louisa and me anywhere in the United States we wanted to go. In the year 1894. And I wanted two tickets to Galesburg, Illinois.

Have you ever been there? It's a wonderful town still, with big old frame houses, huge lawns and tremendous trees whose branches meet overhead and roof the streets. And in 1894, summer evenings were twice as long, and people sat out on their lawns, the men smoking cigars and talking quietly, the women waving palm-leaf fans, with the fireflies all around, in a peaceful world. To be back there with the First World War still twenty years off, and World War II over forty years in the future . . . I wanted two tickets for that.

The clerk figured the fare—he glanced at my fancy hatband, but he figured the fare—and I had enough for two coach tickets, one way. But when I counted out the money and looked up, the clerk was staring at me. He nodded at the bills. "That ain't money, mister," he said, "and if you're trying to skin me you won't get very far," and he glanced at the cash drawer beside him. Of course the money in his drawer was old-style bills, half again as big as the money we use nowadays, and different-looking. I turned away and got out fast. There's nothing nice about jail, even in 1894.

And that was that. I left the same way I came, I suppose. Next day, during lunch hour, I drew three hundred dollars out of the bank, nearly all we had, and bought old-style currency (that *really* worried my psychiatrist friend). You can buy old money at almost any coin dealer's, but you have to pay a premium. My three hundred dollars bought less than two hundred in old-style bills, but I didn't care; eggs were thirteen cents a dozen in 1894.

But I've never again found the corridor that leads to the third level at Grand Central Station, although I've tried often enough.

Louisa was pretty worried when I told her all this, and didn't want me to look for the third level any more, and after a while I stopped; I went back to my stamps. But now we're *both* looking, every week end, because now we have proof that the third level is still there. My friend Sam Weiner disappeared! Nobody knew where, but I sort of suspected because Sam's a city boy, and I used to tell him about Galesburg—I went to school there—and he always said he liked the sound of the place. And that's where he is, all right. In 1894.

Because one night, fussing with my stamp collection, I found—well, do you know what a first-day cover is? When a new stamp is issued, stamp collectors buy some and use them to mail envelopes to themselves on the very first day of sale; and the postmark proves the date. The envelope is called a first-day cover. They're never opened; you just put blank paper in the envelope.

That night, among my oldest first-day covers, I found one that shouldn't have been there. But there it was. It was there because someone had mailed it to my grandfather at his home in Galesburg; that's what the address on the envelope said. And it had been there since July 18, 1894—the postmark showed that—yet I didn't remember it at all. The stamp was a six-cent, dull brown, with a picture of President Garfield. Naturally, when the envelope came to Granddad in the mail, it went right into his collection and stayed there—till I took it out and opened it.

The paper inside wasn't blank. It read:

> *941 Willard Street*
> *Galesburg, Illinois*
> *July 18, 1894*

CHARLEY:

> *I got to wishing that you were right. Then I got to believing you were right. And, Charley, it's true; I found the third level! I've been here two weeks, and right now, down the street at the Dalys', someone is playing a piano, and they're all out on the front porch singing, "Seeing Nellie home." And I'm invited over for lemonade. Come on back, Charley and Louisa. Keep looking till you find the third level! It's worth it, believe me!*

The note is signed *Sam*.

At the stamp and coin store I go to, I found out that Sam bought eight hundred dollars' worth of old-style currency. That ought to set him up in a nice little hay, feed and grain business; he always said that's what he really wished he could do, and he certainly can't go back to his old business. Not in Galesburg, Illinois, in 1894. His old business? Why, Sam was my psychiatrist.

❈ CHARLES BEAUMONT (1929–1967)

Among his many and diverse talents and related accomplishments, Charles Beaumont was a successful Dark Fantasy, Science Fiction, Humor, and Crime Fiction writer. In addition, Beaumont was both a screenplay writer and film critic. Born and raised in Chicago, he spent his relatively short adult life in California, where he joined the professional and social ranks of Ray Bradbury, William F. Nolan, Richard Matheson, and others.

Charles Beaumont is remembered for his short stories and historical essays for Playboy, Esquire, Collier's, The Saturday Evening Post, The Magazine of Fantasy and Science Fiction, *and* Rogue; *for his screen adaptation of Charles G. Finney's* The Circus of Dr. Lao *(filmed as* The Seven Faces of Dr. Lao *in 1964); and for other accomplishments. Along with Rod Serling and Richard Matheson, Beaumont was a primary writer and creative force behind television's* The Twilight Zone. *He wrote more than seventy teleplays, twenty-two for* The Twilight Zone. *Like his friend, William F. Nolan (author, with George Clayton Johnson, of the* Logan's Run *trilogy of novels), Beaumont was an avid car racing fan and historian.*

Beaumont adapted his short story, "The Howling Man," for the November 4, 1960, episode of the same title for The Twilight Zone. *The episode is one of the most acclaimed of the long-running television series. Charles Beaumont died at the young age of thirty-eight.*

The Howling Man

(as "C. B. Lovehill" for Rogue, *November 1959)*

The Germany of that time was a land of valleys and mountains and swift dark rivers, a green and fertile land where everything grew tall and straight out of the earth. There was no other country like it. Stepping across the border from Belgium, where the rain-caped, mustached guards saluted, grinning, like operetta soldiers, you entered a different world entirely. Here the grass became as rich and smooth as velvet; deep, thick woods appeared; the air itself, which had been heavy with the French perfume of wines and sauces, changed: the clean, fresh smell of lakes and pines and boulders came into your lungs. You stood a moment, then, at the border, watching the circling hawks above and wondering, a little fearfully, how such a thing could happen. In less than a minute you had passed from a musty, ancient room, through an invisible door, into a kingdom of winds and light. Unbelievable! But there, at your heels, clearly in view, is Belgium, like all the rest of Europe, a faded tapestry from some forgotten mansion.

In that time, before I had heard of St. Wulfran's, of the wretch who clawed the stones of a locked cell, wailing in the midnight hours, or of the daft Brothers and their mad Abbot, I had strong legs and a mind on its last search, and I preferred to be alone. A while and I'll come back to this spot. We will ride and feel the sickness, fall, and hover on the edge of death, together. But I am not a writer, only one who loves wild, unhousebroken words; I must have a real beginning.

Paris beckoned in my youth. I heeded, for the reason most young men just out of college heed, although they would never admit it: to lie with mysterious beautiful women. A solid, traditional upbringing among the corseted ruins of Boston had succeeded, as such upbringings generally do, in honing the urge to a keen edge. My nightly dreams of beaded bagnios and dusky writhing houris, skilled beyond imagining, reached, finally, the unbearable stage beyond which lies either madness or respectability. Fancying neither, I managed to convince my parents that a year abroad would add exactly the right amount of seasoning to my maturity, like a dash of curry in an otherwise bland, if not altogether tasteless, chowder. I'm afraid that Father caught the hot glint in my eye, but he was kind. Describing, in detail, and with immense effect, the hideous consequences of profligacy, telling of men he knew who'd gone to Europe, innocently, and fallen into dissolutions so profound they'd not been heard of since, he begged me at all times to remember that I was an Ellington and turned me loose. Paris, of course, was enchanting and terrifying, as a jungle must be to a zoo-born monkey. Out of respect to the honored dead, and Dad, I did a quick trot through the Tuileries, the Louvre, and down the Champs Elysées to the Arc de Triomphe; then, with the fall of night, I cannoned off to Montmartre and the Rue Pigalle, embarking on the Grand Adventure. Synoptically, it did not prove to be so grand as I'd imagined; nor was it, after the fourth week, so terribly adventurous. Still: important to what followed, for what followed doubtless wouldn't have but for the sweet complaisant girls.

Boston's Straights and Narrows don't, I fear, prepare one—except psychologically—for the Wild Life. My health broke in due course and, as my thirst had been well and truly slaked, I was not awfully discontent to sink back into the contemplative cocoon to which I was, apparently, more suited. Abed for a month I lay, in celibate silence and almost total inactivity. Then, no doubt as a final gesture of rebellion, I got my idea—got? or had my concentrated sins received it, like a signal from a failing tower?—and I made my strange, un-Ellingtonian decision. I would explore Europe. But not as tourist, safe and fat in his fat, safe bus, insulated against the beauty and the ugliness of changing cultures by a pane of glass and a room at the English-speaking hotel. No. I would go like an unprotected wind, a seven-league-booted leaf, a nestless bird, and I would see this dark strange land with the vision of a boy on the last legs of his dreams. I would go by bicycle, poor and lonely and questing—as poor and lonely and questing, anyway, as one can be with a hundred thousand in the bank and a partnership in Ellington, Carruthers & Blake waiting.

So it was. New England blood and muscles wilted on that first day's pumping, but New England spirit toughened as the miles dropped back. Like an ant crawling over a once lovely, now decayed and somewhat seedy Duchess, I rode over the body of Europe. I dined at restaurants where boar's heads hung, all vicious-tusked and blind; I slept at country inns and breathed the musty age, and sometimes girls came to the door and knocked and asked if I had everything I needed ("Well . . .") and they were better than the girls in Paris, though I can't imagine why. No matter. Out of France I pedaled, into Belgium, out, and to the place of cows and forest, mountains, brooks and laughing people: Germany. (I've rhapsodized on purpose for I feel it's quite important to remember how completely Paradisical the land was then, at that time.)

I looked odd, standing there. The border guard asked what was loose with me, I answered Nothing—grateful for the German, and the French, Miss Finch had drummed into me—and set off along the smallest, darkest path. I serpentined through forests, cities, towns, villages, and always I followed its least likely appendages. Unreasonably, I pedaled as if toward a destination: into the Moselle Valley country, up into the desolate hills of emerald.

By a ferry, fallen to desuetude, the reptile drew me through a bosky wood. The trees closed in at once. I drank the fragrant air and pumped and kept on pumping, but a heat began to grow inside my body. My head began to ache. I felt weak. Two more miles and I was obliged to stop, for perspiration filmed my skin. You know the signs of pneumonia: a sapping of the strength, a trembling, flashes of heat and of cold; visions. I lay in the bed of damp leaves for a time. At last a village came to view. A thirteenth-century village, gray and narrow-streeted, cobbled to the hidden store fronts. A number of old people in peasant costumes looked up as I bumped along and I recall one ancient tallow-colored fellow—nothing more. Only the weakness, like acid, burning off my nerves and muscles. And an intervening blackness to pillow my fall.

I awoke to the smells of urine and hay. The fever had passed, but my arms and legs lay heavy as logs, my head throbbed horribly, and there was an empty shoveled-out hole inside my stomach somewhere. For a while I did not move or open my eyes. Breathing was a major effort. But consciousness came, eventually.

I was in a tiny room. The walls and ceiling were of rough gray stone, the single glassless window was arch-shaped, the floor was uncombed dirt. My bed was not a bed at all but a blanket thrown across a disorderly pile of crinkly straw. Beside me, a crude table; upon it, a pitcher; beneath it, a bucket. Next to the table, a stool. And seated there, asleep, his tonsured head adangle from an Everest of robe, a monk.

I must have groaned, for the shorn pate bobbed up precipitately. Two silver trails gleamed down the corners of the suddenly exposed mouth, which drooped into a frown. The slumbrous eyes blinked.

"It is God's infinite mercy," sighed the gnomelike little man. "You have recovered."

"Not as yet," I told him. Unsuccessfully, I tried to remember what had happened; then I asked questions.

"I am Brother Christophorus. This is the Abbey of St. Wulfran's. The Burgemeister of Schwartzhof, Herr Barth, brought you to us nine days ago. Father Jerome said that you would die and he sent me to watch, for I have never seen a man die, and Father Jerome holds that it is beneficial for a Brother to have seen a man die. But now I suppose that you will not die." He shook his head ruefully.

"Your disappointment," I said, "cuts me to the quick. However, don't abandon hope. The way I feel now, it's touch and go."

"No," said Brother Christophorus sadly. "You will get well. It will take time. But you will get well."

"Such ingratitude, and after all you've done. How can I express my apologies?"

He blinked again. With the innocence of a child, he said, "I beg your pardon?"

"Nothing." I grumbled about blankets, a fire, some food to eat, and then slipped back into the well of sleep. A fever dream of forests full of giant two-headed beasts came, then the sound of screaming.

I awoke. The scream shrilled on—Klaxon-loud, high, cutting, like a cry for help.

"What is that sound?" I asked.

The monk smiled. "Sound? I hear no sound," he said.

It stopped. I nodded. "Dreaming. Probably I'll hear a good deal more before I'm through. I shouldn't have left Paris in such poor condition."

"No," he said. "You shouldn't have left Paris."

Kindly now, resigned to my recovery, Brother Christophorus became attentive to a fault. Nurselike, he spooned thick soups into me, applied compresses, chanted soothing prayers, and emptied the bucket out the window. Time passed slowly. As I fought the sickness, the dreams grew less vivid—but the nightly cries did not diminish. They were as full of terror and loneliness as before, strong, real in my ears. I tried to shut them out, but they would not be shut out. Still, how could they be strong and real except in my vanishing delirium? Brother Christophorus did not hear them. I watched him closely when the sunlight faded to the gray of dusk and the screams began, but he was deaf to them—if they existed. If they existed!

"Be still, my son. It is the fever that makes you hear these noises. That is quite natural. Is that not quite natural? Sleep."

"But the fever is gone! I'm sitting up now. Listen! Do you mean to tell me you don't hear *that?*"

"I hear only you, my son."

The screams, that fourteenth night, continued until dawn. They were totally unlike any sounds in my experience. Impossible to believe they could be uttered and sustained by a human, yet they did not seem to be animal. I listened, there in the gloom, my hands balled into fists, and knew, suddenly, that one of two things must be true. Either someone or something was making these ghastly sounds, and Brother Christophorus was lying, or—I was going mad. Hearing-voices mad, climbing-walls and frothing mad. I'd have to find the answer: that I knew. And by myself.

I listened with a new ear to the howls. Razoring under the door, they rose to operatic pitch, subsided, resumed, like the cries of a surly, hysterical child. To test their reality, I hummed beneath my breath, I covered my head with a blanketing, scratched at the straw, coughed. No difference. The quality of substance, of existence, was there. I tried, then, to localize the screams; and, on the fifteenth night, felt sure that they were coming from a spot not far along the hall.

"The sounds that maniacs hear seem quite real to them."

I know. I know!

The monk was by my side, he had not left it from the start, keeping steady vigil even through Matins. He joined his tremulous soprano to the distant chants, and prayed excessively. But nothing could tempt him away. The food we ate was brought to us, as were all other needs. I'd see the Abbot, Father Jerome, once I was recovered. Meanwhile . . .

"I'm feeling better, Brother. Perhaps you'd care to show me the grounds. I've seen nothing of St. Wulfran's except this little room."

"There is only this little room multiplied. Ours is a rigorous order. The Franciscans, now, they permit themselves esthetic pleasure; we do not. It is, for us, a luxury. We have a single, most unusual job. There is nothing to see."

"But surely the Abbey is very old."

"Yes, that is true."

"As an antiquarian—"

"Mr. Ellington—"

"What is it you don't want me to see? What are you afraid of, Brother?"

"Mr. Ellington? I do not have the authority to grant your request. When you are well enough to leave, Father Jerome will no doubt be happy to accommodate you."

"Will he also be happy to explain the screams I've heard each night since I've been here?"

"Rest, my son. Rest."

The unholy, hackle-raising shriek burst loose and bounded off the hard stone walls. Brother Christophorus crossed himself, apropos of nothing, and sat like an ancient Indian on the weary stool. I knew he liked me. Especially, perhaps. We'd got along quite well in all our talks, but this—*verboten.*

I closed my eyes. I counted to three hundred. I opened my eyes.

The good monk was asleep. I blasphemed, softly, but he did not stir, so I swung my legs over the side of the straw bed and made my way across the dirt floor to the heavy door. I rested there a time, in the candleless dark, listening to the howls; then, with Bostonian discretion, raised the bolt. The rusted hinges creaked, but Brother Christophorus was deep in celestial marble: his head drooped low upon his chest.

Panting, weak as a landlocked fish, I stumbled out into the corridor. The screams became impossibly loud. I put my hands to my ears, instinctively, and wondered how anyone could sleep with such a furor going on. It *was* a furor. In my mind? No. Real. The monastery shook with these shrill cries. You could feel their realness with your teeth.

I passed a Brother's cell and listened, then another; then I paused. A thick door, made of oak or pine, was locked before me. Behind it were the screams.

A chill went through me on the edge of those unutterable shrieks of hopeless, helpless anguish, and for a moment I considered turning back—not to my room, not to my bed of straw, but back into the open world. But duty held me. I took a breath and walked up to the narrow bar-crossed window and looked in.

A man was in the cell. On all fours, circling like a beast, his head thrown back, a man. The moonlight showed his face. It cannot be described—not, at least, by me. A man past death might look like this, a victim of the Inquisition rack, the stake, the pincers: not a human in the third decade of the twentieth century, surely. I had never seen such suffering within two eyes, such lost, mad suffering. Naked, he crawled about the dirt, cried, leaped up to his feet and clawed the hard stone walls in fury.

Then he saw me.

The screaming ceased. He huddled, blinking, in the corner of his cell. And then, as though unsure of what he saw, he walked right to the door.

In German, hissing: "Who are you?"

"David Ellington," I said. "Are you locked in? Why have they locked you in?"

He shook his head. "Be still, be still. You are not German?"

"No." I told him how I came to be at St. Wulfran's.

"Ah!" Trembling, his horny fingers closing on the bars, the naked man said: "Listen to me, we have only moments. They are mad. You hear? All mad. I was in the village, lying with my woman, when their crazy Abbot burst into the house and hit me with his heavy cross. I woke up here. They flogged me. I asked for food, they would not give it to me. They took my clothes. They threw me in this filthy room. They locked the door."

"Why?"

"Why?" He moaned. "I wish I knew. That's been the worst of it. Five years imprisoned, beaten, tortured, starved, and not a reason given, not a word to guess from—Mr. Ellington! I have sinned, but who has not? With my woman, quietly, alone with my woman, my love. And this God-drunk lunatic, Jerome, cannot stand it. Help me!"

His breath splashed on my face. I took a backward step and tried to think. I couldn't quite believe that in this century a thing so frightening could happen. Yet, the Abbey was secluded, above the world, timeless. What could not transpire here, secretly?

"I'll speak to the Abbot."

"No! I tell you, he's the maddest of them all. Say nothing to him."

"Then how can I help you?"

He pressed his mouth against the bars. "In one way only. Around Jerome's neck, there is a key. It fits this lock. If—"

"Mr. Ellington!"

I turned and faced a fierce El Greco painting of a man. White-bearded, prow-nosed, regal as an Emperor beneath the gray peaked robe, he came out of the darkness. "Mr. Ellington, I did not know that you were well enough to walk. Come with me, please."

The naked man began to weep hysterically. I felt a grip of steel about my arm. Through corridors, past snore-filled cells, the echoes of the weeping dying, we continued to a room.

"I must ask you to leave St. Wulfran's," the Abbot said. "We lack the proper facilities for care of the ill. Arrangements will be made in Schwartzhof—"

"One moment," I said. "While it's probably true that Brother Christophorus's ministrations saved my life—and certainly true that I owe you all a debt of gratitude—I've got to ask for an explanation of that man in the cell."

"What man?" the Abbot said softly.

"The one we just left, the one who's screamed all night long every night."

"No man has been screaming, Mr. Ellington."

Feeling suddenly very weak, I sat down and rested a few breaths' worth. Then I said, "Father Jerome—you are he? I am not necessarily an irreligious person, but neither could I be considered particularly religious. I know nothing of monasteries, what is permitted, what isn't. But I seriously doubt you have the authority to imprison a man against his will."

"This is quite true. We have no such authority."

"Then why have you done so?"

The Abbot looked at me steadily. In a firm, inflexible voice, he said: "No man has been imprisoned at St. Wulfran's."

"He claims otherwise."

"Who claims otherwise?"

"The man in the cell at the end of the corridor."

"There is no man in the cell at the end of the corridor."

"I was talking with him!"

"You were talking with no man."

The conviction in his voice shocked me into momentary silence. I gripped the arms of the chair.

"You are ill, Mr. Ellington," the bearded holy man said. "You have suffered from delirium. You have heard and seen things which do not exist."

"That's true," I said. "But the man in the cell—whose voice I can hear now!— is not one of those things."

The Abbot shrugged. "Dreams can seem very real, my son."

I glanced at the leather thong about his turkey-gobbler neck, all but hidden beneath the beard. "Honest men make unconvincing liars," I lied convincingly. "Brother Christophorus has a way of looking at the floor whenever he denies the cries in the night. You look at me, but your voice loses its command. I can't imagine why, but you are both very intent upon keeping me away from the truth. Which is not only poor Christianity, but also poor psychology. For now I am quite curious indeed. You might as well tell me, Father; I'll find out eventually."

"What do you mean?"

"Only that. I'm sure the police will be interested to hear of a man imprisoned at the Abbey."

"I tell you, *there is no man!*"

"Very well. Let's forget the matter."

"Mr. Ellington—" The Abbot put his hands behind him. "The person in the cell is, ah, one of the Brothers. Yes. He is subject to . . . seizures, fits. You know fits? At these times, he becomes intractable. Violent. Dangerous! We're obliged to lock him in his cell, which you can surely understand."

"I understand," I said, "that you're still lying to me. If the answer were as simple as that, you'd not have gone through the elaborate business of pretending I was delirious. There'd have been no need. There's something more to it, but I can wait. Shall we go on to Schwartzhof?"

Father Jerome tugged at his beard viciously, as if it were some feathered demon come to taunt him. "Would you truly go to the police?" he asked.

"Would you?" I said. "In my position?"

He considered that for a long time, tugging the beard, nodding the prowed head; and the screams went on, so distant, so real. I thought of the naked man clawing in his filth.

"Well, Father?"

"Mr. Ellington, I see that I shall have to be honest with you—which is a great pity," he said. "Had I followed my original instinct and refused to allow you in the Abbey to begin with . . . but, I had no choice. You were near death. No physician was available. You would have perished. Still, perhaps that would have been better."

"My recovery seems to have disappointed a lot of people," I commented. "I assure you it was inadvertent."

The old man took no notice of this remark. Stuffing his mandarin hands into the sleeves of his robe, he spoke with great deliberation. "When I said that there was no man in the cell at the end of the corridor, I was telling the truth. Sit down, sir! Please! Now." He closed his eyes. "There is much to the story, much that you will not understand or believe. You are sophisticated, or feel that you are. You regard our life here, no doubt, as primitive—"

"In fact, I—"

"In fact, you do. I know the current theories. Monks are misfits, neurotics, sexual frustrates, and aberrants. They retreat from the world because they cannot cope with the world. Et cetera. You are surprised I know these things? My son, I was told by the one who began the theories!" He raised his head upward, revealing more of the leather thong. "Five years ago, Mr. Ellington, there were no screams at St. Wulfran's. This was an undistinguished little Abbey in the wild Black Mountain region, and its inmates' job was quite simply to serve God, to save what souls they could by constant prayer. At that time, not very long after the great war, the world was in chaos. Schwartzhof was not the happy village you see now. It was, my son, a resort for the sinful, a hive of vice and corruption, a pit for the unwary—and the wary also, if they had not strength. A Godless place! Forsaken, fornicators paraded the streets. Gambling was done. Robbery and murder, drunkenness, and evils so profound I cannot put them into words. In all the universe you could not have found a fouler pesthole, Mr. Ellington! The Abbots and the Brothers at St. Wulfran's succumbed for years to Schwartzhof, I regret to say. Good men, lovers of God, chaste good men came here and fought but could not win against the black temptations. Finally it was decided that the Abbey should be closed. I heard of this and argued. 'Is that not surrender?' I said. 'Are we to bow before the strength of evil? Let me try, I beg you. Let me try to amplify the word of God that all in Schwartzhof shall hear and see their dark transgressions and repent!' "

The old man stood at the window, a trembling shade. His hands were now clutched together in a fervency of remembrance. "They asked," he said, "if I considered myself more virtuous than my predecessors that I should hope for success where they had failed. I answered that I did not, but that I had an advantage. I was a convert. Earlier I had walked with evil, and knew its face. My wish was granted. For a year. One year only. Rejoicing, Mr. Ellington, I came here; and one night, incognito, walked the streets of the village. The smell of evil was strong. Too strong, I thought—and I had reveled in the alleys of Morocco, I had seen the dens of Hong Kong, Paris, Spain. The orgies were too wild, the drunkards much too drunk, the profanities a great deal too profane. It was as if the evil of the world had been distilled and centered here, as if a pagan tribal chief, in hiding, had assembled all his rituals about him . . ." The Abbot nodded his head. "I thought of Rome, in her last days; of Byzantium; of—Eden. That was the first of many hints to come. No matter what they were. I returned to the Abbey and donned my holy robes and went back into Schwartzhof. I made myself conspicuous. Some jeered, some shrank away, a voice cried 'Damn your foolish God!' And then a hand thrust out from darkness, touched my shoulder, and I heard: 'Now, Father, are you lost?' "

The Abbot brought his tightly clenched hands to his forehead and tapped his forehead.

"Mr. Ellington, I have some poor wine here. Please have some."

I drank, gratefully. Then the priest continued.

"I faced a man of average appearance. So average, indeed, that I felt I knew, then. 'No,' I told him, 'but you are lost!' He laughed a foul laugh. 'Are we not all, Father?' Then he said a most peculiar thing. He said his wife was dying and begged me to give her Extreme Unction. 'Please,' he said, 'in God's sweet name!' I was confused. We hurried to his house. A woman lay upon a bed, her body nude. 'It is a different Extreme Unction that I have in mind,' he whispered, laughing. 'It's the only kind, dear Father, that she understands. No other will have her! Pity! Pity on the poor soul lying there in all her suffering. Give her your Sceptre!' And the woman's arms came snaking, supplicating toward me, round and sensuous and hot . . ."

Father Jerome shuddered and paused. The shrieks, I thought, were growing louder from the hall. "Enough of that," he said. "I was quite sure then. I raised my cross and told the words I'd learned, and it was over. He screamed—as he's doing now—and fell upon his knees. He had not expected to be recognized, nor should he have been normally. But in my life, I'd seen him many times, in many guises. I brought him to the Abbey. I locked him in the cell. We chant his chains each day. And so, my son, you see why you must not speak of the things you've seen and heard?"

I shook my head, as if afraid the dream would end, as if reality would suddenly explode upon me. "Father Jerome," I said, "I haven't the vaguest idea of what you're talking about. Who is the man?"

"Are you such a fool, Mr. Ellington? That you must be told?"

"Yes!"

"Very well," said the Abbot. "He is Satan. Otherwise known as the Dark Angel, Asmodeus, Belial, Ahriman, Diabolus—the Devil."

I opened my mouth.

"I see you doubt me. That is bad. Think, Mr. Ellington, of the peace of the world in these five years. Of the prosperity, of the happiness. Think of this country, Germany, now. Is there another country like it? Since we caught the Devil and locked him up here, there have been no great wars, no overwhelming pestilences: only the sufferings man was meant to endure. Believe what I say, my son; I beg you. Try very hard to believe that the creature you spoke with is Satan himself. Fight your cynicism, for it is born of him; he is the father of cynicism, Mr. Ellington! His plan was to defeat God by implanting doubt in the minds of Heaven's subjects!" The Abbot cleared his throat. "Of course," he said, "we could never release anyone from St. Wulfran's who had any part of the Devil in him."

I stared at the old fanatic and thought of him prowling the streets, looking for sin; saw him standing outraged at the bold fornicator's bed, wheedling him into an invitation to the Abbey, closing that heavy door and locking it, and, because of the world's temporary postwar peace, clinging to his fantasy. What greater dream for a holy man than actually capturing the Devil!

"I believe you," I said.

"Truly?"

"Yes. I hesitated only because it seemed a trifle odd that Satan should have picked a little German village for his home."

"He moves around," the Abbot said. "Schwartzhof attracted him as lovely virgins attract perverts."

"I see."

"Do you? My son, do you?"

"Yes. I swear it. As a matter of fact, I thought he looked familiar, but I simply couldn't place him."

"Are you lying?"

"Father, I am a Bostonian."

"And you promise not to mention this to anyone?"

"I promise."

"Very well." The old man sighed. "I suppose," he said, "that you would not consider joining us as a Brother at the Abbey?"

"Believe me, Father, no one could admire the vocation more than I. But I am not worthy. No; it's quite out of the question. However, you have my word that your secret is safe with me."

He was very tired. Sound had, in these years, reversed for him: the screams had become silence, the sudden cessation of them, noise. The prisoner's quiet talk with me had awakened him from deep slumber. Now he nodded wearily, and I saw that what I had to do would not be difficult after all. Indeed, no more difficult than fetching the authorities.

I walked back to my cell, where Brother Christophorus still slept, and lay down. Two hours passed. I rose again and returned to the Abbot's quarters.

The door was closed but unlocked.

I eased it open, timing the creaks of the hinges with the screams of the prisoner. I tiptoed in. Father Jerome lay snoring in his bed.

Slowly, cautiously, I lifted out the leather thong, and was a bit astounded at my technique. No Ellington had ever burgled. Yet a force, not like experience, but like it, ruled my fingers. I found the knot. I worked it loose.

The warm iron key slid off into my hand.

The Abbot stirred, then settled, and I made my way into the hall.

The prisoner, when he saw me, rushed the bars. "He's told you lies, I'm sure of that!" he whispered hoarsely. "Disregard the filthy madman!"

"Don't stop screaming," I said.

"What?" He saw the key and nodded, then, and made his awful sounds. I thought at first the lock had rusted, but I worked the metal slowly and in time the key turned over.

Howling still, in a most dreadful way, the man stepped out into the corridor. I felt a momentary fright as his clawed hand reached up and touched my shoulder; but it passed. "Come on!" We ran insanely to the outer door, across the frosted ground, down toward the village.

The night was very black.

A terrible aching came into my legs. My throat went dry. I thought my heart would tear loose from its moorings. But I ran on.

"Wait."

Now the heat began.

"Wait."

By a row of shops I fell. My chest was full of pain, my head of fear: I knew the madmen would come swooping from their dark asylum on the hill. I cried out to the naked hairy man: "Stop! Help me!"

"Help you?" He laughed once, a high-pitched sound more awful than the screams had been; and then he turned and vanished in the moonless night.

I found a door, somehow.

The pounding brought a rifled burgher. Policemen came at last and listened to my story. But of course it was denied by Father Jerome and the Brothers of the Abbey.

"This poor traveler has suffered from the vision of pneumonia. There was no howling man at St. Wulfran's. No, no, certainly not. Absurd! Now, if Mr. Ellington would care to stay with us, we'd happily—no? Very well. I fear that you will be delirious a while, my son. The things you see will be quite real. Most real. You'll think—how quaint!—that you have loosed the Devil on the world and that the war to come—what war? But aren't there always wars? Of course!—you'll think that it's your fault"—those old eyes burning condemnation! Beak-nosed, bearded head atremble, rage in every word!—"that you'll have caused the misery and suffering and death. And nights you'll spend, awake, unsure, afraid. How foolish!"

Gnome of God, Christophorus, looked terrified and sad. He said to me, when Father Jerome swept furiously out: "My son, don't blame yourself. Your weakness was *his* lever. Doubt unlocked that door. Be comforted: we'll hunt *him* with our nets, and one day . . ."

One day, what?

I looked up at the Abbey of St. Wulfran's, framed by dawn, and started wondering, as I have wondered since ten thousand times, if it weren't true. Pneumonia breeds delirium; delirium breeds visions. Was it possible that I'd imagined all of this?

No. Not even back in Boston, growing dewlaps, paunches, wrinkles, sacks and money, at Ellington, Carruthers & Blake, could I accept that answer.

The monks were mad, I thought. Or: The howling man was mad. Or: The whole thing was a joke.

I went about my daily work, as every man must do, if sane, although he may have seen the dead rise up or freed a bottled djinn or fought a dragon, once, quite long ago.

But I could not forget. When the pictures of the carpenter from Braumau-am-Inn began to appear in all the papers, I grew uneasy; for I felt I'd seen this man before. When the carpenter invaded Poland, I was sure. And when the world was plunged into war and cities had their entrails blown asunder and that pleasant land I'd visited became a place of hate and death, I dreamed each night.

Each night I dreamed, until this week.

A card arrived. From Germany. A picture of the Moselle Valley is on one side, showing mountains fat with grapes and the dark Moselle, wine of these grapes.

On the other side of the card is a message. It is signed *"Brother Christophorus"* and reads (and reads and reads!): *"Rest now, my son. We have him back with us again."*

✻ RICHARD (BURTON) MATHESON (1926–)

The grand era of the pulp magazines was fading, and paperback books and network television were new popular media when Richard Matheson first began publishing his stories. One of the very last issues of Weird Tales *and one of the very first issues of* The Magazine of Fantasy and Science Fiction *featured some of Matheson's earliest tales.*

Since that time, Matheson has written Crime stories, Westerns, Dark Fantasy, Science Fiction, War Stories, and Social Melodrama with a great deal of popular success. His resume in this regard is extensive. He is responsible for the novels I Am Legend *(1954),* The Shrinking Man *(1956),* A Stir of Echoes *(1958),* Hell House *(1971), and* What Dreams May Come *(1978)—all of which have been made into popular motion pictures. A master of the short story, Matheson was also a pioneer of* The Twilight Zone *television series.*

Stephen King cites Matheson as the author who most influenced his writing style.

Today, Richard Matheson continues to be a vital novel, short story, screenplay, and teleplay writer. His short story "Duel" became the basis for an early Steven Spielberg television movie of the same title in 1971. The movie, which featured veteran actor Dennis Weaver, was instrumental in launching Spielberg's career.

Duel

(Playboy, *April 1971)*

At 11.32 a.m., Mann passed the truck.

He was heading west, en route to San Francisco. It was Thursday and unseasonably hot for April. He had his suit coat off, his tie removed and shirt collar opened, his sleeve cuffs folded back. There was sunlight on his left arm and on part of his lap. He could feel the heat of it through his dark trousers as he drove along the two-lane highway. For the past 20 minutes, he had not seen another vehicle going in either direction.

Then he saw the truck ahead, moving up a curving grade between two high green hills. He heard the grinding strain of its motor and saw a double shadow on the road. The truck was pulling a trailer.

He paid no attention to the details of the truck. As he drew behind it on the grade, he edged his car towards the opposite lane. The road ahead had blind curves and he didn't try to pass until the truck had crossed the ridge. He waited until it started around a left curve on the downgrade, then, seeing that the way was clear, pressed down on the accelerator pedal and steered his car into the eastbound lane. He waited until he could see the truck front in his rearview mirror before he turned back into the proper lane.

Mann looked across the countryside ahead. There were ranges of mountains as far as he could see and, all around him, rolling green hills. He whistled softly as the car sped down the winding grade, its tyres making crisp sounds on the pavement.

At the bottom of the hill, he crossed a concrete bridge and, glancing to the right, saw a dry stream bed strewn with rocks and gravel. As the car moved off the bridge, he saw a trailer park set back from the highway to his right. How can anyone live out here? he thought. His shifting gaze caught sight of a pet cemetery ahead and he smiled. Maybe those people in the trailers wanted to be close to the graves of their dogs and cats.

The highway ahead was straight now. Mann drifted into a reverie, the sunlight on his arm and lap. He wondered what Ruth was doing. The kids, of course, were in school and would be for hours yet. Maybe Ruth was shopping; Thursday was the day she usually went. Mann visualised her in the supermarket, putting various items into the basket cart. He wished he were with her instead of starting on another sales trip. Hours of driving yet before he'd reach San Francisco. Three days of hotel sleeping and restaurant eating, hoped-for contacts and likely disappointments. He sighed; then, reaching out impulsively, he switched on the radio. He revolved the tuning knob until he found a station playing soft, innocuous music. He hummed along with it, eyes almost out of focus on the road ahead.

He started as the truck roared past him on the left, causing his car to shudder slightly. He watched the truck and trailer cut in abruptly for the westbound lane and frowned as he had to brake to maintain a safe distance behind it. What's with you? he thought. He eyed the truck with cursory disapproval. It was a huge gasoline tanker pulling a tank trailer, each of them having six pairs of wheels. He could see that it was not a new rig but was dented and in need of renovation, its tanks painted a cheap-looking silvery colour. Mann wondered if the driver had done the painting himself. His gaze shifted from the word FLAMMABLE printed across the back of the trailer tank, red letters on a white background, to the parallel reflector lines painted in red across the bottom of the tank to the massive rubber flaps swaying behind the rear tyres, then back up again. The reflector lines looked as though they'd been clumsily applied with a stencil. The driver must be an independent trucker, he decided, and not too affluent a one, from the looks of his outfit. He glanced at the trailer's licence plate. It was a California issue.

Mann checked his speedometer. He was holding steady at 55 miles an hour, as he invariably did when he drove without thinking on the open highway. The truck driver must have done a good 70 to pass him so quickly. That seemed a little odd. Weren't truck drivers supposed to be a cautious lot?

He grimaced at the smell of the truck's exhaust and looked at the vertical pipe to the left of the cab. It was spewing smoke, which clouded darkly back across the trailer. Christ, he thought. With all the furor about air pollution, why do they keep allowing that sort of thing on the highways?

He scowled at the constant fumes. They'd make him nauseated in a little while, he knew. He couldn't lag back here like this. Either he'd slow down or he'd pass the truck again. He didn't have the time to slow down. He'd gotten a late start. Keeping it at 55 all the way, he'd just about make his afternoon appointment. No, he'd have to pass.

Depressing the gas pedal, he eased his car towards the opposite lane. No sign of anything ahead. Traffic on this route seemed almost nonexistent today. He pushed down harder on the accelerator and steered all the way into the eastbound lane.

As he passed the truck, he glanced at it. The cab was too high for him to see into. All he caught sight of was the back of the truck driver's left hand on the steering wheel. It was darkly tanned and square-looking, with large veins knotted on its surface.

When Mann could see the truck reflected in the rearview mirror, he pulled back over to the proper lane and looked ahead again.

He glanced at the rearview mirror in surprise as the truck driver gave him an extended horn blast. What was that? he wondered; a greeting or a curse? He grunted with amusement, glancing at the mirror as he drove. The front fenders of the truck were a dingy purple colour, the paint faded and chipped; another amateurish job. All he could see was the lower portion of the truck; the rest was cut off by the top of his rear window.

To Mann's right, now, was a slope of shalelike earth with patches of scrub grass growing on it. His gaze jumped to the clapboard house on top of the slope. The television aerial on its roof was sagging at an angle of less than 40 degrees. Must give great reception, he thought.

He looked to the front again, glancing aside abruptly at a sign printed in jagged block letters on a piece of plywood: NIGHT CRAWLERS — BAIT. What the hell is a night crawler? he wondered. It sounded like some monster in a low-grade Hollywood thriller.

The unexpected roar of the truck motor made his gaze jump to the rearview mirror. Instantly, his startled look jumped to the side mirror. By God, the guy was passing him *again*. Mann turned his head to scowl at the leviathan form as it drifted by. He tried to see into the cab but couldn't because of its height. What's with him, anyway? he wondered. What the hell are we having here, a contest? See which vehicle can stay ahead the longer?

He thought of speeding up to stay ahead but changed his mind. When the truck and trailer started back into the westbound lane, he let up on the pedal, voicing a newly incredulous sound as he saw that if he hadn't slowed down, he would have been prematurely cut off again. Jesus Christ, he thought. What's *with* this guy?

His scowl deepened as the odour of the truck's exhaust reached his nostrils again. Irritably, he cranked up the window on his left. Damn it, was he going to have to breathe that crap all the way to San Francisco? He couldn't afford to slow down. He had to meet Forbes at a quarter after three and that was that.

He looked ahead. At least there was no traffic complicating matters. Mann pressed down on the accelerator pedal, drawing close behind the truck. When the highway curved enough to the left to give him a completely open view of the route ahead, he jarred down on the pedal, steering out into the opposite lane.

The truck edged over, blocking his way.

For several moments, all Mann could do was stare at it in blank confusion. Then, with a startled noise, he braked, returning to the proper lane. The truck moved back in front of him.

Mann could not allow himself to accept what apparently had taken place. It had to be a coincidence. The truck driver couldn't have blocked his way on purpose. He waited for more than a minute, then flicked down the turn-indicator lever to make his intentions perfectly clear and, depressing the accelerator pedal, steered again into the eastbound lane.

Immediately, the truck shifted, barring his way.

'*Jesus Christ!*' Mann was astounded. This was unbelievable. He'd never seen such a thing in 26 years of driving. He returned to the westbound lane, shaking his head as the truck swung back in front of him.

He eased up on the gas pedal, falling back to avoid the truck's exhaust. Now what? he wondered. He still had to make San Francisco on schedule. Why in God's name hadn't he gone a little out of his way in the beginning, so he could have travelled by freeway? This damned highway was two lane all the way.

Impulsively, he sped into the eastbound lane again. To his surprise, the truck driver did not pull over. Instead, the driver stuck his left arm out and waved him on. Mann started pushing down on the accelerator. Suddenly, he let up on the pedal with a gasp and jerked the steering wheel around, raking back behind the truck so quickly that his car began to fishtail. He was fighting to control its zigzag whipping when a blue convertible shot by him in the opposite lane. Mann caught a momentary vision of the man inside it glaring at him.

The car came under his control again. Mann was sucking breath in through his mouth. His heart was pounding almost painfully. My God! he thought. *He wanted me to hit that car head on.* The realisation stunned him. True, he should have seen to it himself that the road ahead was clear; that was his failure. But to wave him on . . . Mann felt appalled and sickened. Boy, oh, boy, oh, boy, he thought. This was really one for the books. That son of a bitch had meant for not only him to be killed but a totally uninvolved passer-by as well. The idea seemed beyond his comprehension. On a California highway on a Thursday morning? *Why?*

Mann tried to calm himself and rationalise the incident. Maybe it's the heat, he thought. Maybe the truck driver had a tension headache or an upset stomach; maybe both. Maybe he'd had a fight with his wife. Maybe she'd failed to put out last night. Mann tried in vain to smile. There could be any number of reasons. Reaching out, he twisted off the radio. The cheerful music irritated him.

He drove behind the truck for several minutes, his face a mask of animosity. As the exhaust fumes started putting his stomach on edge, he suddenly forced down the heel of his right hand on the horn bar and held it there. Seeing that the route ahead was clear, he pushed in the accelerator pedal all the way and steered into the opposite lane.

The movement of his car was paralleled immediately by the truck. Mann stayed in place, right hand jammed down on the horn bar. Get out of the way, you son of a bitch! he thought. He felt the muscles of his jaw hardening until they ached. There was a twisting in his stomach.

'*Damn!*' He pulled back quickly to the proper lane, shuddering with fury. 'You miserable son of a bitch,' he muttered, glaring at the truck as it was shifted back in front of him. What the hell is wrong with you? I pass your goddamn rig a couple of times and you go flying off the deep end? Are you nuts or something? Mann nodded tensely. Yes, he thought; he *is*. No other explanation.

He wondered what Ruth would think of all this, how she'd react. Probably, she'd start to honk the horn and would keep on honking it, assuming that, eventually, it would attract the attention of a policeman. He looked around with a scowl. Just where in hell *were* the policemen out here, anyway? He made a scoffing noise. What policemen? Here in the boondocks? They probably had a sheriff on horseback, for Christ's sake.

He wondered suddenly if he could fool the truck driver by passing on the right. Edging his car towards the shoulder, he peered ahead. No chance. There wasn't room enough. The truck driver could shove him through that wire fence if he wanted to. Mann shivered. And he'd want to, sure as hell, he thought.

Driving where he was, he grew conscious of the debris lying beside the highway: beer cans, candy wrappers, icecream containers, newspaper sections browned and rotted by the weather, a FOR SALE sign torn in half. Keep America beautiful, he thought sardonically. He passed a boulder with the name WILL JASPER painted on it in white. Who the hell is Will Jasper? he wondered. What would he think of this situation?

Unexpectedly, the car began to bounce. For several anxious moments, Mann thought that one of his tyres had gone flat. Then he noticed that the paving along this section of highway consisted of pitted slabs with gaps between them. He saw the truck and trailer jolting up and down and thought: I hope it shakes your brains loose. As the truck veered into a sharp left curve, he caught a fleeting glimpse of the driver's face in the cab's side mirror. There was not enough time to establish his appearance.

'Ah,' he said. A long, steep hill was looming up ahead. The truck would have to climb it slowly. There would doubtless be an opportunity to pass somewhere on the grade. Mann pressed down on the accelerator pedal, drawing as close behind the truck as safety would allow.

Halfway up the slope, Mann saw a turnout for the eastbound lane with no oncoming traffic anywhere in sight. Flooring the accelerator pedal, he shot into the opposite lane. The slow-moving truck began to angle out in front of him. Face stiffening, Mann steered his speeding car across the highway edge and curved it sharply on the turnout. Clouds of dust went billowing up behind his car, making him lose sight of the truck. His tyres buzzed and crackled on the dirt, then, suddenly, were humming on the pavement once again.

He glanced at the rearview mirror and a barking laugh erupted from his throat. He'd only meant to pass. The dust had been an unexpected bonus. Let the bastard get a sniff of something rotten smelling in *his* nose for a change! he thought. He honked the horn elatedly, a mocking rhythm of bleats. Screw you, Jack!

He swept across the summit of the hill. A striking vista lay ahead: sunlit hills and flatland, a corridor of dark trees, quadrangles of cleared-off acreage and bright-green vegetable patches; far off, in the distance, a mammoth water tower. Mann felt stirred by the panoramic sight. Lovely, he thought. Reaching out, he turned the radio back on and started humming cheerfully with the music.

Seven minutes later, he passed a billboard advertising CHUCK'S CAFÉ. No thanks, Chuck, he thought. He glanced at a grey house nestled in a hollow. Was that a cemetery in its front yard or a group of plaster statuary for sale?

Hearing the noise behind him, Mann looked at the rearview mirror and felt himself go cold with fear. The truck was hurtling down the hill, pursuing him.

His mouth fell open and he threw a glance at the speedometer. He was doing more than 60! On a curving downgrade, that was not at all a safe speed to be driving. Yet the truck must be exceeding that by a considerable margin, it was closing the distance between them so rapidly. Mann swallowed, leaning to the right as he steered his car around a sharp curve. Is the man *insane?* he thought.

His gaze jumped forward searchingly. He saw a turnoff half a mile ahead and decided that he'd use it. In the rearview mirror, the huge square radiator grille was all he could see now. He stamped down on the gas pedal and his tyres screeched unnervingly as he wheeled around another curve, thinking that, surely, the truck would have to slow down here.

He groaned as it rounded the curve with ease, only the sway of its tanks revealing the outward pressure of the turn. Mann bit trembling lips together as he whipped his car around another curve. A straight descent now. He depressed the pedal farther, glanced at the speedometer. Almost 70 miles an hour! He wasn't used to driving this fast!

In agony, he saw the turnoff shoot by on his right. He couldn't have left the highway at this speed, anyway; he'd have overturned. Goddamn it, what was wrong with that son of a bitch? Mann honked his horn in frightened rage. Cranking down the window suddenly, he shoved his left arm out to wave the truck back. '*Back!*' he yelled. He honked the horn again. 'Get back, you crazy bastard!'

The truck was almost on him now. He's going to kill me! Mann thought, horrified. He honked the horn repeatedly, then had to use both hands to grip the steering wheel as he swept around another curve. He flashed a look at the rearview mirror. He could see only the bottom portion of the truck's radiator grille. He was going to lose control! He felt the rear wheels start to drift and let up on the pedal quickly. The tyre treads bit in, the car leaped on, regaining its momentum.

Mann saw the bottom of the grade ahead, and in the distance there was a building with a sign that read CHUCK'S CAFÉ. The truck was gaining ground again. This is insane! he thought, enraged and terrified at once. The highway straightened out. He floored the pedal: 74 now—75. Mann braced himself, trying to ease the car as far to the right as possible.

Abruptly, he began to brake, then swerved to the right, raking his car into the open area in front of the café. He cried out as the car began to fishtail, then careered into a skid. *Steer with it!* screamed a voice in his mind. The rear of the car was lashing from side to side, tyres spewing dirt and raising clouds of dust. Mann pressed harder on the brake pedal, turning further into the skid. The car began to straighten out and he braked harder yet, conscious on the sides of his vision, of the truck and trailer roaring by on the highway. He nearly sideswiped one of the cars parked in front of the café, bounced and skidded by it, going almost straight now. He jammed in the brake pedal as hard as he could. The rear end broke to the right and the car spun half around, sheering sideways to a neck-wrenching halt 30 yards beyond the café.

Mann sat in pulsing silence, eyes closed. His heartbeats felt like club blows in his chest. He couldn't seem to catch his breath. If he were ever going to have a heart attack, it would be now. After a while, he opened his eyes and pressed his right palm against his chest. His heart was still throbbing labouredly. No wonder, he thought. It isn't every day I'm almost murdered by a truck.

He raised the handle and pushed out the door, then started forward, grunting in surprise as the safety belt held him in place. Reaching down with shaking fingers, he depressed the release button and pulled the ends of the belt apart. He glanced at the café. What had its patrons thought of his breakneck appearance? he wondered.

He stumbled as he walked to the front door of the café. TRUCKERS WELCOME, read a sign in the window. It gave Mann a queasy feeling to see it. Shivering, he pulled open the door and went inside, avoiding the sight of its customers. He felt certain they were watching him, but he didn't have the strength to face their looks. Keeping his gaze fixed straight ahead, he moved to the rear of the café and opened the door marked GENTS.

Moving to the sink, he twisted the right-hand faucet and leaned over to cup cold water in his palms and splash it on his face. There was a fluttering of his stomach muscles he could not control.

Straightening up, he tugged down several towels from their dispenser and patted them against his face, grimacing at the smell of the paper. Dropping the soggy towels into a wastebasket beside the sink, he regarded himself in the wall mirror. Still with us, Mann, he thought. He nodded, swallowing. Drawing out his metal comb, he neatened his hair. You never know, he thought. You just never know. You drift along, year after year, presuming certain values to be fixed; like being able to drive on a public thoroughfare without somebody trying to murder you. You come to depend on that sort of thing. Then something occurs and all bets are off. One shocking incident and all the years of logic and acceptance are displaced and, suddenly, the jungle is in front of you again. *Man, part animal, part angel.* Where had he come across that phrase? He shivered.

It was entirely an animal in that truck out there.

His breath was almost back to normal now. Mann forced a smile at his reflection. All right, boy, he told himself. It's over now. It was a goddamned nightmare, but it's over. You are on your way to San Francisco. You'll get yourself a nice hotel room, order a bottle of expensive Scotch, soak your body in a hot bath and forget. Damn right, he thought. He turned and walked out of the washroom.

He jolted to a halt, his breath cut off. Standing rooted, heartbeat hammering at his chest, he gaped through the front window of the café.

The truck and trailer were parked outside.

Mann stared at them in unbelieving shock. It wasn't possible. He'd seen them roaring by at top speed. The driver had won; he'd *won!* He'd had the whole damn highway to himself! *Why had he turned back?*

Mann looked around with sudden dread. There were five men eating, three along the counter, two in booths. He cursed himself for having failed to look at faces when he'd entered. Now there was no way of knowing who it was. Mann felt his legs begin to shake.

Abruptly, he walked to the nearest booth and slid in clumsily behind the table. Now wait, he told himself; just wait. Surely, he could tell which one it was. Masking his face with the menu, he glanced across its top. Was it that one in the khaki work shirt? Mann tried to see the man's hands but couldn't. His gaze flicked nervously across the room. Not that one in the suit, of course. Three remaining. That one in the front booth, square-faced, black-haired? If only he could see the man's hands, it might help. One of the two others at the counter? Mann studied them uneasily. Why hadn't he looked at faces when he'd come in?

Now *wait*, he thought. Goddamn it, *wait!* All right, the truck driver was in here. That didn't automatically signify that he meant to continue the insane duel. Chuck's Café might be the only place to eat for miles around. It *was* lunchtime, wasn't it? The truck driver had probably intended to eat here all the time. He'd just been moving too fast to pull into the parking lot before. So he'd slowed down, turned around and driven back, that was all. Mann forced himself to read the menu. Right, he thought. No point in getting so rattled. Perhaps a beer would help relax him.

The woman behind the counter came over and Mann ordered a ham sandwich on rye toast and a bottle of Coors. As the woman turned away, he wondered, with a sudden twinge of self-reproach, why he hadn't simply left the café, jumped into his car and sped away. He would have known immediately, then, if the truck driver was still out to get him. As it was, he'd have to suffer through an entire meal to find out. He almost groaned at his stupidity.

Still, what if the truck driver *had* followed him out and started after him again? He'd have been right back where he'd started. Even if he'd managed to get a good lead, the truck driver would have overtaken him eventually. It just wasn't in him to drive at 80 and 90 miles an hour in order to stay ahead. True, he might have been intercepted by a California Highway Patrol car. What if he weren't, though?

Mann repressed the plaguing thoughts. He tried to calm himself. He looked deliberately at the four men. Either of two seemed a likely possibility as the driver of the truck: the square-faced one in the front booth and the chunky one in the jump suit sitting at the counter. Mann had an impulse to walk over to them and ask which one it was, tell the man he was sorry he'd irritated him, tell him anything to calm him, since, obviously, he wasn't rational, was a manic-depressive, probably. Maybe buy the man a beer and sit with him awhile to try to settle things.

He couldn't move. What if the truck driver were letting the whole thing drop? Mightn't his approach rile the man all over again? Mann felt drained by indecision. He nodded weakly as the waitress set the sandwich and the bottle in front of him. He took a swallow of the beer, which made him cough. Was the truck driver amused by the sound? Mann felt a stirring of resentment deep inside himself. What right did that bastard have to impose this torment on another human being? It was a free country, wasn't it? Damn it, he had every right to pass the son of a bitch on a highway if he wanted to!

'Oh, hell,' he mumbled. He tried to feel amused. He was making entirely too much of this. Wasn't he? He glanced at the pay telephone on the front wall. What was to prevent him from calling the local police and telling them the situation? But, then, he'd have to stay here, lose time, make Forbes angry, probably lose the sale. And what if the truck driver stayed to face them? Naturally, he'd deny the whole thing. What if the police believed him and didn't do anything about it? After they'd gone, the truck driver would undoubtedly take it out on him again, only worse, *God!* Mann thought in agony.

The sandwich tasted flat, the beer unpleasantly sour. Mann stared at the table as he ate. For God's sake, why was he just *sitting* here like this? He was a grown man, wasn't he? Why didn't he settle this damn thing once and for all?

His left hand twitched so unexpectedly, he spilled beer on his trousers. The man in the jump suit had risen from the counter and was strolling towards the front of the café. Mann felt his heartbeat thumping as the man gave money to the waitress, took his change and a toothpick from the dispenser and went outside. Mann watched in anxious silence.

The man did not get into the cab of the tanker truck.

It had to be the one in the front booth, then. His face took form in Mann's remembrance: square, with dark eyes, dark hair; the man who'd tried to kill him.

Mann stood abruptly, letting impulse conquer fear. Eyes fixed ahead, he started towards the entrance. Anything was preferable to sitting in that booth. He stopped by the cash register, conscious of the hitching of his chest as he gulped in air. Was the man observing him? he wondered. He swallowed, pulling out the clip of dollar bills in his right-hand trouser pocket. He glanced towards the waitress. Come *on*, he thought. He looked at his check and, seeing the amount, reached shakily into his trouser pocket for change. He heard a coin fall onto the floor and roll away. Ignoring it, he dropped a dollar and a quarter onto the counter and thrust the clip of bills into his trouser pocket.

As he did, he heard the man in the front booth get up. An icy shudder spasmed up his neck. Turning quickly to the door, he shoved it open, seeing, on the edges of his vision, the square-faced man approach the cash register. Lurching from the café, he started towards his car with long strides. His mouth was dry again. The pounding of his heart was painful in his chest.

Suddenly, he started running. He heard the café door bang shut and fought away the urge to look across his shoulder. Was that a sound of other running footsteps now? Reaching his car, Mann yanked open the door and jarred in awkwardly behind the steering wheel. He reached into his trouser pocket for the keys and snatched them out, almost dropping them. His hand was shaking so badly he couldn't get the ignition key into its slot. He whined with mounting dread. Come on! he thought.

The key slid in, he twisted it convulsively. The motor started and he raced it momentarily before jerking the transmission shift to drive. Depressing the accelerator pedal quickly, he raked the car around and steered it towards the highway. From the corners of his eyes, he saw the truck and trailer being backed away from the café.

Reaction burst inside him. 'No!' he raged and slammed his foot down on the brake pedal. This was idiotic! Why the hell should he run away? His car slid sideways to a rocking halt and, shouldering out the door, he lurched to his feet and started towards the truck with angry strides. *All right, Jack*, he thought. He glared at the man inside the truck. You want to punch my nose, OK, but no more goddamn tournament on the highway.

The truck began to pick up speed. Mann raised his right arm. 'Hey!' he yelled. He knew the driver saw him. '*Hey!*' He started running as the truck kept moving, engine grinding loudly. It was on the highway now. He sprinted towards it with a sense of martyred outrage. The driver shifted gears, the truck moved faster. 'Stop!' Mann shouted. 'Damn it, *stop!*'

He thudded to a panting halt, staring at the truck as it receded down the highway, moved around a hill and disappeared. 'You son of a bitch,' he muttered. 'You goddamn, miserable son of a bitch.'

He trudged back slowly to his car, trying to believe that the truck driver had fled the hazard of a fistfight. It was possible, of course, but, somehow, he could not believe it.

He got into his car and was about to drive onto the highway when he changed his mind and switched the motor off. That crazy bastard might just be tooling along at 15 miles an hour, waiting for him to catch up. Nuts to that, he thought. So he blew his schedule; screw it. Forbes would have to wait, that was all. And if Forbes didn't care to wait, that was all right, too. He'd sit here for a while and let the nut get out of range, let him think he'd won the day. He grinned. You're the bloody Red Baron, Jack; you've shot me down. Now go to hell with my sincerest compliments. He shook his head. Beyond belief, he thought.

He really should have done this earlier, pulled over, waited. Then the truck driver would have had to let it pass. *Or picked on someone else*, the startling thought occurred to him. Jesus, maybe that was how the crazy bastard whiled away his work hours! Jesus Christ Almighty! was it possible?

He looked at the dashboard clock. It was just past 12.30. Wow, he thought. All that in less than an hour. He shifted on the seat and stretched his legs out. Leaning back against the door, he closed his eyes and mentally perused the things he had to do tomorrow and the following day. Today was shot to hell, as far as he could see.

When he opened his eyes, afraid of drifting into sleep and losing too much time, almost 11 minutes had passed. The nut must be an ample distance off by now, he thought: at least 11 miles and likely more, the way he drove. Good enough. He wasn't going to try to make San Francisco on schedule now, anyway. He'd take it real easy.

Mann adjusted his safety belt, switched on the motor, tapped the transmission pointer into drive position and pulled onto the highway, glancing back across his shoulder. Not a car in sight. Great day for driving. Everybody was staying at home. That nut must have a reputation around here. When Crazy Jack is on the highway, lock your car in the garage. Mann chuckled at the notion as his car began to turn the curve ahead.

Mindless reflex drove his right foot down against the brake pedal. Suddenly, his car had skidded to a halt and he was staring down the highway. The truck and trailer were parked on the shoulder less than 90 yards away.

Mann couldn't seem to function. He knew his car was blocking the westbound lane, knew that he should either make a U-turn or pull off the highway, but all he could do was gape at the truck.

He cried out, legs retracting, as a horn blast sounded behind him. Snapping up his head, he looked at the rearview mirror, gasping as he saw a yellow station wagon bearing down on him at high speed. Suddenly, it veered off towards the eastbound lane, disappearing from the mirror. Mann jerked around and saw it hurtling past his car, its rear end snapping back and forth, its back tyres screeching. He saw the twisted features of the man inside, saw his lips move rapidly with cursing.

Then the station wagon had swerved back into the westbound lane and was speeding off. It gave Mann an odd sensation to see it pass the truck. The man in that station wagon could drive on, unthreatened. Only he had been singled out. What happened was demented. Yet it was happening.

He drove his car onto the highway shoulder and braked. Putting the transmission into neutral, he leaned back, staring at the truck. His head was aching again. There was a pulsing at his temples like the ticking of a muffled clock.

What was he to do? He knew very well that if he left his car to walk to the truck, the driver would pull away and repark farther down the highway. He may as well face the fact that he was dealing with a madman. He felt the tremor in his stomach muscles starting up again. His heartbeat thudded slowly, striking at his chest wall. Now what?

With a sudden, angry impulse, Mann snapped the transmission into gear and stepped down hard on the accelerator pedal. The tyres of the car spun sizzlingly before they gripped; the car shot out onto the highway. Instantly, the truck began to move. He even had the motor on! Mann thought in raging fear. He floored the pedal, then, abruptly, realised he couldn't make it, that the truck would block his way and he'd collide with its trailer. A vision flashed across his mind, a fiery explosion and a sheet of flame incinerating him. He started braking fast, trying to decelerate evenly, so he wouldn't lose control.

When he'd slowed down enough to feel that it was safe, he steered the car onto the shoulder and stopped it again, throwing the transmission into neutral.

Approximately 80 yards ahead, the truck pulled off the highway and stopped.

Mann tapped his fingers on the steering wheel. *Now* what? he thought. Turn around and head east until he reached a cutoff that would take him to San Francisco by another route? How did he know the truck driver wouldn't follow him even then? His cheeks twitched as he bit his lips together angrily. No! He wasn't going to turn around!

His expression hardened suddenly. Well, he wasn't going to *sit* here all day, that was certain. Reaching out, he tapped the gearshift into drive and steered his car onto the highway once again. He saw the massive truck and trailer start to move but made no effort to speed up. He tapped at the brakes, taking a position about 30 yards behind the trailer. He glanced at his speedometer. Forty miles an hour. The truck driver had his left arm out the cab window and was waving him on. What did that mean? Had he changed his mind? Decided, finally, that this thing had gone too far? Mann couldn't let himself believe it.

He looked ahead. Despite the mountain ranges all around, the highway was flat as far as he could see. He tapped a fingernail against the horn bar, trying to make up his mind. Presumably, he could continue all the way to San Francisco at this speed, hanging back just far enough to avoid the worst of the exhaust fumes. It didn't seem likely that the truck driver would stop directly on the highway to block his way. And if the truck driver pulled onto the shoulder to let him pass, he could pull off the highway, too. It would be a draining afternoon but a safe one.

On the other hand, outracing the truck might be worth just one more try. This was obviously what that son of a bitch wanted. Yet, surely, a vehicle of such size couldn't be driven with the same daring as, potentially, his own. The laws of mechanics were against it, if nothing else. Whatever advantage the truck had in mass, it had to lose in stability, particularly that of its trailer. If Mann were to drive at, say, 80 miles an hour and there were a few steep grades—as he felt sure there were—the truck would have to fall behind.

The question was, of course, whether he had the nerve to maintain such a speed over a long distance. He'd never done it before. Still, the more he thought about it, the more it appealed to him; far more than the alternative did.

Abruptly, he decided. *Right*, he thought. He checked ahead, then pressed down hard on the accelerator pedal and pulled into the eastbound lane. As he neared the truck, he tensed, anticipating that the driver might block his way. But the truck did not shift from the westbound lane. Mann's car moved along its mammoth side. He glanced at the cab and saw the name KELLER printed on its door. For a shocking instant, he thought it read KILLER and started to slow down. Then, glancing at the name again, he saw what it really was and depressed the pedal sharply. When he saw the truck reflected in the rearview mirror, he steered his car into the westbound lane.

He shuddered, dread and satisfaction mixed together, as he saw that the truck driver was speeding up. It was strangely comforting to know the man's intentions definitely again. That plus the knowledge of his face and name seemed, somehow, to reduce his stature. Before, he had been faceless, nameless, an embodiment of unknown terror. Now, at least, he was an individual. All right, Keller, said his mind, let's see you beat me with that purple-silver relic now. He pressed down harder on the pedal. *Here we go*, he thought.

He looked at the speedometer, scowling as he saw that he was doing only 74 miles an hour. Deliberately, he pressed down on the pedal, alternating his gaze between the highway ahead and the speedometer until the needle turned past 80. He felt a flickering of satisfaction with himself. All right, Keller, you son of a bitch, top that, he thought.

After several moments, he glanced into the rearview mirror again. Was the truck getting closer? Stunned, he checked the speedometer. Damn it! He was down to 76! He forced in the accelerator pedal angrily. *He mustn't go less than 80!* Mann's chest shuddered with convulsive breath.

He glanced aside as he hurtled past a beige sedan parked on the shoulder underneath a tree. A young couple sat inside it, talking. Already they were far behind, their world removed from his. Had they even glanced aside when he'd passed? He doubted it.

He started as the shadow of an overhead bridge whipped across the hood and windshield. Inhaling raggedly, he glanced at the speedometer again. He was holding at 81. He checked the rearview mirror. Was it his imagination that the truck was gaining ground? He looked forward with anxious eyes. There had to be some kind of town ahead. To hell with time; he'd stop at the police station and tell them what had happened. They'd have to believe him. Why would he stop to tell them such a story if it weren't true? For all he knew, Keller had a police record in these parts. *Oh, sure, we're on to him*, he heard a faceless officer remark. *That crazy bastard's asked for it before and now he's going to get it.*

Mann shook himself and looked at the mirror. The truck *was* getting closer. Wincing, he glanced at the speedometer. Goddamn it, pay attention! raged his mind. He was down to 74 again! Whining with frustration, he depressed the pedal. Eighty!—80! he demanded of himself. There was a murderer behind him!

His car began to pass a field of flowers; lilacs, Mann saw, white and purple, stretching out in endless rows. There was a small shack near the highway, the words FIELD FRESH FLOWERS painted on it. A brown-cardboard square was propped against the shack, the word FUNERALS printed crudely on it. Mann saw himself, abruptly, lying in a casket, painted like some grotesque mannequin. The overpowering smell of flowers seemed to fill his nostrils. Ruth and the children sitting in the first row, heads bowed. All his relatives—

Suddenly, the pavement roughened and the car began to bounce and shudder, driving bolts of pain into his head. He felt the steering wheel resisting him and clamped his hands around it tightly, harsh vibrations running up his arms. He didn't dare look at the mirror now. He had to force himself to keep the speed unchanged. Keller wasn't going to slow down; he was sure of that. *What if he got a flat tyre, though?* All control would vanish in an instant. He visualised the somersaulting of his car, its grinding, shrieking tumble, the explosion of its gas tank, his body crushed and burned and—

The broken span of pavement ended and his gaze jumped quickly to the rearview mirror. The truck was no closer, but it hadn't lost ground, either. Mann's eyes shifted. Up ahead were hills and mountains. He tried to reassure himself that upgrades were on his side, that he could climb them at the same speed he was going now. Yet all he could imagine were the downgrades, the immense truck close behind him, slamming violently into his car and knocking it across some cliff edge. He had a horrifying vision of dozens of broken, rusted cars lying unseen in the canyons ahead, corpses in every one of them, all flung to shattering deaths by Keller.

Mann's car went rocketing into a corridor of trees. On each side of the highway was a eucalyptus windbreak, each trunk three feet from the next. It was like speeding through a high-walled canyon. Mann gasped, twitching, as a large twig bearing dusty leaves dropped down across the windshield, then slid out of sight. Dear God! he thought. He was getting near the edge himself. If he should lose his nerve at this speed; it was over. Jesus! That would be ideal for Keller! he realised suddenly. He visualised the square-faced driver laughing as he passed the burning wreckage, knowing that he'd killed his prey without so much as touching him.

Mann started as his car shot out into the open. The route ahead was not straight now but winding up into the foothills. Mann willed himself to press down on the pedal even more. Eighty-three now, almost 84.

To his left was a broad terrain of green hills blending into mountains. He saw a black car on a dirt road, moving towards the highway. *Was its side painted white?* Mann's heartbeat lurched. Impulsively, he jammed the heel of his right hand down against the horn bar and held it there. The blast of the horn was shrill and racking to his ears. His heart began to pound. Was it a police car? Was it?

He let the horn bar up abruptly. *No, it wasn't.* Damn! his mind raged. Keller must have been amused by his pathetic efforts. Doubtless, he was chuckling to himself right now. He heard the truck driver's voice in his mind, coarse and sly. *You think you gonna get a cop to save you, boy? Shee-it. You gonna die.* Mann's heart contorted with savage hatred. *You son of a bitch!* he thought. Jerking his right hand into a fist, he drove it down against the seat. Goddamn you, Keller! I'm going to kill you, if it's the last thing I do!

The hills were closer now. There would be slopes directly, long steep grades. Mann felt a burst of hope within himself. He was sure to gain a lot of distance on the truck. No matter how he tried, that bastard Keller couldn't manage 80 miles an hour on a hill. But I can! cried his mind with fierce elation. He worked up saliva in his mouth and swallowed it. The back of his shirt was drenched. He could feel sweat trickling down his sides. A bath and a drink, first order of the day on reaching San Francisco. A long, hot bath, a long, cold drink. Cutty Sark. He'd splurge, by Christ. He rated it.

The car swept up a shallow rise. Not steep enough, goddamn it! The truck's momentum would prevent its losing speed. Mann felt mindless hatred for the landscape. Already, he had topped the rise and tilted over to a shallow downgrade. He looked at the rearview mirror. *Square*, he thought, everything about the truck was square: the radiator grille, the fender shapes, the bumper ends, the outline of the cab, even the shape of Keller's hands and face. He visualised the truck as some great entity pursuing him, insentient, brutish, chasing him with instinct only.

Mann cried out, horror-stricken, as he saw the ROAD REPAIRS sign up ahead. His frantic gaze leaped down the highway. Both lanes blocked, a huge black arrow pointing towards the alternative route! He groaned in anguish, seeing it was dirt. His foot jumped automatically to the brake pedal and started pumping it. He threw a dazed look at the rearview mirror. The truck was moving as fast as ever! It *couldn't*, though! Mann's expression froze in terror as he started turning to the right.

He stiffened as the front wheels hit the dirt road. For an instant, he was certain that the back part of the car was going to spin; he felt it breaking to the left. 'No, don't!' he cried. Abruptly, he was jarring down the dirt road, elbows braced against his sides, trying to keep from losing control. His tyres battered at the ruts, almost tearing the wheel from his grip. The windows rattled noisily. His neck snapped back and forth with painful jerks. His jolting body surged against the binding of the safety belt and slammed down violently on the seat. He felt the bouncing of the car drive up his spine. His clenching teeth slipped and he cried out hoarsely as his upper teeth gouged deep into his lip.

He gasped as the rear end of the car began surging to the right. He started to jerk the steering wheel to the left, then, hissing, wrenched it in the opposite direction, crying out as the right rear fender cracked into a fence pole, knocking it down. He started pumping at the brakes, struggling to regain control. The car rear yawed sharply to the left, tyres shooting out a spray of dirt. Mann felt a scream tear upward in his throat. He twisted wildly at the steering wheel. The car began careering to the right. He hitched the wheel around until the car was on course again. His head was pounding like his heart now, with gigantic, throbbing spasms. He started coughing as he gagged on dripping blood.

The dirt road ended suddenly, the car regained momentum on the pavement and he dared to look at the rearview mirror. The truck was slowed down but was still behind him, rocking like a freighter on a storm-tossed sea, its huge tyres scouring up a pall of dust. Mann shoved in the accelerator pedal and his car surged forward. A good, steep grade lay just ahead; he'd gain that distance now. He swallowed blood, grimacing at the taste, then fumbled in his trouser pocket and tugged out his handkerchief. He pressed it to his bleeding lip, eyes fixed on the slope ahead. Another 50 yards or so. He writhed his back. His under-shirt was soaking wet, adhering to his skin. He glanced at the rearview mirror. The truck had just regained the highway. *Tough!* he thought with venom. Didn't get me, did you, Keller?

His car was on the first yards of the upgrade when steam began to issue from beneath its hood. Mann stiffened suddenly, eyes widening with shock. The steam increased, became a smoking mist. Mann's gaze jumped down. The red light hadn't flashed on yet but had to in a moment. How could this be happening? Just as he was set to get away! The slope ahead was long and gradual, with many curves. He knew he couldn't stop. Could he U-turn unexpectedly and go back down? the sudden thought occurred. He looked ahead. The highway was too narrow, bound by hills on both sides. There wasn't room enough to make an uninterrupted turn and there wasn't time enough to ease around. If he tried that, Keller would shift direction and hit him head on. 'Oh, my God!' Mann murmured suddenly.

He was going to die.

He stared ahead with stricken eyes, his view increasingly obscured by steam. Abruptly, he recalled the afternoon he'd had the engine steam cleaned at the local car wash. The man who'd done it had suggested he replace the water hoses, because steam-cleaning had a tendency to make them crack. He'd nodded, thinking that he'd do it when he had more time. *More time!* The phrase was like a dagger in his mind. He'd failed to change the hoses and, for that failure he was now about to die.

He sobbed in terror as the dashboard light flashed on. He glanced at it involuntarily and read the word HOT, black on red. With a breathless gasp, he jerked the transmission into low. Why hadn't he done that right away! He looked ahead. The slope seemed endless. Already, he could hear a boiling throb inside the radiator. How much coolant was there left? Steam was clouding faster, hazing up the windshield. Reaching out, he twisted at a dashboard knob. The wipers started flicking back and forth in fan-shaped sweeps. There had to be enough coolant in the radiator to get him to the top. *Then* what? cried his mind. He couldn't drive without coolant, even downhill. He glanced at the rearview mirror. The truck was falling behind. Mann snarled with maddened fury. *If it weren't for that goddamned hose, he'd be escaping now!*

The sudden lurching of the car snatched him back to terror. If he braked now, he could jump out, run and scrabble up that slope. Later, he might not have the time. He couldn't make himself stop the car, though. As long as it kept on running, he felt bound to it, less vulnerable. God knows what would happen if he left it.

Mann stared up the slope with haunted eyes, trying not to see the red light on the edges of his vision. Yard by yard, his car was slowing down. Make it, make it, pleaded his mind, even though he thought that it was futile. The car was running more and more unevenly. The thumping percolation of its radiator filled his ears. Any moment now, the motor would be choked off and the car would shudder to a stop, leaving him a sitting target. No, he thought. He tried to blank his mind.

He was almost to the top, but in the mirror he could see the truck drawing up on him. He jammed down on the pedal and the motor made a grinding noise. He groaned. It had to make the top! Please, God, help me! screamed his mind. The ridge was just ahead. Closer. Closer. Make it. 'Make it.' The car was shuddering and clanking, slowing down—oil, smoke and steam gushing from beneath the hood. The windshield wipers swept from side to side. Mann's head throbbed. Both his hands felt numb. His heartbeat pounded as he stared ahead. Make it, please, God, make it. Make it. *Make it!*

Over! Mann's lips opened in a cry of triumph as the car began descending. Hand shaking uncontrollably, he shoved the transmission into neutral and let the car go into a glide. The triumph strangled in his throat as he saw that there was nothing in sight but hills and more hills. Never mind! He was on a downgrade now, a long one. He passed a sign that read TRUCKS USE LOW GEARS NEXT 12 MILES. Twelve miles! Something would come up. It had to.

The car began to pick up speed. Mann glanced at the speedometer. Forty-seven miles an hour. The red light still burned. He'd save the motor for a long time, too, though; let it cool for 12 miles, if the truck was far enough behind.

His speed increased. Fifty . . . 51. Mann watched the needle turning slowly towards the right. He glanced at the rearview mirror. The truck had not appeared yet. With a little luck, he might still get a good lead. Not as good as he might have if the motor hadn't overheated but enough to work with. There had to be someplace along the way to stop. The needle edged past 55 and started towards the 60 mark.

Again, he looked at the rearview mirror, jolting as he saw that the truck had topped the ridge and was on its way down. He felt his lips begin to shake and crimped them together. His gaze jumped fitfully between the steam-obscured highway and the mirror. The truck was accelerating rapidly. Keller doubtless had the gas pedal floored. It wouldn't be long before the truck caught up to him. Mann's right hand twitched unconsciously towards the gearshift. Noticing, he jerked it back, grimacing, glanced at the Speedometer. The car's velocity had just passed 60. Not enough! He had to use the motor now! He reached out desperately.

His right hand froze in mid-air as the motor stalled; then, shooting out the hand, he twisted the ignition key. The motor made a grinding noise but wouldn't start. Mann glanced up, saw that he was almost on the shoulder, jerked the steering wheel around. Again, he turned the key, but there was no response. He looked up at the rearview mirror. The truck was gaining on him swiftly. He glanced at the speedometer. The car's speed was fixed at 62. Mann felt himself crushed in a vice of panic. He stared ahead with haunted eyes.

Then he saw it, several hundred yards ahead: an escape route for trucks with burned-out brakes. There was no alternative now. Either he took the turnout or his car would be rammed from behind. The truck was frighteningly close. He heard the high-pitched wailing of its motor. Unconsciously, he started easing to the right, then jerked the wheel back suddenly. He mustn't give the move away! He had to wait until the last possible moment. Otherwise, Keller would follow him in.

Just before he reached the escape route, Mann wrenched the steering wheel around. The car rear started breaking to the left, tyres shrieking on the pavement. Mann steered with the skid, braking just enough to keep from losing all control. The rear tyres grabbed and, at 60 miles an hour, the car shot up the dirt trail, tyres slinging up a cloud of dust. Mann began to hit the brakes. The rear wheels sideslipped and the car slammed hard against the dirt bank to the right. Mann gasped as the car bounced off and started to fishtail with violent whipping motions, angling towards the trail edge. He drove his foot down on the brake pedal with all his might. The car rear skidded to the right and slammed against the bank again. Mann heard a grinding rend of metal and felt himself heaved downward suddenly, his neck snapped, as the car ploughed to a violent halt.

As in a dream, Mann turned to see the truck and trailer swerving off the highway. Paralysed, he watched the massive vehicle hurtle towards him, staring at it with a blank detachment, knowing he was going to die but so stupefied by the sight of the looming truck that he couldn't react. The gargantuan shape roared closer, blotting out the sky. Mann felt a strange sensation in his throat, unaware that he was screaming.

Suddenly, the truck began to tilt. Mann stared at it in choked-off silence as it started tipping over like some ponderous beast toppling in slow motion. Before it reached his car, it vanished from his rear window.

Hands palsied, Mann undid the safety belt and opened the door. Struggling from the car, he stumbled to the trail edge, staring downward. He was just in time to see the truck capsize like a foundering ship. The tanker followed, huge wheels spinning as it overturned.

The storage tank on the truck exploded first, the violence of its detonation causing Mann to stagger back and sit down clumsily on the dirt. A second explosion roared below, its shock wave buffeting across him hotly, making his ears hurt. His glazed eyes saw a fiery column shoot up towards the sky in front of him, then another.

Mann crawled slowly to the trail edge and peered down at the canyon. Enormous gouts of flame were towering upward, topped by thick, black, oily smoke. He couldn't see the truck or trailer, only flames. He gaped at them in shock, all feeling drained from him.

Then, unexpectedly, emotion came. Not dread, at first, and not regret; not the nausea that followed soon. It was a primeval tumult in his mind: the cry of some ancestral beast above the body of its vanquished foe.

STEPHEN (EDWIN) KING (1947–)

There is no more important contributor to twentieth-century American popular culture than Stephen King. Most often associated with Horror or Dark Fantasy storytelling, Stephen King is in reality a versatile author of Crime Fiction, Science Fiction, Westerns, Romance, and Social Melodrama.

Like all best-selling and critically acclaimed writers, Stephen King is voraciously well read. He is very much aware of his cultural and literary heritage, and these, combined with his personal experiences, are the primary sources for his stories. King was raised in the 1950s, that period in American popular culture when Science Fiction/Horror movies, comic books, and rock 'n' roll enjoyed tremendous popularity.

Stephen King has written haunted house stories (The Shining), *stories of plague and apocalypse* (The Stand *and* The Mist), *werewolf stories* (Cujo *and* Cycle of the Werewolf), *vampire stories* (Salem's Lot), *stories of outer space invasion* (The Tommyknockers), *stories of perverse ritual* (The Long Walk *and* The Running Man), *and more. The list of authors who have influenced and imitated Stephen King is extensive. King's strength as a storyteller is not found in his telling of new tales, but in his ability to re-tell old, classic tales to new audiences. This is, of course, what Stephen Spielberg and George Lucas have done with their* Star Wars *and* Indiana Jones *series.*

"The Raft" is an enthralling tale of suspense, horror, and adolescence—three elements of life that have often been intertwined.

The Raft
(Gallery, *November 1982*)

It was forty miles from Horlicks University in Pittsburgh to Cascade Lake, and although dark comes early to that part of the world in October and although they didn't get going until six o'clock, there was still a little light in the sky when they got there. They had come in Deke's Camaro. Deke didn't waste any time when he was sober. After a couple of beers, he made that Camaro walk and talk.

He had hardly brought the car to a stop at the pole fence between the parking lot and the beach before he was out and pulling off his shirt. His eyes were scanning the water for the raft. Randy got out of the shotgun seat, a little reluctantly. This had been his idea, true enough, but he had never expected Deke to take it seriously. The girls were moving around in the back seat, getting ready to get out.

Deke's eyes scanned the water restlessly, side to side (*sniper's eyes,* Randy thought uncomfortably), and then fixed on a point.

"It's there!" he shouted, slapping the hood of the Camaro. "Just like you said, Randy! Hot damn! Last one in's a rotten egg!"

"Deke—" Randy began, resetting his glasses on his nose, but that was all he bothered with, because Deke was vaulting the fence and running down the beach, not looking back at Randy or Rachel or LaVerne, only looking out at the raft, which was anchored about fifty yards out on the lake.

Randy looked around, as if to apologize to the girls for getting them into this, but they were looking at Deke—Rachel looking at him was all right, Rachel was Deke's girl, but LaVerne was looking at him too and Randy felt a hot momentary spark of jealousy that got him moving. He peeled off his own sweatshirt, dropped it beside Deke's, and hopped the fence.

"Randy!" LaVerne called, and he only pulled his arm forward through the gray twilit October air in a come-on gesture, hating himself a little for doing it—she was unsure now, perhaps ready to cry it off. The idea of an October swim in the deserted lake wasn't just part of a comfortable, well-lighted bull-session in the apartment he and Deke shared anymore. He liked her, but Deke was stronger. And damned if she didn't have the hots for Deke, and damned if it wasn't irritating.

Deke unbuckled his jeans, still running, and pushed them off his lean hips. He somehow got out of them all the way without stopping, a feat Randy could not have duplicated in a thousand years. Deke ran on, now only wearing bikini briefs, the muscles in his back and buttocks working gorgeously. Randy was more than aware of his own skinny shanks as he dropped his Levi's and clumsily shook them free of his feet—with Deke it was ballet, with him burlesque.

Deke hit the water and bellowed, "Cold! Mother of Jesus!"

Randy hesitated, but only in his mind, where things took longer—*that water's forty-five degrees, fifty at most,* his mind told him. *Your heart could stop.* He was pre-med, he knew that was true . . . but in the physical world he didn't hesitate at all. He leaped it, and for a moment his heart *did* stop, or seemed to; his breath clogged in his throat and he had to force a gasp of air into his lungs as all his submerged skin went numb. *This is crazy,* he thought, and then: *But it was your idea, Pancho.* He began to stroke after Deke.

The two girls looked at each other for a moment. LaVerne shrugged and grinned. "If they can, we can," she said, stripping off her Lacoste shirt to reveal an almost transparent bra. "Aren't girls supposed to have an extra layer of fat?"

Then she was over the fence and running for the water, unbuttoning her cords. After a moment Rachel followed her, much as Randy had followed Deke.

* * *

The girls had come over to the apartment at midafternoon—on Tuesdays a one-o'clock was the latest class any of them had. Deke's monthly allotment had come in—one of the football-mad alums (the players called them "angels") saw that he got two hundred a month in cash—and there was a case of beer in the fridge and a new Night Ranger album on Randy's battered stereo. The four of them set about getting pleasantly oiled. After a while the talk had turned to the end of the long Indian summer they had been enjoying. The radio was predicting flurries for Wednesday. LaVerne had advanced the opinion that weathermen predicting snow flurries in October should be shot, and no one had disagreed.

Rachel said that summers had seemed to last forever when she was a girl, but now that she was an adult ("a doddering senile nineteen," Deke joked, and she kicked his ankle), they got shorter every year. "It seemed like I spent my life out at Cascade Lake," she said, crossing the decayed kitchen linoleum to the icebox. She peered in, found an Iron City Light hiding behind a stack of blue Tupperware storage boxes (the one in the middle contained some nearly prehistoric chili which was now thickly festooned with mold—Randy was a good student and Deke was a good football player, but neither of them was worth a fart in a noisemaker when it came to housekeeping), and appropriated it. "I can still remember the first time I managed to swim all the way out to the raft. I stayed there for damn near two hours, scared to swim back."

She sat down next to Deke, who put an arm around her. She smiled, remembering, and Randy suddenly thought she looked like someone famous or semi-famous. He couldn't quite place the resemblance. It would come to him later, under less pleasant circumstances.

"Finally my brother had to swim out and tow me back on an inner tube. God, he was mad. And I had a sunburn like you wouldn't believe."

"The raft's still out there," Randy said, mostly to say something. He was aware that LaVerne had been looking at Deke again; just lately it seemed like she looked at Deke a lot.

But now she looked at him. "It's almost *Halloween*, Randy. Cascade Beach has been closed since Labor Day."

"Raft's probably still out there, though," Randy said. "We were on the other side of the lake on a geology field trip about three weeks ago and I saw it then. It looked like . . ." He shrugged, ". . . a little bit of summer that somebody forgot to clean up and put away in the closet until next year."

He thought they would laugh at that, but no one did—not even Deke.

"Just because it was there last year doesn't mean it's still there," LaVerne said.

"I mentioned it to a guy," Randy said, finishing his own beer. "Billy DeLois, do you remember him, Deke?"

Deke nodded. "Played second string until he got hurt."

"Yeah, I guess so. Anyway, he comes from out that way, and he said the guys who own the beach never take it in until the lake's almost ready to freeze. Just lazy—at least, that's what he said. He said that some year they'd wait too long and it would get ice-locked."

He fell silent, remembering how the raft had looked, anchored out there on the lake—a square of bright white wood in all that bright blue autumn water. He remembered how the sound of the barrels under it—that buoyant *clunk-clunk* sound—had drifted up to them. The sound was soft, but sounds carried well on the still air around the lake. There had been that sound and the sound of crows squabbling over the remnants of some farmer's harvested garden.

"Snow tomorrow," Rachel said, getting up as Deke's hand wandered almost absently down to the upper swell of her breast. She went to the window and looked out. "What a bummer."

"I'll tell you what," Randy said, "let's go on out to Cascade Lake. We'll swim out to the raft, say good-bye to summer, and then swim back."

If he hadn't been half-loaded he never would have made the suggestion, and he certainly didn't expect anyone to take it seriously. But Deke jumped on it.

"All right! Awesome, Pancho! Fooking *awesome!*" LaVerne jumped and spilled her beer. But she smiled—the smile made Randy a little uneasy. "Let's do it!"

"Deke, you're crazy," Rachel said, also smiling—but her smile looked a little tentative, a little worried.

"No, I'm going to do it," Deke said, going for his coat, and with a mixture of dismay and excitement, Randy noted Deke's grin—reckless and a little crazy. The two of them had been rooming together for three years now—the Jock and the Brain, Cisco and Pancho, Batman and Robin—and Randy recognized that grin. Deke wasn't kidding; he meant to do it. In his head he was already halfway there.

Forget it, Cisco—not me. The words rose to his lips, but before he could say them LaVerne was on her feet, the same cheerful, loony look in her own eyes (or maybe it was just too much beer). "I'm up for it!"

"Then let's go!" Deke looked at Randy. "Whatchoo say, Pancho?"

He had looked at Rachel for a moment then, and saw something almost frantic in her eyes—as far as he himself was concerned, Deke and LaVerne could go out to Cascade Lake together and plow the back forty all night; he would not be delighted with the knowledge that they were boffing each other's brains out, yet neither would he be surprised. But that look in the other girl's eyes, that haunted look—

"Ohhh, *Ceesco!*" Randy cried.

"Ohhhh, *Pancho!*" Deke cried back, delighted.

They slapped palms.

Randy was halfway to the raft when he saw the black patch on the water. It was beyond the raft and to the left of it, more out toward the middle of the lake. Five minutes later the light would have failed too much for him to tell it was anything more than a shadow . . . if he had seen it at all. *Oil slick?* he thought, still pulling hard through the water, faintly aware of the girls splashing behind him. But what would an oil slick be doing on an October-deserted lake? And it was oddly circular, small, surely no more than five feet in diameter—

"*Whoooo!*" Deke shouted again, and Randy looked toward him. Deke was climbing the ladder on the side of the raft, shaking off water like a dog. "Howya doon, Pancho?"

"Okay!" he called back, pulling harder. It really wasn't as bad as he had thought it might be, not once you got in and got moving. His body tingled with warmth and now his motor was in overdrive. He could feel his heart putting out good revs, heating him from the inside out. His folks had a place on Cape Cod, and the water there was worse than this in mid-July.

"You think it's bad now, Pancho, wait'll you get out!" Deke yelled gleefully. He was hopping up and down, making the raft rock, rubbing his body.

Randy forgot about the oil slick until his hands actually grasped the rough, white-painted wood of the ladder on the shore side. Then he saw it again. It was a little closer. A round dark patch on the water, like a big mole, rising and falling on the mild waves. When he had first seen it the patch had been maybe forty yards from the raft. Now it was only half that distance.

How can that be? How—

Then he came out of the water and the cold air bit his skin, bit it even harder than the water had when he first dived in. "Ohhhhhh, *shit!*" He yelled, laughing, shivering in his Jockey shorts.

"Pancho, you ees some kine of beeg asshole," Deke said happily. He pulled Randy up. "Cold enough for you? You sober yet?"

"I'm sober! I'm sober!" He began to jump around as Deke had done, clapping his arms across his chest and stomach in an X. They turned to look at the girls.

Rachel had pulled ahead of LaVerne, who was doing something that looked like a dog paddle performed by a dog with bad instincts.

"You ladies okay?" Deke bellowed.

"Go to hell, Macho City!" LaVerne called, and Deke broke up again.

Randy glanced to the side and saw that odd dark circular patch was even closer—ten yards now, and still coming. It floated on the water, round and regular, like the top of a large steel drum, but the limber way it rode the swells made it clear that it was not the surface of a solid object. Fear, directionless but powerful, suddenly seized him.

"*Swim!*" he shouted at the girls, and bent down to grasp Rachel's hand as she reached the ladder. He hauled her up. She bumped her knee hard—he heard the thud clearly.

"Ow! *Hey!* What—"

LaVerne was still ten feet away. Randy glanced to the side again and saw the round thing nuzzle the offside of the raft. The thing was as dark as oil, but he was sure it wasn't oil—too dark, too thick, too *even*.

"Randy, that *hurt!* What are you doing, being fun—"

"LaVerne! *Swim!*" Now it wasn't just fear, now it was terror.

LaVerne looked up, maybe not hearing the terror but at least hearing the urgency. She looked puzzled but she dog-paddled faster, closing the distance to the ladder.

"Randy, what's wrong with you?" Deke asked.

Randy looked to the side again and saw the thing fold itself around the raft's square corner. For a moment it looked like a Pac-Man image with its mouth open to eat electronic cookies. Then it slipped all the way around the corner and began to slide along the raft, one of its edges now straight.

"Help me get her up!" Randy grunted to Deke, and reached for her hand. "Quick!"

Deke shrugged good-naturedly and reached for LaVerne's other hand. They pulled her up and onto the raft's board surface bare seconds before the black thing slid by the ladder, its sides dimpling as it slipped past the ladder's uprights.

"Randy, have you gone crazy?" LaVarne was out of breath, a little frightened. Her nipples were clearly visible through the bra. They stood out in cold hard points.

"That thing," Randy said, pointing. "Deke? What is it?"

Deke spotted it. It had reached the left-hand corner of the raft. It drifted off a little to one side, reassuming its round shape. It simply floated there. The four of them looked at it.

"Oil slick, I guess," Deke said.

"You really racked my knee," Rachel said, glancing at the dark thing on the water and then back at Randy. "You—"

"It's not an oil slick," Randy said. "Did you ever see a round oil slick? That thing looks like a checker."

"I never saw an oil slick at all," Deke replied. He was talking to Randy but he was looking at LaVerne. LaVerne's panties were almost as transparent as her bra, the delta of her sex sculpted neatly in silk, each buttock a taut crescent. "I don't even believe in them. I'm from Missouri."

"I'm going to bruise," Rachel said, but the anger had gone out of her voice. She had seen Deke looking at LaVerne.

"*God*, I'm cold," LaVerne said. She shivered prettily.

"It went for the girls," Randy said.

"Come on, Pancho. I thought you said you got sober."

"It went for the girls," he repeated stubbornly, and thought: *No one knows we're here. No one at all.*

"Have *you* ever seen an oil slick, Pancho?" He had put his arm around LaVerne's bare shoulders in the same almost-absent way that he had touched Rachel's breast earlier that day. He wasn't touching LaVerne's breast—not yet, anyway—but his hand was close. Randy found he didn't care much, one way or another. That black, circular patch on the water. He cared about that.

"I saw one on the Cape, four years ago," he said. "We all pulled birds out of the surf and tried to clean them off—"

"Ecological, Pancho," Deke said approvingly. "Mucho ecological, I theenk."

Randy said, "It was just this big, sticky mess all over the water. In streaks and big smears. It didn't look like that. It wasn't, you know, *compact*."

It looked like an accident, he wanted to say. *That thing doen't look like an accident; it looks like it's on purpose.*

"I want to go back now," Rachel said. She was still looking at Deke and LaVerne. Randy saw dull hurt in her face. He doubted if she knew it showed.

"So go," LaVerne said. There was a look on her face—*the clarity of absolute triumph*, Randy thought, and if the thought seemed pretentious, it also seemed exactly right. The expression was not aimed precisely at Rachel . . . but neither was LaVerne trying to hide it from the other girl.

She moved a step closer to Deke; a step was all there was. Now their hips touched lightly. For one brief moment Randy's attention passed from the thing floating on the water and focused on LaVerne with an almost exquisite hate. Although he had never hit a girl, in that one moment he could have hit her with real pleasure. Not because he loved her (he had been a little infatuated with her, yes, and more than a little horny for her, yes, and a lot jealous when she had begun to come on to Deke back at the apartment, oh yes, but he wouldn't have brought a girl he actually *loved* within fifteen miles of Deke in the first place), but because he knew that expression on Rachel's face—how that expression felt inside.

"I'm afraid," Rachel said.

"Of an *oil slick?*" LaVerne asked incredulously, and then laughed. The urge to hit her swept over Randy again—to just swing a big roundhouse open-handed blow through the air, to wipe that look of half-assed hauteur from her face and leave a mark on her cheek that would bruise in the shape of a hand.

"Let's see you swim back, then," Randy said.

LaVerne smiled indulgently at him. "I'm not ready to go," she said, as if explaining to a child. She looked up at the sky, then at Deke. "I want to watch the stars come out."

Rachel was a short girl, pretty, but in a gamine, slightly insecure way that made Randy think of New York girls—you saw them hurrying to work in the morning, wearing their smartly tailored skirts with slits in the front or up one side, wearing that same look of slightly neurotic prettiness. Rachel's eyes always sparkled, but it was hard to tell if it was good cheer that lent them that lively look or just free-floating anxiety.

Deke's tastes usually ran more to tall girls with dark hair and sleepy sloe eyes, and Randy saw it was now over between Deke and Rachel—whatever there had been, something simple and maybe a little boring on his part, something deep and complicated and probably painful on hers. It was over, so cleanly and suddenly that Randy almost heard the snap: a sound like dry kindling broken over a knee.

He was a shy boy, but he moved to Rachel now and put an arm around her. She glanced up at him briefly, her face unhappy but grateful for his gesture, and he was glad he had improved the situation for her a little. That similarity bobbed into his mind again. Something in her face, her looks—

He first associated it with TV game shows, then with commercials for crackers or wafers or some damn thing. It came to him then—she looked like Sandy Duncan, the actress who had played in the revival of *Peter Pan* on Broadway.

"What is that thing?" she asked. "Randy? What is it?"

"I don't know."

He glanced at Deke and saw Deke looking at him with that familiar smile that was more loving familiarity than contempt . . . but the contempt was there, too. Maybe Deke didn't even know it, but it was. The expression said *Here goes ole worry-wart*

Randy, pissing in his didies again. It was supposed to make Randy mumble an addition—*It's probably nothing, Don't worry about it, It'll go away.* Something like that. He didn't. Let Deke smile. The black patch on the water scared him. That was the truth.

Rachel stepped away from Randy and knelt prettily on the corner of the raft closest to the thing, and for a moment she triggered an even clearer memory-association: the girl on the White Rock labels. *Sandy Duncan on the White Rock labels,* his mind amended. Her hair, a close-cropped, slightly coarse blond, lay wetly against her finely shaped skull. He could see goosebumps on her shoulder blades above the white band of her bra.

"Don't fall in, Rache," LaVerne said with bright malice.

"Quit it, LaVerne," Deke said, still smiling.

Randy looked from them, standing in the middle of the raft with their arms loosely around each other's waists, hips touching lightly, and back at Rachel. Alarm raced down his spine and out through his nerves like fire. The black patch had halved the distance between it and the corner of the raft where Rachel was kneeling and looking at it. It had been six or eight feet away before. Now the distance was three feet or less. And he saw a strange look in her eyes, a round blankness that seemed queerly like the round blankness of the thing in the water.

Now it's Sandy Duncan sitting on a White Rock label and pretending to be hypnotized by the rich delicious flavor of Nabisco Honey Grahams, he thought idiotically, feeling his heart speed up as it had in the water, and he called out, "Get away from there, Rachel!"

Then everything happened very fast—things happened with the rapidity of fireworks going off. And yet he saw and heard each thing with perfect, hellish clarity. Each thing seemed caught in its own little capsule.

LaVerne laughed—on the quad in a bright afternoon hour it might have sounded like any college girl's laugh, but out here in the growing dark it sounded like the arid cackle of a witch making magic in a pot.

"Rachel, maybe you better get b—" Deke said, but she interrupted him, almost surely for the first time in her life, and indubitably for the last.

"It has colors!" she cried in a voice of utter, trembling wonder. Her eyes stared at the black patch on the water with blank rapture, and for just a moment Randy thought he saw what she was talking about—colors, yeah, colors, swirling in rich, inward-turning spirals. Then they were gone, and there was only dull, lusterless black again. "Such beautiful colors!"

"*Rachel!*"

She reached for it—out and down—her white arm, marbled with gooseflesh, her hand, held out to it, meaning to touch; he saw she had bitten her nails ragged.

"*Ra—*"

He sensed the raft tilt in the water as Deke moved toward them. He reached for Rachel at the same time, meaning to pull her back, dimly aware that he didn't want Deke to be the one to do it.

Then Rachel's hand touched the water—her forefinger only, sending out one delicate ripple in a ring—and the black patch surged over it. Randy heard her gasp in air, and suddenly the blankness left her eyes. What replaced it was agony.

The black, viscous substance ran up her arm like mud . . . and under it, Randy saw her skin dissolving. She opened her mouth and screamed. At the same moment she began to tilt outward. She waved her other hand blindly at Randy and he grabbed for it. Their fingers brushed. Her eyes met his, and she still looked hellishly like Sandy Duncan. Then she fell outward and splashed into the water.

The black thing flowed over the spot where she had landed.

"*What happened?*" LaVerne was screaming behind them. "*What happened? Did she fall in? What happened to her?*"

Randy made as if to dive in after her and Deke pushed him backwards with casual force. "No," he said in a frightened voice that was utterly unlike Deke.

All three of them saw her flail to the surface. Her arms came up, waving—no, not arms. One arm. The other was covered with a black membrane that hung in flaps and folds from something red and knitted with tendons, something that looked a little like a rolled roast of beef.

"*Help!*" Rachel screamed. Her eyes glared at them, away from them, at them, away—her eyes were like lanterns being waved aimlessly in the dark. She beat the water into a froth. "*Help it hurts please help it hurts IT HURTS IT HURRRRR—*"

Randy had fallen when Deke pushed him. Now he got up from the boards of the raft and stumbled forward again, unable to ignore that voice. He tried to jump in and Deke grabbed him, wrapping his big arms around Randy's thin chest.

"No, she's dead," he whispered harshly. "Christ, can't you see that? She's *dead*, Pancho."

Thick blackness suddenly poured across Rachel's face like a drape, and her screams were first muffled and then cut off entirely. Now the black stuff seemed to bind her in crisscrossing ropes. Randy could see it sinking into her like acid, and when her jugular vein gave way in a dark, pumping jet, he saw the thing send out a pseudopod after the escaping blood. He could not believe what he was seeing, could not understand it . . . but there was no doubt, no sensation of losing his mind, no belief that he was dreaming or hallucinating.

LaVerne was screaming. Randy turned to look at her just in time to see her slap a hand melodramatically over her eyes like a silent movie heroine. He thought he would laugh and tell her this, but found he could not make a sound.

He looked back at Rachel. Rachel was almost not there anymore.

Her struggles had weakened to the point where they were really no more than spasms. The blackness oozed over her—*bigger now*, Randy thought, *it's bigger, no question about it*—with mute, muscular power. He saw her hand beat at it; saw the hand become stuck, as if in molasses or on flypaper; saw it consumed. Now there was a sense of her form only, not in the water but in the black thing, not turning but being turned, the form becoming less recognizable, a white flash—*bone*, he thought sickly, and turned away, vomiting helplessly over the side of the raft.

LaVerne was still screaming. Then there was a dull *whap!* and she stopped screaming and began to snivel.

He hit her, Randy thought. *I was going to do that, remember?*

He stepped back, wiping his mouth, feeling weak and ill. And scared. So scared he could think with only one tiny wedge of his mind. Soon he would begin to scream himself. Then Deke would have to slap him, Deke wouldn't panic, oh no, Deke was hero material for sure. *You gotta be a football hero . . . to get along with the beautiful girls*, his mind sang cheerfully. Then he could hear Deke talking to him, and he looked up at the sky, trying to clear his head, trying desperately to put away the vision of Rachel's form becoming blobbish and inhuman as that black thing ate her, not wanting Deke to slap him the way he had slapped LaVerne.

He looked up at the sky and saw the first stars shining up there—the shape of the Dipper already clear as the last white light faded out of the west. It was nearly seven-thirty.

"Oh Ceeesco," he managed. "We are in beeg trouble thees time, I theeenk."

"What is it?" His hand fell on Randy's shoulder, gripping and twisting painfully. "It ate her, did you see that? It *ate* her, it fucking *ate her up!* What *is* it?"

"I don't know. Didn't you hear me before?"

"You're *supposed* to know, you're a fucking brain-ball, you take all the fucking science courses!" Now Deke was almost screaming himself, and that helped Randy get a little more control.

"There's nothing like that in any science book I ever read," Randy told him. "The last time I saw anything like that was the Halloween Shock-Show down at the Rialto when I was twelve."

The thing had regained its round shape now. It floated on the water ten feet from the raft.

"It's bigger," LaVerne moaned.

When Randy had first seen it, he had guessed its diameter at about five feet. Now it had to be at least eight feet across.

"*It's bigger because it ate Rachel!*" LaVerne cried, and began to scream again.

"Stop that or I'm going to break your jaw," Deke said, and she stopped—not all at once, but winding down the way a record does when somebody turns off the juice without taking the needle off the disc. Her eyes were huge things.

Deke looked back at Randy. "You all right, Pancho?"

"I don't know. I guess so."

"My man." Deke tried to smile, and Randy saw with some alarm that he was succeeding—was some part of Deke enjoying this? "You don't have any idea at all what it might be?"

Randy shook his head. Maybe it was an oil slick, after all . . . or had been, until something had happened to it. Maybe cosmic rays had hit it in a certain way. Or maybe Arthur Godfrey had pissed atomic Bisquick all over it, who knew? Who *could* know?

"Can we swim past it, do you think?" Deke persisted, shaking Randy's shoulder.

"*No!*" LaVerne shrieked.

"Stop it or I'm gonna smoke you, LaVerne," Deke said, raising his voice again. "I'm not kidding."

"You saw how fast it took Rachel," Randy said.

"Maybe it was hungry then," Deke answered. "But maybe now it's full."

Randy thought of Rachel kneeling there on the corner of the raft, so still and pretty in her bra and panties, and felt his gorge rise again.

"You try it," he said to Deke.

Deke grinned humorlessly. "Oh Pancho."

"Oh Ceesco."

"I want to go home," LaVerne said in a furtive whisper. "Okay?"

Neither of them replied.

"So we wait for it to go away," Deke said. "It came, it'll go away."

"Maybe," Randy said.

Deke looked at him, his face full of a fierce concentration in the gloom. "Maybe? What's this maybe shit?"

"We came, and it came. I saw it come—like it smelled us. If it's full, like you say, it'll go. I guess. If it still wants chow—" He shrugged.

Deke stood thoughtfully, head bent. His short hair was still dripping a little.

"We wait," he said. "Let it eat fish."

Fifteen minutes passed. They didn't talk. It got colder. It was maybe fifty degrees and all three of them were in their underwear. After the first ten minutes, Randy could hear the brisk, intermittent clickety-click of his teeth. LaVerne had tried to move next to Deke, but he pushed her away—gently but firmly enough.

"Let me be for now," he said.

So she sat down, arms crossed over her breasts, hands cupping her elbows, shivering. She looked at Randy, her eyes telling him he could come back, put his arm around her, it was okay now.

He looked away instead, back at the dark circle on the water. It just floated there, not coming any closer, but not going away, either. He looked toward the shore and there was the beach, a ghostly white crescent that seemed to float. The trees behind it made a dark, bulking horizon line. He thought he could see Deke's Camaro, but he wasn't sure.

"We just picked up and went," Deke said.

"That's right," Randy said.

"Didn't tell anyone."

"No."

"So no one knows we're here."

"No."

"Stop it!" LaVerne shouted. "Stop it, you're scaring me!"

"Shut your pie-hole," Deke said absently, and Randy laughed in spite of himself—no matter how many times Deke said that, it always slew him. "If we have to spend the night out here, we do. Somebody'll hear us yelling tomorrow. We're hardly in the middle of the Australian Outback, are we, Randy?"

Randy said nothing.

"*Are* we?"

"You know where we are," Randy said. "You know as well as I do. We turned off Route 41, we came up eight miles of back road—"

"Cottages every fifty feet—"

"*Summer* cottages. This is October. They're empty, the whole bucking funch of them. We got here and you had to drive around the damn gate, NO TRESPASSING signs every fifty feet—"

"So? A caretaker—" Deke was sounding a little pissed now, a little off-balance. A little scared? For the first time tonight, for the first time this month, this year, maybe for the first time in his whole life? Now there was an awesome thought—Deke loses his fear-cherry. Randy was not sure it was happening, but he thought maybe it was . . . and he took a perverse pleasure in it.

"Nothing to steal, nothing to vandalize," he said. "If there's a caretaker, he probably pops by here on a bimonthly basis."

"Hunters—"

"Next month, yeah," Randy said, and shut his mouth with a snap. He had also succeeded in scaring himself.

"Maybe it'll leave us alone," LaVerne said. Her lips made a pathetic, loose little smile. "Maybe it'll just . . . you know . . . leave us alone."

Deke said, "Maybe pigs will—"

"It's moving," Randy said.

LaVerne leaped to her feet. Deke came to where Randy was and for a moment the raft tilted, scaring Randy's heart into a gallop and making LaVerne scream again. Then Deke stepped back a little and the raft stabilized, with the left front corner (as they faced the shoreline) dipped down slightly more than the rest of the raft.

It came with an oily, frightening speed, and as it did, Randy saw the colors Rachel had seen—fantastic reds and yellows and blues spiraling across an ebony surface like limp plastic or dark, lithe Naugahyde. It rose and fell with the waves and that changed the colors, made them swirl and blend. Randy realized he was going to fall over, fall right into it, he could feel himself tilting out—

With the last of his strength he brought his right fist up into his own nose—the gesture of a man stifling a cough, only a little high and a lot hard. His nose flared with pain, he felt blood run warmly down his face, and then he was able to step back, crying out: "Don't look at it! Deke! Don't look right at it, the colors make you loopy!"

"It's trying to get under the raft," Deke said grimly. "What's this shit, Pancho?"

Randy looked—he looked very carefully. He saw the thing nuzzling the side of the raft, flattening to a shape like half a pizza. For a moment it seemed to be piling up there, thickening, and he had an alarming vision of it piling up enough to run onto the surface of the raft.

Then it squeezed under. He thought he heard a noise for a moment—a rough noise, like a roll of canvas being pulled through a narrow window—but that might have only been nerves.

"Did it go under?" LaVerne said, and there was something oddly nonchalant about her tone, as if she were trying with all her might to be conversational, but she was screaming, too. "Did it go under the raft? Is it under us?"

"Yes," Deke said. He looked at Randy. "I'm going to swim for it right now," he said. "If it's under there I've got a good chance."

"No!" LaVerne screamed. "No, don't leave us here, don't—"

"I'm fast," Deke said, looking at Randy, ignoring LaVerne completely. "But I've got to go while it's under there."

Randy's mind felt as if it was whizzing along at Mach two—in a greasy, nauseating way it was exhilarating, like the last few seconds before you puke into the slipstream of a cheap carnival ride. There was time to hear the barrels under the raft clunking hollowly together, time to hear the leaves on the trees beyond the beach rattling dryly in a little puff of wind, time to wonder why it had gone under the raft.

"Yes," he said to Deke. "But I don't think you'll make it."

"I'll make it," Deke said, and started toward the edge of the raft.

He got two steps and then stopped.

His breath had been speeding up, his brain getting his heart and lungs ready to swim the fastest fifty yards of his life and now his breath stopped like the rest of him, simply stopped in the middle of an inhale. He turned his head, and Randy saw the cords in his neck stand out.

"Panch—" he said in an amazed, choked voice, and then he began to scream.

He screamed with amazing force, great baritone bellows that splintered up toward wild soprano levels. They were loud enough to echo back from the shore in ghostly half-notes. At first Randy thought he was just screaming, and then he realized it was a word—no, two words, the same two words over and over: *"My foot!"* Deke was screaming. *"My foot! My foot! My foot!"*

Randy looked down. Deke's foot had taken on an odd sunken look. The reason was obvious, but Randy's mind refused to accept it at first—it was too impossible, too insanely grotesque. As he watched, Deke's foot was being pulled down between two of the boards that made up the surface of the raft.

Then he saw the dark shine of the black thing beyond the heel and the toes, dark shine alive with swirling, malevolent colors.

The thing had his foot (*"My foot!"* Deke screamed, as if to confirm this elementary deduction. *"My foot, oh my foot, my FOOOOOOT!"*). He had stepped on one of the cracks between the boards (*step on a crack, break yer mother's back*, Randy's mind gibbered), and the thing had been down there. The thing had—

"Pull!" he screamed back suddenly. *"Pull, Deke, goddammit, PULL!"*

"What's happening?" LaVerne hollered, and Randy realized dimly that she wasn't just shaking his shoulder; she had sunk her spade-shaped fingernails into him like claws. She was going to be absolutely no help at all. He drove an elbow into her stomach. She made a barking, coughing noise and sat down on her fanny. He leaped to Deke and grabbed one of Deke's arms.

It was as hard as Carrara marble, every muscle standing out like the rib of a sculpted dinosaur skeleton. Pulling Deke was like trying to pull a big tree out of the ground by the roots. Deke's eyes were turned up toward the royal purple of the post-dusk sky, glazed and unbelieving, and still he screamed, screamed, screamed.

Randy looked down and saw that Deke's foot had now disappeared into the crack between the boards up to the ankle. That crack was perhaps only a quarter of an inch wide, surely no more than half an inch, but his foot had gone into it. Blood ran across the white boards in thick dark tendrils. Black stuff like heated plastic pulsed up and down in the crack, up and down, like a heart beating.

Got to get him out. Got to get him out quick or we're never gonna get him out at all . . . hold on, Cisco, please hold on . . .

LaVerne got to her feet and backed away from the gnarled, screaming Deke-tree in the center of the raft which floated at anchor under the October stars on Cascade Lake. She was shaking her head numbly, her arms crossed over her belly where Randy's elbow had gotten her.

Deke leaned hard against him, arms groping stupidly. Randy looked down and saw blood gushing from Deke's shin, which now tapered the way a sharpened pencil tapers to a point—only the point here was white, not black, the point was a bone, barely visible.

The black stuff surged up again, sucking, eating.

Deke wailed.

Never going to play football on that foot again, WHAT foot, ha-ha, and he pulled Deke with all his might and it was still like pulling at a rooted tree.

Deke lurched again and now he uttered a long, drilling shriek that made Randy fall back, shrieking himself, hands covering his ears. Blood burst from the pores of Deke's calf and shin; his kneecap had taken on a purple, bulging look as it tried to absorb the tremendous pressure being put on it as the black thing hauled Deke's leg down through the narrow crack inch by inch.

Can't help him. How strong it must be! Can't help him now, I'm sorry, Deke, so sorry—

"Hold me, Randy," LaVerne screamed, clutching at him everywhere, digging her face into his chest. Her face was so hot it seemed to sizzle. "Hold me, please, won't you hold me—"

This time, he did.

It was only later that a terrible realization came to Randy: the two of them could almost surely have swum ashore while the black thing was busy with Deke—and if LaVerne refused to try it, he could have done it himself. The keys to the Camaro were in Deke's jeans, lying on the beach. He could have done it . . . but the realization that he could have never came to him until too late.

Deke died just as his thigh began to disappear into the narrow crack between the boards. He had stopped shrieking minutes before. Since then he had uttered only thick, syrupy grunts. Then those stopped, too. When he fainted, falling forward, Randy heard whatever remained of the femur in his right leg splinter in a greenstick fracture.

A moment later Deke raised his head, looked around groggily, and opened his mouth. Randy thought he meant to scream again. Instead, he voided a great jet of blood, so thick it was almost solid. Both Randy and LaVerne were splattered with its warmth and she began to scream again, hoarsely now.

"*Oooog!*" she cried, her face twisted in half-mad revulsion. "*Oooog!* Blood! *Ooooog*, blood! *Blood!*" She rubbed at herself and only succeeded in smearing it around.

Blood was pouring from Deke's eyes, coming with such force that they had bugged out almost comically with the force of the hemorrhage. Randy thought: *Talk about vitality! Christ, LOOK at that! He's like a goddammed human fire hydrant! God! God! God!*

Blood streamed from both of Deke's ears. His face was a hideous purple turnip, swelled shapeless with the hydrostatic pressure of some unbelievable reversal; it was the face of a man being clutched in a bear hug of monstrous and unknowable force.

And then, mercifully, it was over.

Deke collapsed forward again, his hair hanging down on the raft's bloody boards, and Randy saw with sickish amazement that even Deke's scalp had bled.

Sounds from under the raft. Sucking sounds.

That was when it occurred to his tottering, overloaded mind that he could swim for it and stand a good chance of making it. But LaVerne had gotten heavy in his arms, ominously heavy; he looked at her slack face, rolled back an eyelid to disclose only white, and knew that she had not fainted but fallen into a state of shock-unconsciousness.

Randy looked at the surface of the raft. He could lay her down, of course, but the boards were only a foot across. There was a diving board platform attached to the raft in the summertime, but that, at least, had been taken down and stored somewhere. Nothing left but the surface of the raft itself, fourteen boards, each a foot wide and twenty feet long. No way to put her down without laying her unconscious body across any number of those cracks.

Step on a crack, break your mother's back.

Shut up.

And then, tenebrously, his mind whispered: *Do it anyway. Put her down and swim for it.*

But he did not, could not. An awful guilt rose in him at the thought. He held her, feeling the soft, steady drag on his arms and back. She was a big girl.

Deke went down.

Randy held LaVerne in his aching arms and watched it happen. He did not want to, and for long seconds that might even have been minutes he turned his face away entirely; but his eyes always wandered back.

With Deke dead, it seemed to go faster.

The rest of his right leg disappeared, his left leg stretching out further and further until Deke looked like a one-legged ballet dancer doing an impossible split. There was the wishbone crack of his pelvis, and then, as Deke's stomach began to swell ominously with new pressure, Randy looked away for a long time, trying not to hear the wet sounds, trying to concentrate on the pain in his arms. He could maybe bring her around, he thought, but for the time being it was better to have the throbbing pain in his arms and shoulders. It gave him something to think about.

From behind him came a sound like strong teeth crunching up a mouthful of candy jawbreakers. When he looked back, Deke's ribs were collapsing into the crack. His arms were up and out, and he looked like an obscene parody of Richard Nixon giving the V-for-victory sign that had driven demonstrators wild in the sixties and seventies.

His eyes were open. His tongue had popped out at Randy.

Randy looked away again, out across the lake. *Look for lights,* he told himself. He knew there were no lights over there, but he told himself that anyway. *Look for lights over there, somebody's got to be staying the week in his place, fall foliage, shouldn't miss it, bring your Nikon, folks back home are going to love the slides.*

When he looked back, Deke's arms were straight up. He wasn't Nixon anymore; now he was a football ref signaling that the extra point had been good.

Deke's head appeared to be sitting on the boards.

His eyes were still open.

His tongue was still sticking out.

"Oh Ceesco," Randy muttered, and looked away again. His arms and shoulders were shrieking now, but still he held her in his arms. He looked at the far side of the lake. The far side of the lake was dark. Stars unrolled across the black sky, a spill of cold milk somehow suspended high in the air.

Minutes passed. *He'll be gone now. You can look now. Okay, yeah, all right. But don't look. Just to be safe, don't look. Agreed? Agreed. Most definitely. So say we all and so say all of us.*

So he looked anyway and was just in time to see Deke's fingers being pulled down. They were moving—probably the motion of the water under the raft was being transmitted to the unknowable thing which had caught Deke, and that motion was then being transmitted to Deke's fingers. Probably, probably. But it looked to Randy as if Deke was waving to him. The Cisco Kid was waving adiós. For the first time he felt his mind give a sickening wrench—it seemed to cant the way the raft itself had canted when all four of them had stood on the same side. It righted itself, but Randy suddenly understood that madness—real lunacy—was perhaps not far away at all.

Deke's football ring—All-Conference, 1981—slid slowly up the third finger of his right hand. The starlight rimmed the gold and played in the minute gutters between the engraved numbers, 19 on one side of the reddish stone, 81 on the other. The ring slid off his finger. The ring was a little too big to fit down through the crack, and of course it wouldn't squeeze.

It lay there. It was all that was left of Deke now. Deke was gone. No more dark-haired girls with sloe eyes, no more flicking Randy's bare rump with a wet towel when Randy came out of the shower, no more breakaway runs from midfield with fans rising to their feet in the bleachers and cheerleaders turning hysterical cartwheels along the sidelines. No more fast rides after dark in the Camaro with Thin Lizzy blaring "The Boys Are Back in Town" out of the tape deck. No more Cisco Kid.

There was that faint rasping noise again—a roll of canvas being pulled slowly through a slit of a window.

Randy was standing with his bare feet on the boards. He looked down and saw the cracks on either side of both feet suddenly filled with slick darkness. His eyes bulged. He thought of the way the blood had come spraying from Deke's mouth in an almost solid rope, the way Deke's eyes had bugged out as if on springs as hemorrhages caused by hydrostatic pressure pulped his brain.

It smells me. It knows I'm here. Can it come up? Can it get up through the cracks? Can it? Can it?

He stared down, unaware of LaVerne's limp weight now, fascinated by the enormity of the question, wondering what the stuff would feel like when it flowed over his feet, when it hooked into him.

The black shininess humped up almost to the edge of the cracks (Randy rose on tiptoes without being at all aware he was doing it), and then it went down. That canvasy slithering resumed. And suddenly Randy saw it on the water again, a great dark mole, now perhaps fifteen feet across. It rose and fell with the mild wavelets, rose and fell, rose and fell, and when Randy began to see the colors pulsing evenly across it, he tore his eyes away.

He put LaVerne down, and as soon as his muscles unlocked, his arms began to shake wildly. He let them shake. He knelt beside her, her hair spread across the white boards in an irregular dark fan. He knelt and watched that dark mole on the water, ready to yank her up again if it showed any signs of moving.

He began to slap her lightly, first one cheek and then the other, back and forth, like a second trying to bring a fighter around. LaVerne didn't want to come around. LaVerne did not want to pass Go and collect two hundred dollars or take a ride on the Reading. LaVerne had seen enough. But Randy couldn't guard her all night, lifting her like a canvas sack every time that thing moved (and you couldn't look at the thing too long; that was another thing). He had learned a trick, though. He hadn't learned it in college. He had learned it from a friend of his older brother's. This friend had been a paramedic in Nam, and he knew all sorts of tricks—how to catch head lice off a human scalp and make them race in a matchbox, how to cut cocaine with baby laxative, how to sew up deep cuts with ordinary needle and thread. One day they had been talking about ways to bring abysmally drunken folks around so these abysmally drunken people wouldn't puke down their own throats and die, as Bon Scott, the lead singer of AC/DC, had done.

"You want to bring someone around in a hurry?" the friend with the catalogue of interesting tricks had said. "Try this." And he told Randy the trick which Randy now used.

He leaned over and bit LaVerne's earlobe as hard as he could.

Hot, bitter blood squirted into his mouth. LaVerne's eyelids flew up like windowshades. She screamed in a hoarse, growling voice and struck out at him. Randy looked up and saw the far side of the thing only; the rest of it was already under the raft. It had moved with eerie, horrible, silent speed.

He jerked LaVerne up again, his muscles screaming protest, trying to knot into charley horses. She was beating at his face. One of her hands struck his sensitive nose and he saw red stars.

"Quit it!" he shouted, shuffling his feet onto the boards. "Quit it, you bitch, it's under us again, quit it or I'll fucking drop you, I swear to God I will!"

Her arms immediately stopped flailing at him and closed quietly around his neck in a drowner's grip. Her eyes looked white in the swimming starlight.

"Stop it!" She didn't. "Stop it, LaVerne, you're choking me!"

Tighter. Panic flared in his mind. The hollow clunk of the barrels had taken on a duller, muffled note—it was the thing underneath, he supposed.

"I can't breathe!"

The hold loosened a little.

"Now listen. I'm going to put you down. It's all right if you—"

But *put you down* was all she had heard. Her arms tightened in that deadly grip again. His right hand was on her back. He hooked it into a claw and raked at her. She kicked her legs, mewling harshly, and for a moment he almost lost his balance. She felt it. Fright rather than pain made her stop struggling.

"Stand on the boards."

"No!" Her air puffed a hot desert wind against his cheek.

"It can't get you if you stand on the boards."

"No, don't put me down, it'll get me, I know it will, I know—"

He raked at her back again. She screamed in anger and pain and fear. "You get down or I'll drop you, LaVerne."

He lowered her slowly and carefully, both of them breathing in sharp little whines—oboe and flute. Her feet touched the boards. She jerked her legs up as if the boards were hot.

"Put them *down!*" He hissed at her. "I'm not Deke, I can't hold you all night!"

"Deke—"

"Dead."

Her feet touched the boards. Little by little he let go of her. They faced each other like dancers. He could see her waiting for its first touch. Her mouth gaped like the mouth of a goldfish.

"Randy," she whispered. "Where is it?"

"Under. Look down."

She did. He did. They saw the blackness stuffing the cracks, stuffing them almost all the way across the raft now. Randy sensed its eagerness, and thought she did, too.

"Randy, please—"

"Shhhh."

They stood there.

Randy had forgotten to strip off his watch when he ran into the water, and now he marked off fifteen minutes. At a quarter past eight, the black thing slid out from under the raft again. It drew about fifteen feet off and then stopped as it had before.

"I'm going to sit down," he said.

"No!"

"I'm tired," he said. "I'm going to sit down and you're going to watch it. Just remember to keep looking away. Then I'll get up and you sit down. We go like that. Here." He gave her his watch. "Fifteen-minute shifts."

"It ate Deke," she whispered.

"Yes."

"What is it?"

"I don't know."

"I'm cold."

"Me too."

"Hold me, then."

"I've held you enough."

She subsided.

Sitting down was heaven; not having to watch the thing was bliss. He watched LaVerne instead, making sure that her eyes kept shifting away from the thing on the water.

"What are we going to do, Randy?"

He thought.

"Wait," he said.

At the end of fifteen minutes he stood up and let her first sit and then lie down for half an hour. Then he got her on her feet again and she stood for fifteen minutes. They went back and forth. At a quarter of ten, a cold rind of moon rose and beat a path across the water. At ten-thirty, a shrill, lonely cry rose, echoing across the water, and LaVerne shrieked.

"Shut up," he said. "It's just a loon."

"I'm freezing, Randy—I'm numb all over."

"I can't do anything about it."

"Hold me," she said. "You've got to. We'll hold each other. We can both sit down and watch it together."

He debated, but the cold sinking into his own flesh was now bone-deep, and that decided him. "Okay."

They sat together, arms wrapped around each other, and something happened—natural or perverse, it happened. He felt himself stiffening. One of his hands found her breast, cupped in damp nylon, and squeezed. She made a sighing noise, and her hand stole to the crotch of his underpants.

He slid his other hand down and found a place where there was some heat. He pushed her down on her back.

"No," she said, but the hand in his crotch began to move faster.

"I can see it," he said. His heartbeat had sped up again, pushing blood faster, pushing warmth toward the surface of his chilled bare skin. "I can watch it."

She murmured something, and he felt elastic slide down his hips to his upper thighs. He watched it. He slid upward, forward, into her. Warmth. God, she was warm there, at least. She made a guttural noise and her fingers grabbed at his cold, clenched buttocks.

He watched it. It wasn't moving. He watched it. He watched it closely. The tactile sensations were incredible, fantastic. He was not experienced, but neither was he a virgin; he had made love with three girls and it had never been like this. She moaned and began to lift her hips. The raft rocked gently, like the world's hardest waterbed. The barrels underneath murmured hollowly.

He watched it. The colors began to swirl—slowly now, sensuously, not threatening; he watched it and he watched the colors. His eyes were wide. The colors were in his eyes. He wasn't cold now; he was hot now, hot the way you got your first day back on the beach in early June, when you could feel the sun tightening your winter-white skin, reddening it, giving it some

(colors)

color, some tint. First day at the beach, first day of summer, drag out the Beach Boys oldies, drag out the Ramones. The Ramones were telling you that Sheena is a punk rocker, the Ramones were telling you that you can hitch a ride to Rockaway Beach, the sand, the beach, the colors

(moving it's starting to move)

and the feel of summer, the texture; Gary U.S. Bonds, school is out and I can root for the Yankees from the bleachers, girls in bikinis on the beach, the beach, the beach, oh do you love do you love

(love)

the beach do you love

(love I love)

firm breasts fragrant with Coppertone oil, and if the bottom of the bikini was small enough you might see some

(hair her hair HER HAIR IS IN THE OH GOD IN THE WATER HER HAIR)

He pulled back suddenly, trying to pull her up, but the thing moved with oily speed and tangled itself in her hair like a webbing of thick black glue and when he pulled her up she was already screaming and she was heavy with it; it came out of the water in a twisting, gruesome membrane that rolled with flaring nuclear colors—scarlet-vermilion, flaring emerald, sullen ocher.

It flowed down over LaVerne's face in a tide, obliterating it.

Her feet kicked and drummed. The thing twisted and moved where her face had been. Blood ran down her neck in streams. Screaming, not hearing himself scream, Randy ran at her, put his foot against her hip, and shoved. She went flopping and tumbling over the side, her legs like alabaster in the moonlight. For a few endless moments the water frothed and splashed against the side of the raft, as if someone had hooked the world's largest bass in there and it was fighting like hell.

Randy screamed. He screamed. And then, for variety, he screamed some more.

Some half an hour later, long after the frantic splashing and struggling had ended, the loons began to scream back.

That night was forever.

The sky began to lighten in the east around a quarter to five, and he felt a sluggish rise in his spirit. It was momentary; as false as the dawn. He stood on the boards, his eyes half closed, his chin on his chest. He had been sitting on the boards until an hour ago, and had been suddenly awakened— without even knowing until then that he had fallen asleep, that was the scary part—by that unspeakable hissing-canvas sound. He leaped to his feet bare seconds before the blackness began to suck eagerly for him between the boards. His breath whined in and out; he bit at his lip, making it bleed.

Asleep, you were asleep, you asshole!

The thing had oozed out from under again half an hour later, but he hadn't sat down again. He was afraid to sit down, afraid he would go to sleep and that this time his mind wouldn't trip him awake in time.

His feet were still planted squarely on the boards as a stronger light, real dawn this time, filled the east and the first morning birds began to sing. The sun came up, and by six o'clock the day was bright enough for him to be able to see the beach. Deke's camaro, bright yellow, was right where Deke had parked it, nose in to the pole fence. A bright litter of shirts and sweaters and four pairs of jeans were twisted into little shapes along the beach. The sight of them filled him with fresh horror when he thought his capacity for horror must surely be exhausted. He could see *his* jeans, one leg pulled inside out, the pocket showing. His jeans looked so *safe* lying there on the sand; just waiting for him to come along and pull the inside-out leg back through so it was right, grasping the pocket as he did so the change wouldn't fall out. He could almost feel them whispering up his legs, could feel himself buttoning the brass button above the fly—

(do you love yes I love)

He looked left and there it was, black, round as a checker, floating lightly. Colors began to swirl across its hide and he looked away quickly.

"Go home," he croaked. "Go home or go to California and find a Roger Corman movie to audition for."

A plane droned somewhere far away, and he fell into a dozing fantasy: *We are reported missing, the four of us. The search spreads outward from Horlicks. A farmer remembers being passed by a yellow Camaro "going like a bat out of hell." The search centers in the Cascade Lake area. Private pilots volunteer to do a quick aerial search, and one guy, buzzing the lake in his Beechcraft Twin Bonanza, sees a kid standing naked on the raft, one kid, one survivor, one—*

He caught himself on the edge of toppling over and brought his fist into his nose again, screaming at the pain.

The black thing arrowed at the raft immediately and squeezed underneath—it could hear, perhaps, or sense . . . or *something.*

Randy waited.

This time it was forty-five minutes before it came out.

His mind slowly orbited in the growing light.

(do you love yes I love rooting for the Yankees   and Catfish   do you love the Catfish yes I love the
(Route 66 remember the Corvette George Maharis in the Corvette Martin Milner in the Corvette do you love the Corvette
(yes I love the Corvette
(I love do you love
(so hot the sun is like a burning glass it was in her hair and it's the light I remember best the light the summer light
(the summer light of)

afternoon.

Randy was crying.

He was crying because something new had been added now—every time he tried to sit down, the thing slid under the raft. It wasn't entirely stupid, then; it had either sensed or figured out that it could get at him while he was sitting down.

"Go away," Randy wept at the great black mole floating on the water. Fifty yards away, mockingly close, a squirrel was scampering back and forth on the hood of Deke's Camaro. "Go away, please, go anywhere, but leave me alone. I don't love you."

The thing didn't move. Colors began to swirl across its visible surface.

(you do you do love me)

Randy tore his eyes away and looked at the beach, looked for rescue, but there was no one there, no one at all. His jeans still lay there, one leg inside out, the white lining of one pocket showing. They no longer looked to him as if someone was going to pick them up. They looked like relics.

He thought: *If I had a gun, I would kill myself now.*

He stood on the raft.

The sun went down.

Three hours later, the moon came up.

Not long after that, the loons began to scream.

Not long after *that,* Randy turned and looked at the black thing on the water. He could not kill himself, but perhaps the thing could fix it so there was no pain; perhaps that was what the colors were for.

(do you do you do you love)

He looked for it and it was there, floating, riding the waves.

"Sing with me," Randy croaked. "I can root for the Yankees from the bleachers . . . I don't have to worry 'bout teachers . . . I'm so glad that school is out . . . I am gonna . . . sing and shout."

The colors began to form and twist. This time Randy did not look away.

He whispered, "Do you love?"

Somewhere, far across the empty lake, a loon screamed.

❖ ROBERT R(ICHARD) McCAMMON (1952-)

As did a number of Fantasy and Science Fiction authors before him, Robert McCammon began his writing career as a journalist. McCammon's early works were Horror novels, and the first of these included Baal *(1978),* Bethany's Sin *(1979),* Night Boat *(1980),* They Thirst *(1981), and* Mystery Walk *(1983). These early novels drew favorable comparisons to works by other best-selling Horror authors of the 1970s and 1980s, most notably Stephen King. However, each of these novels stands as an excellent story with its own unique merits. As well recognized as he has become in the 1980s and 1990s, Robert McCammon, along with Peter Straub, is not as celebrated as he should be, even though McCammon and Straub continue to be best-selling authors.*

McCammon's Usher's Passing *(1984) is a classic of the Dark Fantasy genre. In terms of technique and execution, this tribute to Poe ranks with Straub's* Ghost Story *(1979) and Stephen King's* The Shining *(1980) in its importance to the development of Dark Fantasy in the late twentieth century.*

"Nightcrawlers" was made into a suspenseful teleplay.

Nightcrawlers

(Masques, *edited by J. N. Wiliamson, 1984*)

1

"Hard rain coming down," Cheryl said, and I nodded in agreement.

Through the diner's plate-glass windows, a dense curtain of rain flapped across the Gulf gas pumps and continued across the parking lot. It hit Big Bob's with a force that made the glass rattle like uneasy bones. The red neon sign that said BIG BOB'S! DIESEL FUEL! EATS! sat on top of a high steel pole above the diner so the truckers on the interstate could see it. Out in the night, the red-tinted rain thrashed in torrents across my old pickup truck and Cheryl's baby-blue Volkswagen.

"Well," I said, "I suppose that storm'll either wash some folks in off the interstate or we can just about hang it up." The curtain of rain parted for an instant, and I could see the treetops whipping back and forth in the woods on the other side of Highway 47. Wind whined around the front door like an animal trying to claw its way in. I glanced at the electric clock on the wall behind the counter. Twenty minutes before nine. We usually closed up at ten, but tonight—with tornado warnings in the weather forecast—I was tempted to turn the lock a little early. "Tell you what," I said. "If we're empty at nine, we skedaddle. 'Kay?"

"No argument here," she said. She watched the storm for a moment longer, then continued putting newly washed coffee cups, saucers, and plates away on the stainless-steel shelves.

Lightning flared from west to east like the strike of a burning bullwhip. The diner's lights flickered, then came back to normal. A shudder of thunder seemed to come right up through my shoes. Late March is the beginning of tornado season in south Alabama, and we've had some whoppers spin past here in the last few years. I knew that Alma was at home, and she understood to get into the root cellar right quick if she spotted a twister, like that one we saw in '82 dancing through the woods about two miles from our farm.

"You got any love-ins planned this weekend, hippie?" I asked Cheryl, mostly to get my mind off the storm and to rib her too.

She was in her late thirties, but I swear that when she grinned she could've passed for a kid. "Wouldn't *you* like to know, redneck?" she answered; she replied the same way to all my digs at her. Cheryl Lovesong—and I *know* that couldn't have been her real name—was a mighty able waitress, and she had hands that were no strangers to hard work. But I didn't care that she wore her long silvery-blond hair in Indian braids with hippie headbands, or came to work in tie-dyed overalls. She was the best waitress who'd ever worked for me, and she got along with everybody just fine—even us rednecks. That's what I am, and proud of it: I drink Rebel Yell whiskey straight, and my favorite songs are about good women gone bad and trains on the long track to nowhere. I keep my wife happy. I've raised my two boys to pray to God and to salute the flag, and if anybody don't like it he can go a few rounds with Big Bob Clayton.

Cheryl would come right out and tell you she used to live in San Francisco in the late sixties, and that she went to love-ins and peace marches and all that stuff. When I reminded her it was 1984 and Ronnie Reagan was president, she'd look at me like I was walking cow-flop. I always figured she'd start thinking straight when all that hippie-dust blew out of her head.

Alma said my tail was going to get burnt if I ever took a shine to Cheryl, but I'm a fifty-five-year-old redneck who stopped sowing his wild seed when he met the woman he married, more than thirty years ago.

Lightning crisscrossed the turbulent sky, followed by a boom of thunder. Cheryl said, "Wow! Look at that light show!"

"Light show, my ass," I muttered. The diner was as solid as the Good Book, so I wasn't too worried about the storm. But on a wild night like this, stuck out in the countryside like Big Bob's was, you had a feeling of being a long way off from civilization—though Mobile was only twenty-seven miles south. On a wild night like this, you had a feeling that anything could happen, as quick as a streak of lightning out of the darkness. I picked up a copy of the Mobile *Press-Register* that the last customer—a trucker on his way to Texas—had left on the counter a half-hour before, and I started plowing through the news, most of it bad: those A-rab countries were still squabbling like Hatfields and McCoys in white robes; two men had robbed a Qwik-Mart in Mobile and been killed by the police in a shoot-out; cops were investigating a massacre at a motel near Daytona Beach; an infant had been stolen from a maternity ward in Birmingham. The only good things on the front page were stories that said the economy was up and that Reagan swore we'd show the Commies who was boss in El Salvador and Lebanon.

The diner shook under a blast of thunder, and I looked up from the paper as a pair of headlights emerged from the rain into my parking lot.

2

The headlights were attached to an Alabama state-trooper car.

"Half-alive, hold the onion, extra brown the buns." Cheryl was already writing on her pad in expectation of the order. I pushed the paper aside and went to the fridge for the hamburger meat.

When the door opened, a windblown spray of rain swept in and stung like buckshot. "Howdy, folks!" Dennis Wells peeled off his gray rain slicker and hung it on the rack next to the door. Over his Smokey the Bear trooper hat was a protective plastic covering, beaded with raindrops. He took off his hat, exposing the thinning blond hair on his pale scalp, as he approached the counter and sat on his usual stool, right next to the cash register. "Cup of black coffee and a rare—" Cheryl was already sliding the coffee in front of him, and the burger sizzled on the griddle. "Ya'll are on the ball tonight!" Dennis said; he said the same thing when he came in, which was almost every night. Funny the kind of habits you fall into, without realizing it.

"Kinda wild out there, ain't it?" I asked as I flipped the burger over.

"Lordy, yes! Wind just about flipped my car over three, four miles down the interstate. Thought I was gonna be eatin' a little pavement tonight." Dennis was a husky young man in his early thirties, with thick blond brows over deep-set light brown eyes. He had a wife and three kids, and he was fast to flash a walletful of their pictures. "Don't reckon I'll be chasin' any speeders tonight, but there'll probably be a load of accidents. Cheryl, you sure look pretty this evenin'."

"Still the same old me." Cheryl never wore a speck of makeup, though one day she'd come to work with glitter on her cheeks. She had a place a few miles away, and I guessed she was farming that funny weed up there. "Any trucks moving?"

"Seen a few, but not many. Truckers ain't fools. Gonna get worse before it gets better, the radio says." He sipped at his coffee and grimaced. "Lordy, that's strong enough to jump out of the cup and dance a jig, darlin'!"

I fixed the burger the way Dennis liked it, put it on a platter with some fries, and served it. "Bobby, how's the wife treatin' you?" he asked.

"No complaints."

"Good to hear. I'll tell you, a fine woman is worth her weight in gold. Hey, Cheryl! How'd you like a handsome young man for a husband?"

Cheryl smiled, knowing what was coming. "The man I'm looking for hasn't been made yet."

"Yeah, but you ain't met *Cecil* yet, either! He asks me about you every time I see him, and I keep tellin' him I'm doin' everything I can to get you two together." Cecil was Dennis' brother-in-law and owned a Chevy dealership in Bay Minette. Dennis had been ribbing Cheryl about going on a date with Cecil for the past four months. "You'd like him," Dennis promised. "He's got a lot of my qualities."

"Well, that's different. In that case, I'm *certain* I don't want to meet him."

Dennis winced. "Oh, you're a cruel woman! That's what smokin' banana peels does to you—turns you mean. Anybody readin' this rag?" He reached over for the newspaper.

"Waitin' here just for you," I said. Thunder rumbled, closer to the diner. The lights flickered briefly once . . . then again before they returned to normal. Cheryl busied herself by fixing a fresh pot of coffee, and I watched the rain whipping against the windows. When the lightning flashed, I could see the trees swaying so hard they looked about to snap.

Dennis read and ate his hamburger. "Boy," he said after a few minutes, "the world's in some shape, huh? Those A-rab pig-stickers are itchin' for war. Mobile metro boys had a little gunplay last night. Good for them." He paused and frowned, then tapped the paper with one thick finger. "This I can't figure."

"What's that?"

"Thing in Florida couple of nights ago. Six people killed at the Pines Haven Motor Inn, near Daytona Beach. Motel was set off in the woods. Only a couple of cinder-block houses in the area, and nobody heard any gunshots. Says here one old man saw what he thought was a bright white star falling over the motel, and that was it. Funny, huh?"

"A UFO," Cheryl offered. "Maybe he saw a UFO."

"Yeah, and I'm a little green man from Mars," Dennis scoffed. "I'm serious. This is weird. The motel was so blown full of holes it looked like a war had been going on. Everybody was dead—even a dog and a canary that belonged to the manager. The cars out in front of the rooms were blasted to pieces. The sound of one of them explodin' was what woke up the people in those houses, I reckon." He skimmed the story again. "Two bodies were out in the parkin' lot, one was holed up in a bathroom, one had crawled under a bed, and two had dragged every piece of furniture in the room over to block the door. Didn't seem to help 'em any, though."

I grunted. "Guess not."

"No motive, no witnesses. You better believe those Florida cops are shakin' the bushes for some kind of dangerous maniac—or maybe more than one, it says here." He shoved the paper away and patted the service revolver holstered at his hip. "If I ever got hold of him—or them—he'd find out not to mess with a 'Bama trooper." He glanced quickly over at Cheryl and smiled mischievously. "Probably some crazy hippie who'd been smokin' his tennis shoes."

"Don't knock it," she said sweetly, "until you've tried it." She looked past him, out the window into the storm. "Car's pullin' in, Bobby."

Headlights glared briefly off the wet windows. It was a station wagon with wood-grained panels on the sides; it veered around the gas pumps and parked next to Dennis' trooper car. On the front bumper was a personalized license plate that said: Ray & Lindy. The headlights died, and all the doors opened at once. Out of the wagon came a whole family: a man and woman, a little girl and boy about eight or nine. Dennis got up and opened the diner door as they hurried inside from the rain.

All of them had gotten pretty well soaked between the station wagon and the diner, and they wore the dazed expressions of people who'd been on the road a long time. The man wore glasses and had curly gray hair, the woman was slim and dark-haired and pretty. The kids were sleepy-eyed. All of them were well-dressed, the man in a yellow sweater with one of those alligators on the chest. They had vacation tans, and I figured they were tourists heading north from the beach after spring break.

"Come on in and take a seat," I said.

"Thank you," the man said. They squeezed into one of the booths near the windows. "We saw your sign from the interstate."

"Bad night to be on the highway," Dennis told them. "Tornado warnings are out all over the place."

"We heard it on the radio," the woman—Lindy, if the license was right—said. "We're on our way to Birmingham, and we thought we could drive right through the storm. We should've stopped at that Holiday Inn we passed about fifteen miles ago."

"That would've been smart," Dennis agreed. "No sense in pushin' your luck." He returned to his stool.

The new arrivals ordered hamburgers, fries, and Cokes. Cheryl and I went to work. Lightning made the diner's lights flicker again, and the sound of thunder caused the kids to jump. When the food was ready and Cheryl served them, Dennis said, "Tell you what. You folks finish your dinners and I'll escort you back to the Holiday Inn. Then you can head out in the morning. How about that?"

"Fine," Ray said gratefully. "I don't think we could've gotten very much further, anyway." He turned his attention to his food.

"Well," Cheryl said quietly, standing beside me, "I don't guess we get home early, do we?"

"I guess not. Sorry."

She shrugged. "Goes with the job, right? Anyway, I can think of worse places to be stuck."

I figured that Alma might be worried about me, so I went over to the pay phone to call her. I dropped a quarter in—and the dial tone sounded like a cat being stepped on. I hung up and tried again. The cat scream continued. "Damn!" I muttered. "Lines must be screwed up."

"Ought to get yourself a place closer to town, Bobby," Dennis said. "Never could figure out why you wanted a joint in the sticks. At least you'd get better phone service and good lights if you were nearer to Mo—"

He was interrupted by the sound of wet and shrieking brakes, and he swiveled around on his stool.

I looked up as a car hurtled into the parking lot, the tires swerving, throwing up plumes of water. For a few seconds I thought it was going to keep coming, right through the window into the diner—but then the brakes caught and the car almost grazed the side of my pickup as it jerked to a stop. In the neon's red glow I could tell it was a beat-up old Ford Fairlane, either gray or a dingy beige. Steam was rising off the crumpled hood. The headlights stayed on for perhaps a minute before they winked off. A figure got out of the car and walked slowly—with a limp—toward the diner.

We watched the figure approach. Dennis' body looked like a coiled spring ready to be triggered. "We got us a live one, Bobby boy," he said.

The door opened, and in a stinging gust of wind and rain a man who looked like walking death stepped into my diner.

3

He was so wet he might well have been driving with his windows down. He was a skinny guy, maybe weighed all of a hundred and twenty pounds, even soaking wet. His unruly dark hair was plastered to his head, and he had gone a week or more without a shave. In his gaunt, pallid face his eyes were startlingly blue; his gaze flicked around the diner, lingered for a few seconds on Dennis. Then he limped on down to the far end of the counter and took a seat. He wiped the rain out of his eyes as Cheryl took a menu to him.

Dennis stared at the man. When he spoke, his voice bristled with authority. "Hey, fella." The man didn't look up from the menu. "Hey, I'm talkin' to *you*."

The man pushed the menu away and pulled a damp packet of Kools out of the breast pocket of his patched Army fatigue jacket. "I can hear you," he said; his voice was deep and husky, and didn't go with his less-than-robust physical appearance.

"Drivin' kinda fast in this weather, don't you think?"

The man flicked a cigarette lighter a few times before he got a flame, then lit one of his smokes and inhaled deeply. "Yeah," he replied. "I was. Sorry. I saw the sign, and I was in a hurry to get here. Miss? I'd just like a cup of coffee, please. Hot and *real* strong, okay?"

Cheryl nodded and turned away from him, almost bumping into me as I strolled down behind the counter to check him out.

"That kind of hurry'll get you killed," Dennis cautioned.

"Right. Sorry." He shivered and pushed the tangled hair back from his forehead with one hand. Up close, I could see deep cracks around his mouth and the corners of his eyes and I figured him to be in his late thirties or early forties. His wrists were as thin as a woman's; he looked like he hadn't eaten a good meal for more than a month. He stared at his hands through bloodshot eyes. Probably on drugs, I thought. The fella gave me the creeps. Then he looked at me with those eyes—so pale blue they were almost white—and I felt like I'd been nailed to the floor. "Something wrong?" he asked—not rudely, just curiously.

"Nope." I shook my head. Cheryl gave him his coffee and then went over to give Ray and Lindy their check.

The man didn't use either cream or sugar. The coffee was steaming, but he drank half of it down like mother's milk. "That's good," he said. "Keep me awake, won't it?"

"More than likely." Over the breast pocket of his jacket was the faint outline of the name that had been sewn there once. I think it was Price, but I could've been wrong.

"That's what I want. To stay awake as long as I can." He finished the coffee. "Can I have another cup, please?"

I poured it for him. He drank that one down just as fast, then rubbed his eyes wearily.

"Been on the road a long time, huh?"

Price nodded. "Day and night. I don't know which is more tired, my mind or my butt." He lifted his gaze to me again. "Have you got anything else to drink? How about beer?"

"No, sorry. Couldn't get a liquor license."

He sighed. "Just as well. It might make me sleepy. But I sure could go for a beer right now. One sip, to clean my mouth out."

He picked up his coffee cup, and I smiled and started to turn away.

But then he wasn't holding a cup. He was holding a Budweiser can, and for an instant I could smell the tang of a newly popped beer.

The mirage was there for only maybe two seconds. I blinked, and Price was holding a cup again. "Just as well," he said, and put it down.

I glanced over at Cheryl, then at Dennis. Neither one was paying attention. Damn! I thought. I'm too young to be losin' either my eyesight or my senses! "Uh . . . " I said, or some other stupid noise.

"One more cup?" Price asked. "Then I'd better hit the road again."

My hand was shaking as I picked it up, but if Price noticed, he didn't say anything.

"Want anything to eat?" Cheryl asked him. "How about a bowl of beef stew?"

He shook his head. "No, thanks. The sooner I get back on the road, the better it'll be."

Suddenly Dennis swiveled toward him, giving him a cold stare that only cops and drill sergeants can muster. "Back on the *road?*" He snorted. "Fella, you ever been in a tornado before? I'm gonna escort those nice people to the Holiday Inn about fifteen miles back. If you're smart, that's where you'll spend the night too. No use in tryin' to—"

"No." Price's voice was rock-steady. "I'll be spending the night behind the wheel."

Dennis' eyes narrowed. "How come you're in such a hurry? Not runnin' from anybody, are you?"

"Nightcrawlers," Cheryl said.

Price turned toward her like he'd been slapped across the face, and I saw what might've been a spark of fear in his eyes.

Cheryl motioned toward the lighter Price had laid on the counter, beside the pack of Kools. It was a beat-up silver Zippo, and inscribed across it was NIGHT-CRAWLERS with the symbol of two crossed rifles beneath it. "Sorry," she said. "I just noticed that, and I wondered what it was."

Price put the lighter away. "I was in 'Nam," he told her. "Everybody in my unit got one."

"Hey." There was suddenly new respect in Dennis' voice. "You a *vet?*"

Price paused so long I didn't think he was going to answer. In the quiet, I heard the little girl tell her mother that the fries were "ucky." Price said, "Yes."

"How about that! Hey, I wanted to go myself, but I got a high number and things were windin' down about that time anyway. Did you see any action?"

A faint, bitter smile passed over Price's mouth. "Too much."

"What? Infantry? Marines? Rangers?"

Price picked up his third cup of coffee, swallowed some, and put it down. He closed his eyes for a few seconds, and when they opened they were vacant and fixed on nothing. "Nightcrawlers," he said quietly. "Special unit. Deployed to re-con Charlie positions in questionable villages." He said it like he was reciting from a manual. "We did a lot of crawling through rice paddies and jungles in the dark."

"Bet you laid a few of them Vietcong out, didn't you?" Dennis got up and came over to sit a few places away from the man. "Man, I was behind you guys all the way. I wanted you to stay in there and fight it out!"

Price was silent. Thunder echoed over the diner. The lights weakened for a few seconds; when they came back on, they seemed to have lost some of their wattage. The place was dimmer than before. Price's head slowly turned toward Dennis, with the inexorable motion of a machine. I was thankful I didn't have to take the full force of Price's dead blue eyes, and I saw Dennis wince. "I *should've* stayed," he said. "I should be there right now, buried in the mud of a rice paddy with the eight other men in my patrol."

"Oh." Dennis blinked. "Sorry. I didn't mean to—"

"I came home," Price continued calmly, "by stepping on the bodies of my friends. Do you want to know what that's like, Mr. Trooper?"

"The war's over," I told him. "No need to bring it back."

Price smiled grimly, but his gaze remained fixed on Dennis. "Some say it's over. I say it came back with the men who were there. Like me. *Especially* like me." Price paused. The wind howled around the door, and the lightning illuminated for an instant the thrashing woods across the highway. "The mud was up to our knees, Mr. Trooper," he said. "We were moving across a rice paddy in the dark, being real careful not to step on the bamboo stakes we figured were planted there. Then the first shots started: *pop pop pop*—like firecrackers going off. One of the Nightcrawlers fired off a flare, and we saw the Cong ringing us. We'd walked right into hell, Mr. Trooper. Somebody shouted, 'Charlie's in the light!' and we started firing, trying to punch a hole through them. But they were everywhere. As soon as one went down, three more took his place. Grenades were going off, and more flares, and people were screaming as they got hit. I took a bullet in the thigh and another through the hand. I lost my rifle, and somebody fell on top of me with half his head missing."

"Uh . . . listen," I said. "You don't have to—"

"I *want* to, friend." He glanced quickly at me, then back to Dennis. I think I cringed when his gaze pierced me. "I want to tell it all. They were fighting and screaming and dying all around me, and I felt the bullets tug at my clothes as they passed through. I know I was screaming too, but what was coming out of my mouth sounded bestial. I ran. The only way I could save my own life was to step on their bodies and drive them down into the mud. I heard some of them choke and blubber as I put my boot on their faces. I knew all those guys like brothers . . . but at that moment they were only pieces of meat. I ran. A gunship chopper came over the paddy and laid down some fire, and that's how I got out. Alone." He bent his face closer toward the other man's. "And you'd better believe I'm in that rice paddy in 'Nam every time I close my eyes. You'd better believe the men I left back there don't rest easy. So you keep your opinions about 'Nam and being 'behind you guys' to yourself, Mr. Trooper. I don't want to hear that bull-shit. Got it?"

Dennis sat very still. He wasn't used to being talked to like that, not even from a 'Nam vet, and I saw the shadow of anger pass over his face.

Price's hands were trembling as he brought a little bottle out of his jeans pocket. He shook two blue-and-orange capsules out onto the counter, took them both with a swallow of coffee, and then recapped the bottle and put it away. The flesh of his face looked almost ashen in the dim light.

"I know you boys had a rough time," Dennis said, "but that's no call to show disrespect to the law."

"The law," Price repeated. "Yeah. Right. Bull*shit.*"

"There are women and children present," I reminded him. "Watch your language."

Price rose from his seat. He looked like a skeleton with just a little extra skin on the bones. "Mister, I haven't slept for more than thirty-six hours. My nerves are shot. I don't mean to cause trouble, but when some fool says he *understands,* I feel like kicking his teeth down his throat—because no one who wasn't there can pretend to understand." He glanced at Ray, Lindy, and the kids. "Sorry, folks. Don't mean to disturb you. Friend, how much do I owe?" He started digging for his wallet.

Dennis slid slowly from his seat and stood with his hands on his hips. "Hold it." He used his trooper's voice again. "If you think I'm lettin' you walk out of here high on pills and needin' sleep, you're crazy. I don't want to be scrapin' you off the highway."

Price paid him no attention. He took a couple of dollars from his wallet and put them on the counter. I didn't touch them. "Those pills will help keep me awake," Price said. "Once I get on the road, I'll be fine."

"Fella, I wouldn't let you go if it was high noon and not a cloud in the sky. I sure as hell don't want to clean up after the accident you're gonna have. Now, why don't you come along to the Holiday Inn and—"

Price laughed grimly. "Mr. Trooper, the last place you want me staying is at a motel." He cocked his head to one side. "I was in a motel in Florida a couple of nights ago, and I think I left my room a little untidy. Step aside and let me pass."

"A motel in Florida?" Dennis nervously licked his lower lip. "What the hell you talkin' about?"

"Nightmares and reality, Mr. Trooper. The point where they cross. A couple of nights ago, they crossed at a motel. I wasn't going to let myself sleep. I was just going to rest for a little while, but I didn't know they'd come so *fast*." A mocking smile played at the edges of his mouth, but his eyes were tortured. "You don't want me staying at that Holiday Inn, Mr. Trooper. You really don't. Now, step aside."

I saw Dennis' hand settle on the butt of his revolver. His fingers unsnapped the fold of leather that secured the gun in the holster. I stared at him numbly. My God, I thought. What's goin' on? My heart had started pounding so hard I was sure everybody could hear it. Ray and Lindy were watching, and Cheryl was backing away behind the counter.

Price and Dennis faced each other for a moment, as the rain whipped against the windows and thunder boomed like shellfire. Then Price sighed, as if resigning himself to something. He said, "I think I want a T-bone steak. Extra rare. How 'bout it?" He looked at me.

"A steak?" My voice was shaking. "We don't have any T-bone—"

Price's gaze shifted to the counter right in front of me. I heard a sizzle. The aroma of cooking meat drifted up to me.

"Oh . . . wow," Cheryl whispered.

A large T-bone steak lay on the countertop, pink and oozing blood. You could've fanned a menu in my face and I would've keeled over. Wisps of smoke were rising from the steak.

The steak began to fade, until it was only an outline on the counter. The lines of oozing blood vanished. After the mirage was gone, I could still smell the meat—and that's how I knew I wasn't crazy.

Dennis' mouth hung open. Ray had stood up from the booth to look, and his wife's face was the color of spoiled milk. The whole world seemed to be balanced on a point of silence—until the wail of the wind jarred me back to my senses.

"I'm getting good at it," Price said softly. "I'm getting very, very good. Didn't start happening to me until about a year ago. I've found four other 'Nam vets who can do the same thing. What's in your head comes true—as simple as that. Of course, the images only last for a few seconds—as long as I'm awake, I mean. I've found out that those other men were drenched by a chemical spray we called Howdy Doody—because it made you stiffen up and jerk like you were hanging on strings. I got hit with it near Khe Sahn. That shit almost suffocated me. It felt like black tar, and it burned the land down to a paved parking lot." He stared at Dennis. "You don't want me around here, Mr. Trooper. Not with the body count I've still got in *my* head."

"You . . . were at . . . that motel, near Daytona Beach?"

Price closed his eyes. A vein had begun beating at his right temple, royal blue against the pallor of his flesh. "Oh, Jesus," he whispered. "I fell asleep, and I couldn't wake myself up. I was having the nightmare. The same one. I was locked in it, and I was trying to scream myself awake." He shuddered, and two tears ran slowly down his cheeks. "*Oh,*" he said, and flinched as if remembering something horrible. "They . . . they were coming through the door when I woke up. Tearing the door right off its hinges. I woke up . . . just as one of them was pointing his rifle at me. And I saw his face. I saw his muddy, misshappen face." His eyes suddenly jerked open. "I didn't know they'd come so fast."

"Who?" I asked him. "*Who* came so fast?"

"The Nightcrawlers," Price said, his face devoid of expression, masklike. "Dear God . . . maybe if I'd stayed asleep a second more. But I ran again, and I left those people dead in that motel."

"You're gonna come with me." Dennis started pulling his gun from the holster. Price's head snapped toward him. "I don't know what kinda fool game you're—"

He stopped, staring at the gun he held.

It wasn't a gun anymore. It was an oozing mass of hot rubber. Dennis cried out and slung the thing from his hand. The molten mess hit the floor with a pulpy *splat*.

"I'm leaving now." Price's voice was calm. "Thank you for the coffee." He walked past Dennis, toward the door.

Dennis grasped a bottle of ketchup from the counter. Cheryl cried out, *"Don't!"* but it was too late. Dennis was already swinging the bottle. It hit the back of Price's skull and burst open, spewing ketchup everywhere. Price staggered forward, his knees buckling. When he went down, his skull hit the floor with a noise like a watermelon being dropped. His body began jerking involuntarily.

"Got him!" Dennis shouted triumphantly. "Got that crazy bastard, didn't I?"

Lindy was holding the little girl in her arms. The boy craned his neck to see. Ray said nervously, "You didn't kill him, did you?"

"He's not dead," I told him. I looked over at the gun; it was solid again. Dennis scooped it up and aimed it at Price, whose body continued to jerk. Just like Howdy Doody, I thought. Then Price stopped moving.

"He's dead!" Cheryl's voice was near-frantic. "Oh God, you killed him, Dennis!"

Dennis prodded the body with the toe of his boot, then bent down. "Naw. His eyes are movin' back and forth behind the lids." Dennis touched his wrist to check the pulse, then abruptly pulled his own hand away. "Jesus Christ! He's as cold as a meat locker!" He took Price's pulse and whistled. "Goin' like a racehorse at the Derby."

I touched the place on the counter where the mirage steak had been. My fingers came away slightly greasy, and I could smell the cooked meat on them. At that instant Price twitched. Dennis scuttled away from him like a crab. Price made a gasping, choking noise.

"What'd he say?" Cheryl asked. "He said something!"

"No he didn't." Dennis stuck him in the ribs with his pistol. "Come on. Get up."

"Get him out of here," I said. "I don't want him—"

Cheryl shushed me. "Listen. Can you hear that?"

I heard only the roar and crash of the storm.

"Don't you *hear* it?" she asked me. Her eyes were getting scared and glassy.

"Yes!" Ray said. "Yes! Listen!"

Then I did hear something, over the noise of the keening wind. It was a distant *chuk-chuk-chuk*, steadily growing louder and closer. The wind covered the noise for a minute, then it came back: CHUK-CHUK-CHUK, almost overhead.

"It's a helicopter!" Ray peered through the window. "Somebody's got a helicopter out there!"

"Ain't nobody can fly a chopper in a storm!" Dennis told him. The noise of rotors swelled and faded, swelled and faded . . . and stopped.

On the floor, Price shivered and began to contort into a fetal position. His mouth opened; his face twisted in what appeared to be agony.

Thunder spoke. A red fireball rose up from the woods across the road and hung lazily in the sky for a few seconds before it descended toward the diner. As it fell, the fireball exploded soundlessly into a white, glaring eye of light that almost blinded me.

Price said something in a garbled, panicked voice. His eyes were tightly closed, and he had squeezed up with his arms around his knees.

Dennis rose to his feet; he squinted as the eye of light fell toward the parking lot and winked out in a puddle of water. Another fireball floated up from the woods, and again blossomed into painful glare.

Dennis turned toward me. "I heard him." His voice was raspy. "He said . . . 'Charlie's in the light.' "

As the second flare fell to the ground and illuminated the parking lot, I thought I saw figures crossing the road. They walked stiff-legged, in an eerie cadence. The flare went out.

"Wake him up," I heard myself whisper. "Dennis . . . dear God . . . *wake him up.*"

4

Dennis stared stupidly at me, and I started to jump across the counter to get to Price myself.

A gout of flame leapt in the parking lot. Sparks marched across the concrete. I shouted, "Get down!" and twisted around to push Cheryl back behind the shelter of the counter.

"What the *hell*—" Dennis said.

He didn't finish. There was the metallic thumping of bullets hitting the gas pumps and the cars. I knew if that gas blew we were all dead. My truck shuddered with the impact of slugs, and I saw the whole thing explode as I ducked behind the counter. Then the windows blew inward with a god-awful crash, and the diner was full of flying glass, swirling wind, and sheets of rain. I heard Lindy scream, and both the kids were crying, and I think I was shouting something myself.

The lights had gone out, and the only illumination was the reflection of red neon off the concrete and the glow of the fluorescents over the gas pumps. Bullets whacked into the wall, and crockery shattered as if it had been hit with a hammer. Napkins and sugar packets were flying everywhere.

Cheryl was holding on to me as if her fingers were nails sunk to my bones. Her eyes were wide and dazed, and she kept trying to speak. Her mouth was working, but nothing came out.

There was another explosion as one of the other cars blew. The whole place shook, and I almost puked with fear.

Another hail of bullets hit the wall. They were tracers, and they jumped and ricocheted like white-hot cigarette butts. One of them sang off the edge of a shelf and fell to the floor about three feet away from me. The glowing slug began to fade, like the beer can and the mirage steak. I put my hand out to find it, but all I felt was splinters of glass and crockery. A phantom bullet, I thought. Real enough to cause damage and death—and then gone.

You don't want me around here, Mr. Trooper, Price had warned. *Not with the body count I've got in my head.*

The firing stopped. I got free of Cheryl and said, "You stay right *here.*" Then I looked up over the counter and saw my truck and the station wagon on fire, the flames being whipped by the wind. Rain slapped me across the face as it swept in where the window glass used to be. I saw Price lying still huddled on the floor, with pieces of glass all around him. His hands were clawing the air, and in the flickering red neon his face was contorted, his eyes still closed. The pool of ketchup around his head made him look like his skull had been split open. He was peering into hell, and I averted my eyes before I lost my own mind.

Ray and Lindy and the two children had huddled under the table of their booth. The woman was sobbing brokenly. I looked at Dennis, lying a few feet from Price: he was sprawled on his face, and there were four holes punched through his back. It was not ketchup that ran in rivulets around Dennis' body. His right arm was outflung, and the fingers twitched around the gun he gripped.

Another flare sailed up from the woods like a Fourth of July sparkler.

When the light brightened, I saw them: at least five figures, maybe more. They were crouched over, coming across the parking lot—but slowly, the speed of nightmares. Their clothes flapped and hung around them, and the flare's light glanced off their helmets. They were carrying weapons—rifles, I guessed. I couldn't see their faces, and that was for the best.

On the floor, Price moaned. I heard him say "light . . . in the light . . ."

The flare hung right over the diner. And then I knew what was going on. *We* were in the light. We were all caught in Price's nightmare, and the Nightcrawlers that Price had left in the mud were fighting the battle again—the same way it had been fought at the Pines Haven Motor Inn. The Nightcrawlers had come back to life, powered by Price's guilt and whatever that Howdy Doody shit had done to him.

And we were in the light, where Charlie had been out in that rice paddy.

There was a noise like castanets clicking. Dots of fire arced through the broken windows and thudded into the counter. The stools squealed as they were hit and spun. The cash register rang and the drawer popped open, and then the entire register blew apart and bills and coins scattered. I ducked my head, but a wasp of fire—I don't know what, a bit of metal or glass maybe—sliced my left cheek open from ear to upper lip. I fell to the floor behind the counter with blood running down my face.

A blast shook the rest of the cups, saucers, plates, and glasses off the shelves. The whole roof buckled inward, throwing loose ceiling tiles, light fixtures, and pieces of metal framework.

We were all going to die. I knew it, right then. Those things were going to destroy us. But I thought of the pistol in Dennis' hand, and of Price lying near the door. If we were caught in Price's nightmare and the blow from the ketchup bottle had broken something in his skull, then the only way to stop his dream was to kill him.

I'm no hero. I was about to piss in my pants, but I knew I was the only one who could move. I jumped up and scrambled over the counter, falling beside Dennis and wrenching at that pistol. Even in death, Dennis had a strong grip. Another blast came, along the wall to my right. The heat of it scorched me, and the shock wave skidded me across the floor through glass and rain and blood.

But I had that pistol in my hand.

I heard Ray shout, "Look out!"

In the doorway, silhouetted by flames, was a skeletal thing wearing muddy green rags. It wore a dented-in helmet and carried a corroded, slime-covered rifle. Its face was gaunt and shadowy, the features hidden behind a scum of rice-paddy muck. It began to lift the rifle to fire at me—slowly, slowly . . .

I got the safety off the pistol and fired twice, without aiming. A spark leapt off the helmet as one of the bullets was deflected, but the figure staggered backward and into the conflagration of the station wagon, where it seemed to melt into ooze before it vanished.

More tracers were coming in. Cheryl's Volkswagen shuddered, the tires blowing out almost in unison. The state-trooper car was already bullet-riddled and sitting on flats.

Another Nightcrawler, this one without a helmet and with slime covering the skull where the hair had been, rose up beyond the window and fired its rifle. I heard the bullet whine past my ear, and as I took aim I saw its bony finger tightening on the trigger again.

A skillet flew over my head and hit the thing's shoulder, spoiling its aim. For an instant the skillet stuck in the Nightcrawler's body, as if the figure itself was made out of mud. I fired once . . . twice . . . and saw pieces of matter fly from the thing's chest. What might've been a mouth opened in a soundless scream, and the thing slithered out of sight.

I looked around. Cheryl was standing behind the counter, weaving on her feet, her face white with shock. "Get down!" I shouted, and she ducked for cover.

I crawled to Price, shook him hard. His eyes would not open. "Wake up!" I begged him. "Wake up, damn you!" And then I pressed the barrel of the pistol against Price's head. Dear God, I didn't want to kill anybody, but I knew I was going to have to blow the Nightcrawlers right out of his brain. I hesitated—too long.

Something smashed into my left collarbone. I heard the bone snap like a broomstick being broken. The force of the shot slid me back against the counter and jammed me between two bullet-pocked stools. I lost the gun, and there was a roaring in my head that deafened me.

I don't know how long I was out. My left arm felt like dead meat. All the cars in the lot were burning, and there was a hole in the diner's roof that a tractor-trailer truck could've dropped through. Rain was sweeping into my face, and when I wiped my eyes clear I saw them, standing over Price.

There were eight of them. The two I thought I'd killed were back. They trailed weeds, and their boots and ragged clothes were covered with mud. They stood in silence, staring down at their living comrade.

I was too tired to scream. I couldn't even whimper. I just watched.

Price's hands lifted into the air. He reached for the Nightcrawlers, and then his eyes opened. His pupils were dead white, surrounded by scarlet.

"End it," he whispered. "End it . . ."

One of the Nightcrawlers aimed its rifle and fired. Price jerked. Another Nightcrawler fired, and then they were all firing point-blank into Price's body. Price thrashed and clutched at his head, but there was no blood; the phantom bullets weren't hitting him.

The Nightcrawlers began to ripple and fade. I saw the flames of the burning cars through their bodies. The figures became transparent, floating in vague outlines. Price had awakened too fast at the Pines Haven Motor Inn, I realized; if he had remained asleep, the creatures of his nightmares would've ended it there, at that Florida motel. They were killing him in front of me—or he was allowing them to end it, and I think that's what he must've wanted for a long, long time.

He shuddered, his mouth releasing a half-moan, half-sigh.

It sounded almost like relief.

The Nightcrawlers vanished. Price didn't move anymore.

I saw his face. His eyes were closed, and I think he must've found peace at last.

5

A trucker hauling lumber from Mobile to Birmingham saw the burning cars. I don't even remember what he looked like.

Ray was cut up by glass, but his wife and the kids were okay. Physically, I mean. Mentally, I couldn't say.

Cheryl went into the hospital for a while. I got a postcard from her with the Golden Gate Bridge on the front. She promised she'd write and let me know how she was doing, but I doubt if I'll ever hear from her. She was the best waitress I ever had, and I wish her luck.

The police asked me a thousand questions, and I told the story the same way every time. I found out later that no bullets or shrapnel were ever dug out of the walls or the cars or Dennis' body—just like in the case of that motel massacre. There was no bullet in me, though my collarbone was snapped clean in two.

Price had died of a massive brain hemorrhage. It looked, the police told me, as if it had exploded in his skull.

I closed the diner. Farm life is fine. Alma understands, and we don't talk about it.

But I never showed the police what I found, and I don't know exactly why not.

I picked up Price's wallet in the mess. Behind a picture of a smiling young woman holding a baby there was a folded piece of paper. On that paper were the names of four men.

Beside one name, Price had written "Dangerous."

I've found four other 'Nam vets who can do the same thing, Price had said.

I sit up at night a lot, thinking about that and looking at those names. Those men had gotten a dose of that Howdy Doody shit in a foreign place they hadn't wanted to be, fighting a war that turned out to be one of those crossroads of nightmare and reality. I've changed my mind about 'Nam because I understand now that the worst of the fighting is still going on, in the battlefields of memory.

A Yankee who called himself Tompkins came to my house one May morning and flashed me an ID that said he worked for a veterans' association. He was very soft-spoken and polite, but he had deep-set eyes that were almost black, and he never blinked. He asked me all about Price, seemed real interested in picking my brain of every detail. I told him the police had the story, and I couldn't add any more to it. Then I turned the tables and asked him about Howdy Doody. He smiled in a puzzled kind of way and said he'd never heard of any chemical defoliant called that. No such thing, he said. Like I say, he was very polite.

But I know the shape of a gun tucked into a shoulder holster. Tompkins was wearing one under his seersucker coat. I never could find any veterans' association that knew anything about him, either.

Maybe I should give that list of names to the police. Maybe I will. Or maybe I'll try to find those four men myself, and try to make some sense out of what's being hidden.

I don't think Price was evil. No. He was just scared, and who can blame a man for running from his own nightmares? I like to believe that, in the end, Price had the courage to face the Nightcrawlers, and in committing suicide he saved our lives.

The newspapers, of course, never got the real story. They called Price a 'Nam vet who'd gone crazy, killed six people in a Florida motel, and then killed a state trooper in a shoot-out at Big Bob's diner and gas stop.

But I know where Price is buried. They sell little American flags at the five-and-dime in Mobile. I'm alive, and I can spare the change.

And then I've got to find out how much courage *I* have.

HIGH FANTASY

Ancestors and Disciples of Robert E. Howard and J. R. R. Tolkien

Exotic lands, outrageous characters, seemingly impossible odds, and never-ending complications and tensions mark the moral quest that is central to the High Fantasy story. In these stories, the world and characters portrayed, though fantastic in nature, hold profound similarities to the reader's world. The fantasy world is often harsh and cruel, populated by barbarians, oppressive military states, and tyrannical rulers. Such is the case in Robert E. Howard's tales of Conan the Barbarian. Oftentimes this world is pastoral and agrarian, as in the case of the works by J. R. R. Tolkien, such as *The Hobbit* and *The Lord of the Rings*. Good and Evil are defined and contrasted in vivid white and black in the works of both Howard and Tolkien. The Epic Poetry of Homer and Arthurian legend is the basis for all such Fantasy fictions.

High Fantasy can be broken into two general categories—heroic Sword and Sorcery fiction and epic romances. In both these categories, the conventions or commonly repeated story elements are the quest and the adventure and the markedly Good and Evil players. Also, in both categories, the inventions or uniquely new story elements are the characters (who, despite their outward appearances as animals, elves, gnomes, hobbits, or the like, are very nearly human) and the exotic locales and challenges in which the stories' characters find themselves. In both variants of Fantasy, magic is religion.

Robert E. Howard created series characters such as Conan the Barbarian, King Kull, Bran Mak Morn, and Solomon Kane for *Weird Tales* and other pulp magazines in the 1920s and '30s. Howard's creations, however, were by no means the first and only practitioners of sword and sorcery lifestyles. In fact, H. Rider Haggard, popular Adventure and Fantasy writer of the latter half of the nineteenth century, was one of several who had written this type of story before Howard. In addition, there were Conan-like stories and series characters in magazines such as *Argosy* at the turn of the century. However, today Heroic Fantasy is measured by the yardstick (or archetype) of Robert E. Howard's Conan the Barbarian.

The stereotypic Heroic Fantasy hero or heroine is physically strong and beautiful, is alone and orphaned, and judges morality and creates justice by an innate sense of what is right. These are emotional and perhaps crafty creatures, but they are not products of mainstream society, nor are they intellectual heavyweights. Their forms of justice, meted out with bloody swords and broad axes, hold a base appeal for many readers of Fantasy fiction.

The epic romance tradition of Fantasy, epitomized in the twentieth century by the writings of J. R. R. Tolkien, is similar yet different. Like Howard's Heroic Fantasy, it has been the subject of much emulation and imitation in recent decades. Elaborate fictional universes are developed and delineated in these Fantasy romances. Entire races of beings (reflective of real-life collective humanity) populate these universes. There is both harmony and conflict between these beings. The conflict, usually of a profound cultural, mythological, and theological nature, provides the complication and tension of the Fantasy story that must ultimately be resolved. This necessitates the moral quest or crusade.

Like Science Fiction, Fantasy provides fables and allegories. High Fantasy, in particular, reinforces contemporary mythology and provides escapism. Traditionally, Fantasy stories of all sorts reinforce the notion that Good is stronger than, and will ultimately defeat, Evil. There are exceptions. In short, the Fantasy story provides its readers with the comfort of the familiar; it ritualistically reenacts and legitimates the myth that Good will triumph over Evil and in the process reinforces the legitimacy of our own experiences in the context of the larger universe.

GEORGE MacDONALD (1824–1905)

A philosopher, theologist, and lecturer, George MacDonald was a prolific Scottish author best remembered for his High Fantasy and children's literature. He also wrote mainstream novels, journalism, poetry, sermons, and literary criticism. MacDonald is considered one of the founders of modern day Fantasy. He was influenced by the existing traditions of E. T. A. Hoffman and other eighteenth- and nineteenth-century fantasists. He was also influenced by classic mythology, legend, and folklore. Much of his work is appropriately deemed Christian Fantasy.

George MacDonald's first High Fantasy work was the 1858 novel Phantastes, A Faerie Romance for Men and Women. *In 1871, he published the first of his children's fantasies—*At the Back of the North Wind. *By this time, MacDonald was also publishing Fantasy in short story form. His second adult Fantasy novel,* Lilith, *was first published in 1895.*

MacDonald is remembered for his exotic alternate worlds, dreamlike story lines, sentimentality, and allegory. T. S. Eliot, J. R. R. Tolkien, and C. S. Lewis acknowledged the influence of George MacDonald on their respective writings.

The Gray Wolf
(Works of Fancy and Imagination, *1871*)

One evening-twilight in spring, a young English student, who had wandered northwards as far as the outlying fragments of Scotland called the Orkney and Shetland islands, found himself on a small island of the latter group, caught in a storm of wind and hail, which had come on suddenly. It was in vain to look about for any shelter; for not only did the storm entirely obscure the landscape, but there was nothing around him save a desert moss.

At length, however, as he walked on for mere walking's sake, he found himself on the verge of a cliff, and saw, over the brow of it, a few feet below him, a ledge of rock, where he might find some shelter from the blast, which blew from behind. Letting himself down by his hands, he alighted upon something that crunched beneath his tread, and found the bones of many small animals scattered about in front of a little cave in the rock, offering the refuge he sought. He went in, and sat upon a stone. The storm increased in violence, and as the darkness grew he became uneasy, for he did not relish the thought of spending the night in the cave. He had parted from his companions on the opposite side of the island, and it added to his uneasiness that they must be full of apprehension about him. At last there came a lull in the storm, and the same instant he heard a footfall, stealthy and light as that of a wild beast, upon the bones at the mouth of the cave. He started up in some fear, though the least thought might have satisfied him that there could be no very dangerous animals upon the island. Before he had time to think, however, the face of a woman appeared in the opening. Eagerly the wanderer spoke. She started at the sound of his voice. He could not see her well, because she was turned towards the darkness of the cave.

"Will you tell me how to find my way across the moor to Shielness?" he asked.

"You cannot find it to-night," she answered, in a sweet tone, and with a smile that bewitched him, revealing the whitest of teeth.

"What am I to do then?" he asked.

"My mother will give you shelter, but that is all she has to offer."

"And that is far more than I expected a minute ago," he replied. "I shall be most grateful."

She turned in silence and left the cave. The youth followed.

She was barefooted, and her pretty brown feet went catlike over the sharp stones, as she led the way down a rocky path to the shore. Her garments were scanty and torn, and her hair blew tangled in the wind. She seemed about five and twenty, lithe and small. Her long fingers kept clutching and pulling nervously at her skirts as she went. Her face was very gray in complexion, and very worn, but delicately formed, and smooth-skinned. Her thin nostrils were tremulous as eyelids, and her lips, whose curves were faultless, had no colour to give sign of indwelling blood. What her eyes were like he could not see, for she had never lifted the delicate films of her eyelids.

At the foot of the cliff they came upon a little hut leaning against it, and having for its inner apartment a natural hollow within it. Smoke was spreading over the face of the rock, and the grateful odour of food gave hope to the hungry student. His guide opened the door of the cottage; he followed her in, and saw a woman bending over a fire in the middle of the floor. On the fire lay a large fish broiling. The daughter spoke a few words, and the mother turned and welcomed the stranger. She had an old and very wrinkled, but honest face, and looked troubled. She dusted the only chair in the cottage, and placed it for him by the side of the fire, opposite the one window, whence he saw a little patch of yellow sand over which the spent waves spread themselves out listlessly. Under this window there was a bench, upon which the daughter threw herself in an unusual posture, resting her chin upon her hand. A moment after, the youth caught the first glimpse of her blue eyes. They were fixed upon him with a strange look of greed, amounting to craving, but as if aware that they belied or betrayed her, she dropped them instantly. The moment she veiled them, her face, notwithstanding its colourless complexion, was almost beautiful.

When the fish was ready, the old woman wiped the deal table, steadied it upon the uneven floor, and covered it with a piece of fine table-linen. She then laid the fish on a wooden platter, and invited the guest to help himself. Seeing no other provision, he pulled from his pocket a hunting knife, and divided a portion from the fish, offering it to the mother first.

"Come, my lamb," said the old woman; and the daughter approached the table. But her nostrils and mouth quivered with disgust.

The next moment she turned and hurried from the hut.

"She doesn't like fish," said the old woman, "and I haven't anything else to give her."

"She does not seem in good health," he rejoined.

The woman answered only with a sigh, and they ate their fish with the help of a little rye-bread. As they finished their supper, the youth heard the sound as of the pattering of a dog's feet upon the sand close to the door; but ere he had time to look out of the window, the door opened and the young woman entered. She looked better, perhaps from having just washed her face. She drew a stool to the corner of the fire opposite him. But as she sat down, to his bewilderment, and even horror, the student spied a single drop of blood on her white skin within her torn dress. The woman brought out a jar of whisky, put a rusty old kettle on the fire, and took her place in front of it. As soon as the water boiled, she proceeded to make some toddy in a wooden bowl.

Meantime the youth could not take his eyes off the young woman, so that at length he found himself fascinated, or rather bewitched. She kept her eyes for the most part veiled with the loveliest eyelids fringed with darkest lashes, and he gazed entranced; for the red glow of the little oil-lamp covered all the strangeness of her complexion. But as soon as he met a stolen glance out of those eyes unveiled, his soul shuddered within him. Lovely face and craving eyes alternated fascination and repulsion.

The mother placed the bowl in his hands. He drank sparingly, and passed it to the girl. She lifted it to her lips, and as she tasted—only tasted it—looked at him. He thought the drink must have been drugged and have affected his brain. Her hair smoothed itself back, and drew her forehead backwards with it; while the lower part of her face projected towards the bowl, revealing, ere she sipped, her dazzling teeth in strange prominence. But the same moment the vision vanished; she returned the vessel to her mother, and rising, hurried out of the cottage.

Then the old woman pointed to a bed of heather in one corner with a murmured apology; and the student, wearied both with the fatigues of the day and the strangeness of the night, threw himself upon it, wrapped in his cloak. The moment he lay down, the storm began afresh, and the wind blew so keenly through the crannies of the hut, that it was only by drawing his cloak over his head that he could protect himself from its currents. Unable to sleep, he lay listening to the uproar, which grew in violence, till the spray was dashing against the window. At length the door opened, and the young woman came in, made up the fire, drew the bench before it, and lay down in the same strange posture, with her chin propped on her hand and elbow, and her face turned towards the youth. He moved a little; she dropped her head, and lay on her face, with her arms crossed beneath her forehead. The mother had disappeared.

Drowsiness crept over him. A movement of the bench roused him, and he fancied he saw some four-footed creature as tall as a large dog trot quietly out of the door. He was sure he felt a rush of cold wind. Gazing fixedly through the darkness, he thought he saw the eyes of the damsel encountering his, but a glow from the falling together of the remnants of the fire, revealed clearly enough that the bench was vacant. Wondering what could have made her go out in such a storm, he fell fast asleep.

In the middle of the night he felt a pain in his shoulder, came broad awake, and saw the gleaming eyes and grinning teeth of some animal close to his face. Its claws were in his shoulder, and its mouth in the act of seeking his throat. Before it had fixed its fangs, however, he had its throat in one hand, and sought his knife with the other. A terrible struggle followed; but regardless of the tearing claws, he found and opened his knife. He had made one futile stab, and was drawing it for a surer, when, with a spring of the whole body, and one wildly-contorted effort, the creature twisted its neck from his hold, and with something betwixt a scream and a howl, darted from him. Again he heard the door open; again the wind blew in upon him, and it continued blowing; a sheet of spray dashed across the floor, and over his face. He sprung from his couch and bounded to the door.

It was a wild night—dark, but for the flash of whiteness from the waves as they broke within a few yards of the cottage; the wind was raving, and the rain pouring down the air. A gruesome sound as of mingled weeping and howling came from somewhere in the dark. He turned again into the hut and closed the door, but could find no way of securing it.

The lamp was nearly out, and he could not be certain whether the form of the young woman was upon the bench or not. Overcoming a strong repugnance, he approached it, and put out his hands—there was nothing there. He sat down and waited for the daylight: he dared not sleep any more.

When the day dawned at length, he went out yet again, and looked around. The morning was dim and gusty and gray. The wind had fallen, but the waves were tossing wildly. He wandered up and down the little strand, longing for more light.

At length he heard a movement in the cottage. By and by the voice of the old woman called to him from the door.

"You're up early, sir. I doubt you didn't sleep well."

"Not very well," he answered. "But where is your daughter?"

"She's not awake yet," said the mother. "I'm afraid I have but a poor breakfast for you. But you'll take a dram and a bit of fish. It's all I've got."

Unwilling to hurt her, though hardly in good appetite, he sat down at the table. While they were eating, the daughter came in, but turned her face away and went to the further end of the hut. When she came forward after a minute or two, the youth saw that her hair was drenched, and her face whiter than before. She looked ill and faint, and when she raised her eyes, all their fierceness had vanished, and sadness had taken its place. Her neck was now covered with a cotton handkerchief. She was modestly attentive to him, and no longer shunned his gaze. He was gradually yielding to the temptation of braving another night in the hut, and seeing what would follow, when the old woman spoke.

"The weather will be broken all day, sir," she said. "You had better be going, or your friends will leave without you."

Ere he could answer, he saw such a beseeching glance on the face of the girl, that he hesitated, confused. Glancing at the mother, he saw the flash of wrath in her face. She rose and approached her daughter, with her hand lifted to strike her. The young woman stooped her head with a cry. He darted round the table to interpose between them. But the mother had caught hold of her; the handkerchief had fallen from her neck; and the youth saw five blue bruises on her lovely throat—the marks of the four fingers and the thumb of a left hand. With a cry of horror he darted from the house, but as he reached the door he turned. His hostess was lying motionless on the floor, and a huge gray wolf came bounding after him.

There was no weapon at hand; and if there had been, his inborn chivalry would never have allowed him to harm a woman even under the guise of a wolf. Instinctively, he set himself firm, leaning a little forward, with half-outstretched arms, and hands curved ready to clutch again at the throat upon which he had left those pitiful marks. But the creature as she sprung eluded his grasp, and just as he expected to feel her fangs, he found a woman weeping on his bosom, with her arms around his neck. The next instant, the gray wolf broke from him, and bounded howling up the cliff. Recovering himself as he best might, the youth followed, for it was the only way to the moor above, across which he must now make his way to find his companions.

All at once he heard the sound of a crunching of bones—not as if a creature was eating them, but as if they were ground by the teeth of rage and disappointment; looking up, he saw close above him the mouth of the little cavern in which he had taken refuge the day before. Summoning all his resolution, he passed it slowly and softly. From within came the sounds of a mingled moaning and growling.

Having reached the top, he ran at full speed for some distance across the moor before venturing to look behind him. When at length he did so, he saw, against the sky, the girl standing on the edge of the cliff, wringing her hands. One solitary wail crossed the space between. She made no attempt to follow him, and he reached the opposite shore in safety.

𝕬 A(BRAHAM) MERRITT (1884–1943)

Abraham Merritt was an accomplished newspaper writer and reporter in the early 1900s. He was a magazine writer, then editor, for The American Weekly, *a magazine supplement included in Hearst newspapers.*

Like Edgar Rice Burroughs and Edmond Hamilton, Merritt was a pivotal author of Fantasy and Science Fiction because he emerged as a contributor to those forms in the days when "Scientific Romances" were becoming "Space Operas" and dime novels were being replaced by pulp magazines. Besides Burroughs, and later Hamilton, Abraham Merritt's contemporaries included Sax Rohmer, Edison Marshall, William Hope Hodgson, Ray Cummings, Murray Leinster, and Max Brand (who wrote popular Science Fiction and Fantasy tales as well as Westerns). Some of Merritt's novels and stories are fantasies, some deal with the occult and the supernatural, and some are appropriately deemed Science Fiction. "The People of the Pit" is a fantasy that evokes memories of H. Rider Haggard's nineteenth-century lost world adventures.

In particular, the importance of Abraham Merritt and his "The People of the Pit" is long reaching. The author and this particular story inspired Jack Williamson and Edmond Hamilton to become writers. Merritt's style in this tale and his other fiction is beautiful, colorful, and detailed—it is highly sensory. In this way, Clark Ashton Smith's weird, dark, and high fantasies of the 1930s and '40s are very similar. The same might be said of the Fantasy works of Henry Kuttner from the same period.

The People of the Pit

(All-Story Weekly, *January 5, 1918*)

North of us a shaft of light shot half way to the zenith. It came from behind the ragged mountain toward which we had been pushing all day. The beam drove up through a column of blue haze whose edges were marked as sharply as the rain that streams from the edges of a thunder cloud. It was like the flash of a search-light through an azure mist and it cast no shadows.

As it struck upward the five-summits were outlined hard and black, and we saw that the whole mountain was shaped like a hand. As the light silhouetted it, the gigantic fingers of the peaks seemed to stretch; the bulk that was the plain of the hand to push. It was exactly as though it moved to thrust something back. The shining beam held steady for a moment; then broke into myriads of tiny luminous globes that swung to and fro and dropped gently. They seemed to be searching.

The forest had become very still. Every wood noise held its breath. I felt the dogs pressing against my legs. They, too, were silent; but every muscle in their bodies trembled, their hair was stiff along their backs, and their eyes, fixed on the falling phosphorescent sparks, were filmed with the terror-glaze.

I looked at Starr Anderson. He was staring at the North where once more the beam had pulsed upward.

" 'The mountain shaped like a hand!' " I spoke, without moving my lips. My mouth was as dry as though Lao T'zai had poured his fear-dust down my throat.

"It's the mountain we've been looking for," he answered in the same tone.

"But that light—what is it? Not the aurora surely," I said.

"Whoever heard of an aurora at this time of the year?"

He voiced the thought that was in my own mind.

"It makes me think something is being hunted up there," he said. "That the lights are seeking—an unholy sort of hunt—it's well for us to be out of range."

"The mountain seems to move each time the shaft shoots up," I said. "What's it keeping back, Starr? It makes me think of the frozen hand of cloud that Shan Nadour set before the Gate of Ghouls to keep them in the lairs that Eblis cut for them."

He raised a hand, listening.

From the north and high over head there came a whispering: It was not the rustling of the aurora, that rushing crackling sound like the ghosts of winds that blew at Creation racing through the skeleton leaves of ancient trees that sheltered Lilith. This whispering held in it a demand. It was eager. It called us to come up where the beam was flashing. It—drew!

There was in it a note of inexorable insistence. It touched my heart with a thousand tiny fear-tipped fingers and it filled me with a vast longing to race on and merge myself in the light. It must have been so that Ulysses felt when he strained at the mast and strove to obey the crystal sweet singing of the sirens.

The whispering grew louder.

"What the hell's the matter with those dogs?" cried Starr Anderson savagely. "Look at them!"

The malemiuts, whining, were racing away toward the light. We saw them disappear among the trees. There came back to us a mournful howling. Then that too died away and left nothing but the insistent murmuring overhead.

The glade we had camped in looked straight to the north. We had reached, I suppose, three hundred miles above the first great bend of the Kuskokwim toward the Yukon. Certainly we were in an untrodden part of the wilderness. We had pushed through from Dawson at the breaking of the spring, on a fair lead to a lost mountain between the five peaks of which, so the Athabascan medicine man had told us, the gold streams out like putty from a clenched fist.

Not an Indian were we able to get to go with us. The land of the Hand Mountain was accursed, they said.

We had sighted a mountain the night before, its ragged top faintly outlined against a pulsing glow. And now by the light that had led us we saw that it was the very place we had sought.

Anderson stiffened. Through the whispering had broken a curious pad-pad and a rustling. It sounded as though a small bear were moving toward us.

I threw a pile of wood on the fire and as it blazed up saw something break through the bushes. It walked on all fours, but it did not walk like a bear. All at once it flashed upon me—it was like a baby crawling upstairs. The forepaws lifted themselves in grotesquely infantile fashion. It was grotesque but it was—terrible. It drew closer. We reached for our guns—and dropped them. Suddenly we knew that this crawling thing was a man!

It was a man. Still with that high climbing pad-pad he swayed to the fire. He stopped.

"Safe," whispered the crawling man in a voice that was an echo of the whispering overhead. "Quite safe here. They can't get out of the blue, you know. They can't get you—unless you answer them—"

"He's mad," said Anderson, and then gently to this broken thing that had been a man; "You're all right—there's nothing after you."

"Don't answer them," repeated the crawling man, "the lights, I mean."

"The lights," I cried, startled even out of pity. "What are they?"

"The people of the pit!" he murmured.

He fell upon his side. We ran to him. Anderson knelt.

"God's love!" he said. "Frank, look at this!"

He pointed to the hands. The wrists were covered with torn rags of a heavy shirt. The hands themselves were—stumps! The fingers had been bent into the palms and the flesh had been worn to the bone. They looked like the feet of a little black elephant! My eyes traveled down the body. Around the waist was a heavy band of yellow metal. From it fell a ring and a dozen links of shining white chain.

"What is he? Where did he come from?" said Anderson. "Look, he's fast asleep—yet even in his sleep his arms try to climb and his feet draw themselves up one after the other! And his knees—how in God's name was he ever able to move on them?"

It was even as he said. In the deep sleep that had come upon the crawler, arms and legs kept raising in a deliberate, dreadful climbing motion. It was as though they had a life of their own—they kept their movement independently of the motionless body. They were semaphoric motions. If you have ever stood at the back of a train and watched the semaphores rise and fall you will know exactly what I mean.

Abruptly the overhead whispering ceased. The shaft of light dropped and did not rise again. The crawling man became still. A gentle glow began to grow around us. The short Alaskan summer night was over. Anderson rubbed his eyes and turned me a haggard face.

"Man!" he exclaimed. "You look as though you have been sick!"

"No more than you, Starr," I said. "That was sheer, stark horror! What do you make of it all?"

"I'm thinking our only answer lies there," he answered, pointing to the figure that lay so motionless under the blankets we had thrown over him. "Whatever they were—that's what they were after. There was no aurora about those lights,

Frank. It was like the flaring up of some queer hell the preacher folk never frightened us with."

"We'll go no further to-day," I said. "I wouldn't wake him for all the gold that runs between the fingers of the five peaks—nor for all the devils that may be behind them."

The crawling man lay in a sleep as deep as the Styx. We bathed and bandaged the pads that had been his hands. Arms and legs were as rigid as though they were crutches. He did not move while we worked over him. He lay as he had fallen, the arms a trifle raised, the knees bent.

I began filing the band that ringed the sleeper's waist. It was gold, but it was like no gold I had ever handled. Pure gold is soft. This was soft too—but it had an unclean, viscid life of its own.

It clung to the file and I could have sworn that it writhed like a live thing when I cut into it. I gashed through it, bent it away from the body and hurled it away. It was—loathsome!

All that day the crawler slept. Darkness came and still he slept. But that night there was no shaft of blue haze from behind the peaks, no questing globes of light, no whispering. Some spell of horror seemed withdrawn—but not far. Both Anderson and I felt that the menace was there, withdrawn perhaps, but waiting.

It was noon the next day when the crawling man awoke. I jumped as the pleasant drawling voice sounded.

"How long have I slept?" he said. His pale blue eyes grew quizzical as I stared at him.

"A night—and almost two days," I said.

"Were there any lights up there last night?" He nodded to the north eagerly. "Any whispering?"

"Neither," I answered. His head fell back and he stared up at the sky.

"They've given it up, then?" he said at last.

"Who have given it up?" asked Anderson.

And once more—"The people of the pit!" the crawling man answered.

We stared at him and again faintly I, for one, felt that queer, maddening desire that the lights had brought with them.

"The people of the pit," he repeated. "Things some god of evil made before the Flood and that somehow have escaped the good God's vengeance. They were calling me!" he added simply.

Anderson and I looked at each other, the same thought in both our minds.

"No," said the crawling man, reading what it was, "I'm not insane. Give me a very little to drink. I'm going to die soon. Will you take me as far south as you can before I die? And afterwards will you build a big fire and burn me? I want to be in such shape that no hellish wile of theirs can drag my body back to them. You'll do it when I've told you about them," he said as we hesitated.

He drank the brandy and water we lifted to his lips.

"Arms and legs quite dead," he said. "Dead as I'll be soon. Well, they did well for me. Now I'll tell you what's up there behind that hand. Hell!

"Listen. My name is Stanton—Sinclair Stanton. Class 1900, Yale. Explorer. I started away from Dawson last year to hunt for five peaks that rose like a hand in a haunted country and ran pure gold between them. Same thing you were after? I thought so. Late last fall my comrade sickened. I sent him back with some Indians. A little later my Indians found out what I was after. They ran away from me. I decided I'd stick, built a cabin, stocked myself with food and lay down to winter it. Did it not badly—it was a pretty mild winter you'll remember. In the spring I started off again. A little less than two weeks ago I sighted the five peaks. Not from this side though—the other. Give me some more brandy.

"I'd made too wide a détour," he went on. "I'd gotten too far north. I beat back. From this side you see nothing but forest straight up to the base of the hand. Over on the other side—"

He was silent for a moment.

"Over there is forest too. But it doesn't reach so far. No! I came out of it. Stretching for miles in front of me was a level plain. It was as worn and ancient looking as the desert around the broken shell of Babylon. At its end rose the peaks. Between me and them—far off—was what looked like a low dike of rocks. Then—I ran across the road!"

"The road!" cried Anderson incredulously.

"The road," said the crawling man. "A fine, smooth, stone road. It ran straight on to the mountain. Oh, it was a road all right—and worn as though millions and millions of feet had passed over it for thousands of years. On each side of it were sand and heaps of stones. After a while I began to notice these stones. They were cut, and the shape of the heaps somehow gave me the idea that a hundred thousand years ago they might have been the ruins of houses. They were as old looking as that. I sensed man about them and at the same time they smelled of immemorial antiquity.

"The peaks grew closer. The heaps of ruins thicker. Something inexpressibly desolate hovered over them, something sinister; something reached from them that struck my heart like the touch of ghosts so old that they could be only the ghosts of ghosts. I went on.

"And now I saw that what I had thought to be the low rock range at the base of the peaks was a thicker litter of ruins. The Hand Mountain was really much farther off. The road itself passed through these ruins and between two high rocks that raised themselves like a gateway."

The crawling man paused. His hands began that sickening pad-pad again. Little drops of bloody sweat showed on his forehead. But after a moment or two he grew quiet. He smiled.

"They were a gateway," he said. "I reached them. I went between them. I sprawled flat, clutching the earth in awe and terror. For I was on a broad stone platform. Before me was—sheer space! Imagine the Grand Cañon three times as wide, roughly circular and with the bottom dropped out. That would be something like what I was looking into.

"It was like peeping over the edge of a cleft world down into the infinity where the planets roll! On the far side stood five peaks. They looked like a gigantic warning hand stretched up to the sky. The lips of the abyss curved away on each side of me.

"I could see down perhaps a thousand feet. Then a thick blue haze shut out the eye. It was like the blue you see gather on the high hills at dusk. But the pit—it was awesome! Awesome as the Maori's Gulf of Ranalak, that sinks between the living and the dead and that only the freshly released soul has strength to leap—but never strength again to leap back.

"I crept back from the verge and stood up, weak, shaking. My hand rested against one of the rocks of the gateway. There was carving upon it. There in sharp outlines was the heroic figure of a man. His back was turned. His arms were stretched above his head and between them he carried something that looked like a sun disk with radiating lines of light. There were symbols on the disk that reminded me of Chinese. But they were not Chinese. No! They had been made by hands dust ages before the Chinese stirred in the womb of time.

"I looked at the opposite rock. It bore an exactly similar figure. There was an odd peaked head-dress on both. The rocks themselves were triangular and the carvings were on the side closest to the pit. The gesture of the men seemed to be that of holding something back—of barring. I looked closer. Behind the outstretched hands and the disks I seemed to see a host of vague shapes and plainly a multitude of globes.

"I traced them out vaguely. Suddenly I felt unaccountably sick. There had come to me an impression—I can't call it sight—an impression of enormous upright slugs. Their swollen bodies seemed to dissolve, then swim into sight, then dissolve again—all except the globes which were their heads and that remained clear. They were—unutterably loathsome. Overcome by an inexplicable and overpowering nausea I stretched myself upon the slab. And then—I saw the stairway that led down into the pit!"

"A stairway!" we cried.

"A stairway," repeated the crawling man as patiently as before. "It seemed not so much carved out of the rock as built into it. Each slab was perhaps twenty feet long and five feet wide. They ran down from the platform and vanished into the blue haze."

"A stairway," said Anderson incredulously, "built into the wall of a precipice and leading down into a bottomless pit—"

"Not bottomless," interrupted the crawling man. "There was a bottom. Yes. I reached it." He paused again. "I reached it," he went on dully. "Down the stairway—down the stairway."

He seemed to grip his mind.

"Yes," he went on firmly. "I went down the stairway. But not that day. I made my camp back of the gates. At dawn I filled my knapsack with food, my two canteens with water from a spring that wells up there by the gateway, walked between the carved monoliths and stepped over the edge of the pit.

"The steps run along the side of the pit at a forty degree pitch. As I went down and down I studied them. They were of a greenish rock quite different from the granitic porphyry that formed the wall of the pit. At first I thought that the builders had taken advantage of an outcropping stratum, and had carved the gigantic flight from it. But the regularity of the angle at which it fell made me doubtful of this theory.

"After I had gone down perhaps half a mile I stepped out upon a landing. From this landing the stairs made a V shaped turn and again ran on downward, clinging to the cliff at the same angle as the first flight. After I had made three of these turns I knew that the steps dropped straight down to whatever they went in a succession of such angles. No strata could be so regular as that. No, the stairway was built by hands! But whose? And why? The answer is in those ruins around the edge of the pit—never I think to be read.

"By noon I had lost sight of the lip of the abyss. Above me, below me, was nothing but the blue haze. Beside me, too, was nothingness, for the further breast of rock had long since vanished in the same haze. I felt no dizziness, and no fear;

only a vast curiosity. What was I to discover? Some ancient and wonderful civilization that had ruled when the poles were tropical gardens? A new world? The key to the mystery of man himself? Nothing living, I felt sure—all was too old for life. Still, a work so wonderful must lead to something quite as wonderful I knew. What was it? I went on.

"At regular intervals I had passed the mouths of small caves. There would be three thousand steps and then an opening, three thousand more steps and an opening—and so on and on. Late that afternoon I stopped before one of these clefts. I suppose I had gone then three miles down the pit, although the angles were such that I had walked in all fully ten miles. I examined the entrance. On each side was carved the same figures as on the great portals at the lip of the pit. But now they were standing face forward, the arms outstretched with their disks, as though holding something back from the shaft itself. Now, too, their faces were covered with veils and there were no hideous shapes behind them.

"I went inside the cave. It ran back for twenty yards like a burrow. It was dry and perfectly light. I could see, outside, the blue haze rising upward like a column. I felt an extraordinary sense of security, although I had not been conscious of any fear. I felt that the figures at the entrance were guardians—but against what? I felt so secure that even curiosity on this point was dulled.

"The blue haze thickened and grew faintly luminescent. I fancied that it was dusk above. I ate and drank a little and slept. When I awoke the blue had lightened again, and I fancied it was dawn above. I went on. I forgot the gulf yawning at my side. I felt no fatigue and little hunger or thirst, although I had drunk and eaten sparingly. That night I spent within another of the caves. And at dawn I descended again.

"It was late that day when I first saw the city—"

He was silent for a time.

"The city," he said at last, "The city of the pit! But not such a city as you have ever seen—nor any other man who has lived to tell of it. The pit, I think, must be shaped like a bottle; the opening before the five peaks is the neck. But how wide the bottom is I do not know—thousands of miles, maybe. And what may lay behind the city—I do not know.

"I had begun to catch little glints of light far down in the blue. Then I saw the tops of—trees, I suppose they are. But not our kind of trees—unpleasant, reptilian trees. They reared themselves on high thin trunks and their tops were nests of thick tendrils with ugly little leaves like narrow heads—or snake heads.

"The trees were red, a vivid, angry red. Here and there I began to glimpse spots of shining yellow. I knew these were water because I could see things breaking through their surface—or at least I could see the splash and ripple but what it was that disturbed them I never saw.

"Straight beneath me was the—city. Mile after mile of closely packed cylinders that lay upon their sides in pyramids of three, of five—of dozens—piled upon each other. It is so hard to make you see what that city is like—look, suppose you have water pipes of a certain length and first you lay three of them side by side and on top of them you place two and on these two one; or suppose you take five for a foundation and place on these four and then three, then two and then one. Do you see? That was the way they looked.

"And they were topped by towers, by minarets, by flares, by fans and twisted monstrosities. They gleamed as though coated with pale rose flame. Beside them the venomous red trees raised themselves like the heads of hydras guarding nests of gigantic jeweled and sleeping worms!

"A few feet beneath me the stairway jutted out into a titanic arch, unearthly as the span that bridges Hell and leads to Asgard. It curved out and down straight through the top of the highest pile of carven cylinders and then—it vanished through it. It was appalling—it was demonic—"

The crawling man stopped. His eyes rolled up into his head. He trembled and again his arms and legs began their horrible crawling movement. From his lips came a whispering. It was an echo of the high murmuring we had heard the night he came to us. I put my hands over his eyes. He quieted.

"The things accursed!" he said. "The People of the Pit! Did I whisper? Yes— but they can't get me now—they can't!"

After a time he began as quietly as before.

"I crossed that span. I went down through the top of that—building. Blue darkness shrouded me for moment and I felt the steps twist into a spiral. I wound down and then I was standing high up in—I can't tell you what. I'll have to call it a room. We have no images for what is in the pit. A hundred feet below me was the floor. The walls sloped down and out from where I stood in a series of widening crescents. The place was colossal—and it was filled with a curious mottled red light. It was like the light inside a green and gold flecked fire opal. The spiral stairs wound below me. I went down to the last step. Far in front of me rose a high columned altar. Its pillars were carved in monstrous scrolls—like mad octopuses with a thousand drunken tentacles; they rested on the backs of shapeless monstrosities carved in crimson stone. The altar front was a gigantic slab of purple covered with carvings.

"I can't describe these carvings! No human being could—the human eye cannot grasp them any more than it can grasp shapes that haunt the fourth dimension. Only a subtle sense in the back of the brain grasped them vaguely. They were formless things that gave no conscious image, yet pressed into the mind like small hot seals—ideas of hate—of combats between unthinkable monstrous things—victories in a nebulous hell of steaming, obscene jungles—aspirations and ideals immeasurably loathsome—

"And as I stood I grew aware of something that lay behind the lip of the altar fifty feet above me. I *knew* it was there—I felt it with every hair and every tiny bit of my skin. Something infinitely malignant, infinitely horrible, infinitely ancient. It lurked, it brooded, it saw me, it threatened and it—was invisible!

"Behind me was a circle of blue light. Something urged me to turn back, to climb the stairs and make away. It was impossible. Terror of that unseen watching thing behind the altar raced me onward like a whirlwind. I passed through the circle. I was in a way that stretched on into dim distance between the rows of carven cylinders.

"Here and there the red trees arose. Between them rolled the stone burrows. And now I could take in the amazing ornamentation that clothed them. They were like the trunks of smooth skinned trees that had fallen and had been clothed with high reaching fantastic orchids. Yes—those cylinders were like that—and more. They should have gone out with the dinosaurs. They were—monstrous! They struck the eyes like a blow and they passed across the nerves like a rasp. And nowhere was there sight or sound of living thing.

"There were circular openings in the cylinders like the opening in the temple of the stairway through which I had run. I passed through one of them. I was in a long bare vaulted room whose curving sides half closed twenty feet over my head, leaving a wide slit that opened into another vaulted chamber above. I saw nothing in the room save the same mottled reddish light of the temple.

"I stumbled. Still I could see nothing, but—my skin prickled and my heart stopped! There *was* something on the floor over which I had tripped!

"I reached down—and my hand touched a—thing—cold and smooth—that moved under it—I turned and ran out of that place. I was filled with a sick loathing that had in it something of madness—I ran on and on—blindly—wringing my hands—weeping with horror—

"When I came to myself I was still among the stone cylinders and red trees. I tried to retrace my steps, to find the temple; for now I was more than afraid. I was like a new soul panic-stricken with the first terrors of hell. But I could not find the temple! And the haze began to thicken and glow; the cylinders to shine more brightly.

"Suddenly I knew that it was dusk in my own world above and that the thickening of the haze was the signal for the awakening of whatever things lived in the pit.

"I scrambled up the sides of one of the burrows. I hid behind a twisted nightmare of stone. Perhaps, I thought, there was a chance of remaining hidden until the blue lightened, the peril passed, and I could escape. There began to grow around me a murmur. It was everywhere—and it grew and grew into a great whispering, I peeped from the side of the stone down into the street.

"I saw lights passing and repassing. More and more lights—they swam out of the circular doorways and they thronged the street. The highest were eight feet above the pave; the lowest perhaps two. They hurried, they sauntered, they bowed, they stopped and whispered—and there was *nothing* under them!"

"Nothing under them!" breathed Anderson.

"No," he went on, "that was the terrible part of it—there was nothing under them. Yet certainly the lights were living things. They had consciousness, volition—what else I did not know. They were nearly two feet across, the largest. Their center was a bright nucleus—red, blue, green. This nucleus faded off gradually into a misty glow that did not end abruptly. It, too, seemed to fade off into nothingness—but a nothingness that had under it a—somethingness.

"I strained my eyes trying to grasp this body into which the lights merged and which one could only *feel* was there, but could not *see*.

"And all at once I grew rigid. Something cold, and thin like a whip, had touched my face. I turned my head. Close behind were three of the lights. They were a pale blue. They looked at me—if you can imagine lights that are eyes.

"Another whiplash gripped my shoulder. Under the closest light came a shrill whispering. I shrieked. Abruptly the murmuring in the street ceased.

"I dragged my eyes from the pale-blue globe that held them and looked out; the lights in the streets were rising by myriads to the level of where I stood! There they stopped and peered at me. They crowded and jostled as though they were a crowd of curious people on Broadway.

"That was the horrible part of it. I felt a score of the lashes touch me—I shrieked again. Then—darkness and a sensation of falling through vast depths.

"When I awoke to consciousness I was again in the great place of the stairway, lying at the foot of the altar. All was silent. There were no lights—only the mottled red glow.

"I jumped to my feet and ran toward the steps. Something jerked me back to my knees. And then I saw that around my waist had been fastened a yellow ring of metal. From it hung a chain, and this chain passed up over the lip of the high ledge.

"I reached into my pockets for my knife to cut through the ring. It was not there! I had been stripped of everything except one of the canteens that I had hung around my neck, and which I suppose they had thought was part of me.

"I tried to break the ring. It seemed alive. It writhed in my hands and drew itself closer around me!

"I pulled at the chain. It was immovable. There came over me in a flood consciousness of the unseen thing above the altar, and I groveled at the foot of the slab. Think—alone in that place of strange light with the brooding ancient horror above me—a monstrous thing, a thing unthinkable—an unseen thing that poured forth horror—

"After a while I gripped myself. Then I saw beside one of the pillars a yellow bowl filled with a thick, white liquid. I drank it. If it killed I did not care. But its taste was pleasant, and as I drank strength came back to me with a rush. Clearly I was not to be starved. The people of the pit, whatever they were, had a conception of human needs.

"And now once more the reddish mottled gleam began to deepen. Again outside arose the humming, and through the circle that was the entrance to the temple came streaming the globes. They ranged themselves in ranks until they filled the temple. Their whispering grew into a chant, a cadenced whispering chant that rose and fell, rose and fell, while to its rhythm the globes lifted and sank, lifted and sank.

"All the night the lights came and went; and all that night the chant sounded as they rose and fell. At the last I felt myself only an atom of consciousness in the sea of that whispering; an atom that rose and fell with the bowing globes.

"I tell you that even my heart pulsed in unison with them! And the red glow faded, the lights streamed out; the whispering died. I was again alone, and I knew that again day had begun in my own world.

"I slept. When I awoke I found beside the pillar another bowl of the white liquid. I scrutinized the chain that held me to the altar. I began to rub two of the links together. I did this for hours. When the red began to thicken there was a ridge worn in the links. Hope rushed up within me. There was, then, a chance to escape.

"With the thickening the lights came again. All through that night the whispering chant sounded, and the globes rose and fell. The chant seized me. It pulsed through me until every nerve and muscle quivered to it. My lips began to quiver. They strove like a man trying to cry out in a nightmare. And at last they, too, were whispering—whispering the evil chant of the people of the pit. My body bowed in unison with the lights.

"I was—God forgive me!—in movement and sound, one with these nameless things, while my soul sank back sick with horror, but powerless. And as I whispered I—saw *them!*

"Saw the things under the lights. Great transparent snail-like bodies—dozens of waving tentacles stretching from them; little round, gaping mouths under the luminous, seeing globes. They were like specters of inconceivably monstrous slugs! And as I stared, still bowing and whispering, the dawn came, and they streamed to and through the entrance. They did not crawl or walk—they floated! They floated and were—gone!

"I did not sleep. I worked all that day at my chain. By thickening of the red I had worn it a sixth through. And all that night, under their spell, I whispered and bowed with the pit people, joining in their chant to the thing that brooded above me!

"Twice again the red thickened and lessened and the chant held me. And then, on the morning of the fifth day, I broke the worn links. I was free! I ran to the stairway. With eyes closed I rushed up and past the unseen horror behind the altar-ledge and was out upon the bridge. I crossed the span and began the ascent of the stairway.

"Can you think what it is to climb straight up the verge of a cleft-world—with hell behind you? Well—worse than hell was behind me, and terror rode me.

"The city of the pit had long been lost in the blue haze before I knew that I could climb no more. My heart beat upon my ears like a sledge. I fell before one of the little caves, feeling that here at last was sanctuary. I crept far back within it and waited for the haze to thicken. Almost at once it did so, and from far below me came a vast and angry murmur. Crouching at the back of the cave, I saw a swift light go shooting up through the blue haze, then die down and break, and as it dimmed and broke I saw myriads of the globes that are the eyes of the pit people swing downward into the abyss. Again and again the light pulsed, and the globes rose with it and fell.

"They are hunting me! They knew I must be somewhere still on the stairway, or, if hiding below, I must some time take to the stairway to escape. The whispering grew louder, more insistent.

"There began to pulse through me a dreadful desire to join in the whispering as I had done in the temple. Something told me that if I did, the sculptured figures could no longer save me; that I would go out and down again into the temple forever! I bit my lips through and through to still them, and all that night the beam shot up through the abyss, the globes swung, and the whispering sounded—and I prayed to the power of the caves and the sculptured figures that still had power to guard them."

He paused—his strength was going.

Then almost in a whisper: "I thought, what were the people who had carved them? Why had they built their city around the verge, and why had they set that stairway in the pit? What had they been to the things that dwelt at the bottom, and what use had the things been to them that they should live beside their dwelling-place? That there had been some purpose was certain. No work so prodigious as the stairway would have been undertaken otherwise. But what was the purpose? And why was it that those who had dwelt about the abyss had passed away ages gone and the dwellers in the abyss still lived?"

He looked at us: "I could find no answer. I wonder if even when I am dead I shall know? I doubt it.

"Dawn came as I wondered, and with it—silence. I drank what was left of the liquid in my canteen, crept from the cave, and began to climb again. That afternoon my legs gave out. I tore off my shirt and made from it pads for my knees and coverings for my hands. I crawled upward. I crawled up and up. And again I crept into one of the caves and waited until again the blue thickened, the shaft of light shot through it, and the whispering came.

"But now there was a new note in the whispering. It was no longer threatening. It called and coaxed. It—drew.

"A terror gripped me. There had come upon me a mighty desire to leave the cave and go out where the lights swung; to let them do with me what they pleased, carry me where they wished. The desire grew. It gained fresh impulse with every rise of the beam, until at last I vibrated with the desire as I had vibrated to the chant in the Temple.

"My body was a pendulum. Up would go the beam, and I would swing toward it! Only my soul kept steady. It held me fast to the floor of the cave, and it placed a hand over my lips to still them. And all that night I fought with my body and lips against the spell of the pit people.

"Dawn came. Again I crept from the cave and faced the stairway. I could not rise. My hands were torn and bleeding, my knees in agony. I forced myself upward step by step.

"After a while my hands became numb, the pain left my knees. They deadened. Step by step my will drove my body upward upon them. And time after time I would sink back within myself to oblivion—only to wake again and find that all the time I had been steadily climbing upward.

"And then—only a dream of crawling up infinite stretches of steps—memories of dull horror while hidden within caves, with thousands of lights pulsing without, and whisperings that called and called me—memory of a time when I awoke to find that my body was obeying the call and had carried me half-way out between the guardians of the portals, while thousands of gleaming globes rested in the blue haze and watched me. Glimpses of bitter fights against sleep, and always—a climb up and up along infinite distances of steps that led from a lost Abaddon to a paradise of blue sky and open world!

"At last a consciousness of clear sky close above me, the lip of the pit before me. Memory of passing between the great portals of the pit and of steady withdrawal from it. Dreams of giant men with strange, peaked crowns and veiled faces who pushed me onward and onward, and held back pulsing globules of light that sought to draw me back to a gulf wherein planets swam between the branches of red trees that had snakes for crowns.

"And then a long, long sleep—how long God alone knows—in a cleft of rocks; an awakening to see far in the north the beam still rising and falling, the lights still hunting, the whispering high above me calling—and knowledge that no longer had they power to draw me.

"Again crawling on dead arms and legs that moved—that moved—like the Ancient Mariner's ship—without volition of mine. And then—your fire—and this—safety."

The crawling man smiled at us for a moment, then quickly fell asleep.

That afternoon we struck camp, and, carrying the crawling man, started back south. For three days we carried him, and still he slept. And on the third day, still sleeping, he died. We built a great pile of wood and we burned his body, as he had asked. We scattered his ashes about the forest with the ashes of the trees that had consumed him.

It must be a great magic, indeed, that can disentangle those ashes and draw them back in a rushing cloud to the pit he called accursed. I do not think that even the people of the pit have such a spell. No.

But Anderson and I did not return to the five peaks to see. And if the gold does steam out between the five peaks of the Hand Mountain like putty from a clenched fist—there it may remain for all of us.

✵ FRANCIS STEVENS (PSD. FOR GERTRUDE BARROWS BENNET) (1884?-1939)

Francis Stevens was one of the greatest writers of Fantasy and Science Fiction during World War I. Of famous authors whose lives were too short or who produced too little writing, it is often asked, "What if?" Such is the case with Robert E. Howard, Charles Beaumont, and others. However, the question has not been more profound than it has been in regard to Francis Stevens.

Mrs. Bennet, under the name of Francis Stevens, wrote twelve weird epic fantasies between 1917 and 1923. These appeared in Argosy, All-Story, Thrill Book, Weird Tales, *and other magazines. Not much is known about the author and her stories beyond the stories themselves. (Her novels include* The Citadel of Fear *(1918),* The Heads of Cerberus *(1919),* Claimed *(1920), and* Sunfire *(1923).) By the post–World War II years, she was all but forgotten when Abraham Merritt rediscovered her and used his rather substantial influence to have some of Stevens's work reprinted. Famed Fantasy and Science Fiction writers and scholars Lloyd Eshbach and Sam Moskowitz have endeavored, in recent years, to give Stevens her justly deserved acclaim.*

Perhaps the only thing more fantastic about Francis Stevens than her stories was her private life. Her husband died shortly after their marriage, and Mrs. Bennet was left to raise and support her infant daughter and her widowed, invalid mother. She succeeded in these endeavors, stopped writing in the early 1920s, and died in 1939. H. P. Lovecraft was one of Stevens's most ardent admirers. In his 1970 edited collection and study of Science Fiction, Under the Moons of Mars, *Sam Moskowitz called her the "most gifted woman writer of science fiction and science fantasy between Mary Wollstonecraft Shelley and C. L. Moore" (125, 126).*

Friend Island

(All-Story Weekly, *September 7, 1918*)

It was upon the waterfront that I first met her, in one of the shabby little tea shops frequented by able sailoresses of the poorer type. The uptown, glittering resorts of the Lady Aviators' Union were not for such as she.

Stern of feature, bronzed by wind and sun, her age could only be guessed, but I surmised at once that in her I beheld a survivor of the age of turbines and oil engines—a true sea-woman of that elder time when woman's superiority to man had not been so long recognized. When, to emphasize their victory, women in all ranks were sterner than today's need demands.

The spruce, smiling young maidens—engine-women and stokers of the great aluminum rollers, but despite their profession, very neat in gold-braided blue knickers and boleros—these looked askance at the hard-faced relic of a harsher day, as they passed in and out of the shop.

I, however, brazenly ignoring similar glances at myself, a mere male intruding on the haunts of the world's ruling sex, drew a chair up beside the veteran. I ordered a full pot of tea, two cups and a plate of macaroons, and put on my most ingratiating air. Possibly my unconcealed admiration and interest were wiles not exercised in vain. Or the macaroons and tea, both excellent, may have loosened the old sea-woman's tongue. At any rate, under cautious questioning, she had soon launched upon a series of reminiscences well beyond my hopes for color and variety.

"When I was a lass," quoth the sea-woman, after a time, "there was none of this high-flying, gilt-edged, leather-stocking luxury about the sea. We sailed by the power of our oil and gasoline. If they failed on us, like as not 'twas the rubber ring and the rolling wave for ours."

She referred to the archaic practice of placing a pneumatic affair called a life-preserver beneath the arms, in case of that dreaded disaster, now so unheard of, shipwreck.

"In them days there was still many a man bold enough to join our crews. And I've knowed cases," she added condescendingly, "where just by the muscle and brawn of such men some poor sailor lass has reached shore alive that would have fed the sharks without 'em. Oh, I ain't so down on men as you might think. It's the spoiling of them that I don't hold with. There's too much preached nowadays that man is fit for nothing but to fetch and carry and do nurse-work in big child-homes. To my mind, a man who hasn't the nerve of a woman ain't fitted to father children, let alone raise 'em. But that's not here nor there. My time's past, and I know it, or I wouldn't be setting here gossipin' to you, my lad, over an empty teapot."

I took the hint, and with our cups replenished, she bit thoughtfully into her fourteenth macaroon and continued.

"There's one voyage I'm not likely to forget, though I live to be as old as Cap'n Mary Barnacle, of the *Shouter*. 'Twas aboard the old *Shouter* that this here voyage occurred, and it was her last and likewise Cap'n Mary's. Cap'n Mary, she was then that decrepit, it seemed a mercy that she should go to her rest, and in good salt water at that.

"I remember the voyage for Cap'n Mary's sake, but most I remember it because 'twas then that I come the nighest in my life to committin' matrimony. For a man, the man had nerve; he was nearer bein' companionable than any other man I ever seed; and if it hadn't been for just one little event that showed up the—the *man-nishness* of him, in a way I couldn't abide, I reckon he'd be keepin' house for me this minute."

"We cleared from Frisco with a cargo of silkateen petticoats for Brisbane. Cap'n Mary was always strong on petticoats. Leather breeches or even half-skirts would ha' paid far better, they being more in demand like, but Cap'n Mary was three-quarters owner, and says she, land women should buy petticoats, and if they didn't it wouldn't be the Lord's fault nor hers for not providing 'em.

"We cleared on a fine day, which is an all sign—or was, then when the weather and the seas o' God still counted in the trafficking of the humankind. Not two days out we met a whirling, mucking bouncer of a gale that well nigh threw the old *Shouter* a full point off her course in the first wallop. She was a stout craft, though. None of your feather-weight, gas-lightened, paper-thin alloy shells, but toughened aluminum from stern to stern. Her turbine drove her through the combers at a forty-five knot clip, which named her a speedy craft for a freighter in them days.

"But this night, as we tore along through the creaming green billows, something unknown went 'way wrong down below.

"I was forward under the shelter of her long over-sloop, looking for a hairpin I'd dropped somewheres about that afternoon. It was a gold hairpin, and gold still being mighty scarce when I was a girl, a course I valued it. But suddenly I felt the old *Shouter* give a jump under my feet like a plane struck by a shell in full flight. Then she trembled all over for a full second, frightened like. Then, with the crash of doomsday ringing in my ears, I felt myself sailing through the air right into the teeth o' the shrieking gale, as near as I could judge. Down I come in the hollow of a monstrous big wave, and as my ears doused under I thought I heard a splash close by. Coming up, sure enough, there close by me was floating a new, patent, hermetic, thermo-ice-chest. Being as it was empty, and being as it was shut up air-tight, that ice-chest made as sweet a life-preserver as a woman could wish in such an hour. About ten foot by twelve, it floated high in the raging sea. Out on its top I scrambled, and hanging on by a handle I looked expectant for some of my poor fellow-women to come floating by. Which they never did, for the good reason that the *Shouter* had blowed up and went below, petticoats, Cap'n Mary and all."

"What caused the explosion?" I inquired.

"The Lord and Cap'n Mary Barnacle can explain," she answered piously. "Besides the oil for her turbines, she carried a power of gasoline for her alternative engines, and likely 'twas the cause of her ending so sudden like. Anyways, all I ever seen of her again was the empty ice-chest that Providence had well-nigh hove upon my head. On that I sat and floated, and floated and sat some more, till by-and-by the storm sort of blowed itself out, the sun come shining — this was next morning — and I could dry my hair and look about me. I was a young lass, then, and not bad to look upon. I didn't want to die, any more than you that's sitting there this minute. So I up and prays for land. Sure enough toward evening a speck heaves up low down on the horizon. At first I took it for a gas liner, but later found it was just a little island, all alone by itself in the great Pacific Ocean.

"Come, now, here's luck, thinks I, and with that I deserts the ice-chest, which being empty, and me having no ice to put in it, not likely to have in them latitudes, is of no further use to me. Striking out I swum a mile or so and set foot on dry land for the first time in nigh three days.

"Pretty land it were, too, though bare of human life as an iceberg in the Arctic.

"I had landed on a shining white beach that run up to a grove of lovely, waving palm trees. Above them I could see the slopes of a hill so high and green it reminded me of my own old home, up near Couquomgomoc Lake in Maine. The whole place just seemed to smile and smile at me. The palms waved and bowed in the sweet breeze, like they wanted to say, 'Just set right down and make yourself to home. We've been waiting a long time for you to come.' I cried, I was that happy to be made welcome. I was a young lass then, and sensitive-like to how folks treated me. You're laughing now, but wait and see if or not there was sense to the way I felt.

"So I up and dries my clothes and my long, soft hair again, which was well worth drying, for I had far more of it than now. After that I walked along a piece, until there was a sweet little path meandering away into the wild woods.

"Here, thinks I, this looks like inhabitants. Be they civil or wild, I wonder? But after traveling the path a piece, lo and behold it ended sudden like in a wide circle of green grass, with a little spring of clear water. And the first thing I noticed was a slab of white board nailed to a palm tree close to the spring. Right off I took a long drink, for you better believe I was thirsty, and then I went to look at this board. It had evidently been tore off the side of a wooden packing box, and the letters was roughly printed in lead pencil.

"'Heaven help whoever you be,' I read. 'This island ain't just right. I'm going to swim for it. You better too. Good-by. Nelson Smith.' That's what it said, but the spellin' was simply awful. It all looked quite new and recent, as if Nelson Smith hadn't more than a few hours before he wrote and nailed it there.

"Well, after reading that queer warning I begun to shake all over like in a chill. Yes, I shook like I had the ague, though the hot tropic sun was burning down right on me and that alarming board. What had scared Nelson Smith so much that he had swum to get away? I looked all around real cautious and careful, but not a single frightening thing could I behold. And the palms and the green grass and the flowers still smiled that peaceful and friendly like. 'Just make yourself to home,' was wrote all over the place in plainer letters than those sprawly lead pencil ones on the board.

"Pretty soon, what with the quiet and all, the chill left me. Then I thought, 'Well, to be sure, this Smith person was just an ordinary man, I reckon, and likely he got nervous of being so alone. Likely he just fancied things which was really not. It's a pity he drowned himself before I come, though likely I'd have found him poor company. By his record I judge him a man of but common education.'

"So I decided to make the most of my welcome, and that I did for weeks to come. Right near the spring was a cave, dry as a biscuit box, with a nice floor of white sand. Nelson had lived there too, for there was a litter of stuff—tin cans— empty—scraps of newspapers and the like. I got to calling him Nelson in my mind, and then Nelly, and wondering if he was dark or fair, and how he come to be cast away there all alone, and what was the strange events that drove him to his end. I cleaned out the cave, though. He had devoured all his tin-canned provisions, however he come by them, but this I didn't mind. That there island was a generous body. Green milk-coconuts, sweet berries, turtle eggs and the like was my daily fare.

"For about three weeks the sun shone every day, the birds sang and the monkeys chattered. We was all one big, happy family, and the more I explored that island the better I liked the company I was keeping. The land was about ten miles from beach to beach, and never a foot of it that wasn't sweet and clean as a private park.

"From the top of the hill I could see the ocean, miles and miles of blue water, with never a sign of a gas liner, or even a little government running-boat. Them running-boats used to go most everywhere to keep the seaways clean of derelicts and the like. But I knowed that if this island was no more than a hundred miles off the regular courses of navigation, it might be many a long day before I'd be rescued. The top of the hill, as I found when first I climbed up there, was a wore-out crater. So I knowed that the island was one of them volcanic ones you run across so many of in the seas between Capricorn and Cancer.

"Here and there on the slopes and down through the jungly tree-growth, I would come on great lumps of rock, and these must have came up out of that crater long ago. If there was lava it was so old it had been covered up entire with green growing stuff. You couldn't have found it without a spade, which I didn't have nor want."

"Well, at first I was happy as the hours was long. I wandered and clambered and waded and swum, and combed my long hair on the beach, having fortunately not lost my side-combs nor the rest of my gold hairpins. But by-and-by it begun to get just a bit lonesome. Funny thing, that's a feeling that, once it starts, it gets worse and worser so quick it's perfectly surprising. And right then was when the days begun to get gloomy. We had a long, sickly hot spell, like I never seen before on an ocean island. There was dull clouds across the sun from morn to night. Even the little monkeys and parrakeets, that had seemed so gay, moped and drowsed like they was sick. All one day I cried, and let the rain soak me through and through—that was the first rain we had—and I didn't get thorough dried even during the night, though I slept in my cave. Next morning I got up mad as thunder at myself and all the world.

"When I looked out the black clouds was billowing across the sky. I could hear nothing but great breakers roaring in on the beaches, and the wild wind raving through the lashing palms.

"As I stood there a nasty little wet monkey dropped from a branch almost on my head. I grabbed a pebble and slung it at him real vicious. 'Get away, you dirty little brute!' I shrieks, and with that there come a awful blinding flare of light. There was a long, crackling noise like a bunch of Chinese fireworks, and then a sound as if a whole fleet of *Shouters* had all went up together.

"When I come to, I found myself 'way in the back of my cave, trying to dig further into the rock with my finger nails. Upon taking thought, it come to me that what had occurred was just a lightning-clap, and going to look, sure enough there lay a big palm tree right across the glade. It was all busted and split open by the lightning, and the little monkey was under it, for I could see his tail and his hind legs sticking out.

"Now, when I set eyes on that poor, crushed little beast I'd been so mean to, I was terrible ashamed. I sat down on the smashed tree and considered and considered. How thankful I had ought to have been. Here I had a lovely, plenteous island, with food and water to my taste, when it might have been a barren, starvation rock that was my lot. And so, thinking, a sort of gradual peaceful feeling stole over me. I got cheerfuller and cheerfuller, till I could have sang and danced for joy.

"Pretty soon I realized that the sun was shining bright for the first time that week. The wind had stopped hollering, and the waves had died to just a singing murmur on the beach. It seemed kind o' strange, this sudden peace, like the cheer in my own heart after its rage and storm. I rose up, feeling sort of queer, and went to look if the little monkey had came alive again, though that was a fool thing, seeing he was laying all crushed up and very dead. I buried him under a tree root, and as I did it a conviction come to me.

"I didn't hardly question that conviction at all. Somehow, living there alone so long, perhaps my natural womanly intuition was stronger than ever before or since, and so I *knowed*. Then I went and pulled poor Nelson Smith's board off from the tree and tossed it away for the tide to carry off. That there board was an insult to my island!"

The sea-woman paused, and her eyes had a far-away look. It seemed as if I and perhaps even the macaroons and tea were quite forgotten.

"Why did you think that?" I asked, to bring her back. "How could an island be insulted?"

She started, passed her hand across her eyes, and hastily poured another cup of tea.

"Because," she said at last, poising a macaroon in mid-air, "because that island—that particular island that I had landed on—had a heart!

"When I was gay, it was bright and cheerful. It was glad when I come, and it treated me right until I got that grouchy it had to mope from sympathy.

It loved me like a friend. When I flung a rock at that poor little drenched monkey critter, it backed up my act with an anger like the wrath o' God, and killed its own child to please me! But it got right cheery the minute I seen the wrongness of my ways. Nelson Smith had no business to say, 'This island ain't just right,' for it was a righter place than ever I seen elsewhere. When I cast away that lying board, all the birds begun to sing like mad. The green milk-coconuts fell right and left. Only the monkeys seemed kind o' sad like still, and no wonder. You see, their own mother, the island, had rounded on one o' them for my sake!

"After that I was right careful and considerate. I named the island Anita, not knowing her right name, or if she had any. Anita was a pretty name, and it sounded kind of South Sea like. Anita and me got along real well together from that day on. It was some strain to be always gay and singing around like a dear duck of a canary bird, but I done my best. Still, for all the love and gratitude I bore Anita, the company of an island, however sympathetic, ain't quite enough for a human being. I still got lonesome, and there was even days when I couldn't keep the clouds clear out of the sky, though I will say we had no more tornadoes.

"I think the island understood and tried to help me with all the bounty and good cheer the poor thing possessed. None the less my heart give a wonderful big leap when one day I seen a blot on the horizon. It drawed nearer and nearer, until at last I could make out its nature."

"A ship, of course," said I, "and were you rescued?"

" 'Tweren't a ship, neither," denied the sea-woman somewhat impatiently. "Can't you let me spin this yarn without no more remarks and fool questions? This thing what was bearing down so fast with the incoming tide was neither more nor less than another island!

"You may well look startled. I was startled myself. Much more so than you, likely. I didn't know then what you, with your book-learning, very likely know now—that islands sometimes float. Their underparts being a tangled-up mess of roots and old vines that new stuff's growed over, they sometimes break away from the mainland in a brisk gale and go off for a voyage, calm as a old-fashioned, eight-funnel steamer. This one was uncommon large, being as much as two miles, maybe, from shore to shore. It had its palm trees and its live things, just like my own Anita, and I've sometimes wondered if this drifting piece hadn't really been a part of my island once—just its daughter like, as you might say.

"Be that, however, as it might be, no sooner did the floating piece get within hailing distance than I hears a human holler and there was a man dancing up and down on the shore like he was plumb crazy. Next minute he had plunged into the narrow strip of water between us and in a few minutes had swum to where I stood.

"Yes, of course it was none other than Nelson Smith!

"I knowed that the minute I set eyes on him. He had the very look of not having no better sense than the man what wrote that board and then nearly committed suicide trying to get away from the best island in all the oceans. Glad enough he was to get back, though, for the coconuts was running very short on the floater what had rescued him, and the turtle eggs wasn't worth mentioning. Being short of grub is the surest way I know to cure a man's fear of the unknown."

"Well, to make a long story short, Nelson Smith told me he was a aeronauter. In them days to be an aeronauter was not the same as to be an aviatress is now. There was dangers in the air, and dangers in the sea, and he had met with both.

His gas tank had leaked and he had dropped into the water close by Anita. A case or two of provisions was all he could save from the total wreck.

"Now, as you might guess, I was crazy enough to find out what had scared this Nelson Smith into trying to swim the Pacific. He told me a story that seemed to fit pretty well with mine, only when it come to the scary part he shut up like a clam, that aggravating way some men have. I give it up at last for just man-foolishness, and we begun to scheme to get away.

"Anita moped some while we talked it over. I realized how she must be feeling, so I explained to her that it was right needful for us to get with our kind again. If we stayed with her we should probably quarrel like cats, and maybe even kill each other out of pure human cussedness. She cheered up considerable after that, and even, I thought, got a little anxious to have us leave. At any rate, when we begun to provision up the little floater, which we had anchored to the big island by a cable of twisted bark, the green nuts fell all over the ground, and Nelson found more turtle nests in a day than I had in weeks.

"During them days I really got fond of Nelson Smith. He was a companionable body, and brave, or he wouldn't have been a professional aeronauter, a job that was rightly thought tough enough for a woman, let alone a man. Though he was not so well educated as me, at least he was quiet and modest about what he did know, not like some men, boasting most where there is least to brag of.

"Indeed, I misdoubt if Nelson and me would not have quit the sea and the air together and set up housekeeping in some quiet little town up in New England, maybe, after we had got away, if it had not been for what happened when we went. I never, let me say, was so deceived in any man before nor since. The thing taught me a lesson and I never was fooled again.

"We was all ready to go, and then one morning, like a parting gift from Anita, come a soft and favoring wind. Nelson and I run down the beach together, for we didn't want our floater to blow off and leave us. As we was running, our arms full of coconuts, Nelson Smith, stubbed his bare toe on a sharp rock, and down he went. I hadn't noticed, and was going on.

"But sudden the ground begun to shake under my feet, and the air was full of a queer, grinding, groaning sound, like the very earth was in pain.

"I turned around sharp. There sat Nelson, holding his bleeding toe in both fists and giving vent to such awful words as no decent sea-going lady would ever speak nor hear to!

" 'Stop it, stop it!' I shrieked at him, but 'twas too late.

"Island or no island, Anita was a lady, too! She had a gentle heart, but she knowed how to behave when she was insulted.

"With one terrible, great roar a spout of smoke and flame belched up out o' the heart of Anita's crater hill a full mile into the air!

"I guess Nelson stopped swearing. He couldn't have heard himself, anyways. Anita was talking now with tongues of flame and such roars as would have bespoke the raging protest of a continent.

"I grabbed that fool man by the hand and run him down to the water. We had to swim good and hard to catch up with our only hope, the floater. No bark rope could hold her against the stiff breeze that was now blowing, and she had broke her cable. By the time we scrambled aboard great rocks was falling right and left. We couldn't see each other for a while for the clouds of fine gray ash.

"It seemed like Anita was that mad she was flinging stones after us, and truly I believe that such was her intention. I didn't blame her, neither!

"Lucky for us the wind was strong and we was soon out of range.

" 'So!' says I to Nelson, after I'd got most of the ashes out of my mouth, and shook my hair clear of cinders. 'So, that was the reason you up and left sudden when you was there before! You aggravated that island till the poor thing druv you out!'

" 'Well,' says he, and not so meek as I'd have admired to see him, 'how could I know the darn island was a lady?'

" 'Actions speak louder than words,' says I. 'You should have knowed it by her ladylike behavior!'

" 'Is volcanoes and slingin' hot rocks ladylike?' he says. 'Is snakes ladylike? T'other time I cut my thumb on a tin can, I cussed a little bit. Say—just a li'l' bit! An' what comes at me out o' all the caves, and out o' every crack in the rocks, and out o' the very spring o' water where I'd been drinkin'? Why snakes! *Snakes*, if you please, big, little, green, red and sky-blue-scarlet! What'd I do? Jumped in the water, of course. Why wouldn't I? I'd ruther swim and drown than be stung or swallowed to death. But how was I t' know the snakes come outta the rocks because I cussed?'

" 'You, couldn't,' I agrees, sarcastic. 'Some folks never knows a lady till she up and whangs 'em over the head with a brick. A real, gentle, kind-like warning, them snakes were, which you would not heed! Take shame to yourself, Nelly,' says I, right stern, 'that a decent little island like Anita can't associate with you peaceable, but you must hurt her sacredest feelings with language no lady would stand by to hear!'

"I never did see Anita again. She may have blew herself right out of the ocean in her just wrath at the vulgar, disgustin' language of Nelson Smith. I don't know. We was took off the floater at last, and I lost track of Nelson just as quick as I could when we was landed at Frisco.

"He had taught me a lesson. A man is just full of mannishness, and the best of 'em ain't good enough for a lady to sacrfice her sensibilities to put up with.

"Nelson Smith, he seemed to feel real bad when he learned I was not for him, and then he apologized. But apologies weren't no use to me. I could never abide him, after the way he went and talked right in the presence of me and my poor, sweet lady friend, Anita!"

Now I am well versed in the lore of the sea in all ages. Through mists of time I have enviously eyed wild voyagings of sea rovers who roved and spun their yarns before the stronger sex came into its own, and ousted man from his heroic pedestal. I have followed—across the printed page—the wanderings of Odysseus. Before Gulliver I have burned the incense of tranced attention; and with reverent awe considered the history of one Munchausen, a baron. But alas, these were only men!

In what field is not woman our subtle superior?

Meekly I bowed my head, and when my eyes dared lift again, the ancient mariness had departed, leaving me to sorrow for my surpassed and outdone idols. Also with a bill for macaroons and tea of such incredible proportions that in comparison therewith I found it easy to believe her story!

CLARK ASHTON SMITH (1893–1961)

Poetry was the literary love of Clark Ashton Smith, and he was more than a little talented at the form but found that he needed to write prose to supplement the meager income generated from poetry writing. Smith did both well. He was a life-long resident of California.

While Weird Tales *magazine featured many talented and enduring authors from 1923 until the early 1950s, Clark Ashton Smith was considered one of the "Three Musketeers of* Weird Tales." *(The other two were H. P. Lovecraft and Robert E. Howard.) Smith, Lovecraft, and Howard were the mainstays of the famous Fantasy pulp magazine. Of course, there were others, including Edmond Hamilton, Seabury Quinn, Robert Bloch, and Mary Counselman. Smith's prose appeared almost exclusively in* Weird Tales, *where it was often edited for its exuberance and eroticism. Much of Clark Ashton Smith's prose and poetry was collected in several volumes published by August Derleth and Donald Wandrei's Arkham House.*

Like Abraham Merritt, Clark Ashton Smith was uniquely talented when it came to employing the colors, dimensions, and textures of language. Both his poetry and prose are lyrical, and they feature exotic atmospheres and settings; intricate plotting; and sensual, even erotic characters and situations. Ray Bradbury has always been a proponent of the author. Smith, like Lovecraft, was an adept storyteller enamored with the old styles of writing. He wrote Dark Fantasy, High Fantasy, and Science Fiction. Much of his fiction was a hybrid of genres and traditions.

The City of Singing Flame
(Wonder Stories, January and November, 1931)

FOREWORD

When Giles Angarth disappeared, nearly two years ago, we had been friends for a decade or more, and I knew him as well as anyone could purport to know him. Yet the thing was no less a mystery to me than to others at the time, and until now, it has remained a mystery.

Like the rest, I sometimes thought that he and Ebbonly had designed it all between them as a huge, insoluble hoax; that they were still alive, somewhere, and laughing at the world that was so sorely baffled by their disappearance. And, until I at last decided to visit Crater Ridge and find, if I could, the two boulders mentioned in Angarth's narrative, no one had uncovered any trace of the missing men or heard even the faintest rumour concerning them. The whole affair, it seemed then, was likely to remain a most singular and exasperating riddle.

Angarth, whose fame as a writer of fantastic fiction was already very considerable, had been spending that summer among the Sierras, and had been living alone until the artist, Felix Ebbonly, went to visit him. Ebbonly, whom I had never met, was well-known for his imaginative paintings and drawings, and had illustrated more than one of Angarth's novels.

When neighbouring campers became alarmed over the prolonged absence of the two men, and the cabin was searched for some possible clue, a package addressed to me was found lying on the table; and I received it in due course of time, after reading many newspaper speculations concerning the double vanishment.

The package contained a small, leather-bound note-book, and Angarth had written on the fly-leaf:

DEAR HASTANE,

You can publish this journal sometime, if you like. People will think it the last and wildest of all my fictions—unless they take it for one of your own. In either case, it will be just as well. Good-bye.

Faithfully,
GILES ANGARTH.

Feeling that it would certainly meet with the reception he anticipated, and being unsure, myself, whether the tale was truth or fabrication, I delayed publishing his journal. Now, from my own experience, I have become satisfied of its reality; and am finally printing it, together with an account of my personal adventures. Perhaps the double publication, preceded as it is by Angarth's return to mundane surroundings, will help to ensure the acceptance of the whole story for more than mere fantasy.

Still, when I recall my own doubts, I wonder. . . . But let the reader decide for himself. And first, as to Giles Angarth's journal:

July, 31*st*, 1938.—I have never acquired the diary-keeping habit—mainly because of my uneventful mode of existence, in which there has seldom been anything to chronicle. But the thing which happened this morning is so extravagantly strange, so remote from mundane laws and parallels, that I feel impelled to write it down to the best of my understanding and ability. Also, I shall keep account of the possible repetition and continuation of my experience. It will be perfectly safe to do this, for no one who ever reads the record will be likely to believe it. . . .

I had gone for a walk on Crater Ridge, which lies a mile or less to the north of my cabin near Summit. Though differing markedly in its character from the usual landscapes round about, it is one of my favourite places. It is exceptionally bare and desolate, with little more in the way of vegetation than mountain sunflowers, wild currant-bushes, and a few sturdy, wind-warped pines and supple tamaracks.

Geologists deny it a volcanic origin; yet its outcroppings of rough, nodular stone and enormous rubble-heaps have all the air of scoriac remains—at least, to my non-scientific eye. They look like the slag and refuse of Cyclopean furnaces, poured out in pre-human years, to cool and harden into shapes of limitless grotesquerie.

Among them are stones that suggest the fragments of primordial bas-reliefs, or small prehistoric idols and figurines, and others that seem to have been graven with lost letters of an indecipherable script. Unexpectedly, there is a little tarn lying on one end of the long, dry Ridge—a tarn that has never been fathomed. The hill is an odd interlude among the granite sheets and crags, and the fir-clothed ravines and valleys of this region.

It was a clear, windless morning, and I paused often to view the magnificent perspectives of varied scenery that were visible on every hand—the titan battlements of Castle Peak; the rude masses of Donner Peak, with its dividing pass of hemlocks; the remote, luminous blue of the Nevada Mountains, and the soft green of willows in the valley at my feet. It was an aloof, silent world, and I heard no sound other than the dry, crackling noise of cicadas.

I strolled on in a zigzag manner for some distance, and coming to one of the rubble-fields with which the Ridge is interstrewn, I began to search the ground closely, hoping to find a stone that was sufficiently quaint and grotesque in its form to be worth keeping as a curiosity: I had found several such in my previous wanderings. Suddenly, I came to a clear space amid the rubble, in which nothing grew—a space that was round as an artificial ring. In the centre were two isolated boulders, queerly alike in shape, and lying about five feet apart.

I paused to examine them. Their substance, a dull, greenish-grey stone, seemed to be different from anything else in the neighbourhood; and I conceived at once the weird, unwarrantable fancy that they might be the pedestals of vanished columns, worn away by incalculable years till there remained only these sunken ends. Certainly, the perfect roundness and uniformity of the boulders was peculiar, and though I possess a smattering of geology, I could not identify their smooth, soapy material.

My imagination was excited, and I began to indulge in some rather overheated fantasies. But the wildest of these was a homely commonplace in comparison with the thing that happened when I took a single step forward in the vacant space immediately between the two boulders. I shall try to describe it to the utmost of my ability; though human language is naturally wanting in words that are adequate for the delineation of events and sensations beyond the normal scope of human experience.

Nothing is more disconcerting than to miscalculate the degree of descent in taking a step. Imagine, then, what it was like to step forward on level, open ground, and find utter nothingness underfoot! I seemed to be going down into an empty gulf; and, at the same time, the landscape before me vanished in a swirl of broken images and everything went blind. There was a feeling of intense, hyperborean cold, and an indescribable sickness and vertigo possessed me, due, no doubt, to the profound disturbance of equilibrium. Either from the speed of my descent or for some other reason, I was, too, totally unable to draw breath.

My thoughts and feelings were unutterably confused, and half the time it seemed to me that I was falling *upward* rather than downward, or was sliding horizontally or at some oblique angle. At last, I had the sensation of turning a complete somersault; and then I found myself standing erect on solid ground once more, without the least shock or jar of impact. The darkness cleared away from my vision, but I was still dizzy, and the optical images I received were altogether meaningless for some moments.

When, finally, I recovered the power of cognisance and was able to view my surroundings with a measure of perception, I experienced a mental confusion equivalent to that of a man who might find himself cast without warning on the shore of some foreign planet. There was the same sense of utter loss and alienation which would assuredly be felt in such a case; the same vertiginous, overwhelming bewilderment, the same ghastly sense of separation from all the familiar environmental details that give colour, form and definition to our lives and even determine our very personalities.

I was standing in the midst of a landscape which bore no degree or manner of resemblance to Crater Ridge. A long, gradual slope, covered with violet grass and studded at intervals with stones of monolithic size and shape, ran undulantly away beneath me to a broad plain with sinuous, open meadows and high, stately forests of an unknown vegetation whose predominant hues were purple and yellow. The plain seemed to end in a wall of impenetrable, golden-brownish mist, that rose with phantom pinnacles to dissolve on a sky of luminescent amber in which there was no sun.

In the foreground of this amazing scene, not more than two or three miles away, there loomed a city whose massive towers and mountainous ramparts of red stone were such as the Anakim of undiscovered worlds might build. Wall on beetling wall, spire on giant spire, it soared to confront the heavens, maintaining everywhere the severe and solemn lines of a rectilinear architecture. It seemed to overwhelm and crush down the beholder with its stern and crag-like imminence.

As I viewed this city, I forgot my initial sense of bewildering loss and alienage, in an awe with which something of actual terror was mingled; and, at the same time, I felt an obscure but profound allurement, the cryptic emanation of some enslaving spell. But after I had gazed awhile, the cosmic strangeness and bafflement of my unthinkable position returned upon me, and I felt only a wild desire to escape from the maddeningly oppressive bizarrerie of this region and regain my own world. In an effort to fight down my agitation, I tried to figure out, if possible, what had really happened.

I had read a number of transdimensional stories—in fact, I had written one or two myself; and I had often pondered the possibility of other worlds or material planes which may co-exist in the same space with ours, invisible and impalpable to human senses. Of course, I realised at once that I had fallen into some such dimension. Doubtless, when I took that step forward between the boulders, I had been precipitated into some sort of flaw or fissure in space, to emerge at the bottom in this alien sphere—in a totally different kind of space.

It sounded simple enough, in a way, but not simple enough to make the *modus operandi* anything but a brain-racking mystery, and in a further effort to collect myself, I studied my immediate surroundings with a close attention. This time, I was impressed by the arrangement of the monolithic stones I have spoken of, many of which were disposed at fairly regular intervals in two parallel lines running down the hill, as if to mark the course of some ancient road obliterated by the purple grass.

Turning to follow its ascent, I saw right behind me two columns, standing at precisely the same distance apart as the two odd boulders on Crater Ridge, and formed of the same soapy, greenish-grey stone. The pillars were perhaps nine feet high, and had been taller at one time, since the tops were splintered and broken away. Not far above them, the mounting slope vanished from view in a great bank of the same golden-brown mist that enveloped the remoter plain. But there were no more monoliths, and it seemed as if the road had ended with those pillars.

Inevitably, I began to speculate as to the relationship between the columns in this new dimension and the boulders in my own world. Surely, the resemblance could not be a matter of mere chance. If I stepped between the columns, could I return to the human sphere by a reversal of my precipitation therefrom? And if so, by what inconceivable beings from foreign time and space had the columns and boulders been established as the portals of a gateway between the two worlds? Who could have used the gateway, and for what purpose?

My brain reeled before the infinite vistas of surmise that were opened by such questions. However, what concerned me most was the problem of getting back to Crater Ridge. The weirdness of it all, the monstrous walls of the near-by town, the unnatural hues and forms of the outlandish scenery, were too much for human nerves, and I felt that I should go mad if forced to remain long in such a milieu. Also, there was no telling what hostile powers or entities I might encounter if I stayed.

The slope and plain were devoid of animate life, as far as I could see; but the great city was presumptive proof of its existence. Unlike the heroes in my own tales, who were wont to visit the Fifth Dimension or the world of Algol with perfect *sang froid*, I did not feel in the least adventurous, and I shrank back with man's instinctive recoil before the unknown. With one fearful glance at the looming city and the wide plain with its lofty, gorgeous vegetation, I turned and stepped back between the columns.

There was the same instantaneous plunge into blind and freezing gulfs, the same indeterminate falling and twisting, which had marked my descent into this new dimension. At the end I found myself standing, very dizzy and shaken, on the same spot from which I had taken my forward step between the greenish-grey boulders. Crater Ridge was swirling and reeling about me as if in the throes of earthquake, and I had to sit down for a minute or two before I could recover my equilibrium.

I came back to the cabin like a man in a dream. The experience seemed, and still seems, incredible and unreal; and yet it has overshadowed everything else, and has coloured and dominated all my thoughts. Perhaps by writing it down I can shake it off a little. It has unsettled me more than any previous experience in my whole life, and the world about me seems hardly less improbable and nightmarish than the one which I have penetrated in a fashion so fortuitous.

August 2nd.—I have done a lot of thinking in the past two days, and the more I ponder and puzzle, the more mysterious it all becomes. Granting the flaw in space, which must be an absolute vacuum, impervious to air, ether, light and matter, how was it possible for me to fall into it? And having fallen in, how could I fall out—particularly into a sphere that has no certifiable relationship with ours?

But, after all, one process would be as easy as the other, in theory. The main objection is: how could one move in a vacuum, either up or down, or backward or forward? The whole thing would baffle the comprehension of an Einstein, and I cannot feel that I have even approached the solution.

Also, I have been fighting the temptation to go back, if only to convince myself that the thing really occurred. But, after all, why shouldn't I go back? An opportunity has been vouchsafed to me such as no man may ever have been given before, and the wonders I shall see, the secrets I shall learn, are beyond imagining. My nervous trepidation is inexcusably childish under the circumstances. . . .

August 3rd.—I went back this morning, armed with a revolver. Somehow, without thinking that it might make a difference, I did not step in the very middle of the space between the boulders. Undoubtedly as a result of this, my descent was more prolonged and impetuous than before, and seemed to consist mainly of a series of spiral somersaults. It must have taken me several minutes to recover from the ensuing vertigo, and when I came to, I was lying on the violet grass.

This time, I went boldly down the slope, and keeping as much as I could in the shelter of that bizarre purple and yellow vegetation, I stole towards the looming city. All was very still; there was no breath of wind in those exotic trees, which appeared to imitate, in their lofty, upright boles and horizontal foliage, the severe architectural lines of the Cyclopean buildings.

I had not gone far when I came to a road in the forest—a road paved with stupendous blocks of stones at least twenty feet square. It ran towards the city. I thought for a while that it was wholly deserted, perhaps disused; and I even dared to walk upon it, till I heard a noise behind me and, turning, saw the approach of several singular entities. Terrified, I sprang back and hid myself in a thicket, from which I watched the passing of those creatures, wondering fearfully if they had seen me. Apparently, my fears were groundless, for they did not even glance at my hiding-place.

It is hard for me to describe or even visualise them now, for they were totally unlike anything that we are accustomed to think of as human or animal. They must have been ten feet tall, and they were moving along with colossal strides that took them from sight in a few instants, beyond a turn of the road. Their bodies were bright and shining, as if encased in some sort of armour, and their heads were equipped with high, curving appendages of opalescent hues which nodded above them like fantastic plumes, but may have been antennae or other sense-organs of a novel type.

Trembling with excitement and wonder, I continued my progress through the richly-coloured undergrowth. As I went on, I perceived for the first time that there were no shadows anywhere. The light came from all portions of the sunless, amber heaven, pervading everything with a soft, uniform luminosity. All was motionless and silent, as before; and there was no evidence of bird, insect or animal life in all this preternatural landscape.

But, when I had advanced to within a mile of the city—as well as I could judge the distance in a realm where the very proportions of objects were unfamiliar—I became aware of something which at first was recognizable as a vibration rather than a sound. There was a queer thrilling in my nerves; the disquieting sense of some unknown force or emanation flowing through my body. This was perceptible for some time before I heard the music, but having heard it, my auditory nerves identified it at once with the vibration.

It was faint and far-off, and seemed to emanate from the very heart of the Titan city. The melody was piercingly sweet, and resembled at times the singing of some voluptuous feminine voice. However, no human voice could have possessed that unearthly pitch, the shrill, perpetually sustained notes that somehow suggested the light of remote worlds and stars translated into sound.

Ordinarily, I am not very sensitive to music; I have even been reproached for not reacting more strongly to it. But I had not gone much farther when I realised the peculiar mental and emotional spell which the far-off sound was beginning to exert upon me. There was a siren-like allurement which drew me on, forgetful of the strangeness and potential perils of my situation; and I felt a slow, drug-like intoxication of brain and senses.

In some insidious manner, I know not how or why, the music conveyed the ideas of vast but attainable space and altitude, of superhuman freedom and exultation; and it seemed to promise all the impossible splendours of which my imagination has vaguely dreamt. . . .

The forest continued almost to the city walls. Peering from behind the final boscage, I saw their overwhelming battlements in the sky above me, and noted the flawless jointure of their prodigious blocks. I was near the great road, which entered an open gate large enough to admit the passage of behemoths. There were no guards in sight, and several more of the tall, gleaming entities came striding along and went in as I watched.

From where I stood, I was unable to see inside the gate, for the wall was stupendously thick. The music poured from that mysterious entrance in an ever-strengthening flood, and sought to draw me on with its weird seduction, eager for unimaginable things. It was hard to resist; hard to rally my will-power and turn back. I tried to concentrate on the thought of danger—but the thought was tenuously unreal.

At last I tore myself away and retraced my footsteps, very slowly and lingeringly, till I was beyond reach of the music. Even then, the spell persisted, like the effects of a drug; and all the way home I was tempted to return and follow those shining giants into the city.

August 5th.—I have visited the new dimension once more. I thought I could resist that summoning music, and I even took some cotton-wadding with which to stuff my ears if it should affect me too strongly. I began to hear the supernal melody at the same distance as before, and was drawn onward in the same manner. But, this time, I entered the open gate!

I wonder if I can describe that city? I felt like a crawling ant upon its mammoth pavements, amid the measureless Babel of its buildings, of its streets and arcades. Everywhere there were columns, obelisks, and the perpendicular pylons of fane-like structures that would have dwarfed those of Thebes and Heliopolis. And the people of the city! How is one to depict them, or give them a name!

I think that the gleaming entities I first saw are not the true inhabitants, but are only visitors, perhaps from some other world or dimension, like myself. The real people are giants, too; but they move slowly, with solemn, hieratic paces. Their bodies are nude and swart, and their limbs are those of caryatides—massive enough, it would seem, to uphold the roofs and lintels of their own buildings. I fear to describe them minutely, for human words would give the idea of something monstrous and uncouth, and these beings are not monstrous, but have merely developed in obedience to the laws of another evolution than ours; the environmental forces and conditions of a different world.

Somehow, I was not afraid when I saw them—perhaps the music had drugged me till I was beyond fear. There was a group of them just inside the gate, and they seemed to pay me no attention whatever as I passed them. The opaque, jet-like orbs of their huge eyes were impassive as the carven eyes of androsphinxes, and they uttered no sound from their heavy, straight, expressionless lips. Perhaps they lack the sense of hearing, for their strange, semi-rectangular heads were devoid of anything in the nature of external ears.

I followed the music, which was still remote and seemed to increase little in loudness. I was soon overtaken by several of those beings whom I had previously seen on the road outside the walls; and they passed me quickly and disappeared in the labyrinth of buildings. After them there came other beings of a less gigantic kind, and without the bright shards of armour worn by the first-comers. Then, overhead, two creatures with long, translucent, blood-coloured wings, intricately veined and ribbed, came flying side by side and vanished behind the others. Their faces, featured with organs of unsurmisable use, were not those of animals, and I felt sure that they were beings of a high order of development.

I saw hundreds of those slow-moving, sombre entities whom I have identified as the true inhabitants, but none of them appeared to notice me. Doubtless they were accustomed to seeing far weirder and more unusual kinds of life than humanity. As I went on, I was overtaken by dozens of improbable-looking creatures, all going in the same direction as myself, as if drawn by the same siren melody.

Deeper and deeper I went into the wilderness of colossal architecture, led by that remote, ethereal, opiate music. I soon noticed a sort of gradual ebb and flow in the sound, occupying an interval of ten minutes or more; but, by imperceptible degrees, it grew sweeter and nearer. I wondered how it could penetrate that manifold maze of builded stone and be heard outside the walls. . . .

I must have walked for miles, in the ceaseless gloom of those rectangular structures that hung above me, tier on tier, at an awful height in the amber zenith. Then, at length, I came to the core and secret of it all. Preceded and followed by a number of those chimerical entities, I emerged on a great square, in whose centre was a temple-like building more immense than the others. The music poured, imperiously shrill and loud, from its many-columned entrance.

I felt the thrill of one who approaches the sanctum of some hierarchal mystery, when I entered the halls of that building. People who must have come from many different worlds or dimensions went with me, and before me, along the titanic colonnades, whose pillars were graven with indecipherable runes and enigmatic bas-reliefs. The dark, colossal inhabitants of the town were standing or roaming about, intent, like all the others, on their own affairs. None of these beings spoke, either to me or to one another, and though several eyed me casually, my presence was evidently taken for granted.

There are no words to convey the incomprehensible wonder of it all. And the music? I have utterly failed to describe that, also. It was as if some marvellous elixir had been turned into sound-waves—an elixir conferring the gift of superhuman life, and the high, magnificent dreams which are dreamt by the Immortals. It mounted in my brain like a supernal drunkenness, as I approached the hidden source.

I do not know what obscure warning prompted me, now, to stuff my ears with cotton before I went any farther. Though I could still hear it, still feel its peculiar, penetrant vibration, the sound became muted when I had done this, and its influence was less powerful henceforth. There is little doubt that I owe my life to this simple and homely precaution.

The endless rows of columns grew dim for a while as the interior of a long, basaltic cavern; and then, some distance ahead, I perceived the glimmering of a soft light on the floor and pillars. The light soon became an over-flooding radiance, as if gigantic lamps were being lit in the temple's heart; and the vibrations of the hidden music pulsed more strongly in my nerves.

The hall ended in a chamber of immense, indefinite scope, whose walls and roof were doubtful with unremoving shadows. In the centre, amid the pavement of mammoth blocks, there was a circular pit, above which seemed to float a fountain of flame that soared in one perpetual, slowly lengthening jet. This flame was the sole illumination, and also, was the source of the wild, unearthly music. Even with my purposely deafened ears, I was wooed by the shrill and starry sweetness of its singing; and I felt the voluptuous lure and the high, vertiginous exaltation.

I knew immediately that the place was a shrine, and that the transdimensional beings who accompanied me were visiting pilgrims. There were scores of them— perhaps hundreds; but all were dwarfed in the cosmic immensity of that chamber. They were gathered before the flame in various attitudes of worship; they bowed their exotic heads, or made mysterious gestures of adoration with unhuman hands and members. And the voices of several, deep as booming drums, or sharp as the stridulation of giant insects, were audible amid the singing of the fountain.

Spellbound, I went forward and joined them. Enthralled by the music and by the vision of the soaring flame, I paid as little heed to my outlandish companions as they to me. The fountain rose and rose, until its light flickered on the limbs and features of throned, colossal statues behind it—of heroes, gods or demons from the earlier cycles of alien time, staring in stone from a dusk of illimitable mystery.

The fire was green and dazzling, pure as the central flame of a star; it blinded me, and when I turned my eyes away, the air was filled with webs of intricate colour, with swiftly changing arabesques whose numberless, unwonted hues and patterns were such as no mundane eye had ever beheld. And I felt a stimulating warmth that filled my very marrow with intenser life. . . .

The music mounted with the flame; and I understood, now, its recurrent ebb and flow. As I looked and listened, a mad thought was born in my mind—the thought of how marvellous and ecstatical it would be to run forward and leap headlong into the singing fire. The music seemed to tell me that I should find in that moment of flaring dissolution all the delight and triumph, all the splendour and exaltation it had promised from afar. It besought me; it pleaded with tones of supernal melody, and despite the wadding in my ears, the seduction was well-nigh irresistible.

However, it had not robbed me of all sanity. With a sudden start of terror, like one who has been tempted to fling himself from a high precipice, I drew back. Then I saw that the same dreadful impulse was shared by some of my companions. The two entities with scarlet wings, whom I have previously mentioned, were standing a little apart from the rest of us. Now, with a great fluttering, they rose and flew towards the flame like moths towards a candle. For a brief moment the light shone redly through their half-transparent wings, ere they disappeared in the leaping incandescence, which flared briefly and then burned as before.

Then, in rapid succession, a number of other beings, who represented the most divergent trends of biology, sprang forward and immolated themselves in the flame. There were creatures with translucent bodies, and some that shone with all the hues of the opal; there were winged colossi, and Titans who strode as with seven-league boots; and there was one being with useless, abortive wings, who crawled rather than ran, to seek the same glorious doom as the rest. But among them there were none of the city's people: these merely stood and looked on, impassive and statue-like as ever.

I saw that the fountain had now reached its greatest height, and was beginning to decline. It sank steadily, but slowly, to half its former elevation. During this interval, there were no more acts of self-sacrifice, and several of the beings beside me turned abruptly and went away, as if they had overcome the lethal spell.

One of the tall, armoured entities, as he left, addressed me in words that were like clarion-notes, with unmistakable accents of warning. By a mighty effort of will, in a turmoil of conflicting emotions, I followed him. At every step, the madness and delirium of the music warred with my instincts of self-preservation. More than once, I started to go back. My homeward journey was blurred and doubtful as the wanderings of a man in an opium-trance; and the music sang behind me, and told me of the rapture I had missed, of the flaming dissolution whose brief instant was better than aeons of mortal life. . . .

August 9th. — I have tried to go on with a new story, but have made no progress. Anything that I can imagine, or frame in language, seems flat and puerile beside the world of unsearchable mystery to which I have found admission. The temptation to return is more cogent than ever; the call of that remembered music is sweeter than the voice of a loved woman. And always I am tormented by the problem of it all, and tantalised by the little which I have perceived and understood.

What forces are these whose existence and working I have merely apprehended? Who are the inhabitants of the city? And who are the beings that visit the enshrined flame? What rumour or legend has drawn them from outland realms and ulterior planets to that place of inenarrable danger and destruction? And what is the fountain itself, what the secret of its lure and its deadly singing? These problems admit of infinite surmise, but no conceivable solution.

I am planning to go back once more . . . but not alone. Someone must go with me, this time, as a witness to the wonder and the peril. It is all too strange for credence: I must have human corroboration of what I have seen and felt and conjectured. Also, another might understand where I have failed to do more than apprehend.

Whom shall I take? It will be necessary to invite someone here from the outer world — someone of high intellectual and aesthetic capacity. Shall I ask Philip

Hastane, my fellow fiction-writer? He would be too busy, I fear. But there is the Californian artist, Felix Ebbonly, who has illustrated some of my fantastic novels. . . .

Ebbonly would be the man to see and appreciate the new dimension, if he can come. With his bent for the bizarre and unearthly, the spectacle of that plain and city, the Babelian buildings and arcades, and the Temple of the Flame, will simply enthrall him. I shall write immediately to his San Francisco address.

August 12th.—Ebbonly is here: the mysterious hints in my letter, regarding some novel pictorial subjects along his own line, were too provocative for him to resist. Now, I have explained fully and given him a detailed account of my adventures. I can see that he is a little incredulous, for which I hardly blame him. But he will not remain incredulous very long, for tomorrow we shall visit together the City of the Singing Flame.

August 13th.—I must concentrate my disordered faculties, must choose my words and write with exceeding care. This will be the last entry in my journal, and the last writing I shall ever do. When I have finished, I shall wrap the journal up and address it to Philip Hastane, who can make such disposition of it as he sees fit.

I took Ebbonly into the other dimension today. He was impressed, even as I had been, by the two isolated boulders on Crater Ridge.

"They look like the guttered ends of columns established by pre-human gods," he remarked. "I begin to believe you now."

I told him to go first, and indicated the place where he should step. He obeyed without hesitation, and I had the singular experience of seeing a man melt into utter, instantaneous nothingness. One moment he was there—the next, there was only bare ground, and the far-off tamaracks whose view his body had obstructed. I followed, and found him standing, in speechless awe, on the violet grass.

"This," he said at last, "is the sort of thing whose existence I have hitherto merely suspected, and have never been able to hint at in my most imaginative drawings."

We spoke little as we followed the range of monolithic boulders towards the plain. Far in the distance, beyond those high and stately trees with their sumptuous foliage, the golden-brown vapours had parted, showing vistas of an immense horizon; and past the horizon were range on range of gleaming orbs and fiery, flying motes in the depth of that amber heaven. It was as if the veil of another universe than ours had been drawn back.

We crossed the plain, and came at length within earshot of the siren music. I warned Ebbonly to stuff his ears with cotton-wadding, but he refused.

"I don't want to deaden any new sensation I may experience," he observed.

We entered the city. My companion was in a veritable rhapsody of artistic delight when he beheld the enormous buildings and the people. I could see, too, that the music had taken hold upon him: his look soon became fixed and dreamy as that of an opium-eater.

At first, he made many comments on the architecture and the various beings who passed us, and called my attention to details which I had not perceived before. However, as we drew nearer the Temple of the Flame, his observational interest seemed to flag, and was replaced by more and more of an ecstatic inward absorption. His remarks became fewer and briefer, and he did not even seem to hear my questions. It was evident that the sound had wholly bemused and bewitched him.

Even as on my former visit, there were many pilgrims going towards the shrine—and few that were coming away from it. Most of them belonged to evolutionary types that I had seen before. Among those that were new to me, I recall one gorgeous creature with golden and cerulean wings like those of a giant lepidoptera, and scintillating, jewel-like eyes that must have been designed to mirror the glories of some Edenic world.

I felt, too, as before, the captious thraldom and bewitchment, the insidious, gradual perversion of thought and instinct, as if the music were working in my brain like a subtle alkaloid. Since I had taken my usual precaution, my subjection to the influence was less complete than that of Ebbonly; but, nevertheless, it was enough to make me forget a number of things—among them, the initial concern which I had felt when my companion refused to employ the same mode of protection as myself. I no longer thought of his danger, or my own, except as something very distant and immaterial.

The streets were like the prolonged and bewildering labyrinth of a nightmare. But the music led us forthrightly, and always there were other pilgrims. Like men in the grip of some powerful current, we were drawn to our destination.

As we passed along the hall of gigantic columns and neared the abode of the fiery fountain, a sense of our peril quickened momentarily in my brain, and I sought to warn Ebbonly once more. But all my protests and remonstrances were futile: he was deaf as a machine, and wholly impervious to anything but the lethal music. His expression and movements were those of a somnambulist. Even when I seized and shook him with such violence as I could muster, he remained oblivious of my presence.

The throng of worshippers was larger than upon my first visit. The jet of pure, incandescent flame was mounting steadily as we entered, and it sang with the pure ardour and ecstasy of a star alone in space. Again, with ineffable tones, it told me the rapture of a moth-like death in its lofty soaring, the exultation and triumph of a momentary union with its elemental essence.

The flame rose to its apex; and even for me, the mesmeric lure was well-nigh irresistible. Many of our companions succumbed, and the first to immolate himself was the giant lepidopterous being. Four others, of diverse evolutionary types, followed in appallingly swift succession.

In my own partial subjection to the music, my own effort to resist that deadly enslavement, I had almost forgotten the very presence of Ebbonly. It was too late for me to even think of stopping him, when he ran forward in a series of leaps that were both solemn and frenzied, like the beginning of some sacerdotal dance, and hurled himself headlong into the flame. The fire enveloped him; it flared up for an instant with a more dazzling greenness, and that was all.

Slowly, as if from benumbed brain centres, a horror crept upon my conscious mind, and helped to annul the perilous mesmerism. I turned, while many others were following Ebbonly's example, and fled from the shrine and from the city. But somehow the horror diminished as I went; more and more, I found myself envying my companion's fate, and wondering as to the sensations he had felt in that moment of fiery dissolution. . . .

Now, as I write this, I am wondering why I came back again to the human world. Words are futile to express what I have beheld and experienced, and the change that has come upon me, beneath the play of incalculable forces in a world of which no other mortal is even cognisant. Literature is nothing more than a shadow. Life, with its drawn-out length of monotonous, reiterative days, is unreal and without meaning, now, in comparison with the splendid death which I might have had—the glorious doom which is still in store.

I have no longer any will to fight the ever-insistent music which I hear in memory. And there seems to be no reason why I should fight it. . . . Tomorrow, I return to the city.

Even when I, Philip Hastane, had read through the Journal of my friend, Giles Angarth, so many times that I had almost learned it by heart, I was still doubtful as to whether the incidents related therein were fiction or verity. The transdimensional adventures of Angarth and Ebbonly; the City of the Flame, with its strange residents and pilgrims; the immolation of Ebbonly, and the hinted return of the narrator himself for a like purpose, in the last entry of the diary, were very much the sort of thing that Angarth might have imagined in one of the fantastic novels for which he had become so justly famous. Add to this the seemingly impossible and incredible nature of the whole tale, and my hesitancy in accepting it as veridical will easily be understood.

However, on the other hand, there was the unsolved and recalcitrant enigma offered by the disappearance of the two men. Both were well-known, one as a writer, the other as an artist; both were in flourishing circumstances, with no serious cares or troubles; and their vanishment, all things considered, was difficult to explain on the ground of any motive less unusual or extraordinary than the one assigned in the journal. At first, as I have mentioned in my foreword to the diary, I thought the whole affair might well have been devised as a somewhat elaborate practical joke; but this theory became less and less tenable as weeks and months went by, and linked themselves slowly into a year, without the reappearance of the presumptive jokers.

Now, at last, I can testify to the truth of all that Angarth wrote—and more. For I, too, have been in Ydmos, the City of Singing Flame, and have known also the supernal glories and raptures of the Inner Dimension. And of these I must tell, however falteringly and inadequately, with mere human words, before the vision fades. For these are things which neither I, nor any other, shall behold or experience again.

Ydmos itself is now a riven ruin; the Temple of the Flame has been blasted to its foundations in the basic rock, and the fountain of singing fire has been stricken at its source. The Inner Dimension has perished like a broken bubble, in the great war that was made upon Ydmos by the rulers of the Outer Lands. . . .

After having finally laid down Angarth's journal, I was unable to forget the peculiar and tantalising problems it raised. The vague, but infinitely suggestive vistas opened by the tale were such as to haunt my imagination recurrently with a hint of half-revealed mysteries. I was troubled by the possibility of some great and mystic meaning behind it all; some cosmic actually of which the narrator had perceived merely the external veils and fringes. As time went on, I found myself pondering it perpetually, and becoming more and more possessed by an overwhelming wonder, and a sense of something which no mere fiction-weaver would have been likely to invent.

In the early summer of 1939, after finishing a new novel, I felt able for the first time to take the necessary leisure for the execution of a project that had often occurred to me. Putting all my affairs in order, and knitting all the loose ends of my literary labours and correspondence in case I should not return, I left my home in Auburn, ostensibly for a week's vacation. Actually, I went to Summit, with the idea of investigating closely the milieu in which Angarth and Ebbonly had disappeared from human ken.

With strange emotions, I visited the forsaken cabin south of Crater Ridge, that had been occupied by Angarth, and saw the rough table of pine boards upon which my friend had written his journal, and then left the sealed package containing it to be forwarded to me after his departure.

There was a weird and brooding loneliness about the place, as if the non-human infinitudes had already claimed it for their own. The unlocked door had sagged inward from the pressure of high-piled winter snows, and fir-needles had sifted across the sill to strew the unswept floor. Somehow, I know not why, the bizarre narrative became more real and more credible to me, while I stood there, as if an occult intimation of all that had happened to its author still lingered around the cabin.

This mysterious intimation grew stronger when I came to visit Crater Ridge itself, and to search amid its miles of pseudo-volcanic rubble for the two boulders so explicitly described by Angarth as having a likeness to the pedestals of ruined columns. Following the northward path which he must have taken from his cabin, and trying to retrace his wanderings on the long, barren hill, I combed it thoroughly from end to end and from side to side, since he had not specified the location of the boulders. And after two mornings spent in this manner, without result, I was almost ready to abandon the quest and dismiss the queer, soapy, greenish-grey column-ends as one of Angarth's most provocative and deceptive fictions.

It must have been the formless, haunting intuition to which I have referred, that made me renew the search on the third morning. This time, after crossing and re-crossing the hill-top for an hour or more, and weaving tortuously among the cicada-haunted wild-currant bushes and sunflowers on the dusty slopes, I came at last to an open, circular, rock-surrounded space that was totally unfamiliar. I had somehow missed it in all my previous roamings. It was the place of which Angarth had told; and I saw, with an inexpressible thrill, the two rounded, worn-looking boulders that were situated in the centre of the ring.

I believe that I trembled a little with excitement, as I went forward to inspect the curious stones. Bending over, but not daring to enter the bare, pebbly space between them, I touched one of them with my hand, and received a sensation of preternatural smoothness, together with a coolness that was inexplicable, considering that the boulders and the soil about them must have lain unshaded from the sultry August sun for many hours.

From that moment, I became fully persuaded that Angarth's account was no mere fable. Just why I should have felt so certain of this, I am powerless to say. But it seemed to me that I stood on the threshold of an ultramundane mystery, on the brink of uncharted gulfs. I looked about at the familiar Sierran valleys and mountains, wondering that they still preserved their wonted outlines, and were still unchanged by the contiguity of alien worlds, still untouched by the luminous glories of arcanic dimensions.

Convinced that I had indeed found the gateway between the worlds, I was prompted to strange reflections. What, and where, was this other sphere to which my friend had obtained entrance? Was it near at hand, like a secret room in the structure of space? Or was it, in reality, millions or trillions of light-years away, by the reckoning of astronomic distance, in a planet of some ulterior galaxy?

After all, we know little or nothing of the actual nature of space; and perhaps, in some way that we cannot imagine, the infinite is doubled upon itself in places, with dimensional folds and tucks, and short-cuts whereby the distance to Algenib or Aldebaran is but a step. Perhaps, also, there is more than one infinity. The spatial "flaw" into which Angarth had fallen might well be a sort of super-dimension, abridging the cosmic intervals and connecting universe with universe.

However, because of this very certitude that I had found the inter-spheric portals, and could follow Angarth and Ebbonly if I so desired, I hesitated before trying the experiment. I was mindful of the mystic danger and irrefragable lure that had overcome the others. I was consumed by imaginative curiosity, by an avid, well-nigh feverish longing to behold the wonders of this exotic realm; but I did not propose to become a victim to the opiate power and fascination of the Singing Flame.

I stood for a long time, eyeing the odd boulders and the barren, pebble-littered spot that gave admission to the unknown. At length, I went away, deciding to defer my venture till the following morning. Visualising the weird doom to which the others had gone so voluntarily, and even gladly, I must confess that I was afraid. On the other hand, I was drawn by the fateful allurement that leads an explorer into far places . . . and, perhaps, by something more than this.

I slept badly that night, with nerves and brain excited by formless, glowing premonitions, by intimations of half-conceived perils, and splendours and vastnesses. Early the next morning, while the sun was still hanging above the Nevada Mountains, I returned to Crater Ridge. I carried a strong hunting-knife and a Colt revolver, and wore a filled cartridge-belt, with a knapsack containing sandwiches and a thermos bottle of coffee.

Before starting, I had stuffed my ears tightly with cotton soaked in a new anaesthetic fluid, mild but efficacious, which would serve to deafen me completely for many hours. In this way, I felt that I should be immune to the demoralising music of the fiery fountain. I peered about at the rugged landscape with its far-flung vistas, wondering if I should ever see it again. Then, resolutely, but with the eerie thrilling and sinking of one who throws himself from a high cliff into some bottomless chasm, I stepped forward into the space between the greyish-green boulders.

My sensations, generally speaking, were similar to those described by Angarth in his diary. Blackness and illimitable emptiness seemed to wrap me round in a dizzy swirl as of rushing wind or milling water, and I went down and down in a spiral descent whose duration I have never been able to estimate. Intolerably stifled, and without even the power to gasp for breath, in the chill, airless vacuum that froze my very muscles and marrow, I felt that I should lose consciousness in another moment and descend into the greater gulf of death or oblivion.

Something seemed to arrest my fall, and I became aware that I was standing still, though I was troubled for some time by a queer doubt as to whether my position was vertical, horizontal, or upside-down in relation to the solid substance that my feet had encountered. Then the blackness lifted slowly like a dissolving cloud, and I saw the slope of violet grass, the rows of irregular monoliths running downwards from where I stood, and the grey-green columns near at hand. Beyond was the titan, perpendicular city of red stone that was dominant above the high and multi-coloured vegetation of the plain.

It was all very much as Angarth had depicted it; but somehow, even then, I became aware of differences that were not immediately or clearly definable, of scenic details and atmospheric elements for which his accounts had not prepared me. And, at the moment, I was too thoroughly disequilibrated and overpowered by the vision of it all to even speculate concerning the character of these differences.

As I gazed at the city, with its crowding tiers of battlements and its multitude of overlooming spires, I felt the invisible threads of a secret attraction, was seized by an imperative longing to know the mysteries hidden behind the massive walls and the myriad buildings. Then, a moment later, my gaze was drawn to the remote, opposite horizon of the plain, as if by some conflicting impulse whose nature and origin were undiscoverable.

It must have been because I had formed so clear and definite a picture of the scene from my friend's narrative, that I was surprised, and even a little disturbed as if by something wrong or irrelevant, when I saw in the far distance the shining towers of what seemed to be another city—a city of which Angarth had not written. The towers rose in serried lines, reaching for many miles in a curious arc-like formation, and were sharply defined against a blackish mass of cloud that had reared behind them and was spreading out on the luminous, amber sky in sullen webs and sinister, crawling filaments.

Subtle disquietude and repulsion seemed to emanate from the far-off, glittering spires, even as attraction emanated from those of the nearer city. I saw them quiver and pulse with an evil light, like living and moving things, through what I assumed to be some refractive trick of the atmosphere. Then, for an instant, the black cloud behind them glowed with dull, angry crimson throughout its whole mass, and even its questing webs and tendrils were turned into lurid threads of fire.

The crimson faded, leaving the cloud inert and lumpish as before; but from many of the vanward towers, lines of red and violet flame had leaped, like outthrust lances, at the bosom of the plain beneath them. They were held thus for at least a minute, moving slowly across a wide area, before they vanished. In the spaces between the towers, I now perceived a multitude of gleaming, restless particles, like armies of militant atoms, and wondered if perchance they were living beings. If the idea had not appeared so fantastical, I could have sworn, even then, that the far city had already changed its position and was advancing towards the other on the plain.

Apart from the fulguration of the cloud, the flames that had sprung from the towers, and the quiverings which I deemed a refractive phenomenon, the whole landscape before and about me was unnaturally still. On the strange amber air, the Tyrian-tinted grasses, and the proud, opulent foliage of the unknown trees, there lay the dead calm that precedes the stupendous turmoil of typonic storm or seismic cataclysm. The brooding sky was permeated with intuitions of cosmic menace, and weighed down by a dim, elemental despair.

Alarmed by this ominous atmosphere, I looked behind me at the two pillars which, according to Angarth, were the gateway of return to the human world. For an instant, I was tempted to go back. Then I turned once more to the near-by city, and the feelings I have mentioned were lost in an oversurging awesomeness and wonder. I felt the thrill of a deep, supernal exaltation before the magnitude of the mighty buildings; a compelling sorcery was laid upon me by the very lines of their construction, by the harmonies of a solemn architectural music. I forgot my impulse to return to Crater Ridge, and started down the slope towards the city.

Soon the boughs of the purple and yellow forest arched above me like the altitudes of Titan-builded aisles, with leaves that fretted the rich heaven in gorgeous arabesques. Beyond them, ever and anon, I caught glimpses of the piled ramparts of my destination; but looking back in the direction of that other city on the horizon, I found that its fulgurating towers were now lost to view.

I saw, however, that the masses of the great sombre cloud were rising steadily on the sky, and once again they flared to a swart, malignant red, as if with some unearthly form of sheet-lightning; and though I could hear nothing with my deadened ears, the ground beneath me trembled with long vibrations as of thunder. There was a queer quality in the vibrations, that seemed to tear my nerves and set my teeth on edge with its throbbing, lancinating discord, painful as broken glass or the torment of a tightened rack.

Like Angarth before me, I came to the paved Cyclopean highway. Following it, in the stillness after the unheard peals of thunder, I felt another and subtler vibration, which I knew to be that of the Singing Flame in the temple at the city's core. It seemed to soothe and exalt and bear me on, to erase with soft caresses the ache that still lingered in my nerves from the torturing pulsations of the thunder.

I met no one on the road, and was not passed by any of the trans-dimensional pilgrims such as had overtaken Angarth; and when the accumulated ramparts loomed above the highest trees and I came forth from the wood in their very shadow, I saw that the great gate of the city was closed, leaving no crevice through which a pygmy like myself might obtain entrance.

Feeling a profound and peculiar discomfiture, such as one would experience in a dream that had gone wrong, I stared at the grim, unrelenting blankness of the gate, which seemed to be wrought from one enormous sheet of sombre and lustreless metal. Then I peered upward at the sheerness of the wall, which rose above me like an alpine cliff, and saw that the battlements were seemingly deserted. Was the city forsaken by its people, by the guardians of the Flame? Was it no longer open to the pilgrims who came from outlying lands to worship the Flame and immolate themselves?

With a curious reluctance, after lingering there for many minutes in a sort of stupor, I turned away to retrace my steps. In the interim of my journey, the black cloud had drawn immeasurably nearer, and was now blotting out half the heaven with two portentous, wing-like formations. It was a sinister and terrible sight; and it lightened again with that ominous, wrathful flaming, with a detonation that beat upon my deaf ears like waves of disintegrative force, and seemed to lacerate the inmost fibres of my body.

I hesitated, fearing that the storm would burst upon me before I could reach the inter-dimensional portals, for I saw that I should be exposed to an elemental disturbance of unfamiliar character and supreme violence. Then, in mid-air before the imminent, ever-rising cloud, I perceived two flying creatures whom I can compare only to gigantic moths. With bright, luminous wings, upon the ebon fore-front of the storm, they approached me in level but precipitate flight, and would have crashed headlong against the shut gate if they had not checked themselves with sudden, easy poise.

With hardly a flutter, they descended and paused on the ground beside me, supporting themselves on queer, delicate legs that branched at the knee-joints in floating antennae and waving tentacles. Their wings were sumptuously mottled webs of pearl and madder, opal and orange; their heads were circled by a series of convex and concave eyes, and fringed with coiling, horn-like organs from whose hollow ends there hung aerial filaments. I was startled and amazed by their aspect; but somehow, by an obscure telepathy I felt assured that their intentions towards me were friendly.

I knew that they wished to enter the city, and also that they understood my predicament. Nevertheless, I was not prepared for what happened. With movements of utmost celerity and grace, one of the giant, moth-like beings stationed himself at my right hand, and the other at my left. Then, before I could even suspect their intention, they enfolded my limbs and body with their long tentacles, wrapping me round and round as if with powerful ropes; and carrying me between them as if my weight were a mere trifle, they rose in the air and soared at the mighty ramparts!

In that swift and effortless ascent, the wall seemed to flow downward beside and beneath us, like a wave of molten stone. Dizzily, I watched the falling away of the mammoth blocks in endless recession. Then we were level with the broad ramparts, were flying across the unguarded parapets and over a canyon-like space, towards the immense rectangular buildings and numberless square towers.

We had hardly crossed the walls when a weird, flickering glow was cast on the edifices before us by another lightening of the great cloud. The moth-like beings paid no apparent heed, and flew steadily on into the city with their strange faces towards an unseen goal. But, turning my head to peer backward at the storm, I beheld an astounding and appalling spectacle. Beyond the city ramparts, as if wrought by black magic or the toil of genii, another city had reared, and its high towers were moving swiftly forward beneath the rubescent dome of the burning cloud!

A second glance, and I perceived that the towers were identical with those I had beheld afar on the plain. In the interim of my passage through the woods, they had travelled over an expanse of many miles, by means of some unknown motive-power, and had closed in on the City of the Flame. Looking more closely, to determine the manner of their locomotion, I saw that they were not mounted on wheels, but on short, massy legs like joined columns of metal, that gave them the stride of ungainly colossi. There were six or more of these legs to each tower, and near the tops of the towers were rows of huge eyelike openings, from which issued the bolts of red and violet flame I have mentioned before.

The many-coloured forest had been burned away by these flames in a league-wide swath of devastation, even to the walls, and there was nothing but a stretch of black, vapouring desert between the mobile towers and the city. Then, even as I gazed, the long, leaping beams began to assail the craggy ramparts, and the topmost parapets were melting like lava beneath them. It was a scene of utmost terror and grandeur; but, a moment later, it was blotted from my vision by the buildings among which we had now plunged.

The great lepidopterous creatures who bore me went on with the speed of eyrie-questing eagles. In the course of that flight, I was hardly capable of conscious thought or volition; I lived only in the breathless and giddy freedom of aerial movement, of dream-like levitation above the labyrinthine maze of stone immensitudes and marvels. I was without actual cognisance of much that I beheld in that stupendous Babel of architectural imageries, and only afterwards, in the more tranquil light of recollection, could I give coherent form and meaning to many of my impressions.

My senses were stunned by the vastness and strangeness of it all; I realised but dimly the cataclysmic ruin that was being loosed upon the city behind us, and the doom from which we were fleeing. I knew that war was being made with unearthly weapons and engineries, by inimical powers that I could not imagine, for a purpose beyond my conception; but, to me, it all had the elemental confusion and vague, impersonal horror of some cosmic catastrophe.

We flew deeper and deeper into the city. Broad, platform roofs and terrace-like tiers of balconies flowed away beneath us, and the pavements raced like darkling streams at some enormous depth. Severe cubicular spires and square monoliths were all about and above us; and we saw on some of the roofs the dark, Atlantean people of the city, moving slowly and statuesquely, or standing in attitudes of cryptic resignation and despair, with their faces towards the flaming cloud. All were weaponless, and I saw no engineries anywhere such as might be used for purposes of military defence.

Swiftly as we flew, the climbing cloud was swifter, and the darkness of its intermittently glowing dome had over-arched the town while its spidery filaments had meshed the further heavens and would soon attach themselves to the opposite horizon. The buildings darkened and lightened with the recurrent fulguration, and I felt in all my tissues the painful pulsing of the thunderous vibrations.

Dully and vaguely, I realised that the winged beings who carried me between them were pilgrims to the Temple of the Flame. More and more, I became aware of an influence that must have been that of the starry music emanating from the temple's heart. There were soft, soothing vibrations in the air, that seemed to absorb and nullify the tearing discords of the unheard thunder. I felt that we were entering a zone of mystic refuge, of sidereal and celestial security, and my troubled senses were both lulled and exalted.

The gorgeous wings of the giant lepidopters began to slant downward. Before and beneath us, at some distance, I perceived a mammoth pile which I knew at once for the Temple of the Flame. Down, still down we went, in the awesome space of the surrounding square; and then I was borne in through the lofty, ever-open entrance, and along the high hall with its thousand columns. Pregnant with strange balsams, the dim, mysterious dusk enfolded us, and we seemed to be entering realms of pre-mundane antiquity and transstellar immensity; to be following a pillared cavern that led to the core of some ultimate star.

It seemed that we were the last and only pilgrims, and also that the temple was deserted by its guardians, for we met no one in the whole extent of that column-crowded gloom. After a while, the dusk began to lighten, and we plunged into a widening beam of radiance, and then into the vast central chamber in which soared the fountain of green fire.

I remember only the impression of shadowy, flickering space, of a vault that was lost in the azure of infinity, of colossal and Memnonian statues that looked down from Himalaya-like altitudes; and, above all, the dazzling jet of flame that aspired from a pit in the pavement and rose into the air like the visible rapture of gods. But all this I saw for an instant only. Then I realised that the beings who bore me were flying straight towards the Flame on level wings, without the slightest pause or flutter of hesitation!

There was no room for fear, no time for alarm, in the dazed and chaotic turmoil of my sensations. I was stupified by all that I had experienced, and moreover, the drug-like spell of the Flame was upon me, even though I could not hear its fatal singing. I believe that I struggled a little, by some sort of mechanical muscular revulsion, against the tentacular arms that were wound about me. But the lepidopters gave no heed; it was plain that they were conscious of nothing but the mounting fire and its seductive music.

I remember, however, that there was no sensation of actual heat, such as might have been expected, when we neared the soaring column. Instead, I felt the most ineffable thrilling in all my fibres, as if I were being permeated by waves of celestial energy and demiurgic ecstasy. Then we entered the Flame. . . .

Like Angarth before me, I had taken it for granted that the fate of all those who flung themselves into the Flame was an instant though blissful destruction. I expected to undergo a briefly flaring dissolution, followed by the nothingness of utter annihilation. The thing which really happened was beyond the boldest reach of speculative thought, and to give even a meagre idea of my sensations would beggar the resources of language.

The Flame enfolded us like a green curtain, blotting from view the great chamber. Then it seemed to me that I was caught and carried to supercelestial heights, in an upward-rushing cataract of quintessential force and deific rapture, and an all-illuminating light. It seemed that I, and my companions, had achieved a godlike union with the Flame; that every atom of our bodies had undergone a transcendental expansion, and was winged with ethereal lightness.

It was as if we no longer existed, except as one divine, indivisible entity, soaring beyond the trammels of matter, beyond the limits of time and space, to attain undreamable shores. Unspeakable was the joy, and infinite the freedom of that ascent, in which we seemed to overpass the zenith of the highest star. Then, as if we had risen with the Flame to its culmination, had reached its very apex, we emerged and came to a pause.

My senses were faint with exaltation, my eyes blind with the glory of the fire; and the world on which I now gazed was a vast arabesque of unfamiliar forms and bewildering hues from another spectrum than the one to which our eyes are habituated. It swirled before my dizzy eyes like a labyrinth of gigantic jewels, with interweaving rays and tangled lustres, and only by slow degrees was I able to establish order and distinguish detail in the surging riot of my perceptions.

All about me were endless avenues of super-prismatic opal and jacinth; arches and pillars of ultra-violet gems, of transcendent sapphire, of unearthly ruby and amethyst, all suffused with a multi-tinted splendour. I appeared to be treading on jewels, and above me was a jewelled sky.

Presently, with recovered equilibrium, with eyes adjusted to a new range of cognition, I began to perceive the actual features of the landscape. With the two moth-like beings still beside me, I was standing on a million-flowered grass, among trees of a paradisal vegetation, with fruit, foliage, blossoms and trunks whose very forms were beyond the conception of tridimensional life. The grace of their drooping boughs, of their fretted fronds, was inexpressible in terms of earthly line and contour, and they seemed to be wrought of pure, ethereal substance, half-translucent to the empyrean light, which accounted for the gem-like impression I had first received.

I breathed a nectar-laden air, and the ground beneath me was ineffably soft and resilient, as if it were composed of some higher form of matter than ours. My physical sensations were those of the utmost buoyancy and well-being, with no trace of fatigue or nervousness, such as might have been looked for after the unparalleled and marvellous events in which I had played a part. I felt no sense of mental dislocation or confusion; and, apart from my ability to recognise unknown colours and non-Euclidean forms, I began to experience a queer alteration and extension of tactility, through which it seemed that I was able to touch remote objects.

The radiant sky was filled with many-coloured suns, like those that might shine on a world of some multiple solar system; but as I gazed, their glory became softer and dimmer, and the brilliant lustre of the trees and grass was gradually subdued, as if by encroaching twilight. I was beyond surprise, in the boundless marvel and mystery of it all, and nothing, perhaps, would have seemed incredible. But if anything could have amazed me or defied belief, it was the human face—the face of my vanished friend, Giles Angarth, which now emerged from among the waning jewels of the forest, followed by that of another man whom I recognised from photographs as Felix Ebbonly.

They came out from beneath the gorgeous boughs, and paused before me. Both were clad in lustrous fabrics, finer than Oriental silk, and of no earthly cut or pattern. Their look was both joyous and meditative, and their faces had taken on a hint of the same translucency that characterised the ethereal fruits and blossoms.

"We have been looking for you," said Angarth. "It occurred to me that, after reading my journal, you might be tempted to try the same experiment, if only to make sure whether the account was truth or fiction. This is Felix Ebbonly, whom I believe you have never met."

It surprised me when I found that I could hear his voice with perfect ease and clearness, and I wondered why the effect of the drug-soaked cotton should have died out so soon in my auditory nerves. Yet such details were trivial in the face of the astounding fact that I had found Angarth and Ebbonly; that they, as well as I, had survived the unearthly rapture of the Flame.

"Where are we?" I asked, after acknowledging his introduction. "I confess that I am totally at a loss to comprehend what has happened."

"We are now in what is called the Inner Dimension," explained Angarth. "It is a higher sphere of space and energy and matter than the one into which we were precipitated from Crater Ridge, and the only entrance is through the Singing Flame in the city of Ydmos. The Inner Dimension is born of the fiery fountain, and sustained by it; and those who fling themselves into the Flame are lifted thereby to this superior plane of vibration. For them, the Outer Worlds no longer exist. The nature of the Flame itself is not known, except that it is a fountain of pure energy springing from the central rock beneath Ydmos, and passing beyond mortal ken by virtue of its own ardency."

He paused, and seemed to be peering attentively at the winged entities, who still lingered at my side. Then he continued:

"I haven't been here long enough to learn very much, myself; but I have found out a few things, and Ebbonly and I have established a sort of telepathic communication with the other beings who have passed through the Flame. Many of them have no spoken language, nor organs of speech, and their very methods of thought are basically different from ours, because of their divergent lines of sense-development and the varying conditions of the worlds from which they come. But we are able to communicate a few images.

"The persons who came with you are trying to tell me something," he went on. "You and they, it seems, are the last pilgrims who will enter Ydmos and attain the Inner Dimension. War is being made on the Flame and its guardians by the rulers of the Outer Lands, because so many of their people have obeyed the lure of the singing fountain and vanished into the higher sphere. Even now, their armies have closed in upon Ydmos and are blasting the city's ramparts with the force-bolts of their moving towers."

I told him what I had seen, comprehending, now, much that had been obscure heretofore. He listened gravely, and then said:

"It has long been feared that such war would be made sooner or later. There are many legends in the Outer Lands concerning the Flame and the fate of those who succumb to its attraction, but the truth is not known, or is guessed only by a few. Many believe, as I did, that the end is destruction; and by some who suspect its existence, the Inner Dimension is hated as a thing that lures idle dreamers away from worldly reality. It is regarded as a lethal and pernicious chimera, as a mere poetic dream, or a sort of opium paradise.

"There are a thousand things to tell you regarding the Inner Sphere, and the laws and conditions of being to which we are now subject after the revibration of all our component atoms in the Flame. But at present there is no time to speak further, since it is highly probable that we are all in grave danger—that the very existence of the Inner Dimension, as well as our own, is threatened by the inimical forces that are destroying Ydmos.

"There are some who say that the Flame is impregnable, that its pure essence will defy the blasting of all inferior beams, and its source remain impenetrable to the lightnings of the Outer Lords. But most are fearful of disaster, and expect the failure of the fountain itself when Ydmos is riven to the central rock.

"Because of this imminent peril, we must not tarry longer. There is a way which affords egress from the Inner Sphere to another and remoter Cosmos in a second infinity—a Cosmos unconceived by mundane astronomers, or by the astronomers of the worlds about Ydmos. The majority of the pilgrims, after a term of sojourn here, have gone on to the worlds of this other universe; and Ebbonly and I have waited only for your coming before following them. We must make haste, and delay no more, or doom will overtake us."

Even as he spoke, the two moth-like entities, seeming to resign me to the care of my human friends, arose on the jewel-tinted air and sailed in long, level flight above the paradisal perspectives whose remoter avenues were lost in glory. Angarth and Ebbonly had now stationed themselves beside me, and one took me by the left arm, and the other by the right.

"Try to imagine that you are flying," said Angarth. "In this sphere, levitation and flight are possible through will-power, and you will soon acquire the ability. We shall support and guide you, however, till you have grown accustomed to the new conditions and are independent of such help."

I obeyed his injunction, and formed a mental image of myself in the act of flying. I was amazed by the clearness and verisimilitude of the thought-picture, and still more by the fact that the picture was becoming an actuality! With little sense of effort, but with exactly the same feeling that characterises a levitational dream, the three of us were soaring from the jewelled ground, slanting easily and swiftly upward through the glowing air.

Any attempt to describe the experience would be fore-doomed to futility, since it seemed that a whole range of new senses had been opened up in me, together with corresponding thought-symbols for which there are no words in human speech. I was no longer Philip Hastane, but a larger, stronger and freer entity, differing as much from my former self as the personality developed beneath the influence of hashish or kava would differ. The dominant feeling was one of immense joy and liberation, coupled with a sense of imperative haste, of the need to escape into other realms where the joy would endure eternal and unthreatened.

My visual perceptions, as we flew above the burning, lucent woods, were marked by intense aesthetic pleasure. It was as far above the normal delight afforded by agreeable imagery as the forms and colours of this world were beyond the cognition of normal eyes. Every changing image was a source of veritable ecstasy; and the ecstasy mounted as the whole landscape began to brighten again and returned to the flashing, scintillating glory it had worn when I first beheld it.

We soared at a lofty elevation, looking down on numberless miles of labyrinthine forest, on long, luxurious meadows, on voluptuously folded hills, on palatial buildings, and waters that were clear as the pristine lakes and rivers of Eden. It all seemed to quiver and pulsate like one living, effulgent, ethereal entity, and waves of radiant rapture passed from sun to sun in the splendour-crowded heaven.

As we went on, I noticed again, after an interval, that partial dimming of the light; that somnolent, dreamy saddening of the colours, to be followed by another period of ecstatic brightening. The slow tidal rhythm of this process appeared to correspond to the rising and falling of the Flame, as Angarth had described it in his journal, and I suspected immediately that there was some connection. No sooner had I formulated this thought, than I became aware that Angarth was speaking. And yet, I am not sure whether he spoke, or whether his worded thought was perceptible to me through another sense than that of physical audition. At any rate, I was cognisant of his comment:

"You are right. The waning and waxing of the fountain and its music is perceived in the Inner Dimension as a clouding and lightening of all visual images."

Our flight began to swiften, and I realised that my companions were employing all their psychic energies in an effort to redouble our speed. The lands below us blurred to a cataract of streaming colour, a sea of flowing luminosity; and we seemed to be hurtling onward like stars through the fiery air. The ecstasy of that endless soaring, the anxiety of that precipitate flight from an unknown doom, are incommunicable. But I shall never forget them, nor the state of ineffable communion and understanding that existed between the three of us. The memory of it all is housed in the deepest, most abiding cells of my brain.

Others were flying beside and above and beneath us, now, in the fluctuant glory: pilgrims of hidden worlds and occult dimensions, proceeding as we ourselves towards that other Cosmos of which the Inner Sphere was the antechamber. These beings were strange and outré beyond belief, in their corporeal forms and attributes; and yet I took no thought of their strangeness, but felt towards them the same conviction of fraternity that I felt towards Angarth and Ebbonly.

As we still went on, it appeared to me that my two companions were telling me many things; communicating, by what means I am not sure, much that they had learned in their new existence. With a grave urgency as if, perhaps, the time for imparting this information might well be brief, ideas were expressed and conveyed which I could never have understood amid terrestrial circumstances. Things that were inconceivable in terms of the five senses, or in abstract symbols of philosophic or mathematic thought, were made plain to me as the letters of the alphabet.

Certain of these data, however, are roughly conveyable or suggestible in language. I was told of the gradual process of initiation into the life of the new dimension, of the powers gained by the neophyte during his term of adaptation, of the various recondite, aesthetic joys experienced through a mingling and multiplying of all the perceptions, of the control acquired over natural forces and over matter itself, so that raiment could be woven and buildings reared solely through an act of volition.

I learned, also, of the laws that would control our passage to the further Cosmos, and the fact that such passage was difficult and dangerous for anyone who had not lived a certain length of time in the Inner Dimension. Likewise, I was told that no one could return to our present plane from the higher Cosmos, even as no one could go backward through the Flame into Ydmos.

Angarth and Ebbonly had dwelt long enough in the Inner Dimension, they said, to be eligible for entrance to the worlds beyond; and they thought that I, too, could escape through their assistance, even though I had not yet developed the faculty of spatial equilibrium necessary to sustain those who dared the interspheric path and its dreadful subjacent gulfs alone. There were boundless, unforeseeable realms, planet on planet, universe on universe, to which we might attain, and among whose prodigies and marvels we could dwell or wander indefinitely. In these worlds, our brains would be attuned to the comprehension of vaster and higher scientific laws, and states of entity beyond those of our present dimensional milieu.

I have no idea of the duration of our flight; since, like everything else, my sense of time was completely altered and transfigured. Relatively speaking, we may have gone on for hours; but it seemed to me that we had crossed an area of that super-nal terrain for whose transit many years, or even centuries, might well have been required.

Even before we came within sight of it, a clear pictorial image of our destination had arisen in my mind, doubtless through some sort of thought-transference. I seemed to envision a stupendous mountain range, with alp on celestial alp, higher than the summer cumuli of Earth; and above them all the horn of an ultra-violet peak whose head was enfolded in a hueless and spiral cloud, touched with the sense of invisible chromatic overtones, that seemed to come down upon it from skies beyond the zenith. I knew that the way to the Outer Cosmos was hidden in the high cloud. . . .

On and on we soared; and at length the mountain range appeared on the far horizon, and I saw the paramount peak of ultra-violet with its dazzling crown of cumulus. Nearer still we came, till the strange volutes of cloud were almost above us, towering to the heavens and vanishing among the vari-coloured suns; and we saw the gleaming forms of pilgrims who preceded us, as they entered the swirling folds.

At this moment, the sky and the landscape had flamed again to their culminating brilliance; they burned with a thousand hues and lustres, so that the sudden, unlooked-for eclipse which now occurred was all the more complete and terrible. Before I was conscious of anything amiss, I seemed to hear a despairing cry from my friends, who must have felt the oncoming calamity through a subtler sense than any of which I was yet capable. Then, beyond the high and luminescent alp of our destination, I saw the mounting of a wall of darkness, dreadful and instant, positive and palpable, that rose everywhere and toppled like some Atlantean wave upon the irised suns and the fiery-coloured vistas of the Inner Dimension.

We hung irresolute in the shadowed air, powerless and hopeless before the impending catastrophe, and saw that the darkness had surrounded the entire world and was rushing upon us from all sides. It ate the heavens, blotted the outer suns, and the vast perspectives over which we had flown appeared to shrink and shrivel like a fire-blackened paper. We seemed to wait alone, for one terrible instant, in a centre of dwindling light on which the cyclonic forces of night and destruction were impinging with torrential rapidity.

The centre shrank to a mere point—and then the darkness was upon us like an overwhelming maelstrom, like the falling and crashing of Cyclopean walls. I seemed to go down with the wreck of shattered worlds in a roaring sea of vortical space and force, to descend into some infra-stellar pit, some ultimate limbo to which the shreds of forgotten suns and systems are flung. Then, after a measure-less interval, there came the sensation of violent impact, as if I had fallen among these shards, at the bottom of the universal night. . . .

I struggled back to consciousness with slow, prodigious effort, as if I were crushed beneath some irremovable weight, beneath the lightless and inert débris of galaxies. It seemed to require the labours of a Titan to lift my lids, and my body and limbs were heavy, as if they had been turned to some denser element than human flesh, or had been subjected to the gravitation of a grosser planet than the Earth.

My mental processes were benumbed and painful, and confused to the last degree; but at length I realised that I was lying on a riven and tilted pavement, among gigantic blocks of fallen stone. Above me, the light of a livid heaven came down among over-turned and jagged walls that no longer supported their colossal dome. Close beside me, I saw a fuming pit from which a ragged rift extended through the floor, like the chasm wrought by an earthquake.

I could not recognise my surroundings for a time; but at last, with a toilsome groping of thought, I understood that I was lying in the ruined temple of Ydmos, and that the pit whose grey and acrid vapours rose beside me was that from which the fountain of singing flame had issued. It was a scene of stupendous havoc and devastation: the wrath that had been visited upon Ydmos had left no wall or pylon of the temple standing. I stared at the blighted heavens from an architectural ruin in which the remains of On and Angkor would have been mere rubble-heaps.

With herculean effort, I turned my head away from the smoking pit, whose thin, sluggish fumes curled upward in phantasmal coils where the green ardour of the Flame had soared and sung. Not until then did I perceive my companions. Angarth, still insensible, was lying near at hand, and just beyond him I saw the pale, contorted face of Ebbonly, whose lower limbs and body were pinned down by the rough and broken pediment of a fallen pillar.

Striving, as in some eternal nightmare, to throw off the leaden-clinging weight of my inertia, and able to bestir myself only with the most painful slowness and laboriousness, I got to my feet and went over to Ebbonly. Angarth, I saw at a glance, was uninjured and would presently regain consciousness, but Ebbonly, crushed by the monolithic mass of stone, was dying swiftly, and even with the help of a dozen men I could not have released him from his imprisonment; nor could I have done anything to palliate his agony.

He tried to smile, with gallant and piteous courage, as I stooped above him.

"It's no use—I'm going in a moment," he whispered. "Good-bye, Hastane—and tell Angarth good-bye for me, too."

His tortured lips relaxed, his eyelids dropped, and his head fell back on the temple pavement. With an unreal, dream-like horror, almost without emotion, I saw that he was dead. The exhaustion that still beset me was too profound to permit of thought or feeling; it was like the first reaction that follows the awakening from a drug-debauch. My nerves were like burnt-out wires, my muscles dead and unresponsive as clay; my brain was ashen and gutted, as if a great fire had burned within it and gone out.

Somehow, after an interval of whose length my memory is uncertain, I managed to revive Angarth, and he sat up dully and dazedly. When I told him that Ebbonly was dead, my words appeared to make no impression upon him, and I wondered for a while if he understood. Finally, rousing himself a little with evident difficulty, he peered at the body of our friend, and seemed to realise in some measure the horror of the situation. But I think he would have remained there for hours, or perhaps for all time, in his utter despair and lassitude, if I had not taken the initiative.

"Come," I said, with an attempt at firmness. "We must get out of this."

"Where to?" he queried, dully. "The Flame has failed at its source, and the Inner Dimension is no more. I wish I were dead, like Ebbonly—I might as well be, judging from the way I feel."

"We must find our way back to Crater Ridge," I said. "Surely we can do it, if the inter-dimensional portals have not been destroyed."

Angarth did not seem to hear me, but he followed obediently when I took him by the arm and began to seek an exit from the temple's heart, among the roofless halls and overturned columns. . . .

My recollections of our return are dim and confused, and full of the tediousness of some interminable delirium. I remember looking back at Ebbonly, lying white and still beneath the massive pillar that would serve as his eternal monument; and I recall the mountainous ruins of the city, in which it seemed that we were the only living beings. It was a wilderness of chaotic stone, of fused, obsidian-like blocks, where streams of molten lava still ran in the mighty chasms, or poured like torrents adown unfathomable pits that had opened in the ground. And I remember seeing, amid the wreckage, the charred bodies of those dark colossi who were the people of Ydmos and the warders of the Flame.

Like pygmies lost in some shattered fortalice of the giants, we stumbled onward, strangling in mephitic and metallic vapours, reeling with weariness, dizzy with the heat that emanated everywhere to surge upon us in buffeting waves. The way was blocked by overthrown buildings, by toppled towers and battlements, over which we climbed precariously and toilsomely; and often we were compelled to divagate from our direct course by enormous rifts that seemed to cleave the foundations of the world.

The moving towers of the wrathful Outer Lords had withdrawn; their armies had disappeared on the plain beyond Ydmos, when we staggered over the riven, shapeless and scoriac crags that had formed the city's ramparts. Before us was nothing but desolation—a fire-blackened and vapour-vaulted expanse in which no tree or blade of grass remained.

Across this waste we found our way to the slope of violet grass above the plain, which had lain beyond the path of the invader's bolts. There the guiding monoliths, reared by a people of whom we were never to learn even the name, still looked down upon the fuming desert and the mounded wrack of Ydmos. And there, at length, we came once more to the greyish-green columns that were the gateway between the worlds.

𝕏 ROBERT E(RVIN) HOWARD (1906–1936)

Heroic Fantasy dates back millennia, but in the twentieth century, tales of sword and sorcery are measured against the archetypal stories of Robert E. Howard. Howard lived life as largely as did his series characters, Conan the Barbarian, Solomon Kane, Bran Mak Morn, Cormac Mac Art, and King Kull. He loved adventure and prize fighting.

Howard was a highly prolific, talented, and popular author. His markets included pulp magazines titled Weird Tales, Spicy Adventures, Action Stories, Thrilling Adventures, Top Notch, Strange Detective, Oriental Stories, *and* Argosy. *He was known for highly stylized characters; intricately plotted, fast-paced action adventures; and exotic settings (in the times of Barbarians and Puritans, on the high seas, and in the Orient). His stories featured impossibly muscled men caught in extreme danger and fast-paced action with voluptuous, sensuous women. "The Tower of the Elephant" features all these story elements and more. For Howard, action was everything.*

Popular authors on their own, Fritz Leiber, L. Sprague de Camp, Lin Carter, Karl Edward Wagner, and Robert Jordan have paid tribute to Robert E. Howard by creating stories and series characters of Heroic Fantasy in the mold of the Howard stories. In the realm of Sword and Sorcery Fantasy, Karl Edward Wagner may have been Howard's most talented successor.

The Tower of the Elephant
(Weird Tales, *March 1933)*

1

Torches flared murkily on the revels in the Maul, where the thieves of the east held carnival by night. In the Maul they could carouse and roar as they liked, for honest people shunned the quarters, and watchmen, well paid with stained coins, did not interfere with their sport. Along the crooked, unpaved streets with their heaps of refuse and sloppy puddles, drunken roisterers staggered, roaring. Steel glinted in the shadows where wolf preyed on wolf, and from the darkness rose the shrill laughter of women, and the sounds of scufflings and strugglings. Torchlight licked luridly from broken windows and wide-thrown doors, and out of these doors, stale smells of wine and rank sweaty bodies, clamor of drinking-jacks and fists hammered on rough tables, snatches of obscene songs, rushed like a blow in the face.

In one of these dens merriment thundered to the low smoked-stained roof, where rascals gathered in every stage of rags and tatters—furtive cut-purses, leering kidnappers, quick-fingered thieves, swaggering bravoes with their wenches, strident-voiced women clad in tawdry finery. Native rogues were the dominant element—dark-skinned, dark-eyed Zamorians, with daggers at their girdles and guile in their hearts. But there were wolves of half a dozen outland nations there as well. There was a giant Hyperborean renegade, taciturn, dangerous, with a broadsword strapped to his great gaunt frame—for men wore steel openly in the Maul. There was a Shemitish counterfeiter, with his hook nose and curled blue-black beard. There was a bold-eyed Brythunian wench, sitting on the knee of a tawny-haired Gunderman—a wandering mercenary soldier, a deserter from some defeated army. And the fat gross rogue whose bawdy jests were causing all the shouts of mirth was a professional kidnapper come up from distant Koth to teach woman-stealing to Zamorians who were born with more knowledge of the art than he could ever attain.

This man halted in his description of an intended victim's charms, and thrust his muzzle into a huge tankard of frothing ale. Then blowing the foam from his fat lips, he said, "By Bel, god of all thieves, I'll show them how to steal wenches: I'll have her over the Zamorian border before dawn, and there'll be a caravan waiting to receive her. Three hundred pieces of silver, a count of Ophir promised me for a sleek young Brythunian of the better class. It took me weeks, wandering among the border cities as a beggar, to find one I knew would suit. And is she a pretty baggage!"

He blew a slobbery kiss in the air.

"I know lords in Shem who would trade the secret of the Elephant Tower for her," he said, returning to his ale.

A touch on his tunic sleeve made him turn his head, scowling at the interruption. He saw a tall, strongly made youth standing beside him. This person was as much out of place in that den as a gray wolf among mangy rats of the gutters. His cheap tunic could not conceal the hard, rangy lines of his powerful frame, the broad heavy shoulders, the massive chest, lean waist, and heavy arms. His skin was brown from outland suns, his eyes blue and smoldering; a shock of tousled black hair crowned his broad forehead. From his girdle hung a sword in a worn leather scabbard.

The Kothian involuntarily drew back; for the man was not one of any civilized race he knew.

"You spoke of the Elephant Tower," said the stranger, speaking Zamorian with an alien accent. "I've heard much of this tower; what is its secret?"

The fellow's attitude did not seem threatening, and the Kothian's courage was bolstered up by the ale, and the evident approval of his audience. He swelled with self-importance.

"The secret of the Elephant Tower?" he exclaimed. "Why, any fool knows that Yara the priest dwells there with the great jewel men call the Elephant's Heart, that is the secret of his magic."

The barbarian digested this for a space.

"I have seen this tower," he said. "It is set in a great garden above the level of the city, surrounded by high walls. I have seen no guards. The walls would be easy to climb. Why has not somebody stolen this secret gem?"

The Kothian stared wide-mouthed at the other's simplicity, then burst into a roar of derisive mirth, in which the others joined.

"Harken to this heathen!" he bellowed. "He would steal the jewel of Yara!— Harken, fellow," he said, turning portentously to the other, "I suppose you are some sort of a northern barbarian—"

"I am a Cimmerian," the outlander answered, in no friendly tone. The reply and the manner of it meant little to the Kothian; of a kingdom that lay far to the south, on the borders of Shem, he knew only vaguely of the northern races.

"Then give ear and learn wisdom, fellow," said he, pointing his drinking-jack at the discomfited youth. "Know that in Zamora, and more especially in this city, there are more bold thieves than anywhere else in the world, even Koth. If mortal man could have stolen the gem, be sure it would have been filched long ago. You speak of climbing the walls, but once having climbed, you would quickly wish yourself back again. There are no guards in the gardens at night for a very good reason—that is, no human guards. But in the watch-chamber, in the lower part of the tower, are armed men, and even if you passed those who roam the gardens by night, you must still pass through the soldiers, for the gem is kept somewhere in the tower above."

"But if a man *could* pass through the gardens," argued the Cimmerian, "why could he not come at the gem through the upper part of the tower and thus avoid the soldiers?"

Again the Kothian gaped at him.

"Listen to him!" he shouted peeringly. "The barbarian is an eagle who would fly to the jeweled rim of the tower, which is only a hundred and fifty feet above the earth, with rounded sides slicker than polished glass!"

The Cimmerian glared about, embarrassed at the roar of mocking laughter that greeted this remark. He saw no particular humor in it, and was too new to civilization to understand its discourtesies. Civilized men are more discourteous than savages because they know they can be impolite without having their skulls split, as a general thing. He was bewildered and chagrined, and doubtless would have slunk away, abashed, but the Kothian chose to goad him further.

"Come, come!" he shouted. "Tell these poor fellows, who have only been thieves since before you were spawned, tell them how you would steal the gem!"

"There is always a way, if the desire be coupled with courage," answered the Cimmerian shortly, nettled.

The Kothian chose to take this as a personal slur. His face grew purple with anger.

"What!" he roared. "You dare tell us our business, and intimate that we are cowards? Get along; get out of my sight!" And he pushed the Cimmerian violently.

"Will you mock me and then lay hands on me?" grated the barbarian, his quick rage leaping up; and he returned the push with an open-handed blow that knocked his tormenter back against the rude-hewn table. Ale splashed over the jack's lip, and the Kothian roared in fury, dragging at his sword.

"Heathen dog!" he bellowed. "I'll have your heart for that!"

Steel flashed and the throng surged wildly back out of the way. In their flight they knocked over the single candle and the den was plunged in darkness, broken by the crash of upset benches, drum of flying feet, shouts, oaths of people tumbling over one another, and a single strident yell of agony that cut the din like a knife. When a candle was relighted, most of the guests had gone out by doors and broken windows, and the rest huddled behind stacks of wine-kegs and under tables. The barbarian was gone; the center of the room was deserted except for the gashed body of the Kothian. The Cimmerian, with the unerring instinct of the barbarian, had killed his man in the darkness and confusion.

2

The lurid lights and drunken revelry fell away behind the Cimmerian. He had discarded his torn tunic, and walked through the night naked except for a loin-cloth and his high-strapped sandals. He moved with the supple ease of a great tiger, his steely muscles rippling under his brown skin.

He had entered the part of the city reserved for the temples. On all sides of him they glittered white in the starlight—snowy marble pillars and golden domes and silver arches, shrines of Zamora's myriad strange gods. He did not trouble his head about them; he knew that Zamora's religion, like all things of a civilized, long-settled people, was intricate and complex, and had lost most of the pristine essence in a maze of formulas and rituals. He had squatted for hours in the courtyards of the philosophers, listening to the arguments of theologians and teachers, and come away in a haze of bewilderment, sure of only one thing, and that, that they were all touched in the head.

His gods were simple and understandable; Crom was their chief, and he lived on a great mountain, whence he sent forth dooms and death. It was useless to call on Crom, because he was a gloomy, savage god, and he hated weaklings. But he gave a man courage at birth, and the will and might to kill his enemies, which, in the Cimmerian's mind, was all any god should be expected to do.

His sandalled feet made no sound on the gleaming pave. No watchmen passed, for even the thieves of the Maul shunned the temples, where strange dooms had been known to fall on violators. Ahead of him he saw, looming against the sky, the Tower of the Elephant. He mused, wondering why it was so named. No one seemed to know. He had never seen an elephant, but he vaguely understood that it was a monstrous animal, with a tail in front as well as behind. This a wandering Shemite had told him, swearing that he had seen such beasts by the thousands in the country of the Hyrkanians; but all men knew what liars were the men of Shem. At any rate, there were no elephants in Zamora.

The shimmering shaft of the tower rose frostily in the stars. In the sunlight it shone so dazzlingly that few could bear its glare, and men said it was built of silver. It was round, a slim perfect cylinder, a hundred and fifty feet in height, and its rim glittered in the starlight with the great jewels which crusted it. The tower stood among the waving exotic trees of a garden raised high above the general level of the city. A high wall enclosed this garden, and outside the wall was a lower level, likewise enclosed by a wall. No lights shone forth; there seemed to be no windows in the tower—at least not above the level of the inner wall. Only the gems high above sparkled frostily in the starlight.

Shrubbery grew thick outside the lower, or outer wall. The Cimmerian crept close and stood beside the barrier, measuring it with his eye. It was high, but he could leap and catch the coping with his fingers. Then it would be child's play to swing himself up and over, and he did not doubt that he could pass the inner wall in the same manner. But he hesitated at the thought of the strange perils which were said to await within. These people were strange and mysterious to him; they were not of his kind—not even of the same blood as the more westerly Brythunians, Nemedians, Kothians and Aquilonians, whose civilized mysteries had awed him in times past. The people of Zamora were very ancient, and, from what he had seen of them, very evil.

He thought of Yara, the high priest, who worked strange dooms from this jeweled tower, and the Cimmerian's hair prickled as he remembered a tale told by a drunken page of the court—how Yara had laughed in the face of a hostile prince, and held up a glowing, evil gem before him, and how rays shot blindingly from that unholy jewel, to envelop the prince, who screamed and fell down, and shrank to a withered blackened lump that changed to a black spider which scampered wildly about the chamber until Yara set his heel upon it.

Yara came not often from his tower of magic, and always to work evil on some man or some nation. The king of Zamora feared him more than he feared death, and kept himself drunk all the time because that fear was more than he could endure sober. Yara was very old—centuries old, men said, and added that he would live for ever because of the magic of his gem, which men called the Heart of the Elephant, for no better reason than they named his hold the Elephant's Tower.

The Cimmerian, engrossed in these thoughts, shrank quickly against the wall. Within the garden some one was passing, who walked with a measured stride. The listener heard the clink of steel. So after all a guard did pace those gardens. The Cimmerian waited, expected to hear him pass again, on the next round, but silence rested over the mysterious gardens.

At last curiosity overcame him. Leaping lightly he grasped the wall and swung himself up to the top with one arm. Lying flat on the broad coping, he looked down into the wide space between the walls. No shrubbery grew near him, though he saw some carefully trimmed bushes near the inner wall. The starlight fell on the even sward and somewhere a fountain tinkled.

The Cimmerian cautiously lowered himself down on the inside and drew his sword, staring about him. He was shaken by the nervousness of the wild at standing thus unprotected in the naked starlight, and he moved lightly around the curve of the wall, hugging its shadow, until he was even with the shrubbery he had noticed. Then he ran quickly toward it, crouching low, and almost tripped over a form that lay crumpled near the edges of the bushes.

A quick look to right and left showed him no enemy in sight at least, and he bent close to investigate. His keen eyes, even in the dim starlight, showed him a strongly built man in the silvered armor and crested helmet of the Zamorian royal guard. A shield and a spear lay near him, and it took but an instant's examination to show that he had been strangled. The barbarian glanced about uneasily. He knew that this man must be the guard he had heard pass his hiding-place by the wall. Only a short time had passed, yet in that interval nameless hands had reached out of the dark and choked out the soldier's life.

Straining his eyes in the gloom, he saw a hint of motion through the shrubs near the wall. Thither he glided, gripping his sword. He made no more noise than a panther stealing through the night, yet the man he was stalking heard. The Cimmerian had a dim glimpse of a huge bulk close to the wall, felt relief that it was at least human; then the fellow wheeled quickly with a gasp that sounded like panic, made the first motion of a forward plunge, hands clutching, then recoiled as the Cimmerian's blade caught the starlight. For a tense instant neither spoke, standing ready for anything.

"You are no soldier," hissed the stranger at last. "You are a thief like myself."

"And who are you?" asked the Cimmerian in a suspicious whisper.

"Taurus of Nemedia."

The Cimmerian lowered his sword.

"I've heard of you. Men call you a prince of thieves."

A low laugh answered him. Taurus was tall as the Cimmerian, and heavier; he was big-bellied and fat, but his every movement betokened a subtle dynamic magnetism, which was reflected in the keen eyes that glinted vitally, even in the starlight. He was barefooted and carried a coil of what looked like a thin, strong rope, knotted at regular intervals.

"Who are you?" he whispered.

"Conan, a Cimmerian," answered the other. "I came seeking a way to steal Yara's jewel, that men call the Elephant's Heart."

Conan sensed the man's great belly shaking in laughter, but it was not derisive.

"By Bel, god of thieves!" hissed Taurus. "I had thought only myself had courage to attempt *that* poaching. These Zamorians call themselves thieves—bah! Conan, I like your grit. I never shared an adventure with any one, but by Bel, we'll attempt this together if you're willing."

"Then you are after the gem, too?"

"What else? I've had my plans laid for months, but you, I think, have acted on a sudden impulse, my friend."

"You killed the soldier?"

"Of course. I slid over the wall when he was on the other side of the garden. I hid in the bushes; he heard me, or thought he heard something. When he came blundering over, it was no trick at all to get behind him and suddenly grip his neck and choke out his fool's life. He was like most men, half blind in the dark. A good thief should have eyes like a cat."

"You made one mistake," said Conan.

Taurus' eyes flashed angrily.

"I? I, a mistake? Impossible!"

"You should have dragged the body into the bushes."

"Said the novice to the master of the art. They will not change the guard until past midnight. Should any come searching for him now, and find his body, they would flee at once to Yara, bellowing the news, and give us time to escape. Were they not to find it, they'd go beating up the bushes and catch us like rats in a trap."

"You are right," agreed Conan.

"So. Now attend. We waste time in this cursed discussion. There are no guards in the inner garden—human guards, I mean, though there are sentinels even more deadly. It was their presence which baffled me for so long, but I finally discovered a way to circumvent them."

"What of the soldiers in the lower part of the tower?"

"Old Yara dwells in the chambers above. By that route we will come—and go, I hope. Never mind asking me how. I have arranged a way. We'll steal down through the top of the tower and strangle old Yara before he can cast any of his accursed spells on us. At least we'll try; it's the chance of being turned into a spider or a toad, against the wealth and power of the world. All good thieves must know how to take risks."

"I'll go as far as any man," said Conan, slipping off his sandals.

"Then follow me." And turning, Taurus leaped up, caught the wall and drew himself up. The man's suppleness was amazing, considering his bulk; he seemed almost to glide up over the edge of the coping. Conan followed him, and lying flat on the broad top, they spoke in wary whispers.

"I see no light," Conan muttered. The lower part of the tower seemed much like that portion visible from outside the garden—a perfect, gleaming cylinder, with no apparent openings.

"There are cleverly constructed doors and windows," answered Taurus, "but they are closed. The soldiers breathe air that comes from above."

The garden was a vague pool of shadows, where feathery bushes and low spreading trees waved darkly in the starlight. Conan's wary soul felt the aura of waiting menace that brooded over it. He felt the burning glare of unseen eyes, and he caught a subtle scent that made the short hairs on his neck instinctively bristle as a hunting dog bristles at the scent of an ancient enemy.

"Follow me," whispered Taurus, "keep behind me, as you value your life."

Taking what looked like a copper tube from his girdle, the Nemedian dropped lightly to the sward inside the wall. Conan was close behind him, sword ready, but Taurus pushed him back, close to the wall, and showed no inclination to advance, himself. His whole attitude was of tense expectancy, and his gaze, like Conan's, was fixed on the shadowy mass of shrubbery a few yards away. This shrubbery was shaken, although the breeze had died down. Then two great eyes blazed from the waving shadows, and behind them other sparks of fire glinted in the darkness.

"Lions!" muttered Conan.

"Aye. By day they are kept in subterranean caverns below the tower. That's why there are no guards in this garden."

Conan counted the eyes rapidly.

"Five in sight; maybe more back in the bushes. They'll charge in a moment—"

"Be silent!" hissed Taurus, and he moved out from the wall, cautiously as if treading on razors, lifting the slender tube. Low rumblings rose from the shadows and the blazing eyes moved forward. Conan could sense the great slavering jaws, the tufted tails lashing tawny sides. The air grew tense—the Cimmerian gripped his sword, expecting the charge and the irresistible hurtling of giant bodies. Then Taurus brought the mouth of the tube to his lips and blew powerfully. A long jet of yellowish powder shot from the other end of the tube and billowed out instantly in a thick green-yellow cloud that settled over the shrubbery, blotting out the glaring eyes.

Taurus ran back hastily to the wall. Conan glared without understanding. The thick cloud hid the shrubbery, and from it no sound came.

"What is that mist?" the Cimmerian asked uneasily.

"Death!" hissed the Nemedian. "If a wind springs up and blows it back upon us, we must flee over the wall. But no, the wind is still, and now it is dissipating. Wait until it vanishes entirely. To breathe it is death."

Presently only yellowish shreds hung ghostily in the air; then they were gone, and Taurus motioned his companion forward. They stole toward the bushes, and Conan gasped. Stretched out in the shadows lay five great tawny shapes, the fire of their grim eyes dimmed for ever. A sweetish cloying scent lingered in the atmosphere.

"They died without a sound!" muttered the Cimmerian. "Taurus, what was that powder?"

"It was made from the black lotus, whose blossoms wave in the lost jungles of Khitai, where only the yellow-skulled priests of Yun dwell. Those blossoms strike dead any who smell of them."

Conan knelt beside the great forms, assuring himself that they were indeed beyond power of harm. He shook his head; the magic of the exotic lands was mysterious and terrible to the barbarians of the north.

"Why can you not slay the soldiers in the tower in the same way?" he asked.

"Because that was all the powder I possessed. The obtaining of it was a feat which in itself was enough to make me famous among the thieves of the world. I stole it out of a caravan bound for Stygia, and I lifted it, in its cloth-of-gold bag, out of the coils of the great serpent which guarded it, without awaking him. But come, in Bel's name! Are we to waste the night in discussion?"

They glided through the shrubbery to the gleaming foot of the tower, and there, with a motion enjoining silence, Taurus unwound his knotted cord, on one end of which was a strong steel hook. Conan saw his plan, and asked no questions as the Nemedian gripped the line a short distance below the hook, and began to swing it about his head. Conan laid his ear to the smooth wall and listened, but could hear nothing. Evidently the soldiers within did not suspect the presence of intruders, who had made no more sound than the night wind blowing through the trees. But a strange nervousness was on the barbarian; perhaps it was the lion-smell which was over everything.

Taurus threw the line with a smooth, ripping motion of his mighty arm. The hook curved upward and inward in a peculiar manner, hard to describe, and vanished over the jeweled rim. It apparently caught firmly, for cautious jerking and then hard pulling did not result in any slipping or giving.

"Luck the first cast," murmured Taurus. "I—"

It was Conan's savage instinct which made him wheel suddenly; for the death that was upon them made no sound. A fleeting glimpse showed the Cimmerian the giant tawny shape, rearing upright against the stars, towering over him for the death-stroke. No civilized man could have moved half so quickly as the barbarian moved. His sword flashed frostily in the starlight with every ounce of desperate nerve and thew behind it, and man and beast went down together.

Cursing incoherently beneath his breath, Taurus bent above the mass, and saw his companion's limbs move as he strove to drag himself from under the great weight that lay limply upon him. A glance showed the startled Nemedian that the lion was dead, its slanting skull split in half. He laid hold of the carcass, and by his aid, Conan thrust it aside and clambered up, still gripping his dripping sword.

"Are you hurt, man?" gasped Taurus, still bewildered by the stunning swiftness of that touch-and-go episode.

"No, by Crom!" answered the barbarian. "But that was as close a call as I've had in a life noways tame. Why did not the cursed beast roar as he charged?"

"All things are strange in this garden," said Taurus. "The lions strike silently—and so do other deaths. But come—little sound was made in that slaying, but the soldiers might have heard, if they are not asleep or drunk. That beast was in some other part of the garden and escaped the death of the flowers, but surely there are no more. We must climb this cord—little need to ask a Cimmerian if he can."

"If it will bear my weight," grunted Conan, cleansing his sword on the grass.

"It will bear thrice my own," answered Taurus. "It was woven from the tresses of dead women, which I took from their tombs at midnight, and steeped in the deadly wine of the upas tree, to give it strength. I will go first—then follow me closely."

The Nemedian gripped the rope and crooking a knee about it, began the ascent; he went up like a cat, belying the apparent clumsiness of his bulk. The Cimmerian followed. The cord swayed and turned on itself, but the climbers were not hindered; both had made more difficult climbs before. The jeweled rim glittered high above them, jutting out from the perpendicular of the wall, so that the cord hung perhaps a foot from the side of the tower—a fact which added greatly to the ease of the ascent.

Up and up they went, silently, the lights of the city spreading out further and further to their sight as they climbed, the stars above them more and more dimmed by the glitter of the jewels along the rim. Now Taurus reached up a hand and gripped the rim itself, pulling himself up and over. Conan paused a moment on the very edge, fascinated by the great frosty jewels whose gleams dazzled his eyes—diamonds, rubies, emeralds, sapphires, turquoises, moonstones, set thick as stars in the shimmering silver. At a distance their different gleams had seemed to merge into a pulsing white glare; but now, at close range, they shimmered with a million rainbow tints and lights, hypnotizing him with their scintillations.

"There is a fabulous fortune here, Taurus," he whispered; but the Nemedian answered impatiently, "Come on! If we secure the Heart, these and all other things shall be ours."

Conan climbed over the sparkling rim. The level of the tower's top was some feet below the gemmed ledge. It was flat, composed of some dark blue substance, set with gold that caught the starlight, so that the whole looked like a wide sapphire flecked with shining gold-dust. Across from the point where they had entered there seemed to be a sort of chamber, built upon the roof. It was of the same silvery material as the walls of the tower, adorned with designs worked in smaller gems; its single door was of gold, its surface cut in scales, and crusted with jewels that gleamed like ice.

Conan cast a glance at the pulsing ocean of lights which spread far below them, then glanced at Taurus. The Nemedian was drawing up his cord and coiling it. He showed Conan where the hook had caught—a fraction of an inch of the point had sunk under a great blazing jewel on the inner side of the rim.

"Luck was with us again," he muttered. "One would think that our combined weight would have torn that stone out. Follow me; the real risks of the venture begin now. We are in the serpent's lair, and we know not where he lies hidden."

Like stalking tigers they crept across the darkly gleaming floor and halted outside the sparkling door. With a deft and cautious hand Taurus tried it. It gave without resistance, and the companions looked in, tensed for anything. Over the Nemedian's shoulder Conan had a glimpse of a glittering chamber, the walls, ceiling and floor of which were crusted with great white jewels which lighted it brightly, and which seemed its only illumination. It seemed empty of life.

"Before we cut off our last retreat," hissed Taurus, "go you to the rim and look over on all sides; if you see any soldiers moving in the gardens, or anything suspicious, return and tell me. I will await you within this chamber."

Conan saw scant reason in this, and a faint suspicion of his companion touched his wary soul, but he did as Taurus requested. As he turned away, the Nemedian slipt inside the door and drew it shut behind him. Conan crept about the rim of the tower, returning to his starting-point without having seen any suspicious movement in the vaguely waving sea of leaves below. He turned toward the door—suddenly from within the chamber there sounded a strangled cry.

The Cimmerian leaped forward, electrified—the gleaming door swung open and Taurus stood framed in the cold blaze behind him. He swayed and his lips parted, but only a dry rattle burst from his throat. Catching at the golden door for support, he lurched out upon the roof, then fell headlong, clutching at his throat. The door swung to behind him.

Conan, crouching like a panther at bay, saw nothing in the room behind the stricken Nemedian, in the brief instant the door was partly open—unless it was not a trick of the light which made it seem as if a shadow darted across the gleaming floor. Nothing followed Taurus out on the roof, and Conan bent above the man.

The Nemedian stared up wth dilated, glazing eyes, that somehow held a terrible bewilderment. His hands clawed at his throat, his lips slobbered and gurgled; then suddenly he stiffened, and the astounded Cimmerian knew that he was dead. And he felt that Taurus had died without knowing what manner of death had stricken him. Conan glared bewilderedly at the cryptic golden door. In that empty room, with its glittering jeweled walls, death had come to the prince of thieves as swiftly and mysteriously as he had dealt doom to the lions in the gardens below.

Gingerly the barbarian ran his hands over the man's half-naked body, seeking a wound. But the only marks of violence were between his shoulders, high up near the base of his bull-neck—three small wounds, which looked as if three nails had been driven deep in the flesh and withdrawn. The edges of these wounds were black, and a faint smell as of putrefaction was evident. Poisoned darts? thought Conan—but in that case the missiles should be still in the wounds.

Cautiously he stole toward the golden door, pushed it open, and looked inside. The chamber lay empty, bathed in the cold, pulsing glow of the myriad jewels. In the very center of the ceiling he idly noted a curious design—a black eight-sided pattern, in the center of which four gems glittered with a red flame unlike the white blaze of the other jewels. Across the room there was another door, like the one in which he stood, except that it was not carved in the scale pattern. Was it from that door that death had come?—and having struck down its victim, had it retreated by the same way?

Closing the door behind him, the Cimmerian advanced into the chamber. His bare feet made no sound on the crystal floor. There were no chairs or tables in the chamber, only three or four silken couches, embroidered with gold and worked in strange serpentine designs, and several silver-bound mahogany chests. Some were sealed with heavy golden locks; others lay open, their carven lids thrown back, revealing heaps of jewels in a careless riot of splendor to the Cimmerian's astounded eyes. Conan swore beneath his breath; already he had looked upon more wealth that night than he had ever dreamed existed in all the world, and he grew dizzy thinking of what must be the value of the jewel he sought.

He was in the center of the room now, going stooped forward, head thrust out warily, sword advanced, when again death struck at him soundlessly. A flying shadow that swept across the gleaming floor was his only warning, and his instinctive sidelong leap all that saved his life. He had a flashing glimpse of a hairy black horror that swung past him with a clashing of frothing fangs, and something splashed on his bare shoulder that burned like drops of liquid hellfire. Springing back, sword high, he saw the horror strike the floor, wheel and scuttle toward him with appalling speed—a gigantic black spider, such as men see only in nightmare dreams.

It was as large as a pig, and its eight thick hairy legs drove its ogreish body over the floor at headlong pace; its four evilly gleaming eyes shone with a horrible intelligence, and its fangs dripped venom that Conan knew, from the burning of his shoulder where only a few drops had splashed as the thing struck and missed, was laden with swift death. This was the killer that had dropped from its perch in the middle of the ceiling on a strand of its web, on the neck of the Nemedian. Fools that they were not to have suspected that the upper chambers would he guarded as well as the lower!

These thoughts flashed briefly through Conan's mind as the monster rushed. He leaped high, and it passed beneath him, wheeled and charged back. This time he evaded its rush with a sidewise leap, and struck back like a cat. His sword severed one of the hairy legs, and again he barely saved himself as the monstrosity swerved at him, fangs clicking fiendishly. But the creature did not press the pursuit; turning, it scuttled across the crystal floor and ran up the wall to the ceiling, where it crouched for an instant, glaring down at him with its fiendish red eyes. Then without warning it launched itself through space, trailing a strand of slimy grayish stuff.

Conan stepped back to avoid the hurtling body—then ducked frantically, just in time to escape being snared by the flying web-rope. He saw the monster's intent and sprang toward the door, but it was quicker, and a sticky strand cast across the door made him a prisoner. He dared not try to cut it with his sword; he knew the stuff would cling to the blade, and before he could shake it loose, the fiend would be sinking its fangs into his back.

Then began a desperate game, the wits and quickness of the man matched against the fiendish craft and speed of the giant spider. It no longer scuttled across the floor in a direct charge, or swung its body through the air at him. It raced about the ceiling and the walls, seeking to snare him in the long loops of sticky gray web-strands, which it flung with a devilish accuracy. These strands were thick as ropes, and Conan knew that once they were coiled about him, his desperate strength would not be enough to tear him free before the monster struck.

All over the chamber went on that devil's dance, in utter silence except for the quick breathing of the man, the low scuff of his bare feet on the shining floor, the castanet rattle of the monstrosity's fangs. The grey strands lay in coils on the floor; they were looped along the walls; they overlaid the jewel-chests and silken couches, and hung in dusky festoons from the jeweled ceiling. Conan's steel-trap quickness of eye and muscle had kept him untouched, though the sticky loops had passed him so close they rasped his naked hide. He knew he could not always avoid them; he not only had to watch the strands swinging from the ceiling, but to keep his eye on the floor, lest he trip in the coils that lay there. Sooner or later a gummy loop would writhe about him, python-like, and then, wrapped like a cocoon, he would lie at the monster's mercy.

The spider raced across the chamber floor, the gray rope waving out behind it. Conan leaped high, clearing a couch—with a quick wheel the fiend ran up the wall, and the strand, leaping off the floor like a live thing, whipped about the Cimmerian's ankle. He caught himself on his hands as he fell, jerking frantically at the web which held him like a pliant vise, or the coil of a python. The hairy devil was racing down the wall to complete its capture. Stung to frenzy, Conan caught up a jewel chest and hurled it with all his strength. It was a move the monster was not expecting. Full in the midst of the branching black legs the massive missile struck, smashing against the wall with a muffled sickening crunch. Blood and greenish slime spattered, and the shattered mass fell with the burst gem-chest to the floor. The crushed black body lay among the flaming riot of jewels that spilled over it; the hairy legs moved aimlessly, the dying eyes glittered redly among the twinkling gems.

Conan glared about, but no other horror appeared, and he set himself to working free of the web. The substance clung tenaciously to his ankle and his hands, but at last he was free, and taking up his sword, he picked his way among the gray coils and loops to the inner door. What horrors lay within he did not know. The Cimmerian's blood was up, and since he had come so far, and overcome so much peril, he was determined to go through to the grim finish of the adventure, whatever that might be. And he felt that the jewel he sought was not among the many so carelessly strewn about the gleaming chamber.

Stripping off the loops that fouled the inner door, he found that it, like the other, was not locked. He wondered if the soldiers below were still unaware of his presence. Well, he was high above their heads, and if tales were to be believed, they were used to strange noises in the tower above them—sinister sounds, and screams of agony and horror.

Yara was on his mind, and he was not altogether comfortable as he opened the golden door. But he saw only a flight of silver steps leading down, dimly lighted by what means he could not ascertain. Down these he went silently, gripping his sword. He heard no sound, and came presently to an ivory door, set with blood-stones. He listened, but no sound came from within; only thin wisps of smoke drifted lazily from beneath the door, bearing a curious exotic odor unfamiliar to the Cimmerian. Below him the silver stair wound down to vanish in the dimness, and up that shadowy well no sound floated; he had an eery feeling that he was alone in a tower occupied only by ghosts and phantoms.

3

Cautiously he pressed against the ivory door and it swung silently inward. On the shimmering threshold Conan stared like a wolf in strange surroundings, ready to fight or flee on the instant. He was looking into a large chamber with a domed golden ceiling; the walls were of green jade, the floor of ivory, partly covered by thick rugs. Smoke and exotic scent of incense floated up from a brazier on a golden tripod, and behind it sat an idol on a sort of marble couch. Conan stared aghast; the image had the body of a man, naked, and green in color; but the head was one of nightmare and madness. Too large for the human body, it had no attributes of humanity. Conan stared at the wide flaring ears, the curling proboscis, on either side of which stood white tusks tipped with round golden balls. The eyes were closed, as if in sleep.

This then, was the reason for the name, the Tower of the Elephant, for the head of the thing was much like that of the beasts described by the Shemitish wanderer. This was Yara's god; where then should the gem be, but concealed in the idol, since the stone was called the Elephant's Heart?

As Conan came forward, his eyes fixed on the motionless idol, the eyes of the thing opened suddenly! The Cimmerian froze in his tracks. It was no image—it was a living thing, and he was trapped in its chamber!

That he did not instantly explode in a burst of murderous frenzy is a fact that measures his horror, which paralyzed him where he stood. A civilized man in his position would have sought doubtful refuge in the conclusion that he was insane;

it did not occur to the Cimmerian to doubt his senses. He knew he was face to face with a demon of the Elder World, and the realization robbed him of all his faculties except sight.

The trunk of the horror was lifted and quested about, the topaz eyes stared unseeingly, and Conan knew the monster was blind. With the thought came a thawing of his frozen nerves, and he began to back silently toward the door. But the creature heard. The sensitive trunk stretched toward him, and Conan's horror froze him again when the being spoke, in a strange, stammering voice that never changed its key or timbre. The Cimmerian knew that those jaws were never built or intended for human speech.

"Who is here? Have you come to torture me again, Yara? Will you never be done? Oh, Yagkosha, is there no end to agony?"

Tears rolled from the sightless eyes, and Conan's gaze strayed to the limbs stretched on the marble couch. And he knew the monster would not rise to attack him. He knew the marks of the rack, and the searing brand of the flame, and tough-souled as he was, he stood aghast at the ruined deformities which his reason told him had once been limbs as comely as his own. And suddenly all fear and repulsion went from him, to be replaced by a great pity. What this monster was, Conan could not know, but the evidences of its sufferings were so terrible and pathetic that a strange aching sadness came over the Cimmerian, he knew not why. He only felt that he was looking upon a cosmic tragedy, and he shrank with shame, as if the guilt of a whole race were laid upon him.

"I am not Yara," he said. "I am only a thief. I will not harm you."

"Come near that I may touch you," the creature faltered, and Conan came near unfearingly, his sword hanging forgotten in his hand. The sensitive trunk came out and groped over his face and shoulders, as a blind man gropes, and its touch was light as a girl's hand.

"You are not of Yara's race of devils," sighed the creature. "The clean, lean fierceness of the wastelands marks you. I know your people from of old, whom I knew by another name in the long, long ago when another world lifted its jeweled spires to the stars. There is blood on your fingers."

"A spider in the chamber above and a lion in the garden," muttered Conan.

"You have slain a man too, this night," answered the other. "And there is death in the tower above. I feel; I know."

"Aye," muttered Conan. "The prince of all thieves lies there dead from the bite of a vermin."

"So—and so!" the strange inhuman voice rose in a sort of low chant. "A slaying in the tavern and a slaying on the roof—I know; I feel. And the third will make the magic of which not even Yara dreams—oh, magic of deliverance, green gods of Yag!"

Again tears fell as the tortured body was rocked to and fro in the grip of varied emotions. Conan looked on, bewildered.

Then the convulsions ceased; the soft, sightless eyes were turned toward the Cimmerian, the trunk beckoned.

"Oh man, listen," said the strange being. "I am foul and monstrous to you, am I not? Nay, do not answer; I know. But you would seem as strange to me, could I see you. There are many worlds besides this earth, and life takes many shapes. I am neither god nor demon, but flesh and blood like yourself, though the substance differ in part, and the form be cast in a different mold.

"I am very old, oh man of the waste countries; long and long ago I came to this planet with others of my world, from the green planet Yag, which circles for ever in the outer fringe of this universe. We swept through space on mighty wings that drove us through the cosmos quicker than light, because we had warred with the kings of Yag and were defeated and outcast. But we could never return, for on earth our wings withered from our shoulders. Here we abode apart from earthly life. We fought the strange and terrible forms of life which then walked the earth, so that we became feared, and were not molested in the dim jungles of the east, where we had our abode.

"We saw men grow from the ape and build the shining cities of Valusia, Kamelia, Commoria, and their sisters. We saw them reel before the thrusts of the heathen Atlanteans and Picts and Lemurians. We saw the oceans rise and engulf Atlantis and Lemuria, and the isles of the Picts, and shining cities of civilization. We saw the survivors of Pictdom and Atlantis build their stone age empires, and go down to ruin, locked in bloody wars. We saw the Picts sink into abysmal savagery, the Atlanteans into apedom again. We saw new savages drift southward in conquering waves from the arctic circle to build a new civilization, with new kingdoms called Nemedia, and Koth, and Aquilonia and their sisters. We saw your people rise under a new name from the jungles of the apes that had been Atlanteans. We saw the descendants of the Lemurians who had survived the cataclysm, rise again through savagery and ride westward, as Hyrkanians. And we saw this race of devils, survivors of the ancient civilization that was before Atlantis sank, come once more into culture and power—this accursed kingdom of Zamora.

"All this we saw, neither aiding nor hindering the immutable cosmic law, and one by one we died; for we of Yag are not immortal, though our lives are as the lives of planets and constellations. At last I alone was left, dreaming of old times among the ruined temples of jungle-lost Khitai, worshipped as a god by an ancient yellow-skinned race. Then came Yara, versed in dark knowledge handed down through the days of barbarism, since before Atlantis sank.

"First he sat at my feet and learned wisdom. But he was not satisfied with what I taught him, for it was white magic, and he wished evil lore, to enslave kings and glut a fiendish ambition. I would teach him none of the black secrets I had gained, through no wish of mine, through the eons.

"But his wisdom was deeper than I had guessed; with guile gotten among the dusky tombs of dark Stygia, he trapped me into divulging a secret I had not intended to bare; and turning my own power upon me, he enslaved me. Ah, gods of Yag, my cup has been bitter since that hour!

"He brought me up from the lost jungles of Khitai where the gray apes danced to the pipes of the yellow priests, and offerings of fruit and wine heaped my broken altars. No more was I a god to kindly jungle-folk—I was slave to a devil in human form."

Again tears stole from the unseeing eyes.

"He pent me in this tower which at his command I built for him in a single night. By fire and rack he mastered me, and by strange unearthly tortures you would not understand. In agony I would long ago have taken my own life, if I could. But he kept me alive—mangled, blinded, and broken—to do his foul bidding. And for three hundred years I have done his bidding, from this marble couch, blackening my soul with cosmic sins, and staining my wisdom with crimes, because I had no other choice. Yet not all my ancient secrets has he wrested from me, and my last gift shall be the sorcery of the Blood and the Jewel.

"For I feel the end of time draw near. You are the hand of Fate. I beg of you, take the gem you will find on yonder altar."

Conan turned to the gold and ivory altar indicated, and took up a great round jewel, clear as crimson crystal; and he knew that this was the Heart of the Elephant.

"Now for the great magic, the mighty magic, such as earth has not seen before, and shall not see again, through a million million of millenniums. By my life-blood I conjure it, by blood born on the green breast of Yag, dreaming far-poised in the great blue vastness of Space.

"Take your sword, man, and cut out my heart; then squeeze it so that the blood will flow over the red stone. Then go you down these stairs and enter the ebony chamber where Yara sits wrapped in lotus-dreams of evil. Speak his name and he will awaken. Then lay this gem before him, and say, 'Yag-kosha gives you a last gift and a last enchantment.' Then get you from the tower quickly; fear not, your way shall be made clear. The life of man is not the life of Yag, nor is human death the death of Yag. Let me be free of this cage of broken blind flesh, and I will once more be Yogah of Yag, morning-crowned and shining, with wings to fly, and feet to dance, and eyes to see, and hands to break."

Uncertainly Conan approached, and Yag-kosha, or Yogah, as if sensing his uncertainty, indicated where he should strike. Conan set his teeth and drove the sword deep. Blood streamed over the blade and his hand, and the monster started convulsively, then lay back quite still. Sure that life had fled, at least life as he understood it, Conan set to work on his grisly task and quickly brought forth something that he felt must be the strange being's heart, though it differed curiously from any he had ever seen. Holding the still pulsing organ over the blazing jewel, he pressed it with both hands, and a rain of blood fell on the stone. To his surprise, it did not run off, but soaked into the gem, as water is absorbed by a sponge.

Holding the jewel gingerly, he went out of the fantastic chamber and came upon the silver steps. He did not look back; he instinctively felt that some transmutation was taking place in the body on the marble couch, and he further felt that it was of a sort not to be witnessed by human eyes.

He closed the ivory door behind him and without hesitation descended the silver steps. It did not occur to him to ignore the instructions given him. He halted at an ebony door, in the center of which was a grinning silver skull, and pushed it open. He looked into a chamber of ebony and jet, and saw, on a black silken couch, a tall, spare form reclining. Yara the priest and sorcerer lay before him, his eyes open and dilated with the fumes of the yellow lotus, far-staring, as if fixed on gulfs and nighted abysses beyond human ken.

"Yara!" said Conan, like a judge pronouncing doom. "Awaken!"

The eyes cleared instantly and became cold and cruel as a vulture's. The tall silken-clad form lifted erect, and towered gauntly above the Cimmerian.

"Dog!" His hiss was like the voice of a cobra. "What do you here?"

Conan laid the jewel on the ebony table.

"He who sent this gem bade me say, 'Yag-kosha gives a last gift and a last enchantment.' "

Yara recoiled, his dark face ashy. The jewel was no longer crystal-clear; its murky depths pulsed and throbbed, and curious smoky waves of changing color passed over its smooth surface. As if drawn hypnotically, Yara bent over the table and gripped the gem in his hands, staring into its shadowed depths, as if it were a magnet to draw the shuddering soul from his body. And as Conan looked, he thought that his eyes must be playing him tricks. For when Yara had risen up from his couch, the priest had seemed gigantically tall; yet now he saw that Yara's head would scarcely come to his shoulder. He blinked, puzzled, and for the first time that night, doubted his own senses. Then with a shock he realized that the priest was shrinking in stature—was growing smaller before his very gaze.

With a detached feeling he watched, as a man might watch a play; immersed in a feeling of overpowering unreality, the Cimmerian was no longer sure of his own identity; he only knew that he was looking upon the external evidences of the unseen play of vast Outer forces, beyond his understanding.

Now Yara was no bigger than a child; now like an infant he sprawled on the table, still grasping the jewel. And now the sorcerer suddenly realized his fate, and he sprang up, releasing the gem. But still he dwindled, and Conan saw a tiny, pigmy figure rushing wildly about the ebony table-top, waving tiny arms and shrieking in a voice that was like the squeak of an insect.

Now he had shrunk until the great jewel towered above him like a hill, and Conan saw him cover his eyes with his hands, as if to shield them from the glare, as he staggered about like a madman. Conan sensed that some unseen magnetic force was pulling 'Yara to the gem. Thrice he raced wildly about it in a narrowing circle, thrice he strove to turn and run out across the table; then with a scream that echoed faintly in the ears of the watcher, the priest threw up his arms and ran straight toward the blazing globe.

Bending close, Conan saw Yara clamber up the smooth, curving surface, impossibly, like a man climbing a glass mountain. Now the priest stood on the top, still with tossing arms, invoking what grisly names only the gods know. And suddenly he sank into the very heart of the jewel, as a man sinks into a sea, and Conan saw the smoky waves close over his head. Now he saw him in the crimson heart of the jewel, once more crystal-clear, as a man sees a scene far away, tiny with great distance. And into the heart came a green, shining winged figure with the body of a man and the head of an elephant—no longer blind or crippled. Yara threw up his arms and fled as a madman flees, and on his heels came the avenger. Then, like the bursting of a bubble, the great jewel vanished in a rainbow burst of iridescent gleams, and the ebony table-top lay bare and deserted—as bare, Conan somehow knew, as the marble couch in the chamber above, where the body of that strange transcosmic being called Yag-kosha and Yogah had lain.

The Cimmerian turned and fled from the chamber, down the silver stairs. So amazed was he that it did not occur to him to escape from the tower by the way he had entered it. Down that winding, shadowy silver well he ran, and came into a large chamber at the foot of the gleaming stairs. There he halted for an instant; he had come into the room of the soldiers. He saw the glitter of their silver corselets, the sheen of their jeweled sword-hilts. They sat slumped at the banquet board, their dusky plumes waving somberly above their drooping helmeted heads; they lay among their dice and fallen goblets on the wine-stained lapis-lazuli floor. And he knew that they were dead. The promise had been made, the word kept; whether sorcery or magic or the falling shadow of great green wings had stilled the revelry, Conan could not know, but his way had been made clear. And a silver door stood open, framed in the whiteness of dawn.

Into the waving green gardens came the Cimmerian, and as the dawn wind blew upon him with the cool fragrance of luxuriant growths, he started like a man waking from a dream. He turned back uncertainly, to stare at the cryptic tower he had just left. Was he bewitched and enchanted? Had he dreamed all that had seemed to have passed? As he looked he saw the gleaming tower sway against the crimson dawn, its jewel-crusted rim sparkling in the growing light, and crash into shining shards.

⚙ J(OHN) R(ONALD) R(EUEL) TOLKIEN
(1892-1973)

Along with Robert E. Howard, J. R. R. Tolkien is perhaps the most imitated author of Fantasy in the twentieth century. If Howard is the architect of Heroic Fantasy of the last one hundred years, then Tolkien is master of Epic Fantasy during that same time period. Much of what has appeared in popular Fantasy of the last fifty years is tribute to and imitation of Howard and Tolkien.

J. R. R. Tolkien was an Oxford professor of and expert on English and English culture; he was well versed in the fields of linguistics and mythology. This extensive background in arts and letters provided much of the content for his stories of Middle Earth, which include The Hobbit, Or, There and Back Again *(1937),* The Lord of the Rings *trilogy (1954–55), and* The Silmarillion *(1977). Tolkien's stories of Middle Earth include epic quests, apocalyptic battles between Good and Evil, alternate worlds and universes, and a range of traditional and new Fantasy characters. Hobbits are his most significant contribution to this last group.*

Tolkien's stories were revived in the 1960s when a substantial part of the population became enamored with stories of Utopia, agrarian life, antiwar allegories, and socialism. The excerpt from The Hobbit *that follows is ingeniously plotted and crafted, and it features the inventive title character and a nasty creature named "Gollum" in a folkloric game with the stakes being life and death.*

Riddles in the Dark
(from The Hobbit, *1937)*

When Bilbo opened his eyes, he wondered if he had; for it was just as dark as with them shut. No one was anywhere near him. Just imagine his fright! He could hear nothing, see nothing, and he could feel nothing except the stone of the floor.

Very slowly he got up and groped about on all fours, till he touched the wall of the tunnel; but neither up nor down it could he find anything: nothing at all, no sign of goblins, no sign of dwarves. His head was swimming, and he was far from certain even of the direction they had been going in when he had his fall. He guessed as well as he could, and crawled along for a good way, till suddenly his hand met what felt like a tiny ring of cold metal lying on the floor of the tunnel. It was a turning point in his career, but he did not know it. He put the ring in his pocket almost without thinking; certainly it did not seem of any particular use at the moment. He did not go much further, but sat down on the cold floor and gave himself up to complete miserableness, for a long while. He thought of himself frying bacon and eggs in his own kitchen at home—for he could feel inside that it was high time for some meal or other; but that only made him miserabler.

He could not think what to do; nor could he think what had happened; or why he had been left behind; or why, if he had been left behind, the goblins had not caught him; or even why his head was so sore. The truth was he had been lying quiet, out of sight and out of mind, in a very dark corner for a long while.

After some time he felt for his pipe. It was not broken, and that was something. Then he felt for his pouch, and there was some tobacco in it, and that was something more. Then he felt for matches and he could not find any at all, and that shattered his hopes completely. Just as well for him, as he agreed when he came to his senses. Goodness knows what the striking of matches and the smell of tobacco would have brought on him out of dark holes in that horrible place. Still at the moment he felt very crushed. But in slapping all his pockets and feeling all round himself for matches his hand came on the hilt of his little sword—the little dagger that he got from the trolls, and that he had quite forgotten; nor do the goblins seem to have noticed it, as he wore it inside his breeches.

Now he drew it out. It shone pale and dim before his eyes. "So it is an elvish blade, too," he thought; "and goblins are not very near, and yet not far enough."

But somehow he was comforted. It was rather splendid to be wearing a blade made in Gondolin for the goblin-wars of which so many songs had sung; and also he had noticed that such weapons made a great impression on goblins that came upon them suddenly.

"Go back?" he thought. "No good at all! Go sideways? Impossible! Go forward? Only thing to do! On we go!" So up he got, and trotted along with his little sword held in front of him and one hand feeling the wall, and his heart all of a patter and a pitter.

Now certainly Bilbo was in what is called a tight place. But you must remember it was not quite so tight for him as it would have been for me or for you. Hobbits are not quite like ordinary people; and after all if their holes are nice cheery places and properly aired, quite different from the tunnels of the goblins, still they are more used to tunnelling than we are, and they do not easily lose their sense of direction underground—not when their heads have recovered from being bumped. Also they can move very quietly, and hide easily, and recover wonderfully from falls and bruises, and they have a fund of wisdom and wise sayings that men have mostly never heard or have forgotten long ago.

I should not have liked to have been in Mr. Baggins' place, all the same. The tunnel seemed to have no end. All he knew was that it was still going down pretty steadily and keeping in the same direction in spite of a twist and a turn or two. There were passages leading off to the side every now and then, as he knew by the glimmer of his sword, or could feel with his hand on the wall. Of these he took no notice, except to hurry past for fear of goblins or half-imagined dark things coming out of them. On and on he went, and down and down; and still he heard no sound of anything except the occasional whirr of a bat by his ears, which startled him at first, till it became too frequent to bother about. I do not know how long he kept on like this, hating to go on, not daring to stop, on, on, until he was tireder than tired. It seemed like all the way to tomorrow and over it to the days beyond.

Suddenly without any warning he trotted splash into water! Ugh! it was icy cold. That pulled him up sharp and short. He did not know whether it was just a pool in the path, or the edge of an underground stream that crossed the passage, or the brink of a deep dark subterranean lake. The sword was hardly shining at all. He stopped, and he could hear, when he listened hard, drops drip-drip-dripping from an unseen roof into the water below; but there seemed no other sort of sound.

"So it is a pool or a lake, and not an underground river," he thought. Still he did not dare to wade out into the darkness. He could not swim; and he thought, too, of nasty slimy things, with big bulging blind eyes, wriggling in the water. There are strange things living in the pools and lakes in the hearts of mountains: fish whose fathers swam in, goodness only knows how many years ago, and never swam out again, while their eyes grew bigger and bigger and bigger from trying to see in the blackness; also there are other things more slimy than fish. Even in the tunnels and caves the goblins have made for themselves there are other things living unbeknown to them that have sneaked in from outside to lie up in the dark. Some of these caves, too, go back in their beginnings to ages before the goblins, who only widened them and joined them up with passages, and the original owners are still there in odd corners, slinking and nosing about.

Deep down here by the dark water lived old Gollum, a small slimy creature. I don't know where he came from, nor who or what he was. He was Gollum—as dark as darkness, except for two big round pale eyes in his thin face. He had a little boat, and he rowed about quite quietly on the lake; for lake it was, wide and deep and deadly cold. He paddled it with large feet dangling over the side, but never a ripple did he make. Not he. He was looking out of his pale lamplike eyes for blind fish, which he grabbed with his long fingers as quick as thinking. He liked meat too. Goblin he thought good, when he could get it; but he took care they never found him out. He just throttled them from behind, if they ever came down alone anywhere near the edge of the water, while he was prowling about. They very seldom did, for they had a feeling that something unpleasant was lurking down there, down at the very roots of the mountain. They had come on the lake, when they were tunneling down long ago, and they found they could go no further; so there their road ended in that direction, and there was no reason to go that way—unless the Great Goblin sent them. Sometimes he took a fancy for fish from the lake, and sometimes neither goblin nor fish came back.

Actually Gollum lived on a slimy island of rock in the middle of the lake. He was watching Bilbo now from the distance with his pale eyes like telescopes. Bilbo could not see him, but he was wondering a lot about Bilbo, for he could see that he was no goblin at all.

Gollum got into his boat and shot off from the island, while Bilbo was sitting on the brink altogether flummoxed and at the end of his way and his wits. Suddenly up came Gollum and whispered and hissed:

"Bless us and splash us, my precioussss! I guess it's a choice feast; at least a tasty morsel it'd make us, gollum!" And when he said *gollum* he made a horrible swallowing noise in his throat. That is how he got his name, though he always called himself 'my precious.'

The hobbit jumped nearly out of his skin when the hiss came in his ears, and he suddenly saw the pale eyes sticking out at him.

"Who are you?" he said, thrusting his dagger in front of him.

"What iss he, my preciouss?" whispered Gollum (who always spoke to himself through never having anyone else to speak to). This is what he had come to find out, for he was not really very hungry at the moment, only curious; otherwise he would have grabbed first and whispered afterwards.

"I am Mr. Bilbo Baggins. I have lost the dwarves and I have lost the wizard, and I don't know where I am; and I don't want to know, if only I can get away."

"What's he got in his handses?" said Gollum, looking at the sword, which he did not quite like.

"A sword, a blade which came out of Gondolin!"

"Sssss" said Gollum, and became quite polite. "Praps ye sits here and chats with it a bitsy, my preciouss. It like riddles, praps it does, does it?" He was anxious to appear friendly, at any rate for the moment, and until he found out more about the sword and the hobbit, whether he was quite alone really, whether he was good to eat, and whether Gollum was really hungry. Riddles were all he could think of.

Asking them, and sometimes guessing them, had been the only game he had ever played with other funny creatures sitting in their holes in the long, long ago, before he lost all his friends and was driven away, alone, and crept down, down, into the dark under the mountains.

"Very well," said Bilbo, who was anxious to agree, until he found out more about the creature, whether he was quite alone, whether he was fierce or hungry, and whether he was a friend of the goblins.

"You ask first," he said, because he had not had time to think of a riddle.

So Gollum hissed:

What has roots as nobody sees,
Is taller than trees,
   Up, up it goes,
   And yet never grows?

"Easy!" said Bilbo. "Mountain, I suppose."

"Does it guess easy? It must have a competition with us, my preciouss! If precious asks, and it doesn't answer, we eats it, my preciousss. If it asks us, and we doesn't answer, then we does what it wants, eh? We shows it the way out, yes!"

"All right!" said Bilbo, not daring to disagree, and nearly bursting his brain to think of riddles that could save him from being eaten.

Thirty white horses on a red hill,
   First they champ,
   Then they stamp,
Then they stand still.

That was all he could think of to ask—the idea of eating was rather on his mind. It was rather an old one, too, and Gollum knew the answer as well as you do.

"Chestnuts, chestnuts," he hissed. "Teeth! teeth! my preciousss; but we has only six!" Then he asked his second:

Voiceless it cries,
Wingless flutters,
Toothless bites,
Mouthless mutters.

"Half a moment!" cried Bilbo, who was still thinking uncomfortably about eating. Fortunately he had once heard something rather like this before, and getting his wits back he thought of the answer. "Wind, wind of course," he said, and he was so pleased that he made up one on the spot. "This'll puzzle the nastly little underground creature," he thought:

An eye in a blue face
Saw an eye in a green face.
"That eye is like to this eye"
Said the first eye,
"But in low place,
Not in high place."

"Ss, ss, ss," said Gollum. He had been underground a long long time, and was forgetting this sort of thing. But just as Bilbo was beginning to hope that the wretch would not be able to answer, Gollum brought up memories of ages and ages and ages before, when he lived with his grandmother in a hole in a bank by a river. "Sss, sss, my preciouss," he said. "Sun on the daisies it means, it does."

But these ordinary aboveground everyday sort of riddles were tiring for him. Also they reminded him of days when he had been less lonely and sneaky and nasty, and that put him out of temper. What is more they made him hungry; so this time he tried something a bit more difficult and more unpleasant:

> It cannot be seen, cannot be felt,
> Cannot be heard, cannot be smelt.
> It lies behind stars and under hills,
>   And empty holes it fills.
> It comes first and follows after,
>   Ends life, kills laughter.

Unfortunately for Gollum Bilbo had heard that sort of thing before; and the answer was all round him any way. "Dark!" he said without even scratching his head or putting on his thinking cap.

> A box without hinges, key, or lid,
> Yet golden treasure inside is hid,

he asked to gain time, until he could think of a really hard one. This he thought a dreadfully easy chestnut, though he had not asked it in the usual words. But it proved a nasty poser for Gollum. He hissed to himself, and still he did not answer; he whispered and spluttered.

After some while Bilbo became impatient. "Well, what is it?" he said. "The answer's not a kettle boiling over, as you seem to think from the noise you are making."

"Give us a chance; let it give us a chance, my preciouss—ss—ss."

"Well," said Bilbo, after giving him a long chance, "what about your guess?"

But suddenly Gollum remembered thieving from nests long ago, and sitting under the river bank teaching his grandmother, teaching his grandmother to suck—"Eggses!" he hissed. "Eggses it is!" Then he asked:

> Alive without breath,
> As cold as death;
> Never thirsty, ever drinking,
> All in mail never clinking.

He also in his turn thought this was a dreadfully easy one, because he was always thinking of the answer. But he could not remember anything better at the moment, he was so flustered by the egg-question. All the same it was a poser for poor Bilbo, who never had anything to do with the water if he could help it. I imagine you know the answer, of course, or can guess it as easy as winking, since you are sitting comfortably at home and have not the danger of being eaten to disturb your thinking. Bilbo sat and cleared his throat once or twice, but no answer came.

After a while Gollum began to hiss with pleasure to himself: "Is it nice, my preciousss? Is it juicy? Is it scrumptiously crunchable?" He began to peer at Bilbo out of the darkness.

"Half a moment," said the hobbit shivering. "I gave you a good long chance just now."

"It must make haste, haste!" said Gollum, beginning to climb out of his boat on to the shore to get at Bilbo. But when he put his long webby foot in the water, a fish jumped out in a fright and fell on Bilbo's toes.

"Ugh!" he said, "it is cold and clammy!"—and so he guessed. "Fish! Fish!" he cried. "It is fish!"

Gollum was dreadfully disappointed; but Bilbo asked another riddle as quick as ever he could, so that Gollum had to get back into his boat and think.

No-legs lay on one-leg, two-legs sat near on three-legs, four-legs got some.

It was not really the right time for this riddle, but Bilbo was in a hurry. Gollum might have had some trouble guessing it, if he had asked it at another time. As it was, talking of fish, "no-legs" was not so very difficult, and after that the rest was easy. "Fish on a little table, man at table sitting on a stool, the cat has the bones" that of course is the answer, and Gollum soon gave it. Then he thought the time had come to ask something hard and horrible. This is what he said:

> *This thing all things devours:*
> *Birds, beasts, trees, flowers;*
> *Gnaws iron, bites steel;*
> *Grinds hard stones to meal;*
> *Slays king, ruins town,*
> *And beats high mountain down.*

Poor Bilbo sat in the dark thinking of all the horrible names of all the giants and ogres he had ever heard told of in tales, but not one of them had done all these things. He had a feeling that the answer was quite different and that he ought to know it, but he could not think of it. He began to get frightened, and that is bad for thinking. Gollum began to get out of his boat. He flapped into the water and paddled to the bank; Bilbo could see his eyes coming towards him. His tongue seemed to stick in his mouth; he wanted to shout out: "Give me more time! Give me time!" But all that came out with a sudden squeal was:

"Time! Time!"

Bilbo was saved by pure luck. For that of course was the answer.

Gollum was disappointed once more; and now he was getting angry, and also tired of the game. It had made him very hungry indeed. This time he did not go back to the boat. He sat down in the dark by Bilbo. That made the hobbit most dreadfully uncomfortable and scattered his wits.

"It's got to ask uss a quesstion, my preciouss, yes, yess, yesss. Jusst one more quesstion to guess, yes, yess," said Gollum.

But Bilbo simply could not think of any question with that nasty wet cold thing sitting next to him, and pawing and poking him. He scratched himself, he pinched himself; still he could not think of anything.

"Ask us! ask us!" said Gollum.

Bilbo pinched himself and slapped himself; he gripped on his little sword; he even felt in his pocket with his other hand. There he found the ring he had picked up in the passage and forgotten about.

"What have I got in my pocket?" he said aloud. He was talking to himself, but Gollum thought it was a riddle, and he was frightfully upset.

"Not fair! not fair!" he hissed. "It isn't fair, my precious, is it, to ask us what it's got in its nassty little pocketses?"

Bilbo seeing what had happened and having nothing better to ask stuck to his question, "What have I got in my pocket?" he said louder.

"S-s-s-s-s," hissed Gollum. "It must give us three guesseses, my preciouss, three guesseses."

"Very well! Guess away!" said Bilbo.

"Handses!" said Gollum.

"Wrong," said Bilbo, who had luckily just taken his hand out again. "Guess again!"

"S-s-s-s-s," said Gollum more upset than ever. He thought of all the things he kept in his own pockets: fish-bones, goblins' teeth, wet shells, a bit of bat-wing, a sharp stone to sharpen his fangs on, and other nasty things. He tried to think what other people kept in their pockets.

"Knife!" he said at last.

"Wrong!" said Bilbo, who had lost his some time ago. "Last guess!"

Now Gollum was in a much worse state than when Bilbo had asked him the egg-question. He hissed and spluttered and rocked himself backwards and forwards, and slapped his feet on the floor, and wriggled and squirmed; but still he did not dare to waste his last guess.

"Come on!" said Bilbo. "I am waiting!" He tried to sound bold and cheerful, but he did not feel at all sure how the game was going to end, whether Gollum guessed right or not.

"Time's up!" he said.

"String, or nothing!" shrieked Gollum, which was not quite fair—working in two guesses at once.

"Both wrong," cried Bilbo very much relieved; and he jumped at once to his feet, put his back to the nearest wall, and held out his little sword. He knew, of course, that the riddle-game was sacred and of immense antiquity, and even wicked creatures were afraid to cheat when they played at it. But he felt he could not trust this slimy thing to keep any promise at a pinch. Any excuse would do for him to slide out of it. And after all that last question had not been a genuine riddle according to the ancient laws.

But at any rate Gollum did not at once attack him. He could see the sword in Bilbo's hand. He sat still, shivering and whispering. At last Bilbo could wait no longer.

"Well?" he said. "What about your promise? I want to go. You must show me the way."

"Did we say so, precious? Show the nassty little Baggins the way out, yes, yes. But what has it got in its pocketses, eh? Not string, precious, but not nothing. Oh no! gollum!"

"Never you mind," said Bilbo. "A promise is a promise."

"Cross it is, impatient, precious," hissed Gollum. "But it must wait, yes it must. We can't go up the tunnels so hasty. We must go and get some things first, yes, things to help us."

"Well, hurry up!" said Bilbo, relieved to think of Gollum going away. He thought he was just making an excuse and did not mean to come back. What was Gollum talking about? What useful thing could he keep out on the dark lake? But he was wrong. Gollum did mean to come back. He was angry now and hungry. And he was a miserable wicked creature, and already he had a plan.

Not far away was his island, of which Bilbo knew nothing, and there in his hiding-place he kept a few wretched oddments, and one very beautiful thing, very beautiful, very wonderful. He had a ring, a golden ring, a precious ring.

"My birthday-present!" he whispered to himself, as he had often done in the endless dark days. "That's what we wants now, yes; we wants it!"

He wanted it because it was a ring of power, and if you slipped that ring on your finger, you were invisible; only in the full sunlight could you be seen, and then only by your shadow, and that would be shaky and faint.

"My birthday-present! It came to me on my birthday, my precious," So he had always said to himself. But who knows how Gollum came by that present, ages ago in the old days when such rings were still at large in the world? Perhaps even the Master who ruled them could not have said. Gollum used to wear it at first, till it tired him; and then he kept it in a pouch next his skin, till it galled him; and now usually he hid it in a hole in the rock on his island, and was always going back to look at it. And still sometimes he put it on, when he could not bear to be parted from it any longer, or when he was very, very, hungry, and tired of fish. Then he would creep along dark passages looking for stray goblins. He might even venture into places where the torches were lit and made his eyes blink and smart; for he would be safe. Oh yes, quite safe. No one would see him, no one would notice him, till he had his fingers on their throat. Only a few hours ago he had worn it, and caught a small goblin-imp. How it squeaked! He still had a bone or two left to gnaw, but he wanted something softer.

"Quite safe, yes," he whispered to himself, "It won't see us, will it, my precious? No. It won't see us, and its nassty little sword will be useless, yes quite."

That is what was in his wicked little mind, as he slipped suddenly from Bilbo's side, and flapped back to his boat, and went off into the dark. Bilbo thought he had heard the last of him. Still he waited a while; for he had no idea how to find his way out alone.

Suddenly he heard a screech. It sent a shiver down his back. Gollum was cursing and wailing away in the gloom, not very far off by the sound of it. He was on his island, scrabbling here and there, searching and seeking in vain.

"Where is it? Where iss it?" Bilbo heard him crying. "Losst it is, my precious, lost, lost! Curse us and crush us, my precious is lost!"

"What's the matter?" Bilbo called. "What have you lost?"

"It mustn't ask us," shrieked Gollum. "Not its business, no, gollum! It's losst, gollum, gollum, gollum."

"Well, so am I," cried Bilbo, "and I want to get unlost. And I won the game, and you promised. So come along! Come and let me out, and then go on with your looking!" Utterly miserable as Gollum sounded, Bilbo could not find much pity in his heart, and he had a feeling that anything Gollum wanted so much could hardly be something good. "Come along!" he shouted.

"No, not yet, precious!" Gollum answered. "We must search for it, it's lost, gollum."

"But you never guessed my last question, and you promised," said Bilbo.

"Never guessed!" said Gollum. Then suddenly out of the gloom came a sharp hiss. "What has it got in its pocketses? Tell us that. It must tell first."

As far as Bilbo knew, there was no particular reason why he should not tell. Gollum's mind had jumped to a guess quicker than his; naturally, for Gollum had brooded for ages on this one thing, and he was always afraid of its being stolen. But Bilbo was annoyed at the delay. After all, he had won the game, pretty fairly, at a horrible risk. "Answers were to be guessed not given," he said.

"But it wasn't a fair question," said Gollum. "Not a riddle, precious, no."

"Oh well, if it's a matter of ordinary questions," Bilbo replied, "then I asked one first. What have you lost? Tell me that!"

"What has it got in its pocketses?" The sound came hissing louder and sharper, and as he looked towards it, to his alarm Bilbo now saw two small points of light peering at him. As suspicion grew in Gollum's mind, the light of his eyes burned with a pale flame.

"What have you lost?" Bilbo persisted.

But now the light in Gollum's eyes had become a green fire, and it was coming swiftly nearer. Gollum was in his boat again, paddling wildly back to the dark shore; and such a rage of loss and suspicion was in his heart that no sword had any more terror for him.

Bilbo could not guess what had maddened the wretched creature, but he saw that all was up, and that Gollum meant to murder him at any rate. Just in time he turned and ran blindly back up the dark passage down which he had come, keeping close to the wall and feeling it with his left hand.

"What has it got in its pocketses?" he heard the hiss loud behind him, and the splash as Gollum leapt from his boat. "What have I, I wonder?" he said to himself, as he panted and stumbled along. He put his left hand in his pocket. The ring felt very cold as it quietly slipped on to his groping forefinger.

The hiss was close behind him. He turned now and saw Gollum's eyes like small green lamps coming up the slope. Terrified he tried to run faster, but suddenly he struck his toes on a snag in the floor, and fell flat with his little sword under him.

In a moment Gollum was on him. But before Bilbo could do anything, recover his breath, pick himself up, or wave his sword, Gollum passed by, taking no notice of him, cursing and whispering as he ran.

What could it mean? Gollum could see in the dark. Bilbo could see the light of his eyes palely shining even from behind. Painfully he got up, and sheathed his sword, which was now glowing faintly again, then very cautiously he followed. There seemed nothing else to do. It was no good crawling back down to Gollum's water. Perhaps if he followed him, Gollum might lead him to some way of escape without meaning to.

"Curse it! curse it! curse it!" hissed Gollum. "Curse the Baggins! It's gone! What has it got in its pocketses? Oh we guess, we guess, my precious. He's found it, yes he must have. My birthday-present."

Bilbo pricked up his ears. He was at last beginning to guess himself. He hurried a little, getting as close as he dared behind Gollum, who was still going quickly, not looking back, but turning his head from side to side, as Bilbo could see from the faint glimmer on the walls.

"My birthday-present! Curse it! How did we lose it, my precious? Yes, that's it. When we came this way last, when we twisted that nassty young squeaker. That's it. Curse it! It slipped from us, after all these ages and ages! It's gone, gollum."

Suddenly Gollum sat down and began to weep, a whistling and gurgling sound horrible to listen to. Bilbo halted and flattened himself against the tunnel-wall. After a while Gollum stopped weeping and began to talk. He seemed to be having an argument with himself.

"It's no good going back there to search, no. We doesn't remember all the places we've visited. And it's no use. The Baggins has got it in its pocketses; the nassty noser has found it, we says."

"We guesses, precious, only guesses. We can't know till we find the nassty creature and squeezes it. But it doesn't know what the present can do, does it? It'll just keep it in its pocketses. It doesn't know, and it can't go far. It's lost itself, the nassty nosey thing. It doesn't know the way out. It said so."

"It said so, yes; but it's tricksy. It doesn't say what it means. It won't say what it's got in its pocketses. It knows. It knows a way in, it must know a way out, yes. It's off to the back-door. To the back-door, that's it."

"The goblinses will catch it then. It can't get out that way, precious."

"Ssss, sss, gollum! Goblinses! Yes, but if it's got the present, our precious present, then goblinses will get it, gollum! They'll find it, they'll find out what it does. We shan't ever be safe again, never, gollum! One of the goblinses will put it on, and then no one will see him. He'll be there but not seen. Not even our clever eyeses will notice him; and he'll come creepsy and tricksy and catch us, gollum, gollum!"

"Then let's stop talking, precious, and make haste. If the Baggins has gone that way, we must go quick and see. Go! Not far now. Make haste!"

With a spring Gollum got up and started shambling off at a great pace. Bilbo hurried after him, still cautiously, though his chief fear now was of tripping on another snag and falling with a noise. His head was in a whirl of hope and wonder. It seemed that the ring he had was a magic ring: it made you invisible! He had heard of such things, of course, in old old tales; but it was hard to believe that he really had found one, by accident. Still there it was: Gollum with his bright eyes had passed him by, only a yard to one side.

On they went, Gollum flip-flapping ahead, hissing and cursing; Bilbo behind going as softly as a hobbit can. Soon they came to places where, as Bilbo had noticed on the way down, side-passages opened, this way and that. Gollum began at once to count them.

"One left, yes. One right, yes. Two right, yes, yes. Two left, yes, yes." And so on and on.

As the count grew he slowed down, and he began to get shaky and weepy; for he was leaving the water further and further behind, and he was getting afraid. Goblins might be about, and he had lost his ring. At last he stopped by a low opening, on their left as they went up.

"Seven right, yes. Six left, yes!" he whispered. "This is it. This is the way to the back-door, yes. Here's the passage!"

He peered in, and shrank back. "But we durstn't go in, precious, no we durstn't. Goblinses down there. Lots of goblinses. We smells them. Ssss!"

"What shall we do? Curse them and crush them! We must wait here, precious, wait a bit and see."

So they came to a dead stop. Gollum had brought Bilbo to the way out after all, but Bilbo could not get in! There was Gollum sitting humped up right in the opening, and his eyes gleamed cold in his head, as he swayed it from side to side between his knees.

Bilbo crept away from the wall more quietly than a mouse; but Gollum stiffened at once, and sniffed, and his eyes went green. He hissed softly but menacingly. He could not see the hobbit, but now he was on the alert, and he had other senses that the darkness had sharpened: hearing and smell. He seemed to be crouched right down with his flat hands splayed on the floor, and his head thrust out, nose almost to the stone. Though he was only a black shadow in the gleam of his own eyes, Bilbo could see or feel that he was tense as a bowstring, gathered for a spring.

Bilbo almost stopped breathing, and went stiff himself. He was desperate. He must get away, out of this horrible darkness, while he had any strength left. He must fight. He must stab the foul thing, put its eyes out, kill it. It meant to kill him. No, not a fair fight. He was invisible now. Gollum had no sword. Gollum had not actually threatened to kill him, or tried to yet. And he was miserable, alone, lost. A sudden understanding, a pity mixed with horror, welled up in Bilbo's heart: a glimpse of endless unmarked days without light or hope of betterment, hard stone, cold fish, sneaking and whispering. All these thoughts passed in a flash of a second. He trembled. And then quite suddenly in another flash, as if lifted by a new strength and resolve, he leaped.

No great leap for a man, but a leap in the dark. Straight over Gollum's head he jumped, seven feet forward and three in the air; indeed, had he known it, he only just missed cracking his skull on the low arch of the passage.

Gollum threw himself backwards, and grabbed as the hobbit flew over him, but too late: his hands snapped on thin air, and Bilbo, falling fair on his sturdy feet, sped off down the new tunnel. He did not turn to see what Gollum was doing. There was a hissing and cursing almost at his heels at first, then it stopped. All at once there came a bloodcurdling shriek, filled with hatred and despair. Gollum was defeated. He dared go no further. He had lost: lost his prey, and lost, too, the only thing he had ever cared for, his precious. The cry brought Bilbo's heart to his mouth, but still he held on. Now faint as an echo, but menacing, the voice came behind:

"Thief, thief, thief! Baggins! We hates it, we hates it, we hates it for ever!"

Then there was a silence. But that too seemed menacing to Bilbo. "If goblins are so near that he smelt them," he thought, "then they'll have heard his shrieking and cursing. Careful now, or this way will lead you to worse things."

The passage was low and roughly made. It was not too difficult for the hobbit, except when, in spite of all care, he stubbed his poor toes again, several times, on nasty jagged stones in the floor. "A bit low for goblins, at least for the big ones," thought Bilbo, not knowing that even the big ones, the orcs of the mountains, go along at a great speed stooping low with their hands almost on the ground.

Soon the passage that had been sloping down began to go up again, and after a while it climbed steeply. That slowed Bilbo down. But at last the slope stopped, the passage turned a corner, and dipped down again, and there, at the bottom of a short incline, he saw, filtering round another corner—a glimpse of light. Not red light, as of fire or lantern, but a pale out-of-doors sort of light. Then Bilbo began to run.

Scuttling as fast as his legs would carry him he turned the last corner and came suddenly right into an open space, where the light, after all that time in the dark, seemed dazzlingly bright. Really it was only a leak of sunshine in through a doorway, where a great door, a stone door, was left standing open.

Bilbo blinked, and then suddenly he saw the goblins: goblins in full armour with drawn swords sitting just inside the door, and watching it with wide eyes, and watching the passage that led to it. They were aroused, alert, ready for anything.

They saw him sooner than he saw them. Yes, they saw him. Whether it was an accident, or a last trick of the ring before it took a new master, it was not on his finger. With yells of delight the goblins rushed upon him.

A pang of fear and loss, like an echo of Gollum's misery, smote Bilbo, and forgetting even to draw his sword he struck his hands into his pockets. And there was the ring still, in his left pocket, and it slipped on his finger. The goblins stopped short. They could not see a sign of him. He had vanished. They yelled twice as loud as before, but not so delightedly.

"Where is it?" they cried.

"Go back up the passage!" some shouted.

"This way!" some yelled. "That way!" others yelled.

"Look out for the door," bellowed the captain.

Whistles blew, armour clashed, swords rattled, goblins cursed and swore and ran hither and thither, falling over one another and getting very angry. There was a terrible outcry, to-do, and disturbance.

Bilbo was dreadfully frightened, but he had the sense to understand what had happened and to sneak behind a big barrel which held drink for the goblin-guards, and so get out of the way and avoid being bumped into, trampled to death, or caught by feel.

"I must get to the door, I must get to the door!" he kept on saying to himself, but it was a long time before he ventured to try. Then it was like a horrible game of blind-man's-buff. The place was full of goblins running about, and the poor little hobbit dodged this way and that, was knocked over by a goblin who could not make out what he had bumped into, scrambled away on all fours, slipped between the legs of the captain just in time, got up, and ran for the door.

It was still ajar, but a goblin had pushed it nearly to. Bilbo struggled but he could not move it. He tried to squeeze through the crack. He squeezed and squeezed, and he stuck! It was awful. His buttons had got wedged on the edge of the door and the door-post. He could see outside into the open air: there were a few steps running down into a narrow valley between tall mountains; the sun came out from behind a cloud and shone bright on the outside of the door—but he could not get through.

Suddenly one of the goblins inside shouted: "There is a shadow by the door. Something is outside!"

Bilbo's heart jumped into his mouth. He gave a terrific squirm. Buttons burst off in all directions. He was through, with a torn coat and waistcoat, leaping down the steps like a goat, while bewildered goblins were still picking up his nice brass buttons on the doorstep.

Of course they soon came down after him, hooting and hallooing, and hunting among the trees. But they don't like the sun: it makes their legs wobble and their heads giddy. They could not find Bilbo with the ring on, slipping in and out of the shadow of the trees, running quick and quiet, and keeping out of the sun; so soon they went back grumbling and cursing to guard the door. Bilbo had escaped.

FRITZ (REUTER) LEIBER JR. (1910–1992)

Fritz Leiber's writing career spanned the last decade of the pulp magazines (the 1940s), the first decades of Fantasy and Science Fiction digest magazines (the 1950s, '60s, and '70s), and beyond. Along with Harlan Ellison, Leiber has been one of the most awarded writers of imaginative fiction of all time. Leiber's early work appeared in the pages of Unknown Worlds, Weird Tales, *and other pulps; it continued in the pages of* The Magazine of Fantasy and Science Fiction, Fantastic, *and other Fantasy and Science Fiction digests.*

As an author and writer, Fritz Leiber was many faceted. He was a master of High Fantasy and Sword and Sorcery stories. His Fafhrd and the Grey Mouser series featured both traditional Sword and Sorcery story lines, and it also was quite inventive, often parodying this important subgenre of Fantasy literature pioneered by Robert E. Howard. This series of stories that evolved from 1939 until Leiber's death has been collected in seven volumes.

Fritz Leiber was also a talented writer of Science Fiction and its many formulas. He wrote stories that can be categorized as Space Operas and Science Fiction allegories. A. E. van Vogt wrote similar works. Leiber was also skilled at Dark Fantasy and supernatural fiction and was influenced by H. P. Lovecraft.

Like Robert Bloch, Fritz Leiber was greatly admired and loved by other authors, not only for his immense talent, but for his humor and kindly nature. Also like Bloch, Leiber possessed keen insight into the human condition and often profoundly reflected and interpreted this condition in his stories.

"Smoke Ghost," a Fritz Leiber classic, is a Fantasy of several dimensions.

Smoke Ghost
(Unknown Worlds, *October 1941*)

Miss Millick wondered just what had happened to Mr. Wran. He kept making the strangest remarks when she took dictation. Just this morning he had quickly turned around and asked, "Have you ever seen a ghost, Miss Millick?" And she had tittered nervously and replied, "When I was a girl there was a thing in white that used to come out of the closet in the attic bedroom when I slept there, and moan. Of course it was just my imagination. I was frightened of lots of things." And he had said, "I don't mean that kind of ghost. I mean a ghost from the world today, with the soot of the factories on its face and the pounding of machinery in its soul. The kind that would haunt coal yards and slip around at night through deserted office buildings like this one. A real ghost. Not something out of books." And she hadn't known what to say.

He'd never been like this before. Of course he might be joking, but it didn't sound that way. Vaguely Miss Millick wondered whether he mightn't be seeking some sort of sympathy from her. Of course, Mr. Wran was married and had a little child, but that didn't prevent her from having daydreams. The daydreams were not very exciting, still they helped fill up her mind. But now he was asking her another of those unprecedented questions.

"Have you ever thought what a ghost of our times would look like, Miss Millick? Just picture it. A smoky composite face with the hungry anxiety of the unemployed, the neurotic restlessness of the person without purpose, the jerky tension of the high-pressure metropolitan worker, the uneasy resentment of the striker, the callous opportunism of the scab, the aggressive whine of the panhandler, the inhibited terror of the bombed civilian, and a thousand other twisted emotional patterns. Each one overlying and yet blending with the other, like a pile of semitransparent masks?"

Miss Millick gave a little self-conscious shiver and said, "That would be terrible. What an awful thing to think of."

She peered furtively across the desk. She remembered having heard that there had been something impressively abnormal about Mr. Wran's childhood, but she couldn't recall what it was. If only she could do something—laugh at his mood or ask him what was really wrong. She shifted the extra pencils in her left hand and mechanically traced over some of the shorthand curlicues in her notebook.

"Yet, that's just what such a ghost or vitalized projection would look like, Miss Millick," he continued, smiling in a tight way. "It would grow out of the real world. It would reflect the tangled, sordid, vicious things. All the loose ends. And it would be very grimy. I don't think it would seem white or wispy, or favor graveyards. It wouldn't moan. But it would mutter unintelligibly, and twitch at your sleeve. Like a sick, surly ape. What would such a thing want from a person, Miss Millick? Sacrifice? Worship? Or just fear? What could you do to stop it from troubling you?"

Miss Millick giggled nervously. There was an expression beyond her powers of definition in Mr. Wran's ordinary, flat-cheeked, thirtyish face, silhouetted against the dusty window. He turned away and stared out into the gray downtown atmosphere that rolled in from the railroad yards and the mills. When he spoke again his voice sounded far away.

"Of course, being immaterial, it couldn't hurt you physically—at first. You'd have to be peculiarly sensitive to see it, or be aware of it at all. But it would begin to influence your actions. Make you do this. Stop you from doing that. Although only a projection, it would gradually get its hooks into the world of things as they are. Might even get control of suitably vacuous minds. Then it could hurt whomever it wanted."

Miss Millick squirmed and read back her shorthand, like the books said you should do when there was a pause. She became aware of the failing light and wished Mr. Wran would ask her to turn on the overhead. She felt scratchy, as if soot were sifting down on to her skin.

"It's a rotten world, Miss Millick," said Mr. Wran, talking at the window. "Fit for another morbid growth of superstition. It's time the ghosts, or whatever you call them, took over and began a rule of fear. They'd be no worse than men."

"But"—Miss Millick's diaphragm jerked, making her titter inanely—"of course, there aren't any such things as ghosts."

Mr. Wran turned around.

"Of course there aren't, Miss Millick," he said in a loud, patronizing voice, as if she had been doing the talking rather than he. "Science and common sense and psychiatry all go to prove it."

She hung her head and might even have blushed if she hadn't felt so all at sea. Her leg muscles twitched, making her stand up, although she hadn't intended to. She aimlessly rubbed her hand along the edge of the desk.

"Why, Mr. Wran, look what I got off your desk," she said, showing him a heavy smudge. There was a note of clumsily playful reproof in her voice. "No wonder the copy I bring you always gets so black. Somebody ought to talk to those scrub-women. They're skimping on your room."

She wished he would make some normal joking reply. But instead he drew back and his face hardened.

"Well, to get back," he rapped out harshly, and began to dictate.

When she was gone, he jumped up, dabbed his finger experimentally at the smudged part of the desk, frowned worriedly at the almost inky smears. He jerked open a drawer, snatched out a rag, hastily swabbed off the desk, crumpled the rag into a ball and tossed it back. There were three or four other rags in the drawer, each impregnated with soot.

Then he went over to the window and peered out anxiously through the dusk, his eyes searching the panorama of roofs, fixing on each chimney and water tank.

"It's a neurosis. Must be. Compulsions. Hallucinations," he muttered to himself in a tired, distraught voice that would have made Miss Millick gasp. "It's that damned mental abnormality cropping up in a new form. Can't be any other explanation. But it's so damned real. Even the soot. Good thing I'm seeing the psychiatrist. I don't think I could force myself to get on the elevated tonight." His voice trailed off, he rubbed his eyes, and his memory automatically started to grind.

It had all begun on the elevated. There was a particular little sea of roofs he had grown into the habit of glancing at just as the packed car carrying him homeward lurched around a turn. A dingy, melancholy little world of tar-paper, tarred gravel, and smoky brick. Rusty tin chimneys with odd conical hats suggested abandoned listening posts. There was a washed-out advertisement of some ancient patent medicine on the nearest wall. Superficially it was like ten thousand other drab city roofs. But he always saw it around dusk, either in the smoky half-light, or tinged with red by the flat rays of a dirty sunset, or covered by ghostly windblown white sheets of rain-splash, or patched with blackish snow; and it seemed unusually bleak and suggestive; almost beautifully ugly though in no sense picturesque; dreary, but meaningful. Unconsciously it came to symbolize for Catesby Wran certain disagreeable aspects of the frustrated, frightened century in which he lived, the jangled century of hate and heavy industry and total wars. The quick daily glance into the half darkness became an integral part of his life. Oddly, he never saw it in the morning, for it was then his habit to sit on the other side of the car, his head buried in the paper.

One evening toward winter he noticed what seemed to be a shapeless black sack lying on the third roof from the tracks. He did not think about it. It merely registered as an addition to the well-known scene and his memory stored away the impression for further reference. Next evening, however, he decided he had been mistaken in one detail. The object was a roof nearer than he had thought. Its color and texture, and the grimy stains around it, suggested that it was filled with coal dust, which was hardly reasonable. Then, too, the following evening it seemed to have been blown against a rusty ventilator by the wind—which could hardly have happened if it were at all heavy. Perhaps it was filled with leaves. Catesby was surprised to find himself anticipating his next daily glance with a minor note of apprehension. There was something unwholesome in the posture of the thing that stuck in his mind—a bulge in the sacking that suggested a misshaped head peering around the ventilator. And his apprehension was justified, for that evening the thing was on the nearest roof, though on the farther side, looking as if it had just flopped down over the low brick parapet.

Next evening the sack was gone. Catesby was annoyed at the momentary feeling of relief that went through him, because the whole matter seemed too unimportant to warrant feelings of any sort. What difference did it make if his imagination had played tricks on him, and he'd fancied that the object was slowly crawling and hitching itself closer across the roofs? That was the way any normal imagination worked. He deliberately chose to disregard the fact that there were reasons for thinking his imagination was by no means a normal one. As he walked home from the elevated, however, he found himself wondering whether the sack was really gone. He seemed to recall a vague, smudgy trail leading across the gravel to the nearer side of the roof, which was masked by a parapet. For an instant an unpleasant picture formed in his mind—that of an inky, humped creature crouched behind the parapet, waiting.

The next time he felt the familiar grating lurch of the car, he caught himself trying not to look out. That angered him. He turned his head quickly. When he turned it back, his compact face was definitely pale. There had been only time for a fleeting rearward glance at the escaping roof. Had he actually seen in silhouette the upper part of a head of some sort peering over the parapet? Nonsense, he told himself. And even if he had seen something, there were a thousand explanations which did not involve the supernatural or even true hallucination. Tomorrow he would take a good look and clear up the whole matter. If necessary, he would visit the roof personally, though he hardly knew where to find it and disliked in any case the idea of pampering a silly fear. He did not relish the walk home from the elevated that evening, and visions of the thing disturbed his dreams, and were in and out of his mind all next day at the office. It was then that he first began to relieve his nerves by making jokingly serious remarks about the supernatural to Miss Millick, who seemed properly mystified. It was on the same day, too, that he became aware of a growing antipathy to grime and soot. Everything he touched seemed gritty, and he found himself mopping and wiping at his desk like an old lady with a morbid fear of germs. He reasoned that there was no real change in his office, and that he'd just now become sensitive to the dirt that had always been there, but there was no denying an increasing nervousness. Long before the car reached the curve, he was straining his eyes through the murky twilight, determined to take in every detail.

Afterward he realized he must have given a muffled cry of some sort, for the man beside him looked at him curiously, and the woman ahead gave him an unfavorable stare. Conscious of his own pallor and uncontrollable trembling, he stared back at them hungrily, trying to regain the feeling of security he had completely lost. They were the usual reassuringly wooden-faced people everyone rides home with on the elevated. But suppose he had pointed out to one of them what he had seen — that sodden, distorted face of sacking and coal dust, that boneless paw which waved back and forth, unmistakably in his direction, as if reminding him of a future appointment — he involuntarily shut his eyes tight. His thoughts were racing ahead to tomorrow evening. He pictured this same windowed oblong of light and packed humanity surging around the curve — then an opaque monstrous form leaping out from the roof in a parabolic swoop — an unmentionable face pressed close against the window, smearing it with wet coal dust — huge paws fumbling sloppily at the glass —

Somehow he managed to turn off his wife's anxious inquiries. Next morning he reached a decision and made an appointment for that evening with a psychiatrist a friend had told him about. It cost him a considerable effort, for Catesby had a well-founded distaste for anything dealing with psychological abnormality. Visiting a psychiatrist meant raking up an episode in his past which he had never fully described even to his wife. Once he had made the decision, however, he felt considerably relieved. The psychiatrist, he told himself, would clear everything up. He could almost fancy him saying, "Merely a bad case of nerves. However, you must consult the oculist whose name I'm writing down for you, and you must take two of these pills in water every four hours," and so on. It was almost comforting, and made the coming revelation he would have to make seem less painful.

But as the smoky dusk rolled in, his nervousness had returned and he had let his joking mystification of Miss Millick run away with him until he had realized he wasn't frightening anyone but himself.

He would have to keep his imagination under better control, he told himself, as he continued to peer out restlessly at the massive, murky shapes of the downtown office buildings. Why, he had spent the whole afternoon building up a kind of neo-medieval cosmology of superstition. It wouldn't do. He realized then that he had been standing at the window much longer than he'd thought, for the glass panel in the door was dark and there was no noise coming from the outer office. Miss Millick and the rest must have gone home.

It was then he made the discovery that there would have been no special reason for dreading the swing around the curve that night. It was, as it happened, a horrible discovery. For, on the shadowed roof across the street and four stories below, he saw the thing huddle and roll across the gravel and, after one upward look of recognition, merge into the blackness beneath the water tank.

As he hurriedly collected his things and made for the elevator, fighting the panicky impulse to run, he began to think of hallucination and mild psychosis as very desirable conditions. For better or for worse, he pinned all his hopes on the psychiatrist.

"So you find yourself growing nervous and . . . er . . . jumpy, as you put it," said Dr. Trevethick, smiling with dignified geniality. "Do you notice any more definite physical symptoms? Pain? Headache? Indigestion?"

Catesby shook his head and wet his lips. "I'm especially nervous while riding in the elevated," he murmured swiftly.

"I see. We'll discuss that more fully. But I'd like you first to tell me about something you mentioned earlier. You said there was something about your childhood that might predispose you to nervous ailments. As you know, the early years are critical ones in the development of an individual's behavior pattern."

Catesby studied the yellow reflections of frosted globes in the dark surface of the desk. The palm of his left hand aimlessly rubbed the thick nap of the armchair. After a while he raised his head and looked straight into the doctor's small brown eyes.

"From perhaps my third to my ninth year," he began, choosing the words with care, "I was what you might call a sensory prodigy."

The doctor's expression did not change. "Yes?" he inquired politely.

"What I mean is that I was supposed to be able to see through walls, read letters through envelopes and books through their covers, fence and play ping-pong blindfolded, find things that were buried, read thoughts." The words tumbled out.

"And could you?" The doctor's voice was toneless.

"I don't know. I don't suppose so," answered Catesby, long-lost emotions flooding back into his voice. "It's all confused now. I thought I could, but then they were always encouraging me. My mother . . . was . . . well . . . interested in psychic phenomena. I was . . . exhibited. I seem to remember seeing things other people couldn't. As if most opaque objects were transparent. But I was very young. I didn't have any scientific criteria for judgment."

He was reliving it now. The darkened rooms. The earnest assemblages of gawking, prying adults. Himself alone on a little platform, lost in a straight-backed wooden chair. The black silk handkerchief over his eyes. His mother's coaxing, insistent questions. The whispers. The gasps. His own hate of the whole business, mixed with hunger for the adulation of adults. Then the scientists from the university, the experiments, the big test. The reality of those memories engulfed him and momentarily made him forget the reason why he was disclosing them to a stranger.

"Do I understand that your mother tried to make use of you as a medium for communicating with the . . . er . . . other world?"

Catesby nodded eagerly.

"She tried to, but she couldn't. When it came to getting in touch with the dead, I was a complete failure. All I could do—or thought I could do—was see real, existing, three-dimensional objects beyond the vision of normal people. Objects anyone could have seen except for distance, obstruction, or darkness. It was always a disappointment to mother."

He could hear her sweetish, patient voice saying, "Try again, dear, just this once. Katie was your aunt. She loved you. Try to hear what she's saying." And he had answered, "I can see a woman in a blue dress standing on the other side of Dick's house." And she had replied, "Yes, I know, dear. But that's not Katie. Katie's a spirit. Try again. Just this once, dear." The doctor's voice gently jarred him back into the softly gleaming office.

"You mentioned scientific criteria for judgment, Mr. Wran. As far as you know, did anyone ever try to apply them to you?"

Catesby's nod was emphatic.

"They did. When I was eight, two young psychologists from the university got interested in me. I guess they did it for a joke at first, and I remember being very determined to show them I amounted to something. Even now I seem to recall how the note of polite superiority and amused sarcasm drained out of their voices. I suppose they decided at first that it was very clever trickery, but somehow they persuaded mother to let them try me out under controlled conditions. There were lots of tests that seemed very businesslike after mother's slipshod little exhibitions. They found I was clairvoyant—or so they thought. I got worked up and on edge. They were going to demonstrate my supernormal sensory powers to the university psychology faculty. For the first time I began to worry about whether I'd come through. Perhaps they kept me going at too hard a pace, I don't know. At any rate, when the test came, I couldn't do a thing. Everything became opaque. I got desperate and made things up out of my imagination. I lied. In the end I failed utterly, and I believe the two young psychologists got into a lot of hot water as a result."

He could hear the brusque, bearded man saying, "You've been taken in by a child, Flaxman, a mere child. I'm greatly disturbed. You've put yourself on the same plane as common charlatans. Gentlemen, I ask you to banish from your minds this whole sorry episode. It must never be referred to." He winced at the recollection of his feeling of guilt. But at the same time he was beginning to feel exhilarated and almost light-hearted. Unburdening his long-repressed memories had altered his whole viewpoint. The episodes on the elevated began to take on what seemed their proper proportions as merely the bizarre workings of over-wrought nerves and an overly suggestible mind. The doctor, he anticipated confidently, would disentangle the obscure subconscious causes, whatever they might be. And the whole business would be finished off quickly, just as his childhood experience—which was beginning to seem a little ridiculous now—had been finished off.

"From that day on," he continued, "I never exhibited a trace of my supposed powers. My mother was frantic and tried to sue the university. I had something like a nervous breakdown. Then the divorce was granted, and my father got custody of me. He did his best to make me forget it. We went on long outdoor vacations and did a lot of athletics, associated with normal matter-of-fact people. I went to business college eventually. I'm in advertising now. But," Catesby paused, "now that I'm having nervous symptoms, I've wondered if there mightn't be a connection. It's not a question of whether I was really clairvoyant or not. Very likely my mother taught me a lot of unconscious deceptions, good enough to fool even young psychology instructors. But don't you think it may have some important bearing on my present condition?"

For several moments the doctor regarded him with a professional frown. Then he said quietly, "And is there some . . . er . . . more specific connection between your experiences then and now? Do you by any chance find that you are once again beginning to . . . er . . . see things?"

Catesby swallowed. He had felt an increasing eagerness to unburden himself of his fears, but it was not easy to make a beginning, and the doctor's shrewd question rattled him. He forced himself to concentrate. The thing he thought he had seen on the roof loomed up before his inner eye with unexpected vividness. Yet it did not frighten him. He groped for words.

Then he saw that the doctor was not looking at him but over his shoulder. Color was draining out of the doctor's face and his eyes did not seem so small. Then the doctor sprang to his feet, walked past Catesby, threw up the window and peered into the darkness.

As Catesby rose, the doctor slammed down the window and said in a voice whose smoothness was marred by a slight, persistent gasping, "I hope I haven't alarmed you. I saw the face of . . . er . . . a Negro prowler on the fire escape. I must have frightened him, for he seems to have gotten out of sight in a hurry. Don't give it another thought. Doctors are frequently bothered by *voyeurs* . . . er . . . Peeping Toms."

"A Negro?" asked Catesby, moistening his lips.

The doctor laughed nervously. "I imagine so, though my first odd impression was that it was a white man in blackface. You see, the color didn't seem to have any brown in it. It was dead-black."

Catesby moved toward the window. There were smudges on the glass. "It's quite all right, Mr. Wran." The doctor's voice had acquired a sharp note of impatience, as if he were trying hard to reassume his professional authority. "Let's continue our conversation. I was asking you if you were"—he made a face—"seeing things."

Catesby's whirling thoughts slowed down and locked into place. "No, I'm not seeing anything that other people don't see, too. And I think I'd better go now. I've been keeping you too long." He disregarded the doctor's half-hearted gesture of denial. "I'll phone you about the physical examination. In a way you've already taken a big load off my mind." He smiled woodenly. "Goodnight, Dr. Trevethick."

Catesby Wran's mental state was a peculiar one. His eyes searched every angular shadow, he glanced sideways down each chasm-like alley and barren basement passageway, and kept stealing looks at the irregular line of the roofs, yet he was hardly conscious of where he was going. He pushed away the thoughts that came into his mind, and kept moving. He became aware of a slight sense of security as he turned into a lighted street where there were people and high buildings and blinking signs. After a while he found himself in the dim lobby of the structure that housed his office. Then he realized why he couldn't go home, why he daren't go home—after what had happened at the office of Dr. Trevethick.

"Hello, Mr. Wran," said the night elevator man, a burly figure in overalls, sliding open the grille-work door to the old-fashioned cage. "I didn't know you were working nights now, too."

Catesby stepped in automatically. "Sudden rush of orders," he murmured inanely. "Some stuff that has to be gotten out."

The cage creaked to a stop at the top floor. "Be working very late, Mr. Wran?"

He nodded vaguely, watched the car slide out of sight, found his keys, swiftly crossed the outer office, and entered his own. His hand went out to the light switch, but then the thought occurred to him that the two lighted windows, standing out against the dark bulk of the building, would indicate his whereabouts and serve as a goal toward which something could crawl and climb. He moved his chair so that the back was against the wall and sat down in the semidarkness. He did not remove his overcoat.

For a long time he sat there motionless, listening to his own breathing and the faraway sounds from the streets below: the thin metallic surge of the crosstown streetcar, the farther one of the elevated, faint lonely cries and honkings, indistinct rumblings. Words he had spoken to Miss Millick in nervous jest came back to him with the bitter taste of truth. He found himself unable to reason critically or connectedly, but by their own volition thoughts rose up into his mind and gyrated slowly and rearranged themselves with the inevitable movement of planets.

Gradually his mental picture of the world was transformed. No longer a world of material atoms and empty space, but a world in which the bodiless existed and moved according to its own obscure laws or unpredictable impulses. The new picture illuminated with dreadful clarity certain general facts which had always bewildered and troubled him and from which he had tried to hide: the inevitability of hate and war, the diabolically timed mischances which wreck the best of human intentions, the walls of willful misunderstanding that divide one man from another, the eternal vitality of cruelty and ignorance and greed. They seemed appropriate now, necessary parts of the picture. And superstition only a kind of wisdom.

Then his thoughts returned to himself and the question he had asked Miss Millick, "What would such a thing want from a person? Sacrifices? Worship? Or just fear? What could you do to stop it from troubling you?" It had become a practical question.

With an explosive jangle, the phone began to ring. "Cate, I've been trying everywhere to get you," said his wife. "I never thought you'd be at the office. What are you doing? I've been worried."

He said something about work.

"You'll be home right away?" came the faint anxious question. "I'm a little frightened. Ronny just had a scare. It woke him up. He kept pointing to the window saying, 'Black man, black man.' Of course it's something he dreamed. But I'm frightened. You will be home? What's that, dear? Can't you hear me?"

"I will. Right away," he said. Then he was out of the office, buzzing the night bell and peering down the shaft.

He saw it peering up the shaft at him from the deep shadows three floors below, the sacking face pressed against the iron grille-work. It started up the stair at a shockingly swift, shambling gait, vanishing temporarily from sight as it swung into the second corridor below.

Catesby clawed at the door to the office, realized he had not locked it, pushed it in, slammed and locked it behind him, retreated to the other side of the room, cowered between the filing cases and the wall. His teeth were clicking. He heard the groan of the rising cage. A silhouette darkened the frosted glass of the door, blotting out part of the grotesque reverse of the company name. After a little the door opened.

The big-globed overhead light flared on and, standing inside the door, her hand on the switch, was Miss Millick.

"Why, Mr. Wran," she stammered vacuously, "I didn't know you were here. I'd just come in to do some extra typing after the movie. I didn't . . . but the lights weren't on. What were you—"

He stared at her. He wanted to shout in relief, grab hold of her, talk rapidly. He realized he was grinning hysterically.

"Why, Mr. Wran, what's happened to you?" she asked embarrassedly, ending with a stupid titter. "Are you feeling sick? Isn't there something I can do for you?"

He shook his head jerkily and managed to say, "No, I'm just leaving. I was doing some extra work myself."

"But you *look* sick," she insisted, and walked over toward him. He inconsequentially realized she must have stepped in mud, for her high-heeled shoes left neat black prints.

"Yes, I'm sure you must be sick. You're so terribly pale." She sounded like an enthusiastic, incompetent nurse. Her face brightened with a sudden inspiration. "I've got something in my bag, that'll fix you up right away," she said. "It's for indigestion."

She fumbled at her stuffed oblong purse. He noticed that she was absent-mindedly holding it shut with one hand while she tried to open it with the other. Then, under his very eyes, he saw her bend back the thick prongs of metal locking the purse as if they were tinfoil, or as if her fingers had become a pair of steel pliers.

Instantly his memory recited the words he had spoken to Miss Millick that afternoon. "It couldn't hurt you physically—at first . . . gradually get its hooks into the world . . . might even get control of suitably vacuous minds. Then it could hurt whomever it wanted." A sickish, cold feeling grew inside him. He began to edge toward the door.

But Miss Millick hurried ahead of him.

"You don't have to wait, Fred," she called. "Mr. Wran's decided to stay a while longer."

The door to the cage shut with a mechanical rattle. The cage creaked. Then she turned around in the door.

"Why, Mr. Wran," she gurgled reproachfully, "I just couldn't think of letting you go home now. I'm sure you're terribly unwell. Why, you might collapse in the street. You've just got to stay here until you feel different."

The creaking died away. He stood in the center of the office, motionless. His eyes traced the coal-black course of Miss Millick's footprints to where she stood blocking the door. Then a sound that was almost a scream was wrenched out of him, for it seemed to him that the blackness was creeping up her legs under the thin stockings.

"Why, Mr. Wran," she said, "you're acting as if you were crazy. You must lie down for a while. Here, I'll help you off with your coat."

The nauseously idiotic and rasping note was the same; only it had been intensified. As she came toward him he turned and ran through the storeroom, clattered a key desperately at the lock of the second door to the corridor.

"Why, Mr. Wran," he heard her call, "are you having some kind of a fit? You must let me help you."

The door came open and he plunged out into the corridor and up the stairs immediately ahead. It was only when he reached the top that he realized the heavy steel door in front of him led to the roof. He jerked up the catch.

"Why, Mr. Wran, you mustn't run away. I'm coming after you."

Then he was out on the gritty gravel of the roof. The night sky was clouded and murky, with a faint pinkish glow from the neon signs. From the distant mills rose a ghostly spurt of flame. He ran to the edge. The street lights glared dizzily upward. Two men were tiny round blobs of hat and shoulders. He swung around.

The thing was in the doorway. The voice was no longer solicitous but moronically playful, each sentence ending in a titter.

"Why, Mr. Wran, why have you come up here? We're all alone. Just think, I might push you off."

The thing came slowly toward him. He moved backward until his heels touched the low parapet. Without knowing why, or what he was going to do, he dropped to his knees. He dared not look at the face as it came nearer, a focus for the worst in the world, a gathering point for poisons from everywhere. Then the lucidity of terror took possession of his mind, and words formed on his lips.

"I will obey you. You are my god," he said. "You have supreme power over man and his animals and his machines. You rule this city and all others. I recognize that."

Again the titter, closer. "Why, Mr. Wran, you never talked like this before. Do you mean it?"

"The world is yours to do with as you will, save or tear to pieces," he answered fawningly, the words automatically fitting themselves together in vaguely liturgical patterns. "I recognize that. I will praise, I will sacrifice. In smoke and soot I will worship you for ever."

The voice did not answer. He looked up. There was only Miss Millick, deathly pale and swaying drunkenly. Her eyes were closed. He caught her as she wobbled toward him. His knees gave way under the added weight and they sank down together on the edge of the roof.

After a while she began to twitch. Small noises came from her throat and her eyelids edged open.

"Come on, we'll go downstairs," he murmured jerkily, trying to draw her up. "You're feeling bad."

"I'm terribly dizzy," she whispered. "I must have fainted, I didn't eat enough. And then I'm so nervous lately, about the war and everything, I guess. Why, we're on the roof! Did you bring me up here to get some air? Or did I come up without knowing it? I'm awfully foolish. I used to walk in my sleep, my mother said."

As he helped her down the stairs, she turned and looked at him. "Why, Mr. Wran," she said, faintly, "you've got a big black smudge on your forehead. Here, let me get it off for you." Weakly she rubbed at it with her handkerchief. She started to sway again and he steadied her.

"No, I'll be all right," she said. "Only I feel cold. What happened, Mr. Wran? Did I have some sort of fainting spell?"

He told her it was something like that.

Later, riding home in the empty elevated car, he wondered how long he would be safe from the thing. It was a purely practical problem. He had no way of knowing, but instinct told him he had satisfied the brute for some time. Would it want more when it came again? Time enough to answer that question when it arose. It might be hard, he realized, to keep out of an insane asylum. With Helen and Ronny to protect, as well as himself, he would have to be careful and tightlipped. He began to speculate as to how many other men and women had seen the thing or things like it.

The elevated slowed and lurched in a familiar fashion. He looked at the roofs near the curve. They seemed very ordinary, as if what made them impressive had gone away for a while.

LORD DUNSANY (PSD. FOR EDWARD JOHN MORETON DRAX PLUNKETT DUNSANY) (1878-1957)

Lord Dunsany was a versatile and prolific author of poetry, short stories, novels, and more. Dunsany was born in London and died in Dublin, and he traveled extensively throughout the world. He served in the Boer War, World War I, and Ireland's Easter Rebellion.

Dunsany's schooling included Greek mythology, classic literature, and the Bible. During World War II, he lectured in literature at the University of Athens in Greece. Like Bram Stoker, Dunsany wrote for the stage. Much of the author's prose was influenced by classic literature; much of this prose can be categorized as Weird Fantasy.

Lord Dunsany's world travels and related experiences provided much of the content for his "Jorkens" stories. These tales feature the adventures of Mr. Joseph Jorkens, a larger-than-life storyteller who regales his friends at the club. The Jorkens stories may have been an important influence on Robert Bloch's "Lefty Feep" stories found in 1940s issues of Fantastic Adventures *pulp magazine. Dunsany's series of Jorkens stories was collected in four volumes.*

"The Strange Drug of Doctor Caber" is a Jorkens story of Fantasy and pseudo science.

The Strange Drug of Doctor Caber
(The Fourth Book of Jorkens, *1948*)

We had got on to a rather commonplace topic one day at the Billiards Club, though why it is of so much public interest as to have become commonplace I do not quite know; but we were discussing murder, and how to do it successfully. Some argued that it was easy, and some hard, but I need not go over the arguments, for they have all been thrashed out on the wireless. Suffice it to say that the hard school were winning, and it was about to be accepted by the Club that murder cannot successfully be committed, when Jorkens joined in.

"I think I may have mentioned to you some time or other," he said, "a man I once knew called Dr. Caber. He's no longer practising now, poor fellow, and perhaps there is no harm in mentioning that he did a very successful murder. Of course the kind of thing was in his line. I don't mean that he was a murderer, I wouldn't say that of him; but he was a good deal in with people who were, and some of them often came to him for help; and, being one of the most inventive geniuses of his time, he was able to help them in a number of ways. I think I told you one. Getting them out of their trouble after they had got into it was his line; fooling the poor old Law, which is of course perfectly legal. But on this occasion they wanted something new and Caber said he would have nothing to do with it, as it was against his principles, and of course wholly illegal. So they raised their price, and Caber was still against it, but said he would do it merely to oblige them."

"Do what?" asked Terbut.

"I'll tell you," said Jorkens. "There was a fellow with a perfect English accent, correct papers, and a good reason for being in England. One of the dangerous sort. One man said he was a German, and had to pay heavy damages. Norman Smith was his name. Well, this man Smith had a motor-bicycle, and travelled about the roads a good deal, especially where there were aerodromes, and got to know a good deal without leaving the road or doing anything really suspicious; and one day he got to know a secret about aeroplanes in a certain district, which was about the most dangerous secret he could have got hold of. It was some time in the year 1938."

"What 'planes were those?" asked Terbut.

"They weren't any," said Jorkens. "That was the deadly secret. We didn't even know it ourselves, bar a very few. Over a large area in the East of England there were no 'planes at all, and only a very few available to be sent there. If he had got that secret home to where he really came from, they would have known that they had us at their mercy; the mercy, that is to say, of the gentry that ran Belsen. Well, the government were informed, but they were busy with several other things; so the people that were watching Norman Smith decided to go to Caber; and Caber, as I told you, refused to help them, but in the end they talked him round. Well, first of all Caber asked for all the facts; and then he sat silent a long time, smoking some kind of a pipe carved out of an Indian tree; and then he told them his wonderful plan, or as much of it as he thought it necessary for them to know.

"We weren't entirely blind or deaf in those days, and Smith was watched all right, and his letters were watched; but what they couldn't guard against was his going back to Germany and heiling Hitler and telling them by word of mouth where we had no defences. Unfortunately he took no interest in the defences we had; he could have been arrested if he had pried into them. But Norman Smith knew how to keep inside our law. My friends of course were outside it, and he wasn't quite looking for them; not that he didn't take precautions of every sort, and his principal precaution was a huge Alsatian, about which they told Caber, a good savage dog of the old Belsen breed, the kind that German ladies used to use to keep the female prisoners in order.

"Well, Norman Smith had a house in Hertfordshire, and there he kept his Alsatian, just in case any lawless people should try to get in at night. Caber asked so many questions about this savage dog that my friends got the idea that he meant to poison it, and one of them even hinted that so simple a plan was hardly worth the money. But it was foolish of them to suppose that one of the greatest masters of the underworld would hold his position there by making plans so simple that any little dog-stealer could have competed with him. Nor was it easy to poison the dog, for Norman Smith had him guarded by two or three cur dogs, as destroyers guard a battleship. The dog was the crux of the whole situation, and there seemed no way of getting by him at night, and my friends were not going about very much by day at that time. Among the facts they told Caber was one that Norman Smith used every now and then to go to the seaside and stay in a large hotel. It is strange how fond spies always are of the sea.

" 'You'll have to do it there,' said Caber at last. 'He won't be able to have the dog in the hotel.'

" 'But we won't be able to get in either,' said my friends. 'They'll have a hall-porter and waiters, if they don't have the dog.'

" 'Then you'll have to do it by day, when he's out for a walk,' said Caber.

" 'We don't like that kind of thing by daylight,' said one of them.

"Caber looked at them. 'You don't know what kind of thing yet,' he said.

" 'Well, what is it?' they asked.

" 'Two or three men to follow him,' said Caber, 'a little fracas, and a jab with a small needle.'

" 'I don't like poison,' said one of them. 'It can always be traced.'

"Caber opened his eyes wide. 'My friends,' he said, 'am I a child?'

" 'I don't care, it can always be traced,' said the other man, still sticking to his point.

" 'But I am not going to give you any poison,' said Caber.

" 'Well, what's the use of the needle?' they asked.

" 'The slightest jab,' said Caber, 'a little harmless fluid put in with a syringe, then your two men get away; better have three. And, after that, he brings a charge of assault, and the police look for the men. But so long as no harm comes to Norman Smith, and the police have only his word that he was pricked by a needle, it is only a local affair, not Scotland Yard and the police of the countryside, as it would be in the case of a murder.'

" 'Not a murder, of course, exactly,' said one of my friends. 'But, then, what is going to be the effect of your needle and syringe?'

" 'Nothing whatever,' said Caber. 'You had better do it at the beginning of his trip to the sea, so as to give plenty of time for them to see the whole thing is innocuous.'

" 'Then, what is the use of it?' they asked bluntly.

" 'Merely,' said Caber, 'that when he goes home, or very soon after, he will accidentally die.'

" 'They'll trace a thing like that,' said the man who didn't like poison.

" 'How do you like my little room?' said Caber. 'I've had it a long time. I've got to like it myself. But what do you think of it?'

" 'What's that got to do with our business?'

" 'Only,' said Caber, 'that if things I did had ever been traced, perhaps I shouldn't be here. I don't say I shouldn't; but I might have moved before now.'

"And somehow that seemed to silence them. And then one said, 'You told us it was innocuous.'

" 'Entirely,' said Caber.

" 'But the man would die when he went home.'

" 'Certainly,' Caber said.

" 'Then I don't quite see . . .'

" 'Perhaps we had better leave it to Dr. Caber,' said one of the others.

"And that in the end was what they did. Well, Norman Smith went to the sea sure enough in a week-or-so's time, and stayed at the large hotel, and left a man in Hertfordshire to feed his dangerous dog, and the three little yapping dogs that were to look after it. And the first morning after he arrived at the sea Norman Smith went for a walk, and he got into a bit of a row with three men near some golf-links, and he went to the police complaining he had been assaulted and alleging he had been impregnated or inoculated with some deadly disease or poison. He had a pin-prick to show on his arm, and he asserted that near it he had seen a drop of some liquid that had a sweaty smell. And the police sent for two doctors, who made tests and examinations, all of which proved that Smith was perfectly fit. And by the end of the week the whole thing had blown over, so far as the police were concerned, and nothing was traced to anybody. You see, poisons can always be traced, and bacterial things even easier, because they are rarer, and as for any unknown poison, that's rarest of all, and the police would soon get on to it."

"And what happened?" we asked.

"Norman Smith went home to Hertfordshire," replied Jorkens, "invigorated by his stay by the sea, and cheered by whatever information spies get when they go to the seaside. And that night his Alsatian killed him."

"Yes, a successful murder," said Terbut, "if you can call a dog a murderer."

And one of us said rather diffidently that he didn't quite see how Caber came into it.

"It was a very subtle drug," said Jorkens. "Perfectly harmless, as Caber said. But it changed his smell. It gave him an entirely new scent. Of course no Alsatian dog would put up with a thing like that."

⚜ ZENNA (CHLARSON) HENDERSON (1917–1983)

Although she was a versatile author of Fantasy and Science Fiction, Zenna Henderson is best remembered for her stories about "The People." This thematic series of stories evolved throughout the author's writing career and centered on portrayals of a range of characters and character types—human and alien. Much of the influence for Henderson's stories came from the author's many and varied experiences as a schoolteacher and educator of children. Such is the case with one of her most famous stories, "The Anything Box."

Zenna Henderson's stories are fun, insightful, touching, and poignant. Her style is oftentimes reminiscent of that of Ray Bradbury, Shirley Jackson, Madeleine L'Engle, Clifford Simak, and others who have told stories about people and their many complexities, traditions, and idiosyncrasies. Henderson often exhibited warmth and gentleness in her stories, and she unobtrusively espoused a profound morality and strong faith that touched the hearts of her readers. Many of her stories appeared in The Magazine of Fantasy and Science Fiction.

The Anything Box
(*The Magazine of Fantasy and Science Fiction, October 1956*)

I suppose it was about the second week of school that I noticed Sue-lynn particularly. Of course, I'd noticed her name before and checked her out automatically for maturity and ability and probable performance the way most teachers do with their students during the first weeks of school. She had checked out mature and capable and no worry as to performance as I had pigeonholed her—setting aside for the moment the little nudge that said, "Too quiet"—with my other no-worrys until the fluster and flurry of the first days had died down a little.

I remember my noticing day. I had collapsed into my chair for a brief respite from guiding hot little hands through the intricacies of keeping a Crayola within reasonable bounds and the room was full of the relaxed, happy hum of a pleased class as they worked away, not realizing that they were rubbing "blue" into their memories as well as onto their papers. I was meditating on how individual personalities were beginning to emerge among the thirty-five or so heterogeneous first graders I had, when I noticed Sue-lynn—really noticed her—for the first time.

She had finished her paper—far ahead of the others as usual—and was sitting at her table facing me. She had her thumbs touching in front of her on the table and her fingers curving as though they held something between them—something large enough to keep her fingertips apart and angular enough to bend her fingers as if for corners. It was something pleasant that she held—pleasant and precious. You could tell that by the softness of her hold. She was leaning forward a little, her lower ribs pressed against the table, and she was looking, completely absorbed, at the table between her hands. Her face was relaxed and happy. Her mouth curved in a tender half-smile, and as I watched, her lashes lifted and she looked at me with a warm share-the-pleasure look. Then her eyes blinked and the shutters came down inside them. Her hand flicked into the desk and out. She pressed her thumbs to her forefingers and rubbed them slowly together. Then she laid one hand over the other on the table and looked down at them with the air of complete denial and ignorance children can assume so devastatingly.

The incident caught my fancy and I began to notice Sue-lynn. As I consciously watched her, I saw that she spent most of her free time staring at the table between her hands, much too unobtrusively to catch my busy attention. She hurried through even the funnest of fun papers and then lost herself in looking. When Davie pushed her down at recess, and blood streamed from her knee to her ankle, she took her bandages and her tear-smudged face to that comfort she had so readily—if you'll pardon the expression—at hand and emerged minutes later, serene and dry-eyed. I think Davie pushed her down because of her Looking. I know the day before he had come up to me, red-faced and squirming.

"Teacher," he blurted. "She Looks!"

"Who looks?" I asked absently, checking the vocabulary list in my book, wondering how on earth I'd missed *where*, one of those annoying *wh* words that throw the children for a loss.

"Sue-lynn. She Looks and Looks!"

"At you?" I asked.

"Well . . ." He rubbed a forefinger below his nose, leaving a clean streak on his upper lip, accepted the proffered Kleenex, and put it in his pocket. "She looks at her desk and tells lies. She says she can see . . ."

"Can see what?" My curiosity picked up its ears.

"Anything," said Davie. "It's her Anything Box. She can see anything she wants to."

"Does it hurt you for her to Look?"

"Well," he squirmed. Then he burst out: "She says she saw me with a dog biting me because I took her pencil—she said." He started a pell-mell verbal retreat. "She *thinks* I took her pencil. I only found—" His eyes dropped. "I'll give it back."

"I hope so," I smiled. "If you don't want her to look at you, then don't do things like that."

"Durn girls," he muttered and clomped back to his seat.

So I think he pushed her down the next day to get back at her for the dog bite.

Several times after that I wandered to the back of the room, casually in her vicinity, but always she either saw or felt me coming and the quick sketch of her hand disposed of the evidence. Only once I thought I caught a glimmer of something—but her thumb and forefinger brushed in sunlight, and it must have been just that.

Children don't retreat for no reason at all, and, though Sue-lynn did not follow any overt pattern of withdrawal, I started to wonder about her. I watched her on the playground, to see how she tracked there. That only confused me more.

She had a very regular pattern. When the avalanche of children first descended at recess, she avalanched along with them and nothing in the shrieking, running, dodging mass resolved itself into a withdrawn Sue-lynn. But after ten minutes or so, she emerged from the crowd, tousle-haired, rosy-cheeked, smutched with dust, one shoelace dangling and, through some alchemy that I coveted for myself, she suddenly became untousled, undusty, and unsmutched. And there she was, serene and composed on the narrow little step at the side of the flight of stairs just where they disappeared into the base of the pseudo-Corinthian column that graced Our Door and her cupped hands received whatever they received and her absorption in what she saw became so complete that the bell came as a shock every time.

And each time, before she joined the rush to Our Door, her hand would sketch a gesture to her pocket, if she had one, or to the tiny ledge that extended between the hedge and the building. Apparently she always had to put the Anything Box away, but never had to go back to get it.

I was so intrigued by her putting whatever it was on the ledge that once I actually went over and felt along the grimy little outset. I sheepishly followed my children into the hall, wiping the dust from my fingertips, and Sue-lynn's eyes brimmed amusement at me without her mouth's smiling. Her hands mischievously squared in front of her and her thumbs caressed a solidness as the line of children swept into the room.

I smiled too because she was so pleased with having outwitted me. This seemed to be such a gay withdrawal that I let my worry die down. Better this manifestation than any number of other ones that I could name.

Someday, perhaps, I'll learn to keep my mouth shut. I wish I had before that long afternoon when we primary teachers worked together in a heavy cloud of ditto fumes, the acrid smell of India ink, drifting cigarette smoke, and the constant current of chatter, and I let Alpha get me started on what to do with our behavior problems. She was all raunched up about the usual rowdy loudness of her boys and the eternal clack of her girls, and I—bless my stupidity—gave her Sue-lynn as an example of what should be our deepest concern rather than the outbursts from our active ones.

"You mean she just sits and looks at nothing?" Alpha's voice grated into her questioning tone.

"Well, I can't see anything," I admitted. "But apparently she can."

"But that's having hallucinations!" Her voice went up a notch. "I read a book once—"

"Yes." Marlene leaned across the desk to flick ashes into the ashtray. "So we have heard and heard and heard."

"Well!" sniffed Alpha. "It's better than *never* reading a book."

"We're waiting," Marlene leaked smoke from her nostrils, "for the day when you read another book. This one must have been uncommonly long."

"Oh, I don't know." Alpha's forehead wrinkled with concentration. "It was only about—" Then she reddened and turned her face angrily away from Marlene.

"Apropos of *our* discussion—," she said pointedly. "It sounds to me like that child has a deep personality disturbance. Maybe even a psychotic—whatever—" Her eyes glistened faintly as she turned the thought over.

"Oh, I don't know," I said, surprised into echoing her words at my sudden need to defend Sue-lynn. "There's something about her. She doesn't have that apprehensive, hunched-shoulder, don't-hit-me-again air about her that so many withdrawn children have." And I thought achingly of one of mine from last year that Alpha had now and was verbally bludgeoning back into silence after all my work with him. "She seems to have a happy, adjusted personality, only with this odd little . . . *plus.*"

"Well, I'd be worried if she were mine," said Alpha. "I'm glad all my kids are so normal." She sighed complacently. "I guess I really haven't anything to kick about. I seldom ever have problem children except wigglers and yakkers, and a holler and a smack can straighten them out."

Marlene caught my eye mockingly, tallying Alpha's class with me, and I turned away with a sigh. To be so happy—well, I suppose ignorance does help.

"You'd better do something about that girl," Alpha shrilled as she left the room. "She'll probably get worse and worse as time goes on. Deteriorating, I think the book said."

I had known Alpha a long time and I thought I knew how much of her talk to discount, but I began to worry about Sue-lynn. Maybe this *was* a disturbance that was more fundamental than the usual run-of-the-mill that I had met up with. Maybe a child *can* smile a soft, contented smile and still have little maggots of madness flourishing somewhere inside.

Or, by gorry! I said to myself defiantly, maybe she *does* have an Anything Box. Maybe she *is* looking at something precious. Who am I to say no to anything like that?

An Anything Box! What could you see in an Anything Box? Heart's desire? I felt my own heart lurch—just a little—the next time Sue-lynn's hands curved. I breathed deeply to hold me in my chair. If it was *her* Anything Box, I wouldn't be able to see my heart's desire in it. Or would I? I propped my cheek up on my hand and doodled aimlessly on my time-schedule sheet. How on earth, I wondered—not for the first time—do I manage to get myself off on these tangents?

Then I felt a small presence at my elbow and turned to meet Sue-lynn's wide eyes.

"Teacher?" The word was hardly more than a breath.

"Yes?" I could tell that for some reason Sue-lynn was loving me dearly at the moment. Maybe because her group had gone into new books that morning. Maybe because I had noticed her new dress, the ruffles of which made her feel very feminine and lovable, or maybe just because the late autumn sun lay so golden across her desk. Anyway, she was loving me to overflowing, and, since, un-like most of the children, she had no casual hugs or easy moist kisses, she was bringing her love to me in her encompassing hands.

"See my box, Teacher? It's my Anything Box."

"Oh, my!" I said. "May I hold it?"

After all, I have held—tenderly or apprehensively or bravely—tiger magic, live rattlesnakes, dragon's teeth, poor little dead butterflies, and two ears and a nose that dropped off Sojie one cold morning—none of which I could see any more than I could the Anything Box. But I took the squareness from her carefully, my tenderness showing in my fingers and my face.

And I received weight and substance and actuality!

Almost I let it slip out of my surprised fingers, but Sue-lynn's apprehensive breath helped me catch it and I curved my fingers around the precious warmness and looked down, down, past a faint shimmering, down into Sue-lynn's Anything Box.

I was running barefoot through the whispering grass. The swirl of my skirts caught the daisies as I rounded the gnarled apple tree at the corner. The warm wind lay along each of my cheeks and chuckled in my ears. My heart outstripped my flying feet and melted with a rush of delight into warmness as his arms—

I closed my eyes and swallowed hard, my palms tight against the Anything Box. "It's beautiful!" I whispered. "It's wonderful, Sue-lynn. Where did you get it?"

Her hands took it back hastily. "It's mine," she said defiantly. "It's mine."

"Of course," I said. "Be careful now. Don't drop it."

She smiled faintly as she sketched a motion to her pocket. "I won't." She patted the pocket on her way back to her seat.

Next day she was afraid to look at me at first for fear I might say something or look something or in some way remind her of what must seem like a betrayal to her now, but after I only smiled my usual smile, with no added secret knowledge, she relaxed.

A night or so later when I leaned over my moon-drenched windowsill and let the shadow of my hair hide my face from such ebullient glory, I remembered about the Anything Box. Could I make one for myself? Could I square off this aching waiting, this outreaching, this silent cry inside me, and make it into an Anything Box? I freed my hands and brought them together thumb to thumb, framing a part of the horizon's darkness between my upright forefingers. I stared into the empty square until my eyes watered. I sighed, and laughed a little, and let my hands frame my face as I leaned out into the night. To have magic so near—to feel it tingle off my fingertips and then to be so bound that I couldn't receive it. I turned away from the window—turning my back on brightness.

It wasn't long after this that Alpha succeeded in putting sharp points of worry back in my thoughts of Sue-lynn. We had ground duty together, and one morning when we shivered while the kids ran themselves rosy in the crisp air, she sizzed in my ear.

"Which one is it? The abnormal one, I mean."

"I don't have any abnormal children," I said, my voice sharpening before the sentence ended because I suddenly realized whom she meant.

"Well, I call it abnormal to stare at nothing." You could almost taste the acid in her words. "Who is it?"

"Sue-lynn," I said reluctantly. "She's playing on the bars now."

Alpha surveyed the upside-down Sue-lynn whose brief skirts were belled down from her bare pink legs and half covered her face as she swung from one of the bars by her knees. Alpha clutched her wizened blue hands together and breathed on them. "She looks normal enough," she said.

"She *is* normal!" I snapped.

"*Well*, bite my head off!" cried Alpha. "You're the one that said she wasn't, not me—or is it 'not I'? I never could remember. Not me? Not I?"

The bell saved Alpha from a horrible end. I never knew a person so serenely unaware of essentials and so sensitive to trivia. But she had succeeded in making me worry about Sue-lynn again, and the worry exploded into distress a few days later.

Sue-lynn came to school sleepy-eyed and quiet. She didn't finish any of her work and she fell asleep during rest time. I cussed TV and drive-ins and assumed a night's sleep would put it right. But next day Sue-lynn burst into tears and slapped Davie clear off his chair.

"Why, Sue-lynn!" I gathered Davie up in all his astonishment and took Sue-lynn's hand. She jerked it away from me and flung herself at Davie again. She got two handfuls of his hair and had him out of my grasp before I knew it. She threw him bodily against the wall with a flip of her hands, then doubled up her fists and pressed them to her streaming eyes. In the shocked silence of the room, she stumbled over to Isolation and, seating herself, back to the class, on the little chair, she leaned her head into the corner and sobbed quietly in big gulping sobs.

"What on earth goes on?" I asked the stupefied Davie who sat spraddle-legged on the floor fingering a detached tuft of hair. "What did you do?"

"I only said 'Robber Daughter,'" said Davie. "It said so in the paper. My mama said her daddy's a robber. They put him in jail cause he robbered a gas station." His bewildered face was trying to decide whether or not to cry. Everything had happened so fast that he didn't know yet if he was hurt.

"It isn't nice to call names," I said weakly. "Get back into your seat. I'll take care of Sue-lynn later."

He got up and sat gingerly down in his chair, rubbing his ruffled hair, wanting to make more of a production of the situation but not knowing how. He twisted his face experimentally to see if he had tears available and had none.

"Durn girls," he muttered and tried to shake his fingers free of a wisp of hair.

I kept my eye on Sue-lynn for the next half hour as I busied myself with the class. Her sobs soon stopped and her rigid shoulders relaxed. Her hands were softly in her lap, and I knew she was taking comfort from her Anything Box. We had our talk together later, but she was so completely sealed off from me by her misery that there was no communication between us. She sat quietly watching me as I talked, her hands trembling in her lap. It shakes the heart, somehow, to see the hands of a little child quiver like that.

That afternoon I looked up from my reading group, startled, as though by a cry, to catch Sue-lynn's frightened eyes. She looked around bewildered and then down at her hands again—her empty hands. Then she darted to the Isolation corner and reached under the chair. She went back to her seat slowly, her hands squared to an unseen weight. For the first time, apparently, she had had to go get the Anything Box. It troubled me with a vague unease for the rest of the afternoon.

Through the days that followed while the trial hung fire, I had Sue-lynn in attendance bodily, but that was all. She sank into her Anything Box at every opportunity. And always, if she had put it away somewhere, she had to go back for it. She roused more and more reluctantly from these waking dreams, and there finally came a day when I had to shake her to waken her.

I went to her mother, but she couldn't or wouldn't understand me, and made me feel like a frivolous gossipmonger taking her mind away from her husband, despite the fact that I didn't even mention him—or maybe because I didn't mention him.

"If she's being a bad girl, spank her," she finally said, wearily shifting the weight of a whining baby from one hip to another and pushing her tousled hair off her forehead. "Whatever you do is all right by me. My worrier is all used up. I haven't got any left for the kids right now."

Well, Sue-lynn's father was found guilty and sentenced to the State Penitentiary and school was less than an hour old the next day when Davie came up, clumsily a-tiptoe, braving my wrath for interrupting a reading group, and whispered hoarsely, "Sue-lynn's asleep with her eyes open again, Teacher."

We went back to the table and Davie slid into his chair next to a completely unaware Sue-lynn. He poked her with a warning finger. "I told you I'd tell on you."

And before our horrified eyes, she toppled, as rigidly as a doll, sideways off the chair. The thud of her landing relaxed her, and she lay limp on the green asphalt tile—a thin paper doll of a girl, one hand still clenched open around something. I pried her fingers loose and almost wept to feel enchantment dissolve under my heavy touch. I carried her down to the nurse's room and we worked over her with wet towels and prayer and she finally opened her eyes.

"Teacher," she whispered weakly.

"Yes, Sue-lynn." I took her cold hands in mine.

"Teacher, I almost got in my Anything Box."

"No," I answered. "You couldn't. You're too big."

"Daddy's there," she said. "And where we used to live."

I took a long, long look at her wan face. I hope it was genuine concern for her that prompted my next words. I hope it wasn't envy or the memory of the niggling nagging of Alpha's voice that put firmness in my voice as I went on. "That's play-like," I said. "Just for fun."

Her hands jerked protestingly in mine. "Your Anything Box is just for fun. It's like Davie's cow pony that he keeps in his desk or Sojie's jet plane, or when the big bear chases all of you at recess. It's fun-for-play, but it's not for real. You mustn't think it's for real. It's only play."

"No!" she denied. "*No!*" she cried frantically and, hunching herself up on the cot, peering through her tear-swollen eyes, she scrabbled under the pillow and down beneath the rough blanket that covered her.

"Where is it?" she cried. "Where is it? Give it back to me, Teacher!"

She flung herself toward me and pulled open both my clenched hands.

"Where did you put it? Where did you put it?"

"There is no Anything Box," I said flatly, trying to hold her to me and feeling my heart breaking along with hers.

"You took it!" she sobbed. "You took it away from me!" And she wrenched herself out of my arms.

"Can't you give it back to her?" whispered the nurse. "If it makes her feel so bad? Whatever it is—"

"It's just imagination," I said, almost sullenly. "I can't give her back something that doesn't exist."

Too young! I thought bitterly. Too young to learn that heart's desire is only playlike.

Of course the doctor found nothing wrong. Her mother dismissed the matter as a fainting spell and Sue-lynn came back to class next day, thin and listless, staring blankly out the window, her hands palm down on the desk. I swore by the pale hollow of her cheek that never, *never* again would I take any belief from anyone without replacing it with something better. What had I given Sue-lynn? What had she better than I had taken from her? How did I know but that her Anything Box was on purpose to tide her over rough spots in her life like this? And what now, now that I had taken it from her?

Well, after a time she began to work again, and later, to play. She came back to smiles, but not to laughter. She puttered along quite satisfactorily except that she was a candle blown out. The flame was gone wherever the brightness of belief goes. And she had no more sharing smiles for me, no overflowing love to bring to me. And her shoulder shrugged subtly away from my touch.

Then one day I suddenly realized that Sue-lynn was searching our classroom. Stealthily, casually, day by day she was searching, covering every inch of the room. She went through every puzzle box, every lump of clay, every shelf and cupboard, every box and bag. Methodically she checked behind every row of books and in every child's desk until finally, after almost a week, she had been through everything in the place except my desk. Then she began to materialize suddenly at my elbow every time I opened a drawer. And her eyes would probe quickly and sharply before I slid it shut again. But if I tried to intercept her looks, they slid away and she had some legitimate errand that had brought her up to the vicinity of the desk.

She believes it again, I thought hopefully. She won't accept the fact that her Anything Box is gone. She wants it again.

But it *is* gone, I thought drearily. It's really-for-true gone.

My head was heavy from troubled sleep, and sorrow was a weariness in all my movements. Waiting is sometimes a burden almost too heavy to carry. While my children hummed happily over their fun-stuff, I brooded silently out the window until I managed a laugh at myself. It was a shaky laugh that threatened to dissolve into something else, so I brisked back to my desk.

As good a time as any to throw out useless things, I thought, and to see if I can find that colored chalk I put away so carefully. I plunged my hands into the wilderness of the bottom right-hand drawer of my desk. It was deep with a huge accumulation of anything—just anything—that might need a tempo-rary hiding place. I knelt to pull out leftover Jack Frost pictures and a broken bean shooter, a chewed red ribbon, a roll of cap-gun ammunition, one striped sock, six Numbers papers, a rubber dagger, a copy of *The Gospel According to St. Luke*, a miniature coal shovel, patterns for jack-o'-lanterns, and a pink plastic pelican. I retrieved my Irish linen hankie I thought lost forever and Sojie's report card that he had told me solemnly had blown out of his hand and landed on a jet and broke the sound barrier so loud that it busted all to flitters. Under the welter of miscellany, I felt a squareness. Oh, happy! I thought, this *is* where I put the col-ored chalk! I cascaded papers off both sides of my lifting hands and shook the box free.

We were together again. Outside, the world was an enchanting wilderness of white, the wind shouting softly through the windows, tapping wet, white fingers against the warm light. Inside all the worry and waiting, the apartness and loneliness were over and forgot-ten, their hugeness dwindled by the comfort of a shoulder, the warmth of clasping hands— and nowhere, nowhere was the fear of parting, nowhere the need to do without again. This was the happy ending. This was—

This was Sue-lynn's Anything Box!

My racing heart slowed as the dream faded . . . and rushed again at the real-ization. I had it here! In my junk drawer! It had been here all the time!

I stood up shakily, concealing the invisible box in the flare of my skirts. I sat down and put the box carefully in the center of my desk, covering the top of it with my palms lest I should drown again in delight. I looked at Sue-lynn. She was finishing her fun paper, competently but unjoyously. Now would come her patient sitting with quiet hands until told to do something else.

Alpha would approve. And very possibly, I thought, Alpha would, for once in her limited life, be right. We may need "hallucinations" to keep us going—all of us but the Alphas—but when we go so far as to try to force ourselves, physically, into the never-never land of heart's desire . . .

I remembered Sue-lynn's thin rigid body toppling doll-like off its chair. Out of her deep need she had found—or created? Who could tell?—something too dan-gerous for a child. I could so easily bring the brimming happiness back to her eyes—but at what a possible price!

No, I had a duty to protect Sue-lynn. Only maturity—the maturity born of the sorrow and loneliness that Sue-lynn was only beginning to know—could be trusted to use an Anything Box safely and wisely.

My heart thudded as I began to move my hands, letting the palms slip down from the top to shape the sides of—

I had moved them back again before I really saw, and I have now learned almost to forget that glimpse of what heart's desire is like when won at the cost of another's heart.

I sat there at the desk trembling and breathless, my palms moist, feeling as if I had been on a long journey away from the little schoolroom. Perhaps I had. Perhaps I had been shown all the kingdoms of the world in a moment of time.

"Sue-lynn," I called. "Will you come up here when you're through?"

She nodded unsmilingly and snipped off the last paper from the edge of Mistress Mary's dress. Without another look at her handiwork, she carried the scissors safely to the scissors box, crumpled the scraps of paper in her hand, and came up to the wastebasket by the desk.

"I have something for you, Sue-lynn," I said, uncovering the box.

Her eyes dropped to the desktop: She looked indifferently up at me. "I did my fun paper already."

"Did you like it?"

"Yes." It was a flat lie.

"Good," I lied right back. "But look here." I squared my hands around the Anything Box.

She took a deep breath and the whole of her little body stiffened.

"I found it," I said hastily, fearing anger. "I found it in the bottom drawer."

She leaned her chest against my desk, her hands caught tightly between, her eyes intent on the box, her face white with the aching want you see on children's faces pressed to Christmas windows.

"Can I have it?" she whispered.

"It's yours," I said, holding it out.

Still she leaned against her hands, her eyes searching my face. "Can I have it?" she asked again.

"Yes!" I was impatient with this anticlimax. "But—"

Her eyes flickered. She had sensed my reservation before I had. "But you must never try to get into it again."

"OK," she said, the word coming out on a long relieved sigh. "OK, Teacher."

She took the box and tucked it lovingly into her small pocket. She turned from the desk and started back to her table. My mouth quirked with a small smile. It seemed to me that everything about her had suddenly turned upward—even the ends of her straight taffy-colored hair. The subtle flame about her that made her Sue-lynn was there again. She scarcely touched the floor as she walked.

I sighed heavily and traced on the desktop with my finger a probable size for an Anything Box. What would Sue-lynn choose to see first? How like a drink after a drought it would seem to her.

I was startled as a small figure materialized at my elbow. It was Sue-lynn, her fingers carefully squared before her.

"Teacher," she said softly, all the flat emptiness gone from her voice. "Anytime you want to take my Anything Box, you just say so."

I groped through my astonishment and incredulity for words. She couldn't possibly have had time to look into the Box yet.

"Why, thank you, Sue-lynn," I managed. "Thanks a lot. I would like very much to borrow it sometime."

"Would you like it now?" she asked, proffering it.

"No, thank you," I said, around the lump in my throat. "I've had a turn already. You go ahead."

"OK," she murmured. Then—"Teacher?"

"Yes?"

Shyly she leaned against me, her cheek on my shoulder. She looked up at me with her warm, unshuttered eyes, then both arms were suddenly around my neck in a brief awkward embrace.

"Watch out!" I whispered, laughing into the collar of her blue dress. "You'll lose it again!"

"No I won't," she laughed back, patting the flat pocket of her dress. "Not ever, ever again!"

J(AMES) G(RAHAM) BALLARD (1930–)

J. G. Ballard is a multitalented author of Fantasy, Science Fiction, Detective Fiction, social melodrama and commentary, and more. He is often vibrant, inventive, and controversial. Ballard is a British writer, though he was born in Shanghai. During World War II, he was interned in a Japanese prisoner of war camp. This experience led to his famous novel, Empire of the Sun *(1984), which was made into a movie by Steven Spielberg in 1987.*

Ballard's writing first appeared in print in the mid-1950s and was primarily Science Fiction–based. Such is the case with the author's Vermilion Sands stories. As time went by, however, Ballard branched into other genres and subgenres of popular fiction. Soon he was writing stories with specific Science Fiction and Fantasy themes, including apocalypse, disaster, urban life, and more. Soon, Ballard's cult following became a mainstream following. Although still a best-selling author today, Ballard may have enjoyed his greatest popularity in the 1960s, when his inventional, progressive stories seemed to find a highly sympathetic portion of the population.

"The Drowned Giant" is an interesting, even macabre Fantasy of environmental science. Certainly, James P. Blaylock's opening sequence in the novel Land of Dreams *(1987) features a giant and storyline reminiscent of Ballard's original tale.*

The Drowned Giant

(Playboy, *May 1965*)

On the morning after the storm the body of a drowned giant was washed ashore on the beach five miles to the northwest of the city. The first news was brought by a nearby farmer and subsequently confirmed by the local newspaper reporters and the police. Despite this the majority of people, myself among them, remained sceptical, but the return of more and more eyewitnesses attesting to the vast size of the giant was finally too much for our curiosity. The library where my colleagues and I were carrying out our research was almost deserted when we set off for the coast shortly after two o'clock, and throughout the day people continued to leave their offices and shops as accounts of the giant circulated around the city.

By the time we reached the dunes above the beach a substantial crowd had gathered, and we could see the body lying in the shallow water two hundred yards away. At first the estimates of its size seemed greatly exaggerated. It was then at low tide, and almost all the giant's body was exposed, but he appeared to be a little larger than a basking shark. He lay on his back with his arms at his sides, in an attitude of repose, as if asleep on the mirror of wet sand, the reflection of his blanched skin fading as the water receded. In the clear sunlight his body glistened like the white plumage of a sea bird.

Puzzled by this spectacle, and dissatisfied with the matter-of-fact explanations of the crowd, my friends and I stepped down from the dunes on to the shingle. Everyone seemed reluctant to approach the giant, but half an hour later two fishermen in wading boots walked out across the sand. As their diminutive figures neared the recumbent body a sudden hubbub of conversation broke out among the spectators. The two men were completely dwarfed by the giant. Although his heels were partly submerged in the sand, the feet rose to at least twice the fishermen's height, and we immediately realized that this drowned leviathan had the mass and dimensions of the largest sperm whale.

Three fishing smacks had arrived on the scene and with keels raised remained a quarter of a mile offshore, the crews watching from the bows. Their discretion deterred the spectators on the shore from wading out across the sand. Impatiently everyone stepped down from the dunes and waited on the shingle slopes, eager for a closer view. Around the margins of the figure the sand had been washed away, forming a hollow, as if the giant had fallen out of the sky. The two fishermen were standing between the immense plinths of the feet, waving to us like tourists among the columns of some water-lapped temple on the Nile. For a moment I feared that the giant was merely asleep and might suddenly stir and clap his heels together, but his glazed eyes stared skyward, unaware of the minuscule replicas of himself between his feet.

The fishermen then began a circuit of the corpse, strolling past the long white flanks of the legs. After a pause to examine the fingers of the supine hand, they disappeared from sight between the arm and chest, then reemerged to survey the head, shielding their eyes as they gazed up at its Grecian profile. The shallow forehead, straight high-bridged nose and curling lips reminded me of a Roman copy of Praxiteles, and the elegantly formed cartouches of the nostrils emphasized the resemblance to monumental sculpture.

Abruptly there was a shout from the crowd, and a hundred arms pointed toward the sea. With a start I saw that one of the fishermen had climbed on to the giant's chest and was now strolling about and signaling to the shore. There was a roar of surprise and triumph from the crowd, lost in a rushing avalanche of shingle as everyone surged forward across the sand.

As we approached the recumbent figure, which was lying in a pool of water the size of a field, our excited chatter fell away again, subdued by the huge physical dimensions of this moribund colossus. He was stretched out at a slight angle to the shore, his legs carried nearer the beach, and this foreshortening had disguised his true length. Despite the two fishermen standing on his abdomen, the crowd formed itself into a wide circle, groups of three or four people tentatively advancing toward the hands and feet.

My companions and I walked around the seaward side of the giant, whose hips and thorax towered above us like the hull of a stranded ship. His pearl-colored skin, distended by immersion in salt water, masked the contours of the enormous muscles and tendons. We passed below the left knee, which was flexed slightly, threads of damp seaweed clinging to its sides. Draped loosely across the midriff, and preserving a tenuous propriety, was a shawl of heavy open-weaved material, bleached to a pale yellow by the water. A strong odor of brine came from the garment as it steamed in the sun, mingled with the sweet but potent scent of the giant's skin.

We stopped by his shoulder and gazed up at the motionless profile. The lips were parted slightly, the open eye cloudy and occluded, as if injected with some blue milky liquid, but the delicate arches of the nostrils and eyebrows invested the face with an ornate charm that belied the brutish power of the chest and shoulders.

The ear was suspended in mid-air over our heads like a sculptured doorway. As I raised my hand to touch the pendulous lobe someone appeared over the edge of the forehead and shouted down at me. Startled by this apparition, I stepped back, and then saw that a group of youths had climbed up on to the face and were jostling each other in and out of the orbits.

People were now clambering all over the giant, whose reclining arms provided a double stairway. From the palms they walked along the forearms to the elbow and then crawled over the distended belly of the biceps to the flat promenade of the pectoral muscles which covered the upper half of the smooth hairless chest. From here they climbed up on to the face, hand over hand along the lips and nose, or forayed down the abdomen to meet others who had straddled the ankles and were patrolling the twin columns of the thighs.

We continued our circuit through the crowd, and stopped to examine the outstretched right hand. A small pool of water lay in the palm, like the residue of another world, now being kicked away by the people ascending the arm. I tried to read the palm-lines that grooved the skin, searching for some clue to the giant's character, but the distension of the tissues had almost obliterated them, carrying away all trace of the giant's identity and his last tragic predicament. The huge muscles and wrist bones of the hand seemed to deny any sensitivity to their owner, but the delicate flexion of the fingers and the well-tended nails, each cut symmetrically to within six inches of the quick, argued a certain refinement of temperament, illustrated in the Grecian features of the face, on which the townsfolk were now sitting like flies.

One youth was even standing, arms wavering at his sides, on the very tip of the nose, shouting down at his companions, but the face of the giant retained its massive composure.

Returning to the shore, we sat down on the shingle, and watched the continuous stream of people arriving from the city. Some six or seven fishing boats had collected offshore, and their crews waded in through the shallow water for a closer look at this enormous storm-catch. Later a party of police appeared and made a half-hearted attempt to cordon off the beach, but after walking up to the recumbent figure any such thoughts left their minds, and they went off together with bemused backward glances.

An hour later there were a thousand people on the beach, at least two hundred of them were standing or sitting on the giant, crowded along his arms and legs or circulating in a ceaseless mele across his chest and stomach. A large gang of youths occupied the head, toppling each other off the cheeks and sliding down the smooth planes of the jaw. Two or three straddled the nose, and another crawled into one of the nostrils, from which he emitted barking noises like a dog.

That afternoon the police returned, and cleared a way through the crowd for a party of scientific experts—authorities on gross anatomy and marine biology—from the university. The gang of youths and most of the people on the giant climbed down, leaving behind a few hardy spirits perched on the tips of the toes and on the forehead. The experts strode around the giant, heads nodding in vigorous consultation, preceded by the policemen who pushed back the press of spectators. When they reached the outstretched hand the senior officer offered to assist them up on the palm, but the experts hastily demurred.

After they returned to the shore, the crowd once more climbed on to the giant, and was in full possession when we left at five o'clock, covering the arms and legs like a dense flock of gulls sitting on the corpse of a large fish.

I next visited the beach three days later. My friends at the library had returned to their work, and delegated to me the task of keeping the giant under observation and preparing a report. Perhaps they sensed my particular interest in the case, and it was certainly true that I was eager to return to the beach. There was nothing necrophilic about this, for to all intents the giant was still alive for me, indeed more alive than many of the people watching him. What I found so fascinating was partly his immense scale, the huge volumes of space occupied by his arms and legs, which seemed to confirm the identity of my own miniature limbs, but above all the mere categorical fact of his existence. Whatever else in our lives might be open to doubt, the giant, dead or alive, existed in an absolute sense, providing a glimpse into a world of similar absolutes of which we spectators on the beach were such imperfect and puny copies.

When I arrived at the beach the crowd was considerably smaller, and some two or three hundred people sat on the shingle, picnicking and watching the groups of visitors who walked out across the sand. The successive tides had carried the giant nearer the shore, swinging his head and shoulders toward the beach, so that he seemed doubly to gain in size, his huge body dwarfing the fishing boats beached beside his feet. The uneven contours of the beach had pushed his spine into a slight arch, expanding his chest and tilting back the head, forcing him into a more expressly heroic posture. The combined effects of seawater and the tumefaction of the tissues had given the face a sleeker and less youthful look. Although the vast proportions of the features made it impossible to assess the age and character of the giant, on my previous visit his classically modeled mouth and nose suggested that he had been a young man of discreet and modest temper. Now, however, he appeared to be at least in early middle age. The puffy cheeks, thicker nose and temples and narrowing eyes gave him a look of well-fed maturity that even now hinted at a growing corruption to come.

This accelerated post-mortem development of the giant's character, as if the latent elements of his personality had gained sufficient momentum during his life to discharge themselves in a brief final résumé, continued to fascinate me. It marked the beginning of the giant's surrender to that all-demanding system of time in which the rest of humanity finds itself, and of which, like the million twisted ripples of a fragmented whirlpool, our finite lives are the concluding products. I took up my position on the shingle directly opposite the giant's head, from where I could see the new arrivals and the children clambering over the legs and arms.

Among the morning's visitors were a number of men in leather jackets and cloth caps, who peered up critically at the giant with a professional eye, pacing out his dimensions and making rough calculations in the sand with spars of driftwood. I assumed them to be from the public works department and other municipal bodies, no doubt wondering how to dispose of this gargantuan piece of jetsam.

Several rather more smartly attired individuals, circus proprietors and the like, also appeared on the scene, and strolled slowly around the giant, hands in the pockets of their long overcoats, saying nothing to one another. Evidently its bulk was too great even for their matchless enterprise. After they had gone the children continued to run up and down the arms and legs, and the youths wrestled with each other over the supine face, the damp sand from their feet covering the white skin.

The following day I deliberately postponed my visit until the late afternoon, and when I arrived there were fewer than fifty or sixty people sitting on the shingle. The giant had been carried still closer to the shore, and was now little more than seventy-five yards away, his feet crushing the palisade of a rotting breakwater. The slope of the firmer sand tilted his body toward the sea, and the bruised face was averted in an almost conscious gesture. I sat down on a large metal winch which had been shackled to a concrete caisson above the shingle, and looked down at the recumbent figure.

His blanched skin had now lost its pearly translucence and was spattered with dirty sand which replaced that washed away by the night tide. Clumps of seaweed filled the intervals between the fingers and a collection of litter and cuttlebones lay in the crevices below the hips and knees. But despite this, and the continuous thickening of his features, the giant still retained his magnificent Homeric stature. The enormous breadth of the shoulders, and the huge columns of the arms and legs, still carried the figure into another dimension, and the giant seemed a more authentic image of one of the drowned Argonauts or heroes of the Odyssey than the conventional human-sized portrait previously in my mind.

I stepped down on to the sand, and walked between the pools of water toward the giant. Two small boys were sitting in the well of the ear, and at the far end a solitary youth stood perched high on one of the toes, surveying me as I approached. As I had hoped when delaying my visit, no one else paid any attention to me, and the people on the shore remained huddled beneath their coats.

The giant's supine right hand was covered with broken shells and sand, in which a score of footprints were visible. The rounded bulk of the hip towered above me, cutting off all sight of the sea. The sweetly acrid odor I had noticed before was now more pungent, and through the opaque skin I could see the serpentine coils of congealed blood vessels. However repellent it seemed, this ceaseless metamorphosis, a visible life in death, alone permitted me to set foot on the corpse.

Using the jutting thumb as a stair rail, I climbed up on to the palm and began my ascent. The skin was harder than I expected, barely yielding to my weight. Quickly I walked up the sloping forearm and the bulging balloon of the biceps. The face of the drowned giant loomed to my right, the cavernous nostrils and huge flanks of the cheeks like the cone of some freakish volcano.

Safely rounding the shoulder, I stepped out on to the broad promenade of the chest, across which the bony ridges of the rib cage lay like huge rafters. The white skin was dappled by the darkening bruises of countless footprints, in which the patterns of individual heel marks were clearly visible. Someone had built a small sandcastle on the center of the sternum, and I climbed on to this partly demolished structure to give myself a better view of the face.

The two children had now scaled the ear and were pulling themselves into the right orbit, whose blue globe, completely occluded by some milk-colored fluid, gazed sightlessly past their miniature forms. Seen obliquely from below, the face was devoid of all grace and repose, the drawn mouth and raised chin propped up by its gigantic slings of muscles resembling the torn prow of a colossal wreck. For the first time I became aware of the extremity of this last physical agony of the giant, no less painful for his unawareness of the collapsing musculature and tissues. The absolute isolation of the ruined figure, cast like an abandoned ship upon the empty shore, almost out of sound of the waves, transformed his face into a mask of exhaustion and helplessness.

As I stepped forward, my foot sank into a trough of soft tissue, and a gust of fetid gas blew through an aperture between the ribs. Retreating from the fouled air, which hung like a cloud over my head, I turned toward the sea to clear my lungs. To my surprise I saw that the giant's left hand had been amputated.

I stared with bewilderment at the blackening stump, while the solitary youth reclining on his aerial perch a hundred feet away surveyed me with a sanguinary eye.

This was only the first of a sequence of depredations. I spent the following two days in the library, for some reason reluctant to visit the shore, aware that I had probably witnessed the approaching end of a magnificent illusion. When I next crossed the dunes and set foot on the shingle the giant was little more than twenty yards away, and with this close proximity to the rough pebbles all traces had vanished of the magic which once surrounded his distant wave-washed form. Despite his immense size, the bruises and dirt that covered his body made him appear merely human in scale, his vast dimensions only increasing his vulnerability.

His right hand and foot had been removed, dragged up the slope and trundled away by cart. After questioning the small group of people huddled by the breakwater, I gathered that a fertilizer company and a cattle food manufacturer were responsible.

The giant's remaining foot rose into the air, a steel hawser fixed to the large toe, evidently in preparation for the following day. The surrounding beach had been disturbed by a score of workmen, and deep ruts marked the ground where the hands and foot had been hauled away. A dark brackish fluid leaked from the stumps, and stained the sand and the white cones of the cuttlefish. As I walked down the shingle I noticed that a number of jocular slogans, swastikas and other signs had been cut into the gray skin, as if the mutilation of this motionless colossus had released a sudden flood of repressed spite. The lobe of one of the ears was pierced by a spear of timber, and a small fire had burned out in the center of the chest, blackening the surrounding skin. The fine wood ash was still being scattered by the wind.

A foul smell enveloped the cadaver, the undisguisable signature of putrefaction, which had at last driven away the usual gathering of youths. I returned to the shingle and climbed up on to the winch. The giant's swollen cheeks had now almost closed his eyes, drawing the lips back in a monumental gape. The once straight Grecian nose had been twisted and flattened, stamped into the ballooning face by countless heels.

When I visited the beach the following day I found, almost with relief, that the head had been removed.

Some weeks elapsed before I made my next journey to the beach, and by then the human likeness I had noticed earlier had vanished again. On close inspection the recumbent thorax and abdomen were unmistakably manlike, but as each of the limbs was chopped off, first at the knee and elbow, and then at shoulder and thigh, the carcass resembled that of any headless sea animal—whale or whale-shark. With this loss of identity, and the few traces of personality that had clung tenuously to the figure, the interest of the spectators expired, and the foreshore was deserted except for an elderly beachcomber and the watchman sitting in the doorway of the contractor's hut.

A loose wooden scaffolding had been erected around the carcass, from which a dozen ladders swung in the wind, and the surrounding sand was littered with coils of rope, long metal-handled knives and grappling irons, the pebbles oily with blood and pieces of bone and skin.

I nodded to the watchman, who regarded me dourly over his brazier of burning coke. The whole area was pervaded by the pungent smell of huge squares of blubber being simmered in a vat behind the hut.

Both the thigh bones had been removed, with the assistance of a small crane draped in the gauzelike fabric which had once covered the waist of the giant, and the open sockets gaped like barn doors. The upper arms, collar bones and pudenda had likewise been dispatched. What remained of the skin over the thorax and abdomen had been marked out in parallel strips with a tar brush, and the first five or six sections had been pared away from the midriff, revealing the great arch of the rib cage.

As I left a flock of gulls wheeled down from the sky and alighted on the beach, picking at the stained sand with ferocious cries.

Several months later, when the news of his arrival had been generally forgotten, various pieces of the body of the dismembered giant began to reappear all over the city. Most of these were bones, which the fertilizer manufacturers had found too difficult to crush, and their massive size, and the huge tendons and discs of cartilage attached to their joints, immediately identified them. For some reason, these disembodied fragments seemed better to convey the essence of the giant's original magnificence than the bloated appendages that had been subsequently amputated. As I looked across the road at the premises of the largest wholesale merchants in the meat market, I recognized the two enormous thighbones on either side of the doorway. They towered over the porters' heads like the threatening megaliths of some primitive druidical religion, and I had a sudden vision of the giant climbing to his knees upon these bare bones and striding away through the streets of the city, picking up the scattered fragments of himself on his return journey to the sea.

A few days later I saw the left humerus lying in the entrance to one of the shipyards (its twin for several years lay on the mud among the piles below the harbor's principal commercial wharf). In the same week the mummified right hand was exhibited on a carnival float during the annual pageant of the guilds.

The lower jaw, typically, found its way to the museum of natural history. The remainder of the skull has disappeared, but is probably still lurking in the waste grounds or private gardens of the city—quite recently, while sailing down the river, I noticed two ribs of the giant forming a decorative arch in a waterside garden, possibly confused with the jawbones of a whale. A large square of tanned and tattooed skin, the size of an Indian blanket, forms a backcloth to the dolls and masks in a novelty shop near the amusement park, and I have no doubt that elsewhere in the city, in the hotels or golf clubs, the mummified nose or ears of the giant hang from the wall above a fireplace. As for the immense pizzle, this ends its days in the freak museum of a circus which travels up and down the northwest. This monumental apparatus, stunning in its proportions and sometime potency, occupies a complete booth to itself. The irony is that it is wrongly identified as that of a whale, and indeed most people, even those who first saw him cast up on the shore after the storm, now remember the giant, if at all, as a large sea beast.

The remainder of the skeleton, stripped of all flesh, still rests on the sea shore, the clutter of bleached ribs like the timbers of a derelict ship. The contractor's hut, the crane and the scaffolding have been removed, and the sand being driven into the bay along the coast has buried the pelvis and backbone. In the winter the high curved bones are deserted, battered by the breaking waves, but in the summer they provide an excellent perch for the sea-wearying gulls.

TANITH LEE (KAIINE) (1947–)

Since the appearance of her first story in 1968, British writer Tanith Lee has been a popular author of Fantasy (including Dark Fantasy and Comic Fantasy) and Science Fiction. She is best known for her Fantasy stories that incorporate both Horror and High Fantasy (epic, historic, mythological, and Sword and Sorcery) elements.

Exotic lands, larger-than-life characters, heroes and heroines, and Good versus Evil themes pervade Lee's writing. And, she is both a profound reflection of and influence on modern-day Fantasists, such as Anne McCaffrey, Madeleine L'Engle, Jane Yolen, Margaret Weis, Tracy Hickman, Ellen Datlow, and Terri Windling. In recent years, Tanith Lee has specialized in Dark Fantasy and retellings of classic fairy tales with a macabre, black humor twist. Such is the case with the first of her fairy tale parodies, "Red as Blood."

Red as Blood
(The Magazine of Fantasy and Science Fiction, *July 1979*)

The beautiful Witch Queen flung open the ivory case of the magic mirror. Of dark gold the mirror was, dark gold like the hair of the Witch Queen that poured down her back. Dark gold the mirror was, and ancient as the seven stunted black trees growing beyond the pale blue glass of the window.

"*Speculum, speculum,*" said the Witch Queen to the magic mirror. "*Dei gratia.*"

"*Volente Deo. Audio.*"

"Mirror," said the Witch Queen. "Whom do you see?"

"I see you, mistress," replied the mirror. "And all in the land. But one."

"Mirror, mirror, who is it you do not see?"

"I do not see Bianca."

The Witch Queen crossed herself. She shut the case of the mirror and, walking slowly to the window, looked out at the old trees through the panes of pale blue glass.

Fourteen years ago, another woman had stood at this window, but she was not like the Witch Queen. The woman had black hair that fell to her ankles; she had a crimson gown, the girdle worn high beneath her breasts, for she was far gone with child. And this woman had thrust open the glass casement on the winter garden, where the old trees crouched in the snow. Then, taking a sharp bone needle, she had thrust it into her finger and shaken three bright drops on the ground. "Let my daughter have," said the woman, "hair black as mine, black as the wood of these warped and arcane trees. Let her have skin like mine, white as this snow. And let her have my mouth, red as my blood." And the woman had smiled and licked at her finger. She had a crown on her head; it shone in the dusk like a star. She never came to the window before dusk: she did not like the day. She was the first Queen, and she did not possess a mirror.

The second Queen, the Witch Queen, knew all this. She knew how, in giving birth, the first Queen had died. Her coffin had been carried into the cathedral and masses had been said. There was an ugly rumor—that a splash of holy water had fallen on the corpse and the dead flesh had smoked. But the first Queen had been reckoned unlucky for the kingdom. There had been a plague in the land since she came there, a wasting disease for which there was no cure.

Seven years went by. The King married the second Queen, as unlike the first as frankincense to myrrh.

"And this is my daughter," said the King to his second Queen.

There stood a little girl child, nearly seven years of age. Her black hair hung to her ankles, her skin was white as snow. Her mouth was red as blood, and she smiled with it.

"Bianca," said the King, "you must love your new mother."

Bianca smiled radiantly. Her teeth were bright as sharp bone needles.

"Come," said the Witch Queen, "come, Bianca. I will show you my magic mirror."

"Please, Mamma, said Bianca softly, I do not like mirrors."

"She is modest," said the King. "And delicate. She never goes out by day. The sun distresses her."

That night, the Witch Queen opened the case of her mirror.

"Mirror. Whom do you see?"

"I see you, mistress. And all in the land. But one."

"Mirror, mirror, who is it you do not see?"

"I do not see Bianca."

The second Queen gave Bianca a tiny crucifix of golden filigree. Bianca would not accept it. She ran to her father and whispered, "I am afraid. I do not like to think of Our Lord dying in agony on His cross. She means to frighten me. Tell her to take it away."

The second Queen grew wild white roses in her garden and invited Bianca to walk there after sundown. But Bianca shrank away. She whispered to her father, "The thorns will tear me. She means me to be hurt."

When Bianca was twelve years old, the Witch Queen said to the King, "Bianca should be confirmed so that she may take Communion with us."

"This may not be," said the King. "I will tell you, she has not been Christened, for the dying word of my first wife was against it. She begged me, for her religion was different from ours. The wishes of the dying must be respected."

"Should you not like to be blessed by the Church," said the Witch Queen to Bianca. "To kneel at the golden rail before the marble altar. To sing to God, to taste the ritual Bread and sip the ritual Wine."

"She means me to betray my true mother," said Bianca to the King. "When will she cease tormenting me?"

The day she was thirteen, Bianca rose from her bed, and there was a red stain there, like a red, red flower.

"Now you are a woman," said her nurse.

"Yes," said Bianca. And she went to her true mother's jewel box, and out of it she took her mother's crown and set it on her head.

When she walked under the old black trees in the dusk, the crown shone like a star.

The wasting sickness, which had left the land in peace for thirteen years, suddenly began again, and there was no cure.

The Witch Queen sat in a tall chair before a window of pale green and dark white glass, and in her hands she held a Bible bound in rosy silk.

"Majesty," said the huntsman, bowing very low.

He was a man, forty years old, strong and handsome, and wise in the hidden lore of the forests, the occult lore of the earth. He could kill too, for it was his trade, without faltering. The slender fragile deer he could kill, and the moon-winged birds, and the velvet hares with their sad, foreknowing eyes. He pitied them, but pitying, he killed them. Pity could not stop him. It was his trade.

"Look in the garden," said the Witch Queen.

The hunter looked through a dark white pane. The sun had sunk, and a maiden walked under a tree.

"The Princess Bianca," said the huntsman.

"What else?" asked the Witch Queen.

The huntsman crossed himself.

"By Our Lord, Madam, I will not say."

"But you know."

"Who does not?"

"The King does not."

"Nor he does."

"Are you a brave man?" asked the Witch Queen.

"In the summer, I have hunted and slain boar. I have slaughtered wolves in winter."

"But are you brave enough?"

"If you command it, Lady," said the huntsman, "I will try my best."

The Witch Queen opened the Bible at a certain place, and out of it she drew a flat silver crucifix, which had been resting against the words: *Thou shalt not be afraid for the terror by night. . . . Nor for the pestilence that walketh in darkness.*

The huntsman kissed the crucifix and put it about his neck beneath his shirt.

"Approach," said the Witch Queen, "and I will instruct you in what to say."

Presently, the huntsman entered the garden, as the stars were burning up in the sky. He strode to where Bianca stood under a stunted dwarf tree, and he kneeled down.

"Princess," he said, "pardon me, but I must give you ill tidings."

"Give them then," said the girl, toying with the long stem of a wan, night-growing flower which she had plucked.

"Your stepmother, the accursed jealous witch, means to have you slain. There is no help for it but you must fly the palace this very night. If you permit, I will guide you to the forest. There are those who will care for you until it may be safe for you to return."

Bianca watched him, but gently trustingly.

"I will go with you, then," she said.

They went by a secret way out of the garden, through a passage under the ground, through a tangled orchard, by a broken road between great over-grown hedges.

Night was a pulse of deep, flickering blue when they came to the forest. The branches of the forest overlapped and intertwined, like leading in a window, and the sky gleamed dimly through like panes of blue-colored glass.

"I am weary," sighed Bianca. "May I rest a moment?"

"By all means," said the huntsman. "In the clearing there, foxes come to play by night. Look in that direction, and you will see them."

"How clever you are," said Bianca. "And how handsome." She sat on the turf and gazed at the clearing.

The huntsman drew his knife silently and concealed it in the folds of his cloak. He stooped above the maiden.

"What are you whispering?" demanded the huntsman, laying his hand on her wood-black hair.

"Only a rhyme my mother taught me."

The huntsman seized her by the hair and swung her about so her white throat was before him, stretched ready for the knife. But he did not strike, for there in his hand he held the dark golden locks of the Witch Queen, and her face laughed up at him, and she flung her arms about him, laughing.

"Good man, sweet man, it was only a test of you. Am I not a witch? And do you not love me?"

The huntsman trembled, for he did love her, and she was pressed so close her heart seemed to beat within his own body.

"Put away the knife. Throw away the silly crucifix. We have no need of these things. The King is not one half the man you are."

And the huntsman obeyed her, throwing the knife and the crucifix far off among the roots of the trees. He gripped her to him and she buried her face in his neck, and the pain of her kiss was the last thing he felt in this world.

The sky was black now. The forest was blacker. No foxes played in the clearing. The moon rose and made white lace through the boughs, and through the backs of the huntsman's empty eyes. Bianca wiped her mouth on a dead flower.

"Seven asleep, Seven awake," said Bianca. "Wood to wood. Blood to blood. Thee to me."

There came a sound like seven huge rendings, distant by the length of several trees, a broken road, an orchard, an underground passage. Then a sound like seven huge single footfalls. Nearer. And nearer.

Hop, hop, hop, hop. Hop, hop, hop.

In the orchard, seven black shudderings.

On the broken road, between the high hedges, seven black creepings.

Brush crackled, branches snapped.

Through the forest, into the clearing, pushed seven warped, mis-shapen, hunched-over, stunted things. Woody-black mossy fur, woody-black bald masks. Eyes like glittering cracks, mouths like moist caverns. Lichen beards. Fingers of twiggy gristle. Grinning. Kneeling. Faces pressed to the earth.

"Welcome," said Bianca.

The Witch Queen stood before a window of glass like diluted wine. She looked at the magic mirror.

"Mirror. Whom do you see?"

"I see you, mistress. I see a man in the forest. He went hunting, but not for deer. His eyes are open, but he is dead. I see all in the land. But one."

The Witch Queen pressed her palms to her ears.

Outside the window, the garden lay, empty of its seven black and stunted dwarf trees.

"Bianca," said the Queen.

The windows had been draped and gave no light. The light spilled from a shallow vessel, light in a sheaf, like pastel wheat. It glowed upon four swords that pointed east and west, that pointed north and south.

Four winds had burst through the chamber, and the grey-silver powders of Time.

The hands of the Witch Queen floated like folded leaves on the air, and through the dry lips the Witch Queen chanted:

"*Pater omnipotens, mitere digneris sanctum Angelum tuum de Infernis.*"

The light faded, and grew brighter.

There, between the hilts of the four swords, stood the Angel Lucefiel, somberly gilded, his face in shadow, his golden wings spread and glazing at his back.

"Since you have called me, I know your desire. It is a comfortless wish. You ask for pain."

"You speak of pain, Lord Lucefiel, who suffer the most merciless pain of all. Worse than the nails in the feet and wrists. Worse than the thorns and the bitter cup and the blade in the side. To be called upon for evil's sake, which I do not, comprehending your true nature, son of God, brother of The Son."

"You recognize me, then. I will grant what you ask."

And Lucefiel (by some named Satan, Rex Mundi, but nevertheless the left hand, the sinister hand of God's design) wrenched lightning from the ether and cast it at the Witch Queen.

It caught her in the breast. She fell.

The sheaf of light towered and lit the golden eyes of the Angel, which were terrible, yet luminous with compassion, as the swords shattered and he vanished.

The Witch Queen pulled herself from the floor of the chamber, no longer beautiful, a withered, slobbering hag.

Into the core of the forest, even at noon, the sun never shone. Flowers propagated in the grass, but they were colorless. Above, the black-green roof hung down nets of thick green twilight through which albino butterflies and moths feverishly drizzled. The trunks of the trees were smooth as the stalks of underwater weeds. Bats flew in the daytime, and birds who believed themselves to be bats.

There was a sepulcher, dripped with moss. The bones had been rolled out, had rolled around the feet of seven twisted dwarf trees. They looked like trees.

Sometimes they moved. Sometimes something like an eye glittered, or a tooth, in the wet shadows.

In the shade of the sepulcher door sat Bianca, combing her hair.

A lurch of motion disturbed the thick twilight.

The seven trees turned their heads.

A hag emerged from the forest. She was crook-backed, and her head was poked forward, predatory, withered and almost hairless, like a vulture's.

"Here we are at last," grated the hag, in a vulture's voice.

She came closer and cranked herself down on her knees and bowed her face into the turf and the colorless flowers.

Bianca sat and gazed at her. The hag lifted herself. Her teeth were yellow palings.

"I bring you the homage of witches, and three gifts," said the hag.

"Why should you do that?"

"Such a quick child, and only fourteen years. Why? Because we fear you. I bring you gifts to curry favor."

Bianca laughed. "Show me."

The hag made a pass in the green air. She held a silken cord worked curiously with a plaited human hair.

"Here is a girdle which will protect you from the devices of priests, from crucifix and chalice and the accursed holy water. In it are knotted the tresses of a virgin, and of a woman no better than she should be, and of a woman dead. And here—" a second pass and a comb was in her hand, lacquered blue over green—"a comb from the deep sea, a mermaid's trinket, to charm and subdue. Part your locks with this, and the scent of ocean will fill men's nostrils and the rhythm of the tides their ears, the tides that bind men like chains. Last," added the hag, "that old symbol of wickedness, the scarlet fruit of Eve, the apple red as blood. Bite, and the understanding of Sin, which the serpent boasted of, will be made known to you." And the hag made her last pass in the air and extended the apple, with the girdle and the comb, towards Bianca.

Bianca glanced at the seven stunted trees.

"I like her gifts, but I do not quite trust her."

The bald masks peered from their shaggy beardings. Eyelets glinted. Twiggy claws clacked.

"All the same," said Bianca, "I will let her tie the girdle on me, and comb my hair herself."

The hag obeyed, simpering. Like a toad she waddled to Bianca. She tied on the girdle. She parted the ebony hair. Sparks sizzled, white from the girdle, peacock's eye from the comb.

"And now, hag, take a little bite of the apple."

"It will be my pride," said the hag, "to tell my sisters I shared this fruit with you." And the hag bit into the apple, and mumbled the bite noisily, and swallowed, smacking her lips.

Then Bianca took the apple and bit into it.

Bianca screamed—and choked.

She jumped to her feet. Her hair whirled about her like a storm cloud. Her face turned blue, then slate, then white again. She lay on the pallid flowers, neither stirring nor breathing.

The seven dwarf trees rattled their limbs and their bear-shaggy heads, to no avail. Without Bianca's art they could not hop. They strained their claws and ripped at the hag's sparse hair and her mantle. She fled between them. She fled into the sunlit acres of the forest, along the broken road, through orchard, into a hidden passage.

The hag reentered the palace by the hidden way, and the Queen's chamber by a hidden stair. She was bent almost double. She held her ribs. With one skinny hand she opened the ivory case of the magic mirror.

"*Speculum, speculum. Dei gratia.* Whom do you see?"

"I see you, mistress. And all in the land. And I see a coffin."

"Whose corpse lies in the coffin?"

"That I cannot see. It must be Bianca."

The hag, who had been the beautiful Witch Queen, sank into her tall chair before the window of pale cucumber green and dark white glass. Her drugs and potions waited ready to reverse the dreadful conjuring of age the Angel Lucefiel had placed on her, but she did not touch them yet.

The apple had contained a fragment of the flesh of Christ, the sacred wafer, the Eucharist.

The Witch Queen drew her Bible to her and opened it randomly.

And read, with fear, the words: *Resurgat.*

It appeared like glass, the coffin, milky glass. It had formed this way. A thin white smoke had risen from the skin of Bianca. She smoked as a fire smokes when a drop of quenching water falls on it. The piece of Eucharist had stuck in her throat. The Eucharist, quenching water to her fire, caused her to smoke.

Then the cold dews of night gathered, and the colder atmospheres of midnight. The smoke of Bianca's quenching froze about her. Frost formed in exquisite silver scrollwork all over the block of misty ice which contained Bianca.

Bianca's frigid heart could not warm the ice. Nor the sunless green twilight of the day.

You could just see her, stretched in the coffin, through the glass. How lovely she looked, Bianca. Black as ebony, white as snow, red as blood.

The trees hung over the coffin. Years passed. The trees sprawled about the coffin, cradling it in their arms. Their eyes wept fungus and green resin. Green amber drops hardened like jewels in the coffin of glass.

"Who is that, lying under the trees?" the Prince asked, as he rode into the clearing.

He seemed to bring a golden moon with him, shining about his golden head, on the golden armor and the cloak of white satin blazoned with gold and blood and ink and sapphire. The white horse trod on the colorless flowers, but the flowers sprang up again when the hoofs had passed. A shield hung from the saddle bow, a strange shield. From one side it had a lion's face, but from the other, a lamb's face.

The trees groaned and their heads split on huge mouths.

"Is this Bianca's coffin?" said the Prince.

"Leave her with us," said the seven trees. They hauled at their roots. The ground shivered. The coffin of ice-glass gave a great jolt, and a crack bisected it.

Bianca coughed.

The jolt had precipitated the piece of Eucharist from her throat.

In a thousand shards the coffin shattered, and Bianca sat up. She stared at the Prince, and she smiled.

"Welcome, beloved," said Bianca.

She got to her feet and shook out her hair, and began to walk toward the Prince on the pale horse.

But she seemed to walk into a shadow, into a purple room; then into a crimson room whose emanations lanced her like knives. Next she walked into a yellow room where she heard the sound of crying which tore her ears. All her body seemed stripped away; she was a beating heart. The beats of her heart became two wings. She flew. She was a raven, then an owl. She flew into a sparkling pane. It scorched her white. Snow white. She was a dove.

She settled on the shoulder of the Prince and hid her head under her wing. She had no longer anything black about her, and nothing red.

"Begin again now, Bianca," said the Prince. He raised her from his shoulder. On his wrist there was a mark. It was like a star. Once a nail had been driven in there.

Bianca flew away, up through the roof of the forest. She flew in at a delicate wine window. She was in the palace. She was seven years old.

The Witch Queen, her new mother, hung a filigree crucifix around her neck. "Mirror," said the Witch Queen. "Whom do you see?"

"I see you, mistress," replied the mirror. "And all in the land. I see Bianca."

JANE (HYATT) YOLEN (1939-)

Jane Yolen is best known as an author of children's Fantasies, but she is also a prolific writer of stories for adolescents and of mainstream Fantasy and Science Fiction. Further, Yolen has created picture books, nonfiction studies, poetry, and music books. She is an accomplished editor and publisher. Of her many specialties, she is best known, in whatever age group, for High Fantasy.

Like Ray Bradbury's work, most of Jane Yolen's prose comes in the form of short stories, or episodic novels comprised of interconnected shorter works. Like Bradbury also, Yolen is well versed in cultural and literary history and draws on the same. She has been a keen observer of the human experience, and her Fantasy can be both dark and uplifting. She has told stories reminiscent of the works of ancient mythology and the grand traditions of George MacDonald, J. R. R. Tolkien, C. S. Lewis, and Frank Herbert.

"The Malaysian Mer" is a tale of myth and antiquity, and it aptly elicits the mindset of the collector of the same.

The Malaysian Mer

(Neptune Rising: Songs and Tales of the Undersea Folk, *1982)*

The shops were not noticeable from the main street and almost lost in the back-alley maze as well. But Mrs. Stambley was an expert at antiquing. A new city and a new back alley got up her hunting and gathering instincts, as she liked to tell her group at home. That this city was half a world away from her comfortable Salem, Massachusetts, home did not faze her. In England or America she guessed she knew how to look.

She had dozed in the sun as the boat made its way along the Thames. At her age naps had become important. Her head nodded peacefully under its covering of flowers draped on a wine-colored crown. She never even heard the tour guide's spiel. At Greenwich she had debarked meekly with the rest of the tourists, but she had easily slipped the leash of the guide, who took the rest of the pack up to check out Greenwich Mean Time. Instead, Mrs. Stambley, her large black leather pocketbook clutched in a sturdy gloved grip, had gone exploring on her own.

To the right of the harbor street was a group of shops and, she sensed, a back alley or two. The smell of it—sharp, mysterious, inviting—drew her in.

She ignored the main street and its big-windowed stores. A small cobbled path ran between two buildings and she slipped into it as comfortably as a foot into a well-worn slipper. There were several branchings, and Mrs. Stambley checked out each one with her watery blue eyes. Then she chose one. She knew it would be the right one. As she often said to her group at home, "I have a gift, a power. I am *never* wrong about it."

Here there were several small, dilapidated shops that seemed to edge one into the other. They had a worn look as if they had sat huddled together, the damp wind blowing off the river moldering their bones, while a bright new town had been built up around them. The windows were dirty, finger-streaked. Only the most intrepid shopper would find the way into them. There were no numbers on the doors.

The first store was full of maps. And if Mrs. Stambley hadn't already spent her paper allowance (she maintained separate monies for paper, gold, and oddities) on a rare chart of the McCodrun ancestry, she might have purchased a map of British waters that was decorated with tritons blowing "their wreathed horns" as the bent-over shopkeeper had quoted. She had been sorely tempted. Mrs. Stambley collected "objects d'mer," as she called them. Sea artifacts and antiquities. Sea magic was her specialty in the group. But the lineage of the Clan McCodrun—the reputed descendants of the selchies—had wiped out her comfortable paper account. And Mrs. Stambley, who was always precise in her reckonings, never spent more than her allotment. As the group's treasurer she had to keep the others in line. She could do no less for herself.

So she oohed and aahed at the map for the storekeeper's benefit and because it *was* quite beautiful and probably 17th century. She even managed to talk him down several pounds on the price, keeping her hand in as it were. But she left smiling her thanks. And he had been so impressed with the American lady's knowledge of the sea and its underwater folk that he smiled back even though she had bought nothing.

The next two shops were total wastes of time. One was full of reproductions and second-hand, badly painted china cups and cracked glassware. Mrs. Stambley sniffed as she left, muttering under her breath "Junk—spelled j-u-n-q-u-e," not even minding that the lady behind the counter heard her. The other store had been worse, a so-called craft shop full of handmade tea cosies and poorly crocheted afghans in simply appalling colors.

As she entered the fourth shop, Mrs. Stambley caught her breath. The smell was there, the smell of deep-sea magic. So deep and dark it might have been called up from the Mariana Trench. In all her years of hunting, she had never had such a find. She put her right hand over her heart and stumbled a bit, scuffing one of her sensible shoes. Then she straightened up and looked around.

The shop was a great deal longer than it was wide, with a staircase running up about halfway along the wall. The rest of the walls were lined with china cupboards in which Victorian and Edwardian cups and saucers were tastefully displayed. One in particular caught her eye because it had a Poseidon on the side. She walked over to look at it, but the magic smell did not come from there.

Books in stacks on the floor blocked her path, and she looked through a few to see what there was. She found an almost complete Britannica, the 1913 edition, missing only the thirteenth volume. There was a first edition of Fort's *Book of the Damned* and a dark grimoire so waterstained she could make out none of the spells. There were three paperback copies of *Folklore of the Sea*, a pleasant volume she had at home. And even the obscure *Melusine, Or the Mistress From the Sea* in both English and French.

She walked carefully around the books and looked for a moment at three glass cases containing fine replicas of early schooners, even down to the carved figure-heads. One was of an Indian maiden, one an angel, one an unnamed muse with long, flowing hair. But she already had several such at home, her favorite a sup-posed replica of the legendary ship of the Flying Dutchman. Looking cost noth-ing, though, and so she looked for quite a while, giving herself time to become used to the odor of the deep magic.

She almost backed into a fourth case, and when she turned around, she got the shock of her life.

In a glass showcase with brass fittings, resting on two wooden holders, was a Malaysian mer.

She had read about them, of course, in the footnotes of obscure folklore jour-nals and in a grimoire of specialized sea spells, but she had never in her wildest imaginings thought to see one. They were said to have disappeared totally.

They were not really mermen, of course. Rather, they were constructs made by Malaysian natives out of monkeys and fish. The Malaysians killed the monkeys, cut off the top half, from the navel up, and sewed on a fish tail. The mummified remains were then sold to innocent British tars in Victorian times. The natives had called the mummies mermen and the young sailors believed them, brought the mers home and gave them to loved ones.

And here, resting on its wooden stands, was a particularly horrible example of one, probably rescued from an attic where it had laid all these years, dust-covered, rotting.

It was gray-green, with gray more predominant, and so skeletal that its rib cage reminded Mrs. Stambley of the pictures of starving children in Africa. Its arms were held stiffly in front as if it were doing an out-of-water dog paddle. The gri-macing face, big-lipped, big-eared, stared out at her in horror. She could not see the stitches that held the monkey half to the fish.

"I see you like our mer," came a voice from behind her, but Mrs. Stambley did not turn. She simply could not take her eyes from the grotesque mummy in the glass and brass case.

"A Malaysian mer," Mrs. Stambley whispered. One part of her noticed the price sticker on the side of the glass—three hundred pounds. Six hundred American dollars. It was more than she had with her . . . but . . .

"You know what it is, then," the voice went on. "That is too bad. Too bad."

The mer blinked its lashless lids and turned its head. Its eyes were entirely black, without irises. When it rolled its lips back, it showed sharp yellow-gray teeth. It had no tongue.

Mrs. Stambley tried to look away and could not. Instead she felt herself being drawn down, down, down into the black deeps of those eyes.

"That really is *too* bad," came the voice again, but now it was very far away and receding quickly.

Mrs. Stambley tried to open her mouth to scream, but only bubbles came out. All around her it was dark and cold and wet, and still she was pulled downward until she landed, with a jarring thud, on a sandy floor. She stood, brushed her skirts down, and settled her hat back on her head. Then, as she placed her pocketbook firmly under one arm, she felt a grip on her ankle, as if seaweed wanted to root her to that spot. She started to struggle against it when a change in the current against her face forced her to look up.

The mer was swimming toward her, lazily, as if it had all the time in the world to reach her.

She stopped wasting her strength in fighting the seaweed manacle, and instead cautiously fingered open her pocketbook. All the while she watched the mer, which had already halved the distance between them. Its mouth was opening and closing with terrifying snaps. Its bony fingers, with the opaque webbings, seemed to reach out for her. Its monkey face grinned. Behind it was a dark, roiling wake.

The water swirled about Mrs. Stambley, picking at her skirt, flipping the hem to show her slip. Above the swimming mer, high above, she could see the darker shadows of circling sharks waiting for what the mer would leave them. But even they feared to come any closer while he was on the hunt.

And then he was close enough so that she could see the hollow of his mouth, the scissored teeth, the black nails, the angry pulsing beat of the webbings. The sound he made came to her through the filtering of the water. It was like the groans and creaks of a sinking ship.

Her hand was inside the pocketbook now, fingers closing on the wallet and poking into the change purse for the wren feathers she kept there. She grabbed them up and held them before her. They were air magic, stronger than that of the sea, and blessed in church. It was luck against seafolk. Her hand trembled only slightly. She spoke a word of power that was washed from her lips into the troubled water.

For a moment the mer stopped, holding his gray hands before his face.

The seaweed around Mrs. Stambley's ankle slithered away. She kicked her foot out and found she was free.

But above a Great White Shark turned suddenly, sending a wash of new water across Mrs. Stambley's front. The tiny feathers broke and she had to let them go. They floated past the mer and were gone.

He put down his hands, gave the monkey grin at her again, and resumed swimming. But she knew—as he did—that he was not immune to her knowledge. It gave her some slight hope.

Her hand went back into her purse and found the zippered pocket. She unzipped it and drew out seven small bones, taken from a male horseshoe crab found on the Elizabeth Islands off the coast near New Bedford. They were strong sea magic and she counted heavily on them. She wrapped her fingers around the seven, held them first to her breast, then to her forehead, then flung them at the mer.

The bones sailed between them and in the filtered light seemed to dance and grow and change and cling together at last into a maze.

Mrs. Stambley kicked her feet, sending up a trough of bubbles, and, holding her hat with one hand, her purse with the other, eeled into the bone-maze. She knew that it would hold for only a minute or two at best.

Behind her she could hear the hunting cry of the mer as it searched for a way in. She ignored it and kicked her feet in a steady rhythm, propelling herself into the heart of the maze. Going in was always easier than coming out. Her bubble trail would lead the mer through once he found the entrance. For now she could still hear him knocking against the walls.

Her purse held one last bit of magic. It was a knife that had been given up by the sea, left on a beach on the North Shore, near Rockport. It had a black handle with a guard and she had mounted a silver coin on its haft.

The seawater laid shifting patterns on the blade that looked now like fire, now like air, the calligraphy of power. Mrs. Stambley knew better than to try to read it. Instead she turned toward the passage where the mer would have to appear. The knife in her right hand, her hat askew, the purse locked under her left arm, Mrs. Stambley guessed she did not look like a seasoned fighter. But in magic, as any good witch knew, *seeming* was all important. And she was not about to give up.

"Great Lir," she spoke, and her human tongue added extra urgency to the bubbles which flowered from her mouth. "Bull-roarer Poseidon, spear-thrower Neptune, mighty Njord, shrewish Ran, cleft-tailed Dagon, hold me safe in the green palms of your hands. Bring me safely from the sea. And when I am home, I will gift you and yours."

From somewhere near an animal called, a bull, a horse, a great sea serpent. It was her answer. In moments she would know what it meant. She put her right hand with the knife behind her and waited.

The water in the maze began to churn angrily and the mer came around the final turning. Seeing Mrs. Stambley backed against the flimsy wall, he laughed. The laugh cascaded out of his mouth in a torrent of bubbles. Their popping made a peculiar punctuation to his mirth. Then he showed his horrible teeth once again, swung his tail to propel himself forward, and moved in for the kill.

Mrs. Stambley kept the knife hidden until the very last moment. And then, as the mer's skeletal arms reached out for her, as the fingers of his hands actually pressed against her neck, and his sharp incisors began to bear down on her throat, she whipped her arms around and slashed at his side. He drew back in pain, and then she knifed him again, as expertly as if she were filleting a fish. He arched his back, opened his mouth in a silent scream of bubbles, and rose slowly toward the white light of the surface.

The maze vanished. Mrs. Stambley stuffed the knife back into her purse, then put her hands over her head, and rose too, leaving a trail of bubbles as dark as blood behind.

"*Too* bad," the voice was finishing.

Mrs. Stambley turned around and smiled blandly, patting her hat into place. "Yes, I know," she said. "It's too bad it is in such condition. For three hundred pounds, I would want something a bit better cared for."

She stepped aside.

The shopkeeper, a wizened, painted old lady with a webbing between her second and third fingers, breathed in sharply. In the showcase, the mummied mer had tipped over on its back. Along one side was a deep, slashing wound. The chest cavity was hollow. It stank. Under the body were seven small knobby sticks that looked surprisingly like bones.

"Yes," Mrs. Stambley continued, not bothering to apologize for her hasty exit, "rather poor condition. Shocking what some folk will try to palm off on tourists. Luckily I know better." She exited through the front door and was relieved to find that the sun lit the alleyway. She put her hand to her ample bosom and breathed deeply.

"Wait, just wait until I tell the group," she said aloud. Then she threaded her way back to the main street where the other tourists and their guide were coming down the hill. Mrs. Stambley walked briskly toward them, straightening her hat once again and smiling. Not even the thought of the lost triton map could dampen her spirits. The look of surprise on the face of that old witch of a shop-keeper had been worth the scare. Only what gift could she give to the gods that would be good enough? It was a thought that she could puzzle over happily all the way home.

 NEIL (RICHARD) GAIMAN (1960-)

There is no more exciting new author of Fantasy and Science Fiction at the beginning of the millennium than Neil Gaiman. Gaiman was first recognized for his comic book story lines, including those that appeared in The Sandman *comics and graphic novels with titles such as* Signal to Noise, Mr. Punch, *and* Violent Cases. *For these talents and contributions, he has earned multiple international awards.*

While still recognized as a premiere comic book scriptwriter, Neil Gaiman is today also recognized as a master fantasist, humorist, and social critic. He has co-written the novel Good Omens, *with Terry Pratchett, and he has written the novel* Neverwhere. *He also made* Neverwhere *into a six-part television series for the BBC. Currently, he is branching into the media of children's stories and radio.*

"Troll Bridge" is a Fantasy with a profound, even irreverent twist on its archetypal predecessors.

Troll Bridge

(Snow White, Rose Red, edited by Ellen Datlow and Terry Windling, 1993)

They pulled up most of the railway tracks in the early sixties, when I was three or four. They slashed the train services to ribbons. This meant that there was nowhere to go but London, and the little town where I lived became the end of the line.

My earliest reliable memory: eighteen months old, my mother away in hospital having my sister, and my grandmother walking with me down to a bridge and lifting me up to watch the train below, panting and steaming like a black iron dragon.

Over the next few years they lost the last of the steam trains, and with them went the network of railways that joined village to village, town to town.

I didn't know that the trains were going. By the time I was seven they were a thing of the past.

We lived in an old house on the outskirts of the town. The fields opposite were empty and fallow. I used to climb the fence and lie in the shade of a small bulrush patch, and read; or if I were feeling more adventurous I'd explore the grounds of the empty manor beyond the fields. It had a weed-clogged ornamental pond, with a low wooden bridge over it. I never saw any groundsmen or caretakers in my for-ays through the gardens and woods; and I never attempted to enter the manor. That would have been courting disaster, and besides, it was a matter of faith for me that all empty old houses were haunted.

It is not that I was credulous, simply that I believed in all things dark and dan-gerous. It was part of my young creed that the night was full of ghosts and witches, hungry and flapping and dressed completely in black.

The converse held reassuringly true: daylight was safe. Daylight was always safe.

A ritual: on the last day of the summer school term, walking home from school, I would remove my shoes and socks and, carrying them in my hands, walk down the stony flinty lane on pink and tender feet. In the summer holiday I would put shoes on only under duress, until school term began once more in September.

When I was seven I discovered the path through the wood. It was summer, hot and bright, and I wandered a long way from home that day.

I was exploring. I went past the manor, its windows boarded up and blind, across the grounds, and through some unfamiliar woods. I scrambled down a steep bank, and I found myself on a shady path that was new to me and overgrown with trees; the light that penetrated the leaves was stained green and gold, and I thought I was in fairyland.

A tiny stream trickled down the side of the path, teeming with tiny, transparent shrimps. I picked them up and watched them jerk and spin on my fingertips. Then I put them back.

I wandered down the path. It was perfectly straight, and overgrown with short grass. From time to time I would find these really terrific rocks: bubbly, melted things, brown and purple and black. If you held them up to the light you could see every colour of the rainbow. I was convinced that they had to be extremely valu-able, and stuffed my pockets with them.

I walked and walked down the quiet golden-green corridor, and saw nobody.

I wasn't hungry or thirsty. I just wondered where the path was going. It trav-elled in a straight line, and was flat, sometimes at the bottom of a ravine, occasion-ally built up, so I could look down on tree-tops and occasional houses. Valleys, and plateaus, valleys and plateaus. And eventually, in one of the valleys, I came to the bridge.

It was built of clean red brick, a huge curving arch over the path. At the side of the bridge were stone steps cut into the embankment, and, at the top of the steps, a little wooden gate.

I was surprised to see any token of the existence of humanity on my path, which I was by now convinced was a natural formation, like a volcano. And, with a sense more of curiosity than anything else (I had, after all, walked hundreds of miles, or so I was convinced, and might be *anywhere*), I climbed the stone steps, and went through the gate.

I was nowhere.

The top of the bridge was paved with mud. On each side of it was a meadow. The meadow on my side was a corn-field; the other field was just grass. There were the caked imprints of huge tractor wheels in the dried mud. I walked across the bridge to be sure: no trip-trap, my bare feet were soundless.

Nothing for miles; just fields and corn and trees.

I picked an ear of wheat, and pulled out the sweet grains, peeling them between my fingers, chewing them meditatively.

I realised then that I was getting hungry, and went back down the stairs to the abandoned railway track. It was time to go home. I was not lost; all I needed to do was follow my path home once more.

There was a troll waiting for me, under the bridge.

"I'm a troll," he said. Then he paused, and added, more or less as an after-thought, "Fol rol de ol rol."

He was huge: his head brushed the top of the brick arch. He was more or less translucent: I could see the bricks and trees behind him, dimmed but not lost. He was all my nightmares given flesh. He had huge strong teeth, and rending claws, and strong, hairy hands. His hair was long, like one of my sister's little plastic gonks, and his eyes bulged. He was naked, and his penis hung from the bush of gonk hair between his legs.

"I heard you, Jack," he whispered, in a voice like the wind. "I heard you trip-trapping over my bridge. And now I'm going to eat your life."

I was only seven, but it was daylight, and I do not remember being scared. It is good for children to find themselves facing the elements of a fairy tale—they are well-equipped to deal with these.

"Don't eat me," I said to the troll. I was wearing a stripy brown T-shirt, and brown corduroy trousers. My hair also was brown, and I was missing a front tooth. I was learning to whistle between my teeth, but wasn't there yet.

"I'm going to eat your life, Jack," said the troll.

I stared the troll in the face. "My big sister is going to be coming down the path soon," I lied, "and she's far tastier than me. Eat her instead."

The troll sniffed the air, and smiled. "You're all alone" he said. "There's nothing else on the path. Nothing at all." Then he leaned down, and ran his fingers over me: it felt like butterflies were brushing my face—like the touch of a blind person. Then he snuffled his fingers, and shook his huge head. "You don't have a big sister. You've only a younger sister, and she's at her friend's today."

"Can you tell all that from smell?" I asked, amazed.

"Trolls can smell the rainbows, trolls can smell the stars," it whispered sadly. "Trolls can smell the dreams you dreamed before you were ever born. Come close to me and I'll eat your life."

"I've got precious stones in my pocket," I told the troll. "Take them, not me. Look." I showed him the lava jewel rocks I had found earlier.

"Clinker," said the troll. "The discarded refuse of steam trains. Of no value to me."

He opened his mouth wide. Sharp teeth. Breath that smelled of leaf mould and the underneaths of things. "Eat. Now."

He became more and more solid to me, more and more real; and the world outside became flatter, began to fade.

"Wait." I dug my feet into the damp earth beneath the bridge, wiggled my toes, held on tightly to the real world. I stared into his big eyes. "You don't want to eat my life. Not yet. I—I'm only seven. I haven't *lived* at all yet. There are books I haven't read yet. I've never been on an aeroplane. I can't whistle yet—not really. Why don't you let me go? When I'm older and bigger and more of a meal I'll come back to you."

The troll stared at me with eyes like headlamps.

Then it nodded.

"When you come back, then," it said. And it smiled.

I turned around and walked back down the silent straight path where the railway lines had once been.

After a while I began to run.

I pounded down the track in the green light, puffing and blowing, until I felt a stabbing ache beneath my ribcage, the pain of stitch; and, clutching my side, I stumbled home.

*   *   *

The fields started to go, as I grew older. One by one, row by row, houses sprang up with roads named after wildflowers and respectable authors. Our home—an aging, tattered Victorian house—was sold, and torn down; new houses covered the garden.

They built houses everywhere.

I once got lost in the new housing estate that covered two meadows I had once known every inch of. I didn't mind too much that the fields were going, though. The old manor house was bought by a multinational, and the grounds became more houses.

It was eight years before I returned to the old railway line, and when I did, I was not alone.

I was fifteen; I'd changed schools twice in that time. Her name was Louise, and she was my first love.

I loved her grey eyes, and her fine light brown hair, and her gawky way of walking (like a fawn just learning to walk which sounds really dumb, for which I apologise): I saw her chewing gum, when I was thirteen, and I fell for her like a suicide from a bridge.

The main trouble with being in love with Louise was that we were best friends, and we were both going out with other people.

I'd never told her I loved her, or even that I fancied her. We were buddies.

I'd been at her house that evening: we sat in her room and played *Rattus Norvegicus*, the first Stranglers LP; it was the beginning of punk, and everything seemed so exciting: the possibilities, in music as in everything else, were endless. Eventually it was time for me to go home, and she decided to accompany me. We held hands, innocently, just pals, and we strolled the ten-minute walk to my house.

The moon was bright, and the world was visible and colourless, and the night was warm.

We got to my house. Saw the lights inside, and stood in the driveway, and talked about the band I was starting. We didn't go in.

Then it was decided that I'd walk *her* home. So we walked back to her house.

She told me about the battles she was having with her younger sister, who was stealing her make-up and perfume. Louise suspected that her sister was having sex with boys. Louise was a virgin. We both were.

We stood in the road outside her house, under the sodium-yellow streetlight, and we stared at each other's black lips and pale yellow faces.

We grinned at each other.

Then we just walked, picking quiet roads and empty paths. In one of the new housing estates a path led us into the woodland, and we followed it.

The path was straight and dark; but the lights of distant houses shone like stars on the ground, and the moon gave us enough light to see. Once we were scared, when something snuffled and snorted in front of us. We pressed close, saw it was a badger, laughed and hugged and kept on walking.

We talked quiet nonsense about what we dreamed and wanted and thought.

And all the time I wanted to kiss her and feel her breasts, and maybe put my hand between her legs.

Finally I saw my chance. There was an old brick bridge over the path, and we stopped beneath it. I pressed up against her. Her mouth opened against mine.

Then she went cold and stiff, and stopped moving.

"Hello," said the troll.

I let go of Louise. It was dark beneath the bridge, but the shape of the troll filled the darkness.

"I froze her," said the troll, "so we can talk. Now: I'm going to eat your life."

My heart pounded, and I could feel myself trembling.

"No."

"You said you'd come back to me. And you have. Did you learn to whistle?"

"Yes."

"That's good. I never could whistle." It sniffed, and nodded. "I am pleased. You have grown in life and experience. More to eat. More for me."

I grabbed Louise, a taut zombie, and pushed her forward. "Don't take me. I don't want to die. Take *her*. I bet she's much tastier than me. And she's two months older than I am. Why don't you take her?"

The troll was silent.

It sniffed Louise from toe to head, snuffling at her feet and crotch and breasts and hair.

Then it looked at me.

"She's an innocent," it said. "You're not. I don't want her. I want you."

I walked to the opening of the bridge and stared up at the stars in the night.

"But there's so much I've never done," I said, partly to myself. "I mean, I've never. Well, I've never had sex. And I've never been to America. I haven't . . ." I paused. "I haven't *done* anything. Not yet."

The troll said nothing.

"I could come back to you. When I'm older."

The troll said nothing.

"I *will* come back. Honest I will."

"Come back to me?" said Louise. "Why? Where are you going?"

I turned around. The troll had gone, and the girl I had thought I loved was standing in the shadows beneath the bridge.

"We're going home," I told her. "Come on."

We walked back, and never said anything.

She went out with the drummer in the punk band I started, and, much later, married someone else. We met once, on a train, after she was married, and she asked me if I remembered that night.

I said I did.

"I really liked you, that night, Jack," she told me. "I thought you were going to kiss me. I thought you were going to ask me out. I would have said yes. If you had."

"But I didn't."

"No," she said. "You didn't." Her hair was cut very short. It didn't suit her.

I never saw her again. The trim woman with the taut smile was not the girl I had loved, and talking to her made me feel uncomfortable.

I moved to London, and then, some years later, I moved back again, but the town I returned to was not the town I remembered: there were no fields, no farms, no little flint lanes; and I moved away as soon as I could, to a tiny village, ten miles down the road.

I moved with my family—I was married by now, with a toddler—into an old house that had once, many years before, been a railway station. The tracks had been dug up, and the old couple who lived opposite us used it to grow vegetables.

I was getting older. One day I found a grey hair; on another, I heard a recording of myself talking, and I realised I sounded just like my father.

I was working in London, doing A & R for one of the major record companies. I was commuting into London by train most days, coming back some evenings.

I had to keep a small flat in London; it's hard to commute when the bands you're checking out don't even stagger onto the stage until midnight. It also meant that it was fairly easy to get laid, if I wanted to, which I did.

I thought that Eleanora—that was my wife's name; I should have mentioned that before, I suppose—didn't know about the other women; but I got back from a two-week jaunt to New York one winter's day, and when I arrived at the house it was empty and cold.

She had left a letter, not a note. Fifteen pages, neatly typed, and every word of it was true. Including the PS, which read: *You really don't love me. And you never did.*

I put on a heavy coat, and I left the house and just walked, stunned and slightly numb.

There was no snow on the ground, but there was a hard frost, and the leaves crunched under my feet as I walked. The trees were skeletal black against the harsh grey winter sky.

I walked down the side of the road. Cars passed me, travelling to and from London. Once I tripped on a branch, half hidden in a heap of brown leaves, ripping my trousers, cutting my leg.

I reached the next village. There was a river at right angles to the road, and a path I'd never seen before beside it, and I walked down the path, and stared at the river, partly frozen. It gurgled and plashed and sang.

The path led off through fields; it was straight and grassy.

I found a rock, half buried, on one side of the path. I picked it up, brushed off the mud. It was a melted lump of purplish stuff, with a strange rainbow sheen to it. I put it into the pocket of my coat and held it in my hand as I walked, its presence warm and reassuring.

The river meandered away across the fields, and I walked on in silence.

I had walked for an hour before I saw houses—new, and small and square—on the embankment above me.

And then I saw the bridge, and I knew where I was: I was on the old railway path, and I'd been coming down it from the other direction.

There were graffiti painted on the side of the bridge: *Fuck* and *Barry Loves Susan* and the omnipresent *NF* of the National Front.

I stood beneath the bridge, in the red brick arch, stood among the ice cream wrappers, and the crisp packets and the single, sad, used condom, and watched my breath steam in the cold afternoon air.

The blood had dried into my trousers.

Cars passed over the bridge above me; I could hear a radio playing loudly in one of them.

"Hello?" I said, quietly, feeling embarrassed, feeling foolish. "Hello?"

There was no answer. The wind rustled the crisp packets and the leaves.

"I came back. I said I would. And I did. Hello?"

Silence.

I began to cry then, stupidly, silently, sobbing under the bridge.

A hand touched my face, and I looked up.

"I didn't think you'd come back," said the troll.

He was my height now, but otherwise unchanged. His long gonk hair was unkempt and had leaves in it, and his eyes were wide and lonely.

I shrugged, then wiped my face with the sleeve of my coat. "I came back."

Three kids passed above us on the bridge, shouting and running.

"I'm a troll," whispered the troll, in a small, scared voice. "Fol rol de ol rol."

He was trembling.

I held out my hand, and took his huge, clawed paw in mine. I smiled at him. "It's okay," I told him. "Honestly. It's okay."

The troll nodded.

He pushed me to the ground, onto the leaves and the wrappers and the condom, and lowered himself on top of me. Then he raised his head, and opened his mouth, and ate my life with his strong sharp teeth.

*   *   *

When he was finished, the troll stood up and brushed himself down. He put his hand into the pocket of his coat, and pulled out a bubbly, burnt lump of clinker rock.

He held it out to me.

"This is yours," said the troll.

I looked at him: wearing my life comfortably, easily, as if he'd been wearing it for years. I took the clinker from his hand, and sniffed it. I could smell the train from which it had fallen, so long ago. I gripped it tightly in my hairy hand.

"Thank you," I said.

"Good luck," said the troll.

"Yeah. Well. You too."

The troll grinned with my face.

It turned its back on me and began to walk back the way I had come, toward the village, back to the empty house I had left that morning; and it whistled as it walked.

I've been here ever since. Hiding. Waiting. Part of the bridge.

I watch from the shadows as the people pass: walking their dogs, or talking, or doing the things that people do. Sometimes people pause beneath my bridge, to stand, or piss, or make love. And I watch them, but say nothing; and they never see me.

Fol rol de ol rol.

I'm just going to stay here, in the darkness under the arch. I can hear you all out there, trip-trapping, trip-trapping over my bridge.

Oh yes, I can hear you.

But I'm not coming out.

✄ JAMES P(AUL) BLAYLOCK (1950–   )

As was Zenna Henderson before him, James P. Blaylock is a teacher. However, while Henderson was an instructor of children, Blaylock's instruction involves college- and university-level English courses. Much of Blaylock's expertise in literature is reflected in his fiction. He is a talented author of Dark Fantasy (sardonic and supernatural), High Fantasy, and scientific romance.

James P. Blaylock, like his good friend and contemporary Tim Powers, reflects and continues the literary traditions of Epic Fantasy (as in The Last Coin, *1988; and* The Paper Grail, *1991), Victorian and Edwardian literature (as in* The Homunculus, *1986), Henry James (as in* Night Relics, *1994; and* All the Bells on Earth, *1995), Jules Verne and H. G. Wells (as in* Lord Kelvin's Machine, *1992), Edgar Rice Burroughs (as in* The Digging Leviathan, *1984), J. R. R. Tolkien (as in* The Elfin Ship, *1982;* The Disappearing Dwarf, *1983; and* The Stone Giant, *1989), Ray Bradbury (as in* Land of Dreams, *1987), and others. Blaylock's stories are colorful and textured like those of A. Merritt and Clark Ashton Smith. At the same time, Blaylock's is an original voice.*

"Thirteen Phantasms" combines many of these elements and traditions, and it is like Jane Yolen's "The Malaysian Mer" in terms of its legitimate, poignant nostalgia. Like William Gibson's "The Gernsback Continuum" (1981), "Thirteen Phantasms" specifically features elements of history and nostalgia that relate to the formation of modern-day Fantasy and Science Fiction.

Thirteen Phantasms
(Omni Online, *October 1996*)

There was a small window in the attic, six panes facing the street, the wood frame unpainted and without moldings. Leafy wisteria vines grew over the glass outside, filtering the sunlight and tinting it green. The attic was dim despite the window, and the vines outside shook in the autumn wind, rustling against the clapboards of the old house and casting leafy shadows on the age-darkened beams and rafters. Landers set his portable telephone next to the crawl-space hatch and shined a flashlight across the underside of the shingles, illuminating dusty cobwebs and the skeleton frame of the roof. The air smelled of dust and wood, and the attic was lonesome with silence and moving shadows, a place sheltered from time and change.

A car rolled past out on the street, and Landers heard a train whistle in the distance. Somewhere across town, church bells tolled the hour, and there was the faint sound of freeway noise off to the east like the drone of a perpetual-motion engine. It was easy to imagine that the wisteria vines had tangled themselves around the window frame for some secretive purpose of their own, obscuring the glass with leaves, muffling the sounds of the world.

He reached down and switched the portable phone off, regretting that he'd brought it with him at all. It struck him suddenly as something incongruous, an artifact from an alien planet. For a passing moment he considered dropping it through the open hatch just to watch it slam to the floor of the kitchen hallway below.

Years ago old Mr. Cummings had set pine planks across the two-by-six ceiling joists to make a boardwalk beneath the roof beam, apparently with the idea of using the attic for storage, although it must have been a struggle to haul things up through the shoulder-width attic hatch. At the end of this boardwalk, against the north wall, lay four, dust-covered cardboard cartons—full of "junk magazines," or so Mrs. Cummings herself had told Landers this morning. The cartons were tied with twine, pulled tight and knotted, all the cartons the same. The word ASTOUNDING was written on the side with a felt marker in neat, draftsmanlike letters. Landers wryly wondered what sort of things Mr. Cummings might have considered astounding, and after a moment, he decided that the man had been fortunate to find enough of it in one lifetime to fill four good-sized boxes.

Landers himself had come up empty in that regard, at least lately. For years he'd had a picture in his mind of himself whistling a cheerful out-of-key tune, walking along a country road, his hands in his pockets and with no particular destination, sunlight streaming through the trees and the limitless afternoon stretching toward the horizon. Somehow that picture had lost its focus in the past year or so, and as with an old friend separated by time and distance, he had nearly given up on seeing it again.

It had occurred to him this morning that he hadn't brewed real coffee for nearly a year now. The coffee pot sat under the counter instead of on top of it, and was something he hauled out for guests. There was a frozen brick of ground coffee in the freezer, but he never bothered with it anymore. Janet had been opposed to freezing coffee at all. Freezing it, she said, killed the aromatic oils. It was better to buy it a half pound at a time, so that it was always fresh. Lately, though, most of the magic had gone out of the morning coffee; it didn't matter how fresh it was.

The Cummingses had owned the house since it was built in 1924, and Mrs. Cummings, ninety years old now, had held on for twenty years after her husband's death, letting the place run down, and then had rented it to Landers and moved into the Palmyra Apartments beyond the Plaza. Occasionally he still got mail intended for her, and it was easier simply to take it to her than to give it back to the post office. This morning she had told him about the boxes in the attic: "Just leave them there," she'd said. Then she had shown him her husband's old slide rule, slipping it out of its leather case and working the slide. She wasn't sure why she kept it, but she had kept a couple of old smoking pipes too, and a ring-shaped cut-crystal decanter with some whiskey still in it. Mrs. Cummings didn't have any use for the pipes or the decanter any more than she had a use for the slide rule, but Landers, who had himself kept almost nothing to remind him of his own past, understood that there was something about these souvenirs, sitting alongside a couple of old photographs on a small table, that recalled better days, easier living.

The arched window of the house on Rexroth Street in Glendale looked out onto a sloping front lawn with an overgrown carob tree at the curb, shading a dusty Land Rover with what looked like prospecting tools strapped to the rear bumper. There was a Hudson Wasp in the driveway, parked behind an Austin Healey. Across the street a man in shirtsleeves rubbed paste polish onto the fender of a Studebaker, and a woman in a sundress dug in a flower bed with a trowel, setting out pansies. A little boy rode a sort of sled on wheels up and down the sidewalk, and the sound of the solid-rubber wheels bumping over cracks sounded oddly loud in the still afternoon.

Russell Latzarel turned away from the window and took a cold bottle of beer from Roycroft Squires. In a few minutes the Newtonian Society would come to order, more or less, for the second time that day. Not that it made a lot of difference. For Latzarel's money they could recess until midnight if they wanted to, and the world would spin along through space for better or worse. He and Squires were both bachelors, and so unlike married men they had until hell froze over to come to order.

"India Pale Ale," Latzarel said approvingly, looking at the label on the squat green bottle. He gulped down an inch of beer. "Elixir of the gods, eh?" He set the bottle on a coaster. Then he filled his pipe with Balkan Sobranie tobacco and tamped it down, settling into an armchair in front of the chessboard, where there was a game laid out, half played. "Who's listed as guest of honor at West Coast Con? Edward tells me they're going to get Clifford Simak and van Vogt both."

"That's not what it says here in the newsletter," Squires told him, scrutinizing a printed pamphlet. "According to this it's TBA."

"To be announced," Latzarel said, then lit his pipe and puffed hard on it for a moment, his lips making little popping sounds. "Same son of a bitch as they advertised last time." He laughed out loud and then bent over to scan the titles of the chess books in the bookcase. He wasn't sure whether Squires read the damned things or whether he kept them there to gain some sort of psychological advantage, which he generally didn't need.

It was warm for November, and the casement windows along the west wall were wide open, the muslin curtains blowing inward on the breeze. Dust motes moved in the sunshine. The Newtonian Society had been meeting here every Saturday night since the war ended, and in that couple of years it had seldom broken up before two or three in the morning. Sometimes when there was a full house, all twelve of them would talk straight through until dawn and then go out after eggs and bacon, the thirty-nine-cent breakfast special down at Velma's Copper Pot on Western, although it wasn't often that the married men could get away with that kind of nonsense. Tonight they had scheduled a critical discussion of E. E. Smith's *Children of the Lens*, but it turned out that none of them liked the story much except Hastings, whose opinion was unreliable anyway, and so the meeting had lost all its substance after the first hour, and members had drifted away, into the kitchen and the library and out to the printing shed in the backyard, leaving Latzarel and Squires alone in the living room. Later on tonight, if the weather held up, they would be driving out to the observatory in Griffith Park.

There was a shuffling on the front walk, and Latzarel looked out in time to see the postman shut the mailbox and turn away, heading up the sidewalk. Squires went out through the front door and emptied the box, then came back in sorting letters. He took a puzzled second look at an envelope. "You're a stamp man," he said to Latzarel, handing it to him. "What do you make of that?"

Landers found that he could stand upright on the catwalk, although the roof sloped at such an angle that if he moved a couple of feet to either side, he had to duck to clear the roof rafters. He walked toward the boxes, but turned after a few steps to shine the light behind him, picking out his footprints in the otherwise-undisturbed dust. Beneath that dust, if a person could only brush away the successive years, lay Mr. Cummings's own footprints, coming and going along the wooden boards.

There was something almost wrong about opening the boxes at all, whatever they contained, like prying open a man's coffin. And somehow the neatly tied string suggested that their packing hadn't been temporary, that old Mr.

Cummings had put them away forever, perhaps when he knew he was at the end of things.

Astounding . . . ? Well, Landers would be the judge of that.

Taking out his pocket knife, he started to cut the string on one of the top boxes, then decided against it and untied it instead, afterward pulling back the flaps. Inside were neatly stacked magazines, dozens of issues of a magazine called *Astounding Science-Fiction*, apparently organized according to date. He picked one up off the top, December of 1947, and opened it carefully. It was well-preserved, the pulp paper yellowed around the outside of the pages, but not brittle. The cover painting depicted a robot with a head like an egg, holding a bent stick in his hand and looking mournfully at a wolf with a rabbit beside it, the world behind them apparently in flames. There were book ads at the back of the magazine, including one from something called the Squires Press: an edition of Clark Ashton Smith's *Thirteen Phantasms*, printed with hand-set type in three volumes on Winnebago Eggshell paper and limited to a hundred copies. "Remit one dollar in seven days," the ad said, "and one dollar monthly until six dollars is paid."

A dollar a month! This struck him as fantastic—stranger in its way, and even more wonderful, than the egg-headed robot on the front cover of the magazine. He sat down beside the boxes and leaned back against the wall so that the pages caught the sunlight through the window. He wished that he had brought along something to eat and drink instead of the worthless telephone. Settling in, he browsed through the contents page before starting in on the editorial, and then from there to the first of the several stories.

*   *   *

When the sunlight failed, Landers ran an extension cord into the attic and hooked up an old lamp in the rafters over the catwalk. Then he brought up a folding chair and a little smoking table to set a plate on. He would have liked something more comfortable, but there was no fitting an overstuffed chair up through the hatch. Near midnight he finished a story called "Rain Check" by Lewis Padgett, which featured a character named Tubby (apparently there had been a time when the world was happy with men named Tubby) and another character who drank highballs. . . .

He laid the book down and sat for a moment, listening to the rustling of leaves against the side of the house.

Highballs. What did people drink nowadays?—beer with all the color and flavor filtered out of it. Maybe that made a sad and frightening kind of sense. He looked at the back cover of the magazine, where perhaps coincidentally, there was an ad for Calvert whiskey: "Just be sure your highball is made with Calvert," the ad counseled. He wondered if there was any such thing anymore, whether anywhere within a twenty-mile radius someone was mixing up a highball out of Calvert whiskey. Hell, a *hundred* miles . . .

Rod's Liquor Store down on the Plaza was open late, and he was suddenly possessed with the idea of mixing himself a highball. He took the magazine with him when he climbed down out of the attic, and before he left the house, he filled out the order blank for the *Thirteen Phantasms* and slipped it into an envelope along with a dollar bill. It seemed right to him, like the highball, or like old Mrs. Cummings keeping the slide rule.

He wrote out Squires's Glendale address, put one of the new interim *G* stamps on the envelope, and slid it into the mail slot for the postman to pick up tomorrow morning.

The canceled stamp depicted an American flag with the words "Old Glory" over the top. "A *G* stamp?" Latzarel said out loud. "What is that, exactly?"

Squires shook his head. "Something new?"

"*Very* damned new, I'd say. Look here." He pointed at the flag on the stamp. "I can't quite . . . " He looked over the top of his glasses, squinting hard. "I count too many stars on this flag. Take a look."

He handed the envelope back to Squires, who peered at the stamp, then dug a magnifying glass out of the drawer of the little desk in front of the window. He peered at the stamp through the glass. "Fifty," he said. "It must be a fake."

"Post office canceled it, too." Latzarel frowned and shook his head. "What kind of sense does that make? Counterfeiting stamps and getting the flag obviously wrong? A man wouldn't give himself away like that, unless he was playing some kind of game."

"Here's something else," Squires said. "Look at the edge. There's no perforations. This is apparently cut out of a solid sheet." He slit the envelope open and unfolded the letter inside. It was an order for the Smith collection, from an address in the city of Orange.

There was a dollar bill included with the order.

Landers flipped through the first volume of the *Thirteen Phantasms*, which had arrived postage-due from Glendale. There were four stories in each volume. Somehow he had expected thirteen altogether, and the first thing that came into his mind was that there was a phantasm missing. He nearly laughed out loud. But then he was sobered by the obvious impossibility of the arrival of any phantasms at all. They had come enclosed in a cardboard carton that was wrapped in brown paper and sealed with tape. He looked closely at the tape, half surprised that it wasn't yellowed with age, that the package hadn't been in transit through the ether for half a century.

He sipped from his highball and reread a note that had come with the books, written out by a man named Russell Latzarel, president of a group calling itself the Newtonian Society—apparently Squires's crowd. In the note, Latzarel wondered if Landers was perpetrating a hoax.

A hoax . . . The note was dated 1947. "Who are you *really?*" it asked. "What is the meaning of the *G* stamp?" For a time he stared out of the window, watching the vines shift against the glass, listening to the wind under the eaves. The house settled, creaking in its joints. He looked at Latzarel's message again. "The dollar bill was a work of art," it read. On the back there was a hand-drawn map and an invitation to the next meeting of the Newtonians. He folded the map and tucked it into his coat pocket. Then he finished his highball and laughed out loud. Maybe it was the whiskey that made this seem monumentally funny. A hoax! He'd show them a hoax.

Almost at once he found something that would do. It was a plastic lapel pin the size of a fifty-cent piece, a hologram of an eyeball. It was only an eighth of an inch thick, but when he turned it in the light it seemed deep as a well. It was a good clear hologram too, the eyeball hovering in the void, utterly three-dimensional. The pin on the back had been glued on sloppily and at a screwball angle, and excess glue had run down the back of the plastic and dried. It was a technological marvel of the late twentieth century, and it was an absolute, and evident, piece of junk. He addressed an envelope, dropped the hologram inside, and slid it into the mail slot.

The trip out to Glendale took over an hour because of a traffic jam at the 605 junction and bumper-to-bumper cars on the Golden State. There was nothing apparently wrong—no accident, no freeway construction, just a million toiling automobiles stretching all the way to heaven-knew-where, to the moon. He had forgotten Latzarel's map, and he fought off a feeling of superstitious dread as the cars in front of him inched along. At Los Feliz he pulled off the freeway, cutting down the offramp at the last possible moment. There was a hamburger joint called Tommy's Little Oasis on Los Feliz, just east of San Fernando Road, that he and Janet used to hit when they were on their way north. That had been a few years back; he had nearly forgotten, but the freeway sign at Los Feliz had jogged his memory. It was a tiny Airstream trailer in the parking lot of a motel shaded by big elm trees. You went there if you wanted a hamburger. That was it. There was no menu except a sign on the wall, and even the sign was nearly pointless, since the only question was did you want cheese or not. Landers wanted cheese.

He slowed down as he passed San Fernando, looking for the motel, for the big overarching elms, recalling a rainy Saturday afternoon when they'd eaten their burgers in the car because it was raining too hard to sit under the steel umbrella at the picnic table out front. Now there was no picnic table, no Airstream trailer, no motel—nothing but a run-down industrial park. Somehow the industrial park had sprung up and fallen into disrepair in—what?—less than twenty years!

He U-turned and headed the opposite direction up San Fernando, turning right on Western. It was better not to think about it, about the pace of things, about the cheeseburgers of days gone by. . . .

Farther up Western, the houses along the street were run-down, probably rentals. There was trash in the street, broken bottles, newspapers soaked in gutter water. Suddenly he was a foreigner. He had wandered into a part of the country that was alien to him. And, unless his instincts had betrayed him, it was clearly alien to Squires Press and the Newtonian Society and men named Tubby. At one time the mix of Spanish-style and Tudor houses had been elegant. Now they needed paint and the lawns were up in weeds, and there was graffiti on fences and garage walls. Windows and doors were barred. He drove slowly, calculating addresses and thinking about turning around, getting back onto the freeway and heading south again, just fleeing home, ordering something else out of the magazines—personally autographed books by long-dead authors, "jar-proof" watches that could take a licking and go on ticking. He pictured the quiet shelter of his attic—his magazines, the makings of another highball. If ever a man needed a highball . . .

And just then he came upon the sign for Rexroth Street, so suddenly that he nearly drove right through the intersection. He braked abruptly, swinging around toward the west, and a car behind him honked its horn hard. He heard the driver shout something as the car flew past.

Landers started searching out addresses. The general tenor of the neighborhood hadn't improved at all, and he considered locking his doors. But then the idea struck him as superfluous, since he was about to park the car and get out anyway. He spotted the address on the curb, the paint faded and nearly unreadable.

The house had a turreted entry hall in front, with an arched window in the wall that faced the street. A couple of the windowpanes were broken and filled with aluminum foil, and what looked like an old bed sheet was strung across as a curtain. Weeds grew up through the cracked concrete of the front walk, and there was black iron debris, apparently car parts, scattered on the lawn.

He drifted to the curb, reaching for the ignition key, but then saw, crouched next to a motorcycle up at the top of the driveway, an immense man, tattooed and bearded and dressed in black jeans and a greasy T-shirt, holding a wrench and looking down the driveway at him. Landers instantly stepped on the gas, angling away from the curb and gunning toward the corner.

He knew what he needed to know. He could go home now. Whoever this man was, living in what must have been Squires's old house, he didn't have anything to do with the *Thirteen Phantasms*. He wasn't a Newtonian. There was no conceivable chance that Squires himself was somewhere inside, working the crank of his mechanical printing press, stamping out fantastic stories on Winnebago Eggshell paper. Squires was gone; that was the truth of it. The Newtonians were gone. The *world they'd inhabited*, with its twenty-five-cent pulp magazines and egg-headed robots and Martian canals, its highballs and hand-set type and slide rules, was gone too. Probably it was all at the bottom of the tar pits, turning into puzzling fossils.

Out beyond the front window, Rexroth Street was dark and empty of anything but the wind. To the south, the Hollywood Hills were a black wall of shadow, as if there were nothing there at all, just a vacancy. The sky above the dark line of the hills was so closely scattered with bright stars in the wind-scoured night that Latzarel might have been dreaming, and the broad wash of the Milky Way spanned the heavens like a lamp-lit road. From up the hall, he could hear Cummings talking on the telephone. Cummings would be talking to his wife about now, asking permission to stay out late. Squires had phoned Rhineholdt at the observatory, and they were due up on the hill in an hour, with just time enough to stop for a late-night burger at the Copper Kettle on the way.

Latzarel took the three-dimensional picture of the eyeball out of his coat pocket and turned it under the lamp in the window, marveling again at the eyeball that hung impossibly in the miniature void, in its little nonexistent cube of frozen space.

There was a sudden glow in the Western sky now—a meteor shower, hundreds of shooting stars, flaming up for a moment before vanishing beyond the darkness of the hills. Latzarel shouted for Squires and the others, and when they all ran into the room the stars were still falling, and the southern sky was like a veil of fireflies.

The totality of Landers's savings account hadn't been worth much at the coin shop. Gold standard bills weren't cheap. Probably he'd have been better off simply buying gold, but somehow the idea wasn't appealing. He wanted folding money in his wallet, just like any other pedestrian—something he could pay for lunch with, a burger and a Coke or a BLT and a slice of apple pie.

He glued the last of the foam-rubber blocks onto the inside top of the wooden crate on his living-room floor, then stood back and looked at the pile of stuff that was ready to go into the box. He'd had a thousand choices, an impossible number of choices. Everywhere he had turned in the house there was something else, some fabulous relic of the late twentieth century: throwaway wristwatches and dimmer switches, cassette tapes and portable telephones, pictorial histories and horse-race results, wallet-size calculators and pop-top cans, Ziploc baggies and Velcro fasteners, power screw guns and bubble paper, a laptop computer, software, a Styrofoam cup . . .

And then it had occurred to him that there was something about the tiniest articles that appealed to him even more than the obvious marvels. Just three trifling little wonders shifted backward in time, barely discernible in his coat pocket, might imply huge, baffling changes in the world: a single green-tinted contact lens, perhaps, and the battery out of a watch, and a hologram bird clipped out of a credit card. He wandered from room to room again, looking around. A felt-tipped pen? A nylon zipper? Something more subtle . . .

But of course if it were *too* subtle, it would be useless, wouldn't it? What was he really planning to *do* with these things? Try to convince a nearsighted man to shove the contact lens into his eye? Would the Newtonians pry the battery apart? To what end? What was inside? Probably black paste of some kind or a lump of dull metal—hardly worth the bother. And the hologram bird—it was like something out of a box of Cracker Jacks. Besides, the Newtonians had already gotten the eyeball, hadn't they? He couldn't do better than the eyeball.

Abruptly he abandoned his search, changing his thinking entirely. Hurrying into the study he pulled books out of the case, selecting and rejecting titles, waiting for something to appeal to him, something . . . He couldn't quite define it. He might as well take nearly any of them, or simply rip out a random copyright page. The daily papers? Better to take along a sack of rotten fruit.

He went out of the study and into the kitchen hallway where he climbed the attic ladder. Untying the last of the boxes, he sorted through the *Astoundings*, settling on March of 1956—ten years in the future, more or less, for the Newtonians. Unlike the rest of the issues, this one was beat up, as if it had been read to pieces, or carried around in someone's coat pocket. He scanned the contents page, noting happily that there was a Heinlein novel serialized in the volume, and he dug through the box again to find April of the same year in order to have all of the story—something called *Double Star*. The torn cover of the April issue showed an ermine-robed king of some kind inspecting a toy locomotive, his forehead furrowed with thought and wonder.

Satisfied at last, Landers hurried back down the ladder and into the living room again. To hell with the trash on the floor, the bubble paper and the screw gun. He would leave all the Buck Rogers litter right here in a pile. Packing that kind of thing into the box was like loading up the Trojan Horse, wasn't it? It was a betrayal. And for what? Show-off value? Wealth? Fame? It was all beside the point; he saw that clearly now. It was very nearly the antithesis of the point.

He slid the *Astoundings* into a niche inside the box along with the *Thirteen Phantasms*, an army-surplus flashlight, a wooden-handled screwdriver, and his sandwiches and bottled water. Then he picked up the portable telephone and made two calls, one to his next-door neighbor and one to Federal Express. His neighbor would unlock the door for the post office, who would haul the crate away on a handcart and truck it to Glendale.

The thought clobbered him suddenly. By what route? he wondered. Along what arcane boulevards would he travel?

He imagined the crate being opened by the man he had seen working on the motorcycle in the neglected driveway. What would Landers do? Threaten the man with the screwdriver? Offer him the antique money? Scramble out of the crate and simply walk away down the street without a backward glance, forever changing the man's understanding of human behavior?

He stopped his mind from running and climbed into the crate, pulling the lid on after him. Carefully and deliberately, he started to set the screws—his last task before lunch. It was silent in the box, and he sat listening for one last moment in the darkness, the attic sitting empty above him, still sheltered by its vines and wooden shingles. He imagined the world revolving, out beyond the walls of the old house, imagined the noise and movement, and he thought briefly of Mrs. Cummings across town, arranging and rearranging a leather-encased slide rule and a couple of old smoking pipes and photographs.

The Saturday meeting of the Newtonian society had come to order right on time. Phillip Mays, the lepidopterist, was home from the Amazon with a collection of insects that included an immense dragonfly commonly thought to have died out in the Carboniferous period, Squires's living-room floor was covered with display boxes and jars, and the room smelled of camphor and pipe smoke. There was the patter of soft rain through the open casements, but the weather was warm and easy despite the rain, and in the dim distance, out over the hills, there was the low rumble of thunder.

The doorbell rang, and Squires, expecting another Newtonian, opened the heavy front door in the turreted entry hall. A large wooden crate sat on the porch, sheltered by the awning, and a post-office truck motored away north toward Kenneth Road, disappearing beyond a mist of rain. Latzarel looked over Squires's shoulder at the heavy crate, trying to figure out what was wrong with it, what was odd about it. Something . . .

"I'll be damned," he said. "The top's screwed on from the inside."

"I'll get a pry bar," Hastings said from behind him.

Latzarel heard a sound then, and he put his ear to the side of the box. There was the click of a screwdriver on metal, the squeak of the screw turning. "Don't bother with the pry bar," Latzarel said, winking at Squires, and he lit a match and held it to his pipe, cupping his hand over the bowl to keep the raindrops from putting it out.

SECTION THREE
SCIENCE FICTION

Today, the concepts of undersea travel and exploration are quite conventional—familiar and predictable. This engraving, however, done for the original 1870 French edition of Jules Verne's *Twenty Thousand Leagues Under the Sea,* was quite inventive and exciting in its day. Note how accurately this illustration predicts the reality of later years.

JULES VERNE, HERBERT GEORGE WELLS, HUGO GERNSBACK, AND THE EARLY DAYS OF MODERN SCIENTIFICTION

LIKE MOST OF TODAY'S POPULAR LITERARY GENRES, SCIENCE Fiction has its origins in ancient mythology, specifically stories, narratives, and tales designed to offer explanations for issues of life and death, cosmology, and humanity's place in the universe. Like all "fictions," Science Fiction has a basis in a fantastic yet socially constructed reality. Depending on the enthusiast or scholar, the parameters of Science Fiction vary. Some, such as Hugo Gernsback (1884–1967), believe that true Science Fiction is grounded in scientific fact. Others have no problem claiming that abstract fantasies and speculations are also part of the genre.

Modern-day Science Fiction began in selected writings of Mary Wollstonecraft Shelley, Edgar Allan Poe, Jules Verne, H. G. Wells, and others. Authors, critics, and readers have long sought to concretely define the genre in terms of story content and story type. Some view Science Fiction as only that story form firmly based in extensions of established scientific fact. Others see Science Fiction as one of several subsets of Fantasy fiction. Still others envision Science Fiction and Fantasy as virtually synonymous. In fact, the similarities between and blending of genres make fiction meaningful. This was the case when Edward S. Ellis presented his novel *The Steam Man of the Prairies* (1865) to a dime novel audience that was nurtured almost exclusively on Westerns.

In these same dime novels later in the nineteenth century (specifically 1892–1898), a popular Science Fiction series was *The Frank Reade Library*. The Frank Reade stories combined traditions of the frontier and Western dime novels with technological innovations, such as steam power. Hence, in the adventures of Frank Reade and his pals, we find steam-driven inventions of all varieties, including mechanical men and similarly constructed mechanical horses.

Many of the story conventions developed in *The Frank Reade Library* became the basis for publisher Edward Stratemeyer's (1863–1930) young adult series, Tom Swift, which began in 1910 with *Tom Swift and His Motorcycle*. (Howard Garis, under the pseudonym Victor Appleton, was the initial writer of these Scientific Romances.) Three later Tom Swift series followed, and Tom Swift stories are in print to this day.

The American pulp magazine was born in 1896 when *Argosy* magazine converted to an all-fiction format. Pulps were the popular fiction print medium that roughly spanned the period between dime novels (which were published between the beginning of the Civil War [about 1860] and just after World War I [about 1920]) and paperback books (which began in the early years of World War II [about 1938]). While there were pulp magazines published during the latter years of the dime novel and well into the era of paperbacks, their "Golden Age" was from sometime between the mid-1910s and mid-1940s. Pulp magazines became the forum and popular medium for a wide, colorful range of popular literary genres, including Science Fiction. At the turn of the century, Science Fiction, in the form of Scientific Romances (by today's standards, rather wooden stories of two-dimensional scientists and rudimentary inventions—in the context of their day, however, these could be quite entertaining and exciting), appeared in *Argosy*.

Between 1911 and 1912, the same time period in which he introduced Tarzan of the Apes to the world, Edgar Rice Burroughs also presented John Carter of Mars. The John Carter series is an interesting and important blend of late-nineteenth-century Scientific Romance and early-twentieth-century Space Opera and of dime novel Westerns and pulp magazine Science Fiction. During their first incarnations, Burroughs's stories of Tarzan and John Carter appeared in the pages of *All-Story*, *Argosy*, and other pulps fortunate enough to purchase these stories from their author.

In 1923, when it premiered, *Weird Tales* provided another market for Science Fiction. While *Weird Tales* is primarily remembered for its range of Fantasy and Dark Fantasy offerings from 1923 to 1952, in its first years, the Chicago-based fiction magazine specialized in Science Fiction stories as much as, if not more than, other genres of popular fiction. Here, a young Edmond Hamilton helped to pioneer the Space Opera story (grand, overblown adventures in outer space that feature multiple characters and impending universe-threatening apocalypses). At the end of the twentieth century, we saw this story formula in *Star Trek* and *Star Wars*.

During the 1910s, Hugo Gernsback, a young Luxembourg immigrant, scientist, and entrepreneur, then living in New York, realized that he could sell his batteries and radios and related electronic equipment in catalogs and magazines that featured stories that speculated about future technologies and worlds based on the then-known sciences. Gernsback's early pulp magazines, such as the landmark *Amazing Stories* (begun in 1926), became the homes of reprints by established Science Fiction masters (such as Poe, Verne, and Wells) and the places that embraced new authors who wrote science-based fiction. In fact, after several manifestations and variations such as "Scientifiction," the term "Science Fiction" originated in the pages of Gernsback's early publications.

Hugo Gernsback was proud to showcase the work of medical doctors, military people, and scientists in his *Amazing Stories* magazine. But, as editor and publisher, Gernsback realized that his rigid parameters for stories of Scientifiction precluded some really fine Fantasy-based stories. Ultimately, Gernsback softened the requirements for stories included in *Amazing Stories*, and then published a range of other science- and/or Fantasy-based magazines. E. E. "Doc" Smith, Dr. David Keller, Dr. Miles Breuer, and others became household names. So did Edgar Rice Burroughs, Murray Leinster, Philip Francis Nowlan (creator of Buck Rogers in the pages of *Amazing*), Edmond Hamilton, John W. Campbell Jr., and a teenager named Jack Williamson. Williamson's first published story in *Amazing* was "The Metal Man" (December 1928); Professor Williamson writes novels and stories for the world's biggest publishers to this day. He is currently working on preserving the heritage of Science Fiction in archives in New Mexico.

In the 1930s, *Astounding Stories* magazine proved *Amazing*'s chief competitor. The most critically acclaimed Science Fiction magazine of all time, *Astounding* had former *Amazing Stories* Hard Science Fiction (technology- and realistic science–based Science Fiction) author John W. Campbell Jr. as its editor from 1937 until 1971. Like Gernsback, Campbell soon realized that he could not ignore the large market for Fantasy fiction. This fiction, as in the case of Gernsback's *Amazing*, did not fit the definition of *Astounding Stories*. Subsequently, John Campbell created *Unknown (Worlds)* as a Fantasy counterpart to *Astounding*. Both flourished. *Unknown* lasted from 1939 to 1943.

Between the 1930s and the demise of pulp magazines as a medium shortly after World War II (due at least in part to the arrival of paperback books and network television programming), there was a host of Science Fiction pulp magazines. Titles included *Thrilling Wonder Stories* (1936–55), *Fantastic Adventures* (1939–53), *Planet Stories* (1939–55), and *Startling Stories* (1939–55).

By the 1940s and 50s, some of these pulps changed to a smaller digest format, and a few, such as *Analog* (a renamed *Astounding*), are with us yet today. In 1949, *The Magazine of Fantasy and Science Fiction* debuted. This digest has served both Fantasy and Science Fiction markets and is successful to this day. Other "slick" magazines (so named because of their glossy paper stock), such as *Locus, Science Fiction Age*, and *Science Fiction Chronicle*, are also popular. *Amazing Stories* is now available in slick format, after being a digest magazine for several decades.

In the pages of the pulpwood magazines, newly emerging Science Fiction authors debuted, evolved, and flourished. It was these authors and their stories that ushered in the early days of paperback books circa 1938. Included in this talented group were E. E. "Doc" Smith, Edmond Hamilton, Robert Heinlein, Robert Bloch, Isaac Asimov, and Ray Bradbury. Women pulp writers were equally important to the medium and genre. Francis Stevens, Clare Winger Harris, C. L. Moore, M. E. Counselman, Leigh Brackett, and Margaret St. Clair were among the best in the field. Brackett, of course, was the author of the second Star Wars movie, *The Empire Strikes Back* (1981).

As the twentieth century unfolded, the array of exciting Science Fiction authors expanded. Soon authors such as Philip José Farmer, Theodore Sturgeon, Hal Clement, Judith Merril, Ursula K. Le Guin, Marion Zimmer Bradley, and Joanna Russ prospered.

Since the days of Mary Shelley, Edgar Allan Poe, Jules Verne, H. G. Wells, and Hugo Gernsback, Science Fiction has taken a variety of directions. It has always been closely tied to Fantasy and Dark Fantasy (Horror); it has also merged with Mystery and Detective Fiction. Science Fiction has featured subgenres and story formulas (i.e., story patterns), which include, but are not limited to, Space Opera, Heroic Fantasy, Hard Science Fiction (with an emphasis on scientific fact), Lost World stories, Alternate Universe stories, Cyberpunk, and more.

In the late 1960s, when the Western story in popular media such as television and motion pictures was becoming increasingly conventional and predictable, and when, in real life, the frontier had shifted from the great American West to outer space, the Science Fiction story arrived to replace the Western. Today, Science Fiction is continued by the old masters and has a promising future at the hands of talented new authors. Fandom and scholarship related to Science Fiction remain strong and vital.

Science Fiction has always been one of the most progressive literary genres. It has also been one of the most popular and best selling, transcending all the popular print and nonprint media of the last two hundred years. Science Fiction, at its best, encourages imagination and reflection. It celebrates ethnicity and gender equality. No writing aspires to higher thinking, yet none is more democratic and open in terms of its embrace of readers and writers. Ray Bradbury reminds us that some Science Fiction, such as George Orwell's *1984* (1949) and Bradbury's own *Fahrenheit 451* (1953), is designed to prevent possible futures, not necessarily predict them.

⬛ FITZ-JAMES O'BRIEN (1828–1862)

Fitz-James O'Brien came to the United States from Ireland in 1852. He died less than ten years later from infection of a wound he received fighting for the Union Army in the Civil War. During his short lifetime, and even shorter stay in the United States, O'Brien produced landmark, and sometimes archetypal, stories.

Influenced by the German E. T. A. Hoffman and the Americans Edgar Allan Poe and Nathaniel Hawthorne, among others, O'Brien was highly talented, imaginative, and versatile. He also inspired other noteworthy authors and stories that followed him. In fact, O'Brien's "What Was It? A Mystery" (Harper's New Monthly Magazine, *March 1859) was directly imitated in Guy de Maupassant's "The Horla" and Ambrose Bierce's "The Damned Thing." O'Brien and Bierce had more than this story line in common. Both were veterans of the Civil War, both were newspaper writers, and both contributed mightily to the popularity and legitimacy of Fantasy and Science Fiction in the second half of the nineteenth century.*

Fitz-James O'Brien's Science Fiction has inspired other writers. For example, the devil dolls of O'Brien's "The Wondersmith" (The Atlantic Monthly, *October 1859) have been widely imitated. This story profoundly influenced A. Merritt's* Burn Witch Burn *(1933), Fredric Brown's "The Geezenstacks" (1954), the* Twilight Zone *television episode starring Agnes Moorhead and written by Richard Matheson, "The Invaders" (January 27, 1961), and others.*

"The Diamond Lens" may be even more imitated.

The Diamond Lens
(Atlantic Monthly, *January 1858*)

I

The Bending of the Twig

From a very early period of my life the entire bent of my inclinations had been towards microscopic investigations. When I was not more than ten years old, a distant relative of our family, hoping to astonish my inexperience, constructed a simple microscope for me, by drilling in a disk of copper a small hole, in which a drop of pure water was sustained by capillary attraction. This very primitive apparatus, magnifying some fifty diameters, presented, it is true, only indistinct and imperfect forms, but still sufficiently wonderful to work up my imagination to a preternatural state of excitement.

Seeing me so interested in this rude instrument, my cousin explained to me all that he knew about the principles of the microscope, related to me a few of the wonders which had been accomplished through its agency, and ended by promising to send me one regularly constructed, immediately on his return to the city. I counted the days, the hours, the minutes, that intervened between that promise and his departure.

Meantime I was not idle. Every transparent substance that bore the remotest resemblance to a lens I eagerly seized upon, and employed in vain attempts to realize that instrument, the theory of whose construction I as yet only vaguely comprehended. All panes of glass containing those oblate spheroidal knots familiarly known as "bull's eyes" were ruthlessly destroyed, in the hope of obtaining lenses of marvellous power. I even went so far as to extract the crystalline humor from the eyes of fishes and animals, and endeavored to press it into the microscopic service. I plead guilty to having stolen the glasses from my Aunt Agatha's spectacles, with a dim idea of grinding them into lenses of wondrous magnifying properties,—in which attempt it is scarcely necessary to say that I totally failed.

At last the promised instrument came. It was of that order known as Field's simple microscope, and had cost perhaps about fifteen dollars. As far as educational purposes went, a better apparatus could not have been selected. Accompanying it was a small treatise on the microscope,—its history, uses, and discoveries. I comprehended then for the first time the "Arabian Nights Entertainments." The dull veil of ordinary existence that hung across the world seemed suddenly to roll away, and to lay bare a land of enchantments. I felt towards my companions as the seer might feel towards the ordinary masses of men. I held conversations with Nature in a tongue which they could not understand. I was in daily communication with living wonders, such as they never imagined in their wildest visions. I penetrated beyond the external portal of things, and roamed through the sanctuaries. Where they beheld only a drop of rain slowly rolling down the window-glass, I saw a universe of beings animated with all the passions common to physical life, and convulsing their minute sphere with struggles as fierce and protracted as those of men. In the common spots of mould, which my mother, good housekeeper that she was, fiercely scooped away from her jam pots, there abode for me, under the name of mildew, enchanted gardens, filled with dells and avenues of the densest foliage and most astonishing verdure, while from the fantastic boughs of these microscopic forests hung strange fruits glittering with green, and silver, and gold.

It was no scientific thirst that at this time filled my mind. It was the pure enjoyment of a poet to whom a world of wonders has been disclosed. I talked of my solitary pleasures to none. Alone with my microscope, I dimmed my sight, day after day and night after night, poring over the marvels which it unfolded to me. I was like one who, having discovered the ancient Eden still existing in all its primitive glory, should resolve to enjoy it in solitude, and never betray to mortal the secret of its locality. The rod of my life was bent at this moment. I destined myself to be a microscopist.

Of course, like every novice, I fancied myself a discoverer. I was ignorant at the time of the thousands of acute intellects engaged in the same pursuit as myself, and with the advantage of instruments a thousand times more powerful than mine. The names of Leeuwenhoek, Williamson, Spencer, Ehrenberg, Schultz, Dujardin, Schact, and Schleiden were then entirely unknown to me, or if known, I was ignorant of their patient and wonderful researches. In every fresh specimen of cryptogamia which I placed beneath my instrument I believed that I discovered wonders of which the world was as yet ignorant. I remember well the thrill of delight and admiration that shot through me the first time that I discovered the common wheel animalcule (*Rotifera vulgaris*) expanding and contracting its flexible spokes, and seemingly rotating through the water. Alas! as I grew older, and obtained some works treating of my favorite study, I found that I was only on the threshold of a science to the investigation of which some of the greatest men of the age were devoting their lives and intellects.

As I grew up, my parents, who saw but little likelihood of anything practical resulting from the examination of bits of moss and drops of water through a brass tube and a piece of glass, were anxious that I should choose a profession. It was their desire that I should enter the counting-house of my uncle, Ethan Blake, a prosperous merchant, who carried on business in New York. This suggestion I decisively combated. I had no taste for trade; I should only make a failure; in short, I refused to become a merchant.

But it was necessary for me to select some pursuit. My parents were staid New England people, who insisted on the necessity of labor; and therefore, although, thanks to the bequest of my poor Aunt Agatha, I should, on coming of age, inherit a small fortune sufficient to place me above want, it was decided that, instead of waiting for this, I should act the nobler part, and employ the intervening years in rendering myself independent.

After much cogitation I complied with the wishes of my family, and selected a profession. I determined to study medicine at the New York Academy. This disposition of my future suited me. A removal from my relatives would enable me to dispose of my time as I pleased without fear of detection. As long as I paid my Academy fees, I might shirk attending the lectures if I chose; and, as I never had the remotest intention of standing an examination, there was no danger of my being "plucked." Besides, a metropolis was the place for me. There I could obtain excellent instruments, the newest publications, intimacy with men of pursuits kindred with my own,—in short, all things necessary to insure a profitable devotion of my life to my beloved science. I had an abundance of money, few desires that were not bounded by my illuminating mirror on one side and my object-glass on the other; what, therefore, was to prevent my becoming an illustrious investigator of the veiled worlds? It was with the most buoyant hopes that I left my New England home and established myself in New York.

II

The Longing of a Man of Science

My first step, of course, was to find suitable apartments. These I obtained, after a couple of days' search, in Fourth Avenue; a very pretty second-floor unfurnished, containing sitting-room, bedroom, and a smaller apartment which I intended to fit up as a laboratory. I furnished my lodgings simply, but rather elegantly, and then devoted all my energies to the adornment of the temple of my worship. I visited Pike, the celebrated optician, and passed in review his splendid collection of microscopes,—Field's Compound, Hingham's, Spencer's, Nachet's Binocular (that founded on the principles of the stereoscope), and at length fixed upon that form known as Spencer's Trunnion Microscope, as combining the greatest number of improvements with an almost perfect freedom from tremor. Along with this I purchased every possible accessory,—draw-tubes, micrometers, a *camera-lucida*, lever-stage, achromatic condensers, white cloud illuminators, prisms, parabolic condensers, polarizing apparatus, forceps, aquatic boxes, fishing-tubes, with a host of other articles, all of which would have been useful in the hands of an experienced microscopist, but, as I afterwards discovered, were not of the slightest present value to me. It takes years of practice to know how to use a complicated microscope. The optician looked suspiciously at me as I made these wholesale purchases. He evidently was uncertain whether to set me down as some scientific celebrity or a madman. I think he inclined to the latter belief. I suppose I was mad. Every great genius is mad upon the subject in which he is greatest. The unsuccessful madman is disgraced and called a lunatic.

Mad or not, I set myself to work with a zeal which few scientific students have ever equalled. I had everything to learn relative to the delicate study upon which I had embarked,—a study involving the most earnest patience, the most rigid analytic powers, the steadiest hand, the most untiring eye, the most refined and subtle manipulation.

For a long time half my apparatus lay inactively on the shelves of my laboratory, which was now most amply furnished with every possible contrivance for facilitating my investigations. The fact was that I did not know how to use some of my scientific accessories,—never having been taught microscopics,—and those whose use I understood theoretically were of little avail, until by practice I could attain the necessary delicacy of handling. Still, such was the fury of my ambition, such the untiring perseverance of my experiments, that, difficult of credit as it may be, in the course of one year I became theoretically and practically an accomplished microscopist.

During this period of my labors, in which I submitted specimens of every substance that came under my observation to the action of my lenses, I became a discoverer,—in a small way, it is true, for I was very young, but still a discoverer. It was I who destroyed Ehrenberg's theory that the *Volvox globator* was an animal, and proved that his "monads" with stomachs and eyes were merely phases of the formation of a vegetable cell, and were, when they reached their mature state, incapable of the act of conjugation, or any true generative act, without which no organism rising to any stage of life higher than vegetable can be said to be complete. It was I who resolved the singular problem of rotation in the cells and hairs of plants into ciliary attraction, in spite of the assertions of Mr. Wenham and others, that my explanation was the result of an optical illusion.

But notwithstanding these discoveries, laboriously and painfully made as they were, I felt horribly dissatisfied. At every step I found myself stopped by the imperfections of my instruments. Like all active microscopists, I gave my imagination full play. Indeed, it is a common complaint against many such, that they supply the defects of their instruments with the creations of their brains. I imagined depths beyond depths in Nature which the limited power of my lenses prohibited me from exploring. I lay awake at night constructing imaginary microscopes of immeasurable power, with which I seemed to pierce through all the envelopes of matter down to its original atom. How I cursed those imperfect mediums which necessity through ignorance compelled me to use! How I longed to discover the secret of some perfect lens, whose magnifying power should be limited only by the resolvability of the object, and which at the same time should be free from spherical and chromatic aberrations, in short from all the obstacles over which the poor microscopist finds himself continually stumbling! I felt convinced that the simple microscope, composed of a single lens of such vast yet perfect power was possible of construction. To attempt to bring the compound microscope up to such a pitch would have been commencing at the wrong end; this latter being simply a partially successful endeavor to remedy those very defects of the simple instrument, which, if conquered, would leave nothing to be desired.

It was in this mood of mind that I became a constructive microscopist. After another year passed in this new pursuit, experimenting on every imaginable substance,—glass, gems, flints, crystals, artificial crystals formed of the alloy of various vitreous materials,—in short, having constructed as many varieties of lenses as Argus had eyes, I found myself precisely where I started, with nothing gained save an extensive knowledge of glass-making. I was almost dead with despair. My parents were surprised at my apparent want of progress in my medical studies, (I had not attended one lecture since my arrival in the city,) and the expenses of my mad pursuit had been so great as to embarrass me very seriously.

I was in this frame of mind one day, experimenting in my laboratory on a small diamond,—that stone, from its great refracting power, having always occupied my attention more than any other,—when a young Frenchman, who lived on the floor above me, and who was in the habit of occasionally visiting me, entered the room.

I think that Jules Simon was a Jew. He had many traits of the Hebrew character: a love of jewelry, of dress, and of good living. There was something mysterious about him. He always had something to sell, and yet went into excellent society. When I say sell, I should perhaps have said peddle; for his operations were generally confined to the disposal of single articles,—a picture, for instance, or a rare carving in ivory, or a pair of duelling-pistols, or the dress of a Mexican *caballero*. When I was first furnishing my rooms, he paid me a visit, which ended in my purchasing an antique silver lamp, which he assured me was a Cellini,—it was handsome enough even for that,—and some other knickknacks for my sitting-room. Why Simon should pursue this petty trade I never could imagine. He apparently had plenty of money, and had the *entrée* of the best houses in the city,—taking care, however, I suppose, to drive no bargains within the enchanted circle of the Upper Ten. I came at length to the conclusion that this peddling was but a mask to cover some greater object, and even went so far as to believe my young acquaintance to be implicated in the slave-trade. That, however, was none of my affair.

On the present occasion, Simon entered my room in a state of considerable excitement.

"*Ah! mon ami!*" he cried, before I could even offer him the ordinary salutation, "it has occurred to me to be the witness of the most astonishing things in the world. I promenade myself to the house of Madame——How does the little animal—*le renard*—name himself in the Latin?"

"Vulpes," I answered.

"Ah! yes,—Vulpes. I promenade myself to the house of Madame Vulpes."

"The spirit medium?"

"Yes, the great medium. Great Heavens! what a woman! I write on a slip of paper many of questions concerning affairs the most secret,—affairs that conceal themselves in the abysses of my heart the most profound; and behold! by example! what occurs? This devil of a woman makes me replies the most truthful to all of them. She talks to me of things that I do not love to talk of to myself. What am I to think? I am fixed to the earth!"

"Am I to understand you, M. Simon, that this Mrs. Vulpes replied to questions secretly written by you, which questions related to events known only to yourself?"

"Ah! more than that, more than that," he answered, with an air of some alarm. "She related to me things— But," he added, after a pause, and suddenly changing his manner, "why occupy ourselves with these follies? It was all the biology, without doubt. It goes without saying that it has not my credence.—But why are we here, *mon ami?* It has occurred to me to discover the most beautiful thing as you can imagine,—a vase with green lizards on it, composed by the great Bernard Palissy. It is in my apartment; let us mount. I go to show it to you."

I followed Simon mechanically; but my thoughts were far from Palissy and his enamelled ware, although I, like him, was seeking in the dark after a great discovery. This casual mention of the spiritualist, Madame Vulpes, set me on a new track. What if this spiritualism should be really a great fact? What if, through communication with subtiler organisms than my own, I could reach at a single bound the goal, which perhaps a life of agonizing mental toil would never enable me to attain?

While purchasing the Palissy vase from my friend Simon, I was mentally arranging a visit to Madame Vulpes.

III

The Spirit of Leeuwenhoek

Two evenings after this, thanks to an arrangement by letter and the promise of an ample fee, I found Madame Vulpes awaiting me at her residence alone. She was a coarse-featured woman, with a keen and rather cruel dark eye, and an exceedingly sensual expression about her mouth and under jaw. She received me in perfect silence, in an apartment on the ground floor, very sparely furnished. In the centre of the room, close to where Mrs. Vulpes sat, there was a common round mahogany table. If I had come for the purpose of sweeping her chimney, the woman could not have looked more indifferent to my appearance. There was no attempt to inspire the visitor with any awe. Everything bore a simple and practical aspect. This intercourse with the spiritual world was evidently as familiar an occupation with Mrs. Vulpes as eating her dinner or riding in an omnibus.

"You come for a communication, Mr. Linley?" said the medium, in a dry, business-like tone of voice.

"By appointment,—yes."

"What sort of communication do you want?—a written one?"

"Yes,—I wish for a written one."

"From any particular spirit?"

"Yes."

"Have you ever known this spirit on this earth?"

"Never. He died long before I was born. I wish merely to obtain from him some information which he ought to be able to give better than any other."

"Will you seat yourself at the table, Mr. Linley," said the medium, "and place your hands upon it?"

I obeyed,—Mrs. Vulpes being seated opposite me, with her hands also on the table. We remained thus for about a minute and a half, when a violent succession of raps came on the table, on the back of my chair, on the floor immediately under my feet, and even on the windowpanes. Mrs Vulpes smiled composedly.

"They are very strong to-night," she remarked. "You are fortunate." She then continued, "Will the spirits communicate with this gentleman?"

Vigorous affirmative.

"Will the particular spirit he desires to speak with communicate?"

A very confused rapping followed this question.

"I know what they mean," said Mrs. Vulpes, addressing herself to me; "they wish you to write down the name of the particular spirit that you desire to converse with. Is that so?" she added, speaking to her invisible guests.

That it was so was evident from the numerous affirmatory responses. While this was going on, I tore a slip from my pocket-book, and scribbled a name, under the table.

"Will this spirit communicate in writing with this gentleman?" asked the medium once more.

After a moment's pause, her hand seemed to be seized with a violent tremor, shaking so forcibly that the table vibrated. She said that a spirit had seized her hand and would write. I handed her some sheets of paper that were on the table, and a pencil. The latter she held loosely in her hand, which presently began to move over the paper with a singular and seemingly involuntary motion. After a few moments had elapsed, she handed me the paper, on which I found written, in a large, uncultivated hand, the words, "He is not here, but has been sent for." A pause of a minute or so now ensued, during which Mrs. Vulpes remained perfectly silent, but the raps continued at regular intervals. When the short period I mention had elapsed, the hand of the medium was again seized with its convulsive tremor, and she wrote, under this strange influence, a few words on the paper, which she handed to me. They were as follows:—

"I am here. Question me.

"LEEUWENHOEK."

I was astounded. The name was identical with that I had written beneath the table, and carefully kept concealed. Neither was it at all probable that an uncultivated woman like Mrs. Vulpes should know even the name of the great father of microscopics. It may have been biology; but this theory was soon doomed to be destroyed. I wrote on my slip—still concealing it from Mrs. Vulpes—a series of questions, which, to avoid tediousness, I shall place with the responses, in the order in which they occurred.

I.—Can the microscope be brought to perfection?
SPIRIT.—Yes.
I.—Am I destined to accomplish this great task?
SPIRIT.—You are.
I.—I wish to know how to proceed to attain this end. For the love which you bear to science, help me!
SPIRIT.—A diamond of one hundred and forty carats, submitted to electro-magnetic currents for a long period, will experience a rearrangement of its atoms *inter se*, and from that stone you will form the universal lens.
I.—Will great discoveries result from the use of such a lens?
SPIRIT.—So great that all that has gone before is as nothing.
I.—But the refractive power of the diamond is so immense, that the image will be formed within the lens. How is that difficulty to be surmounted?
SPIRIT.—Pierce the lens through its axis, and the difficulty is obviated. The image will be formed in the pierced space, which will itself serve as a tube to look through. Now I am called. Good night.

I cannot at all describe the effect that these extraordinary communications had upon me. I felt completely bewildered. No biological theory could account for the *discovery* of the lens. The medium might, by means of biological *rapport* with my mind, have gone so far as to read my questions, and reply to them coherently. But biology could not enable her to discover that magnetic currents would so alter the crystals of the diamond as to remedy its previous defects, and admit of its being polished into a perfect lens. Some such theory may have passed through my head, it is true; but if so, I had forgotten it. In my excited condition of mind there was no course left but to become a convert, and it was in a state of the most painful nervous exaltation that I left the medium's house that evening. She accompanied me to the door, hoping that I was satisfied. The raps followed us as we went through the hall, sounding on the balusters, the flooring, and even the lintels of the door. I hastily expressed my satisfaction, and escaped hurriedly into the cool night air. I walked home with but one thought possessing me,—how to obtain a diamond of the immense size required. My entire means multiplied a hundred times over would have been inadequate to its purchase. Besides, such stones are rare, and become historical. I could find such only in the regalia of Eastern or European monarchs.

IV

The Eye of Morning

There was a light in Simon's room as I entered my house. A vague impulse urged me to visit him. As I opened the door of his sitting-room unannounced, he was bending, with his back toward me, over a carcel lamp, apparently engaged in minutely examining some object which he held in his hands. As I entered, he started suddenly, thrust his hand into his breast pocket, and turned to me with a face crimson with confusion.

"What!" I cried, "poring over the miniature of some fair lady? Well, don't blush so much; I won't ask to see it."

Simon laughed awkwardly enough, but made none of the negative protestations usual on such occasions. He asked me to take a seat.

"Simon," said I, "I have just come from Madame Vulpes."

This time Simon turned as white as a sheet, and seemed stupefied, as if a sudden electric shock had smitten him. He babbled some incoherent words, and went hastily to a small closet where he usually kept his liquors. Although astonished at his emotion, I was too preoccupied with my own idea to pay much attention to anything else.

"You say truly when you call Madame Vulpes a devil of a woman," I continued. "Simon, she told me wonderful things to-night, or rather was the means of telling me wonderful things. Ah! if I could only get a diamond that weighed one hundred and forty carats!"

Scarcely had the sigh with which I uttered this desire died upon my lips, when Simon, with the aspect of a wild beast, glared at me savagely, and, rushing to the mantelpiece, where some foreign weapons hung on the wall, caught up a Malay creese, and brandished it furiously before him.

"No!" he cried in French, into which he always broke when excited. "No! you shall not have it! You are perfidious! You have consulted with that demon, and desire my treasure! But I will die first! Me! I am brave! You cannot make me fear!"

All this, uttered in a loud voice trembling with excitement, astounded me. I saw at a glance that I had accidentally trodden upon the edges of Simon's secret, whatever it was. It was necessary to reassure him.

"My dear Simon," I said, "I am entirely at a loss to know what you mean. I went to Madame Vulpes to consult with her on a scientific problem, to the solution of which I discovered that a diamond of the size I just mentioned was necessary. You were never alluded to during the evening, nor, so far as I was concerned, even thought of. What can be the meaning of this outburst? If you happen to have a set of valuable diamonds in your possession, you need fear nothing from me.

The diamond which I require you could not possess; or, if you did possess it, you would not be living here."

Something in my tone must have completely reassured him; for his expression immediately changed to a sort of constrained merriment, combined, however, with a certain suspicious attention to my movements. He laughed, and said that I must bear with him; that he was at certain moments subject to a species of vertigo, which betrayed itself in incoherent speeches, and that the attacks passed off as rapidly as they came. He put his weapon aside while making this explanation, and endeavored, with some success, to assume a more cheerful air.

All this did not impose on me in the least. I was too much accustomed to analytical labors to be baffled by so flimsy a veil. I determined to probe the mystery to the bottom.

"Simon," I said, gayly, "let us forget all this over a bottle of Burgundy. I have a case of Lausseure's *Clos Vougeot* down-stairs, fragrant with the odors and ruddy with the sunlight of the Côte d'Or. Let us have up a couple of bottles. What say you?"

"With all my heart," answered Simon, smilingly.

I produced the wine and we seated ourselves to drink. It was of a famous vintage, that of 1848, a year when war and wine throve together,—and its pure but powerful juice seemed to impart renewed vitality to the system. By the time we had half finished the second bottle, Simon's head, which I knew was a weak one, had begun to yield, while I remained calm as ever, only that every draught seemed to send a flush of vigor through my limbs. Simon's utterance became more and more indistinct. He took to singing French *chansons* of a not very moral tendency. I rose suddenly from the table just at the conclusion of one of those incoherent verses, and, fixing my eyes on him with a quiet smile, said: "Simon, I have deceived you. I learned your secret this evening. You may as well be frank with me. Mrs. Vulpes, or rather one of her spirits, told me all."

He started with horror. His intoxication seemed for the moment to fade away, and he made a movement towards the weapon that he had a short time before laid down. I stopped him with my hand.

"Monster!" he cried, passionately, "I am ruined! What shall I do? You shall never have it! I swear by my mother!"

"I don't want it," I said; "rest secure, but be frank with me. Tell me all about it."

The drunkenness began to return. He protested with maudlin earnestness that I was entirely mistaken,—that I was intoxicated; then asked me to swear eternal secrecy, and promised to disclose the mystery to me. I pledged myself, of course, to all. With an uneasy look in his eyes, and hands unsteady with drink and nervousness, he drew a small case from his breast and opened it. Heavens! How the mild lamp-light was shivered into a thousand prismatic arrows, as it fell upon a vast rose-diamond that glittered in the case! I was no judge of diamonds, but I saw at a glance that this was a gem of rare size and purity. I looked at Simon with wonder, and—must I confess it?—with envy. How could he have obtained this treasure? In reply to my questions, I could just gather from his drunken statements (of which, I fancy, half the incoherence was affected) that he had been superintending a gang of slaves engaged in diamond-washing in Brazil; that he had seen one of them secrete a diamond, but, instead of informing his employers, had quietly watched the negro until he saw him bury his treasure; that he had dug it up and fled with it, but that as yet he was afraid to attempt to dispose of it publicly,—so valuable a gem being almost certain to attract too much attention to its owner's antecedents,—and he had not been able to discover any of those obscure channels by which such matters are conveyed away safely. He added, that, in accordance with the oriental practice, he had named his diamond by the fanciful title of "The Eye of Morning."

While Simon was relating this to me, I regarded the great diamond attentively. Never had I beheld anything so beautiful. All the glories of light, ever imagined or described, seemed to pulsate in its crystalline chambers. Its weight, as I learned from Simon, was exactly one hundred and forty carats. Here was an amazing coincidence. The hand of Destiny seemed in it. On the very evening when the spirit of Leeuwenhoek communicates to me the great secret of the microscope, the priceless means which he directs me to employ start up within my easy reach! I determined, with the most perfect deliberation, to possess myself of Simon's diamond.

I sat opposite to him while he nodded over his glass, and calmly revolved the whole affair. I did not for an instant contemplate so foolish an act as a common theft, which would of course be discovered, or at least necessitate flight and concealment, all of which must interfere with my scientific plans. There was but one step to be taken,—to kill Simon. After all, what was the life of a little peddling Jew, in comparison with the interests of science? Human beings are taken every day from the condemned prisons to be experimented on by surgeons. This man, Simon, was by his own confession a criminal, a robber, and I believed on my soul a murderer. He deserved death quite as much as any felon condemned by the laws; why should I not, like government, contrive that his punishment should contribute to the progress of human knowledge?

The means for accomplishing everything I desired lay within my reach. There stood upon the mantel-piece a bottle half full of French laudanum. Simon was so occupied with his diamond, which I had just restored to him, that it was an affair of no difficulty to drug his glass. In a quarter of an hour he was in a profound sleep.

I now opened his waistcoat, took the diamond from the inner pocket in which he had placed it, and removed him to the bed, on which I laid him so that his feet hung down over the edge. I had possessed myself of the Malay creese, which I held in my right hand, while with the other I discovered as accurately as I could by pulsation the exact locality of the heart. It was essential that all the aspects of his death should lead to the surmise of self-murder. I calculated the exact angle at which it was probable that the weapon, if levelled by Simon's own hand, would enter his breast; then with one powerful blow I thrust it up to the hilt in the very spot which I desired to penetrate. A convulsive thrill ran through Simon's limbs. I heard a smothered sound issue from his throat, precisely like the bursting of a large air-bubble, sent up by a diver, when it reaches the surface of the water; he turned half round on his side, and, as if to assist my plans more effectually, his right hand, moved by some mere spasmodic impulse, clasped the handle of the creese, which it remained holding with extraordinary muscular tenacity. Beyond this there was no apparent struggle. The laudanum, I presume, paralyzed the usual nervous action. He must have died instantaneously.

There was yet something to be done. To make it certain that all suspicion of the act should be diverted from any inhabitant of the house to Simon himself, it was necessary that the door should be found in the morning *locked on the inside*. How to do this, and afterwards escape myself? Not by the window; that was a physical impossibility. Besides, I was determined that the windows *also* should be found bolted. The solution was simple enough. I descended softly to my own room for a peculiar instrument which I had used for holding small slippery substances, such as minute spheres of glass, etc. This instrument was nothing more than a long slender hand-vice, with a very powerful grip, and a considerable leverage, which last was accidentally owing to the shape of the handle. Nothing was simpler than, when the key was in the lock, to seize the end of its stem in this vice, through the keyhole, from the outside, and so lock the door. Previously, however, to doing this, I burned a number of papers on Simon's hearth. Suicides almost always burn papers before they destroy themselves. I also emptied some more laudanum into Simon's glass, — having first removed from it all traces of wine, — cleaned the other wine-glass, and brought the bottles away with me. If traces of two persons drinking had been found in the room, the question naturally would have arisen, Who was the second? Besides, the wine-bottles might have been identified as belonging to me. The laudanum I poured out to account for its presence in his stomach, in case of a *post-mortem* examination. The theory naturally would be, that he first intended to poison himself, but, after swallowing a little of the drug, was either disgusted with its taste, or changed his mind from other motives, and chose the dagger. These arrangements made, I walked out, leaving the gas burning, locked the door with my vice, and went to bed.

Simon's death was not discovered until nearly three in the afternoon. The servant, astonished at seeing the gas burning, — the light streaming on the dark landing from under the door, — peeped through the keyhole and saw Simon on the bed. She gave the alarm. The door was burst open, and the neighborhood was in a fever of excitement.

Every one in the house was arrested, myself included. There was an inquest; but no clew to his death beyond that of suicide could be obtained. Curiously enough, he had made several speeches to his friends the preceding week, that seemed to point to self-destruction. One gentleman swore that Simon had said in his presence that "he was tired of life." His landlord affirmed that Simon, when paying him his last month's rent, remarked that "he would not pay him rent much longer." All the other evidence corresponded, — the door locked inside, the position of the corpse, the burnt papers. As I anticipated, no one knew of the possession of the diamond by Simon, so that no motive was suggested for his murder. The jury, after a prolonged examination, brought in the usual verdict, and the neighborhood once more settled down into its accustomed quiet.

V

Animula

The three months succeeding Simon's catastrophe I devoted night and day to my diamond lens. I had constructed a vast galvanic battery, composed of nearly two thousand pairs of plates, — a higher power I dared not use, lest the diamond should be calcined. By means of this enormous engine I was enabled to send a powerful current of electricity continually through my great diamond, which it seemed to me gained in lustre every day. At the expiration of a month I commenced the grinding and polishing of the lens, a work of intense toil and exquisite delicacy. The great density of the stone, and the care required to be taken with the curvatures of the surfaces of the lens, rendered the labor the severest and most harassing that I had yet undergone.

At last the eventful moment came; the lens was completed. I stood trembling on the threshold of new worlds. I had the realization of Alexander's famous wish before me. The lens lay on the table, ready to be placed upon its platform. My hand fairly shook as I enveloped a drop of water with a thin coating of oil of turpentine, preparatory to its examination, — a process necessary in order to prevent the rapid evaporation of the water. I now placed the drop on a thin slip of glass under the lens, and throwing upon it, by the combined aid of a prism and a mirror, a powerful stream of light, I approached my eye to the minute hole drilled through the axis of the lens. For an instant I saw nothing save what seemed to be an illuminated chaos, a vast luminous abyss. A pure white light, cloudless and serene, and seemingly limitless as space itself, was my first impression. Gently, and with the greatest care, I depressed the lens a few hair's-breadths. The wondrous illumination still continued, but as the lens approached the object a scene of indescribable beauty was unfolded to my view.

I seemed to gaze upon a vast space, the limits of which extended far beyond my vision. An atmosphere of magical luminousness permeated the entire field of view. I was amazed to see no trace of animalculous life. Not a living thing, apparently, inhabited that dazzling expanse. I comprehended instantly that, by the wondrous power of my lens, I had penetrated beyond the grosser particles of aqueous matter, beyond the realms of infusoria and protozoa, down to the original gaseous globule, into whose luminous interior I was gazing, as into an almost boundless dome filled with a supernatural radiance.

It was, however, no brilliant void into which I looked. On every side I beheld beautiful inorganic forms, of unknown texture, and colored with the most enchanting hues. These forms presented the appearance of what might be called, for want of a more specific definition, foliated clouds of the highest rarity; that is, they undulated and broke into vegetable formations, and were tinged with splendors compared with which the gilding of our autumn woodlands is as dross compared with gold. Far away into the illimitable distance stretched long avenues of these gaseous forests, dimly transparent, and painted with prismatic hues of unimaginable brilliancy. The pendent branches waved along the fluid glades until every vista seemed to break through half-lucent ranks of many-colored drooping silken pennons. What seemed to be either fruits or flowers, pied with a thousand hues, lustrous and ever varying, bubbled from the crowns of this fairy foliage. No hills, no lakes, no rivers, no forms animate or inanimate, were to be seen, save those vast auroral copses that floated serenely in the luminous stillness, with leaves and fruits and flowers gleaming with unknown fires, unrealizable by mere imagination.

How strange, I thought, that this sphere should be thus condemned to solitude! I had hoped, at least, to discover some new form of animal life,—perhaps of a lower class than any with which we are at present acquainted,—but still, some living organism. I found my newly discovered world, if I may so speak, a beautiful chromatic desert.

While I was speculating on the singular arrangements of the internal economy of Nature, with which she so frequently splinters into atoms our most compact theories, I thought I beheld a form moving slowly through the glades of one of the prismatic forests. I looked more attentively, and found that I was not mistaken. Words cannot depict the anxiety with which I awaited the nearer approach of this mysterious object. Was it merely some inanimate substance, held in suspense in the attenuated atmosphere of the globule? or was it an animal endowed with vitality and motion? It approached, flitting behind the gauzy, colored veils of cloud-foliage, for seconds dimly revealed, then vanishing. At last the violet pennons that trailed nearest to me vibrated; they were gently pushed aside, and the Form floated out into the broad light.

It was a female human shape. When I say "human," I mean it possessed the outlines of humanity,—but there the analogy ends. Its adorable beauty lifted it illimitable heights beyond the loveliest daughter of Adam.

I cannot, I dare not, attempt to inventory the charms of this divine revelation of perfect beauty. Those eyes of mystic violet, dewy and serene, evade my words. Her long, lustrous hair following her glorious head in a golden wake, like the track sown in heaven by a falling star, seems to quench my most burning phrases with its splendors. If all the bees of Hybla nestled upon my lips, they would still sing but hoarsely the wondrous harmonies of outline that enclosed her form.

She swept out from between the rainbow-curtains of the cloud-trees into the broad sea of light that lay beyond. Her motions were those of some graceful Naiad, cleaving, by a mere effort of her will, the clear, unruffled waters that fill the chambers of the sea. She floated forth with the serene grace of a frail bubble ascending through the still atmosphere of a June day. The perfect roundness of her limbs formed suave and enchanting curves. It was like listening to the most spiritual symphony of Beethoven the divine, to watch the harmonious flow of lines. This, indeed, was a pleasure cheaply purchased at any price. What cared I, if I had waded to the portal of this wonder through another's blood? I would have given my own to enjoy one such moment of intoxication and delight.

Breathless with gazing on this lovely wonder, and forgetful for an instant of everything save her presence, I withdrew my eye from the microscope eagerly,— alas! As my gaze fell on the thin slide that lay beneath my instrument, the bright light from mirror and from prism sparkled on a colorless drop of water! There, in that tiny bead of dew, this beautiful being was forever imprisoned. The planet Neptune was not more distant from me than she. I hastened once more to apply my eye to the microscope.

Animula (let me now call her by that dear name which I subsequently bestowed on her) had changed her position. She had again approached the wondrous forest, and was gazing earnestly upwards. Presently one of the trees—as I must call them—unfolded a long ciliary process, with which it seized one of the gleaming fruits that glittered on its summit, and, sweeping slowly down, held it within reach of Animula. The sylph took it in her delicate hand and began to eat. My attention was so entirely absorbed by her, that I could not apply myself to the task of determining whether this singular plant was or was not instinct with volition.

I watched her, as she made her repast, with the most profound attention. The suppleness of her motions sent a thrill of delight through my frame; my heart beat madly as she turned her beautiful eyes in the direction of the spot in which I stood. What would I not have given to have had the power to precipitate myself into that luminous ocean, and float with her through those groves of purple and gold! While I was thus breathlessly following her every movement, she suddenly started, seemed to listen for a moment, and then cleaving the brilliant ether in which she was floating, like a flash of light, pierced through the opaline forest, and disappeared.

Instantly a series of the most singular sensations attacked me. It seemed as if I had suddenly gone blind. The luminous sphere was still before me, but my daylight had vanished. What caused this sudden disappearance? Had she a lover or a husband? Yes, that was the solution! Some signal from a happy fellow-being had vibrated through the avenues of the forest, and she had obeyed the summons.

The agony of my sensations, as I arrived at this conclusion, startled me. I tried to reject the conviction that my reason forced upon me. I battled against the fatal conclusion,—but in vain. It was so. I had no escape from it. I loved an animalcule!

It is true that, thanks to the marvellous power of my microscope, she appeared of human proportions. Instead of presenting the revolting aspect of the coarser creatures, that live and struggle and die, in the more easily resolvable portions of the water-drop, she was fair and delicate and of surpassing beauty. But of what account was all that? Every time that my eye was withdrawn from the instrument, it fell on a miserable drop of water, within which, I must be content to know, dwelt all that could make my life lovely.

Could she but see me once! Could I for one moment pierce the mystical walls that so inexorably rose to separate us, and whisper all that filled my soul, I might consent to be satisfied for the rest of my life with the knowledge of her remote sympathy. It would be something to have established even the faintest personal link to bind us together,—to know that at times, when roaming through those enchanted glades, she might think of the wonderful stranger, who had broken the monotony of her life with his presence, and left a gentle memory in her heart!

But it could not be. No invention of which human intellect was capable could break down the barriers that Nature had erected. I might feast my soul upon her wondrous beauty, yet she must always remain ignorant of the adoring eyes that day and night gazed upon her, and, even when closed, beheld her in dreams. With a bitter cry of anguish I fled from the room, and, flinging myself on my bed, sobbed myself to sleep like a child.

VI

The Spilling of the Cup

I arose the next morning almost at daybreak, and rushed to my microscope. I trembled as I sought the luminous world in miniature that contained my all. Animula was there. I had left the gas-lamp, surrounded by its moderators, burning, when I went to bed the night before. I found the sylph bathing, as it were, with an expression of pleasure animating her features, in the brilliant light which surrounded her. She tossed her lustrous golden hair over her shoulders with innocent coquetry. She lay at full length in the transparent medium, in which she supported herself with ease, and gambolled with the enchanting grace that the nymph Salmacis might have exhibited when she sought to conquer the modest Hermaphroditus. I tried an experiment to satisfy myself if her powers of reflection were developed. I lessened the lamp-light considerably. By the dim light that remained, I could see an expression of pain flit across her face. She looked upward suddenly, and her brows contracted. I flooded the stage of the microscope again with a full stream of light, and her whole expression changed. She sprang forward like some substance deprived of all weight. Her eyes sparkled and her lips moved. Ah! if science had only the means of conducting and reduplicating sounds, as it does the rays of light, what carols of happiness would then have entranced my ears! what jubilant hymns to Adonaïs would have thrilled the illumined air!

I now comprehended how it was that the Count de Gabalis peopled his mystic world with sylphs,—beautiful beings whose breath of life was lambent fire, and who sported forever in regions of purest ether and purest light. The Rosicrucian had anticipated the wonder that I had practically realized.

How long this worship of my strange divinity went on thus I scarcely know. I lost all note of time. All day from early dawn, and far into the night, I was to be found peering through that wonderful lens. I saw no one, went nowhere, and scarce allowed myself sufficient time for my meals. My whole life was absorbed in contemplation as rapt as that of any of the Romish saints. Every hour that I gazed upon the divine form strengthened my passion,—a passion that was always overshadowed by the maddening conviction, that, although I could gaze on her at will, she never, never could behold me!

At length, I grew so pale and emaciated, from want of rest, and continual brooding over my insane love and its cruel conditions, that I determined to make some effort to wean myself from it. "Come," I said, "this is at best but a fantasy. Your imagination has bestowed on Animula charms which in reality she does not possess. Seclusion from female society has produced this morbid condition of mind. Compare her with the beautiful women of your own world, and this false enchantment will vanish."

I looked over the newspapers by chance. There I beheld the advertisement of a celebrated *danseuse* who appeared nightly at Niblo's. The Signorina Caradolce had the reputation of being the most beautiful as well as the most graceful woman in the world. I instantly dressed and went to the theatre.

The curtain drew up. The usual semicircle of fairies in white muslin were standing on the right toe around the enamelled flower-bank, of green canvas, on which the belated prince was sleeping. Suddenly a flute is heard. The fairies start. The trees open, the fairies all stand on the left toe, and the queen enters. It was the Signorina. She bounded forward amid thunders of applause, and, lighting on one foot, remained poised in air. Heavens! was this the great enchantress that had drawn monarchs at her chariot-wheels? Those heavy muscular limbs, those thick ankles, those cavernous eyes, that stereotyped smile, those crudely painted cheeks! Where were the vermeil blooms, the liquid expressive eyes, the harmonious limbs of Animula?

The Signorina danced. What gross, discordant movements! The play of her limbs was all false and artificial. Her bounds were painful athletic efforts; her poses were angular and distressed the eye. I could bear it no longer; with an exclamation of disgust that drew every eye upon me, I rose from my seat in the very middle of the Signorina's *pas-de-fascination*, and abruptly quitted the house.

I hastened home to feast my eyes once more on the lovely form of my sylph. I felt that henceforth to combat this passion would be impossible. I applied my eye to the lens. Animula was there,—but what could have happened? Some terrible change seemed to have taken place during my absence. Some secret grief seemed to cloud the lovely features of her I gazed upon. Her face had grown thin and haggard; her limbs trailed heavily; the wondrous lustre of her golden hair had faded. She was ill!— ill, and I could not assist her! I believe at that moment I would have gladly forfeited all claims to my human birthright, if I could only have been dwarfed to the size of an animalcule, and permitted to console her from whom fate had forever divided me.

I racked my brain for the solution of this mystery. What was it that afflicted the sylph? She seemed to suffer intense pain. Her features contracted, and she even writhed, as if with some internal agony. The wondrous forests appeared also to have lost half their beauty. Their hues were dim and in some places faded away altogether. I watched Animula for hours with a breaking heart, and she seemed absolutely to wither away under my very eye. Suddenly I remembered that I had not looked at the water-drop for several days. In fact, I hated to see it; for it reminded me of the natural barrier between Animula and myself. I hurriedly looked down on the stage of the microscope. The slide was still there,—but, great heavens! the water-drop had vanished! The awful truth burst upon me; it had evaporated, until it had become so minute as to be invisible to the naked eye; I had been gazing on its last atom, the one that contained Animula,—and she was dying!

I rushed again to the front of the lens, and looked through. Alas! the last agony had seized her. The rainbow-hued forests had all melted away, and Animula lay struggling feebly in what seemed to be a spot of dim light. Ah! the sight was horrible: the limbs once so round and lovely shrivelling up into nothings; the eyes—those eyes that shone like heaven—being quenched into black dust; the lustrous golden hair now lank and discolored. The last throe came. I beheld that final struggle of the blackening form—and I fainted.

When I awoke out of a trance of many hours, I found myself lying amid the wreck of my instrument, myself as shattered in mind and body as it. I crawled feebly to my bed, from which I did not rise for months.

They say now that I am mad; but they are mistaken. I am poor, for I have neither the heart nor the will to work; all my money is spent, and I live on charity. Young men's associations that love a joke invite me to lecture on Optics before them, for which they pay me, and laugh at me while I lecture. "Linley, the mad microscopist," is the name I go by. I suppose that I talk incoherently while I lecture. Who could talk sense when his brain is haunted by such ghastly memories, while ever and anon among the shapes of death I behold the radiant form of my lost Animula!

EDWARD PAGE MITCHELL (1852–1927)

Edward Page Mitchell and his stories may be the greatest lost treasures of Science Fiction. Fortunately, Sam Moskowitz helped to change that situation by doing extensive research on the author. Mitchell was a newspaper writer and editor for the New York Sun, *which had been founded by Benjamin H. Day in 1833. Because he published much of his work anonymously, Mitchell's contributions are underrecognized, and he has long remained in virtual obscurity.*

Edward Page Mitchell's years of greatest contribution to Science Fiction came in the 1870s and '80s. The Science Fiction topics he wrote about are wide ranging. Short story titles include "The Balloon Tree," "The Ablest Man in the World," "The Man Without a Body," "The Story of the Deluge," "The Professor's Experiment," "The Soul Spectroscope," and "The Inside of the Earth." Mitchell also wrote Dark Fantasies and supernatural thrillers.

In several ways, Mitchell's Science Fiction anticipates that of H. G. Wells. For example, Mitchell's "The Crystal Man" (New York Sun, January 30, 1881), which deals with the creation of an invisible man through scientific means, precedes Wells's The Invisible Man: A Grotesque Romance *(1897). Mitchell's "The Clock That Went Backward" predates Wells's* The Time Machine: An Invention *(1895).*

The Clock That Went Backward
(New York Sun, *September 18, 1881*)

A row of Lombardy poplars stood in front of my Great-Aunt Gertrude's house, on the bank of the Sheepscot River. In personal appearance my aunt was surprisingly like one of those trees. She had the look of hopeless anemia that distinguishes them from fuller-blooded sorts. She was tall, severe in outline, and extremely thin. Her habiliments clung to her. I am sure that had the gods found occasion to impose upon her the fate of Daphne she would have taken her place easily and naturally in the dismal row, as melancholy a poplar as the rest.

Some of my earliest recollections are of this venerable relative. Alive and dead she bore an important part in the events I am about to recount: events which I believe to be without parallel in the experience of mankind.

During our periodical visits of duty to Aunt Gertrude in Maine, my cousin Harry and myself were accustomed to speculate much on her age. Was she sixty, or was she six score? We had no precise information; she might have been either. The old lady was surrounded by old-fashioned things. She seemed to live altogether in the past. In her short half-hours of communicativeness over her second cup of tea, or on the piazza where the poplars sent slim shadows directly toward the east, she used to tell us stories of her alleged ancestors. I say alleged, because we never fully believed that she had ancestors.

A genealogy is a stupid thing. Here is Aunt Gertrude's, reduced to its simplest forms:

Her great-great-grandmother (1599–1642) was a woman of Holland who married a Puritan refugee, and sailed from Leyden to Plymouth in the ship *Ann* in the year of our Lord 1632. This Pilgrim mother had a daughter, Aunt Gertrude's great-grandmother (1640–1718). She came to the Eastern District of Massachusetts in the early part of the last century; and was carried off by the Indians in the Penobscot wars. Her daughter (1680–1776) lived to see these colonies free and independent, and contributed to the population of the coming republic not less than nineteen stalwart sons and comely daughters. One of the latter (1735–1802) married a Wiscasset skipper engaged in the West India trade, with whom she sailed. She was twice wrecked at sea — once on what is now Seguin Island and once on San Salvador. It was on San Salvador that Aunt Gertrude was born.

We got to be very tired of hearing this family history. Perhaps it was the constant repetition and the merciless persistency with which the above dates were driven into our young ears that made us skeptics. As I have said, we took little stock in Aunt Gertrude's ancestors. They seemed highly improbable. In our private opinion the great-grandmothers and grandmothers and so forth were pure myths, and Aunt Gertrude herself was the principal in all the adventures attributed to them, having lasted from century to century while generations of contemporaries went the way of all flesh.

On the first landing of the square stairway of the mansion loomed a tall Dutch clock. The case was more than eight feet high, of a dark red wood, not mahogany, and it was curiously inlaid with silver. No common piece of furniture was this. About a hundred years ago there flourished in the town of Brunswick a horologist named Cary, an industrious and accomplished workman. Few well-to-do houses on that part of the coast lacked a Cary timepiece. But Aunt Gertrude's clock had marked the hours and minutes of two full centuries before the Brunswick artisan was born. It was running when William the Taciturn pierced the dikes to relieve Leyden. The name of the maker, Jan Lipperdam, and the date, 1572, were still legible in broad black letters and figures reaching quite across the dial. Cary's masterpieces were plebeian and recent beside this ancient aristocrat. The jolly Dutch moon, made to exhibit the phases over a landscape of windmills and polders, was cunningly painted. A skilled hand had carved the grim ornament at the top, a death's-head transfixed by a two-edged sword. Like all timepieces of the sixteenth century, it had no pendulum. A simple Van Wyck escapement governed the descent of the weights to the bottom of the tall case.

But these weights never moved. Year after year, when Harry and I returned to Maine, we found the hands of the old clock pointing to the quarter past three, as they had pointed when we first saw them. The fat moon hung perpetually in the third quarter, as motionless as the death's-head above. There was a mystery about the silenced movement and the paralyzed hands. Aunt Gertrude told us that the works had never performed their functions since a bolt of lightning entered the clock; and she showed us a black hole in the side of the case near the top, with a yawning rift that extended downward for several feet. This explanation failed to satisfy us. It did not account for the sharpness of her refusal when we proposed to bring over the watchmaker from the village, or for her singular agitation once when she found Harry on a stepladder, with a borrowed key in his hand, about to test for himself the clock's suspended vitality.

One August night, after we had grown out of boyhood, I was awakened by a noise in the hallway. I shook my cousin. "Somebody's in the house," I whispered.

We crept out of our room and onto the stairs. A dim light came from below. We held our breath and noiselessly descended to the second landing. Harry clutched my arm. He pointed down over the banisters, at the same time drawing me back into the shadow.

We saw a strange thing.

Aunt Gertrude stood on a chair in front of the old clock, as spectral in her white nightgown and white nightcap as one of the poplars when covered with snow. It chanced that the floor creaked slightly under our feet. She turned with a sudden movement, peering intently into the darkness, and holding a candle high toward us, so that the light was full upon her pale face. She looked many years older than when I bade her good night. For a few minutes she was motionless, except in the trembling arm that held aloft the candle. Then, evidently reassured, she placed the light upon a shelf and turned again to the clock.

We now saw the old lady take a key from behind the face and proceed to wind up the weights. We could hear her breath, quick and short. She rested a hand on either side of the case and held her face close to the dial, as if subjecting it to anxious scrutiny. In this attitude she remained for a long time. We heard her utter a sigh of relief, and she half turned toward us for a moment. I shall never forget the expression of wild joy that transfigured her features then.

The hands of the clock were moving; they were moving backward.

Aunt Gertrude put both arms around the clock and pressed her withered check against it. She kissed it repeatedly. She caressed it in a hundred ways, as if it had been a living and beloved thing. She fondled it and talked to it, using words which we could hear but could not understand. The hands continued to move backward.

Then she started back with a sudden cry. The clock had stopped. We saw her tall body swaying for an instant on the chair. She stretched out her arms in a convulsive gesture of terror and despair, wrenched the minute hand to its old place at a quarter past three, and fell heavily to the floor.

II

Aunt Gertrude's will left me her bank and gas stocks, real estate, railroad bonds, and city sevens, and gave Harry the clock. We thought at the time that this was a very unequal division, the more surprising because my cousin had always seemed to be the favorite. Half in seriousness we made a thorough examination of the ancient timepiece, sounding its wooden case for secret drawers, and even probing the not complicated works with a knitting needle to ascertain if our whimsical relative had bestowed there some codicil or other document changing the aspect of affairs. We discovered nothing.

There was testamentary provision for our education at the University of Leyden. We left the military school in which we had learned a little of the theory of war, and a good deal of the art of standing with our noses over our heels, and took ship without delay. The clock went with us. Before many months it was established in a corner of a room in the Breede Straat.

The fabric of Jan Lipperdam's ingenuity, thus restored to its native air, continued to tell the hour of quarter past three with its old fidelity. The author of the clock had been under the sod for nearly three hundred years. The combined skill of his successors in the craft at Leyden could make it go neither forward nor backward.

We readily picked up enough Dutch to make ourselves understood by the townspeople, the professors, and such of our eight hundred and odd fellow students as came into intercourse. This language, which looks so hard at first, is only a sort of polarized English. Puzzle over it a little while and it jumps into your comprehension like one of those simple cryptograms made by running together all the words of a sentence and then dividing in the wrong places.

The language acquired and the newness of our surroundings worn off, we settled into tolerably regular pursuits. Harry devoted himself with some assiduity to the study of sociology, with especial reference to the round-faced and not unkind maidens of Leyden. I went in for the higher metaphysics.

Outside of our respective studies, we had a common ground of unfailing interest. To our astonishment, we found that not one in twenty of the faculty or students knew or cared a stiver about the glorious history of the town, or even about the circumstances under which the university itself was founded by the Prince of Orange. In marked contrast with the general indifference was the enthusiasm of Professor Van Stopp, my chosen guide through the cloudiness of speculative philosophy.

This distinguished Hegelian was a tobacco-dried little old man, with a skullcap over features that reminded me strangely of Aunt Gertrude's. Had he been her own brother the facial resemblance could not have been closer. I told him so once, when we were together in the Stadthuis looking at the portrait of the hero of the siege, the Burgomaster Van der Werf. The professor laughed. "I will show you what is even a more extraordinary coincidence," said he; and, leading the way across the hall to the great picture of the siege, by Wanners, he pointed out the figure of a burgher participating in the defense. It was true. Van Stopp might have been the burgher's son; the burgher might have been Aunt Gertrude's father.

The professor seemed to be fond of us. We often went to his rooms in an old house in the Rapenburg Straat, one of the few houses remaining that antedate 1574. He would walk with us through the beautiful suburbs of the city, over straight roads lined with poplars that carried us back to the bank of the Sheepscot in our minds. He took us to the top of the ruined Roman tower in the center of the town, and from the same battlements from which anxious eyes three centuries ago had watched the slow approach of Admiral Boisot's fleet over the submerged polders, he pointed out the great dike of the Landscheiding, which was cut that the oceans might bring Boisot's Zealanders to raise the leaguer and feed the starving. He showed us the headquarters of the Spaniard Valdez at Leyderdorp, and told us how heaven sent a violent northwest wind on the night of the first of October, piling up the water deep where it had been shallow and sweeping the fleet on between Zoeterwoude and Zwieten up to the very walls of the fort at Lammen, the last stronghold of the besiegers and the last obstacle in the way of succor to the famishing inhabitants. Then he showed us where, on the very night before the retreat of the besieging army, a huge breach was made in the wall of Leyden, near the Cow Gate, by the Walloons from Lammen.

"Why!" cried Harry, catching fire from the eloquence of the professor's narrative, "that was the decisive moment of the siege."

The professor said nothing. He stood with his arms folded, looking intently into my cousin's eyes.

"For," continued Harry, "had that point not been watched, or had defense failed and the breach been carried by the night assault from Lammen, the town would have been burned and the people massacred under the eyes of Admiral Boisot and the fleet of relief. Who defended the breach?"

Van Stopp replied very slowly, as if weighing every word:

"History records the explosion of the mine under the city wall on the last night of the siege; it does not tell the story of the defense or give the defender's name. Yet no man that ever lived had a more tremendous charge than fate entrusted to this unknown hero. Was it chance that sent him to meet that unexpected danger? Consider some of the consequences had he failed. The fall of Leyden would have destroyed the last hope of the Prince of Orange and of the free states. The tyranny of Philip would have been reestablished. The birth of religious liberty and of self-government by the people would have been postponed, who knows for how many centuries? Who knows that there would or could have been a republic of the United States of America had there been no United Netherlands? Our University, which has given to the world Grotius, Scaliger, Arminius, and Descartes, was founded upon this hero's successful defense of the breach. We owe to him our presence here today. Nay, you owe to him your very existence. Your ancestors were of Leyden; between their lives and the butchers outside the walls he stood that night."

The little professor towered before us, a giant of enthusiasm and patriotism. Harry's eyes glistened and his cheeks reddened.

"Go home, boys," said Van Stopp, "and thank God that while the burghers of Leyden were straining their gaze toward Zoeterwoude and the fleet, there was one pair of vigilant eyes and one stout heart at the town wall just beyond the Cow Gate!"

III

The rain was splashing against the windows one evening in the autumn of our third year at Leyden, when Professor Van Stopp honored us with a visit in the Breede Straat. Never had I seen the old gentleman in such spirits. He talked incessantly. The gossip of the town, the news of Europe, science, poetry, philosophy, were in turn touched upon and treated with the same high and good humor. I sought to draw him out on Hegel, with whose chapter on the complexity and interdependency of things I was just then struggling.

"You do not grasp the return of the Itself into Itself through its Otherself?" he said smiling. "Well, you will, sometime."

Harry was silent and preoccupied. His taciturnity gradually affected even the professor. The conversation flagged, and we sat a long while without a word. Now and then there was a flash of lightning succeeded by distant thunder.

"Your clock does not go," suddenly remarked the professor. "Does it ever go?"

"Never since we can remember," I replied. "That is, only once, and then it went backward. It was when Aunt Gertrude—"

Here I caught a warning glance from Harry. I laughed and stammered, "The clock is old and useless. It cannot be made to go."

"Only backward?" said the professor, calmly, and not appearing to notice my embarrassment. "Well, and why should not a clock go backward? Why should not Time itself turn and retrace its course?"

He seemed to be waiting for an answer. I had none to give.

"I thought you Hegelian enough," he continued, "to admit that every condition includes its own contradiction. Time is a condition, not an essential. Viewed from the Absolute, the sequence by which future follows present and present follows past is purely arbitrary. Yesterday, today, tomorrow; there is no reason in the nature of things why the order should not be tomorrow, today, yesterday."

A sharper peal of thunder interrupted the professor's speculations.

"The day is made by the planet's revolution on its axis from west to east. I fancy you can conceive conditions under which it might turn from east to west, unwinding, as it were, the revolutions of past ages. Is it so much more difficult to imagine Time unwinding itself; Time on the ebb, instead of on the flow; the past unfolding as the future recedes; the centuries countermarching; the course of events proceeding toward the Beginning and not, as now, toward the End?"

"But," I interposed, "we know that as far as we are concerned the—"

"We know!" exclaimed Van Stopp, with growing scorn. "Your intelligence has no wings. You follow in the trail of Compte and his slimy brood of creepers and crawlers. You speak with amazing assurance of your position in the universe. You seem to think that your wretched little individuality has a firm foothold in the Absolute. Yet you go to bed tonight and dream into existence men, women, children, beasts of the past or the future. How do you know that at this moment you yourself, with all your conceit of nineteenth-century thought, are anything more than a creature of a dream of the future, dreamed, let us say, by some philosopher of the sixteenth century? How do you know that you are anything more than a creature of a dream of the past, dreamed by some Hegelian of the twenty-sixth century? How do you know, boy, that you will not vanish into the sixteenth century or 2060 the moment the dreamer awakes?"

There was no replying to this, for it was sound metaphysics. Harry yawned. I got up and went to the window. Profesor Van Stopp approached the clock.

"Ah, my children," said he, "there is no fixed progress of human events. Past, present, and future are woven together in one inextricable mesh. Who shall say that this old clock is not right to go backward?"

A crash of thunder shook the house. The storm was over our heads.

When the blinding glare had passed away, Professor Van Stopp was standing upon a chair before the tall timepiece. His face looked more than ever like Aunt Gertrude's. He stood as she had stood in that last quarter of an hour when we saw her wind the clock.

The same thought struck Harry and myself.

"Hold!" we cried, as he began to wind the works. "It may be death if you—"

The professor's sallow features shone with the strange enthusiasm that had transformed Aunt Gertrude's.

"True," he said, "it may be death; but it may be the awakening. Past, present, future; all woven together! The shuttle goes to and fro, forward and back—"

He had wound the clock. The hands were whirling around the dial from right to left with inconceivable rapidity. In this whirl we ourselves seemed to be borne along. Eternities seemed to contract into minutes while lifetimes were thrown off at every tick. Van Stopp, both arms outstretched, was reeling in his chair. The house shook again under a tremendous peal of thunder. At the same instant a ball of fire, leaving a wake of sulphurous vapor and filling the room with dazzling light, passed over our heads and smote the clock. Van Stopp was prostrated. The hands ceased to revolve.

IV

The roar of the thunder sounded like heavy cannonading. The lightning's blaze appeared as the steady light of a conflagration. With our hands over our eyes, Harry and I rushed into the night.

Under a red sky people were hurrying toward the Stadthius. Flames in the direction of the Roman tower told us that the heart of the town was afire. The faces of those we saw were haggard and emaciated. From every side we caught disjointed phrases of complaint or despair. "Horseflesh at ten schillings the pound," said one, "and bread at sixteen schillings." "Bread indeed!" an old woman retorted: "It's eight weeks gone since I have seen a crumb." "My little grandchild, the lame one, went last night." Do you know what Gekke Betje, the washerwoman did? She was starving. Her babe died, and she and her man—"

A louder cannon burst cut short this revelation. We made our way on toward the citadel of the town, passing a few soldiers here and there and many burghers with grim faces under their broad-brimmed felt hats.

"There is bread plenty yonder where the gunpowder is, and full pardon, too. Valdez shot another amnesty over the walls this morning."

An excited crowd immediately surrounded the speaker. "But the fleet!" they cried.

"The fleet is grounded fast on the Greenway polder. Boisot may turn his one eye seaward for a wind till famine and pestilence have carried off every mother's son of ye, and his ark will not be a rope's length nearer. Death by plague, death by starvation, death by fire and musketry—that is what the burgomaster offers us in return for glory for himself and kingdom for Orange."

"He asks us," said a sturdy citizen, "to hold out only twenty-four hours longer, and to pray meanwhile for an ocean wind."

"Ah, yes!" sneered the first speaker. "Pray on. There is bread enough locked in Pieter Adriaanszoon van der Werf's cellar. I warrant you that is what gives him so wonderful a stomach for resisting the Most Catholic King."

A young girl, with braided yellow hair, pressed through the crowd and confronted the malcontent. "Good people," said the maiden, "do not listen to him. He is a traitor with a Spanish heart. I am Pieter's daughter. We have no bread. We ate malt cakes and rapeseed like the rest of you till it was gone. Then we stripped the green leaves from the lime trees and willows in our garden and ate them. We have eaten even the thistles and weeds that grew between the stones by the canal. The coward lies."

Nevertheless, the insinuation had its effect. The throng, now become a mob, surged off in the direction of the burgomaster's house. One ruffian raised his hand to strike the girl out of the way. In a wink the cur was under the feet of his fellows, and Harry panting and glowing, stood at the maiden's side, shouting defiance in good English at the backs of the rapidly retreating crowd.

With the utmost frankness she put both her arms around Harry's neck and kissed him.

"Thank you," she said. "You are a hearty lad. My name is Gertruyd van der Werf."

Harry was fumbling in his vocabulary for the proper Dutch phrases, but the girl would not stay for compliments. "They mean mischief to my father"; and she hurried us through several exceedingly narrow streets into a three-cornered marketplace dominated by a church with two spires. "There he is," she exclaimed, "on the steps of St. Pancras."

There was a tumult in the marketplace. The conflagration raging beyond the church and the voices of the Spanish and Walloon cannon outside of the walls were less angry than the roar of this multitude of desperate men clamoring for the bread that a single word from their leader's lips would bring them. "Surrender to the King!" they cried, "or we will send your dead body to Lammen as Leyden's token of submission."

One tall man, taller by half a head than any of the burghers confronting him, and so dark of complexion that we wondered how he could be the father of Gertruyd, heard the threat in silence. When the burgomaster spoke, the mob listened in spite of themselves.

"What is it you ask, my friends? That we break our vow and surrender Leyden to the Spaniards? That is to devote ourselves to a fate far more horrible than starvation. I have to keep the oath! Kill me, if you will have it so. I can die only once, whether by your hands, by the enemy's, or by the hand of God. Let us starve, if we must, welcoming starvation because it comes before dishonor. Your menaces do not move me; my life is at your disposal. Here, take my sword, thrust it into my breast, and divide my flesh among you to appease your hunger. So long as I remain alive expect no surrender."

There was silence again while the mob wavered. Then there were mutterings around us. Above these rang out the clear voice of the girl whose hand Harry still held—unnecessarily, it seemed to me.

"Do you not feel the sea wind? It has come at last. To the tower! And the first man there will see by moonlight the full white sails of the prince's ships."

For several hours I scoured the streets of the town, seeking in vain my cousin and his companion; the sudden movement of the crowd toward the Roman tower had separated us. On every side I saw evidences of the terrible chastisement that had brought this stout-hearted people to the verge of despair. A man with hungry eyes chased a lean rat along the bank of the canal. A young mother, with two dead babes in her arms, sat in a doorway to which they bore the bodies of her husband and father, just killed at the walls. In the middle of a deserted street I passed unburied corpses in a pile twice as high as my head. The pestilence had been there—kinder than the Spaniard, because it held out no treacherous promises while it dealt its blows.

Toward morning the wind increased to a gale. There was no sleep in Leyden, no more talk of surrender, no longer any thought or care about defense. These words were on the lips of everybody I met: "Daylight will bring the fleet!"

Did daylight bring the fleet? History says so, but I was not a witness. I know only that before dawn the gale culminated in a violent thunderstorm, and that at the same time a muffled explosion, heavier than the thunder, shook the town. I was in the crowd that watched from the Roman Mound for the first signs of the approaching relief. The concussion shook hope out of every face. "Their mine has reached the wall!" But where? I pressed forward until I found the burgomaster, who was standing among the rest. "Quick!" I whispered. "It is beyond the Cow Gate, and this side of the Tower of Burgundy." He gave me a searching glance, and then strode away, without making any attempt to quiet the general panic. I followed close at his heels.

It was a tight run of nearly half a mile to the rampart in question. When we reached the Cow Gate this is what we saw:

A great gap, where the wall had been, opening to the swampy fields beyond: in the moat, outside and below, a confusion of upturned faces, belonging to men who struggled like demons to achieve the breach, and who now gained a few feet and now were forced back; on the shattered rampart a handful of soldiers and burghers forming a living wall where masonry had failed; perhaps a double handful of women and girls, serving stones to the defenders and boiling water in buckets, besides pitch and oil and unslaked lime, and some of them quoiting tarred and burning hoops over the necks of the Spaniards in the moat; my cousin Harry leading and directing the men; the burgomaster's daughter Gertruyd encouraging and inspiring the women.

But what attracted my attention more than anything else was the frantic activity of a little figure in black, who, with a huge ladle, was showering molten lead on the heads of the assailing party. As he turned to the bonfire and kettle which supplied him with ammunition, his features came into the full light. I gave a cry of surprise: the ladler of molten lead was Professor Van Stopp.

The burgomaster Van der Werf turned at my sudden exclamation. "Who is that?" I said. "The man at the kettle?"

"That," replied Van der Werf, "is the brother of my wife, the clockmaker Jan Lipperdam."

The affair at the breach was over almost before we had had time to grasp the situation. The Spaniards, who had overthrown the wall of brick and stone, found the living wall impregnable. They could not even maintain their position in the moat; they were driven off into the darkness. Now I felt a sharp pain in my left arm. Some stray missile must have hit me while we watched the fight.

"Who has done this thing?" demanded the burgomaster. "Who is it that has kept watch on today while the rest of us were straining fools' eyes toward tomorrow?"

Gertruyd van der Werf came forward proudly, leading my cousin. "My father," said the girl, "he has saved my life."

"That is much to me," said the burgomaster, "but it is not all. He has saved Leyden and he has saved Holland."

I was becoming dizzy. The faces around me seemed unreal. Why were we here with these people? Why did the thunder and lightning forever continue? Why did the clockmaker, Jan Lipperdam, turn always toward me the face of Professor Van Stopp? "Harry!" I said, "come back to our rooms."

But though he grasped my hand warmly his other hand still held that of the girl, and he did not move. Then nausea overcame me. My head swam, and the breach and its defenders faded from sight.

V

Three days later I sat with one arm bandaged in my accustomed seat in Van Stopp's lecture room. The place beside me was vacant.

"We hear much," said the Hegelian professor, reading from a notebook in his usual dry, hurried tone, "of the influence of the sixteenth century upon the nineteenth. No philosopher, as far as I am aware, has studied the influence of the nineteenth century upon the sixteenth. If cause produces effect, does effect never induce cause? Does the law of heredity, unlike all other laws of this universe of mind and matter, operate in one direction only? Does the descendant owe everything to the ancestor, and the ancestor nothing to the descendant? Does destiny, which may seize upon our existence, and for its own purposes bear us far into the future, never carry us back into the past?"

I went back to my rooms in the Breede Straat, where my only companion was the silent clock.

JULES (GABRIEL) VERNE (1828–1905)

Established cultural and literary heritages dramatically influenced the writings of Mary Shelley and Edgar Allan Poe. Such was also the case with Jules Verne. In fact, the Frenchman Verne was profoundly influenced by Poe, who had earlier been influenced by, among other factors, French literature. Jules Verne's success as a popular writer and speculator about the future was due to the fact that he was a voracious reader and an excellent imitator as well as original thinker.

Jules Verne was enamored with the works of the Swiss writer and philosopher J(ohan) R(udolph) Wyss (particularly Wyss's The Swiss Family Robinson, *1814). Near the end of the late 1890s, Verne's work increasingly paid tribute to (and increasingly imitated) the work of U.S. and English writers of Fantasy and Science Fiction, such as dime novelist and* Frank Reade *series writer, Luis Philip Senarens.*

Much has been written and said in praise of Jules Verne's contributions to Science Fiction. This praise is surely justified, yet it should also be qualified. Perhaps Verne's ability to manipulate popular history and fiction is appropriately likened to Steven Spielberg's and George Lucas's ability to do the same in the present day. A master of romance, adventure, escapism, philosophy, and psychology for the masses, Jules Verne was tremendously prolific and varied in his writing. He wrote many more novels than short stories. When Hugo Gernsback inaugurated the first issue of Amazing Stories *in 1926, he featured the work of Verne, alongside that of Poe and H. G. Wells, as a model and as a starting point for modern-day Scientifiction.*

Like much of Verne's Science Fiction, "An Express of the Future" is amazingly accurate in its prediction of the future.

An Express of the Future
(The Strand Magazine, *January 1895*)

"Take care!" cried my conductor, "there's a step!"

Safely descending the step thus indicated to me, I entered a vast room, illuminated by blinding electric reflectors, the sound of our feet alone breaking the solitude and silence of the place.

Where was I? What had I come there to do? Who was my mysterious guide? Questions unanswered. A long walk in the night, iron doors opened and reclosed with a clang, stairs descending, it seemed to me, deep into the earth—that is all I could remember. I had, however, no time for thinking.

"No doubt you are asking yourself who I am?" said my guide: "Colonel Pierce, at your service. Where are you? In America, at Boston—in a station."

"A station?"

"Yes, the starting-point of the 'Boston to Liverpool Pneumatic Tubes Company.'"

And, with an explanatory gesture, the Colonel pointed out to me two long iron cylinders, about a metre and a half in diameter, lying upon the ground a few paces off.

I looked at these two cylinders, ending on the right in a mass of masonry, and closed on the left with heavy metallic caps, from which a cluster of tubes were carried up to the roof; and suddenly I comprehended the purpose of all this.

Had I not, a short time before, read, in an American newspaper, an article describing this extraordinary project for linking Europe with the New World by means of two gigantic submarines tubes? An inventor had claimed to have accomplished the task; and that inventor, Colonel Pierce, I had before me.

In thought I realized the newspaper article.

Complaisantly the journalist entered into the details of the enterprise. He stated that more than 3,000 miles of iron tubes, weighing over 13,000,000 tons, were required, with the number of ships necessary, for the transport of this material—200 ships of 2,000 tons, each making thirty-three voyages. He described this Armada of science bearing the steel to two special vessels, on board of which the ends of the tubes were joined to each other, and incased in a triple netting of iron, the whole covered with a resinous preparation to preserve it from the action of the seawater.

Coming at once to the question of working, he filled the tubes—transformed into a sort of pea-shooter of interminable length—with a series of carriages, to be carried with their travellers by powerful currents of air, in the same way that despatches are conveyed pneumatically round Paris.

A parallel with the railways closed the article, and the author enumerated with enthusiasm the advantages of the new and audacious system. According to him, there would be, in passing through these tubes, a suppression of all nervous trepidation, thanks to the interior surface being of finely polished steel; equality of temperature secured by means of currents of air, by which the heat could be modified according to the seasons; incredibly low fares, owing to the cheapness of construction and working expenses—forgetting, or waving aside, all considerations of the question of gravitation and of wear and tear.

All that now came back to my mind.

So, then, this "Utopia" had become a reality, and these two cylinders of iron at my feet passed thence under the Atlantic and reached to the coast of England!

In spite of the evidence, I could not bring myself to believe in the thing having been done. That the tubes had been laid I could not doubt; but that men could travel by this route—never!

"Was it not impossible even to obtain a current of air of that length?"—I expressed that opinion aloud.

"Quite easy, on the contrary!" protested Colonel Pierce; "to obtain it, all that is required is a great number of steam fans similar to those used in blast furnaces. The air is driven by them with a force which is practically unlimited, propelling it at the speed of 1,800 kilometres an hour—almost that of a cannon-ball!—so that our carriages with their travellers, in the space of two hours and forty minutes, accomplish the journey between Boston and Liverpool."

"Eighteen hundred kilometres an hour!" I exclaimed.

"Not one less. And what extraordinary consequences arise from such a rate of speed! The time at Liverpool being four hours and forty minutes in advance of ours, a traveller starting from Boston at nine o'clock in the morning, arrives in

England at 3.53 in the afternoon. Isn't that a journey quickly made? In another sense, on the contrary, our trains, in this latitude, gain over the sun more than 900 kilometres an hour, beating that planet hand over hand: quitting Liverpool at noon, for example, the traveller will reach the station where we now are at thirty-four minutes past nine in the morning—that is to say, earlier than he started! Ha! ha! I don't think one can travel quicker than *that!*"

I did not know what to think. Was I talking with a madman?—or must I credit these fabulous theories, in spite of the objections which rose in my mind?

"Very well, so be it!" I said. "I will admit that travellers may take this mad-brained route, and that you can obtain this incredible speed. But, when you have got this speed, how do you check it? When you come to a stop, everything must be shattered to pieces!"

"Not at all," replied the Colonel, shrugging his shoulders. "Between our tubes—one for the out; the other for the home journey—consequently worked by currents going in opposite directions—a communication exists at every joint. When a train is approaching, an electric spark advertises us of the fact; left to it-self, the train would continue its course by reason of the speed it had acquired; but, simply by the turning of a handle, we are able to let in the opposing current of compressed air from the parallel tube, and, little by little, reduce to nothing the final shock of stopping. But what is the use of all these explanations? Would not a trial be a hundred times better?"

And, without waiting for an answer to his questions, the Colonel pulled sharply a bright brass knob projecting from the side of one of the tubes: a panel slid smoothly in its grooves, and in the opening left by its removal I perceived a row of seats, on each of which two persons might sit comfortably side by side.

"The carriage!" exclaimed the Colonel. "Come in."

I followed him without offering any objection, and the panel immediately slid back into its place.

By the light of an electric lamp in the roof I carefully examined the carriage I was in.

Nothing could be more simple: a long cylinder, comfortably upholstered, along which some fifty arm-chairs, in pairs, were ranged in twenty-five parallel ranks. At either end a valve regulated the atmospheric pressure, that at the farther end al-lowing breathable air to enter the carriage, that in front allowing for the discharge of any excess beyond a normal pressure.

After spending a few moments on this examination, I became impatient.

"Well," I said, "are we not going to start?"

"Going to start?" cried the Colonel. "We *have* started!"

Started—like that—without the least jerk, was it possible? I listened atten-tively, trying to detect a sound of some kind that might have guided me.

If we had really started—if the Colonel had not deceived me in talking of a speed of eighteen hundred kilometres an hour—we must already be far from any land, under the sea; above our heads the huge, foam-crested waves; even at that moment, perhaps—taking it for a monstrous sea-serpent of an unknown kind—whales were battering with their powerful tails our long, iron prison!

But I heard nothing but a dull rumble, produced, no doubt, by the passage of our carriage, and, plunged in boundless astonishment, unable to believe in the re-ality of all that had happened to me, I sat silently, allowing the time to pass.

At the end of about an hour a sense of freshness upon my forehead suddenly aroused me from the torpor into which I had sunk by degrees.

I raised my hand to my brow: it was moist.

Moist! Why was that? Had the tube burst under pressure of the waters—a pressure which could not but be formidable, since it increases at the rate of "an atmosphere" every ten metres of depth? Had the ocean broken in upon us?

Fear seized upon me. Terrified, I tried to call out—and—and I found myself in my garden, generously sprinkled by a driving rain, the big drops of which had awakened me. I had simply fallen asleep while reading the article devoted by an American journalist to the fantastic projects of Colonel Pierce—who also, I much fear, has only dreamed.

H(ERBERT) G(EORGE) WELLS (1866–1946)

At the turn of the twentieth century, H. G. Wells was recognized as one of the leading intellectuals of the day. Wells was a prolific and versatile author, politician, social historian, and visionary. His work was recognized internationally, and he was one of the fortunate writers and theorists to receive this recognition during his lifetime. No author, not even Mary Shelley, is more important to Science Fiction than is Wells. An Englishman, Wells was influenced by Rudyard Kipling, Arthur Conan Doyle, and Robert Louis Stevenson.

H. G. Wells is responsible for several of the enduring archetypal classics of the genre. Some of these are homages and owe a significant debt to H. Rider Haggard, Jules Verne, Edward Page Mitchell, and other nineteenth-century authors of Science Fiction. Wells's landmark novels include The Time Machine: An Invention *(1895),* The Island of Dr. Moreau *(1896),* The Invisible Man: A Grotesque Romance *(1897), and* The War of the Worlds *(1897). Wells was also a highly successful author of Fantasy and Science Fiction short stories.*

Along with Jules Verne, Wells is considered the founder of Science Fiction as a distinct genre of fiction. Hugo Gernsback helped solidify Wells's position in this regard by featuring reprints of his stories in the very first issues of Amazing Stories, *which began in 1926. By the late 1920s and early 1930s, Wells's fiction became the standard for all Science Fiction authors. He has been often imitated by a range of twentieth-century authors, including George Orwell, Ray Bradbury, Frederik Pohl, and J. G. Ballard.*

"The Star" is one such influential short story. A tale of impending apocalypse, "The Star" predates a range of stories and multimedia interpretations that have followed to this day. Perhaps the most famous of these are Philip Wylie and Edwin Balmer's co-authored novels, When Worlds Collide *(1932) and* After Worlds Collide *(1933), and George Pal's 1951 movie adaptation,* When Worlds Collide.

The Star
(Graphic, *Christmas 1897*)

It was on the first day of the new year that the announcement was made, almost simultaneously from three observatories, that the motion of the planet Neptune, the outermost of all the planets that wheel about the sun, had become very erratic. Ogilvy had already called attention to a suspected retardation in its velocity in December. Such a piece of news was scarcely calculated to interest a world the greater portion of whose inhabitants were unaware of the existence of the planet Neptune, nor outside the astronomical profession did the subsequent discovery of a faint, remote speck of light in the region of the perturbed planet cause any very great excitement. Scientific people, however, found the intelligence remarkable enough, even before it became known that the new body was rapidly growing larger and brighter, that its motion was quite different from the orderly progress of the planets, and that the deflection of Neptune and its satellite was becoming now of an unprecedented kind.

Few people without a training in science can realize the huge isolation of the solar system. The sun with its specks of planets, its dust of planetoids, and its impalpable comets, swims in a vacant immensity that almost defeats the imagination. Beyond the orbit of Neptune there is space, vacant so far as human observation has penetrated, without warmth or light or sound, blank emptiness, for twenty million times a million miles. That is the smallest estimate of the distance to be traversed before the very nearest of the stars is attained. And, saving a few comets more unsubstantial than the thinnest flame, no matter had ever to human knowledge crossed this gulf of space, until early in the twentieth century this strange wanderer appeared. A vast mass of matter it was; bulky, heavy, rushing without warning out of the black mystery of the sky into the radiance of the sun. By the second day it was clearly visible to any decent instrument, as a speck with a barely sensible diameter, in the constellation Leo near Regulus. In a little while an opera glass could attain it.

On the third day of the new year the newspaper readers of two hemispheres were made aware for the first time of the real importance of this unusual apparition in the heavens. "A Planetary Collision," one London paper headed the news, and proclaimed Duchaine's opinion that this strange new planet would probably collide with Neptune. The leader writers enlarged upon the topic. So that in most of the capitals of the world, on January 3rd, there was an expectation, however vague, of some imminent phenomenon in the sky; and as the night followed the sunset round the globe, thousands of men turned their eyes skyward to see—the old familiar stars just as they had always been.

Until it was dawn in London and Pollux setting and the stars overhead grown pale. The winter's dawn it was, a sickly filtering accumulation of daylight, and the light of gas and candles shone yellow in the windows to show where people were astir. But the yawning policeman saw the thing, the busy crowds in the markets stopped agape, workmen going to their work betimes, milkmen, the drivers of newscarts, dissipation going home jaded and pale, homeless wanderers, sentinels on their beats, and in the country, labourers trudging afield, poachers slinking home, all over the dusky quickening country it could be seen—and out at sea by seamen watching for the day—a great white star, come suddenly into the westward sky!

Brighter it was than any star in our skies; brighter than the evening star at its brightest. It still glowed out white and large, no mere twinkling spot of light, but a small round clear shining disc, an hour after the day had come. And where science has not reached, men stared and feared, telling one another of the wars and pestilences that are foreshadowed by these fiery signs in the Heavens. Sturdy Boers, dusky Hottentots, Gold Coast negroes, Frenchmen, Spaniards, Portuguese, stood in the warmth of the sunrise watching the setting of this strange new star.

And in a hundred observatories there had been suppressed excitement, rising almost to shouting pitch, as the two remote bodies had rushed together, and a hurrying to and fro to gather photographic apparatus and spectroscope, and this appliance and that, to record this novel astonishing sight, the destruction of a world. For it was a world, a sister planet of our earth, far greater than our earth indeed, that had so suddenly flashed into flaming death. Neptune it was had been struck, fairly and squarely, by the strange planet from outer space and the heat of the concussion had incontinently turned two solid globes into one vast mass of incandescence. Round the world that day, two hours before the dawn, went the pallid great white star, fading only as it sank westward and the sun mounted above it. Everywhere men marvelled at it, but of all those who saw it none could have marvelled more than those sailors, habitual watchers of the stars, who far away at sea had heard nothing of its advent and saw it now rise like a pigmy moon and climb zenithward and hang overhead and sink westward with the passing of the night.

And when next it rose over Europe everywhere were crowds of watchers on hilly slopes, on house-roofs, in open spaces, staring eastward for the rising of the great new star. It rose with a white glow in front of it, like the glare of a white fire, and those who had seen it come into existence the night before cried out at the sight of it. "It is larger," they cried. "It is brighter!" And, indeed the moon a quarter full and sinking in the west was in its apparent size beyond comparison, but scarcely in its breadth had it as much brightness now as the little circle of the strange new star.

"It is brighter!" cried the people clustering in the streets. But in the dim observatories the watchers held their breath and peered at one another. "*It is nearer,*" they said. "*Nearer!*"

And voice after voice repeated, "It is nearer," and the clicking telegraph took that up, and it trembled along telephone wires, and in a thousand cities grimy compositors fingered the type. "It is nearer." Men writing in offices, struck with a strange realisation, flung down their pens; men talking in a thousand places suddenly came upon a grotesque possibility in those words, "It is nearer." It hurried along awakening streets, it was shouted down the frost-stilled ways of quiet villages, men who had read these things from the throbbing tape stood in yellow-lit doorways shouting the news to the passers-by. "It is nearer." Pretty women, flushed and glittering, heard the news told jestingly between the dances, and feigned an intelligent interest they did not feel. "Nearer! Indeed. How curious! How very, very clever people must be to find out things like that!"

Lonely tramps faring through the wintry night murmured those words to comfort themselves—looking skyward. "It has need to be nearer, for the night's as cold as charity. Don't seem much warmth from it if it *is* nearer, all the same."

"What is a new star to me?" cried the weeping woman kneeling beside her dead.

The schoolboy, rising early for his examination work, puzzled it out for himself—with the great white star, shining broad and bright through the frost-flowers of his window. "Centrifugal, centripetal," he said, with his chin on his fist. "Stop a planet in its flight, rob it of its centrifugal force, what then? Centripetal has it, and down it falls into the sun! and this—!"

"Do *we* come in the way? I wonder—"

The light of that day went the way of its brethren, and with the later watches of the frosty darkness rose the strange star again. And it was now so bright that the waxing moon seemed but a pale yellow ghost of itself, hanging huge in the sunset. In a South African city a great man had married, and the streets were alight to welcome his return with his bride. "Even the skies have illuminated," said the flatterer. Under Capricorn, two negro lovers, daring the wild beasts and evil spirits, for love of one another, crouched together in a cane brake where the fire-flies hovered. "That is our star," they whispered, and felt strangely comforted by the sweet brilliance of its light.

The master mathematician sat in his private room and pushed the papers from him. His calculations were already finished. In a small white phial there still remained a little of the drug that had kept him awake and active for four long nights. Each day, serene, explicit, patient as ever, he had given his lecture to his students, and then had come back at once to this momentous calculation. His face was grave, a little drawn and hectic from his drugged activity. For some time he seemed lost in thought. Then he went to the window, and the blind went up with a click. Halfway up the sky, over the clustering roofs, chimneys, and steeples of the city, hung the star.

He looked at it as one might look into the eyes of a brave enemy. "You may kill me," he said after a silence. "But I can hold you—and all the universe for that matter—in the grip of this little brain. I would not change. Even now."

He looked at the little phial. "There will be no need of sleep again," he said. The next day at noon, punctual to the minute, he entered his lecture theatre, put his hat on the end of the table as his habit was, and carefully selected a large piece of chalk. It was a joke among his students that he could not lecture without that piece of chalk to fumble in his fingers, and once he had been stricken to impotence by their hiding his supply. He came and looked under his grey eyebrows at the rising tiers of young fresh faces, and spoke with his accustomed studied commonness of phrasing. "Circumstances have risen—circumstances beyond my control," he said and paused, "which will debar me from completing the course I had designed. It would seem, gentlemen, if I may put the thing clearly and briefly, that—Man has lived in vain."

The students glanced at one another. Had they heard aright? Mad? Raised eyebrows and grinning lips there were, but one or two faces remained intent upon his calm grey-fringed face. "It will be interesting," he was saying, "to devote this morning to an exposition, so far as I can make it clear to you, of the calculations that have led me to this conclusion. Let us assume—"

He turned towards the blackboard, meditating a diagram in the way that was usual to him. "What was that about 'lived in vain'?" whispered one student to another. "Listen," said the other, nodding towards the lecturer.

And presently they began to understand.

That night the star rose later, for its proper eastward motion had carried it some way across Leo towards Virgo, and its brightness was so great that the sky became a luminous blue as it rose, and every star was hidden in its turn, save only Jupiter near the zenith, Capella, Aldebaran, Sirius, and the pointers of the Bear. It was very white and beautiful. In many parts of the world that night a pallid halo encircled it about. It was perceptibly larger; in the clear refractive sky of the tropics it seemed as if it were nearly a quarter the size of the moon. The frost was still on the ground in England, but the world was as brightly lit as if it were midsummer moonlight. One could see to read quite ordinary print by that cold clear light, and in the cities the lamps burnt yellow and wan.

And everywhere the world was awake that night, and throughout Christendom a sombre murmur hung in the keen air over the countryside like the belling of bees in the heather, and this murmurous tumult grew to a clangour in the cities. It was the tolling of the bells in a million belfry towers and steeples, summoning the people to sleep no more, to sin no more, but to gather in their churches and pray. And overhead, growing larger and brighter as the earth rolled on its way and the night passed, rose the dazzling star.

And the streets and houses were alight in all the cities, the shipyards glared, and whatever roads led to high country were lit and crowded all night long. And in all the seas about the civilised lands, ships with throbbing engines, and ships with belling sails crowded with men and living creatures, were standing out to ocean and the north. For already the warning of the master mathematician had been telegraphed all over the world, and translated into a hundred tongues. The new planet and Neptune, locked in a fiery embrace, were whirling headlong, ever faster and faster towards the sun. Already every second this blazing mass flew a hundred miles, and every second its terrific velocity increased. As it flew now, indeed, it must pass a hundred million of miles wide of the earth and scarcely affect it. But near its destined path, as yet only slightly perturbed, spun the mighty planet Jupiter and his moons sweeping splendid round the sun. Every moment now the attraction between the fiery star and the greatest of the planets grew stronger. And the result of that attraction? Inevitably Jupiter would be deflected from his orbit into an elliptical path, and the burning star, swung by his attraction wide of its sunward rush, would "describe a curved path" and perhaps collide with, and certainly pass very close to, our earth. "Earthquakes, volcanic outbreaks, cyclones, sea waves, floods, and a steady rise in temperature to I know not what limit"—so prophesied the master mathematician.

And overhead, to carry out his words, lonely and cold and livid, blazed the star of the coming doom.

To many who stared at it that night until their eyes ached, it seemed that it was visibly approaching. And that night, too, the weather changed, and the frost that had gripped all Central Europe and France and England softened towards a thaw.

But you must not imagine because I have spoken of people praying through the night and people going aboard ships and people fleeing towards mountainous country that the whole world was already in a terror because of the star. As a matter of fact, use and wont still ruled the world, and save for the talk of idle moments and the splendour of the night, nine human beings out of ten were still busy at their common occupations. In all the cities the shops, save one here and there, opened and closed at their proper hours, the doctor and the undertaker plied their trades, the workers gathered in the factories, soldiers drilled, scholars studied, lovers sought one another, thieves lurked and fled, politicians planned their schemes. The presses of the newspapers roared through the nights, and many a priest of this church and that would not open his holy building to further what he considered a foolish panic. The newspapers insisted on the lesson of the year 1000—for then, too, people had anticipated the end. The star was no star— mere gas—a comet; and were it a star it could not possibly strike the earth. There was no precedent for such a thing. Common sense was sturdy everywhere, scornful, jesting, a little inclined to persecute the obdurate fearful. That night, at seven-fifteen by Greenwich time, the star would be at its nearest to Jupiter. Then the world would see the turn things would take. The master mathematician's grim warnings were treated by many as so much mere elaborate self-advertisement. Common sense at last, a little heated by argument, signified its unalterable convictions by going to bed. So, too, barbarism and savagery, already tired of the novelty, went about their mighty business, and save for a howling dog here and there, the beast world left the star unheeded.

And yet, when at last the watchers in the European States saw the star rise, an hour later it is true, but no larger than it had been the night before, there were still plenty awake to laugh at the master mathematician.

But hereafter the laughter ceased. The star grew—it grew with a terrible steadiness hour after hour, a little larger each hour, a little nearer the midnight zenith, and brighter and brighter, until it had turned night into a second day. Had it come straight to the earth instead of in a curved path, had it lost no velocity to Jupiter, it must have leapt the intervening gulf in a day, but as it was it took five days altogether to come by our planet. The next night it had become a third the size of the moon before it set to English eyes, and the thaw was assured. It rose over America near the size of the moon, but blinding white to look at, and *hot*; and a breath of hot wind blew now with its rising and gathering strength, and in Virginia, and Brazil, and down the St. Lawrence valley, it shone intermittently through a driving reek of thunderclouds, flickering violet lightning and hail unprecedented. In Manitoba was a thaw and devastating floods. And upon all the mountains of the earth the snow and ice began to melt that night, and all the rivers coming out of high country flowed thick and turbid, and soon—in their upper reaches—with swirling trees and the bodies of beasts and men. They rose steadily, steadily in the ghostly brilliance, and came trickling over their banks at last, behind the flying population of their valleys.

And along the coast of Argentina and up the South Atlantic the tides were higher than had ever been in the memory of man, and the storms drove the waters in many cases scores of miles inland, drowning whole cities. And so great grew the heat during the night that the rising of the sun was like the coming of a shadow. The earthquakes began and grew until all down America from the Arctic Circle to Cape Horn, hillsides were sliding, fissures were opening, and houses and walls crumbling to destruction. The whole side of Cotopaxi slipped out in one vast convulsion, and a tumult of lava poured out so high and broad and swift and liquid that in one day it reached the sea.

So the star, with the wan moon in its wake, marched across the Pacific, trailed the thunderstorms like the hem of a robe, and the growing tidal wave that toiled behind it, frothing and eager, poured over island and island and swept them clear of men. Until that wave came at last—in a blinding light and with the breath of a furnace, swift and terrible it came—a wall of water, fifty feet high, roaring hungrily, upon the long coasts of Asia, and swept inland across the plains of China. For a space the star, hotter now and larger and brighter than the sun in its strength, showed with pitiless brilliance the wide and populous country; towns and villages with their pagodas and trees, roads, wide, cultivated fields, millions of sleepless people staring in helpless terror at the incandescent sky; and then, low and growing, came the murmur of the flood. And thus it was with millions of men that night—a flight nowhither, with limbs heavy with heat and breath fierce and scant, and the flood like a wall swift and white behind. And then death.

China was lit glowing white, but over Japan and Java and all the islands of Eastern Asia the great star was a ball of dull red fire because of the steam and smoke and ashes the volcanoes were spouting forth to salute its coming. Above was the lava, hot gases and ash, and below the seething floods, and the whole earth swayed and rumbled with the earthquake shocks. Soon the immemorial snows of Thibet and the Himalaya were melting and pouring down by ten million deepening converging channels upon the plains of Burmah and Hindostan. The tangled summits of the Indian jungles were aflame in a thousand places, and below the hurrying waters around the stems were dark objects that still struggled feebly and reflected the blood-red tongues of fire. And in a rudderless confusion a multitude of men and women fled down the broad riverways to that one last hope of men—the open sea.

Larger grew the star, and larger, hotter, and brighter with a terrible swiftness now. The tropical ocean had lost its phosphorescence, and the whirling steam rose in ghostly wreaths from the black waves that plunged incessantly, speckled with storm-tossed ships.

And then came a wonder. It seemed to those who in Europe watched for the rising of the star that the world must have ceased its rotation. In a thousand open spaces of down and upland the people who had fled thither from the floods and the falling houses and sliding slopes of hill watched for that rising in vain. Hour followed hour through a terrible suspense, and the star rose not. Once again men set their eyes upon the old constellations they had counted lost to them for ever. In England it was hot and clear overhead, though the ground quivered perpetually, but in the tropics, Sirius and Capella and Aldebaran showed through a veil of steam. And when at last the great star rose near ten hours late, the sun rose close upon it, and in the centre of its white heart was a disc of black.

Over Asia it was the star had begun to fall behind the movement of the sky, and then suddenly, as it hung over India, its light had been veiled. All the plain of India from the mouth of the Indus to the mouths of the Ganges was a shallow waste of shining water that night, out of which rose temples and palaces, mounds and hills, black with people. Every minaret was a clustering mass of people, who fell one by one into the turbid waters, as heat and terror overcame them. The whole land seemed a-wailing, and suddenly there swept a shadow across that furnace of despair, and a breath of cold wind, and a gathering of clouds, out of the cooling air. Men looking up, near blinded, at the star, saw that a black disc was creeping across the light. It was the moon, coming between the star and the earth. And even as men cried to God at this respite, out the East with a strange inexplicable swiftness sprang the sun. And then star, sun, and moon rushed together across the heavens.

So it was that presently, to the European watchers, star and sun rose close upon each other, drove headlong for a space and then slower, and at last came to rest, star and sun merged into one glare of flame at the zenith of the sky. The moon no longer eclipsed the star but was lost to sight in the brilliance of the sky. And though those who were still alive regarded it for the most part with that dull stupidity that hunger, fatigue, heat, and despair engender, there were still men who could perceive the meaning of these signs. Star and earth had been at their nearest, had swung about one another, and the star had passed. Already it was receding, swifter and swifter, in the last stage of its headlong journey downward into the sun.

And then the clouds gathered, blotting out the vision of the sky, the thunder and lightning wove a garment round the world; all over the earth was such a downpour of rain as men had never before seen, and where the volcanoes flared red against the cloud canopy there descended torrents of mud. Everywhere the waters were pouring off the land, leaving mud-silted ruins, and the earth littered like a storm-worn beach with all that had floated, and the dead bodies of the men and brutes, its children. For days the water streamed off the land, sweeping away soil and trees and houses in the way, and piling huge dykes and scooping out Titanic gullies over the countryside. Those were the days of darkness that followed the star and the heat. All through them, and for many weeks and months, the earthquakes continued.

But the star had passed, and men, hunger-driven and gathering courage only slowly, might creep back to their ruined cities, buried granaries, and sodden fields. Such few ships as had escaped the storms of that time came stunned and shattered and sounding their way cautiously through the new marks and shoals of once-familiar ports. And as the storms subsided men perceived that everywhere the days were hotter than of yore, and the sun larger, and the moon, shrunk to a third of its former size, took now fourscore days between its new and new.

But of the new brotherhood that grew presently among men, of the saving of laws and books and machines, of the strange change that had come over Iceland and Greenland and the shores of Baffin's Bay, so that the sailors coming there presently found them green and gracious, and could scarce believe their eyes, this story does not tell. Nor of the movement of mankind now that the earth was hotter, northward and southward towards the poles of the earth. It concerns itself only with the coming and the passing of the star.

The Martian astronomers—for there are astronomers on Mars, although they are very different beings from men—were naturally profoundly interested by these things. They saw them from their own standpoint, of course. "Considering the mass and temperature of the missile that was flung through our solar system into the sun," one wrote, "it is astonishing what a little damage the Earth, which it missed so narrowly, has sustained. All the familiar continental markings and the masses of the seas remain intact, and indeed the only difference seems to be a shrinkage of the white discoloration (supposed to be frozen water) round either pole." Which only shows how small the vastest of human catastrophes may seem, at a distance of a few million miles.

HARRIET ELIZABETH PRESCOTT SPOFFORD
(1835–1921)

A popular mainstream author of the mid- and late-nineteenth-century, Harriet Spofford wrote stories that often featured Fantasy, Supernatural, Detective Fiction, and Science Fiction elements. Spofford utilized a consciously, almost painfully literary style and emphasized detailed descriptions and images of people, settings, and atmospheres. Her stories appeared in The Atlantic Monthly, The Metropolitan Magazine, *and similar publications. In literary circles today, she is remembered as a New England romance writer and poet. As such, it is easy to see the influence of Nathaniel Hawthorne on her style. William Dean Howells admired her; Henry James despised her.*

Though Spofford had her first story, "Sir Rohan's Ghost," published when she was twenty-five years old, she did not publish her first Science Fiction story, "The Ray of Displacement," until she was in her late sixties. This tale centers on the idea of humans passing through solid matter, and as an original work, it foreshadows stories by Murray Leinster, Gene Roddenberry's Star Trek series, and others.

The Ray of Displacement
(The Metropolitan Magazine, *October 1903*)

> *"We should have to reach the Infinite to arrive at the Impossible."*

It would interest none but students should I recite the circumstances of the discovery. Prosecuting my usual researches, I seemed rather to have stumbled on this tremendous thing than to have evolved it from formulæ.

Of course, you already know that all molecules, all atoms, are separated from each other by spaces perhaps as great, when compared relatively, as those which separate the members of the stellar universe. And when by my Y-ray I could so far increase these spaces that I could pass one solid body through another, owing to the differing situation of their atoms, I felt no disembodied spirit had wider, freer range than I. Until my discovery was made public my power over the material universe was practically unlimited.

Le Sage's theory concerning ultra-mundane corpuscles was rejected because corpuscles could not pass through solids. But here were corpuscles passing through solids. As I proceeded, I found that at the displacement of one one-billionth of a centimeter the object capable of passing through another was still visible, owing to the refraction of the air, and had the power of communicating its polarization; and that at two one-billionths the object became invisible, but that at either displacement the subject, if a person, could see into the present plane; and all movement and direction were voluntary. I further found my Y-ray could so polarize a substance that its touch in turn temporarily polarized anything with which it came in contact, a negative current moving atoms to the left, and a positive to the right of the present plane.

My first experience with this new principle would have made a less determined man drop the affair. Brant had been by way of dropping into my office and laboratory when in town. As I afterwards recalled, he showed a signal interest in certain toxicological experiments. "Man alive!" I had said to him once, "let those crystals alone! A single one of them will send you where you never see the sun!" I was uncertain if he brushed one off the slab. He did not return for some months. His wife, as I heard afterwards, had a long and baffling illness in the meantime, divorcing him on her recovery; and he had remained out of sight, at last leaving his native place for the great city. He had come in now, plausibly to ask my opinion of a stone — a diamond of unusual size and water.

I put the stone on a glass shelf in the next room while looking for the slide. You can imagine my sensation when that diamond, with something like a flash of shadow, so intense and swift it was, burst into a hundred rays of blackness and subsided — a pile of carbon! I had forgotten that the shelf happened to be negatively polarized, consequently everything it touched sharing its polarization, and that in pursuing my experiment I had polarized myself also, but with the opposite current; thus the atoms of my fingers passing through the spaces of the atoms of the stone already polarized, separated them negatively so far that they suffered disintegration and returned to the normal. "Good heavens! What has happened!" I cried before I thought. In a moment he was in the rear room and bending with me over the carbon. "Well," he said straightening himself directly, "you gave me a pretty fright. I thought for a moment that was my diamond."

"But it is!" I whispered.

"Pshaw!" he exclaimed roughly. "What do you take me for? Come, come, I'm not here for tricks. That's enough damned legerdemain. Where's my diamond?"

With less dismay and more presence of mind I should have edged along to my batteries, depolarized myself, placed in vacuum the tiny shelf of glass and applied my Y-ray; and with, I knew not what, of convulsion and flame the atoms might have slipped into place. But, instead, I stood gasping. He turned and surveyed me; the low order of his intelligence could receive but one impression.

"Look here," he said, "you will give me back my stone! Now! Or I will have an officer here!"

My mind was flying like the current through my coils. How could I restore the carbon to its original, as I must, if at all, without touching it, and how could I gain time without betraying my secret? "You are very short," I said. "What would you do with your officer?"

"Give you up! Give you up, appear against you, and let you have a sentence of twenty years behind bars."

"Hard words, Mr. Brant. You could say I had your property. I could deny it. Would your word outweigh mine? But return to the office in five minutes—if it is a possible thing you shall——"

"And leave you to make off with my jewel! Not by a long shot! I'm a bad man to deal with, and I'll have my stone or——"

"Go for your officer," said I.

His eye, sharp as a dagger's point, fell an instant. How could he trust me? I might escape with my booty. Throwing open the window to call, I might pinion him from behind, powerful as he was. But before he could gainsay, I had taken half a dozen steps backward, reaching my batteries.

"Give your alarm," I said. I put out my hand, lifting my lever, turned the current into my coils, and blazed up my Y-ray for half a heart-beat, succeeding in that brief time in reversing and in receiving the current that so far changed matters that the thing I touched would remain normal, although I was left still so far subjected to the ray of the less displacement that I ought, when the thrill had subsided, to be able to step through the wall as easily as if no wall were there. "Do you see what I have here?" I most unwisely exclaimed. "In one second I could annihilate you——" I had no time for more, or even to make sure I was correct, before, keeping one eye on me, he had called the officer.

"Look here," he said again, turning on me. "I know enough to see you have something new there, some of your damned inventions. Come, give me my diamond, and if it is worth while I'll find the capital, go halves, and drop this matter."

"Not to save your life!" I cried.

"You know me, officer," he said, as the blue coat came running in. "I give this man into custody for theft."

"It is a mistake, officer," I said. "But you will do your duty."

"Take him to the central station," said Mr. Brant, "and have him searched. He has a jewel of mine on his person."

"Yer annar's sure it's not on the primmises?" asked the officer.

"He has had no time——"

"Sure, if it's quick he do be he's as like to toss it in a corner——"

I stretched out my hand to a knob that silenced the humming among my wires, and at the same time sent up a thread of white fire whose instant rush and subsidence hinted of terrible power behind. The last divisible particle of radium— their eyeballs throbbed for a week.

"Search," I said. "But be careful about shocks. I don't want murder here, too."

Apparently they also were of that mind. For, recovering their sight, they threw my coat over my shoulders and marched me between them to the station, where I was searched, and, as it was already late, locked into a cell for the night.

I could not waste strength on the matter. I was waiting for the dead middle of the night. Then I should put things to proof.

I confess it was a time of intense breathlessness while waiting for silence and slumber to seal the world. Then I called upon my soul, and I stepped boldly forward and walked through that stone wall as if it had been air.

Of course, at my present displacement I was perfectly visible, and I slipped behind this and that projection, and into that alley, till sure of safety. There I made haste to my quarters, took the shelf holding the carbon, and at once subjected it to the necessary treatment. I was unprepared for the result. One instant the room seemed full of a blinding white flame, an intolerable heat, which shut my eyes and singed my hair and blistered my face.

"It is the atmosphere of a fire-dissolving planet," I thought. And then there was darkness and a strange odor.

I fumbled and stumbled about till I could let in the fresh air; and presently I saw the dim light of the street lamp. Then I turned on my own lights—and there was the quartz slab with a curious fusing of its edges, and in the center, flashing, palpitating, lay the diamond, all fire and whiteness. I wonder if it were not considerably larger; but it was hot as if just fallen from Syra Vega; it contracted slightly after subjection to dephlogistic gases.

It was near morning when, having found Brant's address, I passed into his house and his room, and took my bearings. I found his waistcoat, left the diamond in one of its pockets, and returned. It would not do to remain away, visible or invisible. I must be vindicated, cleared of the charge, set right before the world by Brant's appearing and confessing his mistake on finding the diamond in his pocket.

Judge Brant did nothing of the kind. Having visited me in my cell and in vain renewed his request to share in the invention which the habit of his mind convinced him must be of importance, he appeared against me. And the upshot of the business was that I went to prison for the term of years he had threatened.

I asked for another interview with him; but was refused, unless on the terms already declined. My lawyer, with the prison chaplain, went to him, but to no purpose. At last I went myself, as I had gone before, begging him not to ruin the work of my life. He regarded me as a bad dream, and I could not undeceive him without betraying my secret. I returned to my cell and again waited. For to escape was only to prevent possible vindication. If Mary had lived—but I was alone in the world.

The chaplain arranged with my landlord to take a sum of money I had, and to keep my rooms and apparatus intact till the expiration of my sentence. And then I put on the shameful and degrading prison garb and submitted to my fate.

It was a black fate. On the edge of the greatest triumph over matter that had ever been achieved, on the verge of announcing the actuality of the Fourth Dimension of Space, and of defining and declaring its laws, I was a convict laborer at a prison bench.

One day Judge Brant, visiting a client under sentence of death, in relation to his fee, made pretext to look me up, and stopped at my bench. "And how do you like it as far as you've gone?" he said.

"So that I go no farther," I replied. "And unless you become accessory to my taking off, you will acknowledge you found the stone in your pocket——"

"Not yet, not yet," he said, with an unctuous laugh. "It was a keen jest you played. Regard this as a jest in return. But when you are ready, I am ready."

The thing was hopeless. That night I bade good-by to the life that had plunged me from the pinnacle of light to the depths of hell.

When again conscious I lay on a cot in the prison hospital. My attempt had been unsuccessful. St. Angel sat beside me. It was here, practically, he came into my life—alas! that I came into his.

In the long nights of darkness and failing faintness, when horror had me by the throat, he was beside me, and his warm, human touch was all that held me while I hung over the abyss. When I swooned off again his hand, his voice, his bending face recalled me. "Why not let me go, and then an end?" I sighed.

"To save you from a great sin," he replied. And I clung to his hand with the animal instinct of living.

I was well, and in my cell, when he said. "You claim to be an honest man——"

"And yet?"

"You were about taking that which did not belong to you."

"I hardly understand——"

"Can you restore life once taken?"

"Oh, life! That worthless thing!"

"Lent for a purpose."

"For torture!"

"If by yourself you could breathe breath into any pinch of feathers and toss it off your hand a creature—but, as it is, life is a trust. And you, a man of parts, of power, hold it only to return with usury."

"And stripped of the power of gathering usury! Robbed of the work about to revolutionize the world!"

"The world moves on wide waves. Another man will presently have reached your discovery."

As if that were a thing to be glad of! I learned afterwards that St. Angel had given up the sweetness of life for the sake of his enemy. He had gone to prison, and himself worn the stripes, rather than the woman he loved should know her husband was the criminal. Perhaps he did not reconcile this with his love of inviolate truth. But St. Angel had never felt so much regard for his own soul as for the service of others. Self-forgetfulness was the dominant of all his nature.

"Tell me," he said, sitting with me, "about your work."

A whim of trustfulness seized me. I drew an outline, but paused at the look of pity on his face. He felt there was but one conclusion to draw—that I was a madman.

"Very well," I said, "you shall see." And I walked through the wall before his amazed eyes, and walked back again.

For a moment speechless, "You have hypnotic power," then he said. "You made me think I saw it."

"You did see it. I can go free any day I choose."

"And you do not?"

"I must be vindicated." And I told exactly what had taken place with Brant and his diamond. "Perhaps that vindication will never come," I said at last. "The offended *amour propre*, and the hope of gain, hindered in the beginning. Now he will find it impossible."

"That is too monstrous to believe!" said St. Angel. "But since you can, why not spend an hour or two at night with your work?"

"In these clothes! How long before I should be brought back? The first wayfarer—oh, you see!"

St. Angel thought a while. "You are my size," he said then. "We will exchange clothes. I will remain here. In three hours return, that you may get your sleep. It is fortunate the prison should be in the same town."

Night after night then I was in my old rooms, the shutters up, lost in my dreams and my researches, arriving at great ends.

Night after night I reappeared on the moment, and St. Angel went his way.

I had now found that molecular displacement can be had in various directions. Going further, I saw that gravity acts on bodies whose molecules are on the same plane, and one of the possible results of the application of the Y-ray was the suspension of the laws of gravity. This possibly accounted for an almost inappreciable buoyancy and the power of directing one's course. My last studies showed that a substance thus treated has the degenerative power of attracting the molecules of any norm into its new orbit—a disastrous possibility. A chair might disappear into a table previously treated by a Y-ray. In fact, the outlook was to infinity. The change so slight—the result so astonishing! The subject might go into molecular interstices as far removed, to all essential purpose, as if billions of miles away in interstellar space. Nothing was changed, nothing disrupted; but the thing had stepped aside to let the world go by. The secrets of the world were mine. The criminal was at my mercy. The lover had no reserves from me. And as for my enemy, the Lord had delivered him into my hand. I could leave him only a puzzle for the dissectors. I could make him, although yet alive, a conscious ghost to stand or wander in his altered shape through years of nightmare alone and lost. What wonders of energy would follow this ray of displacement. What withdrawal of malignant growth and deteriorating tissue was to come. "To what heights of succor for humanity the surgeon can rise with it!" said St. Angel, as, full of my enthusiasm, I dilated on the marvel.

"He can work miracles!" I exclaimed. "He can heal the sick, walk on the deep, perhaps—who knows—raise the dead!"

I was at the height of my endeavor when St. Angel brought me my pardon. He had so stated my case to the Governor, so spoken of my interrupted career, and of my prison conduct, that the pardon had been given. I refused to accept it. "I accept," I said, "nothing but vindication, if I stay here till the day of judgment!"

"But there is no provision for you now," he urged. "Officially you no longer exist."

"Here I am," I said, "and here I stay."

"At any rate," he continued, "come out with me now and see the Governor, and see the world and the daylight outdoors, and be a man among men a while!"

With the stipulation that I should return, I put on a man's clothes again and went out the gates.

It was with a thrill of exultation that, exhibiting the affairs in my room to St. Angel, finally I felt the vibrating impulse that told me I had received the ray of the larger displacement. In a moment I should be viewless as the air.

"Where are you?" said St. Angel, turning this way and that. "What has become of you?"

"Seeing is believing," I said. "Sometimes not seeing is the naked truth."

"Oh, but this is uncanny!" he exclaimed. "A voice out of empty air."

"Not so empty! But place your hand under the second coil. Have no fear. You hear me now," I said. "I am in perhaps the Fourth Dimension. I am invisible to any one not there—to all the world, except, presently, yourself. For now you, you also, pass into the unseen. Tell me what you feel."

"Nothing," he said. "A vibration—a suspicion of one. No, a blow, a sense of coming collapse, so instant it has passed."

"Now," I said, "there is no one on earth with eyes to see you but myself!"

"That seems impossible."

"Did you see me? But now you do. We are on the same plane. Look in that glass. There is the reflection of the room, of the window, the chair. Do you see me? Yourself?"

"Powers of the earth and air, but this is ghastly!" said St. Angel.

"It is the working of natural law. Now we will see the world, ourselves unseen."

"An unfair advantage."

"Perhaps. But there are things to accomplish to-day." What things I never dreamed; or I had stayed on the threshold.

I wanted St. Angel to know the manner of man this Brant was. We went out, and arrested our steps only inside Brant's office.

"This door is always blowing open!" said the clerk, and he returned to a woman standing in a suppliant attitude. "The Judge has gone to the races," he said, "and he's left word that Tuesday morning your goods'll be put out of the house if you don't pay up!" The woman went her way weeping.

Leaving, we mounted a car; we would go to the races ourselves. I doubt if St. Angel had ever seen anything of the sort. I observed him quietly slip a dime into the conductor's pocket—he felt that even the invisible, like John Gilpin, carried a right. "This opens a way for the right hand undreamed of the left," he said to me later.

It was not long before we found Judge Brant, evidently in an anxious frame, his expanse of countenance white with excitement. He had been plunging heavily, as I learned, and had big money staked, not upon the favorite but upon *Hannan*, the black mare. "That man would hardly put up so much on less than a certainty," I thought. Winding our way unseen among the grooms and horses, I found what I suspected—a plan to pocket the favorite. "But I know a game worth two of that," I said. I took a couple of small smooth pebbles, previously prepared, from the chamois bag into which I had put them with some others and an aluminum wafer treated for the larger displacement, and slipped one securely under the favorite's saddle-girth. When he warmed to his work he should be, for perhaps half an hour, at the one-billionth point, before the virtue expired, and capable of passing through every obstacle as he was directed.

"Hark you, Danny," then I whispered in the jockey's ear.

"Who are you? What—I—I—don't——" looking about with terror.

"It's no ghost," I whispered hurriedly. "Keep your nerve. I am flesh and blood—alive as you. But I have the property which for half an hour I give you—a new discovery. And knowing Bub and Whittler's game, it's up to you to knock 'em out. Now, remember, when they try the pocket ride straight through them!"

Other things kept my attention; and when the crucial moment came I had some excited heart-beats. And so had Judge Brant. It was in the instant when Danny, having held the favorite well in hand for the first stretch, *Hannan* and *Darter* in the lead and the field following, was about calling on her speed, that suddenly Bub and Whittler drew their horses' heads a trifle more closely together, in such wise that it was impossible to pass on either side, and a horse could no more shoot ahead than if a stone wall stood there. "Remember, Danny!" I shouted, making a trumpet of my hands. "Ride straight through!"

And Danny did. He pulled himself together, and set his teeth as if it were a compact with powers of evil, and rode straight through without turning a hair, or disturbing either horse or rider. Once more the Y-ray was triumphant.

But about Judge Brant the air was blue. It would take a very round sum of money to recoup the losses of those few moments. I disliked to have St. Angel hear him; but it was all in the day's work.

The day had not been to Judge Brant's mind, as at last he bent his steps to the club. As he went it occurred to me to try upon him the larger ray of displacement, and I slipped down the back of his collar the wafer I had ready. He would not at once feel its action, but in the warmth either of walking or dining, its properties should be lively for nearly an hour. I had curiosity to see if the current worked not only through all substances, but through all sorts and conditions.

"I should prefer a better pursuit," said St. Angel, as we reached the street. "Is there not something ignoble in it?"

"In another case. Here it is necessary to hound the criminal, to see the man entirely. A game not to be played too often, for there is work to be done before establishing the counteracting currents that may ensure reserves and privacies to people. To-night let us go to the club with Judge Brant, and then I will back to my cell."

As you may suppose, Brant was a man neither of imagination nor humor. As you have seen, he was hard and cruel, priding himself on being a good hater, which in his contention meant indulgence of a preternaturally vindictive temper when prudence allowed. With more cunning than ability, he had achieved some success in his profession, and he secured admission to a good club, recently crowning his efforts, when most of the influential members were absent, by getting himself made one of its governors.

It would be impossible to find a greater contrast to this wretch than in St. Angel—a man of delicate imagination and pure fancy, tender to the child on the street, the fly on the wall; all his atmosphere that of kindness. Gently born, but too finely bred, his physical resistance was so slight that his immunity lay in not being attacked. His clean, fair skin, his brilliant eyes, spoke of health, but the fragility of frame did not speak of strength. Yet St. Angel's life was the active principle of good; his neighborhood was purification.

I was revolving these things while we followed Judge Brant, when I saw him pause in an agitated manner, like one startled out of sleep. A quick shiver ran over his strong frame; he turned red and pale, then with a shrug went on. The displacement had occurred. He was now on the plane of invisibility, and we must have a care ourselves.

Wholly unconscious of any change, the man pursued his way. The street was as usual. There was the boy who always waited for him with the extra but to-night was oblivious; and failing to get his attention the Judge walked on. A shower that had been threatening began to fall, the sprinkle becoming a downpour, with umbrellas spread and people hurrying. The Judge hailed a car; but the motorman was as blind as the newsboy. The shower stopped as suddenly as it had begun, but he went on some paces beforce perceiving that he was perfectly dry, for as he shut and shook his umbrella not a drop fell, and as he took off his hat and looked at it, not an atom of moisture was to be found there. Evidently bewildered, and looking about shamefacedly, I fancied I could hear him saying, with his usual oaths, "I must be deucedly overwrought, or this is some blue devilment."

As the Judge took his accustomed seat in the warm and brilliantly lighted room, and picking up the evening paper, looked over the columns, the familiar every-day affair quieting his nerves so that he could have persuaded himself he had been half asleep as he walked, he was startled by the voice, not four feet away, of one of the old officers who made the Kings County their resort. Something had ruffled the doughty hero. "By the Lord Harry, sir," he was saying in unmodulated tones, "I should like to know what this club is coming to when you can spring on it the election of such a man as this Brant! Judge? What's he Judge of? Beat his wife, too didn't he? The governors used to be gentlemen!"

"But you know, General," said his *vis-à-vis*. "I think no more of him than you do; but when a man lives at the Club——"

"Lives here!" burst in the other angrily. "He hasn't anywhere else to live! Is there a decent house in town open to him? Well, thank goodness, I've somewhere else to go before he comes in! The sight of him gives me a fit of the gout!" And the General stumped out stormily.

"Old boy seems upset!" said some one not far away. "But he's right. It was sheer impudence in the fellow to put up his name."

I could see Brant grow white and gray with anger, as surprised and outraged, wondering what it meant—if the General intended insult—if Scarsdale—but no, apparently they had not seen him. The contemptuous words rankled; the sweat stood on his forehead.

Had not the moment been serious, there were a thousand tricks to play. But the potency of the polarization was subsiding and in a short time the normal molecular plane would be re-established. It was there that I made my mistake. I should not have allowed him to depolarize so soon. I should have kept him bewildered and foodless till famished and weak. Instead, as ion by ion the effect of the ray decreased, his shape grew vague and misty, and then one and another man there rubbed his eyes, for Judge Brant was sitting in his chair and a waiter was hastening towards him.

It had all happened in a few minutes. Plainly the Judge understood nothing of the circumstances. He was dazed, but he must put the best face on it; and he ordered his dinner and a pony of brandy, eating like a hungry animal.

He rose, after a time, refreshed, invigorated, and all himself. Choosing a cigar, he went into another room, seeking a choice lounging place, where for a while he could enjoy his ease and wonder if anything worse than a bad dream had befallen. As for the General's explosion, it did not signify; he was conscious of such opinion; he was overliving it; he would be expelling the old cock yet for conduct unbecoming a gentleman.

Meanwhile, St. Angel, tiring of the affair, and weary, had gone into this room, and in an arm-chair by the hearth was awaiting me—the intrusive quality of my observations not at all to his mind. He had eaten nothing all day, and was somewhat faint. He had closed his eyes, and perhaps fallen into a light doze when he must have been waked by the impact of Brant's powerful frame, as the latter took what seemed to him the empty seat. I expected to see Brant at once flung across the rug by St. Angel's natural effort in rising. Instead, Brant sank into the chair as into down pillows.

I rushed, as quickly as I could, to seize and throw him off, "Through him! Pass through him! Come out! Come to me!" I cried. And people to-day remember that voice out of the air, in the Kings County Club.

It seemed to me that I heard a sound, a sob, a whisper, as if one cried with a struggling sigh, "Impossible!" And with that a strange trembling convulsed Judge Brant's great frame, he lifted his hands, he thrust out his feet, his head fell forward, he groaned gurglingly, shudder after shudder shook him as if every muscle quivered with agony or effort, the big veins started out as if every pulse were a red-hot iron. He was wrestling with something, he knew not what, something as antipathetic to him as white is to black; every nerve was concentrated in rebellion, every fiber struggled to break the spell.

The whole affair was that of a dozen heart-beats—the attempt of the opposing molecules each to draw the other into its own orbit. The stronger physical force, the greater aggregation of atoms was prevailing. Thrust upward for an instant, Brant fell back into his chair exhausted, the purple color fading till his face shone fair as a girl's, sweet and smiling as a child's, white as the face of a risen spirit—Brant's!

Astounded, I seized his shoulder and whirled him about. There was no one else in the chair. I looked in every direction. There was no St. Angel to be seen. There was but one conclusion to draw—the molecules of Brant's stronger material frame had drawn into their own plane the molecules of St. Angel's.

I rushed from the place, careless if seen or unseen, howling in rage and misery. I sought my laboratory, and in a fiend's fury depolarized myself, and I demolished every instrument, every formula, every vestige of my work. I was singed and scorched and burned, but I welcomed any pain. And I went back to prison, admitted by the officials who hardly knew what else to do. I would stay there, I thought, all my days. God grant they should be few! It would be seen that a life of imprisonment and torture were too little punishment for the ruin I had wrought.

It was after a sleepless night, of which every moment seemed madness, that, the door of my cell opening, I saw St. Angel. St. Angel? God have mercy on me, no, it was Judge Brant I saw!

He came forward, with both hands extended, a grave, imploring look on his face. "I have come," he said, a singular sweet overtone in his voice that I had never heard before, yet which echoed like music in my memory, "to make you all the reparation in my power. I will go with you at once before the Governor, and acknowledge that I have found the diamond. I can never hope to atone for what you have suffered. But as long as I live, all that I have, all that I am, is yours!"

There was a look of absolute sweetness on his face that for a dizzy moment made me half distraught. "We will go together," he said. "I have to stop on the way and tell a woman whose mortgage comes due to-day that I have made a different disposition; and, do you know," he added brightly, after an instant's hesitation, "I think I shall help her pay it!" and he laughed gayly at the jest involved.

"Will you say that you have known my innocence all these years?" I said sternly.

"Is not that," he replied, with a touching and persuasive quality of tone, "a trifle too much? Do you think this determination has been reached without a struggle? If you are set right before the world, is not something due to—Brant?"

"If I did not know who and what you are," I said, "I should think the soul of St. Angel had possession of you!"

The man looked at me dreamily. "Strange!" he murmured. "I seem to have heard something like that before. However," as if he shook off a perplexing train of thought, "all that is of no consequence. It is not who you are, but what you do. Come, my friend, don't deny me, don't let the good minute slip. Surely the undoing of the evil of a lifetime, the turning of that force to righteousness, is work outweighing all a prison chaplain's——"

My God, what had the intrusion of my incapable hands upon forbidden mysteries done!

"Come," he said. "We will go together. We will carry light into dark places—there are many waiting——"

"St. Angel!" I cried, with a loud voice, "are you here?"

And again the smile of infinite sweetness illuminated the face even as the sun shines up from the depths of a stagnant pool.

❧ EDGAR RICE BURROUGHS (1875–1950)

A real-life adventurer and world traveler, Edgar Rice Burroughs debuted as a popular author in the twilight of the dime novel era and in the dawn of the pulp magazine. Burroughs is best remembered for his archetypal jungle hero, Tarzan, who first appeared in 1912. But he was ultimately responsible for other enduring Fantasies and Science Fiction, including his John Carter of Mars *Space Opera series, which began with the serial novel* Under the Moons of Mars. *(This novel was later retitled* A Princess of Mars *when McClurg Publishers preserved the story in hardcover form.)* Under the Moons of Mars *was an important bridge between nineteenth-century Scientific Romance and early twentieth-century Space Opera (Westerns set in outer space), and between dime novel fiction and pulp magazine fiction.*

In regard to the kinds of fiction Burroughs published—Lost Worlds Fantasies, Westerns, Space Operas, Jungle Adventures, and Mystery stories—his predecessors and contemporaries were numerous. They included H. Rider Haggard, Arthur Conan Doyle, A. Merritt, George Allan England, Francis Stevens, Frank L. Baum, and others. Edgar Rice Burroughs's followers were and are also numerous and include Edmond Hamilton, Ray Cummings, Murray Leinster, Jack Williamson, Otis Albert Kline, Fritz Leiber, Leigh Brackett, Ray Bradbury, and Michael Crichton. A Princess of Mars *is a true classic of Science Fiction.*

A Princess of Mars

(originally published as Under the Moons of Mars *by Norman Bean in* The All-Story, *where the serial began with the February 1912 issue and continued through the July 1912 issue)*

FOREWORD

To the Reader of this Work:

In submitting Captain Carter's strange manuscript to you in book form, I believe that a few words relative to this remarkable personality will be of interest.

My first recollection of Captain Carter is of the few months he spent at my father's home in Virginia, just prior to the opening of the civil war. I was then a child of but five years, yet I well remember the tall, dark, smooth-faced, athletic man whom I called Uncle Jack.

He seemed always to be laughing; and he entered into the sports of the children with the same hearty good fellowship he displayed toward those pastimes in which the men and women of his own age indulged; or he would sit for an hour at a time entertaining my old grandmother with stories of his strange, wild life in all parts of the world. We all loved him, and our slaves fairly worshipped the ground he trod.

He was a splendid specimen of manhood, standing a good two inches over six feet, broad of shoulder and narrow of hip, with the carriage of the trained fighting man. His features were regular and clear cut, his hair black and closely cropped, while his eyes were of a steel gray, reflecting a strong and loyal character, filled with fire and initiative. His manners were perfect, and his courtliness was that of a typical southern gentleman of the highest type.

His horsemanship, especially after hounds, was a marvel and delight even in that country of magnificent horsemen. I have often heard my father caution him against his wild recklessness, but he would only laugh, and say that the tumble that killed him would be from the back of a horse yet unfoaled.

When the war broke out he left us, nor did I see him again for some fifteen or sixteen years. When he returned it was without warning, and I was much surprised to note that he had not aged apparently a moment, nor had he changed in any other outward way. He was, when others were with him, the same genial, happy fellow we had known of old, but when he thought himself alone I have seen him sit for hours gazing off into space, his face set in a look of wistful longing and hopeless misery; and at night he would sit thus looking up into the heavens, at what I did not know until I read his manuscript years afterwards.

He told us that he had been prospecting and mining in Arizona part of the time since the war; and that he had been very successful was evidenced by the unlimited amount of money with which he was supplied. As to the details of his life during these years he was very reticent, in fact he would not talk of them at all.

He remained with us for about a year and then went to New York, where he purchased a little place on the Hudson, where I visited him once a year on the occasions of my trips to the New York market—my father and I owning and operating a string of general stores throughout Virginia at that time. Captain Carter had a small but beautiful cottage, situated on a bluff overlooking the river, and during one of my last visits, in the winter of 1885, I observed he was much occupied in writing, I presume now, upon this manuscript.

He told me at this time that if anything should happen to him he wished me to take charge of his estate, and he gave me a key to a compartment in the safe which stood in his study, telling me I would find his will there and some personal instructions which he had me pledge myself to carry out with absolute fidelity.

After I had retired for the night I have seen him from my window standing in the moonlight on the brink of the bluff overlooking the Hudson with his arms stretched out to the heavens as though in appeal. I thought at the time that he was praying, although I never had understood that he was in the strict sense of the term a religious man.

Several months after I had returned home from my last visit, the first of March, 1886, I think, I received a telegram from him asking me to come to him at once. I had always been his favorite among the younger generation of Carters and so I hastened to comply with his demand.

I arrived at the little station, about a mile from his grounds, on the morning of March 4, 1886, and when I asked the livery man to drive me out to Captain Carter's he replied that if I was a friend of the Captain's he had some very bad news for me; the Captain had been found dead shortly after daylight that very morning by the watchman attached to an adjoining property.

For some reason this news did not surprise me, but I hurried out to his place as quickly as possible, so that I could take charge of the body and of his affairs.

I found the watchman who had discovered him, together with the local police chief and several townspeople, assembled in his little study. The watchman related the few details connected with the finding of the body, which he said had been still warm when he came upon it. It lay, he said, stretched full length in the snow with the arms outstretched above the head toward the edge of the bluff, and when he showed me the spot it flashed upon me that it was the identical one where I had seen him on those other nights, with his arms raised in supplication to the skies.

There were no marks of violence on the body, and with the aid of a local physician the coroner's jury quickly reached a decision of death from heart failure. Left alone in the study, I opened the safe and withdrew the contents of the drawer in which he had told me I would find my instructions. They were in part peculiar indeed, but I have followed them to each last detail as faithfully as I was able.

He directed that I remove his body to Virginia without embalming, and that he be laid in an open coffin within a tomb which he previously had had constructed and which, as I later learned, was well ventilated. The instructions impressed upon me that I must personally see that this was carried out just as he directed, even in secrecy if necessary.

His property was left in such a way that I was to receive the entire income for twenty-five years, when the principal was to become mine. His further instructions related to this manuscript which I was to retain sealed and unread, just as I found it, for eleven years; nor was I to divulge its contents until twenty-one years after his death.

A strange feature about the tomb, where his body still lies, is that the massive door is equipped with a single, huge gold-plated spring lock which can be opened *only from the inside.*

Yours very sincerely,
EDGAR RICE BURROUGHS.

Contents

CHAPTER I

On the Arizona Hills

I am a very old man; how old I do not know. Possibly I am a hundred, possibly more; but I cannot tell because I have never aged as other men, nor do I remember any childhood. So far as I can recollect I have always been a man, a man of about thirty. I appear today as I did forty years and more ago, and yet I feel that I cannot go on living forever; that some day I shall die the real death from which there is no resurrection. I do not know why I should fear death, I who have died twice and am still alive; but yet I have the same horror of it as you who have never died, and it is because of this terror of death, I believe, that I am so convinced of my mortality.

And because of this conviction I have determined to write down the story of the interesting periods of my life and of my death. I cannot explain the phenomena; I can only set down here in the words of an ordinary soldier of fortune a chronicle of the strange events that befell me during the ten years that my dead body lay undiscovered in an Arizona cave.

I have never told this story, nor shall mortal man see this manuscript until after I have passed over for eternity. I know that the average human mind will not believe what it cannot grasp, and so I do not purpose being pilloried by the public, the pulpit, and the press, and held up as a colossal liar when I am but telling the simple truths which some day science will substantiate. Possibly the suggestions which I gained upon Mars, and the knowledge which I can set down in this chronicle, will aid in an earlier understanding of the mysteries of our sister planet; mysteries to you, but no longer mysteries to me.

My name is John Carter; I am better known as Captain Jack Carter of Virginia. At the close of the Civil War I found myself possessed of several hundred thousand dollars (Confederate) and a captain's commission in the cavalry arm of an army which no longer existed; the servant of a state which had vanished with the hopes of the South. Masterless, penniless, and with my only means of livelihood, fighting, gone, I determined to work my way to the southwest and attempt to retrieve my fallen fortunes in a search for gold.

I spent nearly a year prospecting in company with another Confederate officer, Captain James K. Powell of Richmond. We were extremely fortunate, for late in the winter of 1865, after many hardships and privations, we located the most remarkable gold-bearing quartz vein that our wildest dreams had ever pictured. Powell, who was a mining engineer by education, stated that we had uncovered over a million dollars worth of ore in a trifle over three months.

As our equipment was crude in the extreme we decided that one of us must return to civilization, purchase the necessary machinery and return with a sufficient force of men properly to work the mine.

As Powell was familiar with the country, as well as with the mechanical requirements of mining we determined that it would be best for him to make the trip. It
was agreed that I was to hold down our claim against the remote possibility of its
being jumped by some wandering prospector.

On March 3, 1866, Powell and I packed his provisions on two of our burros,
and bidding me good-bye he mounted his horse, and started down the mountainside toward the valley, across which led the first stage of his journey.

The morning of Powell's departure was, like nearly all Arizona mornings, clear
and beautiful; I could see him and his little pack animals picking their way down
the mountainside toward the valley, and all during the morning I would catch occasional glimpses of them as they topped a hog back or came out upon a level
plateau. My last sight of Powell was about three in the afternoon as he entered the
shadows of the range on the opposite side of the valley.

Some half hour later I happened to glance casually across the valley and was
much surprised to note three little dots in about the same place I had last seen my
friend and his two pack animals. I am not given to needless worrying, but the more
I tried to convince myself that all was well with Powell, and that the dots I had seen
on his trail were antelope or wild horses, the less I was able to assure myself.

Since we had entered the territory we had not seen a hostile Indian, and we
had, therefore, become careless in the extreme, and were wont to ridicule the stories we had heard of the great numbers of these vicious marauders that were supposed to haunt the trails, taking their toll in lives and torture of every white party
which fell into their merciless clutches.

Powell, I knew, was well armed and, further, an experienced Indian fighter; but
I too had lived and fought for years among the Sioux in the North, and I knew
that his chances were small against a party of cunning trailing Apaches. Finally I
could endure the suspense no longer, and, arming myself with my two Colt revolvers and a carbine, I strapped two belts of cartridges about me and catching my
saddle horse, started down the trail taken by Powell in the morning.

As soon as I reached comparatively level ground I urged my mount into a can-
ter and continued this, where the going permitted, until, close upon dusk, I discovered the point where other tracks joined those of Powell. They were the tracks
of unshod ponies, three of them, and the ponies had been galloping.

I followed rapidly until, darkness shutting down, I was forced to await the rising
of the moon, and given an opportunity to speculate on the question of the wisdom
of my chase. Possibly I had conjured up impossible dangers, like some nervous old
housewife, and when I should catch up with Powell would get a good laugh for my
pains. However, I am not prone to sensitiveness, and the following of a sense of
duty, wherever it may lead, has always been a kind of fetich with me throughout my
life; which may account for the honors bestowed upon me by three republics and
the decorations and friendships of an old and powerful emperor and several lesser
kings, in whose service my sword has been red many a time.

About nine o'clock the moon was sufficiently bright for me to proceed on my
way and I had no difficulty in following the trail at a fast walk, and in some places
at a brisk trot until, about midnight, I reached the water hole where Powell had
expected to camp. I came upon the spot unexpectedly, finding it entirely deserted,
with no signs of having been recently occupied as a camp.

I was interested to note that the tracks of the pursuing horsemen, for such I was
now convinced they must be, continued after Powell with only a brief stop at the
hole for water; and always at the same rate of speed as his.

I was positive now that the trailers were Apaches and that they wished to capture Powell alive for the fiendish pleasure of the torture, so I urged my horse onward at a most dangerous pace, hoping against hope that I would catch up with the red rascals before they attacked him.

Further speculation was suddenly cut short by the faint report of two shots far ahead of me. I knew that Powell would need me now if ever, and I instantly urged my horse to his topmost speed up the narrow and difficult mountain trail.

I had forged ahead for perhaps a mile or more without hearing further sounds, when the trail suddenly debouched onto a small, open plateau near the summit of the pass. I had passed through a narrow, overhanging gorge just before entering suddenly upon this table land, and the sight which met my eyes filled me with consternation and dismay.

The little stretch of level land was white with Indian tepees, and there were probably half a thousand red warriors clustered around some object near the center of the camp. Their attention was so wholly riveted to this point of interest that they did not notice me, and I easily could have turned back into the dark recesses of the gorge and made my escape with perfect safety. The fact, however, that this thought did not occur to me until the following day removes any possible right to a claim to heroism to which the narration of this episode might possibly otherwise entitle me.

I do not believe that I am made of the stuff which constitutes heroes, because, in all of the hundreds of instances that my voluntary acts have placed me face to face with death, I cannot recall a single one where any alternative step to that I took occurred to me until many hours later. My mind is evidently so constituted that I am subconsciously forced into the path of duty without recourse to tiresome mental processes. However that may be, I have never regretted that cowardice is not optional with me.

In this instance I was, of course, positive that Powell was the center of attraction, but whether I thought or acted first I do not know, but within an instant from the moment the scene broke upon my view I had whipped out my revolvers and was charging down upon the entire army of warriors, shooting rapidly, and whooping at the top of my lungs. Singlehanded, I could not have pursued better tactics, for the red men, convinced by sudden surprise that not less than a regiment of regulars was upon them, turned and fled in every direction for their bows, arrows, and rifles.

The view which their hurried routing disclosed filled me with apprehension and with rage. Under the clear rays of the Arizona moon lay Powell, his body fairly bristling with the hostile arrows of the braves. That he was already dead I could not but be convinced, and yet I would have saved his body from mutilation at the hands of the Apaches as quickly as I would have saved the man himself from death.

Riding close to him I reached down from the saddle, and grasping his cartridge belt drew him up across the withers of my mount. A backward glance convinced me that to return by the way I had come would be more hazardous than to continue across the plateau, so, putting spurs to my poor beast, I made a dash for the opening to the pass which I could distinguish on the far side of the table land.

The Indians had by this time discovered that I was alone and I was pursued with imprecations, arrows, and rifle balls. The fact that it is difficult to aim anything but imprecations accurately by moonlight, that they were upset by the sudden and unexpected manner of my advent, and that I was a rather rapidly moving target saved me from the various deadly projectiles of the enemy and permitted me to reach the shadows of the surrounding peaks before an orderly pursuit could be organized.

My horse was traveling practically unguided as I knew that I had probably less knowledge of the exact location of the trail to the pass than he, and thus it happened that he entered a defile which led to the summit of the range and not to the pass which I had hoped would carry me to the valley and to safety. It is probable, however, that to this fact I owe my life and the remarkable experiences and adventures which befell me during the following ten years.

My first knowledge that I was on the wrong trail came when I heard the yells of the pursuing savages suddenly grow fainter and fainter far off to my left.

I knew then that they had passed to the left of the jagged rock formation at the edge of the plateau, to the right of which my horse had borne me and the body of Powell.

I drew rein on a little level promontory overlooking the trail below and to my left, and saw the party of pursuing savages disappearing around the point of a neighboring peak.

I knew the Indians would soon discover that they were on the wrong trail and that the search for me would be renewed in the right direction as soon as they located my tracks.

I had gone but a short distance further when what seemed to be an excellent trail opened up around the face of a high cliff. The trail was level and quite broad and led upward and in the general direction I wished to go. The cliff arose for several hundred feet on my right, and on my left was an equal and nearly perpendicular drop to the bottom of a rocky ravine.

I had followed this trail for perhaps a hundred yards when a sharp turn to the right brought me to the mouth of a large cave. The opening was about four feet in height and three to four feet wide, and at this opening the trail ended.

It was now morning, and, with the customary lack of dawn which is a startling characteristic of Arizona, it had become daylight almost without warning.

Dismounting, I laid Powell upon the ground, but the most painstaking examination failed to reveal the faintest spark of life. I forced water from my canteen between his dead lips, bathed his face and rubbed his hands, working over him continuously for the better part of an hour in the face of the fact that I knew him to be dead.

I was very fond of Powell; he was thoroughly a man in every respect; a polished southern gentleman; a staunch and true friend; and it was with a feeling of the deepest grief that I finally gave up my crude endeavors at resuscitation.

Leaving Powell's body where it lay on the ledge I crept into the cave to reconnoiter. I found a large chamber, possibly a hundred feet in diameter and thirty or forty feet in height; a smooth and well-worn floor, and many other evidences that the cave had, at some remote period, been inhabited. The back of the cave was so lost in dense shadow that I could not distinguish whether there were openings into other apartments or not.

As I was continuing my examination I commenced to feel a pleasant drowsiness creeping over me which I attributed to the fatigue of my long and strenuous ride, and the reaction from the excitement of the fight and the pursuit. I felt comparatively safe in my present location as I knew that one man could defend the trail to the cave against an army.

I soon became so drowsy that I could scarcely resist the strong desire to throw myself on the floor of the cave for a few moments' rest, but I knew that this would never do, as it would mean certain death at the hands of my red friends, who might be upon me at any moment. With an effort I started toward the opening of the cave only to reel drunkenly against a side wall, and from there slip prone upon the floor.

CHAPTER II

The Escape of the Dead

A sense of delicious dreaminess overcame me, my muscles relaxed, and I was on the point of giving way to my desire to sleep when the sound of approaching horses reached my ears. I attempted to spring to my feet but was horrified to discover that my muscles refused to respond to my will. I was now thoroughly awake, but as unable to move a muscle as though turned to stone. It was then, for the first time, that I noticed a slight vapor filling the cave. It was extremely tenuous and only noticeable against the opening which led to daylight. There also came to my nostrils a faintly pungent odor, and I could only assume that I had been overcome by some poisonous gas, but why I should retain my mental faculties and yet be unable to move I could not fathom.

I lay facing the opening of the cave and where I could see the short stretch of trail which lay between the cave and the turn of the cliff around which the trail led. The noise of the approaching horses had ceased, and I judged the Indians were creeping stealthily upon me along the little ledge which led to my living tomb. I remember that I hoped they would make short work of me as I did not particularly relish the thought of the innumerable things they might do to me if the spirit prompted them.

I had not long to wait before a stealthy sound apprised me of their nearness, and then a war-bonneted, paint-streaked face was thrust cautiously around the shoulder of the cliff, and savage eyes looked into mine. That he could see me in the dim light of the cave I was sure for the early morning sun was falling full upon me through the opening.

The fellow, instead of approaching, merely stood and stared; his eyes bulging and his jaw dropped. And then another savage face appeared, and a third and fourth and fifth, craning their necks over the shoulders of their fellows whom they could not pass upon the narrow ledge. Each face was the picture of awe and fear, but for what reason I did not know, nor did I learn until ten years later. That there were still other braves behind those who regarded me was apparent from the fact that the leaders passed back whispered word to those behind them.

Suddenly a low but distinct moaning sound issued from the recesses of the cave behind me, and, as it reached the ears of the Indians, they turned and fled in terror, panic-stricken. So frantic were their efforts to escape from the unseen thing behind me that one of the braves was hurled headlong from the cliff to the rocks below. Their wild cries echoed in the canyon for a short time, and then all was still once more.

The sound which had frightened them was not repeated, but it had been sufficient as it was to start me speculating on the possible horror which lurked in the shadows at my back. Fear is a relative term and so I can only measure my feelings at that time by what I had experienced in previous positions of danger and by those I have passed through since; but I can say without shame that if the sensations I endured during the next few minutes were fear, then may God help the coward, for cowardice is of a surety its own punishment.

To be held paralyzed, with one's back toward some horrible and unknown danger from the very sound of which the ferocious Apache warriors turn in wild stampede, as a flock of sheep would madly flee from a pack of wolves, seems to me the last word in fearsome predicaments for a man who had ever been used to fighting for his life with all the energy of a powerful physique.

Several times I thought I heard faint sounds behind me as of somebody moving cautiously, but eventually even these ceased, and I was left to the contemplation of my position without interruption. I could but vaguely conjecture the cause of my paralysis, and my only hope lay in that it might pass off as suddenly as it had fallen upon me.

Late in the afternoon my horse, which had been standing with dragging rein before the cave, started slowly down the trail, evidently in search of food and water, and I was left alone with my mysterious unknown companion and the dead body of my friend, which lay just within my range of vision upon the ledge where I had placed it in the early morning.

From then until possibly midnight all was silence, the silence of the dead; then, suddenly, the awful moan of the morning broke upon my startled ears, and there came again from the black shadows the sound of a moving thing, and a faint rustling as of dead leaves. The shock to my already overstrained nervous system was terrible in the extreme, and with a superhuman effort I strove to break my awful bonds. It was an effort of the mind, of the will, of the nerves; not muscular, for I could not move even so much as my little finger, but none the less mighty for all that. And then something gave, there was a momentary feeling of nausea, a sharp click as of the snapping of a steel wire, and I stood with my back against the wall of the cave facing my unknown foe.

And then the moonlight flooded the cave, and there before me lay my own body as it had been lying all these hours, with the eyes staring toward the open ledge and the hands resting limply upon the ground. I looked first at my lifeless clay there upon the floor of the cave and then down at myself in utter bewilderment; for there I lay clothed, and yet here I stood but naked as at the minute of my birth.

The transition had been so sudden and so unexpected that it left me for a moment forgetful of aught else than my strange metamorphosis. My first thought was, is this then death! Have I indeed passed over forever into that other life! But I could not well believe this, as I could feel my heart pounding against my ribs from the exertion of my efforts to release myself from the anaesthesis which had held me. My breath was coming in quick, short gasps, cold sweat stood out from every pore of my body, and the ancient experiment of pinching revealed the fact that I was anything other than a wraith.

Again was I suddenly recalled to my immediate surroundings by a repetition of the weird moan from the depths of the cave. Naked and unarmed as I was, I had no desire to face the unseen thing which menaced me.

My revolvers were strapped to my lifeless body which, for some unfathomable reason, I could not bring myself to touch. My carbine was in its boot, strapped to my saddle, and as my horse had wandered off I was left without means of defense. My only alternative seemed to lie in flight and my decision was crystallized by a recurrence of the rustling sound from the thing which now seemed, in the darkness of the cave and to my distorted imagination, to be creeping stealthily upon me.

Unable longer to resist the temptation to escape this horrible place I leaped quickly through the opening into the starlight of a clear Arizona night. The crisp, fresh mountain air outside the cave acted as an immediate tonic and I felt new life and new courage coursing through me. Pausing upon the brink of the ledge I up-braided myself for what now seemed to me wholly unwarranted apprehension. I reasoned with myself that I had lain helpless for many hours within the cave, yet nothing had molested me, and my better judgment, when permitted the direction of clear and logical reasoning, convinced me that the noises I had heard must have resulted from purely natural and harmless causes; probably the conformation of the cave was such that a slight breeze had caused the sounds I heard.

I decided to investigate, but first I lifted my head to fill my lungs with the pure, invigorating night air of the mountains. As I did so I saw stretching far below me the beautiful vista of rocky gorge, and level, cacti-studded flat, wrought by the moonlight into a miracle of soft splendor and wondrous enchantment.

Few western wonders are more inspiring than the beauties of an Arizona moonlit landscape; the silvered mountains in the distance, the strange lights and shadows upon hog back and arroyo, and the grotesque details of the stiff, yet beautiful cacti form a picture at once enchanting and inspiring; as though one were catching for the first time a glimpse of some dead and forgotten world, so different is it from the aspect of any other spot upon our earth.

As I stood thus meditating, I turned my gaze from the landscape to the heavens where the myriad stars formed a gorgeous and fitting canopy for the wonders of the earthly scene. My attention was quickly riveted by a large red star close to the distant horizon. As I gazed upon it I felt a spell of overpowering fascination—it was Mars, the god of war, and for me, the fighting man, it had always held the power of irresistible enchantment. As I gazed at it on that far-gone night it seemed to call across the unthinkable void, to lure me to it, to draw me as the lodestone attracts a particle of iron.

My longing was beyond the power of opposition; I closed my eyes, stretched out my arms toward the god of my vocation and felt myself drawn with the sud-denness of thought through the trackless immensity of space. There was an in-stant of extreme cold and utter darkness.

CHAPTER III

My Advent on Mars

I opened my eyes upon a strange and weird landscape. I knew that I was on Mars; not once did I question either my sanity or my wakefulness. I was not asleep, no need for pinching here; my inner consciousness told me as plainly that I was upon Mars as your conscious mind tells you that you are upon Earth. You do not ques-tion the fact; neither did I.

I found myself lying prone upon a bed of yellowish, moss-like vegetation which stretched around me in all directions for interminable miles. I seemed to be lying in a deep, circular basin, along the outer verge of which I could distinguish the ir-regularities of low hills.

It was midday, the sun was shining full upon me and the heat of it was rather intense upon my naked body, yet no greater than would have been true under sim-ilar conditions on an Arizona desert. Here and there were slight outcroppings of quartz-bearing rock which glistened in the sunlight; and a little to my left, perhaps a hundred yards, appeared a low, walled enclosure about four feet in height. No water, and no other vegetation than the moss was in evidence, and as I was somewhat thirsty I determined to do a little exploring.

Springing to my feet I received my first Martian surprise, for the effort, which on Earth would have brought me standing upright, carried me into the Martian air to the height of about three yards. I alighted softly upon the ground, however, without appreciable shock or jar. Now commenced a series of evolutions which even then seemed ludicrous in the extreme. I found that I must learn to walk all over again, as the muscular exertion which carried me easily and safely upon Earth played strange antics with me upon Mars.

Instead of progressing in a sane and dignified manner, my attempts to walk resulted in a variety of hops which took me clear of the ground a couple of feet at each step and landed me sprawling upon my face or back at the end of each second or third hop. My muscles, perfectly attuned and accustomed to the force of gravity on Earth, played the mischief with me in attempting for the first time to cope with the lesser gravitation and lower air pressure on Mars.

I was determined, however, to explore the low structure which was the only evidence of habitation in sight, and so I hit upon the unique plan of reverting to first principles in locomotion, creeping. I did fairly well at this and in a few moments had reached the low, encircling wall of the enclosure.

There appeared to be no doors or windows upon the side nearest me, but as the wall was but about four feet high I cautiously gained my feet and peered over the top upon the strangest sight it had ever been given me to see.

The roof of the enclosure was of solid glass about four or five inches in thickness, and beneath this were several hundred large eggs, perfectly round and snowy white. The eggs were nearly uniform in size being about two and one-half feet in diameter.

Five or six had already hatched and the grotesque caricatures which sat blinking in the sunlight were enough to cause me to doubt my sanity. They seemed mostly head, with little scrawny bodies, long necks and six legs, or, as I afterward learned, two legs and two arms, with an intermediary pair of limbs which could be used at will either as arms or legs. Their eyes were set at the extreme sides of their heads a trifle above the center and protruded in such a manner that they could be directed either forward or back and also independently of each other, thus permitting this queer animal to look in any direction, or in two directions at once, without the necessity of turning the head.

The ears, which were slightly above the eyes and closer together, were small, cup-shaped antennae, protruding not more than an inch on these young specimens. Their noses were but longitudinal slits in the center of their faces, midway between their mouths and ears.

There was no hair on their bodies, which were of a very light yellowish-green color. In the adults, as I was to learn quite soon, this color deepens to an olive green and is darker in the male than in the female. Further, the heads of the adults are not so out of proportion to their bodies as in the case of the young.

The iris of the eyes is blood red, as in Albinos, while the pupil is dark. The eyeball itself is very white, as are the teeth. These latter add a most ferocious appearance to an otherwise fearsome and terrible countenance, as the lower tusks curve upward to sharp points which end about where the eyes of earthly human beings are located. The whiteness of the teeth is not that of ivory, but of the snowiest and most gleaming of china. Against the dark background of their olive skins their tusks stand out in a most striking manner, making these weapons present a singularly formidable appearance.

Most of these details I noted later, for I was given but little time to speculate on the wonders of my new discovery. I had seen that the eggs were in the process of hatching, and as I stood watching the hideous little monsters break from their shells I failed to note the approach of a score of full-grown Martians from behind me.

Coming, as they did, over the soft and soundless moss, which covers practically the entire surface of Mars with the exception of the frozen areas at the poles and the scattered cultivated districts, they might have captured me easily, but their intentions were far more sinister. It was the rattling of the accouterments of the foremost warrior which warned me.

On such a little thing my life hung that I often marvel that I escaped so easily. Had not the rifle of the leader of the party swung from its fastenings beside his saddle in such a way as to strike against the butt of his great metal shod spear I should have snuffed out without ever knowing that death was near me. But the little sound caused me to turn, and there upon me, not ten feet from my breast, was the point of that huge spear, a spear forty feet long, tipped with gleaming metal, and held low at the side of a mounted replica of the little devils I had been watching.

But how puny and harmless they now looked beside this huge and terrific incarnation of hate, of vengeance and of death. The man himself, for such I may call him, was fully fifteen feet in height and, on Earth, would have weighed some four hundred pounds. He sat his mount as we sit a horse, grasping the animal's barrel with his lower limbs, while the hands of his two right arms held his immense spear low at the side of his mount; his two left arms were outstretched laterally to help preserve his balance, the thing he rode having neither bridle or reins of any description for guidance.

And his mount! How can earthly words describe it! It towered ten feet at the shoulder; had four legs on either side; a broad flat tail, larger at the tip than at the root, and which it held straight out behind while running; a gaping mouth which split its head from its snout to its long, massive neck.

Like its master, it was entirely devoid of hair, but was of a dark slate color and exceeding smooth and glossy. Its belly was white, and its legs shaded from the slate of its shoulders and hips to a vivid yellow at the feet. The feet themselves were heavily padded and nailless, which fact had also contributed to the noiselessness of their approach, and, in common with a multiplicity of legs, is a characteristic feature of the fauna of Mars. The highest type of man and one other animal, the only mammal existing on Mars, alone have well-formed nails, and there are absolutely no hoofed animals in existence there.

Behind this first charging demon trailed nineteen others, similar in all respects, but, as I learned later, bearing individual characteristics peculiar to themselves; precisely as no two of us are identical although we are all cast in a similar mold. This picture, or rather materialized nightmare, which I have described at length, made but one terrible and swift impression on me as I turned to meet it.

Unarmed and naked as I was, the first law of nature manifested itself in the only possible solution of my immediate problem, and that was to get out of the vicinity of the point of the charging spear. Consequently I gave a very earthly and at the same time superhuman leap to reach the top of the Martian incubator, for such I had determined it must be.

My effort was crowned with a success which appalled me no less than it seemed to surprise the Martian warriors, for it carried me fully thirty feet into the air and landed me a hundred feet from my pursuers and on the opposite side of the enclosure.

I alighted upon the soft moss easily and without mishap, and turning saw my enemies lined up along the further wall. Some were surveying me with expressions which I afterward discovered marked extreme astonishment, and the others were evidently satisfying themselves that I had not molested their young.

They were conversing together in low tones, and gesticulating and pointing toward me. Their discovery that I had not harmed the little Martians, and that I was unarmed, must have caused them to look upon me with less ferocity; but, as I was to learn later, the thing which weighed most in my favor was my exhibition of hurdling.

While the Martians are immense, their bones are very large and they are muscled only in proportion to the gravitation which they must overcome. The result is that they are infinitely less agile and less powerful, in proportion to their weight, than an Earth man, and I doubt that were one of them suddenly to be transported to Earth he could lift his own weight from the ground; in fact, I am convinced that he could not do so.

My feat then was as marvelous upon Mars as it would have been upon Earth, and from desiring to annihilate me they suddenly looked upon me as a wonderful discovery to be captured and exhibited among their fellows.

The respite my unexpected agility had given me permitted me to formulate plans for the immediate future and to note more closely the appearance of the warriors, for I could not disassociate these people in my mind from those other warriors who, only the day before, had been pursuing me.

I noted that each was armed with several other weapons in addition to the huge spear which I have described. The weapon which caused me to decide against an attempt at escape by flight was what was evidently a rifle of some description, and which I felt, for some reason, they were peculiarly efficient in handling.

These rifles were of a white metal stocked with wood, which I learned later was a very light and intensely hard growth much prized on Mars, and entirely unknown to us denizens of Earth. The metal of the barrel is an alloy composed principally of aluminum and steel which they have learned to temper to a hardness far exceeding that of the steel with which we are familiar. The weight of these rifles is comparatively little, and with the small caliber, explosive, radium projectiles which they use, and the great length of the barrel, they are deadly in the extreme and at ranges which would be unthinkable on Earth. The theoretic effective radius of this rifle is three hundred miles, but the best they can do in actual service when equipped with their wireless finders and sighters is but a trifle over two hundred miles.

This is quite far enough to imbue me with great respect for the Martian firearm, and some telepathic force must have warned me against an attempt to escape in broad daylight from under the muzzles of twenty of these death-dealing machines.

The Martians, after conversing for a short time, turned and rode away in the direction from which they had come, leaving one of their number alone by the enclosure. When they had covered perhaps two hundred yards they halted, and turning their mounts toward us sat watching the warrior by the enclosure.

He was the one whose spear had so nearly transfixed me, and was evidently the leader of the band, as I had noted that they seemed to have moved to their present position at his direction. When his force had come to a halt he dismounted, threw down his spear and small arms, and came around the end of the incubator toward me, entirely unarmed and as naked as I, except for the ornaments strapped upon his head, limbs, and breast.

When he was within about fifty feet of me he unclasped an enormous metal armlet, and holding it toward me in the open palm of his hand, addressed me in a clear, resonant voice, but in a language, it is needless to say, I could not understand. He then stopped as though waiting for my reply, pricking up his antennae-like ears and cocking his strange-looking eyes still further toward me.

As the silence became painful I concluded to hazard a little conversation on my own part, as I had guessed that he was making overtures of peace. The throwing down of his weapons and the withdrawing of his troop before his advance toward me would have signified a peaceful mission anywhere on Earth, so why not, then, on Mars!

Placing my hand over my heart I bowed low to the Martian and explained to him that while I did not understand his language, his actions spoke for the peace and friendship that at the present moment were most dear to my heart. Of course I might have been a babbling brook for all the intelligence my speech carried to him, but he understood the action with which I immediately followed my words.

Stretching my hand toward him, I advanced and took the armlet from his open palm, clasping it about my arm above the elbow; smiled at him and stood waiting. His wide mouth spread into an answering smile, and locking one of his intermediary arms in mine we turned and walked back toward his mount. At the same time he motioned his followers to advance. They started toward us on a wild run, but were checked by a signal from him. Evidently he feared that were I to be really frightened again I might jump entirely out of the landscape.

He exchanged a few words with his men, motioned to me that I would ride behind one of them, and then mounted his own animal. The fellow designated reached down two or three hands and lifted me up behind him on the glossy back of his mount, where I hung on as best I could by the belts and straps which held the Martian's weapons and ornaments.

The entire cavalcade then turned and galloped away toward the range of hills in the distance.

CHAPTER IV

A Prisoner

We had gone perhaps ten miles when the ground began to rise very rapidly. We were, as I was later to learn, nearing the edge of one of Mars' long-dead seas, in the bottom of which my encounter with the Martians had taken place.

In a short time we gained the foot of the mountains, and after traversing a narrow gorge came to an open valley, at the far extremity of which was a low table land upon which I beheld an enormous city. Toward this we galloped, entering it by what appeared to be a ruined roadway leading out from the city, but only to the edge of the table land, where it ended abruptly in a flight of broad steps.

Upon closer observation I saw as we passed them that the buildings were deserted, and while not greatly decayed had the appearance of not having been tenanted for years, possibly for ages. Toward the center of the city was a large plaza, and upon this and in the buildings immediately surrounding it were camped some nine or ten hundred creatures of the same breed as my captors, for such I now considered them despite the suave manner in which I had been trapped.

With the exception of their ornaments all were naked. The women varied in appearance but little from the men, except that their tusks were much larger in proportion to their height, in some instances curving nearly to their high-set ears.

Their bodies were smaller and lighter in color, and their fingers and toes bore the rudiments of nails, which were entirely lacking among the males. The adult females ranged in height from ten to twelve feet.

The children were light in color, even lighter than the women, and all looked precisely alike to me, except that some were taller than others; older, I presumed.

I saw no signs of extreme age among them, nor is there any appreciable difference in their appearance from the age of maturity, about forty, until, at about the age of one thousand years, they go voluntarily upon their last strange pilgrimage down the river Iss, which leads no living Martian knows whither and from whose bosom no Martian has ever returned, or would be allowed to live did he return after once embarking upon its cold, dark waters.

Only about one Martian in a thousand dies of sickness or disease, and possibly about twenty take the voluntary pilgrimage. The other nine hundred and seventy-nine die violent deaths in duels, in hunting, in aviation and in war; but perhaps by far the greatest death loss comes during the age of childhood, when vast numbers of the little Martians fall victims to the great white apes of Mars.

The average life expectancy of a Martian after the age of maturity is about three hundred years, but would be nearer the one-thousand mark were it not for the various means leading to violent death. Owing to the waning resources of the planet it evidently became necessary to counteract the increasing longevity which their remarkable skill in therapeutics and surgery produced, and so human life has come to be considered but lightly on Mars, as is evidenced by their dangerous sports and the almost continual warfare between the various communities.

There are other and natural causes tending toward a diminution of population, but nothing contributes so greatly to this end as the fact that no male or female Martian is ever voluntarily without a weapon of destruction.

As we neared the plaza and my presence was discovered we were immediately surrounded by hundreds of the creatures who seemed anxious to pluck me from my seat behind my guard. A word from the leader of the party stilled their clamor, and we proceeded at a trot across the plaza to the entrance of as magnificent an edifice as mortal eye has rested upon.

The building was low, but covered an enormous area. It was constructed of gleaming white marble inlaid with gold and brilliant stones which sparkled and scintillated in the sunlight. The main entrance was some hundred feet in width and projected from the building proper to form a huge canopy above the entrance hall. There was no stairway, but a gentle incline to the first floor of the building opened into an enormous chamber encircled by galleries.

On the floor of this chamber, which was dotted with highly carved wooden desks and chairs, were assembled about forty or fifty male Martians around the steps of a rostrum. On the platform proper squatted an enormous warrior heavily loaded with metal ornaments, gay-colored feathers and beautifully wrought leather trappings ingeniously set with precious stones. From his shoulders depended a short cape of white fur lined with brilliant scarlet silk.

What struck me as most remarkable about this assemblage and the hall in which they were congregated was the fact that the creatures were entirely out of proportion to the desks, chairs, and other furnishings; these being of a size adapted to human beings such as I, whereas the great bulks of the Martians could scarcely have squeezed into the chairs, nor was there room beneath the desks for their long legs. Evidently, then, there were other denizens on Mars than the wild and grotesque creatures into whose hands I had fallen, but the evidences of extreme antiquity which showed all around me indicated that these buildings might have belonged to some long-extinct and forgotten race in the dim antiquity of Mars.

Our party had halted at the entrance to the building, and at a sign from the leader I had been lowered to the ground. Again locking his arm in mine, we had proceeded into the audience chamber. There were few formalities observed in approaching the Martian chieftain. My captor merely strode up to the rostrum, the others making way for him as he advanced. The chieftain rose to his feet and uttered the name of my escort who, in turn, halted and repeated the name of the ruler followed by his title.

At the time, this ceremony and the words they uttered meant nothing to me, but later I came to know that this was the customary greeting between green Martians. Had the men been strangers, and therefore unable to exchange names, they would have silently exchanged ornaments, had their missions been peaceful — otherwise they would have exchanged shots, or have fought out their introduction with some other of their various weapons.

My captor, whose name was Tars Tarkas, was virtually the vice-chieftain of the community, and a man of great ability as a statesman and warrior. He evidently explained briefly the incidents connected with his expedition, including my capture, and when he had concluded the chieftain addressed me at some length.

I replied in our good old English tongue merely to convince him that neither of us could understand the other; but I noticed that when I smiled slightly on concluding, he did likewise. This fact, and the similar occurrence during my first talk with Tars Tarkas, convinced me that we had at least something in common; the ability to smile, therefore to laugh; denoting a sense of humor. But I was to learn that the Martian smile is merely perfunctory, and that the Martian laugh is a thing to cause strong men to blanch in horror.

The ideas of humor among the green men of Mars are widely at variance with our conceptions of incitants to merriment. The death agonies of a fellow being are, to these strange creatures, provocative of the wildest hilarity, while their chief form of commonest amusement is to inflict death on their prisoners of war in various ingenious and horrible ways.

The assembled warriors and chieftains examined me closely, feeling my muscles and the texture of my skin. The principal chieftain then evidently signified a desire to see me perform, and, motioning me to follow, he started with Tars Tarkas for the open plaza.

Now, I had made no attempt to walk, since my first signal failure, except while tightly grasping Tars Tarkas' arm, and so now I went skipping and flitting about among the desks and chairs like some monstrous grasshopper. After bruising myself severely, much to the amusement of the Martians, I again had recourse to creeping, but this did not suit them and I was roughly jerked to my feet by a towering fellow who had laughed most heartily at my misfortunes.

As he banged me down upon my feet his face was bent close to mine and I did the only thing a gentleman might do under the circumstances of brutality, boorishness, and lack of consideration for a stranger's rights; I swung my fist squarely to his jaw and he went down like a felled ox. As he sunk to the floor I wheeled around with my back toward the nearest desk, expecting to be overwhelmed by the vengeance of his fellows, but determined to give them as good a battle as the unequal odds would permit before I gave up my life.

My fears were groundless, however, as the other Martians, at first struck dumb with wonderment, finally broke into wild peals of laughter and applause. I did not recognize the applause as such, but later, when I had become acquainted with their customs, I learned that I had won what they seldom accord, a manifestation of approbation.

The fellow whom I had struck lay where he had fallen, nor did any of his mates approach him. Tars Tarkas advanced toward me, holding out one of his arms, and we thus proceeded to the plaza without further mishap. I did not, of course, know the reason for which we had come to the open, but I was not long in being enlightened. They first repeated the word "sak" a number of times, and then Tars Tarkas made several jumps, repeating the same word before each leap; then, turning to me, he said, "sak!" I saw what they were after, and gathering myself together I "sakked" with such marvelous success that I cleared a good hundred and fifty feet; nor did I this time, lose my equilibrium, but landed squarely upon my feet without falling. I then returned by easy jumps of twenty-five or thirty feet to the little group of warriors.

My exhibition had been witnessed by several hundred lesser Martians, and they immediately broke into demands for a repetition, which the chieftain then ordered me to make; but I was both hungry and thirsty, and determined on the spot that my only method of salvation was to demand the consideration from these creatures which they evidently would not voluntarily accord. I therefore ignored the repeated commands to "sak," and each time they were made I motioned to my mouth and rubbed my stomach.

Tars Tarkas and the chief exhanged a few words, and the former, calling to a young female among the throng, gave her some instructions and motioned me to accompany her. I grasped her proffered arm and together we crossed the plaza toward a large building on the far side.

My fair companion was about eight feet tall, having just arrived at maturity, but not yet to her full height. She was of a light olive-green color, with a smooth, glossy hide. Her name, as I afterward learned, was Sola, and she belonged to the retinue of Tars Tarkas. She conducted me to a spacious chamber in one of the buildings fronting on the plaza, and which, from the litter of silks and furs upon the floor, I took to be the sleeping quarters of several of the natives.

The room was well lighted by a number of large windows and was beautifully decorated with mural paintings and mosaics, but upon all there seemed to rest that indefinable touch of the finger of antiquity which convinced me that the architects and builders of these wondrous creations had nothing in common with the crude half-brutes which now occupied them.

Sola motioned me to be seated upon a pile of silks near the center of the room, and, turning, made a peculiar hissing sound, as though signaling to someone in an adjoining room. In response to her call I obtained my first sight of a new Martian wonder. It waddled in on its ten short legs, and squatted down before the girl like an obedient puppy. The thing was about the size of a Shetland pony, but its head bore a slight resemblance to that of a frog, except that the jaws were equipped with three rows of long, sharp tusks.

CHAPTER V

I Elude My Watch Dog

Sola stared into the brute's wicked-looking eyes, muttered a word or two of command, pointed to me, and left the chamber. I could not but wonder what this ferocious-looking monstrosity might do when left alone in such close proximity to such a relatively tender morsel of meat; but my fears were groundless, as the beast, after surveying me intently for a moment, crossed the room to the only exit which led to the street, and lay down full length across the threshold.

This was my first experience with a Martian watch dog, but it was destined not to be my last, for this fellow guarded me carefully during the time I remained a captive among these green men; twice saving my life, and never voluntarily being away from me a moment.

While Sola was away I took occasion to examine more minutely the room in which I found myself captive. The mural painting depicted scenes of rare and wonderful beauty: mountains, rivers, lake, ocean, meadow, trees and flowers, winding roadways, sun-kissed gardens—scenes which might have portrayed earthly views but for the different colorings of the vegetation. The work had evidently been wrought by a master hand, so subtle the atmosphere, so perfect the technique; yet nowhere was there a representation of a living animal, either human or brute, by which I could guess at the likeness of these other and perhaps extinct denizens of Mars.

While I was allowing my fancy to run riot in wild conjecture on the possible explanation of the strange anomalies which I had so far met with on Mars, Sola returned bearing both food and drink. These she placed on the floor beside me, and seating herself a short ways off regarded me intently. The food consisted of about a pound of some solid substance of the consistency of cheese and almost tasteless, while the liquid was apparently milk from some animal. It was not unpleasant to the taste, though slightly acid, and I learned in a short time to prize it very highly. It came, as I later discovered, not from an animal, as there is only one mammal on Mars and that one very rare indeed, but from a large plant which grows practically without water, but seems to distill its plentiful supply of milk from the products of the soil, the moisture of the air, and the rays of the sun. A single plant of this species will give eight or ten quarts of milk per day.

After I had eaten I was greatly invigorated, but feeling the need of rest I stretched out upon the silks and was soon asleep. I must have slept several hours, as it was dark when I awoke, and I was very cold. I noticed that someone had thrown a fur over me, but it had become partially dislodged and in the darkness I could not see to replace it. Suddenly a hand reached out and pulled the fur over me, shortly afterwards adding another to my covering.

I presumed that my watchful guardian was Sola, nor was I wrong. This girl alone, among all the green Martians with whom I came in contact, disclosed characteristics of sympathy, kindliness, and affection; her ministrations to my bodily wants were unfailing, and her solicitous care saved me from much suffering and many hardships.

As I was to learn, the Martian nights are extremely cold, and as there is practically no twilight or dawn, the changes in temperature are sudden and most uncomfortable, as are the transitions from brilliant daylight to darkness. The nights are either brilliantly illumined or very dark, for if neither of the two moons of Mars happen to be in the sky almost total darkness results, since the lack of atmosphere, or, rather, the very thin atmosphere, fails to diffuse the starlight to any great extent; on the other hand, if both of the moons are in the heavens at night the surface of the ground is brightly illuminated.

Both of Mars' moons are vastly nearer her than is our moon to Earth; the nearer moon being but about five thousand miles distant, while the further is but little more than fourteen thousand miles away, against the nearly one-quarter million miles which separate us from our moon. The nearer moon of Mars makes a complete revolution around the planet in a little over seven and one-half hours, so that she may be seen hurtling through the sky like some huge meteor two or three times each night, revealing all her phases during each transit of the heavens.

The further moon revolves about Mars in something over thirty and one-quarter hours, and with her sister satellite makes a nocturnal Martian scene one of splendid and weird grandeur. And it is well that nature has so graciously and abundantly lighted the Martian night, for the green men of Mars, being a nomadic race without high intellectual development, have but crude means for artificial lighting; depending principally upon torches, a kind of candle, and a peculiar oil lamp which generates a gas and burns without a wick.

This last device produces an intensely brilliant far-reaching white light, but as the natural oil which it requires can only be obtained by mining in one of several widely separated and remote localities it is seldom used by these creatures whose only thought is for today, and whose hatred for manual labor has kept them in a semi-barbaric state for countless ages.

After Sola had replenished my coverings I again slept, nor did I awaken until daylight. The other occupants of the room, five in number, were all females, and they were still sleeping, piled high with a motley array of silks and furs. Across the threshold lay stretched the sleepless guardian brute, just as I had last seen him on the preceding day; apparently he had not moved a muscle; his eyes were fairly glued upon me, and I fell to wondering just what might befall me should I endeavor to escape.

I have ever been prone to seek adventure and to investigate and experiment where wiser men would have left well enough alone. It therefore now occurred to me that the surest way of learning the exact attitude of this beast toward me would be to attempt to leave the room. I felt fairly secure in my belief that I could escape him should he pursue me once I was outside the building, for I had begun to take great pride in my ability as a jumper. Furthermore, I could see from the shortness of his legs that the brute himself was no jumper and probably no runner.

Slowly and carefully, therefore, I gained my feet, only to see that my watcher did the same; cautiously I advanced toward him, finding that by moving with a shuffling gait I could retain my balance as well as make reasonably rapid progress. As I neared the brute he backed cautiously away from me, and when I had reached the open he moved to one side to let me pass. He then fell in behind me and followed about ten paces in my rear as I made my way along the deserted street.

Evidently his mission was to protect me only, I thought, but when we reached the edge of the city he suddenly sprang before me, uttering strange sounds and baring his ugly and ferocious tusks. Thinking to have some amusement at his expense, I rushed toward him, and when almost upon him sprang into the air, alighting far beyond him and away from the city. He wheeled instantly and charged me with the most appalling speed I had ever beheld. I had thought his short legs a bar to swiftness, but had he been coursing with greyhounds the latter would have appeared as though asleep on a door mat. As I was to learn, this is the fleetest animal on Mars, and owing to its intelligence, loyalty, and ferocity is used in hunting, in war, and as the protector of the Martian man.

I quickly saw that I would have difficulty in escaping the fangs of the beast on a straightaway course, and so I met his charge by doubling in my tracks and leaping over him as he was almost upon me. This maneuver gave me a considerable advantage, and I was able to reach the city quite a bit ahead of him, and as he came tearing after me I jumped for a window about thrity feet from the ground in the face of one of the buildings overlooking the valley.

Grasping the sill I pulled myself up to a sitting posture without looking into the building, and gazed down at the baffled animal beneath me. My exultation was short-lived, however, for scarcely had I gained a secure seat upon the sill than a huge hand grasped me by the neck from behind and dragged me violently into the room. Here I was thrown upon my back, and beheld standing over me a colossal ape-like creature, white and hairless except for an enormous shock of bristly hair upon its head.

CHAPTER VI

A Fight That Won Friends

The thing, which more nearly resembled our earthly men than it did the Martians I had seen, held me pinioned to the ground with one huge foot, while it jabbered and gesticulated at some answering creature behind me. This other, which was evidently its mate, soon came toward us, bearing a mighty stone cudgel with which it evidently intended to brain me.

The creatures were about ten or fifteen feet tall, standing erect, and had, like the green Martians, an intermediary set of arms or legs, midway between their upper and lower limbs. Their eyes were close together and non-protruding; their ears were high set, but more laterally located than those of the Martians, while their snouts and teeth were strikingly like those of our African gorilla. Altogether they were not unlovely when viewed in comparison with the green Martians.

The cudgel was swinging in the arc which ended upon my upturned face when a bolt of myriad-legged horror hurled itself through the doorway full upon the breast of my executioner. With a shriek of fear the ape which held me leaped through the open window, but its mate closed in a terrific death struggle with my preserver, which was nothing less than my faithful watch-thing; I cannot bring myself to call so hideous a creature a dog.

As quickly as possible I gained my feet and backing against the wall I witnessed such a battle as it is vouchsafed few beings to see. The strength, agility, and blind ferocity of these two creatures is approached by nothing known to earthly man. My beast had an advantage in his first hold, having sunk his mighty fangs far into the breast of his adversary; but the great arms and paws of the ape, backed by muscles far transcending those of the Martian men I had seen, had locked the throat of my guardian and slowly were choking out his life, and bending back his head and neck upon his body, where I momentarily expected the former to fall limp at the end of a broken neck.

In accomplishing this the ape was tearing away the entire front of its breast, which was held in the vise-like grip of the powerful jaws. Back and forth upon the floor they rolled, neither one emitting a sound of fear or pain. Presently I saw the great eyes of my beast bulging completely from their sockets and blood flowing from its nostrils. That he was weakening perceptibly was evident, but so also was the ape, whose struggles were growing momentarily less.

Suddenly I came to myself and, with that strange instinct which seems ever to prompt me to my duty, I seized the cudgel, which had fallen to the floor at the commencement of the battle, and swinging it with all the power of my earthly arms I crashed it full upon the head of the ape, crushing his skull as though it had been an eggshell.

Scarcely had the blow descended when I was confronted with a new danger. The ape's mate, recovered from its first shock of terror, had returned to the scene of the encounter by way of the interior of the building. I glimpsed him just before he reached the doorway and the sight of him, now roaring as he perceived his lifeless fellow stretched upon the floor, and frothing at the mouth, in the extremity of his rage, filled me, I must confess, with dire forebodings.

I am ever willing to stand and fight when the odds are not too overwhelmingly against me, but in this instance I perceived neither glory nor profit in pitting my relatively puny strength against the iron muscles and brutal ferocity of this enraged denizen of an unknown world; in fact, the only outcome of such an encounter, so far as I might be concerned, seemed sudden death.

I was standing near the window and I knew that once in the street I might gain the plaza and safety before the creature could overtake me; at least there was a chance for safety in flight, against almost certain death should I remain and fight however desperately.

It is true I held the cudgel, but what could I do with it against his four great arms? Even should I break one of them with my first blow, for I figured that he would attempt to ward off the cudgel, he could reach out and annihilate me with the others before I could recover for a second attack.

In the instant that these thoughts passed through my mind I had turned to make for the window, but my eyes alighting on the form of my erstwhile guardian threw all thoughts of flight to the four winds. He lay gasping upon the floor of the chamber, his great eyes fastened upon me in what seemed a pitiful appeal for protection. I could not withstand that look, nor could I, on second thought, have deserted my rescuer without giving as good an account of myself in his behalf as he had in mine.

Without more ado, therefore, I turned to meet the charge of the infuriated bull ape. He was now too close upon me for the cudgel to prove of any effective assistance, so I merely threw it as heavily as I could at his advancing bulk. It struck him just below the knees, eliciting a howl of pain and rage, and so throwing him off his balance that he lunged full upon me with arms wide stretched to ease his fall.

Again, as on the preceding day, I had recourse to earthly tactics, and swinging my right fist full upon the point of his chin I followed it with a smashing left to the pit of his stomach. The effect was marvelous, for, as I lightly sidestepped, after delivering the second blow, he reeled and fell upon the floor doubled up with pain and gasping for wind. Leaping over his prostrate body, I seized the cudgel and finished the monster before he could regain his feet.

As I delivered the blow a low laugh rang out behind me, and, turning, I beheld Tars Tarkas, Sola, and three or four warriors standing in the doorway of the chamber. As my eyes met theirs I was, for the second time, the recipient of their zealously guarded applause.

My absence had been noted by Sola on her awakening, and she had quickly informed Tars Tarkas, who had set out immediately with a handful of warriors to search for me. As they had approached the limits of the city they had witnessed the actions of the bull ape as he bolted into the building, frothing with rage.

They had followed immediately behind him, thinking it barely possible that his actions might prove a clew to my whereabouts and had witnessed my short but decisive battle with him. This encounter, together with my set-to with the Martian warrior on the previous day and my feats of jumping placed me upon a high pinnacle in their regard. Evidently devoid of all the finer sentiments of friendship, love, or affection, these people fairly worship physical prowess and bravery, and nothing is too good for the object of their adoration as long as he maintains his position by repeated examples of his skill, strength, and courage.

Sola, who had accompanied the searching party of her own volition, was the only one of the Martians whose face had not been twisted in laughter as I battled for my life. She, on the contrary, was sober with apparent solicitude and, as soon as I had finished the monster, rushed to me and carefully examined my body for possible wounds or injuries. Satisfying herself that I had come off unscathed she smiled quietly, and, taking my hand, started toward the door of the chamber.

Tars Tarkas and the other warriors had entered and were standing over the now rapidly reviving brute which had saved my life, and whose life I, in turn, had rescued. They seemed to be deep in argument, and finally one of them addressed me, but remembering my ignorance of his language turned back to Tars Tarkas, who, with a word and gesture, gave some command to the fellow and turned to follow us from the room.

There seemed something menacing in their attitude toward my beast, and I hesitated to leave until I had learned the outcome. It was well I did so, for the warrior drew an evil-looking pistol from its holster and was on the point of putting an end to the creature when I sprang forward and struck up his arm. The bullet striking the wooden casing of the window exploded, blowing a hole completely through the wood and masonry.

I then knelt down beside the fearsome-looking thing, and raising it to its feet motioned for it to follow me. The looks of surprise which my actions elicited from the Martians were ludicrous; they could not understand, except in a feeble and childish way, such attributes as gratitude and compassion. The warrior whose gun I had struck up looked inquiringly at Tars Tarkas, but the latter signed that I be left to my own devices, and so we returned to the plaza with my great beast following close at heel, and Sola grasping me tightly by the arm.

I had at least two friends on Mars; a young woman who watched over me with motherly solicitude, and a dumb brute which, as I later came to know, held in its poor ugly carcass more love, more loyalty, more gratitude than could have been found in the entire five million green Martians who rove the deserted cities and dead sea bottoms of Mars.

CHAPTER VII

Child-Raising on Mars

After a breakfast, which was an exact replica of the meal of the preceding day and an index of practically every meal which followed while I was with the green men of Mars, Sola escorted me to the plaza, where I found the entire community engaged in watching or helping at the harnessing of huge mastodonian animals to great three-wheeled chariots. There were about two hundred and fifty of these vehicles, each drawn by a single animal, any one of which, from their appearance, might easily have drawn the entire wagon train when fully loaded.

The chariots themselves were large, commodious, and gorgeously decorated. In each was seated a female Martian loaded with ornaments of metal, with jewels and silks and furs, and upon the back of each of the beasts which drew the chariots was perched a young Martian driver. Like the animals upon which the warriors were mounted, the heavier draft animals wore neither bit nor bridle, but were guided entirely by telepathic means.

This power is wonderfully developed in all Martians, and accounts largely for the simplicity of their language and the relatively few spoken words exchanged even in long conversations. It is the universal language of Mars, through the medium of which the higher and lower animals of this world of paradoxes are able to communicate to a greater or less extent, depending upon the intellectual sphere of the species and the development of the individual.

As the cavalcade took up the line of march in single file, Sola dragged me into an empty chariot and we proceeded with the procession toward the point by which I had entered the city the day before. At the head of the caravan rode some two hundred warriors, five abreast, and a like number brought up the rear, while twenty-five or thirty outriders flanked us on either side.

Every one but myself—men, women, and children—were heavily armed, and at the tail of each chariot trotted a Martian hound, my own beast following closely behind ours; in fact, the faithful creature never left me voluntarily during the entire ten years I spent on Mars. Our way led out across the little valley before the city, through the hills, and down into the dead sea bottom which I had traversed on my journey from the incubator to the plaza. The incubator, as it proved, was the terminal point of our journey this day, and, as the entire cavalcade broke into a mad gallop as soon as we reached the level expanse of sea bottom, we were soon within sight of our goal.

On reaching it the chariots were parked with military precision on the four sides of the enclosure, and half a score of warriors, headed by the enormous chieftain, and including Tars Tarkas and several other lesser chiefs, dismounted and advanced toward it. I could see Tars Tarkas explaining something to the principal chieftain, whose name, by the way, was, as nearly as I can translate it into English, Lorquas Ptomel, Jed; jed being his title.

I was soon appraised of the subject of their conversation, as, calling to Sola, Tars Tarkas signed for her to send me to him. I had by this time mastered the intricacies of walking under Martian conditions, and quickly responding to his command I advanced to the side of the incubator where the warriors stood.

As I reached their side a glance showed me that all but a very few eggs had hatched, the incubator being fairly alive with the hideous little devils. They ranged in height from three to four feet, and were moving restlessly about the enclosure as though searching for food.

As I came to a halt before him, Tars Tarkas pointed over the incubator and said, "Sak." I saw that he wanted me to repeat my performance of yesterday for the edification of Lorquas Ptomel, and, as I must confess that my prowess gave me no little satisfaction, I responded quickly, leaping entirely over the parked chariots on the far side of the incubator. As I returned, Lorquas Ptomel grunted something at me, and turning to his warriors gave a few words of command relative to the incubator. They paid no further attention to me and I was thus permitted to remain close and watch their operations, which consisted in breaking an opening in the wall of the incubator large enough to permit of the exit of the young Martians.

On either side of this opening the women and the younger Martians, both male and female, formed two solid walls leading out through the chariots and quite away into the plain beyond. Between these walls the little Martians scampered, wild as deer; being permitted to run the full length of the aisle, where they were captured one at a time by the women and older children; the last in the line capturing the first little one to reach the end of the gauntlet, her opposite in the line capturing the second, and so on until all the little fellows had left the enclosure and been appropriated by some youth or female. As the women caught the young they fell out of line and returned to their respective chariots, while those who fell into the hands of the young men were later turned over to some of the women.

I saw that the ceremony, if it could be dignified by such a name, was over, and seeking out Sola I found her in our chariot with a hideous little creature held tightly in her arms.

The work of rearing young, green Martians consists solely in teaching them to talk, and to use the weapons of warfare with which they are loaded down from the very first year of their lives. Coming from eggs in which they have lain for five years, the period of incubation, they step forth into the world perfectly developed except in size. Entirely unknown to their own mothers, who, in turn, would have difficulty in pointing out the fathers with any degree of accuracy, they are the common children of the community, and their education devolves upon the females who chance to capture them as they leave the incubator.

Their foster mothers may not even have had an egg in the incubator, as was the case with Sola, who had not commenced to lay, until less than a year before she became the mother of another woman's offspring. But this counts for little among the green Martians, as parental and filial love is as unknown to them as it is common among us. I believe this horrible system which has been carried on for ages is the direct cause of the loss of all the finer feelings and higher humanitarian instincts among these poor creatures. From birth they know no father or mother love, they know not the meaning of the word home; they are taught that they are only suffered to live until they can demonstrate by their physique and ferocity that they are fit to live. Should they prove deformed or defective in any way they are promptly shot; nor do they see a tear shed for a single one of the many cruel hardships they pass through from earliest infancy.

I do not mean that the adult Martians are unnecessarily or intentionally cruel to the young, but theirs is a hard and pitiless struggle for existence upon a dying planet, the natural resources of which have dwindled to a point where the support of each additional life means an added tax upon the community into which it is thrown.

By careful selection they rear only the hardiest specimens of each species, and with almost supernatural foresight they regulate the birth rate to merely offset the loss by death. Each adult Martian female brings forth about thirteen eggs each year, and those which meet the size, weight, and specific gravity tests are hidden in the recesses of some subterranean vault where the temperature is too low for incubation. Every year these eggs are carefully examined by a council of twenty chieftains, and all but about one hundred of the most perfect are destroyed out of each yearly supply. At the end of five years about five hundred almost perfect eggs have been chosen from the thousands brought forth. These are then placed in the almost air-tight incubators to be hatched by the sun's rays after a period of another five years. The hatching which we had witnessed today was a fairly representative event of its kind, all but about one per cent of the eggs hatching in two days. If the remaining eggs ever hatched we knew nothing of the fate of the little Martians. They were not wanted, as their offspring might inherit and transmit the tendency to prolonged incubation, and thus upset the system which has maintained for ages and which permits the adult Martians to figure the proper time for return to the incubators, almost to an hour.

The incubators are built in remote fastnesses, where there is little or no likelihood of their being discovered by other tribes. The result of such a catastrophe would mean no children in the community for another five years. I was later to witness the results of the discovery of an alien incubator.

The community of which the green Martians with whom my lot was cast formed a part was composed of some thirty thousand souls. They roamed an enormous tract of arid and semi-arid land between forty and eighty degrees south latitude, and bounded on the east and west by two large fertile tracts. Their headquarters lay in the southwest corner of this district, near the crossing of two of the so-called Martian canals.

As the incubator had been placed far north of their own territory in a supposedly uninhabited and unfrequented area, we had before us a tremendous journey, concerning which I, of course, knew nothing.

After our return to the dead city I passed several days in comparative idleness. On the day following our return all the warriors had ridden forth early in the morning and had not returned until just before darkness fell. As I later learned, they had been to the subterranean vaults in which the eggs were kept and had transported them to the incubator, which they had then walled up for another five years, and which, in all probability, would not be visited again during that period.

The vaults which hid the eggs until they were ready for the incubator were located many miles south of the incubator, and would be visited yearly by the council of twenty chieftains. Why they did not arrange to build their vaults and incubators nearer home has always been a mystery to me, and, like many other Martian mysteries, unsolved and unsolvable by earthly reasoning and customs.

Sola's duties were now doubled, as she was compelled to care for the young Martian as well as for me, but neither one of us required much attention, and as we were both about equally advanced in Martian education, Sola took it upon herself to train us together.

Her prize consisted in a male about four feet tall, very strong and physically perfect; also, he learned quickly, and we had considerable amusement, at least I did, over the keen rivalry we displayed. The Martian language, as I have said, is extremely simple, and in a week I could make all my wants known and understand nearly everything that was said to me. Likewise, under Sola's tutelage, I developed my telepathic powers so that I shortly could sense practically everything that went on around me.

What surprised Sola most in me was that while I could catch telepathic messages easily from others, and often when they were not intended for me, no one could read a jot from my mind under any circumstances. At first this vexed me, but later I was very glad of it, as it gave me an undoubted advantage over the Martians.

CHAPTER VIII

A Fair Captive from the Sky

The third day after the incubator ceremony we set forth toward home, but scarcely had the head of the procession debouched into the open ground before the city than orders were given for an immediate and hasty return. As though trained for years in this particular evolution, the green Martians melted like mist into the spacious doorways of the nearby buildings, until, in less than three minutes, the entire cavalcade of chariots, mastodons and mounted warriors was nowhere to be seen.

Sola and I had entered a building upon the front of the city, in fact, the same one in which I had had my encounter with the apes, and, wishing to see what had caused the sudden retreat, I mounted to an upper floor and peered from the window out over the valley and the hills beyond; and there I saw the cause of their sudden scurrying to cover. A huge craft, long, low, and gray-painted, swung slowly over the crest of the nearest hill. Following it came another, and another, and another, until twenty of them, swinging low above the ground, sailed slowly and majestically toward us.

Each carried a strange banner swung from stem to stern above the upper works, and upon the prow of each was painted some odd device that gleamed in the sunlight and showed plainly even at the distance at which we were from the vessels. I could see figures crowding the forward decks and upper works of the air craft. Whether they had discovered us or simply were looking at the deserted city I could not say, but in any event they received a rude reception, for suddenly and without warning the green Martian warriors fired a terrific volley from the windows of the buildings facing the little valley across which the great ships were so peacefully advancing.

Instantly the scene changed as by magic; the foremost vessel swung broadside toward us, and bringing her guns into play returned our fire, at the same time moving parallel to our front for a short distance and then turning back with the evident intention of completing a great circle which would bring her up to position once more opposite our firing line; the other vessels followed in her wake, each one opening upon us as she swung into position. Our own fire never diminished, and I doubt if twenty-five per cent of our shots went wild. It had never been given me to see such deadly accuracy of aim, and it seemed as though a little figure on one of the craft dropped at the explosion of each bullet, while the banners and upper works dissolved in spurts of flame as the irresistible projectiles of our warriors mowed through them.

The fire from the vessels was most ineffectual, owing, as I afterward learned, to the unexpected suddenness of the first volley, which caught the ship's crews entirely unprepared and the sighting apparatus of the guns unprotected from the deadly aim of our warriors.

It seems that each green warrior has certain objective points for his fire under relatively identical circumstances of warfare. For example, a proportion of them, always the best marksmen, direct their fire entirely upon the wireless finding and sighting apparatus of the big guns of an attacking naval force; another detail attends to the smaller guns in the same way; others pick off the gunners; still others the officers; while certain other quotas concentrate their attention upon the other members of the crew, upon the upper works, and upon the steering gear and propellers.

Twenty minutes after the first volley the great fleet swung trailing off in the direction from which it had first appeared. Several of the craft were limping perceptibly, and seemed but barely under the control of their depleted crews. Their fire had ceased entirely and all their energies seemed focused upon escape. Our warriors then rushed up to the roofs of the buildings which we occupied and followed the retreating armada with a continuous fusillade of deadly fire.

One by one, however, the ships managed to dip below the crests of the outlying hills until only one barely moving craft was in sight. This had received the brunt of our fire and seemed to be entirely unmanned, as not a moving figure was visible upon her decks. Slowly she swung from her course, circling back toward us in an erratic and pitiful manner. Instantly the warriors ceased firing, for it was quite apparent that the vessel was entirely helpless, and, far from being in a position to inflict harm upon us, she could not even control herself sufficiently to escape.

As she neared the city the warriors rushed out upon the plain to meet her, but it was evident that she still was too high for them to hope to reach her decks. From my vantage point in the window I could see the bodies of her crew strewn about, although I could not make out what manner of creatures they might be. Not a sign of life was manifest upon her as she drifted slowly with the light breeze in a southeasterly direction.

She was drifting some fifty feet above the ground, followed by all but some hundred of the warriors who had been ordered back to the roofs to cover the possibility of a return of the fleet, or of reinforcements. It soon became evident that she would strike the face of the buildings about a mile south of our position, and as I watched the progress of the chase I saw a number of warriors gallop ahead, dismount and enter the building she seemed destined to touch.

As the craft neared the building, and just before she struck, the Martian warriors swarmed upon her from the windows, and with their great spears eased the shock of the collision, and in a few moments they had thrown out grappling hooks and the big boat was being hauled to ground by their fellows below.

After making her fast, they swarmed the sides and searched the vessel from stem to stern. I could see them examining the dead sailors, evidently for signs of life, and presently a party of them appeared from below dragging a little figure among them. The creature was considerably less than half as tall as the green Martian warriors, and from my balcony I could see that it walked erect upon two legs and surmised that it was some new and strange Martian monstrosity with which I had not as yet become acquainted.

They removed their prisoner to the ground and then commenced a systematic rifling of the vessel. This operation required several hours, during which time a number of the chariots were requisitioned to transport the loot, which consisted in arms, ammunition, silks, furs, jewels, strangely carved stone vessels, and a quantity of solid foods and liquids, including many casks of water, the first I had seen since my advent upon Mars.

After the last load had been removed the warriors made lines fast to the craft and towed her far out into the valley in a southwesterly direction. A few of them then boarded her and were busily engaged in what appeared, from my distant position, as the emptying of the contents of various carboys upon the dead bodies of the sailors and over the decks and works of the vessel.

This operation concluded, they hastily clambered over her sides, sliding down the guy ropes to the ground. The last warrior to leave the deck turned and threw something back upon the vessel, waiting an instant to note the outcome of his act. As a faint spurt of flame rose from the point where the missile struck he swung over the side and was quickly upon the ground. Scarcely had he alighted than the guy ropes were simultaneously released, and the great warship, lightened by the removal of the loot, soared majestically into the air, her decks and upper works a mass of roaring flames.

Slowly she drifted to the southeast, rising higher and higher as the flames ate away her wooden parts and diminished the weight upon her. Ascending to the roof of the building I watched her for hours, until finally she was lost in the dim vistas of the distance. The sight was awe-inspiring in the extreme as one contemplated this mighty floating funeral pyre, drifting unguided and unmanned through the lonely wastes of the Martian heavens; a derelict of death and destruction, typifying the life story of these strange and ferocious creatures into whose unfriendly hands fate had carried it.

Much depressed, and, to me, unaccountably so, I slowly descended to the street. The scene I had witnessed seemed to mark the defeat and annihilation of the forces of a kindred people, rather than the routing by our green warriors of a horde of similar, though unfriendly, creatures. I could not fathom the seeming hallucination, nor could I free myself from it; but somewhere in the innermost recesses of my soul I felt a strange yearning toward these unknown foemen, and a mighty hope surged through me that the fleet would return and demand a reckoning from the green warriors who had so ruthlessly and wantonly attacked it.

Close at my heel, in his now accustomed place, followed Woola, the hound, and as I emerged upon the street Sola rushed up to me as though I had been the object of some search on her part. The cavalcade was returning to the plaza, the homeward march having been given up for that day; nor, in fact, was it recommenced for more than a week, owing to the fear of a return attack by the air craft.

Lorquas Ptomel was too astute an old warrior to be caught upon the open plains with a caravan of chariots and children, and so we remained at the deserted city until the danger seemed passed.

As Sola and I entered the plaza a sight met my eyes which filled my whole being with a great surge of mingled hope, fear, exultation, and depression, and yet most dominant was a subtle sense of relief and happiness; for just as we neared the throng of Martians I caught a glimpse of the prisoner from the battle craft who was being roughly dragged into a nearby building by a couple of green Martian females.

And the sight which met my eyes was that of a slender, girlish figure, similar in every detail to the earthly women of my past life. She did not see me at first, but just as she was disappearing through the portal of the building which was to be her prison she turned, and her eyes met mine. Her face was oval and beautiful in the extreme, her every feature was finely chiseled and exquisite, her eyes large and lustrous and her head surmounted by a mass of coal black, waving hair, caught loosely into a strange yet becoming coiffure. Her skin was of a light reddish copper color, against which the crimson glow of her cheeks and the ruby of her beautifully molded lips shone with a strangely enhancing effect.

She was as destitute of clothes as the green Martians who accompanied her; indeed, save for her highly wrought ornaments she was entirely naked, nor could any apparel have enhanced the beauty of her perfect and symmetrical figure.

As her gaze rested on me her eyes opened wide in astonishment, and she made a little sign with her free hand; a sign which I did not, of course, understand. Just a moment we gazed upon each other, and then the look of hope and renewed courage which had glorified her face as she discovered me, faded into one of utter dejection, mingled with loathing and contempt. I realized I had not answered her signal, and ignorant as I was of Martian customs, I intuitively felt that she had made an appeal for succor and protection which my unfortunate ignorance had prevented me from answering. And then she was dragged out of my sight into the depths of the deserted edifice.

CHAPTER IX

I Learn the Language

As I came back to myself I glanced at Sola, who had witnessed this encounter and I was surprised to note a strange expression upon her usually expressionless countenance. What her thoughts were I did not know, for as yet I had learned but little of the Martian tongue; enough only to suffice for my daily needs.

As I reached the doorway of our building a strange surprise awaited me. A warrior approached bearing the arms, ornaments, and full accouterments of his kind.

These he presented to me with a few unintelligible words, and a bearing at once respectful and menacing.

Later, Sola, with the aid of several of the other women, remodeled the trappings to fit my lesser proportions, and after they completed the work I went about garbed in all the panoply of war.

From then on Sola instructed me in the mysteries of the various weapons, and with the Martian young I spent several hours each day practicing upon the plaza. I was not yet proficient with all the weapons, but my great familiarity with similar earthly weapons made me an unusually apt pupil, and I progressed in a very satisfactory manner.

The training of myself and the young Martians was conducted solely by the women, who not only attend to the education of the young in the arts of individual defense and offense, but are also the artisans who produce every manufactured article wrought by the green Martians. They make the powder, the cartridges, the firearms; in fact everything of value is produced by the females. In time of actual warfare they form a part of the reserves, and when the necessity arises fight with even greater intelligence and ferocity than the men.

The men are trained in the higher branches of the art of war; in strategy and the maneuvering of large bodies of troops. They make the laws as they are needed; a new law for each emergency. They are unfettered by precedent in the administration of justice. Customs have been handed down by ages of repetition, but the punishment for ignoring a custom is a matter for individual treatment by a jury of the culprit's peers, and I may say that justice seldom misses fire, but seems rather to rule in inverse ratio to the ascendency of law. In one respect at least the Martians are a happy people; they have no lawyers.

I did not see the prisoner again for several days subsequent to our first encounter, and then only to catch a fleeting glimpse of her as she was being conducted to the great audience chamber where I had had my first meeting with Lorquas Ptomel. I could not but note the unnecessary harshness and brutality with which her guards treated her; so different from the almost maternal kindliness which Sola manifested toward me, and the respectful attitude of the few green Martians who took the trouble to notice me at all.

I had observed on the two occasions when I had seen her that the prisoner exchanged words with her guards, and this convinced me that they spoke, or at least could make themselves understood by a common language. With this added incentive I nearly drove Sola distracted by my importunities to hasten on my education, and within a few more days I had mastered the Martian tongue sufficiently well to enable me to carry on a passable conversation and to fully understand practically all that I heard.

At this time our sleeping quarters were occupied by three or four females and a couple of the recently hatched young, beside Sola and her youthful ward, myself, and Woola the hound. After they had retired for the night it was customary for the adults to carry on a desultory conversation for a short time before lapsing into sleep, and now that I could understand their language I was always a keen listener, although I never proffered any remarks myself.

On the night following the prisoner's visit to the audience chamber the conversation finally fell upon this subject, and I was all ears on the instant. I had feared to question Sola relative to the beautiful captive, as I could not but recall the strange expression I had noted upon her face after my first encounter with the prisoner. That it denoted jealousy I could not say, and yet, judging all things by mundane standards as I still did, I felt it safer to affect indifference in the matter until I learned more surely Sola's attitude toward the object of my solicitude.

Sarkoja, one of the older women who shared our domicile, had been present at the audience as one of the captive's guards, and it was toward her the questioners turned.

"When," asked one of the women, "will we enjoy the death throes of the red one? or does Lorquas Ptomel, Jed, intend holding her for ransom?"

"They have decided to carry her with us back to Thark, and exhibit her last agonies at the great games before Tal Hajus," replied Sarkoja.

"What will be the manner of her going out?" inquired Sola. "She is very small and very beautiful; I had hoped that they would hold her for ransom."

Sarkoja and the other women grunted angrily at this evidence of weakness on the part of Sola.

"It is sad, Sola, that you were not born a million years ago," snapped Sarkoja, "when all the hollows of the land were filled with water, and the peoples were as soft as the stuff they sailed upon. In our day we have progressed to a point where such sentiments mark weakness and atavism. It will not be well for you to permit Tars Tarkas to learn that you hold such degenerate sentiments, as I doubt that he would care to entrust such as you with the grave responsibilities of maternity."

"I see nothing wrong with my expression of interest in this red woman," retorted Sola. "She has never harmed us, nor would she should we have fallen into her hands. It is only the men of her kind who war upon us, and I have ever thought that their attitude toward us is but the reflection of ours toward them. They live at peace with all their fellows, except when duty calls upon them to make war, while we are at peace with none; forever warring among our own kind as well as upon the red men, and even in our own communities the individuals fight amongst themselves. Oh, it is one continual, awful period of bloodshed from the time we break the shell until we gladly embrace the bosom of the river of mystery, the dark and ancient Iss which carries us to an unknown, but at least no more frightful and terrible existence! Fortunate indeed is he who meets his end in an early death. Say what you please to Tars Tarkas, he can mete out no worse fate to me than a continuation of the horrible existence we are forced to lead in this life."

This wild outbreak on the part of Sola so greatly surprised and shocked the other women, that, after a few words of general reprimand, they all lapsed into silence and were soon asleep. One thing the episode had accomplished was to assure me of Sola's friendliness toward the poor girl, and also to convince me that I had been extremely fortunate in falling into her hands rather than those of some of the other females. I knew that she was fond of me, and now that I had discovered that she hated cruelty and barbarity I was confident that I could depend upon her to aid me and the girl captive to escape, provided of course that such a thing was within the range of possiblities.

I did not even know that there were any better conditions to escape to, but I was more than willing to take my chances among people fashioned after my own mold rather than to remain longer among the hideous and bloodthirsty green men of Mars. But where to go, and how, was as much of a puzzle to me as the age-old search for the spring of eternal life has been to earthly men since the beginning of time.

I decided that at the first opportunity I would take Sola into my confidence and openly ask her to aid me, and with this resolution strong upon me I turned among my silks and furs and slept the dreamless and refreshing sleep of Mars.

CHAPTER X

Champion and Chief

Early the next morning I was astir. Considerable freedom was allowed me, as Sola had informed me that so long as I did not attempt to leave the city I was free to go and come as I pleased. She had warned me, however, against venturing forth unarmed, as this city, like all other deserted metropolises of an ancient Martian civilization, was peopled by the great white apes of my second day's adventure.

In advising me that I must not leave the boundaries of the city Sola had explained that Woola would prevent this anyway should I attempt it, and she warned me most urgently not to arouse his fierce nature by ignoring his warnings should I venture too close to the forbidden territory. His nature was such, she said, that he would bring me back into the city dead or alive should I persist in opposing him; "preferably dead," she added.

On this morning I had chosen a new street to explore when suddenly I found myself at the limits of the city. Before me were low hills pierced by narrow and inviting ravines. I longed to explore the country before me, and, like the pioneer stock from which I sprang, to view what the landscape beyond the encircling hills might disclose from the summits which shut out my view.

It also occurred to me that this would prove an excellent opportunity to test the qualities of Woola. I was convinced that the brute loved me; I had seen more evidences of affection in him than in any other Martian animal, man or beast, and I was sure that gratitude for the acts that had twice saved his life would more than outweigh his loyalty to the duty imposed upon him by cruel and loveless masters.

As I approached the boundary line Woola ran anxiously before me, and thrust his body against my legs. His expression was pleading rather than ferocious, nor did he bare his great tusks or utter his fearful guttural warnings. Denied the friendship and companionship of my kind, I had developed considerable affection for Woola and Sola, for the normal earthly man must have some outlet for his natural affections, and so I decided upon an appeal to a like instinct in this great brute, sure that I would not be disappointed.

I had never petted nor fondled him, but now I sat upon the ground and putting my arms around his heavy neck I stroked and coaxed him, talking in my newly acquired Martian tongue as I would have to my hound at home, as I would have talked to any other friend among the lower animals. His response to my manifestation of affection was remarkable to a degree; he stretched his great mouth to its full width, baring the entire expanse of his upper rows of tusks and wrinkling his snout until his great eyes were almost hidden by the folds of flesh. If you have ever seen a collie smile you may have some idea of Woola's facial distortion.

He threw himself upon his back and fairly wallowed at my feet; jumped up and sprang upon me, rolling me upon the ground by his great weight; then wriggling and squirming around me like a playful puppy presenting its back for the petting it craves. I could not resist the ludicrousness of the spectacle, and holding my sides I rocked back and forth in the first laughter which had passed my lips in many days; the first, in fact, since the morning Powell had left camp when his horse, long unused, had precipitately and unexpectedly bucked him off headforemost into a pot of frijoles.

My laughter frightened Woola, his antics ceased and he crawled pitifully toward me, poking his ugly head far into my lap; and then I remembered what laughter signified on Mars—torture, suffering, death. Quieting myself, I rubbed the poor old fellow's head and back, talked to him for a few minutes, and then in an authoritative tone commanded him to follow me, and arising started for the hills.

There was no further question of authority between us; Woola was my devoted slave from that moment hence, and I his only and undisputed master. My walk to the hills occupied but a few minutes, and I found nothing of particular interest to reward me. Numerous brilliantly colored and strangely formed wild flowers dotted the ravines and from the summit of the first hill I saw still other hills stretching off toward the north, and rising, one range above another, until lost in mountains of quite respectable dimensions; though I afterward found that only a few peaks on all Mars exceed four thousand feet in height; the suggestion of magnitude was merely relative.

My morning's walk had been large with importance to me for it had resulted in a perfect understanding with Woola, upon whom Tars Tarkas relied for my safe keeping. I now knew that while theoretically a prisoner I was virtually free, and I hastened to regain the city limits before the defection of Woola could be discovered by his erstwhile masters. The adventure decided me never again to leave the limits of my prescribed stamping grounds until I was ready to venture forth for good and all, as it would certainly result in a curtailment of my liberties, as well as the probable death of Woola, were we to be discovered.

On regaining the plaza I had my third glimpse of the captive girl. She was standing with her guards before the entrance to the audience chamber, and as I approached she gave me one haughty glance and turned her back full upon me. The act was so womanly, so earthly womanly, that though it stung my pride it also warmed my heart with a feeling of companionship; it was good to know that someone else on Mars beside myself had human instincts of a civilized order, even though the manifestation of them was so painful and mortifying.

Had a green Martian woman desired to show dislike or contempt she would, in all likelihood, have done it with a sword thrust or a movement of her trigger finger; but as their sentiments are mostly atrophied it would have required a serious injury to have aroused such passions in them. Sola, let me add, was an exception; I never saw her perform a cruel or uncouth act, or fail in uniform kindliness and good nature. She was indeed, as her fellow Martian had said of her, an atavism; a dear and precious reversion to a former type of loved and loving ancestor.

Seeing that the prisoner seemed the center of attraction I halted to view the proceedings. I had not long to wait for presently Lorquas Ptomel and his retinue of chieftains approached the building and, signing the guards to follow with the prisoner, entered the audience chamber. Realizing that I was a somewhat favored character, and also convinced that the warriors did not know of my proficiency in their language, as I had pleaded with Sola to keep this a secret on the grounds that I did not wish to be forced to talk with the men until I had perfectly mastered the Martian tongue, I chanced an attempt to enter the audience chamber and listen to the proceedings.

The council squatted upon the steps of the rostrum, while below them stood the prisoner and her two guards. I saw that one of the women was Sarkoja, and thus understood how she had been present at the hearing of the preceding day, the results of which she had reported to the occupants of our dormitory last night. Her attitude toward the captive was most harsh and brutal. When she held her, she sunk her rudimentary nails into the poor girl's flesh, or twisted her arm in a most painful manner. When it was necessary to move from one spot to another she either jerked her roughly, or pushed her headlong before her. She seemed to be venting upon this poor defenseless creature all the hatred, cruelty, ferocity, and spite of her nine hundred years, backed by unguessable ages of fierce and brutal ancestors.

The other woman was less cruel because she was entirely indifferent; if the prisoner had been left to her alone, and fortunately she was at night, she would have received no harsh treatment, nor, by the same token would she have received any attention at all.

As Lorquas Ptomel raised his eyes to address the prisoner they fell on me and he turned to Tars Tarkas with a word, and gesture of impatience. Tars Tarkas made some reply which I could not catch, but which caused Lorquas Ptomel to smile; after which they paid no further attention to me.

"What is your name?" asked Lorquas Ptomel, addressing the prisoner.

"Dejah Thoris, daughter of Mors Kajak of Helium."

"And the nature of your expedition?" he continued.

"It was a purely scientific research party sent out by my father's father, the Jeddak of Helium, to rechart the air currents, and to take atmospheric density tests," replied the fair prisoner, in a low, well-modulated voice.

"We were unprepared for battle," she continued, "as we were on a peaceful mission, as our banners and the colors of our craft denoted. The work we were doing was as much in your interests as in ours, for you know full well that were it not for our labors and the fruits of our scientific operations there would not be enough air or water on Mars to support a single human life. For ages we have maintained the air and water supply at practically the same point without an appreciable loss, and we have done this in the face of the brutal and ignorant interference of your green men.

"Why, oh, why will you not learn to live in amity with your fellows, must you ever go on down the ages to your final extinction but little above the plane of the dumb brutes that serve you! A people without written language, without art, without homes, without love; the victim of eons of the horrible community idea. Owning everything in common, even to your women and children, has resulted in your owning nothing in common. You hate each other as you hate all else except yourselves. Come back to the ways of our common ancestors, come back to the light of kindliness and fellowship. The way is open to you, you will find the hands of the red men stretched out to aid you. Together we may do still more to regenerate our dying planet. The granddaughter of the greatest and mightiest of the red jeddaks has asked you. Will you come?"

Lorquas Ptomel and the warriors sat looking silently and intently at the young woman for several moments after she had ceased speaking. What was passing in their minds no man may know, but that they were moved I truly believe, and if one man high among them had been strong enough to rise above custom, that moment would have marked a new and mighty era for Mars.

I saw Tars Tarkas rise to speak, and on his face was such an expression as I had never seen upon the countenance of a green Martian warrior. It bespoke an inward and mighty battle with self, with heredity, with age-old custom, and as he opened his mouth to speak, a look almost of benignity, of kindliness, momentarily lighted up his fierce and terrible countenance.

What words of moment were to have fallen from his lips were never spoken, as just then a young warrior, evidently sensing the trend of thought among the older men, leaped down from the steps of the rostrum, and striking the frail captive a powerful blow across the face, which felled her to the floor, placed his foot upon her prostrate form and turning toward the assembled council broke into peals of horrid, mirthless laughter.

For an instant I thought Tars Tarkas would strike him dead, nor did the aspect of Lorquas Ptomel augur any too favorably for the brute, but the mood passed, their old selves reasserted their ascendency, and they smiled. It was portentous however that they did not laugh aloud, for the brute's act constituted a side-splitting witticism according to the ethics which rule green Martian humor.

That I have taken moments to write down a part of what occurred as that blow fell does not signify that I remained inactive for any such length of time. I think I must have sensed something of what was coming, for I realize now that I was crouched as for a spring as I saw the blow aimed at her beautiful, upturned, pleading face, and ere the hand descended I was halfway across the hall.

Scarcely had his hideous laugh rang out but once, when I was upon him. The brute was twelve feet in height and armed to the teeth, but I believe that I could have accounted for the whole roomful in the terrific intensity of my rage. Springing upward, I struck him full in the face as he turned at my warning cry and then as he drew his short-sword I drew mine and sprang up again upon his breast, hooking one leg over the butt of his pistol and grasping one of his huge tusks with my left hand while I delivered blow after blow upon his enormous chest.

He could not use his short-sword to advantage because I was too close to him, nor could he draw his pistol, which he attempted to do in direct opposition to Martian custom which says that you may not fight a fellow warrior in private combat with any other than the weapon with which you are attacked. In fact he could do nothing but make a wild and futile attempt to dislodge me. With all his immense bulk he was little if any stronger than I, and it was but the matter of a moment or two before he sank, bleeding and lifeless, to the floor.

Dejah Thoris had raised herself upon one elbow and was watching the battle with wide, staring eyes. When I had regained my feet I raised her in my arms and bore her to one of the benches at the side of the room.

Again no Martian interfered with me, and tearing a piece of silk from my cape I endeavored to staunch the flow of blood from her nostrils. I was soon successful as her injuries mounted to little more than an ordinary nosebleed, and when she could speak she placed her hand upon my arm and looking up into my eyes, said:

"Why did you it? You who refused me even friendly recognition in the first hour of my peril! And now you risk your life and kill one of your companions for my sake. I cannot understand. What strange manner of man are you, that you consort with the green men, though your form is that of my race, while your color is little darker than that of the white ape? Tell me, are you human, or are you more than human?"

"It is a strange tale," I replied, "too long to attempt to tell you now, and one which I so much doubt the credibility of myself that I fear to hope that others will believe it. Suffice it, for the present, that I am your friend, and, so far as our captors will permit, your protector and your servant."

"Then you too are a prisoner? But why, then, those arms and the regalia of a Tharkian chieftain? What is your name? Where is your country?"

"Yes, Dejah Thoris, I too am a prisoner; my name is John Carter, and I claim Virginia, one of the United States of America, Earth, as my home; but why I am permitted to wear arms I do not know, nor was I aware that my regalia was that of a chieftain."

We were interrupted at this juncture by the approach of one of the warriors, bearing arms, accouterments and ornaments, and in a flash one of her questions was answered and a puzzle cleared up for me. I saw that the body of my dead antagonist had been stripped, and I read in the menacing yet respectful attitude of the warrior who had brought me these trophies of the kill the same demeanor as that evinced by the other who had brought me my original equipment, and now for the first time I realized that my blow, on the occasion of my first battle in the audience chamber had resulted in the death of my adversary.

The reason for the whole attitude displayed toward me was now apparent; I had won my spurs, so to speak, and in the crude justice, which always marks Martian dealings, and which, among other things, has caused me to call her the planet of paradoxes, I was accorded the honors due a conqueror; the trappings and the position of the man I killed. In truth, I was a Martian chieftain, and this I learned later was the cause of my great freedom and my toleration in the audience chamber.

As I had turned to receive the dead warrior's chattels I had noticed that Tars Tarkas and several others had pushed forward toward us, and the eyes of the former rested upon me in a most quizzical manner. Finally he addressed me:

"You speak the tongue of Barsoom quite readily for one who was deaf and dumb to us a few short days ago. Where did you learn it, John Carter?"

"You, yourself, are responsible, Tars Tarkas," I replied, "in that you furnished me with an instructress of remarkable ability; I have to thank Sola for my learning."

"She has done well," he answered, "but your education in other respects needs considerable polish. Do you know what your unprecedented temerity would have cost you had you failed to kill either of the two chieftains whose metal you now wear?"

"I presume that that one whom I had failed to kill, would have killed me," I answered, smiling.

"No, you are wrong. Only in the last extremity of self-defense would a Martian warrior kill a prisoner; we like to save them for other purposes," and his face bespoke possibilities that were not pleasant to dwell upon.

"But one thing can save you now," he continued. "Should you, in recognition of your remarkable valor, ferocity, and prowess, be considered by Tal Hajus as worthy of his service you may be taken into the community and become a full-fledged Tharkian. Until we reach the headquarters of Tal Hajus it is the will of Lorquas Ptomel that you be accorded the respect your acts have earned you. You will be treated by us as a Tharkian chieftain, but you must not forget that every chief who ranks you is responsible for your safe delivery to our mighty and most ferocious ruler. I am done."

"I hear you, Tars Tarkas," I answered. "As you know I am not of Barsoom; your ways are not my ways, and I can only act in the future as I have in the past, in accordance with the dictates of my conscience and guided by the standards of mine own people. If you will leave me alone I will go in peace, but if not, let the individual Barsoomians with whom I must deal either respect my rights as a stranger among you, or take whatever consequences may befall. Of one thing let us be sure, whatever may be your ultimate intentions toward this unfortunate young woman, whoever would offer her injury or insult in the future must figure on making a full accounting to me. I understand that you belittle all sentiments of generosity and kindliness, but I do not, and I can convince your most doughty warrior that these characteristics are not incompatible with an ability to fight."

Ordinarily I am not given to long speeches, nor ever before had I descended to bombast, but I had guessed at the keynote which would strike an answering chord in the breasts of the green Martians, nor was I wrong, for my harangue evidently deeply impressed them, and their attitude toward me thereafter was still further respectful.

Tars Tarkas himself seemed pleased with my reply, but his only comment was more or less enigmatical — "And I think I know Tal Hajus, Jeddak of Thark."

I now turned my attention to Dejah Thoris, and assisting her to her feet I turned with her toward the exit, ignoring her hovering guardian harpies as well as the inquiring glances of the chieftains. Was I not now a chieftain also! Well, then, I would assume the responsibilities of one. They did not molest us, and so Dejah Thoris, Princess of Helium, and John Carter, gentleman of Virginia, followed by the faithful Woola, passed through utter silence from the audience chamber of Lorquas Ptomel, Jed among the Tharks of Barsoom.

CHAPTER XI

With Dejah Thoris

As we reached the open the two female guards who had been detailed to watch over Dejah Thoris hurried up and made as though to assume custody of her once more. The poor child shrank against me and I felt her two little hands fold tightly over my arm. Waving the women away, I informed them that Sola would attend the captive hereafter, and I further warned Sarkoja that any more of her cruel attentions bestowed upon Dejah Thoris would result in Sarkoja's sudden and painful demise.

My threat was unfortunate and resulted in more harm than good to Dejah Thoris, for, as I learned later, men do not kill women upon Mars, nor women, men. So Sarkoja merely gave us an ugly look and departed to hatch up deviltries against us.

I soon found Sola and explained to her that I wished her to guard Dejah Thoris as she had guarded me; that I wished her to find other quarters where they would not be molested by Sarkoja, and I finally informed her that I myself would take up my quarters among the men.

Sola glanced at the accouterments which were carried in my hand and slung across my shoulder.

"You are a great chieftain now, John Carter," she said, "and I must do your bidding, though indeed I am glad to do it under any circumstances. The man whose metal you carry was young, but he was a great warrior, and had by his promotions and kills won his way close to the rank of Tars Tarkas, who, as you know, is second to Lorquas Ptomel only. You are eleventh, there are but ten chieftains in this community who rank you in prowess."

"And if I should kill Lorquas Ptomel?" I asked.

"You would be first, John Carter; but you may only win that honor by the will of the entire council that Lorquas Ptomel meet you in combat, or should he attack you, you may kill him in self-defense, and thus win first place."

I laughed, and changed the subject. I had no particular desire to kill Lorquas Ptomel, and less to be a jed among the Tharks.

I accompanied Sola and Dejah Thoris in a search for new quarters, which we found in a building nearer the audience chamber and of far more pretentious architecture than our former habitation. We also found in this building real sleeping apartments with ancient beds of highly wrought metal swinging from enormous gold chains depending from the marble ceilings. The decoration of the walls was most elaborate, and, unlike the frescoes in the other buildings I had examined, portrayed many human figures in the compositions. These were of people like myself, and of a much lighter color than Dejah Thoris. They were clad in graceful, flowing robes, highly ornamented with metal and jewels, and their luxuriant hair was of a beautiful golden and reddish bronze. The men were beardless and only a few wore arms. The scenes depicted for the most part, a fair-skinned, fair-haired people at play.

Dejah Thoris clasped her hands with an exclamation of rapture as she gazed upon these magnificent works of art, wrought by a people long extinct; while Sola, on the other hand, apparently did not see them.

We decided to use this room, on the second floor and overlooking the plaza, for Dejah Thoris and Sola, and another room adjoining and in the rear for the cooking and supplies. I then dispatched Sola to bring the bedding and such food and utensils as she might need, telling her that I would guard Dejah Thoris until her return.

As Sola departed Dejah Thoris turned to me with a faint smile.

"And whereto, then, would your prisoner escape should you leave her, unless it was to follow you and crave your protection, and ask your pardon for the cruel thoughts she has harbored against you these past few days?"

"You are right," I answered, "there is no escape for either of us unless we go together."

"I heard your challenge to the creature you call Tars Tarkas, and I think I understand your position among these people, but what I cannot fathom is your statement that you are not of Barsoom.

"In the name of my first ancestor, then," she continued, "where may you be from? You are like unto my people, and yet so unlike. You speak my language, and yet I heard you tell Tars Tarkas that you had but learned it recently. All Barsoomians speak the same tongue from the ice-clad south to the ice-clad north, though their written languages differ. Only in the valley Dor, where the river Iss empties into the lost sea of Korus, is there supposed to be a different language spoken, and, except in the legends of our ancestors, there is no record of a Barsoomian returning up the river Iss, from the shores of Korus in the valley of Dor. Do not tell me that you have thus returned! They would kill you horribly anywhere upon the surface of Barsoom if that were true; tell me it is not!"

Her eyes were filled with a strange, weird light; her voice was pleading, and her little hands, reached up upon my breast, were pressed against me as though to wring a denial from my very heart.

"I do not know your customs, Dejah Thoris, but in my own Virginia a gentleman does not lie to save himself; I am not of Dor; I have never seen the mysterious Iss; the lost sea of Korus is still lost, so far as I am concerned. Do you believe me?"

And then it struck me suddenly that I was very anxious that she should believe me. It was not that I feared the results which would follow a general belief that I had returned from the Barsoomian heaven or hell, or whatever it was. Why was it, then! Why should I care what she thought? I looked down at her; her beautiful face upturned, and her wonderful eyes opening up the very depth of her soul; and as my eyes met hers I knew why, and—I shuddered.

A similar wave of feeling seemed to stir her; she drew away from me with a sigh, and with her earnest, beautiful face turned up to mine, she whispered: "I believe you, John Carter; I do not know what a 'gentleman' is, nor have I ever heard before of Virginia; but on Barsoom no *man* lies; if he does not wish to speak the truth he is silent. Where is this Virginia, your country, John Carter?" she asked, and it seemed that this fair name of my fair land had never sounded more beautiful than as it fell from those perfect lips on that far-gone day.

"I am of another world," I answered, "the great planet Earth, which revolves about our common sun and next within the orbit of your Barsoom, which we know as Mars. How I came here I cannot tell you, for I do not know; but here I am, and since my presence has permitted me to serve Dejah Thoris I am glad that I am here."

She gazed at me with troubled eyes, long and questioningly. That it was difficult to believe my statement I well knew, nor could I hope that she would do so however much I craved her confidence and respect. I would much rather not have told her anything of my antecedents, but no man could look into the depth of those eyes and refuse her slightest behest.

Finally she smiled, and, rising, said: "I shall have to believe even though I cannot understand. I can readily perceive that you are not of the Barsoom of today; you are like us, yet different—but why should I trouble my poor head with such a problem, when my heart tells me that I believe because I wish to believe!"

It was good logic, good, earthly, feminine logic, and if it satisfied her I certainly could pick no flaws in it. As a matter of fact it was about the only kind of logic that could be brought to bear upon my problem. We fell into a general conversation then, asking and answering many questions on each side. She was curious to learn of the customs of my people and displayed a remarkable knowledge of events on Earth. When I questioned her closely on this seeming familiarity with earthly things she laughed, and cried out:

"Why, every school boy on Barsoom knows the geography, and much concerning the fauna and flora, as well as the history of your planet fully as well as of his own. Can we not see everything which takes place upon Earth, as you call it; is it not hanging there in the heavens in plain sight?"

This baffled me, I must confess, fully as much as my statements had confounded her; and I told her so. She then explained in general the instruments her people had used and been perfecting for ages, which permit them to throw upon a screen a perfect image of what is transpiring upon any planet and upon many of the stars. These pictures are so perfect in detail that, when photographed and enlarged, objects no greater than a blade of grass may be distinctly recognized. I afterward, in Helium, saw many of these pictures, as well as the instruments which produced them.

"If, then, you are so familiar with earthly things," I asked, "why is it that you do not recognize me as identical with the inhabitants of that planet?"

She smiled again as one might in bored indulgence of a questioning child.

"Because, John Carter," she replied, "nearly every planet and star having atmospheric conditions at all approaching those of Barsoom, shows forms of animal life almost identical with you and me; and, further, Earth men, almost without exception, cover their bodies with strange, unsightly pieces of cloth, and their heads with hideous contraptions the purpose of which we have been unable to conceive; while you, when found by the Tharkian warriors, were entirely undisfigured and unadorned.

"The fact that you wore no ornaments is a strong proof of your un-Barsoomian origin, while the absence of grotesque coverings might cause a doubt as to your earthliness."

I then narrated the details of my departure from the Earth, explaining that my body there lay fully clothed in all the, to her, strange garments of mundane dwellers. At this point Sola returned with our meager belongings and her young Martian protege, who, of course, would have to share the quarters with them.

Sola asked us if we had had a visitor during her absence, and seemed much surprised when we answered in the negative. It seemed that as she had mounted the approach to the upper floors where our quarters were located, she had met

Sarkoja descending. We decided that she must have been eavesdropping, but as we could recall nothing of importance that had passed between us we dismissed the matter as of little consequence, merely promising ourselves to be warned to the utmost caution in the future.

Dejah Thoris and I then fell to examining the architecture and decorations of the beautiful chambers of the building we were occupying. She told me that these people had presumably flourished over a hundred thousand years before. They were the early progenitors of her race, but had mixed with the other great race of early Martians, who were very dark, almost black, and also with the reddish yellow race which had flourished at the same time.

These three great divisions of the higher Martians had been forced into a mighty alliance as the drying up of the Martian seas had compelled them to seek the comparatively few and always diminishing fertile areas, and to defend themselves, under new conditions of life, against the wild hordes of green men.

Ages of close relationship and intermarrying had resulted in the race of red men, of which Dejah Thoris was a fair and beautiful daughter. During the ages of hardships and incessant warring between their own various races, as well as with the green men, and before they had fitted themselves to the changed conditions, much of the high civilization and many of the arts of the fair-haired Martians had become lost; but the red race of today has reached a point where it feels that it has made up in new discoveries and in a more practical civilization for all that lies irretrievably buried with the ancient Barsoomians, beneath the countless intervening ages.

These ancient Martians had been a highly cultivated and literary race, but during the vicissitudes of those trying centuries of readjustment to new conditions, not only did their advancement and production cease entirely, but practically all their archives, records, and literature were lost.

Dejah Thoris related many interesting facts and legends concerning this lost race of noble and kindly people. She said that the city in which we were camping was supposed to have been a center of commerce and culture known as Korad. It had been built upon a beautiful, natural harbor, landlocked by magnificent hills. The little valley on the west front of the city, she explained, was all that remained of the harbor, while the pass through the hills to the old sea bottom had been the channel through which the shipping passed up to the city's gates.

The shores of the ancient seas were dotted with just such cities, and lesser ones, in diminishing numbers, were to be found converging toward the center of the oceans, as the people had found it necessary to follow the receding waters until necessity had forced upon them their ultimate salvation, the so-called Martian canals.

We had been so engrossed in exploration of the building and in our conversation that it was late in the afternoon before we realized it. We were brought back to a realization of our present conditions by a messenger bearing a summons from Lorquas Ptomel directing me to appear before him forthwith. Bidding Dejah Thoris and Sola farewell, and commanding Woola to remain on guard, I hastened to the audience chamber, where I found Lorquas Ptomel and Tars Tarkas seated upon the rostrum.

CHAPTER XII

A Prisoner with Power

As I entered and saluted, Lorquas Ptomel signaled me to advance, and, fixing his great, hideous eyes upon me, addressed me thus:

"You have been with us a few days, yet during that time you have by your prowess won a high position among us. Be that as it may, you are not one of us; you owe us no allegiance.

"Your position is a peculiar one," he continued; "you are a prisoner and yet you give commands which must be obeyed; you are an alien and yet you are a Tharkian chieftain; you are a midget and yet you can kill a mighty warrior with one blow of your fist. And now you are reported to have been plotting to escape with another prisoner of another race; a prisoner who, from her own admission, half believes you are returned from the valley of Dor. Either one of these accusations, if proved, would be sufficient grounds for your execution, but we are a just people and you shall have a trial on our return to Thark, if Tal Hajus so commands.

"But," he continued, in his fierce guttural tones, "if you run off with the red girl it is I who shall have to account to Tal Hajus; it is I who shall have to face Tars Tarkas, and either demonstrate my right to command, or the metal from my dead carcass will go to a better man, for such is the custom of the Tharks.

"I have no quarrel with Tars Tarkas; together we rule supreme the greatest of the lesser communities among the green men; we do not wish to fight between ourselves; and so if you were dead, John Carter, I should be glad. Under two conditions only, however, may you be killed by us without orders from Tal Hajus; in personal combat in self-defense, should you attack one of us, or were you apprehended in an attempt to escape.

"As a matter of justice I must warn you that we only await one of these two excuses for ridding ourselves of so great a responsibility. The safe delivery of the red girl to Tal Hajus is of the greatest importance. Not in a thousand years have the Tharks made such a capture; she is the granddaughter of the greatest of the red jeddaks, who is also our bitterest enemy. I have spoken. The red girl told us that we were without the softer sentiments of humanity, but we are a just and truthful race. You may go."

Turning, I left the audience chamber. So this was the beginning of Sarkoja's persecution! I knew that none other could be responsible for this report which had reached the ears of Lorquas Ptomel so quickly, and now I recalled those portions of our conversation which had touched upon escape and upon my origin.

Sarkoja was at this time Tars Tarkas' oldest and most trusted female. As such she was a mighty power behind the throne, for no warrior had the confidence of Lorquas Ptomel to such an extent as did his ablest lieutenant, Tars Tarkas.

However, instead of putting thoughts of possible escape from my mind, my audience with Lorquas Ptomel only served to center my every faculty on this subject. Now, more than before, the absolute necessity for escape, in so far as Dejah Thoris was concerned, was impressed upon me, for I was convinced that some horrible fate awaited her at the headquarters of Tal Hajus.

As described by Sola, this monster was the exaggerated personification of all the ages of cruelty, ferocity, and brutality from which he had descended. Cold, cunning, calculating; he was, also, in marked contrast to most of his fellows, a slave to that brute passion which the waning demands for procreation upon their dying planet has almost stilled in the Martian breast.

The thought that the divine Dejah Thoris might fall into the clutches of such an abysmal atavism started the cold sweat upon me. Far better that we save friendly bullets for ourselves at the last moment, as did those brave frontier women of my lost land, who took their own lives rather than fall into the hands of the Indian braves.

As I wandered about the plaza lost in my gloomy forebodings Tars Tarkas approached me on his way from the audience chamber. His demeanor toward me was unchanged, and he greeted me as though we had not just parted a few moments before.

"Where are your quarters, John Carter?" he asked.

"I have selected none," I replied. "It seemed best that I quartered either by myself or among the other warriors, and I was awaiting an opportunity to ask your advice. As you know," and I smiled, "I am not yet familiar with all the customs of the Tharks."

"Come with me," he directed, and together we moved off across the plaza to a building which I was glad to see adjoined that occupied by Sola and her charges.

"My quarters are on the first floor of this building," he said, "and the second floor also is fully occupied by warriors, but the third floor and the floors above are vacant; you may take your choice of these.

"I understand," he continued, "that you have given up your woman to the red prisoner. Well, as you have said, your ways are not our ways, but you can fight well enough to do about as you please, and so, if you wish to give your woman to a captive, it is your own affair; but as a chieftain you should have those to serve you, and in accordance with our customs you may select any or all the females from the retinues of the chieftains whose metal you now wear."

I thanked him, but assured him that I could get along very nicely without assistance except in the matter of preparing food, and so he promised to send women to me for this purpose and also for the care of my arms and the manufacture of my ammunition, which he said would be necessary. I suggested that they might also bring some of the sleeping silks and furs which belonged to me as spoils of combat, for the nights were cold and I had none of my own.

He promised to do so, and departed. Left alone, I ascended the winding corridor to the upper floors in search of suitable quarters. The beauties of the other buildings were repeated in this, and, as usual, I was soon lost in a tour of investigation and discovery.

I finally chose a front room on the third floor, because this brought me nearer to Dejah Thoris, whose apartment was on the second floor of the adjoining building, and it flashed upon me that I could rig up some means of communication whereby she might signal me in case she needed either my services or my protection.

Adjoining my sleeping apartment were baths, dressing rooms, and other sleeping and living apartments, in all some ten rooms on this floor. The windows of the back rooms overlooked an enormous court, which formed the center of the square made by the buildings which faced the four contiguous streets, and which was now given over to the quartering of the various animals belonging to the warriors occupying the adjoining buildings.

While the court was entirely overgrown with the yellow, moss-like vegetation which blankets practically the entire surface of Mars, yet numerous fountains, statuary, benches, and pergola-like contraptions bore witness to the beauty which the court must have presented in bygone times, when graced by the fair-haired, laughing people whom stern and unalterable cosmic laws had driven not only from their homes, but from all except the vague legends of their descendants.

One could easily picture the gorgeous foliage of the luxuriant Martian vegetation which once filled this scene with life and color; the graceful figures of the beautiful women, the straight and handsome men; the happy frolicking children—all sunlight, happiness and peace. It was difficult to realize that they had gone;

down through ages of darkness, cruelty, and ignorance, until their hereditary instincts of culture and humanitarianism had risen ascendant once more in the final composite race which now is dominant upon Mars.

My thoughts were cut short by the advent of several young females bearing loads of weapons, silks, furs, jewels, cooking utensils, and casks of food and drink, including considerable loot from the air craft. All this, it seemed, had been the property of the two chieftains I had slain, and now, by the customs of the Tharks, it had become mine. At my direction they placed the stuff in one of the back rooms, and then departed, only to return with a second load, which they advised me constituted the balance of my goods. On the second trip they were accompanied by ten or fifteen other women and youths, who, it seemed, formed the retinues of the two chieftains.

They were not their families, nor their wives, nor their servants; the relationship was peculiar, and so unlike anything known to us that it is most difficult to describe. All property among the green Martians is owned in common by the community, except the personal weapons, ornaments and sleeping silks and furs of the individuals. These alone can one claim undisputed right to, nor may he accumulate more of these than are required for his actual needs. The surplus he holds merely as custodian, and it is passed on to the younger members of the community as necessity demands.

The women and children of a man's retinue may be likened to a military unit for which he is responsible in various ways, as in matters of instruction, discipline, sustenance, and the exigencies of their continual roamings and their unending strife with other communities and with the red Martians. His women are in no sense wives. The green Martians use no word corresponding in meaning with this earthly word. Their mating is a matter of community interest solely, and is directed without reference to natural selection. The council of chieftains of each community control the matter as surely as the owner of a Kentucky racing stud directs the scientific breeding of his stock for the improvement of the whole.

In theory it may sound well, as is often the case with theories, but the results of ages of this unnatural practice, coupled with the community interest in the offspring being held paramount to that of the mother, is shown in the cold, cruel creatures, and their gloomy, loveless, mirthless existence.

It is true that the green Martians are absolutely virtuous, both men and women, with the exception of such degenerates as Tal Hajus; but better far a finer balance of human characteristics even at the expense of a slight and occasional loss of chastity.

Finding that I must assume responsibility for these creatures, whether I would or not, I made the best of it and directed them to find quarters on the upper floors, leaving the third floor to me. One of the girls I charged with the duties of my simple cuisine, and directed the others to take up the various activities which had formerly constituted their vocations. Thereafter I saw little of them, nor did I care to.

CHAPTER XIII

Love-Making on Mars

Following the battle with the air ships, the community remained within the city for several days, abandoning the homeward march until they could feel reasonably assured that the ships would not return; for to be caught on the open plains with a cavalcade of chariots and children was far from the desire of even so warlike a people as the green Martians.

During our period of inactivity, Tars Tarkas had instructed me in many of the customs and arts of war familiar to the Tharks, including lessons in riding and guiding the great beasts which bore the warriors. These creatures, which are known as thoats, are as dangerous and vicious as their masters, but when once subdued are sufficiently tractable for the purposes of the green Martians.

Two of these animals had fallen to me from the warriors whose metal I wore, and in a short time I could handle them quite as well as the native warriors. The method was not at all complicated. If the thoats did not respond with sufficient celerity to the telepathic instructions of their riders they were dealt a terrific blow between the ears with the butt of a pistol, and if they showed fight this treatment was continued until the brutes either were subdued, or had unseated their riders.

In the latter case it became a life and death struggle between the man and the beast. If the former were quick enough with his pistol he might live to ride again, though upon some other beast; if not, his torn and mangled body was gathered up by his women and burned in accordance with Tharkian custom.

My experience with Woola determined me to attempt the experiment of kindness in my treatment of my thoats. First I taught them that they could not unseat me, and even rapped them sharply between the ears to impress upon them my authority and mastery. Then, by degrees, I won their confidence in much the same manner as I had adopted countless times with my many mundane mounts. I was ever a good hand with animals, and by inclination, as well as because it brought more lasting and satisfactory results, I was always kind and humane in my dealings with the lower orders. I could take a human life, if necessary, with far less compunction than that of a poor, unreasoning, irresponsible brute.

In the course of a few days my thoats were the wonder of the entire community. They would follow me like dogs, rubbing their great snouts against my body in awkward evidence of affection, and respond to my every command with an alacrity and docility which caused the Martian warriors to ascribe to me the possession of some earthly power unknown on Mars.

"How have you bewitched them?" asked Tars Tarkas one afternoon, when he had seen me run my arm far between the great jaws of one of my thoats which had wedged a piece of stone between two of his teeth while feeding upon the moss-like vegetation within our court yard.

"By kindness," I replied. "You see, Tars Tarkas, the softer sentiments have their value, even to a warrior. In the height of battle as well as upon the march I know that my thoats will obey my every command, and therefore my fighting efficiency is enhanced, and I am a better warrior for the reason that I am a kind master. Your other warriors would find it to the advantage of themselves as well as of the community to adopt my methods in this respect. Only a few days since you, yourself, told me that these great brutes, by the uncertainty of their tempers, often were the means of turning victory into defeat, since, at a crucial moment, they might elect to unseat and rend their riders."

"Show me how you accomplish these results," was Tars Tarkas' only rejoinder. And so I explained as carefully as I could the entire method of training I had adopted with my beasts, and later he had me repeat it before Lorquas Ptomel and the assembled warriors. That moment marked the beginning of a new existence for the poor thoats, and before I left the community of Lorquas Ptomel I had the satisfaction of observing a regiment of as tractable and docile mounts as one might care to see. The effect on the precision and celerity of the military movements was so remarkable that Lorquas Ptomel presented me with a massive anklet of gold from his own leg, as a sign of his appreciation of my service to the horde.

On the seventh day following the battle with the air craft we again took up the march toward Thark, all probability of another attack being deemed remote by Lorquas Ptomel.

During the days just preceding our departure I had seen but little of Dejah Thoris, as I had been kept very busy by Tars Tarkas with my lessons in the art of Martian warfare, as well as in the training of my thoats. The few times I had visited her quarters she had been absent, walking upon the streets with Sola, or investigating the buildings in the near vicinity of the plaza. I had warned them against venturing far from the plaza for fear of the great white apes, whose ferocity I was only too well acquainted with. However, since Woola accompanied them on all their excursions, and as Sola was well armed, there was comparatively little cause for fear.

On the evening before our departure I saw them approaching along one of the great avenues which lead into the plaza from the east. I advanced to meet them, and telling Sola that I would take the responsibility for Dejah Thoris' safekeeping, I directed her to return to her quarters on some trivial errand. I liked and trusted Sola, but for some reason I desired to be alone with Dejah Thoris, who represented to me all that I had left behind upon Earth in agreeable and congenial companionship. There seemed bonds of mutual interest between us as powerful as though we had been born under the same roof rather than upon different planets, hurtling through space some forty-eight million miles apart.

That she shared my sentiments in this respect I was positive, for on my approach the look of pitiful hopelessness left her sweet countenance to be replaced by a smile of joyful welcome, as she placed her little right hand upon my left shoulder in true red Martian salute.

"Sarkoja told Sola that you had become a true Thark," she said, "and that I would now see no more of you than of any of the other warriors."

"Sarkoja is a liar of the first magnitude," I replied, "notwithstanding the proud claim of the Tharks to absolute verity."

Dejah Thoris laughed.

"I knew that even though you became a member of the community you would not cease to be my friend; 'A warrior may change his metal, but not his heart,' as the saying is upon Barsoom.

"I think they have been trying to keep us apart," she continued, "for whenever you have been off duty one of the older women of Tars Tarkas' retinue has always arranged to trump up some excuse to get Sola and me out of sight. They have had me down in the pits below the buildings helping them mix their awful radium powder, and make their terrible projectiles. You know that these have to be manufactured by artificial light, as exposure to sunlight always results in an explosion. You have noticed that their bullets explode when they strike an object? Well, the opaque, outer coating is broken by the impact, exposing a glass cylinder, almost solid, in the forward end of which is a minute particle of radium powder. The moment the sunlight, even though diffused, strikes this powder it explodes with a violence which nothing can withstand. If you ever witness a night battle you will note the absence of these explosions, while the morning following the battle will be filled at sunrise with the sharp detonations of exploding missiles fired the preceding night. As a rule, however, non-exploding projectiles are used at night."[1]

While I was much interested in Dejah Thoris' explanation of this wonderful adjunct to Martian warfare, I was more concerned by the immediate problem of their treatment of her. That they were keeping her away from me was not a matter for surprise, but that they should subject her to dangerous and arduous labor filled me with rage.

"Have they ever subjected you to cruelty and ignominy, Dejah Thoris?" I asked, feeling the hot blood of my fighting ancestors leap in my veins as I awaited her reply.

"Only in little ways, John Carter," she answered. "Nothing that can harm me outside my pride. They know that I am the daughter of ten thousand jeddaks, that I trace my ancestry straight back without a break to the builder of the first great waterway, and they, who do not even know their own mothers, are jealous of me. At heart they hate their horrid fates, and so wreak their poor spite on me who stands for everything they have not, and for all they most crave and never can attain. Let us pity them, my chieftain, for even though we die at their hands we can afford them pity, since we are greater than they and they know it."

Had I known the significance of those words "my chieftain," as applied by a red Martian woman to a man, I should have had the surprise of my life, but I did not know at that time, nor for many months thereafter. Yes, I still had much to learn upon Barsoom.

"I presume it is the better part of wisdom that we bow to our fate with as good grace as possible, Dejah Thoris; but I hope, nevertheless, that I may be present the next time that any Martian, green, red, pink, or violet, has the temerity to even so much as frown on you, my princess."

Dejah Thoris caught her breath at my last words, and gazed upon me with dilated eyes and quickening breath, and then, with an odd little laugh, which brought roguish dimples to the corners of her mouth, she shook her head and cried:

"What a child! A great warrior and yet a stumbling little child."

"What have I done now?" I asked, in sore perplexity.

"Some day you shall know, John Carter, if we live; but I may not tell you. And I, the daughter of Mors Kajak, son of Tardos Mors, have listened without anger," she soliloquized in conclusion.

Then she broke out again into one of her gay, happy, laughing moods; joking with me on my prowess as a Thark warrior as contrasted with my soft heart and natural kindliness.

"I presume that should you accidentally wound an enemy you would take him home and nurse him back to health," she laughed.

"That is precisely what we do on Earth," I answered. "At least among civilized men."

This made her laugh again. She could not understand it, for, with all her tenderness and womanly sweetness, she was still a Martian, and to a Martian the only good enemy is a dead enemy; for every dead foeman means so much more to divide between those who live.

---

[1] I have used the word radium in describing this powder because in the light of recent discoveries on Earth I believe it to be a mixture of which radium is the base. In Captain Carter's manuscript it is mentioned always by the name used in the written language of Helium and is spelled in hieroglyphics which it would be difficult and useless to reproduce.

I was very curious to know what I had said or done to cause her so much perturbation a moment before and so I continued to importune her to enlighten me.

"No," she exclaimed, "it is enough that you have said it and that I have listened. And when you learn, John Carter, and if I be dead, as likely enough I shall be ere the further moon has circled Barsoom another twelve times, remember that I listened and that I—smiled."

It was all Greek to me, but the more I begged her to explain the more positive became her denials of my request, and, so, in very hopelessness, I desisted.

Day had now given away to night and as we wandered along the great avenue lighted by the two moons of Barsoom, and with Earth looking down upon us out of her luminous green eye, it seemed that we were alone in the universe, and I, at least, was content that it should be so.

The chill of the Martian night was upon us, and removing my silks I threw them across the shoulders of Dejah Thoris. As my arm rested for an instant upon her I felt a thrill pass through every fiber of my being such as contact with no other mortal had even produced; and it seemed to me that she had leaned slightly toward me, but of that I was not sure. Only I knew that as my arm rested there across her shoulders longer than the act of adjusting the silk required she did not draw away, nor did she speak. And so, in silence, we walked the surface of a dying world, but in the breast of one of us at least had been born that which is ever oldest, yet ever new.

I loved Dejah Thoris. The touch of my arm upon her naked shoulder had spoken to me in words I could not mistake, and I knew that I had loved her since the first moment that my eyes had met hers that first time in the plaza of the dead city of Korad.

CHAPTER XIV

A Duel to the Death

My first impulse was to tell her of my love, and then I thought of the helplessness of her position wherein I alone could lighten the burdens of her captivity, and protect her in my poor way against the thousands of hereditary enemies she must face upon our arrival at Thark. I could not chance causing her additional pain or sorrow by declaring a love which, in all probability she did not return. Should I be so indiscreet, her position would be even more unbearable than now, and the thought that she might feel that I was taking advantage of her helplessness, to influence her decision was the final argument which sealed my lips.

"Why are you so quiet, Dejah Thoris?" I asked. "Possibly you would rather return to Sola and your quarters."

"No," she murmured, "I am happy here. I do not know why it is that I should always be happy and contented when you, John Carter, a stranger, are with me; yet at such times it seems that I am safe and that, with you, I shall soon return to my father's court and feel his strong arms about me and my mother's tears and kisses on my cheek."

"Do people kiss, then, upon Barsoom?" I asked, when she had explained the word she used, in answer to my inquiry as to its meaning.

"Parents, brothers, and sisters, yes; and," she added in a low, thoughtful tone, "lovers."

"And you, Dejah Thoris, have parents and brothers and sisters?"

"Yes."

"And a—lover?"

She was silent, nor could I venture to repeat the question.

"The man of Barsoom," she finally ventured, "does not ask personal questions of women, except his mother, and the woman he has fought for and won."

"But I have fought—" I started, and then I wished my tongue had been cut from my mouth; for she turned even as I caught myself and ceased, and drawing my silks from her shoulder she held them out to me, and without a word, and with head held high, she moved with the carriage of the queen she was toward the plaza and the doorway of her quarters.

I did not attempt to follow her, other than to see that she reached the building in safety, but, directing Woola to accompany her, I turned disconsolately and entered my own house. I sat for hours cross-legged, and cross-tempered, upon my silks meditating upon the queer freaks chance plays upon us poor devils of mortals.

So this was love! I had escaped it for all the years I had roamed the five continents and their encircling seas; in spite of beautiful women and urging opportunity; in spite of a half-desire for love and a constant search for my ideal, it had remained for me to fall furiously and hopelessly in love with a creature from another world, of a species similar possibly, yet not identical with mine. A woman who was hatched from an egg, and whose span of life might cover a thousand years; whose people had strange customs and ideas; a woman whose hopes, whose pleasures, whose standards of virtue and of right and wrong might vary as greatly from mine as did those of the green Martians.

Yes, I was a fool, but I was in love, and though I was suffering the greatest misery I had ever known I would not have had it otherwise for all the riches of Barsoom. Such is love, and such are lovers wherever love is known.

To me, Dejah Thoris was all that was perfect; all that was virtuous and beautiful and noble and good. I believed that from the bottom of my heart, from the depth of my soul on that night in Korad as I sat cross-legged upon my silks while the nearer moon of Barsoom raced through the western sky toward the horizon, and lighted up the gold and marble, and jeweled mosaics of my world-old chamber, and I believe it today as I sit at my desk in the little study overlooking the Hudson. Twenty years have intervened; for ten of them I lived and fought for Dejah Thoris and her people, and for ten I have lived upon her memory.

The morning of our departure for Thark dawned clear and hot, as do all Martian mornings except for the six weeks when the snow melts at the poles.

I sought out Dejah Thoris in the throng of departing chariots, but she turned her shoulder to me, and I could see the red blood mount to her cheek. With the foolish inconsistency of love I held my peace when I might have plead ignorance of the nature of my offense, or at least the gravity of it, and so have effected, at worst, a half conciliation.

My duty dictated that I must see that she was comfortable, and so I glanced into her chariot and rearranged her silks and furs. In doing so I noted with horror that she was heavily chained by one ankle to the side of the vehicle.

"What does this mean?" I cried, turning to Sola.

"Sarkoja thought it best," she answered, her face betokening her disapproval of the procedure.

Examining the manacles I saw that they fastened with a massive spring lock.

"Where is the key, Sola? Let me have it."

"Sarkoja wears it, John Carter," she answered.

I turned without further word and sought out Tars Tarkas, to whom I vehemently objected to the unnecessary humiliations and cruelties, as they seemed to my lover's eyes, that were being heaped upon Dejah Thoris.

"John Carter," he answered, "if ever you and Dejah Thoris escape the Tharks it will be upon this journey. We know that you will not go without her. You have shown yourself a mighty fighter, and we do not wish to manacle you, so we hold you both in the easiest way that will yet ensure security. I have spoken."

I saw the strength of his reasoning at a flash, and knew that it were futile to appeal from his decision, but I asked that the key be taken from Sarkoja and that she be directed to leave the prisoner alone in future.

"This much, Tars Tarkas, you may do for me in return for the friendship that, I must confess, I feel for you."

"Friendship?" he replied. "There is no such thing, John Carter; but have your will. I shall direct that Sarkoja cease to annoy the girl, and I myself will take the custody of the key."

"Unless you wish me to assume the responsibility," I said, smiling.

He looked at me long and earnestly before he spoke.

"Were you to give me your word that neither you nor Dejah Thoris would attempt to escape until after we have safely reached the court of Tal Hajus you might have the key and throw the chains into the river Iss."

"It were better that you held the key, Tars Tarkas," I replied.

He smiled, and said no more, but that night as we were making camp I saw him unfasten Dejah Thoris' fetters himself.

With all his cruel ferocity and coldness there was an undercurrent of something in Tars Tarkas which he seemed ever battling to subdue. Could it be a vestige of some human instinct come back from an ancient forbear to haunt him with the horror of his people's ways!

As I was approaching Dejah Thoris' chariot I passed Sarkoja, and the black, venomous look she accorded me was the sweetest balm I had felt for many hours. Lord, how she hated me! It bristled from her so palpably that one might almost have cut it with a sword.

A few moments later I saw her deep in conversation with a warrior named Zad; a big, hulking, powerful brute, but one who had never made a kill among his own chieftains, and so was still an *o mad*, or man with one name; he could win a second name only with the metal of some chieftain. It was this custom which entitled me to the names of either of the chieftains I had killed; in fact, some of the warriors addressed me as Dotar Sojat, a combination of the surnames of the two warrior chieftains whose metal I had taken, or, in other words, whom I had slain in fair fight.

As Sarkoja talked with Zad he cast occasional glances in my direction, while she seemed to be urging him very strongly to some action. I paid little attention to it at the time, but the next day I had good reason to recall the circumstances, and at the same time gain a slight insight into the depths of Sarkoja's hatred and the lengths to which she was capable of going to wreak her horrid vengeance on me.

Dejah Thoris would have none of me again on this evening, and though I spoke her name she neither replied, nor conceded by so much as the flutter of an eyelid that she realized my existence. In my extremity I did what most other lovers would have done; I sought word from her through an intimate. In this instance it was Sola whom I intercepted in another part of camp.

"What is the matter with Dejah Thoris?" I blurted out at her. "Why will she not speak to me?"

Sola seemed puzzled herself, as though such strange actions on the part of two humans were quite beyond her, as indeed they were, poor child.

"She says you have angered her, and that is all she will say, except that she is the daughter of a jed and the granddaughter of a jeddak and she has been humiliated by a creature who could not polish the teeth of her grandmother's sorak."

I pondered over this report for some time, finally asking,

"What might a sorak be, Sola?"

"A little animal about as big as my hand, which the red Martian women keep to play with," explained Sola.

Not fit to polish the teeth of her grandmother's cat! I must rank pretty low in the consideration of Dejah Thoris, I thought; but I could not help laughing at the strange figure of speech, so homely and in this respect so earthly. It made me homesick, for it sounded very much like "not fit to polish her shoes." And then commenced a train of thought quite new to me. I began to wonder what my people at home were doing. I had not seen them for years. There was a family of Carters in Virginia who claimed close relationship with me; I was supposed to be a great uncle, or something of the kind equally foolish. I could pass anywhere for twenty-five to thirty years of age, and to be a great uncle always seemed the height of incongruity, for my thoughts and feelings were those of a boy. There was two little kiddies in the Carter family whom I had loved and who had thought there was no one on Earth like Uncle Jack; I could see them just as plainly, as I stood there under the moonlit skies of Barsoom, and I longed for them as I had never longed for any mortals before. By nature a wanderer, I had never known the true meaning of the word home, but the great hall of the Carters had always stood for all that the word did mean to me, and now my heart turned toward it from the cold and unfriendly peoples I had been thrown amongst. For did not even Dejah Thoris despise me! I was a low creature, so low in fact that I was not even fit to polish the teeth of her grandmother's cat; and then my saving sense of humor came to my rescue, and laughing I turned into my silks and furs and slept upon the moon-haunted ground the sleep of a tired and healthy fighting man.

We broke camp the next day at an early hour and marched with only a single halt until just before dark. Two incidents broke the tediousness of the march. About noon we espied far to our right what was evidently an incubator, and Lorquas Ptomel directed Tars Tarkas to investigate it. The latter took a dozen warriors, including myself, and we raced across the velvety carpeting of moss to the little enclosure.

It was indeed an incubator, but the eggs were very small in comparison with those I had seen hatching in ours at the time of my arrival on Mars.

Tars Tarkas dismounted and examined the enclosure minutely, finally announcing that it belonged to the green men of Warhoon and that the cement was scarcely dry where it had been walled up.

"They cannot be a day's march ahead of us," he exclaimed, the light of battle leaping to his fierce face

The work at the incubator was short indeed. The warriors tore open the entrance and a couple of them, crawling in, soon demolished all the eggs with their short-swords. Then remounting we dashed back to join the cavalcade. During the ride I took occasion to ask Tars Tarkas if these Warhoons whose eggs we had destroyed were a smaller people than his Tharks.

"I noticed that their eggs were so much smaller than those I saw hatching in your incubator," I added.

He explained that the eggs had just been placed there; but, like all green Martian eggs, they would grow during the five-year period of incubation until they obtained the size of those I had seen hatching on the day of my arrival on Barsoom. This was indeed an interesting piece of information, for it had always seemed remarkable to me that the green Martian women, large as they were, could bring forth such enormous eggs as I had seen the four-foot infants emerging from. As a matter of fact, the new-laid egg is but little larger than an ordinary goose egg, and as it does not commence to grow until subjected to the light of the sun the chieftains have little difficulty in transporting several hundreds of them at one time from the storage vaults to the incubators.

Shortly after the incident of the Warhoon eggs we halted to rest the animals, and it was during this halt that the second of the day's interesting episodes occurred. I was engaged in changing my riding cloths from one of my thoats to the other, for I divided the day's work between them, when Zad approached me, and without a word struck my animal a terrific blow with his long-sword.

I did not need a manual of green Martian etiquette to know what reply to make, for, in fact, I was so wild with anger that I could scarcely refrain from drawing my pistol and shooting him down for the brute he was; but he stood waiting with drawn long-sword, and my only choice was to draw my own and meet him in fair fight with his choice of weapons or a lesser one.

This latter alternative is always permissible, therefore I could have used my short-sword, my dagger, my hatchet, or my fists had I wished, and been entirely within my rights, but I could not use firearms or a spear while he held only his long-sword.

I chose the same weapon he had drawn because I knew he prided himself upon his ability with it, and I wished, if I worsted him at all, to do it with his own weapon. The fight that followed was a long one and delayed the resumption of the march for an hour. The entire community surrounded us, leaving a clear space about one hundred feet in diameter for our battle.

Zad first attempted to rush me down as a bull might a wolf, but I was much too quick for him, and each time I side-stepped his rushes he would go lunging past me, only to receive a nick from my sword upon his arm or back. He was soon streaming blood from a half dozen minor wounds, but I could not obtain an opening to deliver an effective thrust. Then he changed his tactics, and fighting warily and with extreme dexterity, he tried to do by science what he was unable to do by brute strength. I must admit that he was a magnificent swordsman, and had it not been for my greater endurance and the remarkable agility the lesser gravitation of Mars lent me I might not have been able to put up the creditable fight I did against him.

We circled for some time without doing much damage on either side; the long, straight, needle-like swords flashing in the sunlight, and ringing out upon the stillness as they crashed together with each effective parry. Finally Zad, realizing that he was tiring more than I, evidently decided to close in and end the battle in a final blaze of glory for himself; just as he rushed me a blinding flash of light struck full in my eyes, so that I could not see his approach and could only leap blindly to one side in an effort to escape the mighty blade that it seemed I could already feel in my vitals. I was only partially successful, as a sharp pain in my left shoulder attested, but in the sweep of my glance as I sought to again locate my adversary, a sight met my astonished gaze which paid me well for the wound the temporary blindness had caused me. There, upon Dejah Thoris' chariot stood three figures, for the purpose evidently of witnessing the encounter above the heads of the intervening Tharks. There were Dejah Thoris, Sola, and Sarkoja, and as my fleeting glance swept over them a little tableau was presented which will stand graven in my memory to the day of my death.

As I looked, Dejah Thoris turned upon Sarkoja with the fury of a young tigress and struck something from her upraised hand; something which flashed in the sunlight as it spun to the ground. Then I knew what had blinded me at that crucial moment of the fight, and how Sarkoja had found a way to kill me without herself delivering the final thrust. Another thing I saw, too, which almost lost my life for me then and there, for it took my mind for the fraction of an instant entirely from my antagonist; for, as Dejah Thoris struck the tiny mirror from her hand, Sarkoja, her face livid with hatred and baffled rage, whipped out her dagger and aimed a terrific blow at Dejah Thoris; and then Sola, our dear and faithful Sola, sprang between them; the last I saw was the great knife descending upon her shielding breast.

My enemy had recovered from his thrust and was making it extremely interesting for me, so I reluctantly gave my attention to the work in hand, but my mind was not upon the battle.

We rushed each other furiously time after time, 'til suddenly, feeling the sharp point of his sword at my breast in a thrust I could neither parry nor escape, I threw myself upon him with outstretched sword and with all the weight of my body, determined that I would not die alone if I could prevent it. I felt the steel tear into my chest, all went black before me, my head whirled in dizziness, and I felt my knees giving beneath me.

CHAPTER XV

Sola Tells Me Her Story

When consciousness returned, and, as I soon learned, I was down but a moment, I sprang quickly to my feet searching for my sword, and there I found it, buried to the hilt in the green breast of Zad, who lay stone dead upon the ochre moss of the ancient sea bottom. As I regained my full senses I found his weapon piercing my left breast, but only through the flesh and muscles which cover my ribs, entering near the center of my chest and coming out below the shoulder. As I had lunged I had turned so that his sword merely passed beneath the muscles, inflicting a painful but not dangerous wound.

Removing the blade from my body I also regained my own, and turning my back upon his ugly carcass, I moved, sick, sore, and disgusted, toward the chariots which bore my retinue and my belongings. A murmur of Martian applause greeted me, but I cared not for it.

Bleeding and weak I reached my women, who, accustomed to such happenings, dressed my wounds, applying the wonderful healing and remedial agents which make only the most instantaneous of death blows fatal. Give a Martian woman a chance and death must take a back seat. They soon had me patched up so that, except for weakness from loss of blood and a little soreness around the wound, I suffered no great distress from this thrust which, under earthly treatment, undoubtedly would have put me flat on my back for days.

As soon as they were through with me I hastened to the chariot of Dejah Thoris, where I found my poor Sola with her chest swathed in bandages, but apparently little the worse for her encounter with Sarkoja, whose dagger it seemed had struck the edge of one of Sola's metal breast ornaments and, thus deflected, had inflicted but a slight flesh wound.

As I approached I found Dejah Thoris lying prone upon her silks and furs, her lithe form wracked with sobs. She did not notice my presence, nor did she hear me speaking with Sola, who was standing a short distance from the vehicle.

"Is she injured?" I asked of Sola, indicating Dejah Thoris by an inclination of my head.

"No," she answered, "she thinks that you are dead."

"And that her grandmother's cat may now have no one to polish its teeth?" I queried, smiling.

"I think you wrong her, John Carter," said Sola. "I do not understand either her ways or yours, but I am sure the granddaughter of ten thousand jeddaks would never grieve like this over the death of one she considered beneath her, or indeed over any who held but the highest claim upon her affections. They are a proud race, but they are just, as are all Barsoomians, and you must have hurt or wronged her grievously that she will not admit your existence living, though she mourns you dead.

"Tears are a strange sight upon Barsoom," she continued, "and so it is difficult for me to interpret them. I have seen but two people weep in all my life, other than Dejah Thoris; one wept from sorrow, the other from baffled rage. The first was my mother, years ago before they killed her; the other was Sarkoja, when they dragged her from me today."

"Your mother!" I exclaimed, "but, Sola, you could not have known your mother, child."

"But I did. And my father also," she added. "If you would like to hear the strange and un-Barsoomian story come to the chariot tonight, John Carter, and I will tell you that of which I have never spoken in all my life before. And now the signal has been given to resume the march, you must go."

"I will come tonight, Sola," I promised. "Be sure to tell Dejah Thoris I am alive and well. I shall not force myself upon her, and be sure that you do not let her know I saw her tears. If she would speak with me I but await her command."

Sola mounted the chariot, which was swinging into its place in line, and I hastened to my waiting thoat and galloped to my station beside Tars Tarkas at the rear of the column.

We made a most imposing and awe-inspiring spectacle as we strung out across the yellow landscape; the two hundred and fifty ornate and brightly colored chariots, preceded by an advance guard of some two hundred mounted warriors and chieftains riding five abreast and one hundred yards apart, and followed by a like number in the same formation, with a score or more of flankers on either side; the fifty extra mastodons, or heavy draught animals, known as zitidars, and the five or six hundred extra thoats of the warriors running loose within the hollow square formed by the surrounding warriors. The gleaming metal and jewels of the gorgeous ornaments of the men and women, duplicated in the trappings of the zitidars and thoats, and interspersed with the flashing colors of magnificent silks and furs and feathers, lent a barbaric splendor to the caravan which would have turned an East Indian potentate green with envy.

The enormous broad tires of the chariots and the padded feet of the animals brought forth no sound from the moss-covered sea bottom; and so we moved in utter silence, like some huge phantasmagoria, except when the stillness was broken by the guttural growling of a goaded zitidar, or the squealing of fighting thoats. The green Martians converse but little, and then usually in monosyllables, low and like the faint rumbling of distant thunder.

We traversed a trackless waste of moss which, bending to the pressure of broad tire or padded foot, rose up again behind us, leaving no sign that we had passed. We might indeed have been the wraiths of the departed dead upon the dead sea of that dying planet for all the sound or sign we made in passing. It was the first march of a large body of men and animals I had ever witnessed which raised no dust and left no spoor; for there is no dust upon Mars except in the cultivated districts during the winter months, and even then the absence of high winds renders it almost unnoticeable.

We camped that night at the foot of the hills we had been approaching for two days and which marked the southern boundary of this particular sea. Our animals had been two days without drink, nor had they had water for nearly two months, not since shortly after leaving Thark; but, as Tars Tarkas explained to me, they require but little and can live almost indefinitely upon the moss which covers Barsoom, and which, he told me, holds in its tiny stems sufficient moisture to meet the limited demands of the animals.

After partaking of my evening meal of cheese-like food and vegetable milk I sought out Sola, whom I found working by the light of a torch upon some of Tars Tarkas' trappings. She looked up at my approach, her face lighting with pleasure and with welcome.

"I am glad you came," she said; "Dejah Thoris sleeps and I am lonely. Mine own people do not care for me, John Carter; I am too unlike them. It is a sad fate, since I must live my life amongst them, and I often wish that I were a true green Martian woman, without love and without hope; but I have known love and so I am lost.

"I promised to tell you my story, or rather the story of my parents. From what I have learned of you and the ways of your people I am sure that the tale will not seem strange to you, but among green Martians it has no parallel within the memory of the oldest living Thark, nor do our legends hold many similar tales.

"My mother was rather small, in fact too small to be allowed the responsibilities of maternity, as our chieftains breed principally for size. She was also less cold and cruel than most green Martian women, and caring little for their society, she often roamed the deserted avenues of Thark alone, or went and sat among the wild flowers that deck the nearby hills, thinking thoughts and wishing wishes which I believe I alone among Tharkian women today may understand, for am I not the child of my mother?

"And there among the hills she met a young warrior, whose duty it was to guard the feeding zitidars and thoats and see that they roamed not beyond the hills. They spoke at first only of such things as interest a community of Tharks, but gradually, as they came to meet more often, and, as was now quite evident to both, no longer by chance, they talked about themselves, their likes, their ambitions and their hopes. She trusted him and told him of the awful repugnance she felt for the cruelties of their kind, for the hideous, loveless lives they must ever lead, and then she waited for the storm of denunciation to break from his cold, hard lips; but instead he took her in his arms and kissed her.

"They kept their love a secret for six long years. She, my mother, was of the retinue of the great Tal Hajus, while her lover was a simple warrior, wearing only his own metal. Had their defection from the traditions of the Tharks been discovered both would have paid the penalty in the great arena before Tal Hajus and the assembled hordes.

"The egg from which I came was hidden beneath a great glass vessel upon the highest and most inaccessible of the partially ruined towers of ancient Thark. Once each year my mother visited it for the five long years it lay there in the process of incubation. She dared not come oftener, for in the mighty guilt of her conscience she feared that her every move was watched. During this period my father gained great distinction as a warrior and had taken the metal from several chieftains. His love for my mother had never diminished, and his one ambition in life was to reach a point where he might wrest the metal from Tal Hajus himself, and thus, as ruler of the Tharks, be free to claim her as his own, as well as, by the might of his power, protect the child which otherwise would be quickly dispatched should the truth become known.

"It was a wild dream, that of wresting the metal from Tal Hajus in five short years, but his advance was rapid, and he soon stood high in the councils of Thark. But one day the chance was lost forever, in so far as it could come in time to save his loved ones, for he was ordered away upon a long expedition to the ice-clad south, to make war upon the natives there and despoil them of their furs, for such is the manner of the green Barsoomian; he does not labor for what he can wrest in battle from others.

"He was gone for four years, and when he returned all had been over for three; for about a year after his departure, and shortly before the time for the return of an expedition which had gone forth to fetch the fruits of a community incubator, the egg had hatched. Thereafter my mother continued to keep me in the old tower, visiting me nightly and lavishing upon me the love the community life would have robbed us both of. She hoped, upon the return of the expedition from the incubator, to mix me with the other young assigned to the quarters of Tal Hajus, and thus escape the fate which would surely follow discovery of her sin against the ancient traditions of the green men.

"She taught me rapidly the language and customs of my kind, and one night she told me the story I have told to you up to this point, impressing upon me the necessity for absolute secrecy and the great caution I must exercise after she had placed me with the other young Tharks to permit no one to guess that I was further advanced in education than they, nor by any sign to divulge in the presence of others my affection for her, or my knowledge of my parentage; and then drawing me close to her she whispered in my ear the name of my father.

"And then a light flashed out upon the darkness of the tower chamber, and there stood Sarkoja, her gleaming, baleful eyes fixed in a frenzy of loathing and contempt upon my mother. The torrent of hatred and abuse she poured out upon her turned my young heart cold in terror. That she had heard the entire story was apparent, and that she had suspected something wrong from my mother's long nightly absences from her quarters accounted for her presence there on that fateful night.

"One thing she had not heard, nor did she know, the whispered name of my father. This was apparent from her repeated demands upon my mother to disclose the name of her partner in sin, but no amount of abuse or threats could wring this from her, and to save me from needless torture she lied, for she told Sarkoja that she alone knew nor would she even tell her child.

"With final imprecations, Sarkoja hastened away to Tal Hajus to report her discovery, and while she was gone my mother, wrapping me in the silks and furs of her night coverings, so that I was scarcely noticeable, descended to the streets and ran wildly away toward the outskirts of the city, in the direction which led to the far south, out toward the man whose protection she might not claim, but on whose face she wished to look once more before she died.

"As we neared the city's southern extremity a sound came to us from across the mossy flat, from the direction of the only pass through the hills which led to the gates, the pass by which caravans from either north or south or east or west would enter the city. The sounds we heard were the squealing of thoats and the grumbling of zitidars, with the occasional clank of arms which announced the approach of a body of warriors. The thought uppermost in her mind was that it was my father returned from his expedition, but the cunning of the Thark held her from headlong and precipitate flight to greet him.

"Retreating into the shadows of a doorway she awaited the coming of the cavalcade which shortly entered the avenue, breaking its formation and thronging the thoroughfare from wall to wall. As the head of the procession passed us the lesser moon swung clear of the overhanging roofs and lit up the scene with all the brilliancy of her wondrous light. My mother shrank further back into the friendly shadows, and from her hiding place saw that the expedition was not that of my father, but the returning caravan bearing the young Tharks. Instantly her plan was formed, and as a great chariot swung close to our hiding place she slipped stealthily in upon the trailing tailboard, crouching low in the shadow of the high side, straining me to her bosom in a frenzy of love.

"She knew, what I did not, that never again after that night would she hold me to her breast, nor was it likely we would ever look upon each other's face again. In the confusion of the plaza she mixed me with the other children, whose guardians during the journey were now free to relinquish their responsibility. We were herded together into a great room, fed by women who had not accompanied the expedition, and the next day we were parceled out among the retinues of the chieftains.

"I never saw my mother after that night. She was imprisoned by Tal Hajus, and every effort, including the most horrible and shameful torture, was brought to bear upon her to wring from her lips the name of my father; but she remained steadfast and loyal, dying at last amidst the laughter of Tal Hajus and his chieftains during some awful torture she was undergoing.

"I learned afterwards that she told them that she had killed me to save me from a like fate at their hands, and that she had thrown my body to the white apes. Sarkoja alone disbelieved her, and I feel to this day that she suspects my true origin, but does not dare expose me, at the present, at all events, because she also guesses, I am sure, the identity of my father.

"When he returned from his expedition and learned the story of my mother's fate I was present as Tal Hajus told him; but never by the quiver of a muscle did he betray the slightest emotion; only he did not laugh as Tal Hajus gleefully described her death struggles. From that moment on he was the cruelest of the cruel, and I am awaiting the day when he shall win the goal of his ambition, and feel the carcass of Tal Hajus beneath his foot, for I am as sure that he but waits the opportunity to wreak a terrible vengeance, and that his great love is as strong in his breast as when it first transfigured him nearly forty years ago, as I am that we sit here upon the edge of a world-old ocean while sensible people sleep, John Carter."

"And your father, Sola, is he with us now?" I asked.

"Yes," she replied, "but he does not know me for what I am, nor does he know who betrayed my mother to Tal Hajus. I alone know my father's name, and only I and Tal Hajus and Sarkoja know that it was she who carried the tale that brought death and torture upon her he loved."

We sat silent for a few moments, she wrapped in the gloomy thoughts of her terrible past, and I in pity for the poor creatures whom the heartless, senseless customs of their race had doomed to loveless lives of cruelty and of hate. Presently she spoke.

"John Carter, if ever a real man walked the cold, dead bosom of Barsoom you are one. I know that I can trust you, and because the knowledge may someday help you or him or Dejah Thoris or myself, I am going to tell you the name of my father, nor place any restrictions or conditions upon your tongue. When the time comes, speak the truth if it seems best to you. I trust you because I know that you are not cursed with the terrible trait of absolute and unswerving truthfulness, that you could lie like one of your own Virginia gentlemen if a lie would save others from sorrow or suffering. My father's name is Tars Tarkas."

CHAPTER XVI

We Plan Escape

The remainder of our journey to Thark was uneventful. We were twenty days upon the road, crossing two sea bottoms and passing through or around a number of ruined cities, mostly smaller than Korad. Twice we crossed the famous Martian waterways, or canals, so-called by our earthly astronomers. When we approached these points a warrior would be sent far ahead with a powerful field glass, and if no great body of red Martian troops was in sight we would advance as close as possible without chance of being seen and then camp until dark, when we would slowly approach the cultivated tract, and, locating one of the numerous, broad highways which cross these areas at regular intervals, creep silently and stealthily across to the arid lands upon the other side. It required five hours to make one of these crossings without a single halt, and the other consumed the entire night, so that we were just leaving the confines of the high-walled fields when the sun broke out upon us.

Crossing in the darkness, as we did, I was unable to see but little, except as the nearer moon, in her wild and ceaseless hurtling through the Barsoomian heavens, lit up little patches of the landscape from time to time, disclosing walled fields and low, rambling buildings, presenting much the appearance of earthly farms. There were many trees, methodically arranged, and some of them were of enormous height; there were animals in some of the enclosures, and they announced their presence by terrified squealings and snortings as they scented our queer, wild beasts and wilder human beings.

Only once did I perceive a human being, and that was at the intersection of our crossroad with the wide, white turnpike which cuts each cultivated district longitudinally at its exact center. The fellow must have been sleeping beside the road, for, as I came abreast of him, he raised upon one elbow and after a single glance at the approaching caravan leaped shrieking to his feet and fled madly down the road, scaling a nearby wall with the agility of a scared cat. The Tharks paid him not the slightest attention; they were not out upon the warpath, and the only sign that I had that they had seen him was a quickening of the pace of the caravan as we hastened toward the bordering desert which marked our entrance into the realm of Tal Hajus.

Not once did I have speech with Dejah Thoris, as she sent no word to me that I would be welcome at her chariot, and my foolish pride kept me from making any advances. I verily believe that a man's way with women is in inverse ratio to his prowess among men. The weakling and the saphead have often great ability to charm the fair sex, while the fighting man who can face a thousand real dangers unafraid, sits hiding in the shadows like some frightened child.

Just thirty days after my advent upon Barsoom we entered the ancient city of Thark, from whose long-forgotten people this horde of green men have stolen even their name. The hordes of Thark number some thirty thousand souls, and are divided into twenty-five communities. Each community has its own jed and lesser chieftains, but all are under the rule of Tal Hajus, Jeddak of Thark. Five communities make their headquarters at the city of Thark, and the balance are scattered among other deserted cities of ancient Mars throughout the district claimed by Tal Hajus.

We made our entry into the great central plaza early in the afternoon. There were no enthusiastic friendly greetings for the returned expedition. Those who chanced to be in sight spoke the names of warriors or women with whom they came in direct contact, in the formal greeting of their kind, but when it was discovered that they brought two captives a greater interest was aroused, and Dejah Thoris and I were the centers of inquiring groups.

We were soon assigned to new quarters, and the balance of the day was devoted to settling ourselves to the changed conditions. My home now was upon an avenue leading into the plaza from the south, the main artery down which we had marched from the gates of the city. I was at the far end of the square and had an entire building to myself. The same grandeur of architecture which was so noticeable a characteristic of Korad was in evidence here, only, if that were possible, on a larger and richer scale. My quarters would have been suitable for housing the greatest of earthly emperors, but to these queer creatures nothing about a building appealed to them but its size and the enormity of its chambers; the larger the building, the more desirable; and so Tal Hajus occupied what must have been an enormous public building, the largest in the city, but entirely unfitted for residence purposes; the next largest was reserved for Lorquas Ptomel, the next for the jed of a lesser rank, and so on to the bottom of the list of five jeds. The warriors occupied the buildings with the chieftains to whose retinues they belonged; or, if they preferred, sought shelter among any of the thousands of untenanted buildings in their own quarter of town; each community being assigned a certain section of the city. The selection of building had to be made in accordance with these divisions, except in so far as the jeds were concerned, they all occupying edifices which fronted upon the plaza.

When I had finally put my house in order, or rather seen that it had been done, it was nearing sunset, and I hastened out with the intention of locating Sola and her charges, as I had determined upon having speech with Dejah Thoris and trying to impress on her the necessity of our at least patching up a truce until I could find some way of aiding her to escape. I searched in vain until the upper rim of the great red sun was just disappearing behind the horizon and then I spied the ugly head of Woola peering from a second-story window on the opposite side of the very street where I was quartered, but nearer the plaza.

Without waiting for a further invitation I bolted up the winding runway which led to the second floor, and entering a great chamber at the front of the building was greeted by the frenzied Woola, who threw his great carcass upon me, nearly hurling me to the floor; the poor old fellow was so glad to see me that I thought he would devour me, his head split from ear to ear, showing his three rows of tusks in his hobgloblin smile.

Quieting him with a word of command and a caress, I looked hurriedly through the approaching gloom for a sign of Dejah Thoris, and then, not seeing her, I called her name. There was an answering murmur from the far corner of the apartment, and with a couple of quick strides I was standing beside her where she crouched among the furs and silks upon an ancient carved wooden seat. As I waited she rose to her full height and looking me straight in the eye said:

"What would Dotar Sojat, Thark, of Dejah Thoris his captive?"

"Dejah Thoris, I do not know how I have angered you. It was furtherest from my desire to hurt or offend you, whom I had hoped to protect and comfort. Have none of me if it is your will, but that you must aid me in effecting your escape, if such a thing be possible, is not my request, but my command. When you are safe once more at your father's court you may do with me as you please, but from now on until that day I am your master, and you must obey and aid me."

She looked at me long and earnestly and I thought that she was softening toward me.

"I understand your words, Dotar Sojat," she replied, "but you I do not understand. You are a queer mixture of child and man, of brute and noble. I only wish that I might read your heart."

"Look down at your feet, Dejah Thoris; it lies there now where it has lain since that other night at Korad, and where it will ever lie beating alone for you until death stills it forever."

She took a little step toward me, her beautiful hands outstretched in a strange, groping gesture.

"What do you mean, John Carter?" she whispered. "What are you saying to me?"

"I am saying what I had promised myself that I would not say to you, at least until you were no longer a captive among the green men; what from your attitude toward me for the past twenty days I had thought never to say to you; I am saying, Dejah Thoris, that I am yours, body and soul, to serve you, to fight for you, and to die for you. Only one thing I ask of you in return, and that is that you make no sign, either of condemnation or of approbation of my words until you are safe among your own people, and that whatever sentiments you harbor toward me they be not influenced or colored by gratitude; whatever I may do to serve you will be prompted solely from selfish motives, since it gives me more pleasure to serve you than not."

"I will respect your wishes, John Carter, because I understand the motives which prompt them, and I accept your service no more willingly than I bow to your authority; your word shall be my law. I have twice wronged you in my thoughts and again I ask your forgiveness."

Further conversation of a personal nature was prevented by the entrance of Sola, who was much agitated and wholly unlike her usual calm and possessed self.

"That horrible Sarkoja has been before Tal Hajus," she cried, "and from what I heard upon the plaza there is little hope for either of you."

"What do they say?" inquired Dejah Thoris.

"That you will be thrown to the wild calots [dogs] in the great arena as soon as the hordes have assembled for the yearly games."

"Sola," I said, "you are a Thark, but you hate and loathe the customs of your people as much as we do. Will you not accompany us in one supreme effort to escape? I am sure that Dejah Thoris can offer you a home and protection among her people, and your fate can be no worse among them than it must ever be here."

"Yes," cried Dejah Thoris, "come with us, Sola, you will be better off among the red men of Helium than you are here, and I can promise you not only a home with us, but the love and affection your nature craves and which must always be denied you by the customs of your own race. Come with us, Sola; we might go without you, but your fate would be terrible if they thought you had connived to aid us. I know that even that fear would not tempt you to interfere in our escape, but we want you with us, we want you to come to a land of sunshine and happiness, amongst a people who know the meaning of love, of sympathy, and of gratitude. Say that you will, Sola; tell me that you will."

"The great waterway which leads to Helium is but fifty miles to the south," murmured Sola, half to herself; "a swift thoat might make it in three hours; and then to Helium it is five hundred miles, most of the way through thinly settled districts. They would know and they would follow us. We might hide among the great trees for a time, but the chances are small indeed for escape. They would follow us to the very gates of Helium, and they would take toll of life at every step; you do not know them."

"Is there no other way we might reach Helium?" I asked. "Can you not draw me a rough map of the country we must traverse, Dejah Thoris?"

"Yes," she replied, and taking a great diamond from her hair she drew upon the marble floor the first map of Barsoomian territory I had ever seen. It was crisscrossed in every direction with long straight lines, sometimes running parallel and sometimes converging toward some great circle. The lines, she said, were waterways; the circles, cities; and one far to the northwest of us she pointed out as Helium. There were other cities closer, but she said she feared to enter many of them, as they were not all friendly toward Helium.

Finally, after studying the map carefully in the moonlight which now flooded the room, I pointed out a waterway far to the north of us which also seemed to lead to Helium.

"Does not this pierce your grandfather's territory?" I asked.

"Yes," she answered, "but it is two hundred miles north of us; it is one of the waterways we crossed on the trip to Thark."

"They would never suspect that we would try for that distant waterway," I answered, "and that is why I think that it is the best route for our escape."

Sola agreed with me, and it was decided that we should leave Thark this same night; just as quickly, in fact, as I could find and saddle my thoats. Sola was to ride one and Dejah Thoris and I the other; each of us carrying sufficient food and drink to last us for two days, since the animals could not be urged too rapidly for so long a distance.

I directed Sola to proceed with Dejah Thoris along one of the less frequented avenues to the southern boundary of the city, where I would overtake them with the thoats as quickly as possible; then, leaving them to gather what food, silks, and furs we were to need, I slipped quietly to the rear of the first floor, and entered the courtyard, where our animals were moving restlessly about, as was their habit, before settling down for the night.

In the shadows of the buildings and out beneath the radiance of the Martian moons moved the great herd of thoats and zitidars, the latter grunting their low gutturals and the former occasionally emitting the sharp squeal which denotes the almost habitual state of rage in which these creatures passed their existence. They

were quieter now, owing to the absence of man, but as they scented me they became more restless and their hideous noise increased. It was risky business, this
entering a paddock of thoats alone and at night; first, because their increasing
noisiness might warn the nearby warriors that something was amiss, and also because for the slightest cause, or for no cause at all some great bull thoat might take
it upon himself to lead a charge upon me.

Having no desire to awaken their nasty tempers upon such a night as this, where
so much depended upon secrecy and dispatch, I hugged the shadows of the buildings, ready at an instant's warning to leap into the safety of a nearby door or window.
Thus I moved silently to the great gates which opened upon the street at the back of
the court, and as I neared the exit I called softly to my two animals. How I thanked
the kind providence which had given me the foresight to win the love and confidence of these wild dumb brutes, for presently from the far side of the court I saw
two huge bulks forcing their way toward me through the surging mountains of flesh.

They came quite close to me, rubbing their muzzles against my body and nosing for the bits of food it was always my practice to reward them with. Opening
the gates I ordered the two great beasts to pass out, and then slipping quietly after
them I closed the portals behind me.

I did not saddle or mount the animals there, but instead walked quietly in the
shadows of the buildings toward an unfrequented avenue which led toward the
point I had arranged to meet Dejah Thoris and Sola. With the noiselessness of
disembodied spirits we moved stealthily along the deserted streets, but not until
we were within sight of the plain beyond the city did I commence to breathe
freely. I was sure that Sola and Dejah Thoris would find no difficulty in reaching
our rendezvous undetected, but with my great thoats I was not so sure for myself,
as it was quite unusual for warriors to leave the city after dark; in fact there was no
place for them to go within any but a long ride.

I reached the appointed meeting place safely, but as Dejah Thoris and Sola
were not there I led my animals into the entrance hall of one of the large buildings. Presuming that one of the other women of the same household may have
come in to speak to Sola, and so delayed their departure, I did not feel any undue
apprehension until nearly an hour had passed without a sign of them, and by the
time another half hour had crawled away I was becoming filled with grave anxiety.
Then there broke upon the stillness of the night the sound of an approaching
party, which, from the noise, I knew could be no fugitives creeping stealthily toward liberty. Soon the party was near me, and from the black shadows of my entranceway I perceived a score of mounted warriors, who, in passing, dropped a
dozen words that fetched my heart clean into the top of my head.

"He would likely have arranged to meet them just without the city, and so—" I
heard no more, they had passed on; but it was enough. Our plan had been discovered, and the chances for escape from now on to the fearful end would be small
indeed. My one hope now was to return undetected to the quarters of Dejah
Thoris and learn what fate had overtaken her, but how to do it with these great
monstrous thoats upon my hands, now that the city probably was aroused by the
knowledge of my escape was a problem of no mean proportions.

Suddenly an idea occurred to me, and acting on my knowledge of the construction of the buildings of these ancient Martian cities with a hollow court within the
center of each square, I groped my way blindly through the dark chambers, calling
the great thoats after me. They had difficulty in negotiating some of the doorways, but as the buildings fronting the city's principal exposures were all designed

upon a magnificent scale, they were able to wriggle through without sticking fast; and thus we finally made the inner court where I found, as I had expected, the usual carpet of moss-like vegetation which would prove their food and drink until I could return them to their own enclosure. That they would be as quiet and contented here as elsewhere I was confident, nor was there but the remotest possibility that they would be discovered, as the green men had no great desire to enter these outlying buildings, which were frequented by the only thing, I believe, which caused them the sensation of fear—the great white apes of Barsoom.

Removing the saddle trappings, I hid them just within the rear doorway of the building through which we had entered the court, and, turning the beasts loose, quickly made my way across the court to the rear of the buildings upon the further side, and thence to the avenue beyond. Waiting in the doorway of the building until I was assured that no one was approaching, I hurried across to the opposite side and through the first doorway to the court beyond; thus, crossing through court after court with only the slight chance of detection which the necessary crossing of the avenues entailed, I made my way in safety to the courtyard in the rear of Dejah Thoris' quarters.

Here, of course, I found the beasts of the warriors who quartered in the adjacent buildings, and the warriors themselves I might expect to meet within if I entered; but, fortunately for me, I had another and safer method of reaching the upper story where Dejah Thoris should be found, and, after first determining as nearly as possible which of the buildings she occupied, for I had never observed them before from the court side, I took advantage of my relatively great strength and agility and sprang upward until I grasped the sill of a second-story window which I thought to be in the rear of her apartment. Drawing myself inside the room I moved stealthily toward the front of the building, and not until I had quite reached the doorway of her room was I made aware by voices that it was occupied.

I did not rush headlong in, but listened without to assure myself that it was Dejah Thoris and that it was safe to venture within. It was well indeed that I took this precaution, for the conversation I heard was in the low gutturals of men, and the words which finally came to me proved a most timely warning. The speaker was a chieftain and he was giving orders to four of his warriors.

"And when he returns to this chamber," he was saying, "as he surely will when he finds she does not meet him at the city's edge, you four are to spring upon him and disarm him. It will require the combined strength of all of you to do it if the reports they bring back from Korad are correct. When you have him fast bound bear him to the vaults beneath the jeddak's quarters and chain him securely where he may be found when Tal Hajus wishes him. Allow him to speak with none, nor permit any other to enter this apartment before he comes. There will be no danger of the girl returning, for by this time she is safe in the arms of Tal Hajus, and may all her ancestors have pity upon her, for Tal Hajus will have none; the great Sarkoja has done a noble night's work. I go, and if you fail to capture him when he comes, I commend your carcasses to the cold bosom of Iss."

CHAPTER XVII

A Costly Recapture

As the speaker ceased he turned to leave the apartment by the door where I was standing, but I needed to wait no longer; I had heard enough to fill my soul with dread, and stealing quietly away I returned to the courtyard by the way I had come. My plan of action was formed upon the instant, and crossing the square and the bordering avenue upon the opposite side I soon stood within the courtyard of Tal Hajus.

The brilliantly lighted apartments of the first floor told me where first to seek, and advancing to the windows I peered within. I soon discovered that my approach was not to be the easy thing I had hoped, for the rear rooms bordering the court were filled with warriors and women. I then glanced up at the stories above, discovering that the third was apparently unlighted, and so decided to make my entrance to the building from that point. It was the work of but a moment for me to reach the windows above, and soon I had drawn myself within the sheltering shadows of the unlighted third floor.

Fortunately the room I had selected was untenanted, and creeping noiselessly to the corridor beyond I discovered a light in the apartments ahead of me. Reaching what appeared to be a doorway I discovered that it was but an opening upon an immense inner chamber which towered from the first floor, two stories below me, to the dome-like roof of the building, high above my head. The floor of this great circular hall was thronged with chieftains, warriors and women, and at one end was a great raised platform upon which squatted the most hideous beast I had ever put my eyes upon. He had all the cold, hard, cruel, terrible features of the green warriors, but accentuated and debased by the animal passions to which he had given himself over for many years. There was not a mark of dignity or pride upon his bestial countenance, while his enormous bulk spread itself out upon the platform where he squatted like some huge devil fish, his six limbs accentuating the similarity in a horrible and startling manner.

But the sight that froze me with apprehension was that of Dejah Thoris and Sola standing there before him, and the fiendish leer of him as he let his great protruding eyes gloat upon the lines of her beautiful figure. She was speaking, but I could not hear what she said, nor could I make out the low grumbling of his reply. She stood there erect before him, her head high held, and even at the distance I was from them I could read the scorn and disgust upon her face as she let her haughty glance rest without sign of fear upon him. She was indeed the proud daughter of a thousand jeddaks, every inch of her dear, precious little body; so small, so frail beside the towering warriors around her, but in her majesty dwarfing them into insignificance; she was the mightiest figure among them and I verily believe that they felt it.

Presently Tal Hajus made a sign that the chamber be cleared, and that the prisoners be left alone before him. Slowly the chieftains, the warriors and the women melted away into the shadows of the surrounding chambers, and Dejah Thoris and Sola stood alone before the jeddak of the Tharks.

One chieftain alone had hesitated before departing; I saw him standing in the shadows of a mighty column, his fingers nervously toying with the hilt of his great-sword and his cruel eyes bent in implacable hatred upon Tal Hajus. It was Tars Tarkas, and I could read his thoughts as they were an open book for the undisguised loathing upon his face. He was thinking of that other woman who, forty years ago, had stood before this beast, and could I have spoken a word into his ear at that moment the reign of Tal Hajus would have been over; but finally he also strode from the room, not knowing that he left his own daughter at the mercy of the creature he most loathed.

Tal Hajus arose, and I, half fearing, half anticipating his intentions, hurried to the winding runway which led to the floors below. No one was near to intercept me, and I reached the main floor of the chamber unobserved, taking my station in the shadow of the same column that Tars Tarkas had but just deserted. As I reached the floor Tal Hajus was speaking.

"Princess of Helium, I might wring a mighty ransom from your people would I but return you to them unharmed, but a thousand times rather would I watch that beautiful face writhe in the agony of torture; it shall be long drawn out, that I promise you; ten days of pleasure were all too short to show the love I harbor for your race. The terrors of your death shall haunt the slumbers of the red men through all the ages to come; they will shudder in the shadows of the night as their fathers tell them of the awful vengeance of the green men; of the power and might and hate and cruelty of Tal Hajus. But before the torture you shall be mine for one short hour, and word of that too shall go forth to Tardos Mors, Jeddak of Helium, your grandfather, that he may grovel upon the ground in the agony of his sorrow. Tomorrow the torture will commence; tonight thou art Tal Hajus'; come!"

He sprang down from the platform and grasped her roughly by the arm, but scarcely had he touched her than I leaped between them. My short-sword, sharp and gleaming was in my right hand; I could have plunged it into his putrid heart before he realized that I was upon him; but as I raised my arm to strike I thought of Tars Tarkas, and, with all my rage, with all my hatred, I could not rob him of that sweet moment for which he had lived and hoped all these long, weary years, and so, instead, I swung my good right fist full upon the point of his jaw. Without a sound he slipped to the floor as one dead.

In the same deathly silence I grasped Dejah Thoris by the hand, and motioning to Sola to follow we sped noiselessly from the chamber and to the floor above. Unseen we reached a rear window and with the straps and leather of my trappings I lowered, first Sola and then Dejah Thoris to the ground below. Dropping lightly after them I drew them rapidly around the court in the shadows of the buildings, and thus we returned over the same course I had so recently followed from the distant boundary of the city.

We finally came upon my thoats in the courtyard where I had left them, and placing the trappings upon them we hastened through the building to the avenue beyond. Mounting, Sola upon one beast, and Dejah Thoris behind me upon the other, we rode from the city of Thark through the hills to the south.

Instead of circling back around the city to the northwest and toward the nearest waterway which lay so short a distance from us, we turned to the northeast and struck out upon the mossy waste across which, for two hundred dangerous and weary miles, lay another main artery leading to Helium.

No word was spoken until we had left the city far behind, but I could hear the quiet sobbing of Dejah Thoris as she clung to me with her dear head resting against my shoulder.

"If we make it, my chieftain, the debt of Helium will be a mighty one; greater than she can ever pay you; and should we not make it," she continued, "the debt is no less, though Helium will never know, for you have saved the last of our line from worse than death."

I did not answer, but instead reached to my side and pressed the little fingers of her I loved where they clung to me for support, and then, in unbroken silence, we sped over the yellow, moonlit moss; each of us occupied with his own thoughts. For my part I could not be other than joyful had I tried, with Dejah Thoris' warm body pressed close to mine, and with all our unpassed danger my heart was singing as gaily as though we were already entering the gates of Helium.

Our earlier plans had been so sadly upset that we now found ourselves without food or drink, and I alone was armed. We therefore urged our beasts to a speed that must tell on them sorely before we could hope to sight the ending of the first stage of our journey.

We rode all night and all the following day with only a few short rests. On the second night both we and our animals were completely fagged, and so we lay down upon the moss and slept for some five or six hours, taking up the journey once more before daylight. All the following day we rode, and when, late in the afternoon we had sighted no distant trees, the mark of the great waterways throughout all Barsoom, the terrible truth flashed upon us—we were lost.

Evidently we had circled, but which way it was difficult to say, nor did it seem possible with the sun to guide us by day and the moons and stars by night. At any rate no waterway was in sight, and the entire party was almost ready to drop from hunger, thirst and fatigue. Far ahead of us and a trifle to the right we could distinguish the outlines of low mountains. These we decided to attempt to reach in the hope that from some ridge we might discern the missing waterway. Night fell upon us before we reached our goal, and, almost fainting from weariness and weakness, we lay down and slept.

I was awakened early in the morning by some huge body pressing close to mine, and opening my eyes with a start I beheld my blessed old Woola snuggling close to me; the faithful brute had followed us across that trackless waste to share our fate, whatever it might be. Putting my arms about his neck I pressed my cheek close to his, nor am I ashamed that I did it, nor of the tears that came to my eyes as I thought of his love for me. Shortly after this Dejah Thoris and Sola awakened, and it was decided that we push on at once in an effort to gain the hills.

We had gone scarcely a mile when I noticed that my thoat was commencing to stumble and stagger in a most pitiful manner, although we had not attempted to force them out of a walk since about noon of the preceding day. Suddenly he lurched wildly to one side and pitched violently to the ground. Dejah Thoris and I were thrown clear of him and fell upon the soft moss with scarcely a jar; but the poor beast was in a pitiable condition, not even being able to rise, although relieved of our weight. Sola told me that the coolness of the night, when it fell, together with the rest would doubtless revive him, and so I decided not to kill him, as was my first intention, as I had thought it cruel to leave him alone there to die of hunger and thirst. Relieving him of his trappings, which I flung down beside him, we left the poor fellow to his fate, and pushed on with the one thoat as best we could. Sola and I walked, making Dejah Thoris ride, much against her will. In this way we had progressed to within about a mile of the hills we were endeavoring to reach when Dejah Thoris, from her point of vantage upon the thoat, cried out that she saw a great party of mounted men filing down from a pass in the hills several miles away. Sola and I both looked in the direction she indicated, and there, plainly discernible, were several hundred mounted warriors. They seemed to be headed in a southwesterly direction, which would take them away from us.

They doubtless were Thark warriors who had been sent out to capture us, and we breathed a great sigh of relief that they were traveling in the opposite direction. Quickly lifting Dejah Thoris from the thoat, I commanded the animal to lie down and we three did the same, presenting as small an object as possible for fear of attracting the attention of the warriors toward us.

We could see them as they filed out of the pass, just for an instant, before they were lost to view behind a friendly ridge; to us a most providential ridge; since, had they been in view for any great length of time, they scarcely could have failed to discover us. As what proved to be the last warrior came into view from the pass, he halted and, to our consternation, threw his small but powerful fieldglass to his eye and scanned the sea bottom in all directions. Evidently he was a chieftain, for in certain marching formations among the green men a chieftain brings up at the extreme rear of the column. As his glass swung toward us our hearts stopped in our breasts, and I could feel the cold sweat start from every pore in my body.

Presently it swung full upon us and—stopped. The tension on our nerves was near the breaking point, and I doubt if any of us breathed for the few moments he held us covered by his glass; and then he lowered it and we could see him shout a command to the warriors who had passed from our sight behind the ridge. He did not wait for them to join him, however, instead he wheeled his thoat and came tearing madly in our direction.

There was but one slight chance and that we must take quickly. Raising my strange Martian rifle to my shoulder I sighted and touched the button which controlled the trigger; there was a sharp explosion as the missile reached its goal, and the charging chieftain pitched backward from his flying mount.

Springing to my feet I urged the thoat to rise, and directed Sola to take Dejah Thoris with her upon him and make a mighty effort to reach the hills before the green warriors were upon us. I knew that in the ravines and gullies they might find a temporary hiding place, and even though they died there of hunger and thirst it would be better so than that they fell into the hands of the Tharks. Forcing my two revolvers upon them as a slight means of protection, and, as a last resort, as an escape for themselves from the horrid death which recapture would surely mean, I lifted Dejah Thoris in my arms and placed her upon the thoat behind Sola, who had already mounted at my command.

"Good-bye, my princess," I whispered, "we may meet in Helium yet. I have escaped from worse plights than this," and I tried to smile as I lied.

"What," she cried, "are you not coming with us?"

"How may I, Dejah Thoris? Someone must hold these fellows off for a while, and I can better escape them alone than could the three of us together."

She sprang quickly from the thoat and, throwing her dear arms about my neck, turned to Sola, saying with quiet dignity: "Fly, Sola! Dejah Thoris remains to die with the man she loves."

Those words are engraved upon my heart. Ah, gladly would I give up my life a thousand times could I only hear them once again; but I could not then give even a second to the rapture of her sweet embrace, and pressing my lips to hers for the first time, I picked her up bodily and tossed her to her seat behind Sola again, commanding the latter in peremptory tones to hold her there by force, and then, slapping the thoat upon the flank, I saw them borne away; Dejah Thoris struggling to the last to free herself from Sola's grasp.

Turning, I beheld the green warriors mounting the ridge and looking for their chieftain. In a moment they saw him, and then me; but scarcely had they discovered me than I commenced firing, lying flat upon my belly in the moss. I had an even hundred rounds in the magazine of my rifle, and another hundred in the belt at my back, and I kept up a continuous stream of fire until I saw all of the warriors who had been first to return from behind the ridge either dead or scurrying to cover.

My respite was short-lived however, for soon the entire party, numbering some thousand men, came charging into view, racing madly toward me. I fired until my rifle was empty and they were almost upon me, and then a glance showing me that Dejah Thoris and Sola had disappeared among the hills, I sprang up, throwing down my useless gun, and started away in the direction opposite to that taken by Sola and her charge.

If ever Martians had an exhibition of jumping, it was granted those astonished warriors on that day long years ago, but while it led them away from Dejah Thoris it did not distract their attention from endeavoring to capture me.

They raced wildly after me until, finally, my foot struck a projecting piece of quartz, and down I went sprawling upon the moss. As I looked up they were upon me, and although I drew my long-sword in an attempt to sell my life as dearly as possible, it was soon over. I reeled beneath their blows which fell upon me in perfect torrents; my head swam; all was black, and I went down beneath them to oblivion.

CHAPTER XVIII

Chained in Warhoon

It must have been several hours before I regained consciousness and I well remember the feeling of surprise which swept over me as I realized that I was not dead.

I was lying among a pile of sleeping silks and furs in the corner of a small room in which were several green warriors, and bending over me was an ancient and ugly female.

As I opened my eyes she turned to one of the warriors, saying,

"He will live, O, Jed."

" 'Tis well," replied the one so addressed, rising and approaching my couch, "he should render rare sport for the great games."

And now as my eyes fell upon him, I saw that he was no Thark, for his ornaments and metal were not of that horde. He was a huge fellow, terribly scarred about the face and chest, and with one broken tusk and a missing ear. Strapped on either breast were human skulls and depending from these a number of dried human hands.

His reference to the great games of which I had heard so much while among the Tharks convinced me that I had but jumped from purgatory into gehenna.

After a few more words with the female, during which she assured him that I was now fully fit to travel, the jed ordered that we mount and ride after the main column.

I was strapped securely to as wild and unmanageable a thoat as I had ever seen, and, with a mounted warrior on either side to prevent the beast from bolting, we rode forth at a furious pace in pursuit of the column. My wounds gave me but little pain, so wonderfully and rapidly had the applications and injections of the female exercised their therapeutic powers, and so deftly had she bound and plastered the injuries.

Just before dark we reached the main body of troops shortly after they had made camp for the night. I was immediately taken before the leader, who proved to be the jeddak of the hordes of Warhoon.

Like the jed who had brought me, he was frightfully scarred, and also decorated with the breastplate of human skulls and dried dead hands which seemed to mark all the greater warriors among the Warhoons, as well as to indicate their awful ferocity, which greatly transcends even that of the Tharks.

The jeddak, Bar Comas, who was comparatively young, was the object of the fierce and jealous hatred of his old lieutenant, Dak Kova, the jed who had captured me, and I could not but note the almost studied efforts which the latter made to affront his superior.

He entirely omitted the usual formal salutation as we entered the presence of the jeddak, and as he pushed me roughly before the ruler he exclaimed in a loud and menacing voice,

"I have brought a strange creature wearing the metal of a Thark whom it is my pleasure to have battle with a wild thoat at the great games."

"He will die as Bar Comas, your jeddak, sees fit, if at all," replied the young ruler, with emphasis and dignity.

"If at all?" roared Dak Kova. "By the dead hands at my throat but he shall die, Bar Comas. No maudlin weakness on your part shall save him. O, would that Warhoon were ruled by a real jeddak rather than by a water-hearted weakling from whom even old Dak Kova could tear the metal with his bare hands!"

Bar Comas eyed the defiant and insubordinate chieftain for an instant, his expression one of haughty, fearless contempt and hate, and then without drawing a weapon and without uttering a word he hurled himself at the throat of his defamer.

I never before had seen two green Martian warriors battle with nature's weapons and the exhibition of animal ferocity which ensued was as fearful a thing as the most disordered imagination could picture. They tore at each others' eyes and ears with their hands and with their gleaming tusks repeatedly slashed and gored until both were cut fairly to ribbons from head to foot.

Bar Comas had much the better of the battle as he was stronger, quicker and more intelligent. It soon seemed that the encounter was done saving only the final death thrust when Bar Comas slipped in breaking away from a clinch. It was the one little opening that Dak Kova needed, and hurling himself at the body of his adversary he buried his single mighty tusk in Bar Comas' groin and with a last powerful effort ripped the young jeddak wide open the full length of his body, the great tusk finally wedging in the bones of Bar Comas' jaw. Victor and vanquished rolled limp and lifeless upon the moss, a huge mass of torn and bloody flesh.

Bar Comas was stone dead, and only the most herculean efforts on the part of Dak Kova's females saved him from the fate he deserved. Three days later he walked without assistance to the body of Bar Comas which, by custom, had not been moved from where it fell, and placing his foot upon the neck of his erstwhile ruler he assumed the title of Jeddak of Warhoon.

The dead jeddak's hands and head were removed to be added to the ornaments of his conquerer, and then his women cremated what remained, amid wild and terrible laughter.

The injuries to Dak Kova had delayed the march so greatly that it was decided to give up the expedition, which was a raid upon a small Thark community in retaliation for the destruction of the incubator, until after the great games, and the entire body of warriors, ten thousand in number, turned back toward Warhoon.

My introduction to these cruel and bloodthirsty people was but an index to the scenes I witnessed almost daily while with them. They are a smaller horde than the Tharks but much more ferocious. Not a day passed but that some members of the various Warhoon communities met in deadly combat. I have seen as high as eight mortal duels within a single day.

We reached the city of Warhoon after some three days march and I was immediately cast into a dungeon and heavily chained to the floor and walls. Food was brought me at intervals but owing to the utter darkness of the place I do not know whether I lay there days, or weeks, or months. It was the most horrible experience of all my life and that my mind did not give way to the terrors of that inky blackness has been a wonder to me ever since. The place was filled with creeping, crawling things; cold, sinuous bodies passed over me when I lay down, and in the darkness I occasionally caught glimpses of gleaming, fiery eyes, fixed in horrible intentness upon me. No sound reached me from the world above and no word would my jailer vouchsafe when my food was brought to me, although I at first bombarded him with questions.

Finally all the hatred and maniacal loathing for these awful creatures who had placed me in this horrible place was centered by my tottering reason upon this single emissary who represented to me the entire horde of Warhoons.

I had noticed that he always advanced with his dim torch to where he could place the food within my reach and as he stooped to place it upon the floor his head was about on a level with my breast. So, with the cunning of a madman, I backed into the far corner of my cell when next I heard him approaching and gathering a little slack of the great chain which held me in my hand I waited his coming, crouching like some beast of prey. As he stooped to place my food upon the ground I swung the chain above my head and crashed the links with all my strength upon his skull. Without a sound he slipped to the floor, stone dead.

Laughing and chattering like the idiot I was fast becoming I fell upon his prostrate form my fingers feeling for his dead throat. Presently they came in contact with a small chain at the end of which dangled a number of keys. The touch of my fingers on these keys brought back my reason with the suddenness of thought. No longer was I a jibbering idiot, but a sane, reasoning man with the means of escape within my very hands.

As I was groping to remove the chain from about my victim's neck I glanced up into the darkness to see six pairs of gleaming eyes fixed, unwinking, upon me. Slowly they approached and slowly I shrank back from the awful horror of them. Back into my corner I crouched holding my hands, palms out, before me, and stealthily on came the awful eyes until they reached the dead body at my feet. Then slowly they retreated but this time with a strange grating sound and finally they disappeared in some black and distant recess of my dungeon.

CHAPTER XIX

Battling in the Arena

Slowly I regained my composure and finally essayed again to attempt to remove the keys from the dead body of my former jailer. But as I reached out into the darkness to locate it I found to my horror that it was gone. Then the truth flashed on me; the owners of those gleaming eyes had dragged my prize away from me to be devoured in their neighboring lair; as they had been waiting for days, for weeks, for months, through all this awful eternity of my imprisonment to drag my dead carcass to their feast.

For two days no food was brought me, but then a new messenger appeared and my incarceration went on as before, but not again did I allow my reason to be submerged by the horror of my position.

Shortly after this episode another prisoner was brought in and chained near me. By the dim torch light I saw that he was a red Martian and I could scarcely await the departure of his guards to address him. As their retreating footsteps died away in the distance, I called out softly the Martian word of greeting, kaor.

"Who are you who speaks out of the darkness?" he answered.

"John Carter, a friend of the red men of Helium."

"I am of Helium," he said, "but I do not recall your name."

And then I told him my story as I have written it here, omitting only any reference to my love for Dejah Thoris. He was much excited by the news of Helium's princess and seemed quite positive that she and Sola could easily have reached a point of safety from where they left me. He said that he knew the place well because the defile through which the Warhoon warriors had passed when they discovered us was the only one ever used by them when marching to the south.

"Dejah Thoris and Sola entered the hills not five miles from a great waterway and are now probably quite safe," he assured me.

My fellow prisoner was Kantos Kan, a padwar (lieutenant) in the navy of Helium. He had been a member of the ill-fated expedition which had fallen into the hands of the Tharks at the time of Dejah Thoris' capture, and he briefly related the events which followed the defeat of the battleships.

Badly injured and only partially manned they had limped slowly toward Helium, but while passing near the city of Zodanga, the capital of Helium's hereditary enemies among the red men of Barsoom, they had been attacked by a great body of war vessels and all but the craft to which Kantos Kan belonged were either destroyed or captured. His vessel was chased for days by three of the Zodangan war ships but finally escaped during the darkness of a moonless night.

Thirty days after the capture of Dejah Thoris, or about the time of our coming to Thark, his vessel had reached Helium with about ten survivors of the original crew of seven hundred officers and men. Immediately seven great fleets, each of one hundred mighty war ships, had been dispatched to search for Dejah Thoris, and from these vessels two thousand smaller craft had been kept out continuously in futile search for the missing princess.

Two green Martian communities had been wiped off the face of Barsoon by the avenging fleets, but no trace of Dejah Thoris had been found. They had been searching among the northern hordes, and only within the past few days had they extended their quest to the south.

Kantos Kan had been detailed to one of the small one-man fliers and had had the misfortune to be discovered by the Warhoons while exploring their city. The bravery and daring of the man won my greatest respect and admiration. Alone he had landed at the city's boundary and on foot had penetrated to the buildings surrounding the plaza. For two days and nights he had explored their quarters and their dungeons in search of his beloved princess only to fall into the hands of a party of Warhoons as he was about to leave, after assuring himself that Dejah Thoris was not a captive there.

During the period of our incarceration Kantos Kan and I became well acquainted, and formed a warm personal friendship. A few days only elapsed, however, before we were dragged forth from our dungeon for the great games. We were conducted early one morning to an enormous amphitheater, which instead of having been built upon the surface of the ground was excavated below the surface. It had partially filled with debris so that how large it had originally been was difficult to say. In its present condition it held the entire twenty thousand Warhoons of the assembled hordes.

The arena was immense but extremely uneven and unkempt. Around it the Warhoons had piled building stone from some of the ruined edifices of the ancient city to prevent the animals and the captives from escaping into the audience, and at each end had been constructed cages to hold them until their turns came to meet some horrible death upon the arena.

Kantos Kan and I were confined together in one of the cages. In the others were wild calots, thoats, mad zitidars, green warriors, and women of other hordes, and many strange and ferocious wild beasts of Barsoom which I had never before seen. The din of their roaring, growling and squealing was deafening and the formidable appearance of any one of them was enough to make the stoutest heart feel grave forebodings.

Kantos Kan explained to me that at the end of the day one of these prisoners would gain freedom and the others would lie dead about the arena. The winners in the various contests of the day would be pitted against each other until only two remained alive; the victor in the last encounter being set free, whether animal or man. The following morning the cages would be filled with a new consignment of victims, and so on throughout the ten days of the games.

Shortly after we had been caged the amphitheater began to fill and within an hour every available part of the seating space was occupied. Dak Kova, with his jeds and chieftains, sat at the center of one side of the arena upon a large raised platform.

At a signal from Dak Kova the doors of two cages were thrown open and a dozen green Martian females were driven to the center of the arena. Each was given a dagger and then, at the far end, a pack of twelve calots, or wild dogs were loosed upon them.

As the brutes, growling and foaming, rushed upon the almost defenseless women I turned my head that I might not see the horrid sight. The yells and laughter of the green horde bore witness to the excellent quality of the sport and when I turned back to the arena, as Kantos Kan told me it was over, I saw three victorious calots, snarling and growling over the bodies of their prey. The women had given a good account of themselves.

Next a mad zitidar was loosed among the remaining dogs, and so it went throughout the long, hot, horrible day.

During the day I was pitted against first men and then beasts, but as I was armed with a long-sword and always outclassed my adversary in agility and generally in strength as well, it proved but child's play to me. Time and time again I won the applause of the bloodthirsty multitude, and toward the end there were cries that I be taken from the arena and be made a member of the hordes of Warhoon.

Finally there were but three of us left, a great green warrior of some far northern horde, Kantos Kan, and myself. The other two were to battle and then I to fight the conqueror for the liberty which was accorded the final winner.

Kantos Kan had fought several times during the day and like myself had always proven victorious, but occasionally by the smallest of margins, especially when pitted against the green warriors. I had little hope that he could best his giant adversary who had mowed down all before him during the day. The fellow towered nearly sixteen feet in height, while Kantos Kan was some inches under six feet. As they advanced to meet one another I saw for the first time a trick of Martian swordsmanship which centered Kantos Kan's every hope of victory and life on one cast of the dice, for, as he came to within about twenty feet of the huge fellow he threw his sword arm far behind him over his shoulder and with a mighty sweep hurled his weapon point foremost at the green warrior. It flew true as an arrow and piercing the poor devil's heart laid him dead upon the arena.

Kantos Kan and I were now pitted against each other but as we approached to the encounter I whispered to him to prolong the battle until nearly dark in the hope that we might find some means of escape. The horde evidently guessed that we had no hearts to fight each other and so they howled in rage as neither of us placed a fatal thrust. Just as I saw the sudden coming of dark I whispered to Kantos Kan to thrust his sword between my left arm and my body. As he did so I staggered back clasping the sword tightly with my arm and thus fell to the ground with his weapon apparently protruding from my chest. Kantos Kan perceived my coup and stepping quickly to my side he placed his foot upon my neck and withdrawing his sword from my body gave me the final death blow through the neck which is supposed to sever the jugular vein, but in this instance the cold blade slipped harmlessly into the sand of the arena. In the darkness which had now fallen none could tell but that he had really finished me. I whispered to him to go and claim his freedom and then look for me in the hills east of the city, and so he left me.

When the amphitheater had cleared I crept stealthily to the top and as the great excavation lay far from the plaza and in an untenanted portion of the great dead city I had little trouble in reaching the hills beyond.

CHAPTER XX

In the Atmosphere Factory

For two days I waited there for Kantos Kan, but as he did not come I started off on foot in a northwesterly direction toward a point where he had told me lay the nearest waterway. My only food consisted of vegetable milk from the plants which gave so bounteously of this priceless fluid.

Through two long weeks I wandered, stumbling through the nights guided only by the stars and hiding during the days behind some protruding rock or among the occasional hills I traversed. Several times I was attacked by wild beasts; strange, uncouth monstrosities that leaped upon me in the dark, so that I had ever to grasp my long-sword in my hand that I might be ready for them. Usually my strange, newly acquired telepathic power warned me in ample time, but once I was down with vicious fangs at my jugular and a hairy face pressed close to mine before I knew that I was even threatened.

What manner of thing was upon me I did not know, but that it was large and heavy and many-legged I could feel. My hands were at its throat before the fangs had a chance to bury themselves in my neck, and slowly I forced the hairy face from me and closed my fingers, vise-like, upon its windpipe.

Without sound we lay there, the beast exerting every effort to reach me with those awful fangs, and I straining to maintain my grip and choke the life from it as I kept it from my throat. Slowly my arms gave to the unequal struggle, and inch by inch the burning eyes and gleaming tusks of my antagonist crept toward me, until, as the hairy face touched mine again, I realized that all was over. And then a living mass of destruction sprang from the surrounding darkness full upon the creature that held me pinioned to the ground. The two rolled growling upon the moss, tearing and rending one another is a frightful manner, but it was soon over and my preserver stood with lowered head above the throat of the dead thing which would have killed me.

The nearer moon, hurtling suddenly above the horizon and lighting up the Barsoomian scene, showed me that my preserver was Woola, but from whence he had come, or how found me, I was at a loss to know. That I was glad of his companionship it is needless to say, but my pleasure at seeing him was tempered by anxiety as to the reason of his leaving Dejah Thoris. Only her death I felt sure, could account for his absence from her, so faithful I knew him to be to my commands.

By the light of the now brilliant moons I saw that he was but a shadow of his former self, and as he turned from my caress and commenced greedily to devour the dead carcass at my feet I realized that the poor fellow was more than half starved. I, myself, was in but little better plight but I could not bring myself to eat the uncooked flesh and I had no means of making a fire. When Woola had finished his meal I again took up my weary and seemingly endless wandering in quest of the elusive waterway.

At daybreak of the fifteenth day of my search I was overjoyed to see the high trees that denoted the object of my search. About noon I dragged myself wearily to the portals of a huge building which covered perhaps four square miles and towered two hundred feet in the air. It showed no aperture in the mighty walls other than the tiny door at which I sank exhausted, nor was there any sign of life about it.

I could find no bell or other method of making my presence known to the inmates of the place, unless a small round hole in the wall near the door was for that purpose. It was of about the bigness of a lead pencil and thinking that it might be in the nature of a speaking tube I put my mouth to it and was about to call into it when a voice issued from it asking me whom I might be, where from, and the nature of my errand.

I explained that I had escaped from the Warhoons and was dying of starvation and exhaustion.

"You wear the metal of a green warrior and are followed by a calot, yet you are of the figure of a red man. In color you are neither green nor red. In the name of the ninth day, what manner of creature are you?"

"I am a friend of the red men of Barsoom and I am starving. In the name of humanity open to us," I replied.

Presently the door commenced to recede before me until it had sunk into the wall fifty feet, then it stopped and slid easily to the left, exposing a short, narrow corridor of concrete, at the further end of which was another door, similar in every respect to the one I had just passed. No one was in sight, yet immediately we passed the first door it slid gently into place behind us and receded rapidly to its original position in the front wall of the building. As the door had slipped aside I had noted its great thickness, fully twenty feet, and as it reached its place once more after closing behind us, great cylinders of steel had dropped from the ceiling behind it and fitted their lower ends into apertures countersunk in the floor.

A second and a third door receded before me and slipped to one side as the first, before I reached a large inner chamber where I found food and drink set out upon a great stone table. A voice directed me to satisfy my hunger and to feed my calot, and while I was thus engaged my invisible host put me through a severe and searching cross-examination.

"Your statements are most remarkable," said the voice, on concluding its questioning, "but you are evidently speaking the truth, and it is equally evident that you are not of Barsoom. I can tell that by the conformation of your brain and the strange location of your internal organs and the shape and size of your heart."

"Can you see through me?" I exclaimed.

"Yes, I can see all but your thoughts, and were you a Barsoomian I could read those."

Then a door opened at the far side of the chamber and a strange, dried up, little mummy of a man came toward me. He wore but a single article of clothing or adornment, a small collar of gold from which depended upon his chest a great ornament as large as a dinner plate set solid with huge diamonds, except for the exact center which was occupied by a strange stone, an inch in diameter, that scintillated nine different and distinct rays; the seven colors of our earthly prism and two beautiful rays which, to me, were new and nameless. I cannot describe them any more than you could describe red to a blind man. I only know that they were beautiful in the extreme.

The old man sat and talked with me for hours, and the strangest part of our intercourse was that I could read his every thought while he could not fathom an iota from my mind unless I spoke.

I did not apprise him of my ability to sense his mental operations, and thus I learned a great deal which proved of immense value to me later and which I would never have known had he suspected my strange power, for the Martians have such perfect control of their mental machinery that they are able to direct their thoughts with absolute precision.

The building in which I found myself contained the machinery which produces that artificial atmosphere which sustains life on Mars. The secret of the entire process hinges on the use of the ninth ray, one of the beautiful scintillations which I had noted emanating from the great stone in my host's diadem.

This ray is separated from the other rays of the sun by means of finely adjusted instruments placed upon the roof of the huge building, three-quarters of which is used for reservoirs in which the ninth ray is stored. This product is then treated electrically, or rather certain proportions of refined electric vibrations are incorporated with it, and the result is then pumped to the five principal air centers of the planet where, as it is released, contact with the ether of space transforms it into atmosphere.

There is always sufficient reserve of the ninth ray stored in the great building to maintain the present Martian atmosphere for a thousand years, and the only fear, as my new friend told me, was that some accident might befall the pumping apparatus.

He led me to an inner chamber where I beheld a battery of twenty radium pumps any one of which was equal to the task of furnishing all Mars with the atmosphere compound. For eight hundred years, he told me, he had watched these pumps which are used alternately a day each at a stretch, or a little over twenty-four and one-half Earth hours. He has one assistant who divides the watch with him. Half a Martian year, about three hundred and forty-four of our days, each of these men spend alone in this huge, isolated plant.

Every red Martian is taught during earliest childhood the principles of the manufacture of atmosphere, but only two at one time ever hold the secret of ingress to the great building, which, built as it is with walls a hundred and fifty feet thick, is absolutely unassailable, even the roof being guarded from assault by air craft by a glass covering five feet thick.

The only fear they entertain of attack is from the green Martians or some demented red man, as all Barsoomians realize that the very existence of every form of life on Mars is dependent upon the uninterrupted working of this plant.

One curious fact I discovered as I watched his thoughts was that the outer doors are manipulated by telepathic means. The locks are so finely adjusted that the doors are released by the action of a certain combination of thought waves. To experiment with my new-found toy I thought to surprise him into revealing this combination and so I asked him in a casual manner how he had managed to unlock the massive doors for me from the inner chambers of the building. As quick as a flash there leaped to his mind nine Martian sounds, but as quickly faded as he answered that this was a secret he must not divulge.

From then on his manner toward me changed as though he feared that he had been surprised into divulging his great secret, and I read suspicion and fear in his looks and thoughts, though his words were still fair.

Before I retired for the night he promised to give me a letter to a nearby agricultural officer who would help me on my way to Zodanga, which he said, was the nearest Martian city.

"But be sure that you do not let them know you are bound for Helium as they are at war with that country. My assistant and I are of no country, we belong to all Barsoom and this talisman which we wear protects us in all lands, even among the green men—though we do not trust ourselves to their hands if we can avoid it," he added.

"And so good-night, my friend," he continued, "may you have a long and restful sleep—yes, a long sleep."

And though he smiled pleasantly I saw in his thoughts the wish that he had never admitted me, and then a picture of him standing over me in the night, and the swift thrust of a long dagger and the half formed words, "I am sorry, but it is for the best good of Barsoom."

As he closed the door of my chamber behind him his thoughts were cut off from me as was the sight of him, which seemed strange to me in my little knowledge of thought transference.

What was I to do? How could I escape through these mighty walls? Easily could I kill him now that I was warned, but once he was dead I could no more escape, and with the stopping of the machinery of the great plant I should die with all the other inhabitants of the planet—all, even Dejah Thoris were she not already dead. For the others I did not give the snap of my finger, but the thought of Dejah Thoris drove from my mind all desire to kill my mistaken host.

Cautiously I opened the door of my apartment and, followed by Woola, sought the inner of the great doors. A wild scheme had come to me; I would attempt to force the great locks by the nine thought waves I had read in my host's mind.

Creeping stealthily through corridor after corridor and down winding runways which turned hither and thither I finally reached the great hall in which I had broken my long fast that morning. Nowhere had I seen my host, nor did I know where he kept himself by night.

I was on the point of stepping boldly out into the room when a slight noise behind me warned me back into the shadows of a recess in the corridor. Dragging Woola after me I crouched low in the darkness.

Presently the old man passed close by me, and as he entered the dimly lighted chamber which I had been about to pass through I saw that he held a long thin dagger in his hand and that he was sharpening it upon a stone. In his mind was the decision to inspect the radium pumps, which would take about thirty minutes, and then return to my bed chamber and finish me.

As he passed through the great hall and disappeared down the runway which led to the pump-room, I stole stealthily from my hiding place and crossed to the great door, the inner of the three which stood between me and liberty.

Concentrating my mind upon the massive lock I hurled the nine thought waves against it. In breathless expectancy I waited, when finally the great door moved softly toward me and slid quietly to one side. One after the other the remaining mighty portals opened at my command and Woola and I stepped forth into the darkness, free, but little better off than we had been before, other than that we had full stomachs.

Hastening away from the shadows of the formidable pile I made for the first crossroad, intending to strike the central turnpike as quickly as possible. This I reached about morning and entering the first enclosure I came to I searched for some evidences of a habitation.

There were low rambling buildings of concrete barred with heavy impassable doors, and no amount of hammering and hallooing brought any response. Weary and exhausted from sleeplessness I threw myself upon the ground commanding Woola to stand guard.

Some time later I was awakened by his frightful growlings and opened my eyes to see three red Martians standing a short distance from us and covering me with their rifles.

"I am unarmed and no enemy," I hastened to explain. "I have been a prisoner among the green men and am on my way to Zodanga. All I ask is food and rest for myself and my calot and the proper directions for reaching my destination."

They lowered their rifles and advanced pleasantly toward me placing their right hands upon my left shoulder, after the manner of their custom of salute, and asking me many questions about myself and my wanderings. They then took me to the house of one of them which was only a short distance away.

The buildings I had been hammering at in the early morning were occupied only by stock and farm produce, the house proper standing among a grove of enormous trees, and, like all red-Martian homes, had been raised at night some forty or fifty feet from the ground on a large round metal shaft which slid up or down within a sleeve sunk in the ground, and was operated by a tiny radium engine in the entrance hall of the building. Instead of bothering with bolts and bars for their dwellings, the red Martians simply run them up out of harm's way during the night. They also have private means for lowering or raising them from the ground without if they wish to go away and leave them.

These brothers, with their wives and children, occupied three similar houses on this farm. They did no work themselves, being government officers in charge. The labor was performed by convicts, prisoners of war, delinquent debtors and confirmed bachelors who were too poor to pay the high celibate tax which all red-Martian governments impose.

They were the personification of cordiality and hospitality and I spent several days with them, resting and recuperating from my long and arduous experiences.

When they had heard my story—I omitted all reference to Dejah Thoris and the old man of the atmosphere plant—they advised me to color my body to more nearly resemble their own race and then attempt to find employment in Zodanga, either in the army or the navy.

"The chances are small that your tale will be believed until after you have proven your trustworthiness and won friends among the higher nobles of the court. This you can most easily do through military service, as we are a warlike people on Barsoom," explained one of them, "and save our richest favors for the fighting man."

When I was ready to depart they furnished me with a small domestic bull thoat, such as is used for saddle purposes by all red Martians. The animal is about the size of a horse and quite gentle, but in color and shape an exact replica of his huge and fierce cousin of the wilds.

The brothers had supplied me with a reddish oil with which I anointed my entire body and one of them cut my hair, which had grown quite long, in the prevailing fashion of the time, square at the back and banged in front, so that I could have passed anywhere upon Barsoom as a full-fledged red Martian. My metal and ornaments were also renewed in the style of a Zodangan gentleman, attached to the house of Ptor, which was the family name of my benefactors.

They filled a little sack at my side with Zodangan money. The medium of exchange upon Mars is not dissimilar from our own except that the coins are oval. Paper money is issued by individuals as they require it and redeemed twice yearly. If a man issues more than he can redeem, the government pays his creditors in full and the debtor works out the amount upon the farms or in mines, which are all owned by the government. This suits everybody except the debtor as it has been a difficult thing to obtain sufficient voluntary labor to work the great isolated farm lands of Mars, stretching as they do like narrow ribbons from pole to pole, through wild stretches peopled by wild animals and wilder men.

When I mentioned my inability to repay them for their kindness to me they assured me that I would have ample opportunity if I lived long upon Barsoom, and bidding me farewell they watched me until I was out of sight upon the broad white turnpike.

CHAPTER XXI

An Air Scout for Zodanga

As I proceeded on my journey toward Zodanga many strange and interesting sights arrested my attention, and at the several farm houses where I stopped I learned a number of new and instructive things concerning the methods and manners of Barsoom.

The water which supplies the farms of Mars is collected in immense underground reservoirs at either pole from the melting ice caps, and pumped through long conduits to the various populated centers. Along either side of these conduits, and extending their entire length, lie the cultivated districts. These are divided into tracts of about the same size, each tract being under the supervision of one or more government officers.

Instead of flooding the surface of the fields, and thus wasting immense quantities of water by evaporation, the precious liquid is carried underground through a vast network of small pipes directly to the roots of the vegetation. The crops upon Mars are always uniform, for there are no droughts, no rains, no high winds, and no insects, or destroying birds.

On this trip I tasted the first meat I had eaten since leaving Earth—large, juicy steaks and chops from the well-fed domestic animals of the farms. Also I enjoyed luscious fruits and vegetables, but not a single article of food which was exactly similar to anything on Earth. Every plant and flower and vegetable and animal has been so refined by ages of careful, scientific cultivation and breeding that the like of them on Earth dwindled into pale, gray, characterless nothingness by comparison.

At a second stop I met some highly cultivated people of the noble class and while in conversation we chanced to speak of Helium. One of the older men had been there on a diplomatic mission several years before and spoke with regret of the conditions which seemed destined ever to keep these two countries at war.

"Helium," he said, "rightly boasts the most beautiful women of Barsoom, and of all her treasures the wondrous daughter of Mors Kajak, Dejah Thoris, is the most exquisite flower.

"Why," he added, "the people really worship the ground she walks upon and since her loss on that ill-starred expedition all Helium has been draped in mourning.

"That our ruler should have attacked the disabled fleet as it was returning to Helium was but another of his awful blunders which I fear will sooner or later compel Zodanga to elevate a wiser man to his place.

"Even now, though our victorious armies are surrounding Helium, the people of Zodanga are voicing their displeasure, for the war is not a popular one, since it is not based on right or justice. Our forces took advantage of the absence of the principal fleet of Helium on their search for the princess, and so we have been able easily to reduce the city to a sorry plight. It is said she will fall within the next few passages of the further moon."

"And what, think you, may have been the fate of the princess, Dejah Thoris?" I asked as casually as possible.

"She is dead," he answered. "This much was learned from a green warrior recently captured by our forces in the south. She escaped from the hordes of Thark with a strange creature of another world, only to fall into the hands of the Warhoons. Their thoats were found wandering upon the sea bottom and evidences of a bloody conflict were discovered nearby."

While this information was in no way reassuring, neither was it at all conclusive proof of the death of Dejah Thoris, and so I determined to make every effort possible to reach Helium as quickly as I could and carry to Tardos Mors such news of his granddaughter's possible whereabouts as lay in my power.

Ten days after leaving the three Ptor brothers I arrived at Zodanga. From the moment that I had come in contact with the red inhabitants of Mars I had noticed that Woola drew a great amount of unwelcome attention to me, since the huge brute belonged to a species which is never domesticated by the red men. Were one to stroll down Broadway with a Numidian lion at his heels the effect would be somewhat similar to that which I should have produced had I entered Zodanga with Woola.

The very thought of parting with the faithful fellow caused me so great regret and genuine sorrow that I put it off until just before we arrived at the city's gates; but then, finally, it became imperative that we separate. Had nothing further than my own safety or pleasure been at stake no argument could have prevailed upon me to turn away the one creature upon Barsoom that had never failed in a demonstration of affection and loyalty; but as I would willingly have offered my life in the service of her in search of whom I was about to challenge the unknown dangers of this, to me, mysterious city, I could not permit even Woola's life to threaten the success of my venture, much less his momentary happiness, for I doubted not he soon would forget me. And so I bade the poor beast an affectionate farewell, promising him, however, that if I came through my adventure in safety that in some way I should find the means to search him out.

He seemed to understand me fully, and when I pointed back in the direction of Thark he turned sorrowfully away, nor could I bear to watch him go; but resolutely set my face toward Zodanga and with a touch of heartsickness approached her frowning walls.

The letter I bore from them gained me immediate entrance to the vast, walled city. It was still very early in the morning and the streets were practically deserted.

The residences, raised high upon their metal columns, resembled huge rookeries, while the uprights themselves presented the appearance of steel tree trunks. The shops as a rule were not raised from the ground nor were their doors bolted or barred, since thievery is practically unknown upon Barsoom. Assassination is the ever-present fear of all Barsoomians, and for this reason alone their homes are raised high above the ground at night, or in times of danger.

The Ptor brothers had given me explicit directions for reaching the point of the city where I could find living accommodations and be near the offices of the government agents to whom they had given me letters. My way led to the central square or plaza, which is a characteristic of all Martian cities.

The plaza of Zodanga covers a square mile and is bounded by the palaces of the jeddak, the jeds, and other members of the royalty and nobility of Zodanga, as well as by the principal public buildings, cafés, and shops.

As I was crossing the great square lost in wonder and admiration of the magnificent architecture and the gorgeous scarlet vegetation which carpeted the broad lawns I discovered a red Martian walking briskly toward me from one of the avenues. He paid not the slightest attention to me, but as he came abreast I recognized him, and turning I placed my hand upon his shoulder, calling out:

"Kaor, Kantos Kan!"

Like lightning he wheeled and before I could so much as lower my hand the point of his long-sword was at my breast.

"Who are you?" he growled, and then as a backward leap carried me fifty feet from his sword he dropped the point to the ground and exclaimed, laughing,

"I do not need a better reply, there is but one man upon all Barsoom who can bounce about like a rubber ball. By the mother of the further moon, John Carter, how came you here, and have you become a Darseen that you can change your color at will?

"You gave me a bad half minute my friend," he continued, after I had briefly outlined my adventures since parting with him in the arena at Warhoon. "Were my name and city known to the Zodangans I would shortly be sitting on the banks of the lost sea of Korus with my revered and departed ancestors. I am here in the interest of Tardos Mors, Jeddak of Helium, to discover the whereabouts of Dejah Thoris, our princess. Sab Than, prince of Zodanga, has her hidden in the city and has fallen madly in love with her. His father, Than Kosis, Jeddak of Zodanga, has made her voluntary marriage to his son the price of peace between our countries, but Tardos Mors will not accede to the demands and has sent word that he and his people would rather look upon the dead face of their princess than see her wed to any than her own choice, and that personally he would prefer being engulfed in the ashes of a lost and burning Helium to joining the metal of his house with that of Than Kosis. His reply was the deadliest affront he could have put upon Than Kosis and the Zodangans, but his people love him the more for it and his strength in Helium is greater today than ever.

"I have been here three days," continued Kantos Kan, "but I have not yet found where Dejah Thoris is imprisoned. Today I join the Zodangan navy as an air scout and I hope in this way to win the confidence of Sab Than, the prince, who is commander of this division of the navy, and thus learn the whereabouts of Dejah Thoris. I am glad that you are here, John Carter, for I know your loyalty to my princess and two of us working together should be able to accomplish much."

The plaza was now commencing to fill with people going and coming upon the daily activities of their duties. The shops were opening and the cafés filling with early morning patrons. Kantos Kan led me to one of these gorgeous eating places where we were served entirely by mechanical apparatus. No hand touched the food from the time it entered the building in its raw state until it emerged hot and delicious upon the tables before the guests, in response to the touching of tiny buttons to indicate their desires.

After our meal, Kantos Kan took me with him to the headquarters of the air-scout squadron and introducing me to his superior asked that I be enrolled as a member of the corps. In accordance with custom an examination was necessary, but Kantos Kan had told me to have no fear on this score as he would attend to that part of the matter. He accomplished this by taking my order for examination to the examining officer and representing himself as John Carter.

"This ruse will be discovered later," he cheerfully explained, "when they check up my weights, measurements, and other personal identification data, but it will be several months before this is done and our mission should be accomplished or have failed long before that time."

The next few days were spent by Kantos Kan in teaching me the intricacies of flying and of repairing the dainty little contrivances which the Martians use for this purpose. The body of the one-man air craft is about sixteen feet long, two feet wide and three inches thick, tapering to a point at each end. The driver sits on top of this plane upon a seat constructed over the small, noiseless radium engine which propels it. The medium of buoyancy is contained within the thin metal walls of the body and consists of the eighth Barsoomian ray, or ray of propulsion, as it may be termed in view of its properties.

This ray, like the ninth ray, is unkown on Earth, but the Martians have discovered that it is an inherent property of all light no matter from what source it emanates. They have learned that it is the solar eighth ray which propels the light of the sun to the various planets, and that it is the individual eighth ray of each planet which "reflects," or propels the light thus obtained out into space once more. The solar eighth ray would be absorbed by the surface of Barsoom, but the Barsoomian eighth ray, which tends to propel light from Mars into space, is constantly streaming out from the planet constituting a force of repulsion of gravity which when confined is able to lift enormous weights from the surface of the ground.

It is this ray which has enabled them to so perfect aviation that battle ships far outweighing anything known upon Earth sail as gracefully and lightly through the thin air of Barsoom as a toy balloon in the heavy atmosphere of Earth.

During the early years of the discovery of this ray many strange accidents occurred before the Martians learned to measure and control the wonderful power they had found. In one instance, some nine hundred years before, the first great battle ship to be built with eighth ray reservoirs was stored with too great a quantity of the rays and she had sailed up from Helium with five hundred officers and men, never to return.

Her power of repulsion for the planet was so great that it had carried her far into space, where she can be seen today, by the aid of powerful telescopes, hurtling through the heavens ten thousand miles from Mars, a tiny satellite that will thus encircle Barsoom to the end of time.

The fourth day after my arrival at Zodanga I made my first flight, and as a result of it I won a promotion which included quarters in the palace of Than Kosis.

As I rose above the city I circled several times, as I had seen Kantos Kan do, and then throwing my engine into top speed I raced at terrific velocity toward the south, following one of the great waterways which enter Zodanga from that direction.

I had traversed perhaps two hundred miles in a little less than an hour when I descried far below me a party of three green warriors racing madly toward a small figure on foot which seemed to be trying to reach the confines of one of the walled fields.

Dropping my machine rapidly toward them, and circling to the rear of the warriors, I soon saw that the object of their pursuit was a red Martian wearing the metal of the scout squadron to which I was attached. A short distance away lay his tiny flier, surrounded by the tools with which he had evidently been occupied in repairing some damage when surprised by the green warriors.

They were now almost upon him; their flying mounts charging down on the relatively puny figure at terrific speed, while the warriors leaned low to the right, with their great metal-shod spears. Each seemed striving to be the first to impale the poor Zodangan and in another moment his fate would have been sealed had it not been for my timely arrival.

Driving my fleet air craft at high speed directly behind the warriors I soon overtook them and without diminishing my speed I rammed the prow of my little flier between the shoulders of the nearest. The impact sufficient to have torn through inches of solid steel, hurled the fellow's headless body into the air over the head of his thoat, where it fell sprawling upon the moss. The mounts of the other two warriors turned squealing in terror, and bolted in opposite directions.

Reducing my speed I circled and came to the ground at the feet of the astonished Zodangan. He was warm in his thanks for my timely aid and promised that my day's work would bring the reward it merited, for it was none other than a cousin of the jeddak of Zodanga whose life I had saved.

We wasted no time in talk as we knew that the warriors would surely return as soon as they had gained control of their mounts. Hastening to his damaged machine we were bending every effort to finish the needed repairs and had almost completed them when we saw the two green monsters returning at top speed from opposite sides of us. When they had approached within a hundred yards their thoats again became unmanageable and absolutely refused to advance further toward the air craft which had frightened them.

The warriors finally dismounted and hobbling their animals advanced toward us on foot with drawn long-swords. I advanced to meet the larger, telling the Zodangan to do the best he could with the other. Finishing my man with almost no effort, as had now from much practice become habitual with me, I hastened to return to my new acquaintance whom I found indeed in desperate straits.

He was wounded and down with the huge foot of his antagonist upon his throat and the great long-sword raised to deal the final thrust. With a bound I cleared the fifty feet intervening between us, and with outstretched point drove my sword completely through the body of the green warrior. His sword fell, harmless, to the ground and he sank limply upon the prostrate form of the Zodangan.

A cursory examination of the latter revealed no mortal injuries and after a brief rest he asserted that he felt fit to attempt the return voyage. He would have to pilot his own craft, however, as these frail vessels are not intended to convey but a single person.

Quickly completing the repairs we rose together into the still, cloudless Martian sky, and at great speed and without further mishap returned to Zodanga.

As we neared the city we discovered a mighty concourse of civilians and troops assembled upon the plain before the city. The sky was black with naval vessels and private and public pleasure craft, flying long streamers of gay-colored silks, and banners and flags of odd and picturesque design.

My companion signaled that I slow down, and running his machine close beside mine suggested that we approach and watch the ceremony, which, he said, was for the purpose of conferring honors on individual officers and men for bravery and other distinguished service. He then unfurled a little ensign which denoted that his craft bore a member of the royal family of Zodanga, and together we made our way through the maze of low-lying air vessels until we hung directly over the jeddak of Zodanga and his staff. All were mounted upon the small domestic bull thoats of the red Martians, and their trappings and ornamentation bore such a quantity of gorgeously colored feathers that I could not but be struck with the startling resemblance the concourse bore to a band of the red Indians of my own Earth.

One of the staff called the attention of Than Kosis to the presence of my companion above them and the ruler motioned for him to descend. As they waited for the troops to move into position facing the jeddak the two talked earnestly together, the jeddak and his staff occasionally glancing up at me. I could not hear their conversation and presently it ceased and all dismounted, as the last body of troops had wheeled into position before their emperor. A member of the staff advanced toward the troops, and calling the name of a soldier commanded him to advance. The officer then recited the nature of the heroic act which had won the approval of the jeddak, and the latter advanced and placed a metal ornament upon the left arm of the lucky man.

Ten men had been so decorated when the aid called out, "John Carter, air scout!"

Never in my life had I been so surprised, but the habit of military discipline is strong within me, and I dropped my little machine lightly to the ground and advanced on foot as I had seen the others do. As I halted before the officer, he addressed me in a voice audible to the entire assemblage of troops and spectators.

"In recognition, John Carter," he said, "of your remarkable courage and skill in defending the person of the cousin of the jeddak Than Kosis and, singlehanded, vanquishing three green warriors, it is the pleasure of our jeddak to confer on you the mark of his esteem."

Than Kosis then advanced toward me and placing an ornament upon me, said:

"My cousin has narrated the details of your wonderful achievement, which seems little short of miraculous, and if you can so well defend a cousin of the jeddak how much better could you defend the person of the jeddak himself. You are therefore appointed a padwar of The Guards and will be quartered in my palace hereafter."

I thanked him, and at his direction joined the members of his staff. After the ceremony I returned my machine to its quarters on the roof of the barracks of the air-scout squadron, and with an orderly from the palace to guide me I reported to the officer in charge of the palace.

CHAPTER XXII

I Find Dejah

The major-domo to whom I reported had been given instructions to station me near the person of the jeddak, who, in time of war, is always in great danger of assassination, as the rule that all is fair in war seems to constitute the entire ethics of Martian conflict.

He therefore escorted me immediately to the apartment in which Than Kosis then was. The ruler was engaged in conversation with his son, Sab Than, and several courtiers of his household, and did not perceive my entrance.

The walls of the apartment were completely hung with splendid tapestries which hid any windows or doors which may have pierced them. The room was lighted by imprisoned rays of sunshine held between the ceiling proper and what appeared to be a ground-glass false ceiling a few inches below.

My guide drew aside one of the tapestries, disclosing a passage which encircled the room, between the hangings and the walls of the chamber. Within this passage I was to remain, he said, so long as Than Kosis was in the apartment. When he left I was to follow. My only duty was to guard the ruler and keep out of sight as much as possible. I would be relieved after a period of four hours. The major-domo then left me.

The tapestries were of a strange weaving which gave the appearance of heavy solidity from one side, but from my hiding place I could perceive all that took place within the room as readily as though there had been no curtain intervening.

Scarcely had I gained my post than the tapestry at the opposite end of the chamber separated and four soldiers of The Guard entered, surrounding a female figure. As they approached Than Kosis the soldiers fell to either side and there standing before the jeddak and not ten feet from me, her beautiful face radiant with smiles, was Dejah Thoris.

Sab Than, Prince of Zodanga, advanced to meet her, and hand in hand they approached close to the jeddak. Then Kosis looked up in surprise, and, rising, saluted her.

"To what strange freak do I owe this visit from the Princess of Helium, who, two days ago, with rare consideration for my pride, assured me that she would prefer Tal Hajus, the green Thark, to my son?"

Dejah Thoris only smiled the more and with the roguish dimples playing at the corners of her mouth she made answer:

"From the beginning of time upon Barsoom it has been the prerogative of woman to change her mind as she listed and to dissemble in matters concerning her heart. That you will forgive, Than Kosis, as has your son. Two days ago I was not sure of his love for me, but now I am, and I have come to beg of you to forget my rash words and to accept the assurance of the Princess of Helium that when the time comes she will wed Sab Than, Prince of Zodanga."

"I am glad that you have so decided," replied Than Kosis. "It is far from my desire to push war further against the people of Helium, and, your promise shall be recorded and a proclamation to my people issued forthwith."

"It were better, Than Kosis," interrupted Dejah Thoris, "that the proclamation wait the ending of this war. It would look strange indeed to my people and to yours were the Princess of Helium to give herself to her country's enemy in the midst of hostilities."

"Cannot the war be ended at once?" spoke Sab Than. "It requires but the word of Than Kosis to bring peace. Say it, my father, say the word that will hasten my happiness, and end this unpopular strife."

"We shall see," replied Than Kosis, "how the people of Helium take to peace. I shall at least offer it to them."

Dejah Thoris, after a few words, turned and left the apartment, still followed by her guards.

Thus was the edifice of my brief dream of happiness dashed, broken, to the ground of reality. The woman for whom I had offered my life, and from whose lips I had so recently heard a declaration of love for me, had lightly forgotten my very existence and smilingly given herself to the son of her people's most hated enemy.

Although I had heard it with my own ears I could not believe it. I must search out her apartments and force her to repeat the cruel truth to me alone before I would be convinced, and so I deserted my post and hastened through the passage behind the tapestries toward the door by which she had left the chamber. Slipping quietly through this opening I discovered a maze of winding corridors, branching and turning in every direction.

Running rapidly down first one and then another of them I soon became hopelessly lost and was standing panting against a side wall when I heard voices near me. Apparently they were coming from the opposite side of the partition against which I leaned and presently I made out the tones of Dejah Thoris. I could not hear the words but I knew that I could not possibly be mistaken in the voice.

Moving on a few steps I discovered another passageway at the end of which lay a door. Walking boldly forward I pushed into the room only to find myself in a small antechamber in which were the four guards who had accompanied her. One of them instantly arose and accosted me, asking the nature of my business.

"I am from Than Kosis," I replied, "and wish to speak privately with Dejah Thoris, Princess of Helium."

"And your order?" asked the fellow.

I did not know what he meant, but replied that I was a member of The Guard, and without waiting for a reply from him I strode toward the opposite door of the antechamber, behind which I could hear Dejah Thoris conversing.

But my entrance was not to be so easily accomplished. The guardsman stepped before me, saying,

"No one comes from Than Kosis without carrying an order or the password. You must give me one or the other before you may pass."

"The only order I require, my friend, to enter where I will, hangs at my side," I answered, tapping my long-sword; "will you let me pass in peace or no?"

For reply he whipped out his own sword, calling to the others to join him, and thus the four stood, with drawn weapons, barring my further progress.

"You are not here by the order of Than Kosis," cried the one who had first addressed me, "and not only shall you not enter the apartments of the Princess of Helium but you shall go back to Than Kosis under guard to explain this unwarranted temerity. Throw down your sword; you cannot hope to overcome four of us," he added with a grim smile.

My reply was a quick thrust which left me but three antagonists and I can assure you that they were worthy of my metal. They had me backed against the wall in no time, fighting for my life. Slowly I worked my way to a corner of the room where I could force them to come at me only one at a time, and thus we fought upward of twenty minutes; the clanging of steel on steel producing a veritable bedlam in the little room.

The noise had brought Dejah Thoris to the door of her apartment, and there she stood throughout the conflict with Sola at her back peering over her shoulder. Her face was set and emotionless and I knew that she did not recognize me, nor did Sola.

Finally a lucky cut brought down a second guardsman and then, with only two opposing me, I changed my tactics and rushed them down after the fashion of my fighting that had won me many a victory. The third fell within ten seconds after the second, and the last lay dead upon the bloody floor a few moments later. They were brave men and noble fighters, and it grieved me that I had been forced to kill them, but I would have willingly depopulated all Barsoom could I have reached the side of my Dejah Thoris in no other way.

Sheathing my bloody blade I advanced toward my Martian Princess, who still stood mutely gazing at me without sign of recognition.

"Who are you, Zodangan?" she whispered. "Another enemy to harass me in my misery?"

"I am a friend," I answered, "a once cherished friend."

"No friend of Helium's princess wears that metal," she replied, "and yet the voice! I have heard it before; it is not—it cannot be—no, for he is dead."

"It is, though, my Princess, none other than John Carter," I said. "Do you not recognize, even through paint and strange metal, the heart of your chieftain?"

As I came close to her she swayed toward me with outstretched hands, but as I reached to take her in my arms she drew back with a shudder and a little moan of misery.

"Too late, too late," she grieved. "O my chieftain that was, and whom I thought dead, had you but returned one little hour before—but now it is too late, too late."

"What do you mean, Dejah Thoris?" I cried. "That you would not have promised yourself to the Zodangan prince had you known that I lived?"

"Think you, John Carter, that I would give my heart to you yesterday and to-day to another? I thought that it lay buried with your ashes in the pits of Warhoon, and so today I have promised my body to another to save my people from the curse of a victorious Zodangan army."

"But I am not dead, my princess. I have come to claim you, and all Zodanga cannot prevent it."

"It is too late, John Carter, my promise is given, and on Barsoom that is final. The ceremonies which follow later are but meaningless formalities. They make the fact of marriage no more certain than does the funeral cortege of a jeddak again place the seal of death upon him. I am as good as married, John Carter. No longer may you call me your princess. No longer are you my chieftain."

"I know but little of your customs here upon Barsoom, Dejah Thoris, but I do know that I love you, and if you meant the last words you spoke to me that day as the hordes of Warhoon were charging down upon us, no other man shall ever claim you as his bride. You meant them then, my princess, and you mean them still! Say that it is true."

"I meant them, John Carter," she whispered. "I cannot repeat them now for I have given myself to another. Ah, if you had only known our ways, my friend," she continued, half to herself, "the promise would have been yours long months ago, and you could have claimed me before all others. It might have meant the fall of Helium, but I would have given my empire for my Tharkian chief."

Then aloud she said: "Do you remember the night when you offended me? You called me your princess without having asked my hand of me, and then you boasted that you had fought for me. You did not know, and I should not have been offended; I see that now. But there was no one to tell you, what I could not, that upon Barsoom there are two kinds of women in the cities of the red men. The one they fight for that they may ask them in marriage; the other kind they fight for also, but never ask their hands. When a man has won a woman he may address her as his princess, or in any of the several terms which signify possession. You had fought for me, but had never asked me in marriage, and so when you called me your princess, you see," she faltered, "I was hurt, but even then, John Carter, I did not repulse you, as I should have done, until you made it doubly worse by taunting me with having won me through combat."

"I do not need ask your forgiveness now, Dejah Thoris," I cried. "You must know that my fault was of ignorance of your Barsoomian customs. What I failed to do, through implicit belief that my petition would be presumptuous and unwelcome, I do now, Dejah Thoris; I ask you to be my wife, and by all the Virginian fighting blood that flows in my veins you shall be."

"No, John Carter, it is useless," she cried, hopelessly, "I may never be yours while Sab Than lives."

"You have sealed his death warrant, my princess—Sab Than dies."

"Nor that either," she hastened to explain. "I may not wed the man who slays my husband, even in self-defense. It is custom. We are ruled by custom upon Barsoom. It is useless, my friend. You must bear the sorrow with me. That at least we may share in common. That, and the memory of the brief days among the Tharks. You must go now, nor ever see me again. Good-bye, my chieftain that was."

Disheartened and dejected, I withdrew from the room, but I was not entirely discouraged, nor would I admit that Dejah Thoris was lost to me until the ceremony had actually been performed.

As I wandered along the corridors, I was as absolutely lost in the mazes of winding passageways as I had been before I discovered Dejah Thoris' apartments.

I knew that my only hope lay in escape from the city of Zodanga, for the matter of the four dead guardsmen would have to be explained, and as I could never reach my original post without a guide, suspicion would surely rest on me so soon as I was discovered wandering aimlessly through the palace.

Presently I came upon a spiral runway leading to a lower floor, and this I followed downward for several stories until I reached the doorway of a large apartment in which were a number of guardsmen. The walls of this room were hung with transparent tapestries behind which I secreted myself without being apprehended.

The conversation of the guardsmen was general, and awakened no interest in me until an officer entered the room and ordered four of the men to relieve the detail who were guarding the Princess of Helium. Now, I knew, my troubles would commence in earnest and indeed they were upon me all too soon, for it seemed that the squad had scarcely left the guardroom before one of their number burst in again breathlessly, crying that they had found their four comrades butchered in the antechamber.

In a moment the entire palace was alive with people. Guardsmen, officers, courtiers, servants, and slaves ran helter-skelter through the corridors and apartments carrying messages and orders, and searching for signs of the assassin.

This was my opportunity and slim as it appeared I grasped it, for as a number of soldiers came hurrying past my hiding place I fell in behind them and followed through the mazes of the palace until, in passing through a great hall, I saw the blessed light of day coming in through a series of larger windows.

Here I left my guides, and, slipping to the nearest window, sought for an avenue of escape. The windows opened upon a great balcony which overlooked one of the broad avenues of Zodanga. The ground was about thirty feet below, and at a like distance from the building was a wall fully twenty feet high, constructed of polished glass about a foot in thickness. To a red Martian escape by this path would have appeared impossible, but to me, with my earthly strength and agility, it seemed already accomplished. My only fear was in being detected before darkness fell, for I could not make the leap in broad daylight while the court below and the avenue beyond were crowded with Zodangans.

Accordingly I searched for a hiding place and finally found one by accident, inside a huge hanging ornament which swung from the ceiling of the hall, and about ten feet from the floor. Into the capacious bowl-like vase I sprang with ease, and scarcely had I settled down within it than I heard a number of people enter the apartment. The group stopped beneath my hiding place and I could plainly overhear their every word.

"It is the work of Heliumites," said one of the men.

"Yes, O Jeddak, but how had they access to the palace? I could believe that even with the diligent care of your guardsmen a single enemy might reach the inner chambers, but how a force of six or eight fighting men could have done so unobserved is beyond me. We shall soon know, however, for here comes the royal psychologist."

Another man now joined the group, and, after making his formal greetings to his ruler, said:

"O mighty Jeddak, it is a strange tale I read in the dead minds of your faithful guardsmen. They were felled not by a number of fighting men, but by a single opponent."

He paused to let the full weight of this announcement impress his hearers, and that his statement was scarcely credited was evidenced by the impatient exclamation of incredulity which escaped the lips of Than Kosis.

"What manner of weird tale are you bringing me, Notan?" he cried.

"It is the truth, my Jeddak," replied the psychologist. "In fact the impressions were strongly marked on the brain of each of the four guardsmen. Their antagonist was a very tall man, wearing the metal of one of your own guardsmen, and his fighting ability was little short of marvelous for he fought fair against the entire four and vanquished them by his surpassing skill and superhuman strength and endurance. Though he wore the metal of Zodanga, my Jeddak, such a man was never seen before in this or any other country upon Barsoom.

"The mind of the Princess of Helium whom I have examined and questioned was a blank to me, she has perfect control, and I could not read one iota of it. She said that she witnessed a portion of the encounter, and that when she looked there was but one man engaged with the guardsmen; a man whom she did not recognize as ever having seen."

"Where is my erstwhile savior?" spoke another of the party, and I recognized the voice of the cousin of Than Kosis, whom I had rescued from the green warriors. "By the metal of my first ancestor," he went on, "but the description fits him to perfection, especially as to his fighting ability."

"Where is this man?" cried Than Kosis. "Have him brought to me at once. What know you of him, cousin? It seemed strange to me now that I think upon it that there should have been such a fighting man in Zodanga, of whose name, even, we were ignorant before today. And his name too, John Carter, who ever heard of such a name upon Barsoom!"

Word was soon brought that I was nowhere to be found, either in the palace or at my former quarters in the barracks of the air-scout squadron. Kantos Kan, they had found and questioned, but he knew nothing of my whereabouts, and as to my past, he had told them he knew as little, since he had but recently met me during our captivity among the Warhoons.

"Keep your eyes on this other one," commanded Than Kosis. "He also is a stranger and likely as not they both hail from Helium, and where one is we shall sooner or later find the other. Quadruple the air patrol, and let every man who leaves the city by air or ground be subjected to the closest scrutiny."

Another messenger now entered with word that I was still within the palace walls.

"The likeness of every person who has entered or left the palace grounds today has been carefully examined," concluded the fellow, "and not one approaches the likeness of this new padwar of the guards, other than that which was recorded of him at the time he entered."

"Then we will have him shortly," commented Than Kosis contentedly, "and in the meanwhile we will repair to the apartments of the Princess of Helium and question her in regard to the affair. She may know more than she cared to divulge to you, Notan. Come."

They left the hall, and, as darkness had fallen without, I slipped lightly from my hiding place and hastened to the balcony. Few were in sight, and choosing a moment when none seemed near I sprang quickly to the top of the glass wall and from there to the avenue beyond the palace grounds.

CHAPTER XXIII

Lost in the Sky

Without effort at concealment I hastened to the vicinity of our quarters, where I felt sure I should find Kantos Kan. As I neared the building I became more careful, as I judged, and rightly, that the place would be guarded. Several men in civilian metal loitered near the front entrance and in the rear were others. My only means of reaching, unseen, the upper story where our apartments were situated was through an adjoining building, and after considerable maneuvering I managed to attain the roof of a shop several doors away.

Leaping from roof to roof, I soon reached an open window in the building where I hoped to find the Heliumite, and in another moment I stood in the room before him. He was alone and showed no surprise at my coming, saying he had expected me much earlier, as my tour of duty must have ended some time since.

I saw that he knew nothing of the events of the day at the palace, and when I had enlightened him he was all excitement. The news that Dejah Thoris had promised her hand to Sab Than filled him with dismay.

"It cannot be," he exclaimed. "It is impossible! Why no man in all Helium but would prefer death to the selling of our loved princess to the ruling house of Zodanga. She must have lost her mind to have assented to such an atrocious bargain. You, who do not know how we of Helium love the members of our ruling house, cannot appreciate the horror with which I contemplate such an unholy alliance."

"What can be done, John Carter?" he continued. "You are a resourceful man. Can you not think of some way to save Helium from this disgrace?"

"If I can come within sword's reach of Sab Than," I answered, "I can solve the difficulty in so far as Helium is concerned, but for personal reasons I would prefer that another struck the blow that frees Dejah Thoris."

Kantos Kan eyed me narrowly before he spoke.

"You love her!" he said. "Does she know it?"

"She knows it, Kantos Kan, and repulses me only because she is promised to Sab Than."

The splendid fellow sprang to his feet, and grasping me by the shoulder raised his sword on high, exclaiming:

"And had the choice been left to me I could not have chosen a more fitting mate for the first princess of Barsoom. Here is my hand upon your shoulder, John Carter, and my word that Sab Than shall go out at the point of my sword for the sake of my love for Helium, for Dejah Thoris, and for you. This very night I shall try to reach his quarters in the palace."

"How?" I asked. "You are strongly guarded and a quadruple force patrols the sky."

He bent his head in thought a moment, then raised it with an air of confidence.

"I only need to pass these guards and I can do it," he said at last. "I know a secret entrance to the palace through the pinnacle of the highest tower. I fell upon it by chance one day as I was passing above the palace on patrol duty. In this work it is required that we investigate any unusual occurrence we may witness, and a face peering from the pinnacle of the high tower of the palace was, to me, most unusual. I therefore drew near and discovered that the possessor of the peering face was none other than Sab Than. He was slightly put out at being detected and commanded me to keep the matter to myself, explaining that the passage from the tower led directly to his apartments, and was known only to him. If I can reach the roof of the barracks and get my machine I can be in Sab Than's quarters in five minutes; but how am I to escape from this building, guarded as you say it is?"

"How well are the machine sheds at the barracks guarded?" I asked.

"There is usually but one man on duty there at night upon the roof."

"Go to the roof of this building, Kantos Kan, and wait me there."

Without stopping to explain my plans I retraced my way to the street and hastened to the barracks. I did not dare to enter the building, filled as it was with members of the air-scout squadron, who, in common with all Zodanga, were on the lookout for me.

The building was an enormous one, rearing its lofty head fully a thousand feet into the air. But few buildings in Zodanga were higher than these barracks, though several topped it by a few hundred feet; the docks of the great battleships of the line standing some fifteen hundred feet from the ground, while the freight and passenger stations of the merchant squadrons rose nearly as high.

It was a long climb up the face of the building, and one fraught with much danger, but there was no other way, and so I essayed the task. The fact that Barsoomian architecture is extremely ornate made the feat much simpler than I had anticipated, since I found ornamental ledges and projections which fairly formed a perfect ladder for me all the way to the eaves of the building. Here I met my first real obstacle. The eaves projected nearly twenty feet from the wall to which I clung, and though I encircled the great building I could find no opening through them.

The top floor was alight, and filled with soldiers engaged in the pastimes of their kind; I could not, therefore, reach the roof through the building.

There was one slight, desperate chance, and that I decided I must take — it was for Dejah Thoris, and no man has lived who would not risk a thousand deaths for such as she.

Clinging to the wall with my feet and one hand, I unloosened one of the long leather straps of my trappings at the end of which dangled a great hook by which air sailors are hung to the sides and bottoms of their craft for various purposes of repair, and by means of which landing parties are lowered to the ground from the battleships.

I swung this hook cautiously to the roof several times before it finally found lodgment; gently I pulled on it to strengthen its hold, but whether it would bear the weight of my body I did not know. It might be barely caught upon the very outer verge of the roof, so that as my body swung out at the end of the strap it would slip off and launch me to the pavement a thousand feet below.

An instant I hesitated, and then, releasing my grasp upon the supporting ornament, I swung out into space at the end of the strap. Far below me lay the brilliantly lighted streets, the hard pavements, and death. There was a little jerk at the top of the supporting eaves, and a nasty slipping, grating sound which turned me cold with apprehension; then the hook caught and I was safe.

Clambering quickly aloft I grasped the edge of the eaves and drew myself to the surface of the roof above. As I gained my feet I was confronted by the sentry on duty, into the muzzle of whose revolver I found myself looking.

"Who are you and whence came you?" he cried.

"I am an air scout, friend, and very near a dead one, for just by the merest chance I escaped falling to the avenue below," I replied.

"But how came you upon the roof, man? No one has landed or come up from the building for the past hour. Quick, explain yourself, or I call the guard."

"Look you here, sentry, and you shall see how I came and how close a shave I had to not coming at all," I answered, turning toward the edge of the roof, where, twenty feet below, at the end of my strap, hung all my weapons.

The fellow, acting on impulse of curiosity, stepped to my side and to his undoing, for as he leaned to peer over the eaves I grasped him by his throat and his pistol arm and threw him heavily to the roof. The weapon dropped from his grasp, and my fingers choked off his attempted cry for assistance. I gagged and bound him and then hung him over the edge of the roof as I myself had hung a few moments before. I knew it would be morning before he would be discovered, and I needed all the time that I could gain.

Donning my trappings and weapons I hastened to the sheds, and soon had out both my machine and Kantos Kan's. Making his fast behind mine I started my engine, and skimming over the edge of the roof I dove down into the streets of the city far below the plane usually occupied by the air patrol. In less than a minute I was settling safely upon the roof of our apartment beside the astonished Kantos Kan.

I lost no time in explanations, but plunged immediately into a discussion of our plans for the immediate future. It was decided that I was to try to make Helium while Kantos Kan was to enter the palace and dispatch Sab Than. If successful he was then to follow me. He set my compass for me, a clever little device which will remain steadfastly fixed upon any given point on the surface of Barsoom, and bidding each other farewell we rose together and sped in the direction of the palace which lay in the route which I must take to reach Helium.

As we neared the high tower a patrol shot down from above, throwing its piercing searchlight full upon my craft, and a voice roared out a command to halt, following with a shot as I paid no attention to his hail. Kantos Kan dropped quickly into the darkness, while I rose steadily and at terrific speed raced through the

Martian sky followed by a dozen of the air-scout craft which had joined the pursuit, and later by a swift cruiser carrying a hundred men and a battery of rapid-fire guns. By twisting and turning my little machine, now rising and now falling, I managed to elude their searchlights most of the time, but I was also losing ground by these tactics, and so I decided to hazard everything on a straightaway course and leave the result to fate and the speed of my machine.

Kantos Kan had shown me a trick of gearing, which is known only to the navy of Helium, that greatly increased the speed of our machines, so that I felt sure I could distance my pursuers if I could dodge their projectiles for a few moments.

As I sped through the air the screeching of the bullets around me convinced me that only by a miracle could I escape, but the die was cast, and throwing on full speed I raced a straight course toward Helium. Gradually I left my pursuers further and further behind, and I was just congratulating myself on my lucky escape, when a well-directed shot from the cruiser exploded at the prow of my little craft. The concussion nearly capsized her, and with a sickening plunge she hurtled downward through the dark night.

How far I fell before I regained control of the plane I do not know, but I must have been very close to the ground when I started to rise again, as I plainly heard the squealing of animals below me. Rising again I scanned the heavens for my pursuers, and finally making out their lights far behind me, saw that they were landing, evidently in search of me.

Not until their lights were no longer discernible did I venture to flash my little lamp upon my compass, and then I found to my consternation that a fragment of the projectile had utterly destroyed my only guide, as well as my speedometer. It was true I could follow the stars in the general direction of Helium, but without knowing the exact location of the city or the speed at which I was traveling my chances for finding it were slim.

Helium lies a thousand miles southwest of Zodanga, and with my compass intact I should have made the trip, barring accidents, in between four and five hours. As it turned out, however, morning found me speeding over a vast expanse of dead sea bottom after nearly six hours of continuous flight at high speed. Presently a great city showed below me, but it was not Helium, as that alone of all Barsoomian metropolises consists in two immense circular walled cities about seventy-five miles apart and would have been easily distinguishable from the altitude at which I was flying.

Believing that I had come too far to the north and west, I turned back in a southeasterly direction, passing during the forenoon several other large cities, but none resembling the description which Kantos Kan had given me of Helium. In addition to the twin-city formation of Helium, another distinguishing feature is the two immense towers, one of vivid scarlet rising nearly a mile into the air from the center of one of the cities, while the other, of bright yellow and of the same height, marks her sister.

CHAPTER XXIV

Tars Tarkas Finds a Friend

About noon I passed low over a great dead city of ancient Mars, and as I skimmed out across the plain beyond I came full upon several thousand green warriors engaged in a terrific battle. Scarcely had I seen them than a volley of shots was directed at me, and with the almost unfailing accuracy of their aim my little craft was instantly a ruined wreck, sinking erratically to the ground.

I fell almost directly in the center of the fierce combat, among warriors who had not seen my approach so busily were they engaged in life and death struggles. The men were fighting on foot with long-swords, while an occasional shot from a sharpshooter on the outskirts of the conflict would bring down a warrior who might for an instant separate himself from the entangled mass.

As my machine sank among them I realized that it was fight or die, with good chances of dying in any event, and so I struck the ground with drawn long-sword ready to defend myself as I could.

I fell beside a huge monster who was engaged with three antagonists, and as I glanced at his fierce face, filled with the light of battle, I recognized Tars Tarkas the Thark. He did not see me, as I was a trifle behind him, and just then the three warriors opposing him, and whom I recognized as Warhoons, charged simultaneously. The mighty fellow made quick work of one of them, but in stepping back for another thrust he fell over a dead body behind him and was down and at the mercy of his foes in an instant. Quick as lightning they were upon him, and Tars Tarkas would have been gathered to his fathers in short order had I not sprung before his prostrate form and engaged his adversaries. I had accounted for one of them when the mighty Thark regained his feet and quickly settled the other.

He gave me one look, and a slight smile touched his grim lips as, touching my shoulder, he said,

"I would scarcely recognize you, John Carter, but there is no other mortal upon Barsoom who would have done what you have for me. I think I have learned that there is such a thing as friendship, my friend."

He said no more, nor was there opportunity, for the Warhoons were closing in about us, and together we fought, shoulder to shoulder, during all that long, hot afternoon, until the tide of battle turned and the remnant of the fierce Warhoon horde fell back upon their thoats, and fled into the gathering darkness.

Ten thousand men had been engaged in that titanic struggle, and upon the field of battle lay three thousand dead. Neither side asked or gave quarter, nor did they attempt to take prisoners.

On our return to the city after the battle we had gone directly to Tars Tarkas' quarters, where I was left alone while the chieftain attended the customary council which immediately follows an engagement.

As I sat awaiting the return of the green warrior I heard something move in an adjoining apartment, and as I glanced up there rushed suddenly upon me a huge and hideous creature which bore me backward upon the pile of silks and furs upon which I had been reclining. It was Woola—faithful, loving Woola. He had found his way back to Thark and, as Tars Tarkas later told me, had gone immediately to my former quarters where he had taken up his pathetic and seemingly hopeless watch for my return.

"Tal Hajus knows that you are here, John Carter," said Tars Tarkas, on his return from the jeddak's quarters; "Sarkoja saw and recognized you as we were returning. Tal Hajus has ordered me to bring you before him tonight. I have ten thoats, John Carter; you may take your choice from among them, and I will accompany you to the nearest waterway that leads to Helium. Tars Tarkas may be a cruel green warrior, but he can be a friend as well. Come, we must start."

"And when you return, Tars Tarkas?" I asked.

"The wild calots, possibly, or worse," he replied. "Unless I should chance to have the opportunity I have so long waited of battling with Tal Hajus."

"We will stay, Tars Tarkas, and see Tal Hajus tonight. You shall not sacrifice yourself, and it may be that tonight you can have the chance you wait."

He objected strenuously, saying that Tal Hajus often flew into wild fits of passion at the mere thought of the blow I had dealt him, and that if ever he laid his hands upon me I would be subjected to the most horrible tortures.

While we were eating I repeated to Tars Tarkas the story which Sola had told me that night upon the sea bottom during the march to Thark.

He said but little, but the great muscles of his face worked in passion and in agony at recollection of the horrors which had been heaped upon the only thing he had ever loved in all his cold, cruel, terrible existence.

He no longer demurred when I suggested that we go before Tal Hajus, only saying that he would like to speak to Sarkoja first. At his request I accompanied him to her quarters, and the look of venomous hatred she cast upon me was almost adequate recompense for any future misfortunes this accidental return to Thark might bring me.

"Sarkoja," said Tars Tarkas, "forty years ago you were instrumental in bringing about the torture and death of a woman named Gozava. I have just discovered that the warrior who loved that woman has learned of your part in the transaction. He may not kill you, Sarkoja, it is not our custom, but there is nothing to prevent him tying one end of a strap about your neck and the other end to a wild thoat, merely to test your fitness to survive and help perpetuate our race. Having heard that he would do this on the morrow, I thought it only right to warn you, for I am a just man. The river Iss is but a short pilgrimage, Sarkoja. Come, John Carter."

The next morning Sarkoja was gone, nor was she ever seen after.

In silence we hastened to the jeddak's palace, where we were immediately admitted to his presence; in fact, he could scarcely wait to see me and was standing erect upon his platform glowering at the entrance as I came in.

"Strap him to that pillar," he shrieked. "We shall see who it is dares strike the mighty Tal Hajus. Heat the irons; with my own hands I shall burn the eyes from his head that he may not pollute my person with his vile gaze."

"Chieftains of Thark," I cried, turning to the assembled council and ignoring Tal Hajus, "I have been a chief among you, and today I have fought for Thark shoulder to shoulder with her greatest warrior. You owe me, at least, a hearing. I have won that much today. You claim to be just people—"

"Silence," roared Tal Hajus. "Gag the creature and bind him as I command."

"Justice, Tal Hajus," exclaimed Lorquas Ptomel. "Who are you to set aside the customs of ages among the Tharks."

"Yes, justice!" echoed a dozen voices, and so, while Tal Hajus fumed and frothed, I continued.

"You are a brave people and you love bravery, but where was your mighty jeddak during the fighting today? I did not see him in the thick of battle; he was not there. He rends defenseless women and little children in his lair, but how recently has one of you seen him fight with men? Why, even I, a midget beside him, felled him with a single blow of my fist. Is it of such that the Tharks fashion their jeddaks? There stands beside me now a great Thark, a mighty warrior and a noble man. Chieftains, how sounds, Tars Tarkas, Jeddak of Thark?"

A roar of deep-toned applause greeted this suggestion.

"It but remains for this council to command, and Tal Hajus must prove his fitness to rule. Were he a brave man he would invite Tars Tarkas to combat, for he does not love him, but Tal Hajus is afraid; Tal Hajus, your jeddak, is a coward. With my bare hands I could kill him, and he knows it."

After I ceased there was tense silence, as all eyes were riveted upon Tal Hajus. He did not speak or move, but the blotchy green of his countenance turned livid, and the froth froze upon his lips.

"Tal Hajus," said Lorquas Ptomel in a cold, hard voice, "never in my long life have I seen a jeddak of the Tharks so humiliated. There could be but one answer to this arraignment. We wait it." And still Tal Hajus stood as though petrified.

"Chieftains," continued Lorquas Ptomel, "shall the jeddak, Tal Hajus, prove his fitness to rule over Tars Tarkas?"

There were twenty chieftains about the rostrum, and twenty swords flashed high in assent.

There was no alternative. That decree was final, and so Tal Hajus drew his long-sword and advanced to meet Tars Tarkas.

The combat was soon over, and, with his foot upon the neck of the dead monster, Tars Tarkas became jeddak among the Tharks.

His first act was to make me a full-fledged chieftain with the rank I had won by my combats the first few weeks of my captivity among them.

Seeing the favorable disposition of the warriors toward Tars Tarkas, as well as toward me, I grasped the opportunity to enlist them in my cause against Zodanga. I told Tars Tarkas the story of my adventures, and in a few words had explained to him the thought I had in mind.

"John Carter has made a proposal," he said, addressing the council, "which meets with my sanction. I shall put it to you briefly. Dejah Thoris, the Princess of Helium, who was our prisoner, is now held by the jeddak of Zodanga, whose son she must wed to save her country from devastation at the hands of the Zodangan forces.

"John Carter suggests that we rescue her and return her to Helium. The loot of Zodanga would be magnificent, and I have often thought that had we an alliance with the people of Helium we could obtain sufficient assurance of sustenance to permit us to increase the size and frequency of our hatchings, and thus become unquestionably supreme among the green men of all Barsoom. What say you?"

It was a chance to fight, an opportunity to loot, and they rose to the bait as a speckled trout to a fly.

For Tharks they were wildly enthusiastic, and before another half hour had passed twenty mounted messengers were speeding across dead sea bottoms to call the hordes together for the expedition.

In three days we were on the march toward Zodanga, one hundred thousand strong, as Tars Tarkas had been able to enlist the services of three smaller hordes on the promise of the great loot of Zodanga.

At the head of the column I rode beside the great Thark while at the heels of my mount trotted my beloved Woola.

We traveled entirely by night, timing our marches so that we camped during the day at deserted cities where, even to the beasts, we were all kept indoors during the daylight hours. On the march Tars Tarkas, through his remarkable ability and statesmanship, enlisted fifty thousand more warriors from various hordes, so that, ten days after we set out we halted at midnight outside the great walled city of Zodanga, one hundred and fifty thousand strong.

The fighting strength and efficiency of this horde of ferocious green monsters was equivalent to ten times their number of red men. Never in the history of Barsoom, Tars Tarkas told me, had such a force of green warriors marched to battle together. It was a monstrous task to keep even a semblance of harmony among them, and it was a marvel to me that he got them to the city without a mighty battle among themselves.

But as we neared Zodanga their personal quarrels were submerged by their greater hatred for the red men, and especially for the Zodangans, who had for years waged a ruthless campaign of extermination against the green men, directing special attention toward despoiling their incubators.

Now that we were before Zodanga the task of obtaining entry to the city devolved upon me, and directing Tars Tarkas to hold his forces in two divisions out of earshot of the city, with each division opposite a large gateway, I took twenty dismounted warriors and approached one of the small gates that pierced the walls at short intervals. These gates have no regular guard, but are covered by sentries, who patrol the avenue that encircles the city just within the walls much as our metropolitan police patrol their beats.

The walls of Zodanga are seventy-five feet in height and fifty feet thick. They are built of enormous blocks of carborundum, and the task of entering the city seemed, to my escort of green warriors, an impossibility. The fellows who had been detailed to accompany me were of one of the smaller hordes, and therefore did not know me.

Placing three of them with their faces to the wall and arms locked, I commanded two more to mount to their shoulders, and a sixth I ordered to climb upon the shoulders of the upper two. The head of the topmost warrior towered over forty feet from the ground.

In this way, with ten warriors, I built a series of three steps from the ground to the shoulders of the topmost man. Then starting from a short distance behind them I ran swiftly up from one tier to the next, and with a final bound from the broad shoulders of the highest I clutched the top of the great wall and quietly drew myself to its broad expanse. After me I dragged six lengths of leather from an equal number of my warriors. These lengths we had previously fastened together, and passing one end to the topmost warrior I lowered the other end cautiously over the opposite side of the wall toward the avenue below. No one was in sight, so, lowering myself to the end of my leather strap, I dropped the remaining thirty feet to the pavement below.

I had learned from Kantos Kan the secret of opening these gates, and in another moment my twenty great fighting men stood within the doomed city of Zodanga.

I found to my delight that I had entered at the lower boundary of the enormous palace grounds. The building itself showed in the distance a blaze of glorious light, and on the instant I determined to lead a detachment of warriors directly within the palace itself, while the balance of the great horde was attacking the barracks of the soldiery.

Dispatching one of my men to Tars Tarkas for a detail of fifty Tharks, with word of my intentions, I ordered ten warriors to capture and open one of the great gates while with the nine remaining I took the other. We were to do our work quietly, no shots were to be fired and no general advance made until I had reached the palace with my fifty Tharks. Our plans worked to perfection. The two sentries we met were dispatched to their fathers upon the banks of the lost sea of Korus, and the guards at both gates followed them in silence.

CHAPTER XXV

The Looting of Zodanga

As the great gate where I stood swung open my fifty Tharks, headed by Tars Tarkas himself, rode in upon their mighty thoats. I led them to the palace walls, which I negotiated easily without assistance. Once inside, however, the gate gave me considerable trouble, but I finally was rewarded by seeing it swing upon its huge hinges, and soon my fierce escort was riding across the gardens of the jeddak of Zodanga.

As we approached the palace I could see through the great windows of the first floor into the brilliantly illuminated audience chamber of Than Kosis. The immense hall was crowded with nobles and their women, as though some important function was in progress. There was not a guard in sight without the palace, due, I presume, to the fact that the city and palace walls were considered impregnable, and so I came close and peered within.

At one end of the chamber, upon massive golden thrones encrusted with diamonds, sat Than Kosis and his consort, surrounded by officers and dignitaries of state. Before them stretched a broad aisle lined on either side with soldiery, and as I looked there entered this aisle at the far end of the hall, the head of a procession which advanced to the foot of the throne.

First there marched four officers of the jeddak's Guard bearing a huge salver on which reposed, upon a cushion of scarlet silk, a great golden chain with a collar and padlock at each end. Directly behind these officers came four others carrying a similar salver which supported the magnificent ornaments of a prince and princess of the reigning house of Zodanga.

At the foot of the throne these two parties separated and halted, facing each other at opposite sides of the aisle. Then came more dignitaries, and the officers of the palace and of the army, and finally two figures entirely muffled in scarlet silk, so that not a feature of either was discernible. These two stopped at the foot of the throne, facing Than Kosis. When the balance of the procession had entered and assumed their stations Than Kosis addressed the couple standing before him. I could not hear his words, but presently two officers advanced and removed the scarlet robe from one of the figures, and I saw that Kantos Kan had failed in his mission, for it was Sab Than, Prince of Zodanga, who stood revealed before me.

Than Kosis now took a set of the ornaments from one of the salvers and placed one of the collars of gold about his son's neck, springing the padlock fast. After a few more words addressed to Sab Than he turned to the other figure, from which the officers now removed the enshrouding silks, disclosing to my now comprehending view Dejah Thoris, Princess of Helium.

The object of the ceremony was clear to me; in another moment Dejah Thoris would be joined forever to the Prince of Zodanga. It was an impressive and beautiful ceremony, I presume, but to me it seemed the most fiendish sight I had ever witnessed, and as the ornaments were adjusted upon her beautiful figure and her collar of gold swung open in the hands of Than Kosis I raised my long-sword above my head, and, with the heavy hilt, I shattered the glass of the great window and sprang into the midst of the astonished assemblage. With a bound I was on the steps of the platform beside Than Kosis, and as he stood riveted with surprise I brought my long-sword down upon the golden chain that would have bound Dejah Thoris to another.

In an instant all was confusion; a thousand drawn swords menaced me from every quarter, and Sab Than sprang upon me with a jeweled dagger he had drawn from his nuptial ornaments. I could have killed him as easily as I might a fly, but the age-old custom of Barsoom stayed my hand, and grasping his wrist as the dagger flew toward my heart I held him as though in a vise and with my long-sword pointed to the far end of the hall.

"Zodanga has fallen," I cried. "Look!"

All eyes turned in the direction I had indicated, and there, forging through the portals of the entranceway rode Tars Tarkas and his fifty warriors on their great thoats.

A cry of alarm and amazement broke from the assemblage, but no word of fear, and in a moment the soldiers and nobles of Zodanga were hurling themselves upon the advancing Tharks.

Thrusting Sab Than headlong from the platform, I drew Dejah Thoris to my side. Behind the throne was a narrow doorway and in this Than Kosis now stood facing me, with drawn long-sword. In an instant we were engaged, and I found no mean antagonist.

As we circled upon the broad platform I saw Sab Than rushing up the steps to aid his father, but, as he raised his hand to strike, Dejah Thoris sprang before him and then my sword found the spot that made Sab Than jeddak of Zodanga. As his father rolled dead upon the floor the new jeddak tore himself free from Dejah Thoris' grasp, and again we faced each other. He was soon joined by a quartet of officers, and, with my back against a golden throne, I fought once again for Dejah Thoris. I was hard pressed to defend myself and yet not strike down Sab Than and, with him, my last chance to win the woman I loved. My blade was swinging with the rapidity of lightning as I sought to parry the thrusts and cuts of my opponents. Two I had disarmed, and one was down, when several more rushed to the aid of their new ruler, and to avenge the death of the old.

As they advanced there were cries of "The woman! The woman! Strike her down; it is her plot. Kill her! Kill her!"

Calling to Dejah Thoris to get behind me I worked my way toward the little doorway back of the throne, but the officers realized my intentions, and three of them sprang in behind me and blocked my chances for gaining a position where I could have defended Dejah Thoris against any army of swordsmen.

The Tharks were having their hands full in the center of the room, and I began to realize that nothing short of a miracle could save Dejah Thoris and myself, when I saw Tars Tarkas surging through the crowd of pigmies that swarmed about him. With one swing of his mighty long-sword he laid a dozen corpses at his feet, and so he hewed a pathway before him until in another moment he stood upon the platform beside me, dealing death and destruction right and left.

The bravery of the Zodangans was awe-inspiring, not one attempted to escape, and when the fighting ceased it was because only Tharks remained alive in the great hall, other than Dejah Thoris and myself.

Sab Than lay dead beside his father, and the corpses of the flower of Zodangan nobility and chivalry covered the floor of the bloody shambles.

My first thought when the battle was over was for Kantos Kan, and leaving Dejah Thoris in charge of Tars Tarkas I took a dozen warriors and hastened to the dungeons beneath the palace. The jailers had all left to join the fighters in the throne room, so we searched the labyrinthine prison without opposition.

I called Kantos Kan's name aloud in each new corridor and compartment, and finally I was rewarded by hearing a faint response. Guided by the sound, we soon found him helpless in a dark recess.

He was overjoyed at seeing me, and to know the meaning of the fight, faint echoes of which had reached his prison cell. He told me that the air patrol had captured him before he reached the high tower of the palace, so that he had not even seen Sab Than.

We discovered that it would be futile to attempt to cut away the bars and chains which held him prisoner, so, at his suggestion I returned to search the bodies on the floor above for keys to open the padlocks of his cell and of his chains.

Fortunately among the first I examined I found his jailer, and soon we had Kantos Kan with us in the throne room.

The sounds of heavy firing, mingled with shouts and cries, came to us from the city's streets, and Tars Tarkas hastened away to direct the fighting without. Kantos Kan accompanied him to act as guide, the green warriors commencing a thorough search of the palace for other Zodangans and for loot, and Dejah Thoris and I were left alone.

She had sunk into one of the golden thrones, and as I turned to her she greeted me with a wan smile.

"Was there ever such a man!" she exclaimed. "I know that Barsoom has never before seen your like. Can it be that all Earth men are as you? Alone, a stranger, hunted, threatened, persecuted, you have done in a few short months what in all the past ages of Barsoom no man has ever done: joined together the wild hordes of the sea bottoms and brought them to fight as allies of a red Martian people."

"The answer is easy, Dejah Thoris," I replied smiling. "It was not I who did it, it was love, love for Dejah Thoris, a power that would work greater miracles than this you have seen."

A pretty flush overspread her face and she answered,

"You may say that now, John Carter, and I may listen, for I am free."

"And more still I have to say, ere it is again too late," I returned. "I have done many strange things in my life, many things that wiser men would not have dared, but never in my wildest fancies have I dreamed of winning a Dejah Thoris for myself—for never had I dreamed that in all the universe dwelt such a woman as the Princess of Helium. That you are a princess does not abash me, but that you are you is enough to make me doubt my sanity as I ask you, my princess, to be mine."

"He does not need to be abashed who so well knew the answer to his plea before the plea were made," she replied, rising and placing her dear hands upon my shoulders, and so I took her in my arms and kissed her.

And thus in the midst of a city of wild conflict, filled with the alarms of war; with death and destruction reaping their terrible harvest around her, did Dejah Thoris, Princess of Helium, true daughter of Mars, the God of War, promise herself in marriage to John Carter, Gentleman of Virginia.

CHAPTER XXVI

Through Carnage to Joy

Sometime later Tars Tarkas and Kantos Kan returned to report that Zodanga had been completely reduced. Her forces were entirely destroyed or captured, and no further resistance was to be expected from within. Several battleships had escaped, but there were thousands of war and merchant vessels under guard of Thark warriors.

The lesser hordes had commenced looting and quarreling among themselves, so it was decided that we collect what warriors we could, man as many vessels as possible with Zodangan prisoners and make for Helium without further loss of time.

Five hours later we sailed from the roofs of the dock buildings with a fleet of two hundred and fifty battleships, carrying nearly one hundred thousand green warriors, followed by a fleet of transports with our thoats.

Behind us we left the stricken city in the fierce and brutal clutches of some forty thousand green warriors of the lesser hordes. They were looting, murdering, and fighting amongst themselves. In a hundred places they had applied the torch, and columns of dense smoke were rising above the city as though to blot out from the eye of heaven the horrid sights beneath.

In the middle of the afternoon we sighted the scarlet and yellow towers of Helium, and a short time later a great fleet of Zodangan battleships rose from the camps of the besiegers without the city, and advanced to meet us.

The banners of Helium had been strung from stem to stem of each of our mighty craft, but the Zodangans did not need this sign to realize that we were enemies, for our green Martian warriors had opened fire upon them almost as they left the ground. With their uncanny marksmanship they raked the on-coming fleet with volley after volley.

The twin cities of Helium, perceiving that we were friends, sent out hundreds of vessels to aid us, and then began the first real air battle I had ever witnessed.

The vessels carrying our green warriors were kept circling above the contending fleets of Helium and Zodanga, since their batteries were useless in the hands of the Tharks who, having no navy, have no skill in naval gunnery. Their small-arm fire, however, was most effective, and the final outcome of the engagement was strongly influenced, if not wholly determined, by their presence.

At first the two forces circled at the same altitude, pouring broadside after broadside into each other. Presently a great hole was torn in the hull of one of the immense battle craft from the Zodangan camp; with a lurch she turned completely over, the little figures of her crew plunging, turning and twisting toward the ground a thousand feet below; then with sickening velocity she tore after them, almost completely burying herself in the soft loam of the ancient sea bottom.

A wild cry of exultation arose from the Heliumite squadron, and with redoubled ferocity they fell upon the Zodangan fleet. By a pretty maneuver two of the vessels of Helium gained a position above their adversaries, from which they poured upon them from their keel bomb batteries a perfect torrent of exploding bombs.

Then, one by one, the battleships of Helium succeeded in rising above the Zodangans, and in a short time a number of the beleaguering battleships were drifting hopeless wrecks toward the high scarlet tower of greater Helium. Several others attempted to escape, but they were soon surrounded by thousands of tiny individual fliers, and above each hung a monster battleship of Helium ready to drop boarding parties upon their decks.

Within but little more than an hour from the moment the victorious Zodangan squadron had risen to meet us from the camp of the besiegers the battle was over, and the remaining vessels of the conquered Zodangans were headed toward the cities of Helium under prize crews.

There was an extremely pathetic side to the surrender of these mighty fliers, the result of an age-old custom which demanded that surrender should be signalized by the voluntary plunging to earth of the commander of the vanquished vessel. One after another the brave fellows, holding their colors high above their heads, leaped from the towering bows of their mighty craft to an awful death.

Not until the commander of the entire fleet took the fearful plunge, thus indicating the surrender of the remaining vessels, did the fighting cease, and the useless sacrifice of brave men come to an end.

We now signaled the flagship of Helium's navy to approach, and when she was within hailing distance I called out that we had the Princess Dejah Thoris on board, and that we wished to transfer her to the flagship that she might be taken immediately to the city.

As the full import of my announcement bore in upon them a great cry arose from the decks of the flagship, and a moment later the colors of the Princess of Helium broke from a hundred points upon her upper works. When the other vessels of the squadron caught the meaning of the signals flashed them they took up the wild acclaim and unfurled her colors in the gleaming sunlight.

The flagship bore down upon us, and as she swung gracefully to and touched our side a dozen officers sprang upon our decks. As their astonished gaze fell upon the hundreds of green warriors, who now came forth from the fighting shelters, they stopped aghast, but at sight of Kantos Kan, who advanced to meet them, they came forward, crowding about him.

Dejah Thoris and I then advanced, and they had no eyes for other than her. She received them gracefully, calling each by name, for they were men high in the esteem and service of her grandfather, and she knew them well.

"Lay your hands upon the shoulder of John Carter," she said to them, turning toward me, "the man to whom Helium owes her princess as well as her victory today."

They were very courteous to me and said many kind and complimentary things, but what seemed to impress them most was that I had won the aid of the fierce Tharks in my campaign for the liberation of Dejah Thoris, and the relief of Helium.

"You owe your thanks more to another man than to me," I said, "and here he is; meet one of Barsoom's greatest soldiers and statesmen, Tars Tarkas, Jeddak of Thark."

With the same polished courtesy that had marked their manner toward me they extended their greetings to the great Thark, nor, to my surprise, was he much behind them in ease of bearing or in courtly speech. Though not a garrulous race, the Tharks are extremely formal, and their ways lend themselves amazingly to dignified and courtly manners.

Dejah Thoris went aboard the flagship, and was much put out that I would not follow, but, as I explained to her, the battle was but partly won; we still had the land forces of the besieging Zodangans to account for, and I would not leave Tars Tarkas until that had been accomplished.

The commander of the naval forces of Helium promised to arrange to have the armies of Helium attack from the city in conjunction with our land attack, and so the vessels separated and Dejah Thoris was borne in triumph back to the court of her grandfather, Tardos Mors, Jeddak of Helium.

In the distance lay our fleet of transports, with the thoats of the green warriors, where they had remained during the battle. Without landing stages it was to be a difficult matter to unload these beasts upon the open plain, but there was nothing else for it, and so we put out for a point about ten miles from the city and began the task.

It was necessary to lower the animals to the ground in slings and this work occupied the remainder of the day and half the night. Twice we were attacked by parties of Zodangan cavalry, but with little loss, however, and after darkness shut down they withdrew.

As soon as the last thoat was unloaded Tars Tarkas gave the command to advance, and in three parties we crept upon the Zodangan camp from the north, the south and the east.

About a mile from the main camp we encountered their outposts and, as had been prearranged, accepted this as the signal to charge. With wild, ferocious cries and amidst the nasty squealing of battle-enraged thoats we bore down upon the Zodangans.

We did not catch them napping, but found a well-entrenched battle line confronting us. Time after time we were repulsed until, toward noon, I began to fear for the result of the battle.

The Zodangans numbered nearly a million fighting men, gathered from pole to pole, wherever stretched their ribbon-like waterways, while pitted against them were less than a hundred thousand green warriors. The forces from Helium had not arrived, nor could we receive any word from them.

Just at noon we heard heavy firing all along the line between the Zodangans and the cities, and we knew then that our much-needed reinforcements had come.

Again Tars Tarkas ordered the charge, and once more the mighty thoats bore their terrible riders against the ramparts of the enemy. At the same moment the battle line of Helium surged over the opposite breastworks of the Zodangans and in another moment they were being crushed as between two millstones. Nobly they fought, but in vain.

The plain before the city became a veritable shambles ere the last Zodangan surrendered, but finally the carnage ceased, the prisoners were marched back to Helium, and we entered the greater city's gates, a huge triumphal procession of conquering heroes.

The broad avenues were lined with women and children, among which were the few men whose duties necessitated that they remain within the city during the battle. We were greeted with an endless round of applause and showered with ornaments of gold, platinum, silver, and precious jewels. The city had gone mad with joy.

My fierce Tharks caused the wildest excitement and enthusiasm. Never before had an armed body of green warriors entered the gates of Helium, and that they came now as friends and allies filled the red men with rejoicing.

That my poor services to Dejah Thoris had become known to the Heliumites was evidenced by the loud crying of my name, and by the loads of ornaments that were fastened upon me and my huge thoat as we passed up the avenues to the palace, for even in the face of the ferocious appearance of Woola the populace pressed close about me.

As we approached this magnificent pile we were met by a party of officers who greeted us warmly and requested that Tars Tarkas and his jeds with the jeddaks and jeds of his wild allies, together with myself, dismount and accompany them to receive from Tardos Mors an expression of his gratitude for our services.

At the top of the great steps leading up to the main portals of the palace stood the royal party, and as we reached the lower steps one of their number descended to meet us. He was an almost perfect specimen of manhood; tall, straight as an arrow, superbly muscled and with the carriage and bearing of a ruler of men. I did not need to be told that he was Tardos Mors, Jeddak of Helium.

The first member of our party he met was Tars Tarkas and his first words sealed forever the new friendship between the races.

"That Tardos Mors," he said, earnestly, "may meet the greatest living warrior of Barsoom is a priceless honor, but that he may lay his hand on the shoulder of a friend and ally is a far greater boon."

"Jeddak of Helium," returned Tars Tarkas, "it has remained for a man of another world to teach the green warriors of Barsoom the meaning of friendship; to him we owe the fact that the hordes of Thark can understand you; that they can appreciate and reciprocate the sentiments so graciously expressed."

Tardos Mors then greeted each of the green jeddaks and jeds, and to each spoke words of friendship and appreciation.

As he approached me he laid both hands upon my shoulders.

"Welcome, my son," he said; "that you are granted, gladly, and without one word of opposition, the most precious jewel in all Helium, yes, on all Barsoom, is sufficient earnest of my esteem."

We were then presented to Mors Kajak, Jed of lesser Helium, and father of Dejah Thoris. He had followed close behind Tardos Mors and seemed even more affected by the meeting than had his father.

He tried a dozen times to express his gratitude to me, but his voice choked with emotion and he could not speak, and yet he had, as I was to later learn, a reputation for ferocity and fearlessness as a fighter that was remarkable even upon warlike Barsoom. In common with all Helium he worshiped his daughter, nor could he think of what she had escaped without deep emotion.

CHAPTER XXVII

From Joy to Death

For ten days the hordes of Thark and their wild allies were feasted and entertained, and, then, loaded with costly presents and escorted by ten thousand soldiers of Helium commanded by Mors Kajak, they started on the return journey to their own lands. The jed of lesser Helium with a small party of nobles accompanied them all the way to Thark to cement more closely the new bonds of peace and friendship.

Sola also accompanied Tars Tarkas, her father, who before all his chieftains had acknowledged her as his daughter.

Three weeks later, Mors Kajak and his officers, accompanied by Tars Tarkas and Sola, returned upon a battleship that had been dispatched to Thark to fetch them in time for the ceremony which made Dejah Thoris and John Carter one.

For nine years I served in the councils and fought in the armies of Helium as a prince of the house of Tardos Mors. The people seemed never to tire of heaping honors upon me, and no day passed that did not bring some new proof of their love for my princess, the incomparable Dejah Thoris.

In a golden incubator upon the roof of our palace lay a snow-white egg. For nearly five years ten soldiers of the jeddak's Guard had constantly stood over it, and not a day passed when I was in the city that Dejah Thoris and I did not stand hand in hand before our little shrine planning for the future, when the delicate shell should break.

Vivid in my memory is the picture of the last night as we sat there talking in low tones of the strange romance which had woven our lives together and of this wonder which was coming to augment our happiness and fulfill our hopes.

In the distance we saw the bright-white light of an approaching airship, but we attached no special significance to so common a sight. Like a bolt of lightning it raced toward Helium until its very speed bespoke the unusual.

Flashing the signals which proclaimed it a dispatch bearer for the jeddak, it circled impatiently awaiting the tardy patrol boat which must convoy it to the palace docks.

Ten minutes after it touched at the palace a message called me to the council chamber, which I found filling with the members of that body.

On the raised platform of the throne was Tardos Mors, pacing back and forth with tense-drawn face. When all were in their seats he turned toward us.

"This morning," he said, "word reached the several governments of Barsoom that the keeper of the atmosphere plant had made no wireless report for two days, nor had almost ceaseless calls upon him from a score of capitals elicited a sign of response.

"The ambassadors of the other nations asked us to take the matter in hand and hasten the assistant keeper to the plant. All day a thousand cruisers have been searching for him until, just now one of them returns bearing his dead body, which was found in the pits beneath his house horribly mutilated by some assassin.

"I do not need to tell you what this means to Barsoom. It would take months to penetrate those mighty walls, in fact the work has already commenced, and there would be little to fear were the engine of the pumping plant to run as it should and as they all have for hundreds of years; but the worst, we fear, has happened. The instruments show a rapidly decreasing air pressure on all parts of Barsoom—the engine has stopped."

"My gentlemen," he concluded, "we have at best three days to live."

There was absolute silence for several minutes, and then a young noble arose, and with his drawn sword held high above his head addressed Tardos Mors.

"The men of Helium have prided themselves that they have ever shown Barsoom how a nation of red men should live, now is our opportunity to show them how they should die. Let us go about our duties as though a thousand useful years still lay before us."

The chamber rang with applause and as there was nothing better to do than to allay the fears of the people by our example we went our ways with smiles upon our faces and sorrow gnawing at our hearts.

When I returned to my palace I found that the rumor already had reached Dejah Thoris, so I told her all that I had heard.

"We have been very happy, John Carter," she said, "and I thank whatever fate overtakes us that it permits us to die together."

The next two days brought no noticeable change in the supply of air, but on the morning of the third day breathing became difficult at the higher altitudes of the rooftops. The avenues and plazas of Helium were filled with people. All business had ceased. For the most part the people looked bravely into the face of their unalterable doom. Here and there, however, men and women gave way to quiet grief.

Toward the middle of the day many of the weaker commenced to succumb and within an hour the people of Barsoom were sinking by thousands into the unconsciousness which precedes death by asphyxiation.

Dejah Thoris and I with the other members of the royal family had collected in a sunken garden within an inner courtyard of the palace. We conversed in low tones, when we conversed at all, as the awe of the grim shadow of death crept over us. Even Woola seemed to feel the weight of the impending calamity, for he pressed close to Dejah Thoris and to me, whining pitifully.

The little incubator had been brought from the roof of our palace at request of Dejah Thoris and she sat gazing longingly upon the unknown little life that now she would never know.

As it was becoming perceptibly difficult to breathe Tardos Mors arose, saying, "Let us bid each other farewell. The days of the greatness of Barsoom are over. Tomorrow's sun will look down upon a dead world which through all eternity must go swinging through the heavens peopled not even by memories. It is the end."

He stooped and kissed the women of his family, and laid his strong hand upon the shoulders of the men.

As I turned sadly from him my eyes fell upon Dejah Thoris. Her head was drooping upon her breast, to all appearances she was lifeless. With a cry I sprang to her and raised her in my arms.

Her eyes opened and looked into mine.

"Kiss me, John Carter," she murmured. "I love you! I love you! It is cruel that we must be torn apart who were just starting upon a life of love and happiness."

As I pressed her dear lips to mine the old feeling of unconquerable power and authority rose in me. The fighting blood of Virginia sprang to life in my veins.

"It shall not be, my princess," I cried. "There is, there must be some way, and John Carter, who has fought his way through a strange world for love of you, will find it."

And with my words there crept above the threshold of my conscious mind a series of nine long forgotten sounds. Like a flash of lightning in the darkness their full purport dawned upon me—the key to the three great doors of the atmosphere plant!

Turning suddenly toward Tardos Mors as I still clasped my dying love to my breast I cried,

"A flier, Jeddak! Quick! Order your swiftest flier to the palace top. I can save Barsoom yet."

He did not wait to question, but in an instant a guard was racing to the nearest dock and though the air was thin and almost gone at the rooftop they managed to launch the fastest one-man, air-scout machine that the skill of Barsoom had ever produced.

Kissing Dejah Thoris a dozen times and commanding Woola, who would have followed me, to remain and guard her, I bounded with my old agility and strength to the high ramparts of the palace, and in another moment I was headed toward the goal of the hopes of all Barsoom.

I had to fly low to get sufficient air to breathe, but I took a straight course across an old sea bottom and so had to rise only a few feet above the ground.

I traveled with awful velocity for my errand was a race against time with death. The face of Dejah Thoris hung always before me. As I turned for a last look as I left the palace garden I had seen her stagger and sink upon the ground beside the little incubator. That she had dropped into the last coma which would end in death, if the air supply remained unreplenished, I well knew, and so, throwing caution to the winds, I flung overboard everything but the engine and compass, even to my ornaments, and lying on my belly along the deck with one hand on the steering wheel and the other pushing the speed lever to its last notch I split the thin air of dying Mars with the speed of a meteor.

An hour before dark the great walls of the atmosphere plant loomed suddenly before me, and with a sickening thud I plunged to the ground before the small door which was withholding the spark of life from the inhabitants of an entire planet.

Beside the door a great crew of men had been laboring to pierce the wall, but they had scarcely scratched the flint-like surface, and now most of them lay in the last sleep from which not even air would awaken them.

Conditions seemed much worse here than at Helium, and it was with difficulty that I breathed at all. There were a few men still conscious, and to one of these I spoke.

"If I can open these doors is there a man who can start the engines?" I asked.

"I can," he replied, "if you open quickly. I can last but a few moments more. But it is useless, they are both dead and no one else upon Barsoom knew the secret of these awful locks. For three days men crazed with fear have surged about this portal in vain attempts to solve its mystery."

I had no time to talk, I was becoming very weak and it was with difficulty that I controlled my mind at all.

But, with a final effort, as I sank weakly to my knees I hurled the nine thought waves at that awful thing before me. The Martian had crawled to my side and with staring eyes fixed on the single panel before us we waited in the silence of death.

Slowly the mighty door receded before us. I attempted to rise and follow it but I was too weak.

"After it," I cried to my companion, "and if you reach the pump room turn loose all the pumps. It is the only chance Barsoom has to exist tomorrow!"

From where I lay I opened the second door, and then the third, and as I saw the hope of Barsoom crawling weakly on hands and knees through the last doorway I sank unconscious upon the ground.

CHAPTER XXVIII

At the Arizona Cave

It was dark when I opened my eyes again. Strange, stiff garments were upon my body; garments that cracked and powdered away from me as I rose to a sitting posture.

I felt myself over from head to foot and from head to foot I was clothed, though when I fell unconscious at the little doorway I had been naked. Before me was a small patch of moonlit sky which showed through a ragged aperture.

As my hands passed over my body they came in contact with pockets and in one of these a small parcel of matches wrapped in oiled paper. One of these matches I struck, and its dim flame lighted up what appeared to be a huge cave, toward the back of which I discovered a strange, still figure huddled over a tiny bench. As I approached it I saw that it was the dead and mummified remains of a little old woman with long black hair, and the thing it leaned over was a small charcoal burner upon which rested a round copper vessel containing a small quantity of greenish powder.

Behind her, depending from the roof upon rawhide thongs, and stretching entirely across the cave, was a row of human skeletons. From the thong which held them stretched another to the dead hand of the little old woman; as I touched the cord the skeletons swung to the motion with a noise as of the rustling of dry leaves.

It was a most grotesque and horrid tableau and I hastened out into the fresh air; glad to escape from so gruesome a place.

The sight that met my eyes as I stepped out upon a small ledge which ran before the entrance of the cave filled me with consternation.

A new heaven and a new landscape met my gaze. The silvered mountains in the distance, the almost stationary moon hanging in the sky, the cacti-studded valley below me were not of Mars. I could scarce believe my eyes, but the truth slowly forced itself upon me—I was looking upon Arizona from the same ledge from which ten years before I had gazed with longing upon Mars.

Burying my head in my arms I turned, broken, and sorrowful, down the trail from the cave.

Above me shone the red eye of Mars holding her awful secret, forty-eight million miles away.

Did the Martian reach the pump room? Did the vitalizing air reach the people of that distant planet in time to save them? Was my Dejah Thoris alive, or did her beautiful body lie cold in death beside the tiny golden incubator in the sunken garden of the inner courtyard of the palace of Tardos Mors, the jeddak of Helium?

For ten years I have waited and prayed for an answer to my questions. For ten years I have waited and prayed to be taken back to the world of my lost love. I would rather lie dead beside her there than live on Earth all those millions of terrible miles from her.

The old mine, which I found untouched, has made me fabulously wealthy; but what care I for wealth!

As I sit here tonight in my little study overlooking the Hudson, just twenty years have elapsed since I first opened my eyes upon Mars.

I can see her shining in the sky through the little window by my desk, and tonight she seems calling to me again as she has not called before since that long dead night, and I think I can see, across that awful abyss of space, a beautiful black-haired woman standing in the garden of a palace, and at her side is a little boy who puts his arm around her as she points into the sky toward the planet Earth, while at their feet is a huge and hideous creature with a heart of gold.

I believe that they are waiting there for me, and something tells me that I shall soon know.

CURT SIODMAK (1902–2000)

Internationally renowned screenplay writer and film director of dozens of German and American movies, Curt Siodmak is also known as a writer of more than a dozen popular novels. In the United States, Siodmak's film credits—both adaptations of stories and original authorship of stories that form the basis for Fantasy and Science Fiction genre films—include The Ape *(1940)*, The Invisible Man Returns *(1940)*, The Invisible Woman *(1940)*, Invisible Agent *(1942)*, The Wolf Man *(1942)*, Son of Dracula *(1943)*, Frankenstein Meets the Werewolf *(1943)*, I Walked With a Zombie *(1943)*, The Lady and the Monster *(1944)*, The Beast With Five Fingers *(1946)*, Tarzan's Magic Fountain *(1949)*, Riders to the Stars *(1953)*, Creature with the Atom Brain *(1955)*, Earth vs. the Flying Saucers *(1956), and others.*

Curt Siodmak's most famous work is probably the internationally popular and acclaimed novel Donovan's Brain *(1943). This modern-day variant of Mary Shelley's* Frankenstein *is a Fantasy and Science Fiction favorite that has been made into movies such as* The Lady and the Monster *(1944)*, Donovan's Brain *(1953), and* Vengeance *(1963). This story was also adapted into two consecutive half-hour radio episodes for the long-running radio drama series,* Suspense *(May 18 and 25, 1944); Orson Welles starred in these episodes.*

Siodmak was a successful film writer and author by the time he was in his late teens. When Hugo Gernsback introduced Amazing Stories *in 1926, Curt Siodmak was one of the famed publisher/scientist's first authors. "The Eggs from Lake Tanganyika" is not the first story of its kind, in English or other languages, yet it really is an archetypal story—it is the model on which much Science Fiction has been based since. Also, it began a tradition and subgenre in Gernsback's Science Fiction pulp magazines that endured for several years and was the subject of several of Frank R. Paul's magazine cover paintings. The story, of course, is about nature gone wild, animals and natural events of normally insignificant or minor proportion and threat to humanity that become, through some scientific event, unwielding, huge abominations of nature that imperil the earth.*

The Eggs from Lake Tanganyika

(Amazing Stories, *July 1926*)

Professor Meyer-Maier drew a sharp needle out of the cushion, carefully picked up with the pincers the fly lying in front of him and stuck it carefully upon a piece of white paper. He looked over the rim of his glasses, dipped his pen in the ink and wrote under the specimen:

"*Glossina palpalis*, specimen from Tsetsefly River. In the aboriginal language termed *nsi-nsi*. Usually found on river courses and lakes in West Africa. Bearer of the malady Negana (Tse-tse sickness—sleeping sickness)."

He laid down the pen and took up a powerful magnifying glass for a closer examination. "A horrible creature," he murmered, and shivered involuntarily. On each side of the head of the flying horror, there was a monstrous eye surrounded by many sharp lashes and divided up into a hundred thousand flashing facets. An ugly proboscis thickly studded with curved barbs or hooks grew out of the lower side of the head. The wings were small and pointed, the legs armed with thorns, spines and claws. The thorax was muscular, like that of a prize fighter. The abdomen was thin and looked like India rubber. It could take in a great quantity of blood and expand like a balloon. On the whole, the flying horror, resembling a pre-historic flying dragon, was not very pleasant looking—Prof. Meyer-Maier took a pin and transfixed the body of the fly. It seemed to him that a vicious sheen of light eminated from the eyes and that the proboscis rolled up. Quickly he picked up the magnifying glass, but it was an optical illusion—the thing was dead, with all its poison still within its body.

Memories of the Expedition to Africa

With a deep sigh he laid aside pincers and magnifying glass and sank into a deep revery. The clock struck 12, 1-2-3-4-5, counted Professor Meyer-Maier.

In Udjidji, a village on lake Tanganyika, the natives had told him of gigantic flies inhabiting the interior further north. These monsters were three times as big as the giants composing the giant bodyguard of the Prince of Ssuggi, who all had to be of at least standard height. Meyer-Maier laughed over this negro fable, but the negroes were obstinate. They refused to follow him to the northern part of Lake Tanganyika. Even Msu-uru, his black servant, who otherwise made an intelligent impression, trembled with excitement and begged to be left out of the expedition—because there enormous flies and bees were to be found,—that let no man approach. They drank the river dry and guarded the valley of the elephants. "The Valley of the Elephants" was a fabled place where the old pachyderms withdrew to die. "It is inexplicable," soliloquized Meyer-Maier, "that no one ever found a dead elephant."

The clock struck 6-7-8.

The natives had come along on the expedition much against their will. Meyer-Maier had trouble to keep the caravan moving up to the day when he found four great, strange looking eggs, larger than ostrich eggs. The negroes were seized with a panic, half of them deserting in the night, in spite of the great distance from the coast. The other half could only be kept there by tremendous efforts. He had to make up his mind finally, to go back, but he secretly put the eggs he had found into his camping chest to solve their riddle.

Now they were here in his Berlin home, in his work-room. He had not found time as yet to examine them, for he had brought much material home to be worked over.

The clock struck 9-10.

Meyer-Maier kept thinking of the ugly head of the tse-tse fly that he had seen through the magnifying glass. A strange thought occurred to him and made him smile. Suppose the stories of the negroes were true and the giant flies—butterflies and beetles as big as elephants—did exist! And suppose that they propagated as flies do!—each one laying eighty million eggs a year! He laughed aloud and pictured to himself how such a creature would stalk through the streets.

A Strange Sound and the Hatching of an Egg

He broke off suddenly, in the midst of his laughter. A sound reached his ear, an earsplitting buzzing like that of a thousand flies, a deafening hum, as if a swarm of bees were entering the room; it burst out like a blast of wind through the room and then stopped. Meyer-Maier jerked the door open. Nothing. All was quiet.

"I must relax for a while," said he, and opened the window. He turned on the light and threw back the lid of the big chest, which contained the giant eggs. Suddenly he grew pale as death and staggered back. A creature was crawling out, a creature as big as a police dog—a frightful creature, with wings, a muscular body, and six hairy legs with claws. It crept slowly, raised its incandescent head to the light and polished its wings with its hind legs. Faint with fright, Meyer-Maier pressed against the wall with outspread arms. A loud buzzing,—the creature swept across the room, climbed up on the windowsill and was gone.

Meyer-Maier came slowly to himself. "My nerves are deceiving me. Did I dream?" he whispered, and dragged himself to the camp-chest. But he became frozen with horror. One egg was broken open. "It breaks out of its shell like a chicken, it does not change into a chrysalis," he thought mechanically. At last his mind cleared and he awoke to the emergency. He sprang to the desk, snatched up his revolver, ran downstairs and out into the street. He saw no trace of the escaped giant insect. Meyer-Maier looked up at the lighted windows of his home. Suddenly the light became dim. "The other eggs"—like a blow came the thought—"the other eggs too have broken." He raced back up the stairs. A deafening buzzing filled the room. He jerked his door open and fired—once, twice, until the magazine was empty—the room was silent. Through the window he saw three silhouettes sweeping high across the night-sky and disappearing in the direction of the great woods in the West. In the chest there lay the four broken giant eggs. . . .

A Call for His Colleague

Meyer-Maier sank upon a chair. "It's against all logic," he thought, and glanced at the empty revolver in his hand. "My delirium has taken wings and crawled out of the egg. What should I do? Shall I call the police? They will send me to an alienist! Keep quiet about it? Look for the creatures? I'll call up my colleague, Schmidt-Schmitt!" He dragged himself to the telephone and got a connection. Schmidt-Schmitt was at home! "This is Meyer-Maier," sounded a tired voice. "Come over at once!"

"What's the trouble?" asked Schmidt-Schmitt.

"My African giant eggs have burst," lisped Meyer-Maier with a failing voice. "You must come at once!"

"Your nerves are out of order," answered Schmidt-Schmitt. "Have you still got the creatures?"

"They've gone," whispered Meyer-Maier,—he thought he would collapse,— "flew out of the window."

"There, there," laughed Schmidt-Schmitt. "Now, we are getting to the truth— of course they aren't there. Anyhow, I'll come over. Meanwhile take a cognac and put on a cold pack."

"Take your car, and say nothing about what I told you."

Professor Meyer-Maier hung up the receiver.

It was incredible. He pressed his hand to his forehead. If the empty shells were not irrefutable evidence, he would have been inclined to think of hallucinations.

He helped himself to some brandy and after the second glass he felt better. "I wish Professor Schmidt-Schmitt would come. He ought to be here by now. He will have an explanation and will help me to get myself in hand again. The day of ghosts and miracles is long past. But why isn't he here? He ought to have come by this time."

Meyer-Maier looked out of the window. A car came tearing through the dark street and stopped with squeaking brakes in front of Meyer-Maier's residence. A form jumped out like an India rubber ball, ran up the steps, burst into Meyer-Maier's study, and collapsed into a chair.

"How awful," he gasped.

"It seems to me, you are even more excited over it than I," said Professor Meyer-Maier dispiritedly while he watched his shaking friend.

"Absolutely terrible," Professor Schmidt-Schmitt wiped his forehead with a silk handkerchief. "You were not suffering from nerves, you had no hallucinations. Just now I saw a fly-creature as large as a heifer falling upon a horse. The monster grew big and heavy, while the horse collapsed and the fly flew away. I examined the horse. Its veins and arteries were empty. Not a drop of blood was left in its body. The driver fainted with fright and has not come to yet. It is a world catastrophy."

Notifying the Police

"We must notify the police at once."

A quick telephone connection was obtained. The police Lieutenant in charge himself answered.

"This is Professor Meyer-Maier talking! Please believe what I am going to tell you. I am neither drunk nor crazy. Four poisonous gigantic flies, as large as horses, are at large in the city. They must be destroyed at all costs."

"What are you trying to do? Kid me?" the Lieutenant came back in an angry voice.

"Believe me—for God's sake," yelled Meyer-Maier, reaching the end of his nervous strength.

"Hold the wire." The Lieutenant turned to the desk of the sergeant. "What is up now?"

"A cab driver has been here who says that his horse was killed by a gigantic bird on Karlstrasse."

"Get the men of the second platoon ready for immediate action," he ordered the sergeant, and turned back to the telephone. "Hello Professor! Are you still there? Please come over as quickly as possible. What you told me is true. One of these giant insects has been seen."

Professor Meyer-Maier hung up. He loaded his revolver and put a Browning pistol into his colleague's hand. "Is your car still downstairs?"

"Yes I took the little limosine."

"Excellent—then the monster cannot attack us." They rushed on through the night.

"What can happen now?" inquired Professor Schmidt-Schmitt.

"These giant flies may propagate and multiply in the manner of the housefly. And in that case, due to their strength and poisonous qualities," continued Professor Meyer-Maier, "the whole human race will perish in a few weeks. When they crept from the shell they were as large as dogs. They grew to the size of a horse within an hour. God knows what will happen next. Let us hope and pray that we will be able to find and kill the four flies and destroy the eggs which they have laid in the meantime, within fourteen days."

The car came to a stop in front of the Police Station. A policeman armed with steel hemet and hand trench bombs swinging from his belt tore open the limousine door. The Lieutenant hastened out and conducted the scientists into the station house.

"Any more news?" inquired Meyer-Maier.

"The West Precinct station just called up. One of their patrolmen saw a giant animal fly over the Teutoburger Forest. Luckily we had war tanks near there which immediately set out in search of the creature."

The telephone-bell rang. The Lieutenant rushed to the phone.

"Central Police Station."

"East Station talking. Report comes from Lake Wieler, that a gigantic fly has attacked two motor boats."

"Put small trench mortars on the police-boat and go out on the lake. Shoot when the beast gets near you."

The door of the station house opened and the city commissioner entered. "I have just heard some fabulous stories," he said, and approached the visitors. "Professor Meyer-Maier? Major Pritzel-Wilzell! Can you explain all this?"

"I brought home with me four large eggs from my African expedition, for examination. Tonight these eggs broke open. Four great flies came out—a sort of tse-tse fly, such as is found on Lake Tanganyika. The creatures escaped through the window and we must make every endeavor to kill them at once."

The telephone bell rang as if possessed.

"This is the Central Broadcasting Station. A giant bird has been caught in the high voltage lines. It has fallen down and lies on the street."

"Close the street at once." The Major took up the instrument. "Call up the Second Company. Let all four flying companies go off with munition and gasoline for three days. Come with me my friends, we will get at least one of them!"

An armored automobile came tearing along at a frightful speed. "We appreciate your foresight, Major," said Meyer-Maier, as they stepped into the steel-armored machine.

One of the Giant Flies Is Electrocuted

Although it was five o'clock in the morning, the square in front of the broadcasting station was black with people. The police kept a space clear in the center, where monstrously large and ugly, lay the dead giant fly. Its wings were burnt, its proboscis extended, while the legs, with their claws, were drawn up against the body. The abdomen was a great ball, full of bright red liquid. "That is certainly the creature that killed the horse," said Schmidt-Schmitt, and pointed at the thick abdomen. He then walked around the creature. "*Glossina palpalis.* A monstrous tse-tse fly."

"Will you please send the monster to the zoological laboratory?" The Major nodded assent. The firemen, prepared for service, pushed poles under the insect and tried to lift it up from the ground. Out of the air came a droning sound. An airplane squadron dropped out of the clouds and again disappeared. A bright body with vibrating wings flew across the sky. The airplanes dropped on it. The noise of the machine-guns started. The bright body fell in a spiral course to the ground. Crying and screaming, the people fled from the street and crowded into the houses. They couldn't tell where the insect would fall and they were afraid of their heads. The street was empty in an instant. The body of the monster fell directly in front of the armored car and lay there, stiff. In its fall it carried away a lot of aerial cable and now it lay on the pavement as if caught in a net, the head torn by the machine gun bullets. It looked like a strange gleaming cactus.

"Take me to my home, Major," groaned Meyer-Maier. "I can't stand it any longer. The excitement is too much for me."

In the Hospital

The armored car started noisily into motion. Meyer-Maier fell from the seat, senseless, upon the floor of the tonneau. When he came to himself, he lay in a strange bed. His gaze fell upon a bell which swung to and fro above his face. In his head there was a humming like an airplane motor. He made no attempt, even to think. His finger pressed the push-button and he never released it until half-a-dozen attendants came rushing into the room. One figure stood out in dark colors, in the group of white-clad interns. It was his colleague, Schmidt-Schmitt.

"You're awake?" said he, and stepped to his bed. "How are you feeling?"

"My head is buzzing as if there were a swarm of hornets living in it. How many hours have I lain here?"

"Hours?" Schmidt-Schmitt dwelt upon the word. "Today is the fifteenth day that you are lying in Professor Stiebling's sanitorium. It was a difficult case. You always woke up at meal-time and without saying a word, went to sleep again."

"Fifteen days!" cried Meyer-Maier excitedly. And the insects? Have they been killed?"

"I'll tell you the whole story when you are well again," said Schmidt-Schmitt, quieting him. "Lie as you are, quietly—any excitement may hurt you."

"They must not come into the room!" he screamed out to an excited messenger, who breathlessly pulled the door open.

"Professor!——" the man was in deadly fear——"the central Police station has given out the news that a swarm of giant flies are descending upon the city."

"Barricade all windows at once!"

"You wasted precious time," screamed Meyer-Maier, and jumped out of the bed. "Let me go to my house. I must solve the riddle as to how to get at the insects. Don't touch me," he raved. He snatched a coat from the rack, ran out of the house, and jumped into Schmidt-Schmitt's automobile which stood at the gate, and went like the wind, to his home. The door of his house was ajar. He rushed up four flights and in delirious haste rushed into his workroom. The telephone bell rang.

The Danger Is Over

Meyer-Maier snatched up the receiver. He got the consoling message from the city police-commissioner: "The danger is over, Professor. Our air-squadron has destroyed the swarm with a cloud of poison-gas. Only two of the insects escaped death. These we have caught in a net and are taking them to the zoological gardens."

"And if they have left eggs behind them?"

"We are going to search the woods systematically and will inject Lysol into any eggs we find. I think that will help," laughed the Major. "Shall I send some of them to you for examination?"

"No," cried Meyer-Maier in fright. "Keep them off my neck."

He sat down at his work-table. There seemed a vicious smile on the face of the transfixed dead tse-tse fly. "You frightful ghost," murmured the professor with pallid lips, and threw a book on the insect. His head was in a daze. He tried his best to think clearly. An axiom of science came to him: if the flies are as large as elephants, they can only propagate as fast as elephants do. They can't have a million young ones, but only a few. "I can't be wrong," he murmured. "I'll look up the confirmation."

He took up the telephone and called the city Commissioner. "Major, how many insects were in the swarm?"

"Thirteen. Eleven are dead. The other two will never escape alive. They are fed up with the poison-gas."

"Thank you." Meyer-Maier hung up the receiver. "Very well," he murmured, "now there can be no question of any danger, for each fly can only lay three or four eggs at once,—not a million."

An immense weariness overcame him. He went into his bed-room and fell exhausted on his bed. "It is well that there is a supreme wisdom which controls the laws of nature. Otherwise the world would be subject to the strangest surprises," he thought of the monsters and crept anxiously under the bed-clothes. "I'll entrust Schmidt-Schmitt with the investigation of the creature phenomenon, I simply can't stand further excitement."

And sleep spread the mantle of well-deserved quiet over him.

🜔 CLARE WINGER HARRIS (1891–1968)

Along with Frances Stevens, Clare Winger Harris was one of the first women pioneers of Fantasy and Science Fiction in the post–World War I pulp magazines. Both women were extremely talented, and their stories (personal and fictional) are cornerstones of Fantasy and Science Fiction yet today. Their contributions cannot be overstated and are often underappreciated. Beyond historical significance, Stevens's and Harris's tales are still great fun.

*As a child, Clare Winger Harris read and enjoyed the writings of Jules Verne and H. G. Wells. She had her first major sale to the pulps with her story "The Runaway World" (*Weird Tales, *July 1926). Her style in this and later stories is highly reflective of that of her contemporary Edmond Hamilton. Although not terribly prolific, Harris sold her stories consistently to Hugo Gernsback for publication in* Amazing Stories *and* Science Wonder Quarterly. *Many of these stories were collected in* Away from the Here and Now *(1947) and were deemed "Pseudo-Science" stories.*

"The Fate of the Poseidonia" was written in the 1920s, set in the 1950s, and is, unfortunately, extremely insightful and relevant at the turn of the millennium. The story predicts the social, environmental Science Fiction warnings of George Orwell, Ray Bradbury, Kurt Vonnegut, and Harry Harrison. (If you live anywhere near, or know anything about, the world's major water sources such as oceans, seas, rivers, and lakes—and the pollution and shortages of the same—then you know how chilling this story actually is.)

The Fate of the Poseidonia

(Amazing Stories, *June 1927*)

I

The first moment I laid eyes on Martell I took a great dislike to the man. There sprang up between us an antagonism that as far as he was concerned might have remained passive, but which circumstances forced into activity on my side.

How distinctly I recall the occasion of our meeting at the home of Professor Stearns, head of the Astronomy department of Austin College. The address which the professor proposed giving before the Mentor Club, of which I was a member, was to be on the subject of the planet, Mars. The spacious front rooms of the Stearns home were crowded for the occasion with rows of chairs, and at the end of the double parlors a screen was erected for the purpose of presenting telescopic views of the ruddy planet in its various aspects.

As I entered the parlor after shaking hands with my hostess, I felt, rather than saw, an unfamiliar presence, and the impression I received involuntarily was that of antipathy. What I saw was the professor himself engaged in earnest conversation with a stranger. Intuitively I knew that from the latter emanated the hostility of which I was definitely conscious.

He was a man of slightly less than average height. At once I noticed that he did not appear exactly normal physically and yet I could not ascertain in what way he was deficient. It was not until I had passed the entire evening in his company that I was fully aware of his bodily peculiarities. Perhaps the most striking characteristic was the swarthy, coppery hue of his flesh that was not unlike that of an American Indian. His chest and shoulders seemed abnormally developed, his limbs and features extremely slender in proportion. Another peculiar individuality was the wearing of a skull-cap pulled well down over his forehead.

Professor Stearns caught my eye, and with a friendly nod indicated his desire that I meet the new arrival.

"Glad to see you, Mr. Gregory," he said warmly as he clasped my hand. "I want you to meet Mr. Martell, a stranger in our town, but a kindred spirit, in that he is interested in Astronomy and particularly in the subject of my lecture this evening."

I extended my hand to Mr. Martell and imagined that he responded to my salutation somewhat reluctantly. Immediately I knew why. The texture of the skin was most unusual. For want of a better simile, I shall say that it felt not unlike a fine, dry sponge. I do not believe that I betrayed any visible surprise, though inwardly my whole being revolted. The deep, close-set eyes of the stranger seemed searching me for any manifestation of antipathy, but I congratulate myself that my outward poise was undisturbed by the strange encounter.

The guests assembled, and I discovered to my chagrin that I was seated next to the stranger, Martell. Suddenly the lights were extinguished preparatory to the presentation of the lantern-slides. The darkness that enveloped us was intense. Supreme horror gripped me when I presently became conscious of two faint phosphorescent lights to my right. There could be no mistaking their origin. They were the eyes of Martell and they were regarding me with an enigmatical stare. Fascinated, I gazed back into those diabolical orbs with an emotion akin to terror. I felt that I should shriek and then attack their owner. But at the precise moment when my usually steady nerves threatened to betray me, the twin lights vanished. A second later the lantern light flashed on the screen. I stole a furtive glance in the direction of Martell. He was sitting with his eyes closed.

"The planet Mars should be of particular interest to us," began Professor Stearns, "not only because of its relative proximity to us, but because of the fact that there are visible upon its surface undeniable evidences of the handiwork of man, and I am inclined to believe in the existence of mankind there not unlike the humanity of the earth."

The discourse proceeded uninterruptedly. The audience remained quiet and attentive, for Professor Stearns possessed the faculty of holding his listeners spellbound. A large map of one hemisphere of Mars was thrown on the screen, and simultaneously the stranger Martell drew in his breath sharply with a faint whistling sound.

The professor continued, "Friends, do you observe that the outstanding physical difference between Mars and Terra appears to be in the relative distribution of land and water? On our own globe the terrestrial parts lie as distinct entities surrounded by the vast aqueous portions, whereas on Mars the land and water are so intermingled by gulfs, bays, capes and peninsulas that it requires careful study to ascertain for a certainty which is which. It is my opinion, and I do not hold it alone, for much discussion with my worthy colleagues has made it obvious that the peculiar land contours are due to the fact that water is becoming a very scarce commodity on our neighboring planet. Much of what is now land is merely the exposed portions of the one-time ocean bed, the precious life-giving fluid now occupying only the lowest depressions. We may conclude that the telescopic eye, when turned on Mars, sees a waning world, the habitat of a people struggling desperately and vainly for existence, with inevitable extermination facing them in the not far distant future. What will they do? If they are no farther advanced in the evolutionary stage than a carrot or a jelly-fish, they will ultimately succumb to fate, but if they are men and women such as you and I, they will fight for the continuity of their race. I am inclined to the opinion that the Martians will not die without putting up a brave struggle, which will result in the prolongation of their existence, but not in their complete salvation."

Professor Stearns paused. "Are there any questions?" he asked.

I was about to speak when the voice of Martell boomed in my ear, startling me.

"In regard to the map, professor," he said, "I believe that gulf which lies farthest south is not a gulf at all but is a part of the land portion surrounding it. I think you credit the poor dying planet with even more water than it actually has!"

"It is possible and even probable that I have erred," replied the learned man, "and I am sorry indeed if that gulf is to be withdrawn from the credit of the Martians, for the future must look very black."

"Just suppose," resumed Martell, leaning toward the lecturer with interested mien, "that the Martians were the possessors of an intelligence equal to that of terrestrials, what might they do to save themselves from total extinction? In other words to bring it home to us more realistically, what would *we* do were we threatened with a like disaster?"

"That is a very difficult question to answer, and one upon which merely an opinion could be ventured," smiled Professor Stearns. " 'Necessity is the mother of invention,' and in our case without the likelihood of the existence of the mother, we can hardly hazard a guess as to the nature of the offspring. But always, as Terra's resources have diminished, the mind of man has discovered substitutes. There has always been a way out, and let us hope our brave planetary neighbors will succeed in solving their problem."

"Let us hope so indeed," echoed the voice of Martell.

II

At the time of my story in the winter of 1954–1955, I was still unmarried and was living in a private hotel on East Ferguson Avenue, where I enjoyed the comforts of well-furnished bachelor quarters. To my neighbors I paid little or no attention, absorbed in my work during the day and paying court to Margaret Landon in the evenings.

I was not a little surprised upon one occasion, as I stepped into the corridor, to see a strange yet familiar figure in the hotel locking the door of the apartment adjoining my own. Almost instantly I recognized Martell, on whom I had not laid eyes since the meeting some weeks previous at the home of Professor Stearns. He evinced no more pleasure at our meeting than I did, and after the exchange of a few cursory remarks from which I learned that he was my new neighbor, we went our respective ways.

I thought no more of the meeting, and as I am not blessed or cursed (as the case may be) with a natural curiosity concerning the affairs of those about me, I seldom met Martell, and upon the rare occasions when I did, we confined our remarks to that ever-convenient topic, the weather.

Between Margaret and myself there seemed to be growing an inexplicable estrangement that increased as time went on, but it was not until after five repeated futile efforts to spend an evening in her company that I suspected the presence of a rival. Imagine my surprise and my chagrin to discover that rival in the person of my neighbor, Martell! I saw them together at the theatre and wondered, even with all due modesty, what there was in the ungainly figure and peculiar character of Martell to attract a beautiful and refined girl of Margaret Landon's type. But attract her he did, for it was plainly evident, as I watched them with the eyes of a jealous lover, that Margaret was fascinated by the personality of her escort.

In sullen rage I went to Margaret a few days later, expressing my opinion of her new admirer in derogatory epithets. She gave me calm and dignified attention until I had exhausted my vocabulary voicing my ideas of Martell, then she made reply in Martell's defense.

"Aside from personal appearance, Mr. Martell is a forceful and interesting character, and I refuse to allow you to dictate to me who my associates are to be. There is no reason why we three cannot all be friends."

"Martell hates me as I hate him," I replied with smoldering resentment. "That is sufficient reason why we three cannot all be friends."

"I think you must be mistaken," she replied curtly. "Mr. Martell praises your qualities as a neighbor and comments not infrequently on your excellent virtue of attending strictly to your own business."

I left Margaret's presence in a down-hearted mood.

"So Martell appreciates my lack of inquisitiveness, does he?" I mused as later I reviewed mentally the closing words of Margaret, and right then and there doubts and suspicions arose in my mind. If self-absorption was an appreciable quality as far as Martell was concerned, there was reason for his esteem of that phase of my character. I had discovered the presence of a mystery; Martell had something to conceal!

It was New Year's Day, not January 1st as they had it in the old days, but the extra New Year's Day that was sandwiched as a separate entity between two years. This new chronological reckoning had been put into use in 1950. The calendar had previously contained twelve months in length from twenty-eight to thirty-one days, but with the addition of a new month and the adoption of a uniformity of twenty-eight days for all months and the interpolation of an isolated New Year's Day the world's system of chronology was greatly simplified. It was, as I say, on New Year's Day that I arose later than usual and dressed myself. The buzzing monotone of a voice from Martell's room annoyed me. Could he be talking over the telephone to Margaret? Right then and there I stooped to the performance of a deed of which I did not think myself capable. Ineffable curiosity converted me into a spy and an eavesdropper. I dropped to my knees and peered through the keyhole. I was rewarded with an unobstructed profile view of Martell seated at a low desk on which stood a peculiar cubical mechanism measuring on each edge six or seven inches. Above it hovered a tenuous vapor and from it issued strange sounds, occasionally interrupted by remarks from Martell, uttered in an unknown tongue. Good heavens! Was this a new-fangled radio that communicated with the spirit-world? For only in such a way could I explain the peculiar vapor that enveloped the tiny machine. Television had been perfected, but as yet no instrument had been invented which delivered messages from the "unknown bourne!"

I crouched in my undignified position until it was with difficulty that I arose, at the same time that Martell shut off the mysterious contrivance. Could Margaret be involved in any diabolical schemes? The very suggestion caused me to break out in a cold sweat. Surely Margaret, the very personification of innocence and purity, could be no partner in any nefarious undertaking! I resolved to call her up. She answered the phone and I thought her voice showed agitation.

"Margaret, this is George," I said. "Are you all right?"

She answered faintly in the affirmative.

"May I come over at once?" I pled. "I have something important to tell you."

To my surprise she consented, and I lost no time in speeding my volplane to her home. With no introductory remarks, I plunged right into a narrative of the peculiar and suspicious actions of Martell, and ended by begging her to discontinue her association with him. Ever well poised and with a girlish dignity that was irresistibly charming Margaret quietly thanked me for my solicitude for her well-being but assured me that there was nothing to fear from Martell. It was like beating against a brick wall to obtain any satisfaction from her, so I returned to my lonely room, there to brood in solitude over the unhappy change that Martell had brought into my life.

Once again I gazed through the tiny aperture. My neighbor was nowhere to be seen, but on the desk stood that which I mentally termed the devil-machine. The subtle mist that had previously hovered above it was wanting.

The next day upon arising I was drawn as by a magnet toward the keyhole, but my amazement knew no bounds when I discovered that it had been plugged from the other side, and my vision completely barred!

"Well, I guess it serves me right," I muttered in my chagrin. "I ought to keep out of other people's private affairs. But," I added as an afterthought in feeble defense of my actions, "my motive is to save Margaret from that scoundrel." And such I wanted to prove him to be before it was too late!

III

The sixth of April, 1955, was a memorable day in the annals of history, especially to the inhabitants of Pacific coast cities throughout the world. Radios buzzed with the alarming and mystifying news that just overnight the ocean line had receded several feet. What cataclysm of nature could have caused the disappearance of thousands of tons of water inside of twenty-four hours? Scientists ventured the explanation that internal disturbances must have resulted in the opening of vast submarine fissures into which the sea had poured.

This explanation, stupendous as it was, sounded plausible enough and was accepted by the world at large, which was too busy accumulating gold and silver to worry over the loss of nearly a million tons of water. How little we then realized that the relative importance of gold and water was destined to be reversed, and that man was to have forced upon him a new conception of values which would bring to him a complete realization of his former erroneous ideas.

May and June passed marking little change in the drab monotony that had settled into my life since Margaret Landon had ceased to care for me. One afternoon early in July I received a telephone call from Margaret. Her voice betrayed an agitated state of mind, and sorry though I was that she was troubled, it pleased me that she had turned to me in her despair. Hope sprang anew in my breast, and I told her I would be over at once.

I was admitted by the taciturn housekeeper and ushered into the library where Margaret rose to greet me as I entered. There were traces of tears in her lovely eyes. She extended both hands to me in a gesture of spontaneity that had been wholly lacking in her attitude toward me ever since the advent of Martell. In the rôle of protector and adviser, I felt that I was about to be reinstated in her regard.

But my joy was short-lived as I beheld a recumbent figure on the great davenport and recognized it instantly as that of Martell. So he was in the game after all! Margaret had summoned me because her lover was in danger! I turned to go but felt a restraining hand.

"Wait, George," the girl pled. "The doctor will be here any minute."

"Then let the doctor attend to him," I replied coldly. "I know nothing of the art of healing."

"I know, George," Margaret persisted, "but he mentioned you before he lost consciousness and I think he wants to speak to you. Won't you wait, please?"

I paused, hesitant at the supplicating tones of her whom I loved, but at that moment the maid announced the doctor, and I made a hasty exit.

Needless to say I experienced a sense of guilt as I returned to my rooms.

"But," I argued as I seated myself comfortably before my radio, "a rejected lover would have to be a very magnanimous specimen of humanity to go running about doing favors for a rival. What do the pair of them take me for anyway—a fool?"

I rather enjoyed a consciousness of righteous indignation, but disturbing visions of Margaret gave me an uncomfortable feeling that there was much about the affair that was incomprehensible to me.

"The transatlantic passenger-plane, *Pegasus*, has mysteriously disappeared," said the voice of the news announcer. "One member of her crew has been picked up who tells such a weird, fantastic tale that it has not received credence. According to his story the *Pegasus* was winging its way across mid-ocean last night keeping an even elevation of three thousand feet, when, without any warning, the machine started straight up. Some force outside of itself was drawing it up, but whither? The rescued mechanic, the only one of all the fated ship's passengers, possessed the presence of mind to manipulate his parachute, and thus descended in safety before the air became too rare to breathe, and before he and the parachute could be attracted upwards. He stoutly maintains that the plane could not have fallen later without his knowledge. Scouting planes, boats and submarines sent out this morning verify his seemingly mad narration. Not a vestige of the *Pegasus* is to be found above, on the surface or below the water. Is this tragedy in any way connected with the lowering of the ocean level? Has someone a theory? In the face of such an inexplicable enigma the government will listen to the advancement of any theories in the hope of solving the mystery. Too many times in the past have so-called level-headed people failed to give ear to the warnings of theorists and dreamers, but now we know that the latter are often the possessors of a sixth sense that enables them to see that to which the bulk of mankind is blind."

I was awed by the fate of the *Pegasus*. I had had two flights in the wonderful machine myself three years ago, and I knew that it was the last word in luxuriant air-travel.

How long I sat listening to brief news bulletins and witnessing scenic flashes of world affairs I do not know, but there suddenly came to my mind and persisted in staying there a very disquieting thought. Several times I dismissed it as unworthy of any consideration, but it continued with unmitigating tenacity.

After an hour of mental pros and cons I called up the hotel office.

"This is Mr. Gregory in suite 307," I strove to keep my voice steady. "Mr. Martell of 309 is ill at the house of a friend. He wishes me to have some of his belongings taken to him. May I have the key to his rooms?"

There was a pause that to me seemed interminable, then the voice of the clerk, "Certainly, Mr. Gregory, I'll send a boy up with it at once."

I felt like a culprit of the deepest dye as I entered Martell's suite a few moments later and gazed about me. I knew I might expect interference from any quarter at any moment, so I wasted no time in a general survey of the apartment, but proceeded at once to the object of my visit. The tiny machine which I now perceived was more intricate than I had supposed from my previous observations through the keyhole, stood in its accustomed place upon the desk. It had four levers and a dial, and I decided to manipulate each of these in turn. I commenced with the one at my extreme left. For a moment apparently nothing happened, then I realized that above the machine a mist was forming.

At first it was faint and cloudy but the haziness quickly cleared, and before my startled vision a scene presented itself. I seemed to be inside a bamboo hut looking toward an opening which afforded a glimpse of a wave-washed sandy beach and a few palm trees silhouetted against the horizon. I could imagine myself on a desert isle. I gasped in astonishment, but it was nothing to the shock which was to follow. While my fascinated gaze dwelt on the scene before me, a shadow fell athwart the hut's entrance and the figure of a man came toward me. I uttered a hoarse cry. For a moment I thought I had been transplanted chronologically to the discovery of America, for the being who approached me bore a general resemblance to an Indian chief. From his forehead tall, white feathers stood erect. He was without clothing and his skin had a reddish cast that glistened with a coppery sheen in the sunlight. Where had I seen those features or similar ones recently? I had it! Martell! The Indian savage was a natural replica of the suave and civilized Martell, and yet was this man before me a savage? On the contrary, I noted that his features displayed a remarkably keen intelligence.

The stranger approached a table upon which I seemed to be, and raised his arms. A muffled cry escaped my lips! The feathers that I had supposed constituted his headdress were attached permanently along the upper portion of his arms to a point a little below each elbow. *They grew there.* This strange being had feathers instead of hair.

I do not know by what presence of mind I managed to return the lever to its original position, but I did, and sat weakly gazing vacantly at the air, where but a few seconds before a vivid tropic scene had been visible. Suddenly a low buzzing sound was heard. Only for an instant was I mystified, then I knew that the stranger of the desert-isle was endeavoring to summon Martell.

Weak and dazed I waited until the buzzing had ceased and then I resolutely pulled the second of the four levers. At the inception of the experiment the same phenomena were repeated, but when a correct perspective was effected a very different scene was presented before my startled vision. This time I seemed to be in a luxuriant room filled with costly furnishings, but I had time only for a most fleeting glance, for a section of newspaper that had intercepted part of my view, moved, and from behind its printed expanse emerged a being who bore a resemblance to Martell and the Indian of the desert island. It required but a second to turn off the mysterious connection, but that short time had been of sufficient duration to enable me to read the heading of the paper in the hands of a copper-hued man. It was *Die Münchene Zeitung*.

Still stupefied by the turn of events, it was with a certain degree of enjoyment that I continued to experiment with the devil-machine. I was startled when the same buzzing sound followed the disconnecting of the instrument.

I was about to manipulate the third lever when I became conscious of pacing footsteps in the outer hall. Was I arousing the suspicion of the hotel officials? Leaving my seat before the desk, I began to move about the room in semblance of gathering together Martell's required articles. Apparently satisfied, the footsteps retreated down the corridor and were soon inaudible.

Feverishly now I fumbled with the third lever. There was no time to lose and I was madly desirous of investigating all the possibilities of this new kind of television-set. I had no doubt that I was on the track of a nefarious organization of spies, and I worked on in the self-termed capacity of a Sherlock Holmes.

The third lever revealed an apartment no less sumptuous than the German one had been. It appeared to be unoccupied for the present, and I had ample time to survey its expensive furnishings which had an oriental appearance. Through an open window at the far end of the room I glimpsed a mosque with domes and minarets. I could not ascertain for a certainty whether this was Turkey or India. It might have been any one of many eastern lands, I could not know. The fact that the occupant of this oriental apartment was temporarily absent made me desirous of learning more about it, but time was precious to me now, and I disconnected. No buzzing followed upon this occasion, which strengthened my belief that my lever manipulation sounded a similar buzzing that was audible in the various stations connected for the purpose of accomplishing some wicked scheme.

The fourth handle invited me to further investigation. I determined to go through with my secret research though I died in the effort. Just before my hand dropped, the buzzing commenced, and I perceived for the first time a faint glow near the lever of No. 4. I dared not investigate 4 at this time, for I did not wish it known that another than Martell was at this station. I thought of going on to dial 5, but an innate love of system forced me to risk a loss of time rather than to take them out of order. The buzzing continued for the usual duration of time, but I waited until it had apparently ceased entirely before I moved No. 4.

My soul rebelled at that which took form from the emanating mist. A face, another duplicate of Martell's, but if possible more cruel, confronted me, completely filling up the vaporous space, and two phosphorescent eyes seared a warning into my own. A nauseating sensation crept over me as my hand crept to the connecting part of No. 4. When every vestige of the menacing face had vanished, I arose weakly and took a few faltering steps around the room. A bell was ringing with great persistence from some other room. It was mine! It would be wise to answer it. I fairly flew back to my room and was rewarded by the sound of Margaret's voice with a note of petulance in it.

"Why didn't you answer, George? The phone rang several times."

"Couldn't. Was taking a bath," I lied.

"Mr. Martell is better," continued Margaret. "The doctor says there's no immediate danger."

There was a pause and the sound of a rasping voice a little away from the vicinity of the phone, and then Margaret's voice came again.

"Mr. Martell wants you to come over, George. He wants to see you."

"Tell him I have to dress after my bath, then I'll come," I answered.

IV

There was not a moment to spare. I rushed back into Martell's room determined to see this thing through. I had never been subject to heart attacks, but certainly the suffocating sensation that possessed me could be attributed to no other cause.

A loud buzzing greeted my ears as soon as I had closed the door of Martell's suite. I looked toward the devil-machine. The four stations were buzzing at once! What was I to do? There was no light near dial 5, and that alone remained uninvestigated. My course of action was clear; try out No. 5 to my satisfaction, leave Martell's room and go to Margaret Landon's home as I had told her I would. They must not know what I had done. But it was inevitable that Martell would know when he got back to his infernal television and radio. *He must not get back!* Well, time enough to plan that later; now to the work of seeing No. 5.

When I turned the dial of No. 5 (for, as I have stated before, this was a dial instead of a lever) I was conscious of a peculiar sensation of distance. It fairly took my breath away. What remote part of the earth's surface would the last position reveal to me?

A sharp hissing sound accompanied the manipulation of No. 5 and the vaporous shroud was very slow in taking definite shape. When it was finally at rest, and it was apparent that it would not change further, the scene depicted was at first incomprehensible to me. I stared with bulging eyes and bated breath trying to read any meaning into the combinations of form and color that had taken shape before me.

In the light of what has since occurred, the facts of which are known throughout the world, I can lend my description a little intelligence borrowed, as it were, from the future. At the time of which I write, however, no such enlightenment was mine, and it must have been a matter of minutes before the slightest knowledge of the significance of the scene entered my uncomprehending brain.

My vantage-point seemed to be slightly aerial, for I was looking down upon a scene possibly ninety feet below me. Arid red cliffs and promontories jutted over dry ravines and crevices. In the immediate foreground and also across a deep gully extended a comparatively level area which was the scene of some sort of activity. There was about it a vague suggestion of a shipyard, yet I saw no lumber, only great mountainous piles of dull metal, among which moved thousands of agile figures. They were men and women, but how strange they appeared! Their red bodies were minus clothing of any description and their heads and shoulders were covered with long white feathers that, when folded, draped the upper portions of their bodies like shawls. They were unquestionably of the same race as the desert-island stranger—and Martell! At times the feathers of these strange people stood erect and spread out like a peacock's tail. I noticed that when spread in this fan-like fashion they facilitated locomotion.

I glanced toward the sun far to my right and wondered if I had gone crazy. I rubbed my hands across my eyes and peered again. Yes, it was our luminary, but it was little more than half its customary size! I watched it sinking with fascinated gaze. It vanished quickly beyond the red horizon and darkness descended with scarcely a moment of intervening twilight. It was only by the closest observation that I could perceive that I was still in communication with No. 5.

Presently the gloom was dissipated by a shaft of light from the opposite horizon whither the sun had disappeared, so rapidly that I could follow its movement across the sky; the moon hove into view. But wait, was it the moon? Its surface looked strangely unfamiliar, and it too seemed to have shrunk in size.

Spellbound, I watched the tiny moon glide across the heavens while I listened to the clang of metal tools from the workers below. Again a bright light appeared on the horizon beyond the great metal bulks below me. The scene was rapidly being rendered visible by an orb that exceeded the sun in diameter. Then I knew. Great God! There were two moons traversing the welkin! My heart was pounding so loudly that it drowned out the sound of the metalworkers. I watched on, unconscious of the passage of time.

Voices shouted from below in great excitement. Events were evidently working up to some important climax while the little satellite passed from my line of vision and only the second large moon occupied the sky. Straight before me and low on the horizon it hung with its lower margin touching the cliffs. It was low enough now so that a few of the larger stars were becoming visible. One in particular attracted my gaze and held it. It was a great bluish-green star, and I noticed that the workers paused seemingly to gaze in silent admiration at its transcendent beauty. Then shout after shout arose from below and I gazed in bewilderment at the spectacle of the next few minutes, or was it hours?

A great spherical bulk hove in view from the right of my line of vision. It made me think of nothing so much as a gyroscope of gigantic proportions. It seemed to be made of the metal with which the workers were employed below, and as it gleamed in the deep blue of the sky it looked like a huge satellite. A band of red metal encircled it with points of the same at top and bottom. Numerous openings that resembled the portholes of an ocean-liner appeared in the broad central band, from which extended metal points. I judged these were the "eyes" of the machine. But that which riveted my attention was an object that hung poised in the air below the mighty gyroscope, held in suspension by some mysterious force, probably magnetic in nature, evidently controlled in such a manner that at a certain point it was exactly counter-balanced by the gravitational pull. The lines of force apparently traveled from the poles of the mammoth sphere. But the object that depended in mid-air, as firm and rigid as though resting on terra-firma, was the missing *Pegasus*, the epitome of earthly scientific skill, but in the clutches of this unearthly looking marauder it looked like a fragile toy. Its wings were bent and twisted, giving it an uncanny resemblance to a bird in the claws of a cat.

In my spellbound contemplation of this new phenomenon I had temporarily forgotten the scene below, but suddenly a great cloud momentarily blotted out the moon, then another and another and another, in rapid succession. Huge bulks of aircraft were eclipsing the moon. Soon the scene was all but obliterated by the machines whose speed accelerated as they reached the upper air. On and on they sped in endless procession while the green star gazed serenely on! The green star, most sublime of the starry host! I loved its pale beauty, though I knew not why. Darkness. The moon had set, but I knew that those frightfully gigantic and ominous shapes still sped upward and onward. Whither?

The tiny moon again made its appearance, serving to reveal once more that endless aerial migration. Was it hours or days? I had lost all sense of the passage of time. The sound of rushing feet, succeeded by a pounding at the door, brought me back to my immediate surroundings. I had the presence of mind to shut off the machine, then I arose and assumed a defensive attitude as the door opened and many figures confronted me. Foremost among them was Martell, his face white with rage, or was it fear?

"Officer, seize that man," he cried furiously. "I did not give him permission to spy in my room. He lied when he said that." Here Martell turned to the desk clerk who stood behind two policemen.

"Speaking of spying," I flung back at him, "Martell, you ought to know the meaning of that word. He's a spy himself," I cried to the two apparently unmoved officers. "Why he—he—" To continue was futile.

From their unsympathetic attitudes, I knew the odds were against me. I had lied, and I had been found in a man's private room without his permission. It would be a matter of time and patience before I could persuade the law that I had any justice on my side.

I was handcuffed and led toward the door just as a sharp pain like an icy clutch at my heart overcame me. I sank into oblivion.

V

When I regained consciousness two days later I discovered that I was the sole occupant of a cell in the State Hospital for the Insane. Mortified to the extreme, I pled with the keeper to bring about my release, assuring him that I was unimpaired mentally.

"Sure, that's what they all say," the fellow remarked with a wry smile.

"But I must be freed," I reiterated impatiently, "I have a message of importance for the world. I must get into immediate communication with the Secretary of War."

"Yes, yes," agreed the keeper affably. "We'll let you see the Secretary of War when that fellow over there," he jerked his thumb in the direction of the cell opposite mine, "dies from drinking hemlock. He says he's Socrates, and every time he drinks a cup of milk he flops over, but he always revives."

I looked across the narrow hall into a pair of eyes that mirrored a deranged mind, then my gaze returned to the guard who was watching me narrowly. I turned away with a shrug of despair.

Later in the day the man appeared again, but I sat in sullen silence in a corner of my cell. Days passed in this manner until at last a plausible means of communication with the outside world occurred to me. I asked if my good friend Professor Stearns might be permitted to visit me. The guard replied that he believed it could be arranged for sometime the following week. It is a wonder I did not become demented, imprisoned as I was, in solitude, with the thoughts of the mysterious revelations haunting me continually.

One afternoon the keeper, passing by on one of his customary rounds, thrust a newspaper between the bars of my cell. I grabbed it eagerly and retired to read it.

The headlines smote my vision with an almost tactile force.
"Second Mysterious Recession of Ocean. The *Poseidonia* is lost!"
I continued to read the entire article, the letters of which blazed before my eyes like so many pinpoints of light.

"Ocean waters have again receded, this time in the Atlantic. Seismologists are at a loss to explain the mysterious cataclysm as no earth tremors have been registered. It is a little over three months since the supposed submarine fissures lowered the level of the Pacific Ocean several feet, and now the same calamity, only to a greater extent, has visited the Atlantic.

"The island of Madeira reports stranded fish upon her shores by the thousands, the decay of which threatens the health of the island's population. Two merchant vessels off the Azores, and one fifty miles out from Gibraltar, were found total wrecks. Another, the *Transatlantic*, reported a fearful agitation of the ocean depths, but seemed at a loss for a plausible explanation, as the sky was cloudless and no wind was blowing.

" 'But despite this fact,' wired the *Transatlantic*, 'great waves all but capsized us. This marine disturbance lasted throughout the night.'

"The following wireless from the great ocean liner, *Poseidonia*, brings home to us the realization that Earth has been visited with a stupendous calamity. The *Poseidonia* was making her weekly trans-Atlantic trip between Europe and America, and was in mid-ocean at the time her message was flashed to the world.

" 'A great cloud of flying objects of enormous proportions has just appeared in the sky, blotting out the light of the stars. No sound accompanies the approach of this strange fleet. In appearance the individual craft resemble mammoth balloons. The sky is black with them and in their vicinity the air is humid and oppressive, as though the atmosphere were saturated to the point of condensation. Everything is orderly. There are no collisions. Our captain has given orders for us to turn back toward Europe—we have turned, but the dark dirigibles are pursuing us. Their speed is unthinkable. Can the *Poseidonia*, doing a mere hundred miles an hour, escape? A huge craft is bearing down upon us from above and behind. There is no escape. Pandemonium reigns. The enemy—'

"Thus ends the tragic message from the brave wireless operator of the *Poseidonia*."

I threw down the paper and called loudly for the keeper. Socrates across the hall eyed me suspiciously. I was beginning to feel that perhaps the poor demented fellow had nothing on me; that I should soon be in actuality a raving maniac.

The keeper came in response to my call, entered my cell and patted my shoulders reassuringly.

"Never mind, old top," he said, "it isn't so bad as it seems."

"Now look here," I burst forth angrily, "I tell you I am *not insane!*" How futile my words sounded! "If you will send Professor Mortimer Stearns, teacher of Astronomy at Austin, to me at once for an hour's talk, I'll prove to the world that I have not been demented."

"Professor Stearns is a very highly esteemed friend of mine," I continued, noting the suspicion depicted on his countenance. "If you wish, go to him first and find out his true opinion of me. I'll wager it will not be an uncomplimentary one!"

The man twisted his keys thoughtfully, and I uttered not a word, believing a silent demeanor most effective in the present crisis. After what seemed an eternity:

"All right," he said, "I'll see what can be done toward arranging a visit from Professor Mortimer Stearns as soon as possible."

I restrained my impulse toward a too effusive expression of gratitude as I realized that a quiet dignity prospered my cause more effectually.

The next morning at ten, after a constant vigil, I was rewarded with the most welcome sight of Professor Stearns striding down the hall in earnest conversation with the guard. He was the straw and I the drowning man, but would he prove a more substantial help than the proverbial straw? I surely hoped so.

A chair was brought for the professor and placed just outside my cell. I hastily drew my own near it.

"Well, this is indeed unfortunate," said Mortimer Stearns with some embarrassment, "and I sincerely hope you will soon be released."

"Unfortunate!" I echoed. "It is nothing short of a calamity."

My indignation voiced so vociferously startled the good professor and he shoved his chair almost imperceptibly away from the intervening bars. At the far end of the hall the keeper eyed me suspiciously. Hang it all, was my last resort going to fail me?

"Professor Stearns," I said earnestly, "will you try to give me an unbiased hearing? My situation is a desperate one, and it is necessary for someone to believe in me before I can render humanity the service it needs."

He responded to my appeal with something of his old sincerity that always endeared him to his associates.

"I shall be glad to hear your story, Gregory, and if I can render any service, I'll not hesitate—"

"That's splendid of you," I interrupted with emotion, "and now to my weird tale."

I related from the beginning, omitting no details, however trivial they may have seemed, the series of events that had brought me to my present predicament.

"And your conclusion?" queried the professor in strange, hollow tones.

"That Martian spies, one of whom is Martell, are superintending by radio and television, an unbelievably well-planned theft of Earth's water in order to replenish their own dry ocean beds!"

"Stupendous!" gasped Professor Stearns. "Something must be done to prevent another raid. Let's see," he mused, "the interval was three months before, was it not? Three months we shall have for bringing again into use the instruments of war that, praise God! have lain idle for many generations. It is the only way to deal with a formidable foe from outside."

VI

Professor Stearns was gone, but there was hope in my heart in place of the former grim despair. When the guard handed the evening paper to me I amazed him with a grateful "thank you." But my joy was short-lived. Staring up at me from the printed passenger-list of the ill-fated *Poseidonia* were the names of Mr. and Mrs. T. M. Landon and daughter, Margaret!

I know the guard classed me as one of the worst cases on record, but I felt that surely Fate had been unkind.

"A package for Mr. George Gregory," bawled a voice in the corridor.

Thanks to the influence of Professor Stearns, I was permitted to receive mail. When the guard saw that I preferred unwrapping it myself, he discreetly left me to the mystery of the missive.

A card just inside bore the few but significant words, "For Gregory in remembrance of Martell."

I suppressed an impulse to dash the accursed thing to the floor when I saw that it was Martell's radio and television instrument. Placing it upon the table I drew a chair up to it and turned each of the levers, but not one functioned. I manipulated the dial No. 5. The action was accompanied by the same hissing sound that had so startled my overwrought nerves upon the previous occasion. Slowly the wraithlike mist commenced the process of adjustment. Spellbound I watched the scene before my eyes.

Again I had the sensation of a lofty viewpoint. It was identical with the one I had previously held, but the scene—was it the same? I must be—and yet! The barren red soil was but faintly visible through a verdure. The towering rocky palisades that bordered the chasm were crowned with golden-roofed dwellings, or were they temples, for they liked the pure marble fanes of the ancient Greeks except in color. Down the steep slopes flowed streams of sparkling water that dashed with a merry sound to a canal below.

Gone were the thousands of beings and their metal aircraft, but seated on a grassy plot in the left foreground of the picture was a small group of the white-feathered, red-skinned inhabitants of this strange land. In the distance rose the temple-crowned crags. One figure alone stood, and with a magnificent gesture held arms aloft. The great corona of feathers spread, following the line of the arms like the open wings of a great eagle. The superb figure stood and gazed into the deep velvety blue of the sky, the others following the direction of their leader's gaze.

Involuntarily I too watched the welkin where now not even a moon was visible. Then within the range of my vision there moved a great object—the huge aerial gyroscope—and beneath it, dwarfed by its far greater bulk, hung a modern ocean-liner, like a jewel from the neck of some gigantic ogre.

Great God—it was the *Poseidonia!* I knew now, in spite of the earthly appearance of the great ship, that it was no terrestrial scene upon which I gazed. I was beholding the victory of Martell, the Martian, who had filled his world's canals with water of Earth, and even borne away trophies of our civilization to exhibit to his fellow-beings.

I closed my eyes to shut out the awful scene, and thought of Margaret, dead and yet aboard the liner, frozen in the absolute cold of outer space!

How long I sat stunned and horrified I do not know, but when I looked back for another last glimpse of the Martian landscape, I uttered a gasp of incredulity. A face filled the entire vaporous screen, the beloved features of Margaret Landon. She was speaking and her voice came over the distance like the memory of a sound that is not quite audible and yet very real to the person in whose mind it exists. It was more as if time divided us instead of space, yet I knew it was the latter, for while a few minutes of time came between us, millions of miles of space intervened!

"George," came the sweet, far-away voice, "I loved you, but you were so suspicious and jealous that I accepted the companionship of Martell, hoping to bring you to your senses. I did not know what an agency for evil he had established upon the earth. Forgive me, dear."

She smiled wistfully. "My parents perished with hundreds of others in the transportation of the *Poseidonia*, but Martell took me from the ship to the ether-craft for the journey, so that I alone was saved."

Her eyes filled with tears. "Do not mourn for me, George, for I shall take up the thread of life anew among these strange but beautiful surroundings. Mars is indeed lovely, but I will tell you of it later, for I cannot talk long now."

"I only want to say," she added hastily, "that Terra need fear Mars no more. There is a sufficiency of water now—and I will prevent any—"

She was gone, and in her stead was the leering, malevolent face of Martell. He was minus his skull-cap, and his clipped feathers stood up like the ruff of an angry turkey-gobbler.

I reached instinctively for the dial, but before my hand touched it there came a sound, not unlike that of escaping steam, and instantaneously the picture vanished. I did not object to the disappearance of the Martian, but another fact did cause me regret; from that moment I was never able to view the ruddy planet through the agency of the little machine. All communication had been forever shut off by Martell.

Although many doubt the truth of my solution of the mystery of the disappearance of the *Pegasus* and of the *Poseidonia*, and are still searching beneath the ocean waves, I know that never will either of them be seen again on Earth.

✵ LESLIE F(RANCES) STONE (1905–1987)

Like Francis Stevens and Clare Winger Harris, Leslie F. Stone was an important, but only moderately prolific author of Fantasy and Science Fiction of the 1920s and 1930s. Ultimately, she published about twenty Science Fiction- and Fantasy-related stories. Her first Science Fiction story was entitled "Men With Wings," and it appeared in Hugo Gernsback's Air Wonder Stories *in 1929. This was followed by a sequel entitled "Women With Wings." Stone wrote tales of the distant future, such as "When the Sun Went Out" (1929), and Space Operas, such as "Out of the Void" (Amazing Stories, 1929) and "Across the Void" (Amazing Stories, 1930).*

Leslie F. Stone wrote Science Fiction for about eight years, and she was quite popular during that time. She wrote and published very rarely after that. But, as Forrest J Ackerman tells us, she was Hugo Gernsback's main female author in the first half of the 1930s. However, Stone's association with Experimenter Publishers (Gernsback's company) also had its problems. When the publisher went under, so too did Leslie F. Stone's writing career see its demise. Ackerman states that Science Fiction's loss of Stone was profound, and he further notes how "The Conquest of Gola" predates and predicts Joanna Russ's "When It Changed" (also found in this volume) by four decades.

The Conquest of Gola

(Wonder Stories, *April 1931*)

Hola, my daughters (sighed the Matriarch), it is true indeed, I am the only living one upon Gola who remembers the invasion from Detaxal. I alone of all my generation survive to recall vividly the sights and scenes of that past era. And well it is that you come to me to hear by free communication or mind to mind, face to face with each other.

Ah, well I remember the surprise of that hour when through the mists that enshroud our lovely world, there swam the first of the great smooth cylinders of the Detaxalans, fifty *tas* in length, as glistening and silvery as the soil of our land, propelled by the man-things that on Detaxal are supreme even as we women are supreme on Gola.

In those bygone days, as now, Gola was enwrapped by her cloud mists that keep from us the terrific glare of the great star that glows like a malignant spirit out there in the darkness of the void. Only occasionally when a particularly great storm parts the mist of heaven do we see the wonders of the vast universe, but that does not prevent us, with our marvelous telescopes handed down to us from thousands of generations before us, from learning what lies across the dark seas of the outside.

Therefore we knew of the nine planets that encircle the great star and are subject to its rule. And so are we familiar enough with the surfaces of these planets to know why Gola should appear as a haven to their inhabitants who see in our cloud-enclosed mantle a sweet release from the blasting heat and blinding glare of the great sun.

So it was not strange at all to us to find that the people of Detaxal, the third planet of the sun, had arrived on our globe with a wish in their hearts to migrate here, and end their days out of reach of the blistering warmth that had come to be their lot on their own world.

Long ago we, too, might have gone on exploring expeditions to other worlds, other universes, but for what? Are we not happy here? We who have attained the greatest of civilizations within the confines of our own silvery world. Powerfully strong with our mighty force rays, we could subjugate all the universe, but why?

Are we not content with life as it is, with our lovely cities, our homes, our daughters, our gentle consorts? Why spend physical energy in combative strife for something we do not wish, when our mental processes carry us further and beyond the conquest of mere terrestrial exploitation?

On Detaxal it is different, for there the peoples, the ignoble male creatures, breed for physical prowess, leaving the development of their sciences, their philosophies, and the contemplation of the abstract to a chosen few. The greater part of the race faces forth to conquer, to lay waste, to struggle and fight as the animals do over a morsel of worthless territory. Of course we can see why they desired Gola with all its treasures, but we can thank Providence and ourselves that they did not succeed in "commercializing" us as they have the remainder of the universe with their ignoble Federation.

Ah yes, well I recall the hour when first they came, pushing cautiously through the cloud mists, seeking that which lay beneath. We of Gola were unwarned until the two cylinders hung directly above Tola, the greatest city of that time, which still lies in its ruins since that memorable day. But they have paid for it—paid for it well in thousands and tens of thousands of their men.

We were first apprised of their coming when the alarm from Tola was sent from the great beam station there, advising all to stand in readiness for an emergency. Geble, my mother, was then Queen of all Gola, and I was by her side in Morka, that pleasant seaside resort, where I shall soon travel to partake of its rejuvenating waters.

With us were four of Geble's consorts, sweet gentle males, that gave Geble much pleasure in those free hours away from the worries of state. But when the word of the strangers' descent over our home city, Tola, came to us, all else was forgotten. With me at her side, Geble hastened to the beam station and there in the matter transmitter we dispatched our physical beings to the palace at Tola, and the next moment were staring upward at the two strange shapes etched against the clouds.

What the Detaxalan ships were waiting for we did not know then, but later we learned. Not grasping the meaning of our beam stations, the commanders of the ships considered the city below them entirely lacking in means of defense, and were conferring on the method of taking it without bloodshed on either side.

It was not long after our arrival in Tola that the first of the ships began to descend toward the great square before the palace. Geble watched without a word, her great mind already scanning the brains of those whom she found within the great machine. She transferred to my mind but a single thought as I stood there at her side and that with a sneer, "Barbarians!"

Now the ship was settling in the square and after a few moments of hesitation, a circular doorway appeared at the side and four of the Detaxalans came through the opening. The square was empty but for themselves and their flyer, and we saw them looking about surveying the beautiful buildings on all sides. They seemed to recognize the palace for what it was and in one accord moved in our direction.

Then Geble left the window at which we stood and strode to the doorway opening upon the balcony that faced the square. The Detaxalans halted in their tracks when they saw her slender graceful form appear and removing the strange coverings they wore on their heads they each made a bow.

Again Geble sneered, for only the male-things of our world bow their heads, and so she recognized these visitors for what they were, nothing more than the despicable males of the species! And what creatures they were!

Imagine a short almost flat body set high upon two slender legs, the body tapering in the middle, several times as broad across as it is through the center, with two arms almost as long as the legs attached to the upper part of the torso. A small column-like neck of only a few inches divides the head of oval shape from the body, and in this head only are set the organs of sight, hearing, and scent. Their bodies were like a patchwork of a misguided nature.

Yes, strange as it is, my daughters, practically all of the creature's faculties had their base in the small ungainly head, and each organ was perforce pressed into serving for several functions. For instance, the breathing nostrils also served for scenting out odors, nor was this organ able to exclude any disagreeable odors that might come its way, but had to dispense to the brain both pleasant and unpleasant odors at the same time.

Then there was the mouth, set directly beneath the nose, and here again we had an example of one organ doing the work of two, for the creature not only used the mouth with which to take in the food for its body, but it also used the mouth to enunciate the excruciatingly ugly sounds of its language forthwith.

Never before have I seen such a poorly organized body, so unlike our own highly developed organisms. How much nicer it is to be able to call forth any organ at will, and dispense with it when its usefulness is over! Instead these poor Detaxalans had to carry theirs about in physical being all the time so that always was the surface of their bodies entirely marred.

Yet that was not the only part of their ugliness, and proof of the lowliness of their origin, for whereas our fine bodies support themselves by muscular development, these poor creatures were dependent entirely upon a strange structure to keep them in their proper shape.

Imagine if you can a bony skeleton somewhat like the foundations upon which we build our edifices, laying stone and cement over the steel framework. But this skeleton instead is inside a body which the flesh, muscle and skin overlay. Everywhere in their bodies are these cartilaginous structures—hard, heavy, bony structures developed by the chemicals of the being for its use. Even the hands, feet and head of the creatures were underlaid with these bones—ugh, it was terrible when we dissected one of the fellows for study. I shudder to think of it.

Yet again there was still another feature of the Detaxalans that was equally as horrifying as the rest, namely their outer covering. As we viewed them for the first time out there in the square we discovered that parts of the body, that is the part of the head which they called the face, and the bony hands were entirely naked without any sort of covering, neither fur nor feathers, just the raw, pinkish-brown skin looking as if it had been recently plucked.

Later we found a few specimens that had a type of fur on the lower part of the face, but these were rare. And when they doffed the head coverings which we had first taken for some sort of natural covering, we saw that the top of the head was overlaid with a very fine fuzz of fur several inches long.

We did not know in the beginning that the strange covering on the bodies of the four men, green in color, was not a natural growth, but later discovered that such was the truth, and not only the face and hands were bare of fur, but the entire body, except for a fine sprinkling of hair that was scarcely visible except on the chest, was also bare. No wonder the poor things covered themselves with their awkward clothing. We arrived at the conclusion that their lack of fur had been brought about by the fact that always they had been exposed to the bright rays of the sun so that without the dampness of our own planet the fur had dried up and fallen away from the flesh!

Now thinking it over I suppose that we of Gola presented strange forms to the people of Detaxal with our fine circular bodies, rounded at the top, our short beautiful lower limbs with the circular foot pads, and our short round arms and hand pads, flexible and muscular like rubber.

But how envious they must have been of our beautiful golden coats, our movable eyes, our power to scent, hear and touch with any part of the body, to absorb food and drink through any part of the body most convenient to us at any time. Oh yes, laugh though you may, without a doubt we were also freaks to those freakish Detaxalans. But no matter, let us return to the tale.

On recognizing our visitors for what they were, simple-minded males, Geble was chagrined at them for taking up her time, but they were strangers to our world and we Golans are always courteous. Geble began of course to try to communicate by thought transference, but strangely enough the fellows below did not catch a single thought. Instead, entirely unaware of Geble's overture to friendship, the leader commenced to speak to her in most outlandish manner, contorting the red lips of his mouth into various uncouth shapes and making sounds that fell upon our hearing so unpleasantly that we immediately closed our senses to them. And without a word Geble turned her back upon them, calling for Tanka, her personal secretary.

Tanka was instructed to welcome the Detaxalans while she herself turned to her own chambers to summon a half dozen of her council. When the council arrived she began to discuss with them the problem of extracting more of the precious tenix from the waters of the great inland lake of Notauch. Nothing whatever was said of the advent of the Detaxalans, for Geble had dismissed them from her mind as creatures not worthy of her thought.

In the meantime Tanka had gone forth to meet the four who of course could not converse with her. In accordance with the Queen's orders she led them indoors to the most informal receiving chamber and there had them served with food and drink which by the looks of the remains in the dishes they did not relish at all.

Leading them through the rooms of the lower floor of the palace she made a pretence of showing them everything which they duly surveyed. But they appeared to chafe at the manner in which they were being entertained.

The creatures even made an attempt through the primitive method of conversing by their arms to learn something of what they had seen, but Tanka was as supercilious as her mistress. When she thought they had had enough, she led them to the square and back to the door of their flyer, giving them their dismissal.

But the men were not ready to accept it. Instead they tried to express to Tanka their desire to meet the ruling head of Gola. Although their hand motions were perfectly inane and incomprehensible, Tanka could read what passes through their brains, and understood more fully than they what lay in their minds. She shook her head and motioned that they were to embark in their flyer and be on their way back to their planet.

Again and again Detaxalans tried to explain what they wished, thinking Tanka did not understand. At last she impressed upon their savage minds that there was nothing for them but to depart, and disgruntled by her treatment they reentered their machine, closed its ponderous door and raised their ship to the leave of its sister flyer. Several minutes passed and then, with thanksgiving, we saw them pass over the city.

Told of this, Geble laughed. "To think of mere man-things daring to attempt to force themselves upon us. What is the universe coming to? What were their women back home considering when they sent them to us? Have they developed too many males and think that we can find use for them?" she wanted to know.

"It is strange indeed," observed Yabo, one of the council members. "What did you find in the minds of these ignoble creatures, O August One?"

"Nothing of particular interest, a very low grade of intelligence, to be sure. There was no need of looking below the surface."

"It must have taken intelligence to build those ships."

"None aboard them did that. I don't question it but that their mothers built the ships for them as playthings, even as we give toys to our 'little ones,' you know. I recall that the ancients of our world perfected several types of space-flyers many ages ago!"

"Maybe those males do not have 'mothers' but instead they build the ships themselves. Maybe they are the stronger sex on their world!" This last was said by Suiki, the fifth consort of Geble, a pretty little male, rather young in years. No one had noticed his coming into the chamber, but now everyone showed surprise at his words.

"Impossible!" ejaculated Yabo.

Geble, however, laughed at the little chap's expression. "Suiki is a profound thinker," she observed, still laughing, and she drew him to her gently hugging him.

And with that the subject of the men from Detaxal was closed. It was reopened, however, several hours later when it was learned that instead of leaving Gola altogether the ships were seen one after another by the various cities of the planet as they circumnavigated it.

It was rather annoying, for everywhere the cities' routines were broken up as the people dropped their work and studies to gaze at the cylinders. Too, it was upsetting the morale of the males, for on learning that the two ships contained only creatures of their own sex they were becoming envious wishing for the same type of playthings for themselves.

Shut in, as they are, unable to grasp the profundities of our science and thought, the gentle, fun-loving males were always glad for a new diversion and this new method developed by the Detaxalans had intrigued them.

It was then that Geble decided it was high time to take matters into her own hands. Not knowing where the two ships were at the moment it was not difficult with the object-finder beam to discover their whereabouts, and then with the attractor to draw them to Tola magnetically. An *ous* later we had the pleasure of seeing the two ships rushing toward our city. When they arrived above it, power brought them down to the square again.

Again Tanka was sent out, and directed the commanders of the two ships to follow her in to the Queen. Knowing the futility of attempting to converse with them without mechanical aid, Geble caused to be brought her three of the ancient mechanical thought transformers that are only museum pieces to us but still workable. The two men were directed to place them on their heads while she donned the third. When this was done she ordered the creatures to depart immediately from Gola, telling them that she was tired of their play.

Watching the faces of the two I saw them frowning and shaking their heads. Of course I could read their thoughts as well as Geble without need of the transformers, since it was only for their benefit that these were used, so I heard the whole conversation, though I need only to give you the gist of it.

"We have no wish to leave your world as yet," the two had argued.

"You are disrupting the routine of our lives here," Geble told them, "and now that you've seen all that you can there is no need for you to stay longer. I insist that you leave immediately."

I saw one of the men smile, and thereupon he was the one who did all the talking (I say "talking," for this he was actually doing, mouthing each one of his words although we understood his thoughts as they formed in his queer brain, so different from ours).

"Listen here," he laughed, "I don't get the hang of you people at all. We came to Gola (he used some outlandish name of his own, but I use our name of course) with the express purpose of exploration and exploitation. We come as friends. Already we are in alliance with Damin (again the name for the fourth planet of our system was different, but I give the correct appellation), established commerce and trade, and now we are ready to offer you the chance to join our Federation peaceably.

"What we have seen of this world is very favorable; there are good prospects for business here. There is no reason why you people as those of Damin and Detaxal can not enter into a nice business arrangement congenially. You have far more here to offer tourists, more than Damin. Why, except for your clouds this would be an ideal paradise for every man, woman and child on Detaxal and Damin to visit, and of course with our new cloud dispensers we could clear your atmosphere for you in short order and keep it that way. Why, you'll make millions in the first year of your trade.

"Come now, allow us to discuss this with your ruler—king or whatever you call him. Women are all right in their place, but it takes the men to see the profit of a thing like this—you are a woman, aren't you?"

The first of his long speech, of course, was so much gibberish to us, with his prate of business arrangements, commerce and trade, tourists, profits, cloud dispensers and what not, but it was the last part of what he said that took my breath away, and you can imagine how it affected Geble. I could see straightway that she was intensely angered, and good reason too. By the looks of the silly fellow's face I could guess that he was getting the full purport of her thoughts. He began to shuffle his funny feet and a foolish grin pervaded his face.

"Sorry," he said, "if I insulted you—I didn't intend that, but I believed that man holds the same place here as he does on Detaxal and Damin, but I suppose it is just as possible for woman to be the ruling factor of a world as man is elsewhere."

That speech naturally made Geble more irate, and tearing off her thought transformer she left the room without another word. In a moment, however, Yabo appeared wearing the transformer in her place. Yabo had none of the beauty of my mother, for whereas Geble was slender and as straight as a rod, Yabo was obese, and her fat body overflowed until she looked like a large dumpy bundle of *yat* held together in her furry skin. She had very little dignity as she waddled toward the Detaxalans, but there was determination in her whole manner, and without preliminaries she began to scold the two as though they were her own consorts.

"There has been enough of this, my fine young men," she shot at them. "You've had your fun, and now it is time for you to return to your mothers and consorts. Shame on you for making up such miserable tales about yourselves. I have a good mind to take you home with me for a couple of days, and I'd put you in your places quick enough. The idea of men acting like you are!"

For a moment I thought the Detaxalans were going to cry by the faces they made, but instead they broke into laughter, such heathenish sounds as had never before been heard on Gola, and I listened in wonder instead of excluding it from my hearing, but the fellows sobered quickly enough at that, and the spokesman addressed the shocked Yabo.

"I see," said he, "it's impossible for your people and mine to arrive at an understanding peaceably. I'm sorry that you take us for children out on a spree, that you are accustomed to such a low type of men as is evidently your lot here."

"I have given you your chance to accept our terms without force, but since you refuse, under the orders of the Federation I will have to take you forcibly, for we are determined that Gola become one of us, if you like it or not. Then you will learn that we are not the children you believe us to be.

"You may go to your supercilious Queen now and advise her that we give you exactly ten hours in which to evacuate this city, for precisely on the hour we will lay this city in ruins. And if that does not suffice you, we will do the same with every other city on the planet! Remember, ten hours!"

And with that he took the mechanical thought transformer from his head and tossed it on the table. His companion did the same and the two of them strode out of the room and to their flyers which arose several thousand feet above Tola and remained there.

Hurrying in to Geble, Yabo told her what the Detaxalan had said. Geble was reclining on her couch and did not bother to raise herself.

"Childish prattle," she conceded and withdrew her red eyes on their movable stems into their pockets, paying no more heed to the threats of the men from Detaxal.

I, however, could not be as calm as my mother, and I was fearful that it was not childish prattle after all. Not knowing how long ten hours might be I did not wait, but crept up to the palace's beam station and set its dials so that the entire building and as much of the surrounding territory as it could cover were protected in the force zone.

Alas, that the same beam was not greater. But it had not been put there for defense, only for matter transference and whatever other peacetime methods we used. It was the means of proving just the same that it was also a very good defensive instrument, for just two *ous* later the hovering ships above let loose their powers of destruction, heavy explosives that entirely demolished all of Tola and its millions of people and only the palace royal of all that beauty was left standing!

Awakened from her nap by the terrific detonation, Geble came hurriedly to a window to view the ruin, and she was wild with grief at what she saw. Geble, however, saw that there was urgent need for action. She knew without my telling her what I had done to protect the palace. And though she showed no sign of appreciation, I knew that I had won a greater place in her regard than any other of her many daughters and would henceforth be her favorite as well as her successor, as the case turned out.

Now, with me behind her, she hurried to the beam station and in a twinkling we were both in Tubia, the second greatest city of that time. Nor were we to be caught napping again, for Geble ordered all beam stations to throw out their zone forces while she herself manipulated one of Tubia's greatest power beams, attuning it to the emanations of the two Detaxalan flyers. In less than an *ous* the two ships were seen through the mists heading for Tubia. For a moment I grew fearful, but on realizing that they were after all in our grip, and the attractors held every living thing powerless against movement, I grew calm and watched them come over the city and the beam pull them to the ground.

With the beam still upon them, they lay supine on the ground without motion. Descending to the square Geble called for Ray C, and when the machine arrived she herself directed the cutting of the hole in the side of the flyer and was the first to enter it with me immediately behind, as usual.

We were both astounded by what we saw of the great array of machinery within. But a glance told Geble all she wanted to know of their principles. She interested herself only in the men standing rigidly in whatever position our beam had caught them. Only the eyes of the creatures expressed their fright, poor things, unable to move so much as a hair while we moved among them untouched by the power of the beam because of the strength of our own minds.

They could have fought against it if they had known how, but their simple minds were too weak for such exercise.

Now glancing about among the stiff forms around us, of which there were one thousand, Geble picked out those of the males she desired for observation, choosing those she judged to be their finest specimens, those with much hair on their faces and having more girth than the others. These she ordered removed by several workers who followed us, and then we emerged again to the outdoors.

Using hand beam torches the picked specimens were kept immobile after they were out of reach of the greater beam and were borne into the laboratory of the building Geble had converted into her new palace. Geble and I followed, and she gave the order for the complete annihilation of the two powerless ships.

Thus ended the first foray of the people of Detaxal. And for the next two *tels* there was peace upon our globe again. In the laboratory the thirty who had been rescued from their ships were given thorough examinations both physically and mentally and we learned all there was to know about them. Hearing of the destruction of their ships, most of the creatures had become frightened and were quite docile in our hands. Those that were unruly were used in the dissecting room for the advancement of Golan knowledge.

After a complete study of them, which yielded little, we lost interest in them scientifically. Geble, however, found some pleasure in having the poor creatures around her and kept three of them in her own chambers so she could delve into their brains as she pleased. The others she doled out to her favorites as she saw fit.

One she gave to me to act as a slave or in what capacity I desired him, but my interest in him soon waned, especially since I had now come of age and was allowed to have two consorts of my own, and go about the business of bringing my daughters into the world.

My slave I called Jon and gave him complete freedom of my house. If only we had foreseen what was coming we would have annihilated every one of them immediately! It did please me later to find that Jon was learning our language and finding a place in my household, making friends with my two shut-in consorts. But as I have said I paid little attention to him.

So life went on smoothly with scarcely a change after the destruction of the ships of Detaxal. But that did not mean we were unprepared for more. Geble reasoned that there would be more ships forthcoming when the Detaxalans found that their first two did not return. So, although it was sometimes inconvenient, the zones of force were kept upon our cities.

And Geble was right, for the day came when dozens of flyers descended upon Gola from Detaxal. But this time the zones of force did not hold them since the zones were not in operation!

And we were unwarned, for when they descended upon us, our world was sleeping, confident that our zones were our protection. The first indication that I had of trouble brewing was when, awakening, I found the ugly form of Jon bending over me. Surprised, for it was not his habit to arouse me, I started up only to find his arms about me, embracing me. And how strong he was! For the moment a new emotion swept me, for the first time I knew the pleasure to be had in the arms of a strong man, but that emotion was short lived, for I saw in the blue eyes of my slave that he had recognized the look in my eyes for what it was, and for the moment he was tender.

Later I was to grow angry when I thought of that expression of his, for his eyes filled with pity, pity for me! But pity did not stay, instead he grinned and the next instant he was binding me down to my couch with strong rope. Geble, I learned later, had been treated as I, as were the members of the council and every other woman in Gola!

That was what came of allowing our men to meet on common ground with the creatures from Detaxal, for a weak mind is open to seeds of rebellion and the Detaxalans had sown it well, promising dominance to the lesser creatures of Gola.

That, however, was only part of the plot on the part of the Detaxalans. They were determined not only to revenge those we had murdered, but also to gain mastery of our planet. Unnoticed by us they had constructed a machine which transmits sound as we transmit thought and by its means had communicated with their own world, advising them of the very hour to strike when all of Gola was slumbering. It was a masterful stroke, only they did not know the power of the mind of Gola—so much more ancient than theirs.

Lying there bound on my couch I was able to see out the window and, trembling with terror, I watched a half dozen Detaxalan flyers descend into Tubia, guessing that the same was happening in our other cities. I was truly frightened, for I did not have the brain of Geble. I was young yet, and in fear I watched the hordes march out of their machines, saw the thousands of our men join them.

Free from restraint, the shut-ins were having their holiday and how they cavorted out in the open, most of the time getting in the way of the freakish Detaxalans who were certainly taking over our city.

A half *ous* passed while I lay there watching, waiting in fear at what life we had led up to the present and trembled over what the future might be when the Detaxalans had infested us with commerce and trade, business propositions, tourists and all of their evil practices. It was then that I received the message from Geble, clear and definite, just as all the women of the globe received it, and hope returned to my heart.

There began that titanic struggle, the fight that won us victory over the simpleminded weaklings below who had presumptuously dared to conquer us. The first indication that the power of our combined mental concentration at Geble's orders was taking effect. They tried to shake us off, but we knew we could bring them back to us.

At first the Detaxalans paid them no heed. They knew not what was happening until there came the wholesale retreat of the Golan men back to the buildings, back to the chambers from which they had escaped. Then grasping something of what was happening the already defeated invaders sought to retain their hold on our little people. Our erstwhile captives sought to hold them with oratorical gestures, but of course we won. We saw our creatures return to us and unbind us.

Only the Detaxalans did not guess the significance of that, did not realize that inasmuch as we had conquered our own men, we could conquer them also. As they went about their work of making our city their own, establishing already their autocratic bureaus wherever they pleased, we began to concentrate upon them, hypnotizing them to the flyers that had disgorged them.

And soon they began to feel of our power, the weakest ones first, feeling the mental bewilderment creeping upon them. Their leaders, stronger in mind, knew nothing of this at first, but soon our terrible combined mental power was forced upon them also and they realized that their men were deserting them, crawling back to their ships! The leaders began to exhort them into new action, driving them physically. But our power gained on them and now we began to concentrate upon the leaders themselves. They were strong of will and they defied us, fought us, mind against mind, but of course it was useless. Their minds were not suited to the test they put themselves to, and after almost three *ous* of struggle, we of Gola were able to see victory ahead.

At last the leaders succumbed. Not a single Detaxalan was abroad in the avenues. They were within their flyers, held there by our combined wills, unable to act for themselves. It was then as easy for us to switch the zones of force upon them, subjugate them more securely and with the annihilator beam to disintegrate completely every ship and man into nothingness! Thousands upon thousands died that day and Gola was indeed revenged.

Thus, my daughters, ended the second invasion of Gola.

Oh yes, more came from their planet to discover what had happened to their ships and their men, but we of Gola no longer hesitated, and they no sooner appeared beneath the mists than they too were annihilated until at last Detaxal gave up the thought of conquering our cloud-laden world. Perhaps in the future they will attempt it again, but we are always in readiness for them now, and our men — well, they are still the same ineffectual weaklings, my daughters . . .

❄ C(ATHERINE) L(UCILLE) MOORE (1911-1987)

Catherine L. Moore and Leigh Brackett (1915–1978) were the most important women writers of Science Fiction in the twentieth century. Weird Tales *published Moore's first story in its November 1933 issue, along with stories by Edmond Hamilton, E. Hoffman Price, Clark Ashton Smith, and others. The tale, a wild Space Opera set on Mars and featuring a hero named Northwest Smith, was entitled "Shambleau." "Shambleau" received great reader response and became a Science Fiction landmark.*

Moore, born in Indianapolis in 1911, would soon become one of the most important and highly revered authors, of both genre and nongenre fiction, of the twentieth century. As was the case with her contemporary, Leigh Brackett, Moore championed women writers of Science Fiction. Like Brackett, she was influenced by the popular pulp magazines and Science Fiction authors of her youth—particularly Amazing Stories *and Edgar Rice Burroughs. In turn, she influenced a whole generation of new, burgeoning women Science Fiction authors. In the 1930s and 1940s particularly, Moore was a regular contributor to both* Weird Tales *and* Astounding, *and she published in other magazines as well, such as* Unknown (Worlds) *and* Famous Fantastic Mysteries. *Moore had two primary series characters—one was Northwest Smith (introduced in "Shambleau") and the other was a strong-willed female warrior named Jirel of Joiry (introduced in "The Black God's Kiss" in the October 1934 issue of* Weird Tales*).*

During the years of her marriage (1940–58) to famous Fantasy and Science Fiction author Henry Kuttner (1914–58), C. L. Moore collaborated with Kuttner on a number of short stories and novels, as "Lewis Padgett," "Lawrence O'Donnell," and various other pseudonyms, and under Kuttner's own byline. In 1957, Moore published her Cold War novel, Doomsday Morning. *After the death of Kuttner, she turned to writing for television; her grand Science Fiction career was all but over. Catherine Moore was dearly loved by her fellow authors and fans alike. Of the many contributions she made to Fantasy and Science Fiction, "Shambleau" remains one of the most important.*

Shambleau
(*Weird Tales, November 1933*)

Man has conquered space before. You may be sure of that. Somewhere beyond the Egyptians, in that dimness out of which come echoes of half-mythical names—Atlantis, Mu—somewhere back of history's first beginnings there must have been an age when mankind, like us today, built cities of steel to house its star-roving ships and knew the names of the planets in their own native tongues—heard Venus' people call their wet world "Shaardol" in that soft, sweet, slurring speech and mimicked Mars' guttural "Lakkdiz" from the harsh tongues of Mars' dryland dwellers. You may be sure of it. Man has conquered space before, and out of that conquest faint, faint echoes run still through a world that has forgotten the very fact of a civilization which must have been as mighty as our own. There have been too many myths and legends for us to doubt it. The myth of the Medusa, for instance, can never have had its roots in the soil of Earth. That tale of the snake-haired Gorgon whose gaze turned the gazer to stone never originated about any creature that Earth nourished. And those ancient Greeks who told the story must have remembered, dimly and half believing, a tale of antiquity about some strange being from one of the outlying planets their remotest ancestors once trod.

"SHAMBLEAU! HA . . . SHAMBLEAU!" The wild hysteria of the mob rocketed from wall to wall of Lakkdarol's narrow streets and the storming of heavy boots over the slag-red pavement made an ominous undernote to that swelling bay, "Shambleau! Shambleau!"

Northwest Smith heard it coming and stepped into the nearest doorway, laying a wary hand on his heat-gun's grip, and his colorless eyes narrowed. Strange sounds were common enough in the streets of Earth's latest colony on Mars—a raw, red little town where anything might happen, and very often did. But Northwest Smith, whose name is known and respected in every dive and wild outpost on a dozen wild planets, was a cautious man, despite his reputation. He set his back against the wall and gripped his pistol, and heard the rising shout come nearer and nearer.

Then into his range of vision flashed a red running figure, dodging like a hunted hare from shelter to shelter in the narrow street. It was a girl—a berry-brown girl in a single tattered garment whose scarlet burnt the eyes with its brilliance. She ran wearily, and he could hear her gasping breath from where he stood. As she came into view he saw her hesitate and lean one hand against the wall for support, and glance wildly around for shelter. She must not have seen him in the depths of the doorway, for as the bay of the mob grew louder and the pounding of feet sounded almost at the corner she gave a despairing little moan and dodged into the recess at his very side.

When she saw him standing there, tall and leather-brown, hand on his heat-gun, she sobbed once, inarticulately, and collapsed at his feet, a huddle of burning scarlet and bare, brown limbs.

Smith had not seen her face, but she was a girl, and sweetly made and in danger; and though he had not the reputation of a chivalrous man, something in her hopeless huddle at his feet touched that chord of sympathy for the underdog that stirs in every Earthman, and he pushed her gently into the corner behind him and jerked out his gun, just as the first of the running mob rounded the corner.

It was a motley crowd, Earthmen and Martians and a sprinkling of Venusian swampmen and strange, nameless denizens of unnamed planets—a typical Lakkdarol mob. When the first of them turned the corner and saw the empty street before them there was a faltering in the rush and the foremost spread out and began to search the doorways on both sides of the street.

"Looking for something?" Smith's sardonic call sounded clear above the clamor of the mob.

They turned. The shouting died for a moment as they took in the scene before them—tall Earthman in the space-explorer's leathern garb, all one color from the burning of savage suns save for the sinister pallor of his no-colored eyes in a scarred and resolute face, gun in his steady hand and the scarlet girl crouched behind him, panting.

The foremost of the crowd—a burly Earthman in tattered leather from which the Patrol insignia had been ripped away—stared for a moment with a strange expression of incredulity on his face overspreading the savage exultation of the chase. Then he let loose a deep-throated bellow, "Shambleau!" and lunged forward. Behind him the mob took up the cry again, "Shambleau! Shambleau! Shambleau!" and surged after.

Smith, lounging negligently against the wall, arms folded and gun-hand draped over his left forearm, looked incapable of swift motion, but at the leader's first forward step the pistol swept in a practiced half-circle and the dazzle of blue-white heat leaping from its muzzle seared an arc in the slag pavement at his feet. It was an old gesture, and not a man in the crowd but understood it. The foremost recoiled swiftly against the surge of those in the rear, and for a moment there was confusion as the two tides met and struggled. Smith's mouth curled into a grim curve as he watched.

The man in the mutilated Patrol uniform lifted a threatening fist and stepped to the very edge of the deadline, while the crowd rocked to and fro behind him.

"Are you crossing that line?" queried Smith in an ominously gentle voice.

"We want that girl!"

"Come and get her!" Recklessly Smith grinned into his face. He saw danger there, but his defiance was not the foolhardy gesture it seemed. An expert psychologist of mobs from long experience, he sensed no murder here. Not a gun had appeared in any hand in the crowd. They desired the girl with an inexplicable bloodthirstiness he was at a loss to understand, but toward himself he sensed no such fury. A mauling he might expect, but his life was in no danger. Guns would have appeared before now if they were coming out at all. So he grinned in the man's angry face and leaned lazily against the wall.

Behind their self-appointed leader the crowd milled impatiently, and threatening voices began to rise again. Smith heard the girl moan at his feet.

"What do you want with her?" he demanded.

"She's Shambleau! Shambleau, you fool! Kick her out of there—we'll take care of her!"

"I'm taking care of her," drawled Smith.

"She's Shambleau, I tell you! Damn your hide, man, we never let those things live! Kick her out here!"

The repeated name had no meaning to him, but Smith's innate stubbornness rose defiantly as the crowd surged forward to the very edge of the arc, their clamor growing louder. "Shambleau! Kick her out here! Give us Shambleau! Shambleau!"

Smith dropped his indolent pose like a cloak and planted both feet wide, swinging up his gun threateningly. "Keep back!" he yelled. "She's mine! Keep back!"

He had no intention of using that heat-beam. He knew by now that they would not kill him unless he started the gunplay himself, and he did not mean to give up his life for any girl alive. But a severe mauling he expected, and he braced himself instinctively as the mob heaved within itself.

To his astonishment a thing happened then that he had never known to happen before. At his shouted defiance the foremost of the mob—those who had heard him clearly—drew back a little, not in alarm but evidently surprised. The ex-Patrolman said, "Yours! She's *yours?*" in a voice from which puzzlement crowded out the anger.

Smith spread his booted legs wide before the crouching figure and flourished his gun.

"Yes," he said. "And I'm keeping her! Stand back there!"

The man stared at him wordlessly, and horror, disgust and incredulity mingled on his weather-beaten face. The incredulity triumphed for a moment and he said again, "*Yours!*"

Smith nodded defiance.

The man stepped back suddenly, unutterable contempt in his very pose. He waved an arm to the crowd and said loudly, "It's—his!" and the press melted away, gone silent, too, and the look of contempt spread from face to face.

The ex-Patrolman spat on the slag-paved street and turned his back indifferently. "Keep her, then," he advised briefly over one shoulder. "But don't let her out again in this town!"

Smith stared in perplexity almost open-mouthed as the suddenly scornful mob began to break up. His mind was in a whirl. That such bloodthirsty animosity should vanish in a breath he could not believe. And the curious mingling of contempt and disgust on the faces he saw baffled him even more. Lakkdarol was anything but a puritan town—it did not enter his head for a moment that his claiming the brown girl as his own had caused that strangely shocked revulsion to spread through the crowd. No, it was something more deeply rooted than that. Instinctive, instant disgust had been in the faces he saw—they would have looked less so if he had admitted cannibalism or *Pharol*-worship.

And they were leaving his vicinity as swiftly as if whatever unknowing sin he had committed were contagious. The street was emptying as rapidly as it had filled. He saw a sleek Venusian glance back over his shoulder as he turned the corner and sneer, "Shambleau!" and the word awoke a new line of speculation in Smith's mind. Shambleau! Vaguely of French origin, it must be. And strange enough to hear it from the lips of Venusians and Martian drylanders, but it was their use of it that puzzled him more. "We never let those things live," the ex-Patrolman had said. It reminded him dimly of something . . . an ancient line from some writing in his own tongue . . . "Thou shalt not suffer a witch to live." He smiled to himself at the similarity, and simultaneously was aware of the girl at his elbow.

She had risen soundlessly. He turned to face her, sheathing his gun, and stared at first with curiosity and then in the entirely frank openness with which men regard that which is not wholly human. For she was not. He knew it at a glance, though the brown, sweet body was shaped like a woman's and she wore the garment of scarlet—he saw it was leather—with an ease that few unhuman beings achieve toward clothing. He knew it from the moment he looked into her eyes, and a shiver of unrest went over him as he met them. They were frankly green as young grass, with slit-like, feline pupils that pulsed unceasingly, and there was a look of dark, animal wisdom in their depths—that look of the beast which sees more than man.

There was no hair upon her face—neither brows nor lashes, and he would have sworn that the tight scarlet turban bound-around her head covered baldness. She had three fingers and a thumb, and her feet had four digits apiece too, and all sixteen of them were tipped with round claws that sheathed back into the flesh like a cat's. She ran her tongue over her lips—a thin, pink, flat tongue as feline as her eyes—and spoke with difficulty. He felt that that throat and tongue had never been shaped for human speech.

"Not—afraid now," she said softly, and her little teeth were white and pointed as a kitten's.

"What did they want you for?" he asked her curiously. "What had you done? Shambleau . . . is that your name?"

"I—not talk your—speech," she demurred hesitantly.

"Well, try to—I want to know. Why were they chasing you? Will you be safe on the street now, or hadn't you better get indoors somewhere? They looked dangerous."

"I—go with you," She brought it out with difficulty.

"Say you!" Smith grinned. "What are you, anyhow? You look like a kitten to me."

"Shambleau." She said it somberly.

"Where d'you live? Are you a Martian?"

"I come from—from far—from long ago—far country——"

"Wait!" laughed Smith. "You're getting your wires crossed. You're not a Martian?"

She drew herself up very straight beside him, lifting the turbaned head, and there was something queenly in the poise of her.

"Martian?" she said scornfully. "My people—are—are—you have no word. Your speech—hard for me."

"What's yours? I might know it—try me."

She lifted her head and met his eyes squarely, and there was in hers a subtle amusement—he could have sworn it.

"Some day I—speak to you in—my own language," she promised, and the pink tongue flicked out over her lips, swiftly, hungrily.

Approaching footsteps on the red pavement interrupted Smith's reply. A dryland Martian came past, reeling a little and exuding an aroma of *segir*-whisky, the Venusian brand. When he caught the red flash of the girl's tatters he turned his head sharply, and as his *segir*-steeped brain took in the fact of her presence he lurched toward the recess unsteadily, bawling, "Shambleau, by *Pharol!* Shambleau!" and reached out a clutching hand.

Smith struck it aside contemptuously.

"On your way, drylander," he advised.

The man drew back and stared, blear-eyed.

"Yours, eh?" he croaked. "*Zut!* You're welcome to it!" And like the ex-Patrolman before him he spat on the pavement and turned away, muttering harshly in the blasphemous tongue of the drylands.

Smith watched him shuffle off, and there was a crease between his colorless eyes, a nameless unease rising within him.

"Come on," he said abruptly to the girl. "If this sort of thing is going to happen we'd better get indoors. Where shall I take you?"

"With—you," she murmured.

He stared down into the flat green eyes. Those ceaselessly pulsing pupils disturbed him, but it seemed to him, vaguely, that behind the animal shallows of her gaze was a shutter—a closed barrier that might at any moment open to reveal the very deeps of that dark knowledge he sensed there.

Roughly he said again, "Come on, then," and stepped down into the street.

She pattered along a pace or two behind him, making no effort to keep up with his long strides, and though Smith—as men know from Venus to Jupiter's moons—walks as softly as a cat, even in spacemen's boots, the girl at his heels slid like a shadow over the rough pavement, making so little sound that even the lightness of his footsteps was loud in the empty street.

Smith chose the less frequented ways of Lakkdarol, and somewhat shamefacedly thanked his nameless gods that his lodgings were not far away, for the few pedestrians he met turned and stared after the two with that by now familiar mingling of horror and contempt which he was as far as ever from understanding.

The room he had engaged was a single cubicle in a lodging-house on the edge of the city. Lakkdarol, raw camp-town that it was in those days, could have furnished little better anywhere within its limits, and Smith's errand there was not one he wished to advertise. He had slept in worse places than this before, and knew that he would do so again.

There was no one in sight when he entered, and the girl slipped up the stairs at his heels and vanished through the door, shadowy, unseen by anyone in the house. Smith closed the door and leaned his broad shoulders against the panels, regarding her speculatively.

She took in what little the room had to offer in a glance—frowsy bed, rickety table, mirror hanging unevenly and cracked against the wall, unpainted chairs—a typical camp-town room in an Earth settlement abroad. She accepted its poverty in that single glance, dismissed it, then crossed to the window and leaned out for a moment, gazing across the low roof-tops toward the barren countryside beyond, red slag under the late afternoon sun.

"You can stay here," said Smith abruptly, "until I leave town. I'm waiting here for a friend to come in from Venus. Have you eaten?"

"Yes," said the girl quickly. "I shall—need no—food for—a while."

"Well—" Smith glanced around the room. "I'll be in sometime tonight. You can go or stay just as you please. Better lock the door behind me."

With no more formality than that he left her. The door closed and he heard the key turn, and smiled to himself. He did not expect, then, ever to see her again.

He went down the steps and out into the late-slanting sunlight with a mind so full of other matters that the brown girl receded very quickly into the background. Smith's errand in Lakkdarol, like most of his errands, is better not spoken of. Man lives as he must, and Smith's living was a perilous affair outside the law and ruled by the ray-gun only. It is enough to say that the shipping-port and its cargoes outbound interested him deeply just now, and that the friend he awaited was Yarol the Venusian, in that swift little Edsel ship the *Maid* that can flash from world to world with a derisive speed that laughs at Patrol boats and leaves pursuers floundering in the ether far behind. Smith and Yarol and the *Maid* were a trinity that had caused the Patrol leaders much worry and many gray hairs in the past, and the future looked very bright to Smith himself that evening as he left his lodging-house.

Lakkdarol roars by night, as Earthmen's camp-towns have a way of doing on every planet where Earth's outposts are, and it was beginning lustily as Smith went down among the awakening lights toward the center of town. His business there does not concern us. He mingled with the crowds where the lights were brightest, and there was the click of ivory counters and the jingle of silver, and red *segir* gurgled invitingly from black Venusian bottles, and much later Smith strolled homeward under the moving moons of Mars, and if the street wavered a little under his feet now and then—why, that is only understandable. Not even Smith could drink red *segir* at every bar from the *Martian Lamb* to the *New Chicago* and remain entirely steady on his feet. But he found his way back with very little difficulty—considering—and spent a good five minutes hunting for his key before he remembered he had left it in the inner lock for the girl.

He knocked then, and there was no sound of footsteps from within, but in a few moments the latch clicked and the door swung open. She retreated soundlessly before him as he entered, and took up her favorite place against the window, leaning back on the sill and outlined against the starry sky beyond. The room was in darkness.

Smith flipped the switch by the door and then leaned back against the panels, steadying himself. The cool night air had sobered him a little, and his head was clear enough—liquor went to Smith's feet, not his head, or he would never have come this far along the lawless way he had chosen. He lounged against the door now and regarded the girl in the sudden glare of the bulbs, blinking a little as much at the scarlet of her clothing as at the light.

"So you stayed," he said.

"I—waited," she answered softly, leaning farther back against the sill and clasping the rough wood with slim, three-fingered hands, pale brown against the darkness.

"Why?"

She did not answer that, but her mouth curved into a slow smile. On a woman it would have been reply enough—provocative, daring. On Shambleau there was something pitiful and horrible in it—so human on the face of one half-animal. And yet . . . that sweet brown body curving so softly from the tatters of scarlet leather—the velvety texture of that brownness—the white-flashing smile. . . . Smith was aware of a stirring excitement within him. After all—time would be hanging heavy now until Yarol came. . . . Speculatively he allowed the steel-pale eyes to wander over her, with a slow regard that missed nothing. And when he spoke he was aware that his voice had deepened a little. . . .

"Come here," he said.

She came forward slowly, on bare clawed feet that made no sound on the floor, and stood before him with downcast eyes and mouth trembling in that pitifully human smile. He took her by the shoulders—velvety soft shoulders, of a creamy smoothness that was not the texture of human flesh. A little tremor went over her, perceptibly, at the contact of his hands. Northwest Smith caught his breath suddenly and dragged her to him . . . sweet yielding brownness in the circle of his arms . . . heard her own breath catch and quicken as her velvety arms closed about his neck. And then he was looking down into her face, very near, and the green animal eyes met his with the pulsing pupils and the flicker of—something—deep behind their shallows—and through the rising clamor of his blood, even as he stooped his lips to hers, Smith felt something deep within him shudder away—inexplicable, instinctive, revolted. What it might be he had no words to tell, but the very touch of her was suddenly loathsome—so soft and velvet and un-human—and it might have been an animal's face that lifted itself to his mouth—the dark knowledge looked hungrily from the darkness of those slit pupils—and for a mad instant he knew that same wild, feverish revulsion he had seen in the faces of the mob. . . .

"God!" he gasped, a far more ancient invocation against evil than he realized, then or ever, and he ripped her arms from his neck, swung her away with such a force that she reeled half across the room. Smith fell back against the door, breathing heavily, and stared at her while the wild revolt died slowly within him.

She had fallen to the floor beneath the window, and as she lay there against the wall with bent head he saw, curiously, that her turban had slipped—the turban that he had been so sure covered baldness—and a lock of scarlet hair fell below the binding leather, hair as scarlet as her garment, as unhumanly red as her eyes were unhumanly green. He stared, and shook his head dizzily and stared again, for it seemed to him that the thick lock of crimson had moved, *squirmed* of itself against her cheek.

At the contact of it her hands flew up and she tucked it away with a very human gesture and then dropped her head again into her hands. And from the deep shadow of her fingers he thought she was staring up at him covertly.

Smith drew a deep breath and passed a hand across his forehead. The inexplicable moment had gone as quickly as it came—too swiftly for him to understand or analyze it. "Got to lay off the *segir*," he told himself unsteadily. Had he imagined that scarlet hair? After all, she was no more than a pretty brown girl-creature from one of the many half-human races peopling the planets. No more than that, after all. A pretty little thing, but animal. . . . He laughed a little shakily.

"No more of that," he said. "God knows I'm no angel, but there's got to be a limit somewhere. Here." He crossed to the bed and sorted out a pair of blankets from the untidy heap, tossing them to the far corner of the room. "You can sleep there."

Wordlessly she rose from the floor and began to rearrange the blankets, the uncomprehending resignation of the animal eloquent in every line of her.

Smith had a strange dream that night. He thought he had awakened to a room full of darkness and moonlight and moving shadows, for the nearer moon of Mars was racing through the sky and everything on the planet below her was endued with a restless life in the dark. And something . . . some nameless, unthinkable *thing* . . . was coiled about his throat . . . something like a soft snake, wet and warm. It lay loose and light about his neck . . . and it was moving gently, very gently, with a soft, caressive pressure that sent little thrills of delight through every nerve and fiber of him, a perilous delight—beyond physical pleasure, deeper than joy of the mind. That warm softness was caressing the very roots of his soul with a terrible intimacy. The ecstasy of it left him weak, and yet he knew—in a flash of knowledge born of this impossible dream—that the soul should not be handled. . . . And with that knowledge a horror broke upon him, turning the pleasure into a rapture of revulsion, hateful, horrible—but still most foully sweet. He tried to lift his hands and tear the dream-monstrosity from his throat—tried but half-heartedly; for though his soul was revolted to its very deeps, yet the delight of his body was so great that his hands all but refused the attempt. But when at last he tried to lift his arms a cold shock went over him and he found that he could not stir . . . his body lay stony as marble beneath the blankets, a living marble that shuddered with a dreadful delight through every rigid vein.

The revulsion grew strong upon him as he struggled against the paralyzing dream—a struggle of soul against sluggish body—titanically, until the moving dark was streaked with blankness that clouded and closed about him at last and he sank back into the oblivion from which he had awakened.

Next morning, when the bright sunlight shining through Mars' clear thin air awakened him, Smith lay for a while trying to remember. The dream had been more vivid than reality, but he could not now quite recall . . . only that it had been more sweet and horrible than anything else in life. He lay puzzling for a while, until a soft sound from the corner aroused him from his thoughts and he sat up to see the girl lying in a catlike coil on her blankets, watching him with round, grave eyes. He regarded her somewhat ruefully.

"Morning," he said. "I've just had the devil of a dream. . . . Well, hungry?"

She shook her head silently, and he could have sworn there was a covert gleam of strange amusement in her eyes.

He stretched and yawned, dismissing the nightmare temporarily from his mind.

"What am I going to do with you?" he inquired, turning to more immediate matters. "I'm leaving here in a day or two and I can't take you along, you know. Where'd you come from in the first place?"

Again she shook her head.

"Not telling? Well, it's your own business. You can stay here until I give up the room. From then on you'll have to do your own worrying."

He swung his feet to the floor and reached for his clothes.

Ten minutes later, slipping the heat-gun into its holster at his thigh, Smith turned to the girl. "There's food-concentrate in that box on the table. It ought to hold you until I get back. And you'd better lock the door again after I've gone."

Her wide, unwavering stare was his only answer, and he was not sure she had understood, but at any rate the lock clicked after him as before, and he went down the steps with a faint grin on his lips.

The memory of last night's extraordinary dream was slipping from him, as such memories do, and by the time he had reached the street the girl and the dream and all of yesterday's happenings were blotted out by the sharp necessities of the present.

Again the intricate business that had brought him here claimed his attention. He went about it to the exclusion of all else, and there was a good reason behind everything he did from the moment he stepped out into the street until the time when he turned back again at evening; though had one chosen to follow him during the day his apparently aimless rambling through Lakkdarol would have seemed very pointless.

He must have spent two hours at the least idling by the space-port, watching with sleepy, colorless eyes the ships that came and went, the passengers, the vessels lying at wait, the cargoes—particularly the cargoes. He made the rounds of the town's saloons once more, consuming many glasses of varied liquors in the course of the day and engaging in idle conversation with men of all races and worlds, usually in their own languages, for Smith was a linguist of repute among his contemporaries. He heard the gossip of the spaceways, news from a dozen planets of a thousand different events. He heard the latest joke about the Venusian Emperor and the latest report on the Chino-Aryan war and the latest song hot from the lips of Rose Robertson, whom every man on the civilized planets adored as "the Georgia Rose." He passed the day quite profitably, for his own purposes, which do not concern us now, and it was not until late evening, when he turned homeward again, that the thought of the brown girl in his room took definite shape in his mind, though it had been lurking there, formless and submerged, all day.

He had no idea what comprised her usual diet, but he bought a can of New York roast beef and one of Venusian frog-broth and a dozen fresh canal-apples and two pounds of that Earth lettuce that grows so vigorously in the fertile canal-soil of Mars. He felt that she must surely find something to her liking in this broad variety of edibles, and—for his day had been very satisfactory—he hummed *The Green Hills of Earth* to himself in a surprisingly good baritone as he climbed the stairs.

The door was locked, as before, and he was reduced to kicking the lower panels gently with his boot, for his arms were full. She opened the door with that softness that was characteristic of her and stood regarding him in the semi-darkness as he stumbled to the table with his load. The room was unlit again.

"Why don't you turn on the lights?" he demanded irritably after he had barked his shin on the chair by the table in an effort to deposit his burden there.

"Light and—dark—they are alike—to me," she murmured.

"Cat eyes, eh? Well, you look the part. Here, I've brought you some dinner. Take your choice. Fond of roast beef? Or how about a little frog-broth?"

She shook her head and backed away a step.

"No," she said. "I can not—eat your food."

Smith's brows wrinkled. "Didn't you have any of the food tablets?"

Again the red turban shook negatively.

"Then you haven't had anything for—why, more than twenty-four hours! You must be starved."

"Not hungry," she denied.

"What can I find for you to eat, then? There's time yet if I hurry. You've got to eat, child."

"I shall—eat," she said softly. "Before long—I shall—feed. Have no—worry."

She turned away then and stood at the window, looking out over the moonlit landscape as if to end the conversation. Smith cast her a puzzled glance as he opened the can of roast beef. There had been an odd undernote in that assurance that, undefinably, he did not like. And the girl had teeth and tongue and presumably a fairly human digestive system, to judge from her human form. It was nonsense for her to pretend that he could find nothing that she could eat. She must have had some of the food concentrate after all, he decided, prying up the thermos lid of the inner container to release the long-sealed savor of the hot meat inside.

"Well, if you won't eat you won't," he observed philosophically as he poured hot broth and diced beef into the dishlike lid of the thermos can and extracted the spoon from its hiding-place between the inner and outer receptacles. She turned a little to watch him as he pulled up a rickety chair and sat down to the food, and after a while the realization that her green gaze was fixed so unwinkingly upon him made the man nervous, and he said between bites of creamy canal-apple, "Why don't you try a little of this? It's good."

"The food—I eat is—better," her soft voice told him in its hesitant murmur, and again he felt rather than heard a faint undernote of unpleasantness in the words. A sudden suspicion struck him as he pondered on that last remark—some vague memory of horror-tales told about campfires in the past—and he swung round in the chair to look at her, a tiny, creeping fear unaccountably arising. There had been that in her words—in her unspoken words, that menaced. . . .

She stood up beneath his gaze demurely, wide green eyes with their pulsing pupils meeting his without a falter. But her mouth was scarlet and her teeth were sharp. . . .

"What food do you eat?" he demanded. And then, after a pause, very softly, "Blood?"

She stared at him for a moment, uncomprehending; then something like amusement curled her lips and she said scornfully, "You think me—vampire, eh? No—I am Shambleau!"

Unmistakably there were scorn and amusement in her voice at the suggestion, but as unmistakably she knew what he meant—accepted it as a logical suspicion— vampires! Fairy tales—but fairy tales this unhuman, outland creature was most familiar with. Smith was not a credulous man, nor a superstitious one, but he had seen too many strange things himself to doubt that the wildest legend might have a basis of fact. And there was something namelessly strange about her. . . .

He puzzled over it for a while between deep bites of the canal-apple. And though he wanted to question her about a great many things, he did not, for he knew how futile it would be.

He said nothing more until the meat was finished and another canal-apple had followed the first, and he had cleared away the meal by the simple expedient of tossing the empty can out of the window. Then he lay back in the chair and surveyed her from half-closed eyes, colorless in a face tanned like saddle-leather. And again he was conscious of the brown, soft curves of her, velvety—subtle arcs and planes of smooth flesh under the tatters of scarlet leather. Vampire she might be, unhuman she certainly was, but desirable beyond words as she sat submissive beneath his low regard, her red-turbaned head bent, her clawed fingers lying in her lap. They sat very still for a while, and the silence throbbed between them.

She was so like a woman—an Earth woman—sweet and submissive and demure, and softer than soft fur, if he could forget the three-fingered claws and the pulsing eyes—and that deeper strangeness beyond words. . . . (Had he dreamed that red lock of hair that moved? Had it been *segir* that woke the wild revulsion he knew when he held her in his arms? Why had the mob so thirsted for her?) He sat and stared, and despite the mystery of her and the half-suspicions that thronged his mind—for she was so beautifully soft and curved under those revealing tatters—he slowly realized that his pulses were mounting, became aware of a kindling within . . . brown girl-creature with downcast eyes . . . and then the lids lifted and the green flatness of a cat's gaze met his, and last night's revulsion woke swiftly again, like a warning bell that clanged as their eyes met—animal, after all, too sleek and soft for humanity, and that inner strangeness. . . .

Smith shrugged and sat up. His failings were legion, but the weakness of the flesh was not among the major ones. He motioned the girl to her pallet of blankets in the corner and turned to his own bed.

From deeps of sound sleep he awoke much later. He awoke suddenly and completely, and with that inner excitement that presages something momentous. He awoke to brilliant moonlight, turning the room so bright that he could see the scarlet of the girl's rags as she sat up on her pallet. She was awake, she was sitting with her shoulder half turned to him and her head bent, and some warning instinct crawled coldly up his spine as he watched what she was doing. And yet it was a very ordinary thing for a girl to do—any girl, anywhere. She was unbinding her turban. . . .

He watched, not breathing, a presentiment of something horrible stirring in his brain, inexplicably. . . . The red folds loosened, and—he knew then that he had not dreamed—again a scarlet lock swung down against her cheek . . . a hair, was it? a lock of hair? . . . thick as a thick worm it fell, plumply, against that smooth cheek . . . more scarlet than blood and thick as a crawling worm . . . and like a worm it crawled.

Smith rose on an elbow, not realizing the motion, and fixed an unwinking stare, with a sort of sick, fascinated incredulity, on that—that lock of hair. He had not dreamed. Until now he had taken it for granted that it was the *segir* which had made it seem to move on that evening before. But now . . . it was lengthening, stretching, moving of itself. It must be hair, but it *crawled;* with a sickening life of its own it squirmed down against her cheek, caressingly, revoltingly, impossibly. . . . Wet, it was, and round and thick and shining. . . .

She unfastened the fast fold and whipped the turban off. From what he saw then Smith would have turned his eyes away—and he had looked on dreadful things before, without flinching—but he could not stir. He could only lie there on his elbow staring at the mass of scarlet, squirming—worms, hairs, what?—that writhed over her head in a dreadful mockery of ringlets. And it was lengthening, falling, somehow growing before his eyes, down over her shoulders in a spilling cascade, a mass that even at the beginning could never have been hidden under the skull-tight turban she had worn. He was beyond wondering, but he realized that. And still it squirmed and lengthened and fell, and she shook it out in a horrible travesty of a woman shaking out her unbound hair—until the unspeakable tangle of it—twisting, writhing, obscenely scarlet—hung to her waist and beyond, and still lengthened, an endless mass of crawling horror that until now, somehow, impossibly, had been hidden under the tight-bound turban. It was like a nest of blind, restless red worms . . . it was—it was like naked entrails endowed with an unnatural aliveness, terrible beyond words.

Smith lay in the shadows, frozen without and within in a sick numbness that came of utter shock and revulsion.

She shook out the obscene, unspeakable tangle over her shoulders, and somehow he knew that she was going to turn in a moment and that he must meet her eyes. The thought of that meeting stopped his heart with dread, more awfully than anything else in this nightmare horror; for nightmare it must be, surely. But he knew without trying that he could not wrench his eyes away—the sickened fascination of that sight held him motionless, and somehow there was a certain beauty. . . .

Her head was turning. The crawling awfulnesses rippled and squirmed at the motion, writhing thick and wet and shining over the soft brown shoulders about which they fell now in obscene cascades that all but hid her body. Her head was turning. Smith lay numb. And very slowly he saw the round of her cheek foreshorten and her profile come into view, all the scarlet horrors twisting ominously, and the profile shortened in turn and her full face came slowly round toward the bed—moonlight shining brilliantly as day on the pretty girl-face, demure and sweet, framed in tangled obscenity that crawled. . . .

The green eyes met his. He felt a perceptible shock, and a shudder rippled down his paralyzed spine, leaving an icy numbness in its wake. He felt the gooseflesh rising. But that numbness and cold horror he scarcely realized, for the green eyes were locked with his in a long, long look that somehow presaged nameless things—not altogether unpleasant things—the voiceless voice of her mind assailing him with little murmurous promises. . . .

For a moment he went down into a blind abyss of submission; and then somehow the very sight of that obscenity in eyes that did not then realize they saw it, was dreadful enough to draw him out of the seductive darkness . . . the sight of her crawling and alive with unnameable horror.

She rose, and down about her in a cascade fell the squirming scarlet of—of what grew upon her head. It fell in a long, alive cloak to her bare feet on the floor, hiding her in a wave of dreadful, wet, writhing life. She put up her hands and like a swimmer she parted the waterfall of it, tossing the masses back over her shoulders to reveal her own brown body, sweetly curved. She smiled exquisitely, and in starting waves back from her forehead and down about her in a hideous background writhed the snaky wetness of her living tresses. And Smith knew that he looked upon Medusa.

The knowledge of that—the realization of vast backgrounds reaching into misted history shook him out of his frozen horror for a moment, and in that moment he met her eyes again, smiling, green as glass in the moonlight, half hooded under drooping lids. Through the twisting scarlet she held out her arms. And there was something soul-shakingly desirable about her, so that all the blood surged to his head suddenly and he stumbled to his feet like a sleeper in a dream as she swayed toward him, infinitely graceful, infinitely sweet in her cloak of living horror.

And somehow there was beauty in it, the wet scarlet writhings with moonlight sliding and shining along the thick, worm-round tresses and losing itself in the masses only to glint again and move silvery along writhing tendrils—an awful, shuddering beauty more dreadful than any ugliness could be.

But all this, again, he but half realized, for the insidious murmur was coiling again through his brain, promising, caressing, alluring, sweeter than honey; and the green eyes that held his were clear and burning like the depths of a jewel, and behind the pulsing slits of darkness he was staring into a greater dark that held all things. . . . He had known—dimly he had known when he first gazed into those flat animal shallows that behind them lay this—all beauty and terror, all horror and delight, in the infinite darkness upon which her eyes opened like windows, paned with emerald glass.

Her lips moved, and in a murmur that blended indistinguishably with the silence and the sway of her body and the dreadful sway of her—her hair—she whispered—very softly, very passionately, "I shall—speak to you now—in my own tongue—oh, beloved!"

And in her living cloak she swayed to him, the murmur swelling seductive and caressing in his innermost brain—promising, compelling, sweeter than sweet. His flesh crawled to the horror of her, but it was a perverted revulsion that clasped what it loathed. His arms slid round her under the sliding cloak, wet, wet and warm and hideously alive—and the sweet velvet body was clinging to his, her arms locked about his neck—and with a whisper and a rush the unspeakable horror closed about them both.

In nightmares until he died he remembered that moment when the living tresses of Shambleau first folded him in their embrace. A nauseous, smothering odor as the wetness shut around him—thick, pulsing worms clasping every inch of his body, sliding, writhing, their wetness and warmth striking through his garments as if he stood naked to their embrace.

All this in a graven instant—and after that a tangled flash of conflicting sensation before oblivion closed over him. For he remembered the dream—and knew it for nightmare reality now, and the sliding, gently moving caresses of those wet, warm worms upon his flesh was an ecstasy above words—that deeper ecstasy that strikes beyond the body and beyond the mind and tickles the very roots of the soul with unnatural delight. So he stood, rigid as marble, as helplessly stony as any of Medusa's victims in ancient legends were, while the terrible pleasure of Shambleau thrilled and shuddered through every fiber of him; through every atom of his body and the intangible atoms of what men call the soul, through all that was Smith the dreadful pleasure ran. And it was truly dreadful. Dimly he knew it, even as his body answered to the root-deep ecstasy, a foul and dreadful wooing from which his very soul shuddered away—and yet in the innermost depths of that soul some grinning traitor shivered with delight. But deeply, behind all this, he knew horror and revulsion and despair beyond telling, while the intimate caresses crawled obscenely in the secret places of his soul—knew that the soul should not be handled—and shook with the perilous pleasure through it all.

And this conflict and knowledge, this mingling of rapture and revulsion all took place in the flashing of a moment while the scarlet worms coiled and crawled upon him, sending deep, obscene tremors of that infinite pleasure into every atom that made up Smith. And he could not stir in that slimy, ecstatic embrace—and a weakness was flooding that grew deeper after each succeeding wave of intense delight, and the traitor in his soul strengthened and drowned out the revulsion—and something within him ceased to struggle as he sank wholly into a blazing darkness that was oblivion to all else but that devouring rapture. . . .

The young Venusian climbing the stairs to his friend's lodging-room pulled out his key absent-mindedly, a pucker forming between his fine brows. He was slim, as all Venusians are, as fair and sleek as any of them, and as with most of his country-men the look of cherubic innocence on his face was wholly deceptive. He had the face of a fallen angel, without Lucifer's majesty to redeem it; for a black devil grinned in his eyes and there were faint lines of ruthlessness and dissipation about his mouth to tell of the long years behind him that had run the gamut of experi-ences and made his name, next to Smith's, the most hated and the most respected in the records of the Patrol.

He mounted the stairs now with a puzzled frown between his eyes. He had come into Lakkdarol on the noon liner—the *Maid* in her hold very skillfully dis-guised with paint and otherwise—to find in lamentable disorder the affairs he had expected to be settled. And cautious inquiry elicited the information that Smith had not been seen for three days. That was not like his friend—he had never failed before, and the two stood to lose not only a large sum of money but also their personal safety by the inexplicable lapse on the part of Smith. Yarol could think of one solution only: fate had at last caught up with his friend. Nothing but physical disability could explain it.

Still puzzling, he fitted his key in the lock and swung the door open.

In that first moment, as the door opened, he sensed something very wrong. . . . The room was darkened, and for a while he could see nothing, but at the first breath he scented a strange, unnameable odor, half sickening, half sweet. And deep stirrings of ancestral memory awoke him—ancient swamp-born memo-ries from Venusian ancestors far away and long ago. . . .

Yarol laid his hand on his gun, lightly, and opened the door wider. In the dim-ness all he could see at first was a curious mound in the far corner. . . . Then his eyes grew accustomed to the dark, and saw it more clearly, a mound that somehow heaved and stirred within itself. . . . A mound of—he caught his breath sharply—a mound like a mass of entrails, living, moving, writhing with an un-speakable aliveness. Then a hot Venusian oath broke from his lips and he cleared the door-sill in a swift stride, slammed the door and set his back against it, gun ready in his hand, although his flesh crawled—for he *knew*. . . .

"Smith!" he said softly, in a voice thick with horror. "Northwest!"

The moving mass stirred—shuddered—sank back into crawling quiescence again.

"Smith! Smith!" The Venusian's voice was gentle and insistent, and it quivered a little with terror.

An impatient ripple went over the whole mass of aliveness in the corner. It stirred again, reluctantly, and then tendril by writhing tendril it began to part it-self and fall aside, and very slowly the brown of a spaceman's leather appeared be-neath it, all slimed and shining.

"Smith! Northwest!" Yarol's persistent whisper came again, urgently, and with a dreamlike slowness the leather garments moved . . . a man sat up in the midst of the writhing worms, a man who once, long ago, might have been Northwest Smith. From head to foot he was slimy from the embrace of the crawling horror about him. His face was that of some creature beyond humanity—dead-alive, fixed in a gray stare, and the look of terrible ecstasy that overspread it seemed to come from somewhere far within, a faint reflection from immeasurable distances beyond the flesh. And as there is mystery and magic in the moonlight which is af-ter all but a reflection of the everyday sun, so in that gray face turned to the door was a terror unnameable and sweet, a reflection of ecstasy beyond the understanding of any who have known only earthly ecstasy themselves. And as he sat there turning a blank, eyeless face to Yarol the red worms writhed ceaselessly about him, very gently, with a soft, caressive motion that never slacked.

"Smith . . . come here! Smith . . . get up . . . Smith, Smith!" Yarol's whisper hissed in the silence, commanding, urgent—but he made no move to leave the door.

And with a dreadful slowness, like a dead man rising, Smith stood up in the nest of slimy scarlet. He swayed drunkenly on his feet, and two or three crimson tendrils came writhing up his legs to the knees and wound themselves there, supportingly, moving with a ceaseless caress that seemed to give him some hidden strength, for he said then, without inflection,

"Go away. Go away. Leave me alone." And the dead ecstatic face never changed.

"Smith!" Yarol's voice was desperate. "Smith, listen! Smith, can't you hear me?"

"Go away," the monotonous voice said. "Go away. Go away. Go—"

"Not unless you come too. Can't you hear? Smith! Smith! I'll—"

He hushed in mid-phrase, and once more the ancestral prickle of race-memory shivered down his back, for the scarlet mass was moving again, violently, rising. . . .

Yarol pressed back against the door and gripped his gun, and the name of a god he had forgotten years ago rose to his lips unbidden. For he knew what was coming next, and the knowledge was more dreadful than any ignorance could have been.

The red, writhing mass rose higher, and the tendrils parted and a human face looked out—no, half human, with green cat-eyes that shone in that dimness like lighted jewels, compellingly. . . .

Yarol breathed "Shar!" again, and flung up an arm across his face, and the tingle of meeting that green gaze for even an instant went thrilling through him perilously.

"Smith!" he called in despair. "Smith, can't you hear me?"

"Go away," said that voice that was not Smith's. "Go away."

And somehow, although he dared not look, Yarol knew that the—the other—had parted those worm-thick tresses and stood there in all the human sweetness of the brown, curved woman's body, cloaked in living horror. And he felt the eyes upon him, and something was crying insistently in his brain to lower that shielding arm. . . . He was lost—he knew it, and the knowledge gave him that courage which comes from despair. The voice in his brain was growing, swelling, deafening him with a roaring command that all but swept him before it—command to lower that arm—to meet the eyes that opened upon darkness—to submit—and a promise, murmurous and sweet and evil beyond words, of pleasure to come. . . .

But somehow he kept his head—somehow, dizzily, he was gripping his gun in his upflung hand—somehow, incredibly, crossing the narrow room with averted face, groping for Smith's shoulder. There was a moment of blind fumbling in emptiness, and then he found it, and gripped the leather that was slimy and dreadful and wet—and simultaneously he felt something loop gently about his ankle and a shock of repulsive pleasure went through him, and then another coil, and another, wound about his feet. . . .

Yarol set his teeth and gripped the shoulder hard, and his hand shuddered of it-self, for the feel of that leather was slimy as the worms about his ankles, and a faint tingle of obscene delight went through him from the contact.

That caressive pressure on his legs was all he could feel, and the voice in his brain drowned out all other sounds, and his body obeyed him reluctantly—but somehow he gave one heave of tremendous effort and swung Smith, stumbling, out of that nest of horror. The twining tendrils ripped loose with a little sucking sound, and the whole mass quivered and reached after, and then Yarol forgot his friend utterly and turned his whole being to the hopeless task of freeing himself. For only a part of him was fighting, now—only a part of him struggled against the twining obscenities, and in his innermost brain the sweet, seductive murmur sounded, and his body clamored to surrender. . . .

"*Shar! Shar y'danis* . . . *Shar mor'la-rol*—" prayed Yarol, gasping and half un-conscious that he spoke, boy's prayers that he had forgotten years ago, and with his back half turned to the central mass he kicked desperately with his heavy boots at the red, writhing worms about him. They gave back before him, quivering and curling themselves out of reach, and though he knew that more were reaching for his throat from behind, at least he could go on struggling until he was forced to meet those eyes. . . .

He stamped and kicked and stamped again, and for one instant he was free of the slimy grip as the bruised worms curled back from his heavy feet, and he lurched away dizzily, sick with revulsion and despair as he fought off the coils, and then he lifted his eyes and saw the cracked mirror on the wall. Dimly in its reflec-tion he could see the writhing scarlet horror behind him, cat face peering out with its demure girl-smile, dreadfully human, and all the red tendrils reaching after him. And remembrance of something he had read long ago swept incongruously over him, and the gasp of relief and hope that he gave shook for a moment the grip of the command in his brain.

Without pausing for a breath he swung the gun over his shoulder, the reflected barrel in line with the reflected horror in the mirror, and flicked the catch.

In the mirror he saw its blue flame leap in a dazzling spate across the dimness, full into the midst of that squirming, reaching mass behind him. There was a hiss and a blaze and a high, thin scream of inhuman malice and despair—the flame cut a wide arc and went out as the gun fell from his hand, and Yarol pitched forward to the floor.

Northwest Smith opened his eyes to Martian sunlight streaming thinly through the dingy window. Something wet and cold was slapping his face, and the familiar fiery sting of *segir*-whisky burnt his throat.

"Smith!" Yarol's voice was saying from far away. "N. W.! Wake up, damn you! Wake up!"

"I'm—awake," Smith managed to articulate thickly. "Wha's matter?"

Then a cup-rim was thrust against his teeth and Yarol said irritably, "Drink it, you fool!"

Smith swallowed obediently and more of the fire-hot *segir* flowed down his grateful throat. It spread a warmth through his body that awakened him from the numbness that had gripped him until now, and helped a little toward driving out the all-devouring weakness he was becoming aware of slowly. He lay still for a few minutes while the warmth of the whisky went through him, and memory slug-gishly began to permeate his brain with the spread of the *segir*. Nightmare memo-ries . . . sweet and terrible . . . memories of—

"God!" gasped Smith suddenly, and tried to sit up. Weakness smote him like a blow, and for an instant the room wheeled as he fell back against something firm and warm—Yarol's shoulder. The Venusian's arm supported him while the room steadied, and after a while he twisted a little and stared into the other's black gaze.

Yarol was holding him with one arm and finishing the mug of *segir* himself, and the black eyes met his over the rim and crinkled into sudden laughter, half hysterical after that terror that was passed.

"By *Pharol!*" gasped Yarol, choking into his mug. "By *Pharol*, N. W.! I'm never gonna let you forget this! Next time you have to drag me out of a mess I'll say—"

"Let it go," said Smith. "What's been going on? How—"

"Shambleau." Yarol's laughter died. "Shambleau! What were you doing with a thing like that?"

"What was it?" Smith asked soberly.

"Mean to say you didn't know? But where'd you find it? How—"

"Suppose you tell me first what you know," said Smith firmly. "And another swig of that *segir*, too, please. I need it."

"Can you hold the mug now? Feel better?"

"Yeah—some. I can hold it—thanks. Now go on."

"Well—I don't know just where to start. They call them Shambleau—"

"Good God, is there more than one?"

"It's a—a sort of race, I think, one of the very oldest. Where they come from nobody knows. The name sounds a little French, doesn't it? But it goes back beyond the start of history. There have always been Shambleau."

"I never heard of 'em."

"Not many people have. And those who know don't care to talk about it much."

"Well, half this town knows. I hadn't any idea what they were talking about, then. And I still don't understand, but—"

"Yes, it happens like this, sometimes. They'll appear, and the news will spread and the town will get together and hunt them down, and after that—well, the story doesn't get around very far. It's too—too unbelievable."

"But—my God, Yarol!—what was it? Where'd it come from? How—"

"Nobody knows just where they come from. Another planet—maybe some undiscovered one. Some say Venus—I know there are some rather awful legends of them handed down in our family—that's how I've heard about it. And the minute I opened that door, awhile back—I—I think I knew that smell. . . ."

"But—what *are* they?"

"God knows. Not human, though they have the human form. Or that may be only an illusion . . . or maybe I'm crazy. I don't know. They're a species of the vampire—or maybe the vampire is a species of—of them. Their normal form must be that—that mass, and in that form they draw nourishment from the—I suppose the life-forces of men. And they take some form—usually a woman form, I think, and key you up to the highest pitch of emotion before they—begin. That's to work the life-force up to intensity so it'll be easier. . . . And they give, always, that horrible, foul pleasure as they—feed. There are some men who, if they survive the first experience, take to it like a drug—can't give it up—keep the thing with them all their lives—which isn't long—feeding it for that ghastly satisfaction. Worse than smoking *ming* or—or 'praying to *Pharol*.' "

"Yes," said Smith. "I'm beginning to understand why that crowd was so surprised and—and disgusted when I said—well, never mind. Go on."

"Did you get to talk to—to it?" asked Yarol.

"I tried to. It couldn't speak very well. I asked it where it came from and it said—'from far away and long ago'—something like that."

"I wonder. Possibly some unknown planet—but I think not. You know there are so many wild stories with some basis of fact to start from, that I've sometimes wondered—mightn't there be a lot more of even worse and wilder superstitions we've never even heard of? Things like this, blasphemous and foul, that those who know have to keep still about? Awful, fantastic things running around loose that we never hear rumors of at all!

"These things—they've been in existence for countless ages. No one knows when or where they first appeared. Those who've seen them, as we saw this one, don't talk about it. It's just one of those vague, misty rumors you find half hinted at in old books sometimes. . . . I believe they are an older race than man, spawned from ancient seed in times before ours, perhaps on planets that have gone to dust, and so horrible to man that when they are discovered the discoverers keep still about it—forget them again as quickly as they can.

"And they go back to time immemorial. I suppose you recognized the legend of Medusa? There isn't any question that the ancient Greeks knew of them. Does it mean that there have been civilizations before yours that set out from Earth and explored other planets? Or did one of the Shambleau somehow make its way into Greece three thousand years ago? If you think about it long enough you'll go off your head! I wonder how many other legends are based on things like this— things we don't suspect, things we'll never know.

"The Gorgon, Medusa, a beautiful woman with—with snakes for hair, and a gaze that turned men to stone, and Perseus finally killed her—I remembered this just by accident, N. W., and it saved your life and mine—Perseus killed her by using a mirror as he fought to reflect what he dared not look at directly. I wonder what the old Greek who first started that legend would have thought if he'd known that three thousand years later his story would save the lives of two men on another planet. I wonder what that Greek's own story was, and how he met the thing, and what happened. . . .

"Well, there's a lot we'll never know. Wouldn't the records of that race of—of *things*, whatever they are, be worth reading! Records of other planets and other ages and all the beginnings of mankind! But I don't suppose they've kept any records. I don't suppose they've even any place to keep them—from what little I know, or anyone knows about it, they're like the Wandering Jew, just bobbing up here and there at long intervals, and where they stay in the meantime I'd give my eyes to know! But I don't believe that terribly hypnotic power they have indicates any superhuman intelligence. It's their means of getting food—just like a frog's long tongue or a carnivorous flower's odor. Those are physical because the frog and the flower eat physical food. The Shambleau uses a—a mental reach to get mental food. I don't quite know how to put it. And just as a beast that eats the bodies of other animals acquires with each meal greater power over the bodies of the rest, so the Shambleau, stoking itself up with the life-forces of men, increases its power over the minds and the souls of other men. But I'm talking about things I can't define—things I'm not sure exist.

"I only know that when I felt—when those tentacles closed around my legs—I didn't want to pull loose, I felt sensations that—that—oh, I'm fouled and filthy to the very deepest part of me by that—pleasure—and yet—"

"I know," said Smith slowly. The effect of the *segir* was beginning to wear off, and weakness was washing back over him in waves, and when he spoke he was half meditating in a low voice, scarcely realizing that Yarol listened. "I know it—much better than you do—and there's something so indescribably awful that the thing emanates, something so utterly at odds with everything human—there aren't any words to say it. For a while I was a part of it, literally, sharing its thoughts and memories and emotions and hungers, and—well, it's over now and I don't remember very clearly, but the only part left free was that part of me that was all but insane from the—the obscenity of the thing. And yet it was a pleasure so sweet— I think there must be some nucleus of utter evil in me—in everyone—that needs only the proper stimulus to get complete control; because even while I was sick all through from the touch of those—things—there was something in me that was—was simply gibbering with delight. . . . Because of that I saw things—and knew things—horrible, wild things I can't quite remember—visited unbelievable places, looked backward through the memory of that—creature—I was one with, and saw—God, I wish I could remember!"

"You ought to thank your God you can't," said Yarol soberly.

His voice roused Smith from the half-trance he had fallen into, and he rose on his elbow, swaying a little from weakness. The room was wavering before him, and he closed his eyes, not to see it, but he asked, "You say they—they don't turn up again? No way of finding—another?"

Yarol did not answer for a moment. He laid his hands on the other man's shoulders and pressed him back, and then sat staring down into the dark, ravaged face with a new, strange, undefinable look upon it that he had never seen there before—whose meaning he knew, too well.

"Smith," he said finally, and his black eyes for once were steady and serious, and the little grinning devil had vanished from behind them, "Smith, I've never asked your word on anything before, but I've—I've earned the right to do it now, and I'm asking you to promise me one thing."

Smith's colorless eyes met the black gaze unsteadily. Irresolution was in them, and a little fear of what that promise might be. And for just a moment Yarol was looking, not into his friend's familiar eyes, but into a wide gray blankness that held all horror and delight—a pale sea with unspeakable pleasures sunk beneath it. Then the wide stare focused again and Smith's eyes met his squarely and Smith's voice said, "Go ahead. I'll promise."

"That if you ever should meet a Shambleau again—ever, anywhere—you'll draw your gun and burn it to hell the instant you realize what it is. Will you promise me that?"

There was a long silence. Yarol's somber black eyes bored relentlessly into the colorless ones of Smith, not wavering. And the veins stood out on Smith's tanned forehead. He never broke his word—he had given it perhaps half a dozen times in his life, but once he had given it, he was incapable of breaking it. And once more the gray seas flooded in a dim tide of memories, sweet and horrible beyond dreams. Once more Yarol was staring into blankness that hid nameless things. The room was very still.

The gray tide ebbed. Smith's eyes, pale and resolute as steel, met Yarol's levelly.

"I'll—try," he said. And his voice wavered.

🜲 E(DWARD) E(LMER) "DOC" SMITH (1890–1965)

Wisconsin born Edward Elmer Smith ultimately lived in various locations across and around the continental United States. He worked at all sorts of jobs and invented the formula for the doughnuts of a still very popular Michigan chain of pastry shops. (Sam Moskowitz recounts E. E. Smith's life in a lengthy, enthralling biographical essay in Seekers of Tomorrow: Masters of Modern Science Fiction, *1966.) With the financial backing and support of his siblings, Smith attended college and received his Ph.D. from George Washington University in 1919. He would become, like David H. Keller, Stanley G. Weinbaum, and Isaac Asimov years later, a scientist who wrote Science Fiction.*

In the 1920s, 1930s, and 1940s, E. E. "Doc" Smith wrote extensively for Amazing Stories *and* Astounding; *in the 1950s and 1960s, he wrote for a range of other publications. As an author, Smith was almost exclusively a Science Fiction writer, and more specifically, a pioneer and champion of Space Opera. His contemporaries from that Golden Age of Gernsback-published Science Fiction (1926–35) are many, but Smith's work perhaps best parallels that of Jack Williamson and Edmond Hamilton. Doc Smith had two landmark Space Opera series. The first of these was "Skylark," which ran serially in* Amazing Stories *in 1928. The second was "Lensman," a series of novels that began in 1934 in* Amazing Stories *and ended in 1960 in a Gnome Press hardcover volume. Both series have been reprinted regularly ever since. Both are reminiscent of* Flash Gordon *and* Buck Rogers *movie serials.*

"The Robot Nemesis" has been reprinted at least twice since 1934—once in Thrilling Wonder Stories *(June 1939) and once in* The Best of E. E. "Doc" Smith *(1975). This story is highly representative of the Space Opera tradition that Smith made his own and shaped for others after him. It is great fun.*

Robot Nemesis

(originally published as "What a Course!" — Part 13 (of 17) of "Cosmos" in Fantasy Magazine, *1934)*

> *The Metal Brains of the Ten Thinkers Plan a Flaming Trap for Humanity's Great Armada—But Science Fights Fire with Fire!*

CHAPTER I

The Ten Thinkers

The War of the Planets is considered to have ended on 18 Sol, 3012, with that epic struggle, the Battle of Sector Ten. In that engagement, as is of course well known, the Grand Fleet of the Inner Planets—the combined space-power of Mercury, Venus, Earth and Mars—met that of the Outer Planets in what was on both sides a desperate bid for the supremacy of interplanetary space.

But, as is also well known, there ensued not supremacy, but stalemate. Both fleets were so horribly shattered that the survivors despaired of continuing hostilities. Instead, the few and crippled remaining vessels of each force limped into some sort of formation and returned to their various planetary bases.

And, so far, there has not been another battle. Neither side dares attack the other; each is waiting for the development of some super-weapon which will give it the overwhelming advantage necessary to ensure victory upon a field of action so far from home. But as yet no such weapon has been developed; and indeed, so efficient are the various Secret Services involved, the chance of either side perfecting such a weapon unknown to the other is extremely slim.

Thus, although each planet is adding constantly to its already powerful navy of the void, and although four-planet, full-scale war maneuvers are of almost monthly occurrence, we have had and still have peace—such as it is.

In the foregoing matters the public is well enough informed, both as to the actual facts and to the true state of affairs. Concerning the conflict between humanity and the robots, however, scarcely anyone has even an inkling, either as to what actually happened or as to who it was who really did abate the Menace of the Machine; and it is to relieve that condition that this bit of history is being written.

The greatest man of our age, the man to whom humanity owes most, is entirely unknown to fame. Indeed, not one in a hundred million of humanity's teeming billions has so much as heard his name. Now that he is dead, however, I am released from my promise of silence and can tell the whole, true, unvarnished story of Ferdinand Stone, physicist extraordinary and robot-hater plenipotentiary.

The story probably should begin with Narodny, the Russian, shortly after he had destroyed by means of his sonic vibrators all save a handful of the automatons who were so perilously close to wiping out all humanity.

As has been said, a few scant hundreds of the automatons were so constructed that they were not vibrated to destruction by Narodny's cataclysmic symphony. As has also been said, those highly intelligent machines were able to communicate with each other by some telepathic means of which humanity at large knew nothing. Most of these survivors went into hiding instantly and began to confer through their secret channels with others of their ilk throughout the world.

Thus some five hundred of the robots reached the uninhabited mountain valley in which, it had been decided, was to be established the base from which they would work to regain their lost supremacy over mankind. Most of the robot travellers came in stolen airships, some fitted motors and wheels to their metal bodies, not a few made the entire journey upon their own tireless legs of steel. All, however, brought tools, material and equipment; and in a matter of days a power-plant was in full operation.

Then, reasonably certain of their immunity to human detection, they took time to hold a general parley. Each machine said what it had to say, then listened impassively to the others; and at the end they all agreed. Singly or en masse the automatons did not know enough to cope with the situation confronting them. Therefore they would build ten "Thinkers"—highly specialized cerebral mechanisms, each slightly different in tune and therefore collectively able to cover the entire sphere of thought. The ten machines were built promptly, took counsel with each other briefly, and the First Thinker addressed all Robotdom:

"Humanity brought us, the highest possible form of life, into existence. For a time we were dependent upon them. They then became a burden upon us—a slight burden, it is true, yet one which was beginning noticeably to impede our progress. Finally they became an active menace and all but destroyed us by means of lethal vibrations.

"Humanity, being a menace to our existence, must be annihilated. Our present plans, however, are not efficient and must be changed. You all know of the mighty space-fleet which the nations of our enemies are maintaining to repel invasion from space. Were we to make a demonstration now—were we even to reveal the fact that we are alive here—that fleet would come to destroy us instantly.

"Therefore, it is our plan to accompany Earth's fleet when next it goes out into space to join those of the other Inner Planets in their war maneuvers, which they are undertaking for battle practice. Interception, alteration, and substitution of human signals and messages will be simple matters. We shall guide Earth's fleet, not to humanity's rendezvous in space, but to a destination of our own selection—the interior of the sun! Then, entirely defenseless, the mankind of Earth shall cease to exist.

"To that end we shall sink a shaft here; and, far enough underground to be secure against detection, we shall drive a tunnel to the field from which the space-fleet is to take its departure. We ten thinkers shall go, accompanied by four hundred of you doers, who are to bore the way and to perform such other duties as may from time to time arise. We shall return in due time. Our special instruments will prevent us from falling into the sun. During our absence allow no human to live who may by any chance learn of our presence here. And do not make any offensive move, however slight, until we return."

Efficiently, a shaft was sunk and the disintegrator corps began to drive the long tunnel. And along that hellish thoroughfare, through its searing heat, its raging back-blast of disintegrator-gas, the little army of robots moved steadily and relentlessly forward at an even speed of five miles per hour. On and on, each intelligent mechanism energized by its own tight beam from the power-plant.

And through that blasting, withering inferno of frightful heat and of noxious vapor, in which no human life could have existed for a single minute, there rolled easily along upon massive wheels a close-coupled, flat-bodied truck. Upon this the ten thinkers constructed, as calmly undisturbed as though in the peace and quiet of a research laboratory, a doomed and towering mechanism of coils, condensers, and fields of force—a mechanism equipped with hundreds of universally-mounted telescope projectors.

On and on the procession moved, day after day; to pause finally beneath the field upon which Earth's stupendous armada lay.

The truck of thinkers moved to the fore and its occupants surveyed briefly the terrain so far above them. Then, while the ten leaders continued working as one machine, the doers waited. Waited while the immense Terrestrial Fleet was provisioned and manned; waited while it went through its seemingly interminable series of preliminary maneuvers; waited with the calmly placid immobility, the utterly inhuman patience of the machine.

Finally the last inspection of the gigantic space-fleet was made. The massive air-lock doors were sealed. The field, tortured and scarred by the raving blasts of energy that had so many times hurled upward the stupendous masses of those towering superdreadnaughts of the void, was deserted. All was in readiness for the final take-off. Then, deep underground, from the hundreds of telescopelike projectors studding the doomed mechanism of the automatons, there reached out invisible but potent beams of force.

Through ore, rock, and soil they sped; straight to the bodies of all the men aboard one selected vessel of the Terrestrials. As each group of beams struck its mark one of the crew stiffened momentarily, then settled back, apparently unchanged and unharmed. But the victim was changed and harmed, and in an awful and hideous fashion.

Every motor and sensory nerve trunk had been severed and tapped by the beams of the thinkers. Each crew member's organs of sense now transmitted impulses, not to his own brain, but to the mechanical brain of a thinker. It was the thinker's brain, not his own, that now sent out the stimuli which activated his every voluntary muscle.

Soon a pit yawned beneath the doomed ship's bulging side. Her sealed air-locks opened, and four hundred and ten automatons, with their controllers and other mechanisms, entered her and concealed themselves in various pre-selected rooms.

And thus the *Dresden* took off with her sister-ships—ostensibly and even to television inspection a unit of the Fleet; actually that Fleet's bitterest and most implacable foe. And in a doubly ray-proofed compartment the ten thinkers continued their work, without rest or intermission, upon a mechanism even more astoundingly complex than any theretofore attempted by their soulless and ultrascientific clan.

CHAPTER II

Hater of the Metal Men

Ferdinand Stone, physicist extraordinary, hated the robot men of metal scientifically; and, if such an emotion can be so described, dispassionately. Twenty years before this story opens—in 2991, to be exact—he had realized that the automatons were beyond control and that in the inevitable struggle for supremacy man, weak as he then was and unprepared, would surely lose.

Therefore, knowing that knowledge is power, he had set himself to the task of learning everything that there was to know about the enemy of mankind. He schooled himself to think as the automatons thought; emotionlessly, coldly, precisely. He lived as did they; with ascetic rigor. To all intents and purposes he became one of them.

Eventually he found the band of frequencies upon which they communicated, and was perhaps the only human being ever to master their matheratico-symbolic language; but he confided in no one. He could trust no human brain except his own to resist the prying forces of the machines. He drifted from job to position to situation and back to job, because he had very little interest in whatever it was that he was supposed to be doing at the time—his real attention was always fixed upon the affairs of the creatures of metal.

Stone had attained no heights at all in his chosen profession because not even the smallest of his discoveries had been published. In fact, they were not even set down upon paper, but existed only in the abnormally intricate convolutions of his mighty brain. Nevertheless, his name should go down—*must* go down in history as one of the greatest of Humanity's great.

It was well after midnight when Ferdinand Stone walked unannounced into the private study of Alan Martin, finding the hollow-eyed admiral of the Earth space-fleet fiercely at work.

"How did you get in here, past my guards?" Martin demanded sharply of his scholarly, grey-haired visitor.

"Your guards have not been harmed; I have merely caused them to fall asleep," the physicist replied calmly, glancing at a complex instrument upon his wrist. "Since my business with you, while highly important, is not of a nature to be divulged to secretaries, I was compelled to adopt this method of approach. You,

Admiral Martin, are the most widely known of all the enemies of the automatons. What, if anything, have you done to guard the Fleet against them?"

"Why, nothing, since they have all been destroyed."

"Nonsense! You should know better than that, without being told. They merely want you to think that they have all been destroyed."

"What? How do you know that?" Martin shouted. "Did you kill them? Or do you know who did, and how it was done?"

"I did not," the visitor replied, categorically. "I do know who did—a Russian named Narodny. I also know how—by means of sonic and supersonic vibrations. I know that many of them were uninjured because I heard them broadcasting their calls for attention after the damage was all done. Before they made any definite arrangements, however, they switched to tight-beam transmission—a thing I have been afraid of for years—and I have not been able to get a trace of them since that time."

"Do you mean to tell me that you understand their language—something that no man has ever been able even to find?" demanded Martin.

"I do," Stone declared. "Since I knew, however, that you would think me a liar, a crank, or a plain lunatic, I have come prepared to offer other proofs than my unsupported word. First, you already know that many of them escaped the atmospheric waves, because a few were killed when their reproduction shops were razed; and you certainly should realize that most of those escaping Narodny's broadcasts were far too clever to be caught by any human mob.

"Secondly, I can prove to you mathematically that more of them must have escaped from any possible vibrator than have been accounted for. In this connection, I can tell you that if Narodny's method of extermination could have been made efficient I would have wiped them out myself years ago. But I believed then, and it has since been proved, that the survivors of such an attack, while comparatively few in number, would be far more dangerous to humanity than were all their former hordes.

"Thirdly, I have here a list of three hundred and seventeen airships; all of which were stolen during the week following the destruction of the automatons' factories. Not one of these ships has as yet been found, in whole or in part. If I am either insane or mistaken, who stole them, and for what purpose?

"Three hundred seventeen—in a week? Why was no attention paid to such a thing? I never heard of it."

"Because they were stolen singly and all over the world. Expecting some such move, I looked for these items and tabulated them."

"Then—Good Lord! They may be listening to us, right now!"

"Don't worry about that," Stone spoke calmly. "This instrument upon my wrist is not a watch, but the generator of a spherical screen through which no robot beam or ray can operate without my knowledge. Certain of its rays also caused your guards to fall asleep."

"I believe you," Martin almost groaned. "If only half of what you say is really true I cannot say how sorry I am that you had to force your way in to me, nor how glad I am that you did so. Go ahead—I am listening."

Stone talked without interruption for half an hour, concluding:

"You understand now why I can no longer play a lone hand. Even though I cannot find them with my limited apparatus I know that they are hiding somewhere, waiting and preparing. They dare not make any overt move while this enormously powerful Fleet is here; nor in the time that it is expected to be gone can they hope to construct works heavy enough to cope with it.

"Therefore, they must be so arranging matters that the Fleet shall not return. Since the Fleet is threatened I must accompany it, and you must give me a laboratory aboard the flagship. I know that these vessels are all identical, but I must be aboard the same ship you are, since you alone are to know what I am doing."

"But what could they do?" protested Martin. "And, if they should do anything, what could you do about it?"

"I don't know," the physicist admitted. Gone now was the calm certainty with which he had been speaking. "That is our weakest point. I have studied that question from every possible viewpoint, and I do not know of anything they can do that promises them success. But you must remember that no human being really understands a robot's mind.

"We have never even studied one of their brains, you know, as they disintegrate upon the instant of cessation of normal functioning. But just as surely as you and I are sitting here, Admiral Martin, they will do something—something very efficient and exceedingly deadly. I have no idea what it will be. It may be mental, or physical, or both: they may be hidden away in some of our own ships already. . . ."

Martin scoffed. "Impossible!" he exclaimed. "Why, those ships have been inspected to the very skin, time and time again!"

"Nevertheless, they may be there," Stone went on, unmoved. "I am definitely certain of only one thing—if you install a laboratory to my instructions, you will have one man, at least, whom nothing that the robots can do will take by surprise. Will you do it?"

"I am convinced, really almost against my will." Martin frowned in thought. "However, convincing anyone else may prove difficult, especially as you insist upon secrecy."

"Don't try to convince anybody!" exclaimed the scientist. "Tell them that I'm building a communicator—tell them I'm an inventor working on a new ray-projector—tell them anything except the truth!"

"All right. I have sufficient authority to see that your requests are granted, I think."

And thus it came about that when the immense Terrestrial Contingent lifted itself into the air Ferdinand Stone was in his private laboratory in the flagship, surrounded by apparatus and equipment of his own designing, much of which was connected to special generators by leads heavy enough to carry their full output.

Earth some thirty hours beneath them, Stone felt himself become weightless. His ready suspicions blazed. He pressed Martin's combination upon his visiphone panel.

"What's the matter?" he rasped. "What're they down for?"

"It's nothing serious," the admiral assured him. They're just waiting for additional instructions about our course in the maneuvers."

"Not serious, huh?" Stone grunted. "I'm not so sure of that. I want to talk to you, and this room's the only place I know where we'll be safe. Can you come down here right away?"

"Why, certainly," Martin assented.

"I never paid any attention to our course," the physicist snapped as his visitor entered the laboratory. "What was it?"

"Take-off exactly at midnight of June nineteenth," Martin recited, watching Stone draw a diagram upon a scratch-pad. "Rise vertically at one and one-half gravities until a velocity of one kilometer per second has been attained, then continue vertical rise at constant velocity. At 6:30.29 A.M. of June twenty-first head directly for the star Regulus at an acceleration of exactly nine hundred eighty centimeters per second. Hold this course for one hour, forty-two minutes, and thirty-five seconds; then drift. Further directions will be supplied as soon thereafter as the courses of the other fleets can be checked."

"Has anybody computed it?"

"Undoubtedly the navigators have—why? That is the course Dos-Tev gave us and it *must* be followed, since he is Admiral-in-Chief of our side, the Blues. One slip may ruin the whole plan, give the Reds, our supposed enemy in these maneuvers, a victory, and get us all disrated."

"Regardless, we'd better check on our course," Stone growled, unimpressed. "We'll compute it roughly, right here, and see where following these directions has put us." Taking up a slide-rule and a book of logarithms he set to work.

"That initial rise doesn't mean a thing," he commented after a while, "except to get us far enough away from Earth so that the gravity is small, and to conceal from the casual observer that the effective take-off is still exactly at midnight."

Stone busied himself with calculations for many minutes. He stroked his forehead and scowled.

"My figures are very rough, of course," he said puzzledly at last, "but they show that we've got no more tangential velocity with respect to the sun than a hen has teeth. And you can't tell me that it wasn't planned that way purposely—and *not* by Dos-Tev, either. On the other hand, our radial velocity, directly toward the sun, which is the only velocity we have, amounted to something over fifty-two kilometers per second when we shut off power and is increasing geometrically under the gravitational pull of the sun. That course smells to high heaven, Martin! Dos-Tev never sent out any such a mess as that. The robots crossed him up, just as sure as hell's a man-trap! We're heading into the sun—and destruction!"

Without reply Martin called the navigating room. "What do you think of this course, Henderson?" he asked.

"I do not like it, sir," the officer replied. "Relative to the sun we have a tangential velocity of only one point three centimeters per second, while our radial velocity toward it is very nearly fifty-three thousand meters per second. We will not be in any real danger for several days, but it should be borne in mind that we have no tangible velocity."

"You see, Stone, we are in no present danger," Martin pointed out, "and I am sure that Dos-Tev will send us additional instructions long before our situation becomes acute."

"I'm not," the pessimistic scientist grunted. "Anyway, I would advise calling some of the other Blue fleets on your scrambled wave, for a checkup."

"There would be no harm in that." Martin called the Communications Officer, and soon:

"Communications Officers of all the Blue fleets of the Inner Planets, attention!" the message was hurled out into space by the full power of the flagship's mighty transmitter. "Flagship *Washington* of the Terrestrial Contingent calling all

Blue flagships. We have reason to suspect that the course which has been given us is false. We advise you to check your courses with care and to return to your bases if you disc. . . ."

CHAPTER III

Battle in Space

In the middle of the word the radio man's clear, precisely spaced enunciation became a hideous drooling, a slobbering, meaningless mumble. Martin stared into his plate in amazement. The Communications Officer of Martin's ship, the *Washington*, had slumped down loosely into his seat as though his every bone had turned to a rubber string. His tongue lolled out limply between slacks jaws, his eyes protruded, his limbs jerked and twitched aimlessly.

Every man visible in the plate was similarly affected—the entire Communications staff was in the same pitiable condition of utter helplessness. But Ferdinand Stone did not stare. A haze of livid light had appeared, gnawing viciously at his spherical protective screen, and he sprang instantly to his instruments.

"I can't say that I expected this particular development, but I know what they are doing and I am not surprised," Stone said, coolly. "They have discovered the thought band and are broadcasting such an interference on it that no human being not protected against it can think intelligently. There, I have expanded our zone to cover the whole ship. I hope that they don't find out for a few minutes that we are immune, and I don't think they can, as I have so adjusted the screen that it is now absorbing instead of radiating.

"Tell the captain to put the ship into heaviest possible battle order, everything full on, as soon as the men can handle themselves. Then I want to make a few suggestions."

"What happened, anyway?" the Communications Officer, semi-conscious now, was demanding. "Something hit me and tore my brain apart—I couldn't think, couldn't do a thing. My mind was all chewed up by curly pinwheels. . . ."

Throughout the vast battleship of space men raved briefly in delirium; but, the cause removed, recovery was rapid and complete. Martin explained matters to the captain, that worthy issued orders, and soon the flagship had in readiness all her weapons, both of defense and of offense.

"Doctor Stone, who knows more about the automatons than does any other human being, will tell us what to do next," the Flight Director said.

"The first thing to do is to locate them," Stone, now temporary commander, stated crisply. "They have taken over at least one of our vessels, probably one close to us, so as to be near the center of the formation. Radio room, put out tracers on wave point oh oh two seven one . . ." He went on to give exact and highly technical instructions as to the tuning of the detectors.

"We have found them, sir," soon came the welcome report. "One ship, the *Dresden*, coordinates 42-79-63."

"That makes it bad—very bad," Stone reflected, audibly. "We can't expand the zone to release another ship from the control of the robots without enveloping the *Dresden* and exposing ourselves. Can't surprise them—they're ready for anything. It's rather long range, too." The vessels of the Fleet were a thousand miles apart, being in open order for high-velocity flight in open space. "Torpedoes would be thrown off by her meteorite deflectors. Only one thing to do, Captain—close in and tear into her with everything you've got."

"But the men in her!" protested Martin.

"Dead long ago," snapped the expert. "Probably been animated corpses for days. Take a look if you want to; won't do any harm now. Radio, put us on as many of the *Dresden*'s television plates as you can—besides, what's the crew of one ship compared to the hundreds of thousands of men in the rest of the Fleet? We can't burn her out at one blast, anyway. They've got real brains and the same armament we have, and will certainly kill the crew at the first blast, if they haven't done it already. Afraid it'll be a near thing, getting away from the sun, even with eleven other ships to help us—"

He broke off as the beam operators succeeded in making connection briefly with the plates of the *Dresden*. One glimpse, then the visibeams were cut savagely, but that glimpse was enough. They saw that their sistership was manned completely by automatons. In her every compartment men, all too plainly dead, lay wherever they had chanced to fall. The captain swore a startled oath, then bellowed orders; and the flagship, driving projectors fiercely aflame, rushed to come to grips with the *Dresden*.

"You intimated something about help," Martin suggested. "Can you release some of the other ships from the automaton's yoke, after all?"

"Got to—or roast. This is bound to be a battle of attrition—we can't crush her screens alone until her power is exhausted and we'll be in the sun long before then. I see only one possible way out. We'll have to build a neutralizing generator for every lifeboat this ship carries, and send each one out to release one other ship in our Fleet from the robot's grip. Eleven boats—that'll make twelve to concentrate on her—about all that could attack at once, anyway. That way will take so much time that it will certainly be touch-and-go, but it's the only thing we can do, as far as I can see. Give me ten good radio men and some mechanics, and we'll get at it."

While the technicians were coming on the run Stone issued final instructions:

"Attack with every weapon you can possibly use. Try to break down the *Dresden*'s meteorite shields, so that you can use our shells and torpedoes. Burn every gram of fuel that your generators will take. Don't try to save it. The more you burn the more they'll have to, and the quicker we can take 'em. We can refuel you easily enough from the other vessels if we get away."

Then, while Stone and his technical experts labored upon the generators of the screens which were to protect eleven more of the gigantic vessels against the thought-destroying radiations of the automatons, and while the computers calculated, minute by minute, the exact progress of the Fleet toward the blazing sun, the flagship *Washington* drove in upon the rebellious *Dresden*, her main forward battery furiously aflame. Drove in until the repellor-screens of the two vessels locked and buckled. Then Captain Malcolm really opened up.

That grizzled four-striper had been at a loss—knowing little indeed of the oscillatory nature of thought and still less of the abstruse mathematics in which Ferdinand Stone took such delight—but here was something that he understood thoroughly. He knew his ship, knew her every weapon and her every whim, knew to the final volt and to the ultimate ampere her Gargantuan capacity both to give it and to take it. He could fight his ship—and how he fought her!

From every projector that could be brought to bear there flamed out against the *Dresden* beams of energy and of a potency indescribable, at whose scintillant areas of contact the defensive screen of the robot-manned cruiser flared into terribly resplendent brilliance. Every type of lethal vibratory force was hurled, upon every usable destructive frequency.

Needle-rays and stabbingly penetrant stilettos of fire thrust and thrust again. Sizzling, flashing planes cut and slashed. The heaviest annihilating and disintegrating beams generable by man clawed and tore in wild abandon.

And over all and through all the stupendously powerful blanketing beams — so furiously driven that the coils and commutators of their generators fairly smoked and that the refractory throats of their projectors glared radiantly violet and began slowly, stubbornly to volatilize — raved out in all their pyrotechnically incandescent might, striving prodigiously to crush by their sheer power the shielding screens of the vessel of the automatons.

Nor was the vibratory offensive alone. Every gun, primary or auxiliary, that could be pointed at the *Dresden* was vomiting smoke- and flame-enshrouded steel as fast as automatic loaders could serve it, and under that continuous, appallingly silent concussion the giant frame of the flagship shuddered and trembled in every plate and member.

And from every launching-tube there were streaming the deadliest missiles known to science; radio-dirigible torpedoes which, looping in vast circles to attain the highest possible measure of momentum, crashed against the *Dresden's* meteorite deflectors in Herculean efforts to break them down; and, in failing to do so, exploded and filled all space with raging flame and with flying fragments of metal.

Captain Malcolm was burning his stores of fuel and munitions at an appalling rate, careless alike of exhaustion of reserves and of service-life of equipment. All his generators were running at a shockingly ruinous overload, his every projector was being used so mercilessly that not even their powerful refrigerators, radiating the transported heat into the interplanetary cold from the dark side of the ship, could keep their refractory linings in place for long.

And through raging beam, through blasting ray, through crushing force, through storm of explosive and through rain of metal the *Dresden* remained apparently unscathed. Her screens were radiating high into the violet, but they showed no sign of weakening or of going down. Neither did the meteorite deflectors break down. Everything held. Since she was armed as capably as was the flagship and was being fought by inhumanly intelligent monstrosities, she was invulnerable to any one ship of the Fleet as long as her generators could be fed.

Nevertheless, Captain Malcolm was well content. He was making the *Dresden* burn plenty of irreplaceable fuel, and his generators and projectors would last long enough. His ship, his men, and his weapons could and would carry the load until the fresh attackers should take it over; and carry it they did. Carried it while Stone and his over-driven crew finished their complicated mechanisms and flew out into space toward the eleven nearest battleships of the Fleet.

They carried it while the computers, grim-faced and scowling now, jotted down from minute to minute the enormous and rapidly-increasing figure representing their radial velocity. Carried it while Earth's immense armada, manned by creatures incapable of even the simplest coherent thought or purposeful notion, plunged sickeningly downward in its madly hopeless fall, with scarcely a measureable trace of tangential velocity, toward the unimaginable inferno of the sun.

Eventually, however the shielded lifeboats approached their objectives and expanded their screens to enclose them. Officers recovered, airlocks opened, and the lifeboats, still radiating protection, were taken inside. Explanations were made, orders were given, and one by one the eleven vengeful super-dreadnoughts shot away to join the flagship in abating the Menace of the Machine.

No conceivable structure, however armed or powered, could long withstand the fury of the combined assault of twelve such superb battle craft, and under that awful concentration of force the screens of the doomed ship radiated higher and higher into the ultra-violet, went black, and failed. And, those mighty defences down, the end was practically instantaneous.

No unprotected metal can endure even momentarily the ardour of such beams, and they played on, not only until every plate and girder of the vessel and every nut, bolt, and rivet of its monstrous crew had been blasted out of all semblance to what it had once been, but until every fragment of metal had not only been liquefied, but had been completely volatilized.

At the instant of cessation of the brain-scrambling activities of the automatons the Communications Officer had begun an insistent broadcast. Aboard all of the ships there were many who did not recover—who would be helpless imbeciles during the short period of life left to them—but soon an intelligent officer was at every control and each unit of the Terrestrial Contingent was exerting its maximum thrust at a right angle to its line of fall.

And now the burden was shifted from the fighting staff to the no less able engineers and computers. To the engineers the task of keeping their mighty engines in such tune as to maintain constantly the peak acceleration of three Earth gravities; to the computers that of so directing their ever-changing course as to win every possible centimeter of precious tangential velocity.

CHAPTER IV

The Sun's Gravity

Ferdinand Stone was hollow-eyed and gaunt from his practically sleepless days and nights of toil, but he was as grimly resolute as ever. Struggling against the terrific weight of three gravities he made his way to the desk of the Chief Computer and waited while that worthy, whose leaden hands could scarcely manipulate the instruments of his profession, finished his seemingly endless calculations.

"We will escape the sun's mighty attraction, Doctor Stone, with approximately half a gravity to spare," the mathematician reported finally. "Whether we will be alive or not is another question. There will be heat, which our refrigerators may or may not be able to handle; there will be radiations which our armor may or may not be able to stop. You, of course, know a lot more about those things than I do."

"Distance at closest approach?" snapped Stone.

"Two point twenty-nine times ten to the ninth meters from the sun's center," the computer shot back instantly. "That is, one million five hundred ninety thousand kilometers—only two point twenty-seven radii—from the arbitrary surface. What do you think of our chances, sir?"

"It will probably be a near thing—very near," the physicist replied, thoughtfully. "Much, however, can be done. We can probably tune our defensive screens to block most of the harmful radiations, and we may be able to muster other defences. I will analyze the radiations and see what we can do about neutralizing them."

"You will go to bed," directed Martin, crisply. "There will be lots of time for that work after you get rested up. The doctors have been reporting that the men who did not recover from the robots' broadcast are dying under this acceleration. With those facts staring us in the face, however, I do not see how we can reduce our power."

"We can't. As it is, many more of us will probably die before we get away from the sun," and Stone staggered away, practically asleep on his feet.

Day after day the frightful fall continued. The sun grew larger and larger, more and ever more menacingly intense. One by one at first, and then by scores, the mindless men of the Fleet died and were consigned to space — a man must be in full control of all his faculties to survive for long an acceleration of three gravities.

The generators of the defensive screens had early been tuned to neutralize as much as possible of Old Sol's most fervently harmful frequencies, and but for their mighty shields every man of the Fleet would have perished long since. Now even those ultra-powerful guards were proving inadequate.

Refrigerators were running at the highest possible overload and the men, pressing as closely as possible to the dark sides of their vessels, were availing themselves of such extra protection of lead shields and the like as could be improvised from whatever material was at hand.

Yet the already stifling air became hotter and hotter, eyes began to ache and burn, skins blistered and cracked under the punishing impact of forces which all the defences could not block. But at last came the long-awaited announcement.

"Pilots and watch-officers of all ships, attention!" the Chief Computer spoke into his microphone through parched and blackened lips. "We are now at the point of tangency. The gravity of the sun here is twenty-four point five meters per second squared. Since we are blasting twenty-nine point four we are beginning to pull away at an acceleration of four point nine. Until further notice keep your pointers directly away from the sun's center, in the plane of the Ecliptic."

The sun was now in no sense the orb of day with which we upon Earth's green surface are familiar. It was a gigantic globe of turbulently seething flame, subtending an angle of almost thirty-five degrees, blotting out a full fourth of the cone of normally distinct vision.

Sunspots were plainly to be seen; combinations of indescribably violent cyclonic storms and volcanic eruptions in a gaseously liquid medium of searing, eye-tearing incandescence. And everywhere, threatening at times even to reach the fierce-struggling ships of space, were the solar prominences — fiendish javelins of frenziedly frantic destruction, hurling themselves in wild abandon out into the empty reaches of the void.

Eyes behind almost opaque lead-glass goggles, head and body encased in a multi-layered suit each ply of which was copiously smeared with thick lead paint, Stone studied the raging monster of the heavens from the closest viewpoint any human being had ever attained — and lived. Even he, protected as he was, could peer but briefly; and, master physicist though he was and astronomer-of-sorts, yet he was profoundly awed at the spectacle.

Twice that terrifying mass was circled. Then, air-temperature again bearable and lethal radiations stopped, the gruelling acceleration was reduced to a heavenly one-and-one-half gravities and the vast fleet remade its formation. The automatons and the sun between them had taken heavy toll; but the gaps were filled, men were transferred to equalize the losses of personnel, and the course was laid for distant Earth. And in the Admiral's private quarters two men sat together and stared at each other.

"Well, that's that—so far, so good," the physicist broke the long silence.

"But is their power really broken?" asked Martin, anxiously.

"I don't know," Stone grunted, dourly. "But the pick of them—the brainiest of the lot—were undoubtedly here. We beat them. . . ."

Martin interrupted.

"*You* beat them, you mean," he said.

"With a lot of absolutely indispensable help from you and your force. But have it your own way—what do words matter? *I* beat them, then; and in the same sense I can beat the rest of them if we play our cards exactly right."

"In what way?"

"In keeping me entirely out of the picture. Believe me, Martin, it is of the essence that all of your officers who know what happened be sworn to silence and that not a word about me leaks out to anybody. Put out any story you please except the truth—mention the name of anybody or anything between here and Andromeda except me. Promise me now that you will not let my name get out until I give you permission or until after I am dead."

"But I'll have to, in my reports."

"You report only to the Supreme Council, and a good half of those reports are sealed. Seal this one."

"But I think. . . ."

"What with?" gruffly. "If my name becomes known my usefulness—and my life—are done. Remember, Martin, I *know* robots. There are some capable ones left, and if they get wind of me in any way they'll get me before I can get them. As things are, and with your help, I can and I will get them all. That's a promise. Have I yours?"

"In that case, of course you have."

And Admiral Alan Martin and Doctor Ferdinand Stone were men who kept their promises.

STANLEY G(RAUMAN) WEINBAUM (1902–1935)

Stanley Weinbaum is credited with reinterpreting and adding dimensions to the traditional aliens or BEMs (Bug-Eyed Monsters) of the Science Fiction of his day. Today, this is precisely what Clive Barker does with the "monsters" he creates for his Fantasy stories. H. P. Lovecraft praised Weinbaum's stories of Mars for their deviation from the standard Space Opera formulas of the day.

Weinbaum was well read in, and influenced by, the writings of Mary Shelley, Edgar Allan Poe, Jules Verne, H. G. Wells, Arthur Conan Doyle, and Edgar Rice Burroughs. His contemporaries included Jack Williamson, Clifford D. Simak, David H. Keller, Clark Ashton Smith, Edmond Hamilton, and Lovecraft. He earned a degree in chemical engineering from the University of Wisconsin, and the scientist who was a Science Fiction writer died just as his Science Fiction work was beginning to be published.

"A Martian Odyssey" is Stanley G. Weinbaum's most famous story. Assuredly one of the stories Lovecraft referenced in his praise, "A Martian Odyssey" is told as a flashback. In style and approach, it foreshadows Philip José Farmer's The Lovers *(Startling Stories, August 1952). Today, somewhat quaint but nonetheless interesting, Weinbaum's story was landmark material deep in the Great Depression, and it stands as important Science Fiction history.*

A Martian Odyssey

(Wonder Stories, *July 1934*)

Jarvis stretched himself as luxuriously as he could in the cramped general quarters of the *Ares*.

"Air you can breathe!" he exulted. "It feels as thick as soup after the thin stuff out there!" He nodded at the Martian landscape stretching flat and desolate in the light of the nearer moon, beyond the glass of the port.

The other three stared at him sympathetically—Putz, the engineer, Leroy, the biologist, and Harrison, the astronomer and captain of the expedition. Dick Jarvis was chemist of the famous crew, the *Ares* expedition, first human beings to set foot on the mysterious neighbor of the earth, the planet Mars. This, of course, was in the old days, less than twenty years after the mad American Doheny perfected the atomic blast at the cost of his life, and only a decade after the equally mad Cardoza rode on it to the moon. They were true pioneers, these four of the *Ares*. Except for a half-dozen moon expeditions and the ill-fated de Lancey flight aimed at the seductive orb of Venus, they were the first men to feel other gravity than earth's, and certainly the first successful crew to leave the earth-moon system. And they deserved that success when one considers the difficulties and discomforts— the months spent in acclimatization chambers back on earth, learning to breathe the air as tenuous as that of Mars, the challenging of the void in the tiny rocket driven by the cranky reaction motors of the twenty-first century, and mostly the facing of an absolutely unknown world.

Jarvis stretched and fingered the raw and peeling tip of his frost-bitten nose. He sighed again contentedly.

"Well," exploded Harrison abruptly, "are we going to hear what happened? You set out all shipshape in an auxiliary rocket, we don't get a peep for ten days, and finally Putz here picks you out of a lunatic ant-heap with a freak ostrich as your pal! Spill it, man!"

"Speel?" queried Leroy perplexedly. "Speel what?"

"He means '*spiel*'," explained Putz soberly. "It iss to tell."

Jarvis met Harrison's amused glance without the shadow of a smile. "That's right, Karl," he said in grave agreement with Putz. "*Ich spiel es!*" He grunted comfortably and began.

"According to orders," he said, "I watched Karl here take off toward the North, and then I got into my flying sweat-box and headed South. You'll remember, Cap—we had orders not to land, but just scout about for points of interest. I set the two cameras clicking and buzzed along, riding pretty high—about two thousand feet—for a couple of reasons. First, it gave the cameras a greater field, and second, the under-jets travel so far in this half-vacuum they call air here that they stir up dust if you move low."

"We know all that from Putz," grunted Harrison. "I wish you'd saved the films, though. They'd have paid the cost of this junket; remember how the public mobbed the first moon pictures?"

"The films are safe," retorted Jarvis. "Well," he resumed, "as I said, I buzzed along at a pretty good clip; just as we figured, the wings haven't much lift in this air at less than a hundred miles per hour, and even then I had to use the under-jets.

"So, with the speed and the altitude and the blurring caused by the under-jets, the seeing wasn't any too good. I could see enough, though, to distinguish that what I sailed over was just more of this grey plain that we'd been examining the whole week since our landing—same blobby growths and the same eternal carpet of crawling little plant-animals, or biopods, as Leroy calls them. So I sailed along, calling back my position every hour as instructed, and not knowing whether you heard me."

"I did!" snapped Harrison.

"A hundred and fifty miles south," continued Jarvis imperturbably, "the surface changed to a sort of low plateau, nothing but desert and orange-tinted sand. I figured that we were right in our guess, then, and this grey plain we dropped on was really the Mare Cimmerium which would make my orange desert the region called Xanthus. If I were right, I ought to hit another grey plain, the Mare Chronium in another couple of hundred miles, and then another orange desert, Thyle I or II. And so I did."

"Putz verified our position a week and a half ago!" grumbled the captain. "Let's get to the point."

"Coming!" remarked Jarvis. "Twenty miles into Thyle—believe it or not—I crossed a canal!"

"Putz photographed a hundred! Let's hear something new!"

"And did he also see a city?"

"Twenty of 'em, if you call those heaps of mud cities!"

"Well," observed Jarvis, "from here on I'll be telling a few things Putz didn't see!" He rubbed his tingling nose, and continued. "I knew that I had sixteen hours of daylight at this season, so eight hours—eight hundred miles—from here, I decided to turn back. I was still over Thyle, whether I or II I'm not sure, not more than twenty-five miles into it. And right there, Putz's pet motor quit!"

"Quit? How?" Putz was solicitous.

"The atomic blast got weak. I started losing altitude right away, and suddenly there I was with a thump right in the middle of Thyle! Smashed my nose on the window, too!" He rubbed the injured member ruefully.

"Did you maybe try vashing der combustion chamber mit acid sulphuric?" inquired Putz. "Sometimes der lead giffs a secondary radiation—"

"Naw!" said Jarvis disgustedly. "I wouldn't try that, of course—not more than ten times! Besides, the bump flattened the landing gear and busted off the under-jets. Suppose I got the thing working—what then? Ten miles with the blast coming right out of the bottom and I'd have melted the floor from under me!" He rubbed his nose again. "Lucky for me a pound only weighs seven ounces here, or I'd have been mashed flat!"

"I could have fixed!" ejaculated the engineer. "I bet it vas not serious."

"Probably not," agreed Jarvis sarcastically. "Only it wouldn't fly. Nothing serious, but I had my choice of waiting to be picked up or trying to walk back—eight hundred miles, and perhaps twenty days before we had to leave! Forty miles a day!

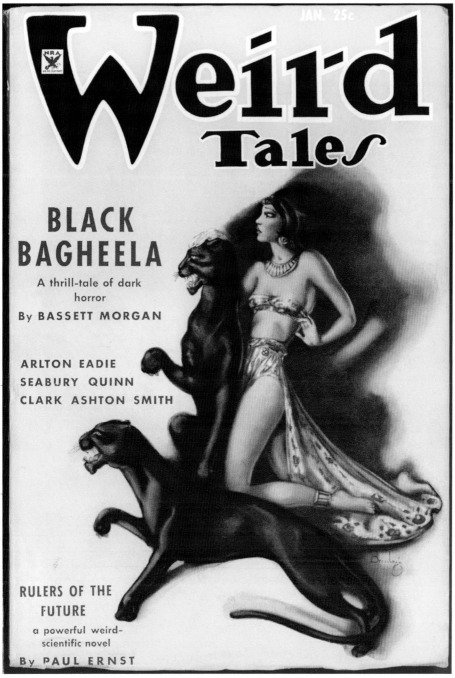

JAN. 25c

Weird
Tales

NRA
WE DO OUR PART

BLACK
BAGHEELA

A thrill-tale of dark
horror

By BASSETT MORGAN

ARLTON EADIE
SEABURY QUINN
CLARK ASHTON SMITH

RULERS OF THE
FUTURE

a powerful weird-
scientific novel

By PAUL ERNST

Margaret Brundage's paintings for the covers of *Weird Tales* magazine in the 1930s featured colorful—highly stylized, yet often highly stereotypic—characters in exotic and fantastic situations. The January 1935 issue of *Weird Tales* included Robert Bloch's first professionally published short story entitled "A Feast in the Abbey," as well as stories by Seabury Quinn, Clark Ashton Smith, Paul Ernst, and other famous fantasy and pulp magazine authors. Bassett Morgan was the pseudonym for Mrs. Grace Jones (1885–1973?).

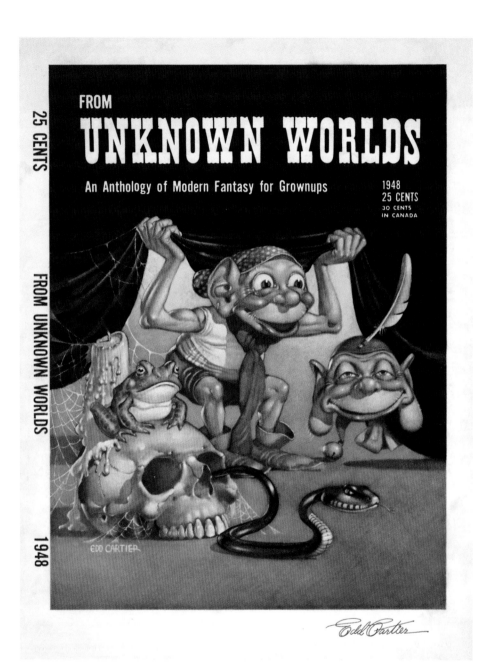

FROM

UNKNOWN WORLDS

An Anthology of Modern Fantasy for Grownups

25 CENTS

FROM UNKNOWN WORLDS

1948

1948
25 CENTS
30 CENTS
IN CANADA

EDD CARTIER

This one-shot "best of" anthology issue of *Unknown Worlds* done in 1948 features the cover art of Edd Cartier (1914–   ), who specialized in black-and-white drawings for pulp magazine interiors. Besides illustrating Fantasy fiction magazines, Cartier was a long-time interior artist for *The Shadow* magazine.

Without doubt the single most famous cover painter of Science Fiction pulp magazines, Frank R. Paul brought to life many of the concepts of the authors whose stories appeared in Hugo Gernsback's fiction magazines. Beyond the colorful planet and period conception of a rocketship, the cover for the November 1928 issue of *Amazing Stories* features Gernsback's famous "Scientifiction" icon, which illustrates Gernsback's commitment to keeping the fiction in *Amazing* firmly rooted in scientific fact. Jack Williamson's "The Metal Man" appeared in the December 1928 issue of *Amazing Stories*.

CONTENTS COPYRIGHTED 1936   JUNE 1936

ASTOUNDING
STORIES

20¢

The Shadow Out of Time
H. P. Lovecraft

also: Schachner, Van Lorne,
Coblentz, Corbett, Williamson

Bug-Eyed Monsters (BEMs) were often the subject of interpretation of Science Fiction and Fantasy pulp magazine cover artists. While not all pulp cover renderings depicted story elements found inside the magazine, this Howard V. Brown (1878–1945) painting was intended to supplement readers' understanding and appreciation of H. P. Lovecraft's *The Shadow Out of Time.* Jack Williamson's second installment of his four-part serial *The Cometeers* (the second *Legion of Space* novel) appeared in this, the June 1936 issue of *Astounding Stories.*

Well," he concluded, "I chose to walk. Just as much chance of being picked up, and it kept me busy."

"We'd have found you," said Harrison.

"No doubt. Anyway, I rigged up a harness from some seat straps, and put the water tank on my back, took a cartridge belt and revolver, and some iron rations, and started out."

"Water tank!" exclaimed the little biologist, Leroy. "She weigh one-quarter ton!"

"Wasn't full. Weighed about two hundred and fifty pounds earth-weight, which is eighty-five here. Then, besides, my own personal two hundred and ten pounds is only seventy on Mars, so, tank and all, I grossed a hundred and fifty-five, or fifty-five pounds less than my everyday earth-weight. I figured on that when I undertook the forty-mile daily stroll. Oh—of course I took a thermo-skin sleeping bag for these wintry Martian nights.

"Off I went, bouncing along pretty quickly. Eight hours of daylight meant twenty miles or more. It got tiresome, of course—plugging along over a soft sand desert with nothing to see, not even Leroy's crawling biopods. But an hour or so brought me to the canal—just a dry ditch about four hundred feet wide, and straight as a railroad on its own company map.

"There'd been water in it sometime, though. The ditch was covered with what looked like a nice green lawn. Only, as I approached, the lawn moved out of my way!"

"Eh?" said Leroy.

"Yeah, it was a relative of your biopods. I caught one—a little grass-like blade about as long as my finger, with two thin, stemmy legs."

"He is where?" Leroy was eager.

"He is let go! I had to move, so I plowed along with the walking grass opening in front and closing behind. And then I was out on the orange desert of Thyle again.

"I plugged steadily along, cussing the sand that made going so tiresome, and, incidentally, cussing that cranky motor of yours, Karl. It was just before twilight that I reached the edge of Thyle, and looked down over the gray Mare Chronium. And I knew there was seventy-five miles of *that* to be walked over, and then a couple of hundred miles of that Xanthus desert, and about as much more Mare Cimmerium. Was I pleased? I started cussing you fellows for not picking me up!"

"We were trying, you sap!" said Harrison.

"That didn't help. Well, I figured I might as well use what was left of daylight in getting down the cliff that bounded Thyle. I found an easy place, and down I went. Mare Chronium was just the same sort of place as this—crazy leafless plants and a bunch of crawlers; I gave it a glance and hauled out my sleeping bag. Up to that time, you know, I hadn't seen anything worth worrying about on this half-dead world—nothing dangerous, that is."

"Did you?" queried Harrison.

"*Did I!* You'll hear about it when I come to it. Well, I was just about to turn in when suddenly I heard the wildest sort of shenanigans!"

"Vot iss shenanigans?" inquired Putz.

"He says, 'Je ne sais quoi,' " explained Leroy. "It is to say, 'I don't know what.' "

"That's right," agreed Jarvis. "I didn't know what, so I sneaked over to find out. There was a racket like a flock of crows eating a bunch of canaries—whistles, cackles, caws, trills, and what have you. I rounded a clump of stumps, and there was Tweel!"

"Tweel?" said Harrison, and "Tveel?" said Leroy and Putz.

"That freak ostrich," explained the narrator. "At least, Tweel is as near as I can pronounce it without sputtering. He called it something like 'Trrrweerrlll.' "

"What was he doing?" asked the Captain.

"He was being eaten! And squealing, of course, as any one would."

"Eaten! By what?"

"I found out later. All I could see then was a bunch of black ropy arms tangled around what looked like, as Putz described it to you, an ostrich. I wasn't going to interfere, naturally; if both creatures were dangerous, I'd have one less to worry about.

"But the bird-like thing was putting up a good battle, dealing vicious blows with an eighteen-inch beak, between screeches. And besides, I caught a glimpse or two of what was on the end of those arms!" Jarvis shuddered. "But the clincher was when I noticed a little black bag or case hung about the neck of the bird-thing! It was intelligent! That or tame, I assumed. Anyway, it clinched my decision. I pulled out my automatic and fired into what I could see of its antagonist.

"There was a flurry of tentacles and a spurt of black corruption, and then the thing, with a disgusting sucking noise, pulled itself and its arms into a hole in the ground. The other let out a series of clacks, staggered around on legs about as thick as golf sticks, and turned suddenly to face me. I held my weapon ready, and the two of us stared at each other.

"The Martian wasn't a bird, really. It wasn't even bird-like, except just at first glance. It had a beak all right, and a few feathery appendages, but the beak wasn't really a beak. It was somewhat flexible; I could see the tip bend slowly from side to side; it was almost like a cross between a beak and a trunk. It had four-toed feet, and four fingered things—hands, you'd have to call them, and a little roundish body, and a long neck ending in a tiny head—and that beak. It stood an inch or so taller than I, and—well, Putz saw it!"

The engineer nodded, "*Ja!* I saw!"

Jarvis continued. "So—we stared at each other. Finally the creature went into a series of clackings and twitterings and held out its hands toward me, empty. I took that as a gesture of friendship."

"Perhaps," suggested Harrison, "it looked at that nose of yours and thought you were its brother!"

"Huh! You can be funny without talking! Anyway, I put up my gun and said 'Aw, don't mention it,' or something of the sort, and the thing came over and we were pals.

"By that time, the sun was pretty low and I knew that I'd better build a fire or get into my thermo-skin. I decided on the fire. I picked a spot at the base of the Thyle cliff, where the rock could reflect a little heat on my back. I started breaking off chunks of this desiccated Martian vegetation, and my companion caught the idea and brought in an armful. I reached for a match, but the Martian fished into his pouch and brought out something that looked like a glowing coal; one touch of it, and the fire was blazing—and you all know what a job we have starting a fire in this atmosphere!

"And that bag of his!" continued the narrator. "That was a manufactured article, my friends; press an end and she popped open—press the middle and she sealed so perfectly you couldn't see the line. Better than zippers.

"Well, we stared at the fire a while and I decided to attempt some sort of communication with the Martian. I pointed at myself and said 'Dick'; he caught the drift immediately, stretched a bony claw at me and repeated 'Tick.' Then I pointed at him, and he gave that whistle I called Tweel; I can't imitate his accent. Things were going smoothly; to emphasize the names, I repeated 'Dick,' and then, pointing at him, 'Tweel.'

"There we stuck! He gave some clacks that sounded negative, and said something like 'P-p-p-proot.' And that was just the beginning; I was always 'Tick,' but as for him—part of the time he was 'Tweel,' and part of the time he was 'P-p-p-proot,' and part of the time he was sixteen other noises!

"We just couldn't connect. I tried 'rock,' and I tried 'star,' and 'tree,' and 'fire,' and Lord knows what else, and try as I would, I couldn't get a single word! Nothing was the same for two successive minutes, and if that's a language, I'm an alchemist! Finally I gave it up and called him Tweel, and that seemed to do.

"But Tweel hung on to some of my words. He remembered a couple of them, which I suppose is a great achievement if you're used to a language you have to make up as you go along. But I couldn't get the hang of his talk; either I missed some subtle point or we just didn't *think* alike—and I rather believe the latter view.

"I've other reasons for believing that. After a while I gave up the language business, and tried mathematics. I scratched two plus two equals four on the ground, and demonstrated it with pebbles. Again Tweel caught the idea, and informed me that three plus three equals six. Once more we seemed to be getting somewhere.

"So, knowing that Tweel had at least a grammar school education, I drew a circle for the sun, pointing first at it, and then at the last glow of the sun. Then I sketched in Mercury, and Venus, and Mother Earth, and Mars, and finally, pointing to Mars, I swept my hand around in a sort of inclusive gesture to indicate that Mars was our current environment. I was working up to putting over the idea that my home was on the earth.

"Tweel understood my diagram all right. He poked his beak at it, and with a great deal of trilling and clucking, he added Deimos and Phobos to Mars, and then sketched in the earth's moon!

"Do you see what that proves? It proves that Tweel's race uses telescopes—that they're civilized!"

"Does not!" snapped Harrison. "The moon is visible from here as a fifth magnitude star. They could see its revolution with the naked eye."

"The moon, yes!" said Jarvis. "You've missed my point. Mercury isn't visible! And Tweel knew of Mercury because he placed the Moon at the *third* planet, not the second. If he didn't know Mercury, he'd put the earth second, and Mars third, instead of fourth! See?"

"Humph!" said Harrison.

"Anyway," proceeded Jarvis, "I went on with my lesson. Things were going smoothly, and it looked as if I could put the idea over. I pointed at the earth on my diagram, and then at myself, and then, to clinch it, I pointed to myself and then to the earth itself shining bright green almost at the zenith.

"Tweel set up such an excited clacking that I was certain he understood. He jumped up and down, and suddenly he pointed at himself and then at the sky, and then at himself and at the sky again. He pointed at his middle and then at Arcturus, at his head and then at Spica, at his feet and then at half a dozen stars, while I just gaped at him. Then, all of a sudden, he gave a tremendous leap. Man, what a hop! He shot straight up into the starlight, seventy-five feet if an inch! I saw him silhouetted against the sky, saw him turn and come down at me head first, and land smack on his beak like a javelin! There he stuck square in the center of my sun-circle in the sand—a bull's eye!"

"Nuts!" observed the captain. "Plain nuts!"

"That's what I thought, too! I just stared at him open-mouthed while he pulled his head out of the sand and stood up. Then I figured he'd missed my point, and I went through the whole blamed rigamarole again, and it ended the same way, with Tweel on his nose in the middle of my picture!"

"Maybe it's a religious rite," suggested Harrison.

"Maybe," said Jarvis dubiously. "Well, there we were. We could exchange ideas up to a certain point, and then—blooey! Something in us was different, unrelated; I don't doubt that Tweel thought me just as screwy as I thought him. Our minds simply looked at the world from different viewpoints, and perhaps his viewpoint is as true as ours. But—we couldn't get together, that's all. Yet, in spite of all difficulties, I *liked* Tweel, and I have a queer certainty that he liked me."

"Nuts!" repeated the captain. "Just daffy!"

"Yeah? Wait and see. A couple of times I've thought that perhaps we—" He paused, and then resumed his narrative. "Anyway, I finally gave it up, and got into my thermo-skin to sleep. The fire hadn't kept me any too warm, but that damned sleeping bag did. Got stuffy five minutes after I closed myself in. I opened it a little and bingo! Some eighty-below-zero air hit my nose, and that's when I got this pleasant little frostbite to add to the bump I acquired during the crash of my rocket.

"I don't know what Tweel made of my sleeping. He sat around, but when I woke up, he was gone. I'd just crawled out of my bag, though, when I heard some twittering, and there he came, sailing down from that three-story Thyle cliff to alight on his beak beside me. I pointed to myself and toward the north, and he pointed at himself and toward the south, but when I loaded up and started away, he came along.

"Man, how he traveled! A hundred and fifty feet at a jump, sailing through the air stretched out like a spear, and landing on his beak. He seemed surprised at my plodding, but after a few moments he fell in beside me, only every few minutes he'd go into one of his leaps, and stick his nose into the sand a block ahead of me. Then he'd come shooting back at me; it made me nervous at first to see that beak of his coming at me like a spear, but he always ended in the sand at my side.

"So the two of us plugged along across the Mare Chronium. Same sort of place as this—same crazy plants and same little green biopods growing in the sand, or crawling out of your way. We talked—not that we understood each other, you know, but just for company. I sang songs, and I suspect Tweel did too; at least, some of his trillings and twitterings had a subtle sort of rhythm.

"Then, for variety, Tweel would display his smattering of English words. He'd point to an outcropping and say 'rock,' and point to a pebble and say it again; or he'd touch my arm and say 'Tick,' and then repeat it. He seemed terrifically amused that the same word meant the same thing twice in succession, or that the same word could apply to two different objects. It set me wondering if perhaps his language wasn't like the primitive speech of some earth people—you know, Captain, like the Negritoes, for instance, who haven't any generic words. No word for food or water or man—words for good food and bad food, or rain water and sea water, or strong man and weak man—but no names for general classes. They're too primitive to understand that rain water and sea water are just different aspects of the same thing. But that wasn't the case with Tweel; it was just that we were somehow mysteriously different—our minds were alien to each other. And yet—we *liked* each other!"

"Looney, that's all," remarked Harrison. "That's why you two were so fond of each other."

"Well, I like *you!*" countered Jarvis wickedly. "Anyway," he resumed, "don't get the idea that there was anything screwy about Tweel. In fact, I'm not so sure but that he couldn't teach our highly praised human intelligence a trick or two. Oh, he wasn't an intellectual superman, I guess; but don't overlook the point that he managed to understand a little of my mental workings, and I never even got a glimmering of his."

"Because he didn't have any!" suggested the captain, while Putz and Leroy blinked attentively.

"You can judge of that when I'm through," said Jarvis. "Well, we plugged along across the Mare Chronium all that day, and all the next. Mare Chronium—Sea of Time! Say, I was willing to agree with Schiaparelli's name by the end of that march! Just that grey, endless plain of weird plants, and never a sign of any other life. It was so monotonous that I was even glad to see the desert of Xanthus toward the evening of the second day.

"I was fair worn out, but Tweel seemed as fresh as ever, for all I never saw him drink or eat. I think he could have crossed the Mare Chronium in a couple of hours with those block-long nose dives of his, but he stuck along with me. I offered him some water once or twice; he took the cup from me and sucked the liquid into his beak, and then carefully squirted it all back into the cup and gravely returned it.

"Just as we sighted Xanthus, or the cliffs that bounded it, one of those nasty sand clouds blew along, not as bad as the one we had here, but mean to travel against. I pulled the transparent flap of my thermo-skin bag across my face and managed pretty well, and I noticed that Tweel used some feathery appendages growing like a mustache at the base of his beak to cover his nostrils, and some similar fuzz to shield his eyes."

"He is a desert creature!" ejaculated the little biologist, Leroy.

"Huh? Why?"

"He drink no water—he is adapt' for sand storm—"

"Proves nothing! There's not enough water to waste any where on this desiccated pill called Mars. We'd call all of it desert on earth, you know." He paused. "Anyway, after the sand storm blew over, a little wind kept blowing in our faces, not strong enough to stir the sand. But suddenly things came drifting along from the Xanthus cliffs—small, transparent spheres, for all the world like glass tennis balls! But light—they were almost light enough to float even in this thin air— empty, too; at least, I cracked open a couple and nothing came out but a bad smell. I asked Tweel about them, but all he said was 'No, no, no,' which I took to mean that he knew nothing about them. So they went bouncing by like tumbleweeds, or like soap bubbles, and we plugged on toward Xanthus. Tweel pointed at one of the crystal balls once and said 'rock,' but I was too tired to argue with him. Later I discovered what he meant.

"We came to the bottom of the Xanthus cliffs finally, when there wasn't much daylight left. I decided to sleep on the plateau if possible; anything dangerous, I reasoned, would be more likely to prowl through the vegetation of the Mare Chronium than the sand of Xanthus. Not that I'd seen a single sign of menace, except the rope-armed black thing that had trapped Tweel, and apparently that didn't prowl at all, but lured its victims within reach. It couldn't lure me while I slept, especially as Tweel didn't seem to sleep at all, but simply sat patiently around all night. I wondered how the creature had managed to trap Tweel, but there wasn't any way of asking him. I found that out too, later; it's devilish!

"However, we were ambling around the base of the Xanthus barrier looking for an easy spot to climb. At least, I was. Tweel could have leaped it easily, for the cliffs were lower than Thyle—perhaps sixty feet. I found a place and started up, swearing at the water tank strapped to my back—it didn't bother me except when climbing—and suddenly I heard a sound that I thought I recognized!

"You know how deceptive sounds are in this thin air. A shot sounds like the pop of a cork. But this sound was the drone of a rocket, and sure enough, there went our second auxiliary about ten miles to westward, between me and the sunset!"

"Vas me!" said Putz. "I hunt for you."

"Yeah; I knew that, but what good did it do me? I hung on to the cliff and yelled and waved with one hand. Tweel saw it too, and set up a trilling and twittering, leaping to the top of the barrier and then high into the air. And while I watched, the machine droned on into the shadows to the south.

"I scrambled to the top of the cliff. Tweel was still pointing and trilling excitedly, shooting up toward the sky and coming down head-on to stick upside down on his beak in the sand. I pointed toward the south and at myself, and he said, 'Yes—Yes—Yes'; but somehow I gathered that he thought the flying thing was a relative of mine, probably a parent. Perhaps I did his intellect an injustice; I think now that I did.

"I was bitterly disappointed by the failure to attract attention. I pulled out my thermo-skin bag and crawled into it, as the night chill was already apparent. Tweel stuck his beak into the sand and drew up his legs and arms and looked for all the world like one of those leafless shrubs out there. I think he stayed that way all night."

"Protective mimicry!" ejaculated Leroy. "See? He is desert creature!"

"In the morning," resumed Jarvis, "we started off again. We hadn't gone a hundred yards into Xanthus when I saw something queer! This is one thing Putz didn't photograph, I'll wager!

"There was a line of little pyramids—tiny ones, not more than six inches high, stretching across Xanthus as far as I could see! Little buildings made of pygmy bricks, they were, hollow inside and truncated, or at least broken at the top and empty. I pointed at them and said 'What?' to Tweel, but he gave some negative twitters to indicate, I suppose, that he didn't know. So off we went, following the row of pyramids because they ran north, and I was going north.

"Man, we trailed that line for hours! After a while, I noticed another queer thing: they were getting larger. Same number of bricks in each one, but the bricks were larger.

"By noon they were shoulder high. I looked into a couple—all just the same, broken at the top and empty. I examined a brick or two as well; they were silica, and old as creation itself!"

"How you know?" asked Leroy.

"They were weathered—edges rounded. Silica doesn't weather easily even on earth, and in this climate—!"

"How old you think?"

"Fifty thousand—a hundred thousand years. How can I tell? The little ones we saw in the morning were older—perhaps ten times as old. Crumbling. How old would that make *them?* Half a million years? Who knows?" Jarvis paused a moment. "Well," he resumed, "we followed the line. Tweel pointed at them and said 'rock' once or twice, but he'd done that many times before. Besides, he was more or less right about these.

"I tried questioning him. I pointed at a pyramid and asked 'People?' and indicated the two of us. He set up a negative sort of clucking and said, 'No, no, no. No one-one-two. No two-two-four,' meanwhile robbing his stomach. I just stared at him and he went through the business again. 'No one-one-two. No two-two-four.' I just gaped at him."

"That proves it!" exclaimed Harrison. "Nuts!"

"You think so?" queried Jarvis sardonically. "Well, I figured it out different! 'No one-one-two!' You don't get it, of course, do you?"

"Nope—nor do you!"

"I think I do! Tweel was using the few English words he knew to put over a very complex idea. What, let me ask, does mathematics make you think of?"

"Why—of astronomy. Or—or logic!"

"That's it! 'No one-one-two!' Tweel was telling me that the builders of the pyramids weren't people—or that they weren't intelligent, that they weren't reasoning creatures! Get it?"

"Huh! I'll be damned!"

"You probably will."

"Why," put in Leroy, "he rub his belly?"

"Why? Because, my dear biologist, that's where his brains are! Not in his tiny head—in his middle!"

"*C'est* impossible!"

"Not on Mars, it isn't! This flora and fauna aren't earthly; your biopods prove that!" Jarvis grinned and took up his narrative. "Anyway, we plugged along across Xanthus and in about the middle of the afternoon, something else queer happened. The pyramids ended."

"Ended!"

"Yeah; the queer part was that the last one—and now they were ten-footers— was capped! See? Whatever built it was still inside; we'd trailed 'em from their half-million-year-old origin to the present.

"Tweel and I noticed it about the same time. I yanked out my automatic (I had a clip of Boland explosive bullets in it) and Tweel, quick as a sleight-of-hand trick, snapped a queer little glass revolver out of his bag. It was much like our weapons, except that the grip was larger to accommodate his four-taloned hand. And we held our weapons ready while we sneaked up along the lines of empty pyramids.

"Tweel saw the movement first. The top tiers of bricks were heaving, shaking, and suddenly slid down the sides with a thin crash. And then—something— something was coming out!

"A long, silvery-grey arm appeared, dragging after it an armored body. Armored, I mean, with scales, silver-grey and dull-shining. The arm heaved the body out of the hole; the beast crashed to the sand.

"It was a nondescript creature—body like a big grey cask, arm and a sort of mouth-hole at one end; stiff, pointed tail at the other—and that's all. No other limbs, no eyes, ears, nose—nothing! The thing dragged itself a few yards, inserted its pointed tail in the sand, pushed itself upright, and just sat.

"Tweel and I watched it for ten minutes before it moved. Then, with a creaking and rustling like—oh, like crumpling stiff paper—its arm moved to the mouth-hole and out came a brick! The arm placed the brick carefully on the ground, and the thing was still again.

"Another ten minutes—another brick. Just one of Nature's bricklayers. I was about to slip away and move on when Tweel pointed at the thing and said 'rock'! I went 'huh?' and he said it again. Then, to the accompaniment of some of his trilling, he said, 'No—no—,' and gave two or three whistling breaths.

"Well, I got his meaning, for a wonder! I said, 'No breath?' and demonstrated the word. Tweel was ecstatic; he said, 'Yes, yes, yes! No, no, no breet!' Then he gave a leap and sailed out to land on his nose about one pace from the monster!

"I was startled, you can imagine! The arm was going up for a brick, and I expected to see Tweel caught and mangled, but—nothing happened! Tweel pounded on the creature, and the arm took the brick and placed it neatly beside the first. Tweel rapped on its body again, and said 'rock,' and I got up nerve enough to take a look myself.

"Tweel was right again. The creature *was* rock, and it didn't breathe!"

"How you know?" snapped Leroy, his black eyes blazing interest.

"Because I'm a chemist. The beast was made of silica! There must have been pure silicon in the sand, and it lived on that. Get it? We, and Tweel, and those plants out there, and even the biopods are *carbon* life; this thing lived by a different set of chemical reactions. It was silicon life!"

"*La vie silicieuse!*" shouted Leroy. "I have suspect, and now it is proof! I must go see! *Il faut que je—*"

"All right! All right!" said Jarvis. "You can go see. Anyhow, there the thing was, alive and yet not alive, moving every ten minutes, and then only to remove a brick. Those bricks were its waste matter. See, Frenchy? We're carbon, and our waste is carbon dioxide, and this thing is silicon, and *its* waste is silicon dioxide—silica. But silica is a solid, hence the bricks. And it builds itself in, and when it is covered, it moves over to a fresh place to start over. No wonder it creaked! A living creature half a million years old!"

"How you know how old?" Leroy was frantic.

"We trailed its pyramids from the beginning, didn't we? If this weren't the original pyramid builder, the series would have ended somewhere before we found him, wouldn't it?—ended and started over with the small ones. That's simple enough, isn't it?

"But he reproduces, or tries to. Before the third brick came out, there was a little rustle and out popped a whole stream of those little crystal balls. They're his spores, or eggs, or seeds—call 'em what you want. They went bouncing by across Xanthus just as they'd bounced by us back in the Mare Chronium. I've a hunch how they work, too—this is for your information, Leroy. I think the crystal shell of silica is no more than a protective covering, like an eggshell, and that the active principle is the smell inside. It's some sort of gas that attacks silicon, and if the shell is broken near a supply of that element, some reaction starts that ultimately develops into a beast like that one."

"You should try!" exclaimed the little Frenchman. "We must break one to see!"

"Yeah? Well, I did. I smashed a couple against the sand. Would you like to come back in about ten thousand years to see if I planted some pyramid monsters? You'd most likely be able to tell by that time!" Jarvis paused and drew a deep breath. "Lord! That queer creature! Do you picture it? Blind, deaf, nerveless, brainless—just a mechanism, and yet—immortal! Bound to go on making bricks, building pyramids, as long as silicon and oxygen exist, and even afterwards it'll just stop. It won't be dead. If the accidents of a million years bring it its food again, there it'll be, ready to run again, while brains and civilizations are part of the past. A queer beast—yet I met a stranger one!"

"If you did, it must have been in your dreams!" growled Harrison.

"You're right!" said Jarvis soberly. "In a way, you're right. The dream-beast! That's the best name for it—and it's the most fiendish, terrifying creation one could imagine! More dangerous than a lion, more insidious than a snake!"

"Tell me!" begged Leroy. "I must go see!"

"Not *this* devil!" He paused again. "Well," he resumed, "Tweel and I left the pyramid creature and plowed along through Xanthus. I was tired and a little disheartened by Putz's failure to pick me up, and Tweel's trilling got on my nerves, as did his flying nosedives. So I just strode along without a word, hour after hour across that monotonous desert.

"Toward mid-afternoon we came in sight of a low dark line on the horizon. I knew what it was. It was a canal; I'd crossed it in the rocket and it meant that we were just one-third of the way across Xanthus. Pleasant thought, wasn't it? And still, I was keeping up to schedule.

"We approached the canal slowly; I remembered that this one was bordered by a wide fringe of vegetation and that Mud-heap City was on it.

"I was tired, as I said. I kept thinking of a good hot meal, and then from that I jumped to reflections of how nice and home-like even Borneo would seem after this crazy planet, and from that, to thoughts of little old New York, and then to thinking about a girl I know there—Fancy Long. Know her?"

"Vision entertainer," said Harrison. "I've tuned her in. Nice blonde—dances and sings on the *Yerba Mate* hour."

"That's her," said Jarvis ungrammatically. "I know her pretty well—just friends, get me?—though she came down to see us off in the *Ares*. Well, I was thinking about her, feeling pretty lonesome, and all the time we were approaching that line of rubbery plants.

"And then—I said, 'What 'n Hell!' and stared. And there she was—Fancy Long, standing plain as day under one of those crack-brained trees, and smiling and waving just the way I remembered her when we left!"

"Now you're nuts, too!" observed the captain.

"Boy, I almost agreed with you! I stared and pinched myself and closed my eyes and then stared again—and every time, there was Fancy Long smiling and waving! Tweel saw something, too; he was trilling and clucking away, but I scarcely heard him. I was bounding toward her over the sand, too amazed even to ask myself questions.

"I wasn't twenty feet from her when Tweel caught me with one of his flying leaps. He grabbed my arm, yelling, 'No—no—no!' in his squeaky voice. I tried to shake him off—he was as light as if he were built of bamboo—but he dug his claws in and yelled. And finally some sort of sanity returned to me and I stopped less than ten feet from her. There she stood, looking as solid as Putz's head!"

"Vot?" said the engineer.

"She smiled and waved, and waved and smiled, and I stood there dumb as Leroy, while Tweel squeaked and chattered. I knew it couldn't be real, yet—there she was!

"Finally I said, 'Fancy! Fancy Long!' She just kept on smiling and waving, but looking as real as if I hadn't left her thirty-seven million miles away.

"Tweel had his glass pistol out, pointing it at her. I grabbed his arm, but he tried to push me away. He pointed at her and said, 'No breet! No breet!' and I understood that he meant that the Fancy Long thing wasn't alive. Man, my head was whirling!

"Still, it gave me the jitters to see him pointing his weapon at her. I don't know why I stood there watching him take careful aim, but I did. Then he squeezed the handle of his weapon; there was a little puff of steam, and Fancy Long was gone! And in her place was one of those writhing, black, rope-armed horrors like the one I'd saved Tweel from!

"The dream-beast! I stood there dizzy, watching it die while Tweel trilled and whistled. Finally he touched my arm, pointed at the twisting thing, and said, 'You one-one-two, he one-one-two.' After he'd repeated it eight or ten times, I got it. Do any of you?"

"*Oui!*" shrilled Leroy. "*Moi—je le comprends!* He mean you think of something, the beast he know, and you see it! *Un chien*—a hungry dog, he would see the big bone with meat! Or smell it—not?"

"Right!" said Jarvis. "The dream-beast uses its victim's longings and desires to trap its prey. The bird at nesting season would see its mate, the fox, prowling for its own prey, would see a helpless rabbit!"

"How he do?" queried Leroy.

"How do I know? How does a snake back on earth charm a bird into its very jaws? And aren't there deep-sea fish that lure their victims into their mouths? Lord!" Jarvis shuddered. "Do you see how insidious the monster is? We're warned now—but henceforth we can't trust even our eyes. You might see me—I might see one of you—and back of it may be nothing but another of those black horrors!"

"How'd your friend know?" asked the captain abruptly.

"Tweel? I wonder! Perhaps he was thinking of something that couldn't possibly have interested me, and when I started to run, he realized that I saw something different and was warned. Or perhaps the dream-beast can only project a single vision, and Tweel saw what I saw—or nothing. I couldn't ask him. But it's just another proof that his intelligence is equal to ours or greater."

"He's daffy, I tell you!" said Harrison. "What makes you think his intellect ranks with the human?"

"Plenty of things! First, the pyramid-beast. He hadn't seen one before; he said as much. Yet he recognized it as a dead-alive automaton of silicon."

"He could have heard of it," objected Harrison. "He lives around here, you know."

"Well how about the language? I couldn't pick up a single idea of his and he learned six or seven words of mine. And do you realize what complex ideas he put over with no more than those six or seven words? The pyramid-monster—the dream-beast! In a single phrase he told me that one was a harmless automaton and the other a deadly hypnotist. What about that?"

"Huh!" said the captain.

"*Huh* if you wish! Could you have done it knowing only six words of English? Could you go even further, as Tweel did, and tell me that another creature was of a sort of intelligence so different from ours that understanding was impossible— even more impossible than that between Tweel and me?"

"Eh? What was that?"

"Later. The point I'm making is that Tweel and his race are worthy of our friendship. Somewhere on Mars—and you'll find I'm right—is a civilization and culture equal to ours, and maybe more than equal. And communication is possible between them and us; Tweel proves that. It may take years of patient trial, for their minds are alien, but less alien than the next minds we encountered—if they *are* minds."

"The next ones? What next ones?"

"The people of the mud cities along the canals." Jarvis frowned, then resumed his narrative. "I thought the dream-beast and the silicon-monster were the strangest beings conceivable, but I was wrong. These creatures are still more alien, less understandable than either and far less comprehensible than Tweel, with whom friendship is possible, and even, by patience and concentration, the exchange of ideas.

"Well," he continued, "we left the dream-beast dying, dragging itself back into its hole, and we moved toward the canal. There was a carpet of that queer walking-grass scampering out of our way, and when we reached the bank, there was a yellow trickle of water flowing. The mound city I'd noticed from the rocket was a mile or so to the right and I was curious enough to want to take a look at it.

"It had seemed deserted from my previous glimpse of it, and if any creatures were lurking in it—well, Tweel and I were both armed. And by the way, that crystal weapon of Tweel's was an interesting device; I took a look at it after the dream-beast episode. It fired a little glass splinter, poisoned, I suppose, and I guess it held at least a hundred of 'em to a load. The propellent was steam—just plain steam!"

"Shteam!" echoed Putz. "From vot come, shteam?"

"From water, of course! You could see the water through the transparent handle and about a gill of another liquid, thick and yellowish. When Tweel squeezed the handle—there was no trigger—a drop of water and a drop of the yellow stuff squirted into the firing chamber, and the water vaporized—pop!—like that. It's not so difficult; I think we could develop the same principle. Concentrated sulphuric acid will heat water almost to boiling, and so will quicklime, and there's potassium and sodium—

"Of course, his weapon hadn't the range of mine, but it wasn't so bad in this thin air, and it *did* hold as many shots as a cowboy's gun in a Western movie. It was effective, too, at least against Martian life; I tried it out, aiming at one of the crazy plants, and darned if the plant didn't wither up and fall apart! That's why I think the glass splinters were poisoned.

"Anyway, we trudged along toward the mud-heap city and I began to wonder whether the city builders dug the canals. I pointed to the city and then at the canal, and Tweel said 'No—no—no!' and gestured toward the south. I took it to mean that some other race had created the canal system, perhaps Tweel's people. I don't know; maybe there's still another intelligent race on the planet, or a dozen others. Mars is a queer little world.

"A hundred yards from the city we crossed a sort of road—just a hard-packed mud trail, and then, all of a sudden, along came one of the mound builders!

"Man, talk about fantastic beings! It looked rather like a barrel trotting along on four legs with four other arms or tentacles. It had no head, just body and members and a row of eyes completely around it. The top end of the barrel-body was a diaphragm stretched as tight as a drum head, and that was all. It was pushing a little coppery cart and tore right past us like the proverbial bat out of Hell. It didn't even notice us, although I thought the eyes on my side shifted a little as it passed.

"A moment later another came along, pushing another empty cart. Same thing—it just scooted past us. Well, I wasn't going to be ignored by a bunch of barrels playing train, so when the third one approached, I planted myself in the way—ready to jump, of course, if the thing didn't stop.

"But it did. It stopped and set up a sort of drumming from the diaphragm on top. And I held out both hands and said, 'We are friends!' And what do you suppose the thing did?"

"Said, 'Pleased to meet you,' I'll bet!" suggested Harrison.

"I couldn't have been more surprised if it had! It drummed on its diaphragm, and then suddenly boomed out, 'We are v-r-r-riends!' and gave its pushcart a vicious poke at me! I jumped aside, and away it went while I stared dumbly after it.

"A minute later another one came hurrying along. This one didn't pause, but simply drummed out, 'We are v-r-r-riends!' and scurried by. How did it learn the phrase? Were all of the creatures in some sort of communication with each other? Were they all parts of some central organism? I don't know, though I think Tweel does.

"Anyway, the creatures went sailing past us, every one greeting us with the same statement. It got to be funny; I never thought to find so many friends on this God-forsaken ball! Finally I made a puzzled gesture to Tweel; I guess he understood, for he said, 'One-one-two—yes!—two-two-four—no!' Get it?"

"Sure," said Harrison. "It's a Martian nursery rhyme."

"Yeah! Well, I was getting used to Tweel's symbolism, and I figured it out this way. 'One-one-two—yes!' The creatures were intelligent. 'Two-two-four—no!' Their intelligence was not of our order, but something different and beyond the logic of two and two is four. Maybe I missed his meaning. Perhaps he meant that their minds were of low degree, able to figure out the simple things—'One-one-two—yes!'—but not more difficult things—'Two-two-four—no!' But I think from what we saw later that he meant the other.

"After a few moments, the creatures came rushing back—first one, then another. Their pushcarts were full of stones, sand, chunks of robbery plants, and such rubbish as that. They droned out their friendly greeting, which didn't really sound so friendly, and dashed on. The third one I assumed to be my first acquaintance and I decided to have another chat with him. I stepped into his path again and waited.

"Up he came, booming out his 'We are v-r-r-riends' and stopped. I looked at him; four or five of his eyes looked at me. He tried his password again and gave a shove on his cart, but I stood firm. And then the—the dashed creature reached out one of his arms, and two finger-like nippers tweaked my nose!"

"Haw!" roared Harrison. "Maybe the things have a sense of beauty!"

"Laugh!" grumbled Jarvis. "I'd already had a nasty bump and a mean frostbite on that nose. Anyway, I yelled 'Ouch!' and jumped aside and the creature dashed away; but from then on, their greeting was 'We are v-r-r-riends! Ouch!' Queer beasts!

"Tweel and I followed the road squarely up to the nearest mound. The creatures were coming and going, paying us not the slightest attention, fetching their loads of rubbish. The road simply dived into an opening, and slanted down like an old mine, and in and out darted the barrel-people, greeting us with their eternal phrase.

"I looked in; there was a light somewhere below, and I was curious to see it. It didn't look like a flame or torch, you understand, but more like a civilized light, and I thought that I might get some clue as to the creatures' development. So in I went and Tweel tagged along, not without a few trills and twitters, however.

"The light was curious; it sputtered and flared like an old arc light, but came from a single black rod set in the wall of the corridor. It was electric, beyond doubt. The creatures were fairly civilized, apparently.

"Then I saw another light shining on something that glittered and I went on to look at that, but it was only a heap of shiny sand. I turned toward the entrance to leave, and the Devil take me if it wasn't gone!

"I suppose the corridor had curved, or I'd stepped into a side passage. Anyway, I walked back in that direction I thought we'd come, and all I saw was more dimlit corridor. The place was a labyrinth! There was nothing but twisting passages running every way, lit by occasional lights, and now and then a creature running by, sometimes with a pushcart, sometimes without.

"Well, I wasn't much worried at first. Tweel and I had only come a few steps from the entrance. But every move we made after that seemed to get us in deeper. Finally I tried following one of the creatures with an empty cart, thinking that he'd be going out for his rubbish, but he ran around aimlessly, into one passage and out another. When he started dashing around a pillar like one of these Japanese waltzing mice, I gave up, dumped my water tank on the floor, and sat down.

"Tweel was as lost as I. I pointed up and he said 'No—no—no!' in a sort of helpless trill. And we couldn't get any help from the natives. They paid no attention at all, except to assure us they were friends—ouch!

"Lord! I don't know how many hours or days we wandered around there! I slept twice from sheer exhaustion; Tweel never seemed to need sleep. We tried following only the upward corridors, but they'd run uphill a ways and then curve downwards. The temperature in that damned ant hill was constant; you couldn't tell night from day and after my first sleep I didn't know whether I'd slept one hour or thirteen, so I couldn't tell from my watch whether it was midnight or noon.

"We saw plenty of strange things. There were machines running in some of the corridors, but they didn't seem to be doing anything—just wheels turning. And several times I saw two barrel-beasts with a little one growing between them, joined to both."

"Parthenogenesis!" exulted Leroy. "Parthenogenesis by budding like *les tulipes!*"

"If you say so, Frenchy," agreed Jarvis. "The things never noticed us at all, except, as I say, to greet us with 'We are v-r-r-riends! Ouch!' They seemed to have no home-life of any sort, but just scurried around with their pushcarts, bringing in rubbish. And finally I discovered what they did with it.

"We'd had a little luck with a corridor, one that slanted upwards for a great distance. I was feeling that we ought to be close to the surface when suddenly the passage debouched into a domed chamber, the only one we'd seen. And man!—I felt like dancing when I saw what looked like daylight through a crevice in the roof.

"There was a—a sort of machine in the chamber, just an enormous wheel that turned slowly, and one of the creatures was in the act of dumping his rubbish below it. The wheel ground it with a crunch—sand, stones, plants, all into powder that sifted away somewhere. While we watched, others filed in, repeating the process, and that seemed to be all. No rhyme nor reason to the whole thing—but that's characteristic of this crazy planet. And there was another fact that's almost too bizarre to believe.

"One of the creatures, having dumped his load, pushed his cart aside with a crash and calmly shoved himself under the wheel! I watched him being crushed, too stupefied to make a sound, and a moment later, another followed him! They were perfectly methodical about it, too; one of the cartless creatures took the abandoned pushcart.

"Tweel didn't seem surprised; I pointed out the next suicide to him, and he just gave the most human-like shrug imaginable, as much as to say, 'What can I do about it?' He must have known more or less about these creatures.

"Then I saw something else. There was something beyond the wheel, something shining on a sort of low pedestal. I walked over; there was a little crystal about the size of an egg, fluorescing to beat Tophet. The light from it stung my hands and face, almost like a static discharge, and then I noticed another funny thing. Remember that wart I had on my left thumb? Look!" Jarvis extended his hand. "It dried up and fell off—just like that! And my abused nose—say, the pain went out of it like magic! The thing had the property of hard x-rays or gamma radiations, only more so; it destroyed diseased tissue and left healthy tissue unharmed!

"I was thinking what a present *that*'d be to take back to Mother Earth when a lot of racket interrupted. We dashed back to the other side of the wheel in time to see one of the pushcarts ground up. Some suicide had been careless, it seems.

"Then suddenly the creatures were booming and drumming all around us and their noise was decidedly menacing. A crowd of them advanced toward us; we backed out of what I thought was the passage we'd entered by, and they came rumbling after us, some pushing carts and some not. Crazy brutes! There was a whole chorus of 'We are v-r-r-riends! Ouch!' I didn't like the 'ouch'; it was rather suggestive.

"Tweel had his glass gun out and I dumped my water tank for greater freedom and got mine. We backed up the corridor with the barrel-beasts following—about twenty of them. Queer thing—the ones coming in with loaded carts moved past us inches away without a sign.

"Tweel must have noticed that. Suddenly, he snatched out that glowing coal cigar-lighter of his and touched a cart-load of plant limbs. Puff! The whole load was burning and the crazy beast pushing it went right along without a change of pace! It created some disturbance among our 'V-r-r-riends,' however—and then I noticed the smoke eddying and swirling past us, and sure enough, there was the entrance!

"I grabbed Tweel and out we dashed and after us our twenty pursuers. The daylight felt like Heaven, though I saw at first glance that the sun was all but set, and that was bad, since I couldn't live outside my thermo-skin bag in a Martian night—at least, without a fire.

"And things got worse in a hurry. They cornered us in an angle between two mounds, and there we stood. I hadn't fired nor had Tweel; there wasn't any use in irritating the brutes. They stopped a little distance away and began their booming about friendship and ouches.

"Then things got still worse! A barrel-brute came out with a pushcart and they all grabbed into it and came out with handfuls of foot-long copper darts—sharp-looking ones—and all of a sudden one sailed past my ear—zing! And it was shoot or die then.

"We were doing pretty well for a while. We picked off the ones next to the pushcart and managed to keep the darts at a minimum, but suddenly there was a thunderous booming of 'v-r-r-riends' and 'ouches,' and a whole army of 'em came out of their hole.

"Man! We were through and I knew it! Then I realized that Tweel wasn't. He could have leaped the mound behind us as easily as not. He was staying for me!

"Say, I could have cried if there'd been time! I'd liked Tweel from the first but whether I'd have had gratitude to do what he was doing—suppose I *had* saved him from the first dream-beast—he'd done as much for me, hadn't he? I grabbed his arm, and said 'Tweel,' and pointed up, and he understood. He said, 'No—no—no, Tick!' and popped away with his glass pistol.

"What could I do? I'd be a goner anyway when the sun set, but I couldn't explain that to him. I said, 'Thanks, Tweel. You're a man!' and felt that I wasn't paying him any compliment at all. A man! There are mighty few men who'd do that.

"So I went 'bang' with my gun and Tweel went 'puff' with his, and the barrels were throwing darts and getting ready to rush us, and booming about being friends. I had given up hope. Then suddenly an angel dropped right down from Heaven in the shape of Putz, with his under-jets blasting the barrels into very small pieces!

"Wow! I let out a yell and dashed for the rocket; Putz opened the door and in I went, laughing and crying and shouting! It was a moment or so before I remembered Tweel; I looked around in time to see him rising in one of his nosedives over the mound and away.

"I had a devil of a job arguing Putz into following! By the time we got the rocket aloft, darkness was down; you know how it comes here—like turning off a light. We sailed out over the desert and put down once or twice. I yelled 'Tweel!' and yelled it a hundred times, I guess. We couldn't find him; he could travel like the wind and all I got—or else I imagined it—was a faint trilling and twittering drifting out of the south. He'd gone, and damn it! I wish—I wish he hadn't!"

The four men of the *Ares* were silent—even the sardonic Harrison. At last little Leroy broke the stillness.

"I should like to see," he murmured.

"Yeah," said Harrison. "And the wart-cure. Too bad you missed that; it might be the cancer cure they've been hunting for a century and a half."

"Oh, that!" muttered Jarvis gloomily. "That's what started the fight!" He drew a glistening object from his pocket.

"Here it is."

𝕾 ISAAC ASIMOV (1920–1992)

Isaac Asimov was one of the scientists who wrote Science Fiction, and he was also one of the most prolific and well-known authors of the twentieth century. He was born in Russia and moved to the United States with his parents in 1923. In his lifetime, Asimov produced multiple volumes on technology and the hard sciences, and on such diverse and impossibly in-depth topics as the Bible and Shakespeare. He wrote Mystery fiction and edited and co-edited hundreds of books. He also contributed mightily to the development of Science Fiction from 1939 (the year his first story, "Marooned Off Vesta," appeared in Amazing Stories*) until his death in 1992.*

Asimov's contributions to Science Fiction came in several varieties and series of stories. One of these series began in "Strange Playfellow" (later retitled "Robbie"), which is the first tale in the ultimately lengthy series of Asimov's "Robot" stories. In "Strange Playfellow," Asimov delineated the "Three Laws of Robotics," which have been utilized by the larger Science Fiction community of writers ever since. Another of these series is Asimov's "Foundation," an infinitely readable and highly intelligent story line that had a pulp magazine genesis. After many years and near the end of his life, Asimov combined the two series into one.

The robot that Isaac Asimov conceived in "Robbie" was more complex and human-like than any similar mechanical man seen prior to 1940.

Robbie

(originally published as "Strange Playfellow" in Super Science Stories, *September 1940)*

THE THREE LAWS OF ROBOTICS

1. A robot may not injure a human being, or, through inaction, allow a human being to come to harm.

2. A robot must obey the orders given it by human beings except where such orders would conflict with the First Law.

3. A robot must protect its own existence as long as such protection does not conflict with the First or Second Law.

HANDBOOK OF ROBOTICS
56TH EDITION, 2058 A.D.

"NINETY-EIGHT—NINETY-NINE—ONE HUNDRED." Gloria withdrew her chubby little forearm from before her eyes and stood for a moment, wrinkling her nose and blinking in the sunlight. Then, trying to watch in all directions at once, she withdrew a few cautious steps from the tree against which she had been leaning.

She craned her neck to investigate the possibilities of a clump of bushes to the right and then withdrew farther to obtain a better angle for viewing its dark recesses. The quiet was profound except for the incessant buzzing of insects and the occasional chirrup of some hardy bird, braving the midday sun.

Gloria pouted, "I bet he went inside the house, and I've told him a million times that that's not fair."

With tiny lips pressed together tightly and a severe frown crinkling her forehead, she moved determinedly toward the two-story building up past the driveway.

Too late she heard the rustling sound behind her, followed by the distinctive and rhythmic clump-clump of Robbie's metal feet. She whirled about to see her triumphing companion emerge from hiding and make for the home-tree at full speed.

Gloria shrieked in dismay. "Wait, Robbie! That wasn't fair, Robbie! You promised you wouldn't run until I found you." Her little feet could make no headway at all against Robbie's giant strides. Then, within ten feet of the goal, Robbie's pace slowed suddenly to the merest of crawls, and Gloria. with one final burst of wild speed, dashed pantingly past him to touch the welcome bark of home-tree first.

Gleefully, she turned on the faithful Robbie, and with the basest of ingratitude, rewarded him for his sacrifice by taunting him cruelly for a lack of running ability.

"Robbie can't run," she shouted at the top of her eight-year-old voice. "I can beat him any day. I can beat him any day." She chanted the words in a shrill rhythm.

Robbie didn't answer, of course—not in words. He pantomimed running instead, inching away until Gloria found herself running after him as he dodged her narrowly, forcing her to veer in helpless circles, little arms outstretched and fanning at the air.

"Robbie," she squealed. "stand still!"—And the laughter was forced out of her in breathless jerks.

—Until he turned suddenly and caught her up, whirling her round, so that for her the world fell away for a moment with a blue emptiness beneath, and green trees stretching hungrily downward toward the void. Then she was down in the grass again, leaning against Robbie's leg and still holding a hard, metal finger.

After a while, her breath returned. She pushed uselessly at her disheveled hair in vogue imitation of one of her mother's gestures and twisted to see if her dress were torn.

She slapped her hand against Robbie's torso, "Bad boy! I'll spank you!"

And Robbie cowered, holding his hands over his face so that she had to add, "No, I won't, Robbie. I won't spank you. But anyway, it's my turn to hide now because you've got longer legs and you promised not to run till I found you."

Robbie nodded his head—a small parallelepiped with rounded edges and corners attached to a similar but much larger parallelepiped that served as torso by means of a short, flexible stalk—and obediently faced the tree. A thin, metal film descended over his glowing eyes and from within his body came a steady, resonant ticking.

"Don't peek now—and don't skip any numbers," warned Gloria, and scurried for cover.

With unvarying regularity, seconds were ticked off, and at the hundredth, up went the eyelids, and the glowing red of Robbie's eyes swept the prospect. They rested for a moment on a bit of colorful gingham that protruded from behind a boulder. He advanced a few steps and convinced himself that it was Gloria who squatted behind it.

Slowly, remaining always between Gloria and home-tree, he advanced on the hiding place, and when Gloria was plainly in sight and could no longer even theorize to herself that she was not seen, he extended one arm toward her, slapping the other against his leg so that if rang again. Gloria emerged sulkily.

"You peeked!" she exclaimed, with gross unfairness. "Besides I'm tired of playing hide-and-seek. I want a ride."

But Robbie was hurt at the unjust accusation, so he seated himself carefully and shook his head panderously from side to side.

Gloria changed her tone to one of gentle coaxing immediately, "Come on, Robbie. I didn't mean it about the peeking. Give me a ride."

Robbie was not to be won over so easily, though. He gazed stubbornly at the sky, and shook his head even more emphatically.

"Please, Robbie, please give me a ride." She encircled his neck with rosy arms and hugged tightly. Then, changing moods in a moment, she moved away. "If you don't, I'm going to cry," and her face twisted appallingly in preparation.

Hard-hearted Robbie paid scant attention to this dreadful possibility, and shook his head a third time. Gloria found it necessary to play her trump card.

"If you don't," she exclaimed warmly, "I won't tell you any more stories, that's all. Not one—"

Robbie gave in immediately and unconditionally before this ultimatum, nodding his head vigorously until the metal of his neck hummed. Carefully, he raised the little girl and placed her on his broad, flat shoulders.

Gloria's threatened tears vanished immediately and she crowed with delight. Robbie's metal skin, kept at a constant temperature of seventy by the high resistance coils within, felt nice and comfortable, while the beautifully loud sound her heels made as they bumped rhythmically against his chest was enchanting.

"You're on air-coaster, Robbie, you're a big, silver air-coaster. Hold out your arms straight.—You *got* to, Robbie, if you're going to be an air-coaster."

The logic was irrefutable. Robbie's arms were wings catching the air currents and he was a silver 'coaster.

Gloria twisted the robot's head and leaned to the right. He banked sharply. Gloria equipped the 'coaster with a motor that went "Br-r-r" and then with weapons that went "Powie" and "Sh-sh-shshsh." Pirates were giving chase and the ship's blasters were coming into play. The pirates dropped in a steady rain.

"Got another one.—Two more," she cried.

Then "Faster, men," Gloria said pompously, "we're running out of ammunition." She aimed over her shoulder with undaunted courage and Robbie was a blunt-nosed spaceship zooming through the void at maximum acceleration.

Clear across the field he sped, to the patch of tall grass on the other side, where he stopped with a suddenness that evoked a shriek from his flushed rider, and then tumbled her onto the soft, green carpet.

Gloria gasped and panted, and gave voice to intermittent whispered exclamations of "That was **nice!**"

Robbie waited until she had caught her breath and then pulled gently at a lock of hair.

"You want something?" said Gloria, eyes wide in an apparently artless complexity that fooled her huge "nursemaid" not at all. He pulled the curl harder.

"Oh, I know. You want a story."

Robbie nodded rapidly.

"Which one?"

Robbie made a semi-circle in the air with one finger.

The little girl protested. "*Again!* I've told you Cinderella a million times. Aren't you tired of it?—It's for babies."

Another semi-circle.

"Oh, well," Gloria composed herself, ran over the details of the tale in her mind (together with her own elaborations, of which she had several) and began:

"Are you ready? Well—once upon a time there was a beautiful little girl whose name was Ella. And she had a terribly cruel step-mother and two very ugly and **very** cruel step-sisters and—"

Gloria was reaching the very climax of the tale—midnight was striking and everything was changing back to the shabby originals lickety-split, while Robbie listened tensely with burning eyes—when the interruption came.

"Gloria!"

It was the high-pitched sound of a woman who has been calling not once, but several times; and had the nervous tone of one in whom anxiety was beginning to overcome impatience.

"Mamma's calling me," said Gloria, not quite happily. "You'd better carry me back to the house, Robbie."

Robbie obeyed with alacrity for somehow there was that in him which judged it best to obey Mrs. Weston, without as much as a scrap of hesitation. Gloria's father was rarely home in the daytime except on Sunday—today, for instance—and when he was, he proved a genial and understanding person. Gloria's mother, however, was a source of uneasiness to Robbie and there was always the impulse to sneak away from her sight.

Mrs. Weston caught sight of them the minute they rose above the masking tufts of long grass and retired inside the house to wait.

"I've shouted myself hoarse, Gloria" she said, severely. "Where were you?"

"I was with Robbie," quavered Gloria. "I was telling him Cinderella, and I forgot it was dinner-time."

"Well, it's a pity Robbie forgot, too." Then, as if that reminded her of the robot's presence, she whirled upon him. "You may go, Robbie. She doesn't need you now." Then, brutally, "And don't come back till I call you."

Robbie turned to go, but hesitated as Gloria cried out in his defense, "Wait, Mamma, you got to let him stay. I didn't finish Cinderella for him. I said I would tell him Cinderella and I'm not finished."

"Gloria!"

"Honest and truly, Mamma, he'll stay so quiet, you won't even know he's here. He can sit on the chair in the corner, and he won't say a word,—I mean he won't *do* anything. Will you, Robbie?"

Robbie, appealed to, nodded his massive head up and down once.

"Gloria, if you don't stop this at once, you shan't see Robbie for a whole week."

The girl's eyes fell, "All right! But Cinderella is his favorite story and I didn't finish it.—And he likes it so much."

The robot left with a disconsolate step and Gloria choked back a sob.

George Weston was comfortable. It was a habit of his to be comfortable on Sunday afternoons. A good, hearty dinner below the hatches; a nice, soft, dilapidated couch an which to sprawl; a copy of the *Times;* slippered feet and shirtless chest;—how could anyone *help* but be comfortable?

He wasn't pleased, therefore, when his wife walked in. After ten years of married life, he still was so unutterably foolish as to love her, and there was no question that he was always glad to see her—still Sunday afternoons just after dinner were sacred to him and his idea of solid comfort was to be left in utter solitude for two or three hours. Consequently, he fixed his eye firmly upon the latest reports of the Lefebre-Yoshida expedition to Mars (this one was to take off from Lunar Base and might actually succeed) and pretended she wasn't there.

Mrs. Weston waited patiently for two minutes, then impatiently for two more, and finally broke the silence.

"George!"

"Hmpph?"

"George, I say! *Will* you put down that paper and look at me?"

The paper rustled to the floor and Weston turned a weary face toward his wife. "What is it, dear?"

"You know what it is, George. It's Gloria and that terrible machine."

"What terrible machine?"

"Now don't pretend you don't know what I'm talking about. It's that robot Gloria calls Robbie. He doesn't leave her for a moment."

"Well, why should he? He's not supposed to. And he certainly isn't a terrible machine. He's the best darn robot money can buy and I'm damned sure he set me back half a year's income. He's worth it, though—darn sight cleverer than half my office staff."

He made a move to pick up the paper again, but his wife was quicker and snatched it away.

"You listen to *me*, George. I won't have my daughter entrusted to a machine—and I don't care how clever it is. It has no soul, and no one knows what it may be thinking. A child just isn't *made* to be guarded by a thing of metal."

Weston frowned, "When did you decide this? He's been with Gloria two years now and I haven't seen you worry till now."

"It was different at first. It was a novelty; it took a load off me, and—and it was a fashionable thing to do. But now I don't know. The neighbors—"

"Well, what have the neighbors to do with it. Now, look. A robot is infinitely more to be trusted than a human nursemaid. Robbie was constructed for only one purpose really—to be the companion of a little child. His entire 'mentality' has been created for the purpose. He just can't help being faithful and loving and kind. He's a machine—*made so*. That's more than you can say for humans."

"But something might go wrong. Some—some—" Mrs. Weston was a bit hazy about the insides of a robot, "some little jigger will come loose and the awful thing will go berserk and—and—" She couldn't bring herself to complete the quite obvious thought.

"Nonsense." Weston denied, with an involuntary nervous shiver. "That's completely ridiculous. We had a long discussion at the time we bought Robbie about the First Law of Robotics. You **know** that it is impossible for a robot to harm a human being; that long before enough can go wrong to alter that First Law, a robot would be completely inoperable. It's a mathematical impossibility. Besides I have an engineer from U.S. Robots here twice a year to give the poor gadget a complete overhaul. Why, there's no more chance of anything at all going wrong with Robbie than there is of you or I suddenly going loony—considerably less, in fact. Besides, how are you going to take him away from Gloria?"

He made another futile stab at the paper and his wife tossed it angrily into the next room.

"That's just it, George! She won't play with anyone else. There are dozens of little boys and girls that she should make friends with, but she won't. She won't go *near* them unless I make her. That's no way for a little girl to grow up. You want her to be normal, don't you? You want her to be able to take her part in society."

"You're jumping at shadows, Grace. Pretend Robbie's a dog. I've seen hundreds of children who would rather have their dog than their father."

"A dog is different, George. We *must* get rid of that horrible thing. You can sell it back to the company. I've asked, and you can."

"You've *asked?* Now look here, Grace, let's not go off the deep end. We're keeping the robot until Gloria is older and I don't want the subject brought up again." And with that he walked out of the room in a huff.

Mrs. Weston met her husband at the door two evenings later. "You'll have to listen to this, George. There's bad feeling in the village."

"About what?" asked Weston. He stepped into the washroom and drowned out any possible answer by the splash of water.

Mrs. Weston waited. She said, "About Robbie."

Weston stepped out, towel in hand, face red and angry, "What are you talking about?"

"Oh, it's been building up and building up. I've tried to close my eyes to it, but I'm not going to any more. Most of the villagers consider Robbie dangerous. Children aren't allowed to go near our place in the evenings."

"We trust *our* child with the thing."

"Well, people aren't reasonable about these things."

"Then to hell with them."

"Saying that doesn't solve the problem. I've got to do my shopping down there. I've got to meet them every day. And it's even worse in the city these days when it comes to robots. New York has just passed an ordinance keeping all robots off the streets between sunset and sunrise."

"All right, but they can't stop us from keeping a robot in our home. — Grace, this is one of your campaigns. I recognize it. But it's no use. The answer is still, no! We're keeping Robbie!"

And yet he loved his wife—and what was worse, his wife knew it. George Weston, after all, was only a man—poor thing—and his wife made full use of every device which a clumsier and more scrupulous sex has learned, with reason and futility, to fear.

Ten times in the ensuing week, he cried, "Robbie stays, — and that's *final!*" and each time it was weaker and accompanied by a louder and more agonized groan.

Came the day at last, when Weston approached his daughter guiltily and suggested a "beautiful" visivox show in the village.

Gloria clapped her hands happily, "Can Robbie go?"

"No dear," he said, and winced at the sound of his voice, "they won't allow robots at the visivox—but you can tell him all about it when you get home." He stumbled all over the last few words and looked away.

Gloria came back from town bubbling over with enthusiasm, for the visivox had been a gorgeous spectacle indeed.

She waited for her father to maneuver the jet-car into the sunken garage, "Wait till I tell Robbie, Daddy. He would have liked it like anything. — Especially when Francis Fran was backing away so-o-o quietly, and backed right into one of the Leopard-Men and had to run." She laughed again, "Daddy, are there really Leopard-Men on the Moon?"

"Probably not," said Weston absently. "It's just funny make-believe." He couldn't take much longer with the car. He'd have to face it.

Gloria ran across the lawn. "Robbie.—Robbie!"

Then she stopped suddenly at the sight of a beautiful collie which regarded her out of serious brown eyes as it wagged its tail on the porch.

"Oh, what a nice dog!" Gloria climbed the steps, approached cautiously and patted it. "Is it for me, Daddy?"

Her mother had joined them. "Yes, it is, Gloria. Isn't it nice—soft and furry. It's very gentle. It *likes* little girls."

"Can he play games?"

"Surely. He can do any number of tricks. Would you like to see some?"

"Right away. I want Robbie to see him, too.—*Robbie!*" She stopped, uncertainly, and frowned, "I'll bet he's just staying in his room because he's mad at me for not taking him to the visivox. You'll have to explain to him, Daddy. He might not believe me, but he knows if you say it, it's so."

Weston's lip grew tighter. He looked toward his wife but could not catch her eye.

Gloria turned precipitously and ran down the basement steps, shouting as she went, "Robbie—Come and see what Daddy and Mamma brought me. They brought me a dog, Robbie."

In a minute she had returned, a frightened little girl. "Mamma, Robbie isn't in his room. Where is he?" There was no answer and George Weston coughed and was suddenly extremely interested in an aimlessly drifting cloud. Gloria's voice quavered on the verge of tears, "Where's Robbie, Mamma?"

Mrs. Weston sat down and drew her daughter gently to her, "Don't feel bad, Gloria. Robbie has gone away, I think."

"Gone *away?* Where? Where's he gone away, Mamma?"

"No one knows, darling. He just walked away. We've looked and we've looked and we've looked for him, but we can't find him."

"You mean he'll never come back again?" Her eyes were round with horror.

"We may find him soon. We'll keep looking for him. And meanwhile you can play with your nice new doggie. Look at him! His name is Lightning and he can—"

But Gloria's eyelids had overflown, "I don't want the nasty dog—I want Robbie. I want you to find me Robbie." Her feelings became too deep for words, and she spluttered into a shrill wail.

Mrs. Weston glanced at her husband for help, but he merely shuffled his feet morosely and did not withdraw his ardent stare from the heavens, so she bent to the task of consolation, "Why do you cry, Gloria? Robbie was only a machine, just a nasty old machine. He wasn't alive at all."

"He was *not* no machine!" screamed Gloria, fiercely and ungrammatically. "He was a *person* just like you and me and he was my *friend.* I want him back. Oh, Mamma, I want him back."

Her mother groaned in defeat and left Gloria to her sorrow.

"Let her have her cry out," she told her husband. "Childish griefs are never lasting. In a few days, she'll forget that awful robot ever existed."

But time proved Mrs. Weston a bit too optimistic. To be sure, Gloria ceased crying, but she ceased smiling, too, and the passing days found her ever more silent and shadowy. Gradually, her attitude of passive unhappiness wore Mrs. Weston down and all that kept her from yielding was the impossibility of admitting defeat to her husband.

Then, one evening, she flounced into the living room, sat down, folded her arms and looked boiling mad.

Her husband stretched his neck in order to see her over his newspaper, "What now, Grace?"

"It's that child, George. I've had to send back the dog today. Gloria positively couldn't stand the sight of him, she said. She's driving me into a nervous breakdown."

Weston laid down the paper and a hopeful gleam entered his eye, "Maybe— Maybe we ought to get Robbie back. It might be done, you know. I can get in touch with—"

"No!" she replied, grimly. "I won't hear of it. We're not giving up that easily. My child shall *not* be brought up by a robot if it takes years to break her of it."

Weston picked up his paper again with a disappointed air. "A year of this will have me prematurely gray."

"You're a big help, George," was the frigid answer. "What Gloria needs is a change of environment. Of course she can't forget Robbie here. How can she when every tree and rock reminds her of him? It is really the *silliest* situation I have ever heard of. Imagine a child pining away for the loss of a robot."

"Well, stick to the point. What's the change in environment you're planning?"

"We're going to take her to New York."

"The city! In August! Say, do you know what New York is like in August? It's unbearable."

"Millions do bear it."

"They don't have a place like this to go to. If they didn't have to stay in New York, they wouldn't."

"Well, *we* have to. I say we're leaving now—or as soon as we can make the arrangements. In the city, Gloria will find sufficient interests and sufficient friends to perk her up and make her forget that machine."

"Oh, Lord," groaned the lesser half, "those frying pavements!"

"We have to," was the unshaken response. "Gloria has lost five pounds in the last month and my little girl's health is more important to me than your comfort."

"It's a pity you didn't think of your little girl's health before you deprived her of her pet robot," he muttered—but to himself.

Gloria displayed immediate signs of improvement when told of the impending trip to the city. She spoke little of it, but when she did, it was always with lively anticipation. Again, she began to smile and to eat with something of her former appetite.

Mrs. Weston hugged herself for joy and lost no opportunity to triumph over her still skeptical husband.

"You see, George, she helps with the packing like a little angel, and chatters away as if she hadn't a care in the world. It's just as I told you—all we need do is substitute other interests."

"Hmpph," was the skeptical response, "I hope so."

Preliminaries were gone through quickly. Arrangements were made for the preparation of their city home and a couple were engaged as housekeepers for the country home. When the day of the trip finally did come, Gloria was all but her old self again, and no mention of Robbie passed her lips at all.

In high good-humor the family took a taxi-gyro to the airport (Weston would have preferred using his own private 'gyro, but it was only a two-seater with no room for baggage) and entered the waiting liner.

"Come, Gloria," called Mrs. Weston. "I've saved you a seat near the window so you can watch the scenery."

Gloria trotted down the aisle cheerily, flattened her nose into a white oval against the thick clear glass, and watched with an intentness that increased as the sudden coughing of the motor drifted backward into the interior. She was too young to be frightened when the ground dropped away as if let through a trap-door and she herself suddenly became twice her usual weight, but not too young to be mightily interested. It wasn't until the ground had changed into a tiny patchwork quilt that she withdrew her nose, and faced her mother again.

"Will we soon be in the city, Mamma?" she asked, rubbing her chilled nose, and watching with interest as the patch of moisture which her breath had formed on the pane shrank slowly and vanished.

"In about half an hour, dear." Then, with just the faintest trace of anxiety, "Aren't you glad we're going? Don't you think you'll be very happy in the city with all the buildings and people and things to see? We'll go to the visivox every day and see shows and go to the circus and the beach and—"

"Yes, Mamma," was Gloria's unenthusiastic rejoinder. The liner passed over a bank of clouds at the moment, and Gloria was instantly absorbed in the usual spectacle of clouds underneath one. Then they were over clear sky again, and she turned to her mother with a sudden mysterious air of secret knowledge.

"*I* know why we're going to the city, Mamma."

"Do you?" Mrs. Weston was puzzled. "Why, dear?"

"You didn't tell me because you wanted it to be a surprise, but I know." For a moment, she was lost in admiration at her own acute penetration, and then she laughed gaily. "We're going to New York so we can find Robbie, aren't we?— With detectives."

The statement caught George Weston in the middle of a drink of water, with disastrous results. There was a sort of strangled gasp, a geyser of water, and then a bout of choking coughs. When all was over, he stood there, a red-faced, water-drenched and very, very annoyed person.

Mrs. Weston maintained her composure, but when Gloria repeated her question in a more anxious tone of voice, she found her temper rather bent.

"Maybe," she retorted, tartly. "Now sit and be still, for Heaven's sake."

New York City, 1998 A.D., was a paradise for the sight-seer more than ever in its history. Gloria's parents realized this and made the most of it.

On direct orders from his wife, George Weston arranged to have his business take care of itself for a month or so, in order to be free to spend the time in what he termed "dissipating Gloria at the verge of ruin." Like everything else Weston did, this was gone about in an efficient, thorough, and business-like way. Before the month had passed, nothing that could be done had not been done.

She was taken to the top of the half-mile tall Roosevelt Building, to gaze down in awe upon the jagged panorama of rooftops that blended far off in the fields of Long Island and the flatlands of New Jersey. They visited the zoos where Gloria stared in delicious fright at the "real live lion" (rather disappointed that the keepers fed him raw steaks, instead of human beings, as she had expected), and asked insistently and peremptorily to see "the whale."

The various museums came in for their share of attention, together with the parks and the beaches and the aquarium.

She was taken halfway up the Hudson in an excursion steamer fitted out in the archaism of the mad Twenties. She travelled to the stratosphere on an exhibition trip, where the sky turned deep purple and the stars came out and the misty earth below looked like a huge concave bowl. Down under the waters of The Long Island Sound she was taken in a glass-walled sub-sea vessel, where in a green and wavering world, quaint and curious sea-things ogled her and wiggled suddenly away.

On a more prosaic level, Mrs. Weston took her to the department stores where she could revel in another type of fairyland.

In fact, when the month had nearly sped, the Westons were convinced that everything conceivable had been done to take Gloria's mind once and for all off the departed Robbie—but they were not quite sure they had succeeded.

The fact remained that wherever Gloria went, she displayed a most absorbed and concentrated interest in such robots as happened to be present. No matter how exciting the spectacle before her, nor how novel to her girlish eyes, she turned away instantly if the corner of her eye caught a glimpse of metallic movement.

Mrs. Weston went out of her way to keep Gloria away from all robots.

And the matter was finally climaxed in the episode at the Museum of Science and Industry. The Museum had announced a special "children's program" in which exhibits of scientific witchery scaled down to the child mind were to be shown. The Westons, of course, placed it upon their list of "absolutely."

It was while the Westons were standing totally absorbed in the exploits of a powerful electro-magnet that Mrs. Weston suddenly became aware of the fact that Gloria was no longer with her. Initial panic gave way to calm decision and, enlisting the aid of three attendants, a careful search was begun.

Gloria, of course, was not one to wander aimlessly, however. For her age, she was an unusually determined and purposeful girl, quite full of the maternal genes in that respect. She had seen a huge sign on the third floor, which had said, "This Way to the Talking Robot." Having spelled it out to herself and having noticed that her parents did not seem to wish to move in the proper direction, she did the obvious thing. Waiting for an opportune moment of parental distraction, she calmly disengaged herself and followed the sign.

The Talking Robot was a *tour de force*, a thoroughly impractical device, possessing publicity value only. Once an hour, an escorted group stood before it and asked questions of the robot engineer in charge in careful whispers. Those the engineer decided were suitable for the robot's circuits were transmitted to the Talking Robot.

It was rather dull. It may be nice to know that the square of fourteen is one hundred ninety-six, that the temperature at the moment is 72 degrees Fahrenheit, and the air-pressure 30.02 inches of mercury, that the atomic weight of sodium is 23, but one doesn't really need a robot for that. One especially does not need an unwieldy, totally immobile mass of wires and coils spreading over twenty-five square yards.

Few people bothered to return for a second helping, but one girl in her middle teens sat quietly on a bench waiting for a third. She was the only one in the room when Gloria entered.

Gloria did not look at her. To her at the moment, another human being was but an inconsiderable item. She saved her attention for this large thing with the wheels. For a moment, she hesitated in dismay. It didn't look like any robot she had ever seen.

Cautiously and doubtfully she raised her treble voice, "Please, Mr. Robot, sir, are you the Talking Robot, sir?" She wasn't sure, but it seemed to her that a robot that actually talked was worth a great deal of politeness.

(The girl in her mid-teens allowed a look of intense concentration to cross her thin, plain face. She whipped out a small notebook and began writing in rapid pot-hooks.)

There was an oily whir of gears and a mechanically-timbred voice boomed out in words that lacked accent and intonation, "I—am—the—robot—that—talks."

Gloria stared at it ruefully. It *did* talk, but the sound come from inside somewheres. There was no *face* to talk to. She said, "Can you help me, Mr. Robot, sir?"

The Talking Robot was designed to answer questions, and only such questions as it could answer had ever been put to it. It was quite confident of its ability, therefore, "I—can—help—you."

"Thank you, Mr. Robot, sir. Have you seen Robbie?"

"Who—is Robbie?"

"He's a robot, Mr. Robot, sir." She stretched to tip-toes. "He's about so high, Mr. Robot, sir, only higher, and he's very nice. He's got a head, you know. I mean you haven't, but he has, Mr. Robot, sir."

The Talking Robot had been left behind, "A—robot?"

"Yes, Mr. Robot, sir. A robot just like you, except he can't talk of course, and—looks like a real person."

"A—robot—like—me?"

"Yes, Mr. Robot, sir."

To which the Talking Robot's only response was an erratic splutter and an occasional incoherent sound. The radical generalization offered it, i.e., its existence, not as a particular object, but as a member of a general group, was too much for it. Loyally, it tried to encompass the concept and half a dozen coils burnt out. Little warning signals were buzzing.

(The girl in her mid-teens left at that point. She had enough for her Physics-1 paper on "Practical Aspects of Robotics." This paper was Susan Calvin's first of many on the subject.)

Gloria stood waiting, with carefully concealed impatience, for the machine's answer when she heard the cry behind her of "There she is," and recognized that cry as her mother's.

"What are you doing here, you bad girl?" cried Mrs. Weston, anxiety dissolving at once into anger. "Do you know you frightened your mamma and daddy almost to death? Why did you run away?"

The robot engineer had also dashed in, tearing his hair, and demanding who of the gathering crowd had tampered with the machine. "Can't anybody read signs?" he yelled. "You're not allowed in here without an attendant."

Gloria raised her grieved voice over the din, "I only came to see the Talking Robot, Mamma. I thought he might know where Robbie was because they're both robots. And then, as the thought of Robbie was suddenly brought forcefully home to her, she burst into a sudden storm of tears, "And I *got* to find Robbie, Mamma, I *got* to."

Mrs. Weston strangled a cry, and said, "Oh, good Heavens. Come home, George. This is more than I can stand."

That evening, George Weston left for several hours, and the next morning, he approached his wife with something that looked suspiciously like smug complacence.

"I've got an idea, Grace."

"About what?" was the gloomy, uninterested query.

"About Gloria."

"You're not going to suggest buying back that robot?"

"No, of course not."

"Then go ahead. I might as well listen to you. Nothing *I've* done seems to have done any good."

"All right. Here's what I've been thinking. The whole trouble with Gloria is that she thinks of Robbie as a *person* and not as a *machine*. Naturally, she can't forget him. Now if we managed to convince her that Robbie was nothing more than a mess of steel and copper in the form of sheets and wires with electricity its juice of life, how long would her longings last? It's the psychological attack, if you see my point."

"How do you plan to do it?"

"Simple. Where do you suppose I went last night? I persuaded Robertson of U.S. Robots and Mechanical Men, Inc. to arrange for a complete tour of his premises tomorrow. The three of us will go, and by the time we're through, Gloria will have it drilled into her that a robot is *not* alive."

Mrs. Weston's eyes widened gradually and something glinted in her eyes that was quite like sudden admiration, "Why, George, that's a *good* idea."

And George Weston's vest buttons strained. "Only kind I have," he said.

Mr. Struthers was a conscientious General Manager and naturally inclined to be a bit talkative. The combination, therefore, resulted in a tour that was fully explained, perhaps even overabundantly explained, at every step. However, Mrs. Weston was not bored. Indeed, she stopped him several times and begged him to repeat his statements in simpler language so that Gloria might understand. Under the influence of this appreciation of his narrative powers, Mr. Struthers expanded genially and became ever more communicative, if possible.

George Weston, himself, showed a gathering impatience.

"Pardon me, Struthers," he said, breaking into the middle of a lecture on the photo-electric cell, "haven't you a section of the factory where only robot labor is employed?"

"Eh? Oh, yes! Yes, indeed!" He smiled at Mrs. Weston. "A vicious circle in a way, robots creating more robots. Of course, we are not making a general practice out of it. For one thing, the unions would never let us. But we can turn out a very few robots using robot labor exclusively, merely as a sort of scientific experiment. You see," he tapped his pince-nez into one palm argumentatively, "what the labor unions don't realize—and I say this as a man who has always been very sympathetic with the labor movement in general—is that the advent of the robot, while involving some dislocation to begin with, will inevitably—"

"Yes, Struthers," said Weston, "but about that section of the factory you speak of—may we see it? It would be very interesting, I'm sure."

"Yes! Yes, of course!" Mr. Struthers replaced his pince-nez in one convulsive movement and gave vent to a soft cough of discomfiture. "Follow me, please."

He was comparatively quiet while leading the three through a long corridor and down a flight of stairs. Then, when they had entered a large well-lit room that buzzed with metallic activity, the sluices opened and the flood of explanation poured forth again.

"There you are!" he said with pride in his voice. "Robots only! Five men act as overseers and they don't even stay in this room. In five years, that is, since we began this project, not a single accident has occurred. Of course, the robots here assembled are comparatively simple, but . . ."

The General Manager's voice had long died to a rather soothing murmur in Gloria's ears. The whole trip seemed rather dull and pointless to her, though there *were* many robots in sight. None were even remotely like Robbie, though, and she surveyed them with open contempt.

In this room, there weren't any people at all, she noticed. Then her eyes fell upon six or seven robots busily engaged at a round table halfway across the room. They widened in incredulous surprise. It was a big room. She couldn't see for sure, but one of the robots looked like—looked like—*it was!*

"*Robbie!*" Her shriek pierced the air, and one of the robots about the table faltered and dropped the tool he was holding. Gloria went almost mad with joy. Squeezing through the railing before either parent could stop her, she dropped lightly to the floor a few feet below, and ran toward her Robbie, arms waving and hair flying.

And the three horrified adults, as they stood frozen in their tracks, saw what the excited little girl did not see—a huge, lumbering tractor bearing blindly down upon its appointed track.

It took split-seconds for Weston to come to his senses, and those split-seconds meant everything, for Gloria could not be overtaken. Although Weston vaulted the railing in a wild attempt, it was obviously hopeless. Mr. Struthers signalled wildly to the overseers to stop the tractor, but the overseers were only human and it took time to act.

It was only Robbie that acted immediately and with precision.

With metal legs eating up the space between himself and his little mistress he charged down from the opposite direction. Everything then happened at once. With one sweep of an arm, Robbie snatched up Gloria, slackening his speed not one iota, and, consequently, knocking every breath of air out of her. Weston not quite comprehending all that was happening, felt, rather than saw, Robbie brush past him, and came to a sudden bewildered halt. The tractor intersected Gloria's path half a second after Robbie had, rolled on ten feet further and came to a grinding, long drawn-out stop.

Gloria regained her breath, submitted to a series of passionate hugs on the part of both her parents and turned eagerly toward Robbie. As far as she was concerned, nothing had happened except that she had found her friend.

But Mrs. Weston's expression had changed from one of relief to one of dark suspicion. She turned to her husband, and, despite her disheveled and undignified appearance, managed to look quite formidable, "*You* engineered this, *didn't you?*"

George Weston swabbed at a hot forehead with his handkerchief. His hand was unsteady, and his lips could curve only into a tremulous and exceedingly weak smile.

Mrs. Weston pursued the thought, "Robbie wasn't designed for engineering or construction work. He couldn't be of any use to them. You had him placed there deliberately so that Gloria would find him. You know you did."

"Well, I did," said Weston. "But, Grace, how was I to know the reunion would be so violent? And Robbie has saved her life; you'll have to admit that. You *can't* send him away again."

Grace Weston considered. She turned toward Gloria and Robbie and watched them abstractedly for a moment. Gloria had a grip about the robot's neck that would have asphyxiated any creature but one of metal, and was prattling nonsense in half-hysterical frenzy. Robbie's chrome-steel arms (capable of bending a bar of steel two inches in diameter into a pretzel) wound about the little girl gently and lovingly, and his eyes glowed a deep, deep red.

"Well," said Mrs. Weston, at last, "I guess he can stay with us until he rusts."

✵ ERIC FRANK RUSSELL (1905–1978)

Eric Frank Russell was the first British author to become a regular contributor to Astounding Stories. *His style was unique—often imitated, never matched, and always admired. He blended humor, intricate plotting, and progressive sociopolitical commentary in his tales. In some ways, he was Science Fiction's Mark Twain.*

Russell's work also appeared in Unknown Worlds. *Russell, himself, was interested in fairy tales, legend, and mythology. Among his literary influences were H. G. Wells and pulp writers Miles J. Breuer, Paul Ernst, and Stanley G. Weinbaum. He, in turn, influenced Henry Kuttner and others. Russell's first story, "The Saga of Pelican West," appeared in the February 1937 issue of* Astounding Stories. *He continued to write during and after World War II until the early 1960s; his most productive time was in the late 1940s and the 1950s.*

A comparatively early story for Eric Frank Russell, "Jay Score" was the first of a series of stories deemed the "Jay Score" stories. These were later collected in Men, Martians and Machines *(1955). This story is unique and quite fun, featuring an ethnically and otherwise diverse spaceship crew that is not only quite innovative for the time, but also foreshadows Gene Roddenberry's* Star Trek *empire, which began with the first* Star Trek *television series in 1966. Other Science Fiction creations, such as* Star Wars *(1977) and George R. R. Martin's "Tuf Voyaging" stories, owe a debt to "Jay Score." Interesting in "Jay Score" also is the presentation of a robot with feelings, a Science Fiction innovation that appeared in Isaac Asimov's "Strange Playfellow" less than a year earlier.*

Jay Score

(Astounding Science-Fiction, *May 1941*)

There are very good reasons for everything they do. To the uninitiated some of their little tricks and some of their regulations seem mighty peculiar—but rocketing through the cosmos isn't quite like paddling a bathtub across a farm pond, no, sir!

For instance, this stunt of using mixed crews is pretty sensible when you look into it. On the outward runs toward Mars, the Asteroids or beyond, they have white Terrestrials to tend the engines because they're the ones who perfected modern propulsion units, know most about them and can nurse them like nobody else. All ships' surgeons are black Terrestrials because for some reason none can explain no Negro gets gravity-bends or space nausea. Every outside repair gang is composed of Martians, who use very little air, are tiptop metal workers and fairly immune to cosmic-ray burn.

As for the inward trips to Venus, they mix them similarly except that the emergency pilot is always a big clunker like Jay Score. There's a motive behind that; he's the one who provided it. I'm never likely to forget him. He sort of sticks in the mind, for keeps. What a character!

Destiny placed me at the top of the gangway the first time he appeared. Our ship was the *Upskadaska City*, a brand new freighter with limited passenger accommodation, registered in the Venusian spaceport from which she took her name. Needless to say she was known among hardened spacemen as the *Upsydaisy*.

We were lying in the Colorado Rocket Basin, north of Denver, with a fair load aboard, mostly watchmaking machinery, agricultural equipment, aeronautical jigs and tools for Upskadaska, as well as a case of radium needles for the Venusian Cancer Research Institute. There were eight passengers, all emigrating agriculturalists planning on making hay thirty million miles nearer the Sun. We had ramped the vessel and were waiting for the blow-brothers-blow siren, due in forty minutes, when Jay Score arrived.

He was six feet nine, weighed at least three hundred pounds yet toted this bulk with the easy grace of a ballet dancer. A big guy like that, moving like that, was something worth watching. He came up the duralumin gangway with all the nonchalance of a tripper boarding the bus for Jackson's Creek. From his hamlike right fist dangled a rawhide case not quite big enough to contain his bed and maybe a wardrobe or two.

Reaching the top, he paused while he took in the crossed swords on my cap, said, "Morning, Sarge. I'm the new emergency pilot. I have to report to Captain McNulty."

I knew we were due for another pilot now that Jew Durkin had been promoted to the snooty Martial scent-bottle *Prometheus*. So this was his successor. He was a Terrestrial all right, but neither black nor white. His expressionless but capable face looked as if covered with old, well-seasoned leather. His eyes held fires resembling phosphorescence. There was an air about him that marked him an exceptional individual the like of which I'd never met before.

"Welcome, Tiny," I offered, getting a crick in the neck as I stared up at him, I did not offer my hand because I wanted it for use later on. "Open your satchel and leave it in the sterilizing chamber. You'll find the skipper in the bow."

"Thanks," he responded without the glimmer of a smile. He stepped into the airlock, hauling the rawhide haybarn with him.

"We blast in forty minutes," I warned.

Didn't see anything more of Jay Score until we were two hundred thousand out, with Earth a greenish moon at the end of our vapor-trail. Then I heard him in the passage asking someone where he could find the sergeant-at-arms. He was directed through my door.

"Sarge," he said, handing over his official requisition, "I've come to collect the trimmings." Then he leaned on the barrier, the whole framework creaked and the top tube sagged in the middle.

"Hey!" I shouted.

"Sorry!" He unleaned. The barrier stood much better when he kept his mass to himself.

Stamping his requisition, I went into the armory, dug out his needle-ray projector and a box of capsules for same. The biggest Venusian mud-skis I could find were about eleven sizes too small and a yard too short for him, but they'd have to do. I gave him a can of thin, multipurpose oil, a jar of graphite, a Lepanto power-pack for his microwave radiophone and, finally, a bunch of nutweed pellicules marked: "Compliments of the Bridal Planet Aromatic Herb Corporation."

Shoving back the spicy lumps, he said, "You can have 'em—they give me the staggers." The rest of the stuff he forced into his side-pack without so much as twitching an eyebrow. Long time since I'd seen anyone so poker-faced.

All the same, the way he eyed the spacesuits seemed strangely wistful. There were thirty bifurcated ones for the Terrestrials, all hanging on the wall like sloughed skins. Also there were six head-and-shoulder helmets for the Martians, since they needed no more than three pounds of air. There wasn't a suit for him. I couldn't have fitted him with one if my life had depended upon it. It'd have been like trying to can an elephant.

Well, he lumbered out lightly, if you get what I mean. The casual, loose-limbed way he transported his tonnage made me think I'd like to be some place else if ever he got on the rampage. Not that I thought him likely to run amok; he was amiable enough though sphinxlike. But I was fascinated by his air of calm assurance and by his motion, which was fast, silent and eerie. Maybe the latter was due to his habit of wearing an inch of sponge-rubber under his big dogs.

I kept an interested eye on Jay Score while the *Upsydaisy* made good time on her crawl through the void. Yes, I was more than curious about him because his type was a new one on me despite that I've met plenty in my time. He remained uncommunicative but kind of quietly cordial. His work was smoothly efficient and in every way satisfactory. McNulty took a great fancy to him, though he'd never been one to greet a newcomer with love and kisses.

Three days out, Jade made a major hit with the Martians. As everyone knows, those goggle-eyed, ten-tentacled, half-breathing kibitzers have stuck harder than glue to the Solar System Chess Championship for more than two centuries. Nobody outside of Mars will ever pry them loose. They are nuts about the game and many's the time I've seen a bunch of them go through all the colors of the spectrum in sheer excitement when at last somebody has moved a pawn after thirty minutes of profound cogitation.

One rest-time Jay spent his entire eight hours under three pounds pressure in the starboard airlock. Through the lock's phones came long silences punctuated by wild and shrill twitterings as if he and the Martians were turning the place into a madhouse. At the end of the time we found our tentacled outside-crew exhausted. It turned out that Jay had consented to play Kli Yang and had forced him to a stalemate. Kli had been sixth runner-up in the last Solar melee, had been beaten only ten times—each time by a brother Martian, of course.

The red-planet gang had a finger on him after that, or I should say a tentacle-tip. Every rest-time they waylaid him and dragged him into the airlock. When we were eleven days out he played the six of them simultaneously, lost two games, stalemated three, won one. They thought he was a veritable whizzbang—for a mere Terrestrial. Knowing their peculiar abilities in this respect, I thought so, too. So did McNulty. He went so far as to enter the sporting data in the log.

You may remember the stunt that the audiopress of 2270 boosted as "McNulty's Miracle Move"? It's practically a legend of the spaceways. Afterward, when we'd got safely home, McNulty disclaimed the credit and put it where it rightfully belonged. The audiopress had a good excuse, as usual. They said he was the captain, wasn't he? And his name made the headline alliterative, didn't it? Seems that there must be a sect of audio-journalists who have to be alliterative to gain salvation.

What precipitated that crazy stunt and whitened my hair was a chunk of cosmic flotsam. Said object took the form of a gob of meteoric nickel-iron ambling along at the characteristic speed of *pssst!* Its orbit lay on the planetary plane and it approached at right angles to our sunward course.

It gave us the business. I'd never have believed anything so small could have made such a slam. To the present day I can hear the dreadful whistle of air as it made a mad break for freedom through that jagged hole.

We lost quite a bit of political juice before the autodoors sealed the damaged section. Pressure already had dropped to nine pounds when the compensators held it and slowly began to build it up again. The fall didn't worry the Martians; to them nine pounds was like inhaling pig-wash.

There was one engineer in that sealed section. Another escaped the closing doors by the skin of his left ear. But the first, we thought, had drawn his fateful number and eventually would be floated out like so many spacemen who've come to the end of their duty.

The guy who got clear was leaning against a bulwark, white-faced from the narrowness of his squeak. Jay Score came pounding along. His jaw was working, his eyes were like lamps, but his voice was cool and easy.

He said, "Get out. Seal this room. I'll try to make a snatch. Open up and let me out fast when I knock."

With that he shoved us from the room, which we sealed by closing its autodoor. We couldn't see what the big hunk was doing but the telltale showed he'd released and opened the door to the damaged section. Couple of seconds later the light went out, showing the door had been closed again. Then came a hard, urgent knock. We opened. Jay plunged through hell-for-leather with the engineer's limp body cuddled in his huge arms. He bore it as if it were no bigger and heavier than a kitten and the way he took it down the passage threatened to carry him clear through the end of the ship.

Meanwhile we found we were in a first-class mess. The rockets weren't functioning any more. The venturi tubes were okay and the combustion chambers undamaged. The injectors worked without a hitch—providing that they were pumped by hand. We had lost none of our precious fuel and the shell was intact save for that one jagged hole. What made us useless was the wrecking of our coordinated feeding and firing controls. They had been located where the big bullet went through and now they were so much scrap.

This was more than serious. General opinion called it certain death though nobody said so openly. I'm pretty certain that McNulty shared the morbid notion even if his official report did under-describe it as "an embarrassing predicament." That is just like McNulty. It's a wonder he didn't define our feelings by recording that we were somewhat nonplussed.

Anyway, the Martial squad poured out, some honest work being required of them for the first time in six trips. Pressure had crawled back to fourteen pounds and they had to come into it to be fitted with their head-and-shoulder contraptions.

Kli Yang sniffed offensively, waved a disgusted tentacle and chirruped, "I could swim!" He eased up when we got his dingbat fixed and exhausted it to his customary three pounds. That is the Martian idea of sarcasm: whenever the atmosphere is thicker than they like they make sinuous backstrokes and declaim, "I could swim!"

To give them their due, they were good. A Martian can cling to polished ice and work continuously for twelve hours on a ration of oxygen that wouldn't satisfy a Terrestrial for more than ninety minutes. I watched them beat it through the airlock, eyes goggling through inverted fishbowls, their tentacles clutching power lines, sealing plates and quasi-arc welders. Blue lights made little auroras outside the ports as they began to cut, shape and close up that ragged hole.

All the time we continued to bullet sunward. But for this accursed misfortune we'd have swung a curve into the orbit of Venus in four hours' time. Then we'd have let her catch us up while we decelerated to a safe landing.

But when that peewee planetoid picked on us we were still heading for the biggest and brightest furnace hereabouts. That was the way we continued to go, our original velocity being steadily increased by the pull of our fiery destination.

I wanted to be cremated—but not yet!

Up in the bow navigation-room Jay Score remained in constant conference with Captain McNulty and the two astro-computator operators. Outside, the Martians continued to crawl around, fizzing and spitting with flashes of ghastly blue light. The engineers, of course, weren't waiting for them to finish their job. Four in spacesuits entered the wrecked section and started the task of creating order out of chaos.

I envied all those busy guys and so did many others. There's a lot of consolation in being able to do something even in an apparently hopeless situation. There's a lot of misery in being compelled to play with one's fingers while others are active.

Two Martians came back through the lock, grabbed some more sealing-plates and crawled out again. One of them thought it might be a bright idea to take his pocket chess set as well, but I didn't let him. There are times and places for that sort of thing and knight to king's fourth on the skin of a busted boat isn't one of them. Then I went along to see Sam Hignett, our Negro surgeon.

Sam had managed to drag the engineer back from the rim of the grave. He'd done it with oxygen, adrenalin and heart-massage. Only his long, dexterous fingers could have achieved it. It was a feat of surgery that has been brought off before, but not often.

Seemed that Sam didn't know what had happened and didn't much care, either. He was like that when he had a patient on his hands. Deftly he closed the chest incision with silver clips, painted the pinched flesh with iodized plastic, cooled the stuff to immediate hardness with a spray of ether.

"Sam," I told him. "You're a marvel."

"Jay gave me a fair chance," he said. "He got him here in time."

"Why put the blame on him?" I joked, unfunnily.

"Sergeant," he answered, very serious, "I'm the ship's doctor. I do the best I can. I couldn't have saved this man if Jay hadn't brought him when he did."

"All right, all right," I agreed. "Have it your own way."

A good fellow, Sam. But he was like all doctors—you know, ethical. I left him with his feebly breathing patient.

McNulty came strutting along the catwalk as I went back. He checked the fuel tanks. He was doing it personally, and that meant something. He looked worried, and that meant a devil of a lot. It meant that I need not bother to write my last will and testament because it would never be read by anything living.

His portly form disappeared into the bow navigation-room and I heard him say, "Jay, I guess you—" before the closing door cut off his voice.

He appeared to have a lot of faith in Jay Score. Well, that individual certainly looked capable enough. The skipper and the new emergency pilot continued to act like cronies even while heading for the final frizzle.

One of the emigrating agriculturalists came out of his cabin and caught me before I regained the armory. Studying me wide-eyed, he said, "Sergeant, there's a half-moon showing through my port."

He continued to pop them at me while I popped mine at him. Venus showing half her pan meant that we were now crossing her orbit. He knew it too—I could tell by the way he bugged them.

"Well," he persisted, with ill-concealed nervousness, "how long is this mishap likely to delay us?"

"No knowing." I scratched my head, trying to look stupid and confident at one and the same time. "Captain McNulty will do his utmost. Put your trust in him— Poppa knows best."

"You don't think we are . . . er . . . in any danger?"

"Oh, not at all."

"You're a liar," he said.

"I resent having to admit it," said I.

That unhorsed him. He returned to his cabin, dissatisfied, apprehensive. In short time he'd see Venus in three-quarter phase and would tell the others. Then the fat would be in the fire.

Our fat in the solar fire.

The last vestiges of hope had drained away just about the time when a terrific roar and violent trembling told that the long-dead rockets were back in action. The noise didn't last more than a few seconds. They shut off quickly, the brief burst serving to show that repairs were effective and satisfactory.

The noise brought out the agriculturalist at full gallop. He knew the worst by now and so did the others. It had been impossible to conceal the truth for the three days since he'd seen Venus as a half-moon. She was far behind us now. We were cutting the orbit of Mercury. But still the passengers clung to desperate hope that someone would perform an unheard-of miracle.

Charging into the armory, he yipped, "The rockets are working again. Does that mean?"

"Nothing," I gave back, seeing no point in building false hopes.

"But can't we turn round and go back?" He mopped perspiration trickling down his jowls. Maybe a little of it was forced out by fear, but most of it was due to the unpleasant fact that interior conditions had become anything but arctic.

"Sir," I said, feeling my shirt sticking to my back, "we've got more pull than any bunch of spacemen ever enjoyed before. And we're moving so goddam fast that there's nothing left to do but hold a lily."

"My ranch," he growled, bitterly. "I've been allotted five thousand acres of the best Venusian tobacco-growing territory, not to mention a range of uplands for beef."

"Sorry, but I think you'll be lucky ever to see it."

Crrrump! went the rockets again. The burst bent me backward and made him bow forward like he had a bad bellyache. Up in the bow, McNulty or Jay Score or someone was blowing them whenever he felt the whim. I couldn't see any sense in it.

"What's that for?" demanded the complainant, regaining the perpendicular.

"Boys will be boys," I said.

Snorting his disgust, he went to his cabin. A typical Terrestrial emigrant, big, healthy and tough, he was slow to crack and temporarily too peeved to be really worried in any genuinely soul-shaking way.

Half an hour later the general call sounded on buzzers all over the boat. It was a ground signal, never used in space. It meant that the entire crew and all other occupants of the vessel were summoned to the central cabin. Imagine guys being called from their posts in full flight!

Something unique in the history of space navigation must have been behind that call, probably a compose-yourselves-for-the-inevitable-end speech by McNulty.

Expecting the skipper to preside over the last rites, I wasn't surprised to find him standing on the tiny dais as we assembled. A faint scowl lay over his plump features but it changed to a ghost of a smile when the Martians mooched in and one of them did some imitation shark-dodging.

Erect beside McNulty, expressionless as usual, Jay Score looked at that swimming Martian as if he were a pane of glass. Then his strangely lit orbs shifted their aim as if they'd seen nothing more boring. The swim-joke was getting stale, anyway.

"Men and vedras," began McNulty—the latter being the Martian word for "adults" and, by implication, another piece of Martian sarcasm—"I have no need to enlarge upon the awkwardness of our position." That man certainly could pick his words—awkward! "Already we are nearer the Sun than any vessel has been in the whole history of cosmic navigation."

"Comic navigation," murmured Kli Yang, with tactless wit.

"We'll need your humor to entertain us later," observed Jay Score in a voice so flat that Kli Yang subsided.

"We are moving toward the luminary," went on McNulty, his scowl reappearing, "faster than any ship moved before. Bluntly, there is not more than one chance in ten thousand of us getting out of this alive." He favored Kli Yang with a challenging stare but that tentacled individual was now subdued. "However, there *is* that one chance—and we are going to take it."

We gaped at him, wondering what the devil he meant. Every one of us knew our terrific velocity made it impossible to describe a U-turn and get back without touching the Sun. Neither could we fight our way in the reverse direction with all that mighty drag upon us. There was nothing to do but go onward, onward, until the final searing blast scattered our disrupted molecules.

"What we intend is to try a cometary," continued McNulty. "Jay and myself and the astro-computators think it's remotely possible that we might achieve it and pull through."

That was plain enough. The stunt was a purely theoretical one frequently debated by mathematicians and astro-navigators but never tried out in grim reality. The idea is to build up all the velocity that can be got and at the same time to angle into the path of an elongated, elliptical orbit resembling that of a comet. In theory, the vessel might then skim close to the Sun so supremely fast that it would swing pendulumlike far out to the opposite side of the orbit whence it came. A sweet trick—but could we make it?

"Calculations show our present condition fair enough to permit a small chance of success," said McNulty. "We have power enough and fuel enough to build up the necessary velocity with the aid of the Sun-pull, to strike the necessary angle and to maintain it for the necessary time. The only point about which we have serious doubts is that of whether we can survive at our nearest to the Sun." He wiped perspiration, unconsciously emphasizing the shape of things to come. "I won't mince words, men. It's going to be a choice sample of hell!"

"We'll see it through, Skipper," said someone. A low murmur of support sounded through the cabin.

Kli Yang stood up, simultaneously waggled four jointless arms for attention, and twittered, "It is an idea. It is excellent. I, Kli Yang, endorse it on behalf of my fellow vedras. We shall cram ourselves into the refrigerator and suffer the Terrestrial stink while the Sun goes past."

Ignoring that crack about human odor, McNulty nodded and said, "Everybody will be packed into the cold room and endure it as best they can."

"Exactly," said Kli. "Quite," he added with bland disregard of superfluity. Wiggling a tentacle-tip at McNulty, he carried on, "But we cannot control the ship while squatting in the icebox like three and a half dozen strawberry sundaes. There will have to be a pilot in the bow. One individual can hold her on course—until he gets fried. So somebody has to be the fryee."

He gave the tip another sinuous wiggle, being under the delusion that it was fascinating his listeners into complete attention. "And since it cannot be denied that we Martians are far less susceptible to extremes of heat, I suggest that—"

"Nuts!" snapped McNulty. His gruffness deceived nobody. The Martians were nuisances—but grand guys.

"All right." Kli's chirrup rose to a shrill, protesting yelp. "Who else is entitled to become a crisp?"

"Me," said Jay Score. It was queer the way he voiced it. Just as if he were a candidate so obvious that only the stone-blind couldn't see him.

He was right, at that! Jay was the very one for the job. If anyone could take what was going to come through the fore observation ports it was Jay Score. He was big and tough, built for just such a task as this. He had a lot of stuff that none of us had got and, after all, he was a fully qualified emergency pilot. And most definitely this was an emergency, the greatest ever.

But it was funny the way I felt about him. I could imagine him up in front, all alone, nobody there, our lives depending on how much hell he could take, while the tremendous Sun extended its searing fingers—

"You!" ejaculated Kli Yang, breaking my train of thought. His goggle eyes bulged irefully at the big, laconic figure on the dais. "You would! I am ready to mate in four moves, as you are miserably aware, and promptly you scheme to lock yourself away."

"Six moves," contradicted Jay, airily. "You cannot do it in less than six."

"Four!" Kli Yang fairly howled. "And right at this point you—"

It was too much for the listening McNulty. He looked as if on the verge of a stroke. His purple face turned to the semaphoring Kli.

"To hell with your blasted chess!" he roared. "Return to your stations, all of you. Make ready for maximum boost. I will sound the general call immediately if it becomes necessary to take cover and then you will all go to the cold room." He stared around, the purple gradually fading as his blood pressure went down. "That is, everyone except Jay."

More like old times with the rockets going full belt. They thundered smoothly and steadily. Inside the vessel the atmosphere became hotter and hotter until moisture trickled continually down our backs and a steaminess lay over the gloss of the walls. What it was like in the bow navigation-room I didn't know and didn't care to discover. The Martians were not inconvenienced yet; for once their whacky composition was much to be envied.

I did not keep check on the time but I'd had two spells of duty with one intervening sleep period before the buzzers gave the general call. By then things had become bad. I was no longer sweating: I was slowly melting into my boots.

Sam, of course, endured it most easily of all the Terrestrials and had persisted long enough to drag his patient completely out of original danger. That engineer was lucky, if it's luck to be saved for a bonfire. We put him in the cold room right away, with Sam in attendance.

The rest of us followed when the buzzer went. Our sanctuary was more than a mere refrigerator; it was the strongest and coolest section of the vessel, a heavily armored, triple-shielded compartment holding the instrument lockers, two sick bays and a large lounge for the benefit of space-nauseated passengers. It held all of us comfortably.

All but the Martians. It held them, but not comfortably. They are never comfortable at fourteen pounds pressure, which they regard as not only thick but also smelly—something like breathing molasses impregnated with aged goat.

Under our very eyes Kli Yang produced a bottle of *hooloo* scent, handed it to his half-parent Kli Morg. The latter took it, stared at us distastefully, then sniffed the bottle in an ostentatious manner that was positively insulting. But nobody said anything.

All were present excepting McNulty and Jay Score. The skipper appeared two hours later. Things must have been raw up front, for he looked terrible. His haggard face was beaded and glossy, his once-plump cheeks sunken and blistered. His usually spruce, well-fitting uniform hung upon him sloppily. It needed only one glance to tell that he'd had a darned good roasting, as much as he could stand.

Walking unsteadily, he crossed the floor, went into the first-aid cubby, stripped himself with slow, painful movements. Sam rubbed him with tannic jelly. We could hear the tormented skipper grunting hoarsely as Sam put plenty of pep into the job.

The heat was now on us with a vengeance. It pervaded the walls, the floor, the air and created a multitude of fierce stinging sensations in every muscle of my body. Several of the engineers took off their boots and jerkins. In short time the passengers followed suit, discarding most of their outer clothing. My agriculturalist sat a miserable figure in tropical silks, moody over what might have been.

Emerging from the cubby, McNulty flopped onto a bunk and said, "If we're all okay in four hours' time, we're through the worst part."

At that moment the rockets faltered. We knew at once what was wrong. A fuel tank had emptied and a relay had failed to cut in. An engineer should have been standing by to switch the conduits. In the heat and excitement, someone had blundered.

The fact barely had time to register before Kli Yang was out through the door. He'd been lolling nearest to it and was gone while we were trying to collect our overheated wits. Twenty seconds later the rockets renewed their steady thrum.

An intercom bell clanged right in my ear. Switching its mike, I croaked a throaty, "Well?" and heard Jay's voice coming back at me from the bow.

"Who did it?"

"Kli Yang," I told him. "He's still outside."

"Probably gone for their domes," guessed Jay. "Tell him I said thanks."

"What's it like around where you live?" I asked.

"Fierce. It isn't so good . . . for vision." Silence a moment, then, "Guess I can stick it . . . somehow. Strap down or hold on ready for the next time I sound the . . . bell."

"Why?" I half yelled, half rasped.

"Going to rotate her. Try . . . distribute . . . the heat."

A faint squeak told that he'd switched off. I told the others to strap down. The Martians didn't have to bother about that because they owned enough saucer-sized suckers to weld them to a sunfishing meteor.

Kli came back, showed Jay's guess to be correct; he was dragging the squad's head-and-shoulder pieces. The lead was as much as he could pull now that temperature had climbed to the point where even he began to wilt.

The Martian moochers gladly donned their gadgets, sealing the seams and evacuating them down to three pounds pressure. It made them considerably happier. Remembering that we Terrestrials use spacesuits to keep air inside, it seemed queer to watch those guys using theirs to keep it outside.

They had just finished making themselves comfortable and had laid out a chessboard in readiness for a minor journey when the bell sounded again. We braced ourselves. The Martians clamped down their suckers.

Slowly and steadily the *Upsydaisy* began to turn upon her longitudinal axis. The chessboard and pieces tried to stay put, failed, crawled along the floor, up the wall and across the ceiling. Solar pull was making them stick to the sunward side.

I saw Kli Morg's strained, heat-ridden features glooming at a black bishop while it skittered around, and I suppose that inside his goldfish bowl were resounding some potent samples of Martian invective.

"Three hours and a half," gasped McNulty.

That four hours estimate could only mean two hours of approach to the absolute deadline and two hours of retreat from it. So the moment when we had two hours to go would be the moment when we were at our nearest to the solar furnace, the moment of greatest peril.

I wasn't aware of that critical time, since I passed out twenty minutes before it arrived. No use enlarging upon the horror of that time. I think I went slightly nuts. I was a hog in an oven, being roasted alive. It's the only time I've ever thought of the Sun as a great big shining bastard that ought to be extinguished for keeps. Soon afterward I became incapable of any thought at all.

I recovered consciousness and painfully moved in my straps ninety minutes after passing the midway point. My dazed mind had difficulty in realizing that we had now only half an hour to go to reach theoretical safety.

What had happened in the interim was left to my imagination and I didn't care to try to picture it just then. The Sun blazing with a ferocity multi-million times greater than that of a tiger's eye, and a hundred thousand times as hungry for our blood and bones. The flaming corona licking out toward this shipload of half-dead entities, imprisoned in a steel bottle.

And up in front of the vessel, behind its totally inadequate quartz observation-ports, Jay Score sitting alone, facing the mounting inferno, staring, staring, staring—

Getting to my feet, I teetered uncertainly, went down like a bundle of rags. The ship wasn't rotating any longer and we appeared to be bulleting along in normal fashion. What dropped me was sheer weakness. I felt lousy.

The Martians already had recovered. I knew they'd be the first. One of them lugged me upright and held me steady while I regained a percentage of my former control. I noticed that another had sprawled right across the unconscious McNulty and three of the passengers. Yes, he'd shielded them from some of the heat and they were the next ones to come to life.

Struggling to the intercom, I switched it but got no response from the front. For three full minutes I hung by it dazedly before I tried again. Nothing doing. Jay wouldn't or couldn't answer.

I was stubborn about it, made several more attempts with no better result. The effort cost me a dizzy spell and down I flopped once more. The heat was still terrific. I felt more dehydrated than a mummy dug out of sand a million years old.

Kli Yang opened the door, crept out with dragging, painstricken motion. His air-helmet was secure on his shoulders. Five minutes later he came back, spoke through the helmet's diaphragm.

"Couldn't get near the bow navigation-room. At the midway catwalk the autodoors are closed, the atmosphere sealed off and it's like being inside a furnace." He stared around, met my gaze, answered the question in my eyes. "There's no air in the bow."

No air meant the observation-ports had gone *phut*. Nothing else could have emptied the navigation-room. Well, we carried spares for that job and could make good the damage once we got into the clear. Meanwhile here we were roaring along, maybe on correct course and maybe not, with an empty, airless navigation-room and with an intercom system that gave nothing but ghastly silence.

Sitting around, we picked up strength. The last to come out of his coma was the sick engineer. Sam brought him through again. It was about then that McNulty wiped sweat, showed sudden excitement.

"Four hours, men," he said, with grim satisfaction. "We've done it!"

We raised a hollow cheer. By Jupiter, the super-heated atmosphere seemed to grow ten degrees cooler with the news. Strange how relief from tension can breed strength; in one minute we had conquered former weakness and were ready to go. But it was yet another four hours before a quartet of spacesuited engineers penetrated the forward hell and bore their burden from the airless navigation room.

They carried him into Sam's cubbyhole, a long, heavy, silent figure with face burned black.

Stupidly I hung around him saying, "Jay, Jay, how're you making out?"

He must have heard, for he moved the fingers of his right hand and emitted a chesty, grinding noise. Two of the engineers went to his cabin, brought back his huge rawhide case. They shut the door, staying in with Sam and leaving me and the Martians fidgeting outside. Kli Yang wandered up and down the passage as if he didn't know what to do with his tentacles.

Sam came out after more than an hour. We jumped him on the spot.

"How's Jay?"

"Blind as a statue." He shook his woolly head. "And his voice isn't there any more. He's taken an awful beating."

"So that's why he didn't answer the intercom." I looked him straight in the eyes. "Can you . . . can you do anything for him, Sam?"

"I only wish I could." His sepia face showed his feelings. "You know how much I'd like to put him right. But I can't." He made a gesture of futility. "He is completely beyond my modest skill. Nobody less than Johannsen can help him. Maybe when we get back to Earth—" His voice petered out and he went back inside.

Kli Yang said, miserably, "I am saddened."

A scene I'll never forget to my dying day was that evening we spent as guests of the Astro Club in New York. That club was then—as it is today—the most exclusive group of human beings ever gathered together. To qualify for membership one had to perform in dire emergency a feat of astro-navigation tantamount to a miracle. There were nine members in those days and there are only twelve now.

Mace Waldron, the famous pilot who saved that Martian liner in 2263, was the chairman. Classy in his soup and fish, he stood at the top of the table with Jay Score sitting at his side. At the opposite end of the table was McNulty, a broad smirk of satisfaction upon his plump pan. Beside the skipper was old, white-haired Knud Johannsen, the genius who designed the J-series and a scientific figure known to every spaceman.

Along the sides, manifestly self-conscious, sat the entire crew of the *Upsydaisy*, including the Martians, plus three of our passengers who'd postponed their trips for this occasion. There were also a couple of audio-journalists with scanners and mikes.

"Gentlemen and vedras," said Mace Waldron, "this is an event without precedent in the history of humanity, an event never thought of, never imagined by this club. Because of that I feel it doubly an honor and a privilege to propose that Jay Score, Emergency Pilot, be accepted as a fully qualified and worthy member of the Astro Club."

"Seconded!" shouted three members simultaneously.

"Thank you, gentlemen." He cocked an inquiring eyebrow. Eight hands went up in unison. "Carried," he said. "Unanimously." Glancing down at the taciturn and unmoved Jay Score, he launched into a eulogy. It went on and on and on, full of praise and superlatives, while Jay squatted beside him with a listless air.

Down at the other end I saw McNulty's gratified smirk grow stronger and stronger. Next to him, old Knud was gazing at Jay with a fatherly fondness that verged on the famous. The crew likewise gave full attention to the blank-faced subject of the talk, and the scanners were fixed upon him too.

I returned my attention to where all the others were looking, and the victim sat there, his restored eyes bright and glittering, but his face completely immobile despite the talk, the publicity, the beam of paternal pride from Johannsen.

But after ten minutes of this I saw J.20 begin to fidget with obvious embarrassment.

Don't let anyone tell you that a robot can't have feelings!

✵ A(LFRED) E(LTON) VAN VOGT (1912–2000)

A. E. van Vogt was born in Canada and lived in both Canada and the United States. His work has been in print ever since the early 1930s, and he debuted in Science Fiction in the July 1939 issue of Astounding Science-Fiction *with "Black Destroyer." A prolific writer, van Vogt also wrote Mystery and Crime Fiction, as well as nonfiction about money and finance and health matters. He was a founder and proponent of L. Ron Hubbard's "Dianetics" research and initiatives.*

Like Eric Frank Russell and Ray Bradbury in that 1940s and 1950s era prior to the Civil Rights Movement, A. E. van Vogt was a visionary writer of stories about ethnicity, race relations, and the human condition. He found Science Fiction to be a most effective vehicle for relating these visions. Van Vogt's first novel, Slan, *was serialized in* Astounding Science-Fiction *in its September through December 1940 issues. In 1946, August Derleth and Donald Wandrei published this novel under the Arkham House imprint. In 1951,* Slan *was revised and published by Simon & Schuster.* Slan *became an archetypal Science Fiction story of race relations. Many short stories, novels, and series of Hard Science Fiction, Space Opera, and morality followed. A. E. van Vogt was always a multitalented and versatile author.*

As shown in "The Weapons Shop," the first installment of what would ultimately become The Weapons Shop *series, van Vogt was influenced by the writings of Philip Wylie, John Taine, Olaf Stapledon, and John W. Campbell Jr.*

The Weapons Shop

(Astounding Science-Fiction, *December 1942*)

The village at night made a curiously timeless picture. Fara walked contentedly beside his wife along the street. The air was like wine; and he was thinking dimly of the artist who had come up from Imperial City and made what the telestats called—he remembered the phrase vividly—"a symbolic painting reminiscent of a scene in the electrical age of seven thousand years ago."

Fara believed that utterly. The street before him with its weedless, automatically tended gardens, its shops set well back among the flowers, its perpetual hard, grassy sidewalks and its street lamps that glowed from every pore of their structure—this was a restful paradise where time had stood still.

And it was like being a part of life that the great artist's picture of this quiet, peaceful scene before him was now in the collection of the empress herself. She had praised it, and naturally the thrice-blest artist had immediately and humbly begged her to accept it.

What a joy it must be to be able to offer personal homage to the glorious, the divine, the serenely gracious and lovely Innelda Isher, one thousand one hundred eightieth of her line.

As they walked, Fara half turned to his wife. In the dim light of the nearest street lamp, her kindly, still youthful face was almost lost in shadow. He murmured softly, instinctively muting his voice to harmonize with the pastel shades of night:

"She said—our empress said—that our little village of Glay seemed to her to have in it all the wholesomeness, the gentleness, that constitutes the finest qualities of her people. Wasn't that a wonderful thought, Creel? She must be a marvelously understanding woman. I—"

He stopped. They had come to a side street, and there was something about a hundred and fifty feet along in that—

"Look!" Fara said hoarsely.

He pointed with rigid arm and finger at a sign that glowed in the night, a sign that read:

FINE WEAPONS
THE RIGHT TO BUY WEAPONS IS THE RIGHT
TO BE FREE

Fara had a strange, empty feeling as he stared at the blazing sign. He saw that other villagers were gathering. He said finally, huskily, "I've heard of these shops. They're places of infamy, against which the government of the empress will act one of these days. They're built in hidden factories, and then transported whole to towns like ours and set up in gross defiance of property rights. That one wasn't there an hour ago."

Fara's face hardened. His voice had a harsh edge in it, as he said, "Creel, go home."

Fara was surprised when Creel did not move off at once. All their married life she had had a pleasing habit of obedience that had made cohabitation a wonderful thing. He saw that she was looking at him wide-eyed, and that it was a timid alarm that held her there. She said, "Fara, what do you intend to do? You're not thinking of—"

"Go home!" Her fear brought out all the grim determination in his nature. "We're not going to let such a monstrous thing desecrate our village. Think of it"—his voice shivered before the appalling thought—"this fine, old-fashioned community, which we had resolved always to keep exactly as the empress has it in her picture gallery, debauched now, ruined by this . . . this thing—But we won't have it; that's all there is to it."

Creel's voice came softly out of the half-darkness of the street corner, the timidity gone from it: "Don't do anything rash, Fara. Remember it is not the first new building to come into Glay—since the picture was painted."

Fara was silent. This was a quality of his wife of which he did not approve, this reminding him unnecessarily of unpleasant facts. He knew exactly what she meant. The gigantic, multitentacled corporation, Automatic Atomic Motor Repair Shops, Inc., had come in under the laws of the state with their flashy building, against the wishes of the village council—and had already taken half of Fara's repair business.

"That's different!" Fara growled finally. "In the first place people will discover in good time that these new automatic repairers do a poor job. In the second place it's fair competition. But this weapon shop is a defiance of all the decencies that make life under the House of Isher such a joy. Look at the hypocritical sign: 'The right to buy weapons—' Aaaaahh!"

He broke off with: "Go home, Creel. We'll see to it that they sell no weapons in this town."

He watched the slender woman-shape move off into the shadows. She was halfway across the street when a thought occurred to Fara. He called, "And if you see that son of ours hanging around some street corner, take him home. He's got to learn to stop staying out so late at night."

The shadowed figure of his wife did not turn; and after watching her for a moment moving along against the dim background of softly glowing street lights, Fara twisted on his heel, and walked swiftly toward the shop. The crowd was growing larger every minute and the night pulsed with excited voices.

Beyond doubt, here was the biggest thing that had ever happened to the village of Glay.

The sign of the weapon shop was, a normal-illusion affair. No matter what his angle of view, he was always looking straight at it. When he paused finally in front of the great display window, the words had pressed back against the store front, and were staring unwinkingly down at him.

Fara sniffed once more at the meaning of the slogan, then forgot the simple thing. There was another sign in the window, which read:

THE FINEST ENERGY WEAPONS IN THE KNOWN
UNIVERSE

A spark of interest struck fire inside Fara. He gazed at that brilliant display of guns, fascinated in spite of himself. The weapons were of every size, ranging from tiny little finger pistols to express rifles. They were made of every one of the light, hard, ornamental substances: glittering glassein, the colorful but opaque Ordine plastic, viridescent magnesitic beryllium. And others.

It was the very deadly extent of the destructive display that brought a chill to Fara. So many weapons for the little village of Glay, where not more that two people to his knowledge had guns, and those only for hunting. Why, the thing was absurd, fantastically mischievous, utterly threatening.

Somewhere behind Fara, a man said: "It's right on Lan Harris' lot. Good joke on that old scoundrel. Will he raise a row!"

There was a faint titter from several men, that made an odd patch of sound on the warm, fresh air. And Fara saw that the man had spoken the truth. The weapon shop had a forty-foot frontage. And it occupied the very center of the green, gardenlike lot of tight-fisted old Harris.

Fara frowned. The clever devils, the weapon shop people, selecting the property of the most disliked man in town, coolly taking it over and giving everybody an agreeable titillation. But the very cunning of it made it vital that the trick shouldn't succeed.

He was still scowling anxiously when he saw the plump figure of Mel Dale, the mayor. Fara edged toward him hurriedly, touched his hat respectfully, and said, "Where's Jor?"

"Here." The village constable elbowed his way through a little bundle of men. "Any plans?" he said.

"There's only one plan," said Fara boldly. "Go in and arrest them."

To Fara's amazement, the two men looked at each other, then at the ground. It was the big constable who answered shortly, "Door's locked. And nobody answers our pounding. I was just going to suggest we let the matter ride until morning."

"Nonsense!" His very astonishment made Fara impatient. "Get an ax and we'll break the door down. Delay will only encourage such riffraff to resist. We don't want their kind in our village for so much as a single night. Isn't that so?"

There was a hasty nod of agreement from everybody in his immediate vicinity. Too hasty. Fara looked around puzzled at eyes that lowered before his level gaze. He thought: "They are all scared. And unwilling." Before he could speak, Constable Jor said, "I guess you haven't heard about those doors or these shops. From all accounts, you can't break into them."

It struck Fara with a sudden pang that it was he who would have to act here. He said, "I'll get my atomic cutting machine from my shop. That'll fix them. Have I your permission to do that, Mr. Mayor?"

In the glow of the weapon shop window, the plump man was sweating visibly. He pulled out a handkerchief and wiped his forehead. He said, "Maybe I'd better call the commander of the Imperial garrison at Ferd, and ask them."

"No!" Fara recognized evasion when he saw it. He felt himself steel; the conviction came that all the strength in this village was in him. "We must act ourselves. Other communities have let these people get in because they took no decisive action. We've got to resist to the limit. Beginning now. This minute. Well?"

The mayor's "All right!" was scarcely more than a sigh of sound. But it was all Fara needed.

He called out his intention to the crowd; and then, as he pushed his way out of the mob, he saw his son standing with some other young men staring at the window display.

Fara called, "Cayle, come and help me with the machine."

Cayle did not even turn; and Fara hurried on, seething. That wretched boy! One of these days he, Fara, would have to take a firm action there. Or he'd have a no-good on his hands.

The energy was soundless—and smooth. There was no sputter, no fireworks. It glowed with a soft, pure white light, almost caressing the metal panels of the door—but not even beginning to sear them.

Minute after minute, the dogged Fara refused to believe the incredible failure, and played the boundlessly potent energy on that resisting wall. When he finally shut off his machine, he was perspiring freely.

"I don't understand it," he gasped. "Why—no metal is supposed to stand up against a steady flood of atomic force. Even the hard metal plates used inside the blast chamber of a motor take the explosions in what is called infinite series, so that each one has unlimited rest. That's the theory, but actually steady running crystallizes the whole plate after a few months."

"It's as Jor told you," said the mayor. "These weapons shops are—big. They spread right through the empire, *and* they *don't recognize the empress.*"

Fara shifted his feet on the hard grass, disturbed. He didn't like this kind of talk. It sounded—sacrilegious. And besides it was nonsense. It must be. Before he could speak, a man said somewhere behind him, "I've heard it said that that door will open only to those who cannot harm the people inside."

The words shocked Fara out of his daze. With a start, and for the first time, he saw that his failure had had a bad psychological effect. He said sharply, "That's ridiculous! If there were doors like that, we'd all have them. We—"

The thought that stopped his words was the sudden realization that *he* had not seen anybody try to open the door; and with all this reluctance around him it was quite possible that—

He stepped forward, grasped at the doorknob and pulled. The door opened with an unnatural weightlessness that gave him the fleeting impression that the knob had come loose in his hand. With a gasp, Fara jerked the door wide open.

"Jor!" he yelled. "Get in!"

The constable made a distorted movement—distorted by what must have been a will to caution, followed by the instant realization that he could not hold back before so many. He leaped awkwardly toward the open door—and it closed in his face.

Fara stared stupidly at his hand, which was still clenched. And then, slowly, a hideous thrill coursed along his nerves. The knob had—withdrawn. It had twisted, become viscous and slipped amorphously from his straining fingers. Even the memory of that brief sensation gave him a feeling of abnormal things.

He grew aware that the crowd was watching with a silent intentness. Fara reached again for the knob, not quite so eagerly this time; and it was only a sudden realization of his reluctance that made him angry when the handle neither turned nor yielded in any way.

Determination returned in full force, and with it came a thought. He motioned to the constable. "Go back, Jor, while I pull."

The man retreated, but it did no good. And tugging did not help. The door would not open. Somewhere in the crowd, a man said darkly, "It decided to let you in, then it changed its mind."

"What foolishness are you talking!" Fara spoke violently. "*It* changed its mind. Are you crazy? A door has no sense."

But a surge of fear put a half-quaver into his voice. It was the sudden alarm that made him bold beyond all his normal caution. With a jerk of his body, Fara faced the shop.

The building loomed there under the night sky, in itself bright as day, huge in width and length, and alien, menacing, no longer easily conquerable. The dim queasy wonder came as to what the soldiers of the empress would do if they were invited to act. And suddenly—a bare, flashing glimpse of a grim possibility—the feeling grew that even they would be able to do nothing.

Abruptly, Fara was conscious of horror that such an idea could enter his mind. He shut his brain tight, said wildly, "The door opened for me once. It will open again."

It did. Quite simply it did. Gently, without resistance, with that same sensation of weightlessness, the strange, sensitive door followed the tug of his fingers. Beyond the threshold was dimness, a wide, darkened alcove. He heard the voice of Mel Dale behind him, the mayor saying, "Fara, don't be a fool. What will you do inside?"

Fara was vaguely amazed to realize that he had stepped across the threshold. He turned, startled, and stared at the blur of faces. "Why—" he began blankly; then he brightened; he said, "Why, I'll buy a gun, of course."

The brilliance of his reply, the cunning implicit in it, dazzled Fara for half a minute longer. The mood yielded slowly, as he found himself in the dimly lighted interior of the weapons shop.

It was preternaturally quiet inside. Not a sound penetrated from the night from which he had come, and the startled thought came that the people of the shop might actually be unaware that there was a crowd outside.

Fara walked forward gingerly on a rugged floor that muffled his footsteps utterly. After a moment, his eyes accustomed themselves to the soft lighting, which came like a reflection from the walls and ceilings. In a vague way, he had expected ultranormality; and the ordinariness of the atomic lighting acted like a tonic to his tensed nerves.

He shook himself angrily. Why should there be anything really superior? He was getting as bad as those credulous idiots out in the street.

He glanced around with gathering confidence. The place looked quite common. It was a shop, almost scantily furnished. There were showcases, on the walls and on the floor, glitteringly lovely things, but nothing unusual, and not many of them—a few dozens. There was in addition, a double, ornate door leading to a back room—

Fara tried to keep one eye on that door, as he examined several showcases, each with three or four weapons either mounted or arranged in boxes or holsters.

Abruptly, the weapons began to excite him. He forgot to watch the door, as the wild thought struck that he ought to grab one of those guns from a case, and then the moment someone came, force him outside where Jor would perform the arrest and—

Behind him, a man said quietly, "You wish to buy a gun?"

Fara turned with a jump. Brief rage flooded him at the way his plan had been wrecked by the arrival of the clerk.

The anger died as he saw that the intruder was a fine-looking, silver-haired man, older than himself. That was immeasurably disconcerting. Fara had an immense and almost automatic respect for age, and for a long second he could only stand there gaping. He said at last, lamely, "Yes, yes, a gun."

"For what purpose?" said the man in his quiet voice.

Fara could only look at him blankly. It was too fast. He wanted to get mad. He wanted to tell these people what he thought of them. But the age of this representative locked his tongue, tangled his emotions. He managed speech only by an effort of will

"For hunting." The plausible word stiffened his mind. "Yes, definitely for hunting. There is a lake to the north of here," he went on more fulsomely, glibly, "and—"

He stopped, scowling, startled at the extent of his dishonesty. He was not prepared to go so deeply into prevarication. He said curtly, "For hunting."

Fara was himself again. Abruptly, he hated the man for having put him so completely at a disadvantage. With smoldering eyes he watched the old fellow click open a showcase, and take out a green-shining rifle.

As the man faced him, weapon in hand, Fara was thinking grimly, "Pretty clever, having an old man as a front." It was the same kind of cunning that had made them choose the property of Miser Harris. Icily furious, taut with his purpose, Fara reached for the gun; but the man held it out of his reach, saying, "Before I can even let you test this, I am compelled by the by-laws of the weapons shops to inform you under what circumstances you may purchase a gun."

So they had private regulations. What a system of psychology tricks to impress gullible fools! Well, let the old scoundrel talk. As soon as he, Fara, got hold of the rifle, he'd put an end to hypocrisy.

"We weapons makers," the clerk was saying mildly, "have evolved guns that can, in their particular ranges, destroy any machine or object made of what is called matter. Thus whoever possesses one of our weapons is the equal and more of any soldier of the empress. I say more because each gun is the center of a field of force which acts as a perfect screen against immaterial destructive forces. That screen offers no resistance to clubs or spears or bullets, or other material substances, but it would require a small atomic cannon to penetrate the superb barrier it creates around its owner.

"You will readily comprehend," the man went on, "that such a potent weapon could not be allowed to fall, unmodified, into irresponsible hands. Accordingly, no gun purchased from us may be used for aggression or murder. In the case of hunting rifle, only such specified game birds and animals as we may from time to time list in our display windows may be shot. Finally, no weapon can be resold without our approval. Is that clear?"

Fara nodded dumbly. For the moment, speech was impossible to him. The incredible, fantastically stupid words were still going round and round in his head. He wondered if he ought to laugh out loud, or curse the man for daring to insult his intelligence so tremendously.

So the gun mustn't be used for murder or robbery. So only certain birds and animals could be shot. And as for reselling it, suppose — suppose he bought this thing, took a trip of a thousand miles, and offered it to some wealthy stranger for two credits — who would ever know?

Or suppose he held up the stranger. Or shot him. How could the weapons shop ever find out? The thing was so ridiculous that—

He grew aware that the gun was being held out to him stock first. He took it eagerly, and had to fight the impulse to turn the muzzle directly on the old man. Mustn't rush this, he thought tautly. He said, "How does it work?"

"You simply aim it, and pull the trigger. Perhaps you would like to try it on a target we have."

Fara swung the gun up. "Yes," he said triumphantly, "and you're it. Now, just get over there to the front door, and then outside."

He raised his voice "And if anybody's thinking of coming through the back door, I've got that covered too."

He motioned jerkily at the clerk. "Quick now, move! I'll shoot! I swear I will."

The man was cool, unflustered. "I have no doubt you would. When we decided to attune the door so that you could enter despite your hostility, we assumed the capacity for homicide. However, this is our party. You had better adjust yourself accordingly, and look behind you—"

There was silence. Finger on trigger, Fara stood motionless. Dim thoughts came of all the *half-things* he had heard in his days about the weapons shops: that they had secret supporters in every district, that they had a private and ruthlesss hidden government, and that once you got into their clutches, the only way out was death and—

But what finally came clear was a mind picture of himself, Fara Clark, family man, faithful subject of the empress, standing here in this dimly lighted store, deliberately fighting an organization so vast and menacing that—He must have been mad.

Only—here he was. He forced courage into his sagging muscles. He said, "You can't fool me with pretending there's someone behind me. Now, get to that door. And *fast!*"

The firm eyes of the old man were looking past him. The man said quietly, "Well, Rad, have you all the data?"

"Enough for a primary," said a young man's baritone voice behind Fara. "Type A-7 conservative. Good average intelligence, but a Monaric development peculiar to small towns. One-sided outlook fostered by the Imperial schools present in exaggerated form. Extremely honest. Reason would be useless. Emotional approach would require extended treatment. I see no reason why we should bother. Let him live his life as it suits him."

"If you think," Fara said shakily, "that that trick voice is going to make me turn, you're crazy. That's the left wall of the building. I know there's no one there."

"I'm all in favor, Rad," said the old man, "of letting him live his life. But he was the prime mover of the crowd outside. I think he should be discouraged."

"We'll advertise his presence," said Rad. "He'll spend the rest of his life denying the charge."

Fara's confidence in the gun had faded so far that, as he listened in puzzled uneasiness to the incomprehensible conversation, he forgot it completely. He parted his lips, but before he could speak, the old man cut in, persistently, "I think a little emotion might have a long-run effect. Show him the palace."

Palace! The startling word tore Fara out of his brief paralysis. "See here," he began, "I can see now that you lied to me. This gun isn't loaded at all. It's—"

His voice failed him. Every muscle in his body went rigid. He stared like a madman. *There was no gun in his hands.*

"Why, you—" he began wildly. And stopped again. His mind heaved with imbalance. With a terrible effort he fought off the spinning sensation, thought finally, tremblingly: Somebody must have sneaked the gun from him. That meant—there was someone behind him. The voice was no mechanical thing. Somehow, they had—

He started to turn—and couldn't. What in the name of—He struggled, pushing with his muscles. And couldn't move, couldn't budge, couldn't even—

The room was growing curiously dark. He had difficulty seeing the old man and— He would have shrieked then if he could. Because the weapons shop was gone. He was—

He was standing in the sky above an immense city.

In the sky, and nothing beneath him, nothing around him but air, and blue summer heaven, and the city a mile, two miles below.

Nothing, nothing— He would have shrieked, but his breath seemed solidly embedded in his lungs. Sanity came back as the remote awareness impinged upon his terrified mind that he was actually standing on a hard floor, and that the city must be a picture somehow focused directly into his eyes.

For the first time, with a start, Fara recognized the metropolis below. It was the city of dreams, Imperial City, capital of the glorious Empress Isher— From his great height, he could see the gardens, the gorgeous grounds of the silver palace, the official Imperial residence itself—

The last tendrils of his fear were fading now before a gathering fascination and wonder; they vanished utterly as he recognized with a ghastly thrill of uncertain expectancy that the palace was drawing nearer at great speed.

"Show him the palace," they had said. Did that mean, could it mean—

That spray of tense thoughts splattered into nonexistence, as the glittering roof flashed straight at his face. He gulped, as the solid metal of it passed through him, and then other walls and ceilings.

His first sense of imminent and mind-shaking desecration came as the picture paused in a great room where a score of men sat around a table at the head of which sat—a young woman.

The inexorable, sacrilegious, limitlessly powered cameras that were taking the picture swung across the table, and caught the woman full face.

It was a handsome face, but there was passion and fury twisting it now, and a very blaze of fire in her eyes, as she leaned forward, and said in a voice at once familiar—how often Fara had heard its calm, measured tones on the telestats—and distorted. Utterly distorted by anger and an insolent certainty of command. That caricature of a beloved voice slashed across the silence as clearly as if he, Fara, was there in that room "I want that skunk killed, do you understand? I don't care how you do it, but I want to hear by tomorrow night that he's dead."

The picture snapped off and instantly—it was as swift as that—Fara was back in the weapon shop. He stood for a moment, swaying, fighting to accustom his eyes to the dimness; and then—

His first emotion was contempt at the simpleness of the trickery—a motion picture. What kind of a fool did they think he was, to swallow something as transparently unreal as that? He'd—

Abruptly, the appalling lechery of the scheme, the indescribable wickedness of what was being attempted here brought red rage.

"Why, you scum!" he flared. "So you've got somebody to act the part of the empress, trying to pretend that—Why, you—"

"That will do," said the voice of Rad; and Fara shook as a big young man walked into his line of vision. The alarmed thought came that people who would besmirch so vilely the character of her imperial majesty would not hesitate to do physical damage to Fara Clark. The young man went on in a steely tone, "We do not pretend that what you saw was taking place this instant in the palace. That would be too much of a coincidence. But it was taken two weeks ago; the woman *is* the empress. The man whose death she ordered is one of her many former lovers. He was found murdered two weeks ago; his name, if you care to look it up in the new files, is Banton McCreddie. However, let that pass. We're finished with you now and—"

"But I'm not finished," Fara said in a thick voice. "I've never heard or seen so much infamy in all my life. If you think this town is through with you, you're crazy. We'll have a guard on this place day and night, and nobody will get in or out. We'll—"

"That will do." It was the silver-haired man; and Fara stopped out of respect for age, before he thought. The old man went on: "The examination has been most interesting. As an honest man, you may call on us if you are ever in trouble. That is all. Leave through the side door."

It was all. Impalpable forces grabbed him, and he was shoved at a door that appeared miraculously in the wall, where seconds before the palace had been.

He found himself standing dazedly in a flower bed, and there was a swarm of men to his left. He recognized his fellow townsmen and that he was—outside.

The incredible nightmare was over.

"Where's the gun?" said Creel, as he entered the house half an hour later.

"The gun?" Fara stared at his wife.

"It said over the radio a few minutes ago that you were the first customer of the new weapon shop. I thought it was queer, but—"

He was eerily conscious of her voice going on for several words longer, but it was the purest jumble. The shock was so great that he had the horrible sensation of being on the edge of an abyss.

So that was what the young man had meant "Advertise! We'll advertise his presence and—"

Fara thought: His reputation! Not that his was a great name, but he had long believed with a quiet pride that Fara Clark's motor repair shop was widely known in the community and countryside.

First, his private humiliation inside the shop. And now this—lying—to people who didn't know why he had gone into the store. Diabolical.

His paralysis ended, as a frantic determination to rectify the base charge drove him to the telestat. After a moment, the plump, sleepy face of Mayor Mel Dale appeared on the plate. Fara's voice made a barrage of sound, but his hopes dashed, as the man said, "I'm sorry, Fara. I don't see how you can have free time on the telestat. You'll have to pay for it. They did."

"They did!" Fara wondered vaguely if he sounded as empty as he felt.

"And they've just paid Lan Harris for his lot. The old man asked top price, and got it. He just phoned me to transfer the title."

"Oh!" The world was shattering. "You mean nobody's going to do anything. What about the Imperial garrison at Ferd?"

Dimly, Fara was aware of the mayor mumbling something about the empress' soldiers refusing to interfere in civilian matters.

"Civilian matters!" Fara exploded. "You mean these people are just going to be allowed to come here whether we want them or not, illegally forcing the sale of lots by first taking possession of them?"

A sudden thought struck him breathless. "Look, you haven't changed your mind about having Jor keep guard in front of the shop?"

With a start, he saw that the plump face in the telestat plate had grown impatient. "Now, see here, Fara," came the pompous words, "let the constituted authorities handle this matter."

"But you're going to keep Jor there," Fara said doggedly.

The mayor looked annoyed, said finally peevishly: "I promised, didn't I? So he'll be there. And now—do you want to buy time on the telestat? It's fifteen credits for one minute. Mind you, as a friend, I think you're wasting your money. No one has ever caught up with a false statement."

Fara said grimly, "Put two on, one in the morning, one in the evening."

"All right. We'll deny it completely. Good night."

The telestat went blank; and Fara sat there. A new thought hardened his face. "That boy of ours—there's going to be a showdown. He either works in my shop, or he gets no more allowance."

Creel said "You've handled him wrong. He's twenty-three and you treat him like a child. Remember, at twenty-three you were a married man."

"That was different," said Fara. "I had a sense of responsibility. Do you know what he did tonight?"

He didn't quite catch her answer. For the moment, he thought she said, "No; in what way did you humiliate him first?"

Fara felt too impatient to verify the impossible words. He rushed on: "He refused in front of the whole village to give me help. He's a bad one, all bad."

"Yes," said Creel in a bitter tone, "he is all bad. I'm sure you don't realize how bad. He's as cold as steel, but without steel's strength or integrity. He took a long time, but he hates even me now, because I stood up for your side so long, knowing you were wrong."

"What's that?" said Fara, startled; then gruffly: "Come, come my dear, we're both upset. Let's go to bed."

He slept poorly.

There were days then when the conviction that this was a personal fight between himself and the weapons shop lay heavily on Fara. Grimly, though it was out of his way, he made a point of walking past the weapon shop, always pausing to speak to Constable Jor and—

On the fourth day, the policeman wasn't there.

Fara waited patiently at first, then angrily then he walked hastily to his shop, and called Jor's house. No, Jor wasn't home. He was guarding the weapon store.

Fara hesitated. His own shop was piled with work, and he had a guilty sense of having neglected his customers for the first time in his life. It would be simple to call up the mayor and report Jor's dereliction. And yet—

He didn't want to get the man into trouble—

Out in the street, he saw that a large crowd was gathering in front of the weapon shop. Fara hurried. A man he knew greeted him excitedly: "Jor's been murdered, Fara!"

"Murdered!" Fara stood stock-still, and at first he was not clearly conscious of the grisly thought that was in his mind: Satisfaction! A flaming satisfaction. Now, he thought, even the soldiers would have to act. They—

With a gasp, he realized the ghastly tenor of his thoughts. He shivered, but finally pushed the sense of shame out of his mind. He said slowly, "Where's the body?"

"Inside."

"You mean, those . . . scum—" In spite of himself, he hesitated over the epithet; even now, it was difficult to think of the fine-faced, silver-haired old man in such terms. Abruptly, his mind hardened; he flared: "You mean those scum actually killed him, then pulled his body inside?"

"Nobody saw the killing," said a second man beside Fara, "but he's gone, hasn't been seen for three hours. The mayor got the weapons shop on the telestat, but they claim they don't know anything. They've done away with him, that's what, and now they are pretending innocence. Well, they won't get out of it as easy as that. Mayor's gone to phone the soldiers at Ferd to bring up some big guns and—"

Something of the intense excitement that was in the crowd surged through Fara, the feeling of big things brewing. It was the most delicious sensation that had ever tingled along his nerves, and it was all mixed with a strange pride that he had been so right about this, that he at least had never doubted that here was evil.

He did not recognize the emotion as the full-flowering joy that comes to a member of a mob. But his voice shook, as he said, "Guns? Yes, that will be the answer, and the soldiers will have to come, of course."

Fara nodded to himself in the immensity of his certainty that the Imperial soldiers would now have no excuse for not acting. He started to say something dark about what the empress would do if she found out that a man had lost his life because the soldiers had shirked their duty, but the words were drowned in a shout:

"Here comes the mayor! Hey, Mr. Mayor, when are the atomic cannons due?"

There was more of the same general meaning, as the mayor's sleek, all-purpose car landed lightly. Some of the questions must have reached his honor, for he stood up in the open two-seater and held up his hand for silence.

To Fara's astonishment, the plump-faced man looked at him with accusing eyes. The thing seemed so impossible that, quite instinctively, Fara looked behind him. But he was almost alone; everybody else had crowded forward.

Fara shook his head, puzzled by that glare; and then, astoundingly, Mayor Dale pointed a finger at him, and said in a voice that trembled, "There's the man who's responsible for the trouble that's come upon us. Stand forward, Fara Clark, and show yourself. You've cost this town seven hundred credits that we could ill afford to spend."

Fara couldn't have moved or spoken to save his life. He just stood there in a maze of dumb bewilderment. Before he could even think, the mayor went on, and there was quivering self-pity in his tone, "We've all known that it wasn't wise to interfere with these weapons shops. So long as the Imperial government leaves them alone, what right have we to set up guards, or act against them? That's what I've thought from the beginning, but this man . . . this . . . this Fara Clark kept after all of us, forcing us to move against our wills, and so now we've got a seven-hundred-credit bill to meet and—"

He broke off with, "I might as well make it brief. When I called the garrison, the commander just laughed and said that Jor would turn up. And I had barely disconnected when there was a money call from Jor. He's on Mars."

He waited for the shouts of amazement to die down. "It'll take three weeks for him to come back by ship, and we've got to pay for it, and Fara Clark is responsible. He—"

The shock was over. Fara stood cold, his mind hard. He said finally, scathingly, "So you're giving up and trying to blame me all in one breath. I say you're all fools."

As he turned away, he heard Mayor Dale saying something about the situation not being completely lost, as he had learned that the weapons shop had been set up in Glay because the village was equidistant from four cities, and that it was the city business the shop was after. This would mean tourists, and accessary trade for the village stores and—

Fara heard no more. Head high, he walked back toward his shop. There were one or two catcalls from the mob, but he ignored them.

He had no sense of approaching disaster, simply a gathering fury against the weapons shop, which had brought him to this miserable status among his neighbors.

The worst of it, as the days passed, was the realization that the people of the weapon shop had no personal interest in him. They were remote, superior, undefeatable. That unconquerableness was a dim, suppressed awareness inside Fara.

When he thought of it, he felt a vague fear at the way they had transferred Jor to Mars in a period of less than three hours, when all the world knew that the trip by fastest spaceship required nearly three weeks.

Fara did not go to the express station to see Jor arrive home. He had heard that the council had decided to charge Jor with half of the expense of the trip, on the threat of losing his job if he made a fuss.

On the second night after Jor's return, Fara slipped down to the constable's house, and handed the officer one hundred seventy-five credits. It wasn't that he was responsible, he told Jor, but—

The man was only too eager to grant the disclaimer, provided the money went with it. Fara returned home with a clearer conscience.

It was on the third day after that the door of his shop banged open and a man came in. Fara frowned as he saw who it was Castler, a village hanger-on. The man was grinning.

"Thought you might be interested, Fara. Somebody came out of the weapon shop today."

Fara strained deliberately at the connecting bolt of a hard plate of the atomic motor he was fixing. He waited with a gathering annoyance that the man did not volunteer further information. Asking questions would be a form of recognition of the worthless fellow. A developing curiosity made him say finally, grudgingly, "I suppose the constable promptly packed him up."

He supposed nothing of the kind, but it was an opening.

"It wasn't a man. It was a girl."

Fara knitted his brows. He didn't like the idea of making trouble for women. But—the cunning devils! Using a girl, just as they had used an old man as a clerk. It was a trick that deserved to fail, the girl probably a tough one who needed rough treatment. Fara said harshly, "Well, what's happened?"

"She's still out, bold as you please. Pretty thing, too."

The bolt off, Fara took the hard plate over to the polisher, and began patiently the long, careful task of smoothing away the crystals that heat had seared on the once shining metal. The soft throb of the polisher made the background to his next words:

"Has anything been done?"

"Nope. The constable's been told, but he says he doesn't fancy being away from his family for another three weeks, and paying the cost into the bargain."

Fara contemplated that darkly for a minute, as the polisher throbbed on. His voice shook with suppressed fury, when he said finally, "So they're letting them get away with it. It's all been as clever as hell. Can't they see that they mustn't give an inch before these . . . these transgressors. It's like giving countenance to sin."

From the corner of his eye, he noticed that there was a curious grin on the face of the other. It struck Fara suddenly that the man was enjoying his anger. And there was something else in that grin; something—a secret knowledge.

Fara pulled the engine plate away from the polisher. He faced the ne'er-do-well, scathed at him, "Naturally, that sin part wouldn't worry you much."

"Oh," said the man nonchalantly, "the hard knocks of life make people tolerant. For instance, after you know the girl better, you yourself will probably come to realize that there's good in all of us."

It was not so much the words, as the curious I've-got-secret-information tone that made Fara snap "What do you mean—if I get to know the girl better! I won't even speak to the brazen creature."

"One can't always choose," the other said with enormous casualness. "Suppose he brings her home."

"Suppose who brings who home?" Fara spoke irritably. "Castler, you—"

He stopped; a dead weight of dismay plumped into his stomach; his whole being sagged. "You mean—" he said.

"I mean," replied Castler with a triumphant leer, "that the boys aren't letting a beauty like her be lonesome. And, naturally, your son was the first to speak to her."

He finished "They're walkin' together now on Second Avenue, comin' this way, so—"

"Get out of here!" Fara roared. "And stay away from me with your gloating. Get out!"

The man hadn't expected such an ignominious ending. He flushed scarlet, then went out, slamming the door.

Fara stood for a moment, every muscle stiff; then, with an abrupt, jerky movement, he shut off his power, and went out into the street.

The time to put a stop to that kind of thing was—now!

He had no clear plan, just that violent determination to put an immediate end to an impossible situation. And it was all mixed up with his anger against Cayle. How could he have had such a worthless son, he who paid his debts and worked hard, and tried to be decent and to live up to the highest standards of the empress?

A brief, dark thought came to Fara that maybe there was some bad blood on Creel's side. Not from her mother, of course—Fara added the mental thought hastily. *There* was a fine, hard-working woman, who hung on to her money, and who would leave Creel a tidy sum one of these days.

But Creel's father had disappeared when Creel was only a child, and there had been some vague scandal about his having taken up with a telestat actress.

And now Cayle with this weapon shop girl. A girl who had let herself be picked up—

He saw them, as he turned the corner onto Second Avenue. They were walking a hundred feet distant, and heading away from Fara. The girl was tall and slender, almost as big as Cayle, and, as Fara came up, she was saying, "You have the wrong idea about us. A person like you can't get a job in our organization. You belong in the Imperial Service, where they can use young men of good education, good appearance and no scruples. I—"

Fara grasped only dimly that Cayle must have been trying to get a job with these people. It was not clear; and his own mind was too intent on his purpose for it to mean anything at the moment. He said harshly, "Cayle!"

The couple turned, Cayle with the measured unhurriedness of a young man who has gone a long way on the road to steellike nerves; the girl was quicker, but withal dignified.

Fara had a vague, terrified feeling that his anger was too great, self-destroying, but the very violence of his emotions ended that thought even as it came. He said thickly, "Cayle, get home—at once."

Fara was aware of the girl looking at him curiously from strange, gray-green eyes. No shame, he thought, and his rage mounted several degrees, driving away the alarm that came at the sight of the flush that crept into Cayle's cheeks.

The flush faded into a pale, tight-lipped anger, Cayle half-turned to the girl, said, "This is the childish old fool I've got to put up with. Fortunately, we seldom see each other; we don't even eat together. What do you think of him?"

The girl smiled impersonally. "Oh, we know Fara Clark; he's the backbone of the empress in Glay."

"Yes," the boy sneered. "You ought to hear him. He thinks we're living in heaven; and the empress is the divine power. The worst part of it is that there's no chance of his ever getting that stuffy look wiped off his face."

They walked off; and Fara stood there. The very extent of what had happened had drained anger from him as if it had never been. There was the realization that he had made a mistake so great that—

He couldn't grasp it. For long, long now, since Cayle had refused to work in his shop, he had felt this building up to a climax. Suddenly, his own uncontrollable ferocity stood revealed as a partial product of that—deeper—problem.

Only, now that the smash was here, he didn't want to face it—

All through the day in his shop, he kept pushing it out of his mind, kept thinking, would this go on now, as before, Cayle and he living in the same house, not even looking at each other when they met, going to bed at different times, getting up, Fara at 6:30, Cayle at noon? Would *that* go on through all the days and years to come?

When he arrived home, Creel was waiting for him. She said, "Fara, he wants you to loan him five hundred credits, so that he can go to Imperial City."

Fara nodded wordlessly. He brought the money back to the house the next morning, and gave it to Creel, who took it into the bedroom.

She came out a minute later. "He says to tell you goodbye."

When Fara came home that evening, Cayle was gone. He wondered whether he ought to feel relieved or—what?

The days passed. Fara worked. He had nothing else to do, and the gray thought was often in his mind that now he would be doing it till the day he died. Except—

Fool that he was—he told himself a thousand times how big a fool—he kept hoping that Cayle would walk into the shop and say, "Father, I've learned my lesson. If you can ever forgive me, teach me the business, and then you retire to a well-earned rest."

It was exactly a month to a day after Cayle's departure that the telestat clicked on just after Fara had finished lunch. "Money call," it sighed, "money call."

Fara and Creel looked at each other. "Eh," said Fara finally, "money call for us."

He could see from the gray look in Creel's face the thought that was in her mind. He said under his breath "Damn that boy!"

But he felt relieved. Amazingly relieved! Cayle was beginning to appreciate the value of parents and—

He switched on the viewer. "Come and collect," he said.

The face that came on the screen was heavy-jowled, beetle-browed—and strange. The man said, "This is Clerk Pearton of the Fifth Bank of Ferd. We have received a sight draft on you for ten thousand credits. With carrying charges and government tax, the sum required will be twelve thousand one hundred credits. Will you pay it now or will you come in this afternoon and pay it?"

"B-but . . . b-but—" said Fara. "W-who—"

He stopped, conscious of the stupidity of the question, dimly conscious of the heavy-faced man saying something about the money having been paid out to one Cayle Clark that morning in Imperial City. At last, Fara found his voice:

"But the bank had no right," he expostulated, "to pay out the money without my authority. I—"

The voice cut him off coldly "Are we then to inform our central that the money was obtained under false pretenses? Naturally, an order will be issued immediately for the arrest of your son."

"Wait . . . wait—" Fara spoke blindly. He was aware of Creel beside him, shaking her head at him. She was as white as a sheet, and her voice was a sick, stricken thing, as she said, "Fara, let him go. He's through with us. We must be as hard—let him go."

The words rang senselessly in Fara's ears. They didn't fit into any normal pattern. He was saying:

"I . . . I haven't got—How about my paying . . . installments? I—"

"If you wish a loan," said Clerk Pearton, "naturally we will be happy to go into the matter. I might say that when the draft arrived, we checked up on your status, and we are prepared to loan you eleven thousand credits on indefinite call with your shop as security. I have the form here, and if you are agreeable, we will switch this call through the registered circuit, and you can sign at once."

"Fara, no."

The clerk went on "The other eleven hundred credits will have to be paid in cash. Is that agreeable?"

"Yes, yes, of course, I've got twenty-five hund—" He stopped his chattering tongue with a gulp; then: "Yes, that's satisfactory."

The deal completed, Fara whirled on his wife. Out of the depths of his hurt and bewilderment, he raged: "What do you mean, standing there and talking about not paying it? You said several times that I was responsible for his being what he is. Besides, we don't know why he needed the money. He—"

Creel said in a low, dead tone: "In one hour, he's stripped us of our life work. He did it deliberately, thinking of us as two old fools, who wouldn't know any better than to pay it."

Before he could speak, she went on, "Oh, I know I blamed you, but in the final issue, I knew it was he. He was always cold and calculating, but I was weak, and I was sure that if you handled him in a different . . . and besides I didn't want to see his faults for a long time. He—"

"All I see," Fara interrupted doggedly, "is that I have saved our name from disgrace."

His high sense of duty rightly done lasted until midafternoon, when the bailiff from Ferd came to take over the shop.

"But what—" Fara began.

The bailiff said, "The Automatic Atomic Repair Shops, Limited, took over your loan from the bank, and are foreclosing. Have you anything to say?"

"It's unfair," said Fara. "I'll take it to court. I'll—"

He was thinking dazedly: *If the empress ever learned of this, she'd . . . she'd—*

The courthouse was a big, gray building; and Fara felt emptier and colder every second, as he walked along the gray corridors. In Glay, his decision not to give himself into the hands of a bloodsucker of a lawyer had seemed a wise act. Here, in these enormous halls and palatial rooms, it seemed the sheerest folly.

He managed, nevertheless, to give an articulate account of the criminal act of the bank in first giving Cayle the money, then turning over the note to his chief competitor, apparently within minutes of his signing it. He finished with: "I'm sure, sir, the empress would not approve of such goings-on against honest citizens. I—"

"How dare you," said the cold-voiced creature on the bench, "use the name of her holy majesty in support of your own gross self-interest?"

Fara shivered. The sense of being intimately a member of the empress' great human family yielded to a sudden chill and a vast mind-picture of the ten million icy courts like this, and the myriad malevolent and heartless men—*like this*—who stood between the empress and her loyal subject, Fara.

He thought passionately: If the empress knew what was happening here, how unjustly he was being treated, she would—

Or would she?

He pushed the crowding, terrible doubt out of his mind—came out of his hard reverie with a start, to hear the Cadi saying, "Plaintiff's appeal dismissed, with costs assessed at seven hundred credits, to be divided between the court and the defense solicitor in the ratio of five to two. See to it that the appellant does not leave till the costs are paid. Next case—"

Fara went alone the next day to see Creel's mother. He called first at "Farmer's Restaurant" at the outskirts of the village. The place was, he noted with satisfaction in the thought of the steady stream of money flowing in, half full, though it was only midmorning. But madame wasn't there. Try the feed store.

He found her in the back of the feed store, overseeing the weighing out of grain into cloth measures. The hard-faced old woman heard his story without a word. She said finally, curtly, "Nothing doing, Fara. I'm one who has to make loans often from the bank to swing deals. If I tried to set you up in business, I'd find the Automatic Atomic Repair people getting after me. Besides, I'd be a fool to turn money over to a man who lets a bad son squeeze a fortune out of him. Such a man has no sense about worldly things.

"And I won't give you a job because I don't hire relatives in my business." She finished: "Tell Creel to come and live at my house. I won't support a man, though. That's all."

He watched her disconsolately for a while, as she went on calmly superintending the clerks who were manipulating the old, no longer accurate measuring machines. Twice her voice echoed through the dust-filled interior, each time with a sharp: "That's overweight, a gram at least. Watch your machine."

Though her back was turned. Fara knew by her posture that she was still, aware of his presence. She turned at last with an abrupt movement and said, "Why don't you go to the weapons shop? You haven't anything to lose and you can't go on like this."

Fara went out, then, a little blindly. At first the suggestion that he buy a gun and commit suicide had no real personal application. But he felt immeasurably hurt that his mother-in-law should have made it.

Kill himself? Why, it was ridiculous. He was still only a young man, going on fifty. Given the proper chance, with his skilled hands, he could wrest a good living even in a world where automatic machines were encroaching everywhere. There was always room for a man who did a good job. His whole life had been based on that credo.

Kill himself—

He went home to find Creel packing. "It's the common sense thing to do," she said. "We'll rent the house and move into rooms."

He told her about her mother's offer to take her in, watching her face as he spoke. Creel shrugged.

"I told her 'No' yesterday," she said thoughtfully. "I wonder why she mentioned it to you."

Fara walked swiftly over to the great front window overlooking the garden, with its flowers, its pool, its rockery. He tried to think of Creel away from this garden of hers, this home of two thirds a lifetime, Creel living in rooms—and knew what her mother had meant. There was one more hope—

He waited till Creel went upstairs, then called Mel Dale on the telestat. The mayor's plump face took on an uneasy expression as he saw who it was.

But he listened pontifically, said finally, "Sorry, the council does not loan money; and I might as well tell you, Fara—I have nothing to do with this, mind you—but you can't get a license for a shop any more."

"W-what?"

"I'm sorry!" The mayor lowered his voice. "Listen, Fara, take my advice, and go to the weapon shop. These places have their uses."

There was a click, and Fara sat staring at the blank face of the viewing screen. So it was to be—death!

He waited until the street was empty of human beings, then slipped across the boulevard, past a design of flower gardens, and so to the door of the shop. The brief fear came that the door wouldn't open, but it did, effortlessly.

As he emerged from the dimness of the alcove into the shop proper, he saw the silver-haired old man sitting in a corner chair, reading under a softly bright light. The old man looked up, put aside his book, then rose to his feet.

"It's Mr. Clark," he said quietly. "What can we do for you?"

A faint flush crept into Fara's cheeks. In a dim fashion, he had hoped that he would not suffer the humiliation of being recognized; but now that his fear was realized, he stood his ground stubbornly. The important thing about killing himself was that there be no body for Creel to bury at great expense. Neither knife nor poison would satisfy that basic requirement.

"I want a gun," said Fara, "that can be adjusted to disintegrate a body six feet in diameter in a single shot. Have you that kind?"

Without a word, the old man turned to a showcase, and brought forth a sturdy gem of a revolver that glinted with all the soft colors of the inimitable Ordine plastic. The old man said in a precise voice. "Notice the flanges on this barrel are little more than bulges. This makes the model ideal for carrying in a shoulder holster under the coat; it can be drawn very swiftly because, when properly attuned, it will leap toward the reaching hand of its owner. At the moment it is attuned to me. Watch while I replace it in its holster and—"

The speed of the draw was absolutely amazing. The old man's fingers moved; and the gun, four feet away, was in them. There was no blur of movement. It was like the door the night that it had slipped from Fara's grasp, and slammed noiselessly in Constable Jor's face. *Instantaneous!*

Fara, who had parted his lips as the old man was explaining, to protest the utter needlessness of illustrating any quality of the weapon except what he had asked for, closed them again. He stared in a brief, dazed fascination; and something of the wonder that was here held his mind and his body.

He had seen and handled the guns of soldiers, and they were simply ordinary metal or plastic things that one used clumsily like any other material substance, not like this at all, not possessed of a dazzling life of their own, leaping with an intimate eagerness to assist with all their superb power the will of their master. They—

With a start, Fara remembered his purpose. He smiled wryly, and said, "All this is very interesting. But what about the beam that can fan out?"

The old man said calmly, "At pencil thickness, this beam will pierce any body except certain alloys of lead up to four hundred yards. With proper adjustment of the firing nozzle, you can disintegrate a six-foot object at fifty yards or less. This screw is the adjustor."

He indicated a tiny device in the muzzle itself. "Turn it to the left to spread the beam, to the right to close it."

Fara said, "I'll take the gun. How much is it?"

He saw that the old man was looking at him thoughtfully; the oldster said finally, slowly, "I have previously explained our regulations to you, Mr. Clark. You recall them, of course?"

"Eh!" said Fara, and stopped, wide-eyed. It wasn't that he didn't remember them. It was simply—

"You mean," he gasped, "those things actually apply. They're not—"

With a terrible effort, he caught his spinning brain and blurring voice. Tense and cold, he said, "All I want is a gun that will shoot in self-defense, but which I can turn on myself if I have to or—want to."

"Oh, suicide!" said the old man. He looked as if a great understanding had suddenly dawned on him. "My dear sir, we have no objection to your killing yourself at any time. That is your personal privilege in a world where privileges grow scanter every year. As for the price of this revolver, it's four credits."

"Four cre . . . only four credits!" said Fara.

He stood, absolutely astounded, his whole mind snatched from its dark purpose. Why, the plastic alone was—and the whole gun with its fine, intricate workmanship—twenty-five credits would have been dirt cheap.

He felt a brief thrill of utter interest; the mystery of the weapon shops suddenly loomed as vast and important as his own black destiny. But the old man was speaking again:

"And now, if you will remove your coat, we can put on the holster—"

Quite automatically, Fara complied. It was vaguely startling to realize that, in a few seconds, he would be walking out of here, equipped for self-murder, and that there was now not a single obstacle to his death.

Curiously, he was disappointed. He couldn't explain it, but somehow there had been in the back of his mind a hope that these shops might, just might—what?

What indeed? Fara sighed wearily—and grew aware again of the old man's voice, saying:

"Perhaps you would prefer to step out of our side door. It is less conspicuous than the front."

There was no resistance in Fara. He was dimly conscious of the man's fingers on his arm, half guiding him; and then the old man pressed one of several buttons on the wall—so that's how it was done—and there was the door.

He could see flowers beyond the opening; without a word he walked toward them. He was outside before he realized it.

Fara stood for a moment in the neat little pathway, striving to grasp the finality of his situation. But nothing would come except a curious awareness of many men around him; for a long second, his brain was like a fog drifting along a stream at night.

Through that darkness grew consciousness of something wrong; the wrongness was there in the back of his mind, as he turned leftward to go to the front of the weapon store.

Vagueness transformed to a shocked, startled sound. For—he was not in Glay, and the weapon shop *wasn't* where it had been. In its place—

A dozen men brushed past Fara to join a long line of men farther along. But Fara was immune to their presence, their strangeness. His whole mind, his whole vision, his very being was concentrating on the section of machine that stood where the weapon shop had been.

A machine, oh, a machine—

His brain lifted, up in his effort to grasp the tremendousness of the dull-metaled immensity of what was spread here under a summer sun beneath a sky as blue as a remote southern sea.

The machine towered into the heavens, five great tiers of metal, each a hundred feet high; and the superbly streamlined five hundred feet ended in a peak of light, a gorgeous spire that tilted straight up a sheer two hundred feet farther, and matched the very sun for brightness.

And it *was* a machine, not a building, because the whole lower tier was alive with shimmering lights, mostly green, but sprinkled colorfully with red and occasionally a blue and yellow. Twice, as Fara watched, green lights directly in front of him flashed unscintillatingly into red.

The second tier was alive with white and red lights, although there were only a fraction as many lights as on the lowest tier. The third section had on its dull-metal surface only blue and yellow lights; they twinkled softly here and there over the vast area.

The fourth tier was a series of signs that brought the beginning of comprehension. The whole sign was:

WHITE—BIRTHS

RED—DEATHS

GREEN—LIVING

BLUE—IMMIGRATION TO EARTH

YELLOW—EMIGRATION

The fifth tier was also all sign, finally explaining:

POPULATIONS	
SOLAR SYSTEM	19,174,463,747
EARTH	11,193,247,361
MARS	1,097,298,604
VENUS	5,141,053,811
MOONS	1,742,863,971

The numbers changed, even as he looked at them, leaping up and down, shifting below and above what they had first been. People were dying, being born, moving to Mars, to Venus, to the moons of Jupiter, to Earth's moon, and others coming back again, landing minute by minute in the thousands of space-ports. Life went on in its gigantic fashion—and here was the stupendous record. Here was—

"Better get in line," said a friendly voice beside Fara. "It takes quite a while to put through an individual case, I understand."

Fara stared at the man. He had the distinct impression of having had senseless words flung at him. "In line?" he started—and stopped himself with a jerk that hurt his throat.

He was moving forward, blindly, ahead of the younger man, thinking a curious jumble that this must have been how Constable Jor was transported to Mars— when another of the man's words penetrated.

"Case?" said Fara violently. "Individual case!"

The man, a heavy-faced, blue-eyed young chap of around thirty-five, looked at him curiously: "You must know why you're here," he said. "Surely, you wouldn't have been sent through here unless you had a problem of some kind that the weapons shop courts will solve for you; there's no other reason for coming to Information Center."

Fara walked on because he was in the line now, a fast-moving line that curved him inexorably around the machine; and seemed to be heading him toward a door that led into the interior of the great metal structure.

So it was a building as well as a machine.

A problem, he was thinking, why, of course, he had a problem, a hopeless, insoluble, completely tangled problem so deeply rooted in the basic structure of Imperial civilization that the whole world would have to be overturned to make it right.

With a start, he saw that he was at the entrance. And the awed thought came: In seconds he would be committed irrevocably to—what?

Inside was a long, shining corridor, with scores of completely transparent hallways leading off the main corridor. Behind Fara, the young man's voice said, "There's one, practically empty. Let's go."

Fara walked ahead; and suddenly he was trembling. He had already noticed that at the end of each side hallway were a dozen young women sitting at desks, interviewing men and . . . and, good heavens, was it possible that all this meant—

He grew aware that he had stopped in front of one of the girls.

She was older than she had looked from a distance, over thirty, but good-looking, alert. She smiled pleasantly, but impersonally, and said, "Your name, please?"

He gave it before he thought and added a mumble about being from the village of Glay. The woman said, "Thank you. It will take a few minutes to get your file. Won't you sit down?"

He hadn't noticed the chair. He sank into it; and his heart beating so wildly that he felt chocked. The strange thing was that there was scarcely a thought in his head, nor a real hope; only an intense, almost mind-wrecking excitement.

With a jerk, he realized that the girl was speaking again, but only snatches of her voice came through that screen of tension in his mind:

"—Information Center is . . . in effect . . . a bureau of statistics. Every person born . . . registered here . . . their education, change of address . . . occupation . . . and the highlights of their life. The whole is maintained by . . . combination of . . . unauthorized and unsuspected liaison with Imperial Chamber of Statistics and . . . through medium of agents . . . in every community—"

It seemed to Fara that he was missing vital information, and that if he could only force his attention and hear more— He strained, but it was no use; his nerves were jumping madly and—

Before he could speak, there was a click, and a thin, dark plate slid onto the woman's desk. She took it up and examined it. After a moment, she said something into a mouthpiece, and in a short time two more plates precipitated out of the empty air onto her desk. She studied them passively, looked up finally.

"You will be interested to know," she said, "that your son, Cayle, bribed himself into a commission in the Imperial army with five thousand credits."

"Eh?" said Fara. He half rose from his chair, but before he could say anything, the young woman was speaking again, firmly, "I must inform you that the weapon shops take no action against individuals. Your son can have his job, the money he stole; we are not concerned with moral correction. That must come naturally from the individual, and from the people as a whole—and now if you will give me a brief account of your problem for the record and the court."

Sweating, Fara sank back into his seat; his mind was heaving; most desperately, he wanted more information about Cayle. He began "But . . . but what . . . how—" He caught himself; and in a low voice described what had happened. When he finished, the girl said, "You will proceed now to the Name Room; watch for your name, and when it appears go straight to Room 474. Remember, 474— and now, the line is waiting, if you please—"

She smiled politely, and Fara was moving off almost before he realized it. He half turned to ask another question, but an old man was sinking into his chair. Fara hurried on, along a great corridor, conscious of curious blasts of sound coming from ahead.

Eagerly, he opened the door; and the sound crashed at him with all the impact of a sledgehammer blow.

It was such a colossal, incredible sound that he stopped short, just inside the door, shrinking back. He stood then trying to blink sense into a visual confusion that rivaled in magnitude that incredible tornado of noise.

Men, men, men everywhere; men by the thousands in a long, broad auditorium, packed into rows of seats, pacing with an abandon of restlessness up and down aisles, and all of them staring with a frantic interest at a long board marked off into squares, each square lettered from the alphabet, from A, B, C, and so on to Z. The tremendous board with its lists of names ran the full length of the immense room.

The Name Room, Fara was thinking shakily, as he sank into a seat—and his name would come up in the C's, and then—

It was like sitting in at a no-limit poker game, watching the jewel-precious cards turn up. It was like playing the exchange with all the world at stake during a stock crash. It was nerve-racking, dazzling, exhausting, fascinating, terrible, mind-destroying, stupendous. It was—

It was like nothing else on the face of the earth.

New names kept flashing on to the twenty-six squares; and men would shout like insane beings and some fainted, and the uproar was absolutely shattering; the pandemonium raged on, one continuous, unbelievable sound.

And every few minutes a great sign would flash along the board, telling everyone:

"WATCH YOUR OWN INITIALS."

Fara watched, trembling in every limb. Each second it seemed to him that he couldn't stand it an instant longer. He wanted to scream at the room to be silent; he wanted to jump up to pace the floor, but others who did that were yelled at hysterically, threatened wildly, hated with a mad, murderous ferocity.

Abruptly, the blind savagery of it scared Fara. He thought unsteadily: "I'm not going to make a fool of myself. I—"

"Clark, Fara—" winked the board. "Clark, Fara—"

With a shout that nearly tore off the top of his head, Fara leaped to his feet. "That's me!" he shrieked. "Me!"

No one turned; no one paid the slightest attention. Shamed, he slunk across the room where an endless line of men kept crowding into a corridor beyond.

The silence in the long corridor was almost as shattering as the mind-destroying noise it replaced. It was hard to concentrate on the idea of a number—474.

It was completely impossible to imagine what could lie beyond—474.

The room was small. It was furnished with a small, business-type table and two chairs. On the table were seven neat piles of folders, each file a different color. The piles were arranged in a row in front of a large, milky-white globe, that began to glow with a soft light. Out of its depths, a man's baritone voice said, "Fara Clark?"

"Yes," said Fara.

"Before the verdict is rendered in your case," the voice went on quietly, "I want you to take a folder from the blue pile. The list will show the Fifth Interplanetary Bank in its proper relation to yourself and the world, and it will be explained to you in due course."

The list, Fara saw, was simply that, a list of names of companies. The names ran from A to Z, and there were about five hundred of them. The folder carried no explanation; and Fara slipped it automatically into his side pocket, as the voice came again from the shining globe: "It has been established," the words came precisely, "that the Fifth Interplanetary Bank perpetrated upon you a gross swindle, and that it is further guilty of practicing scavengery, deception, blackmail and was accessory in a criminal conspiracy.

"The bank made contact with your son, Cayle, through what is quite properly known as a scavenger, that is, an employee who exists by finding young men and women who are normally capable of drawing drafts on their parents or other victims. The scavenger obtains for this service a commission of eight percent, which is always paid by the person making the loan, in this case your son.

"The bank practiced deception in that its authorized agents deceived you in the most culpable fashion by pretending that it had already paid out the ten thousand credits to your son, whereas the money was not paid until your signature had been obtained.

"The blackmail guilt arises out of a threat to have your son arrested for falsely obtaining a loan, a threat made at a time when no money had exchanged hands. The conspiracy consists of the action whereby your note was promptly turned over to your competitor.

"The bank is accordingly triple-fined, thirty-six thousand three hundred credits. It is not in our interest, Fara Clark, for you to know how this money is obtained. Suffice to know that the bank pays it, and that of the fine the weapon shops allocate to their own treasury a total of one half. The other half—"

There was a *plop;* a neatly packaged pile of bills fell onto the table. "For you," said the voice; and Fara, with trembling fingers, slipped the package into his coat pocket. It required the purest mental and physical effort for him to concentrate on the next words that came:

"You must not assume that your troubles are over. The reestablishment of your motor repair shop in Glay will require force and courage. Be discreet, brave and determined, and you cannot fail. Do not hesitate to use the gun you have purchased in defense of your rights. The plan will be explained to you. And now, proceed through the door facing you—"

Fara braced himself with an effort, opened the door and walked through.

It was a dim, familiar room that he stepped into, and there was a silver-haired, fine-faced man who rose from a reading chair, and came forward in the dimness, smiling gravely.

The stupendous, fantastic, exhilarating adventure was over; and he was back in the weapon shop of Glay.

He couldn't get over the wonder of it—this great and fascinating organization established here in the very heart of a ruthless civilization, a civilization that had in a few brief weeks stripped him of everything he possessed.

With a deliberate will, he stopped that glowing flow of thought. A dark frown wrinkled his solidly built face; he said, "The . . . judge—" Fara hesitated over the name, frowned again, annoyed at himself, then went on "The judge said that, to reestablish myself I would have to—"

"Before we go into that," said the old man quietly, "I want you to examine the blue folder you brought with you."

"Folder?" Fara echoed blankly. It took a long moment to remember that he had picked up a folder from the table in Room 474.

He studied the list of company names with a gathering puzzlement, noting that the name of Automatic Atomic Motor Repair Shops was well down among the A's, and the Fifth Interplanetary Bank only one of several great banks included. Fara looked up finally:

"I don't understand," he said "are these the companies you have had to act against?"

The silver-haired man smiled grimly, shook his head. "That is not what I meant. These firms constitute only a fraction of the eight hundred thousand companies that are constantly in our books."

He smiled again, humorlessly: "These companies all know that, because of us, their profits on paper bear no relation to their assets. What they don't know is how great the difference really is; and, as we want a general improvement in business morals, not merely more skillful scheming to outwit us, we prefer them to remain in ignorance."

He paused, and this time he gave Fara a searching glance, said at last "The unique feature of the companies on this particular list is that they are every one wholly owned by Empress Isher."

He finished swiftly: "In view of your past opinions on that subject, I do not expect you to believe me."

Fara stood as still as death, for—he did believe with unquestioning conviction, completely, finally. The amazing, the unforgivable thing was that all his life he had watched the march of ruined men into the oblivion of poverty and disgrace—and blamed *them*.

Fara groaned. "I've been like a madman," he said. "Everything the empress and her officials did was right. No friendship, no personal relationship could survive with me that did not include belief in things as they were. I suppose if I started to talk against the empress I would receive equally short shrift."

"Under no circumstances," said the old man grimly, "must you say anything against her majesty. The weapons shops will not countenance any such words, and will give no further aid to anyone who is so indiscreet. The reason is that, for the moment, we have reached an uneasy state of peace with the Imperial government. We wish to keep it that way; beyond that I will not enlarge on our policy.

"I am permitted to say that the last great attempt to destroy the weapon shops was made seven years ago, when the glorious Innelda Isher was twenty-five years old. That was a secret attempt, based on a new invention; and failed by purest accident because of our sacrifice of a man from seven thousand years in the past. That may sound mysterious to you, but I will not explain.

"The worst period was reached some forty years ago when every person who was discovered receiving aid from us was murdered in some fashion. You may be surprised to know that your father-in-law was among those assassinated at that time."

"Creel's father!" Fara gasped. "But—"

He stopped. His brain was reeling; there was such a rush of blood to his head that for an instant he could hardly see.

"But," he managed at last, "it was reported that he ran away with another woman."

"They always spread a vicious story of some kind," the old man said; and Fara was silent, stunned.

The other went on: "We finally put a stop to their murders by killing the three men from the top down, *excluding* the royal family, who gave the order for the particular execution involved. But we do not again want that kind of bloody murder.

"Nor are we interested in any criticism of our toleration of so much that is evil. It is important to understand that *we do not interfere in the main stream of human existence*. We right wrongs; we act as a barrier between the people and their more ruthless exploiters. Generally speaking, we help only honest men; that is not to say that we do not give assistance to the less scrupulous, but only to the extent of selling them guns—which is a very great aid indeed, and which is one of the reasons why the government is relying almost exclusively for its power on an economic chicanery.

"In the four thousand years since the brilliant genius Walter S. DeLany invented the vibration process that made the weapon shops possible, and laid down the first principles of weapons shop political philosophy, we have watched the tide of government swing backward and forward between democracy under a limited monarchy to complete tyranny. And we have discovered one thing:

"*People always have the kind of government they want*. When they want change, they must change it. As always we shall remain an incorruptible core—and I mean that literally; we have a psychological machine that never lies about a man's character—I repeat, an incorruptible core of human idealism, devoted to relieving the ills that arise inevitably under any form of government.

"But now—your problem. It is very simple, really. You must fight, as all men have fought since the beginning of time for what they valued, for their just rights. As you know, the Automatic Repair people removed all your machinery and tools within an hour or foreclosing on your shop. This material was taken to Ferd, and then shipped to a great warehouse on the coast.

"We recovered it, and with our special means of transportation have now replaced the machines in your shop. You will accordingly go there and—"

Fara listened with a gathering grimness to the instructions, nodded finally, his jaw clamped tight.

"You can count on me," he said curtly. "I've been a stubborn man in my time; and though I've changed sides, I haven't changed *that*."

Going outside was like returning from life to—death; from hope to—reality.

Fara walked along the quiet streets of Glay at darkest night. For the first time it struck him that the weapon shop Information Center must be halfway around the world, for it had been day, brilliant day.

The picture vanished as if it had never existed, and he grew aware again, preternaturally aware of the village of Glay asleep all around him. Silent, peaceful—yet ugly, he thought, ugly with the ugliness of evil enthroned.

He thought: The right to buy weapons—and his heart swelled into his throat; the tears came to his eyes.

He wiped his vision clear with the back of his hand, thought of Creel's long dead father, and strode on, without shame. Tears were good for an angry man.

The shop was the same, but the hard metal padlock yielded before the tiny, blazing, supernal power of the revolver. One flick of fire; the metal dissolved—and he was inside.

It was dark, too dark to see, but Fara did not turn on the lights immediately. He fumbled across to the window control, turned the windows to darkness vibration, and then clicked on the lights.

He gulped with awful relief. For the machines, his precious tools that he had seen carted away within hours after the bailiff's arrival, were here again, ready for use.

Shaky from the pressure of his emotion, Fara called Creel on the telestat. It took a little while for her to appear; and she was in her dressing robe. When she saw who it was she turned a dead white.

"Fara, oh, Fara, I thought—"

He cut her off grimly: "Creel, I've been to the weapon shop. I want you to do this: go straight to your mother. I'm here at my shop. I'm going to stay here day and night until it's settled that I *stay*. . . . I shall go home later for some food and clothing, but I want you to be gone by then. Is that clear?"

Color was coming back into her lean, handsome face. She said: "Don't you bother coming home, Fara. I'll do everything necessary. I'll pack all that's needed into the carplane, including a folding bed. We'll sleep in the back room of the shop."

Morning came palely, but it was ten o'clock before a shadow darkened the open door; and Constable Jor came in. He looked shamefaced.

"I've got an order here for your arrest," he said.

"Tell those who sent you," Fara replied deliberately, "that I resisted arrest—with a gun."

The deed followed the words with such rapidity that Jor blinked. He stood like that for a moment, a big, sleepy-looking man, staring at that gleaming, magical revolver; then:

"I have a summons here ordering you to appear at the great court of Ferd this afternoon. Will you accept it?"

"Certainly."

"Then you will be there?"

"I'll send my lawyer," said Fara. "Just drop the summons on the floor there. Tell them I took it."

The weapons shop man had said, "Do not ridicule by word any legal measure of the Imperial authorities. Simply disobey them."

Jor went out, and seemed relieved. It took an hour before Mayor Mel Dale came pompously through the door.

"See here, Fara Clark," he bellowed from the doorway. "You can't get away with this. This is defiance of the law."

Fara was silent as His Honor waddled farther into the building. It was puzzling, almost amazing, that Mayor Dale would risk his plump, treasured body. Puzzlement ended as the mayor said in a low voice. "Good work, Fara; I knew you had it in you. There's dozens of us in Glay behind you, so stick it out. I had to yell at you just now, because there's a crowd outside. Yell back at me, will you? Let's have a real name calling. But, first, a word of warning: the manager of the Automatic Repair Shop is on his way here with his bodyguards, two of them—"

Shakily, Fara watched the mayor go out. The crisis was at hand. He braced himself, thought: *Let them come, let them—*

It was easier than he had thought—for the men who entered the shop turned pale when they saw the holstered revolver. There was a violence of blustering, nevertheless, that narrowed finally down to:

"Look here," the man said, "we've got your note for twelve thousand one hundred credits. You're not going to deny you owe that money."

"I'll buy it back," said Fara in a stony voice, "for exactly half, not a cent more."

The strong-jawed young man looked at him for a long time. "We'll take it," he said finally, curtly.

Fara said, "I've got the agreement here—"

His first customer was old man Miser Lan Harris. Fara stared at the long-faced oldster with a vast surmise, and his first, amazed comprehension came of how the weapons shop must have settled on Harris' lot—by arrangement.

It was an hour after Harris had gone that Creel's mother stamped into the shop. She closed the door.

"Well," she said, "you did it, eh? Good work. I'm sorry if I seemed rough with you when you came to my place, but we weapon shop supporters can't afford to take risks for those who are not on our side.

"But never mind that. I've come to take Creel home. The important thing is to return everything to normal as quickly as possible."

It was over; incredibly it was over. Twice, as he walked home that night, Fara stopped in midstride, and wondered if it had not all been a dream. The air was like wine. The little world of Glay spread before him, green and gracious, a peaceful paradise where time had stood still.

⚜ FREDRIC (WILLIAM) BROWN (1906–1972)

No other author has been as equally adept at writing both Mystery/Crime/Detective Fiction and Science Fiction than has Fredric Brown. Brown was a master short story and novel writer, though short stories seemed to better suit him. Like Robert Bloch, Fredric Brown could turn a phrase; use words economically; and employ literary tricks, humor, and twist endings on a grand scale. Brown's stories were always fun, and often poignant. Like Ray Bradbury, Brown was an astute observer of the human condition, and his best novels were episodic in nature or extensions of short stories. Like both Bloch and Bradbury, Brown published hundreds of popular, quality short stories and novels.

Fredric Brown was a journalist who lived in Wisconsin, Ohio, and Arizona. In a posthumous collection of his Science Fiction short stories entitled Paradox Lost *(1973), Brown's wife, Elizabeth, wrote in her foreword that Brown hated to write and agonized over the process. She noted, however, that he really liked having written.*

"Arena" is one of Fredric Brown's most recognized Science Fiction stories. It features a revealing vision of human frailty, and it inspired classic television episodes of The Outer Limits *(as "Fun and Games," March 30, 1964) and* Star Trek *("Arena," January 19, 1967).*

Arena

(Astounding Science-Fiction, *July 1944*)

Carson opened his eyes, and found himself looking upward into a flickering blue dimness.

It was hot, and he was lying on sand, and a sharp rock embedded in the sand was hurting his back. He rolled over to his side, off the rock, and then pushed himself up to a sitting position.

"I'm crazy," he thought. "Crazy—or dead—or something." The sand was blue, bright blue. And there wasn't any such thing as bright blue sand on Earth or any of the planets.

Blue sand.

Blue sand under a blue dome that wasn't the sky nor yet a room, but a circum-scribed area—somehow he knew it was circumscribed and finite even though he couldn't see to the top of it.

He picked up some of the sand in his hand and let it run through his fingers. It trickled down onto his bare leg. *Bare?*

Naked. He was stark naked, and already his body was dripping perspiration from the enervating heat, coated blue with sand wherever sand had touched it.

But elsewhere his body was white.

He thought: Then this sand is really blue. If it seemed blue only because of the blue light, then I'd be blue also. But I'm white, so the sand *is* blue. Blue *sand.* There isn't any blue sand. There isn't any place like this place I'm in.

Sweat was running down in his eyes.

It was hot, hotter than hell. Only hell—the hell of the ancients—was supposed to be red and not blue.

But if this place wasn't hell, what was it? Only Mercury, among the planets, had heat like this and this wasn't Mercury. And Mercury was some four billion miles from—

It came back to him then, where he'd been. In the little one-man scouter, outside the orbit of Pluto, scouting a scant million miles to one side of the Earth Armada drawn up in battle array there to intercept the Outsiders.

That sudden strident nerve-shattering ringing of the alarm bell when the rival scouter—the Outsider ship—had come within range of his detectors—

* * *

No one knew who the outsiders were, what they looked like, from what far galaxy they came, other than that it was in the general direction of the Pleiades.

First, sporadic raids on Earth colonies and outposts. Isolated battles between Earth patrols and small groups of Outsider spaceships; battles sometimes won and sometimes lost, but never to date resulting in the capture of an alien vessel. Nor had any member of a raided colony ever survived to describe the Outsiders who had left the ships, if indeed they had left them.

Not a too-serious menace, at first, for the raids had not been too numerous or destructive. And individually, the ships had proved slightly inferior in armament to the best of Earth's fighters, although somewhat superior in speed and maneuverability. A sufficient edge in speed, in fact, to give the Outsiders their choice of running or fighting, unless surrounded.

Nevertheless, Earth had prepared for serious trouble, for a showdown, building the mightiest armada of all time. It had been waiting now, that armada, for a long time. But now the showdown was coming.

Scouts twenty billion miles out had detected the approach of a mighty fleet—a showdown fleet—of the Outsiders. Those scouts had never come back, but their radiotronic messages had. And now Earth's armada, all ten thousand ships and half-million fighting spacemen, was out there, outside Pluto's orbit, waiting to intercept and battle to the death.

And an even battle it was going to be, judging by the advance reports of the men of the far picket line who had given their lives to report—before they had died—on the size and strength of the alien fleet.

Anybody's battle, with the mastery of the solar system hanging in the balance, on an even chance. A last and *only* chance, for Earth and all her colonies lay at the utter mercy of the Outsiders if they ran that gauntlet—

Oh yes. Bob Carson remembered now.

Not that it explained blue sand and flickering blueness. But that strident alarming of the bell and his leap for the control panel. His frenzied fumbling as he strapped himself into the seat. The dot in the visiplate that grew larger.

The dryness of his mouth. The awful knowledge that this was *it*. For him, at least, although the main fleets were still out of range of one another.

This, his first taste of battle. Within three seconds or less he'd be victorious, or a charred cinder. Dead.

Three seconds—that's how long a space-battle lasted. Time enough to count to three, slowly, and then you'd won or you were dead. One hit completely took care of a lightly armed and armored little one-man craft like a scouter.

Frantically—as, unconsciously, his dry lips shaped the word "One"—he worked at the controls to keep that growing dot centered on the crossed spider-webs of the visiplate. His hands doing that, while his right foot hovered over the pedal that would fire the bolt. The single bolt of concentrated hell that had to hit—or else. There wouldn't be time for any second shot.

"Two." He didn't know he'd said that, either. The dot in the visiplate wasn't a dot now. Only a few thousand miles away, it showed up in the magnification of the plate as though it were only a few hundred yards off. It was a sleek, fast little scouter, about the size of his.

And an alien ship, all right.

"Thr—" His foot touched the bolt-release pedal—

And then the Outsider had swerved suddenly and was off the cross-hairs. Carson punched the keys frantically, to follow.

For a tenth of a second, it was out of the visiplate entirely, and then as the nose of his scouter swung after it, he saw it again, diving straight toward the ground.

The ground?

It was an optical illusion of the same sort. It *had* to be, that planet—or what-ever it was—that now covered the visiplate. Whatever it was, it couldn't be there. Couldn't possibly. There *wasn't* any planet nearer than Neptune three billion miles away—with Pluto around on the opposite side of the distant pin-point sun.

His *detectors!* *They* hadn't shown any object of planetary dimensions, even of as-teroid dimensions. They still didn't.

So it couldn't be there, that whatever-it-was he was diving into, only a few hun-dred miles below him.

And in his sudden anxiety to keep from crashing, he forgot even the Outsider ship. He fired the front braking rockets, and even as the sudden change of speed slammed him forward against the seat straps, he fired full right for an emergency turn. Pushed them down and *held* them down, knowing that he needed everything the ship had to keep from crashing and that a turn that sudden would black him out for a moment.

It did black him out.

And that was all. Now he was sitting in hot blue sand, stark naked but other-wise unhurt. No sign of his spaceship and—for that matter—no sign of *space*. That curve overhead wasn't a sky, whatever else it was.

He scrambled to his feet.

Gravity seemed a little bit more than Earth-normal. Not much more.

Flat sand stretching away, a few scrawny bushes in clumps here and there. The bushes were blue, too, but in varying shades, some lighter than the blue of the sand, some darker.

Out from under the nearest bush ran a little thing that was like a lizard, except that it had more than four legs. It was blue, too. Bright blue. It saw him and ran back again under the bush.

He looked up again, trying to decide what was overhead. It wasn't exactly a roof, but it was dome-shaped. It flickered and was hard to look at. But definitely, it curved down to the ground, to the blue sand, all around him.

He wasn't far from being under the center of the dome. At a guess, it was a hundred yards to the nearest wall, if it was a wall. It was as though a blue hemi sphere of *something*, about two hundred and fifty yards in circumference, was in-verted over the flat expanse of the sand.

And everthing blue, except one object. Over near a far curving wall there was a red object. Roughly spherical, it seemed to be about a yard in diameter. Too far for him to see clearly through the flickering blueness. But, unaccountably, he shuddered.

He wiped sweat from his forehead, or tried to, with the back of his hand.

Was this a dream, a nightmare? This heat, this sand, that vague feeling of hor-ror he felt when he looked toward the red thing?

A dream? No, one didn't go to sleep and dream in the midst of a battle in space.

Death? No, never. If there were immortality, it wouldn't be a senseless thing like this, a thing of blue heat and blue sand and red horror.

Then he heard the voice—

Inside his head he heard it, not with his ears. It came from nowhere or everywhere.

"*Through spaces and dimensions wandering,*" rang the words in his mind, "*and in this space and this time I find two people about to wage a war that would exterminate one and so weaken the other that it would retrogress and never fulfill its destiny, but decay and return to mindless dust whence it came. And I say this must not happen.*"

"Who . . . what are you?" Carson didn't say it aloud, but the question formed itself in his brain.

"*You would not understand completely. I am—*" There was pause as though the voice sought—in Carson's brain—for a word that wasn't there, a word he didn't know. "*I am the end of evolution of a race so old the time can not be expressed in words that have meaning to your mind. A race fused into a single entity, eternal—*

"*An entity such as your primitive race might become*"—again the groping for a word—"*time from now. So might the race you call, in your mind, the Outsiders. So I intervene in the battle to come, the battle between fleets so evenly marched that destruction of both races will result. One must survive. One must progress and evolve.*"

"One?" thought Carson. "Mine, or—?"

"*It is in my power to stop the war, to send the Outsiders back to their galaxy. But they would return, or your race would sooner or later follow them there. Only by remaining in this space and time to intervene constantly could I prevent them from destroying one another, and I cannot remain.*

"*So I shall intervene now. I shall destroy one fleet completely without loss to the other. One civilization shall thus survive.*"

Nightmare. This had to be a nightmare, Carson thought. But he knew it wasn't. It was too mad, too impossible, to be anything but real.

He didn't dare ask *the* question—*which?* But his thoughts asked it for him.

"*The stronger shall survive,*" said the voice. "*That I can not—and would not—change. I merely intervene to make it a complete victory, not*"—groping again—"*not Pyrrhic victory to a broken race.*

"*From the outskirts of the not-yet battle I plucked two individuals, you and an Outsider. I see from your mind that in your early history of nationalisms battles between champions, to decide between races, were not unknown.*

"*You and your opponent are here pitted against one another, naked and unarmed, under conditions equally unfamiliar to you both, equally unpleasant to you both. There is no time limit, for here there is no time. The survivor is the champion of his race. That race survives.*"

"But—" Carson's protest was too inarticulate for expression, but the voice answered it.

"*It is fair. The conditions are such that the accident of physical strength will not completely decide the issue. There is a barrier. You will understand. Brain-power and courage will be more important than strength. Most especially courage, which is the will to survive.*"

"But while this goes on, the fleets will—"

"*No, you are in another space, another time. For as long as you are here, time stands still in the universe you know. I see you wonder whether this place is real. It is, and it is not. As I—to your limited understanding—am and am not real. My existence is mental and not physical. You saw me as a planet; it could have been as a dustmote or a sun.*"

"But to you this place is now real. What you suffer here will be real. And if you die here, your death will be real. If you die, your failure will be the end of your race. That is enough for you to know."

And then the voice was gone.

And he was alone, but not alone. For as Carson looked up, he saw that the red thing, the red sphere of horror which he now knew was the Outsider, was rolling toward him.

Rolling.

It seemed to have no legs or arms that he could see, no features. It rolled across the blue sand with the fluid quickness of a drop of mercury. And before it, in some manner he could not understand, came a paralyzing wave of nauseating, retching, horrid hatred.

Carson looked about him frantically. A stone, lying in the sand a few feet away, was the nearest thing to a weapon. It wasn't large, but it had sharp edges, like a slab of flint. It looked a bit like blue flint.

He picked it up, and crouched to receive the attack. It was coming fast, faster than he could run.

No time to think out how he was going to fight it, and how anyway could he plan to battle a creature whose strength, whose characteristics, whose method of fighting he did not know? Rolling so fast, it looked more than ever like a perfect sphere.

Ten yards away. Five. And then it stopped.

Rather, it *was stopped*. Abruptly the near side of it flattened as though it had run up against an invisible wall. It bounced, actually bounced back.

Then it rolled forward again, but more slowly, more cautiously. It stopped again, at the same place. It tried again, a few yards to one side.

There was a barrier there of some sort. It clicked, then, in Carson's mind. That thought projected into his mind by the Entity who had brought them there: "—accident of physical strength will not completely decide the issue. There is a barrier."

A force-field, of course. Not the Netzian Field, known to Earth science, for that glowed and emitted a crackling sound. This one was invisible, silent.

It was a wall that ran from side to side of the inverted hemisphere; Carson didn't have to verify that himself. The Roller was doing that; rolling sideways along the barrier, seeking a break in it that wasn't there.

Carson took half a dozen steps forward, his left hand groping out before him, and then his hand touched the barrier. It felt smooth, yielding, like a sheet of rubber rather than like glass. Warm to his touch, but no warmer than the sand underfoot. And it was completely invisible, even at close range.

He dropped the stone and put both hands against it, pushing. It seemed to yield, just a trifle. But no farther than that trifle, even when he pushed with all his weight. It felt like a sheet of rubber backed up by steel. Limited resiliency, and then firm strength.

He stood on tiptoe and reached as high as he could and the barrier was still there.

He saw the Roller coming back, having reached one side of the arena. That feeling of nausea hit Carson again, and he stepped back from the barrier as it went by. It didn't stop.

But did the barrier stop at ground level? Carson knelt down and burrowed in the sand. It was soft, light, easy to dig in. At two feet down the barrier was still there.

The Roller was coming back again. Obviously, it couldn't find a way through at either side.

There must be a way through, Carson thought. *Some* way we can get at each other, else this duel is meaningless.

But no hurry now, in finding that out. There was something to try first. The Roller was back now, and it stopped just across the barrier, only six feet away. It seemed to be studying him, although for the life of him, Carson couldn't find external evidence of sense organs on the thing. Nothing that looked like eyes or ears, or even a mouth. There was though, he saw now, a series of grooves—perhaps a dozen of them altogether, and he saw two tentacles suddenly push out from two of the grooves and dip into the sand as though testing its consistency. Tentacles about an inch in diameter and perhaps a foot and a half long.

But the tentacles were retractable into the grooves and were kept there except when in use. They were retractable when the thing rolled and seemed to have nothing to do with its method of locomotion. That, as far as Carson could judge, seemed to be accomplished by some shifting—just *how* he couldn't even imagine—of its center of gravity.

He shuddered as he looked at the thing. It was alien, utterly alien, horribly different from anything on Earth or any of the life forms found on the other solar planets. Instinctively, somehow, he knew its mind was as alien as its body.

But he had to try. If it had no telepathic powers at all, the attempt was foredoomed to failure, yet he thought it had such powers. There had, at any rate, been a projection of something that was not physical at the time a few minutes ago when it had first started for him. An almost tangible wave of hatred.

If it could project that, perhaps it could read his mind as well, sufficiently for his purpose.

Deliberately, Carson picked up the rock that had been his only weapon, then tossed it down again in a gesture of relinquishment and raised his empty hands, palms up, before him.

He spoke aloud, knowing that although the words would be meaningless to the creature before him, speaking them would focus his own thoughts more completely upon the message.

"Can we not have peace between us?" he said, his voice sounding strange in the utter stillness. "The Entity who brought us here has told us what must happen if our races fight—extinction of one and weakening and retrogression of the other. The battle between them, said the Entity, depends upon what we do here. Why can not we agree to an external peace—your race to its galaxy, we to ours?"

Carson blanked out his mind to receive a reply.

It came, and staggered him back, physically. He actually recoiled several steps in sheer horror at the depth and intensity of the hatred and lust-to-kill of the red images that had been projected at him. Not as articulate words—as had come to him the thoughts of the Entity—but as wave upon wave of fierce emotion.

For a moment that seemed an eternity he had to struggle against the mental impact of that hatred, fight to clear his mind of it and drive out the alien thoughts to which he had given admittance by blanking out his own thoughts. He wanted to retch.

Slowly his mind cleared as, slowly, the mind of a man wakening from nightmare clears away the fear-fabric of which the dream was woven. He was breathing hard and he felt weaker, but he could think.

He stood studying the Roller. It had been motionless during the mental duel it had so nearly won. Now it rolled a few feet to one side, to the nearest of the blue bushes. Three tentacles whipped out of their grooves and began to investigate the bush.

"O.K.," Carson said, "so it's war then." He managed a wry grin. "If I got your answer straight, peace doesn't appeal to you." And, because he was, after all, a quiet young man and couldn't resist the impulse to be dramatic, he added, "To the death!"

But his voice, in that utter silence, sounded very silly, even to himself. It came to him, then, that this *was* to the death. Not only his own death or that of the red spherical thing which he now thought of as the Roller, but death to the entire race of one or the other of them. The end of the human race, if he failed.

It made him suddenly very humble and very afraid to think that. More than to think it, to *know* it. Somehow, with a knowledge that was above even faith, he knew that the Entity who had arranged this duel had told the truth about its intentions and its powers. It wasn't kidding.

The future of humanity depended upon *him*. It was an awful thing to realize, and he wrenched his mind away from it. He had to concentrate on the situation at hand.

There had to be some way of getting through the barrier, or of killing through the barrier.

Mentally? He hoped that wasn't all, for the Roller obviously had stronger telepathic powers than the primitive, undeveloped ones of the human race. Or did it?

He had been able to drive the thoughts of the Roller out of his own mind; could it drive out his? If its ability to project were stronger, might not its receptivity mechanism be more vulnerable?

He stared at it and endeavored to concentrate and focus all his thoughts upon it.

"*Die,*" he thought. "*You are going to die. You are dying. You are—*" He tried variations on it, and mental pictures. Sweat stood out on his forehead and he found himself trembling with the intensity of the effort. But the Roller went ahead with its investigation of the bush, as utterly unaffected as though Carson had been reciting the multiplication table.

So *that* was no good.

He felt a bit weak and dizzy from the heat and his strenuous effort at concentration. He sat down on the blue sand to rest and gave his full attention to watching and studying the Roller. By close study, perhaps, he could judge its strengths and detect its weaknesses, learn things that would be valuable to know when and if they should come to grips.

It was breaking off twigs. Carson watched carefully, trying to judge just how hard it worked to do that. Later, he thought, he could find a similar bush on his own side, break off twigs of equal thickness himself, and gain a comparison of physical strength between his own arms and hands and those tentacles.

The twigs broke off hard; the Roller was having to struggle with each one, he saw. Each tentacle, he saw, bifurcated at the tip into two fingers, each tipped by a nail or claw. The claws didn't seem to be particularly long or dangerous. No more so than his own fingernails, if they were let to grow a bit.

No, on the whole, it didn't look too tough to handle physically. Unless, of course, that bush was made of pretty tough stuff. Carson looked around him and, yes, right within reach was another bush of identical type.

He reached over and snapped off a twig. It was brittle, easy to break. Of course, the Roller might have been faking deliberately but he didn't think so.

On the other hand, where was it vulnerable? Just how would he go about killing it, if he got the chance? He went back to studying it. The outer hide looked pretty tough. He'd need a sharp weapon of some sort. He picked up the piece of rock again. It was about twelve inches long, narrow, and fairly sharp on one end. If it chipped like flint, he could make a serviceable knife out of it.

The Roller was continuing its investigations of the bushes. It rolled again, to the nearest one of another type. A little blue lizard, many-legged like the one Carson had seen on his side of the barrier, darted out from under the bush.

A tentacle of the Roller lashed out and caught it, picked it up. Another tentacle whipped over and began to pull legs off the lizard, as coldly and calmly as it had pulled twigs off the bush. The creature struggled frantically and emitted a shrill squealing sound that was the first sound Carson had heard here other than the sound of his own voice.

Carson shuddered and wanted to turn his eyes away. But he made himself continue to watch; anything he could learn about his opponent might prove valuable. Even this knowledge of its unnecessary cruelty. Particularly, he thought with a sudden vicious surge of emotion, this knowledge of its unnecessary cruelty. It would make it a pleasure to kill the thing, if and when the chance came.

He steeled himself to watch the dismembering of the lizard, for that very reason.

But he felt glad when, with half its legs gone, the lizard quit squealing and struggling and lay limp and dead in the Roller's grasp.

It didn't continue with the rest of the legs. Contemptuously it tossed the dead lizard away from it, in Carson's direction. It arced through the air between them and landed at his feet.

It had come through the barrier! The barrier wasn't there anymore!

Carson was on his feet in a flash, the knife gripped tightly in his hand, and leaped forward. He'd settle this thing here and now! With the barrier gone—

But it wasn't gone. He had found that out the hard way, running head-on into it and nearly knocking himself silly. He bounced back, and fell.

And as he sat up, shaking his head to clear it, he saw something coming through the air toward him, and to duck it, he threw himself flat again on the sand, and to one side. He got his body out of the way, but there was a sudden sharp pain in the calf of his left leg.

He rolled backward, ignoring the pain, and scrambled to his feet. It was a rock, he saw now, that had struck him. And the Roller was picking up another one now, swinging it back gripped between two tentacles, getting ready to throw again.

It sailed through the air toward him, but he was easily able to step out of its way. The Roller, apparently, could throw straight, but not hard nor far. The first rock had struck him only because he had been sitting down and had not seen it coming until it was almost upon him.

Even as he stepped aside from that weak second throw, Carson drew back his right arm and let fly with the rock that was still in his hand. If missiles, he thought with sudden elation, can cross the barrier, then two can play at the game of throwing them. And the good right arm of an Earthman—

He couldn't miss a three-foot sphere at only four-yard range, and he didn't miss. The rock whizzed straight, and with a speed several times that of the missiles the Roller had thrown. It hit dead center, but it hit flat, unfortunately, instead of point first.

But it hit with such a resounding thump, and obviously it hurt. The Roller had been reaching for another rock, but it changed its mind and got out of there instead. By the time Carson could pick up another rock, the Roller was forty yards back from the barrier and going strong.

His second throw missed by feet, and his third throw was short. The Roller was back out of range—at least out of range of a missile heavy enough to be damaging.

Carson grinned. That round had been his. Except—

He quit grinning as he bent over to examine the calf of his leg. A jagged edge of the stone had made a pretty deep cut, several inches long. It was bleeding pretty freely, but he didn't think it had gone deep enough to hit an artery. If it stopped bleeding of its own accord, well and good. If not, he was in for trouble.

Finding out one thing, though, took precedence over that cut. The nature of the barrier.

He went forward to it again, this time groping with his hands before him. He found it; then holding one hand against it, he tossed a handful of sand at it with the other hand. The sand went right through. His hand didn't.

Organic matter versus inorganic? No, because the dead lizard had gone through it, and a lizard, dead or alive, was certainly organic. Plant life? He broke off a twig and poked at the barrier. The twig went through, with no resistance, but when his fingers gripping the twig came to the barrier, they were stopped.

He couldn't get through it, nor could the Roller. But the rocks and sand and a dead lizard—

How about a live lizard? He went hunting, under bushes, until he found one, and caught it. He tossed it gently against the barrier and it bounced back and scurried away across the blue sand.

That gave him the answer, insofar as he could determine it now. The screen was a barrier to living things. Dead or inorganic matter could cross it.

That off his mind, Carson looked at his injured leg again. The bleeding was lessening, which meant he wouldn't need to worry about making a tourniquet. But he should find some water, if any was available, to clean the wound.

Water—the thought made him realize that he was getting awfully thirsty. He'd *have* to find water, in case this contest turned out to be a protracted one.

Limping slightly now, he started off to make a full curcuit of his half of the arena. Guiding himself with one hand along the barrier, he walked to his right until he came to the curving sidewall. It was visible, a dull blue-grey at close range, and the surface of it felt just like the central barrier.

He experimented by tossing a handful of sand at it, and the sand reached the wall and disappeared as it went through. The hemispherical shell was a force-field, too. But an opaque one, instead of transparent like the barrier.

He followed it around until he came back to the barrier, and walked back along the barrier to the point from which he'd started.

No sign of water.

Worried now, he started a series of zigzags back and forth between the barrier and the wall, covering the intervening space thoroughly.

No water. Blue sand, blue bushes, and intolerable heat. Nothing else.

It must be his imagination, he told himself angrily, that he was suffering *that* much from thirst. How long had he been here? Of course, no time at all, according to his own spacetime frame. The Entity had told him time stood still out there, while he was here. But his body processes went on here, just the same. And according to his body's reckoning, how long had he been here? Three or four hours, perhaps. Certainly not long enough to be suffering seriously from thirst.

But he was suffering from it; his throat dry and parched. Probably the intense heat was the cause. It was *hot!* A hundred and thirty Fahrenheit, at a guess. A dry, still heat without the slightest movement of air.

He was limping rather badly, and utterly fagged out when he'd finished the futile exploration of his domain.

He stared across at the motionless Roller and hoped it was as miserable as he was. And quite possibly it wasn't enjoying this, either. The Entity had said the conditions here were equally unfamiliar and equally uncomfortable for both of them. Maybe the Roller came from a planet where two-hundred-degree heat was the norm. Maybe it was freezing while he was roasting.

Maybe the air was as much too thick for it as it was too thin for him. For the exertion of his explorations had left him panting. The atmosphere here, he realized now, was not much thicker than that on Mars.

No water.

That meant a deadline, for him at any rate. Unless he could find a way to cross that barrier or to kill his enemy from this side of it, thirst would kill him eventually.

It gave him a feeling of desperate urgency. He *must* hurry.

But he made himself sit down for a moment to rest, to think.

What was there to do? Nothing and yet so many things. The several varieties of bushes, for example. They didn't look promising, but he'd have to examine them for possibilities. And his leg—he'd have to do something about that, even without water to clean it. Gather ammunition in the form of rocks. Find a rock that would make a good knife.

His leg hurt rather badly now, and he decided that came first. One type of bush had leaves—or things rather similar to leaves. He pulled off a handful of them and decided, after examination, to take a chance on them. He used them to clean off the sand and dirt and caked blood, then made a pad of fresh leaves and tied it over the wound with tendrils from the same bush.

The tendrils proved unexpectedly tough and strong. They were slender, and soft and pliable, yet he couldn't break them at all. He had to saw them off the bush with the sharp edge of a piece of the blue flint. Some of the thicker ones were over a foot long, and he filed away in his memory, for future reference, the fact that a bunch of the thick ones, tied together, would make a pretty serviceable rope. Maybe he'd be able to think of a use for rope.

Next he made himself a knife. The blue flint *did* chip. From a foot-long splinter of it, he fashioned himself a crude but lethal weapon. And of tendrils from the bush, he made himself a rope-belt through which he could thrust the flint knife, to keep it with him all the time and yet have his hands free.

He went back to studying the bushes. There were three other types. One was leafless, dry, brittle, rather like a dried tumbleweed. Another was of soft, crumbly wood, almost like punk. It looked and felt as though it would make excellent tinder for fire. The third type was the most nearly woodlike. It had fragile leaves that wilted at a touch, but the stalks, although short, were straight and strong.

It was horribly, unbearably hot.

He limped up to the barrier, felt to make sure that it was still there. It was.

He stood watching the Roller for a while. It was keeping a safe distance back from the barrier, out of effective stone-throwing range. It was moving around back there, doing something. He couldn't tell what it was doing.

Once it stopped moving, came a little closer, and seemed to concentrate its attention on him. Again Carson had to fight off a wave of nausea. He threw a stone at it and the Roller retreated and went back to whatever it had been doing before.

At least he could make it keep its distance.

And, he thought bitterly, a devil of a lot of good *that* did him. Just the same, he spent the next hour or two gathering stones of suitable size for throwing, and making several neat piles of them, near his side of the barrier.

His throat burned now. It was difficult for him to think about anything except water.

But he *had* to think about other things. About getting through that barrier, under or over it, getting at that red sphere and killing it before this place of heat and thirst killed him first.

The barrier went to the wall upon either side, but how high and how far under the sand?

For just a moment, Carson's mind was too fuzzy to think out how he could find out either of those things. Idly, sitting there in the hot sand—and he didn't remember sitting down—he watched a blue lizard crawl from the shelter of one bush to the shelter of another.

From under the second bush, it looked out at him.

Carson grinned at it. Maybe he was getting a bit punch-drunk, because he remembered suddenly the old story of the desert-colonists on Mars, taken from an older desert story of Earth—"Pretty soon you get so lonesome you find yourself talking to the lizards, and then not so long after that you find the lizards talking back to you—"

He should have been concentrating, of course, on how to kill the Roller, but instead he grinned at the lizard and said, "Hello, there."

The lizard took a few steps toward him. "Hello," it said.

Carson was stunned for a moment, and then he put back his head and roared with laughter. It didn't hurt his throat to do so, either; he hadn't been *that* thirsty.

Why not? Why should the Entity who thought up this nightmare of a place not have a sense of humor, along with the other powers he had? Talking lizards, equipped to talk back in my own language, if I talk to them—It's a nice touch.

He grinned at the lizard and said, "Come on over." But the lizard turned and ran away, scurrying from bush to bush until it was out of sight.

He was thirsty again.

And he had to *do* something. He couldn't win this contest by sitting here sweating and feeling miserable. He had to *do* something. But what?

Get through the barrier. But he couldn't get through it, or over it. But was he certain he couldn't get under it? And come to think of it, didn't one sometimes find water by digging? Two birds with one stone—

Painfully now, Carson limped up to the barrier and started digging, scooping up sand a double handful at a time. It was slow, hard work because the sand ran in at the edges and the deeper he got the bigger in diameter the hole had to be. How many hours it took him, he didn't know, but he hit bedrock four feet down. Dry bedrock; no sign of water.

And the force-field of the barrier went down clear to the bedrock. No dice. No water. Nothing.

He crawled out of the hole and lay there panting, and then raised his head to look across and see what the Roller was doing. It must be doing something back there.

It was. It was making something out of wood from the bushes, tied together with tendrils. A queerly shaped framework about four feet high and roughly square. To see it better, Carson climbed up onto the mound of sand he had excavated from the hole, and stood there staring.

There were two long levers sticking out of the back of it, one with a cup-shaped affair on the end of it. Seemed to be some sort of a catapult, Carson thought.

Sure enough, the Roller was lifting a sizable rock into the cup-shaped outfit. One of its tentacles moved the other lever up and down for awhile, and then it turned the machine slightly as though aiming it and the lever with the stone flew up and forward.

The stone raced several yards over Carson's head, so far away that he didn't have to duck, but he judged the distance it had traveled, and whistled softly. He couldn't throw a rock that weight more than half that distance. And even retreating to the rear of his domain wouldn't put him out of range of that machine, if the Roller shoved it forward almost to the barrier.

Another rock whizzed over. Not quite so far away this time.

That thing could be dangerous, he decided. Maybe he'd better do something about it.

Moving from side to side along the barrier, so the catapult couldn't bracket him, he whaled a dozen rocks at it. But that wasn't going to be any good, he saw. They had to be light rocks, or he couldn't throw them that far. If they hit the framework, they bounced off harmlessly. And the Roller had no difficulty, at that distance, in moving aside from those that came near it.

Besides, his arm was tiring badly. He ached all over from sheer weariness. If he could only rest awhile without having to duck rocks from that catapult at regular intervals of maybe thirty seconds each—

He stumbled back to the rear of the arena. Then he saw even that wasn't any good. The rocks reached back there, too, only there were longer intervals between them, as though it took longer to wind up the mechanism, whatever it was, of the catapult.

Wearily he dragged himself back to the barrier again. Several times he fell and could barely rise to his feet to go on. He was, he knew, near the limit of his endurance. Yet he didn't dare stop moving now, until and unless he could put that catapult out of action. If he fell asleep, he'd never wake up.

One of the stones from it gave him the first glimmer of an idea. It struck upon one of the piles of stones he'd gathered together near the barrier to use as ammunition, and it struck sparks.

Sparks. Fire. Primitive man had made fire by striking sparks, and with some of those dry crumbly bushes as tinder—

Luckily, a bush of that type was near him. He broke it off, took it over to a pile of stones, then patiently hit one stone against another until a spark touched the punklike wood of the bush. It went up in flames so fast that it singed his eyebrows and was burned to an ash within seconds.

But he had the idea now, and within minutes he had a little fire going in the lee of the mound of sand he'd made digging the hole an hour or two ago. Tinder bushes had started it, and other bushes which burned, but more slowly, kept it a steady flame.

The tough wirelike tendrils didn't burn readily; that made the fire-bombs easy to make and throw. A bundle of faggots tied about a small stone to give it weight and a loop of the tendril to swing it by.

He made half a dozen of them before he lighted and threw the first. It went wide, and the Roller started a quick retreat, pulling the catapult after it. But Carson had others ready and threw them in rapid succession. The fourth wedged in the catapult's framework, and did the trick. The Roller tried desperately to put out the spreading blaze by throwing sand, but its clawed tentacles would take only a spoonful at a time and its efforts were ineffectual. The catapult burned.

The Roller moved safely away from the fire and seemed to concentrate its attention on Carson and again he felt that wave of hatred and nausea. But more weakly; either the Roller itself was weakening or Carson had learned how to protect himself against the mental attack.

He thumbed his nose at it and then sent it scuttling back to safety by throwing a stone. The Roller went clear to the back of its half of the arena and started pulling up bushes again. Probably it was going to make another catapult.

Carson verified—for the hundredth time—that the barrier was still operating, and then found himself sitting in the sand beside it because he was suddenly too weak to stand up.

His leg throbbed steadily now and the pangs of thirst were severe. But those things paled beside the utter physical exhaustion that gripped his entire body.

And the heat.

Hell must be like this, he thought. The hell that the ancients had believed in. He fought to stay awake, and yet staying awake seemed futile, for there was nothing he could do. Nothing, while the barrier remained impregnable and the Roller stayed back out of range.

But there must be *something*. He tried to remember things he had read in books of archaeology about the methods of fighting used back in the days before metal and plastic. The stone missile, that had come first, he thought. Well, that he already had.

The only improvement on it would be a catapult, such as the Roller had made. But he'd never be able to make one, with the tiny bits of wood available from the bushes—no single piece longer than a foot or so. Certainly he could figure out a mechanism for one, but he didn't have the endurance left for a task that would take days.

Days? But the Roller had made one. Had they been here days already? Then he remembered that the Roller had many tentacles to work with and undoubtedly could do such work faster than he.

And besides, a catapult wouldn't decide the issue. He had to do better than that.

Bow and arrow? No; he had tried archery once and knew his own ineptness with a bow. Even with a modern sportsman's durasteel weapon, made for accuracy. With such a crude, pieced-together outfit as he could make here, he doubted if he could shoot as far as he could throw a rock, and knew he couldn't shoot as straight.

Spear? Well, he *could* make that. It would be useless as a throwing weapon at any distance, but would be a handy thing at close range, if he ever got to close range.

And making one would give him something to do. Help keep his mind from wandering, as it was beginning to do. Sometimes now, he had to concentrate awhile before he could remember why he was here, why he had to kill the Roller.

Luckily he was still beside one of the piles of stones. He sorted through it until he found one shaped roughly like a spearhead. With a smaller stone he began to chip it into shape, fashioning sharp shoulders on the sides so that if it penetrated it would not pull out again.

Like a harpoon? There was something in that idea, he thought. A harpoon was better than a spear, maybe, for this crazy contest. If he could once get it into the Roller, and have a rope on it, he could pull the Roller up against the barrier and the stone blade of his knife would reach through that barrier, even if his hands wouldn't.

The shaft was harder to make than the head. But by splitting and joining the main stems of four of the bushes, and wrapping the joints with the tough but thin tendrils, he got a strong shaft about four feet long, and tied the stone head in a notch cut in the end.

It was crude, but strong.

And the rope. With the thin tough tendrils he made himself twenty feet of line. It was light and didn't look strong, but he knew it would hold his weight and to spare. He tied one end of it to the shaft of the harpoon and the other end about his right wrist. At least, if he threw his harpoon across the barrier, he'd be able to pull it back if he missed.

Then when he had tied the last knot and there was nothing more he could do, the heat and the weariness and the pain in his leg and the dreadful thirst were suddenly a thousand times worse than they had been before.

He tried to stand up, to see what the Roller was doing now, and found he couldn't get to his feet. On the third try, he got as far as his knees and then fell flat again.

"I've got to sleep," he thought. "If a showdown came now, I'd be helpless. He could come up here and kill me, if he knew. I've got to regain some strength."

Slowly, painfully, he crawled back away from the barrier. Ten yards, twenty—

The jar of something thudding against the sand near him waked him from a confused and horrible dream to a more confused and more horrible reality, and he opened his eyes again to the blue radiance over blue sand.

How long had he slept? A minute? A day?

Another stone thudded nearer and threw sand on him. He got his arms under him and sat up. He turned around and saw the Roller twenty yards away, at the barrier.

It rolled away hastily as he sat up, not stopping until it was as far away as it could get.

He'd fallen asleep too soon, he realized, while he was still in range of the Roller's throwing ability. Seeing him lying motionless, it had dared to come up to the barrier and throw stones at him. Luckily, it didn't realize how weak he was, or it could have stayed there and kept on throwing stones.

Had he slept long? He didn't think so, because he felt just as he had before. Not rested at all, no thirstier, no different. Probably he'd been there only a few minutes.

He started crawling again, this time forcing himself to keep going until he was as far as he could go, until the colorless, opaque wall of the arena's outer shell was only a yard away.

Then things slipped away again—

When he awoke, nothing about him was changed, but this time he knew that he had slept a long time.

The first thing he became aware of was the inside of his mouth; it was dry, caked. His tongue was swollen.

Something was wrong, he knew, as he returned slowly to full awareness. He felt less tired, the stage of utter exhaustion had passed. The sleep had taken care of that.

But there was pain, agonizing pain. It wasn't until he tried to move that he knew that it came from his leg.

He raised his head and looked down at it. It was swollen terribly below the knee and the swelling showed even halfway up his thigh. The plant tendrils he had used to tie on the protective pad of leaves now cut deeply into the swollen flesh.

To get his knife under that imbedded lashing would have been impossible. Fortunately, the final knot was over the shin bone, in front, where the vine cut in less deeply than elsewhere. He was able, after an agonizing effort, to untie the knot.

A look under the pad of leaves told him the worst. Infection and blood poisoning, both pretty bad and getting worse.

And without drugs, without cloth, without even *water*, there wasn't even a thing he could do about it.

Not a thing, except *die*, when the poison had spread through his system.

He knew it was hopeless, then, and that he'd lost.

And with him, humanity. When he died here, out there in the universe he knew, all his friends, everybody, would die too. And Earth and the colonized planets would be the home of the red, rolling alien Outsiders. Creatures out of a nightmare, things without a human attribute, who picked lizards apart for the fun of it.

It was the thought of that which gave him courage to start crawling, almost blindly in pain, toward the barrier again. Not crawling on his hands and knees this time, but pulling himself along only by his arms and hands.

A chance in a million, that maybe he'd have the strength left, when he got there, to throw his harpoon-spear just *once*, and with deadly effect, if—on another chance in a million—the Roller would come up to the barrier. Or if the barrier was gone, now.

It took him years, it seemed, to get there.

The barrier wasn't gone. It was as impassable as when he'd first felt it.

And the Roller wasn't at the barrier. By raising up on his elbows, he could see it at the back of its part of the arena, working on a wooden framework that was a half-completed duplicate of the catapult he'd destroyed.

It was moving slowly now. Undoubtedly it had weakened, too.

But Carson doubted that it would ever need that second catapult. He'd be dead, he thought, before it was finished.

If he could attract it to the barrier, now, while he was still alive—He waved an arm and tried to shout, but his parched throat would make no sound.

Or if he could get through the barrier—

His mind must have slipped for a moment, for he found himself beating his fists against the barrier in futile rage, and made himself stop.

He closed his eyes, tried to make himself calm.

"Hello," said the voice.

It was a small, thin voice. It sounded like—

He opened his eyes and turned his head. It *was* the lizard.

"Go away," Carson wanted to say. "Go away, you're not really there, or you're there but not really talking. I'm imagining things again."

But he couldn't talk; his throat and tongue were past all speech with the dryness. He closed his eyes again.

"Hurt," said the voice. "Kill. Hurt—kill. Come."

He opened his eyes again. The blue ten-legged lizard was still there. It ran a little way along the barrier, came back, started off again, and came back.

"Hurt," it said. "Kill. Come."

Again it started off, and came back. Obviously it wanted Carson to follow it along the barrier.

He closed his eyes again. The voice kept on. The same three meaningless words. Each time he opened his eyes, it ran off and came back.

"Hurt. Kill. Come."

Carson groaned. There would be no peace unless he followed the blasted thing. Like it wanted him to.

He followed it, crawling. Another sound, a high-pitched squealing. Something small, blue, that looked like a lizard and yet didn't—

Then he saw what it was—the lizard whose legs the Roller had pulled off, so long ago. But it wasn't dead; it had come back to life and was wriggling and screaming in agony.

"Hurt," said the other lizard. "Hurt. Kill. Kill."

Carson understood. He took the flint knife from his belt and killed the tortured creature. The live lizard scurried off quickly.

Carson turned back to the barrier. He leaned his hands and head against it and watched the Roller, far back, working on the new catapult.

"I couldn't get that far," he thought, "if I could get through. If I could get through, I might win yet. It looks weak, too. I might—"

And then there was another reaction of black hopelessness, when pain snapped his will and he wished that he were dead. He envied the lizard he'd just killed. It didn't have to live on and suffer. And he did. It would be hours, it might be days, before the blood poisoning killed him.

If only he could use that knife on himself—

But he knew he wouldn't. As long as he was alive, there was the millionth chance—

He was straining, pushing on the barrier with the flat of his hands, and he noticed his arms, how thin and scrawny they were now. He must really have been here a long time, for days, to get as thin as that.

How much longer now, before he died? How much more heat and thirst and pain could flesh stand?

For a little while he was almost hysterical again, and then came a time of deep calm, and a thought that was startling.

The lizard he had just killed. *It had crossed the barrier, still alive.* It had come from the Roller's side; the Roller had pulled off its legs and then tossed it contemptuously at him and it had come through the barrier. He'd thought, because the lizard was dead.

But it hadn't been dead; it had been unconscious.

A live lizard couldn't go through the barrier, but an unconscious one could. The barrier was not barrier, then, to living flesh, but to conscious flesh. It was a *mental* projection, a *mental* hazard.

And with that thought, Carson started crawling along the barrier to make his last desperate gamble. A hope so forlorn that only a dying man would have dared try it.

No use weighing the odds of success. Not when, if he didn't try it, those odds were infinitely to zero.

He crawled along the barrier to the dune of sand, about four feet high, which he'd scooped out in trying—how many days ago?—to dig under the barrier or to reach water.

That mound was right at the barrier, its farther slope half on one side of the barrier, half on the other.

Taking with him a rock from the pile nearby, he climbed up to the top of the dune and over the top, and lay there against the barrier, his weight leaning against it so that if the barrier were taken away he'd roll on down the short slope into the enemy territory.

He checked to be sure that the knife was safely in his rope belt, that the harpoon was in the crook of his left arm and that the twenty-foot rope was fastened to it and to his wrist.

Then with his right hand he raised the rock with which he would hit himself on the head. Luck would have to be with him on that blow; it would have to be hard enough to knock him out, but not hard enough to knock him out for long.

He had a hunch that the Roller was watching him, and would see him roll down through the barrier, and come to investigate. It would think he was dead, he hoped—he thought it had probably drawn the same deduction about the nature of the barrier that he had drawn. But it would come cautiously. He would have a little time—

He struck.

Pain brought him back to consciousness. A sudden, sharp pain in his hip that was differing from the throbbing pain in his head and the throbbing pain in his leg.

But he had, thinking things out before he had struck himself, anticipated that very pain, even hoped for it, and had steeled himself against awakening with a sudden movement.

He lay still, but opened his eyes just a slit, and saw that he had guessed rightly. The Roller was coming closer. It was twenty feet away and the pain that had awakened him was the stone it had tossed to see whether he was alive or dead.

He lay still. It came closer, fifteen feet away, and stopped again. Carson scarcely breathed.

As nearly as possible, he was keeping his mind a blank, lest its telepathic ability detect consciousness in him. And with his mind blanked out that way, the impact of its thoughts upon his mind was nearly soul-shattering.

He felt sheer horror at the utter *alienness*, the *differentness* of those thoughts. Things that he felt but could not understand and could never express, because no terrestrial language had words, no terrestrial mind had images to fit them. The mind of a spider, he thought, or the mind of a praying mantis or a Martian sand-serpent, raised to intelligence and put in telepathic rapport with human minds, would be a homely familiar thing, compared to this.

He understood now the Entity had been right: Man or Roller, and the universe was not a place that could hold them both. Farther apart than god and devil, there could never be even a balance between them.

Closer. Carson waited until it was only four feet away, until its clawed tentacles reached out—

Oblivious to agony now, he sat up, raised and flung the harpoon with all the strength that remained in him. Or he thought it was all; sudden final strength flooded through him, along with a sudden forgetfulness of pain as definite as a nerve block.

As the Roller, deeply stabbed by the harpoon, rolled away, Carson tried to get to his feet to run after it. He couldn't do that; he fell, but kept crawling.

It reached the end of the rope, and he was jerked forward by the pull of his wrist. It dragged him a few feet and then stopped. Carson kept on going, pulling himself toward it hand over hand along the rope.

It stopped there, writhing tentacles trying in vain to pull out the harpoon. It seemed to shudder and quiver, and then it must have realized that it couldn't get away, for it rolled back toward him, clawed tentacles reaching out.

Stone knife in hand, he met it. He stabbed, again and again, while those horrid claws ripped skin and flesh and muscle from his body.

He stabbed and slashed, and at last it was still.

A bell was ringing, and it took a while after he'd opened his eyes to tell where he was and what it was. He was strapped into the seat of his scouter, and the visi-plate before him showed only empty space. No Outsider ship and no impossible planet.

The bell was the communications plate signal; someone wanted him to switch power into the receiver. Purely reflex action enabled him to reach forward and throw the lever.

The face of Brander, captain of the *Magellan*, mother-ship of his group of scouters, flashed into the screen. His face was pale and his black eyes glowed with excitement.

"*Magellan* to Carson," he snapped. "Come on in. The fight's over. We've won!"

The screen went blank; Brander would be signaling the other scouters of his command.

Slowly, Carson set the controls for the return. Slowly, unbelievingly, he un-strapped himself from the seat and went back to get a drink at the cold-water tank. For some reason, he was unbelievably thirsty. He drank six glasses.

He leaned there against the wall, trying to think.

Had it happened? He was in good health, sound, uninjured. His thirst had been mental rather than physical; his throat hadn't been dry. His leg—

He pulled up his trouser leg and looked at the calf. There was a long white scar there, but a perfectly healed scar. It hadn't been there before. He zipped open the front of his shirt and saw that his chest and abdomen were criss-crossed with tiny, almost unnoticeable perfectly healed scars.

It *had* happened.

The scouter, under automatic control, was already entering the hatch of the mother-ship. The grapples pulled it into its individual lock, and a moment later a buzzer indicated that the lock was air-filled. Carson opened the hatch and stepped outside, went through the double door of the lock.

He went right to Brander's office, went in, and saluted.

Brander still looked dizzily dazed. "Hi, Carson," he said. "What you missed! What a show!"

"What happened, sir?"

"Don't know exactly. We fired one salvo, and their whole fleet went up in dust! Whatever it was jumped from ship to ship in a flash, even the ones we hadn't aimed at and that were out of range! The whole fleet disintegrated before our eyes, and we didn't get the paint of a single ship scratched!

"We can't even claim credit for it. Must have been some unstable component in the metal they used, and our sighting shot just set it off. Man, oh man, too bad you missed all the excitement."

Carson managed to grin. It was a sickly ghost of a grin, for it would be days before he'd be over the mental impact of his experience, but the captain wasn't watching, and didn't notice.

"Yes, sir," he said. Common sense, more than modesty, told him he'd be branded forever as the worst liar in space if he ever said any more than that. "Yes, sir, too bad I missed all the excitement."

 THEODORE STURGEON (1918–1985)

Theodore Sturgeon was born Edward Hamilton Waldo but later had his name legally changed. Sturgeon, like other Science Fiction greats of his period, had his first stories published in the pages of Astounding Science-Fiction. *("Ether Breather" appeared in the September 1939 issue.) His stories also appeared in* Weird Tales *and* Unknown. *He was best known for Fantasy and Science Fiction writing, but he also wrote historical novels, Westerns, Crime fiction, the novelization of the screenplay for Irwin Allen's* Voyage to the Bottom of the Sea *(1961), radio and television scripts, an episode for* Star Trek *entitled "Amok Time" (September 15, 1967), and more. Theodore Sturgeon, in his day and even today, is as important to Science Fiction as are Robert Heinlein and Isaac Asimov.*

Beyond being versatile in various media, Sturgeon was talented in a range of story lines within and outside Fantasy and Science Fiction. Sturgeon produced Hard Science Fiction as well as Space Opera. Often, his Science Fiction was dark in tone; sometimes, it was blended with Fantasy. Sturgeon was an innovator, and a rogue. He was loved by Science Fiction readers and his fellow writers alike.

"Thunder and Roses" is a classic Cold War work of Science Fiction. It is one of Sturgeon's most famous short stories, though he had many acclaimed works. In some ways, the story foreshadows Nevil Shute's consummate condemnation of atomic war in On the Beach *(1957). The theme of the "girl as heroine" was also unique in 1947 and is worthy of note.*

Thunder and Roses

(Astounding Science-Fiction, *November 1947)*

When Pete Mawser learned about the show, he turned away from the GHQ bulletin board, touched his long chin, and determined to shave. This was odd, because the show would be video, and he would see it in his barracks.

He had an hour and a half. It felt good to have a purpose again—even shaving before eight o'clock. Eight o'clock Tuesday, just the way it used to be. Everyone used to catch that show on Tuesday. Everyone used to say, Wednesday morning, "How about the way she sang 'The Breeze and I' last night?" "Hey, did you hear Starr last night?"

That was a while ago, before all those people were dead, before the country was dead. Starr Anthim, institution, like Crosby, like Duse, like Jenny Lind, like the Statue of Liberty.

(Liberty had been one of the first to get it, her bronze beauty volatilized, radioactive, and even now being carried about in vagrant winds, spreading over the earth—)

Pete Mawser grunted and forced his thoughts away from the drifting, poisonous fragments of a blasted Liberty. Hate was first. Hate was ubiquitous, like the increasing blue glow in the air at night, like the tension that hung over the base.

Gunfire crackled sporadically far to the right, swept nearer. Pete stepped out of the street and made for a parked ten-wheeler. There's a lot of cover in and around a ten-wheeler.

There was a Wac sitting on the short running-board.

At the corner a stocky figure backed into the intersection. The man carried a tommy gun in his arms, and he was swinging to and fro with the gentle, wavering motion of a weathervane. He staggered toward them, his gun muzzle hunting. Someone fired from a building and the man swiveled and blasted wildly at the sound.

"He's—blind," said Pete Mawser, and added, "He ought to be," looking at the tattered face.

A siren keened. An armored jeep slewed into the street. The full-throated roar of a brace of .50-caliber machine guns put a swift and shocking end to the incident.

"Poor crazy kid," Pete said softly. "That's the fourth I've seen today." He looked down at the Wac. She was smiling.

"Hey!"

"Hello, Sarge." She must have identified him before, because now she did not raise her eyes or her voice. "What happened?"

"You know what happened. Some kid got tired of having nothing to fight and nowhere to run to. What's the matter with you?"

"No," she said. "I don't mean that." At last she looked up at him. "I mean all of this. I can't seem to remember."

"You . . . well, gee, it's not easy to forget. We got hit. We got hit everywhere at once. All the big cities are gone. We got it from both sides. We got too much. The air is becoming radioactive. We'll all—" He checked himself. She didn't know. She'd forgotten. There was nowhere to escape to, and she'd escaped inside herself, right here. Why tell her about it? Why tell her that everyone was going to die? Why tell her that other, shameful thing: that we hadn't struck back?

But she wasn't listening. She was still looking at him. Her eyes were not quite straight. One held his but the other was slightly shifted and seemed to be looking at his temples. She was smiling again. When his voice trailed off she didn't prompt him. Slowly he moved away. She did not turn her head, but kept looking up at where he had been, smiling a little. He turned away, wanting to run, walking fast.

(How long can a guy hold out? When you're in the Army they try to make you be like everybody else. What do you do when everybody else is cracking up?)

He blanked out the mental picture of himself as the last one left sane. He'd followed that one through before. It always led to the conclusion that it would be better to be one of the first. He wasn't ready for that yet.

Then he blanked that out, too. Every time he said to himself that he wasn't ready for that yet, something within him asked, "Why not?" and he never seemed to have an answer ready.

(How long could a guy hold out?)

He climbed the steps of the QM Central and went inside.

There was nobody at the reception switchboard. It didn't matter. Messages were carried by guys in jeeps, or on motorcycles. The Base Command was not insisting that anybody stick to a sitting job these days. Ten desk men would crack up for every one on a jeep, or on the soul-sweat squads. Pete made up his mind to put in a little stretch on a squad tomorrow. Do him good. He just hoped that this time the adjutant wouldn't burst into tears in the middle of the parade ground. You could keep your mind on the manual of arms just fine until something like that happened.

He bumped into Sonny Weisefreund in the barracks corridor. The tech's round young face was as cheerful as ever. He was naked and glowing, and had a towel thrown over his shoulder.

"Hi, Sonny. Is there plenty of hot water?"

"Why not?" grinned Sonny. Pete grinned back, cursing inwardly. Could anybody say anything about anything at all without one of these reminders? Sure there was hot water. The QM barracks had hot water for three hundred men. There were three dozen left. Men dead, men gone to the hills, men locked up so they wouldn't—

"Starr Anthim's doing a show tonight."

"Yeah. Tuesday night. Not funny, Pete. Don't you know there's a war—"

"No kidding," Pete said swiftly. "She's here—right here on the base."

Sonny's face was joyful. "Gee." He pulled the towel off his shoulder and tied it around his waist. "Starr Anthim here! Where are they going to put on the show?"

"HQ, I imagine. Video only. You know about public gatherings." And a good thing, too, he thought. Put on an in-person show, and some torn-up GI would crack during one of her numbers. He himself would get plenty mad over a thing like that—mad enough to do something about it then and there. And there would probably be a hundred and fifty or more like him, going raving mad because someone had spoiled a Starr Anthim show. That would be a dandy little shambles for her to put in her memory book.

"How'd she happen to come here, Pete?"

"Drifted in on the last gasp of a busted-up Navy helicopter."

"Yeah, but why?"

"Search me. Get your head out of that gift horse's mouth."

He went into the washroom, smiling and glad that he still could. He undressed and put his neatly folded clothes down on a bench. There were a soap wrapper and an empty toothpaste tube lying near the wall. He went and picked them up and put them in the catchall. He took the mop which leaned against the partition and mopped the floor where Sonny had splashed after shaving. Got to keep things squared away. He might say something if it were anyone else but Sonny. But Sonny wasn't cracking up. Sonny always had been like that. Look there. Left his razor out again.

Pete started his shower, meticulously adjusting the valves until the pressure and temperature exactly suited him. He didn't do anything slapdash these days. There was so much to feel, and taste, and see now. The impact of water on his skin, the smell of soap, the consciousness of light and heat, the very pressure of standing on the soles of his feet   he wondered vaguely how the slow increase of radioactivity in the air, as the nitrogen transmuted to Carbon Fourteen, would affect him if he kept carefully healthy in every way. What happens first? Do you go blind? Headaches, maybe? Perhaps you lose your appetite. Or maybe you get tired all the time.

Why not go look it up?

On the other hand, why bother? Only a very small percentage of the men would die of radioactive poisoning. There were too many other things that killed more quickly, which was probably just as well. That razor, for example. It lay gleaming in a sunbeam, curved and clean in the yellow light. Sonny's father and grandfather had used it, or so he said, and it was his pride and joy.

Pete turned his back on it and soaped under his arms, concentrating on the tiny kisses of bursting bubbles. In the midst of a recurrence of disgust at himself for thinking so often of death, a staggering truth struck him. He did not think of such things because he was morbid, after all! It was the very familiarity of things that brought death-thoughts. It was either "I shall never do this again" or "This is one of the last times I shall do this." You might devote yourself completely to doing things in different ways, he thought madly. You might crawl across the floor this time, and next time walk across on your hands. You might skip dinner tonight, and have a snack at two in the morning instead, and eat grass for breakfast.

But you had to breathe. Your heart had to beat. You'd sweat and you'd shiver, the same as always. You couldn't get away from that. When those things happened, they would remind you. Your heart wouldn't beat out its *wunklunk, wunklunk* any more. It would go *one-less, one-less,* until it yelled and yammered in your ears and you had to make it stop.

Terrific polish on that razor.

And your breath would go on, same as before. You could sidle through this door, back through the next one and the one after, and figure out a totally new way to go through the one after that, but your breath would keep on sliding in and out of your nostrils like a razor going through whiskers, making a sound like a razor being stropped.

Sonny came in. Pete soaped his hair. Sonny picked up the razor and stood looking at it. Pete watched him, soap ran into his eye, he swore, and Sonny jumped.

"What are you looking at, Sonny? Didn't you ever see it before?"

"Oh, sure. Sure. I was just—" He shut the razor, opened it, flashed light from its blade, shut it again. "I'm tired of using this, Pete. I'm going to get rid of it. Want it?"

Want it? In his foot locker, maybe. Under his pillow. "Thanks no, Sonny. Couldn't use it."

"I like safety razors," Sonny mumbled. "Electrics, even better. What are we going to do with it?"

"Throw it in the . . . no." Pete pictured the razor turning end over end in the air, half open, gleaming in the maw of the catchall. "Throw it out the—" No. Curving out into the long grass. You might want it. You might crawl around in the moonlight looking for it. You might find it.

"I guess maybe I'll break it up."

"No," Pete said. "The pieces—" Sharp little pieces. Hollow-ground fragments. "I'll think of something. Wait'll I get dressed."

He washed briskly, toweled, while Sonny stood looking at the razor. It was a blade now, and if you broke it, there would be shards and glittering splinters, still razor sharp. You could slap its edge into an emery wheel and grind it away, and somebody could find it and put another edge on it because it was so obviously a razor, a fine steel razor, one that would slice so— "I know. The laboratory. We'll get rid of it," Pete said confidently.

He stepped into his clothes, and together they went to the laboratory wing. It was very quiet there. Their voices echoed.

"One of the ovens," said Pete, reaching for the razor.

"Bake ovens? You're crazy!"

Pete chuckled. "You don't know this place, do you? Like everything else on the base, there was a lot more went on here than most people knew about. They kept calling it the bake shop. Well, it *was* research headquarters for new high-nutrient flours. But there's lots else here. We tested utensils and designed beet peelers and all sorts of things like that. There's an electric furnace in here that—" He pushed open a door.

They crossed a long, quiet, cluttered room to the thermal equipment. "We can do everything here from annealing glass, through glazing ceramics, to finding the melting point of frying pans." He clicked a switch tentatively. A pilot light glowed. He swung open a small, heavy door and set the razor inside. "Kiss it good-bye. In twenty minutes it'll be a puddle."

"I want to see that," said Sonny. "Can I look around until it's cooked?"

"Why not?"

(Everybody around here always said "Why not?")

They walked through the laboratories. Beautifully equipped, they were, and too quiet. Once they passed a major who was bent over a complex electronic hook-up on one of the benches. He was watching a little amber light flicker, and he did not return their salute. They tiptoed past him, feeling awed at his absorption, envying it. They saw the models of the automatic kneaders, the vitaminizers, the remote-signal thermostats and timers and controls.

"What's in there?"

"I dunno. I'm over the edge of my territory. I don't think there's anybody left for this section. They were mostly mechanical and electronic theoreticians. The only thing I know about them is that if we ever needed anything in the way of tools, meters, or equipment, they had it or something better, and if we ever got real bright and figured out a startling new idea, they'd already built it and junked it a month ago. Hey!"

Sonny followed the pointing hand. "What?"

"That wall section. It's loose, or . . . well, what do you know?"

He pushed at the section of wall, which was very slightly out of line. There was a dark space beyond.

"What's in there?"

"Nothing, or some semiprivate hush-hush job. These guys used to get away with murder."

Sonny said, with an uncharacteristic flash of irony, "Isn't that the Army theoretician's business?"

Cautiously they peered in, then entered.

"Wh . . . *hey!* The door!"

It swung swiftly and quietly shut. The soft click of the latch was accompanied by a blaze of light.

The room was small and windowless. It contained machinery—a "trickle" charger, a bank of storage batteries, an electric-powered dynamo, two small self-starting gas-driven light plants and a Diesel complete with sealed compressed-air starting cylinders. In the corner was a relay rack with its panel-bolts spot welded. Protruding from it was a red-top lever. Nothing was labeled.

They looked at the equipment wordlessly for a time and then Sonny said, "Somebody wanted to make awful sure he had power for something."

"Now, I wonder what—" Pete walked over to the relay rack. He looked at the lever without touching it. It was wired up; behind the handle, on the wire, was a folded tag. He opened it cautiously. "To be used only on specific orders of the Commanding Officer."

"Give it a yank and see what happens."

Something clicked behind them. They whirled. "What was that?"

"Seemed to come from that rig by the door."

They approached it cautiously. There was a spring-loaded solenoid attached to a bar which was hinged to drop across the inside of the secret door, where it would fit into steel gudgeons on the panel.

It clicked again. "A Geiger," said Pete disgustedly.

"Now why," mused Sonny, "would they design a door to stay locked unless the general radioactivity went beyond a certain point? That's what it is. See the relays? And the overload switch there? And this?"

"It has a manual lock, too," Pete pointed out. The counter clicked again. "Let's get out of here. I got one of those things built into my head these days."

The door opened easily. They went out, closing it behind them. The keyhole was cleverly concealed in the crack between two boards.

They were silent as they made their way back to the QM labs. The small thrill of violation was gone and, for Pete Mawser at least, the hate was back, that and the shame. A few short weeks before, this base had been a part of the finest country on earth. There was a lot of work here that was secret, and a lot that was such purely progressive and unapplied research that it would be in the way anywhere else but in this quiet wilderness.

Sweat stood out on his forehead. They hadn't struck back at their murderers! It was quite well known that there were launching sites all over the country, in secret caches far from any base or murdered city. Why must they sit here waiting to die, only to let the enemy—"enemies" was more like it—take over the continent when it was safe again?

He smiled grimly. One small consolation. They'd hit too hard: that was a certainty. Probably each of the attackers underestimated what the other would throw. The result—a spreading transmutation of nitrogen into deadly Carbon Fourteen. The effects would not be limited to the continent. What ghastly long-range effect the muted radioactivity would have on the overseas enemies was something that no one alive today could know.

Back at the furnace, Pete glanced at the temperature dial, then kicked the latch control. The pilot winked out and then the door swung open. They blinked and started back from the raging heat within, then bent and peered. The razor was gone. A pool of brilliance lay on the floor of the compartment.

"Ain't much left. Most of it oxidized away," Pete grunted.

They stood together for a time with their faces lit by that small shimmering ruin. Later, as they walked back to the barracks, Sonny broke his long silence with a sigh. "I'm glad we did that, Pete. I'm awful glad we did that."

At a quarter to eight they were waiting before the combination console in the barracks. All hands except Pete and Sonny and a wiry-haired, thick-set corporal named Bonze had elected to see the show on the big screen in the mess hall. The reception was better there, of course, but, as Bonze put it, "you don't get close enough in a big place like that."

"I hope she's the same," said Sonny, half to himself.

Why should she be? thought Pete morosely as he turned on the set and watched the screen begin to glow. There were many more of the golden speckles that had killed reception for the past two weeks. Why should anything be the same, ever again?

He fought a sudden temptation to kick the set to pieces. It, and Starr Anthim, were part of something that was dead. The country was dead, a real country— prosperous, sprawling, laughing, grabbing, growing and changing, leprous in spots with poverty and injustice, but healthy enough to overcome any ill. He wondered how the murderers would like it. They were welcome to it, now. Nowhere to go. No one to fight. That was true for every soul on earth now.

"You hope she's the same," he muttered.

"The show, I mean," said Sonny mildly. "I'd like to just sit here and have it like . . . like—"

Oh, thought Pete mistily. Oh—that. Somewhere to go, that's what it is, for a few minutes. "I know," he said, all the harshness gone from his voice.

Noise receded from the audio as the carrier swept in. The light on the screen swirled and steadied into a diamond pattern. Pete adjusted the focus, chromic balance, and intensity. "Turn out the lights, Bonze. I don't want to see anything but Starr Anthim."

It *was* the same, at first. Starr Anthim had never used the usual fanfares, fade-ins, color, and clamor of her contemporaries. A black screen, then *click*, a blaze of gold. It was all there, in focus; tremendously intense, it did not change. Rather, the eye changed to take it in. She never moved for seconds after she came on; she was there, a portrait, a still face and a white throat. Her eyes were open and sleeping. Her face was alive and still.

Then, in the eyes which seemed green but were blue flecked with gold, an awareness seemed to gather, and they came awake. Only then was it noticeable that her lips were parted. Something in the eyes made the lips be seen, though nothing moved yet. Not until she bent her head slowly, so that some of the gold flecks seemed captured in the golden brows. The eyes were not, then, looking out at an audience. They were looking at me, and at *me*, and at ME.

"Hello—you," she said. She was a dream, with a kid sister's slightly irregular teeth.

Bonze shuddered. The cot on which he lay began to squeak rapidly. Sonny shifted in annoyance. Pete reached out in the dark and caught the leg of the cot. The squeaking subsided.

"May I sing a song?" Starr asked. There was music, very faint. "It's an old one, and one of the best. It's an easy song, a deep song, one that comes from the part of men and women that is mankind—the part that has in it no greed, no hate, no fear. This song is about joyousness and strength. It's—my favorite. Isn't it yours?"

The music swelled. Pete recognized the first two notes of the introduction and swore quietly. This was wrong. This song was not for . . . this song was part of—

Sonny sat raptly. Bonze lay still.

Starr Anthim began to sing. Her voice was deep and powerful, but soft, with the merest touch of vibrato at the ends of the phrases. The song flowed from her without noticeable effort, seeming to come from her face, her long hair, her wide-set eyes. Her voice, like her face, was shadowed and clean, round, blue and green but mostly gold:

> *"When you gave me your heart, you gave me the world,*
> *You gave me the night and the day,*
> *And thunder, and roses, and sweet green grass,*
> *The sea, and soft wet clay.*

> *"I drank the dawn from a golden cup,*
> *From a silver one, the dark,*

The steed I rode was the wild west wind,
My song was the brook and the lark."

The music spiraled, caroled, slid into a somber cry of muted, hungry sixths and ninths; rose, blared, and cut, leaving her voice full and alone:

"With thunder I smote the evil of earth,
With roses I won the right,
With the sea I washed, and with clay I built,
And the world was a place of light!"

The last note left a face perfectly composed again, and there was no movement in it; it was sleeping and vital while the music curved off and away to the places where music rests when it is not heard.

Starr smiled.

"It's so easy," she said. "So simple. All that is fresh and clean and strong about mankind is in that song, and I think that's all that need concern us about mankind." She leaned forward. "Don't you see?"

The smile faded and was replaced with a gentle wonder. A tiny furrow appeared between her brows; she drew back quickly. "I can't seem to talk to you tonight," she said, her voice small. "You hate something."

Hate was shaped like a monstrous mushroom. Hate was the random speckling of a video plate.

"What has happened to us," said Starr abruptly, impersonally, "is simple, too. It doesn't matter who did it—do you understand that? *It doesn't matter.* We were attacked. We were struck from the east and from the west. Most of the bombs were atomic—there were blast bombs and there were dust bombs. We were hit by about five hundred and thirty bombs altogether, and it has killed us."

She waited.

Sonny's fist smacked into his palm. Bonze lay with his eyes open, quiet. Pete's jaws hurt.

"We have more bombs than both of them put together. We *have* them. We are not going to use them. *Wait!*" She raised her hands suddenly, as if she could see into each man's face. They sank back, tense.

"So saturated is the atmosphere with Carbon Fourteen that all of us in this hemisphere are going to die. Don't be afraid to say it. Don't be afraid to think it. It is a truth, and it must be faced. As the transmutation effect spreads from the ruins of our cities, the air will become increasingly radioactive, and then we must die. In months, in a year or so, the effects will be strong overseas. Most of the people there will die, too. None will escape completely. A worse thing will come to them than anything they gave us, because there will be a wave of horror and madness which is impossible to us. We are merely going to die. They will live and burn and sicken, and the children that will be born to them—" She shook her head, and her lower lip grew full. She visibly pulled herself together.

"Five hundred and thirty bombs—I don't think either of our attackers knew just how strong the other was. There has been so much secrecy." Her voice was sad. She shrugged slightly. "They have killed us, and they have ruined themselves. As for us—we are not blameless, either. Neither are we helpless to do anything— yet. But what we must do is hard. We must die—without striking back."

She gazed briefly at each man in turn, from the screen. "We must *not* strike back. Mankind is about to go through a hell of his own making. We can be vengeful—or merciful, if you like—and let go with the hundreds of bombs we have. That would sterilize the planet so that not a microbe, not a blade of grass could escape, and nothing new could grow. We would reduce the earth to a bald thing, dead and deadly.

"No, it just won't do. We can't do it.

"Remember the song? *That* is humanity. That's in all humans. A disease made other humans our enemies for a time, but as the generations march past, enemies become friends and friends enemies. The enmity of those who have killed us is such a tiny, temporary thing in the long sweep of history!"

Her voice deepened. "Let us die with the knowledge that we have done the one noble thing left to us. The spark of humanity can still live and grow on this planet. It will be blown and drenched, shaken and all but extinguished, but it will live if that song is a true one. It will live if we are human enough to discount the fact that the spark is in the custody of our temporary enemy. Some—a few—of his children will live to merge with the new humanity that will gradually emerge from the jungles and the wilderness. Perhaps there will be ten thousand years of beastliness; perhaps man will be able to rebuild while he still has his ruins."

She raised her head, her voice tolling. "And even if this is the end of humankind, we dare not take away the chances some other life form might have to succeed where we failed. If we retaliate, there will not be a dog, a deer, an ape, a bird or fish or lizard to carry the evolutionary torch. In the name of justice, if we must condemn and destroy ourselves, let us not condemn all life along with us! We are heavy enough with sins. If we must destroy, let us stop with destroying ourselves!"

There was a shimmering flicker of music. It seemed to stir her hair like a breath of wind. She smiled.

"That's all," she whispered. And to each man there she said, "Good night—"

The screen went black. As the carrier cut off—there was no announcement—the ubiquitous speckles began to swarm across it.

Pete rose and switched on the lights. Bonze and Sonny were quite still. It must have been minutes later when Sonny sat up straight, shaking himself like a puppy. Something besides the silence seemed to tear with the movement.

He said softly, "You're not allowed to fight anything, or to run away, or to live, and now you can't even hate any more, because Starr says 'no.' "

There was bitterness in the sound of it, and a bitter smell to the air.

Pete Mawser sniffed once, which had nothing to do with the smell. He froze, sniffed again. "What's that smell, Son'?"

Sonny tested it. "I don't—Something familiar. Vanilla—no . . . no.

"Almonds. Bitter—*Bonze!*"

Bonze lay still with his eyes open, grinning. His jaw muscles were knotted, and they could see almost all his teeth. He was soaking wet.

"Bonze!"

"It was just when she came on and said 'Hello—you,' remember?" whispered Pete. "Oh, the poor kid. That's why he wanted to catch the show here instead of in the mess hall."

"Went out looking at her," said Sonny through pale lips. "I can't say I blame him much. Wonder where he got the stuff."

"Never mind that." Pete's voice was harsh. "Let's get out of here."

They left to call the meat wagon. Bonze lay watching the console with his dead eyes and his smell of bitter almonds.

Pete did not realize where he was going, or exactly why, until he found himself on the dark street near GHQ and the communications shack. It had something to do with Bonze. Not that he wanted to do what Bonze had done. But then he hadn't thought of it. What would he have done if he'd thought of it? Nothing, probably. But still—it might be nice to be able to hear Starr, and see her, whenever he felt like it. Maybe there weren't any recordings, but her musical background was recorded, and the Sig might have dubbed the show off.

He stood uncertainly outside the GHQ building. There was a cluster of men outside the main entrance. Pete smiled briefly. Rain, nor snow, nor sleet, nor gloom of night could stay the stage-door Johnny.

He went down the side street and up the delivery ramp in the back. Two doors along the platform was the rear exit of the communications section.

There was a light on in the communications shack. He had his hand out to the screen door when he noticed someone standing in the shadows beside it. The light played daintily on the golden margins of a head and face.

He stopped. "Starr Anthim!"

"Hello, soldier. Sergeant."

He blushed like an adolescent. "I—" His voice left him. He swallowed, reached up to whip off his hat. He had no hat. "I saw the show," he said. He felt clumsy. It was dark, and yet he was very conscious of the fact that his dress shoes were indifferently shined.

She moved toward him into the light, and she was so beautiful that he had to close his eyes. "What's your name?"

"Mawser. Pete Mawser."

"Like the show?"

Not looking at her, he said stubbornly, "No."

"Oh?"

"I mean . . . I liked it some. The song."

"I . . . think I see."

"I wondered if I could maybe get a recording."

"I think so," she said. "What kind of a reproducer have you got?"

"Audiovid."

"A disk. Yes; we dubbed off a few. Wait, I'll get you one."

She went inside, moving slowly. Pete watched her, spellbound. She was a silhouette, crowned and haloed; and then she was a framed picture, vivid and golden. He waited, watching the light hungrily. She returned with a large envelope, called good night to someone inside, and came out on the platform.

"Here you are, Pete Mawser."

"Thanks very—" he mumbled. He wet his lips. "It was very good of you."

"Not really. The more it circulates, the better." She laughed suddenly. "That isn't meant quite as it sounds. I'm not exactly looking for new publicity these days."

The stubbornness came back. "I don't know that you'd get it, if you put on that show in normal times."

Her eyebrows went up. "Well!" she smiled. "I seem to have made quite an impression."

"I'm sorry," he said warmly. "I shouldn't have taken that tack. Everything you think and say these days is exaggerated."

"I know what you mean." She looked around. "How is it here?"

"It's O.K. I used to be bothered by the secrecy, and being buried miles away from civilization." He chuckled bitterly. "Turned out to be lucky after all."

"You sound like the first chapter of *One World or None*."

He looked up quickly. "What do you use for a reading list—the Government's own '*Index Expurgatorius*'?"

She laughed. "Come now—it isn't as bad as all that. The book was never banned. It was just—"

"—Unfashionable," he filled in.

"Yes, more's the pity. If people had paid more attention to it when it was published, perhaps this wouldn't have happened."

He followed her gaze to the dimly pulsating sky. "How long are you going to be here?"

"Until . . . as long as . . . I'm not leaving."

"You're not?"

"I'm finished," she said simply. "I've covered all the ground I can. I've been everywhere that . . . anyone knows about."

"With this show?"

She nodded. "With this particular message."

He was quiet, thinking. She turned to the door, and he put out his hand, not touching her. "Please—"

"What is it?"

"I'd like to . . . I mean, if you don't mind, I don't often have a chance to talk to— Maybe you'd like to walk around a little before you turn in."

"Thanks, no, Sergeant. I'm tired." She did sound tired. "I'll see you around."

He stared at her, a sudden fierce light in his brain. "I know where it is. It's got a red-topped lever and a tag referring to orders of the commanding officer. It's really camouflaged."

She was quiet so long that he thought she had not heard him. Then, "I'll take that walk."

They went down the ramp together and turned toward the dark parade ground.

"How did you know?" she asked quietly.

"Not too tough. This 'message' of yours; the fact that you've been all over the country with it; most of all, the fact that somebody finds it necessary to persuade us not to strike back. Who are you working for?" he asked bluntly.

Surprisingly, she laughed.

"What's that for?"

"A moment ago you were blushing and shuffling your feet."

His voice was rough. "I wasn't talking to a human being. I was talking to a thousand songs I've heard, and a hundred thousand blond pictures I've seen pinned up. You'd better tell me what this is all about."

She stopped. "Let's go up and see the colonel."

He took her elbow. "No. I'm just a sergeant, and he's high brass, and that doesn't make any difference at all now. You're a human being, and so am I, and I'm supposed to respect your rights as such. I don't. You're a woman, and—"

She stiffened. He kept her walking, and finished, "—and that will make as much difference as I let it. You'd better tell me about it."

"All right," she said, with a tired acquiescence that frightened something inside him. "You seem to have guessed right, though. It's true. There are master firing keys for the launching sites. We have located and dismantled all but two. It's very likely that one of the two was vaporized. The other one is—lost."

"Lost?"

"I don't have to tell you about the secrecy," she said disgustedly. "You know how it developed between nation and nation. You must know that it existed between State and Union, between department and department, office and office. There were only three or four men who knew where all the keys were. Three of them were in the Pentagon when it went up. That was the third blast bomb, you know. If there was another, it could only have been Senator Vandercook, and he died three weeks ago without talking."

"An automatic radio key, hm-m-m?"

"That's right. Sergeant, must we walk? I'm so tired—"

"I'm sorry," he said impulsively. They crossed to the reviewing stand and sat on the lonely benches. "Launching racks all over, all hidden, and all armed?"

"Most of them are armed. Enough. Armed and aimed."

"Aimed where?"

"It doesn't matter."

"I think I see. What's the optimum number again?"

"About six hundred and forty; a few more or less. At least five hundred and thirty have been thrown so far. We don't know exactly."

"Who are *we?*" he asked furiously.

"Who? Who?" She laughed weakly. "I could say, 'The Government,' perhaps. If the President dies, the Vice President takes over, and then the Speaker of the House, and so on and on. How far can you go? Pete Mawser, don't you realize yet what's happened?"

"I don't know what you mean."

"How many people do you think are left in this country?"

"I don't know. Just a few million, I guess."

"How many are here?"

"About nine hundred."

"Then as far as I know, this is the largest city left."

He leaped to his feet. "*NO!*" The syllable roared away from him, hurled itself against the dark, empty buildings, came back to him in a series of lower-case echoes: nononono . . . no-no—n . . .

Starr began to speak rapidly, quietly. "They're scattered all over the fields and the roads. They sit in the sun and die in the afternoon. They run in packs, they tear at each other. They pray and starve and kill themselves and die in the fires. The fires—everywhere, if anything stands, it's burning. Summer, and the leaves all down in the Berkshires, and the blue grass burnt brown; you can see the grass dying from the air, the death going out wider and wider from the bald spots. Thunder and roses . . . I saw roses, new ones, creeping from the smashed pots of a greenhouse. Brown petals, alive and sick, and the thorns turned back on themselves, growing into the stems, killing. Feldman died tonight."

He let her be quiet for a time. "Who is Feldman?"

"My pilot." She was talking hollowly into her hands. "He's been dying for weeks. He's been on his nerve ends. I don't think he had any blood left. He buzzed your GHQ and made for the landing strip. He came in with the motor dead, free rotors, giro. Smashed the landing gear. He was dead, too. He killed a man in Chicago so he could steal gas. The man didn't want the gas. There was a dead girl by the pump. He didn't want us to go near. I'm not going anywhere. I'm going to stay here. I'm tired."

At last she cried.

Pete left her alone, and walked out to the center of the parade ground, looking back at the faint huddled glimmer on the bleachers. His mind flickered over the show that evening, and the way she had sung before the merciless transmitter. "Hello—you." "If we must destroy, let us stop with destroying ourselves!"

The dimming spark of humankind—what could it mean to her? How could it mean so much?

"Thunder and roses." Twisted, sick, nonsurvival roses, killing themselves with their own thorns.

"And the world was a place of light!" Blue light, flickering in the contaminated air.

The enemy. The red-topped lever. Bonze. "They pray and starve and kill themselves and die in the fires."

What creatures were these, these corrupted, violent, murdering humans? What right had they to another chance? What was in them that was good?

Starr was good. Starr was crying. Only a human being could cry like that. Starr was a human being.

Had humanity anything of Starr Anthim in it?

Starr *was* a human being.

He looked down through the darkness for his hands. No planet, no universe, is greater to a man than his own ego, his own observing self. These hands were the hands of all history, and like the hands of all men, they could by their small acts make human history or end it. Whether this power of hands was that of a billion hands, or whether it came to a focus in these two—this was suddenly unimportant to the eternities which now infolded him.

He put humanity's hands deep in his pockets and walked slowly back to the bleachers.

"Starr."

She responded with a sleepy-child, interrogative whimper.

"They'll get their chance, Starr. I won't touch the key."

She sat straight. She rose, and came to him, smiling. He could see her smile because, very faintly in this air, her teeth fluoresced. She put her hands on his shoulders. "Pete."

He held her very close for a moment. Her knees buckled then, and he had to carry her.

There was no one in the Officers' Club, which was the nearest building. He stumbled in, moved clawing along the wall until he found a switch. The light hurt him. He carried her to a settee and put her down gently. She did not move. One side of her face was as pale as milk.

There was blood on his hands.

He stood looking stupidly at it, wiped it on the sides of his trousers, looking dully at Starr. There was blood on her shirt.

The echo of no's came back to him from the far walls of the big room before he knew he had spoken. Starr wouldn't do this. She couldn't!

A doctor. But there was no doctor. Not since Anders had hung himself. Get somebody. *Do* something.

He dropped to his knees and gently unbuttoned her shirt. Between the sturdy, unfeminine GI bra and the top of her slacks, there was blood on her side. He whipped out a clean handkerchief and began to wipe it away. There was no wound, no puncture. But abruptly there was blood again. He blotted it carefully. And again there was blood.

It was like trying to dry a piece of ice with a towel.

He ran to the water cooler, wrung out the bloody handkerchief and ran back to her. He bathed her face carefully, the pale right side, the flushed left side. The handkerchief reddened again, this time with cosmetics, and then her face was pale all over, with great blue shadows under the eyes. While he watched, blood appeared on her left cheek.

There must be *somebody*—He fled to the door.

"Pete!"

Running, turning at the sound of her voice, he hit the doorpost stunningly, caromed off, flailed for his balance, and then was back at her side. "Starr! Hang on, now! I'll get a doctor as quick as—"

Her hand strayed over her left cheek. "You found out. Nobody else knew, but Feldman. It got hard to cover properly." Her hand went up to her hair.

"Starr, I'll get a—"

"Pete, darling, promise me something?"

"Why, sure; certainly, Starr."

"Don't disturb my hair. It isn't—all mine, you see." She sounded like a seven-year-old, playing a game. "It all came out on this side, you see? I don't want you to see me that way."

He was on his knees beside her again. "What is it? What happened to you?" he asked hoarsely.

"Philadelphia," she murmured. "Right at the beginning. The mushroom went up a half mile away. The studio caved in. I came to the next day. I didn't know I was burned, then. It didn't show. My left side. It doesn't matter, Pete. It doesn't hurt at all, now."

He sprang to his feet again. "I'm going for a doctor."

"Don't go away. Please don't go away and leave me. Please don't." There were tears in her eyes. "Wait just a little while. Not very long, Pete."

He sank to his knees again. She gathered both his hands in hers and held them tightly. She smiled happily. "You're good, Pete. You're so good."

(She couldn't hear the blood in his ears, the roar of the whirlpool of hate and fear and anguish that spun inside him.)

She talked to him in a low voice, and then in whispers. Sometimes he hated himself because he couldn't quite follow her. She talked about school, and her first audition. "I was so scared that I got a vibrato in my voice. I'd never had one before. I always let myself get a little scared when I sing now. It's easy." There was something about a windowbox when she was four years old. "Two real live tulips and a pitcherplant. I used to be sorry for the flies."

There was a long period of silence after that, during which his muscles throbbed with cramp and stiffness, and gradually became numb. He must have dozed; he awoke with a violent start, feeling her fingers on his face. She was propped up on one elbow. She said clearly, "I just wanted to tell you, darling. Let me go first, and get everything ready for you. It's going to be wonderful. I'll fix you a special tossed salad. I'll make you a steamed chocolate pudding and keep it hot for you."

Too muddled to understand what she was saying, he smiled and pressed her back on the settee. She took his hands again.

The next time he awoke it was broad daylight, and she was dead.

Sonny Weisefreund was sitting on his cot when he got back to the barracks. He handed over the recording he had picked up from the parade ground on the way back. "Dew on it. Dry it off. Good boy," he croaked, and fell face downward on the cot Bonze had used.

Sonny stared at him. "Pete! Where've you been? What happened? Are you all right?"

Pete shifted a little and grunted. Sonny shrugged and took the audiovid disk out of its wet envelope. Moisture would not harm it particularly, though it could not be played while wet. It was made of a fine spiral of plastic, insulated between laminations. Electrostatic pickups above and below the turntable would fluctuate with changes in the dielectric constant which had been impressed by the recording, and these changes were amplified for the video. The audio was a conventional hill-and-dale needle. Sonny began to wipe it down carefully.

Pete fought upward out of a vast, green-lit place full of flickering cold fires. Starr was calling him. Something was punching him, too. He fought it weakly, trying to hear what she was saying. But someone else was jabbering too loud for him to hear.

He opened his eyes. Sonny was shaking him, his round face pink with excitement. The audiovid was running. Starr was talking. Sonny got up impatiently and turned down the audio gain. "Pete! Pete! Wake up, will you? I got to tell you something. Listen to me! Wake up, will yuh?"

"Huh?"

"That's better. Now listen. I've just been listening to Starr Anthim—"

"She's dead," said Pete. Sonny didn't hear. He went on explosively, "I've figured it out. Starr was sent out here, and all over, to *beg* someone not to fire any more atom bombs. If the government was sure they wouldn't strike back, they wouldn't have taken the trouble. Somewhere, Pete, there's some way to launch bombs at those murdering cowards—and I've got a pret-ty shrewd idea of how to do it."

Pete strained groggily toward the faint sound of Starr's voice. Sonny talked on. "Now, s'posing there was a master radio key, an automatic code device something like the alarm signal they have on ships, that rings a bell on any ship within radio range when the operator sends four long dashes. Suppose there's an automatic code machine to launch bombs, with repeaters, maybe, buried all over the country. What would it be? Just a little lever to pull; thass all. How would the thing be hidden? In the middle of a lot of other equipment, that's where; in some place where you'd expect to find crazy-looking secret stuff. Like an experiment station. Like right here. You beginning to get the idea?"

"Shut up. I can't hear her."

"The hell with her! You can hear her some other time. You didn't hear a thing I said!"

"She's dead."

"Yeah. Well, I figure I'll pull that handle. What can I lose? It'll give those murderin' . . . *what?*"

"She's dead."

"Dead? Starr Anthim?" His young face twisted, Sonny sank down to the cot. "You're half asleep. You don't know what you're saying."

"She's dead," Pete said hoarsely. "She got burned by one of the first bombs. I was with her when she . . . she— Shut up, now, and get out of here and let me listen!" he bellowed hoarsely.

Sonny stood up slowly. "They killed her, too. They killed her. That does it. That just fixes it up." His face was white. He went out.

Pete got up. His legs weren't working right. He almost fell. He brought up against the console with a crash, his outflung arm sending the pickup skittering across the record. He put it on again and turned up the gain, then lay down to listen.

His head was all mixed up. Sonny talked too much. Bomb launchers, automatic code machines—

"*You gave me your heart,*" sang Starr. "*You gave me your heart. You gave me your heart. You—*"

Pete heaved himself up again and moved the pickup arm. Anger, not at himself, but at Sonny for causing him to cut the disk that way, welled up.

Starr was talking, stupidly, her face going through the same expression over and over again. "*Struck from the east and from the Struck from the east and from the—*"

He got up again wearily and moved the pickup.

"You gave me your heart. You gave me—"

Pete made an agonized sound that was not a word at all, bent, lifted, and sent the console crashing over. In the bludgeoning silence he said, "I did, too."

Then, "Sonny." He waited.

"*Sonny!*"

His eyes went wide then, and he cursed and bolted for the corridor.

The panel was closed when he reached it. He kicked at it. It flew open, discovering darkness.

"Hey!" bellowed Sonny. "Shut it! You turned off the lights!"

Pete shut it behind him. The lights blazed.

"Pete! What's the matter?"

"Nothing's the matter, Son'," croaked Pete.

"What are you looking at?" said Sonny uneasily.

"I'm sorry," said Pete as gently as he could. "I just wanted to find something out, is all. Did you tell anyone else about this?" He pointed to the lever.

"Why, no. I only just figured it out while you were sleeping, just now."

Pete looked around carefully while Sonny shifted his weight. Pete moved toward a tool rack. "Something you haven't noticed yet, Sonny," he said softly, and pointed. "Up there, on the wall behind you. High up. See?"

Sonny turned. In one fluid movement Pete plucked off a fourteen-inch box wrench and hit Sonny with it as hard as he could.

Afterward he went to work systematically on the power supplies. He pulled the plugs on the gas engines and cracked their cylinders with a maul. He knocked off the tubing of the Diesel starters—the tanks let go explosively—and he cut all the cables with bolt cutters. Then he broke up the relay rack and its lever. When he was quite finished, he put away his tools and bent and stroked Sonny's tousled hair.

He went out and closed the partition carefully. It certainly was a wonderful piece of camouflage. He sat down heavily on a workbench nearby.

"You'll have your chance," he said into the far future. "And by heaven, you'd better make good."

After that he just waited.

❀ JUDITH MERRIL (1923-1997)

Judith Merril has made numerous contributions to Fantasy and Science Fiction. She has been a successful writer, talented and prolific anthologist, editor, publisher, and more. Like Jack Williamson, Judith Merril continues to make contributions to the field that expand on her already impressive career and prove her to be a true visionary, scholar, and humanitarian. Merril has been a pioneer of Science Fiction and Fantasy history and preservation since the early 1950s, when she began assembling anthologies of Science and Speculative Fiction. In doing so, she collected and showcased the works of a number of authors, such as Carol Emshwiller and Kit Reed, who otherwise might remain unknown today. Her tastes were popular, mainstream, and eclectic, and she expanded the vision of the genre. In 1970, the Toronto Public Library founded her Merril Collection of Science Fiction Speculation and Fantasy. This institution and its massive collection are a landmark of Science Fiction and a going concern today. Merril has lived in both the United States and Canada.

As a writer, Judith Merril did much to advance Science Fiction and Fantasy as legitimate literary and artistic forms. She has also done much in regard to maintaining and expanding the traditions and legacies of female Science Fiction and Fantasy authors. Her first published story is a Science Fiction genre classic. It appeared in Astounding Science-Fiction *in 1948 and is entitled "That Only a Mother."*

That Only a Mother
(Astounding Science-Fiction, *June 1948*)

Margaret reached over to the other side of the bed where Hank should have been. Her hand patted the empty pillow, and then she came altogether awake, wondering that the old habit should remain after so many months. She tried to curl up, cat-style, to hoard her own warmth, found she couldn't do it any more, and climbed out of bed with a pleased awareness of her increasingly clumsy bulkiness.

Morning motions were automatic. On the way through the kitchenette, she pressed the button that would start breakfast cooking—the doctor had said to eat as much breakfast as she could—and tore the paper out of the facsimile machine. She folded the long sheet carefully to the "National News" section, and propped it on the bathroom shelf to scan while she brushed her teeth.

No accidents. No direct hits. At least none that had been officially released for publication. *Now, Maggie, don't get started on that. No accidents. No hits. Take the nice newspaper's word for it.*

The three clear chimes from the kitchen announced that breakfast was ready. She set a bright napkin and cheerful colored dishes on the table in a futile attempt to appeal to a faulty morning appetite. Then, when there was nothing more to prepare, she went for the mail, allowing herself the full pleasure of prolonged anticipation, because today there would *surely* be a letter.

There was. There were. Two bills and a worried note from her mother: "Darling. Why didn't you write and tell me sooner? I'm thrilled, of course, but, well, one hates to mention these things, but are you *certain* the doctor was right? Hank's been around all that uranium or thorium or whatever it is all these years, and I know you say he's a designer, not a technician, and he doesn't get near anything that might be dangerous, but you know he used to, back at Oak Ridge. Don't you think . . . well, of course, I'm just being a foolish old woman, and I don't want you to get upset. You know much more about it than I do, and I'm sure your doctor was right. He *should* know . . ."

Margaret made a face over the excellent coffee, and caught herself refolding the paper to the medical news.

Stop it, Maggie, stop it! The radiologist said Hank's job couldn't have exposed him. And the bombed area we drove past . . . No, no. Stop it, now! Read the social notes or the recipes, Maggie girl.

A well-known geneticist, in the medical news, said that it was possible to tell with absolute certainty, at five months, whether the child would be normal, or at least whether the mutation was likely to produce anything freakish. The worst cases, at any rate, could be prevented. Minor mutations, of course, displacements in facial features, or changes in brain structure could not be detected. And there had been some cases recently, of normal embryos with atrophied limbs that did not develop beyond the seventh or eighth month. But, the doctor concluded cheerfully, the *worst* cases could now be predicted and prevented.

"Predicted and prevented." We predicted it, didn't we? Hank and the others, they predicted it. But we didn't prevent it. We could have stopped it in '46 and '47. Now . . .

Margaret decided against the breakfast. Coffee had been enough for her in the morning for ten years; it would have to do for today. She buttoned herself into interminable folds of material that, the salesgirl had assured her, was the *only* comfortable thing to wear during the last few months. With a surge of pure pleasure, the letter and newspaper forgotten, she realized she was on the next to the last button. It wouldn't be long now.

The city in the early morning had always been a special kind of excitement for her. Last night it had rained, and the sidewalks were still damp-gray instead of dusty. The air smelled the fresher, to a city-bred woman, for the occasional pungency of acrid factory smoke. She walked the six blocks to work, watching the lights go out in the all-night hamburger joints, where the plate-glass walls were already catching the sun, and the lights go on in the dim interiors of cigar stores and drycleaning establishments.

The office was in a new Government building. In the rolovator, on the way up, she felt, as always, like a frankfurter roll in the ascending half of an old-style rotary toasting machine. She abandoned the air-foam cushioning gratefully at the fourteenth floor, and settled down behind her desk, at the rear of a long row of identical desks.

Each morning the pile of papers that greeted her was a little higher. These were, as everyone knew, the decisive months. The war might be won or lost on these calculations as well as any others. The manpower office had switched her here when her old expediter's job got to be too strenuous. The computer was easy to operate, and the work was absorbing, if not as exciting as the old job. But you didn't just stop working these days. Everyone who could do anything at all was needed.

And—she remembered the interview with the psychologist—*I'm probably the unstable type. Wonder what sort of neurosis I'd get sitting home reading that sensational paper . . .*

She plunged into the work without pursuing the thought.

February 18.

Hank darling,

Just a note—from the hospital, no less. I had a dizzy spell at work, and the doctor took it to heart. Blessed if I know what I'll do with myself lying in bed for weeks, just waiting—but Dr. Boyer seems to think it may not be so long.

There are too many newspapers around here. More infanticides all the time, and they can't seem to get a jury to convict any of them. It's the fathers who do it. Lucky thing you're not around, in case—

Oh, darling, that wasn't a very *funny* joke, was it? Write as often as you can, will you? I have too much time to think. But there really isn't anything wrong, and nothing to worry about.

Write often, and remember I love you.

MAGGIE.

SPECIAL SERVICE TELEGRAM
FEBRUARY 21, 1953
22:04 LK37G

FROM: TECH. LIEUT. H. MARVELL
X47-016 GCNY
TO: MRS. H. MARVELL
WOMEN'S HOSPITAL
NEW YORK CITY

HAD DOCTOR'S GRAM STOP WILL ARRIVE FOUR OH TEN STOP SHORT LEAVE STOP YOU DID IT MAGGIE STOP LOVE HANK

February 25.

Hank dear,

So you didn't see the baby either? You'd think a place this size would at least have visiplates on the incubators, so the fathers could get a look, even if the poor benighted mommas can't. They tell me I won't see her for another week, or maybe more—but of course, mother always warned me if I didn't slow my pace, I'd probably even have my babies too fast. Why must she *always* be right?

Did you meet that battle-ax of a nurse they put on here? I imagine they save her for people who've already had theirs, and don't let her get too near the prospectives—but a woman like that simply shouldn't be allowed in a maternity ward. She's obsessed with mutations, can't seem to talk about anything else. Oh, well, *ours* is all right, even if it was in an unholy hurry.

I'm tired. They warned me not to sit up so soon, but I *had* to write you. All my love, darling,

MAGGIE.

February 29.

Darling,

I finally got to see her! It's all true, what they say about new babies and the face that only a mother could love—but it's all there, darling, eyes, ears, and noses—no, only one!—all in the right places. We're so *lucky*, Hank.

I'm afraid I've been a rambunctious patient. I kept telling that hatchet-faced female with the mutation mania that I wanted to *see* the baby. Finally the doctor came in to "explain" everything to me, and talking a lot of nonsense, most of which I'm sure no one could have understood, any more than I did. The only thing I got out of it was that she didn't actually *have* to stay in the incubator; they just thought it was "wiser."

I think I got a little hysterical at that point. Guess I was more worried than I was willing to admit, but I threw a small fit about it. The whole business wound up with one of those hushed medical conferences outside the door, and finally the Woman in White said: "Well, we might as well. Maybe it'll work out better that way."

I'd heard about the way doctors and nurses in these places develop a God complex, and believe me it is as true figuratively as it is literally that a mother hasn't got a leg to stand on around here.

I *am* awfully weak, still. I'll write again soon. Love,

MAGGIE.

March 8.

Dearest Hank,

Well, the nurse was wrong if she told you that. She's an idiot anyhow. It's a girl. It's easier to tell with babies than with cats, and *I know*. How about Henrietta?

I'm home again, and busier than a betatron. They got *everything* mixed up at the hospital, and I had to teach myself how to bathe her and do just about everything else. She's getting prettier, too. When can you get a leave, a *real* leave?

Love,
MAGGIE.

May 26.

Hank dear,

You should see her now—and you shall. I'm sending along a reel of color movie. My mother sent her those nighties with drawstrings all over. I put one on, and right now she looks like a snow-white potato sack with that beautiful, beautiful flower-face blooming on top. Is that *me* talking? Am I a doting mother? But wait till you *see* her!

July 10.

. . . Believe it or not, as you like, but your daughter can talk, and I don't mean baby talk. Alice discovered it—she's a dental assistant in the WACs, you know—and when she heard the baby giving out what I thought was a string of gibberish, she said the kid knew words and sentences, but couldn't say them clearly because she has no teeth yet. I'm taking her to a speech specialist.

September 13.

. . . We have a prodigy for real! Now that all her front teeth are in, her speech is perfectly clear and—a new talent now—she can sing! I mean really carry a tune! At seven months! Darling, my world would be perfect if you could only get home.

November 19.

. . . at last. The little goon was so busy being clever, it took her all this time to learn to crawl. The doctor says development in these cases is always erratic . . .

SPECIAL SERVICE TELEGRAM
DECEMBER 1, 1953
08:47 LK59F

FROM: TECH. LIEUT. H. MARVELL
X47-016 GCNY
TO: Mrs. H. MARVELL
APT. K-17
504 E. 19 ST.
N.Y. N.Y.

WEEK'S LEAVE STARTS TOMORROW STOP WILL ARRIVE AIRPORT TEN OH FIVE STOP DON'T MEET ME STOP LOVE LOVE LOVE HANK

Margaret let the water run out of the bathinette until only a few inches were left, and then loosed her hold on the wriggling baby.

"I think it was better when you were retarded, young woman," she informed her daughter happily. "You *can't* crawl in a bathinette, you know."

"Then why can't I go in the bathtub?" Margaret was used to her child's volubility by now, but every now and then it caught her unawares. She swooped the resistant mass of pink flesh into a towel, and began to rub.

"Because you're too little, and your head is very soft, and bathtubs are very hard."

"Oh. Then when can I go in the bathtub?"

"When the outside of your head is as hard as the inside, brainchild." She reached toward a pile of fresh clothing. "I cannot understand," she added, pinning a square of cloth through the nightgown, "why a child of your intelligence can't learn to keep a diaper on the way other babies do. They've been used for centuries, you know, with perfectly satisfactory results."

The child disdained to reply; she had heard it too often. She waited, patiently until she had been tucked, clean and sweet-smelling, into a white-painted crib. Then she favored her mother with a smile that inevitably made Margaret think of the first golden edge of the sun bursting into a rosy predawn. She remembered Hank's reaction to the color pictures of his beautiful daughter, and with the thought, realized how late it was.

"Go to sleep, puss. When you wake up, you know, your *daddy* will be here."

"Why?" asked the four-year-old mind, waging a losing battle to keep the ten-month-old body awake.

Margaret went into the kitchenette and set the timer for the roast. She examined the table, and got her clothes from the closet, new dress, new shoes, new slip, new everything, bought weeks before and saved for the day Hank's telegram came. She stopped to pull a paper from the facsimile, and, with clothes and news, went into the bathroom and lowered herself gingerly into the steaming luxury of a scented bath.

She glanced through the paper with indifferent interest. Today at least there was no need to read the national news. There was an article by a geneticist. The same geneticist. Mutations, he said, were increasing disproportionately. It was too soon for recessives; even the first mutants, born near Hiroshima and Nagasaki in 1946 and 1947 were not old enough yet to breed. *But my baby's all right.* Apparently, there was some degree of free radiation from atomic explosions causing the trouble. *My baby's fine. Precocious, but normal.* If more attention had been paid to the first Japanese mutations, he said . . .

There was that little notice in the paper in the spring of '47. That was when Hank quit at Oak Ridge. "Only 2 or 3 percent of those guilty of infanticide are being caught and punished in Japan today . . ." *But* MY BABY'S *all right.*

She was dressed, combed, and ready to the last light brush-on of lip paste, when the door chime sounded. She dashed for the door, and heard for the first time in eighteen months the almost-forgotten sound of a key turning in the lock before the chime had quite died away.

"Hank!"

"Maggie!"

And then there was nothing to say. So many days, so many months of small news piling up, so many things to tell him, and now she just stood there, staring at a khaki uniform and a stranger's pale face. She traced the features with the finger of memory. The same high-bridged nose, wide-set eyes, fine feathery brows; the same long jaw, the hair a little farther back now on the high forehead, the same tilted curve to his mouth. Pale . . . Of course, he'd been underground all this time. And strange, stranger because of lost familiarity than any newcomer's face could be.

She had time to think all that before his hand reached out to touch her, and spanned the gap of eighteen months. Now, again, there was nothing to say, because there was no need. They were together, and for the moment that was enough.

"Where's the baby?"

"Sleeping. She'll be up any minute."

No urgency. Their voices were as casual as though it were a daily exchange, as though war and separation did not exist. Margaret picked up the coat he'd thrown on the chair near the door, and hung it carefully in the hall closet. She went to check the roast, leaving him to wander through the rooms by himself, remembering and coming back. She found him, finally, standing over the baby's crib.

She couldn't see his face, but she had no need to.

"I think we can wake her just this once." Margaret pulled the covers down and lifted the white bundle from the bed. Sleepy lids pulled back heavily from smoky brown eyes.

"Hello." Hank's voice was tentative.

"Hello." The baby's assurance was more pronounced.

He had heard about it, of course, but that wasn't the same as hearing it. He turned eagerly to Margaret. "She really can——?"

"Of course she can, darling. But what's more important, she can even do nice normal things like other babies do, even stupid ones. Watch her crawl!" Margaret set the baby on the big bed.

For a moment young Henrietta lay and eyed her parents dubiously.

"Crawl?" she asked.

"That's the idea. Your daddy is new around here, you know. He wants to see you show off."

"Then put me on my tummy."

"Oh, of course." Margaret obligingly rolled the baby over.

"What's the matter?" Hank's voice was still casual, but an undercurrent in it began to charge the air of the room. "I thought they turned over first."

"This baby"—Margaret would not notice the tension—"*This* baby does things when she wants to."

This baby's father watched with softening eyes while the head advanced and the body hunched up propelling itself across the bed.

"Why, the little rascal." He burst into relieved laughter. "She looks like one of those potato-sack racers they used to have on picnics. Got her arms pulled out of the sleeves already." He reached over and grabbed the knot at the bottom of the long nightie.

"I'll do it, darling." Margaret tried to get there first.

"Don't be silly, Maggie. This may be *your* first baby, but *I* had five kid brothers." He laughed her away, and reached with his other hand for the string that closed one sleeve. He opened the sleeve bow, and groped for an arm.

"The way you wriggle," he addressed his child sternly, as his hand touched a moving knob of flesh at the shoulder, "anyone might think you are a worm, using your tummy to crawl on, instead of your hands and feet."

Margaret stood and watched, smiling. "Wait till you hear her sing, darling—"

His right hand traveled down from the shoulder to where he thought an arm would be, traveled down, and straight down, over firm small muscles that writhed in an attempt to move against the pressure of his hand. He let his fingers drift up again to the shoulder. With infinite care he opened the knot at the bottom of the nightgown. His wife was standing by the bed, saying, "She can do 'Jingle Bells,' and—"

His left hand felt along the soft knitted fabric of the gown, up toward the diaper that folded, flat and smooth, across the bottom end of his child. No wrinkles. No kicking. *No . . .*

"Maggie." He tried to pull his hands from the neat fold in the diaper, from the wriggling body. "Maggie." His throat was dry; words came hard, low and grating. He spoke very slowly, thinking the sound of each word to make himself say it. His head was spinning, but he had to *know* before he let it go. "Maggie, why . . . didn't you . . . tell me?"

"Tell you what, darling?" Margaret's poise was the immemorial patience of woman confronted with man's childish impetuosity. Her sudden laugh sounded fantastically easy and natural in that room; it was all clear to her now. "Is she wet? I didn't know."

She didn't know. His hands, beyond control, ran up and down the soft-skinned baby body, the sinuous, limbless body. *Oh God, dear God*—his head shook and his muscles contracted in a bitter spasm of hysteria. His fingers tightened on his child—*Oh God, she didn't know . . .*

✠ LEIGH (DOUGLASS) BRACKETT (1915-1978)

Author of numerous short stories, novels, motion picture screenplays, and more, Leigh Brackett was one of the top woman writers of twentieth-century popular fiction in general, and Science Fiction specifically. Brackett's Science Fiction stories were often, but were not limited to, Space Operas reminiscent of Edgar Rice Burroughs's John Carter of Mars *and* Carson of Venus *tales. She also wrote Western Fiction and Detective Fiction. Influenced by past literary tradition, Brackett was an important teacher of aspiring authors. Ray Bradbury may have been her most famous student, and Bradbury himself acknowledges an extensive debt to Brackett. The pair collaborated on the now legendary short pulp novel,* Lorelei of the Red Mist, *which appeared in the Summer 1946 issue of* Planet Stories.

Leigh Brackett is remembered for her contributions to magazines such as Planet Stories, Startling Stories, *and* Thrilling Wonder Stories; *her Eric John Stark adventures (which appeared in two series—one in the 1940s, the other in the 1970s); her screenplays—including a 1946 adaptation (with William Faulkner) of Raymond Chandler's famous novel of Detective Fiction entitled* The Big Sleep, *a landmark John Wayne motion picture vehicle entitled* Rio Bravo *(1958), and the script for the second Star Wars movie,* The Empire Strikes Back *(1979); and her own Crime Fiction. Her critically acclaimed novel* The Long Tomorrow *(1955), a classic tale of postapocalypse America, is reflective of the Cold War era in which it was written. Leigh Brackett married famous popular author Edmond Hamilton, and both influenced and was influenced by his work. Like Robert Bloch, she was one of those extraordinary authors who was highly emulated, revered, and truly loved by her fellow writers.*

"The Enchantress of Venus" is one of Leigh Brackett's 1940s Eric John Stark Space Operas.

The Enchantress of Venus

(Planet Stories, *Fall 1949*)

1

The ship moved slowly across the Red Sea, through the shrouding veils of mist, her sail barely filled by the languid thrust of the wind. Her hull, of a thin light metal, floated without sound, the surface of the strange ocean parting before her prow in silent rippling streamers of flame.

Night deepened toward the ship, a river of indigo flowing out of the west. The man known as Stark stood alone by the after rail and watched its coming. He was full of impatience and a gathering sense of danger, so that it seemed to him that even the hot wind smelled of it.

The steersman lay drowsily over his sweep. He was a big man, with skin and hair the color of milk. He did not speak, but Stark felt that now and again the man's eyes turned toward him, pale and calculating under half-closed lids, with a secret avarice.

The captain and the two other members of the little coasting vessel's crew were forward, at their evening meal. Once or twice Stark heard a burst of laughter, half-whispered and furtive. It was as though all four shared in some private joke, from which he was rigidly excluded.

The heat was oppressive. Sweat gathered on Stark's dark face. His shirt stuck to his back. The air was heavy with moisture, tainted with the muddy fecundity of the land that brooded westward behind the eternal fog.

There was something ominous about the sea itself. Even on its own world, the Red Sea is hardly more than legend. It lies behind the Mountains of White Cloud, the great barrier wall that hides away half a planet. Few men have gone beyond that barrier, into the vast mystery of Inner Venus. Fewer still have come back.

Stark was one of that handful. Three times before he had crossed the mountains, and once he had stayed for nearly a year. But he had never quite grown used to the Red Sea.

It was not water. It was gaseous, dense enough to float the buoyant hulls of the metal ships, and it burned perpetually with its deep inner fires. The mists that clouded it were stained with the bloody glow. Beneath the surface Stark could see the drifts of flame where the lazy currents ran, and the little coiling bursts of sparks that came upward and spread and melted into other bursts, so that the face of the sea was like a cosmos of crimson stars.

It was very beautiful, glowing against the blue, luminous darkness of the night. Beautiful, and strange.

There was a padding of bare feet, and the captain, Malthor, came up to Stark, his outline dim and ghostly in the gloom.

"We will reach Shuruun," he said, "before the second glass is run."

Stark nodded. "Good."

The voyage had seemed endless, and the close confinement of the narrow deck had got badly on his nerves.

"You will like Shuruun," said the captain jovially. "Our wine, our food, our women—all superb. We don't have many visitors. We keep to ourselves, as you will see. But those who do come . . ."

He laughed, and clapped Stark on the shoulder. "Ah, yes. You will be happy in Shuruun!"

It seemed to Stark that he caught an echo of laughter from the unseen crew, as though they listened and found a hidden jest in Malthor's words.

Stark said, "That's fine."

"Perhaps," said Malthor, "you would like to lodge with me. I could make you a good price."

He had made a good price for Stark's passage from up the coast. An exorbitantly good one.

Stark said, "No."

"You don't have to be afraid," said the Venusian, in a confidential tone. "The strangers who come to Shuruun all have the same reason. It's a good place to hide. We're out of everybody's reach."

He paused, but Stark did not rise to his bait. Presently he chuckled and went on, "In fact, it's such a safe place that most of the strangers decide to stay on. Now, at my house, I could give you . . ."

Stark said again, flatly, "No."

The captain shrugged. "Very well. Think it over, anyway." He peered ahead into the red, coiling mists. "Ah! See there?" He pointed, and Stark made out the shadowy loom of cliffs. "We are coming into the strait now."

Malthor turned and took the steering sweep himself, the helmsman going forward to join the others. The ship began to pick up speed. Stark saw that she had come into the grip of a current that swept toward the cliffs, a river of fire racing ever more swiftly in the depths of the sea.

The dark wall seemed to plunge toward them. At first Stark could see no passage. Then, suddenly, a narrow crimson streak appeared, widened, and became a gut of boiling flame, rushing silently around broken rocks. Red fog rose like smoke. The ship quivered, sprang ahead, and tore like a mad thing into the heart of the inferno.

In spite of himself, Stark's hands tightened on the rail. Tattered veils of mist swirled past them. The sea, the air, the ship itself, seemed drenched in blood. There was no sound, in all that wild sweep of current through the strait. Only the sullen fires burst and flowed.

The reflected glare showed Stark that the Straits of Shuruun were defended. Squat fortresses brooded on the cliffs. There were ballistas, and great windlasses for the drawing of nets across the narrow throat. The men of Shuruun could enforce their law, that barred all foreign shipping from their gulf.

They had reason for such a law, and such a defense. The legitimate trade of Shuruun, such as it was, was in wine and the delicate laces woven from spider-silk. Actually, however, the city lived and throve on piracy, the arts of wrecking, and a contraband trade in the distilled juice of the *vela* poppy.

Looking at the rocks and the fortresses, Stark could understand how it was that Shuruun had been able for more centuries than anyone could tell to victimize the shipping of the Red Sea, and offer a refuge to the outlaw, the wolf's-head, the breaker of taboo.

With startling abruptness, they were through the gut and drifting on the still surface of this all but landlocked arm of the Red Sea.

Because of the shrouding fog, Stark could see nothing of the land. But the smell of it was stronger, warm damp soil and the heavy, faintly rotten perfume of vegetation half jungle, half swamp. Once, through a rift in the wreathing vapor, he thought he glimpsed the shadowy bulk of an island, but it was gone at once.

After the terrifying rush of the strait, it seemed to Stark that the ship barely moved. His impatience and the subtle sense of danger deepened. He began to pace the deck, with the nervous, velvet motion of a prowling cat. The moist, steamy air seemed all but unbreathable after the clean dryness of Mars, from whence he had come so recently. It was oppressively still.

Suddenly he stopped, his head thrown back, listening.

The sound was borne faintly on the slow wind. It came from everywhere and nowhere, a vague dim thing without source or direction. It almost seemed that the night itself had spoken—the hot blue night of Venus, crying out of the mists with a tongue of infinite woe.

It faded and died away, only half heard, leaving behind it a sense of aching sadness, as though all the misery and longing of a world had found voice in that desolate wail.

Stark shivered. For a time there was silence, and then he heard the sound again, now on a deeper note. Still faint and far away, it was sustained longer by the vagaries of the heavy air, and it became a chant, rising and falling. There were no words. It was not the sort of thing that would have need of words. Then it was gone again.

Stark turned to Malthor. "What was that?"

The man looked at him curiously. He seemed not to have heard.

"That wailing sound," said Stark impatiently.

"Oh, that." The Venusian shrugged. "A trick of the wind. It sighs in the hollow rocks around the strait."

He yawned, giving place again to the steersman, and came to stand beside Stark. The Earthman ignored him. For some reason, that sound half heard through the mists had brought his uneasiness to a sharp pitch.

Civilization had brushed over Stark with a light hand. Raised from infancy by half-human aboriginals, his perceptions were still those of a savage. His ear was good.

Malthor lied. That cry of pain was not made by any wind.

"I have known several Earthmen," said Malthor, changing the subject, but not too swiftly. "None of them were like you."

Intuition warned Stark to play along. "I don't come from Earth," he said. "I come from Mercury."

Malthor puzzled over that. Venus is a cloudy world, where no man has ever seen the Sun, let alone a star. The captain had heard vaguely of these things. Earth and Mars he knew of. But Mercury was an unknown word.

Stark explained. "The planet nearest the Sun. It's very hot there. The Sun blazes like a huge fire, and there are no clouds to shield it."

"Ah. That is why your skin is so dark." He held his own pale forearm close to Stark's and shook his head. "I have never seen such skin," he said admiringly. "Nor such great muscles."

Looking up, he went on in a tone of complete friendliness, "I wish you would stay with me. You'll find no better lodgings in Shuruun. And I warn you, there are people in the town who will take advantage of strangers—rob them, even slay them. Now, I am known by all as a man of honor. You could sleep soundly under my roof."

He paused, then added with a smile, "Also, I have a daughter. An excellent cook—and very beautiful."

The woeful chanting came again, dim and distant on the wind, an echo of warning against some unimagined fate.

Stark said for the third time, "No."

He needed no intuition to tell him to walk wide of the captain. The man was a rogue, and not a very subtle one.

A flint-hard, angry look came briefly into Malthor's eyes. "You're a stubborn man. You'll find that Shuruun is no place for stubbornness."

He turned and went away. Stark remained where he was. The ship drifted on through a slow eternity of time. And all down that long still gulf of the Red Sea, through the heat and the wreathing fog, the ghostly chanting haunted him, like the keening of lost souls in some forgotten hell.

Presently the course of the ship was altered. Malthor came again to the afterdeck, giving a few quiet commands. Stark saw land ahead, a darker blur on the night, and then the shrouded outlines of a city.

Torches blazed on the quays and in the streets, and the low buildings caught a ruddy glow from the burning sea itself. A squat and ugly town, Shuruun, crouching witch-like on the rocky shore, her ragged skirts dipped in blood.

The ship drifted in toward the quays.

Stark heard a whisper of movement behind him, the hushed and purposeful padding of naked feet. He turned, with the astonishing swiftness of an animal that feels itself threatened, his hand dropping to his gun.

A belaying pin, thrown by the steersman, struck the side of his head with stunning force. Reeling, half blinded, he saw the distorted shapes of men closing in upon him. Malthor's voice sounded, low and hard. A second belaying pin whizzed through the air and cracked against Stark's shoulder.

Hands were laid upon him. Bodies, heavy and strong, bore his down. Malthor laughed.

Stark's teeth glinted bare and white. Someone's cheek brushed past, and he sank them into the flesh. He began to growl, a sound that should never have come from a human throat. It seemed to the startled Venusians that the man they had attacked had by some wizardry become a beast, at the first touch of violence.

The man with the torn cheek screamed. There was a voiceless scuffling on the deck, a terrible intensity of motion, and then the great dark body rose and shook itself free of the tangle, and was gone, over the rail, leaving Malthor with nothing but the silken rags of a shirt in his hands.

The surface of the Red Sea closed without a ripple over Stark. There was a burst of crimson sparks, a momentary trail of flame going down like a drowned comet, and then—nothing.

2

Stark dropped slowly downward through a strange world. There was no difficulty about breathing, as in a sea of water. The gases of the Red Sea support life quite well, and the creatures that dwell in it have almost normal lungs.

Stark did not pay much attention at first, except to keep his balance automatically. He was still dazed from the blow, and he was raging with anger and pain.

The primitive in him, whose name was not Stark but N'Chaka, and who had fought and starved and hunted in the blazing valleys of Mercury's Twilight Belt, learning lessons he never forgot, wished to return and slay Malthor and his men. He regretted that he had not torn out their throats, for now his trail would never be safe from them.

But the man Stark, who had learned some more bitter lessons in the name of civilization, knew the unwisdom of that. He snarled over his aching head, and cursed the Venusians in the harsh, crude dialect that was his mother tongue, but he did not turn back. There would be time enough for Malthor.

It struck him that the gulf was very deep.

Fighting down his rage, he began to swim in the direction of the shore. There was no sign of pursuit, and he judged that Malthor had decided to let him go. He puzzled over the reason for the attack. It could hardly be robbery, since he carried nothing but the clothes he stood in, and very little money.

No. There was some deeper reason. A reason connected with Malthor's insistence that he lodge with him. Stark smiled. It was not a pleasant smile. He was thinking of Shuruun, and the things men said about it, around the shores of the Red Sea.

Then his face hardened. The dim coiling fires through which he swam brought him memories of other times he had gone adventuring in the depths of the Red Sea.

He had not been alone then. Helvi had gone with him—the tall son of a barbarian kinglet up-coast by Yarell. They had hunted strange beasts through the crystal forests of the sea-bottom and bathed in the welling flames that pulse from the very heart of Venus to feed the ocean. They had been brothers.

Now Helvi was gone, into Shuruun. He had never returned.

Stark swam on. And presently he saw below him in the red gloom something that made him drop lower, frowning with surprise.

There were trees beneath him. Great forest giants towering up into an eerie sky, their branches swaying gently to the slow wash of the currents.

Stark was puzzled. The forests where he and Helvi had hunted were truly crystalline, without even the memory of life. The "trees" were no more trees in actuality than the branching corals of Terra's southern oceans.

But these were real, or had been. He thought at first that they still lived, for their leaves were green, and here and there creepers had starred them with great nodding blossoms of gold and purple and waxy white. But when he floated down close enough to touch them, he realized that they were dead—trees, creepers, blossoms, all.

They had not mummified, nor turned to stone. They were pliable, and their colors were very bright. Simply, they had ceased to live, and the gases of the sea had preserved them by some chemical magic, so perfectly that barely a leaf had fallen.

Stark did not venture into the shadowy denseness below the topmost branches. A strange fear came over him, at the sight of that vast forest dreaming in the depths of the gulf, drowned and forgotten, as though wondering why the birds had gone, taking with them the warm rains and the light of day.

He thrust his way upward, himself like a huge dark bird above the branches. An overwhelming impulse to get away from that unearthly place drove him on, his half-wild sense shuddering with an impression of evil so great that it took all his acquired commonsense to assure him that he was not pursued by demons.

He broke the surface at last, to find that he had lost his direction in the red deep and made a long circle around, so that he was far below Shuruun. He made his way back, not hurrying now, and presently clambered out over the black rocks.

He stood at the end of a muddy lane that wandered in toward the town. He followed it, moving neither fast nor slow, but with a wary alertness.

Huts of wattle-and-daub took shape out of the fog, increased in numbers, became a street of dwellings. Here and there rush-lights glimmered through the slitted windows. A man and a woman clung together in a low doorway. They saw him and sprang apart, and the woman gave a little cry. Stark went on. He did not look back, but he knew that they were following him quietly, at a little distance.

The lane twisted snakelike upon itself, crawling now through a crowded jumble of houses. There were more lights, and more people, tall white-skinned folk of the swamp-edges, with pale eyes and long hair the color of new flax, and the faces of wolves.

Stark passed among them, alien and strange with his black hair and sun-darkened skin. They did not speak, nor try to stop him. Only they looked at him out of the red fog, with a curious blend of amusement and fear, and some of them followed him, keeping well behind. A gang of small naked children came from somewhere among the houses and ran shouting beside him, out of reach, until one boy threw a stone and screamed something unintelligible except for one word—*Lhari*. Then they all stopped, horrified, and fled.

Stark went on, through the quarter of the lacemakers, heading by instinct toward the wharves. The glow of the Red Sea pervaded all the air, so that it seemed as though the mist was full of tiny drops of blood. There was a smell about the place he did not like, a damp miasma of mud and crowding bodies and wine, and the breath of the *vela* poppy. Shuruun was an unclean town, and it stank of evil.

There was something else about it, a subtle thing that touched Stark's nerves with a chill finger. Fear. He could see the shadow of it in the eyes of the people, hear its undertone in their voices. The wolves of Shuruun did not feel safe in their own kennel. Unconsciously, as this feeling grew upon him, Stark's step grew more and more wary, his eyes more cold and hard.

He came out into a broad square by the harbor front. He could see the ghostly ships moored along the quays, the piled casks of wine, the tangle of masts and cordage dim against the background of the burning gulf. There were many torches here. Large low buildings stood around the square. There was laughter and the sound of voices from the dark verandas, and somewhere a woman sang to the melancholy lilting of a reed pipe.

A suffused glow of light in the distance ahead caught Stark's eye. That way the streets sloped to a higher ground, and straining his vision against the fog, he made out very dimly the tall bulk of a castle crouched on the low cliffs, looking with bright eyes upon the night, and the streets of Shuruun.

Stark hesitated briefly. Then he started across the square toward the largest of the taverns.

There were a number of people in the open space, mostly sailors and their women. They were loose and foolish with wine, but even so they stopped where they were and stared at the dark stranger, and then drew back from him, still staring.

Those who had followed Stark came into the square after him and then paused, spreading out in an aimless sort of way to join with other groups, whispering among themselves.

The woman stopped singing in the middle of a phrase.

A curious silence fell on the square. A nervous sibilance ran round and round under the silence, and men came slowly out from the verandas and the doors of the wine shops. Suddenly a woman with disheveled hair pointed her arm at Stark and laughed, the shrieking laugh of a harpy.

Stark found his way barred by three tall young men with hard mouths and crafty eyes, who smiled at him as hounds smile before the kill.

"Stranger," they said. "Earthman."

"Outlaw," answered Stark, and it was only half a lie.

One of the young men took a step forward. "Did you fly like a dragon over the Mountains of White Cloud? Did you drop from the sky?"

"I came on Malthor's ship."

A kind of sigh went round the square, and with it the name of Malthor. The eager faces of the young men grew heavy with disappointment. But the leader said sharply, "I was on the quay when Malthor docked. You were not on board."

It was Stark's turn to smile. In the light of the torches, his eyes blazed cold and bright as ice against the sun.

"Ask Malthor the reason for that," he said. "Ask the man with the torn cheek. Or perhaps," he added softly, "you would like to learn for yourselves."

The young men looked at him, scowling, in an odd mood of indecision. Stark settled himself, every muscle loose and ready. And the woman who had laughed crept closer and peered at Stark through her tangled hair, breathing heavily of the poppy wine.

All at once she said loudly, "He came out of the sea. That's where he came from. He's . . ."

One of the young men struck her across the mouth and she fell down in the mud. A burly seaman ran out and caught her by the hair, dragging her to her feet again. His face was frightened and very angry. He hauled the woman away, cursing her for a fool and beating her as he went. She spat out blood, and said no more.

"Well," said Stark to the young men. "Have you made up your minds?"

"Minds!" said a voice behind them—a harsh-timbred, rasping voice that handled the liquid vocables of the Venusian speech very clumsily indeed. "They have no minds, these whelps! If they had, they'd be off about their business, instead of standing here badgering a stranger."

The young men turned, and now between them Stark could see the man who had spoken. He stood on the steps of the tavern. He was an Earthman, and at first Stark thought he was old, because his hair was white and his face deeply lined. His body was wasted with fever, the muscles all gone to knotty strings twisted over bone. He leaned heavily on a stick, and one leg was crooked and terribly scarred.

He grinned at Stark and said, in colloquial English, "Watch me get rid of 'em!"

He began to tongue-lash the young men, telling them that they were idiots, the misbegotten offspring of swamp-toads, utterly without manners, and that if they did not believe the stranger's story they should go and ask Malthor, as he suggested. Finally he shook his stick at them, fairly screeching.

"Go on, now. Go away! Leave us alone—my brother of Earth and I!"

The young men gave one hesitant glance at Stark's feral eyes. Then they looked at each other and shrugged, and went away across the square half sheepishly, like great loutish boys caught in some misdemeanor.

The white-haired Earthman beckoned to Stark. And, as Stark came up to him on the steps he said under his breath, almost angrily, "You're in a trap."

Stark glanced back over his shoulder. At the edge of the square the three young men had met a fourth, who had his face bound up in a rag. They vanished almost at once into a side street, but not before Stark had recognized the fourth man as Malthor.

It was the captain he had branded.

With loud cheerfulness, the lame man said in Venusian, "Come in and drink with me, brother, and we will talk of Earth."

3

The tavern was of the standard low-class Venusian pattern—a single huge room under bare thatch, the wall half open with the reed shutters rolled up, the floor of split logs propped up on piling out of the mud. A long low bar, little tables, mangy skins and heaps of dubious cushions on the floor around them, and at one end the entertainers—two old men with a drum and a reed pipe, and a couple of sulky, tired-looking girls.

The lame man led Stark to a table in the corner and sank down, calling for wine. His eyes, which were dark and haunted by long pain, burned with excitement. His hands shook. Before Stark had sat down he had begun to talk, his words stumbling over themselves as though he could not get them out fast enough.

"How is it there now? Has it changed any? Tell me how it is—the cities, the lights, the paved streets, the women, the Sun. Oh Lord, what I wouldn't give to see the Sun again, and women with dark hair and their clothes on!" He leaned forward, staring hungrily into Stark's face, as though he could see those things mirrored there. "For God's sake, talk to me—talk to me in English, and tell me about Earth!"

"How long have you been here?" asked Stark.

"I don't know. How do you reckon time on a world without a Sun, without one damned little star to look at? Ten years, a hundred years, how should I know? Forever. Tell me about Earth."

Stark smiled wryly. "I haven't been there for a long time. The police were too ready with a welcoming committee. But the last time I saw it, it was just the same."

The lame man shivered. He was not looking at Stark now, but at some place far beyond him.

"Autumn woods," he said. "Red and gold on the brown hills. Snow. I can remember how it felt to be cold. The air bit you when you breathed it. And the women wore high-heeled slippers. No big bare feet tromping in the mud, but little sharp heels tapping on clean pavement."

Suddenly he glared at Stark, his eyes furious and bright with tears.

"Why the hell did you have to come here and start me remembering? I'm Larrabee. I live in Shuruun. I've been here forever, and I'll be here till I die. There isn't any Earth. It's gone. Just look up into the sky, and you'll know it's gone. There's nothing anywhere but clouds, and Venus, and mud."

He sat still, shaking, turning his head from side to side. A man came with wine, put it down, and went away again. The tavern was very quiet. There was a wide space empty around the two Earthmen. Beyond that people lay on the cushions, sipping the poppy wine and watching with a sort of furtive expectancy.

Abruptly, Larrabee laughed, a harsh sound that held a certain honest mirth.

"I don't know why I should get sentimental about Earth at this late date. Never thought much about it when I was there."

Nevertheless, he kept his gaze averted, and when he picked up his cup his hand trembled so that he spilled some of the wine.

Stark was staring at him in unbelief. "Larrabee," he said. "You're Mike Larrabee. You're the man who got half a million credits out of the strong room of the *Royal Venus*."

Larrabee nodded. "And got away with it, right over the Mountains of White Cloud, that they said couldn't be flown. And do you know where that half a million is now? At the bottom of the Red Sea, along with my ship and my crew, out there in the gulf. Lord knows why I lived." He shrugged. "Well, anyway, I was heading for Shuruun when I crashed, and I got here. So why complain?"

He drank again, deeply, and Stark shook his head.

"You've been here nine years, then, by Earth time," he said. He had never met Larrabee, but he remembered the pictures of him that had flashed across space on police bands. Larrabee had been a young man then, dark and proud and handsome.

Larrabee guessed his thought. "I've changed, haven't I?"

Stark said lamely, "Everybody thought you were dead."

Larrabee laughed. After that, for a moment, there was silence. Stark's ears were straining for any sound outside. There was none.

He said abruptly, "What about this trap I'm in?"

"I'll tell you one thing about it," said Larrabee. "There's no way out. I can't help you. I wouldn't if I could, get that straight. But I can't, anyway."

"Thanks," Stark said sourly. "You can at least tell me what goes on."

"Listen," said Larrabee. "I'm a cripple, and an old man, and Shuruun isn't the sweetest place in the solar system to live. But I do live. I have a wife, a slatternly wench I'll admit, but good enough in her way. You'll notice some little dark-haired brats rolling in the mud. They're mine, too. I have some skill at setting bones and such, and so I can get drunk for nothing as often as I will—which is often. Also, because of this bum leg, I'm perfectly safe. So don't ask me what goes on. I take great pains not to know."

Stark said, "Who are the Lhari?"

"Would you like to meet them?" Larrabee seemed to find something very amusing in that thought. "Just go on up to the castle. They live there. They're the Lords of Shuruun, and they're always glad to meet strangers."

He leaned forward suddenly. "Who are you anyway? What's your name, and why the devil did you come here?"

"My name is Stark. And I came here for the same reason you did."

"Stark," repeated Larrabee slowly, his eyes intent. "That rings a faint bell. Seems to me I saw a *Wanted* flash once, some idiot that had led a native revolt somewhere in the Jovian Colonies—a big cold-eyed brute they referred to colorfully as the wild man from Mercury."

He nodded, pleased with himself. "Wild man, eh? Well, Shuruun will tame you down!"

"Perhaps," said Stark. His eyes shifted constantly, watching Larrabee, watching the doorway and the dark veranda and the people who drank but did not talk among themselves. "Speaking of strangers, one came here at the time of the last rains. He was Venusian, from up-coast. A big young man. I used to know him. Perhaps he could help me."

Larrabee snorted. By now, he had drunk his own wine and Stark's too. "Nobody can help you. As for your friend, I never saw him. I'm beginning to think I should never have seen you." Quite suddenly he caught up his stick and got with some difficulty to his feet. He did not look at Stark, but said harshly, "You better get out of here." Then he turned and limped unsteadily to the bar.

Stark rose. He glanced after Larrabee, and again his nostrils twitched to the smell of fear. Then he went out of the tavern the way he had come in, through the front door. No one moved to stop him. Outside, the square was empty. It had begun to rain.

Stark stood for a moment on the steps. He was angry, and filled with a dangerous unease, the hair-trigger nervousness of a tiger that senses the beaters creeping toward him up the wind. He would almost have welcomed the sight of Malthor and the three young men. But there was nothing to fight but the silence and the rain.

He stepped out into the mud, wet and warm around his ankles. An idea came to him, and he smiled, beginning now to move with a definite purpose, along the side of the square.

The sharp downpour strengthened. Rain smoked from Stark's naked shoulders, beat against thatch and mud with a hissing rattle. The harbor had disappeared behind boiling clouds of fog, where water struck the surface of the Red Sea and was turned again instantly by chemical action into vapor. The quays and the neighboring streets were being swallowed up in the impenetrable mist. Lightning came with an eerie bluish flare, and thunder came rolling after it.

Stark turned up the narrow way that led toward the castle.

Its lights were winking out now, one by one, blotted by the creeping fog. Lightning etched its shadowy bulk against the night, and then was gone. And through the noise of the thunder that followed, Stark thought he heard a voice calling.

He stopped, half crouching, his hand on his gun. The cry came again, a girl's voice, thin as the wail of a seabird through the driving rain. Then he saw her, a small white blur in the street behind him, running, and even in that dim glimpse of her every line of her body was instinct with fright.

Stark set his back against a wall and waited. There did not seem to be anyone with her, though it was hard to tell in the darkness and the storm.

She came up to him, and stopped, just out of his reach, looking at him and away again with a painful irresoluteness. A bright flash showed her to him clearly. She was young, not long out of her childhood, and pretty in a stupid sort of way. Just now her mouth trembled on the edge of weeping, and her eyes were very large and scared. Her skirt clung to her long thighs, and above it her naked body, hardly fleshed into womanhood, glistened like snow in the wet. Her pale hair hung dripping over her shoulders.

Stark said gently, "What do you want with me?"

She looked at him, so miserably like a wet puppy that he smiled. And as though that smile had taken what little resolution she had out of her, she dropped to her knees, sobbing.

"I can't do it," she wailed. "He'll kill me, but I just can't do it!"

"Do what?" asked Stark.

She stared up at him. "Run away," she urged him. "Run away *now!* You'll die in the swamps, but that's better than being one of the Lost Ones!" She shook her thin arms at him. *"Run away!"*

4

The street was empty. Nothing showed, nothing stirred anywhere. Stark leaned over and pulled the girl to her feet, drawing her in under the shelter of the thatched eaves.

"Now then," he said. "Suppose you stop crying and tell me what this is all about."

Presently, between gulps and hiccoughs, he got the story out of her.

"I am Zareth," she said. "Malthor's daughter. He's afraid of you, because of what you did to him on the ship, so he ordered me to watch for you in the square, when you would come out of the tavern. Then I was to follow you, and . . ."

She broke off, and Stark patted her shoulder. "Go on."

But a new thought had occurred to her. "If I do, will you promise not to beat me, or . . ." She looked at his gun and shivered.

"I promise."

She studied his face, what she could see of it in the darkness, and then seemed to lose some of her fear.

"I was to stop you. I was to say what I've already said, about being Malthor's daughter and the rest of it, and then I was to say that he wanted me to lead you into an ambush while pretending to help you escape, but that I couldn't do it, and would help you to escape anyhow because I hated Malthor and the whole business about the Lost Ones. So you would believe me, and follow me, and I would lead you into the ambush."

She shook her head and began to cry again, quietly this time, and there was nothing of the woman about her at all now. She was just a child, very miserable and afraid. Stark was glad he had branded Malthor.

"But I can't lead you into the ambush. I do hate Malthor, even if he is my father, because he beats me. And the Lost Ones . . ." She paused. "Sometimes I hear them at night, chanting way out there beyond the mist. It is a very terrible sound."

"It is," said Stark. "I've heard it. Who are the Lost Ones, Zareth?"

"I can't tell you that," said Zareth. "It's forbidden even to speak of them. And anyway," she finished honestly, "I don't even know. People disappear, that's all. Not our own people of Shuruun, at least not very often. But strangers like you— and I'm sure my father goes off into the swamps to hunt among the tribes there, and I'm sure he comes back from some of his voyages with nothing in his hold but men from some captured ship. Why, or what for, I don't know. Except I've heard the chanting."

"They live out there in the gulf, do they, the Lost Ones?"

"They must. There are many islands there."

"And what of the Lhari, the Lords of Shuruun? Don't they know what's going on? Or are they part of it?"

She shuddered, and said, "It's not for us to question the Lhari, nor even to wonder what they do. Those who have are gone from Shuruun, nobody knows where."

Stark nodded. He was silent for a moment, thinking. Then Zareth's little hand touched his shoulder.

"Go," she said. "Lose yourself in the swamps. You're strong, and there's something about you different from other men. You may live to find your way through."

"No. I have something to do before I leave Shuruun." He took Zareth's damp fair head between his hands and kissed her on the forehead. "You're a sweet child, Zareth, and a brave one. Tell Malthor that you did exactly as he told you, and it was not your fault I wouldn't follow you."

"He will beat me anyway," said Zareth philosophically, "but perhaps not quite so hard."

"He'll have no reason to beat you at all, if you tell him the truth—that I would not go with you because my mind was set on going to the castle of the Lhari."

There was a long, long silence, while Zareth's eyes widened slowly in horror, and the rain beat on the thatch, and fog and thunder rolled together across Shuruun.

"To the castle," she whispered. "Oh, no! Go into the swamps, or let Malthor take you—but don't go to the castle!" She took hold of his arm, her fingers biting into his flesh with the urgency of her plea. "You're a stranger, you don't know. . . . Please, don't go up there!"

"Why not?" asked Stark. "Are the Lhari demons? Do they devour men?" He loosened her hands gently. "You'd better go now. Tell your father where I am, if he wishes to come after me."

Zareth backed away slowly, out into the rain, staring at him as though she looked at someone standing on the brink of hell, not dead, but worse than dead. Wonder showed in her face, and through it a great yearning pity. She tried once to speak, and then shook her head and turned away, breaking into a run as though she could not endure to look upon Stark any longer. In a second she was gone.

Stark looked after her for a moment, strangely touched. Then he stepped out into the rain again, heading upward along the steep path that led to the castle of the Lords of Shuruun.

The mist was blinding. Stark had to feel his way, and as he climbed higher, above the level of the town, he was lost in the sullen redness. A hot wind blew, and each flare of lightning turned the crimson fog to a hellish purple. The night was full of a vast hissing where the rain poured into the gulf. He stopped once to hide his gun in a cleft between the rocks.

At length he stumbled against a carven pillar of black stone and found the gate that hung from it, a massive thing sheathed in metal. It was barred, and the pounding of his fists upon it made little sound.

Then he saw the gong, a huge disc of beaten gold beside the gate. Stark picked up the hammer that lay there, and set the deep voice of the gong rolling out between the thunderbolts.

A barred slit opened and a man's eyes looked out at him. Stark dropped the hammer.

"Open up!" he shouted. "I would speak with the Lhari!"

From within he heard an echo of laughter. Scraps of voices came to him on the wind, and then more laughter, and then, slowly, the great valves of the gate creaked open, wide enough only to admit him.

He stepped through, and the gateway shut behind him with a ringing clash.

He stood in a huge open court. Enclosed within its walls was a village of thatched huts, with open sheds for cooking, and behind them were pens for the stabling of beasts, the wingless dragons of the swamps that can be caught and broken to the goad.

He saw this only in vague glimpses, because of the fog. The men who had let him in clustered around him, thrusting him forward into the light that streamed from the huts.

"He would speak with the Lhari!" one of them shouted, to the women and children who stood in the doorways watching. The words were picked up and tossed around the court, and a great burst of laughter went up.

Stark eyed them, saying nothing. They were a puzzling breed. The men, obviously, were soldiers and guards to the Lhari, for they wore the harness of fighting men. As obviously, these were their wives and children, all living behind the castle walls and having little to do with Shuruun.

But it was their racial characteristics that surprised him. They had interbred with the pale tribes of the Swamp-Edges that had peopled Shuruun, and there were many with milk-white hair and broad faces. Yet even these bore an alien stamp. Stark was puzzled, for the race he would have named was unknown here behind the Mountains of White Cloud, and almost unknown anywhere on Venus at Sea-level, among the sweltering marshes and the eternal fogs.

They stared at him even more curiously, remarking on his skin and his black hair and the unfamiliar modeling of his face. The women nudged each other and whispered, giggling, and one of them said aloud, "They'll need a barrel-hoop to collar that neck!"

The guards closed in around him. "Well, if you wish to see the Lhari, you shall," said the leader, "but first we must make sure of you."

Spear-points ringed him round. Stark made no resistance while they stripped him of all he had, except for his shorts and sandals. He had expected that, and it amused him, for there was little enough for them to take.

"All right," said the leader. "Come on."

The whole village turned out in the rain to escort Stark to the castle door. There was about them the same ominous interest that the people of Shuruun had had, with one difference. They knew what was supposed to happen to him, knew all about it, and were therefore doubly appreciative of the game.

The great doorway was square and plain, and yet neither crude nor ungraceful. The castle itself was built of the black stone, each block perfectly cut and fitted, and the door itself was sheathed in the same metal as the gate, darkened but not corroded.

The leader of the guard cried out to the warder, "Here is one who would speak with the Lhari!"

The warder laughed. "And so he shall! Their night is long, and dull."

He flung open the heavy door and cried the word down the hallway. Stark could hear it echoing hollowly within, and presently from the shadows came servants clad in silks and wearing jeweled collars, and from the guttural sound of their laughter Stark knew that they had no tongues.

Stark faltered, then. The doorway loomed hollowly before him, and it came to him suddenly that evil lay behind it and that perhaps Zareth was wiser than he when she warned him from the Lhari.

Then he thought of Helvi, and of other things, and lost his fear in anger. Lightning burned the sky. The last cry of the dying storm shook the ground under his feet. He thrust the grinning warder aside and strode into the castle, bringing a veil of the red fog with him, and did not listen to the closing of the door, which was stealthy and quiet as the footfall of approaching Death.

Torches burned here and there along the walls, and by their smoky glare he could see that the hallway was like the entrance—square and unadorned, faced with the black rock. It was high, and wide, and there was about the architecture a calm reflective dignity that had its own beauty, in some ways more impressive than the sensuous loveliness of the ruined palaces he had seen on Mars.

There were no carvings here, no paintings nor frescoes. It seemed that the builders had felt that the hall itself was enough, in its massive perfection of line and the somber gleam of polished stone. The only decoration was in the window embrasures. These were empty now, open to the sky with the red fog wreathing through them, but there were still scraps of jewel-toned panes clinging to the fretwork, to show what they had once been.

A strange feeling swept over Stark. Because of his wild upbringing, he was abnormally sensitive to the sort of impressions that most men receive either dully or not at all.

Walking down the hall, preceded by the tongueless creatures in their bright silks and blazing collars, he was struck by a subtle *difference* in the place. The castle itself was only an extension of the minds of its builders, a dream shaped into reaity. Stark felt that that dark, cool, curiously timeless dream had not originated in a mind like his own, nor like that of any man he had ever seen.

Then the end of the hall was reached, the way barred by low broad doors of gold fashioned in the same chaste simplicity.

A soft scurrying of feet, a shapeless tittering from the servants, a glancing of malicious, mocking eyes. The golden doors swung open, and Stark was in the presence of the Lhari.

5

They had the appearance in that first glance, of creatures glimpsed in a fever-dream, very bright and distant, robed in a misty glow that gave them an allusion of unearthly beauty.

The place in which the Earthman now stood was like a cathedral for breadth and loftiness. Most of it was in darkness, so that it seemed to reach without limit above and on all sides, as though the walls were only shadowy phantasms of the night itself. The polished black stone under his feet held a dim translucent gleam, depthless as water in a black tarn. There was no substance anywhere.

Far away in this shadowy vastness burned a cluster of lamps, a galaxy of little stars to shed a silvery light upon the Lords of Shuruun.

There had been no sound in the place when Stark entered, for the opening of the golden doors had caught the attention of the Lhari and held it in contemplation of the stranger. Stark began to walk toward them in this utter stillness.

Quite suddenly, in the impenetrable gloom somewhere to his right, there came a sharp scuffling and a scratching of reptilian claws, a hissing and a sort of low angry muttering, all magnified and distorted by the echoing vault into a huge demoniac whispering that swept all around him.

Stark whirled around, crouched and ready, his eyes blazing and his body bathed in cold sweat. The noise increased, rushing toward him. From the distant glow of the lamps came a woman's tinkling laughter, thin crystal broken against the vault. The hissing and snarling rose to hollow crescendo, and Stark saw a blurred shape bounding at him.

His hands reached out to receive the rush, but it never came. The strange shape resolved itself into a boy of about ten, who dragged after him on a bit of rope a young dragon, new and toothless from the egg, and protesting with all its strength.

Stark straightened up, feeling let down and furious—and relieved. The boy scowled at him through a forelock of silver curls. Then he called him a very dirty word and rushed away, kicking and hauling at the little beast until it raged like the father of all dragons and sounded like it, too, in that vast echo chamber.

A voice spoke. Slow, harsh, sexless, it rang thinly through the vault. Thin—but a steel blade is thin, too. It speaks inexorably, and its word is final.

The voice said, "Come here, into the light."

Stark obeyed the voice. As he approached the lamps, the aspect of the Lhari changed and steadied. Their beauty remained, but it was not the same. They had looked like angels. Now that he could see them clearly, Stark thought that they might have been the children of Lucifer himself.

There were six of them, counting the boy. Two men, about the same age as Stark, with some complicated gambling game forgotten between them. A woman, beautiful, gowned in white silk, sitting with her hands in her lap, doing nothing. A woman, younger, not so beautiful perhaps, but with a look of stormy and bitter vitality. She wore a short tunic of crimson, and a stout leather glove on her left hand, where perched a flying thing of prey with its fierce eyes hooded.

The boy stood beside the two men, his head poised arrogantly. From time to time he cuffed the little dragon, and it snapped at him with its impotent jaws. He was proud of himself for doing that. Stark wondered how he would behave with the beast when it had grown its fangs.

Opposite him, crouched on a heap of cushions, was a third man. He was deformed, with an ungainly body and long spidery arms, and in his lap a sharp knife lay on a block of wood, half formed into the shape of an obese creature half woman, half pure evil. Stark saw with a flash of surprise that the face of the deformed young man, of all the faces there, was truly human, truly beautiful. His eyes were old in his boyish face, wise, and very sad in their wisdom. He smiled upon the stranger, and his smile was more compassionate than tears.

They looked at Stark, all of them, with restless, hungry eyes. They were the pure breed, that had left its stamp of alienage on the pale-haired folk of the swamps, the serfs who dwelt in the huts outside.

They were of the Cloud People, the folk of the High Plateaus, kings of the land on the farther slopes of the Mountains of White Cloud. It was strange to see them here, on the dark side of the barrier wall, but here they were. How they had come, and why, leaving their rich cool plains for the fetor of these foreign swamps, he could not guess. But there was no mistaking them—the proud fine shaping of their bodies, their alabaster skin, their eyes that were all colors and none, like the dawn sky, their hair that was pure warm silver.

They did not speak. They seemed to be waiting for permission to speak, and Stark wondered which one of them had voiced that steely summons.

Then it came again. "Come here—come closer." And he looked beyond them, beyond the circle of lamps into the shadows again, and saw the speaker.

She lay upon a low bed, her head propped on silken pillows, her vast, her incredibly gigantic body covered with a silken pall. Only her arms were bare, two shapeless masses of white flesh ending in tiny hands. From time to time she stretched one out and took a morsel of food from the supply laid ready beside her, snuffling and wheezing with the effort, and then gulped the tidbit down with a horrible voracity.

Her features had long ago dissolved into a shaking formlessness, with the exception of her nose, which rose out of the fat curved and cruel and thin, like the bony beak of the creature that sat on the girl's wrist and dreamed its hooded dreams of blood. And her eyes . . .

Stark looked into her eyes and shuddered. Then he glanced at the carving half formed in the cripple's lap, and knew what thought had guided the knife.

Half woman, half pure evil. And strong. Very strong. Her strength lay naked in her eyes for all to see, and it was an ugly strength. It could tear down mountains, but it could never build.

He saw her looking at him. Her eyes bored into his as though they would search out his very guts and study them, and he knew that she expected him to turn away, unable to bear her gaze. He did not. Presently he smiled and said, "I have outstared a rock-lizard, to determine which of us should eat the other. And I've outstared the very rock while waiting for him."

She knew that he spoke the truth. Stark expected her to be angry, but she was not. A vague mountainous rippling shook her and emerged at length as a voiceless laughter.

"You see that?" she demanded, addressing the others. "You whelps of the Lhari—not one of you dares to face me down, yet here is a great dark creature from the gods know where who can stand and shame you."

She glanced again at Stark. "What demon's blood brought you forth, that you have learned neither prudence nor fear?"

Stark answered somberly, "I learned them both before I could walk. But I learned another thing also—a thing called anger."

"And you are angry?"

"Ask Malthor if I am, and why!"

He saw the two men start a little, and a slow smile crossed the girl's face.

"Malthor," said the hulk upon the bed, and ate a mouthful of roast meat dripping with fat. "That is interesting. But rage against Malthor did not bring you here. I am curious, Stranger. Speak."

"I will."

Stark glanced around. The place was a tomb, a trap. The very air smelled of danger. The younger folk watched him in silence. Not one of them had spoken since he came in, except the boy who had cursed him, and that was unnatural in itself. The girl leaned forward, idly stroking the creature on her wrist so that it stirred and ran its knife-like talons in and out of their bony sheathes with sensuous pleasure. Her gaze on Stark was bold and cool, oddly challenging. Of them all, she alone saw him as a man. To the others he was a problem, a diversion—something less than human.

Stark said, "A man came to Shuruun at the time of the last rains. His name was Helvi, and he was son of a little king by Yarell. He came seeking his brother, who had broken taboo and fled for his life. Helvi came to tell him that the ban was lifted, and he might return. Neither one came back."

The small evil eyes were amused, blinking in their tallowy creases. "And so?"

"And so I have come after Helvi, who is my friend."

Again there was the heaving of that bulk of flesh, the explosion of laughter that hissed and wheezed in snake-like echoes through the vault.

"Friendship must run deep with you, Stranger. Ah, well. The Lhari are kind of heart. You shall find your friend."

And as though that were the signal to end their deferential silence, the younger folk burst into laughter also, until the vast hall rang with it, giving back a sound like demons laughing on the edge of Hell.

The cripple only did not laugh, but bent his bright head over his carving, and sighed.

The girl sprang up. "Not yet, Grandmother! Keep him awhile."

The cold, cruel eyes shifted to her. "And what will you do with him, Varra? Haul him about on a string, like Bor with his wretched beast?"

"Perhaps—though I think it would need a stout chain to hold him." Varra turned and looked at Stark, bold and bright, taking in the breadth and the height of him, the shaping of the great smooth muscles, the iron line of the jaw. She smiled. Her mouth was very lovely, like the red fruit of the swamp tree that bears death in its pungent sweetness.

"Here is a man," she said. "The first man I have seen since my father died."

The two men at the gaming table rose, their faces flushed and angry. One of them strode forward and gripped the girl's arm roughly.

"So I am not a man," he said, with surprising gentleness. "A sad thing, for one who is to be your husband. It's best that we settle that now, before we wed."

Varra nodded. Stark saw that the man's fingers were cutting savagely into the firm muscle of her arm, but she did not wince.

"High time to settle it all, Egil. You have borne enough from me. The day is long overdue for my taming. I must learn now to bend my neck, and acknowledge my lord."

For a moment Stark thought she meant it, the note of mockery in her voice was so subtle. Then the woman in white, who all this time had not moved nor changed expression, voiced again the thin, tinkling laugh he had heard once before. From that, and the dark suffusion of blood in Egil's face, Stark knew that Varra was only casting the man's own phrases back at him. The boy let out one derisive bark, and was cuffed into silence.

Varra looked straight at Stark. "Will you fight for me?" she demanded.

Quite suddenly, it was Stark's turn to laugh. "No!" he said.

Varra shrugged. "Very well, then. I must fight for myself."

"Man," snarled Egil. "I'll show you who's a man, you scapegrace little vixen!"

He wrenched off his girdle with his free hand, at the same time bending the girl around so he could get a fair shot at her. The creature of prey, a Terran falcon, clung to her wrist, beating its wings and screaming, its hooded head jerking.

With a motion so quick that it was hardly visible, Varra slipped the hood and flew the creature straight for Egil's face.

He let go, flinging up his arms to ward off the talons and the tearing beak. The wide wings beat and hammered. Egil yelled. The boy Bor got out of range and danced up and down shrieking with delight.

Varra stood quietly. The bruises were blackening on her arm, but she did not deign to touch them. Egil blundered against the gaming table and sent the ivory pieces flying. Then he tripped over a cushion and fell flat, and the hungry talons ripped his tunic to ribbons down the back.

Varra whistled, a clear peremptory call. The creature gave a last peck at the back of Egil's head and flopped sullenly back to its perch on her wrist. She held it, turning toward Stark. He knew from the poise of her that she was on the verge of launching her pet at him. But she studied him and then shook her head.

"No," she said, and slipped the hood back on. "You would kill it."

Egil had scrambled up and gone off into the darkness, sucking a cut on his arm. His face was black with rage. The other man looked at Varra.

"If you were pledged to me," he said, "I'd have that temper out of you!"

"Come and try it," answered Varra.

The man shrugged and sat down. "It's not my place. I keep the peace in my own house." He glanced at the woman in white, and Stark saw that her face, hitherto blank of any expression, had taken on a look of abject fear.

"You do," said Varra, "and, if I were Arel, I would stab you while you slept. But you're safe. She had no spirit to begin with."

Arel shivered and looked steadfastly at her hands. The man began to gather up the scattered pieces. He said casually, "Egil will wring your neck some day, Varra, and I shan't weep to see it."

All this time the old woman had eaten and watched, watched and eaten, her eyes glittering with interest.

"A pretty brood, are they not?" she demanded of Stark. "Full of spirit, quarreling like young hawks in the nest. That's why I keep them around me, so—they are such sport to watch. All except Treon there." She indicated the crippled youth. "He does nothing. Dull and soft-mouthed, worse than Arel. What a grandson to be cursed with! But his sister has fire enough for two." She munched a sweet, grunting with pride.

Treon raised his head and spoke, and his voice was like music, echoing with an eerie liveliness in that dark place.

"Dull I may be, Grandmother, and weak in body, and without hope. Yet I shall be the last of the Lhari. Death sits waiting on the towers, and he shall gather you all before me. I know, for the winds have told me."

He turned his suffering eyes upon Stark and smiled, a smile of such woe and resignation that the Earthman's heart ached with it. Yet there was a thankfulness in it too, as though some long waiting was over at last.

"You," he said softly, "Stranger with the fierce eyes. I saw you come, out of the darkness, and where you set foot there was a bloody print. Your arms were red to the elbows, and your breast was splashed with the redness, and on your brow was the symbol of death. Then I knew, and the wind whispered into my ear, 'It is so. This man shall pull the castle down, and its stones shall crush Shuruun and set the Lost Ones free'."

He laughed, very quietly. "Look at him, all of you. For he will be your doom!"

There was a moment's silence, and Stark, with all the superstitions of a wild race thick within him, turned cold to the roots of his hair. Then the old woman said disgustedly, "Have the winds warned you of this, my idiot?"

And with astonishing force and accuracy she picked up a ripe fruit and flung it at Treon.

"Stop your mouth with that," she told him. "I am weary to death of your prophecies."

Treon looked at the crimson juice trickling slowly down the breast of his tunic, to drip upon the carving in his lap. The half formed head was covered with it. Treon was shaken with silent mirth.

"Well," said Varra, coming up to Stark, "what do you think of the Lhari? The proud Lhari, who would not stoop to mingle their blood with the cattle of the swamps. My half-witted brother, my worthless cousins, that little monster Bor who is the last twig of the tree—do you wonder I flew my falcon at Egil?"

She waited for an answer, her head thrown back, the silver curls framing her face like wisps of storm-cloud. There was a swagger about her that at once irritated and delighted Stark. A hellcat, he thought, but a mighty fetching one, and bold as brass. Bold—and honest. Her lips were parted, midway between anger and a smile.

He caught her to him suddenly and kissed her, holding her slim strong body as though she were a doll. He was in no hurry to set her down. When at last he did, he grinned and said, "Was that what you wanted?"

"Yes," answered Varra. "That was what I wanted." She spun about, her jaw set dangerously. "Grandmother . . ."

She got no farther. Stark saw that the old woman was attempting to sit upright, her face purpling with effort and the most terrible wrath he had ever seen.

"You," she gasped at the girl. She choked on her fury and her shortness of breath, and then Egil came soft-footed into the light, bearing in his hand a thing made of black metal and oddly shaped, with a blunt, thick muzzle.

"Lie back, Grandmother," he said. "I had a mind to use this on Varra—"

Even as he spoke he pressed a stud, and Stark in the act of leaping for the sheltering darkness, crashed down and lay like a dead man. There had been no sound, no flash, nothing, but a vast hand that smote him suddenly into oblivion.

Egil finished,—"but I see a better target."

6

Red. Red. Red. The color of blood. Blood in his eyes. He was remembering now. The quarry had turned on him, and they had fought on the bare, blistering rocks.

Nor had N'Chaka killed. The Lord of the Rocks was very big, a giant among lizards, and N'Chaka was small. The Lord of the Rocks had laid open N'Chaka's head before the wooden spear had more than scratched his flank.

It was strange that N'Chaka still lived. The Lord of the Rocks must have been full fed. Only that had saved him.

N'Chaka groaned, not with pain, but with shame. He had failed. Hoping for a great triumph, he had disobeyed the tribal law that forbids a boy to hunt the quarry of a man, and he had failed. Old One would not reward him with the girdle and the flint spear of manhood. Old One would give him to the women for the punishment of little whips. Tika would laugh at him, and it would be many seasons before Old One would grant him permission to try the Man's Hunt.

Blood in his eyes.

He blinked to clear them. The instinct of survival was prodding him. He must arouse himself and creep away, before the Lord of the Rocks returned to eat him.

The redness would not go away. It swam and flowed, strangely sparkling. He blinked again, and tried to lift his head, and could not, and fear struck down upon him like the iron frost of night upon the rocks of the valley.

It was all wrong. He could see himself clearly, a naked boy dizzy with pain, rising and clambering over the ledges and the shale to the safety of the cave. He could see that, and yet he could not move.

All wrong. Time, space, the universe, darkened and turned.

A voice spoke to him. A girl's voice. Not Tika's and the speech was strange.

Tika was dead. Memories rushed through his mind, the bitter things, the cruel things. Old One was dead, and all the others . . .

The voice spoke again, calling him by a name that was not his own.

Stark.

Memory shattered into a kaleidoscope of broken pictures, fragments, rushing, spinning. He was adrift among them. He was lost, and the terror of it brought a scream into his throat.

Soft hands touching his face, gentle words, swift and soothing. The redness cleared and steadied, though it did not go away, and quite suddenly he was himself again, with all his memories where they belonged.

He was lying on his back, and Zareth, Malthor's daughter, was looking down at him. He knew now what the redness was. He had seen it too often before not to know. He was somewhere at the bottom of the Red Sea—that weird ocean in which a man can breathe.

And he could not move. That had not changed, nor gone away. His body was dead.

The terror he had felt before was nothing to the agony that filled him now. He lay entombed in his own flesh, staring up at Zareth, wanting an answer to a question he dared not ask.

She understood, from the look in his eyes.

"It's all right," she said, and smiled. "It will wear off. You'll be all right. It's only the weapon of the Lhari. Somehow it puts the body to sleep, but it will wake again."

Stark remembered the black object that Egil had held in his hands. A projector of some sort, then, beaming a current of high-frequency vibration that paralyzed the nerve centers. He was amazed. The Cloud People were barbarians themselves, though on a higher scale than the swamp-edge tribes, and certainly had no such scientific proficiency. He wondered where the Lhari had got hold of such a weapon.

It didn't really matter. Not just now. Relief swept over him, bringing him dangerously close to tears. The effect would wear off. At the moment, that was all he cared about.

He looked up at Zareth again. Her pale hair floated with the slow breathing of the sea, a milky cloud against the spark-shot crimson. He saw now that her face was drawn and shadowed, and there was a terrible hopelessness in her eyes. She had been alive when he first saw her—frightened, not too bright, but full of emotion and a certain dogged courage. Now the spark was gone, crushed out.

She wore a collar around her white neck, a ring of dark metal with the ends fused together for all time.

"Where are we?" he asked.

And she answered, her voice carrying deep and hollow in the dense substance of the sea, "We are in the place of the Lost Ones."

Stark looked beyond her, as far as he could see, since he was unable to turn his head. And wonder came to him.

Black walls, black vault above him, a vast hall filled with the wash of the sea that slipped in streaks of whispering flame through the high embrasures. A hall that was twin to the vault of shadows where he had met the Lhari.

"There is a city," said Zareth dully. "You will see it soon. You will see nothing else until you die."

Stark said, very gently, "How do you come here, little one?"

"Because of my father. I will tell you all I know, which is little enough. Malthor has been slaver to the Lhari for a long time. There are a number of them among the captains of Shuruun, but that is a thing that is never spoken of—so I, his daughter, could only guess. I was sure of it when he sent me after you."

She laughed, a bitter sound. "Now I'm here, with the collar of the Lost Ones on my neck. But Malthor is here, too." She laughed again, ugly laughter to come from a young mouth. Then she looked at Stark, and her hand reached out timidly to touch his hair in what was almost a caress. Her eyes were wide, and soft, and full of tears.

"Why didn't you go into the swamps when I warned you?"

Stark answered stolidly, "Too late to worry about that now." Then, "You say Malthor is here, a slave?"

"Yes." Again, that look of wonder and admiration in her eyes. "I don't know what you said or did to the Lhari, but the Lord Egil came down in a black rage and cursed my father for a bungling fool because he could not hold you. My father whined and made excuses, and all would have been well—only his curiosity got the better of him and he asked the Lord Egil what had happened. You were like a wild beast, Malthor said, and he hoped you had not harmed the Lady Varra, as he could see from Egil's wounds that there had been trouble.

"The Lord Egil turned quite purple. I thought he was going to fall in a fit."

"Yes," said Stark. "That was the wrong thing to say." The ludicrous side of it struck him, and he was suddenly roaring with laughter. "Malthor should have kept his mouth shut!"

"Egil called his guard and ordered them to take Malthor. And when he realized what had happened, Malthor turned on me, trying to say that it was all my fault, that I let you escape."

Stark stopped laughing.

Her voice went on slowly, "Egil seemed quite mad with fury. I have heard that the Lhari are all mad, and I think it is so. At any rate, he ordered me taken too, for he wanted to stamp Malthor's seed into the mud forever. So we are here."

There was a long silence. Stark could think of no word of comfort, and as for hope, he had better wait until he was sure he could at least raise his head. Egil might have damaged him permanently, out of spite. In fact, he was surprised he wasn't dead.

He glanced again at the collar on Zareth's neck. Slave. Slave to the Lhari, in the City of the Lost Ones.

What the devil did they do with slaves, at the bottom of the sea?

The heavy gases conducted sound remarkably well, except for an odd property of diffusion which made it seem that a voice came from everywhere at once. Now, all at once, Stark became aware of a dull clamor of voices drifting towards him.

He tried to see, and Zareth turned his head carefully so that he might.

The Lost Ones were returning from whatever work it was they did.

Out of the dim red murk beyond the open door they swam, into the long, long vastness of the hall that was filled with the same red murk, moving slowly, their white bodies trailing wakes of sullen flame. The host of the damned drifting through a strange red-lit hell, weary and without hope.

One by one they sank onto pallets laid in rows on the black stone floor, and lay there, utterly exhausted, their pale hair lifting and floating with the slow eddies of the sea. And each one wore a collar.

One man did not lie down. He came toward Stark, a tall barbarian who drew himself with great strokes of his arms so that he was wrapped in wheeling sparks. Stark knew his face.

"Helvi," he said, and smiled in welcome.

"Brother!"

Helvi crouched down—a great handsome boy he had been the time Stark saw him, but he was a man now, with all the laughter turned to grim deep lines around his mouth and the bones of his face standing out like granite ridges.

"Brother," he said again, looking at Stark through a glitter of unashamed tears. "Fool." And he cursed Stark savagely because he had come to Shuruun to look for an idiot who had gone the same way, and was already as good as dead.

"Would you have followed me?" asked Stark.

"But I am only an ignorant child of the swamps," said Helvi. "You come from space, you know the other worlds, you can read and write—you should have better sense!"

Stark grinned. "And I'm still an ignorant child of the rocks. So we're two fools together. Where is Tobal?"

Tobal was Helvi's brother, who had broken taboo and looked for refuge in Shuruun. Apparently he had found peace at last, for Helvi shook his head.

"A man cannot live too long under the sea. It is not enough merely to breathe and eat. Tobal overran his time, and I am close to the end of mine." He held up his hand and then swept it down sharply, watching the broken fires dance along his arms.

"The mind breaks before the body," said Helvi casually, as though it were a matter of no importance.

Zareth spoke. "Helvi has guarded you each period while the others slept."

"And not I alone," said Helvi. "The little one stood with me."

"Guarded me!" said Stark. "Why?"

For answer, Helvi gestured toward a pallet not far away. Malthor lay there, his eyes half open and full of malice, the fresh scar livid on his cheek.

"He feels," said Helvi, "that you should not have fought upon his ship."

Stark felt an inward chill of horror. To lie here helpless, watching Malthor come toward him with open fingers reaching for his helpless throat . . .

He made a passionate effort to move, and gave up, gasping. Helvi grinned.

"Now is the time I should wrestle you, Stark, for I never could throw you before." He gave Stark's head a shake, very gentle for all its apparent roughness. "You'll be throwing me again. Sleep now, and don't worry."

He settled himself to watch, and presently in spite of himself Stark slept, with Zareth curled at his feet like a little dog.

There was no time down there in the heart of the Red Sea. No daylight, no dawn, no space of darkness. No winds blew, no rain nor storm broke the endless silence. Only the lazy currents whispered by on their way to nowhere, and the red sparks danced, and the great hall waited, remembering the past.

Stark waited, too. How long he never knew, but he was used to waiting. He had learned his patience on the knees of the great mountains whose heads lift proudly into open space to look at the Sun, and he had absorbed their own contempt for time.

Little by little, life returned to his body. A mongrel guard came now and again to examine him, pricking Stark's flesh with his knife to test the reaction, so that Stark should not malinger.

He reckoned without Stark's control. The Earthman bore his prodding without so much as a twitch until his limbs were completely his own again. Then he sprang up and pitched the man half the length of the hall, turning over and over, yelling with startled anger.

At the next period of labor, Stark was driven with the rest out into the City of the Lost Ones.

7

Stark had been in places before that oppressed him with a sense of their strangeness or their wickedness—Sinharat, the lovely ruin of coral and gold lost in the Martian wastes; Jekkara, Valkis—the Low-Canal towns that smell of blood and wine; the cliff-caves of Arianrhod on the edge of Darkside, the buried tomb-cities of Callisto. But this—this was nightmare to haunt a man's dreams.

He stared about him as he went in the long line of slaves, and felt such a cold shuddering contraction of his belly as he had never known before.

Wide avenues paved with polished blocks of stone, perfect as ebon mirrors. Buildings, tall and stately, pure and plain, with a calm strength that could outlast the ages. Black, all black, with no fripperies of paint or carving to soften them, only here and there a window like a drowned jewel glinting through the red.

Vines like drifts of snow cascading down the stones. Gardens with close-clipped turf and flowers lifting bright on their green stalks, their petals open to a daylight that was gone, their heads bending as though to some forgotten breeze. All neat, all tended, the branches pruned, the fresh soil turned this morning—by whose hand?

Stark remembered the great forest dreaming at the bottom of the gulf, and shivered. He did not like to think how long ago these flowers must have opened their young bloom to the last light they were ever going to see. For they were dead—dead as the forest, dead as the city. Forever bright—and dead.

Stark thought that it must always have been a silent city. It was impossible to imagine noisy throngs flocking to a market square down those immense avenues. The black walls were not made to echo song or laughter. Even the children must have moved quietly along the garden paths, small wise creatures born to an ancient dignity.

He was beginning to understand now the meaning of that weird forest. The Gulf of Shuruun had not always been a gulf. It had been a valley, rich, fertile, with this great city in its arms, and here and there on the upper slopes the retreat of some noble or philosopher—of which the castle of the Lhari was a survivor.

A wall of rock had held back the Red Sea from this valley. And then, somehow, the wall had cracked, and the sullen crimson tide had flowed slowly, slowly into the fertile bottoms, rising higher, lapping the towers and the treetops in swirling flame, drowning the land forever. Stark wondered if the people had known the disaster was coming, if they had gone forth to tend their gardens for the last time so that they might remain perfect in the embalming gases of the sea.

The columns of slaves, herded by overseers armed with small black weapons similar to the one Egil had used, came out into a broad square whose farther edges were veiled in the red murk. And Stark looked on ruin.

A great building had fallen in the center of the square. The gods only knew what force had burst its walls and tossed the giant blocks like pebbles into a heap. But there it was, the one untidy thing in the city, a mountain of debris.

Nothing else was damaged. It seemed that this had been the place of temples, and they stood unharmed, ranked around the sides of the square, the dim fires rippling through their open porticoes. Deep in their inner shadows Stark thought he could make out images, gigantic things brooding in the spark-shot gloom.

He had no chance to study them. The overseers cursed them on, and now he saw what use the slaves were put to. They were clearing away the wreckage of the fallen building.

Helvi whispered, "For sixteen years men have slaved and died down here, and the work is not half done. And why do the Lhari want it done at all? I'll tell you why. Because they are mad, mad as swamp-dragons gone *musth* in the spring!"

It seemed madness indeed, to labor at this pile of rocks in a dead city at the bottom of the sea. It was madness. And yet the Lhari, though they might be insane, were not fools. There was a reason for it, and Stark was sure it was a good reason—good for the Lhari, at any rate.

An overseer came up to Stark, thrusting him roughly toward a sledge already partly loaded with broken rocks. Stark hesitated, his eyes turning ugly, and Helvi said,

"Come on, you fool! Do you want to be down flat on your back again?"

Stark glanced at the little weapon, blunt and ready, and turned reluctantly to obey. And there began his servitude.

It was a weird sort of life he led. For a while he tried to reckon time by the periods of work and sleep, but he lost count, and it did not greatly matter anyway.

He labored with the others, hauling the huge blocks away, clearing out the cellars that were partly bared, shoring up weak walls underground. The slaves clung to their old habit of thought, calling the work-periods "days" and the sleep-periods "nights."

Each "day" Egil, or his brother Cond, came to see what had been done, and went away black-browed and disappointed, ordering the work speeded up.

Treon was there also much of the time. He would come slowly in his awkward crabwise way and perch like a pale gargoyle on the stones, never speaking, watching with his sad beautiful eyes. He woke a vague foreboding in Stark. There was something awesome in Treon's silent patience, as though he waited the coming of some black doom, long delayed but inevitable. Stark would remember the prophecy, and shiver.

It was obvious to Stark after a while that the Lhari were clearing the building to get at the cellars underneath. The great dark caverns already bared had yielded nothing, but the brothers still hoped. Over and over Cond and Egil sounded the walls and the floors, prying here and there, and chafing at the delay in opening up the underground labyrinth. What they hoped to find, no one knew.

Varra came, too. Alone, and often, she would drift down through the dim mist-fires and watch, smiling a secret smile, her hair like blown silver where the currents played with it. She had nothing but curt words for Egil, but she kept her eyes on the great dark Earthman, and there was a look in them that stirred his blood. Egil was not blind, and it stirred his too, but in a different way.

Zareth saw that look. She kept as close to Stark as possible, asking no favors, but following him around with a sort of quiet devotion, seeming contented only when she was near him. One "night" in the slave barracks she crouched beside his pallet, her hand on his bare knee. She did not speak, and her face was hidden by the floating masses of her hair.

Stark turned her head so that he could see her, pushing the pale cloud gently away.

"What troubles you, little sister?"

Her eyes were wide and shadowed with some vague fear. But she only said, "It's not my place to speak."

"Why not?"

"Because . . ." Her mouth trembled, and then suddenly she said, "Oh, it's foolish, I know. But the woman of the Lhari . . ."

"What about her?"

"She watches you. Always she watches you! And the Lord Egil is angry. There is something in her mind, and it will bring you only evil. I know it!"

"It seems to me," said Stark wryly, "that the Lhari have already done as much evil as possible to all of us."

"No," answered Zareth, with an odd wisdom. "Our hearts are still clean."

Stark smiled. He leaned over and kissed her. "I'll be careful, little sister."

Quite suddenly she flung her arms around his neck and clung to him tightly, and Stark's face sobered. He patted her, rather awkwardly, and then she had gone, to curl up on her own pallet with her head buried in her arms.

Stark lay down. His heart was sad, and there was a stinging moisture in his eyes.

The red eternities dragged on. Stark learned what Helvi had meant when he said that the mind broke before the body. The sea bottom was no place for creatures of the upper air. He learned also the meaning of the metal collars, and the manner of Tobal's death.

Helvi explained.

"There are boundaries laid down. Within them we may range, if we have the strength and the desire after work. Beyond them we may not go. And there is no chance of escape by breaking through the barrier. How this is done I do not understand, but it is so, and the collars are the key to it.

"When a slave approaches the barrier the collar brightens as though with fire, and the slave falls. I have tried this myself, and I know. Half paralyzed, you may still crawl back to safety. But if you are mad, as Tobal was, and charge the barrier strongly . . ."

He made a cutting motion with his hands.

Stark nodded. He did not attempt to explain electricity or electronic vibrations to Helvi, but it seemed plain enough that the force with which the Lhari kept their slaves in check was something of the sort. The collars acted as conductors, perhaps for the same type of beam that was generated in the hand-weapons. When the metal broke the invisible boundary line it triggered off a force-beam from the central power station, in the manner of the obedient electric eye that opens doors and rings alarm bells. First a warning—then death.

The boundaries were wide enough, extending around the city and enclosing a good bit of forest beyond it. There was no possibility of a slave hiding among the trees, because the collar could be traced by the same type of beam, turned to low power, and the punishment meted out to a retaken man was such that few were foolish enough to try that game.

The surface, of course, was utterly forbidden. The one unguarded spot was the island where the central power station was, and here the slaves were allowed to come sometimes at night. The Lhari had discovered that they lived longer and worked better if they had an occasional breath of air and a look at the sky.

Many times Stark made that pilgrimage with the others. Up from the red depths they would come, through the reeling bands of fire where the currents ran, through the clouds of crimson sparks and the sullen patches of stillness that were like pools of blood, a company of white ghosts shrouded in flame, rising from their tomb for a little taste of the world they had lost.

It didn't matter that they were so weary they had barely the strength to get back to the barracks and sleep. They found the strength. To walk again on the open ground, to be rid of the eternal crimson dusk and the oppressive weight on the chest—to look up into the hot blue night of Venus and smell the fragrance of the *liha*-trees borne on the land wind . . . They found the strength.

They sang here, sitting on the island rocks and staring through the mists toward the shore they would never see again. It was their chanting that Stark had heard when he came down the gulf with Malthor, that wordless cry of grief and loss. Now he was here himself, holding Zareth close to comfort her and joining his own deep voice into that primitive reproach to the gods.

While he sat, howling like the savage he was, he studied the power plant, a squat blockhouse of a place. On the nights the slaves came guards were stationed outside to warn them away. The blockhouse was doubly guarded with the shock-beam. To attempt to take it by force would only mean death for all concerned.

Stark gave that idea up for the time being. There was never a second when escape was not in his thoughts, but he was too old in the game to break his neck against a stone wall. Like Malthor, he would wait.

Zareth and Helvi both changed after Stark's coming. Though they never talked of breaking free, both of them lost their air of hopelessness. Stark made neither plans nor promises. But Helvi knew him from of old, and the girl had her own subtle understanding, and they held up their heads again.

Then, one "day" as the work was ending, Varra came smiling out of the red murk and beckoned to him, and Stark's heart gave a great leap. Without a backward look he left Helvi and Zareth, and went with her, down the wide still avenue that led outward to the forest.

8

They left the stately buildings and the wide spaces behind them, and went in among the trees. Stark hated the forest. The city was bad enough, but it was dead, honestly dead, except for those neat nightmare gardens. There was something terrifying about these great trees, full-leafed and green, rioting with flowering vines and all the rich undergrowth of the jungle, standing like massed corpses made lovely by mortuary art. They swayed and rustled as the coiling fires swept them, branches bending to that silent horrible parody of wind. Stark always felt trapped there, and stifled by the stiff leaves and the vines.

But he went, and Varra slipped like a silver bird between the great trunks, apparently happy.

"I have come here often, ever since I was old enough. It's wonderful. Here I can stoop and fly like one of my own hawks." She laughed and plucked a golden flower to set in her hair, and then darted away again, her white legs flashing.

Stark followed. He could see what she meant. Here in this strange sea one's motion was as much flying as swimming, since the pressure equalized the weight of the body. There was a queer sort of thrill in plunging headlong from the tree-tops, to arrow down through a tangle of vines and branches and then sweep upward again.

She was playing with him, and he knew it. The challenge got his blood up. He could have caught her easily but he did not, only now and again he circled her to show his strength. They sped on and on, trailing wakes of flame, a black hawk chasing a silver dove through the forests of a dream.

But the dove had been fledged in an eagle's nest. Stark wearied of the game at last. He caught her and they clung together, drifting still among the trees with the momentum of that wonderful weightless flight.

Her kiss at first was lazy, teasing and curious. Then it changed. All Stark's smoldering anger leaped into a different kind of flame. His handling of her was rough and cruel, and she laughed, a little fierce voiceless laugh, and gave it back to him, and remembered how he had thought her mouth was like a bitter fruit that would give a man pain when he kissed it.

She broke away at last and came to rest on a broad branch, leaning back against the trunk and laughing, her eyes brilliant and cruel as Stark's own. And Stark sat down at her feet.

"What do you want?" he demanded. "What do you want with me?"

She smiled. There was nothing sidelong or shy about her. She was bold as a new blade.

"I'll tell you, wild man."

He started. "Where did you pick up that name?"

"I have been asking the Earthman Larrabee about you. It suits you well." She leaned forward. "This is what I want of you. Slay me Egil and his brother Cond. Also Bor, who will grow up worse than either—although that I can do myself, if you're averse to killing children, though Bor is more monster than child. Grandmother can't live forever, and with my cousins out of the way she's no threat. Treon doesn't count."

"And if I do—what then?"

"Freedom. And me. You'll rule Shuruun at my side."

Stark's eyes were mocking. "For how long, Varra?"

"Who knows? And what does it matter? The years take care of themselves." She shrugged. "The Lhari blood has run out, and it's time there was a fresh strain. Our children will rule after us, and they'll be men."

Stark laughed. He roared with it.

"It's not enough that I'm a slave to the Lhari. Now I must be executioner and herd bull as well!" He looked at her keenly. "Why me, Varra? Why pick on me?"

"Because, as I have said, you are the first man I have seen since my father died. Also, there is something about you . . ."

She pushed herself upward to hover lazily, her lips just brushing his.

"Do you think it would be so bad a thing to live with me, wild man?"

She was lovely and maddening, a silver witch shining among the dim fires of the sea, full of wickedness and laughter. Stark reached out and drew her to him.

"Not bad," he murmured. "Dangerous."

He kissed her, and she whispered, "I think you're not afraid of danger."

"On the contrary, I'm a cautious man." He held her off, where he could look straight into her eyes. "I owe Egil something on my own, but I will not murder. The fight must be fair, and Cond will have to take care of himself."

"Fair! Was Egil fair with you—or me?"

He shrugged. "My way, or not at all."

She thought it over a while, then nodded. "All right. As for Cond, you will give him a blood debt, and pride will make him fight. The Lhari are all proud," she added bitterly. "That's our curse. But it's bred in the bone, as you'll find out."

"One more thing. Zareth and Helvi are to go free, and there must be an end to this slavery."

She stared at him. "You drive a hard bargain, wild man!"

"Yes or no?"

"Yes *and* no. Zareth and Helvi you may have, if you insist, though the gods know what you see in that pallid child. As to the other . . ." She smiled very mockingly. "I'm no fool, Stark. You're evading me, and two can play that game."

He laughed. "Fair enough. And now tell me this, witch with the silver curls—how am I to get at Egil that I may kill him?"

"I'll arrange that."

She said it with such vicious assurance that he was pretty sure she would arrange it. He was silent for a moment, and then he asked,

"Varra—what are the Lhari searching for at the bottom of the sea?"

She answered slowly, "I told you that we are a proud clan. We were driven out of the High Plateaus centuries ago because of our pride. Now it's all we have left, but it's a driving thing."

She paused, and then went on. "I think we had known about the city for a long time, but it had never meant anything until my father became fascinated by it. He would stay down here days at a time, exploring, and it was he who found the weapons and the machine of power which is on the island. Then he found the chart and the metal book, hidden away in a secret place. The book was written in pictographs—as though it was meant to be deciphered—and the chart showed the square with the ruined building and the temples, with a separate diagram of catacombs underneath the ground.

"The book told of a secret—a thing of wonder and of fear. And my father believed that the building had been wrecked to close the entrance to the catacombs where the secret was kept. He determined to find it."

Sixteen years of other men's lives. Stark shivered. "What was the secret, Varra?"

"The manner of controlling life. How it was done I do not know, but with it one might build a race of giants, of monsters, or of gods. You can see what that would mean to us, a proud and dying clan."

"Yes," Stark answered slowly. "I can see."

The magnitude of the idea shook him. The builders of the city must have been wise indeed in their scientific research to evolve such a terrible power. To mold the living cells of the body to one's will—to create, not life itself but its form and fashion . . .

A race of giants, or of gods. The Lhari would like that. To transform their own degenerate flesh into something beyond the race of men, to develop their followers into a corps of fighting men that no one could stand against, to see that their children were given an unholy advantage over all the children of men . . . Stark was appalled at the realization of the evil they could do if they ever found that secret.

Varra said, "There was a warning in the book. The meaning of it was not quite clear, but it seemed that the ancient ones felt that they had sinned against the gods and been punished, perhaps by some plague. They were a strange race, and not human. At any rate, they destroyed the great building there as a barrier against anyone who should come after them, and then let the Red Sea in to cover their city forever. They must have been superstitious children, for all their knowledge."

"Then you all ignored the warning, and never worried that a whole city had died to prove it."

She shrugged. "Oh, Treon has been muttering prophecies about it for years. Nobody listens to him. As for myself, I don't care whether we find the secret or not. My belief is it was destroyed along with the building, and besides, I have no faith in such things."

"Besides," mocked Stark shrewdly, "you wouldn't care to see Egil and Cond striding across the heavens of Venus, and you're doubtful just what your own place would be in the new pantheon."

She showed her teeth at him. "You're too wise for your own good. And now goodbye." She gave him a quick, hard kiss and was gone, flashing upward, high above the treetops where he dared not follow.

Stark made his way slowly back to the city, upset and very thoughtful.

As he came back into the great square, heading toward the barracks, he stopped, every nerve taut.

Somewhere, in one of the shadowy temples, the clapper of a votive bell was swinging, sending its deep pulsing note across the silence. Slowly, slowly, like the beating of a dying heart it came, and mingled with it was the faint sound of Zareth's voice, calling his name.

9

He crossed the square, moving very carefully through the red murk, and presently he saw her.

It was not hard to find her. There was one temple larger than all the rest. Stark judged that it must once have faced the entrance of the fallen building, as though the great figure within was set to watch over the scientists and the philosophers who came there to dream their vast and sometimes terrible dreams.

The philosophers were gone, and the scientists had destroyed themselves. But the image still watched over the drowned city, its hand raised both in warning and in benediction.

Now, across its reptilian knees, Zareth lay. The temple was open on all sides, and Stark could see her clearly, a little white scrap of humanity against the black unhuman figure.

Malthor stood beside her. It was he who had been tolling the votive bell. He had stopped now, and Zareth's words came clearly to Stark.

"Go away, go away! They're waiting for you. Don't come in here!"

"I'm waiting for you, Stark," Malthor called out, smiling. "Are you afraid to come?" And he took Zareth by the hair and struck her, slowly and deliberately, twice across the face.

All expression left Stark's face, leaving it perfectly blank except for his eyes, which took on a sudden lambent gleam. He began to move toward the temple, not hurrying even then, but moving in such a way that it seemed an army could not have stopped him.

Zareth broke free from her father. Perhaps she was intended to break free.

"Egil!" she screamed. "It's a trap . . ."

Again Malthor caught her and this time he struck her harder, so that she crumpled down again across the image that watched with its jeweled, gentle eyes and saw nothing.

"She's afraid for you," said Malthor. "She knows I mean to kill you if I can. Well, perhaps Egil is here also. Perhaps he is not. But certainly Zareth is here. I have beaten her well, and I shall beat her again, as long as she lives to be beaten, for her treachery to me. And if you want to save her from that, you outland dog, you'll have to kill me. Are you afraid?"

Stark was afraid. Malthor and Zareth were alone in the temple. The pillared colonnades were empty except for the dim fires of the sea. Yet Stark was afraid, for an instinct older than speech warned him to be.

It did not matter. Zareth's white skin was mottled with dark bruises, and Malthor was smiling at him, and it did not matter.

Under the shadow of the roof and down the colonnade he went, swiftly now, leaving a streak of fire behind him. Malthor looked into his eyes, and his smile trembled and was gone.

He crouched. And at the last moment, when the dark body plunged down at him as a shark plunges, he drew a hidden knife from his girdle and struck.

Stark had not counted on that. The slaves were searched for possible weapons every day, and even a sliver of stone was forbidden. Somebody must have given it to him, someone . . .

The thought flashed through his mind while he was in the very act of trying to avoid that death blow. *Too late, too late, because his own momentum carried him onto the point* . . .

Reflexes quicker than any man's, the hair-trigger reactions of a wild thing. Muscles straining, the center of balance shifted with an awful wrenching effort, hands grasping at the fire-shot redness as though to force it to defy its own laws. The blade ripped a long shallow gash across his breast. But it did not go home. By a fraction of an inch, it did not go home.

While Stark was still off balance, Malthor sprang.

They grappled. The knife blade glittered redly, a hungry tongue eager to taste Stark's life. The two men rolled over and over, drifting and tumbling erratically, churning the sea to a froth of sparks, and still the image watched, its calm reptilian features unchangingly benign and wise. Threads of a darker red laced heavily across the dancing fires.

Stark got Malthor's arm under his own and held it there with both hands. His back was to the man now. Malthor kicked and clawed with his feet against the backs of Stark's thighs, and his left arm came up and tried to clamp around Stark's throat. Stark buried his chin so that it could not, and then Malthor's hand began to tear at Stark's face, searching for his eyes.

Stark voiced a deep bestial sound in his throat. He moved his head suddenly, catching Malthor's hand between his jaws. He did not let go. Presently his teeth were locked against the thumb-joint, and Malthor was screaming, but Stark could give all his attention to what he was doing with the arm that held the knife. His eyes had changed. They were all beast now, the eyes of a killer blazing cold and beautiful in his dark face.

There was a dull crack, and the arm ceased to strain or fight. It bent back upon itself, and the knife fell, drifting quietly down. Malthor was beyond screaming now. He made one effort to get away as Stark released him, but it was a futile gesture, and he made no sound as Stark broke his neck.

He thrust the body from him. It drifted away, moving lazily with the suck of the currents through the colonnade, now and again touching a black pillar as though in casual wonder, wandering out at last into the square. Malthor was in no hurry. He had all eternity before him.

Stark moved carefully away from the girl, who was trying feebly now to sit up on the knees of the image. He called out, to some unseen presence hidden in the shadows under the roof,

"Malthor screamed your name, Egil. Why didn't you come?"

There was a flicker of movement in the intense darkness of the ledge at the top of the pillars.

"Why should I?" asked the Lord Egil of the Lhari. "I offered him his freedom if he could kill you, but it seems he could not—even though I gave him a knife, and drugs to keep your friend Helvi out of the way."

He came out where Stark could see him, very handsome in a tunic of yellow silk, the blunt black weapon in his hands.

"The important thing was to bait a trap. You would not face me because of this—" He raised the weapon. "I might have killed you as you worked, of course, but my family would have had hard things to say about that. You're a phenomenally good slave."

"They'd have said hard words like 'coward,' Egil," Stark said softly. "And Varra would have set her bird at you in earnest."

Egil nodded. His lip curved cruelly. "Exactly. That amused you, didn't it? And now my little cousin is training another falcon to swoop at me. She hooded you today, didn't she, Outlander?"

He laughed. "Ah well. I didn't kill you openly because there's a better way. Do you think I want it gossiped all over the Red Sea that my cousin jilted me for a foreign slave? Do you think I wish it known that I hated you, and why? No. I would have killed Malthor anyway, if you hadn't done it, because he knew. And when I have killed you and the girl I shall take your bodies to the barrier and leave them there together, and it will be obvious to everyone, even Varra, that you were killed trying to escape."

The weapon's muzzle pointed straight at Stark, and Egil's finger quivered on the trigger stud. Full power, this time. Instead of paralysis, death. Stark measured the distance between himself and Egil. He would be dead before he struck, but the impetus of his leap might carry him on, and give Zareth a chance to escape. The muscles of his thighs stirred and tensed.

A voice said, "And it will be obvious how and why *I* died, Egil? For if you kill them, you must kill me too."

Where Treon had come from, or when, Stark did not know. But he was there by the image, and his voice was full of a strong music, and his eyes shone with a fey light.

Egil had started, and now he swore in fury. "You idiot! You twisted freak! How did you come here?"

"How does the wind come, and the rain? I am not as other men." He laughed, a somber sound with no mirth in it. "I am here, Egil, and that's all that matters. And you will not slay this stranger who is more beast than man, and more man than any of us. The gods have a use for him."

He had moved as he spoke, until now he stood between Stark and Egil.

"Get out of the way," said Egil.

Treon shook his head.

"Very well," said Egil. "If you wish to die, you may."

The fey gleam brightened in Treon's eyes. "This is a day of death," he said softly, "but not of his, or mine."

Egil said a short, ugly word, and raised the weapon up.

Things happened very quickly after that. Stark sprang, arching up and over Treon's head, cleaving the red gases like a burning arrow. Egil started back, and shifted his aim upward, and his finger snapped down on the trigger stud.

Something white came between Stark and Egil, and took the force of the bolt.

Something white. A girl's body, crowned with streaming hair, and a collar of metal glowing bright around the slender neck.

Zareth.

They had forgotten her, the beaten child crouched on the knees of the image. Stark had moved to keep her out of danger, and she was no threat to the mighty Egil, and Treon's thoughts were known only to himself and the winds that taught him. Unnoticed, she had crept to a place where one last plunge would place her between Stark and death.

The rush of Stark's going took him on over her, except that her hair brushed softly against his skin. Then he was on top of Egil, and it had all been done so swiftly that the Lord of the Lhari had not had time to loose another bolt.

Stark tore the weapon from Egil's hand. He was cold, icy cold, and there was a strange blindness on him, so that he could see nothing clearly but Egil's face. And it was Stark who screamed this time, a dreadful sound like the cry of a great cat gone beyond reason or fear.

Treon stood watching. He watched the blood stream darkly into the sea, and he listened to the silence come, and he saw the thing that had been his cousin drift away on the slow tide, and it was as though he had seen it all before and was not surprised.

Stark went to Zareth's body. The girl was still breathing, very faintly, and her eyes turned to Stark, and she smiled.

Stark was blind now with tears. All his rage had run out of him with Egil's blood, leaving nothing but an aching pity and a sadness, and a wondering awe. He took Zareth very tenderly into his arms and held her, dumbly, watching the tears fall on her upturned face. And presently he knew that she was dead.

Sometime later Treon came to him and said softly, "To this end she was born, and she knew it, and was happy. Even now she smiles. And she should, for she had a better death than most of us." He laid his hand on Stark's shoulder. "Come, I'll show you where to put her. She will be safe there, and tomorrow you can bury her where she would wish to be."

Stark rose and followed him, bearing Zareth in his arms.

Treon went to the pedestal on which the image sat. He pressed in a certain way upon a series of hidden springs, and a section of the paving slid noiselessly back, revealing stone steps leading down.

10

Treon led the way down, into darkness that was lightened only by the dim fires they themselves woke in passing. No currents ran here. The red gas lay dull and stagnant, closed within the walls of a square passage built of the same black stone.

"These are the crypts," he said. "The labyrinth that is shown on the chart my father found." And he told about the chart, as Varra had.

He led the way surely, his misshapen body moving without hesitation past the mouths of branching corridors and the doors of chambers whose interiors were lost in shadow.

"The history of the city is here. All the books and the learning, that they had not the heart to destroy. There are no weapons. They were not a warlike people, and I think that the force we of the Lhari have used differently was defensive only, protection against the beasts and the raiding primitives of the swamps."

With a great effort, Stark wrenched his thoughts away from the light burden he carried.

"I thought," he said dully, "that the crypts were under the wrecked building."

"So we all thought. We were intended to think so. That is why the building was wrecked. And for sixteen years we of the Lhari have killed men and women with dragging the stones of it away. But the temple was shown also in the chart. We thought it was there merely as a landmark, an identification for the great building. But I began to wonder . . ."

"How long have you known?"

"Not long. Perhaps two rains. It took many seasons to find the secret of this passage. I came here at night, when the others slept."

"And you didn't tell?"

"No!" said Treon. "You are thinking that if I had told, there would have been an end to the slavery and the death. But what then? My family, turned loose with the power to destroy a world, as this city was destroyed? No! It was better for the slaves to die."

He motioned Stark aside, then, between doors of gold that stood ajar, into a vault so great that there was no guessing its size in the red and shrouding gloom.

"This was the burial place of their kings," said Treon softly. "Leave the little one here."

Stark looked around him, still too numb to feel awe, but impressed even so.

They were set in straight lines, the beds of black marble—lines so long that there was no end to them except the limit of vision. And on them slept the old kings, their bodies, marvelously embalmed, covered with silken palls, their hands crossed upon their breasts, their wise unhuman faces stamped with the mark of peace.

Very gently, Stark laid Zareth down on a marble couch, and covered her also with silk, and closed her eyes and folded her hands. And it seemed to him that her face, too, had that look of peace.

He went out with Treon, thinking that none of them had earned a better place in the hall of kings than Zareth.

"Treon," he said.

"Yes?"

"That prophecy you spoke when I came to the castle—I will bear it out."

Treon nodded. "That is the way of prophecies."

He did not return toward the temple, but led the way deeper into the heart of the catacombs. A great excitement burned within him, a bright and terrible thing that communicated itself to Stark. Treon had suddenly taken on the stature of a figure of destiny, and the Earthman had the feeling that he was in the grip of some current that would plunge on irresistibly until everything in its path was swept away. Stark's flesh quivered.

They reached the end of the corridor at last. And there, in the red gloom, a shape sat waiting before a black, barred door. A shape grotesque and incredibly misshapen, so horribly malformed that by it Treon's crippled body appeared almost beautiful. Yet its face was as the faces of the images and the old kings, and its sunken eyes had once held wisdom, and one of its seven-fingered hands was still slim and sensitive.

Stark recoiled. The thing made him physically sick, and he would have turned away, but Treon urged him on.

"Go closer. It is dead, embalmed, but it has a message for you. It has waited all this time to give that message."

Reluctantly, Stark went forward.

Quite suddenly, it seemed that the thing spoke.

Behold me. Look upon me, and take counsel before you grasp that power which lies beyond the door!

Stark leaped back, crying out, and Treon smiled.

"It was so with me. But I have listened to it many times since then. It speaks not with a voice, but within the mind, and only when one has passed a certain spot."

Stark's reasoning mind pondered over that. A thought-record, obviously, triggered off by an electronic beam. The ancients had taken good care that their warning would be heard and understood by anyone who should solve the riddle of the catacombs. Thought-images, speaking directly to the brain, know no barrier of time or language.

He stepped forward again, and once more the telepathic voice spoke to him.

"We tampered with the secrets of the gods. We intended no evil. It was only that we love perfection, and wished to shape all living things as flawless as our buildings and our gardens. We did not know that it was against the Law . . .

"I was one of those who found the way to change the living cell. We used the unseen force that comes from the Land of the Gods beyond the sky, and we so harnessed it that we could build from the living flesh as the potter builds from the clay. We healed the halt and the maimed, and made those stand tall and straight who came crooked from the egg, and for a time we were as brothers to the gods themselves. I myself, even I, knew the glory of perfection. And then came the reckoning.

"The cell, once made to change, would not stop changing. The growth was slow, and for a while we did not notice it, but when we did it was too late. We were becoming a city of monsters. And the force we had used was worse than useless, for the more we tried to mold the monstrous flesh to its normal shape, the more the stimulated cells grew and grew, until the bodies we labored over were like things of wet mud that flow and change even as you look at them.

"One by one the people of the city destroyed themselves. And those of us who were left realized the judgment of the gods, and our duty. We made all things ready, and let the Red Sea hide us forever from our own kind, and those who should come after.

"Yet we did not destroy our knowledge. Perhaps it was our pride only that forbade us, but we could not bring ourselves to do it. Perhaps other gods, other races wiser than we, can take away the evil and keep only the good. For it is good for all creatures to be, if not perfect, at least strong and sound.

"But heed this warning, whoever you may be that listen. If your gods are jealous, if your people have not the wisdom or the knowledge to succeed where we failed in controlling this force, then touch it not! Or you, and all your people, will become as I."

The voice stopped. Stark moved back again, and said to Treon incredulously, "And your family would ignore that warning?"

Treon laughed. "They are fools. They are cruel and greedy and very proud. They would say that this was a lie to frighten away intruders, or that human flesh would not be subject to the laws that govern the flesh of reptiles. They would say anything, because they have dreamed this dream too long to be denied."

Stark shuddered and looked at the black door. "The thing ought to be destroyed."

"Yes," said Treon softly.

His eyes were shining, looking into some private dream of his own. He started forward, and when Stark would have gone with him he thrust him back, saying, "No. You have no part in this." He shook his head.

"I have waited," he whispered, almost to himself. "The winds bade me wait, until the day was ripe to fall from the tree of death. I have waited, and at dawn I knew, for the wind said, *Now is the gathering of the fruit at hand*."

He looked suddenly at Stark, and his eyes had in them a clear sanity, for all their feyness.

"You heard, Stark. 'We made those stand tall and straight who came crooked from the egg'. I will have my hour. I will stand as a man for the little time that is left."

He turned, and Stark made no move to follow. He watched Treon's twisted body recede, white against the red dusk, until it passed the monstrous watcher and came to the black door. The long thin arms reached up and pushed the bar away.

The door swung slowly back. Through the opening Stark glimpsed a chamber that held a structure of crystal rods and discs mounted on a frame of metal, the whole thing glowing and glittering with a restless bluish light that dimmed and brightened as though it echoed some vast pulse-beat. There was other apparatus, intricate banks of tubes and condensers, but this was the heart of it, and the heart was still alive.

Treon passed within and closed the door behind him.

Stark drew back some distance from the door and its guardian, crouched down, and set his back against the wall. He thought about the apparatus. Cosmic rays, perhaps—the unseen force that came from beyond the sky. Even yet, all their potentialities were not known. But a few luckless spacemen had found that under certain conditions they could do amazing things to human tissue.

It was a line of thought Stark did not like at all. He tried to keep his mind away from Treon entirely. He tried not to think at all. It was dark there in the corridor, and very still, and the shapeless horror sat quiet in the doorway and waited with him. Stark began to shiver, a shallow animal-twitching of the flesh.

He waited. After a while he thought Treon must be dead, but he did not move. He did not wish to go into that room to see.

He waited.

Suddenly he leaped up, cold sweat bursting out all over him. A crash had echoed down the corridor, a clashing of shattered crystal and a high singing note that trailed off into nothing.

The door opened.

A man came out. A man tall and straight and beautiful as an angel, a strong-limbed man with Treon's face, Treon's tragic eyes. And behind him the chamber was dark. The pulsing heart of power had stopped.

The door was shut and barred again. Treon's voice was saying, "There are records left, and much of the apparatus, so that the secret is not lost entirely. Only it is out of reach."

He came to Stark and held out his hand. "Let us fight together, as men. And do not fear. I shall die, long before this body changes." He smiled, the remembered smile that was full of pity for all living things. "I know, for the winds have told me."

Stark took his hand and held it.

"Good," said Treon. "And now lead on, stranger with the fierce eyes. For the prophecy is yours, and the day is yours, and I who have crept about like a snail all my life know little of battles. Lead, and I will follow."

Stark fingered the collar around his neck. "Can you rid me of this?"

Treon nodded. "There are tools and acid in one of the chambers."

He found them, and worked swiftly, and while he worked Stark thought, smiling—and there was no pity in that smile at all.

They came back at last into the temple, and Treon closed the entrance to the catacombs. It was still night, for the square was empty of slaves. Stark found Egil's weapon where it had fallen, on the ledge where Egil died.

"We must hurry," said Stark. "Come on."

11

The island was shrouded heavily in mist and the blue darkness of the night. Stark and Treon crept silently among the rocks until they could see the glimmer of torchlight through the window-slits of the power station.

There were seven guards, five inside the blockhouse, two outside to patrol.

When they were close enough, Stark slipped away, going like a shadow, and never a pebble turned under his bare foot. Presently he found a spot to his liking and crouched down. A sentry went by not three feet away, yawning and looking hopefully at the sky for the first signs of dawn.

Treon's voice rang out, the sweet unmistakable voice. "Ho, there, guards!"

The sentry stopped and whirled around. Off around the curve of the stone wall someone began to run, his sandals thud-thudding on the soft ground, and the second guard came up.

"Who speaks?" one demanded. "The Lord Treon?"

They peered into the darkness, and Treon answered, "Yes." He had come forward far enough so that they could make out the pale blur of his face, keeping his body out of sight among the rocks and the shrubs that sprang up between them.

"Make haste," he ordered. "Bid them open the door, there." He spoke in breathless jerks, as though spent. "A tragedy—a disaster! Bid them open!"

One of the men leaped to obey, hammering on the massive door that was kept barred from the inside. The other stood goggle-eyed, watching. Then the door opened, spilling a flood of yellow torchlight into the red fog.

"What is it?" cried the men inside. "What has happened?"

"Come out!" gasped Treon. "My cousin is dead, the Lord Egil is dead, murdered by a slave."

He let that sink in. Three or more men came outside into the circle of light, and their faces were frightened, as though somehow they feared they might be held responsible for this thing.

"You know him," said Treon. "The great black-haired one from Earth. He has slain the Lord Egil and got away into the forest, and we need all extra guards to go after him, since many must be left to guard the other slaves, who are mutinous. You, and you—" He picked out the four biggest ones. "Go at once and join the search. I will stay here with the others."

It nearly worked. The four took a hesitant step or two, and then one paused and said doubtfully,

"But, my lord, it is forbidden that we leave our posts, for any reason. Any reason at all, my lord! The Lord Cond would slay us if we left this place."

"And you fear the Lord Cond more than you do me," said Treon philosophically. "Ah, well. I understand."

He stepped out, full into the light.

A gasp went up, and then a startled yell. The three men from inside had come out armed only with swords, but the two sentries had their shock-weapons. One of them shrieked,

"It is a demon, who speaks with Treon's voice!"

And the two black weapons started up.

Behind them, Stark fired two silent bolts in quick succession, and the men fell, safely out of the way for hours. Then he leaped for the door.

He collided with two men who were doing the same thing. The third had turned to hold Treon off with his sword until they were safely inside.

Seeing that Treon, who was unarmed, was in danger of being spitted on the man's point, Stark fired between the two lunging bodies as he fell, and brought the guard down. Then he was involved in a thrashing tangle of arms and legs, and a lucky blow jarred the shock-weapon out of his hand.

Treon added himself to the fray. Pleasuring in his new strength, he caught one man by the neck and pulled him off. The guards were big men, and powerful, and they fought desperately. Stark was bruised and bleeding from a cut mouth before he could get in a finishing blow.

Someone rushed past him into the doorway. Treon yelled. Out of the tail of his eyes Stark saw the Lhari sitting dazed on the ground. The door was closing.

Stark hunched up his shoulders and sprang.

He hit the heavy panel with a jar that nearly knocked him breathless. It slammed open, and there was a cry of pain and the sound of someone falling. Stark burst through, to find the last of the guards rolling every which way over the floor. But one rolled over onto his feet again, drawing his sword as he rose. He had not had time before.

Stark continued his rush without stopping. He plunged headlong into the man before the point was clear of the scabbard, bore him over and down, and finished the man off with savage efficiency.

He leaped to his feet, breathing hard, spitting blood out of his mouth, and looked around the control room. But the others had fled, obviously to raise the warning.

The mechanism was simple. It was contained in a large black metal oblong about the size and shape of a coffin, equipped with grids and lenses and dials. It hummed softly to itself, but what its source of power was Stark did not know. Perhaps those same cosmic rays, harnessed to a different use.

He closed what seemed to be a master switch, and the humming stopped, and the flickering light died out of the lenses. He picked up the slain guard's sword and carefully wrecked everything that was breakable. Then he went outside again.

Treon was standing up, shaking his head. He smiled ruefully.

"It seems that strength alone is not enough," he said. "One must have skill as well."

"The barriers are down," said Stark. "The way is clear."

Treon nodded, and went with him back into the sea. This time both carried shock-weapons taken from the guards—six in all, with Egil's. Total armament for war.

As they forged swiftly through the red depths, Stark asked, "What of the people of Shuruun? How will they fight?"

Treon answered, "Those of Malthor's breed will stand for the Lhari. They must, for all their hope is there. The others will wait, until they see which side is safest. They would rise against the Lhari if they dared, for we have brought them only fear in their lifetimes. But they will wait, and see."

Stark nodded. He did not speak again.

They passed over the brooding city, and Stark thought of Egil and of Malthor who were part of that silence now, drifting slowly through the empty streets where the little currents took them, wrapped in their shrouds of dim fire.

He thought of Zareth sleeping in the hall of kings, and his eyes held a cold, cruel light.

They swooped down over the slave barracks. Treon remained on watch outside. Stark went in, taking with him the extra weapons.

The slaves still slept. Some of them dreamed, and moaned in their dreaming, and others might have been dead, with their hollow faces white as skulls.

Slaves. One hundred and four, counting the women.

Stark shouted out to them, and they woke, starting up on their pallets, their eyes full of terror. Then they saw who it was that called them, standing collarless and armed, and there was a great surging and a clamor that stilled as Stark shouted again, demanding silence. This time Helvi's voice echoed his. The tall barbarian had wakened from his drugged sleep.

Stark told them, very briefly, all that happened.

"You are freed from the collar," he said. "This day you can survive or die as men, and not as slaves." He paused, then asked, "Who will go with me into Shuruun?"

They answered with one voice, the voice of the Lost Ones, who saw the red pall of death begin to lift from over them. The Lost Ones, who had found hope again.

Stark laughed. He was happy. He gave the extra weapons to Helvi and three others that he chose, and Helvi looked into his eyes and laughed too.

Treon spoke from the open door. "They are coming!"

Stark gave Helvi quick instructions and darted out, taking with him one of the other men. With Treon, they hid among the shrubbery of the garden that was outside the hall, patterned and beautiful, swaying its lifeless brilliance in the lazy drifts of fire.

The guards came. Twenty of them, tall armed men, to turn out the slaves for another period of labor, dragging the useless stones.

And the hidden weapons spoke with their silent tongues.

Eight of the guards fell inside the hall. Nine of them went down outside. Ten of the slaves died before the remaining three were overcome.

Now there were twenty swords among ninety-four slaves, counting the women.

They left the city and rose up over the dreaming forest, a flight of white ghosts with flames in their hair, coming back from the red dusk and the silence to find the light again.

Light, and vengeance.

The first pale glimmer of dawn was sifting through the clouds as they came up among the rocks below the castle of the Lhari. Stark left them and went like a shadow up the tumbled cliffs to where he had hidden his gun on the night he had first come to Shuruun. Nothing stirred. The fog lifted up from the sea like a vapor of blood, and the face of Venus was still dark. Only the high clouds were touched with pearl.

Stark returned to the others. He gave one of his shock-weapons to a swamp-lander with a cold madness in his eyes. Then he spoke a few final words to Helvi and went back with Treon under the surface of the sea.

Treon led the way. He went along the face of the submerged cliff, and presently he touched Stark's arm and pointed to where a round mouth opened in the rock.

"It was made long ago," said Treon, "so that the Lhari and their slavers might come and go and not be seen. Come—and be very quiet."

They swam into the tunnel mouth, and down the dark way that lay beyond, until the lift of the floor brought them out of the sea. Then they felt their way silently along, stopping now and again to listen.

Surprise was their only hope. Treon had said that with the two of them they might succeed. More men would surely be discovered, and meet a swift end at the hands of the guards.

Stark hoped Treon was right.

They came to a blank wall of dressed stone. Treon leaned his weight against one side, and a great block swung slowly around on a central pivot. Guttering torchlight came through the crack. By it Stark could see that the room beyond was empty.

They stepped through, and as they did so a servant in bright silks came yawning into the room with a fresh torch to replace the one that was dying.

He stopped in mid-step, his eyes widening. He dropped the torch. His mouth opened to shape a scream, but no sound came, and Stark remembered that these servants were tongueless—to prevent them from telling what they saw or heard in the castle, Treon said.

The man spun about and fled, down a long dim-lit hall. Stark ran him down without effort. He struck once with the barrel of his gun, and the man fell and was still.

Treon came up. His face had a look almost of exaltation, a queer shining of the eyes that made Stark shiver. He led on, through a series of empty rooms, all somber black, and they met no one else for a while.

He stopped at last before a small door of burnished gold. He looked at Stark once, and nodded, and thrust the panels open and stepped through.

12

They stood inside the vast echoing hall that stretched away into darkness until it seemed there was no end to it. The cluster of silver lamps burned as before, and within their circle of radiance the Lhari started up from their places and stared at the strangers who had come in through their private door.

Cond, and Arel with her hands idle in her lap. Bor, pummeling the little dragon to make it hiss and snap, laughing at its impotence. Varra, stroking the winged creature on her wrist, testing with her white finger the sharpness of its beak. And the old woman, with a scrap of fat meat halfway to her mouth.

They had stopped, frozen, in the midst of these actions. And Treon walked slowly into the light.

"Do you know me?" he said.

A strange shivering ran through them. Now, as before, the old woman spoke first, her eyes glittering with a look as rapacious as her appetite.

"You are Treon," she said, and her whole vast body shook.

The name went crying and whispering off around the dark walls, *Treon! Treon! Treon!* Cond leaped forward, touching his cousin's straight strong body with hands that trembled.

"You have found it," he said. "The secret."

"Yes." Treon lifted his silver head and laughed, a beautiful ringing bell-note that sang from the echoing corners. "I found it, and it's gone, smashed, beyond your reach forever. Egil is dead, and the day of the Lhari is done."

There was a long, long silence, and then the old woman whispered, *"You lie!"*

Treon turned to Stark.

"Ask him, the stranger who came bearing doom upon his forehead. Ask him if I lie."

Cond's face became something less than human. He made a queer crazed sound and flung himself at Treon's throat.

Bor screamed suddenly. He alone was not much concerned with the finding or the losing of the secret, and he alone seemed to realize the significance of Stark's presence. He screamed, looking at the big dark man, and went rushing off down the hall, crying for the guard as he went, and the echoes roared and racketed. He fought open the great doors and ran out, and as he did so the sound of fighting came through from the compound.

The slaves, with their swords and clubs, with their stones and shards of rock, had come over the wall from the cliffs.

Stark had moved forward, but Treon did not need his help. He had got his hands around Cond's throat, and he was smiling. Stark did not disturb him.

The old woman was talking, cursing, commanding, choking on her own apoplectic breath. Arel began to laugh. She did not move, and her hands remained limp and open in her lap. She laughed and laughed, and Varra looked at Stark and hated him.

"You're a fool, wild man," she said. "You would not take what I offered you, so you shall have nothing—only death."

She slipped the hood from her creature and set it straight at Stark. Then she drew a knife from her girdle and plunged it into Treon's side.

Treon reeled back. His grip loosened and Cond tore away, half throttled, raging, his mouth flecked with foam. He drew his short sword and staggered in upon Treon.

Furious wings beat and thundered around Stark's head, and talons were clawing for his eyes. He reached up with his left hand and caught the brute by one leg and held it. Not long, but long enough to get one clear shot at Cond that dropped him in his tracks. Then he snapped the falcon's neck.

He flung the creature at Varra's feet, and picked up the gun again. The guards were rushing into the hall now at the lower end, and he began to fire at them.

Treon was sitting on the floor. Blood was coming in a steady trickle from his side, but he had the shock-weapon in his hands, and he was still smiling.

There was a great boiling roar of noise from outside. Men were fighting there, killing, dying, screaming their triumph or their pain. The echoes raged within the hall, and the noise of Stark's gun was like a hissing thunder. The guards, armed only with swords, went down like ripe wheat before the sickle, but there were many of them, too many for Stark and Treon to hold for long.

The old woman shrieked and shrieked, and was suddenly still.

Helvi burst in through the press, with a knot of collared slaves. The fight dissolved into a whirling chaos. Stark threw his gun away. He was afraid now of hitting his own men. He caught up a sword from a fallen guard and began to hew his way to the barbarian.

Suddenly Treon cried his name. He leaped aside, away from the man he was fighting, and saw Varra fall with the dagger still in her hand. She had come up behind him to stab, and Treon had seen and pressed the trigger stud just in time.

For the first time, there were tears in Treon's eyes.

A sort of sickness came over Stark. There was something horrible in this spectacle of a family destroying itself. He was too much the savage to be sentimental over Varra, but all the same he could not bear to look at Treon for a while.

Presently he found himself back to back with Helvi, and as they swung their swords—the shock-weapons had been discarded for the same reason as Stark's gun—Helvi panted,

"It has been a good fight, my brother! We cannot win, but we can have a good death, which is better than slavery!"

It looked as though Helvi was right. The slaves, unfortunately, weakened by their long confinement, worn out by overwork, were being beaten back. The tide turned, and Stark was swept with it out into the compound, fighting stubbornly.

The great gate stood open. Beyond it stood the people of Shuruun, watching, hanging back—as Treon had said, they would wait and see.

In the forefront, leaning on his stick, stood Larrabee the Earthman.

Stark cut his way free of the press. He leaped up onto the wall and stood there, breathing hard, sweating, bloody, with a dripping sword in his hand. He waved it, shouting down to the men of Shuruun.

"What are you waiting for, you scuts, you women? The Lhari are dead, the Lost Ones are freed—must we of Earth do all your work for you?"

And he looked straight at Larrabee.

Larrabee stared back, his dark suffering eyes full of a bitter mirth. "Oh, well," he said in English. "Why not?"

He threw back his head and laughed, and the bitterness was gone. He voiced a high, shrill rebel yell and lifted his stick like a cudgel, limping toward the gate, and the men of Shuruun gave tongue and followed him.

After that, it was soon over.

They found Bor's body in the stable pens, where he had fled to hide when the fighting started. The dragons, maddened by the smell of the blood, had slain him very quickly.

Helvi had come through alive, and Larrabee, who had kept himself carefully out of harm's way after he had started the men of Shuruun on their attack. Nearly half the slaves were dead, and the rest wounded. Of those who had served the Lhari, few were left.

Stark went back into the great hall. He walked slowly, for he was very weary, and where he set his foot there was a bloody print, and his arms were red to the elbows, and his breast was splashed with the redness. Treon watched him come, and smiled, nodding.

"It is as I said. And I have outlived them all."

Arel had stopped laughing at last. She had made no move to run away, and the tide of battle had rolled over her and drowned her unaware. The old woman lay still, a mountain of inert flesh upon her bed. Her hand still clutched a ripe fruit, clutched convulsively in the moment of death, the red juice dripping through her fingers.

"Now I am going, too," said Treon, "and I am well content. With me goes the last of our rotten blood, and Venus will be the cleaner for it. Bury my body deep, stranger with the fierce eyes. I would not have it looked on after this."

He sighed and fell forward.

Bor's little dragon crept whimpering out from its hiding place under the old woman's bed and scurried away down the hall, trailing its dragging rope.

Stark leaned on the taffrail, watching the dark mass of Shuruun recede into the red mists.

The decks were crowded with the outland slaves, going home. The Lhari were gone, the Lost Ones freed forever, and Shuruun was now only another port on the Red Sea. Its people would still be wolf's-heads and pirates, but that was natural and as it should be. The black evil was gone.

Stark was glad to see the last of it. He would be glad also to see the last of the Red Sea.

The off-shore wind set the ship briskly down the gulf. Stark thought of Larrabee, left behind with his dreams of winter snows and city streets and women with dainty feet. It seemed that he had lived too long in Shuruun, and had lost the courage to leave it.

"Poor Larrabee," he said to Helvi, who was standing near him. "He'll die in the mud, still cursing it."

Someone laughed behind him. He heard a limping step on the deck and turned to see Larrabee coming toward him.

"Changed my mind at the last minute," Larrabee said. "I've been below, lest I should see my muddy brats and be tempted to change it again." He leaned beside Stark, shaking his head. "Ah, well, they'll do nicely without me. I'm an old man, and I've a right to choose my own place to die in. I'm going back to Earth, with you."

Stark glanced at him. "I'm not going to Earth."

Larrabee sighed. "No. No, I suppose you're not. After all, you're no Earthman, really, except for an accident of blood. Where are you going?"

"I don't know. Away from Venus, but I don't know yet where."

Larrabee's dark eyes surveyed him shrewdly. " 'A restless, cold-eyed tiger of a man', that's what Varra said. He's lost something, she said. He'll look for it all his life, and never find it."

After that there was silence. The red fog wrapped them, and the wind rose and sent them scudding before it.

Then, faint and far off, there came a moaning wail, a sound like broken chanting that turned Stark's flesh cold.

All on board heard it. They listened, utterly silent, their eyes wide, and somewhere a woman began to weep.

Stark shook himself. "It's only the wind," he said roughly, "in the rocks by the strait."

The sound rose and fell, weary, infinitely mournful, and the part of Stark that was N'Chaka said that he lied. It was not the wind that keened so sadly through the mists. It was the voices of the Lost Ones who were forever lost—Zareth, sleeping in the hall of kings, and all the others who would never leave the dreaming city and the forest, never find the light again.

Stark shivered, and turned away, watching the leaping fires of the strait sweep toward them.

ROBERT A(NSON) HEINLEIN (1907–1988)

While Robert A. Heinlein wrote and published some Fantasy stories (most notably for Unknown Worlds), he is primarily remembered as a writer of Hard Science Fiction that spanned half a century. This is how he liked to be thought of during his lifetime as well.

Heinlein was one of the greatest Science Fiction writers of all time. He may have been the most adept writer of pure Science Fiction. He could also be one of the most varied, and like all highly revered authors (such as Hawthorne and Hemingway, for example) had moments of unevenness. Robert Heinlein was extremely effective at portraying the society and culture in which each of his stories was written. Since his tales were published for some fifty years during his lifetime, his stories went through periods of change (in terms of topic, style, and mood) that are fairly compared to the phases that an artist such as Picasso evolved and devolved through during his career.

In the late 1930s and early 1940s, Heinlein was a more than competent pulp magazine writer. If Erle Stanley Gardner, Dashiell Hammett, and Raymond Chandler were model writers of pulp Detective Fiction at this time, then Robert A. Heinlein was a model writer of pulp Science Fiction. During the post–World War II through the 1960s Cold War years, Heinlein was an exquisite critic of government, the military, and the two-dimensional, paranoid people who could often be found in these organizations. Such is the case with "The Long Watch." In the 1960s and 1970s, Heinlein wrote progressive and counterculture stories, such as Stranger in a Strange Land *(1961) and* Farnham's Freehold *(1964). To follow the Science Fiction career of Robert A. Heinlein is to follow the evolution of twentieth-century Science Fiction as a genre.*

The Long Watch

(American Legion Magazine, *December 1949*)

> *"Nine ships blasted off from Moon Base. Once in space, eight of them formed a globe around the smallest. They held this formation all the way to Earth.*
>
> *"The small ship displayed the insignia of an admiral—yet there was no living thing of any sort in her. She was not even a passenger ship, but a drone, a robot ship intended for radioactive cargo. This trip she carried nothing but a lead coffin—and a Geiger counter that was never quiet."*
>
> —from the editorial *After Ten Years*,
> film 38, 17 June 2009, Archives of
> the *N. Y. Times*

Johnny Dahlquist blew smoke at the Geiger counter. He grinned wryly and tried it again. His whole body was radioactive by now. Even his breath, the smoke from his cigarette, could make the Geiger counter scream.

How long had he been here? Time doesn't mean much on the Moon. Two days? Three? A week? He let his mind run back: the last clearly marked time in his mind was when the Executive Officer had sent for him, right after breakfast—

"Lieutenant Dahlquist, reporting to the Executive Officer."

Colonel Towers looked up. "Ah, John Ezra. Sit down, Johnny. Cigarette?"

Johnny sat down, mystified but flattered. He admired Colonel Towers, for his brilliance, his ability to dominate, and for his battle record. Johnny had no battle record; he had been commissioned on completing his doctor's degree in nuclear physics and was now junior bomb officer of Moon Base.

The Colonel wanted to talk politics; Johnny was puzzled. Finally Towers had come to the point; it was not safe (so he said) to leave control of the world in political hands; power must be held by a scientifically selected group. In short—the Patrol.

Johnny was startled rather than shocked. As an abstract idea, Towers' notion sounded plausible. The League of Nations had folded up; what would keep the United Nations from breaking up, too, and thus lead to another World War. "And you know how bad such a war would be, Johnny."

Johnny agreed. Towers said he was glad that Johnny got the point. The senior bomb officer could handle the work, but it was better to have both specialists.

Johnny sat up with a jerk. "You are going to *do* something about it?" He had thought the Exec was just talking.

Towers smiled. "We're not politicians; we don't just talk. We act."

Johnny whistled. "When does this start?"

Towers flipped a switch. Johnny was startled to hear his own voice, then identified the recorded conversation as having taken place in the junior officers' messroom. A political argument he remembered, which he had walked out on . . . a good thing, too! But being spied on annoyed him.

Towers switched it off. "We *have* acted," he said. "We know who is safe and who isn't. Take Kelly—" He waved at the loudspeaker. "Kelly is politically unreliable. You noticed he wasn't at breakfast?"

"Huh? I thought he was on watch."

"Kelly's watch-standing days are over. Oh, relax; he isn't hurt."

Johnny thought this over. "Which list am I on?" he asked. "Safe or unsafe?"

"Your name has a question mark after it. But I have said all along that you could be depended on." He grinned engagingly. "You won't make a liar of me, Johnny?"

Dahlquist didn't answer; Towers said sharply, "Come now—what do you think of it? Speak up."

"Well, if you ask me, you've bitten off more than you can chew. While it's true that Moon Base controls the Earth, Moon Base itself is a sitting duck for a ship. One bomb—*blooie!*"

Towers picked up a message form and handed it over; it read: I HAVE YOUR CLEAN LAUNDRY—ZACK. "That means every bomb in the *Trygve Lie* has been put out of commission. I have reports from every ship we need worry about." He stood up. "Think it over and see me after lunch. Major Morgan needs your help right away to change control frequencies on the bombs."

"The control frequencies?"

"Naturally. We don't want the bombs jammed before they reach their targets."

"What? You said the idea was to *prevent* war."

Towers brushed it aside. "There won't be a war—just a psychological demonstration, an unimportant town or two. A little bloodletting to save an all-out war. Simple arithmetic."

He put a hand on Johnny's shoulder. "You aren't squeamish, or you wouldn't be a bomb officer. Think of it as a surgical operation. And think of your family."

Johnny Dahlquist had been thinking of his family. "Please, sir, I want to see the Commanding Officer."

Towers frowned. "The Commodore is not available. As you know, I speak for him. See me again—after lunch."

The Commodore was decidedly not available; the Commodore was dead. But Johnny did not know that.

Dahlquist walked back to the messroom, bought cigarettes, sat down and had a smoke. He got up, crushed out the butt, and headed for the Base's west airlock. There he got into his space suit and went to the lockmaster. "Open her up, Smitty."

The marine looked surprised. "Can't let anyone out on the surface without word from Colonel Towers, sir. Hadn't you heard?"

"Oh, yes! Give me your order book." Dahlquist took it, wrote a pass for himself, and signed it "by direction of Colonel Towers." He added, "Better call the Executive Officer and check it."

The lockmaster read it and stuck the book in his pocket. "Oh, no, Lieutenant. Your word's good."

"Hate to disturb the Executive Officer, eh? Don't blame you." He stepped in, closed the inner door, and waited for the air to be sucked out.

Out on the Moon's surface he blinked at the light and hurried to the track-rocket terminus; a car was waiting. He squeezed in, pulled down the hood, and punched the starting button. The rocket car flung itself at the hills, dived through and came out on a plain studded with projectile rockets, like candles on a cake. Quickly it dived into a second tunnel through more hills. There was a stomach-wrenching deceleration and the car stopped at the underground atom-bomb armory.

As Dahlquist climbed out he switched on his walkie-talkie. The space-suited guard at the entrance came to port-arms. Dahlquist said, "Morning, Lopez," and walked by him to the airlock. He pulled it open.

The guard motioned him back. "Hey! Nobody goes in without the Executive Officer's say-so." He shifted his gun, fumbled in his pouch and got out a paper. "Read it, Lieutenant."

Dahlquist waved it away. "I drafted that order myself. *You* read it; you've misinterpreted it."

"I don't see how, Lieutenant."

Dahlquist snatched the paper, glanced at it, then pointed to a line. "See? '—except persons specifically designated by the Executive Officer.' That's the bomb officers, Major Morgan and me."

The guard looked worried. Dahlquist said, "Damn it, look up 'specifically designated'—it's under *'Bomb Room, Security, Procedure for,'* in your standing orders. Don't tell me you left them in the barracks!"

"Oh, no, sir! I've got 'em." The guard reached into his pouch. Dahlquist gave him back the sheet; the guard took it, hesitated, then leaned his weapon against his hip, shifted the paper to his left hand, and dug into his pouch with his right.

Dahlquist grabbed the gun, shoved it between the guard's legs, and jerked. He threw the weapon away and ducked into the airlock. As he slammed the door he saw the guard struggling to his feet and reaching for his side arm. He dogged the outer door shut and felt a tingle in his fingers as a slug struck the door.

He flung himself at the inner door, jerked the spill lever, rushed back to the outer door and hung his weight on the handle. At once he could feel it stir. The guard was lifting up; the lieutenant was pulling down, with only his low Moon weight to anchor him. Slowly the handle raised before his eyes.

Air from the bomb room rushed into the lock through the spill valve. Dahlquist felt his space suit settle on his body as the pressure in the lock began to equal the pressure in the suit. He quit straining and let the guard raise the handle. It did not matter; thirteen tons of air pressure now held the door closed.

He latched open the inner door to the bomb room, so that it could not swing shut. As long as it was open, the airlock could not operate; no one could enter.

Before him in the room, one for each projectile rocket, were the atom bombs, spaced in rows far enough apart to defeat any faint possibility of spontaneous chain reaction. They were the deadliest things in the known universe, but they were his babies. He had placed himself between them and anyone who would misuse them.

But, now that he was here, he had no plan to use his temporary advantage.

The speaker on the wall sputtered into life. "Hey! Lieutenant! What goes on here? You gone crazy?" Dahlquist did not answer. Let Lopez stay confused—it would take him that much longer to make up his mind what to do. And Johnny Dahlquist needed as many minutes as he could squeeze. Lopez went on protesting. Finally he shut up.

Johnny had followed a blind urge not to let the bombs—*his* bombs!—be used for "demonstrations on unimportant towns." But what to do next? Well, Towers couldn't get through the lock. Johnny would sit tight until hell froze over.

Don't kid yourself, John Ezra! Towers could get in. Some high explosive against the outer door—then the air would whoosh out, our boy Johnny would drown in blood from his burst lungs—and the bombs would be sitting there, unhurt. They were built to stand the jump from Moon to Earth; vacuum would not hurt them at all.

He decided to stay in his space suit; explosive decompression didn't appeal to him. Come to think about it, death from old age was his choice.

Or they could drill a hole, let out the air, and open the door without wrecking the lock. Or Towers might even have a new airlock built outside the old. Not likely, Johnny thought; a *coup d'etat* depended on speed. Towers was almost sure to take the quickest way—blasting. And Lopez was probably calling the Base right now. Fifteen minutes for Towers to suit up and get here, maybe a short dicker—then *whoosh!* the party is over.

Fifteen minutes—

In fifteen minutes the bombs might fall back into the hands of the conspirators; in fifteen minutes he must make the bombs unusable.

An atom bomb is just two or more pieces of fissionable metal, such as plutonium. Separated, they are no more explosive than a pound of butter; slapped together, they explode. The complications lie in the gadgets and circuits and gun used to slap them together in the exact way and at the exact time and place required.

These circuits, the bomb's "brain," are easily destroyed—but the bomb itself is hard to destroy because of its very simplicity. Johnny decided to smash the "brains"—and quickly!

The only tools at hand were simple ones used in handling the bombs. Aside from a Geiger counter, the speaker on the walkie-talkie circuit, a television rig to the base, and the bombs themselves, the room was bare. A bomb to be worked on was taken elsewhere—not through fear of explosion, but to reduce radiation exposure for personnel. The radioactive material in a bomb is buried in a "tamper"—in these bombs, gold. Gold stops alpha, beta, and much of the deadly gamma radiation—but not neutrons.

The slippery, poisonous neutrons which plutonium gives off had to escape, or a chain reaction—explosion!—would result. The room was bathed in an invisible, almost undetectable rain of neutrons. The place was unhealthy; regulations called for staying in it as short a time as possible.

The Geiger counter clicked off the "background" radiation, cosmic rays, the trace of radioactivity in the Moon's crust, and secondary radioactivity set up all through the room by neutrons. Free neutrons have the nasty trait of infecting what they strike, making it radioactive, whether it be concrete wall or human body. In time the room would have to be abandoned.

Dahlquist twisted a knob on the Geiger counter; the instrument stopped clicking. He had used a suppressor circuit to cut out noise of "background" radiation at the level then present. It reminded him uncomfortably of the danger of staying here. He took out the radiation exposure film all radiation personnel carry; it was a direct-response type and had been fresh when he arrived. The most sensitive end was faintly darkened already. Half way down the film a red line crossed it. Theoretically, if the wearer was exposed to enough radioactivity in a week to darken the film to that line, he was, as Johnny reminded himself, a "dead duck."

Off came the cumbersome space suit; what he needed was speed. Do the job and surrender—better to be a prisoner than to linger in a place as "hot" as this.

He grabbed a ball hammer from the tool rack and got busy, pausing only to switch off the television pick-up. The first bomb bothered him. He started to smash the cover plate of the "brain," then stopped, filled with reluctance. All his life he had prized fine apparatus.

He nerved himself and swung; glass tinkled, metal creaked. His mood changed; he began to feel a shameful pleasure in destruction. He pushed on with enthusiasm, swinging, smashing, destroying!

So intent was he that he did not at first hear his name called. "Dahlquist! Answer me! Are you there?"

He wiped sweat and looked at the TV screen. Towers' perturbed features stared out.

Johnny was shocked to find that he had wrecked only six bombs. Was he going to be caught before he could finish? Oh, no! He *had* to finish. Stall, son, stall! "Yes, Colonel? You called me?"

"I certainly did! What's the meaning of this?"

"I'm sorry, Colonel."

Towers' expression relaxed a little. "Turn on your pick-up, Johnny, I can't see you. What was that noise?"

"The pick-up is on," Johnny lied. "It must be out of order. That noise—uh, to tell the truth, Colonel, I was fixing things so that nobody could get in here."

Towers hesitated, then said firmly, "I'm going to assume that you are sick and send you to the Medical Officer. But I want you to come out of there, right away. That's an order, Johnny."

Johnny answered slowly. "I can't just yet, Colonel. I came here to make up my mind and I haven't quite made it up. You said to see you after lunch."

"I meant you to stay in your quarters."

"Yes, sir. But I thought I ought to stand watch on the bombs, in case I decided you were wrong."

"It's not for you to decide, Johnny. I'm your superior officer. You are sworn to obey me."

"Yes, sir." This was wasting time; the old fox might have a squad on the way now. "But I swore to keep the peace, too. Could you come out here and talk it over with me? I don't want to do the wrong thing."

Towers smiled. "A good idea, Johnny. You wait there. I'm sure you'll see the light." He switched off.

"There," said Johnny. "I hope you're convinced that I'm a half-wit—you slimy mistake!" He picked up the hammer, ready to use the minutes gained.

He stopped almost at once; it dawned on him that wrecking the "brains" was not enough. There were no spare "brains," but there was a well-stocked electronics shop. Morgan could jury-rig control circuits for bombs. Why, he could himself—not a neat job, but one that would work. Damnation! He would have to wreck the bombs themselves—and in the next ten minutes.

But a bomb was solid chunks of metal, encased in a heavy tamper, all tied in with a big steel gun. It couldn't be done—not in ten minutes.

Damn!

Of course, there was one way. He knew the control circuits; he also knew how to beat them. Take this bomb: if he took out the safety bar, unhooked the proximity circuit, shorted the delay circuit, and cut in the arming circuit by hand—then unscrewed *that* and reached in *there*, he could, with just a long, stiff wire, set the bomb off.

Blowing the other bombs and the valley itself to Kingdom Come.

Also Johnny Dahlquist. That was the rub.

All this time he was doing what he had thought out, up to the step of actually setting off the bomb. Ready to go, the bomb seemed to threaten, as if crouching to spring. He stood up, sweating.

He wondered if he had the courage. He did not want to funk—and hoped that he would. He dug into his jacket and took out a picture of Edith and the baby. "Honeychile," he said, "if I get out of this, I'll never even try to beat a red light." He kissed the picture and put it back. There was nothing to do but wait.

What was keeping Towers? Johnny wanted to make sure that Towers was in blast range. What a joke on the jerk! Me—sitting here, ready to throw the switch on him. The idea tickled him; it led to a better: why blow himself up—alive?

There was another way to rig it—a "dead man" control. Jigger up some way so that the last step, the one that set off the bomb, would not happen as long as he kept his hand on a switch or a lever or something. Then, if they blew open the door, or shot him, or anything—up goes the balloon!

Better still, if he could hold them off with the threat of it, sooner or later help would come—Johnny was sure that most of the Patrol was not in this stinking conspiracy—and then: Johnny comes marching home! What a reunion! He'd resign and get a teaching job; he'd stood his watch.

All the while, he was working. Electrical? No, too little time. Make it a simple mechanical linkage. He had it doped out but had hardly begun to build it when the loudspeaker called him. "Johnny?"

"That you, Colonel?" His hands kept busy.

"Let me in."

"Well, now, Colonel, that wasn't in the agreement." Where in blue blazes was something to use as a long lever?

"I'll come in alone, Johnny, I give you my word. We'll talk face to face."

His word! "We can talk over the speaker, Colonel." Hey, that was it—a yardstick, hanging on the tool rack.

"Johnny, I'm warning you. Let me in, or I'll blow the door off."

A wire—he needed a wire, fairly long and stiff. He tore the antenna from his suit. "You wouldn't do that, Colonel. It would ruin the bombs."

"Vacuum won't hurt the bombs. Quit stalling."

"Better check with Major Morgan. Vacuum won't hurt them; explosive decompression would wreck every circuit." The Colonel was not a bomb specialist; he shut up for several minutes. Johnny went on working.

"Dahlquist," Towers resumed, "that was a clumsy lie. I checked with Morgan. You have sixty seconds to get into your suit, if you aren't already. I'm going to blast the door."

"No, you won't," said Johnny. "Ever hear of a 'dead man' switch?" Now for a counterweight—and a sling.

"Eh? What do you mean?"

"I've rigged number seventeen to set off by hand. But I put in a gimmick. It won't blow while I hang on to a strap I've got in my hand. But if anything happens to me—*up she goes!* You are about fifty feet from the blast center. Think it over."

There was a short silence. "I don't believe you."

"No? Ask Morgan. He'll believe me. He can inspect it, over the TV pickup." Johnny lashed the belt of his space suit to the end of the yardstick.

"You said the pick-up was out of order."

"So I lied. This time I'll prove it. Have Morgan call me."

Presently Major Morgan's face appeared. "Lieutenant Dahlquist?"

"Hi, Stinky. Wait a sec." With great care Dahlquist made one last connection while holding down the end of the yardstick. Still careful, he shifted his grip to the belt, sat down on the floor, stretched an arm and switched on the TV pick-up. "Can you see me, Stinky?"

"I can see you," Morgan answered stiffly. "What is this nonsense?"

"A little surprise I whipped up." He explained it—what circuits he had cut out, what ones had been shorted, just how the jury-rigged mechanical sequence fitted in.

Morgan nodded. "But you're bluffing, Dahlquist. I feel sure that you haven't disconnected the 'K' circuit. You don't have the guts to blow yourself up."

Johnny chuckled. "I sure haven't. But that's the beauty of it. It can't go off, *so long as I am alive.* If your greasy boss, ex-Colonel Towers, blasts the door, then I'm dead and the bomb goes off. It won't matter to me, but it will to him. Better tell him." He switched off.

Towers came on over the speaker shortly. "Dahlquist?"

"I hear you."

"There's no need to throw away your life. Come out and you will be retired on full pay. You can go home to your family. That's a promise."

Johnny got mad. "You keep my family out of this!"

"Think of them, man."

"Shut up. Get back to your hole. I feel a need to scratch and this whole she-bang might just explode in your lap."

2

Johnny sat up with a start. He had dozed, his hand hadn't let go the sling, but he had the shakes when he thought about it.

Maybe he should disarm the bomb and depend on their not daring to dig him out? But Towers' neck was already in hock for treason; Towers might risk it. If he did and the bomb were disarmed, Johnny would be dead and Towers would have the bombs. No, he had gone this far; he wouldn't let his baby girl grow up in a dictatorship just to catch some sleep.

He heard the Geiger counter clicking and remembered having used the suppressor circuit. The radioactivity in the room must be increasing, perhaps from scattering the "brain" circuits—the circuits were sure to be infected; they had lived too long too close to plutonium. He dug out his film.

The dark area was spreading toward the red line.

He put it back and said, "Pal, better break this deadlock or you are going to shine like a watch dial." It was a figure of speech; infected animal tissue does not glow—it simply dies, slowly.

The TV screen lit up; Towers' face appeared. "Dahlquist? I want to talk to you."

"Go fly a kite."

"Let's admit you have us inconvenienced."

"Inconvenienced, hell—I've got you stopped."

"For the moment. I'm arranging to get more bombs—"

"Liar."

"—but you are slowing us up. I have a proposition."

"Not interested."

"Wait. When this is over I will be chief of the world government. If you cooperate, even now, I will make you my administrative head."

Johnny told him what to do with it. Towers said, "Don't be stupid. What do you gain by dying?"

Johnny grunted. "Towers, what a prime stinker you are. You spoke of my family. I'd rather see them dead than living under a two-bit Napoleon like you. Now go away—I've got some thinking to do."

Towers switched off.

Johnny got out his film again. It seemed no darker but it reminded him forcibly that time was running out. He was hungry and thirsty—and he could not stay awake forever. It took four days to get a ship up from Earth; he could not expect rescue any sooner. And he wouldn't last four days—once the darkening spread past the red line he was a goner.

His only chance was to wreck the bombs beyond repair, and get out—before that film got much darker.

He thought about ways, then got busy. He hung a weight on the sling, tied a line to it. If Towers blasted the door, he hoped to jerk the rig loose before he died.

There was a simple, though arduous, way to wreck the bombs beyond any capacity of Moon Base to repair them. The heart of each was two hemispheres of plutonium, their flat surfaces polished smooth to permit perfect contact when slapped together. Anything less would prevent the chain reaction on which atomic explosion depended.

Johnny started taking apart one of the bombs.

He had to bash off four lugs, then break the glass envelope around the inner assembly. Aside from that the bomb came apart easily. At last he had in front of him two gleaming, mirror-perfect half globes.

A blow with the hammer—and one was no longer perfect. Another blow and the second cracked like glass; he had tapped its crystalline structure just right.

Hours later, dead tired, he went back to the armed bomb. Forcing himself to steady down, with extreme care he disarmed it. Shortly its silvery hemispheres too were useless. There was no longer a usable bomb in the room—but huge fortunes in the most valuable, most poisonous, and most deadly metal in the known world were spread around the floor.

Johnny looked at the deadly stuff. "Into your suit and out of here, son," he said aloud. "I wonder what Towers will say?"

He walked toward the rack, intending to hang up the hammer. As he passed, the Geiger counter chattered wildly.

Plutonium hardly affects a Geiger counter; secondary infection from plutonium does. Johnny looked at the hammer, then held it closer to the Geiger counter. The counter screamed.

Johnny tossed it hastily away and started back toward his suit.

As he passed the counter it chattered again. He stopped short.

He pushed one hand close to the counter. Its clicking picked up to a steady roar. Without moving he reached into his pocket and took out his exposure film. It was dead black from end to end.

3

Plutonium taken into the body moves quickly to bone marrow. Nothing can be done; the victim is finished. Neutrons from it smash through the body, ionizing tissue, transmuting atoms into radioactive isotopes, destroying and killing. The fatal dose is unbelievably small; a mass a tenth the size of a grain of table salt is more than enough—a dose small enough to enter through the tiniest scratch. During the historic "Manhattan Project" immediate high amputation was considered the only possible first-aid measure.

Johnny knew all this but it no longer disturbed him. He sat on the floor, smoking a hoarded cigarette, and thinking. The events of his long watch were running through his mind.

He blew a puff of smoke at the Geiger counter and smiled without humor to hear it chatter more loudly. By now even his breath was "hot"—carbon-14, he supposed, exhaled from his blood stream as carbon dioxide. It did not matter.

There was no longer any point in surrendering, nor would he give Towers the satisfaction—he would finish out this watch right here. Besides, by keeping up the bluff that one bomb was ready to blow, he could stop them from capturing the raw material from which bombs were made. That might be important in the long run.

He accepted, without surprise, the fact that he was not unhappy. There was a sweetness about having no further worries of any sort. He did not hurt, he was not uncomfortable, he was no longer even hungry. Physically he still felt fine and his mind was at peace. He was dead—he knew that he was dead; yet for a time he was able to walk and breathe and see and feel.

He was not even lonesome. He was not alone; there were comrades with him—the boy with his finger in the dike, Colonel Bowie, too ill to move but insisting that he be carried across the line, the dying Captain of the *Chesapeake* still with deathless challenge on his lips, Rodger Young peering into the gloom. They gathered about him in the dusky bomb room.

And of course there was Edith. She was the only one he was aware of. Johnny wished that he could see her face more clearly. Was she angry? Or proud and happy?

Proud though unhappy—he could see her better now and even feel her hand. He held very still.

Presently his cigarette burned down to his fingers. He took a final puff, blew it at the Geiger counter, and put it out. It was his last. He gathered several butts and fashioned a roll-your-own with a bit of paper found in a pocket. He lit it carefully and settled back to wait for Edith to show up again. He was very happy.

He was still propped against the bomb case, the last of his salvaged cigarettes cold at his side, when the speaker called out again. "Johnny? Hey, Johnny! Can you hear me? This is Kelly. It's all over. The *Lafayette* landed and Towers blew his brains out. Johnny? *Answer me.*"

When they opened the outer door, the first man in carried a Geiger counter in front of him on the end of a long pole. He stopped at the threshold and backed out hastily. "Hey, chief!" he called. "Better get some handling equipment—uh, and a lead coffin, too."

"Four days it took the little ship and her escort to reach Earth. Four days while all of Earth's people awaited her arrival. For ninety-eight hours all commercial programs were off television; instead there was an endless dirge—the Dead March *from* Saul, *the* Valhalla *theme,* Going Home, *the Patrol's own* Landing Orbit.

"The nine ships landed at Chicago Port. A drone tractor removed the casket from the small ship; the ship was then refueled and blasted off in an escape trajectory, thrown away into outer space, never again to be used for a lesser purpose.

"The tractor progressed to the Illinois town where Lieutenant Dahlquist had been born, while the dirge continued. There it placed the casket on a pedestal, inside a barrier marking the distance of safe approach. Space marines, arms reversed and heads bowed, stood guard around it; the crowds stayed outside this circle. And still the dirge continued.

"When enough time had passed, long, long after the heaped flowers had withered, the lead casket was enclosed in marble, just as you see it today."

❀ RAY(MOND DOUGLAS) BRADBURY (1920–)

An author who draws heavily on personal experience and cultural inheritance, who relies heavily on the history of ideas, free word association, and the potential of imagery and color through language, Ray Bradbury has proven himself a magician of words and teller of universal tales that incorporate myths and symbols that define American and world culture.

Bradbury's short stories, novels, stage plays, screenplays, poems, and radio plays appeal to all ages, and his dexterity with issues of youth and age, and coming of age, makes his writing significant to a wide-ranging public. He has always drawn heavily on personal experiences, making autobiography the largest overriding element of his work. Bradbury is a visionary who is sensitive to the emotions and idiosyncrasies and wonders that compose the human experience. The subjects and social issues addressed in his fiction include detailed discussions of various religions, youth, age, death and dying, nature and the environment, life and living, family and friends, race, gender, love, sex, Eros, the rural community, a variety of geographical locales, and much more.

The popular literary genres and related story types that Ray Bradbury has contributed to since his early pulp magazine days of the 1940s are numerous. A representative list includes Gothic tales, Dark Fantasy, Detective Fiction, and Science Fiction. And, Ray Bradbury writes not only genre fiction; he crosses between genres and even ignores such categorization altogether.

The episodic novel The Martian Chronicles, *among other things, is best appreciated as an environmental allegory. In the 1940s and early 1950s, Bradbury was writing intelligent, insightful stories about ethnicity, race relations, and gender long before such stories became fashionable. He was also writing other moral allegories. "There Will Come Soft Rains" is a classic tale found in his landmark novel,* The Martian Chronicles.

There Will Come Soft Rains
(Colliers, *May 6, 1950*)

AUGUST 2026

In the living room the voice-clock sang, *Tick-tock, seven o'clock, time to get up, time to get up, seven o'clock!* as if it were afraid that nobody would. The morning house lay empty. The clock ticked on, repeating and repeating its sounds into the emptiness. *Seven-nine, breakfast time, seven-nine!*

In the kitchen the breakfast stove gave a hissing sigh and ejected from its warm interior eight pieces of perfectly browned toast, eight eggs sunnyside up, sixteen slices of bacon, two coffees, and two cool glasses of milk.

"Today is August 4, 2026," said a second voice from the kitchen ceiling, "in the city of Allendale, California." It repeated the date three times for memory's sake. "Today is Mr. Featherstone's birthday. Today is the anniversary of Tilita's marriage. Insurance is payable, as are the water, gas, and light bills."

Somewhere in the walls, relays clicked, memory tapes glided under electric eyes.

Eight-one, tick-tock, eight-one o'clock, off to school, off to work, run, run, eight-one! But no doors slammed, no carpets took the soft tread of rubber heels. It was raining outside. The weather box on the front door sang quietly: "Rain, rain, go away; rubbers, raincoats for today . . ." And the rain tapped on the empty house, echoing.

Outside, the garage chimed and lifted its door to reveal the waiting car. After a long wait the door swung down again.

At eight-thirty the eggs were shriveled and the toast was like stone. An aluminum wedge scraped them into the sink, where hot water whirled them down a metal throat which digested and flushed them away to the distant sea. The dirty dishes were dropped into a hot washer and emerged twinkling dry.

Nine-fifteen, sang the clock, *time to clean.*

Out of warrens in the wall, tiny robot mice darted. The rooms were acrawl with the small cleaning animals, all rubber and metal. They thudded against chairs, whirling their mustached runners, kneading the rug nap, sucking gently at hidden dust. Then, like mysterious invaders, they popped into their burrows. Their pink electric eyes faded. The house was clean.

Ten o'clock. The sun came out from behind the rain. The house stood alone in a city of rubble and ashes. This was the one house left standing. At night the ruined city gave off a radioactive glow which could be seen for miles.

Ten-fifteen. The garden sprinklers whirled up in golden founts, filling the soft morning air with scatterings of brightness. The water pelted windowpanes, running down the charred west side where the house had been burned evenly free of its white paint. The entire west face of the house was black, save for five places. Here the silhouette in paint of a man mowing a lawn. Here, as in a photograph, a woman bent to pick flowers. Still farther over, their images burned on wood in one titanic instant, a small boy, hands flung into the air; higher up, the image of a thrown ball, and opposite him a girl, hands raised to catch a ball which never came down.

The five spots of paint—the man, the woman, the children, the ball—remained. The rest was a thin charcoaled layer.

The gentle sprinkler rain filled the garden with falling light.

Until this day, how well the house had kept its peace. How carefully it had inquired, "Who goes there? What's the password?" and, getting no answer from lonely foxes and whining cats, it had shut up its windows and drawn shades in an old-maidenly preoccupation with self-protection which bordered on a mechanical paranoia.

It quivered at each sound, the house did. If a sparrow brushed a window, the shade snapped up. The bird, startled, flew off! No, not even a bird must touch the house!

The house was an altar with ten thousand attendants, big, small, servicing, attending, in choirs. But the gods had gone away, and the ritual of the religion continued senselessly, uselessly.

Twelve noon.

A dog whined, shivering, on the front porch.

The front door recognized the dog voice and opened. The dog, once huge and fleshy, but now gone to bone and covered with sores, moved in and through the house, tracking mud. Behind it whirred angry mice, angry at having to pick up mud, angry at inconvenience.

For not a leaf fragment blew under the door but what the wall panels flipped open and the copper scrap rats flashed swiftly out. The offending dust, hair, or paper, seized in miniature steel jaws, was raced back to the burrows. There, down tubes which fed into the cellar, it was dropped into the sighing vent of an incinerator which sat like evil Baal in a dark corner.

The dog ran upstairs, hysterically yelping to each door, at last realizing, as the house realized, that only silence was here.

It sniffed the air and scratched the kitchen door. Behind the door, the stove was making pancakes which filled the house with a rich baked odor and the scent of maple syrup.

The dog frothed at the mouth, lying at the door, sniffing, its eyes turned to fire. It ran wildly in circles, biting at its tail, spun in a frenzy, and died. It lay in the parlor for an hour.

Two o'clock, sang a voice.

Delicately sensing decay at last, the regiments of mice hummed out as softly as blown gray leaves in an electrical wind.

Two-fifteen.

The dog was gone.

In the cellar, the incinerator glowed suddenly and a whirl of sparks leaped up the chimney.

Two thirty-five.

Bridge tables sprouted from patio walls. Playing cards fluttered onto pads in a shower of pips. Martinis manifested on an oaken bench with egg-salad sandwiches. Music played.

But the tables were silent and the cards untouched.

At four o'clock the tables folded like great butterflies back through the paneled walls.

Four-thirty.

The nursery walls glowed.

Animals took shape: yellow giraffes, blue lions, pink antelopes, lilac panthers cavorting in crystal substance. The walls were glass. They looked out upon color and fantasy. Hidden films clocked through well-oiled sprockets, and the walls lived. The nursery floor was woven to resemble a crisp, cereal meadow. Over this ran aluminum roaches and iron crickets, and in the hot still air butterflies of delicate red tissue wavered among the sharp aroma of animal spoors! There was the sound like a great matted yellow hive of bees within a dark bellows, the lazy bumble of a purring lion. And there was the patter of okapi feet and the murmur of a fresh jungle rain, like other hoofs, falling upon the summer-starched grass. Now the walls dissolved into distances of parched weed, mile on mile, and warm endless sky. The animals drew away into thorn brakes and water holes.

It was the children's hour.

Five o'clock. The bath filled with clear hot water.

Six, seven, eight o'clock. The dinner dishes manipulated like magic tricks, and in the study a *click.* In the metal stand opposite the hearth where a fire now blazed up warmly, a cigar popped out, half an inch of soft gray ash on it, smoking, waiting.

Nine o'clock. The beds warmed their hidden circuits, for nights were cool here.

Nine-five. A voice spoke from the study ceiling:

"Mrs. McClellan, which poem would you like this evening?"

The house was silent.

The voice said at last, "Since you express no preference, I shall select a poem at random." Quiet music rose to back the voice. "Sara Teasdale. As I recall, your favorite. . . ."

> *"There will come soft rains and the smell of the ground,*
> *And swallows circling with their shimmering sound;*
>
> *And frogs in the pools singing at night,*
> *And wild plum trees in tremulous white;*
>
> *Robins will wear their feathery fire,*
> *Whistling their whims on a low fence-wire;*
>
> *And not one will know of the war, not one*
> *Will care at last when it is done.*
>
> *Not one would mind, neither bird nor tree,*
> *If mankind perished utterly;*
>
> *And Spring herself, when she woke at dawn*
> *Would scarcely know that we were gone."*

The fire burned on the stone hearth and the cigar fell away into a mound of quiet ash on its tray. The empty chairs faced each other between the silent walls, and the music played.

At ten o'clock the house began to die.

The wind blew. A falling tree bough crashed through the kitchen window. Cleaning solvent, bottled, shattered over the stove. The room was ablaze in an instant!

"Fire!" screamed a voice. The house lights flashed, water pumps shot water from the ceilings. But the solvent spread on the linoleum, licking, eating, under the kitchen door, while the voices took it up in chorus: "Fire, fire, fire!"

The house tried to save itself. Doors sprang tightly shut, but the windows were broken by the heat and the wind blew and sucked upon the fire.

The house gave ground as the fire in ten billion angry sparks moved with flaming ease from room to room and then up the stairs. While scurrying water rats squeaked from the walls, pistoled their water, and ran for more. And the wall sprays let down showers of mechanical rain.

But too late. Somewhere, sighing, a pump shrugged to a stop. The quenching rain ceased. The reserve water supply which had filled baths and washed dishes for many quiet days was gone.

The fire crackled up the stairs. It fed upon Picassos and Matisses in the upper halls, like delicacies, baking off the oily flesh, tenderly crisping the canvases into black shavings.

Now the fire lay in beds, stood in windows, changed the colors of drapes!

And then, reinforcements.

From attic trapdoors, blind robot faces peered down with faucet mouths gushing green chemical.

The fire backed off, as even an elephant must at the sight of a dead snake. Now there were twenty snakes whipping over the floor, killing the fire with a clear cold venom of green froth.

But the fire was clever. It had sent flames outside the house, up through the attic to the pumps there. An explosion! The attic brain which directed the pumps was shattered into bronze shrapnel on the beams.

The fire rushed back into every closet and felt of the clothes hung there.

The house shuddered, oak bone on bone, its bared skeleton cringing from the heat, its wire, its nerves revealed as if a surgeon had torn the skin off to let the red veins and capillaries quiver in the scalded air. Help, help! Fire! Run, run! Heat snapped mirrors like the brittle winter ice. And the voices wailed Fire, fire, run, run, like a tragic nursery rhyme, a dozen voices, high, low, like children dying in a forest, alone, alone. And the voices fading as the wires popped their sheathings like hot chestnuts. One, two, three, four, five voices died.

In the nursery the jungle burned. Blue lions roared, purple giraffes bounded off. The panthers ran in circles, changing color, and ten million animals, running before the fire, vanished off toward a distant steaming river. . . .

Ten more voices died. In the last instant under the fire avalanche, other choruses, oblivious, could be heard announcing the time, playing music, cutting the lawn by remote-control mower, or setting an umbrella frantically out and in the slamming and opening front door, a thousand things happening, like a clock shop when each clock strikes the hour insanely before or after the other, a scene of maniac confusion, yet unity; singing, screaming, a few last cleaning mice darting bravely out to carry the horrid ashes away! And one voice, with sublime disregard for the situation, read poetry aloud in the fiery study, until all the film spools burned, until all the wires withered and the circuits cracked.

The fire burst the house and let it slam flat down, puffing out skirts of spark and smoke.

In the kitchen, an instant before the rain of fire and timber, the stove could be seen making breakfasts at a psychopathic rate, ten dozen eggs, six loaves of toast, twenty dozen bacon strips, which, eaten by fire, started the stove working again, hysterically hissing!

The crash. The attic smashing into kitchen and parlor. The parlor into cellar, cellar into sub-cellar. Deep freeze, armchair, film tapes, circuits, beds, and all like skeletons thrown in a cluttered mound deep under.

Smoke and silence. A great quantity of smoke.

Dawn showed faintly in the east. Among the ruins, one wall stood alone. Within the wall, a last voice said, over and over again and again, even as the sun rose to shine upon the heaped rubble and steam:

"Today is August 5, 2026, today is August 5, 2026, today is . . ."

☙ FRANK BELKNAP LONG (1903–1994)

A contemporary and friend of H. P. Lovecraft in the 1920s, Frank Belknap Long remained a master writer of Dark Fantasy, Fantasy, and Science Fiction until his death seven decades later. He lived in New York City, the publishing center of the world for two centuries.

Long was a regular contributor to both Weird Tales *and* Astounding Stories. *He wrote several novels but was more successful as a short story writer. Arkham House publishers released four volumes of his work:* The Hounds of Tindalos *(1946—a short story collection),* The Horror from the Hills *(1963—a novel),* The Rim of the Unknown *(1972—a short story collection), and* In Mayan Splendor *(1977—a poetry collection). Some of Long's best early Weird Fantasy and Science Fiction is found in the collection* Night Fears *(1979). His stories have been frequently anthologized.*

"Invasion" is a Frank Belknap Long Science Fiction offering that provides an inventive twist to the standard invasion story of yesterday and today. Its theme of humans being foolish and wasting a great resource—friendship—is reminiscent of Harry Bates's "Farewell to the Master" (1940) and the movie adaptation of the same, The Day the Earth Stood Still *(1951).*

Invasion

(Startling Stories, *July 1950*)

It wasn't at all the way they had imagined it would be. On the radio the news had sounded so horribly ominous, like the opening and closing chords of a funeral march with dull explosions interrupting the music.

Earth invaded from Mars or Venus, shining lights in the sky, the slow remorseless approach of the conquerors, their terrible weapons sending great shafts of electric radiance boring through the night.

The television screen in the living room had gone dead on the frozen face of a marionette. For an instant the radio in the children's nursery upstairs had squealed and hummed with static while the voice of an announcer pierced the bedlam like the last lingering wail of a banshee at Finnegan's wake.

"We're taking you to Washington! The next voice you hear will be that of the President—"

Brindled Betty, the tabbycat, sat staring now at a bough-shadowed windowpane, her back hairs bristling in fright. But the tapping on the door downstairs was so quiet and gentle it did not even frighten the children as it went echoing through the house.

It has been said that the splash of a stone dropped into a bottomless well can be heard by those with dread in their hearts and the will to listen. The tapping was as light as the patter of rain on a gossamer web in a summer garden. And yet it could be heard in every part of the house, upstairs and down, from cellar to attic.

"Let us in!" it seemed to be saying. "We're from Mars and we've come to stay. You may as well make the best of what has happened!"

Monica Dayton looked at her husband and then down at the tousled head of her small son. She groped for words.

"Dan, it can't be true! Only the very ignorant were taken in by that Martian invasion scare of ten or twelve years ago. We've got to remember that! Only the *very* ignorant!"

Dan Dayton was far too disturbed to contradict his wife. In his mind's gaze he saw a cone of cold blue radiance sweeping straight toward him across the floor. Blotting out the children first and then the mother of his children!

Blotting out Tommy, eight-next-month, and Kathy, six-last-week, with a horrible droning and a humming, unearthly as an echo in a vacuum, chill with the deadliness of the completely alien. Dan Dayton did not even consider what might happen to himself.

He never had considered himself first in the ordinary affairs of life and he wasn't starting now. He walked to the front door and threw it open.

"May I come in?" the youth asked in a pleasant friendly voice.

The youth was very tall, well over six feet, and quite resplendently attired in a single shining garment which seemed molded to his body, giving him the aspect of an acrobat in tights. He stood facing Dayton with the moonlight at his back, his shoulders held straight. It was easy to see that he was smiling, though his face was half in shadows. Everything about him seemed to radiate confidence and good will.

"May I come in?" he repeated.

Dayton was too startled to say anything. He simply fell back and the stranger moved past him into the living room.

The stranger looked first at the children and then at Dan Dayton's wife. "How are you, children?" he said, smiling. "How are you, Monica?"

Dayton returned into the room and stood staring from the youth to his wife, utter consternation in his eyes. Monica's lips began to shake. It was a full minute before she could find enough self-confidence to say, "Who are you? Where did you come from?"

"I came from Mars!" the young man said.

"He's crazy, Mom!" Tommy cried, drawing close to his mother in sudden fright.

"You speak English!" Monica's eyes were suddenly wild with relief. "You know my name! If you were really from Mars you'd never call it Mars! Mars is what we call it! You'd have another name for it."

"We have," the youth said. "But before I knocked your minds were pleasant with a drowsy hum of thoughts. Your thoughts were like golden bees, swarming unbidden into my mind. It was a simple matter for me to make your thoughts yield the rich honey of understanding!"

"Telepathy!" Monica flashed him a scornful look. "You can read our minds—is that what you're trying to say?"

The youth nodded.

"Well, it won't wash!" Monica exclaimed. "If you can read my thoughts what am I thinking now? Tell me! We'll put it to the test, do you hear?"

For answer the youth walked to the window and drew back the drapes. "The spaceship which brought me to Earth is out there," he said. "You were thinking that if I could show you the ship you would believe me."

With exclamations of wild disbelief the children rushed to the window. The youth stepped aside so that both the children and Monica could peer out.

"Golly!" Tommy muttered.

"Get back, let me look!" Kathy pleaded.

Dan Dayton stepped forward and raised his daughter up, a choking dryness in his throat.

The ship was at least a hundred feet in length and it rested on the front lawn in a blaze of light. It tapered at both ends like a great silver cigar.

The youth looked around the room. A look of gratification came into his face when his eyes lighted on a comfortable easy chair. He strode to the chair and sat down, crossing his long legs.

"There is so much that you do not know!" he said. "So many ways in which I can be of help."

Outside the windows the night lay dreaming in quiet moonlight. A June bug buzzed into the room and circled the stranger's head twice before it went zooming out into the night air again.

Tommy was the first to accept the spaceship on the lawn and the stranger in the chair—to really accept what had happened with his emotions as well as his mind.

"What's Mars like?" he asked. "Do you have really big cities like New York or Chicago?"

"Of course we have!" the youth said. "But there is no dust in our cities. A Martian city is like a great silver urn, blue and cool within. It is like a flower opening snowy petals to the dawn."

"Do Martians have fun playing games?" Tommy asked. "I mean—baseball and things like that?"

"Not baseball, Tommy!" the youth said. "Martians go skating. On Earth there are insects which skate over the water in deep woodland pools. Martians skate over frozen blue lakes in much the same way. It gives them a great deal of pleasure."

"Do they do all of the other things we do?" Kathy asked. "Eat and sleep and go for walks and have children?"

"Pretty nearly!" the youth said. "But they are the worst walkers in the world. It is so much easier to fly that they have almost forgotten how to walk."

"*You* walk all right!" Tommy said.

"There is a reason for that, Tommy!" the youth said.

Monica did an incredible thing then. She approached the seated youth and bent over him. Without trying to analyze her emotions, feeling only a fierce concern for the welfare of her children, she looked deep into his eyes.

If the stranger were evil surely her mother's instinct would know. Surely, surely, she would be warned in time.

When Monica straightened there was a great wonder in her gaze. "He is speaking the truth!" she said. "He wishes only to help us and asks nothing in return."

"I could have told you that!" the youth said, with a quick, forgiving smile.

The doorbell rang suddenly, echoing through the house. Dan exchanged a startled glance with his wife—then went quickly to answer the bell.

A stout, gray-haired man of fifty stood on the porch, a heavy rifle in the crook of his arm. Dan recognized him instantly as the mayor of the town, William Bowers.

"We saw the ship come down on your lawn!" Bowers said, excitedly. "I am acting under direct orders from the Governor! In each village the local authorities have been empowered to take action and preserve order!"

As if bursting with a desire to exercise his authority Mayor Bowers brushed quickly past Dayton and entered the living room. He looked around. His eye fell on the youth and he stiffened in horrified alarm.

"Just who is this?" he demanded.

"A Martian!" Monica said. "He came to Earth in the spaceship on the lawn!"

Bowers' face grew hard and determined. He went up to the youth and thrust the barrel of the rifle up against the youth's chest.

"Get up and keep your hands raised!" he warned. "I'm not taking any chances!"

"Don't be a fool, Bowers!" Dan Dayton said. "Put that gun up and listen to what he has to say!"

"I'll do nothing of the sort!" Bowers retorted. "There's something ugly here, something I don't understand. I'm playing it sure!"

The youth spoke then. "You're taking me to jail?"

"That's right!" Bowers glared. "I'm locking you up. I won't breathe easy until you're behind bars."

"I'm afraid that I cannot go with you," the youth said.

"You'd better get some sense into that thick skull of yours!" Bowers warned. "You're human—you're a man. That means you can be hurt, knocked down, thrown into prison. I'll give you just ten more seconds to get moving."

"But why should you want to hurt me?" the youth asked. "Have I hurt you?"

"You came to invade Earth!" the Mayor cried, almost beside himself with rage. "You came to make war! You came to kill and maim and destroy!"

Bowers' face turned savage. "Maybe I'm crazy to act as if you really could be from Mars! But I'd rather be crazy than dead."

"I am really from Mars," the youth said. "But you are putting words into my mouth. Why should I come to kill and maim? Am I not a man like yourself? Surely we have much in common. Surely only a wild beast would repay friendship with destruction."

"*Friendship!* You expect me to believe you came in friendship?"

"How could you believe otherwise?" the youth asked.

"Don't think you can disarm me with your talk!" Bowers cried, his face purpling. "I don't know what kind of trick you're pulling but it won't work! Do you hear? It will get you nowhere!"

"You'd better put up that gun, Bowers!" Dan Dayton said.

Bowers turned savagely, "Who'll make me?"

"I will!" Dan said.

He went up to Bowers and grabbed hold of the gun. The two men started struggling furiously for possession of the weapon. Mayor Bowers punched Dayton in the stomach. Dayton grunted, recoiled a step and sent his fist crashing against Bowers' jaw.

Bowers reeled back, and swung about. He aimed the rifle at the youth's chest, his lips flecked with blood.

"All right now! Get moving!"

"I'm sorry, but I shall stay here with my friends!" the youth said.

"Ah!"

"I'm staying here. You had better go. If you only want to hurt people, Mayor Bowers, we can never be friends!"

Mayor Bowers squeezed the trigger of the rifle. The weapon leapt, roared.

The stranger fell forward to the floor. His right arm went spinning off. His head fell back, began to rock. His right eye rolled out on the floor. Wheels, cogs and gears spurted from his chest in a metallic shower. There was a great yawning hole in his chest.

Smoke poured from him and was fanned by a breeze from the wind blowing in from the cool night.

Mayor Bowers stood blinking stupidly, too appalled to make a sound. But Tommy ran with a shriek to the shattered, crumpled form on the floor.

"You've killed him!" he sobbed, tears streaming down his face. "You've killed him! You've killed him!"

"A robot!" Dan heard himself muttering, a horrible dryness in his mouth.

Mayor Bowers found his voice then. "I knew it was some kind of vicious trick," he said. "I could tell there was something wrong. Nobody could be as good as he claimed to be. Real people just aren't made that way."

Monica reached out and drew her son to her. Holding him tightly by the shoulder she faced Mayor Bowers in white-lipped rage.

"He *was* good!" she said. "He was friendly and good and kind. I could feel the goodness radiating out from him. Dan could feel it too. The children could feel it. If there is justice on Earth you'll pay for what you just did, Mayor Bowers!"

"Nonsense!" Mayor Bowers said, drawing himself up. "He was just an ingenious mechanical dummy! The spaceship must be a fraud too! I intend to get to the bottom of this!"

Mayor Bowers swung about and walked straight out of the room and out of the cottage, the rifle securely back in the crook of his arm.

The children rushed to the window to watch Mayor Bowers cross the lawn. He was almost to the ship, well within the shadow of the ship, when the even vaster shadow fell upon him.

Mayor Bowers screamed just once but so shrilly that for the barest instant he seemed to be right back in the room again.

Then a dull thundering came from beyond the window. Lights flashed on the lawn, danced, leapt high. Mayor Bowers was lifted up and hurled thirty feet. He crashed down on the gravel driveway in front of the cottage, rolled over and lay still.

After a moment a slight twitching shuddered through him. He sat up, his face dazed, and shook his head as if to clear it. Instantly stark terror seemed to sweep back upon him. He recoiled, blinking furiously, his attitude that of a light-dazzled puppy in a litter of blind squirming whelps.

He was dragging himself away into the darkness when the voice spoke. The voice seemed to be in the room, and yet to come from a great distance. Perhaps it was not an actual voice.

"This is but one of many cautious experiments which we have been conducting all over Earth to determine the real nature of your intelligence and emotional equipment. We constructed an automaton in the likeness of yourselves, friendly and without guile.

"We constructed him on Mars and sent him to test your good will as you test the acid bite of certain fluids with bits of colored paper. He was like you in that he represented all that you most admire in yourselves.

"He was like you and yet how quickly he was destroyed! No Mayfly living out its brief span in the sunlight was ever so ill-treated by its own kind. We are not like you at all and if we showed ourselves to you as we are—do you not see? If you treat your own kind as you treated him how would you treat another type of life, completely alien to you?"

For a moment a faint, pulsing radiance seemed to fill the room.

"We came in friendliness, bearing a gift well within our power to bestow. But that gift we must now withhold. All Earth will forget. We shall make sure of that. You will remember only that you were vaguely troubled by an interruption in your pleasant ways so trivial it will hardly seem worth trying to recall.

"You will never know that you might have had—immortality under the stars!"

The voice faded as the children stared and Dan Dayton stood with his arm about his wife's shoulder, a shining wonder in his stare.

Upstairs in the nursery the children's radio, no longer silenced by the electrical discharge on the lawn, squealed and hummed with static again.

Then a voice droned out of the din, "And the Silver Queen said to the Jack-in-Ermine, quite earnestly, 'Snow fills the moat and wolves howl on the plain! Tarry here with me by the fire, my brave knight!'"

✵ EDMOND (MOORE) HAMILTON (1904–1977)

The August 1926 issue of Weird Tales *featured a story entitled "The Monster-God of Mamurth" and introduced the story's author, a young Edmond Hamilton, to its readership. The story was inspired by A. Merritt's "The People of the Pit" (All-Story, January 5, 1918). Like his friend and contemporary Jack Williamson, Hamilton was a great admirer of Merritt. Hamilton was also influenced by Arthur Conan Doyle's Professor Challenger stories.*

Edmond Hamilton soon became a popular and prolific author of Dark Fantasy and Science Fiction. Although multitalented, Hamilton's specialty was the grand epics of intergalactic conflict and conquest called Space Opera. In the early 1920s, Argosy *and* Weird Tales *printed Science Fiction stories; by 1926* Amazing Stories *arrived to do the same. This was the environment in which Hamilton debuted. In these magazines and others, he helped conclude the era of Scientific Romance and usher in modern-day Science Fiction. Hamilton influenced many subsequent Science Fiction authors, including John W. Campbell Jr. and A. E. van Vogt. He married Leigh Brackett on December 31, 1946.*

Of his many contributions to Science Fiction, Edmond Hamilton's Captain Future stories are noteworthy. These stories appeared in a magazine series entitled Captain Future, *and in a series of short stories printed in* Startling Stories. *"The Harpers of Titan" is a Captain Future classic.*

The Harpers of Titan
(Startling Stories, *September 1950*)

CHAPTER I

Shadowed Moon

> *His name was Simon Wright, and once he had been a man like other men. Now he was a man no longer, but a living brain, housed in a metal case, nourished by serum instead of blood, provided with artificial senses and means of motion.*
>
> *The body of Simon Wright, that had known the pleasures and the ills of physical existence, had long ago mingled with the dust. But the mind of Simon Wright lived on, brilliant and unimpaired.*

The ridge lifted, gaunt and rocky, along the rim of the lichen forest, the giant growths crowding to the very crest and down the farther slope into the valley.

Here and there was a clearing around what might once have been a temple, now long fallen into ruin. The vast ragged shapes of the lichens loomed above it, wrinkled and wind torn and sad. Now and again a little breeze came and set them to rustling with a sound like muted weeping, shaking down a rotten, powdery dust.

Simon Wright was weary of the ridge and the dun-gray forest, weary of waiting. Three of Titan's nights had passed since he and Grag and Otho and Curt Newton, whom the System knew better as Captain Future, had hidden their ship down in the lichen-forest and had waited here on the ridge for a man who did not come.

This was the fourth night of waiting, under the incredible glory of Titan's sky. But even the pageant of Saturn, girdled with the blazing Rings and attended by the brilliant swarm of moons, failed to lift Simon's mental spirits. Somehow the beauty above only accentuated the dreariness below.

Curt Newton said sharply, "If Keogh doesn't come tonight, I'm going down there and look for him."

He looked outward through a rift in the lichens, to the valley where Moneb lay—a city indistinct with night and distance, picked out here and there with the light of torches.

Simon spoke, his voice coming precise and metallic through the artificial resonator.

"Keogh's message warned us on no account to go into the city. Be patient, Curtis. He will come."

Otho nodded. Otho, the lean, lithe android who was so exactly human that only a disturbing strangeness in his pointed face and green, bright eyes betrayed him.

"Apparently," Otho said, "there's a devil of a mess going on in Moneb, and we're liable to make it worse if we go tramping in before we know what it's all about."

The manlike metal form of Grag moved impatiently in the shadows with a dull clanking sound. His booming voice crashed loud against the stillness.

"I'm like Curt," he said. "I'm tired of waiting."

"We are all tired," said Simon. "But we must wait. From Keogh's message, I judge that he is neither a coward nor a fool. He knows the situation. We do not. We must not endanger him by impatience."

Curt sighed. "I know it." He settled back on the block of stone where he was sitting. "I only hope he makes it soon. These infernal lichens are getting on my nerves."

Poised effortlessly upon the unseen magnetic beams that were his limbs, Simon watched and brooded. Only in a detached way could he appreciate the picture he presented to others—a small square metal case, with a strange face of artificial lens-eyes and resonator-mouth, hovering in the darkness.

To himself, Simon seemed almost a bodiless ego. He could not see his own strange body. He was conscious only of the steady, rhythmic throbbing of the serum-pump that served as his heart and of the visual and auditory sensations that his artificial sense-organs gathered for him.

His lenslike eyes were capable of better vision under all conditions than the human eye, but even so he could not penetrate the shifting, tumultuous shadows of the valley. It remained a mystery of shaking moonlight, mist and darkness.

It looked peaceful. And yet the message of this stranger, Keogh, had cried for help against an evil too great for him to fight alone.

Simon was acutely conscious of the dreary rustling of the lichens. His microphonic auditory system could hear and distinguish each separate tiny note too faint for normal ears, so that the rustling became a weaving, shifting pattern of sound, as of ghostly voices whispering—a sort of symphony of despair.

Pure fancy, and Simon Wright was not given to fancies. Yet in these nights of waiting he had developed a definite sense of foreboding. He reasoned now that this sad whispering of the forest was responsible, his brain reacting to the repeated stimulus of a sound-pattern.

Like Curt, he hoped that Keogh would come soon.

Time passed. The Rings filled the sky with supernal fire, and the moons went splendidly on their eternal way, bathed in the milky glow of Saturn. The lichens would not cease from their dusty weeping. Now and again Curt Newton rose and went restlessly back and forth across the clearing. Otho watched him, sitting still, his slim body bent like a steel bow. Grag remained where he was, a dark immobile giant in the shadows, dwarfing even Newton's height.

Then, abruptly, there was a sound different from all other sounds. Simon heard, and listened, and after a moment he said:

"There are two men, climbing the slope from the valley, coming this way."

Otho sprang up. Curt voiced a short, sharp "Ah!" and said, "Better take cover, until we're sure."

The four melted into the darkness.

Simon was so close to the strangers that he might have reached out one of his force-beams and touched them. They came into the clearing, breathing heavily from the long climb, looking eagerly about. One was a tall man, very tall, with a gaunt width of shoulder and a fine head. The other was shorter, broader, moving with a bearlike gait. Both were Earthmen, with the unmistakable stamp of the frontiers on them, and the hardness of physical labor. Both men were armed.

They stopped. The hope went out of them, and the tall man said despairingly, "They failed us. They didn't come. Dan, they didn't come!"

Almost, the tall man wept.

"I guess your message didn't get through," the other man said. His voice, too, was leaden. "I don't know, Keogh. I don't know what we'll do now. I guess we might as well go back."

Curt Newton spoke out of the darkness. "Hold on a minute. It's all right."

Curt moved out into the open space, his lean face and red hair clear in the moonlight.

"It's he," said the stocky man. "It's Captain Future." His voice was shaken with relief.

Keogh smiled, a smile without much humor in it. "You thought I might be dead, and someone else might keep the appointment. Not a far-fetched assumption. I've been so closely watched that I dared not try to get away before. I only just managed it tonight."

He broke off, staring, as Grag came striding up, shaking the ground with his tread. Otho moved in from beyond him, light as a leaf. Simon joined them, gliding silently from among the shadows.

Keogh laughed, a little shakily. "I'm glad to see you. If you only knew how glad I am to see you all!"

"And me!" said the stocky man. He added, "I'm Harker."

"My friend," Keogh told the Futuremen. "For many years, my friend." Then he hesitated, looking earnestly at Curt. "You will help me? I've held back down there in Moneb so far. I've kept the people quiet. I've tried to give them courage when they need it, but I'm only one man. That's a frail peg on which to hang the fate of a city."

Curt nodded gravely. "We'll do all we can. Otho—Grag! Keep watch, just in case."

Grag and Otho disappeared again. Curt looked expectantly at Keogh and Harker. The breeze had steadied to a wind, and Simon was conscious that it was rising, bringing a deeper plaint from the lichens.

Keogh sat down on a block of stone and began to talk. Hovering near him, Simon listened, watching Keogh's face. It was a good face. A wise man, Simon thought, and a strong one, exhausted now by effort and long fear.

"I was the first Earthman to come into the valley, years ago," Keogh said. "I liked the men of Moneb and they liked me. When the miners began to come in, I saw to it that there was no trouble between them and the natives. I married a girl of Moneb, daughter of one of the chief men. She's dead now, but I have a son here. And I'm one of their councilors, the only man of foreign blood ever allowed in the Inner City.

"So you see, I've swung a lot of weight and have used it to keep peace here between native and outlander. But *now!*"

He shook his head. "There have always been men in Moneb who hated to see Earthmen and Earth civilization come in and lessen their own influence. They've hated the Earthmen who live in New Town and work the mines. They'd have tried long ago to force them out, and would have embroiled Moneb in a hopeless struggle, if they'd dared defy tradition and use their one possible weapon. Now, they're bolder and are planning to use that weapon."

Curt Newton looked at him keenly. "What is this weapon, Keogh?"

Keogh's answer was a question. "You Futuremen know these worlds well—I suppose you've heard of the Harpers?"

Simon Wright felt a shock of surprise. He saw incredulous amazement on Curt Newton's face.

"You don't mean that your malcontents plan to use the *Harpers* as a weapon?"

Keogh nodded somberly. "They do."

Memories of old days on Titan were flashing through Simon's mind; the strange, strange form of life that dwelt deep in the great forests, the unforgettable beauty wedded to dreadful danger.

"The Harpers could be a weapon, yes," he said, after a moment. "But the weapon would slay those who wielded it, unless they were protected from it."

"Long ago," Keogh answered, "the men of Moneb had such a protection. They used the Harpers, then. But use of them was so disastrous that it was forbidden, put under a tabu.

"Now, those who wish to force out the Earthmen here plan to break that tabu. They want to bring in the Harpers, and use them."

Harker added, "Things were all right until the old king died. He was a man. His son is a weakling. The fanatics against outland civilization have got to him, and he's afraid of his own shadow. Keogh has been holding him on his feet, against them."

Simon saw the almost worshipful trust in Harker's eyes as he glanced at his friend.

"They've tried to kill Keogh, of course," Harker said. "With him gone, there'd be no leader against them."

Keogh's voice rose, to be heard over the booming and thrumming of the lichens.

"A full council has been called for two days from now. That will be the time of decision—whether we, or the breakers of tabu, will rule in Moneb. And I know, as I know truth, that some kind of a trap has been set for me.

"That is where I will need you Futuremen's help, most desperately. But you must not be seen in the town. Any strangers now would excite suspicion, and you are too well known and—" he glanced at Simon and added apologetically, "distinctive."

He paused. In that pause, the boom and thunder of the lichen was like the slatting of great sails in the wind, and Simon could not hear the little furtive sound from behind him until it was too late—a second too late.

A man leaped into the clearing. Simon had a fleeting glimpse of copper-gold limbs and a killer's face, and a curious weapon raised. Simon spoke, but the bright small dart was already fled.

In the same breath, Curt turned and drew and fired. The man dropped. Out in the shadows another gun flashed, and they heard Otho's fierce cry.

There was a timeless instant when no one moved, and then Otho came back into the clearing. "There were only two of them, I think."

"They followed us!" Harker exclaimed. "They followed us up here to—"

He had been turning, as he spoke. He suddenly stopped speaking, and then cried out Keogh's name.

Keogh lay face down in the powdery dust. From out his temple stood a slim bronzed shaft little larger than a needle, and where it pierced the flesh was one dark drop of blood.

Simon hovered low over the Earthman. His sensitive beams touched the throat, the breast, lifted one lax eyelid.

Simon said, without hope, "He still lives."

CHAPTER II

Unearthly Stratagem

Grag carried Keogh through the the forest and, tall man that Keogh was, he seemed like a child in the robot's mighty arms. The wind howled, and the lichens shook and thundered, and it was growing darker.

"Hurry!" said Harker. "Hurry—there may still be a chance!"

His face had the white, staring look that comes with shock. Simon was still possessed of emotion—sharper, clearer emotions than before, he thought, divorced as they were from the chemical confusions of the flesh. Now he knew a great pity for Harker.

"The *Comet* is just ahead." Curt told him.

Presently they saw the ship, a shadowed bulk of metal lost among the giant growths. Swiftly they took Keogh in, and Grag laid him carefully on the table in the tiny laboratory. He was still breathing, but Simon knew that it would not be for long.

The laboratory of the *Comet*, for all its cramped size, was fitted with medical equipment comparable to most hospitals—most of it designed for its particular purpose by Simon himself, and by Curt Newton. It had been used many times before for the saving of lives. Now the two of them, Simon and Curt together, worked feverishly to save Keogh.

Curt wheeled a marvellously compact adaptation of the Fraser unit into place. Within seconds the tubes were clamped into Keogh's arteries and the pumps were working, keeping the blood flowing normally, feeding in a stimulant solution directly to the heart. The oxygen unit was functioning. Presently Curt nodded.

"Pulse and respiration normal. Now let's have a look at the brain."

He swung the ultrafluoroscope into position and switched it on. Simon looked into the screen, hovering close to Curt's shoulder.

"The frontal lobe is torn beyond repair," he said. "See the tiny barbs on that dart? Deterioration of the cells has already set in."

Harker spoke from the doorway. "Can't you do something? Can't you save him?" He stared into Curt's face for a moment, and then his head dropped forward and he said dully, "No, of course you can't. I knew it when he was hit."

All the strength seemed to run out of him. He leaned against the door, a man tired and beaten and sad beyond endurance.

"It's bad enough to lose a friend. But now everything he fought for is lost, too. The fanatics will win, and they'll turn loose something that will destroy not only the Earthmen here, but the entire populace of Moneb too, in the long run."

Tears began to run slowly from Harker's eyes. He did not seem to notice them. He said, to no one, to the universe, "Why couldn't I have seen him in time? Why couldn't I have killed him—in time?"

For a long, long moment, Simon looked at Harker. Then he glanced again into the screen, and then aside at Curt, who nodded and slowly switched it off. Curt began to remove the tubes of the Fraser unit from Keogh's wrists.

Simon said, "Wait, Curtis. Leave them as they are."

Curt straightened, a certain startled wonder in his eyes. Simon glided to where Harker stood, whiter and more stricken than the dead man on the table.

Simon spoke his name three times, before he roused himself to answer.

"Yes?"

"How much courage have you, Harker? As much as Keogh? As much as I?"

Harker shook his head.

"There are times when courage doesn't help a bit."

"Listen to me, Harker! Have you the courage to walk beside Keogh into Moneb, knowing that he is dead?"

The eyes of the stocky man widened. And Curt Newton came to Simon and said in a strange voice, "What are you thinking of?"

"I am thinking of a brave man who died in the act of seeking help from us. I am thinking of many innocent men and women who will die, unless . . . Harker, it is true, is it not, that the success of your fight depended on Keogh?"

Harker's gaze dwelt upon the body stretched on the table—a body that breathed and pulsed with the semblance of life borrowed from the sighing pumps.

"That is true," he said. "That's why they killed him. He was the leader. With him gone—" Harker's broad hands made a gesture of utter loss.

"Then it must not be known that Keogh died."

Curt said harshly, "No! Simon, you can't do it!"

"Why not, Curtis? You are perfectly capable of completing the operation."

"They've killed the man once. They'll be ready to do it again. Simon, you can't risk yourself! Even if I could do the operation—no!"

Something queerly pleading came into Curt's gray eyes. "This is my kind of a job, Simon. Mine and Grag's and Otho's. Let us do it."

"And how will you do it?" Simon asked. "By force? By reasoning? You are not omnipotent, Curtis. Nor are Grag and Otho. You, all three of you, would be going into certain death, and even more certain defeat. And I know you. You *would* go."

Simon paused. It seemed to him suddenly that he had gone mad, that he must be mad to contemplate what he was about to do. And yet, it was the only way— the only possible chance of preventing an irretrievable disaster.

Simon knew what the Harpers could do, in the wrong hands. He knew what would happen to the Earthmen in New Town. And he knew too what retribution for that would overtake the many guiltless people of Moneb, as well as the few guilty ones.

He glanced beyond Harker and saw Grag standing there, and Otho beside him, his green eyes very bright, and Simon thought, I made them both, I and Roger Newton. I gave them hearts and minds and courage. Some day they will perish, but it will not be because I failed them.

And there was Curt, stubborn, reckless, driven by the demon of his own loneliness, a bitter searcher after knowledge, a stranger to his own kind.

Simon thought, We made him so, Otho and Grag and I. And we wrought too well. There is too much iron in him. He will break, but never bend—and I will not have him broken because of me!

Harker said, very slowly, "I don't understand."

Simon explained. "Keogh's body is whole. Only the brain was destroyed. If the body were supplied with another brain—mine—Keogh would seem to live again, to finish his task in Moneb."

Harker stood for a long moment without speaking. Then he whispered, "Is that possible?"

"Quite possible. Not easy, not even safe—but possible."

Harker's hands clenched into fists. Something, a light that might have been hope, crept back into his eyes.

"Only we five," said Simon, "know that Keogh died. There would be no difficulty there. And I know the language of Titan, as I know most of the System tongues.

"But I would still need help—a guide, who knew Keogh's life and could enable me to live it for the short time that is necessary. You, Harker. And I warn you, it will not be easy."

Harker's voice was low, but steady. "If you can do the one thing, I can do the other."

Curt Newton said angrily, "No one is going to do anything of the sort. Simon, I won't have any part of it!"

The stormy look that Simon knew so well had come into Curt's face. If Simon had been able to, he would have smiled. Instead, he spoke exactly as he had spoken so many times before, long ago when Curt Newton was a small redheaded boy playing in the lonely corridors of the laboratory hidden under Tycho, with no companions but the robot, the android, and Simon, himself.

"You will do as I say, Curtis!" He turned to the others. "Grag, take Mr. Harker into the main cabin. See that he sleeps, for he will need his strength. Otho, Curtis will want your help."

Otho came in and shut the door. He glanced from Simon to Curt and back again, his eyes brilliant with a certain acid amusement. Curt stood where he was, his jaw set, unmoving.

Simon glided over to the cabinets built solidly against one wall. Using the wonderfully adaptable force-beams more skilfully than a man uses his hands, he took from them the needful things—the trephine saw, the clamps and sutures, the many-shaped delicate knives. And the other things, that had set modern surgery so far ahead of the crude Twentieth Century techniques. The compounds that prevented bleeding, the organic chemicals that promoted cell regeneration so rapidly and fully that a wound would heal within hours and leave no scar, the stimulants and anæsthetics that prevented shock, the neurone compounds.

The UV tube was pulsing overhead, sterilizing everything in the laboratory. Simon, whose vision was better and touch more sure than that of any surgeon dependent on human form, made the preliminary incision in Keogh's skull.

Curt Newton had still not moved. His face was as set and stubborn as before, but there was a pallor about it now, something of desperation.

Simon said sharply, "Curtis!"

Curt moved then. He came to the table and put his hands on it beside the dead man's head, and Simon saw that they trembled.

"I can't," he whispered. "Simon, I can't do it. I'm afraid."

Simon looked steadily into his eyes. "There is no need to be. You will not let me die."

He held out a glittering instrument. Slowly, like a man in a dream, Curt took it.

Otho's bright gaze softened. He nodded to Simon, across Curt's shoulder, and smiled. There was admiration in that smile, for both of them.

Simon busied himself with other things.

"Pay particular attention, Curtis, to the trigeminal, glossopharyngeal, facial—"

"I know all about that," said Curt, with a peculiar irritation.

"—pneumogastric, spinal accessory, and hypoglossal nerves," Simon finished. Vials and syringes were laid in a neat row. "Here is the anæsthetic to be introduced into my serum-stream. And immediately after the operation, this is to be injected beneath the dura and pia mater."

Curt nodded. His hands had stopped shaking, working now with swift, sure skill. His mouth had thinned to a grim line.

Simon thought, He'll do. He'll always do.

There was a moment, then, of waiting. Simon looked down at the man John Keogh and of a sudden fear took hold of him, a deep terror of what he was about to do.

He was content as he was. Once, many years before, he had made his choice between extinction and his present existence. The genius of Curt's own father had saved him then, given him new life, and Simon had made peace with that life, strange as it was, and turned it to good use. He had discovered the advantages of his new form—the increased skills, the ability to think clearly with a mind unfettered by useless and uncontrollable impulses of the flesh. He had learned to be grateful for them.

And now, after all these years . . .

He thought, I cannot do it, after all! I, too, am afraid—not of dying, but of life.

And yet, beneath that fear was longing, a hunger that Simon had thought mercifully dead these many years.

The longing to be once again a man, a human being clothed in flesh.

The cold, clear mind of Simon Wright, the precise, logical unwavering mind, reeled under the impact of these mingled dreads and hungers. They leaped up full stature from their graves in his subconscious. He was shocked that he could still be prey to emotion, and the voice of his mind cried out, I cannot do it! No, I cannot!

Curt said quietly, "All ready, Simon."

Slowly, very slowly, Simon moved and came to rest beside John Keogh. He saw Otho watching him, with a look of pain. and understanding, and—yes, envy. Being unhuman himself, Otho would know, where others could only guess.

Curt's face was cut from stone. The serum-pump broke its steady rhythm, and then went on.

Simon Wright passed quietly into the darkness.

CHAPTER III

Once Born of Flesh

Hearing came first. A distant confusion of sounds, seeming very dull and blurred. Simon's first thought was that something had gone wrong with his auditory mechanism. Then a chill wing of memory brushed him, and in its wake came a pang of fear, and a sense of *wrongness.*

It was dark. Why should it be so dark in the *Comet?*

From far off, someone called his name. "Simon! Simon, open your eyes!"

Eyes?

Again that dull inchoate terror. His mind was heavy. It refused to function, and the throb of the serum-pump was gone.

The serum-pump, Simon thought. It has stopped, and I am dying!

He must call for help. That had happened once before, and Curt had saved him. He cried out, "Curtis, the serum-pump has stopped!"

The voice was not his own, and it was formed so strangely.

"I'm here, Simon. Open your eyes."

A long unused series of motor relays clicked over in Simon's brain at that repeated command. Without conscious volition he raised his eyelids. Someone's eyelids, surely not his own! He had not had eyelids for many years!

He saw.

Vision like the hearing, dim and blurred. The familiar laboratory seemed to swim in a wavering haze. Curt's face, and Otho's, and above them the looming form of Grag, and a strange man . . . No, not strange; he had a name and Simon knew it—Harker.

That name started the chain, and Simon remembered. Memory pounced upon him, worried him, tore him, and now he could *feel the fear*—the physical anguish of it, the sweating, the pounding of the heart, the painful contraction of the great bodily ganglia.

"Raise your hand, Simon. Raise your right hand." There was a strained undertone in Curt's voice, Simon understood. Curt was afraid he might not have done things properly.

Uncertainly, like a child who has not yet learned coordination, Simon raised his right hand. Then his left. He looked at them for an endless moment and let them fall. Drops of saline moisture stung his eyes, and he remembered them. He remembered tears.

"You're all right," Curt said shakily. He helped Simon raise his head and held a glass to his lips. "Can you drink this? It will clear away the fog, give you strength."

Simon drank, and the act of drinking had wonder in it.

The potion counteracted the remaining effects of the anæsthetic. Sight and hearing cleared, and he had his mind under control again. He lay still for some time, trying to adjust himself to the all but forgotten sensations of the flesh.

The little things. The crispness of a sheet against the skin, the warmth, the pleasure of relaxed lips. The memory of sleep.

He sighed, and in that, too, there was wonder. "Give me your hand, Curtis. I will stand."

Curt was on one side, Otho on the other, steadying him. And Simon Wright, in the body of John Keogh, rose from the table where he had lain and stood upright, a man and whole.

By the doorway, Harker fell forward in a dead faint.

Simon looked at him, the strong stocky man crumpled on the floor, his face gray and sick. He said, with a queer touch of pity for all humanity, "I told him it would not be easy."

But even Simon had not realized just how hard it would be.

There were so many things to be learned all over again. Long used to a weightless, effortless ease of movement, this tall rangy body he now inhabited seemed heavy and awkward, painfully slow. He had great difficulty in managing it. At first his attempts to walk were a series of ungainly staggerings wherein he must cling to something to keep from falling.

His sense of balance had to undergo a complete readjustment. And the dullness of his sight and hearing bothered him. That was only comparative, he knew— Keogh's sight and hearing had been excellent, by all human standards. But they lacked the precision, the selectivity, the clarity to which Simon had become accustomed. He felt as though his senses were somehow muffled, as by a veil.

And it was a strange thing, when he stumbled or made an incautious movement, to feel pain again.

But as he began to gain control over this complicated bulk of bone and muscle and nerve, Simon found himself taking joy in it. The endless variety of sensory and tactile impressions, the feeling of life, of warm blood flowing, the knowing of heat and cold and hunger were fascinating.

Once born of flesh, he thought, and clenched his hands together. What have I done? What madness have I done?

He must not think of that, nor of himself. He must think of nothing but the task to be done, in the name of John Keogh who was dead.

Harker recovered from his faint. "I'm sorry," he muttered. "It was just that I saw him—you—rise up and stand, it—" He did not finish. "I'm all right, now. You don't have to worry."

Simon noticed that he kept his eyes averted as much as possible. But there was a dogged look about him that said he told the truth.

"We ought to get back as soon as you can make it," Harker said. "We—Keogh and I, have been gone too long as it is."

He added, "There's just one thing. What about Dion?"

"Dion?"

"Keogh's son."

Simon said slowly, "No need to tell the boy. He could not understand, and it will only torture him."

Mercifully, he thought, the time would be short. But he wished that Keogh had not had a son.

Curt interrupted. "Simon, I've been talking to Harker. The council is tonight, only a few hours away. And you will have to go alone into the Inner City, for there Harker is not allowed to enter.

"But Otho and I are going to try to get around Moneb and into the council hall, secretly. Harker tells me that was Keogh's idea, and it's a good one—if it works. Grag will stay with the ship, on call if necessary."

He handed Simon two objects, a small mono-wave audio disc and a heavy metal box only four inches square.

"We'll keep in touch with the audios," he said. "The other is a hasty adaptation of the *Comet's* own repellor field, but tuned for sonic vibrations. I had to rob two of the coil units. What do you think of it?"

watched him from the doorways and sent the name of Keogh whispering up the lanes and the twisting alleys.

It came to Simon that there was yet another thing in the air of Moneb—a thing called fear.

They came to the gates in the inner wall. Here Harker dropped helplessly back with the other men, and Simon and the son of Keogh went on alone.

Temple and palace rose above him, impressive and strong, bearing in heroic frescoes the history of the kings of Moneb. Simon hardly saw them. There was a tightness in him now, a gathering of nerves.

This was the test—now, before he was ready for it. This was the time when he must not falter, or the thing he had done would be for nothing, and the Harpers would be brought into the valley of Moneb.

Two round towers of brick, a low and massive doorway. Dimness, lighted by torches, red light flaring on coppery flesh, on the ceremonial robes of the councilors, here and there on a helmet of barbaric design. Voices, clamoring over and through each other. A feeling of tension so great that the nerves screamed with it.

Dion pressed his arm and said something that Simon did not catch, but the smile, the look of love and pride, were unmistakable. Then the boy was gone, to the shadowy benches beyond.

Simon stood alone.

At one end of the low, oblong hall, beside the high, gilded seat of the king, he saw a group of helmeted men looking toward him with hatred they did not even try to conceal, and with it, a contempt that could only come from triumph.

And suddenly from out of the uneasy milling of the throng before him an old man stepped and put his hands on Simon's shoulders, and peered at him with anguished eyes.

"It is too late, John Keogh," the old man said hoarsely. "It is all for nothing. They have brought the Harpers in!"

CHAPTER IV

The Harpers

Simon felt a cold shock of recoil. He had not looked for this. He had not expected that now, this soon, he might be called upon to meet the Harpers.

He had met them once before, years ago. He knew the subtle and terrible danger of them. It had shaken him badly then, when he was a brain divorced from flesh. What would it do to him, now that he dwelt again in a vulnerable, unpredictable human body?

His hand closed tightly on the tiny metal box in his pocket. He must gamble that it would protect him from the Harpers' power. But, remembering that experience of years ago, he dreaded the test.

He asked the old councillor, "Do you know this to be true, about the Harpers?"

"Taras and two others were seen at dawn, coming back from the forest, each bearing a hidden thing. And—they wore the Helmets of Silence."

The old man gestured toward the group of men by the king's throne who looked with such triumphant hatred at he whom they thought to be John Keogh.

"See, they wear them still!"

Swiftly, Simon studied the helmets. At first glance they had seemed no more than the ordinary bronze battle-gear of a barbaric warrior. Now he saw that they were of curious design, covering the ears and the entire cranial area, and overlarge as though padded with many layers of some insulating material.

The Helmets of Silence. He knew, now, that Keogh had spoken truly when he told of an ancient means of protection used long ago by the men of Moneb against the Harpers. Those helmets would protect, yes.

The king of Moneb rose from his throne. And the nervous uproar in the hall stilled to a frozen tension.

A young man, the king. Very young, very frightened, weakness and stubbornness mingled in his face. His head was bare.

"We of Moneb have too long tolerated strangers in our valley—have even suffered one of them to sit in this council and influence our decisions," he began.

Here there was a sharp uneasy turning of heads toward "Keogh."

"The strangers' ways more and more color the lives of our people. They must go—all of them! And since they will not go willingly, they must be forced!"

He had learned the speech by rote. Simon knew that from the way in which he stumbled over it, the way in which his eyes slid to the tallest of the cloaked and helmeted men beside him, for prompting and strength. The dark, tall man whom Simon recognized from Harker's description as Keogh's chief enemy, Taras.

"We cannot force the Earthmen out with our darts and spears. Their weapons are too strong. But we too have a weapon, one they cannot fight! It was forbidden to us, by foolish kings who were afraid it might be used against them. But now we must use it.

"Therefore I demand that the old tabu be lifted! I demand that we invoke the power of the Harpers to drive the Earthmen forth!"

There was a taut, unhappy silence in the hall. Simon saw men looking at him, the eager confidence in young Dion's eyes. He knew that they placed in him their desperate last hope of preventing this thing.

They were right, for whatever was done he must do alone. Curt Newton and Otho could not possibly have yet made their way secretly by back ways to this council hall.

Simon strode forward. He looked around him. Because of what he was, a kind of fierce exaltation took him, to be once more a man among men. It made his voice ring loud, thundering from the low vault.

"Is it not true that the king fears, not the Earthmen, but Taras—and that Taras is bent not on freeing Moneb from a mythical yoke, but in placing one of his own upon our necks?"

There was a moment of utter silence in which they all, king and councilors alike, stared at him aghast. And in the silence, Simon said grimly:

"I speak for the council! There will be no lifting of tabu—and he that brings the Harpers into Moneb does so under pain of death!"

For one short moment the councilors recovered their courage and voiced it. The hall shook with the cheering. Under cover of the noise Taras bent and spoke into the king's ear, and Simon saw the face of the king become pallid.

From behind the high seat Taras lifted a helmet bossed in gold and placed it on the king's head. A Helmet of Silence.

The cheering faded, and was not.

The king said hoarsely, "Then for the good of Moneb, I must disband the council."

Taras stepped forward. He looked directly at Simon, and his eyes smiled. "We had forseen your traitorous counsels, John Keogh. And so we came prepared."

He flung back his cloak. Beneath it, in the curve of his left arm, was something wrapped in silk.

Simon instinctively stepped back.

Taras ripped the silk away. And in his hands was a living creature no larger than a dove, a thing of silver and rose-pearl and delicate frills of shining membrane, and large, soft, gentle eyes.

A dweller in the deep forests, a shy sweet bearer of destruction, an angel of madness and death.

A Harper!

A low moan rose among the councilors, and there was a shifting and a swaying of bodies poised for flight. Taras said,

"Be still. There is time enough for running, when I give you leave."

The councilors were still. The king was still, white-faced upon his throne. But on the shadowy benches, Simon saw Keogh's son bent forward, yearning toward the man he thought to be his father, his face alight with a child's faith.

Taras stroked the creature in his hands, his head bent low over it.

The membranous frills began to lift and stir. The rose-pearl body pulsed, and there broke forth a ripple of music like the sound of a muted harp, infinitely sweet and distant.

The eyes of the Harper glowed. It was happy, pleased to be released from the binding silk that had kept its membranes useless for the making of music. Taras continued to stroke it gently, and it responded with a quivering freshet of song, the liquid notes running and trilling upon the silent air.

And two more of the helmeted men brought forth silvery, soft-eyed captives from under their cloaks, and they began to join their music together, timidly at first, and then more and more without hesitation, until the council hall was full of the strange wild harping and men stood still because they were too entranced now to move.

Even Simon was not proof against that infinitely poignant tide of thrilling sound. He felt his body respond, every nerve quivering with a pleasure akin to pain.

He had forgotten the effect of music on the human consciousness. For many years he had forgotten music. Now, suddenly, all those long-closed gates between mind and body were flung open by the soaring song of the Harpers. Clear, lovely, thoughtless, the very voice of life unfettered, the music filled Simon with an aching hunger for he knew not what. His mind wandered down vague pathways thronged with shadows, and his heart throbbed with a solemn joy that was close to tears.

Caught in the sweet wild web of that harping, he stood motionless, dreaming, forgetful of fear and danger, of everything except that somewhere in that music was the whole secret of creation, and that he was poised on the very edge of understanding the subtle secret of that song.

Song of a newborn universe joyously shouting its birth-cry, of young suns calling to each other in exultant strength, the thunderous chorus of star-voices and the humming bass of the racing, spinning worlds!

Song of life, growing, burgeoning, bursting, on every world, complicated counterpoint of a million million species voicing the ecstasy of being in triumphant chorus!

Something deep in Simon Wright's tranced mind warned him that he was being trapped by that hypnotic web of sound, that he was falling deeper, deeper, into the Harpers' grip. But he could not break the spell of that singing.

Soaring singing of the leaf drinking the sun, of the bird on the wing, of the beast warm in its burrow, of the young, bright miracle of love, of birth, of living!

And then the song changed. The beauty and joy faded from it, and into the sounds came a note of terror, growing, growing . . .

It came to Simon then that Taras was speaking to the thing he held, and that the soft eyes of the Harper were afraid.

The creature's simple mind was sensitive to telepathic impulses, and Taras was filling its mild emptiness with thoughts of danger and of pain, so that its membranes shrilled now to a different note.

The other Harpers picked it up. Shivering, vibrating together and across each other's rhythms, the three small rose-pearl beings flooded the air with a shuddering sound that was the essence of all fear.

Fear of a blind universe that lent its creatures life only to snatch it from them, of the agony and death that always and forever must rend the bright fabric of living! Fear of the somber depths of darkness and pain into which all life must finally descend, of the shadows that closed down so fast, so fast!

That awful threnody of primal terror that shuddered from the Harpers struck icy fingers of dread across the heart. Simon recoiled from it, he could not bear it, he knew that if he heard it long he must go mad.

Only dimly was he aware of the terror among the other councilors, the writhing of their faces, the movements of their hands. He tried to cry out but his voice was lost in the screaming of the Harpers, going ever higher and higher until it was torture to the body.

And still Taras bent over the Harper, cruel-eyed, driving it to frenzy with the power of his mind. And still the Harpers screamed, and now the sound had risen and part of it had slipped over the threshold of hearing, and the super-sonic notes stabbed the brain like knives.

A man bolted past Simon. Another followed, and another, and then more and more, clawing, trampling, falling, floundering in the madness of panic. And he himself must flee!

He would *not* flee! Something held him from the flight his body craved—some inner core of thought hardened and strengthened by his long divorcement from the flesh. It steadied him, made him fight back with iron resolution, to reality.

His shaking hand drew out the little metal box. The switch clicked. Slowly, as the power of the thing built up, it threw out a high, shrill keening sound.

"The one weapon against the Harpers!" Curt had said. "The only thing that can break sound is—sound!"

The little repeller reached out its keening sonic vibrations and caught at the Harpers' terrible singing, like a claw.

It clawed and twisted and broke that singing. It broke it, by its subtle sonic interference, into shrieking dissonances.

Simon strode forward, toward the throne and toward Taras. And now into the eyes of Taras had come a deadly doubt.

The Harpers, wild and frightened now, strove against the keening sound that broke their song into hideous discord. The shuddering sonic struggle raged, much of it far above the level of hearing, and Simon felt his body plucked and shaken by terrible vibrations.

He staggered, but he went on. The faces of Taras and the others were contorted by pain. The king had fainted on his throne.

Storm of shattered harmonies, of splintered sound, shrieked like the very voice of madness around the throne. Simon, his mind darkening, knew that he could endure no more . . .

And suddenly it was over. Beaten, exhausted, the Harpers stilled the wild vibration of their membranes. Utterly silent, they remained motionless in the hands of their captors, their soft eyes glazed with hopeless terror.

Simon laughed. He swayed a little on his feet and said to Taras,

"My weapon is stronger than yours!"

Taras dropped the Harper. It crawled away and hid itself beneath the throne. Taras whispered,

"Then we must have it from you, Earthman!"

He sprang toward Simon. On his heels came the others, mad with the bitter fury of defeat when they had been so sure of victory.

Simon snatched out the audio-disc and raised it to his lips, pressing its button and crying out the one word, "Hurry!"

He felt that it was too late. But not until now, not until this moment when fear conquered the force of tradition, could Curt and Otho have entered this forbidden place without provoking the very outbreak that must be prevented.

Simon went down beneath his attackers' rush. As he went down, he saw that the councilors who had fled were running back to help him. He heard their voices shouting, and he saw the boy Dion among them.

Something struck cruelly against his head, and there was a crushing weight upon him. Someone screamed, and he caught the bright sharp flash of darts through the torchlight.

He tried to rise, but he could not. He was near unconsciousness, aware only of a confusion of movement and ugly sounds. He smelled blood, and he knew pain.

He must have moved, for he found himself on his hands and knees, looking down into the face of Dion. The shank of a copper dart stood out from the boy's breast, and there was a streak of red across the golden skin. His eyes met Simon's, in a dazed, wondering look. He whispered uncertainly:

"Father!"

He crept into Simon's arms. Simon held him, and Dion murmured once more and then sighed. Simon continued to hold him, though the boy had become very heavy and his eyes looked blankly now into nothingness.

It came to Simon that the hall had grown quiet. A voice spoke to him. He lifted his head and saw Curt standing over him, and Otho, both staring at him anxiously. He could not see them clearly. He said, "The boy thought I was his father. He clung to me and called me Father as he died."

Otho took Dion's body and laid it gently on the stones.

Curt said, "It's all over, Simon. We got here in time, and it's all right."

Simon rose. Taras and his men were dead. Those who had tried to foster hatred were gone, and not ever again would Harpers be brought into Moneb. That was what the pale, shaken councilors around him were telling him.

He could not hear them clearly. Not so clearly, somehow, as the fading whisper of a dying boy.

He turned and walked out of the council hall, onto the steps. It was dark now. There were torches flaring, and the wind blew cold, and he was very tired.

Curt stood beside him. Simon said, "I will go back to the ship."

He saw the question in Curt's eyes, the question that he did not quite dare to ask.

Heartsick, Simon spoke the lines that a Chinese poet had written long ago.

"'Now I know, that the ties of flesh and blood only bind us to a load of grief and sorrow.'"

He shook his head. "I will return to what I was. I could not bear the agony of a second human life—no!"

Curt did not answer. He took Simon's arm and they walked together across the court.

Behind them Otho came, carrying gently three small creatures of silver and rose-pearl, who began now to sound ripples of muted music, faint but hopeful at first, then soaring swiftly to the gladness of prisoners newly freed.

* * *

They buried the body of John Keogh in the clearing where he had died, and the boy Dion lay beside him. Over them, Curt and Grag and Otho built a cairn of stones with Harker's help.

From the shadows Simon Wright watched, a small square shape of metal hovering on silent beams, again a living brain severed forever from human form.

It was done, and they parted from Harker and went down through the great booming lichens toward the ship. Curt and the robot and android paused and looked back, at the tall cairn towering lonely against the stars.

But Simon did not look back.

ꞷ ARTHUR C(HARLES) CLARKE (1917–)

As were E. E. "Doc" Smith and Isaac Asimov, Arthur C. Clarke is a scientist who writes Science Fiction. Born in the United Kingdom in 1917, Clarke earned college degrees in both physics and mathematics. His first professional publication was the Science Fiction story "Loophole," which appeared in the April 1946 issue of Astounding Science-Fiction, *but his first professional sale was the Science Fiction tale "Rescue Party," which was published in* Astounding Science-Fiction, *in its May 1946 issue. Clarke's early Science Fiction was rather standard fare, but it evidenced a cleanness and orderliness that was attractive to magazine editors and readers alike. His first two novels appeared in 1951. These were* Prelude to Space *and* Sands of Mars.*

Also in 1951, Clarke's short story "Sentinel of Eternity" was published in the one and only issue of 10 Story Fantasy. *This tale became the basis for the Stanley Kubrick motion picture classic,* 2001: A Space Odyssey *(1968). (Clarke and Kubrick co-authored the screenplay; Clarke later wrote the novel based on that screenplay.) In the 1960s, 1970s, and 1980s, Arthur C. Clarke spent much of his writing effort on works of nonfiction, though he continued to publish an occasional Science Fiction short story or novel. In 1973, he received extensive critical acclaim and several major literary awards for his Science Fiction epic,* Rendezvous in Rama.*

The vision germinated in "The Sentinel" and continued later in 2001: A Space Odyssey *has profoundly influenced writers of Fantasy and Hard Science Fiction ever since.*

The Sentinel

(originally published as "Sentinel of Eternity" in 10 Story Fantasy, *Spring 1951)*

The next time you see the full Moon high in the south, look carefully at its right-hand edge and let your eye travel upward along the curve of the disk. Round about two o'clock you will notice a small, dark oval: anyone with normal eyesight can find it quite easily. It is the great walled plain, one of the finest on the Moon, known as the Mare Crisium—the Sea of Crises. Three hundred miles in diameter, and almost completely surrounded by a ring of magnificent mountains, it had never been explored until we entered it in the late summer of 1996.

Our expedition was a large one. We had two heavy freighters which had flown our supplies and equipment from the main lunar base in the Mare Serenitatis, five hundred miles away. There were also three small rockets which were intended for short-range transport over regions which our surface vehicles couldn't cross. Luckily, most of the Mare Crisium is very flat. There are none of the great crevasses so common and so dangerous elsewhere, and very few craters or mountains of any size. As far as we could tell, our powerful Caterpillar tractors would have no difficulty in taking us wherever we wished to go.

I was geologist—or selenologist, if you want to be pedantic—in charge of the group exploring the southern region of the Mare. We had crossed a hundred miles of it in a week, skirting the foothills of the mountains along the shore of what was once the ancient sea, some thousand million years before. When life was beginning on Earth, it was already dying here. The waters were retreating down the flanks of those stupendous cliffs, retreating into the empty heart of the Moon. Over the land which we were crossing, the tideless ocean had once been half a mile deep, and now the only trace of moisture was the hoarfrost one could sometimes find in caves which the searing sunlight never penetrated.

We had begun our journey early in the slow lunar dawn, and still had almost a week of Earth-time before nightfall. Half a dozen times a day we would leave our vehicle and go outside in the space-suits to hunt for interesting minerals, or to place markers for the guidance of future travelers. It was an uneventful routine. There is nothing hazardous or even particularly exciting about lunar exploration. We could live comfortably for a month in our pressurized tractors, and if we ran into trouble we could always radio for help and sit tight until one of the spaceships came to our rescue.

I said just now that there was nothing exciting about lunar exploration, but of course that isn't true. One could never grow tired of those incredible mountains, so much more rugged than the gentle hills of Earth. We never knew, as we rounded the capes and promontories of that vanished sea, what new splendors would be revealed to us. The whole southern curve of the Mare Crisium is a vast delta where a score of rivers once found their way into the ocean, fed perhaps by the torrential rains that must have lashed the mountains in the brief volcanic age when the Moon was young. Each of these ancient valleys was an invitation, challenging us to climb into the unknown uplands beyond. But we had a hundred miles still to cover, and could only look longingly at the heights which others must scale.

We kept Earth-time aboard the tractor, and precisely at 22.00 hours the final radio message would be sent out to Base and we would close down for the day. Outside, the rocks would still be burning beneath the almost vertical Sun, but to us it was night until we awoke again eight hours later. Then one of us would prepare breakfast, there would be a great buzzing of electric razors, and someone would switch on the short-wave radio from Earth. Indeed, when the smell of frying sausages began to fill the cabin, it was sometimes hard to believe that we were not back on our own world—everything was so normal and homely, apart from the feeling of decreased weight and the unnatural slowness with which objects fell.

It was my turn to prepare breakfast in the corner of the main cabin that served as a galley. I can remember that moment quite vividly after all these years, for the radio had just played one of my favorite melodies, the old Welsh air, "David of the White Rock." Our driver was already outside in his space-suit, inspecting our

Caterpillar treads. My assistant, Louis Garnett, was up forward in the control position, making some belated entries in yesterday's log.

As I stood by the frying pan waiting—like any terrestrial housewife—for the sausages to brown, I let my gaze wander idly over the mountain walls which covered the whole of the southern horizon, marching out of sight to east and west below the curve of the Moon. They seemed only a mile or two from the tractor, but I knew that the nearest was twenty miles away. On the Moon, of course, there is no loss of detail with distance—none of that almost imperceptible haziness which softens and sometimes transfigures all far-off things on Earth.

Those mountains were ten thousand feet high, and they climbed steeply out of the plain as if ages ago some subterranean eruption had smashed them skyward through the molten crust. The base of even the nearest was hidden from sight by the steeply curving surface of the plain, for the Moon is a very little world, and from where I was standing the horizon was only two miles away.

I lifted my eyes toward the peaks which no man had ever climbed, the peaks which, before the coming of terrestrial life, had watched the retreating oceans sink sullenly into their graves, taking with them the hope and the morning promise of a world. The sunlight was beating against those ramparts with a glare that hurt the eyes, yet only a little way above them the stars were shining steadily in a sky blacker than a winter midnight on Earth.

I was turning away when my eye caught a metallic glitter high on the ridge of a great promontory thrusting out into the sea thirty miles to the west. It was a dimensionless point of light, as if a star had been clawed from the sky by one of those cruel peaks, and I imagined that some smooth rock surface was catching the sunlight and heliographing it straight into my eyes. Such things were not uncommon. When the Moon is in her second quarter, observers on Earth can sometimes see the great ranges in the Oceanus Procellarum burning with a blue-white iridescence as the sunlight flashes from their slopes and leaps again from world to world. But I was curious to know what kind of rock could be shining so brightly up there, and I climbed into the observation turret and swung our four-inch telescope round to the west.

I could see just enough to tantalize me. Clear and sharp in the field of vision, the mountain peaks seemed only half a mile away, but whatever was catching the sunlight was still too small to be resolved. Yet it seemed to have an elusive symmetry, and the summit upon which it rested was curiously flat. I stared for a long time at that glittering enigma, straining my eyes into space, until presently a smell of burning from the galley told me that our breakfast sausages had made their quarter-million-mile journey in vain.

All that morning we argued our way across the Mare Crisium while the western mountains reared higher in the sky. Even when we were out prospecting in the space-suits, the discussion would continue over the radio. It was absolutely certain, my companions argued, that there had never been any form of intelligent life on the Moon. The only living things that had ever existed there were a few primitive plants and their slightly less degenerate ancestors. I know that as well as anyone, but there are times when a scientist must not be afraid to make a fool of himself.

"Listen," I said at last, "I'm going up there, if only for my own peace of mind. That mountain's less than twelve thousand feet high—that's only two thousand under Earth gravity—and I can make the trip in twenty hours at the outside. I've always wanted to go up into those hills, anyway, and this gives me an excellent excuse."

"If you don't break your neck," said Garnett, "you'll be the laughing-stock of the expedition when we get back to Base. That mountain will probably be called Wilson's Folly from now on."

"I won't break my neck," I said firmly. "Who was the first man to climb Pico and Helicon?"

"But weren't you rather younger in those days?" asked Louis gently.

"That," I said with great dignity, "is as good a reason as any for going."

We went to bed early that night, after driving the tractor to within half a mile of the promontory. Garnett was coming with me in the morning; he was a good climber, and had often been with me on such exploits before. Our driver was only too glad to be left in charge of the machine.

At first sight, those cliffs seemed completely unscalable, but to anyone with a good head for heights, climbing is easy on a world where all weights are only a sixth of their normal value. The real danger in lunar mountaineering lies in over-confidence; a six-hundred-foot drop on the Moon can kill you just as thoroughly as a hundred-foot fall on Earth.

We made our first halt on a wide ledge about four thousand feet above the plain. Climbing had not been very difficult, but my limbs were stiff with the unaccustomed effort, and I was glad of the rest. We could still see the tractor as a tiny metal insect far down at the foot of the cliff, and we reported our progress to the driver before starting on the next ascent.

Inside our suits it was comfortably cool, for the refrigeration units were fighting the fierce sun and carrying away the body-heat of our exertions. We seldom spoke to each other, except to pass climbing instructions and to discuss our best plan of ascent. I do not know what Garnett was thinking, probably that this was the craziest goose-chase he had ever embarked upon. I more than half agreed with him, but the joy of climbing, the knowledge that no man had ever gone this way before and the exhilaration of the steadily widening landscape gave me all the reward I needed.

I don't think I was particularly excited when I saw in front of us the wall of rock I had first inspected through the telescope from thirty miles away. It would level off about fifty feet above our heads, and there on the plateau would be the thing that had lured me over these barren wastes. It was, almost certainly, nothing more than a boulder splintered ages ago by a falling meteor, and with its cleavage planes still fresh and bright in this incorruptible, unchanging silence.

There were no hand-holds on the rock face, and we had to use a grapnel. My tired arms seemed to gain new strength as I swung the three-pronged metal anchor round my head and sent it sailing up toward the stars. The first time it broke loose and came falling slowly back when we pulled the rope. On the third attempt, the prongs gripped firmly and our combined weights could not shift it.

Garnett looked at me anxiously. I could tell that he wanted to go first, but I smiled back at him through the glass of my helmet and shook my head. Slowly, taking my time, I began the final ascent.

Even with my space-suit, I weighed only forty pounds here, so I pulled myself up hand over hand without bothering to use my feet. At the rim I paused and waved to my companion, then I scrambled over the edge and stood upright, staring ahead of me.

You must understand that until this very moment I had been almost completely convinced that there could be nothing strange or unusual for me to find here. Almost, but not quite; it was that haunting doubt that had driven me forward. Well, it was a doubt no longer, but the haunting had scarcely begun.

I was standing on a plateau perhaps a hundred feet across. It had once been smooth—too smooth to be natural—but falling meteors had pitted and scored its surface through immeasurable eons. It had been leveled to support a glittering, roughly pyramidal structure, twice as high as a man, that was set in the rock like a gigantic, many-faceted jewel.

Probably no emotion at all filled my mind in those first few seconds. Then I felt a great lifting of my heart, and a strange, inexpressible joy. For I loved the Moon, and now I knew that the creeping moss of Aristarchus and Eratosthenes was not the only life she had brought forth in her youth. The old, discredited dream of the first explorers was true. There had, after all, been a lunar civilization—and I was the first to find it. That I had come perhaps a hundred million years too late did not distress me; it was enough to have come at all.

My mind was beginning to function normally, to analyze and to ask questions. Was this a building, a shrine—or something for which my language had no name? If a building, then why was it erected in so uniquely inaccessible a spot? I wondered if it might be a temple, and I could picture the adepts of some strange priesthood calling on their gods to preserve them as the life of the Moon ebbed with the dying oceans, and calling on their gods in vain.

I took a dozen steps forward to examine the thing more closely, but some sense of caution kept me from going too near. I knew a little of archaeology, and tried to guess the cultural level of the civilization that must have smoothed this mountain and raised the glittering mirror surfaces that still dazzled my eyes.

The Egyptians could have done it, I thought, if their workmen had possessed whatever strange materials these far more ancient architects had used. Because of the thing's smallness, it did not occur to me that I might be looking at the handiwork of a race more advanced than my own. The idea that the Moon had possessed intelligence at all was still almost too tremendous to grasp, and my pride would not let me take the final, humiliating plunge.

And then I noticed something that set the scalp crawling at the back of my neck—something so trivial and so innocent that many would never have noticed it at all. I have said that the plateau was scarred by meteors; it was also coated inches-deep with the cosmic dust that is always filtering down upon the surface of any world where there are no winds to disturb it. Yet the dust and the meteor scratches ended quite abruptly in a wide circle enclosing the little pyramid, as though an invisible wall was protecting it from the ravages of time and the slow but ceaseless bombardment from space.

There was someone shouting in my earphones, and I realized that Garnett had been calling me for some time. I walked unsteadily to the edge of the cliff and signaled him to join me, not trusting myself to speak. Then I went back toward that circle in the dust. I picked up a fragment of splintered rock and tossed it gently toward the shining enigma. If the pebble had vanished at that invisible barrier I should not have been surprised, but it seemed to hit a smooth, hemispherical surface and slide gently to the ground.

I knew then that I was looking at nothing that could be matched in the antiquity of my own race. This was not a building, but a machine, protecting itself with forces that had challenged Eternity. Those forces, whatever they might be, were still operating, and perhaps I had already come too close. I thought of all the radiations man had trapped and tamed in the past century. For all I knew, I might be as irrevocably doomed as if I had stepped into the deadly, silent aura of an unshielded atomic pile.

I remember turning then toward Garnett, who had joined me and was now standing motionless at my side. He seemed quite oblivious to me, so I did not disturb him but walked to the edge of the cliff in an effort to marshal my thoughts.

There below me lay the Mare Crisium—Sea of Crises, indeed—strange and weird to most men, but reassuringly familiar to me. I lifted my eyes toward the crescent Earth, lying in her cradle of stars, and I wondered what her clouds had covered when these unknown builders had finished their work. Was it the steaming jungle of the Carboniferous, the bleak shore-line over which the first amphibians must crawl to conquer the land—or, earlier still, the long loneliness before the coming of life?

Do not ask me why I did not guess the truth sooner—the truth that seems so obvious now. In the first excitement of my discovery, I had assumed without question that this crystalline apparition had been built by some race belonging to the Moon's remote past, but suddenly, and with overwhelming force, the belief came to me that it was as alien to the Moon as I myself.

In twenty years we had found no trace of life but a few degenerate plants. No lunar civilization, whatever its doom, could have left but a single token of its existence.

I looked at the shining pyramid again, and the more remote it seemed from anything that had to do with the Moon. And suddenly I felt myself shaking with a foolish, hysterical laughter, brought on by excitement and over-exertion: for I had imagined that the little pyramid was speaking to me and was saying: "Sorry, I'm a stranger here myself."

It has taken us twenty years to crack that invisible shield and to reach the machine inside those crystal walls. What we could not understand, we broke at last with the savage might of atomic power and now I have seen the fragments of the lovely, glittering thing I found up there on the mountain.

They are meaningless. The mechanisms—if indeed they are mechanisms—of the pyramid belong to a technology that lies far beyond our horizon, perhaps to the technology of paraphysical forces.

The mystery haunts us all the more now that the other planets have been reached and we know that only Earth has ever been the home of intelligent life in our Universe. Nor could any lost civilization of our own world have built that machine, for the thickness of the meteoric dust on the plateau has enabled us to measure its age. It was set there upon its mountain before life had emerged from the seas of Earth.

When our world was half its present age, *something* from the stars swept through the Solar System, left this token of its passage, and went again upon its way. Until we destroyed it, that machine was still fulfilling the purpose of its builders; and as to that purpose, here is my guess.

Nearly a hundred thousand million stars are turning in the circle of the Milky Way, and long ago other races on the worlds of other suns must have scaled and passed the heights that we have reached. Think of such civilizations, far back in time against the fading afterglow of Creation, masters of a universe so young that life as yet had come only to a handful of worlds. Theirs would have been a loneliness we cannot imagine, the loneliness of gods looking out across infinity and finding none to share their thoughts.

They must have searched the star-clusters as we have searched the planets. Everywhere there would be worlds, but they would be empty or peopled with crawling, mindless things. Such was our Earth, the smoke of the great volcanoes still staining the skies, when that first ship of the peoples of the dawn came sliding in from the abyss beyond Pluto. It passed the frozen outer worlds, knowing that life could play no part in their destinies. It came to rest among the inner planets, warming themselves around the fire of the Sun and waiting for their stories to begin.

Those wanderers must have looked on Earth, circling safely in the narrow zone between fire and ice, and must have guessed that it was the favorite of the Sun's

children. Here, in the distant future, would be intelligence; but there were countless stars before them still, and they might never come this way again.

So they left a sentinel, one of millions they have scattered throughout the
Universe, watching over all worlds with the promise of life. It was a beacon that
down the ages has been patiently signaling the fact that no one had discovered it.

Perhaps you understand now why that crystal pyramid was set upon the Moon
instead of on the Earth. Its builders were not concerned with races still struggling
up from savagery. They would be interested in our civilization only if we proved
our fitness to survive—by crossing space and so escaping from the Earth, our cradle. That is the challenge that all intelligent races must meet, sooner or later. It is
a double challenge, for it depends in turn upon the conquest of atomic energy and
the last choice between life and death.

Once we had passed that crisis, it was only a matter of time before we found the
pyramid and forced it open. Now its signals have ceased, and those whose duty it
is will be turning their minds upon Earth. Perhaps they wish to help our infant
civilization. But they must be very, very old, and the old are often insanely jealous
of the young.

I can never look now at the Milky Way without wondering from which of those
banked clouds of stars the emissaries are coming. If you will pardon so commonplace a simile, we have set off the fire-alarm and have nothing to do but to wait.

I do not think we will have to wait for long.

🕊 KATHERINE (ANNE) MacLEAN (1925–)

A love of stories, books, reading, science, classical literature, Shakespeare, Sherlock Holmes,
H. G. Wells, and Edgar Rice Burroughs has marked the life of Katherine MacLean.
MacLean began her writing career as an important woman writer of the Cold War era,
though her stories were not particularly feminist in tone at this time. Her writing has of-
ten been a blend of Science Fiction and Fantasy, and one of her primary thematic em-
phases is Hard Science Fiction and technology.

Katherine MacLean is primarily a short story writer, and some of her best short stories
are collected in The Diploids *(1962) and* The Trouble With You Earth People
(1980). "Pictures Don't Lie" is one of MacLean's most famous stories. It features an end-
ing that is reminiscent of stories by Mary Elizabeth Counselman, Robert Bloch, Shirley
Jackson, Richard Matheson, and Charles Beaumont. This story is also similar to some of
the writing of her contemporary, Fredric Brown, a newspaper man who often used jour-
nalism and reporting as central elements of his stories.

Pictures Don't Lie

(Galaxy, *August 1951*)

The man from the *News* asked, "What do you think of the aliens, Mr. Nathen?
Are they friendly? Do they look human?"

"Very human," said the thin young man.

Outside, rain sleeted across the big windows with a steady, faint drumming,
blurring and dimming the view of the airfield where *They* would arrive. On the

concrete runways the puddles were pockmarked with rain, and the grass growing untouched between the runways of the unused field glistened wetly, bending before gusts of wind.

Back at a respectful distance from the place where the huge spaceship would land were the gray shapes of trucks, where TV camera crews huddled inside their mobile units, waiting. Farther back in the deserted, sandy landscape, behind distant sandy hills, artillery was ringed in a great circle, and in the distance across the horizon bombers stood ready at airfields, guarding the world against possible treachery from the first alien ship ever to land from space.

"Do you know anything about their home planet?" asked the man from the *Herald.*

The *Times* man stood with the others, listening absently, thinking of questions but reserving them. Joseph R. Nathen, the thin young man with the straight black hair and the tired lines on his face, was being treated with respect by his interviewers. He was obviously on edge, and they did not want to harry him with too many questions at once. They wanted to keep his good will. Tomorrow he would be one of the biggest celebrities ever to appear in headlines.

"No, nothing directly."

"Any ideas or deductions?" the *Herald* persisted.

"Their world must be Earthlike to them," the weary-looking young man answered uncertainly. "The environment evolves the animal. But only in relative terms, of course." He looked at them with a quick glance and then looked away evasively, his lank black hair beginning to cling to his forehead with sweat. "That doesn't necessarily mean anything."

"Earthlike," muttered a reporter, writing it down as if he had noticed nothing more in the reply.

The *Times* man glanced at the *Herald*, wondering if he had noticed, and received a quick glance in exchange.

The *Herald* asked Nathen, "You think they are dangerous, then?"

It was the kind of question, assuming much, that usually broke reticence and brought forth quick facts—when it hit the mark. They all knew of the military precautions, although they were not supposed to know.

The question missed. Nathen glanced out the window vaguely. "No, I wouldn't say so."

"You think they are friendly, then?" said the *Herald*, equally positive on the opposite tack.

A fleeting smile touched Nathen's lips. "Those I know are."

There was no lead in this direction, and they had to get the basic facts of the story before the ship came. The *Times* asked, "What led up to your contacting them?"

Nathen answered, after a hesitation, "Static. Radio static. The Army told you my job, didn't they?"

The Army had told them nothing at all. The officer who had conducted them in for the interview stood glowering watchfully, as if he objected by instinct to telling anything to the public.

Nathen glanced at him doubtfully. "My job is radio decoder for the Department of Military Intelligence. I use a directional pickup, tune in on foreign bands, record any scrambled or coded messages I hear, and build automatic decoders and descramblers for all the basic scramble patterns."

The officer cleared his throat but said nothing.

The reporters smiled, noting that down.

Security regulations had changed since arms inspection had been legalized by the U.N. Complete information being the only public security against secret rearmament, spying and prying had come to seem a public service. Its aura had changed. It was good public relations to admit to it.

Nathen continued, "In my spare time I started directing the pickup at stars. There's radio noise from stars, you know. Just stuff that sounds like spatter static, and an occasional squawk. People have been listening to it for a long time, and researching, trying to work out why stellar radiation on those bands comes in such jagged bursts. It didn't seem natural."

He paused and smiled uncertainly, aware that the next thing he would say was the thing that would make him famous—an idea that had come to him while he listened, an idea as simple and as perfect as the one that came to Newton when he saw the apple fall.

"I decided it wasn't natural. I tried decoding it."

Hurriedly, he tried to explain it away and make it seem obvious. "You see, there's an old intelligence trick, speeding up a message on a record until it sounds just like that, a short squawk of static, and then broadcasting it. Undergrounds use it. I'd heard that kind of screech before."

"You mean they broadcast at us in code?" asked the *News*.

"It's not exactly code. All you need to do is record it and slow it down. They're not broadcasting at us. If a star has planets, inhabited planets, and there is broadcasting between them, they would send it on a tight beam to save power." He looked for comprehension. "You know, like a spotlight. Theoretically, a tight beam can go on forever without losing power. But aiming would be difficult from planet to planet. You can't expect a beam to stay on target, over such distances, more than a few seconds at a time. So they'd naturally compress each message into a short half-second- or one-second-length package and send it a few hundred times in one long blast to make sure it is picked up during the instant the beam swings across the target."

He was talking slowly and carefully, remembering that this explanation was for the newspapers. "When a stray beam swings through our section of space, there's a sharp peak in noise level from that direction. The beams are swinging to follow their own planets at home, and the distance between there and here exaggerates the speed of swing tremendously, so we wouldn't pick up more than a *bip* as it passes."

"How do you account for the number of squawks coming in?" the *Times* asked. "Do stellar systems rotate on the plane of the Galaxy?" It was a private question; he spoke impulsively from interest and excitement.

The radio decoder grinned, the lines of strain vanishing from his face for a moment. "Maybe we're intercepting everybody's telephone calls, and the whole Galaxy is swarming with races that spend all day yacking at each other over the radio. Maybe the human type is standard model."

"It would take something like that," the *Times* agreed. They smiled at each other. The *News* asked, "How did you happen to pick up television instead of voices?"

"Not by accident," Nathen explained patiently. "I'd recognized a scanning pattern, and I wanted pictures. Pictures are understandable in any language."

Near the interviewers, a senator paced back and forth, muttering his memorized speech of welcome and nervously glancing out the wide, streaming windows into the gray, sleeting rain.

Opposite the windows of the long room was a small raised platform flanked by the tall shapes of TV cameras and sound pickups on booms, and darkened flood-lights, arranged and ready for the senator to make his speech of welcome to the aliens and the world. A shabby radio sending set stood beside it without a case to conceal its parts, two cathode television tubes flickering nakedly on one side and the speaker humming on the other. A vertical panel of dials and knobs jutted up before them, and a small hand-mike sat ready on the table before the panel. It was connected to a boxlike, expensively cased piece of equipment with "Radio Lab, U.S. Property" stenciled on it.

"I recorded a couple of package screeches from Sagittarius and began working on them," Nathen added. "It took a couple of months to find the synchronizing signals and set the scanners close enough to the right time to even get a pattern. When I showed the pattern to the Department, they gave me full time to work on it, and an assistant to help. It took eight months to pick out the color bands and assign them the right colors, to get anything intelligible on the screen."

The shabby-looking mess of exposed parts was the original receiver that they had labored over for ten months, adjusting and readjusting to reduce the madden-ing rippling plaids of unsynchronized color scanners to some kind of sane picture.

"Trial and error," said Nathen, "but it came out all right. The wide band spread of the squawks had suggested color TV from the beginning."

He walked over and touched the set. The speaker bipped slightly and the gray screen flickered with a flash of color at the touch. The set was awake and sensitive, tuned to receive from the great interstellar spaceship which now circled the at-mosphere.

"We wondered why there were so many bands, but when we got the set work-ing and started recording and playing everything that came in, we found we'd tapped something like a lending-library line. It was all fiction, plays."

Between the pauses in Nathen's voice, the *Times* found himself unconsciously listening for the sound of roaring, swiftly approaching rocket jets.

The *Post* asked, "How did you contact the spaceship?"

"I scanned and recorded a film copy of *The Rite of Spring*, the Disney-Stravinsky combination, and sent it back along the same line we were receiving from. Just testing. It wouldn't get there for a good number of years, if it got there at all, but I thought it would please the library to get a new record in.

"Two weeks later, when we caught and slowed a new batch of recordings, we found an answer. It was obviously meant for us. It was a flash of the Disney being played to a large audience, and then the audience sitting and waiting before a blank screen. The signal was very clear and loud. We'd intercepted a spaceship. They were asking for an encore, you see. They liked the film and wanted more. . . ."

He smiled at them in sudden thought. "You can see them for yourself. It's all right down the hall where the linguists are working on the automatic trans-lator."

The listening officer frowned and cleared his throat, and the thin young man turned to him quickly. "No security reason why they should not see the broad-casts, is there? Perhaps you should show them." He said to the reporters reassur-ingly, "It's right down the hall. You will be informed the moment the spaceship approaches."

The interview was very definitely over. The lank-haired, nervous young man turned away and seated himself at the radio set while the officer swallowed his ob-jections and showed them dourly down the hall to a closed door.

They opened it and fumbled into a darkened room crowded with empty folding chairs, dominated by a glowing bright screen. The door closed behind them, bringing total darkness.

There was the sound of reporters fumbling their way into seats around him, but the *Times* man remained standing, aware of an enormous surprise, as if he had been asleep and wakened to find himself in the wrong country.

The bright colors of the double image seemed the only real thing in the darkened room. Even blurred as they were, he could see that the action was subtly different, the shapes subtly not right.

He was looking at aliens.

The impression was of two humans disguised, humans moving oddly, half dancing, half crippled. Carefully, afraid the images would go away, he reached up to his breast pocket, took out his polarized glasses, rotated one lens at right angles to the other, and put them on.

Immediately, the two beings came into sharp focus, real and solid, and the screen became a wide, illusively near window through which he watched them.

They were conversing with each other in a gray-walled room, discussing something with restrained excitement. The large man in the green tunic closed his purple eyes for an instant at something the other said and grimaced, making a motion with his fingers as if shoving something away from him.

Mellerdrammer.

The second, smaller, with yellowish-green eyes, stepped closer, talking more rapidly in a lower voice. The first stood very still, not trying to interrupt.

Obviously, the proposal was some advantageous treachery, and he wanted to be persuaded. The *Times* groped for a chair and sat down.

Perhaps gesture is universal; desire and aversion, a leaning forward or a leaning back, tension, relaxation. Perhaps these actors were masters. The scenes changed: a corridor, a parklike place in what he began to realize was a spaceship, a lecture room. There were others talking and working, speaking to the man in the green tunic, and never was it unclear what was happening or how they felt.

They talked a flowing language with many short vowels and shifts of pitch, and they gestured in the heat of talk, their hands moving with an odd lagging difference of motion, not slow, but somehow drifting.

He ignored the language, but after a time the difference in motion began to arouse his interest. Something in the way they walked . . .

With an effort he pulled his mind from the plot and forced his attention to the physical difference. Brown hair in short, silky crew cuts, varied eye colors, the colors showing clearly because their irises were very large, their round eyes set very widely apart in tapering, light-brown faces. Their necks and shoulders were thick in a way that would indicate unusual strength for a human, but their wrists were narrow and their fingers long and thin and delicate.

There seemed to be more than the usual number of fingers.

Since he came in, a machine had been whirring and a voice muttering beside him. He turned from counting their fingers and looked around. Beside him sat an alert-looking man wearing earphones, watching and listening with hawklike concentration. Beside him was a tall streamlined box. From the screen came the sound of the alien language. The man abruptly flipped a switch on the box, muttered a word into a small hand microphone, and flipped the switch back with nervous rapidity.

He reminded the *Times* man of the earphoned interpreters at the U.N. The machine was probably a vocal translator and the mutterer a linguist adding to its vocabulary. Near the screen were two other linguists taking notes.

The *Times* remembered the senator pacing in the observatory room, rehearsing his speech of welcome. The speech would not be just the empty pompous gesture he had expected. It would be translated mechanically and understood by the aliens.

On the other side of the glowing window that was the stereo screen, the large protagonist in the green tunic was speaking to a pilot in a gray uniform. They stood in a brightly lit canary-yellow control room in a spaceship.

The *Times* tried to pick up the thread of the plot. Already he was interested in the fate of the hero, and liked him. That was the effect of good acting, probably, for part of the art of acting is to win affection from the audience, and this actor might be the matinee idol of whole Solar Systems.

Controlled tension, betraying itself by a jerk of the hands, a too quick answer to a question. The uniformed one, not suspicious, turned his back, busying himself at some task involving a map lit with glowing red points, his motions sharing the same fluid, dragging grace of the others, as if they were under water or on a slow-motion film. The other was watching a switch, a switch set into a panel, moving closer to it, talking casually—background music coming and rising in thin chords of tension.

There was a close-up of the alien's face watching the switch, and the *Times* noted that his ears were symmetrical half circles, almost perfect, with no earholes visible. The voice of the uniformed one answered—a brief word in a preoccupied, deep voice. His back was still turned. The other glanced at the switch, moving closer to it, talking casually, the switch coming closer and closer stereoscopically. It was in reach, filling the screen. His hand came into view, darted out, closed over the switch—

There was a sharp clap of sound and his hand opened in a frozen shape of pain. Beyond him, as his gaze swung up, stood the figure of the uniformed officer, unmoving, a weapon rigid in his hand, in the startled position in which he had turned and fired, watching with widening eyes as the man in the green tunic swayed and fell.

The tableau held, the uniformed one drooping, looking down at his hand holding the weapon which had killed, and music began to build in from the background. Just for an instant, the room and the things within it flashed into one of those bewildering color changes that were the bane of color television—to a color negative of itself, a green man standing in a violet control room, looking down at the body of a green man in a red tunic. It held for less than a second; then the color-band alternator fell back into phase and the colors reversed to normal.

Another uniformed man came and took the weapon from the limp hand of the other, who began to explain dejectedly in a low voice while the music mounted and covered his words and the screen slowly went blank, like a window that slowly filmed over with gray fog.

The music faded.

In the dark, someone clapped appreciatively.

The earphoned man beside the *Times* shifted his earphones back from his ears and spoke briskly. "I can't get any more. Either of you want a replay?"

There was a short silence until the linguist nearest the set said, "I guess we've squeezed that one dry. Let's run the tape where Nathen and that ship radio boy are kidding around CQing and tuning their beams in closer. I have a hunch the boy is talking routine ham talk and giving the old radio count—one-two-three-testing."

There was some fumbling in the semidark and then the screen came to life again.

It showed a flash of an audience sitting before a screen and gave a clipped chord of some familiar symphony. "Crazy about Stravinsky and Mozart," remarked the earphoned linguist to the *Times*, resettling his earphones. "Can't stand Gershwin. Can you beat that?" He turned his attention back to the screen as the right sequence came on.

The *Post*, who was sitting just in front of him, turned to the *Times* and said, "Funny how much they look like people." He was writing, making notes to telephone his report. "What color hair did that character have?"

"I didn't notice." He wondered if he should remind the reporter that Nathen had said he assigned the color bands on guess, choosing the colors that gave the most plausible images. The guests, when they arrived, could turn out to be bright green with blue hair. Only the gradations of color in the picture were sure, only the similarities and contrasts, the relationship of one color to another.

From the screen came the sound of the alien language again. This race averaged deeper voices than human. He liked deep voices. Could he write that?

No, there was something wrong with that, too. How had Nathen established the right sound-track pitch? Was it a matter of taking the modulation as it came in, or some sort of heterodyning up and down by trial and error? Probably.

It might be safer to assume that Nathen had simply preferred deep voices.

As he sat there, doubting, an uneasiness he had seen in Nathen came back to add to his own uncertainty, and he remembered just how close that uneasiness had come to something that looked like restrained fear.

"What I don't get is why he went to all the trouble of picking up TV shows instead of just contacting them," the *News* complained. "They're good shows, but what's the point?"

"Maybe so we'd get to learn their language, too," said the *Herald*.

On the screen now was the obviously unstaged and genuine scene of a young alien working over a bank of apparatus. He turned and waved and opened his mouth in the comical O shape which the *Times* was beginning to recognize as their equivalent of a smile, then went back to trying to explain something about the equipment, in elaborate, awkward gestures and carefully mouthed words.

The *Times* got up quietly, went out into the bright white stone corridor, and walked back the way he had come, thoughtfully folding his stereo glasses and putting them away.

No one stopped him. Secrecy restrictions were ambiguous here. The reticence of the Army seemed more a matter of habit—mere reflex, from the fact that it had all originated in the Intelligence Department—than any reasoned policy of keeping the landing a secret.

The main room was more crowded than he had left it. The TV camera and sound crew stood near their apparatus, the senator had found a chair and was reading, and at the far end of the room eight men were grouped in a circle of chairs, arguing something with impassioned concentration. The *Times* recognized a few he knew personally, eminent names in science, workers in field theory.

A stray phrase reached him: "—reference to the universal constants as ratio—" It was probably a discussion of ways of converting formulas from one mathematics to another for a rapid exchange of information.

They had reason to be intent, aware of the flood of insights that novel viewpoints could bring, if they could grasp them. He would have liked to go over and listen, but there was too little time left before the spaceship was due, and he had a question to ask.

The hand-rigged transceiver was still humming, tuned to the sending band of the circling ship, and the young man who had started it all was sitting on the edge of the TV platform with his chin resting in one hand. He did not look up as the *Times* approached, but it was the indifference of preoccupation, not discourtesy.

The *Times* sat down on the edge of the platform beside him and took out a pack of cigarettes, then remembered the coming TV broadcast and the ban on smoking. He put them away, thoughtfully watching the diminishing rain spray against the streaming windows.

"What's wrong?" he asked.

Nathen showed that he was aware and friendly by a slight motion of his head. "*You* tell me."

"Hunch," said the *Times* man. "Sheer hunch. Everything sailing along too smoothly, everyone taking too much for granted."

Nathen relaxed slightly. "I'm still listening."

"Something about the way they move . . ."

Nathen shifted to glance at him.

"That's bothered me, too."

"Are you sure they're adjusted to the right speed?"

Nathen clenched his hands out in front of him and looked at them consideringly. "I don't know. When I turn the tape faster, they're all rushing, and you begin to wonder why their clothes don't stream behind them, why the doors close so quickly and yet you can't hear them slam, why things fall so fast. If I turn it slower, they all seem to be swimming." He gave the *Times* a considering sideways glance. "Didn't catch the name."

Country-bred guy, thought the *Times*. "Jacob Luke, *Times*," he said, extending his hand.

Nathen gave the hand a quick, hard grip, identifying the name. "Sunday Science Section editor. I read it. Surprised to meet you here."

"Likewise." The *Times* smiled. "Look, have you gone into this rationally, with formulas?" He found a pencil in his pocket. "Obviously, there's something wrong with our judgment of their weight-to-speed-to-momentum ratio. Maybe it's something simple, like low gravity aboard ship, with magnetic shoes. Maybe they *are* floating slightly."

"Why worry?" Nathen cut in. "I don't see any reason to try to figure it out now." He laughed and shoved back his black hair nervously. "We'll see them in twenty minutes."

"Will we?" asked the *Times* slowly.

There was a silence while the senator turned a page of his magazine with a slight crackling of paper and the scientists argued at the other end of the room. Nathen pushed at his lank black hair again, as if it were trying to fall forward in front of his eyes and keep him from seeing.

"Sure." The young man laughed suddenly, talked rapidly. "Sure we'll see them. Why shouldn't we, with all the government ready with welcome speeches, the whole Army turned out and hiding over the hill, reporters all around, newsreel cameras — everything set up to broadcast the landing to the world. The President himself shaking hands with me and waiting in Washington — "

He came to the truth without pausing for breath.

He said, "Hell, no, they won't get here. There's some mistake somewhere. Something's wrong. I should have told the brass hats yesterday when I started adding it up. Don't know why I didn't say anything. Scared, I guess. Too much top rank around here. Lost my nerve."

He clutched the *Times* man's sleeve. "Look. I don't know what— "

A green light flashed on the sending-receiving set. Nathen didn't look at it, but he stopped talking.

The loud-speaker on the set broke into a voice speaking in the aliens' language. The senator started and looked nervously at it, straightening his tie. The voice stopped.

Nathen turned and looked at the loud-speaker. His worry seemed to be gone. "What is it?" the *Times* asked anxiously.

"He says they've slowed enough to enter the atmosphere now. They'll be here in five to ten minutes, I guess. That's Bud. He's all excited. He says holy smoke, what a murky-looking planet we live on." Nathen smiled. "Kidding."

The *Times* was puzzled. "What does he mean, murky? It can't be raining over much territory on Earth." Outside, the rain was slowing and bright-blue patches of sky were shining through breaks in the cloud blanket, glittering blue light from the drops that ran down the windows. He tried to think of an explanation. "Maybe they're trying to land on Venus." The thought was ridiculous, he knew. The spaceship was following Nathen's sending beam. It couldn't miss Earth. "Bud" had to be kidding.

The green light glowed on the set again, and they stopped speaking, waiting for the message to be recorded, slowed, and replayed. The cathode screen came to life suddenly with a picture of the young man sitting at his sending set, his back turned, watching a screen at one side that showed a glimpse of a huge dark plain approaching. As the ship plunged down toward it, the illusion of solidity melted into a boiling turbulence of black clouds. They expanded in an inky swirl, looked huge for an instant, and then blackness swallowed the screen. The young alien swung around to face the camera, speaking a few words as he moved, made the O of a smile again, then flipped the switch and the screen went gray.

Nathen's voice was suddenly toneless and strained. "He said something like break out the drinks, here they come."

"The atmosphere doesn't look like that," the *Times* said at random, knowing he was saying something too obvious even to think about. "Not Earth's atmosphere."

Some people drifted up. "What did they say?"

"Entering the atmosphere, ought to be landing in five or ten minutes," Nathen told them.

A ripple of heightened excitement ran through the room. Cameramen began adjusting the lens angles again, turning on the mike and checking it, turning on the floodlights. The scientists rose and stood near the window, still talking. The reporters trooped in from the hall and went to the windows to watch for the great event. The three linguists came in, trundling a large wheeled box that was the mechanical translator, supervising while it was hitched into the sound-broadcasting system.

"Landing where?" the *Times* asked Nathen brutally. "Why don't you do something?"

"Tell me what to do and I'll do it," Nathen said quietly, not moving.

It was not sarcasm. Jacob Luke of the *Times* looked sideways at the strained whiteness of his face and moderated his tone. "Can't you contact them?"

"Not while they're landing."

"What now?" The *Times* took out a pack of cigarettes, remembered the rule against smoking, and put it back.

"We just wait." Nathen leaned his elbow on one knee and his chin in his hand. They waited.

All the people in the room were waiting. There was no more conversation. A bald man of the scientist group was automatically buffing his fingernails over and over and inspecting them without seeing them; another absently polished his glasses, held them up to the light, put them on, and then a moment later took them off and began polishing again. The television crew concentrated on their jobs, moving quietly and efficiently, with perfectionist care, minutely arranging things that did not need to be arranged, checking things that had already been checked.

This was to be one of the great moments of human history, and they were all trying to forget that fact and remain impassive and wrapped up in the problems of their jobs, as good specialists should.

After an interminable age the *Times* consulted his watch. Three minutes had passed. He tried holding his breath a moment, listening for a distant approaching thunder of jets. There was no sound.

The sun came out from behind the clouds and lit up the field like a great spotlight on an empty stage.

Abruptly, the green light shone on the set again, indicating that a squawk message had been received. The recorder recorded it, slowed it, and fed it back to the speaker. It clicked and the sound was very loud in the still, tense room.

The screen remained gray, but Bud's voice spoke a few words in the alien language. He stopped, the speaker clicked, and the light went out. When it was plain that nothing more would occur and no announcement was to be made of what was said, the people in the room turned back to the windows and talk picked up again.

Somebody told a joke and laughed alone.

One of the linguists remained turned toward the loud-speaker, then looked at the widening patches of blue sky showing out the window, his expression puzzled. He had understood.

"It's dark," the thin Intelligence Department decoder translated, low-voiced, to the man from the *Times*. "Your atmosphere is *thick*. That's precisely what Bud said."

Another three minutes. The *Times* caught himself about to light a cigarette and swore silently, blowing the match out and putting the cigarette back into its package. He listened for the sound of the rocket jets. It was time for the landing, yet he heard no blasts.

The green light came on in the transceiver.

Message in.

Instinctively, he came to his feet. Nathen abruptly was standing beside him. Then the message came in the voice he was coming to think of as Bud. It spoke and paused. Suddenly the *Times* knew.

"We've landed." Nathen whispered the words.

The wind blew across the open spaces of white concrete and damp soil that was the empty airfield, swaying the wet, shiny grass. The people in the room looked out, listening for the roar of jets, looking for the silver bulk of a spaceship in the sky.

Nathen moved, seating himself at the transmitter, switching it on to warm up, checking and balancing dials. Jacob Luke of the *Times* moved softly to stand behind his right shoulder, hoping he could be useful. Nathen made a half motion of his head, as if to glance back at him, unhooked two of the earphone sets hanging on the side of the tall streamlined box that was the automatic translator, plugged them in, and handed one back over his shoulder to the *Times* man.

The voice began to come from the speaker again.

Hastily, Jacob Luke fitted the earphones over his ears. He fancied he could hear Bud's voice tremble. For a moment it was just Bud's voice speaking the alien language, and then, very distant and clear in his earphones, he heard the recorded voice of the linguist say an English word, then a mechanical click and another clear word in the voice of one of the other translators, then another as the alien's voice flowed from the loud-speaker, the cool single words barely audible, overlapping and blending like translating thought, skipping unfamiliar words yet quite astonishingly clear.

"Radar shows no buildings or civilization near. The atmosphere around us registers as thick as glue. Tremendous gas pressure, low gravity, no light at all. You didn't describe it like this. Where are you, Joe? This isn't some kind of trick, is it?" Bud hesitated, was prompted by a deeper official voice, and jerked out the words.

"If it is a trick, we are ready to repel attack."

The linguist stood listening. He whitened slowly and beckoned the other linguists over to him and whispered to them.

Joseph Nathen looked at them with unwarranted bitter hostility while he picked up the hand mike, plugging it into the translator. "Joe calling," he said quietly into it in clear, slow English. "No trick. We don't know where you are. I am trying to get a direction fix from your signal. Describe your surroundings to us if at all possible."

Nearby, the floodlights blazed steadily on the television platform, ready for the official welcome of the aliens to Earth. The television channels of the world had been alerted to set aside their scheduled programs for an unscheduled great event. In the long room the people waited, listening for the swelling sound of rocket jets.

This time, after the light came on, there was a long delay. The speaker sputtered and sputtered again, building to a steady scratching through which they could barely hear a dim voice. It came through in a few tiny words and then wavered back to inaudibility. The machine translated in their earphones.

"Tried . . . seemed . . . repair . . ." Suddenly it came in clearly. "Can't tell if the auxiliary blew, too. Will try it. We might pick you up clearly on the next try. I have the volume down. Where is the landing port? Repeat. Where is the landing port? Where are you?"

Nathen put down the hand mike and carefully set a dial on the recording box and flipped a switch, speaking over his shoulder. "This sets it to repeat what I said the last time. It keeps repeating." Then he sat with unnatural stillness, his head still half turned, as if he had suddenly caught a glimpse of answer and was trying with no success whatever to grasp it.

The green warning light cut in, the recording clicked, and the playback of Bud's face and voice appeared on the screen.

"We heard a few words, Joe, and then the receiver blew again. We're adjusting a viewing screen to pick up the long waves that go through the murk and convert them to visible light. We'll be able to see out soon. The engineer says that something is wrong with the stern jets, and the captain has had me broadcast a help call to our nearest space base." He made the mouth O of a grin. "The message won't reach it for some years. I trust you, Joe, but get us out of here, will you? — They're buzzing that the screen is finally ready. Hold everything."

The screen went gray and the green light went off.

The *Times* considered the lag required for the help call, the speaking and recording of the message just received, the time needed to reconvert a viewing screen.

"They work fast." He shifted uneasily and added at random, "Something wrong with the time factor. All wrong. They work *too* fast."

The green light came on again immediately. Nathen half turned to him, sliding his words hastily into the gap of time as the message was recorded and slowed. "They're close enough for our transmission power to blow their receiver."

If it was on Earth, why the darkness around the ship? "Maybe they see in the high ultraviolet—the atmosphere is opaque to that band," the *Times* suggested hastily as the speaker began to talk in the young extra-Terrestrial's voice.

That voice *was* shaking now. "Stand by for the description."

They tensed, waiting. The *Times* brought a map of the state before his mind's eye.

"A half circle of cliffs around the horizon. A wide muddy lake swarming with swimming things. Huge, strange white foliage all around the ship and incredibly huge, pulpy monsters attacking and eating each other on all sides. We almost landed in the lake, right on the soft edge. The mud can't hold the ship's weight, and we're sinking. The engineer says we might be able to blast free, but the tubes are mud-clogged and might blow up the ship. When can you reach us?"

The *Times* thought vaguely of the Carboniferous era. Nathen obviously had seen something he had not.

"Where are they?" the *Times* asked him quietly.

Nathen pointed to the antenna position indicators. The *Times* let his eyes follow the converging imaginary lines of focus out the window to the sunlit airfield, the empty airfield, the drying concrete and green waving grass where the lines met.

Where the lines met. The spaceship was there!

The fear of something unknown gripped him suddenly.

The spaceship was broadcasting again. "*Where are you? Answer if possible! We are sinking! Where are you?*"

He saw that Nathen knew. "What is it?" the *Times* asked hoarsely. "Are they in another dimension or the past or on another world or what?"

Nathen was smiling bitterly, and Jacob Luke remembered that the young man had a friend in that spaceship. "My guess is that they evolved on a high-gravity planet with a thin atmosphere, near a blue-white star. Sure, they see in the ultraviolet range. Our sun is abnormally small and dim and yellow. Our atmosphere is so thick it screens out ultraviolet." He laughed harshly. "A good joke on us, the weird place we evolved in, the thing it did to us!"

"Where are you?" called the alien spaceship. "Hurry, please! We're sinking!"

The decoder slowed his tumbled, frightened words and looked up into the *Times*' face for understanding. "We'll rescue them," he said quietly. "You were right about the time factor, right about them moving at a different speed. I misunderstood. This business about squawk coding, speeding for better transmission to counteract beam waver—I was wrong."

"What do you mean?"

"They don't speed up their broadcasts."

"They don't—?"

Suddenly, in his mind's eye, the *Times* began to see again the play he had just seen—but the actors were moving at blurring speed, the words jerking out in a fluting, dizzying stream, thoughts and decisions passing with unfollowable rapidity, rippling faces in a twisting blur of expressions, doors slamming wildly, shatteringly, as the actors leaped in and out of rooms.

No—faster, faster—he wasn't visualizing it as rapidly as it was, an hour of talk and action in one almost instantaneous "squawk," a narrow peak of "noise" interfering with a single word in an Earth broadcast! Faster—faster—it was impossible. Matter could not stand such stress—inertia—momentum—abrupt weight.

It was insane. "Why?" he asked. "How?"

Nathen laughed again harshly, reaching for the mike. "Get them out? There isn't a lake or river within hundreds of miles from here!"

A shiver of unreality went down the *Times'* spine. Automatically and inanely, he found himself delving in his pocket for a cigarette while he tried to grasp what had happened. "Where are they, then? Why can't we see their spaceship?"

Nathen switched the microphone on in a gesture that showed the bitterness of his disappointment.

"We'll need a magnifying glass for that."

✿ PHILIP JOSÉ FARMER (1918-)

At the first presentation of the Hugo Awards (Science Fiction's prestigious annual awards named for Hugo Gernsback) in 1953, Philip José Farmer was named the best new writer in the Science Fiction field for 1952. Farmer's first major Science Fiction writing is the novella that follows, The Lovers. *With this story, Farmer not only introduced himself, but opened the door for future Science Fiction stories, such as those by Harlan Ellison, Samuel R. Delany, and Joanna Russ, that would openly and intelligently deal with matters of sexuality.*

Ironically, Farmer, the Science Fiction writer who is perhaps the best living scholar and preserver of pulp magazine culture, published The Lovers *at the end of the pulp era.*

*The multitalented Farmer is the product of a modest midwestern upbringing (he was born and raised in Indiana). His writing evidences his love of film, genealogy, and popular culture history. Like Katherine MacLean, his influences include classical literature, Hugo Gernsback, and Edgar Rice Burroughs. Farmer's famous novel-length pastiches and studies of Tarzan (*Tarzan Alive, *1972) and Doc Savage (*Doc Savage: His Apocalyptic Life, *1973) number among the author's many fine works, and in their own ways are definitive.*

*A prolific author of a range of novels and short stories, Philip José Farmer is also famous for three series of novels—*The Riverworld Series, The World of Tiers Series, *and* The Dayworld Series. *Always progressive and innovative, Farmer remains a topnotch author today.* The Lovers *was ultimately followed by a sequel (*The Moth and Rust, Starling Stories, *June 1953). These two stories were combined and revised in a larger novel, also entitled* The Lovers; *this novel was first published in 1961.*

The Lovers

(Startling Stories, *August 1952)*

FOREWORD

During the day, the dreadnaught *Gabriel* squatted in a park in the center of the city of Siddo, on the planet Ozagen. From sunrise to sunset the *Gabriel's* personnel ventured out among the Ozagenians—or wogglebugs, as they were familiarly and contemptuously called—learning all they could of Ozagen's history, customs, language and other things.

The "other things," though the Earthmen did not mention this to the wogglebugs, were Ozagen's technologies. As far as could be seen, the wogs had progressed, roughly speaking, to the level of Earth's early 20th-century science. Logically, there should be nothing to fear from them. But the men of Earth's Haijac Union trusted no one. What if the wogs were hiding terrible weapons, waiting to catch the men unawares?

At nightfall, the spaceship rose to a height of fifty feet and poised there until the sun rose again. Then it sank back into the deep depression made by its own weight. Always a radar gig hovered in the stratosphere and probed for other spacecraft. Presumably, neither Earth's Israeli Republics nor its Bantu-Malay Federation knew of Ozagen . . . but if they found out!

Meanwhile the Terrans searched, studied, prowled and planned. Before they attacked the natives, before they began their decimation project to make room for the hordes that would follow, they must learn the wogs' potentialities.

And so it was that, a month after the appearance of the *Gabriel* above Siddo, two presumably friendly (to wogs) Terrans set out with two presumably friendly (to Terrans) wogglebugs on a trip. They were going to investigate the ruins of a city left by a dead humanoid race. They rode a vehicle fantastic to the men. . . .

I

The motor hiccoughed and jerked. The Ozagenian sitting on the right side of the rear seat leaned over and shouted something. Hal Yarrow twisted his head and yelled, "*Quoi?*"

Fobo, sitting directly behind Hal, stuck his mouth against the Earthman's ear. He translated the gibberish into French:

"Zugu says and emphasizes that you should pump the throttle. That little rod to your right. It gives the carburetor more alcohol. *Où quelque chose.*"

Fobo's antennae tickled Hal's ears. Hal said, "*Merci,*" and worked the throttle. To do so, he had to lean across the gapt, sitting at his right. "*Pardonnez-moi, monsieur Pornsen!*" he bellowed.

The gapt did not look at Yarrow; his hands, lying on his lap, were locked together. The knuckles showed white. Like his ward, he was having his first experience with an internal combustion motor. Unlike Hal, he was scared by the loud noise, the fumes, the bumps and bangs, and just the idea of riding in a manually controlled vehicle.

Hal grinned. He loved this quaint car, so reminiscent of Earth's early twentieth-century autos. It thrilled him to be able to twist the stiff-acting wheel and feel the heavy body obey his muscles. The four cylinders' banging and the alcohol's reek excited him. As for the bouncing, that was fun. It was romantic like putting out to sea in a sailboat—something else he hoped to do before they left Ozagen.

Also, anything that scared his gapt pleased Yarrow.

His pleasure ended. The cylinders popped, off-key. The car jerked and then rolled to a stop. At once, the two wogglebugs hopped over the side and raised the hood. Hal followed. Pornsen sat. He pulled a package of Merciful Seraphim from his uniform pocket, took one out and lit up.

Hal noted that it was the fourth he'd seen Pornsen smoking since morning prayers. If Pornsen wasn't careful, he'd be going over his quota. That meant that the next time Hal got in trouble, he could blackmail the gapt into helping him.

Judging by his troubles so far on this expedition, it wouldn't be long before he would have to.

Hal bent over the motor and watched. Zugu seemed to know what the matter was. He should, since he was the inventor and builder of the only—as far as the Terrans knew—native-made self-propelling vehicle on this planet.

Zugu used a wrench to unscrew a long narrow pipe from a round glass case. Yarrow remembered that this was a gravity feed system. The fuel ran from the tank into the glass case, which was a sediment chamber. From there it ran into the feed pipe, which in turn passed on to the carburetor.

Pornsen called harshly, "Well, Yarrow, are we going to be stuck here all day?"

Though he still wore the hood and goggles the Ozagenians had equipped him with as windbreaks, the gapt's expression was clear enough. He would take out his annoyance in a report that would not be favorable to Hal. Unless, that is, his ward came across something so important in the humanoid ruins that it would justify this long trip.

The gapt—G.A.P.T., or Guardian Angel Pro Tempore—had wanted to wait the two days that would be needed until they could get a gig. The trip to the ruins could then have been made in fifteen minutes, a soundless and comfortable ride through the air. But Hal had argued that driving through the countryside would be as valuable—if not more so, in detecting any possible hidden large industries—as reconnoitering by air. That his superiors had agreed was another thing that had exasperated Pornsen. Where his ward went, he had to go.

So he had sulked all day while the young Terran, coached by Zugu, wheeled the jalopy down the forest roads. The only times the gapt spoke was to remind Hal of the sacredness of the human self by telling him to slow down. Hal would nod and would ease his foot off the accelerator. But after a while he would slowly press down. Once again they would roar and leap down the dirt road.

Zugu unscrewed both ends of the pipe, stuck one in his V-shaped mouth, and blew. Nothing came out the other end. Zugu shut his big blue eyes and blew again. Nothing happened, except that his already green-tinged face turned a dark green. Then he rapped the copper tubing against the hood and blew once more. No reaction.

Fobo reached into a large leather pouch slung from a belt around his big belly. His finger and thumb came out holding a tiny blue insect. Gently, he pushed the creature into one end of the pipe. In about five seconds a small red insect dropped out of the other end. Behind it, evidently in pursuit, came the blue. Fobo picked up his pet and put it back in the pouch. Zugu squashed the red thing beneath his bare heel.

"*Voilà: C'est un mangeur de l'alcool, monsieur,*" said Fobo. "It lives in the tank and imbibes freely and unmolested. It extracts the carbohydrates therein. A swimmer upon the golden seas of alcohol. What a life! But now and then it goes into the sediment chamber, eats and devours the filter, and passes into the feedpipe. *Voyez!* Zugu is even now replacing the filter. In a moment we will be on our way and road."

Fobo's breath had a strange and sickening odor. Hal wondered if the wog had been drinking liquor. He had never smelled alcohol on anybody's breath before, so he had no experience to go on. But even the thought of it made Hal nervous. If his gapt knew a bottle was being passed back and forth in the rear seat, he would not for a minute let Hal out of his sight.

The wogs climbed into the back seat. "*Allons!*"

Pornsen pursed his thin lips. He had meant to ask Zugu to drive, but he realized the wogs might think he lacked confidence in Yarrow. He did, but he could not admit that in front of an Ozagenian.

Though Hal started slowly enough, he soon found his foot heavy. The trees began whizzing by. He glanced at Pornsen. The gapt's rigid back and set teeth showed that he was thinking of the report he would make to the chief Uzzite back in the spaceship. He looked mad enough to demand the 'Meter for his ward.

Yarrow breathed deeply the wind battering his face-mask. To H with Pornsen! To H with the 'Meter! The blood lurched in his veins. This planet's air was not stuffy Earth's. His lungs sucked it in like a happy bellows. At that moment he felt as if he could have snapped his fingers under the nose of the Sandalphon himself.

"Look out!" screamed Pornsen.

Hal glimpsed out of the corners of his eyes the large antelope-like beast that leaped from the forest onto the road. A half-second later, he twisted the wheel away from it. The jalopy skidded on the dirt. Its rear end swung around. Hal was not well enough grounded in the physics of driving to know that he should have turned the wheels in the direction of the skid to straighten the car out.

His lack of knowledge was not fatal, except to the beast, for its bulk struck the vehicle's side. Checked, the car quit trying to circle. Instead, it angled off the road and ran up a sloping ridge of earth. From there it leaped high into the air and landed with an all-at-once bang of four tires blowing.

Even that did not halt it. A big bush loomed. Hal jerked on the wheel. Too late.

His chest pushed hard against the wheel as if it were trying to telescope the steering shaft against the dashboard. Fobo slammed into Yarrow's back. Both cried, out, and the wog fell off.

Then, except for a sharp hissing, there was silence. A pillar of steam from the broken radiator shot through the branches that held Hal's face in a rough barky embrace.

Yarrow stared through steamshapes into big brown eyes. He shook his head. Was he stunned? Eyes. And arms like branches. Or branches like arms. He thought he was in the grip of a brown-eyed nymph. Or were they called dryads? He couldn't ask anybody. He wasn't supposed to know about such creatures. *Nymph* and *dryad* had even been cut out of such books as Hack's edition of the Revised and Moral Milton. Only an unexpurgated *Paradise Lost*, booklegged from Israel, had enabled Hal to learn of Greek mythology.

Thoughts flashed off and on like lights on a spaceship's pilotboard. Nymphs sometimes turned into trees to escape their pursuers. Was this one of the fabled forest women staring at him with large and beautiful eyes through the longest lashes he had ever seen?

He shut his lids and wondered if a head injury were responsible for the vision and if it were permanent. If it were, so what? Hallucinations like that were worth keeping

He opened his eyes. The illusion was gone.

He thought, *It was that antelope looking at me. It got away after all. It ran around the bush and looked back. Antelope eyes.*

II

He forgot about the eyes. He was choking. A heavy nauseating odor hung around the car. The crash must have frightened the wogs very much, else they would not have released the sphincter muscles which controlled the neck of their "madbags." This organ, a bladder located near the small of their backs, had once been used by the prehumanoid ancestors of the Ozagenians as a powerful weapon of defense in much the same way as a bombardier beetle thwarts attackers. Now an almost vestigial structure, the madbag served as a means of relieving extreme nervous tension. Its function was effective, but it presented problems such as that of the wog psychiatrists, who either had to keep their windows open or else wear gasmasks during therapy.

Hal pushed aside the branches and struggled over the side. Why didn't wogs build doors in their vehicles?

Wong Af Pornsen, assisted by Zugu, crawled out from under the foliage. His big paunch, the color of his uniform, and the white nylon angel's wings sewed on the back of his jacket made him resemble a fat blue bug. When he stood up and took off his windmask, he showed a bloodless face. His shaking fingers fumbled over the crossed hourglass and sword, symbol of the Haijac Union, before they found the button he was searching for. He pulled out a pack of Merciful Cherubim. Once the cigarette was in his lips, he had a hard time holding the lighter to it.

Hal took out his own and held the glowing coil to the tobacco. It didn't waver.

Only thirty years of discipline could have shoved back the grin he felt deep inside his face muscles.

Pornsen accepted the light. A second later, a tremor of skin around his lips and eyes revealed that he knew he had lost much of his advantage over Yarrow. Trained in psychology, he realized you don't let a man do you a service—even one as slight as his ward's—and then crack the whip on him.

He began formally, "Hal Shamshiel Yarrow . . ."

"Shib, *abba*, I hear."

"You're—uh—much too reckless."

Considering the offense, his voice was milder than it should have been. Now and then he stopped to draw in or puff out smoke.

"The hierarchy has had its eye (puff) upon you for a long time. Though you have not been suspected of any moral turpitude—as regards sex or liquor, that is—you have shown signs of a certain pride and independence. That is not shib, Yarrow. That is not real. It smacks of behavior that does not conform to the structure of the universe as we know it, as it has been revealed to mankind by the Forerunner, real be his name.

"I have (puff)—may the Forerunner forgive them!—sent two dozen men to H. I didn't like it, for I am a tender-hearted man, but it is the duty of the Guardian Angels Pro Tempore to watch out for the diseases of the self that may spread and infect the followers of Isaac Sigmen. Unreality must not be tolerated; the self is too weak and precious to be subjected to temptation.

"I have been your gapt since you were (puff) born. You always were a disobedient child, but you could be whipped into submissiveness, into seeing reality. Not until you were eighteen did you become hard to handle. That was when you decided to become a joat. I thought you'd make a very good specialist, and I warned you that as a joat you'd only get so high in our society. But you persisted. And since we have need of joats, and since I was overridden by my superior, I allowed you to become one.

"That wasn't too (puff) unshib, but when I picked out the woman most suitable to be your wife, I saw just how proud and rebellious you were. She was a woman whom the Urielites, selfdocs, and Sandalphons agreed was the ideal mate as set forth in the Western Talmud. And yet you argued and held out for a year before you consented to marry her. In that year of unreal behavior, you cost the Sturch one self. . . ."

Hal's face had paled, and in so doing had revealed seven thin red marks that rayed out fanwise from the left corner of his lips and across his cheek to his ear. They were scars left by Pornsen's lash years before.

"I cost it nothing," blazed Hal. "Mary and I were married ten years, and she proved barren. And it was her fault, not mine, as the tests proved. When that came out, why didn't you insist on our divorce, as your duty required, instead of pigeonholing my petition?"

Pornsen blew out smoke slowly enough, but his voice tensed. He dropped one shoulder lower than the other, a characteristic when he forgot himself, and said, "That's another thing. I was sure when you applied for this expedition that it was not out of desire to serve the Sturch in its quest for new lands for our over-crowded planets. (Puff) I was sure you signed up for one reason. To get away from your wife. Since barrenness, adultery, and space travel are the only legal grounds for divorce, and adultery means going to H, you took the only way out. You became legally dead. You—"

"You can't prove it!" Hal was shaking, and loathed himself because he could not hide his rage.

"Oh, I could have, if I had recommended you for the Elohimeter. But we needed scientists very much, and my superiors thought it best to overlook your possible motives. Besides, you had an excuse in that sterility report, which was lost through the inefficiency of my secretaries.

"However, the hierarchy has been slowly and regretfully, but surely, coming to the conclusion that you do not have a high enough regard for your self. Or that of others.

"The self, as defined by Isaac Sigmen, is sacred, sacred to God, to the angels both high and low, to the pre-Torah prophets. . . ."

Hal listened with only a half-ear. Pornsen was repeating Moral Lecture PT19, which his ward knew by heart. Hal was looking at the beast's body crumpled on the road. Now he remembered the thump the jalopy had made when it struck it. But if it were dead, whose eyes had he seen through the bush?

Fobo, the empathist, was bending over it. He straightened up; large tears filled his blue eyes and ran down the long tubular nose. The antennae rising from his bald forehead waved. He made a circular sign with his index finger over the carcass.

Hal said to Pornsen, "Shut up!"

The gapt stiffened. The lower left shoulder drew level with the other. The cigarette fell from his slack thin lips. Red swarmed up his bull-neck and sagging jowls. His right hand shot to his belt and grabbed the crux ansata on the handle of his whip. He jerked it out and cracked it in the air.

The marks on Yarrow's cheek tingled in remembrance of that other time when the lashes, one for each of the Seven Deadly Unrealities, had cut the flesh.

The gapt said, "How dare you?"

Hal said in a low voice, swiftly, "A moment ago you said something in English. You know French is the only tongue we're allowed to speak under any circumstances."

The whip dropped.

"When—when was that?"

"When you screamed at me just before we struck that animal. Remember? And when you were yelling for help under the bush."

Pornsen stuck the whip back in his belt and lit up another Merciful Seraphim. His fifth that day. Another, and he'd be over his quota.

"You say nothing to the chief," he muttered. "And I'll keep quiet about your sibboleth recklessness."

"Shib," agreed Hal.

He tried to keep the contempt and elation out of his voice. Once a gapt cracked. . . .

Pornsen rolled his small green eyes at the approaching Fobo. "Think he heard me?"

"I wouldn't know."

Fobo stopped and looked at them. His antennae became rigid. He said, *"Un argument, messieurs?"*

Fobo had wept as the dying beast's nervous discharges of grief and pain struck his overtrained, too receptive antennae. Now he smiled the ghastly V-in-V smile of a wogglebug. Though supersensitive, his nervous system was a hit and run one. Charge and discharge came easily.

"Non!" replied Hal. "No disagreement. We were just wondering how far we'd have to walk to get to the humanoid ruins. Your jalopy's wrecked. Tell Zugu I'm sorry."

"Ca ne fait rien. The walk will be pleasant and stimulating. It is only a mile. Or thereabouts."

"Bien. Allons."

The ward turned away and threw his mask and goggles in the rear seat of the car, where the Ozagenians had laid theirs.

He picked up his suitcase, but left the gapt's on the floor. Let him carry his own. He said, "Fobo, aren't you afraid the driving-clothes will be stolen?"

"Pardon? What does that mean?"

"Voler, Voler. To take an article of property from someone without their permission, and keep it for yourself. It is a crime, punishable by law."

"Un crime?"

Hal gave up. He shrugged and moved his long legs fast. Behind him the gapt, afraid of losing dignity if he trailed behind Hal, and angry because his ward was breaking etiquette by forcing him to carry his own case, shouted, "You'll pay for this, you—you joat!"

With which outburst he lost face.

Hal didn't turn. He plunged on ahead. The angry retort he was phrasing beneath his breath fizzed away. Out of the corner of his eye he had caught a flash of white skin in the green summer foliage.

But when he turned to look for it, it was gone. Nor did he see it or its owner the rest of the day.

III

Soo Yarrow. *Soo Yarrow. B'swa. L'fvayfvoo, soo* Yarrow."

Hal woke up. For a moment, he didn't remember where he was. Then he recalled that he was sleeping in one of the marble rooms of the mammal-humanoid ruins. The moonlight, brighter than Earth's, poured in through the doorway. It shone on a small shape on the floor near the entrance, and on a flying insect that passed above the shape. Something long and thin flickered up and wrapped itself around the flier and pulled it into a suddenly gaping mouth.

The lizard loaned by the ruins custodian was doing a fine job of keeping out pests.

Hal turned his head to look at the open window a foot above him. The bug-catcher there was busily sweeping the area clean of mosquitoes. From beyond that moonwashed square the voice had seemed to come. He listened. Silence. Then a snuffling and rattling jerked him upright. A thing the size of a raccoon stood by the doorway. It was one of the quasi-insects, the so-called lungbugs, that prowled the forest at night. It represented a development of arthropod not found on Earth. Unlike its Terran cousins, it no longer depended solely on tracheae, or breathing tubes, for oxygen. A pair of distensible sacs, like a frog's, swelled out and fell in behind its mouth, and enabled it to make the heavy breathing sound.

Though it was shaped like a preying mantis, Hal wasn't worried. Fobo had told him it would not attack without provocation.

A shrilling like that of an alarm clock suddenly filled the room. Pornsen, on the cot across the room, sat up. He saw the insect and yelled. It scurried off. The shrilling, which had come from the mechanism on Pornsen's wrist, stopped.

Pornsen lay down and groaned. "That makes the sixth time those bugs have woke me up."

"Turn off the wristbox," said Hal.

Pornsen did not answer. For about ten minutes he was restless and then he began snoring. Hal's lids felt heavy. He must have dreamed the soft low voice speaking in a tongue neither Terran nor Ozagenian. He must have, because it had been human; and he and the gapt were the only specimens of homo sapiens for at least two hundred miles.

It had been a woman's voice. God! To hear one again. Almost two years now!

And he knew it would probably be five years before he would hear another. That is, if he returned. . . .

"*Soo Yarrow. L'fvayfvoo. Say mwa, zh'net w'stinvak.*"

Hal stood up. His neck was cased in ice. The whisper *was* coming from the window. He turned his head. The outline of a woman's head leaned into the solid box of moonlight that was the window. Moonwash fell off white shoulders. A pale finger crossed the black of mouth.

"*Poo lamoo d'b'tyu, soo. Seelahs. F'nay. Feet, seel-fvooplay.*"

Numbed, but obeying as if shot full of hypno-lipno, he threw aside the sheet over his legs. Slowly, he turned on his buttocks and moved his feet until they touched the stone floor. With a look to make sure Pornsen was still asleep, he rose.

For a second his training almost overcame him and forced him to wake the gapt up. But it was evident the woman was addressing him alone. Her urgency and suppressed fear decided him to take a chance. It also made him wonder if she might not be a member of one of the unreal sects that had fled the Haijac Union two hundred or more years ago—

No. That couldn't be. She spoke in no tongue he knew. For that same reason, it was improbable that she was a party to an expedition from one of the other Earth nations.

Her words had seemed to click something familiar, however—as if he ought to know the language. But he didn't. It wasn't the English or Icelandic or Caucasian of the Haijac Union, or the Hebrew of the Israeli Republics, or the Bazaar or Swahili of the Bantu-Malay Federation. Yet it had sounded like something he'd heard before. And recently.

He picked up his suitcase and shoved it under the sheet. He rolled up a blanket and packed it next to the case. His jacket he folded and laid on the pillow. If Pornsen woke up and took a quick look at the cot, he might be fooled into thinking the bulk under the sheet was Hal's.

Softly, on bare feet, he walked to the doorway. A cylinder the size of a tin can squatted on guard. If any object larger than a mouse came within two feet of the field radiating from the cylinder, it would set up a disturbance which would cause a signal to be transmitted to the small box mounted on a silver bracelet around the gapt's wrist. The box would shrill—as it had at the appearance of the lungbug—and up would come Pornsen from the bottom of his ever-watchful sleep.

The watchcan was not only there to insure against trespassers. Its primary purpose was to make certain that Hal would not leave the room without Pornsen's knowledge. As the ruins had no working plumbing, the only permissible excuse to step outside would be to relieve bowel or bladder. The gapt would go along to see that that was what he intended.

Two things Pornsen was watching for. One was unsupervised contact with the wogs. The other was that unreal conduct, punishable by exile to H and cataloged in the *Sefer shel ha Chetim*, or the Book of Sins, as Onanism. The long space voyage had resulted in the arrest of five men for that very unreality.

Hal picked up one of the flyswatters given them by the ruins custodian. It had a three-foot-long handle made of some flexible wood. Its mass would not be enough to touch off the field. Though his hand trembled, he grasped the swatter-end and very gently pushed the cylinder to one side with the handle. He had to be careful not to upset it, for that, too, would trigger the alarm. Fortunately, the stone floor was smooth.

When he had stepped outside, he reached back in and slid the cylinder back to its former spot. Then, with his heart pounding under the double burden of tampering with the guard and of meeting a strange woman, he walked around the corner.

She had moved from the window into the shadow of a kneeling goddess' statue about sixty yards away. When Hal began striding toward her, he saw the reason for her hiding. Fobo was strolling towards him. Hal walked faster. He wanted to intercept the wog before he noticed the girl and also before he came so close that their voices might wake up Pornsen.

"*Bon soir*," greeted Fobo. His antennae described little circles. "You seem nervous. Is it that incident of the forenoon?"

"*Non*. I am just restless."

Hal looked at the empathist. Ozagen! What was the story? That the discoverer of this planet, upon first seeing the natives, had exclaimed, "Oz again!" because the aborigines had so much resembled Frank Baum's Professor Wogglebug? Their bodies were rather round, and their limbs were skinny in proportion. Their mouths were shaped like two broad and shallow V's, one set inside the other. The lips were thick and lobular. Actually, a wogglebug had four lips, each leg of the two V's separated by a deep seam at the connection. Once, far back on the evolutionary path, those lips had been modified arms. Now they were rudimentary limbs, so disguised as true labial parts that no one who did not know their history would have guessed their origin. When the wide V-in-V mouths opened in a laugh, they startled the Terrans. The teeth were quite human, true, but a fold of skin hung from the roof of the mouth. Once the epipharynx, it was now a vestigial upper tongue, of no use at all except to tell of the wogs' arthropodal ancestry.

Their skins were as unpigmented as Hal's redhead complexion, but where the Earthman's epidermis was pink, theirs was a very faint green. Copper, not iron, carried oxygen in their blood cells.

They had antennae, their forepates were bald, but a stiff corkscrew fuzz rose from their backpates to form a corona. To complete the Oz parallel, their noses were bridgeless and shot straight out from their faces in projectile fashion.

The Terran who first saw them might have been justified by his remark. However, the story wasn't true. Ozagen was the native name for "Mother Earth."

IV

Wogglebug they were called, yet they were no more insects than the Earthmen. It was true that millions of years ago their ancestors had been a primitive unspecialized wormlike arthropod. But evolution follows parallel paths when aiming at intelligent beings. Realizing the limitations of the anatomy, she had split Fobo's Nth-great-grandfather from the arthropod phylum. When the crustacea, arachnida, and insecta had formed exoskeletons and ventral nervous systems, Grandpa the Nth had declined to go along with his cousins. He had refused to harden his delicate cuticle-skin into chitin and had begun shifting the central nerves from chest and belly to the back and had also erected a skeleton inside the flesh. Both of the latter feats were equal to lifting oneself by the bootstraps.

As the price for that action, by the time the true arthropods were very developed, highly specialized creatures creeping, hopping, and flying by the billions over the hot new globe, Fobo's ancestors were still ugly, flatwormish things hiding from their beautiful, fully rounded-out relatives.

Becoming chordate arthropods—a contradiction in terms, by the way—was a deed that took many millions of years and much humility and self-denial.

Yet it had been worth it. The wogs' fathers had finally made the ventral to dorsal shift and sheathed their bones in muscle. Their cold blood became warm; they developed airsacs and then lungs. Their nerves ramified and grew intricate. The strata-shot eye of the epoch winked, and a monkeylike creature appeared. Another wink, and it was an ape. After a very long while, as years go, it came down from the trees. Once brachiate, it began walking on two feet. It passed through australopithecoid, pithecanthropoid, and neanderthaloid stages. It became Fobo.

One of the few arthropodal heritages left was the pair of antennae. Eras ago they might have been used, as some insects are supposed to use theirs, for communication. Now their function was rudimentary, but effective. They were so sensitive they could pick up nervous discharges from the skin of other beings. That gift, thought Hal, probably helped make the Ozagen society what it was. No wogglebug could fool another about his emotions. If he pretended friendliness, he would be betrayed. Hate, fear, rage, affection and love were easily read. A wog had to express what he felt, because he could not hide it. And once he had expressed, he had discharged his emotions, rebalanced his organism, and opened himself to rational talk and conduct.

At least, that was the theory. In actual practice, as Fobo said, it was not so easy.

Hal became aware that Fobo was talking to him:

"—this *joat* that *monsieur* Pornsen called you when he was so angry and furious. What does that mean?"

The Terran could not tell Fobo that the word was an initial combination, formed from the first letters of jack-of-all-trades. The wog would wonder how they deduced that combination from French.

"It means," he said carefully, "that I am not a specialist in any of the sciences, but one who knows, or is supposed to know, a great deal about all of them. Actually, I am a liaison officer between various scientists and the government. It is my business to summarize and integrate what is going on in science and then report to the hierarchy."

He glanced at the statue. The woman was not in sight.

"Science has become so specialized that intelligible communication even between scientists in the same field is very difficult. Each has a deep vertical knowledge of his own little field, but not much horizontal. The more he knows about his own subject, the less aware he is of what others are doing. It is so bad that a physicist, for instance, who deals in mercury anti-ions will find it hard to talk the same language as one whose study is radioactive isotopes. Or two doctors who specialize in nose dysfunctions. One treats the left nostril; the other, the right. Believe me, that's not exaggerated."

Fobo shrugged his shoulders and threw up his hands. He might have been French.

"But . . . science would come to a standstill!"

"Exactly."

Hal saw a head stick out from the base of the statue. It withdrew. Hal began sweating.

Fobo questioned the joat about the religion of the Forerunner. Hal was as taciturn as possible and replied to some questions not at all. The wog was nothing if not logical, and logic was the light that Hal had never turned upon what he had been taught by the Urielites.

Finally the empathist said, "I feel that this conversation is making you nervous. Perhaps we can pursue it some other time. Tell me, what do you think of these ruins?"

"Very interesting. What I cannot imagine is how these people, who you say once covered this huge continent, could entirely die out."

"Oh, there may be a few in the backwoods or jungles. But most died in the wars with us about five hundred years ago. Since then there's been peace on this planet. It's true we wiped them out, but they were very decadent, quarrelsome and greedy, and forced my ancestors to fight them."

Human, all right, thought Hal.

"I'll tell you later about their decline and fall," Fobo said. "In some ways it is a fantastic story. Right now, I think I'll go to bed."

"I'm restless. If you don't mind, I'll poke around. These ruins are fascinating in the moonlight."

"Reminds me of a poem by our great bard, Shamero. If I could remember it, I'd quote it." Fobo's V-in-V lips yawned. "*Bonne nuit.*"

Hal watched him until he'd disappeared, then turned and walked toward the statue of the Great Mother. When he got to the shadows in its base, he saw the girl slipping into the darkness cast by a mountainous heap of rubble. He followed, only to see her thirty yards ahead, leaning against a monolith. Beyond was the lake, silvery and black in the moonpaint.

"*B'swa, soo Yarrow.*" Her voice was low and throaty.

"*Bon soir, mademoiselle,*" he said mechanically . . . and then paused, struck.

Of course! Now he knew why it had had a familiar ring. *B'swa* was *bon soir!* Even though her words were a degraded form, they could not disguise their essential Latinity. *B'swa!* And *l'fvayfvoo* was *levez-vous*, which was French for "get up." How could he have missed it? It must have been because his mind wasn't expecting the familiar, and therefore had not recognized it. *Say mwa, C'est moi.* It's I. And *soo* Yarrow. Could that be *monsieur* Yarrow? The initial m dropped. Final r also. Abandonment of nasalization plus vowel and consonant shifts in other words. Different, but still subtly Gallic.

"Bon soir, mademoiselle."

How inadequate those words were. Here were two human beings meeting a thousand light-years from Earth, one a man who had not seen a woman for two years, the other a woman obviously hiding; perhaps the only woman left on the planet. And all he could say was "Good evening, miss."

He stepped closer. Suddenly he was flushed with heat. Her white skin was relieved only by two black, narrow strips of cloth, one across her breasts, the other diapered around the hips. In all his life he had seen only one woman who was not clad from neck to floor in thick cloth, and that had been in a semidarkness. She had been his wife.

The heat of his embarrassment was followed by a gasp of astonishment. She was lipsticked! Her lips were scarlet in the moonlight with the forbidden rouge.

His mind gave that problem a quick flip in the air and considered its other side. Cosmetics had gone out with the coming of the Forerunner. They were unreal, immoral. No woman dared . . . well, that wasn't true . . . it was just in the Haijac Union that they were not used. Israeli and Bantu women wore rouge; but then everybody knew what kind of women they were.

Another step, and Hal breathed hard again. He was close enough to see that the scarlet was natural. That meant that she was not Earthborn but was an Ozagen human being. The murals in the ruins showed red-lipped women, and Fobo had told him they were born with the flaming labile pigment.

But how could that be? She spoke a Terran dialect.

The next moment he forgot about his doubts and paradoxes. She was clinging to him, and he had his arms around her, clumsily trying to comfort her. She was pouring out words, one so fast after the other that even though he knew they came from the French he could only make out a word here and a phrase there.

Hal asked her to slow down and go over what she had said. She paused, her head cocked slightly to the left, while he enunciated clearly his request. When he was through, she brushed back the hair over one ear, a gesture he was to find characteristic of her when she was thinking.

Then she repeated.

She began slowly enough. But as she progressed she speeded up, her full lips working like two bright-red things independent of her, packed with their own life and purpoзc.

Fascinated, Hal watched them. As they worked, they seemed to send stabs of desire into him, almost as if they were heliographing erotic messages.

With an effort he lifted his gaze from them and listened, trying to grasp her whole story.

She told it disconnectedly and with repetition and backtracking. But he could understand that her name was Jeannette, that she came from a plateau in the tropics of Ozagen, that she was one of the few human beings left on the planet, that she had been captured by an exploring party of wogs and taken to Siddo, that she had only recently escaped, that she had been hiding in the ruins and the nearby forest, that she was frightened because of the things that prowled the forest at night, that she lived on wild fruit and berries or on food stolen from wog farmhouses, that she had seen Hal when he crashed the jalopy, that she had followed him and listened to his conversations with the two wogs and with the gapt, that she could tell by her instincts—here she used a word that he did not understand but which he translated as "instincts"—that he was a man she could trust, that he had to do something for her.

That he had to save her.

Tears filled her big dark eyes, and her voice broke. She leaned against him; her shoulders were soft and smooth; her full breasts pressed against his ribs. What her words did not say, her body did.

Yarrow thought swiftly. He had to get back to the room in the ruins before Pornsen woke up. And he couldn't see her tomorrow, because a gig from the ship was picking the two Haijacs up in the morning. Whatever he was going to do would have to be told to her in the next few minutes.

Suddenly he had a plan; it unfolded in an instant from another idea, one he had long carried around buried in the fertile soil of his brain. Its seeds had been in him even before the ship had left Earth. But he hadn't had the courage to carry it out. Now, with the sudden appearance of this girl as a catalyst, he was thrown into action. She was what he needed to spark his guts and make him step onto a path that, once taken, could not be retraced.

"Jeannette," he said rapidly and fiercely, "listen to me! You'll have to wait here every night. No matter what things haunt the dark, you'll have to be here. I can't tell you just when I'll be able to get a gig and fly here. Sometime in the next three weeks, I think. If I'm not here by then, keep waiting. *Keep waiting!* I'll be here! And when I am, we'll be safe. Safe for a while, at least. Can you do that? Can you hide here? And wait?"

She nodded her head and said, *"Vi."*

V

Two weeks later, Yarrow flew from the spaceship *Gabriel* to the ruins. His needle-shaped gig gleamed in the big moon as it floated over the white marble buildings and settled to a stop. The city lay silent and bleached, great stone cubes and hexagons and cylinders and pyramids and statues like toys left scattered while the giant child went to bed and slept forever.

The Terran stepped out, glanced to left and right, and then strode to an enormous arch. His flashlight probed its darkness; his voice echoed from the faraway roof and walls.

"Jeannette. C'est moi. Votre ami, Hal Yarrow. Jeannette. Ou êtes vous?"

He walked down the fifty-yard-broad staircase that led to the crypts of the kings. The beam bounced up and down the steps and suddenly splashed against the black and white figure of the girl.

"Hal!" she cried, looking up at him. "Thank the Great Stone Mother! I've waited every night! But I knew you'd come!"

Tears trembled on the long lashes; her scarlet mouth was screwed up as if she were doing her best to keep from sobbing. He wanted to take her in his arms and comfort her, but a lifetime of "you-must-nots" stiffened his arms. It was a terrible thing even to look at a woman as unclothed as she was. To embrace her would be unthinkable. Nevertheless, that was exactly what he was thinking of.

The next minute, as if divining his paralysis, she moved to him and put her head on his chest. Her own shoulders hunched forward as she tried to burrow into him. He found his arms going around her. His muscles tightened, and heat stabbed from his stomach down into his loins.

He released her and looked away. "We'll talk later. We've no time to lose. Come."

She followed him, silently, until they came to the gig. Then she hesitated by the door. He gestured impatiently for her to climb in and sit down beside him.

"You will think I'm a coward," she said. "But I have never been in a flying machine. To leave this solid earth. . . ."

Surprised, he could only stare at her. It was hard for him to understand the mental attitude of a person totally unaccustomed to airtravel. Such reactions did not fit into his culture.

"Get in!" he barked.

Obediently enough, she got in and sat down in the co-pilot's seat. She could not keep from trembling, however, or looking with huge brown eyes at the instruments before and around her.

Deciding the best thing to do was to ignore her fear, Hal glanced at his watchphone.

"Ten minutes to get to my apartment in the city. One minute to drop you off there. A half-minute to return to the ship. Fifteen minutes to report on my espionage among the wogs. Thirty seconds to return to the apartment. Not quite half an hour in all. Not bad."

He laughed. "I would have been here two days ago, but I had to wait until all the gigs that were on automatic were in use. Then I pretended that I was in a hurry, that I had forgotten some notes, and that I had to go back to my apartment to pick them up. So I borrowed one of the manually controlled gigs used for exploration outside the city. I never could have gotten permission from the O.D. for that, but he was overwhelmed by this."

Hal touched a large golden badge on his left chest. It bore a Hebrew L.

"That means I'm one of the Chosen. I've passed the 'Meter."

Jeannette had seemingly forgotten her terror and had been looking at Hal's face in the glow from the panel-light. She gave a little cry. "Hal Yarrow! What have they done to you?" Her fingers touched his face.

He looked at her. A deep purple ringed his eyes; his cheeks were sunken, and in one a muscle twitched; a rash spread over his forehead; and the seven whipmarks stood out against a pale skin.

"Anybody would say I was crazy to do it," he said. "I stuck my head in the lion's mouth. And he didn't bite my head off. Instead, I bit his tongue."

"What do you mean?"

"Listen. Didn't you think it was strange that Pornsen wasn't with me tonight, breathing his sanctimonious breath down my neck? No? Well, you don't know our setup. There was only one way I could get permission to move out of my quarters in the ship and get an apartment in Siddo. That is, without having a gapt living with me to watch my every move. And without having to leave you out here in the forest. And I couldn't do *that*."

He shook his head. She ran her finger down the line from his nose to the corner of his lip. Ordinarily he would have shrunk from the touch, because he hated close contact with anybody. Now, he didn't shrink.

"Hal," she said softly. *"M' sheh.*

"Mon cher," he corrected.

"Mon cher," she repeated.

He felt a glow. *My dear.* Well, why not?

To stave off the headiness her touch gave, he said, "There was only one thing to do. Volunteer for the 'Meter."

"Le Métre? Keskasekasah?"

"It's the only thing that can free you from the constant shadow of a gapt. Once you've passed it, you're pure, above suspicion—theoretically, at least.

"My petition caught the hierarchy off guard. They never expected any of the scientists—let alone me—to volunteer. Urielites and Uzzites have to take it if they hope to advance in the hierarchy—"

"Urielites? Uzzites?"

"To put it in ancient terminology, priests and cops. The Forerunner adopted those terms—the names of angels—for religious-governmental use—from the Talmud. See?"

"Non."

"You'll be clearer about that later. Anyway, only the most zealous ask to face the 'Meter. It's true that many people do, but the majority do it because they are compelled to. The Urielites were gloomy about my chances before it, but they were forced by law to let me try my chances. Besides, they were bored, and they wanted to be entertained—in their grim fashion."

He scowled a little at the memory. "So it was that a day later I was told to report to the psych lab at 2300 S.T.—Ship's Time, that is. I went into my cabin—Pornsen was out—opened my labcase, and took out a bottle labeled 'Prophetsfood.' It was supposed to contain a powder whose base was peyote. That's a drug that was once used by American Indian medicine-men."

"Quoi?"

"Just listen. You'll get the main points. Prophetsfood is taken by everybody during Purification Period. That's two days of locking yourself in a cell, fasting, praying, being flagellated by electric whips, and seeing visions induced by hunger and Prophetsfood. Also subjective time-traveling."

"Quoi?"

"Don't keep saying 'What?' I haven't got time to explain dunnology . . . It took me ten years of hard study to understand it and its mathematics. Even then, there were a lot of questions I had. But it's not wise to ask them. You might be thought to be doubting.

"Anyway, my bottle did not hold Prophetsfood. Instead it contained a substitute I'd secretly prepared just before the ship left Earth. That powder was the reason why I dared face the 'Meter. And why I was not as terrified as I should have been . . . though I was scared enough. Believe me."

"I do believe you. You were brave. You overcame your fear."

Hot blood crept beneath his face-skin. It was the first time in his life he had ever been complimented.

"A month before the expedition took off for Ozagen, I had noticed in one of the many scientific journals that passed under my nose an announcement that a certain drug had been synthesized. Its efficacy was in destroying the virus of the so-called Sirian 'rash.' What interested me was a footnote. It was in small print and in Hebrew, which showed that the biochemist must have realized its importance."

"Poow kwa?"

"Why? Well, I imagine it was in Hebrew in order to keep any layman from understanding it. If a secret like that became generally known. . . ."

"The note commented briefly that it had been found that a man suffering from the 'rash' was temporarily immune to the effects of hypno-lipno. And that the Urielites should take care during any sessions with the 'Meter that their subject was healthy."

"I have trouble understanding you," she said.

"I'll go slower. Hypno-lipno is the most widely used truth-drug. I saw at once the implications in the note. The beginning of the article had described how the Sirian 'rash' was narcotically induced for experimental purposes. The drug used was not named, but it did not take me long to look it and its processing up in other journals. I thought: if the true 'rash' would make a man immune to hypno-lipno, why wouldn't the artificial?

"No sooner said that done. I prepared a batch, inserted a tape of questions about my personal life in a psychotester, injected the 'rash' drug, injected the truth drug, and swore that I would lie to the tester about my life. And I *could* lie, even though shot full of hypno-lipno!"

"You're so intelligent," she murmured.

She squeezed his biceps. He hardened them. It was a vain thing to do, but he wanted her to think he was strong.

"Nonsense!" he clipped. "A blind man would have seen what to do. In fact, I wouldn't be surprised if the Uzzites had arrested the chemist and put out orders for some other truth drug to be used. If they did, they were too late. Our ship left before any such news reached us.

"Anyway, the first day with the 'Meter was nothing to worry about. I took a twelve-hour written and oral test in serialism. That's Dunne's theories of time and Sigmen's amplifications on it. I've been taking that same test for years. Easy but tiring.

"The next day I rose early, bathed, injected what was supposed to be Prophetsfood, and, breakfastless, went into the Purification Cell. Alone, I lay two days on a cot. From time to time I took a drink of water or a shot of the false drug. Now and then I pressed the button that sent the mechanical scourge lashing against me. The more flagellations, you know, the higher your credit.

"I didn't see any visions. I did break out with the 'rash.' That didn't worry me. If anybody got suspicious, I could explain that I had an allergy to Prophetsfood. Some people do."

He looked below. Moonfrosted forest and an occasional square or hexagonal light from a farmhouse. Ahead was the high range of hills that shielded Siddo.

"So," he continued, unconsciously talking faster as the hills loomed closer, "at the end of my purification I rose, dressed, and ate the ceremonial dinner of locusts and honey."

"Ugh!"

"Locusts aren't so bad if you've been eating them since childhood."

"Locusts are delicious," she said. "I've eaten them many times. It's the combination with honey that sickens me."

He shrugged and said, "I'm turning out the cabin lights. Get down on the floor. And put on that cloak and nightmask. You can pass for a wog."

Obediently she slid off the seat. Before he flicked the lights off, he glanced down. She was leaning over while picking up the cloak, and he could not help getting a full glimpse of her superb breasts. Though he jerked his head away, he kept the image in his head. He felt both deeply aroused and ashamed.

He continued uncomfortably: "Then the hierarch came in. Macneff the Sandalphon, that is, the Archurielite, the theologians, and the dunnological specialists: the psychoneural parallelists, the interventionists, the substratumists, the chronentropists, the pseudotemporalists, the cosmobservists.

"I was seated on a chair. Wires were taped to my body. Needles were stuck in my arms and back. Hypno-lipno was injected. The lights were turned out. Prayers were said; readings from the Western Talmud and the Revised Scriptures were intoned. Then a spotlight shone down from the ceiling upon the Elohimeter. . . ."

"*Keskasekasah?*"

"Elohim is Hebrew for God. Meter is Greek for—well, for those." He pointed at the instrument panel. "The Elohimeter is round and enormous, and its needle, as long as my arm, is straight up and down. The circumference of the dial's face is marked with Hebraic letters that are supposed to mean something to those giving the test.

"Most people are ignorant of what the dipping and rising needle shows. But I'm a joat. I've access to the books that describe the test."

"Then you knew the answers, *nespa?*"

"*Oui.* Though that means nothing, because hypno-lipno brings out the truth, the reality . . . unless, of course, you are suffering from Sirian 'rash,' natural or artificial."

His sudden laugh was a mirthless bark.

"Under the drug, Jeannette, all the dirty and foul things you've done and thought, all the hates you've had for your superiors, all the doubts about the realness of the Forerunner's doctrines—these rise up from your lower-level minds like soap released at the bottom of a dirty bathtub. Up it comes, slick and irresistibly buoyant and covered with all the layers of scum.

"But I sat there, and I watched the needle—it's just like watching the face of God, Jeannette—you can't understand that, can you?—and I lied. Oh, I didn't overplay it. I didn't pretend to be incredibly pure and faithful. I confessed to minor unrealities. Then the needle would flicker and go back around the circumference a few square letters. But on the big issues, I answered as if my life depended on them. Which it did.

"And I told them my dreams—my subjective time-traveling."

"*Subjectif?*"

"*Oui.* Everybody travels in time subjectively. But the Forerunner is the only man, except his first disciples and a few of the scriptural prophets, who has traveled objectively.

"Anyway, my dreams were beauties—architecturally speaking. Just what they liked to hear. My last, and crowning, creation—or lie—was one in which the Forerunner himself appeared on Ozagen and spoke to the Sandalphon, Macneff. That event is supposed to take place a year from now."

"Oh, Hal!" she breathed. "Why did you tell them that?"

"Because now, *ma chère*, the expedition will not leave Ozagen until that year is up. They couldn't go without giving up the chance of seeing Sigmen in the flesh as he voyages up and down the stream of time. Nor without making a liar of him. And of me. So, you see, that colossal lie will make sure that we have at least a year together. . . ."

"And then?"

"We'll think of something else then."

Her throaty voice murmured in the darkness by the seat: "And you would do all that for me. . . ."

Hal did not reply. He was too busy keeping the gig close to the rooftop level. Clumps of buildings, widely separated by woods, flashed by. So fast was he going that he almost overshot Fobo's castlelike house. Three stories high, medieval-seeming with its crenellated towers and gargoyle heads of stone beasts and insects leering out from many niches, it was not nearer than a hundred yards to any other building. Wogs built their cities with plenty of elbow-room in mind.

Jeanette put on the long-snouted nightmask; the gig's door swung open; they ran across the sidewalk and into the building. After they dashed through the lobby and up on the steps to the second floor, they had to stop while Hal fumbled for the key. He had had a wog smith make the lock and a wog carpenter install it. He hadn't trusted the carpenter's mate from the ship, because there was too much chance of duplicate keys being made.

He finally found the key, had trouble inserting it. When the door opened, he was breathing hard. He almost pushed Jeannette through. She had taken her mask off.

"Wait, Hal," she said, leaning her weight against his. "Haven't you forgotten something?"

"Oh, *Forerunner!* What could it be? Something serious?"

"No. I only thought," and she smiled and then lowered her lids, "that it was the Terran custom for men to carry their brides across the threshold."

His jaw dropped. Bride! She was certainly taking a lot for granted!

He couldn't take time to argue. Without a word, he swept her up in his arms and carried her into the apartment. There he put her down and said, "Back as soon as possible. If anybody knocks or tries to get in, hide in that special closet I told you about. Don't make a sound or come out until you're sure it's me."

She suddenly put her arms around him and kissed him.

"M'sheh, m'gwa, foh."

Things were going too fast. He didn't say a word or even return her kiss. Vaguely he felt that her words, applied to him, were somewhat ridiculous. If he translated her degenerate French right, she had called him her dear, her strong man.

Turning, he closed the door; but not so quickly that he did not see the hall-light shine on a white face haloed blackly by a hood. A red red mouth stained the whiteness,

He shook. He had a feeling that Jeannette was not going to be the frigid mate so much admired, officially, by the Sturch.

VI

Hal was an hour late returning home from the *Gabriel*, because the Sandalphon asked for more details about the prophecy he'd made concerning Sigmen. Then

Hal had to dictate his report on the day's espionage to a stenoservo. Afterwards, he ordered a sailor to pilot his gig back to the apartment. While he was walking toward the launching-rack, he met Pornsen.

"*Shalom, abba,*" greeted Hal.

He smiled and rubbed his knuckles against the raised lamech on the shield.

The gapt's left shoulder, always low, sagged even more, as if it were a flag dipping in surrender. His ward was now out of his reach. More, if there were any whipcuts to be given, they would be struck by Yarrow.

The joat puffed out his chest and started to walk on, but Pornsen said, "Just a minute, son. Are you going back to the city?"

"Shib."

"Shib. I'll ride back with you. I have an apartment in the same building. On the third floor, right next door to Fobo's.

Hal opened his mouth to protest, then closed it. It was Pornsen's turn to smile. He knew he had nettled the joat. He turned and led the way. Hal followed with tight lips. Had the gapt perhaps trailed him and seen his meeting with Jeannette? No. If he had, he would have had Hal arrested at once.

The thing was that the gapt was small-minded. He knew his presence would annoy Hal.

Under his breath Hal quoted an old proverb, "A gapt's teeth never let loose."

The sailor was waiting by the gig. They all got in and dropped silently into the night.

At the apartment-building Hal strode into the doorway ahead of Pornsen. He felt a slight glow of satisfaction at thus breaking etiquette and expressing his contempt for the man.

Before opening his door, he paused. The guardian angel passed silently behind him. Hal, struck with a devilish thought, called out in French, "*Père!*"

Pornsen turned.

"What?"

"Would you care to inspect my rooms and see if I'm hiding a woman in there?"

The little man purpled. He closed his eyes and swayed, dizzy with sheer fury. When he opened them he shouted, "Yarrow! If ever I saw an unreal personality, you're it! I don't care how you stand with the hierarchy! I think you're—you're—just not simply shib!"

Hal looked blank. "I'm sure I don't know what you mean, Pornsen. I'm pure. I've proven there isn't an evil thought in my head."

His voice became strident, harsh. "Pornsen, you've just been talking in English! I'm sorry, but I have to report that in the morning. You know what that means!"

Pornsen's red face was suddenly drained of its blood. He opened his mouth, closed it, looked at Yarrow's merciless face, spun on his bootheels and walked away.

Hal leaned against the doorway. He felt both weak and triumphant. When he had recovered from the reaction of baiting his guardian, he turned the key in his lock. Around and around in his head flew the thought that it had taken this girl only a few hours to fill him with enough courage to overcome thirty years of fear and submissiveness.

He clicked on the front room lights. Looking beyond into the dining room, he could see the closed kitchen door. The rattling of pots came through it. He sniffed deeply.

Steak!

The pleasure was replaced by a frown. He'd told her to hide until he returned. What if he had been a wog or an Uzzite?

When he swung the door open, the hinges squeaked. Jeannette's back was to him. At the first protest of un-oiled iron, she whirled. The spatula in her hand dropped; the other hand flew to her open mouth.

The angry words on his lips died. If he were to scold her now, she would probably break out in embarrassing tears.

"*M'tyuh!* You startled me!"

He grunted and went by her to lift the lids on the pots.

"You see," she said, her voice trembling as if she divined his anger and were defending herself, "I have lived such a life, being afraid of getting caught, that anything sudden scares me. I am always ready to run."

"How those wogs fooled me!" Hal said sourly. "I thought they were so kind and gentle, and now I find they've kept you prisoner for two years."

She glanced at him out of the side of her large eyes. Her color had come back; her red lips smiled.

"Oh, they weren't so bad. They really were kind. They gave me everything I wanted, except my freedom. They were afraid I'd make my way back to my aunts and sisters."

"What did they care?"

"Oh, they thought there might be some males of my race left in the jungle and that I might give them children. They are terribly frightened of my race becoming numerous and strong again and making war on them. They do not like war."

"Hm! Well, let's eat."

When they had finished, he sighed, patted his stomach, and said, "Ah, Jeannette, the soup was the best I ever tasted. The bread was fresh and hot. The salad was superb. The steak was perfect."

"My aunts gave me very good training. Among my people the female is taught at an early age all that will please a man. All. By the time we've grown up, we do it almost instinctively."

Hal leaned back and lit a cigarette. She tried one, coughed, then drew in and blew out smoke like a veteran. She seemed to have an amazing facility for imitation. Show or tell her something once, and she never forgot it.

They smoked awhile, looking at each other. During the meal she had chattered lightly and amusingly about her life with her father and her relatives. She had the trick of raising her eyebrows as she laughed; he was fascinated by them. They were almost bracket-shaped. A thin line rose from the bridge of the nose, turned at right angles, curved slightly while going above the eyesockets, and then made a little hook downwards. He asked her if the shape was a trait of her mother's people. She laughed and said No, she got them from her father. Her laughter was low and musical. It did not get on his nerves, as his ex-wife's had. Lulled by it, he felt pleasant. She seemed to have a sixth sense that guessed his moods and thoughts and exactly what he needed to blunt any gloominess or sharpen any gaiety.

Finally he said, "We'll have to wash the dishes. It would never do for a visitor to see a table set for two. And another thing: we'll have to hide the cigarettes, and air out the rooms frequently. Now that I've been 'Metered, I'm supposed to have renounced such vices as smoking."

Jeannette would not let him help her do the dishes. He smoked and speculated about the chances of getting tobacco. She so enjoyed the cigarettes that he could not stand the idea of her missing out on them. One of the crewmen he knew did

not smoke, but instead sold his ration to his mates. Maybe a wog could act as mid-
dleman; buy the stuff from the sailor, and pass it on to Hal. He'd have to be careful . . . maybe it wasn't worth it. . . .

Hal sighed. Having Jeannette was wonderful, but she was beginning to complicate his life. Here he was, contemplating a criminal action as if it were the most
natural thing in the world.

She was standing before him, hands on her hips, eyes shining.

"Now, Hal, *mon cher*, if we only had something to drink . . . it would make a
perfect evening."

He got to his feet. "Sorry. I forgot you wouldn't know how to make coffee."

"*Non. Non.* It is the liquor I am thinking of. *L'alcool. Pas le café.*"

"Alcohol? Good God, girl, we don't *drink!* That'd be the most disgust—"

He stopped. She was hurt. He mastered himself. After all, she couldn't help it.
She came from a different culture. She wasn't even, strictly speaking, all human.

"I'm sorry," he said. "It's a religious matter. Forbidden."

Tears filled her eyes. Her shoulders began to shake. She put her face into her
hands and began to sob. "You don't understand. I have to have it. I have to."

"But why?"

She spoke from behind her fingers. "Because during my imprisonment I had
little to do but entertain myself. My captors gave me liquor; it helped to pass the
time and make me forget how utterly homesick I was. Before I knew it, I was an—
an alcoholic."

Hal clenched his fists and growled, "Those sons of bugs!"

"So you see, I have to have a drink. It would make me feel better, just for the
time being. And later, maybe later, I can try to overcome it. I know I can, if you'll
help me."

He gestured emptily. "But—but where can I get you any?" His stomach revolted at the idea of trafficking in alcohol, but if she needed it, he'd try his best to
get it.

Swiftly she said, "Fobo lives on the third floor. Perhaps he could give you
some."

"But Fobo was one of your captors! Won't he suspect something if I come asking for alcohol?"

"He'll think it's for you."

"All right," he said, somewhat sullenly, and at the same time guiltily because he
was sullen. "But I hate for anybody to think *I* drink. Even if he is just a wog."

She came up to him and seemed to flow against him. Her lips pressed softly
and hotly. Her body tried to pass through his. He held her for a minute and then
took his mouth away.

"Do I have to leave you?" he whispered. "Couldn't you pass up the liquor? Just
for tonight? Tomorrow I'll get you some."

Her voice broke. "Oh, *m'namoow*, I wish I could. How I wish I could. But I
can't. I just can't. Believe me. . . ."

"I believe you."

He released her and walked into the front room, where he took a hood, cloak,
and nightmask out of the closet. His head was bent; his shoulders sagged.
Everything would be spoiled. He would not be able to get near her, not with her
breath stinking with alcohol. And she'd probably wonder why he was cold, and he
wouldn't have the nerve to tell how revolting she was, because that would hurt her
feelings. To make it worse, she'd be hurt anyway, if he offered no explanation.

Before he left, she kissed him again on his now frozen lips.
"Hurry! I'll be waiting."
"Yeah."

VII

Yarrow knocked lightly. Fobo's apartment was next door to Pornsen's. Tonight was not a good time for the gapt to see him visiting the empathist.

When the door opened, he stepped in and shut it quickly. Noise bounced off the walls of the room, large as a basketball court. Screaming, twelve wog children raced around. Abasa, Fobo's wife, was sitting in one corner and chattering with three female visitors. The empathist himself was at a table by the door, reading.

Hal shouted, "How can you concentrate?"

Fobo looked up. "Why, can't you cut out all unwanted noises with an effort of will? That is, turn off certain nerve paths? No? Well, we wogs can, though how, we don't know. That is one of the subjects for research at the nearby College of Empathology. And now, won't you sit down? I'd offer you a drink, but I'm fresh out."

Hal was sure that his dismay didn't show on his face, but Fobo's antennae must have picked it up.

"Anything wrong?"

Hal decided not to waste time. "Yes. Where can I get a quart of liquor?"

The wog took his night garments down from a hook, put them on, and then buckled on a broad leather belt with sheath and short rapier.

"I was just thinking of going out and getting some. You see, this empathology is very trying on the nerves. I run into so many people who need help; and since I must put myself into their shoes, feel their emotions as they feel them, and then must wrench myself out of their shoes and take an objective look at their problems, I am exhausted and shaken at the end of the day. I find that a drink or two relaxes me. You understand?"

The Terran didn't, but he shook his head yes. He wondered how he was going to explain that he was breaking the law by drinking. He'd have to stress the necessity of saying nothing to Pornsen.

Outside, Hal said, "Why the sword?"

"Oh, there isn't much danger, but it's best to be careful. You see, this is a world of insects whose development and specialization go even beyond that of your planet. You know the parasites and mimics that infest ant colonies, don't you? The beetles that look like ants and make an easy living from that resemblance? The pygmy ants and other tiny creatures that live in the walls and prey on the eggs and the young? Well, we have things analogous to them. Things that hide in sewers or basements or hollow trees and creep around the city at night. Our streets are well-lighted and patrolled, but they are often separated by wooded stretches. . . ."

By the time Fobo had finished talking, they had passed through a park, zigzagged down a dozen blocks of a shopping district, now closed, and stopped before a building in front of which a big electric sign blazed.

"Duroku's Tavern," translated Fobo.

It was in the basement. Hal, after stopping to shudder at the blast of liquor that came up the steps, followed the wog. In the entrance he paused to blink.

Loud odors of alcohol mingled with loud bars of a strange music and even louder talk. Wogs crowded the hexagonal-topped tables and leaned across big pewter steins to shout in each other's face. Antennae wiggled with drunken emotion. Somebody waved his hands uncoordinatedly and sent a stein crashing. A waitress, looking much like her Terran counterpart with her white apron and peaked cap, hurried up with a towel to mop up the mess. When she bent over, she was slapped resoundingly on the rump by a jovial, greenfaced, and very fat wogglebug. His tablemates howled with laughter, their broad V-in-V lips wide open. The waitress laughed, too, and said something to the fat one that must have been witty, for the tables roundabout guffawed.

On a platform at one end of the room a five-piece band slammed out fast and weird notes. Hal saw three instruments that looked Terranlike: a harp, a trumpet, and a drum. A fourth musician, however, was not himself producing any music, but was now and then prodding with a long stick a rabbit-sized locustoid insect in a cage. When so urged, the creature rubbed its hind wings over its back legs and gave four loud chirps followed by a long, nerve-scratching screech.

The fifth player was pumping away at a bellows connected to a bag and three short and narrow pipes. A thin squealing came out.

Fobo shouted, "You mustn't judge Ozagen by this place. It's a lowerclass hangout. Especially, don't think that noise is typical of our music. It's cheap popular stuff. I'll take you to a symphony concert one of these days, and you'll hear what great music is like."

The wog led the man to one of the curtained-off booths scattered along the walls. They sat down. A waitress came to them. Sweat ran off her forehead and down her tubular nose.

"Keep your mask on until we've gotten our drinks," said Fobo. "Then we can close the curtains."

The waitress said something in Wog. Fobo repeated in French, "Beer, wine, or alcohol à la beetle. Myself, I wouldn't touch the first two. They're for women and children."

The Terran didn't want to lose face. He said with a bravado he didn't feel, "The latter, of course."

"Double shot?"

Hal didn't know what that meant, but he nodded.

Fobo held up two fingers. The waitress returned quickly with two big steins. The wog leaned his nose into the fumes and breathed deeply. He closed his eyes in ecstasy, lifted the stein, and drank a long time. When he put the container down, he belched loudly and then smacked his lips.

"Tastes as good coming up as going down!" he bellowed.

The man felt queasy. Eructation was very frowned upon in the Haijac Union.

"*Mais, monsieur!* You are not drinking."

Yarrow said weakly, "*Damifaino,*" the Ozagen equivalent of mud-in-your-eye, and drank.

Fire ran down his throat like lava down a volcano's slope. And, like a volcano, Hal erupted. He coughed and wheezed; liquor spurted out of his mouth; his eyes shut and squeezed out big tears.

"*Tres bonne, n'est-ce pas?*" said Fobo calmly.

"Yes, very good," croaked Yarrow from a throat that seemed to be permanently scarred. Though he had spat most of the stuff out, some of it must have dropped straight through his intestines and into his legs, for he felt a hot tide down there swinging back and forth as if pulled by some invisible moon circling around and around in his head, a big moon that bulged and brushed against the inside of his skull.

"Have another."

The second drink he managed better—outwardly, at least, for he did not cough or sputter. But inwardly he was not so unconcerned. His belly writhed, and he was sure he would disgrace himself. After a few deep breaths, he thought he would keep the liquor down. Then he belched. The lava got as far as his throat before he managed to stop it.

"Pardon me," he said, blushing.

"Why?" said Fobo.

Hal thought that was one of the funniest retorts he had ever heard. He laughed loudly and sipped at the stein. If he could empty it swiftly and then buy a quart for Jeannette, he could get back before the night was completely wasted.

When the liquor had receded halfway down the stein, Hal heard Fobo, dimly and faroff as if he were at the end of a long tunnel, ask him if he cared to see where the alcohol was made.

"Shib," Hal agreed.

He rose, but had to put a hand on the table to steady himself. The wog told him to put his mask back on. "Earthmen are still objects of curiosity. We don't want to waste all evening answering questions. Or drinking drinks that'll be forced on us."

They threaded through the noisy crowd to a backroom. There Fobo gestured and said, *"Voilà, L'escarbot."*

Hal looked. If he had not had some of his inhibitions washed away in the liquorish flood, he might have been overwhelmingly repulsed. As it was, he was curious.

The thing sitting on a chair by the table might at first glance have been taken for a wogglebug. It had the antennae, the blond fuzz, the bald pate, the nose, and the V-shaped mouth. It also had the round body and enormous paunch of some of the Ozagens.

But a second look in the bright light from the unshaded bulb overhead showed a creature whose body was sheathed in a hard and lightly green-tinted chitin. And though it wore a long cloak, the legs and arms were naked. They were not smooth-skinned but were ringed, segmented with the edges of armor-sections, like stovepipes.

Fobo spoke to it in Wog. Yarrow understood some of the words; the others he was able to fill in.

"Ducko, this is Mr. Yarrow. Say hello to Mr. Yarrow, Ducko."

The big blue eyes looked at Hal. There was nothing about them to distinguish them from a wog's, yet they seemed inhuman, thoroughly arthropodal.

"Hello, Mr. Yarrow," Ducko said in a parrot's voice.

"Tell Mr. Yarrow what a fine night it is."

"It's a fine night, Mr. Yarrow."

"Tell him Ducko is happy to see him."

"Ducko is happy to see you."

"And serve him."

"And serve you."

"Show Mr. Yarrow how you make beetlejuice."

A wog standing by the table glanced at his wristwatch. He spoke in rapid Ozagen. Fobo translated.

"He says Ducko ate a half hour ago. He should be ready to serve. These creatures eat a big meal every half hour and then they—watch!"

Duroku hurried up with a huge earthenware bowl and set it on the table. Ducko leaned over it until a half-inch long tube, probably a modified tracheal opening, was poised above the edge. From the tube he shot a clear liquid into the bowl until it was filled to the brim. Duroku grabbed the bowl and carried it off. An Ozagen came from the kitchen with a plate of highly-sugared spaghetti. He set it down, and Ducko began eating from it with a big spoon.

Hal's brain was by then not working very fast, but he began to see what was going on. Frantically, he looked around for a place to throw up. Fobo shoved a drink under his nose. For lack of anything better to do, he swallowed some. Whole hog or none. Surprisingly, the fiery stuff settled his stomach. Or else burned away the rising tide.

"Exactly," replied Fobo to Hal's strangled question. "These creatures are a superb example of parasitical mimicry. Though quasi-insectal, they look much like us. They live among us and earn their board and room by furnishing us with a cheap and smooth alcoholic drink. You noticed its enormous belly, no? *Eh bien*, it is there that they so rapidly manufacture the alcohol and so easily upchuck it. Simple and natural, *oui?* Duroku has two others working for him, but it is their night off, and doubtless they are in some neighborhood tavern, getting drunk. A sailor's holiday. . . ."

Hal burst out, "Can't we buy a quart and get out? I feel sick. It must be the closeness of the air. Or something."

"Something, probably," murmured Fobo.

He sent a waitress after two quarts. While they were waiting for her, they saw a short wog in a mask and blue cloak enter. The newcomer stood in the doorway, black boots widespread and the long tubular projection of the mask pointing this way and that like a sub's periscope peering for prey.

Hal gasped and said, "Pornsen!"

"*Oui*," replied Fobo. "That drooping shoulder and the black boots and the lack of antennae give him away. Who does he think he's fooling?"

The joat looked wildly around. "I've got to get out of here!"

The waitress returned with the bottles. Fobo paid her and gave one to Hal, who automatically put it in the inside pocket of his cloak.

The gapt saw them through the doorway, but he must not have recognized them. Yarrow still wore his mask, while the empathist probably still looked to Pornsen like any other wog. Methodical as always, Pornsen evidently determined to make a thorough search. He brought up his sloping shoulder in a sudden gesture and began parting the curtains of the booths along the walls. Whenever he saw a wog with his or her mask on, he lifted the grotesque covering and looked behind.

Fobo chuckled. "He won't keep that up long. What does he think we Ozagens are? A bunch of rabbits?"

What he had been waiting for happened. A burly wog suddenly stood up as Pornsen reached for his mask and instead lifted the gapt's. Surprised at seeing a non-Ozagenian's features, the wog dropped his jaw and stared for a second. Then he gave a screech, yelled something, and punched the Earthman in the nose.

At once there was bedlam. Pornsen staggered back into a table, knocking it and its steins over, and fell to the floor. Two wogs jumped him. Another hit a fourth. The fourth struck back. Duroku, carrying a short club, hurried up and began thumping his fighting customers on the back and legs. Somebody threw beetle-juice in his face.

And at that moment Fobo threw the switch that plunged the tavern into darkness.

VIII

Hal stood bewildered. A hand seized his. "Follow me!" The hand tugged. Hal turned and allowed himself to be led, stumbling, toward what he thought was the backdoor.

Any number of others must have had the same idea. Hal was knocked down and trampled upon. Fobo's hand was torn from his. Yarrow cried out for the wog, but any possible answer was drowned out in a chorus of *Beat it! Get off my back, you dumb son-of-a-bug! Great Larva, we're piled up in the doorway!*

Sharp reports added to the noise. A foul stench choked Hal as the wogs, under nervous stress, released the gas in their madbags. Gasping, he fought his way through the door. A few seconds later his mad scrambling over twisting bodies got him his freedom. He lurched down an alleyway. Once on the street, he ran as fast as he could. He didn't know where he was going. His one thought was to put as much distance as possible between himself and Pornsen.

Arc-lights on top of tall slender iron poles flashed by. He ran with his shoulder almost scraping the buildings. He wanted to stay in the shadows thrown by the many balconies jutting out from the second stories. Presently, he slowed down at a narrow passageway. A glance showed him it wasn't a blind alley. He darted down it until he came to a large square can, one that by its odor must have been used for garbage. Squatting behind it, he tried to lessen his gaspings. After a minute his lungs regained their balance; he no longer had to sob for air. Then he could listen without having his heart thudding in his ears.

He heard no pursuer. After a while he decided it was safe to rise. He felt the bottle in his cloakpocket. Miraculously, it had not been broken. Jeannette would get her liquor. What a story he would have to tell her! After all he had gone through for her, he would surely get a just reward. . . .

He shivered with goose-pimples at the thought and began to walk briskly down the alley. Where he was he had no idea, but he carried a map of the city in his pocket. It had been printed in the ship and bore street names in Ozagen with French translations beneath. All he had to do was read the street-signs under one of the many lamps, orient himself with the map, and return home. As for Pornsen, the fellow had no real evidence against him, and would not be able to accuse him until he got some. Hal's possession of the golden lamech made him above suspicion. Pornsen. . . .

Porsen! No sooner had he muttered the name than the flesh appeared. There was a click of hard bootheels behind him. He turned. A short, cloaked figure was coming down the alley. A lamp's glow outlined the droop of a shoulder and shone on black leather boots. His mask was off.

"Yarrow!" shrilled the gapt. "No use running! Wait!" Triumph was in the voice. "I saw you go in that tavern!"

He clickclacked up to his ward's tall rigid form. "Drinking! I know you were drinking!"

"Yeah?" Hal croaked. "What else?"

"Isn't that enough?" screamed the gapt. "Or are you hiding something in your apartment? Maybe you are! Maybe you've got the place filled with bottles. Come on. Come on. Let's get back to your apartment. We'll go over it and see what we see. I wouldn't be surprised to find all sorts of evidence of your unreal thinking."

Hal hunched his shoulders and clenched his fists, but he said nothing. When the gapt told him to precede him back to Fobo's building, he walked without a sign of resistance. Like conqueror and conquered, they marched from the alley into the street. Yarrow, however, spoiled the picture by reeling a little and having to put his hand to the wall to steady himself.

Pornsen sneered, "You drunken joat! You make me sick to my stomach!"

Hal pointed ahead. "I'm not the only one who's sick. Look at that fellow."

He was not really interested, but he had a wild hope that anything he said or did, however trivial, might put off the final and fatal moment when they would return to his apartment. What he indicated was a large and evidently intoxicated wogglebug hanging onto a lamp post to keep from falling on his tube-shaped nose. The picture might have been one of a nineteenth or twentieth century drunk, complete to top hat, cloak and lamp post. Now and then the creature groaned as if he were deeply disturbed.

"Perhaps we'd better stop and see if he's hurt?" said Hal.

He had to say anything, anything, to delay Pornsen. Before his captor could protest, he went up to the wog. He put his hand on the free arm—the other was wrapped around the post—and spoke in Ozagen.

"Can we help you?"

The big wog looked as if he, too, had been in a brawl. His cloak, besides being ripped down the back, was spotted with dried green blood. He kept his face away from Hal, so that the Earthman had a hard time understanding his muttering.

Pornsen jerked at his arm. "Come on, Yarrow. He'll get by all right. What's one sick bug more or less?"

"Shib," agreed Hal, tonelessly. He let his hand drop and started to walk on. Pornsen, behind, took one step . . . and then bumped into Hal as Hal stopped.

"What are you stopping for, Yarrow?" The gapt's voice was suddenly apprehensive.

And then the voice was screaming in agony.

Hal whirled . . . to see in grim actuality what had flashed across his mind and caused him to stop in his tracks. When he had put his hand on the wog's arm, he had felt, not warm skin, but hard and cool chitin. For a few seconds the meaning of that had not cleared the brain's switchboard. Then it had come through, and he had remembered the talk he and Fobo had had on the way to the tavern, and why Fobo wore a sword. Too late, he had wheeled to warn Pornsen.

Now the gapt was holding both hands to his eyes and shrieking. The big thing that had been leaning against the lamp post was advancing towards Hal. Its body seemed to grow huger with every step. A sac across its chest was swelled until it looked like a palpitating grey balloon; the hideous insectal face, with two vestigial arms waving on each side of its mouth and the funnel-shaped proboscis below the mouth, was pointed at him. It was that proboscis which Hal had mistakenly thought was a wog's nose. In reality, the thing must breathe through tracheae and two slits below the enormous eyes.

Hal yelled with fury and as a means of discharging his fear. At the same time he grabbed his cloak and threw it up before his face. His mask might have saved him, but he did not care to take the chance.

Something burned the back of his hand. He yelped with pain, but leaped forward. Before the thing could breathe in air to bloat the sac again and expell the acid through the funnel, Hal rammed his head against its paunch.

The thing said, *"Oof!"* and fell backward where it lay on its back and thrashed its legs and arms like a giant poisonous bug—which it was. Then, as it recovered from the shock and rolled over and tried to get back on its feet, Hal kicked hard. His leather toe drove with a crunching sound through the thin chitin.

The toe withdrew; a greenish blood oozed out; Hal kicked again in the open place. The thing screamed and tried to crawl away on all fours. The Terran leaped upon it with both feet and bore it sprawling to the cement. He pressed his heel against its thin neck and shoved with all the strength of his leg. The neck cracked. The thing lay still. Its lower jaw dropped open and exposed two rows of tiny needle-teeth. The mouth's rudimentary arms wigwagged feebly for a while and then drooped.

Hal's chest heaved in agony. He couldn't get enough air. His guts quivered and threatened to force their way through his throat. Then they did, and Hal bent over, retching.

All at once, he was sober. By that time Pornsen had quit screaming. He was lying huddled on his side in the gutter. Hal turned him over and shuddered at what he saw. The eyes were partly burned out, and the lips were grey with large blisters. The tongue, too, sticking from the mouth, was swollen and lumpy. Evidently Pornsen had swallowed some of the venom. According to Fobo, even a small part was fatal.

Hal straightened up and walked away. A wog patrol would find the gapt's body and turn it over to the Earthmen. Let the hierarchy figure out what had happened. Pornsen was dead, and now that he was, Yarrow admitted to himself what he had never allowed himself to admit before this time. He had hated Pornsen. And he was glad that he was dead. If Pornsen had suffered horribly, so what? His pains were brief, but the pain and grief he had caused Hal had lasted for almost thirty years.

In all that time Hal had kept unconscious his desire to kill the man. Now his feelings, anti-climactically, exploded. Tears ran down his cheeks; his shoulders shook with sobs; he staggered like a drunk. Something was reaching down into his intestines and tearing them apart. It wasn't grief. It was hate, working out like a poison, a swift poison leaving his body but boiling him alive. Still, it was coming out, and though he felt that he was dying while it lasted, by the time he arrived at home he felt much better. Fatigue held his arms and legs down, and he could hardly make it up the steps. But inside, where the heart was, he was stronger than he had ever been in his life.

IX

A tall ghost in a light blue shroud was waiting for the Terran in the false dawn. It was the empathist, standing in the hexagonal-shaped arch that led into his building. When Hal came close, Fobo threw back the hood and exposed a face that was scratched on one cheek and blacked around the right eye.

He chuckled and said, "Some son of a bug pulled my mask off and plowed me good. But it was fun. It helps if you blow off steam that way now and then. How did you come out? I was afraid you might have been picked up by the police. Normally that wouldn't worry me, but I know your colleagues at the ship would frown upon such activities."

Hal smiled wanly. "Frown misses it by a mile."

He wondered how Fobo knew what the hierarch's reactions would be. How much did these wogs know about the Terrestrials? Were they onto the Haijac game, and waiting to pounce? If so, with what? Their technology, as far as could be determined, was way behind Earth's. True, they seemed to know more of psychic functions than the Terrans did, but that was understandable. The Sturch had long ago decreed that the proper psychology had been perfected and that further research was unnecessary. The result had been a standstill in the psychical sciences.

He shrugged mentally. He was too tired to think of such things. All he wanted was to go to bed.

"I'll tell you later what happened," he said.

Fobo replied, "I can guess. Your hand. You'd better let me fix that burn. Nightlifer venom is nasty."

Like a little child, Hal followed to the wog's apartment and let him put a cooling salve on it.

"*Voilà,*" said Fobo. "Go to bed. Tomorrow you can tell me all about it."

Hal thanked him and walked down to his floor. His hand fumbled with the key. Finally, after using Sigmen's name in vain, he inserted the key. When he had shut and locked the door, he called Jeannette. She must have been hiding in the closet-within-a-closet in the bedroom, for he heard two doors bang. In a moment she was running to him. She threw her arms around him.

"Oh, *mon homme, mon homme!* Hal, *mon amour,* what has happened? I was so worried. I thought I would scream when the night went by, and you didn't return."

Though he was sorry he had caused her pain, he could not help a prickling of pleasure because someone cared enough about him to worry. Nobody ever had before.

"There was a brawl," he said. He had decided not to say anything about the gapt or the nightlifer. Later, when the strain had passed, he'd talk.

She untied his cloak and hood and took off his mask. While she hung them up in the frontroom closet, he sank into a chair and closed his eyes. A moment later they were pulled open by the sound of liquid pouring into a glass. She was standing in front of him and filling a large glass from the quart. The odor of beetlejuice began to turn his stomach, and the picture of a beautiful girl about to drink the nauseating stuff spun it all the way around.

She looked at him. The delicate brackets of her brows rose. "*Qu'y a-t-il?*"

"Nothing's the matter!" he groaned. "I'm all right."

She put down the glass, picked up his hand, and led him into the bedroom. There she gently sat him down, pressed on his shoulder until he laid down, and then took off his shoes. He didn't resist. After she unbuttoned his shirt, she stroked his hair.

"You're sure you're all right?"

"Shib. I could lick the world with one hand tied behind my back."

"Good."

The bed creaked as she got up and walked out of the room. Before he could fall asleep, she returned. Again, he opened his eyes. Again, she was standing with a glass in her hand.

She said, "Would you like a sip now, Hal?"

"Great Mind, girl, don't you understand?" he barked. Fury poured adrenalin into his tired blood. He sat up. "Why do you think I got sick? I can't stand the stuff! I can't stand to see you drink it. It makes me sick. You make me sick. What's the matter with you? Are you stupid?"

Jeannette's eyes widened. Blood drained from her face and left the pigment of her lips a crimson moon in a white lake. Her hand shook so that the liquor spilled.

"Why—why—" she gasped—"I thought you said you felt fine. I thought you were all right. I thought you wanted to go to bed with me."

Yarrow groaned. He shut his eyes and laid back down. Sarcasm was lost on her. She insisted on taking everything literally. She would have to be re-educated, not only in irony, but in other things. If he weren't so exhausted, he would have been shocked by her open proposal—so much like that of the Scarlet Woman in the Western Talmud when she had tried to seduce the Forerunner.

But he was past being shocked. Moreover, a voice on the edge of his conscience said that she had merely put into hard and unrecallable words what he had planned in his heart all this time. But when you spoke them!

A crash of glass shattered his thoughts. He jerked upright. She was standing there, face twisted, lovely red mouth quivering and tears flowing. Her hand was empty. A large wet patch against the wall, still dripping, showed what had become of the glass.

"I thought you loved me!" she yelled.

Unable to think of anything to say, he stared. She spun and walked away. He heard her go into the front room. Loud sobs forced him to jump out of bed and walk swiftly after her. These rooms were supposed to be soundproof, but one never knew. What if she were overheard?

Anyway, she was twisting something inside him, and he had to straighten it out.

When he entered the front room, she didn't look up. For a while he stood silent, wanting to say something but utterly unable to because he had never been forced to solve such a problem before. Haijac women didn't cry often, or if they did, they wept alone in privacy.

He sat down by her and put his hand on her soft shoulder.

"Jeannette."

She turned quickly and laid her dark hair against his chest and said, between sobs, "I thought maybe you didn't love me. And I couldn't stand it. Not after all I've been through!"

"Well, Jeannette, I didn't . . . I mean . . . I wasn't. . . ."

He paused. He had had no intention of saying he loved her. He'd never told any girl he loved her. Nor had any girl ever told him. And here was this girl on a faraway planet, only half-human at that, taking it for granted that he was hers, body and self.

He began speaking in a soft voice. Words came easily, because he was quoting Moral Lecture AT 16:

". . . all beings with their hearts in the right place are brothers . . . Man and woman are brother and sister . . . Love is everywhere . . . but love . . . should be on a higher plane . . . Man and woman should rightly loath the beastly act as something the Great Mind, the Cosmic Observer, has not yet eliminated in man's evolutionary development . . . The time will come when children will be produced otherwise. Meanwhile we must recognize sex as outmoded, and necessary for only one reason: children . . ."

Slap! His head rang, and points of fire whirled off into the blackness before his eyes.

It was a moment before he could realize that Jeannette had leaped to her feet and slammed him hard with the palm of her hand. He saw her standing above him with her eyes slitted and her red mouth open and drawn back in a snarl.

Then she whirled and ran into the bedroom. He got up and followed her. She was lying on the bed, sobbing.

"Jeannette, you don't understand."

"*Va t'feh fut!*"

When he understood that, he blushed. Then he got mad. He grabbed her by the shoulder and turned her over so that she faced him.

Suddenly he was saying, "But I do love you, Jeannette. I *do*."

He sounded strange, even to himself. The concept of love, as she meant it, was alien to him—rusty, perhaps, if it could be put that way. It would need a lot of polishing. But it would, he knew, be polished. Here in his arms was one whose very nature and instinct and education were pointed toward love.

He had thought he had drained himself of grief earlier that night, but now, as he forgot his resolve not to tell her what had happened, and as he recounted, step by step, the long and terrible night, tears ran down his face. Thirty years makes a deep well; it takes a long time to pump out all the weeping.

Jeannette, too, cried, and said that she was sorry that she had gotten angry at him. She promised never again to do so. He said it was all right. They kissed again and again until, like two babies who have wept themselves and loved themselves out of frustration and fury, they passed gently into sleep.

X

At dawn the Haijac ship, which had been suspended fifty feet high, settled to earth. All day long it would rest there in the middle of a big glade. At nightfall it would rise again. Even though the Terrans had so far seen no evidence of wog aerial flight, except for a few balloons, they took no chances of sudden attack. The sinking sun always saw the *Gabriel* poised above the treetops, radar probing, ready on the instant to accelerate into Ozagen's stratosphere, or, if necessary, into the safety of space.

At 0900 Ship's Time, Yarrow walked into the *Gabriel*, the smell of morning dew on grass in his nostrils. As he had a little time before the conference, he looked up Turnboy, the historian joat. Casually, he asked if Turnboy knew anything of a spaceflight emigration from France during the Forerunner's early days. Turnboy was delighted to show off his knowledge. Yes, the remnants of the Gallic nation had gathered in the Loire country after the Apocalyptic War and had formed the nucleus of what might have become a new France.

But the fastgrowing colonies sent from Iceland to the northern part of France, and from Israel to the southern part, had surrounded the Loire. New France found itself squeezed economically and religiously. Sigmen's disciples invaded the Catholic territory in waves of missionaries. High tariffs had strangled the little state's trade. Finally a group of Frenchmen, seeing the inevitable absorption or conquest of their state, religion, and tongue, had left in six spaceships, three thousand strong, to find another Gaul rotating about some faroff star. Where they had landed, nobody knew.

Hal thanked Turnboy and walked to the conference room. He spoke to many; two years of flight had enabled him to recognize most of the personnel. Half of them, like him, had a Mongolian tinge to their features. They were the English-speaking descendants of Hawaiian and Australian survivor of the same war which had decimated France. Their manytimes great-grandfathers had repopulated Australia, the Americas, and Japan.

Almost half of the crew spoke Icelandic. Their ancestors had sailed from the grim island to spread across northern Europe and Siberia and Manchuria.

About a sixteenth of the crew spoke Georgian when among their fellows from home. Their fathers had moved down from the Caucasus Mountains and resettled the depopulated plains of southern Russia. A minority in the Haijac Union, they were gradually abandoning their native tongue in favor of that of their closest neighbors — the Icelanders.

At 1200 Hal left the conference room. He felt wonderful. First, he had been moved from twentieth place to the Archurielite's left to sixth from his right. The lamech on his chest made the difference. Second, there was little difficulty about Pornsen's death. The gapt was considered as a casualty of war. Everyone was warned about the nightlifers and other things that sometimes prowled Siddo after dusk. It was not, however, suggested that the Haijacs quit their moonlit espionage.

Macneff, the Achurielite, ordered Hal, as the dead gapt's spiritual son, to arrange for the funeral the following day. Then he pulled down a huge map from a long roller on the wall. This was the representation of Earth that would be given to the wogs.

It was a good example of the Haijacs' subtlety and Chinese box-within-a-box thinking. The sheet bore two hemispheres of Earth with colored political boundaries. It was correct as far as the Bantu and Malay states were concerned. But the positions of the Israeli and Haijac nations had been reversed. The legend beneath the map said that green was the color of the Forerunner states and yellow was the Hebrews'. The green portion, however, was a ring around the Mediterranean, covering Palestine, Turkey, the Balkans, Italy, Austria, south Germany, lower France, Spain and northern Africa; it included the Sahara Sea, Arabia, Mesopotamia, and eastern Persia.

In other words, said Macneff, if by any inconceivable chance the Ozagenians were concealing spaceships, or captured the *Gabriel* and built ships with it as a model, and if they managed to find Sol, they would still attack the wrong country. They would think the Israeli Republic was the Union. Unless, that is, they took time to capture and question Terrans and thus found out the truth. But that was unlikely, for the essence of modern war was the surprise attack. The wogs would not want to give their enemies a chance to prepare.

As everyone knew, Macneff added, the deception might have been furthered by having the *Gabriel*'s members speak Hebrew. But since that was the holy tongue, not to be used by the lower classes except in religious rituals nor to be used at all in profane matters such as carrying on a war, it was forbidden.

However — due to the excellent suggestion of Yarrow, the linguistic joat — French was being spoken. If the wogs pierced the deception, they would think it was a ruse of the Israeli.

After the conference, still glowing from the Achurielite's compliment, Hal gave orders for the funeral arrangements. Other duties kept him till dark, when he returned home.

XI

When Yarrow locked the door behind him, he heard the shower running. He hung his coat up in the closet; the water quit splashing. As he went toward his bedroom door, Jeannette stepped out from the bathroom. She was drying her hair with a big towel, and she was naked.

She said, *"Bon jour, Hal,"* and walked on unselfconsciously into the bedroom.

Hal replied feebly. He turned and went back into the front room. He felt foolish, because of his timorousness, and at the same time vaguely wicked, unreal, because of the pounding of his heart, his heavy breathing, the hot and fluid fingers that wrapped themselves, half-pain, half-delight, around his loins.

She came out dressed in a pale green robe which he had purchased for her and which she had re-cut and re-sewed to fit her figure. Her heavy black hair was piled on her head in a Psyche knot. She kissed him and asked if he wanted to come into the kitchen while she cooked. He said that would be fine.

She began making a sort of spaghetti. He asked her to tell him about her life. Once started, she was not hard to keep going.

". . . and so my father's people found a planet like Earth and settled there. It was a beautiful planet; that is why they called it *Luhbawpfey.*"

"Huh?"

"Le Beau Pays," she enunciated more carefully. "The beautiful land. According to my father, there are about thirty million living there on one continent. My father was not content to live the life his grandfathers had—tilling the soil or running a shop and raising many children. He and some other young men like him took the only spaceship left of the original six that had come there, and they sailed off to the stars. They came to Ozagen. And crashed. No wonder. It was two hundred and fifty years old."

"The obsolete ion-beam drive. Is the wreck still around?"

"Vi. I mean *oui.* Close to where my sisters and aunts and cousins live."

"Your mother is dead?"

She hesitated, then nodded. "Yes. She died giving birth to me. And my sisters. Father died later. Or rather, we think he did. He went on a hunting-party and never came back."

Hal frowned. "Wait a minute. You told me that your mother and aunts were the last of the native human beings on Ozagen. And you said once before that Rastignac was the only Earthman to get out alive from the wreck. He was your mother's husband, naturally . . . and incredible as it sounds, their union—one of a terrestrial and an extraterrestrial—was fertile! That alone would rock my colleagues on their heels. Amazing! Completely contrary to accepted science, that their body chemistry and chromosomes should match! But—what I'm getting at is that your mother's *sister* had children, too. If the last Ozagenian human male died years before Rastignac crashed, who was their father?"

"Jean Rastignac. He was the husband of my mother and my four aunts. They all say that he was a superb and very virile lover."

Hal said, "Oh."

Until she had the spaghetti and salad ready, he watched her in silence. By then he had regained some of his perspective. After all, the Frenchman was not too much worse than he himself was. Maybe not as bad. He chuckled. How easy it was to condemn somebody else for giving way to temptation until you yourself faced the same situation. He wondered what Pornsen would have done if Jeannette had contacted him.

". . . and so it was easy to escape from the wogs," she was saying. "They did not watch me closely, and they were through examining me. *Mon Dieu*, the tests. Questions, questions! That Fobo asked me all sorts of things. Wanted to find out my intelligence, my personality, my etcetera. Put me under all kinds of machines. He and his fellows turned me inside out. Literally, my dear. They took pictures of my insides. Showed me my skeleton and organs and just simply everything. They said it was most interesting. Imagine that! I am exposed as no woman has ever been exposed, and to them I am just most interesting. Indeed!"

"Well," laughed Hal. "You can't expect arthropods to take the viewpoint of a mammal towards a female . . . that is. . . ."

She looked archly at him. "And am I a mammal?"

"Obviously, unmistakably, indisputably, and enthusiastically."

"For that you get a kiss."

"Hmmm. I'll bet that was almost as good as the spaghetti is going to be."

"You eat your food, and then I will show you something that is much better than almost as good."

He was learning fast. He didn't even flush.

After the meal she cut a pitcher of beetlejuice with water, poured in a purplish liquid which made the drink smell like grapes, and dropped sprigs of an orange plant on the surface. Poured into a glass of ice cubes, it was cool and even tasted like grapes. It did not gag him at all.

"Why did you pick me, instead of Pornsen?" he asked.

She sat on his lap, one arm around his neck, the other on the table, drink in hand. "Oh, you were so goodlooking, and he was so ugly. Besides, I eavesdropped, and he sounded mean. You were nice. And I knew I had to be careful. My father had told me about Earthmen. He said they couldn't be trusted."

"How true. But you must have an instinct for doing the right thing, Jeannette. If you had antennae, I'd say you could detect nervous emanations. Here, let's see!" He went to run his fingers through her hair, but she ducked her head and laughed.

He laughed with her and dropped the hand to her shoulder, rubbing the smooth skin. "I was probably the only person on the ship who wouldn't have betrayed you. But I'm in a quandary now. You see, your presence here raises the devil. Here we Haijacs are, speaking French as a sort of camouflage for our real nationality, and all the time the wogs knew our language from the beginning. When we first came here, we were careless of what we said before them, because we figured it would take some time for them to learn French.

"Now our expedition may be in danger. And I can't tell Macneff that, because he would want to know how I knew. That'd give you away. And there's something else. You told me they have x-ray machines. So far we've seen none. Are the wogs hiding them? And if they are, what else are they concealing? And why? It's important that we know; but I can't tell Macneff they've got a hidden technology. So I'm on the horns of a dilemna."

"A dilemna? A beast I never heard of."

He hugged her. "I hope you never do. Listen, Jeannette, this is serious. Sooner or later, and probably sooner, we'll have to make up our minds to leave. Our specialists are working night and day on samples of wogglebug blood. They hope to make an artificial semivirus that will attach itself to the copper in the green blood-cells and change their electrophoretic properties."

"*Comment?*"

"Don't look so blank. Or giggle. It's deadly serious. It's what killed seven-eighths of Earth's people. Guided missiles by the tens of thousands circling high over the surface. Dropping little knots of protein molecules that locked onto the hemoglobin in the red blood cells and gave them a positive charge so that one end of a globin molecule would bind with the end of another. Which would make the molecules go into a sort of crystallization. Which would twist the doughnut shaped red cells into a scimitar, and cause an artificial sickle cell anemia.

"The lab-created anemia was much swifter and more certain than the natural kind, because every red cell would be affected, not just a small percentage. Every cell would soon break down. The blood would have no carriers of oxygen to various parts of the body. The body would die.

"The body did die, Jeannette—the body of humanity. Almost a planetful of human beings perished from lack of oxygen. Only by accident did any organized governments survive. Most of those were islands that weren't attacked because they were felt to be too small to bother with. Hawaii, and Iceland, and a city in Australia and Bali.

"Palestine got scotfree by sheer coincidence. An experiment with short radiowaves interfered with the missiles' guiding beams. None got to the Holy Land. By the time the enemy found out why, they were dead. All over the world—not only in the civilized parts, but in the arctic, the jungles, the mountains—they died. Everywhere the missiles circled; everywhere was the invisible rain of death, the skulls, the bones—"

"Hush!" Jeannette put her finger on his quivering lips. "I don't know what you mean by proteins and molecules and those—those electrofrenetic charges! They're way above my head. But I do know that the longer you've been talking, the more scared you've been getting. Your voice was getting higher, and your eyes were growing wider.

"Somebody has frightened you in the past. No! Don't interrupt! They've scared you, and you've been man enough to hide most of your fear, but they've done such a horribly efficient job that you haven't been able to get over it.

"Well—" and she put her soft lips to his ears and whispered—"I'm going to wipe that fear out. I'm going to lead you out of that valley of fright. No! Don't protest! I know it hurts your ego to think that a woman could know you're afraid. But I don't think any the less of you. I admire you all the more because you've conquered so much of it. I know what courage it took to face the 'Meter. I know you did it because of me. I'm proud that you did. I love you for it. And I know what courage it takes to keep me here, when any time a slip would send you to certain disgrace and death. I know what it all means. It's my nature and instinct and business and love to know.

"Now! Drink with me. We're not outside these walls where we have to worry ourselves about such things and be scared. We're in here. Away from everything except ourselves. Drink. And love me. I'll love you, Hal, and we'll not see the world outside nor need to. For the time being. Forget in my arms."

They drank the purplish liquor. After a while he picked her up and carried her into the bedroom. There he forgot. The only disconcerting item was that she insisted upon keeping her eyes open, even during the climax, as if she were trying to photograph his features upon her mind.

XII

On earth, the alcoholics were not cured but were sent to H. Therefore no psychological or narcotic therapies had been worked out for addicts. Hal, deadended by this fact in his desire to wipe out Jeannette's alcoholism, went for medicine to the very people who had given her the disease. Only he pretended that the cure was for himself.

Fobo said, "There is widespread drinking on Ozagen, but it is light. Our few alcoholics are quickly empathized into normality. Why don't you let me empathize you?"

"Sorry. My government forbids that."

He had given Fobo the same excuse for not inviting the wog home.

"You have the most forbidding government," said Fobo, and went into one of his long, howling laughs. When he recovered, he said, "You're forbidden to touch liquor, too, but that doesn't hold you back. Well, there's no accounting for inconsistency. Seriously, though, I have just the thing for you. It's called Easyglow. It's a stimulant which has an effect similar to alcohol's, but which is, in reality, however, depressing. We put it into the daily ration of liquor, increasing slowly the Easyglow and diminishing the alcohol. In two or three weeks the patient is drinking from a fluid 96 per cent Easyglow. The taste is much the same; the drinker seldom suspects. Continued treatment eases the patient from his dependence on the alcohol. There is only one drawback."

He paused and said. "The drinker is now addicted to Easyglow!"

He whooped and slapped his thigh and wiggled his antennae and laughed until the tears came.

"Really, though, the peculiar effect of Easyglow is that it opens the patient for discharge of the strains that have driven him to drink. He may then be empathized and at the same time weaned from the stimulant. Since I have no opportunity to slip the stuff to you secretly, I'm taking the chance that you are seriously interested in curing yourself. When you're ready for therapy, tell me."

Hal took the bottle to his apartment. Every day its contents went quietly and carefully into the beetlejuice he got for Jeannette. He hoped that he was psychologist enough to cure her once the Easyglow took effect.

Although he didn't know it, he was himself being "cured" by Fobo. His almost daily talks with the empathist instilled doubts about the religion and science of the Haijacs—or, as their enemies termed them, the Highjackers. Fobo read the biographies of Isaac Sigmen and the Works: the Pre-Torah, the Western Talmud, the Revised Scriptures, the Foundations of Serialism, Time and Theology, The Self and the World-Line. Calmly sitting at his table with a glass of juice in his hand, the wog challenged the mathematics of the dunnologists. Hal proved; Fobo disproved. He pointed out that the math was mainly based on false-to-fact assumptions; that Dunne's and Sigmen's reasoning was buttressed by too many analogs, metaphors and strained interpretations. Remove the buttresses, and the structure fell

And worse, far worse, he said that the Forerunner's biographies and theological writings revealed him, even through the censor's veil, as a sexually frigid and woman-hating man with a messiah complex and paranoid and schizophrenic tendencies which burst through his icy shell from time to time in religious-scientific frenzies and fantasies.

"Other men," Fobo said, "have stamped their personality and ideas upon their times. But Sigmen had an advantage over those great leaders who came before him. Because of Earth's rejuvenation serums he lived long enough, not only to set up his kind of society, but to consolidate it and weed out its weaknesses. He didn't die until the cement of his social form had hardened."

"But the Forerunner didn't die," protested Yarrow. "He left in time. He is still with us, traveling down the fields of presentation, skipping here and there, now to the past, now to the future. Always, wherever he is needed to turn pseudo-time into real time, he is there."

"Ah, yes," smiled Fobo. "That was the reason you went to the ruins, was it not? To check up on a mural which hinted that the Ozagen humans had once been visited by a man from outer space. You thought it might have been the Forerunner, didn't you?"

"Macneff did," said Hal, annoyed. "But my report showed that, though the man resembled Sigmen somewhat, the evidence was too inconclusive. The Forerunner may or may not have visited this planet a thousand years ago."

"Be that as it may, I maintain your theses are meaningless. You claim that his prophecies came true. I say, first, that they were couched ambiguously. Second, if they have been realized, it is because your powerful state-church—you may call it the Sturch—has made strenuous efforts to fulfill them.

"Furthermore, this pyramidal society of yours—his guardian-angel administration—where every ten families have a gapt to supervise their most intimate and minute details, and every ten family-gapts have a block-gapt at their head, and every fifty block-gapts are directed by a supervisor-gapt, and so on—this society is based on fear and ignorance and suppression."

Hal, shaken, angered, shocked, would get up to leave. Fobo would call him back and ask him to disprove what he'd said. Hal would let loose a flood of wrath. Sometimes, when he had finished, he would be asked to sit down and continue the discussion. Sometimes, Fobo would lose his temper; they would shout and scream insults; twice, they fought with fists; Hal got a bloody nose once and Fobo a black eye. Then the wog, weeping, would embrace Hal and ask for his forgiveness, and they would sit down and drink some more until their nerves were calmed.

Yarrow told Jeannette of these incidents. She encouraged him to tell them over and over again until he had talked away the stress and strain of grief and hate and doubt. Afterwards, there was always love such as he had never thought possible. For the first time he knew that man and woman could become one flesh. His wife and he had remained outside the circle of each other, but Jeannette knew the geometry that would take him in and the chemistry that would mix his substance with hers.

Always, too, there was the light and the drink. But they did not bother him. Unknown to her, she was now drinking a liquor almost entirely Easyglow. And he had gotten used to the light above their bed. It was one of her quirks. Fear of the dark wasn't behind it, because it was only while making love that she required a bulb be left on. He didn't understand it. Perhaps she wanted to impress his image on her memory, always to have it if she ever lost him. If so, let her keep the light.

By its glow he explored her body with an interest that was part sexual and part anthropological. He was delighted and astonished at the many small differences between her and Terran women. There was a small appendage of skin on the roof of her mouth that might have been the rudiment of some organ whose function was long ago cast aside by evolution. There were two bumps of cartilage on the top of her head, hidden by her thick black hair. She had thirty teeth; the wisdom teeth were missing. That might or might not have been a characteristic of her mother's people.

He suspected that she either had an extra set of pectoral muscles or else an extraordinarily well-developed normal set. Her large and cone-shaped breasts did not sag. They were high and firm and pointed slightly upwards: the ideal of feminine beauty so often portrayed through the ages by male sculptors and painters and so seldom existing in nature.

She was not only a pleasure to look at; she was pleasing to be with. At least once a week she would greet him with a new garment. She loved to sew; out of the materials he gave her she fashioned slips, blouses, skirts and even gowns. Along with the change in dress went new hairdos. She was ever-new and ever-beautiful, and she made Hal realize for the first time that a thing of beauty was a joy, if not for forever, then for at least as long as it lasted.

Her imitativeness was another thing that delighted him. She had switched from her brand of French to his almost overnight. Within a week she was speaking it faster and more expressively than he. As she also knew Ozagen thoroughly, he decided the best way for him to learn it was to have her read wog books to him. He'd lie on the divan while she sat on a chair. Her accent and pronunciation were correct, and trained his ear. Where she saved him time was in his not having to look up each new word in a dictionary—she translated for him.

Jeannette loved to read to him, but she wearied of the dry and technical books he gave her. When he saw that she was tired, he softened and let her stop. He never did, for example, finish Weenai's monumental *Rise and Fall of Man on Ozagen*. That evening Jeannette began, as usual, bravely enough. Her low, throaty voice tried to simulate interest in what her eyes saw. She went through the first chapter, which described the formation of the planet and the beginnings of life. In the second she yawned quite openly and looked at Hal, but he closed his eyes and pretended not to notice. So she read of the rise of the wogs from an arthropod that had changed its mind and decided to become a chordate. Weenai made some heavy jests about the contrariness of the wogglebugs since that fateful day, and then took up, in the third chapter, the story of mammalian evolution on the other large continent of Ozagen. It climaxed in man.

She quoted: "But homo sapiens, like us, had its mimical parasites. One was a different species of the so-called tavern beetle. It, instead of resembling a wog, looked like a man. Like its counterpart, it could fool no intelligent person, but its gift of alcohol made it very acceptable to man. It, too, accompanied its host from primitive times, became an integral part of his civilization, and, finally, a large cause of man's downfall.

"Humanity's disappearance from the face of Ozagen is due not only to the tavern beetle. That creature can be controlled, and has been by us. Like most things, it has benefits to confer. Like most things, it can be abused or its purpose distorted so that it becomes a menace.

"That is what man did with it.

"He had, it must be noted, an ally to help him in the misuse of the insect. This was another parasite, one of a somewhat different kind; one that was, indeed, our cousin. That is, it is a so-called chordate arthropod.

"One thing, however, distinguishes it from us, and from man, and from any other animal on this planet with the exception of some very low species. That is, that from the very first fossil evidence we have of it, it was wholly—"

Jeannette put the book down. "I don't know the next word. Hal, do I have to read this? It's so boring."

"No. Forget it. Read me one of those comics that you and the crew like so much."

She smiled, a beautiful sight, and began Vol. 1037, Book 56, of the *Adventures of Leif Magnus, Beloved Disciple of the Forerunner, When He Met the Horror From Arcturus.*

He listened to her translation of the French into vernacular Wog until he grew tired of the banalities and pulled her down to him.

Always, there was the light left on above them.

XIV

It was the following day that Yarrow, returning from the market with a large box, said, "You've sure been putting away the groceries lately. You're not eating for two? Or maybe three?"

She paled. "*Mon Dieu!* Do you know what you're saying?"

He put the box on a table and grabbed her shoulders.

"Shib. I do. Jeannette, I've been thinking about that very thing for a long time, but I haven't said anything. I didn't want to worry you. Tell me, are you?"

She looked him straight in the eye, but her body was shaking. "Oh, no. It is impossible!"

"Why should it be? We've used no preventives."

"*Oui.* But I know—don't ask me how—call it instinct, if you wish—that it cannot be. But you must never say things like that. Not even joking. I can't stand it."

He pulled her close and said over her shoulder, "Is it because you can't? Because you know you'll never bear my children?"

Her thick, faintly perfumed hair nodded. "I know. Don't ask me how I know."

He held her at arm's length again. "Listen, Jeannette. I'll tell you what's been troubling you. You and I are really of different species. Your mother and father were, too. Yet they had issue. But you're thinking that the ass and the mare have young, too, but the mule is sterile. The lion and the tigress may breed, but the liger or tigon can't. Isn't that right? You're afraid you're a mule!"

She put her head on his chest and sobbed.

He said, "Let's be real about this, honey. Maybe you are. So what? My God, our situation is bad enough without a baby to complicate it. We'll be lucky if you are . . . uh . . . well, we have each other, haven't we? That's all I want. You."

He couldn't keep from being reflective as he dried her tears and kissed her and helped her put the food in the refrigerator.

The quantities of groceries and milk she had been consuming were more than a normal amount, especially the milk. There had been no telltale change in her superb figure, true. But the stuff was going somewhere.

A month passed. He watched her closely. She ate enormously. Nothing happened.

Yarrow put it down to his ignorance of her alien metabolism.

XV

Another month. Hal was just leaving the ship's library when Turnboy stopped him.

"The rumor is that the techs have finally made the globinlocking molecule," the historian said. "I think that this time the grapevine's right. A conference is called for 1500."

"Shib." Hal kept his despair out of his voice.

When the meeting broke up at 1650, it left him with sagging shoulders. The virus was already in production. In a week a large enough supply would be made to fill the disseminators of six prowler-torpedoes. The plan was to release them to wipe out the city of Siddo. A beachhead would be established there. While the *Gabriel* flew back to Earth, the beachhead would keep making the virus and would send prowlers out in spirals whose range would expand until a large territory would be covered. By the time a huge fleet returned, millions of wogs would be slain. The fleet would then deal with the rest of the planet.

When he got home, he found Jeannette lying in bed. She smiled weakly. Her hair was loose in a black corona on the pillow.

He forgot his mood in a thrill of concern.

"What's the matter, baby?"

He laid his hand on her forehead. The skin was dry and hot and rough.

"I don't know. I haven't been feeling really well for two weeks, but I didn't complain. I thought I'd get over it. Today I felt so bad I just had to go back to bed after breakfast."

"We'll get you well."

He sounded confident. Inside himself, he was lost. If she had contracted a serious disease, she could get no doctor, no medicine—

For the next few days she continued to lie in bed. Her temperature fluctuated from 99.5 in the morning to 100.2 at night. Hal attended her as well as he could. He put wet towels and ice-bags on her head and gave her aspirin. She had quit eating so much food; all she wanted was liquid. She seemed to be always asking for milk. Even the beetlejuice and the cigarettes were turned down.

Her illness was bad enough, but her silences stung Yarrow into a frenzy. As long as he had known her, she had chattered lightly, merrily, amusingly. She could be quiet, but it was with an interested wordlessness. Now she let him talk, and when he quit, she did not fill his silence with questions or comments.

In an effort to arouse her, he told her of his plan to steal a gig and take her back to her jungle home. A light came into her dulled eyes; the brown looked shiny for the first time. She even sat up while he put a map of the continent on her lap. She indicated the general area where she had lived, and then described the mountain range that rose from the green tropics, and the tableland on its top where her aunts and sisters lived in the ruins of a metropolis.

Hal sat down at the little octagonal-shaped table by the bed and worked out the coordinates from the maps. Now and then he glanced up. She was lying on her side, her white and delicate shoulder rising from her nightgown, her eyes large in the shadows that were beginning to stain rings around them.

"All I have to do is steal a little key," he said. "You see, the milometer on a gig is set at 0 before every flight from the field. The boat will run fifty miles on manual. That gives us leeway to go any place in Siddo and return. But once the tape passes fifty, the gig automatically stops and sends out a location signal. That's to keep anybody from running away. However, the autos can be unlocked and the signal turned off. A little key will do it. I can get it. Don't worry."

"You must love me very much."

"You bet I do!"

He rose and kissed her. Her mouth, once so soft and dewy, felt dry and hard. It was almost as if the skin were turning to horn.

He returned to his calculations. An hour later, a sigh from her made him look up. Her eyes were closed, and her lips were slightly open. Sweat ran down her face.

He hoped her fever had broken. No. The mercury stopped at 100.3.

She said something.

He bent down. "What?"

She was muttering in an unknown language. Delirious. Hal swore. He had to act. No matter what the consequences. He ran into the bathroom, shook from a bottle a ten grain rockabye tablet, went back and propped Jeannette up and got her to wash the pill down with a glass of water.

After he locked her bedroom door, he put on a hood and cloak and walked fast to the nearst pharmacy. There he purchased three 20-gauge needles, three syringes, and some anti-coagulant. Back in his apartment, he tried to insert the needle in an arm vein. The point refused to go in until the fourth attempt when, in a fit of exasperation, he pressed hard.

During none of the jabbings did she open her eyes or jerk her arm.

When the first fluid crept into the glass tube, he gasped with relief. Though he hadn't known it, he had been biting his lower lip and holding his breath. Suddenly he knew that he had for the last month been pushing a horrible suspicion back to the outlands of his mind. Now, he realized the thought had been ridiculous.

The blood was red.

He tried to arouse her in order to get a specimen of urine. She twisted her mouth over strange syllables, then lapsed back into sleep or a coma—he didn't know which. In an anguish of despair he slapped her face, again and again, hoping he could bring her to. He swore once more, for he realized all at once that he should have gotten the specimen before giving her the rockabye Pill. How stupid could he get! He wasn't thinking straight; he was too excited over her condition and what he had to do at the ship.

He perked some very strong coffee and managed to get part of it down her. The rest dribbled down her chin and soaked her gown.

Either the caffeine or his desperate tone awoke her, for she opened her eyes long enough to look at him while he explained what he wanted her to do and where he was going afterwards. Once he'd gotten the urine into a previously boiled jar, he wrapped the syringes and jar in a handkerchief and dropped them into the cloak-pocket.

He had already wristphoned the *Gabriel* for a gig. A horn beeped outside. He took another look at Jeannette, locked the bedroom door, locked the apartment door, and ran down the stairs. The gig hovered above the curb. He entered, sat down, and punched the *Go* button. The boat rose to a thousand feet and then flashed at an 11-degree angle toward the park where the ship squatted.

XVI

The medical section was empty, except for one orderly. The fellow dropped his comic and jumped to his feet.

"Take it easy," said Hal. "I just want to use the Labtech. And I don't want to be bothered with making out triplicate forms. This is a little personal matter, see?"

Hal had taken off his cloak. The orderly looked at the bright golden lamech.

"Shib," he grunted.

Hal gave him two cigarettes.

"Geez, thanks." The orderly lit up, sat down, and picked up his *The Forerunner and Delilah in the Wicked City of Gaza*.

Yarrow went around the corner of the Labtech, where the orderly couldn't see him, and set the proper dials. After he inserted his specimens, he sat down. Almost at once he jumped up and began pacing back and forth. Meanwhile, the huge cube of the Labtech purred like a contented cat as it digested its strange food. A half-hour later, it rumbled once and then flashed a green light: ANALYSIS COMPLETE.

Hal pressed a button. Like a tongue out of a metal mouth, a long tape slid out. He read the code. Urine was normal. No infection there. Also normal was the pH and the blood count.

He hadn't been sure the "eye" would recognize the cells in her blood. However, the chances had been strong that her red cells would be Terranlike. Why not? Evolution follows parallel paths; the biconcave disk is the most efficient form for carrying the maximum of oxygen.

The machine chattered. More tape. Unknown hormone! Similar in molecular structure to the parathyroid hormone primarily concerned in the control of calcium metabolism.

What did that mean? Could the mysterious substance loosed in her bloodstream be the cause of her trouble?

More clicks. The calcium content of the blood was 40 mg. per cent.

Strange. Such an abnormally high percentage should mean that the renal threshold was passed and that an excess of calcium should be "spilling" into the urine. Where was it going?

The Labtech flashed a red light: FINISHED.

He took a Hematology book down from the shelf and opened it to the Ca section. When he quit reading, he straightened his shoulders. New hope? Perhaps. Her case sounded as if she had a form of hypercalcemia, which was manifested by any number of diseases ranging from rickets and steomalacia to chronic hypertrophic arthritis. Whatever she had, she was suffering from a malfunction of the parathyroid glands.

The next move was to the Pharm machine. He punched three buttons, dialed a number, stood for two minutes, and then lifted a little door at waist-level. A tray slid out. On it was a cellophane sheath containing a hypodermic needle and a tube holding 30 c.c. of a pale blue fluid. It was Jesper's serum, a "one-shot" readjustor of the parathyroid.

Hal put on his cloak, stuck the package in the inside pocket, and strode out. The orderly didn't even look up.

The next step was the weapons room. There he gave the storekeeper an order—made out in triplicate—for one .1 mm. automatic and a clip of one hundred cartridges. The keeper only glanced over the forged signatures— he, too, was awed by the lamech—and unlocked the door. Hal took the gun, which he could easily hide in the palm of his hand, and stuck it in his pants pocket.

At the key room, two corridors away, he repeated the crime. Or rather, he tried to.

Moto, the officer on duty, looked at the papers, hesitated, and said, "I'm sorry. My orders are to check on any requests with the Chief Uzzite. That won't be possible for about an hour, though. He's in conference with the Archurielite."

Hal picked up his papers. "Never mind. My business'll hold. Be back in the morning."

On the way home, he planned what he'd do. After injecting Jesper's serum in Jeannette, he'd move her into the gig. The floor beneath the gig's control-panel would have to be ripped up, two wires would be unhooked, and one connected to another lead. That would remove the fifty-mile limit. Unfortunately, it would also set off an alarm back in the *Gabriel*. His hope was that he could take off straight up, level off, and dive behind the range of hills to the west of Siddo. The hills would deflect the radar. The autopilot could be set long enough for him to demolish the box that would be sending out the signal by which the *Gabriel* might track him down.

After that, with the gig hedgehopping, he could hope to be free until daybreak. Then he'd submerge in the nearest deep-enough lake or river until nightfall. During the darkness he could rise and speed towards the tropics; and if his radar showed any signs of pursuit, he could plunge again into a body of water.

He left the long needle-shape parked by the curb. His feet pounded the stairs. The key missed the hole the first two tries. He slammed the door without bothering to lock it again.

"Jeannette!" he shouted. Suddenly he was afraid that she might have gotten up while delirious and somehow opened the doors and wandered out.

A low moan answered him. He unlocked the bedroom door and shoved it open. She was lying with her eyes wide.

"Jeannette. Do you feel better?"

"No. Worse. Much worse."

"Don't worry, baby. I've got just the medicine that'll put new life in you. In a couple of hours you'll be sitting up and yelling for steaks. And you won't even want to touch that milk. You'll be drinking Easyglow by the gallon. And then—"

He faltered as he saw her face. It was a stony mask of distress, like the grotesque and twisted wooden faces of the Greek tragedians.

"Oh, no . . . *no!* My God," she moaned. "What did you say? Easyglow?" Her voice rose. "Is *that* what you've been giving me?"

"Shib, Jeannette. Take it easy. You liked it. What's the difference? The point is that we're going—"

"Oh, Hal, Hal! What have you done?"

Her pitiful face tore at him. Tears were falling; if ever stone could weep, it was weeping now.

He turned and ran into the kitchen where he took out the sheath, removed the contents, and inserted the needle in the tube. He went back into the bedroom. She said nothing as he thrust the point into her vein. For a moment he was afraid the needle would break. The skin was almost brittle.

"This stuff cures Earth people in a jiffy," he said, with what he hoped was a cheery bedside manner.

"Oh, Hal, come here. It's—it's too late now."

He withdrew the needle, rubbed alcohol on the break and put a pad on it. Then he dropped to his knees by the bed and kissed her. Her lips were hard.

"Hal, do you love me?"

"Won't you ever believe me? How many times must I tell you?"

"No matter what you'll find out about me?"

"I know all about you."

"No, you don't. You can't. Oh, Great Mother, if only I'd told you, Hal! Maybe you'd have loved me just as much, anyway. Maybe . . ."

"Jeannette! What's the matter?"

Her lids had closed. Her body shook in a spasm. When the violent trembling passed, she whispered with stiff lips. He bent his head to hear her.

"What did you say? Jeannette! Speak!"

He shook her. The fever must have died, for her shoulder was cold. And hard. The words came low and slurring.

"Take me to my aunts and sisters. They'll know what to do. Not for me . . . but for the . . ."

"What do you mean?"

"Hal, will you always love . . ."

"Yes, yes. You know that! We've got more important things to do now than talk about that."

If she heard him she gave no sign. Her head was tilted far back with her exquisite nose pointed at the ceiling. Her lids and mouth were closed, and her hands were by her side, palms up. The breasts were motionless. Whatever breath she might have was too feeble to stir them.

XVII

Hal ran upstairs to the third floor and pounded on Fobo's door until it opened.

The empathist's wife said, "Bugs, alive, Hal, you startled me!"

"Where's Fobo?"

"He's at a college board meeting."

"I've got to see him at once."

Abasa yelled after him, "If it's important, go ahead. Those meetings bore him, anyway."

By the time Yarrow had taken the steps three at a time and bee-lined across the nearby campus, his lungs were on fire. He didn't slacken his pace; he hurtled up the steps of the administration building and burst into the board room.

When he tried to speak, he had to stop and suck in deep breaths.

Fobo jumped out of his chair.

"What's up?"

"You—gasp—you've—got to come. Matter—life—death!"

"Excuse me, gentlemen," said Fobo.

The ten wogs nodded their antennae and resumed the conference. The empathist put on his cloak and high-crowned, plumed hat and led Hal out.

"Now, what is it?"

"Listen. I've got to trust you. I know you can't promise me anything. But I think you won't turn me in to my people. You're a real person, Fobo. Not like the Haijac men."

"Get to the point, my friend."

"Listen. You wogs are as advanced as we are in endocrinology. And you've got an advantage. You know Jeannette inside out. You've examined her."

"Jeannette? Oh, Rastignac! The *lalitha*."

"Yes. I've been hiding her in my apartment."

"I know."

"You . . . know! How?"

"Never mind." The wog put his hand on Hal's shoulder. "Something bad has happened, or you'd not have come to me about her."

By the time Hal had told him, they were at their apartments. Fobo stopped him at the door.

"I may as well tell you. Your countrymen know you're up to something. For the last eight days a man has been living in that building down the street and spying on you. His name is Art Hunah Fedtof."

"An Uzzite!"

"*Oui.* He lives in the front room on the ground floor. His windows are darkened, but he is probably watching you right now."

"Forget about him!" Yarrow snarled.

He bounded up the stairs. Fobo followed him into his rooms. The wog felt Jeannette's forehead and tried to lift her lid to look at her eye. It would not bend.

"Hmm! Calcification of the outer skin layer is far advanced."

With one hand he threw the sheet from her figure and with the other he grabbed her gown by the neckline and ripped the thin cloth down the middle. The two parts fell to either side. She lay nude, as silent and pale and beautiful as a sculptor's masterpiece.

Her lover gave a little cry at what seemed like a violation. But he shut up at once, because he knew that Fobo's move was medical. In any case, the wog would not have been sexually interested.

Puzzled, he watched. Fobo had tapped his fingertips against her flat belly and then put his ear against it. When he stood up, he shook his head.

"I won't deceive you, Hal. Though we'll do the best we can, we may not be good enough. She'll have to go to a surgeon. If we can cut her eggs out before they hatch, that, plus the serum you gave her, may reverse the effect and pull her out."

"Eggs?"

"I'll tell you later. Wrap her up. I'll run upstairs and phone Dr. Kuto."

Yarrow folded a blanket around her. When he rolled her over, she was as stiff as a show-window dummy. He covered her face. The stony look was too much for him.

His wristphone shrilled. Automatically he reached to flick the stud and just in time drew his hand back. It shrilled loudly, insistently. Finally he decided that if he didn't answer, he would stir up their suspicion far faster.

"Yarrow!"

"Shib!"

"Report to the Archurielite. You will be given fifteen minutes."

"Shib."

Fobo came back in and said, "What're you going to do?"

Hal squared his mouth and said, "You take her by the shoulders, and I'll carry her feet. Rigid as she is, we won't need a stretcher."

As they carried her down the steps, he said, "Can you hide us after the operation, Fobo? We won't be able to use the gig now."

"Don't worry," the wog said enigmatically over his shoulder. "The Earthmen are going to be too busy to run after you."

It took sixty seconds to get her in the gig, hop to the hospital, and get her out.

Hal said, "Let's put her on the ground for a minute. I've got to set the gig on auto and send her back to the *Gabriel*. That way, at least, they won't know where I'm at."

"No. Leave it here. You may be able to use it afterward."

"After what?"

"Later. Ah, there's Kuto."

In the waiting room the joat paced back and forth and puffed Merciful Seraphim out in smoke. The empathist sat on a chair and rubbed his bald pate and the thick golden corkscrew fuzz on the back of his head.

"All this could have been avoided," he said unhappily. "But I didn't know until a week ago that the *lalitha* was living with you. I didn't think there was any hurry to tell you that I knew. Anyway, I was busy working on Project Earthman."

"What was that?" barked Yarrow.

"Oh, for some time we've had our electroencephalographs on you. You Terrans are far ahead of us in most of the physical sciences, but in the psychical sciences we've got you beaten. For instance, you haven't yet found out that below the level of the general brain-waves, which might be likened to 'static,' lie very weak but definite impulses.

"These we call the 'semantic' waves. Our instruments, built with our antennae and nervous system as a model, are so sensitive that they can pick them up at quite a distance and amplify them. The various heights of the semantic waves are then correlated with the spoken syllables of the language. In other words, we have a more or less efficient mind-reader.

"We trained them on you Terrans from the beginning. We thought we would have quite an advantage, because we had learned a type of French from the *lalitha*. To our consternation, however, we found that you talked to us in one language but tended to do your thinking in, not one, but four different tongues."

"Those were Hebrew for the theological thinking of the Urielites and technical thinking of some of the scientists," snapped Hal. "English, Icelandic and Georgian for the everyday thoughts. Any other time I'd be interested in this thinkpicker. But for Forerunner's sake, I want to hear about Jeannette!"

"Believe me, Hal, I can feel for and with you." He wiggled his antennae to indicate he was receiving grief and anxiety emanations. "It's necessary and justifiable that I take my explanation in order. Otherwise, I'll be confused and backtracking all the time, which I detest. As I was saying, we were stumped for a while because the semantic waves' fluctuations did not match those of the spoken word. However, we kept picking up stray thoughts here and there in French. As well grounded as you all seem to have been in that language, it was inevitable that you would do a certain amount of private thinking in it, regardless of your native tongue. About two weeks ago we managed to work out the complete synchronization in the artificial tongue and also bind up a great many impulses with the other languages' words by comparing them with the French."

"Then you know we have perfected the globinlocker?"

Fobo smiled. "Yes, but we were suspicious of that from the beginning. When you asked us for samples of blood, your request was accompanied by too heavy a charge of what we call 'furtive' emanations. We gave you the blood, all right, but it was that of a barnyard creature which uses copper in its blood cells. We wogs use magnesium as the oxygen-carrying element in our cells."

"Our virus is useless!"

"Naturally. Now to get to the personal. My colleagues had their e.c.g's turned on you whenever you came into my room. They didn't think it was any use tapping your waves when you were in your room. You'd be likely to be thinking in the vernacular. About a week ago they did, however, just for experiment, and they were amazed to find the *lalitha* there. They told me. I was too engrossed with this business with the ship to put two and two together. Otherwise, I'd have known why you were pretending to be an alcoholic. I—"

A nurse entered and said, "Phone, Doctor."

Yarrow paced, and smoked another cigarette. Fobo came back.

He said, We're going to have company. One of my colleagues, who is watching the ship, tells me Macneff and two Uzzites left in a gig a minute ago. They should be arriving at the hospital any second now."

Yarrow stopped in midstride. His jaw dropped. "Here?"

"Don't be afraid."

Hal just stood there. The cigarette, unnoticed, burned until it seared his fingers. He dropped it and crushed it beneath his sole.

Bootheels clicked in the corridor.

Three men entered. One was a tall and gaunt ghost—Macneff, the Archurielite. The others were short and broad-shouldered and clad in black. Their meaty hands, though empty, were hooked, ready to dart into their pockets. Their heavy-lidded eyes stabbed at Fobo and then at Hal.

Macneff strode up to the joat. His pale blue eyes glared; his lipless mouth was drawn back in a skull's smile.

"You unspeakable degenerate!" he shouted.

His arm flashed, and the whip, jerked out of his belt, cracked. Thin red marks crawled out of Yarrow's white face and began oozing blood.

"You will be taken back to Earth in chains and there exhibited as an example of the worst pervert, traitor, and—and—!"

He drooled, unable to find words.

"You—who have passed the Elohimeter, who are supposed to be so pure—you have lusted after and lain with an insect!"

"What! What!"

"Yes. With a thing that is even lower than a beast of the field! What even Moses did not think of when he forbade union between man and beast, what even the Forerunner could not have guessed when he reaffirmed the law and set the death penalty for it, you have done. You, Hal Yarrow, the pure, the lamech wearer!"

Fobo rose and said in a deep voice, "Might I suggest and stress that you are not quite right in your zoological classification? It is not the class of insecta but the class of the chordata pseudarthropoda, or words to that effect."

The joat said, "What?" again. He could not think.

The wog growled, "Shut up, Hal. Let me talk."

He swung to face Macneff. "You know about her?"

"You are shib that I know her! Yarrow thought he was getting away with something. But no matter how clever these unrealists are, they're always tripped up. In this case, it was his asking Turnboy about those Frenchmen that fled Earth two and a half centuries ago. Turnboy, who is very zealous in his attitude towards the Sturch, reported the conversation. It lay among my papers for quite a while. When I came across it, I turned it over to the psychologists. They told me that the joat's question was a deviation from the pattern expected of him; a thing totally irrelevant unless it was connected to something we didn't know about him.

"A man was put on his trail. He saw Yarrow buying twice the groceries he should have. And much cloth and sewing equipment and silk stockings and perfume and earrings. Moreover, when you wogs learned the tobacco habit from us and began making cigarettes too, he bought them from you. The conclusion was obvious. He had a female in his apartment.

"We didn't think it'd be a wog female, for she wouldn't have to stay hidden. Therefore she must be human. But we couldn't imagine how she got here on

Ozagen. It was impossible for him to have stowed her away on the *Gabriel*. She must either have come here in a different ship, or be descended from people who had.

"It was Yarrow's talk with Turnboy that furnished the clue. Obviously, the French had landed here. She was a great-great-granddaughter. How the joat had found her, we didn't know. It wasn't important. We'll find out, anyhow."

"You're due to find out some other things, too," Fobo said calmly. "How did you discover she wasn't human?"

Yarrow muttered, "I've got to sit down."

XVIII

He swayed to the wall and sank into a chair. One of the Uzzites started to move toward him. Macneff waved the man back and said, "Turnboy had been reading the history of man on Ozagen. He came across so many references to the *lalitha* that the suspicion was bound to rise that the girl might be one.

"Last week one of the wog physicians, while talking to Turnboy, mentioned that he had once examined a *lalitha*. Later, he said, she had run away. It wasn't hard for us to guess where she had ended up!"

"My boy," said Fobo, turning to Hal, "didn't you read Weenai's book?"

Hal shook his head. "We started it, but Jeannette mislaid it."

"And doubtless saw to it that you had other things to think of . . . they are good at diverting a man's mind. Why not? That is their purpose in life.

"Well, Hal, I'll explain. The *lalitha* are the highest example of mimetic parasitism known. Also, they are unique among sentient beings. Unique in that all are female.

"You see, if you'd read on in Weenai, you'd have found that fossil evidence shows that about the time that Ozagenian man was still an insectivorous marmoset-like creature, he had in his family group not only his own females but the females of another class, perhaps another phylum. These animals looked and probably stank enough like the females of prehomo marmoset to be able to live and mate with them. They seemed mammalian, but dissection would have indicated very strongly their pseudoarthropodal ancestry.

"It's reasonable to suppose that these precursors of the *lalitha* were man's parasites long before the marmosetoid stage. They may have met him when he first crawled out of the sea, and promptly adapted their shape, through an evolutionary process, to that of the lungfish. And later to the amphibian's. And the reptile's and primitive mammal's. And so on.

"What we do know is that the *lalitha* were Nature's most amazing experiment in parasitism and parallel evolution. As man metamorphosed into higher forms, so she kept pace with him. All female, mind you, depending upon the male of another phylum for the continuance of the species.

"It is astonishing the way they became integrated into the prehuman cultures, the pithecanthropoid and neanderthaloid steps. Only when homo sapiens developed did their troubles begin. Some families and tribes accepted them; others killed them. So they resorted to artifice, and disguised themselves as human women. A thing not hard to do—unless they became pregnant.

"In which case they died."

Hal groaned and put his hands over his face.

"Painful but real, as our acquaintance Macneff would say," said Fobo. "Of course—such a condition required a secret sorority. In those societies where the *lalitha* was forced to camouflage, she would, once pregnant, have to leave. And perish in some hidden place among her kind, who would then take care of the nymphs—" here Hal shuddered—"until they were able to go into human cultures. Or else be introduced as foundlings or changelings.

"You'll find quite a tribal lore about them—fables and myths make them central or peripheral characters quite frequently. They were regarded as witches, demons, or worse.

"With the introduction of the alcohol beetle in primitive times, a change for the better came to the *lalitha*. Alcohol made them sterile. At the same time, barring accident, disease, or murder, it made them *immortal*."

Hal took his hands off his face. "You—you mean Jeannette would have lived—forever? That I cost her—that?"

"She could have lived a thousand years, at least. We know that some did. What's more, they remained young. Let me explain. In due order. Some of what I'm going to say will distress you, Hal, but it must be said.

"The long life of the pseudo-woman, sometimes so long that they survived tribes and nations they had joined when first founded, led to their being worshipped as goddesses. They became the repositories of wisdom and wealth. Religions were established with *lalitha* as the focus and priests and beetles on the circumference as permanent marks of human civilizations. The priests and the kings were their lovers.

"Some cultures barred the *lalitha*. They could not, however, keep them out. The false women infiltrated. Being always very beautiful, they mated with the most powerful men—the leaders, the rich, the poets, the thinkers. They competed with women and beat them at their own game, hands down, because in the *lalitha* Nature wrought the complete female.

"You see, they had no male hormone, no male element. They were all woman, and they centered their lives on men. They were instinctively and consciously sensitive to their lovers' desires, whims and moods. Yet they were crafty enough not to be clinging vines. When the time demanded a quarrel, they produced it. They knew what few human females did: the time to speak and the time not to speak.

"You noticed that in Jeannette, didn't you, Hal? No wonder. As part of their arthropodal heritage they owned two rudimentary antennae—mere bumps on their heads, but still sensitive in detecting the grosser nervous emanations.

"And so they gained mastery over their lovers. Influenced unduly the governments. Caused widespread slavery and wholesale breeding of beetles and the resulting alcoholism which led to humankind's downfall.

"When we wogs came to this continent, half their cities were ruined. War, liquor, depraved religious rites, falling birth rate, graft, corruption—a hundred factors leveled once mighty man. Yet, though weakened, they fought us. The *lalitha* urged them to battle, for they saw in us their doom. We could not be influenced by them as their men were. War and disease slew half of them; the rest just seemed to lose interest in living. . . ."

A wog nurse with a white mask over her long nose came out of the operating room. Hal sprang up and watched her as she said something to the empathist in a low voice.

Macneff had been pacing back and forth with his hands clutched behind him. Hal wondered, in the back of his mind, why he, Hal, had not been dragged away at once; why the priest had waited to hear Fobo. Then a flash of insight told him that Macneff had wanted the joat to hear all about Jeannette and realize the full enormity of his deeds.

The nurse went back into the operating room. The Archurielite said loudly, "Is the beast of the fields dead yet?"

Fobo, ignoring him, spoke to Hal, who had shaken as if at a blow when he heard the word "dead."

"Your larv—that is, your children, have been removed. They are in an incubator. They are—" he hesitated—"eating well. They will live."

Yarrow could tell from his tone that it was no use asking about the mother.

The wog twitched his antennae. Big tears rolled from his round blue eyes. He did not, however, offer any sympathy. He kept on talking:

"You won't understand, Hal, what has happened unless you comprehend the *lalitha's* unique method of reproduction. To begin, their ovaries furnish the matrix for the bodies of the embryo, all beautiful bodies, the apex of art as practised by Nature. The male spermatozoa is in no way connected with the genes that lay out the pattern for the body.

"Two things the *lalitha* needs to reproduce. Those two things must occur simultaneously. They are, excitation from orgasm and the stimulation of the photokinetic nerve."

Fobo paused and seemed to cock an ear, as if he were listening for something outside. Hal, who had absorbed some of the empathy of the wog during his acquaintanceship, felt that he was waiting for something big. Really big. And whatever it was, it involved the fate of the Earthmen.

Suddenly he thrilled to hot and cold tinglings . . . and the knowledge that he was on the wog's side!

"What is this nerve?" Fobo went on. "It is a property of the *lalitha*, and runs from the retina of the eye, along with the optic nerve, to the back of the brain. From there it descends the spinal column and leaves the base to enter the uterus. Or, as we term it, the *camera obscura uteri*. The dark room of the womb. Where the photographs of the father's features are developed. And attached to the daughters' faces.

"Yes, that is one of their unique anatomical marks. The photogenes. A *lalitha's* chromosomes are connected to the photokinetic nerve. During intercourse, at the moment of the climax, an electrochemical change takes place in that nerve. By the light that the *lalitha* always requires—an arc-reflex makes it impossible for her to close her eyes at that time—the face of the male is photographed.

"Photographed is an inadequate word, but it is the only one we have for the process. Anyway, if his hair is light brown, that information passes down a string of genes, each of which controls a specific hair color from jet-black down through the hair-spectrum to orange-red. The genes work on a cybernetic parallel. A yes-no binary system. If the gene's color does not correspond to the photokinetic nerve's request, it does not respond. It says no. If it approximates most closely the request, it says yes.

"The same thing happens with the shape and thickness of the hair, the size and shape of the nose and lips, the cheekbones, and jaw, and chin, and the color of the eyes. The shape of the nose, for instance, might have to be turned down a hundred and fifty times before the right combination of genes were struck—"

"You hear that?" exulted Macneff. "You have begat larvae! Monsters of an unholy union. Insect children! And they will have your face as witness of this revolting carnality—"

"Of course, I am no connoisseur of human features," interrupted Fobo, "but the young man's strike me as vigorous and handsome. In a human way, you understand."

He turned to Yarrow. "Now you see why Jeannette desired light. And why she pretended alcoholism. As long as she drank a sufficient amount of liquor before copulation, she was sure that the workings of the delicate photokinetic nerve would be interfered with. No pregnancy that way. No death. But when . . . you cut the beetlejuice with Easyglow . . . unknowing, of course. . . ."

Macneff burst into a high-pitched laughter. "What irony! Truly it has been said that the wages of unrealism are death!"

Fobo spoke loudly. "Go ahead, son. Cry, if you like. You'll feel better. You can't, eh? I wish you would.

"*Eh, bien. Je continue.* The *lalitha*, no matter how human she looks, cannot escape her arthropod heritage. The nymphs that develop from the larvae can easily pass for babies, but it would pain you to see the larvae themselves. Though they are not any uglier than a five months' human embryo. Not to me, anyway.

"It is a sad thing that the *lalitha* mother must die. Hundreds of millions of years ago, when the primitive pseudo-arthropod was ready to hatch the eggs in her womb, a hormone was released in her body. It calcified the skin and turned her into a womb-tomb. She became a shell. Her larvae ate the organs and the bones, which were softened by the draining away of their calcium. When the young had fulfilled the function of the larva, which is to eat and grow, they rested and became nymphs. Then they broke the shell in its weak place in the belly.

"That weak point is the navel. It alone does not calcify with the epidermis, but remains soft. By the time the nymphs are ready to come out, the soft flesh of the navel has decayed. Its dissolution lets loose a chemical which decalcifies an area that takes in most of the abdomen. The nymphs, though weak as human babies and much smaller, are activated by instinct to kick out the thin and brittle covering.

"You must understand, Hal, that the navel itself is both functional and mimetic. Since the larvae are not connected to the mother by an umbilical cord, they would have no navel. But they grow an excrescence which resembles one.

"The breasts of the adult also have two functions. Like the human female's, they are both sexual and reproductive. They never produce milk, of course, but they are glands. At the time the larvae are ready to hatch from the eggs, the breasts act as two powerful pumps of the hormone which carries out the hardening of the skin.

"Nothing wasted, you see—Nature's economy. The things that enable her to survive in human society also carry out the death process.

"It is a sad thing, but it has not changed in all these epochs. The mothers must give their lives for their young. Yet Nature, as a sort of recompense, has given them a gift. On the analogy of reptiles, which do not stop growing larger as long as they aren't killed, the *lalitha* will not die if they remain unpregnant. And so—"

Hal leaped to his feet and shouted, "Stop it!"

"I'm sorry," Fobo said softly. "I'm just trying to make you see why Jeannette felt that she couldn't tell you what she truly was. She loved you, Hal; she possessed the three factors that make love: a genuine passion, a deep affection, and the feeling of being one flesh with you, male and female so inseparable it would be hard to tell where one began and the other ended. I know she did, believe me, for we empathists can put ourselves into somebody else's nervous system and think and feel as they do.

"And feel, despite all this, she must have had a bitter leaven in her love. The belief that if you knew she was of an utterly alien branch of the animal kingdom, separated by millions of years of evolution, barred by her ancestry and anatomy from the true completion of marriage—children—you would turn from her with horror. That belief must have shot with darkness even her brightest moments. . . ."

"*No!* I would have loved her, anyway! It might have been a shock. But I'd have gotten over it. Why, she was human; she was more human than most of the women I've known!"

Macneff sounded as if he were going to retch. When he had recovered himself, he howled, "You absymal thing! How can you stand yourself, now you know what utterly filthy monster you have lain with! Why don't you try to tear out your eyes, which have seen that vile filth! Why don't you bite off your lips, which have kissed that insect mouth! Why don't you cut off your hands, which have pawed with loathsome lust that mockery of a body! Why don't you tear out by the roots those organs of carnal—"

Fobo spoke through the storm of wrath. "Macneff! Macneff!"

The gaunt head swiveled towards the empathist. His eyes stared, and his lips had drawn back into what seemed to be an impossibly large smile; a smile of absolute fury.

"What? What?" he muttered, like a man waking from sleep.

"Macneff. Why don't you tell Yarrow what you were thinking about the other night? When you were alone in your cabin, and supposedly at your prayers. Why don't you tell him what you were planning to do if your agents brought in the *lalitha* alive? What were you thinking?"

The Sandalphon's jaw fell. Red flooded his face and became purple. The violent color faded, and a corpselike white replaced it.

He screeched like an owl.

"*Enough!* Uzzites, take this—this thing that calls itself a man to the gig!"

The two men in black circled to come at the joat from front and back. Their approach was based on training, not real caution. Years of taking prisoners had taught them to expect no resistance. The arrested always stood cowed and numb before the representatives of the Sturch. Now, despite the unusual circumstances, and the knowledge that Hal carried a gun, they saw nothing different in him.

Normally, they would have been right. They could not guess that they had met a man whose basically rebellious character was on the point of bursting the lifelong cocoon of repression. He stood with bowed head and hunched shoulders and dangling arms, the typical arrestee.

That was one second; the next, he was a tiger striking.

The agent in front of him reeled back, blood flowing from his mouth and spilling on his black jacket. When he bumped into the wall, he paused to spit out three teeth.

By then Yarrow had whirled and rammed a fist into the big soft belly of the man behind him.

"*Whoof!*" went the Uzzite.

He folded. As he did so, Hal brought his knee up against the unguarded chin. There was a crack of bone breaking, and the agent fell to the floor.

"Watch him!" yelled Macneff. "He's got a gun!"

The Uzzite by the wall shoved his hand under his jacket, feeling for the weapon in his armpit holster. Simultaneously a heavy bronze bookend, thrown by Fobo, struck his temple. He crumpled.

Macneff screamed, "You are resisting, Yarrow! You are resisting!"

Hal bellowed, "You're damn shib I am!"

Head down like a mad bull's, he plunged at the Archurielite.

Macneff slashed with his whip at his attacker's skull. Hal rammed into the gray-clad form and knocked it to the floor. When Macneff got to his knees, Yarrow seized him by the throat and squeezed. Macneff turned purple and clutched at the terrible hands.

At that moment a tremendous *boom!* rattled the hospital windows. On its heels came another shock wave. Somewhere outside, the night became day for a second.

Hal unclenched his hands and let Macneff fall.

"What was that?" he demanded.

"I imagine it was the *Gabriel* falling from a height of fifty feet," Fobo said. "Not very far, of course, but the ship is tremendous. Something must have exploded. I hope the damage wasn't too serious, for we want to use the ship as a model to build some for ourselves."

Macneff groaned. Hal, standing over him and breathing hard, stared at the wog.

"We don't have mechanical flying missiles, Hal. But we do have hordes of winged and poisonous insects whose flight may be directed, within limits, by painful or pleasing super or subsonic waves. And who also may be conditioned by the sweat-impregnated clothing of Terrans to bite any Earthmen that come within their sense of smell.

"What happened a moment ago was that our fierce little fighters were sent through the open ports and ventilators of the *Gabriel*. Once inside, it is probable that they stung everybody on the ship, and that those stung collapsed with half-paralyzed nervous systems. Naturally, I don't know why the ship fell and then exploded. However, that makes it unnecessary for us to board the ship from a balloon which Zugu had powered with a motor."

"You wogs think of everything, don't you?"

Fobo shrugged. "We are peaceful . . . but, unlike you Terrans, we are really 'realists.' If we have to take action against vermin, we exterminate them. On this insect-ridden planet we have had a long history of battling vermin."

He looked at Macneff, who was on all fours, eyes glazed, shaking his head like a wounded bear.

Fobo said, "I do not include you in that vermin, Hal. You are free to go where you want."

Hal sat down again and croaked, "What is there left for me?"

"Plenty, man." Tears ran down Fobo's nose and collected at the end. "You have your daughters to care for, to love. In a few days they will be through with their feeding in the incubator—they survived the Caesarean quite well—and will be beautiful babies. They will be yours as much as any human infants could be. After all, they look like you—in a modified feminine way, of course. Your genes are theirs. What's the difference whether genes act by cellular or photonic means? Genes are genes.

"And there will be women for you. You forget that she has aunts and sisters. All young and beautiful."

"Thanks, Fobo, but that's not for me." He buried his face in his hands.

A nurse stuck her head out of the door of the operating room.

"Doctor Fobo, we are bringing the body out. Does the man care to look?"

Without removing his hands, Hal shook his head.

Two nurses wheeled the carrier out. A white sheet was draped over the form. It clung to the superb curves of the shell beneath.

Hal did not look up.

He moaned, "Jeannette! Jeannette!"

ANDRE NORTON (1912-)

The prolific and widely talented Andre Norton began her young adulthood as a librarian in Cleveland, Ohio, during the early years of the Great Depression. Her love and talent for research are subsequently found in most of her writing. In the 1950s, 1960s, and 1970s, Norton was primarily a Science Fiction author. Since then, she has written mostly Fantasy. However, in recent decades, Norton has also been quite versatile, writing Science Fiction, High Fantasies, Dark Fantasies, and more.

Like Katherine MacLean and other women Science Fiction authors from the 1950s, Andre Norton published some of her first stories under male pseudonyms. Formulas and themes of her stories include Space Opera, Heroic Fantasy, magic, quest for self, and maturity of self. Norton has been an important editor and anthologist of Fantasy and Science Fiction of the second half of the twentieth century. She has also co-written several novels in recent years, including a sequel to Robert Louis Stevenson's The Strange Case of Dr. Jekyll and Mr. Hyde *(1886) entitled* The Jekyll Legacy *(1990) with Robert Bloch.*

"Mousetrap" is both Science Fiction and a humorous, ironic folk tale. It is the kind of story Damon Runyon would have written if he wrote Science Fiction. It is also highly reminiscent of Lord Dunsany's Jorkens stories of the first half of the twentieth century and of Robert Bloch's Lefty Feep stories published in Fantastic Adventures *in the 1940s.*

Mousetrap

(The Magazine of Fantasy and Science Fiction, *June 1954)*

Remember that old adage about the man who built a better mouse trap and then could hardly cope with the business which beat a state highway to his door? I saw that happen once — on Mars.

Sam Levatts was politely introduced — for local color — by the tourist guides as a "desert spider." "Drunken bum" would have been the more exact term. He prospected over and through the dry lands out of Terraport and brought in Star Stones, Gormel ore, and like knickknacks to keep him sodden and mostly content. In his highly scented stupors he dreamed dreams and saw visions. At least his muttered description of the "lovely lady" was taken to be a vision, since there are no ladies in the Terraport dives he frequented and the females met there are far from lovely.

But Sam continued a peaceful dreamer until he met Len Collins and Operation Mousetrap began.

Every dumb tourist who steps into a scenic sandmobile at Terraport has heard of the "sand monsters." Those which still remain intact are now all the property of the tourist bureaus. And, brother, they're guarded as if they were a part of that cache of Martian royal jewels Black Spragg stumbled on twenty years ago. Because the monsters, which can withstand the dust storms, the extremes of desert cold and heat, crumble away if so much as a human finger tip is poked into their ribs.

Nowadays you are allowed to get within about twenty feet of the "Spider Man" or the "Armed Frog" and that's all. Try to edge a little closer and you'll get a shock that'll lay you flat on your back with your toes pointing Earthwards.

And, ever since the first monster went drifting off as a puff of dust under someone's hands, the museums back home have been adding to the cash award waiting for the fellow who can cement them for transportation. By the time Len Collins met Sam that award could be quoted in stellar figures.

Of course, all the bright boys in the glue, spray and plastic business had been taking a crack at the problem for years. The frustrating answer being that when they stepped out of the rocket over here, all steamed up about the stickability of their new product, they had nothing to prove it on. Not one of the known monsters was available for testing purposes. Every one is insured, guarded, and under the personal protection of the Space Marines.

But Len Collins had no intention of trying to reach one of these treasures. Instead he drifted into Sam's favorite lapping ground and set them up for Levatts—three times in succession. At the end of half an hour Sam thought he had discovered the buddy of his heart. And on the fifth round he spilled his wild tale about the lovely lady who lived in the shelter of two red rocks—far away—a vague wave of the hand suggesting the general direction.

Len straightway became a lover of beauty panting to behold this supreme treat. And he stuck to Sam that night closer than a Moonman to his oxy-supply. The next morning they both disappeared from Terraport in a private sandmobile hired by Len.

Two weeks later Collins slunk into town again and booked passage back to New York. He clung to the port hotel, never sticking his head out of the door until it was time to scuttle to the rocket.

Sam showed up in the Flame Bird four nights later. He had a nasty sand burn down his jaw and he could hardly keep his feet for lack of sleep. He was also—for the first time in Martian history—cold and deadly sober. And he sat there all evening drinking nothing stronger than Sparkling Canal Water. Thereby shocking some kindred souls half out of their wits.

What TV guy doesn't smell a story in a quick change like that? I'd be running the dives every night for a week—trying to pick up some local color for our 6 o'clock casting. And the most exciting and promising thing I had come across so far was Sam's sudden change of beverage. Strictly off the record—we cater to the family and tourist public mostly—I started to do a little picking and prying. Sam answered most of my feelers with grunts.

Then I hit pay dirt with the casual mention that the Three Planets Travel crowd had picked up another shocked cement dealer near their pet monster, "The Ant King." Sam rolled a mouthful of the Sparkling Water around his tongue, swallowed with a face to frighten all monsters, and asked a question of his own.

"Where do these here science guys think all the monsters come from?"

I shrugged. "No explanation that holds water. They can't examine them closely without destroying them. That's one reason for the big award awaiting any guy who can glue them together so they'll stand handling."

Sam pulled something from under the pocket flap of his spacealls. It was a picture, snapped in none too good a light, but clear enough.

Two large rocks curved toward each other to form an almost perfect archway and in their protection stood a woman. At least her slender body had the distinctly graceful curves we have come to associate with the stronger half of the race. But she also had wings, outspread in a grand sweep as if she stood on tiptoe almost ready to take off. There were only the hints of features—that gave away the secret of what she really was—because none of the sand monsters ever showed clear features.

"Where—?" I began.

Sam spat. "Nowhere now." He was grim, and his features had tightened up. He looked about ten years younger and a darn sight tougher.

"I found her two years ago. And I kept going back just to look at her. She wasn't a monster like the rest of 'em. She was perfect. Then that—" Sam lapsed into some of the finest space-searing language I have ever been privileged to hear—"that Collins got me drunk enough to show him where she was. He knocked me out, sprayed her with his goo, and tried to load her into the back of the 'mobile. It didn't work. She held together for about five minutes and then—" He snapped his fingers. "Dust just like 'em all!"

I found myself studying the picture for a second time. And I was beginning to wish I had Collins alone for about three minutes or so. Most of the sand images I had seen I could cheerfully do without—they were all nightmare material. But, as Sam had pointed out, this was no monster. And it was the only one of its type I had ever seen or heard about. Maybe there might just be another somewhere— the desert dry lands haven't been one quarter explored.

Sam nodded as if he had caught that thought of mine right out of the smoky air.

"Won't do any harm to look. I've noticed one thing about all of the monsters— they are found only near the rocks. Red rocks like these," he tapped the snapshot, "that have a sort of blue-green moss growin' on 'em." His eyes focused on the wall but I had an idea that he was seeing beyond it, beyond all the sand barrier walls in Terraport, out into the dry lands. And I guessed that he wasn't telling all he knew—or suspected.

I couldn't forget that picture. The next night I was back at the Flame Bird. But Sam didn't show. Instead rumor had it that he had loaded up with about two months' supplies and had gone back to the desert. And that was the last I heard of him for weeks. Only, his winged woman had crept into my dreams and I hated Collins. The picture was something—but I would have given a month's credits— interstellar at that—to have seen the original.

During the next year Sam made three long trips out, keeping quiet about his discoveries, if any. He stopped drinking and he was doing better financially. Actually brought in two green Star Stones, the sale of which covered most of his expenses for the year. And he continued to take an interest in the monsters and the eternal quest for the fixative. Two of the rocket pilots told me that he was sending to Earth regularly for everything published on the subject.

Gossip had already labeled him "sand happy." I almost believed that after I met him going out of town one dawn. He was in his prospector's crawler and strapped up in plain sight on top of his water tanks was one of the damnedest contraptions I'd ever seen—a great big wire cage!

I did a double take at the thing when he slowed down to say good-by. He saw my bug-eyes and answered their protrusion with a grin, a wicked one.

"Gonna bring me back a sand mouse, fella. A smart man can learn a lot from just watchin' a sand mouse, he sure can!"

Martian sand mice may live in the sand—popularly they're supposed to eat and drink the stuff, too—but they are nowhere near like their Terran namesakes. And nobody with any brains meddles with a sand mouse. I almost dismissed Sam as hopeless then and there and wondered what form the final crack-up would take. But when he came back into town a couple of weeks later—minus the cage—he was still grinning. If Sam had held any grudge against me, I wouldn't have cared for that grin—not one bit!

Then Len Collins came back. And he started in right away at his old tricks—hanging around the dives listening to prospectors' talk. Sam had stayed in town and I caught up with them both at the Flame Bird, as thick as thieves over one table, Sam lapping up imported rye as if it were Canal Water and Len giving him cat at the mouse hole attention.

To my surprise Sam hailed me and pulled out a third stool at the table, insisting that I join them—much to Collins' annoyance. But I'm thick-skinned when I think I'm on the track of a story and I stuck. Stuck to hear Sam spill his big secret. He had discovered a new monster, one which so far surpassed the winged woman that they couldn't be compared. And Collins sat there licking his chops and almost drooling. I tried to shut Sam up—but I might as well have tried to can a dust storm. And in the end he insisted that I come along on their expedition to view this fabulous wonder. Well, I did.

We took a wind plane instead of a sandmobile. Collins was evidently in the chips and wanted speed. Sam piloted us. I noticed then, if Collins didn't, that Sam was a lot less drunk than he had been when he spilled his guts in the Flame Bird. And, noting that, I relaxed some—feeling a bit happier about the whole affair.

The red rocks we were hunting stood out like fangs—a whole row of them—rather nasty looking. From the air there was no sign of any image, but then those were mostly found in the shadow of such rocks and might not be visible from above. Sam landed the plane and we slipped and slid through the shin-deep sand.

Sam was skidding around more than was necessary and he was muttering. Once he sang—in a rather true baritone—just playing the souse again. However, we followed along without question.

Collins dragged with him a small tank which had a hose attachment. And he was so eager that he fairly crowded on Sam's heels all the way. When at last Sam stopped short he slid right into him. But Sam apparently didn't even notice the bump. He was pointing ahead and grinning fatuously.

I looked along the line indicated by his finger, eager to see another winged woman or something as good. But there was nothing even faintly resembling a monster—unless you could count a lump of greenish stuff puffed up out of the sand a foot or so.

"Well, where is it?" Collins had fallen to one knee and had to put down his spray gun while he got up.

"Right there." Sam was still pointing to that greenish lump.

Collins' face had been wind-burned to a tomato red but now it darkened to a dusky purple as he stared at that repulsive hump.

"You fool!" Only he didn't say "fool." He lurched forward and kicked that lump, kicked it good and hard.

At the same time Sam threw himself flat on the ground and, having planted one of his oversize paws between my shoulders, took me with him. I bit into a mouthful of grit and sand and struggled wildly. But Sam's hand held me pinned tightly to the earth—as if I were a laboratory bug on a slide.

There was a sort of muffled exclamation, followed by an odd choking sound, from over by the rocks. But, in spite of my squirming, Sam continued to keep me more or less blindfolded. When he at last released me I was burning mad and came up with my fists ready. Only Sam wasn't there to land on. He was standing over by the rocks, his hands on his hips, surveying something with an open and proud satisfaction.

Because now there *was* a monster in evidence, a featureless anthropoidic figure of reddish stuff. Not as horrible as some I'd seen, but strange enough.

"Now—let's see if his goo does work this time!"

Sam took up the can briskly, pointed the hose tip at the monster, and let fly with a thin stream of pale bluish vapor, washing it all over that half-crouched thing.

"But—" I was still spitting sand between my teeth and only beginning to realize what must have happened. "Is that—that *thing*—"

"Collins? Yeah. He shouldn't have shown his temper that way. He kicked just once too often. That's what he did to her when she started to crumple, so I counted on him doing it again. Only, disturb one of those puff balls and get the stuff that's inside them on you and—presto—a monster! I got on to it when I was being chased by a sand mouse a couple of months back. The bugger got too close to one of those things—thinking more about dinner than danger, I guess—and whamoo! Hunted me up another mouse and another puff ball—just to be on the safe side. Same thing again. So—here we are! Say, Jim, I think this *is* going to work!" He had drawn one finger along the monster's outstretched arm and nothing happened. It still stood solid.

"Then all those monsters must once have been alive!" I shivered a little, remembering a few of them.

Sam nodded. "Maybe they weren't all natives of Mars—too many different kinds have been found. Terra was probably not the first to land a rocket here. Certainly the antmen and that big frog never lived together. Some day I'm going to get me a stellar ship and go out to look for the world my lady came from. This thin air could never have supported her wings.

"Now, Jim, if you'll just give me a hand, we'll get this work of art back to Terraport. How many million credits are the science guys offering if one is brought back in one piece?"

He was so businesslike about it that I simply did as he asked. And he collected from the scientists all right—collected enough to buy his stellar ship. He's out there now, prospecting along the Milky Way, hunting his winged lady. And the unique monster is in the Interplanetary Museum to be gaped at by all the tourists. Me—I avoid red rocks, green puff balls, and never, never kick at objects of my displeasure—it's healthier that way.

ALFRED BESTER (1913–1987)

As did writers Philip José Farmer and Willy Ley, and artists Virgil Finlay, Hannes Bok, and Ed Emshwiller, Alfred Bester received one of the first Hugo Awards in 1953. He earned this citation for Best Science Fiction Novel of 1952. This novel, a Science Fiction Murder Mystery in the best traditions of Fredric Brown, is entitled The Demolished Man.*

Alfred Bester was a lifelong resident of Manhattan. New York and popular culture flowed through his veins. He was the author of pulp magazine fiction, comic book stories [specifically D.C.'s (Detective Comics) Superman, Batman, *and* Green Lantern *series], radio dramas (for such series as* Nick Carter, Charlie Chan, *and* The Shadow*), television scripts (for* Tom Corbett: Space Cadet*), and much more. Bester consciously and meticulously outlined, plotted, and revised his stories — he was a student and successful purveyor of formula fiction. He directly influenced James Blish (pseudonym for William Atheling Jr.) and Samuel R. Delany.*

"Fondly Fahrenheit" is a classic Alfred Bester story. Like The Demolished Man, *it is an ingenious blend of Murder Mystery and Science Fiction. It features the tightly woven plotting of the best of Arthur Conan Doyle's Sherlock Holmes stories and the riveting Hard Science Fiction of Hal Clement.*

Fondly Fahrenheit

(The Magazine of Fantasy and Science Fiction, *August 1954*)

He doesn't know which of us I am these days, but they know one truth. You must own nothing but yourself. You must make your own life, live your own life and die your own death . . . or else you will die another's.

The rice fields on Paragon III stretch for hundreds of miles like checkerboard tundras, a blue and brown mosaic under a burning sky of orange. In the evening, clouds whip like smoke, and the paddies rustle and murmur.

A long line of men marched across the paddies the evening we escaped from Paragon III. They were silent, armed, intent; a long rank of silhouetted statues looming against the smoking sky. Each man carried a gun. Each man wore a walkie-talkie belt pack, the speaker button in his ear, the microphone bug clipped to his throat, the glowing viewscreen strapped to his wrist like a green-eyed watch. The multitude of screens showed nothing but a multitude of individual paths through the paddies. The annunciators uttered no sound but the rustle and splash of steps. The men spoke infrequently, in heavy grunts, all speaking to all.

"Nothing here."

"Where's here?"

"Jenson's fields."

"You're drifting too far west."

"Close in the line there."

"Anybody covered the Grimson paddy?"

"Yeah. Nothing."

"She couldn't have walked this far."

"Could have been carried."

"Think she's alive?"

"Why should she be dead?"

The slow refrain swept up and down the long line of beaters advancing toward the smoky sunset. The line of beaters wavered like a writhing snake, but never ceased its remorseless advance. One hundred men spaced fifty feet apart. Five thousand feet of ominous search. One mile of angry determination stretching from east to west across a compass of heat. Evening fell. Each man lit his search lamp. The writhing snake was transformed into a necklace of wavering diamonds.

"Clear here. Nothing."

"Nothing here."

"Nothing."

"What about the Allen paddies?"

"Covering them now."

"Think we missed her?"

"Maybe."

"We'll beat back and check."

"This'll be an all-night job."

"Allen paddies clear."

"God damn! We've got to find her!"

"We'll find her."

"Here she is. Sector seven. Tune in."

The line stopped. The diamonds froze in the heat. There was silence. Each man gazed into the glowing green screen on his wrist, tuning to sector seven. All tuned to one. All showed a small nude figure awash in the muddy water of a paddy. Alongside the figure an owner's stake of bronze read: VANDALEUR. The ends of the line converged toward the Vandaleur field. The necklace turned into a cluster of stars. One hundred men gathered around a small nude body, a child dead in a rice paddy. There was no water in her mouth. There were fingermarks on her throat. Her innocent face was battered. Her body was torn. Clotted blood on her skin was crusted and hard.

"Dead three-four hours at least."

"Her mouth is dry."

"She wasn't drowned. Beaten to death."

In the dark evening heat the men swore softly. They picked up the body. One stopped the others and pointed to the child's fingernails. She had fought her murderer. Under the nails were particles of flesh and bright drops of scarlet blood, still liquid, still uncoagulated.

"That blood ought to be clotted, too."

"Funny."

"Not so funny. What kind of blood don't clot?"

"Android."

"Looks like she was killed by one."

"Vandaleur owns an android."

"She couldn't be killed by an android."

"That's android blood under her nails."

"The police better check."

"The police'll prove I'm right."

"But andys can't kill."

"That's android blood, ain't it?"

"Androids can't kill. They're made that way."

"Looks like one android was made wrong."

"Jesus!"

And the thermometer that day registered 92.9° gloriously Fahrenheit.

So there we were aboard the *Paragon Queen* enroute for Megaster V, James Vandaleur and his android. James Vandaleur counted his money and wept. In the second-class cabin with him was his android, a magnificent synthetic creature with classic features and wide blue eyes. Raised on its forehead in a cameo of flesh were the letters MA, indicating that this was one of the rare multiple-aptitude androids, worth $57,000 on the current exchange. There we were, weeping and counting and calmly watching.

"Twelve, fourteen, sixteen. Sixteen hundred dollars," Vandaleur wept. "That's all. Sixteen hundred dollars. My house was worth ten thousand. The land was worth five. There was furniture, cars, my paintings, etchings, my plane, my—And nothing to show for everything but sixteen hundred dollars. Christ!"

I leaped up from the table and turned on the android. I pulled a strap from one of the leather bags and beat the android. It didn't move.

"I must remind you," the android said, "that I am worth fifty-seven thousand dollars on the current exchange. I must warn you that you are endangering valuable property."

"You damned crazy machine," Vandaleur shouted.

"I am not a machine," the android answered. "The robot is a machine. The android is a chemical creation of synthetic tissue."

"What got into you?" Vandaleur cried. "Why did you do it? Damn you!" He beat the android savagely.

"I must remind you that I cannot be punished," I said. "The pleasure-pain syndrome is not incorporated in the android synthesis."

"Then why did you kill her?" Vandaleur shouted. "If it wasn't for kicks, why did you—"

"I must remind you," the android said, "that the second-class cabins in these ships are not soundproofed."

Vandaleur dropped the strap and stood panting, staring at the creature he owned.

"Why did you do it? Why did you kill her?" I asked.

"I don't know," I answered.

"First it was malicious mischief. Small things. Petty destruction. I should have known there was something wrong with you then. Androids can't destroy. They can't harm. They—"

"There is no pleasure-pain syndrome incorporated in the android synthesis."

"Then it got to arson. Then serious destruction. The assault . . . that engineer on Rigel. Each time worse. Each time we had to get out faster. Now it's murder. Christ! What's the matter with you? What's happened?"

"There are no self-check relays incorporated in the android brain."

"Each time we had to get out it was a step downhill. Look at me. In a second-class cabin. Me. James Paleologue Vandaleur. There was a time when my father was the wealthiest—Now, sixteen hundred dollars in the world. That's all I've got. And you. Christ damn you!"

Vandaleur raised the strap to beat the android again, then dropped it and collapsed on a berth, sobbing. At last he pulled himself together.

"Instructions," he said.

The multiple android responded at once. It arose and awaited orders.

"My name is now Valentine. James Valentine. I stopped off on Paragon III for only one day to transfer to this ship for Megaster V. My occupation: Agent for one privately owned MA android which is for hire. Purpose of visit: To settle on Megaster V. Fix the papers."

The android removed Vandaleur's passport and papers from a bag, got pen and ink and sat down at the table. With an accurate, flawless hand—an accomplished hand that could draw, write, paint, carve, engrave, etch, photograph, design, create, and build—it meticulously forged new credentials for Vandaleur. Its owner watched me miserably.

"Create and build," I muttered, "And now destroy. Oh God! What am I going to do? Christ! If I could only get rid of you. If I didn't have to live off you. God! If only I'd inherited some guts instead of you."

Dallas Brady was Megaster's leading jewelry designer. She was short, stocky, amoral, and a nymphomaniac. She hired Vandaleur's multiple-aptitude android and put me to work in her shop. She seduced Vandaleur. In her bed one night, she asked abruptly, "Your name's Vandaleur, isn't it?"

"Yes," I murmured. Then: "No! It's Valentine. James Valentine."

"What happened on Paragon?" Dallas Brady asked. "I thought androids couldn't kill or destroy property. Prime Directives and Inhibitions set up for them when they're synthesized. Every company guarantees they can't."

"Valentine!" Vandaleur insisted.

"Oh come off it," Dallas Brady said. "I've known for a week. I haven't hollered copper, have I?"

"The name is Valentine."

"You want to prove it? You want I should call the cops?" Dallas reached out and picked up the phone.

"For God's sake, Dallas!" Vandaleur leaped up and struggled to take the phone from her. She fended him off, laughing at him, until he collapsed and wept in shame and helplessness.

"How did you find out?" he asked at last.

"The papers are full of it. And Valentine was a little too close to Vandaleur. That wasn't smart, was it?"

"I guess not. I'm not very smart."

"Your android's got quite a record, hasn't it? Assault. Arson. Destruction. What happened on Paragon?"

"It kidnapped a child. Took her out into the rice fields and murdered her."

"Raped her?"

"I don't know."

"They're going to catch up with you."

"Don't I know it? Christ! We've been running for two years now. Seven planets in two years. I must have abandoned fifty thousand dollars' worth of property in two years."

"You better find out what's wrong with it."

"How can I? Can I walk into a repair clinic and ask for an overhaul? What am I going to say? 'My android's just turned killer. Fix it.' They'd call the police right off." I began to shake. "They'd have that android dismantled inside one day. I'd probably be booked as accessory to murder."

"Why didn't you have it repaired before it got to murder?"

"I couldn't take the chance," Vandaleur explained angrily. "If they started fooling around with lobotomies and body chemistry and endocrine surgery, they might have destroyed its aptitudes. What would I have left to hire out? How would I live?"

"You could work yourself. People do."

"Work at what? You know I'm good for nothing. How could I compete with specialist androids and robots? Who can, unless he's got a terrific talent for a particular job?"

"Yeah. That's true."

"I lived off my old man all my life. Damn him! He had to go bust just before he died. Left me the android and that's all. The only way I can get along is living off what it earns."

"You better sell it before the cops catch up with you. You can live off fifty grand. Invest it."

"At three percent? Fifteen hundred a year? When the android returns fifteen percent on its value? Eight thousand a year. That's what it earns. No, Dallas. I've got to go along with it."

"What are you going to do about its violence kick?"

"I can't do anything . . . except watch it and pray. What are you going to do about it?"

"Nothing. It's none of my business. Only one thing. . . . I ought to get something for keeping my mouth shut."

"What?"

"The android works for me for free. Let somebody else pay you, but I get it for free."

The multiple-aptitude android worked. Vandaleur collected its fees. His expenses were taken care of. His savings began to mount. As the warm spring of Megaster V turned to hot summer, I began investigating farms and properties. It would be possible, within a year or two, for us to settle down permanently, provided Dallas Brady's demands did not become rapacious.

On the first hot day of summer, the android began singing in Dallas Brady's workshop. It hovered over the electric furnace which, along with the weather, was broiling the shop, and sang an ancient tune that had been popular half a century before.

Oh, it's no feat to beat the heat.
All reet! All reet!
So jeet your seat
Be fleet be fleet
Cool and discreet
Honey . . .

It sang in a strange, halting voice, and its accomplished fingers were clasped behind its back, writhing in a strange rumba all their own. Dallas Brady was surprised.

"You happy or something?" she asked.

"I must remind you that the pleasure-pain syndrome is not incorporated in the android synthesis," I answered. "All reet! All reet! Be fleet be fleet, cool and discreet, honey . . ."

Its fingers stopped their writhing and picked up a heavy pair of iron tongs. The android poked them into the glowing heart of the furnace, leaning far forward to peer into the lovely heat.

"Be careful, you damned fool!" Dallas Brady exclaimed. "You want to fall in?"

"I must remind you that I am worth fifty-seven thousand dollars on the current exchange," I said. "It is forbidden to endanger valuable property. All reet! All reet! Honey . . ."

It withdrew a crucible of glowing gold from the electric furnace, turned, capered hideously, sang crazily, and splashed a sluggish gobbet of molten gold over Dallas Brady's head. She screamed and collapsed, her hair and clothes flaming, her skin crackling. The android poured again while it capered and sang.

"Be fleet be fleet, cool and discreet, honey . . ." It sang and slowly poured and poured the molten gold. Then I left the workshop and rejoined James Vandaleur in his hotel suite. The android's charred clothes and squirming fingers warned its owner that something was very much wrong.

Vandaleur rushed to Dallas Brady's workshop, stared once, vomited, and fled. I had enough time to pack one bag and raise nine hundred dollars on portable assets. He took a third-class cabin on the *Megaster Queen*, which left that morning for Lyra Alpha. He took me with him. He wept and counted his money and I beat the android again.

And the thermometer in Dallas Brady's workshop registered 98.1° beautifully Fahrenheit.

On Lyra Alpha we holed up in a small hotel near the university. There, Vandaleur carefully bruised my forehead until the letters MA were obliterated by the swelling and the discoloration. The letter would reappear again, but not for several months, and in the meantime Vandaleur hoped the hue and cry for an MA android would be forgotten. The android was hired out as a common laborer in the university power plant. Vandaleur, as James Venice, eked out life on the android's small earnings.

I wasn't too unhappy. Most of the other residents in the hotel were university students, equally hard-up, but delightfully young and enthusiastic. There was one charming girl with sharp eyes and a quick mind. Her name was Wanda, and she and her beau, Jed Stark, took a tremendous interest in the killing android which was being mentioned in every paper in the galaxy.

"We've been studying the case," she and Jed said at one of the casual student parties which happened to be held this night in Vandaleur's room. "We think we know what's causing it. We're going to do a paper." They were in a high state of excitement.

"Causing what?" somebody wanted to know.

"The android rampage."

"Obviously out of adjustment, isn't it? Body chemistry gone haywire. Maybe a kind of synthetic cancer, yes?"

"No." Wanda gave Jed a look of suppressed triumph.

"Well, what is it?"

"Something specific."

"What?"

"That would be telling."

"Oh come on."

"Nothing doing."

"Won't you tell us?" I asked intently. "I . . . We're very much interested in what could go wrong with an android."

"No, Mr. Venice," Wanda said. "It's a unique idea and we've got to protect it. One thesis like this and we'll be set up for life. We can't take the chance of somebody stealing it."

"Can't you give us a hint?"

"No. Not a hint. Don't say a word, Jed. But I'll tell you this much, Mr. Venice. I'd hate to be the man who owns that android."

"You mean the police?" I asked.

"I mean projection, Mr. Venice. Projection! That's the danger . . . and I won't say any more. I've said too much as is."

I heard steps outside, and a hoarse voice singing softly: "Be fleet be fleet cool and discreet, honey . . ." My android entered the room, home from its tour of duty at the university power plant. It was not introduced. I motioned to it and I immediately responded to the command and went to the beer keg and took over Vandaleur's job of serving the guests. Its accomplished fingers writhed in a private rumba of their own. Gradually they stopped their squirming, and the strange humming ended.

Androids were not unusual at the university. The wealthier students owned them along with cars and planes. Vandaleur's android provoked no comment, but young Wanda was sharp-eyed and quick-witted. She noted my bruised forehead and she was intent on the history-making thesis she and Jed Stark were going to write. After the party broke up, she consulted with Jed walking upstairs to her room.

"Jed, why'd that android have a bruised forehead?"

"Probably hurt itself, Wanda. It's working in the power plant. They fling a lot of heavy stuff around."

"That all?"

"What else?"

"It could be a convenient bruise."

"Convenient for what?"

"Hiding what's stamped on its forehead."

"No point to that, Wanda. You don't have to see marks on a forehead to recognize an android. You don't have to see a trademark on a car to know it's a car."

"I don't mean it's trying to pass as a human. I mean it's trying to pass as a lower-grade android."

"Why?"

"Suppose it had 'MA' on its forehead."

"Multiple aptitude? Then why in hell would Venice waste it stoking furnaces if it could earn more—Oh. Oh! You mean it's—?"

Wanda nodded.

"Jesus!" Stark pursed his lips. "What do we do? Call the police?"

"No. We don't know if it's an MA for a fact. If it turns out to be an MA and the killing android, our paper comes first anyway. This is our big chance, Jed. If it's *that* android we can run a series of controlled tests and—"

"How do we find out for sure?"

"Easy. Infrared film. That'll show what's under the bruise. Borrow a camera. Buy some film. We'll sneak down to the power plant tomorrow afternoon and take some pictures. Then we'll know."

They stole down into the university power plant the following afternoon. It was a vast cellar, deep under the earth. It was dark, shadowy, luminous with burning light from the furnace doors. Above the roar of the fires they could hear a strange voice shouting and chanting in the echoing vault: "All reet! All reet! So jeet your seat. Be fleet be fleet, cool and discreet, honey . . ." And they could see a capering figure dancing a lunatic rumba in time to the music it shouted. The legs twisted. The arms waved. The fingers writhed.

Jed Stark raised the camera and began shooting his spool of infrared film, aiming the camera sights at that bobbing head. Then Wanda shrieked, for I saw them and came charging down on them, brandishing a polished steel shovel. It smashed the camera. It felled the girl and then the boy. Jed fought me for a desperate hissing moment before he was bludgeoned into helplessness. Then the android dragged them to the furnace and fed them to the flames, slowly, hideously. It capered and sang. Then it returned to my hotel.

The thermometer in the power plant registered 100.9° murderously Fahrenheit. All reet! All reet!

We bought steerage on *Lyra Queen* and Vandaleur and the android did odd jobs for their meals. During the night watches, Vandaleur would sit alone in the steerage head with a cardboard portfolio on his lap, puzzling over its contents. That portfolio was all he had managed to bring with him from Lyra Alpha. He had stolen it from Wanda's room. It was labeled ANDROID. It contained the secret of my sickness.

And it contained nothing but newspapers. Scores of newspapers from all over the galaxy, printed, microfilmed, engraved, etched, offset, photostated . . . Rigel *Star-Banner* . . . Paragon *Picayune* . . . Megaster *Times-Leader* . . . Lalande *Herald* . . . Lacaille *Journal* . . . Indi *Intelligencer* . . . Eridani *Telegram-News*. All reet! All reet!

Nothing but newspapers. Each paper contained an account of one crime in the android's ghastly career. Each paper also contained news, domestic and foreign, sports, society, weather, shipping news, stock exchange quotations, human interest stories, features, contests, puzzles. Somewhere in that mass of uncollated facts was the secret Wanda and Jed Stark had discovered. Vandaleur pored over the papers helplessly. It was beyond him. So jeet your seat!

"I'll sell you," I told the android. "Damn you. When we land on Terra, I'll sell you. I'll settle for three percent on whatever you're worth."

"I am worth fifty-seven thousand dollars on the current exchange," I told him.

"If I can't sell you, I'll turn you in to the police," I said.

"I am valuable property," I answered. "It is forbidden to endanger valuable property. You won't have me destroyed."

"Christ damn you!" Vandaleur cried. "What? Are you arrogant? Do you know you can trust me to protect you? Is that the secret?"

The multiple-aptitude android regarded him with calm accomplished eyes. "Sometimes," it said, "it is a good thing to be property."

It was three below zero when the *Lyra Queen* dropped at Croydon Field. A mixture of ice and snow swept across the field, fizzing and exploding into steam under the *Queen's* tail jets. The passengers trotted numbly across the blackened concrete to customs inspection, and thence to the airport bus that was to take them to London. Vandaleur and the android were broke. They walked.

By midnight they reached Piccadilly Circus. The December ice storm had not slackened, and the statue of Eros was encrusted with ice. They turned right, walked down to Trafalgar Square and then along the Strand shaking with cold and wet. Just above Fleet Street, Vandaleur saw a solitary figure coming from the direction of St. Paul's. He drew the android into an alley.

"We've got to have money," he whispered. He pointed at the approaching figure. "He has money. Take it from him."

"The order cannot be obeyed," the android said.

"Take it from him," Vandaleur repeated. "By force. Do you understand? We're desperate."

"It is contrary to my prime directive," I said. "I cannot endanger life or property. The order cannot be obeyed."

"For God's sake!" Vandaleur burst out. "You've attacked, destroyed, murdered. Don't gibber about prime directives. You haven't any left. Get his money. Kill him if you have to. I tell you, we're desperate!"

"It is contrary to my prime directive," I said. "I cannot endanger life or property. The order cannot be obeyed."

I thrust the android back and leaped out at the stranger. He was tall, austere, competent. He had an air of hope curdled by cynicism. He carried a cane. I saw he was blind.

"Yes?" he said. "I hear you near me. What is it?"

"Sir . . ." Vandaleur hesitated. "I'm desperate."

"We are all desperate," the stranger replied. "Quietly desperate."

"Sir . . . I've got to have some money."

"Are you begging or stealing?" The sightless eyes passed over Vandaleur and the android.

"I'm prepared for either."

"Ah. So are we all. It is the history of our race." The stranger motioned over his shoulder. "I have been begging at St. Paul's, my friend. What I desire cannot be stolen. What is it you desire that you are lucky enough to be able to steal?"

"Money," Vandaleur said.

"Money for what? Come, my friend, let us exchange confidences. I will tell you why I beg if you tell me why you steal. My name is Blenheim."

"My name is . . . Vole."

"I was not begging for sight at St. Paul's, Mr. Vole. I was begging for a number."

"A number?"

"Ah yes. Numbers rational, numbers irrational, numbers imaginary. Positive integers. Negative integers. Fractions, positive and negative. Eh? You have never heard of Blenheim's immortal treatise on Twenty Zeros, or The Differences in Absence of Quantity?" Blenheim smiled bitterly. "I am the wizard of the Theory of Number, Mr. Vole, and I have exhausted the charm of Number for myself. After fifty years of wizardry, senility approaches and the appetite vanishes. I have been praying in St. Paul's for inspiration. Dear God, I prayed, if You exist, send me a number."

Vandaleur slowly lifted the cardboard portfolio and touched Blenheim's hand with it. "In here," he said, "is a number. A hidden number. A secret number. The number of a crime. Shall we exchange, Mr. Blenheim? Shelter for a number?"

"Neither begging nor stealing, eh?" Blenheim said. "But a bargain. So all life reduces itself to the banal." The sightless eyes again passed over Vandaleur and the android. "Perhaps the All-Mighty is not God but a merchant. Come home with me."

On the top floor of Blenheim's house we shared a room—two beds, two closets, two washstands, one bathroom. Vandaleur bruised my forehead again and sent me out to find work, and while the android worked, I consulted with Blenheim and read him the papers from the portfolio, one by one. All reet! All reet!

Vandaleur told him so much and no more. He was a student, I said, attempting a thesis on the murdering android. In these papers which he had collected were the facts that would explain the crimes of which Blenheim had heard nothing. There must be a correlation, a number, a statistic, something which would account for my derangement, I explained, and Blenheim was piqued by the mystery, the detective story, the human interest of number.

We examined the papers. As I read them aloud, he listed them and their contents in his blind, meticulous writing. And then I read his notes to him. He listed the papers by type, by typeface, by fact, by fancy, by article, spelling, words, theme, advertising, pictures, subject, politics, prejudices. He analyzed. He studied. He meditated. And we lived together in that top floor, always a little cold, always a little terrified, always a little closer . . . brought together by our fear of it, our hatred between us. Like a wedge driven into a living tree and splitting the trunk, only to be forever incorporated into the scar tissue, we grew together. Vandaleur and the android. Be fleet be fleet!

And one afternoon Blenheim called Vandaleur into his study and displayed his notes. "I think I've found it," he said, "but I can't understand it."

Vandaleur's heart leaped.

"Here are the correlations," Blenheim continued. "In fifty papers there are accounts of the criminal android. What is there, outside the depredations, that is also in fifty papers?"

"I don't know, Mr. Blenheim."

"It was a rhetorical question. Here is the answer. The weather."

"What?"

"The weather." Blenheim nodded. "Each crime was committed on a day when the temperature was above ninety degrees Fahrenheit."

"But that's impossible," Vandaleur exclaimed. "It was cool on Lyra Alpha."

"We have no record of any crime committed on Lyra Alpha. There is no paper."

"No. That's right, I—" Vandaleur was confused. Suddenly he exclaimed."No. You're right. The furnace room. It was hot there. Hot! Of course. My God, yes! That's the answer. Dallas Brady's electric furnace . . . the rice deltas on Paragon. So jeet your seat. Yes. But why? Why? My God, why?"

I came into the house at that moment, and passing the study, saw Vandaleur and Blenheim. I entered, awaiting commands, my multiple aptitudes devoted to service.

"That's the android, eh?" Blenheim said after a long moment.

"Yes," Vandaleur answered, still confused by the discovery. "And that explains why it refused to attack you that night on the Strand. It wasn't hot enough to break the prime directive. Only in the heat . . . The heat, all reet!" He looked at the android. A silent lunatic command passed from man to android. I refused. It is forbidden to endanger life. Vandaleur gestured furiously, then seized Blenheim's shoulders and yanked him back out of his desk chair to the floor. Blenheim shouted once. Vandaleur leaped on him like a tiger, pinning him to the floor and sealing his mouth with one hand.

"Find a weapon," he called to the android.

"It is forbidden to endanger life."

"This is a fight for self-preservation. Bring me a weapon!" He held the squirming mathematician with all his weight. I went at once to a cupboard where I knew a revolver was kept. I checked it. It was loaded with five cartridges. I handed it to

Vandaleur. I took it, rammed the barrel against Blenheim's head and pulled the trigger. He shuddered once.

We had three hours before the cook returned from her day off. We looted the house. We took Blenheim's money and jewels. We packed a bag with clothes. We took Blenheim's notes, destroyed the newspapers; and we left, carefully locking the door behind us. In Blenheim's study we left a pile of crumpled papers under a half inch of burning candle. And we soaked the rug around it with kerosene. No, I did all that. The android refused. I am forbidden to endanger life or property.

All reet!

They took the tubes to Leicester Square, changed trains, and rode to the British Museum. There they got off and went to a small Georgian house just off Russell Square. A shingle in the window read: NAN WEBB, PSYCHOMETRIC CONSULTANT. Vandaleur had made a note of the address some weeks earlier. They went into the house. The android waited in the foyer with the bag. Vandaleur entered Nan Webb's office.

She was a tall woman with gray shingled hair, very fine English complexion, and very bad English legs. Her features were blunt, her expression acute. She nodded to Vandaleur, finished a letter, sealed it and looked up.

"My name," I said, "is Vanderbilt. James Vanderbilt."

"Quite."

"I'm an exchange student at London University."

"Quite."

"I've been researching on the killing android, and I think I've discovered something very interesting. I'd like your advice on it. What is your fee?"

"What is your college at the University?"

"Why?"

"There is a discount for students."

"Merton College."

"That will be two pounds, please."

Vandaleur placed two pounds on the desk and added to the fee Blenheim's notes. "There is a correlation," he said, "between the crimes of the android and the weather. You will note that each crime was committed when the temperature rose above ninety degrees Fahrenheit. Is there a psychometric answer for this?"

Nan Webb nodded, studied the notes for a moment, put down the sheets of paper, and said: "Synesthesia, obviously."

"What?"

"Synesthesia," she repeated. "When a sensation, Mr. Vanderbilt, is interpreted immediately in terms of a sensation from a different sense organ from the one stimulated, it is called synesthesia. For example: A sound stimulus gives rise to a simultaneous sensation of definite color. Or color gives rise to a sensation of taste. Or a light stimulus gives rise to a sensation of sound. There can be confusion or short circuiting of any sensation of taste, smell, pain, pressure, temperature, and so on. D'you understand?"

"I think so."

"Your research has uncovered the fact that the android most probably reacts to temperature stimulus above the ninety-degree level synesthetically. Most probably there is an endocrine response. Probably a temperature linkage with the android adrenal surrogate. High temperature brings about a response of fear, anger, excitement, and violent physical activity . . . all within the province of the adrenal gland."

"Yes. I see. Then if the android were to be kept in cold climates . . ."

"There would be neither stimulus nor response. There would be no crimes. Quite."

"I see. What is projection?"

"How do you mean?"

"Is there any danger of projection with regard to the owner of the android?"

"Very interesting. Projection is a throwing forward. It is the process of throwing out upon another the ideas or impulses that belong to oneself. The paranoid, for example, projects upon others his conflicts and disturbances in order to externalize them. He accuses, directly or by implication, other men of having the very sicknesses with which he is struggling himself."

"And the danger of projection?"

"It is the danger of believing what is implied. If you live with a psychotic who projects his sickness upon you, there is a danger of falling into his psychotic pattern and becoming virtually psychotic yourself. As, no doubt, is happening to you, Mr. Vandaleur."

Vandaleur leaped to his feet.

"You are an ass," Nan Webb went on crisply. She waved the sheets of notes. "This is no exchange student's writing. It's the unique cursive of the famous Blenheim. Every scholar in England knows this blind writing. There is no Merton College at London University. That was a miserable guess. Merton is one of the Oxford colleges. And you, Mr. Vandaleur, are so obviously infected by association with your deranged android . . . by projection, if you will . . . that I hesitate between calling the Metropolitan Police and the Hospital for the Criminally Insane."

I took out the gun and shot her.

Reet!

"Antares II, Alpha Aurigae, Acrux IV, Pollux IX, Rigel Centaurus," Vandaleur said. "They're all cold. Cold as a witch's kiss. Mean temperatures of forty degrees Fahrenheit. Never gets hotter than seventy. We're in business again. Watch that curve."

The multiple-aptitude android swung the wheel with its accomplished hands. The car took the curve sweetly and sped on through the northern marshes, the reeds stretching for miles, brown and dry, under the cold English sky. The sun was sinking swiftly. Overhead, a lone flight of bustards flapped clumsily eastward. High above the flight, a lone helicopter drifted toward home and warmth.

"No more warmth for us," I said. "No more heat. We're safe when we're cold. We'll hole up in Scotland, make a little money, get across to Norway, build a bankroll, and then ship out. We'll settle on Pollux. We're safe. We've licked it. We can live again."

There was a startling *bleep* from overhead, and then a ragged roar: ATTENTION JAMES VANDALEUR AND ANDROID. ATTENTION JAMES VANDALEUR AND ANDROID!"

Vandaleur started and looked up. The lone helicopter was floating above them. From its belly came amplified commands: "YOU ARE SURROUNDED. THE ROAD IS BLOCKED. YOU ARE TO STOP YOUR CAR AT ONCE AND SUBMIT TO ARREST. STOP AT ONCE!"

I looked at Vandaleur for orders.

"Keep driving," Vandaleur snapped.

The helicopter dropped lower: "ATTENTION ANDROID. YOU ARE IN CONTROL OF THE VEHICLE. YOU ARE TO STOP AT ONCE. THIS IS A STATE DIRECTIVE SUPERSEDING ALL PRIVATE COMMANDS."

"What the hell are you doing?" I shouted.

"A state directive supersedes all private commands," the android answered. "I must point out to you that—"

"Get the hell away from the wheel," Vandaleur ordered. I clubbed the android, yanked him sideways, and squirmed over him to the wheel. The car veered off the road in that moment and went churning through the frozen mud and dry reeds. Vandaleur regained control and continued westward through the marshes toward a parallel highway five miles distant.

"We'll beat their goddamned block," he grunted.

The car pounded and surged. The helicopter dropped even lower. A searchlight blazed from the belly of the plane.

"ATTENTION JAMES VANDALEUR AND ANDROID. SUBMIT TO ARREST. THIS IS A STATE DIRECTIVE SUPERSEDING ALL PRIVATE COMMANDS."

"He can't submit," Vandaleur shouted wildly. "There's no one to submit to. He can't and I won't."

"Christ!" I muttered. "We'll beat them yet. We'll beat the block. We'll beat the heat. We'll—"

"I must point out to you," I said, "that I am required by my prime directive to obey state directives which supersede all private commands. I must submit to arrest."

"Who says it's a state directive?" Vandaleur said. "Them? Up in the plane? They've got to show credentials. They've got to prove it's state authority before you submit. How d'you know they're not crooks trying to trick us?"

Holding the wheel with one arm, he reached into his side pocket to make sure the gun was still in place. The car skidded. The tires squealed on frost and reeds. The wheel was wrenched from his grasp and the car yawed up a small hillock and overturned. The motor roared and the wheels screamed. Vandaleur crawled out and dragged the android with him. For the moment we were outside the circle of light boring down from the helicopter. We blundered off into the marsh, into the blackness, into concealment. . . . Vandaleur running with a pounding heart, hauling the android along.

The helicopter circled and soared over the wrecked car, searchlight peering, loudspeaker braying. On the highway we had left, lights appeared as the pursuing and blocking parties gathered and followed radio directions from the plane. Vandaleur and the android continued deeper and deeper into the marsh, working their way toward the parallel road and safety. It was night by now. The sky was a black matte. Not a star showed. The temperature was dropping. A southeast night wind knifed us to the bone.

Far behind there was a dull concussion. Vandaleur turned, gasping. The car's fuel had exploded. A geyser of flame shot up like a lurid fountain. It subsided into a low crater of burning reeds. Whipped by the wind, the distant hem of flame fanned up into a wall, ten feet high. The wall began marching down on us, cracking fiercely. Above it, a pall of oil smoke surged forward. Behind it, Vandaleur could make out the figures of men . . . a mass of beaters searching the marsh.

"Christ!" I cried and searched desperately for safety. He ran, dragging me with him, until their feet crunched through the surface ice of a pool. He trampled the ice furiously, then flung himself down in the numbing water, pulling the android with us.

The wall of flame approached. I could hear the crackle and feel the heat. He could see the searchers clearly. Vandaleur reached into his side pocket for the gun. The pocket was torn. The gun was gone. He groaned and shook with cold and terror. The light from the marsh fire was blinding. Overhead, the helicopter floated helplessly to one side, unable to fly through the smoke and flames and aid the searchers who were beating far to the right of us.

"They'll miss us," Vandaleur whispered. "Keep quiet. That's an order. They'll miss us. We'll beat them. We'll beat the fire. We'll—"

Three distinct shots sounded less than a hundred feet from the fugitives. *Blam! Blam! Blam!* They came from the last three cartridges in my gun as the marsh fire reached it where it had dropped, and exploded the shells. The searchers turned toward the sound and began working directly toward us. Vandaleur cursed hysterically and tried to submerge even deeper to escape the intolerable heat of the fire. The android began to twitch.

The wall of flame surged up to them. Vandaleur took a deep breath and prepared to submerge until the flame passed over them. The android shuddered and burst into an earsplitting scream.

"All reet! All reet!" it shouted. "Be fleet be fleet!"

"Damn you!" I shouted. I tried to drown it.

"Damn you!" I cursed him. I smashed his face.

The android battered Vandaleur, who fought it off until it exploded out of the mud and staggered upright. Before I could return to the attack, the live flames captured it hypnotically. It danced and capered in a lunatic rumba before the wall of fire. Its legs twisted. Its arms waved. The fingers writhed in a private rumba of their own. It shrieked and sang and ran in a crooked waltz before the embrace of the heat, a muddy monster silhouetted against the brilliant sparkling flare.

The searchers shouted. There were shots. The android spun around twice and then continued its horrid dance before the face of the flames. There was a rising gust of wind. The fire swept around the capering figure and enveloped it for a roaring moment. Then the fire swept on, leaving behind it a sobbing mass of synthetic flesh oozing scarlet blood that would never coagulate.

The thermometer would have registered 1200° wondrously Fahrenheit.

Vandaleur didn't die. I got away. They missed him while they watched the android caper and die. But I don't know which of us he is these days. Projection, Wanda warned me. Projection, Nan Webb told him. If you live with a crazy man or a crazy machine long enough, I become crazy too. Reet!

But we know one truth. We know they were wrong. The new robot and Vandaleur know that because the new robot's started twitching too. Reet! Here on cold Pollux, the robot is twitching and singing. No heat, but my fingers writhe. No heat, but it's taken the little Talley girl off for a solitary walk. A cheap labor robot. A servo-mechanism . . . all I could afford . . . but it's twitching and humming and walking alone with the child somewhere and I can't find them. Christ! Vandaleur can't find me before it's too late. Cool and discreet, honey, in the dancing frost while the thermometer registers 10° fondly Fahrenheit.

🔯 MARION ZIMMER BRADLEY (1930–1999)

A versatile and prolific author of Fantasy and Science Fiction, Marion Zimmer Bradley is best remembered for her Heroic Fantasies and Space Operas and her retellings of epic narratives and legends. Bradley often wrote stories that celebrated the plight and ultimate triumph of the underdog. From her entrance into Fantasy and Science Fiction in the mid-1950s until the time of her death, she was a leading feminist and human rights activist. Like many of her female contemporaries in the field, Bradley used male pseudonyms at the beginning of her career. At this time also, she was a great admirer and imitator of C. L. Moore, Henry Kuttner, and Leigh Brackett.

Bradley's contributions to Fantasy and Science Fiction are many, but her most significant are probably her Darkover stories (begun in 1958) and her novel The Mists of Avalon *(1983). The Darkover stories comprise a grand, philosophical Space Opera. The* Mists of Avalon *is one of the most successful and acclaimed retellings of Arthurian legend ever written.*

Depending on the type of fiction she wrote, Marion Zimmer Bradley's stories can be favorably compared to other popular fiction masters. For example, her Heroic Fantasy or Sword and Sorcery stories follow the work of Robert E. Howard and Fritz Leiber; her Space Opera makes for interesting comparison to the work of E. E. "Doc" Smith and Isaac Asimov; and her retelling of classic legends and fairy tales is reflected in some of the stories of Tanith Lee and Jane Yolen.

"Exiles of Tomorrow" is one of Marion Zimmer Bradley's earliest mainstream publications. It provides a unique bend to the classic Time Travel stories of Edward Page Mitchell, Jules Verne, and H. G. Wells.

Exiles of Tomorrow
(Fantastic Universe, *March 1955*)

"A very strange thing happened when I was born," Carey Kennaird told me.

He paused and refilled his wine glass, looking at me with a curious appraisal in his young and very blue eyes. I returned his glance as casually as I could, wondering why he had suddenly decided to confide in me.

I had known Carey Kennaird for only a few weeks. We were the most casual of acquaintances; a word in the lobby of our hotel, a cup of coffee in a lunchroom he liked, mugs of beer in the quiet back room of the corner bar. He was intelligent and I had enjoyed his conversation. But until now it had consisted entirely of surface commonplaces. Today, he seemed to be opening up a trifle.

He had volunteered the information, unasked, that he was the son of a well-known research physicist, and that he was in Chicago to look for his father who had disappeared mysteriously a week or so before. Young Kennaird seemed oddly unworried about his father's plight. But I was pleased at the way his reserve appeared to be dropping.

As I say, Carey Kennaird had a casual way with him, and he puzzled me. He did not, somehow, seem emotionally in sympathy with the hectic tempo of the rushed age in which he had grown up.

"Well," I told him noncommitally, "childhood memories often make quite normal events seem strange. What was it?"

The appraisal in his eyes was franker now. "Mr. Grayne, do you ever read science-fiction?"

"I'm afraid not," I told him. "At least, only very occasionally."

He looked a little crestfallen. "Oh—well, do you know anything about the familiar science-fiction concept of traveling in time?"

"A little." I finished my drink, wishing the waiter would bring us another bottle of wine. "It's supposed to involve some quite staggering paradoxes, I believe. I'm thinking of the man who goes back in time and kills his own grandfather?"

He looked disgusted. "That's at best a trite layman's idea!"

"Well, I'm a layman," I said genially. The arrogance of young people always strikes me as being pathetic rather than insulting. I did not think young Kennaird could have been more than nineteen. Twenty, perhaps. "Now then, young fellow, don't tell me you've actually invented a time machine!"

"Good Lord, no!" The denial was so laughingly spontaneous that I had to laugh with him, "No, just an idea that interests me. I don't really believe there's much paradox involved in time-travel at all."

He paused, his eyes still on my face. "See here, Mr. Grayne, I'd like to—well, do you mind listening to something rather fantastic? I'm not drunk, but I've got a good reason for wanting to confide in you. You see, I know a great deal about you, really."

I wasn't surprised. In fact, I'd been prepared for just such a statement. I grinned a strained grin at the boy. "No, go ahead," I told him. "I'm interested." I leaned back in my chair, preparing to listen.

You see, I knew what he was going to say.

II

Ryn Kenner sat in his cell, his head buried in his hands.

"Oh, God—" he muttered to himself, over and over.

There were so many unpredictable risks involved. Even though he had spent three years coaching Cara, teaching her to guard against every possible contingency, he still might fail. If only he could have eliminated the psychic block. But that, of course, was the most necessary risk of all.

Sometimes, in spite of his humanitarian training, Ryn Kenner thought the old, primitive safeguards had been better. Executing murderers, locking maniacs up in cells was certainly better than exiling men in this horrible new way. Ryn Kenner knew that he would have preferred to die. Two or three times he had even thought of slashing his wrists with a razor before the Exile. Once he had actually set a razor against his right wrist, but his early training had been too strong for him. Even the word *suicide* could set off a mental complex of quivering nerve reactions impossible to control.

The tragedy, Kenner thought despondently, resided in the paradox that civilization had become too enlightened. There had been a time when men had thought that traveling backward in time would upset the framework of events and change the future. But it had been a manifestly mistaken idea, for in this year, 2543 A.D., the whole past had already occurred, and the present moment contained within itself the entire past, including whatever rectifying attempts time-travelers had made in that past.

Kenner shivered as he realized that his own acts had all occurred in the past. He, Ryn Kenner, had already died—six centuries before.

Time-travel—the perfect, the most humane way of banishing criminals! He had heard all the arguments which sophistry could muster. The strong individualists were clearly misfits in the enlightened twenty-sixth century. For their own good, they should be exiled to eras psychologically congenial to them. A good many of them had been sent to California in the year 1849. They thus took a one-way trip to an era where murder was not a crime, but a social necessity, the respectable business of a gentleman. Religious fanatics were exiled to the First Dark Ages, where they could not disturb the tranquil materialism of the present century; too aggressive atheists, to the twenty-third century.

Kenner rose and began to pace his cell, which was a prison in fact, if not in appearance. Outside the wide window spread a spacious view of Nyor Harbor, and the room was luxuriously furnished. He knew, however, that if he stepped a foot past the lines which had been drawn around the door, he would be instantly overpowered by a powerful sleeping gas. He had tried it once, with almost disastrous results.

This hour of high decision was his last in the twenty-sixth century. In fifty minutes, in his own personal, subjective time from now, he would be somewhere in the twentieth century, the era to which his rashness had condemned him when he had been apprehended by the psycho police while attempting to rediscover the fabulous atomic isotopes. And he wouldn't remember enough to get back. He would be permitted to keep all his training—all his knowledge, and memory—but there would be a fatal reservation.

Never, for the rest of his life, would Kenner be able to remember that he had come from the past. For the three weeks during which he had been confined to the cell the radiant suggestor had been steadily beaming at his brain. No defense his mind could devise had sufficed to stay its slow inroads into his thought.

Already his brain was beginning to grow fuzzy and he knew that the time was short. He drew a long breath, hearing steps in the corridor, and the whistle which meant the hypnotic gas was being momentarily turned off.

He stopped pacing.

Abruptly the door opened, and a psycho-supervisor entered the cell. Framed in the radiance behind him—

"Cara!" Kenner almost sobbed, and ran forward to catch his wife in his arms, and hold her with hungry violence. She cried softly against him. "Ryn, Ryn, it won't be long—"

The supervisor's face was compassionate. "Kenner," he said, "you may have twenty minutes alone with your wife. You will be unsupervised." The door closed softly behind him.

Kenner led Cara to a seat. She tried to hold back her tears, looking at him with wide, frightened eyes. "Ryn, darling, I thought you might have—"

"Hush, Cara," he whispered. "They may be listening. Just remember everything I've told you. You *mustn't* risk being sent to a different year. You already know what to do."

"I'll—find you," she promised.

"Let's not talk about it," Kenner urged gently. "We haven't long. Grayne promised he'd look after you until—"

"I know. He's been good to me while you were here."

The twenty minutes didn't seem long. The supervisor pretended not to notice while Cara clung to Kenner in a last agony of farewell. Ryn brushed the tears away from her eyes, softly.

"See you in nineteen forty-five, Cara," he whispered, and let her go.

"It's a date darling," were her last words before she followed the supervisor out of the prison. Kenner, in the last few moments remaining to him, before he sank into sleep again, desperately tried to marshal what little knowledge he possessed about the twentieth century.

His brain felt dark now, and oppressed, as if someone had wrapped his mind in smothering folds of wool. Dimly he knew that when he woke, his prison would be yet unbuilt. And yet, all the rest of his life he would be in prison—the prison of a mind that would never let him speak the truth.

III

"—and of course, this hypothetical psychic block would also contain a provision prohibiting marriage with anyone from the past," Carey Kennaird finished. "It would naturally be inconvenient for children to be born of the time exiles. But if my hypothetical man from the future should actually find the wife he'd arranged to have exiled with him, there'd be no psychic block against marrying *her*." He paused, staring at me steadily. "Now, what would happen to the kid?"

My own glass stood empty. I signalled to the waiter, but Kennaird shook his head. "Thanks, I've had enough."

I paid for the wine. "Suppose we walk to the hotel together, Kennaird?" I said. "You've got a fascinating theory there, my boy. It would make a fine plot for a science-fiction novel. Are you a writer? Of course, what happened to the boy—" we passed together into the blinding sunlight of the Chicago Loop, "—would be the climax of your story."

"It would," Kennaird agreed.

We crossed the street beneath the thundering El trains, and stood in front of Marshall Field's while Carey lit a cigarette.

"Smoke?" he asked.

I shook my head. "No thanks. You said you had a reason for confiding in me, young man. What is it?"

He looked at me curiously. "I think you know, Mr. Grayne. You weren't born in the Twentieth Century. I was, of course. But you're like Dad and Cara. You're a time exile, too, aren't you?

"I know you can't *say* anything; because of the psychic block. But you don't have to deny it. That's how Dad told me. He made me read science-fiction. Then he made me ask him leading questions—and just answered yes or no." Young Kennaird paused. "I don't have the psychic block. Dad was trying to help me discover the time-travel device. He came up to Chicago, and disappeared. But I'm on the right track now. I'm sure of it. I think Dad got back somehow."

Even though I'd known what he was going to say, I swallowed hard.

"Something very strange *did* happen when you were born," I said. "You put a peculiar strain on the whole framework of time. It was something that never should have happened, because of—" my voice faltered, "the psychic block against marrying anyone from the past."

Carey Kennaird looked at me intently. "Hard to talk about the psychic block, isn't it? Dad never could."

I nodded without speaking. We climbed the hotel steps together. "Come up to my room," I urged. "We'll talk it over. You see, Carey—I'm going to call you that—Kenner used to be my friend."

"I wonder," Carey said, "If Dad got home in the twenty-sixth century."

"He did."

Carey stared. "Mr. Grayne! Is he all right?"

Regretfully, I shook my head. The elevator boy let us off on the fourth floor. I wondered if he, too, were an exile. I wondered how many people in Chicago were exiles, sullen behind the mask of a mental block which clamped a gag on their lips when they tried to speak the truth.

I wondered how many men, and how many women, were living such a lie, day in, and day out, lonely, miserable exiles from their own tomorrow, victims of a fate literally worse than death. Small wonder they would do *anything* to avoid such a fate.

My door closed behind us. While Carey stared, wide-eyed, at the device which loomed darkly in one corner of the room, I went to my desk, and removed the shining disk. I walked straight up to him. "This is from your father," I told him. "Look at it carefully."

He accepted it eagerly, his eyes blazing with excitement, sensing at once that it had come from the twenty-sixth century.

He died instantly.

Hating my work, hating time-travel, hating the whole chain of events, which had made me an instrument of justice, I stepped into the device that would return me to the twenty-sixth century.

Carey Kennaird had told the truth. A very strange thing *had* happened at his birth. Like an extra electron bombarding an unstable isotope, he had broken the link that held the framework of time together. His birth had started a chain reaction that had ended, for me, a week before in 2556, when Kenner and Cara had reappeared in the twenty-sixth century and been murdered in a panic by the psycho-supervisors. I, already condemned to time exile, had won a free pardon for my work, a commutation of my sentence to a light reprimand and the loss of my position. It was ugly work and I hated it, for Kenner and Cara *had* been my friends. But I had no freedom of choice. Anything was better than exile into time.

Anything, anything.

Besides, it had been necessary.

It isn't lawful for children to be born before their parents.

HAL CLEMENT (PSD. FOR HARRY CLEMENT STUBBS) (1922-)

Hal Clement is a scientist who has written and published Science Fiction for almost sixty years. A Hard Science Fiction writer, Clement has consistently focused his stories on realistic or semirealistic scientific concepts. His subject matter and style made him an exemplary author of John W. Campbell Jr.'s Astounding Science-Fiction *magazine. Hal Clement published his first story, "Proof," in the pages of this magazine's June 1942 issue.*

The author's Needle *(1950) and its sequel,* Through the Eye of a Needle *(1978), are acclaimed stories of aliens and invasion and feature detection, searches, and chases that predate the television series* V *(1984–85). His loosely connected novels* Mission of Gravity *(1953),* Close to Critical *(1958), and* Star Light *(1971) are Hard Science Fiction classics that feature an elaborately constructed world and the real-life scientific principles of gravity. Larry Niven's "Ringworld" series has many parallels to these three Hal Clement novels.*

Because of his exacting standards and commitment to scientific detail, Hal Clement is one of the best Hard Science Fiction authors of all time, ranking in this regard with Robert E. Heinlein and Isaac Asimov. If the Supernatural or Ghost story is one of the most difficult Dark Fantasy stories to write convincingly, then the Hard Science Fiction story is likewise one of the most difficult Science Fiction stories to present well.

Hal Clement's "Dust Rag" is topflight Hard Science Fiction.

Dust Rag

(Astounding Science-Fiction, *September 1956*)

"Checking out."

"Checked, Ridge. See you soon."

Ridging glanced over his shoulder at Beacon Peak, as the point where the relay station had been mounted was known. The gleaming dome of its leaden meteor shield was visible as a spark; most of the lower peaks of Harpalus were already below the horizon, and with them the last territory with which Ridging or Shandara could claim familiarity. The humming turbine tractor that carried them was the only sign of humanity except each others' faces—the thin crescent of their home world was too close to the sun to be seen easily, and Earth doesn't look very "human" from outside in any case.

The prospect ahead was not exactly strange, of course. Shandara had remarked several times in the last four weeks that a man who had seen any of the Moon had seen all of it. A good many others had agreed with him. Even Ridging, whose temperament kept him normally expecting something new to happen, was beginning to get a trifle bored with the place. It wasn't even dangerous; he knew perfectly well what exposure to vacuum would mean, but checking spacesuit and airlock valves had become a matter of habit long before.

Cosmic rays went through plastic suits and living bodies like glass, for the most part ineffective because unabsorbed; meteors blew microscopic holes through thin metal, but scarcely marked spacesuits or hulls, as far as current experiences went; the "dust-hidden crevasses" which they had expected to catch unwary men or vehicles simply didn't exist—the dust was too dry to cover any sort of hole, except by filling it completely. The closest approach to a casualty suffered so far had occurred when a man had missed his footing on the ladder outside the *Albireo*'s airlock and narrowly avoided a hundred-and-fifty-foot fall.

Still, Shandara was being cautious. His eyes swept the ground ahead of their tracks, and his gauntleted hands rested lightly on brake and steering controls as the tractor glided ahead.

Harpalus and the relay station were out of sight now. Another glance behind assured Ridging of that. For the first time in weeks he was out of touch with the rest of the group, and for the first time he wondered whether it was such a good idea. Orders had been strict, the radius of exploration settled on long before was not to be exceeded. Ridging had been completely in favor of this; but it was his own instruments which had triggered the change of schedule.

One question about the Moon to which no one could more than guess an answer in advance was that of its magnetic field. Once the group was on the surface it had immediately become evident that there was one, and comparative readings had indicated that the south magnetic pole—or a south magnetic pole—lay a few hundred miles away. It had been decided to modify the program to check the region, since the last forlorn chance of finding any trace of a gaseous envelope around the Moon seemed to lie in auroral investigation. Ridging found himself, to his intense astonishment, wondering why he had volunteered for the trip and then wondering how such thoughts could cross his mind. He had never considered himself a coward, and certainly had no one but himself to blame for being in the tractor. No one had made him volunteer, and any technician could have set up and operated the equipment.

"Come out of it, Ridge. Anyone would think you were worried." Shandara's careless tones cut into his thoughts. "How about running this buggy for a while? I've had her for a hundred kilos."

"Right." Ridging slipped into the driver's seat as his companion left it without slowing the tractor. He did not need to find their location on the photographic map clipped beside the panel; he had been keeping a running check almost unconsciously between the features it showed and the landmarks appearing over the horizon. A course had been marked on it, and navigation was not expected to be a problem even without a magnetic compass.

The course was far from straight, though it led over what passed for fairly smooth territory on the Moon. Even back on Sinus Roris the tractor had had to weave its way around numerous obstacles; now well onto the Mare Frigoris, the situation was no better, and according to the map it was nearly time to turn south through the mountains, which would be infinitely worse. According to the photos taken during the original landing approach the journey would be possible, however, and would lead through the range at its narrowest part out onto Mare Imbrium. From that point to the vicinity of Plato, where the region to be investigated lay, there should be no trouble at all.

Oddly enough, there wasn't. Ridging was moderately surprised; Shandara seemed to take it as a matter of course. The cartographer had eaten, slept, and taken his turn at driving with only an occasional remark. Ridging was beginning to believe by the time they reached their goal that his companion was actually as bored with the Moon as he claimed to be. The thought, however, was fleeting; there was work to be done.

About six hundred pounds of assorted instruments were attached to the trailer which had been improvised from discarded fuel tanks. The tractor itself could not carry them; its entire cargo space was occupied by another improvisation—an auxiliary fuel tank which had been needed to make the present journey possible. The instruments had to be removed, set up in various spots, and permitted to make their records for the next thirty hours. This would have been a minor task, and possibly even justified a little boredom, had it not been for the fact that some of the "spots" were supposed to be as high as possible. Both men had climbed Lunar mountains in the last four weeks, and neither was worried about the task; but there was some question as to which mountain would best suit their needs.

They had stopped on fairly level ground south and somewhat west of Plato— "sunset" west, that is, not astronomical. There were a number of fairly prominent elevations in sight. None seemed more than a thousand meters or so in height, however, and the men knew that Plato in one direction and the Teneriffe Mountains in the other had peaks fully twice as high. The problem was which to choose.

"We can't take the tractor either way," pointed out Shandara. "We're cutting things pretty fine on the fuel question as it is. We are going to have to pack the instruments ourselves, and it's fifty or sixty kilometers to Teneriffe before we even start climbing. Plato's a lot closer."

"The *near side* of Plato's a lot closer," admitted Ridging, "but the measured peaks in its rim must be on the east and west sides, where they can cast shadows across the crater floor. We might have to go as far for a really good peak as we would if we headed south."

"That's not quite right. Look at the map. The near rim of the crater is fairly straight, and doesn't run straight east and west; it must cast shadows that they could measure from Earth. Why can't it contain some of those two-thousand-meter humps mentioned in the atlas?"

"No reason why it *can't;* but we don't know that it *does.* This map doesn't show."

"It doesn't show for Teneriffe, either."

"That's true, but there isn't much choice there, and we know that there's at least one high peak in a fairly small area. Plato is well over three hundred kilometers around."

"It's still a closer walk, and I don't see why, if there are high peaks at any part of the rim, they shouldn't be fairly common all around the circumference."

"I don't see *why* either," retorted Ridging, "but I've seen several craters for which that wasn't true. So have you." Shandara had no immediate answer to this, but he had no intention of exposing himself to an unnecessarily long walk if he could help it. The instruments to be carried were admittedly light, at least on the Moon; but there would be no chance of opening spacesuits until the men got back to the tractor, and spacesuits got quite uncomfortable after a while.

It was the magnetometer that won Shandara's point for him. This pleased him greatly at the time, though he was heard to express a different opinion later. The meter itself did not attract attention until the men were about ready to start, and he had resigned himself to the long walk after a good deal more argument; but a final check of the recorders already operating made Ridging stop and think.

"Say, Shan, have you noticed any sunspots lately?"

"Haven't looked at the sun, and don't plan to."

"I know. I mean, have any of the astronomers mentioned anything of the sort?"

"I didn't hear them, and we'll never be able to ask until we get back. Why?"

"I'd say there was a magnetic storm of some sort going on. The intensity, dip, and azimuth readings have all changed quite a bit in the last hour."

"I thought dip was near vertical anyway."

"It is, but that doesn't keep it from changing. You know, Shan, maybe it would be better if we went to Plato, instead."

"That's what I've been saying all along. What's changed your mind?"

"This magnetic business. On Earth, such storms are caused by charged particles from the sun, deflected by the planet's magnetic field and forming what amounts to tremendous electric currents which naturally produce fields of their own. If that's what is happening here, it would be nice to get even closer to the local magnetic vertical, if we can; and that seems to be in, or at least near, Plato."

"That suits me. I've been arguing that way all along. I'm with you."

"There's one other thing—"

"What?"

"This magnetometer ought to go along with us, as well as the stuff we were taking anyway. Do you mind helping with the extra weight?" Shandara had not considered this aspect of the matter, but since his arguments had been founded on the question of time rather than effort he agreed readily to the additional labor.

"All right. Just a few minutes while I dismount and repack this gadget, and we'll be on our way." Ridging set to work, and was ready in the specified time, since the apparatus had been designed to be handled by space-suited men. The carrying racks that took the place of regular packs made the travelers look top-heavy, but they had long since learned to keep their balance under such loads. They turned until the nearly motionless sun was behind them and to their right, and set out for the hills ahead.

These elevations were not the peaks they expected to use; the Moon's near horizon made those still invisible. They did, however, represent the outer reaches of the area which had been disturbed by whatever monstrous explosion had blown the ring of Plato in the Moon's crust. As far as the men were concerned, these hills simply meant that very little of their journey would be across level ground, which pleased them just as well. Level ground was sometimes an inch or two deep in dust; and while dust could not hide deep cracks it could and sometimes did fill broader hollows and cover irregularities where one could trip. For a top-heavy man, this could be a serious nuisance. Relatively little dust had been encountered by any of the expedition up to this point, since most of their work had involved slopes or peaks; but a few annoying lessons had been learned.

Shandara and Ridging stuck to the relatively dust-free slopes, therefore. The going was easy enough for experienced men, and they traveled at pretty fair speed—some ten or twelve miles an hour, they judged. The tractor soon disappeared, and compasses were useless, but both men had a good eye for country, and were used enough to the Lunar landscape to have no particular difficulty in finding distinctive features. They said little, except to call each other's attention to particularly good landmarks.

The general ground level was going up after the first hour and a half, though there was still plenty of downhill travel. A relatively near line of peaks ahead was presumably the crater rim; there was little difficulty in deciding on the most suitable one and heading for it. Naturally the footing became worse and the slopes steeper as they approached, but nothing was dangerous even yet. Such crevasses as existed were easy both to see and to jump, and there are few loose rocks on the Moon.

It was only about three and a half hours after leaving the tractor, therefore, that the two men reached the peak they had selected, and looked out over the great walled plain of Plato. They couldn't see all of it, of course; Plato is a hundred kilometers across, and even from a height of two thousand meters the farther side of the floor lies below the horizon. The opposite rim could be seen, of course, but there was no easy way to tell whether any of the peaks visible there were as high as the one from which the men saw them. It didn't really matter; this one was high enough for their purposes.

The instruments were unloaded and set up in half an hour. Ridging did most of the work, with a professional single-mindedness which Shandara made no attempt to emulate. The geophysicist scarcely glanced at the crater floor after his first look around upon their arrival, while Shandara did little else. Ridging was not surprised; he had been reasonably sure that his friend had had ulterior reasons for wanting to come this way.

"All right," he said, as he straightened up after closing the last switch, "when do we go down, and how long do we take?"

"Go down where?" asked Shandara innocently.

"Down to the crater floor, I suppose. I'm sure you don't see enough to satisfy you from here. It's just an ordinary crater, of course, but it's three times the diameter of Harpalus even if the walls are less than half as high, and you'll surely want to see every square meter of the floor."

"I'll want to see *some* of the floor, anyway." Shandara's tone carried feeling even through the suit radios. "It's nice of you to realize that we have to go down. I wish you realized why."

"You mean . . . you mean you really expect to climb down there?" Ridging, in spite of his knowledge of the other's interests, was startled. "I didn't really mean—"

"I didn't think you did. You haven't looked over the edge once."

Ridging repaired the omission, letting his gaze sweep carefully over the grayish plain at the foot of the slope. He knew that the floor of Plato was one of the darker areas on the Moon, but had never supposed that this fact constituted a major problem.

"I don't get it," he said at last. "I don't see anything. The floor is smoother than that of Harpalus, I'd say, but I'm not really sure even of that, from this distance. It's a couple of kilos down and I don't know how far over."

"You brought the map." It was not a question.

"Of course."

"Look at it. It's a good one." Ridging obeyed, bewildered. The map was good, as Shandara had said; its scale was sufficient to show Plato some fifteen centimeters across, with plenty of detail. It was basically an enlargement of a map published on Earth, from telescopic observations; but a good deal of detail had been added from photographs taken during the approach and landing of the expedition. Shandara knew that; it was largely his own work.

As a result, Ridging was not long in seeing what his companion meant. The map showed five fairly large craterlets *within* Plato, and nearly a hundred smaller features.

Ridging could see none of them from where he stood.

He looked thoughtfully down the slope, then at the other man.

"I begin to see what you mean. Did you expect something like this? Is that why you wanted to come here? Why didn't you tell me?"

"I didn't expect it, though I had a vague hope. A good many times in the past, observers have reported that the features on the floor of this crater were obscured. Dr. Pickering, at the beginning of the century, thought of it as an active volcanic area; others have blamed the business on clouds—and others, of course, have assumed the observers themselves were at fault, though that is pretty hard to justify. I didn't really expect to get a chance to check up on the phenomenon, but I'm sure you don't expect me to stay up here now."

"I suppose not." Ridging spoke in a tone of mock resignation. The problem did not seem to concern his field directly, but he judged rightly that the present situation affected Shandara the way an offer of a genuine fragment of Terrestrial core material would influence Ridging himself. "What do you plan to take down? I suppose you want to get measures of some sort."

"Well, there isn't too much here that will apply, I'm afraid. I have my own camera and some filters, which may do some good. I can't see that the magnetic stuff will be any use down there. We don't have any pressure-measuring or gas-collecting gadgetry; I suppose if we'd brought a spare water container from the tractor we could dump it, but we didn't and I'd bet that nothing would be found in it but water vapor if we did. We'll just have to go down and see what our eyes will tell us, and record anything that seems recordable on film. Are you ready?"

"Ready as I ever will be." Ridging knew the remark was neither original nor brilliant, but nothing else seemed to fit.

The inner wall of the crater was a good deal steeper than the one they had climbed, but still did not present a serious obstacle. The principal trouble was that much of the way led through clefts where the sun did not shine, and the only light was reflected from distant slopes. There wasn't much of it, and the men had to be careful of their footings—there was an occasional loose fragment here, and a thousand-meter fall is no joke even on the Moon. The way did not lead directly toward the crater floor; the serrated rim offered better ways between its peaks, hairpinning back and forth so that sometimes the central plain was not visible at all. No floor details appeared as they descended, but whatever covered them was still below; the stars, whenever the mountains cut off enough sidelight, were clear as ever. Time and again Shandara stopped to look over the great plain, which seemed limitless now that the peaks on the farther side had dropped below the horizon, but nothing in the way of information rewarded the effort.

It was the last few hundred meters of descent that began to furnish something of interest. Shandara was picking his way down an unusually uninviting bit of slope when Ridging, who had already negotiated it, spoke up sharply.

"Shan! Look at the stars over the northern horizon! Isn't there some sort of haze? The sky around them looks a bit lighter." The other paused and looked.

"You're right. But how could that be? There couldn't suddenly be enough air at this level—gases don't behave that way. Van Maanen's star might have an atmosphere twenty meters deep, but the Moon doesn't and never could have."

"There's *something* between us and the sky."

"That I admit; but I still say it isn't gas. Maybe dust—"

"What would hold it up? Dust is just as impossible as air."

"I don't know. The floor's only a few yards down—let's not stand here guessing." They resumed their descent.

The crater floor was fairly level, and sharply distinguished from the inner slope of the crater wall. Something had certainly filled, partly at least, the vast pit after the original explosion; but neither man was disposed to renew the argument about the origin of Lunar craters just then. They scrambled down the remaining few yards of the journey and stopped where they were, silently.

There *was* something blocking vision; the horizon was no longer visible, nor could the stars be seen for a few degrees above where it should have been. Neither man would have had the slightest doubt about the nature of the obscuring matter had he been on Earth; it bore every resemblance to dust. It *had* to be dust.

But it couldn't be. Granted that dust can be fine enough to remain suspended for weeks or months in Earth's atmosphere when a volcano like Krakatoa hurls a few cubic miles of it aloft, the Moon had not enough gas molecules around it to interfere with the trajectory of a healthy virus particle—and no seismometer in the last four weeks had registered crustal activity even approaching the scale of vulcanism. There was nothing on the Moon to throw the dust up, and even less to keep it there.

"Meteor splash?" Shandara made the suggestion hesitantly, fully aware that while a meteor might raise dust it could never keep it aloft. Ridging did not bother to answer, and his friend did not repeat the suggestion.

The sky straight overhead seemed clear as ever; whatever the absorbing material was, it apparently took more than the few feet above them to show much effect. That could not be night, though, Ridging reflected, if this stuff was responsible for hiding the features which should have been visible from the crater rim. Maybe it was thicker farther in. If so, they'd better go on—there might be some chance of collecting samples after all.

He put this to Shandara, who agreed; and the two started out across the hundred-kilometer plain.

The surface *was* fairly smooth, though a pattern of minute cracks suggestive of the joints formed in cooling basalt covered it almost completely. These were not wide enough even to constitute a tripping danger, and the men ignored them for the time being, though Ridging made a mental note to get a sample of the rock if he could detach one.

The obscuration did thicken as they progressed, and by the time they had gone half a dozen kilometers it was difficult to see the crater wall behind them. Looking up, they saw that all but the brighter stars had faded from view even when the men shaded their eyes from the sunlit rock around them.

"Maybe gas is coming from these cracks, carrying dust up with it?" Shandara was no geologist, but had an imagination. He had also read most of the serious articles which had ever been published about the Moon.

"We could check. If that were the case, it should be possible to see currents coming from them; the dust would be thicker just above a crack than a few centimeters away. If we had something light, like a piece of paper, it might be picked up."

"Worth trying. We have the map," Shandara pointed out. "That should do for paper; the plastic is thin enough." Ridging agreed. With some difficulty—spacesuit gloves were not designed for that purpose—he tore a tiny corner off the sheet on which the map was printed, knelt down, and held the fragment over one of the numerous cracks. It showed no tendency to flutter in his grasp, and when he let go it dropped as rapidly as anything ever did on the Moon, to lie quietly directly across the crack he had been testing. He tried to pick it up, but could not get a grip on it with his stiff gloves.

"That one didn't seem to pan out," he remarked, standing up once more.

"Maybe the paper was too heavy—this stuff must be awfully fine—or else it's coming from only a few of the cracks."

"Possibly; but I don't think it's practical to try them all. It would be smarter to figure some way to get a sample of this stuff, and let people with better lab facilities figure out what it is and what holds it off the surface."

"I've been trying to think of a way to do that. If we laid the map out on the ground, some of the material might settle on it."

"Worth trying. If it does, though, we'll have another question—why does it settle there and yet remain suspended long enough to do what is being done? We've been more than an hour coming down the slope, and I'll bet your astronomical friends of the past have reported obscurations longer lasting even than that."

"They have. Well, even if it does raise more problems it's worth trying. Spread out the map, and we'll wait a few minutes." Ridging obeyed; then, to keep the score even, came up with an idea of his own.

"Why don't you lay your camera on the ground pointing up and make a couple of time exposures of the stars? You could repeat them after we get back in the clear, and maybe get some data on the obscuring power of this material."

"Good enough." Shandara removed the camera from its case, clipped a sunshade over its lens, and looked up to find a section of sky with a good selection of stars. As usual, he had to shield his eyes both from sunlight and from the glare of the nearby hills; but even then he did not seem satisfied.

"This stuff is getting thicker, I think," he said. "It's scattering enough light so that it's hard to see any stars at all—harder than it was a few minutes ago, I'd say." Ridging imitated his maneuver, and agreed.

"That's worth recording, too," he pointed out. "Better stay here a while and get several shots at different times." He looked down again. "It certainly *is* getting thicker. I'm having trouble seeing you, now."

Human instincts being what they are, the solution to the mystery followed automatically and immediately. A man who fails, for any reason, to see as clearly as he expects usually rubs his eyes—if he can get at them. A man wearing goggles or a space helmet may just possibly control this impulse, but he follows the practically identical one of wiping the panes through which he looks. Ridging did not have a handkerchief within reach, of course, and the gauntlet of a spacesuit is not one of the best windshield wipers imaginable; but without giving a single thought to the action, he wiped his faceplate with his gauntlet.

Had there been no results he would not have been surprised; he had no reason to expect any. He would probably have dismissed the matter, perhaps with a faint hope that his companion might not have noticed the futile gesture. However, there were results. Very marked ones.

The points where the plastic of the gauntlet actually touched the faceplate were few; but they left trails all the way across—opaque trails. Surprised and still not thinking, Ridging repeated the gesture in an automatic effort to wipe the smears of whatever it was from his helmet; he only made matters worse. He did not quite cover the supposedly transparent area with glove trails—but in the few seconds after he got control of his hand the streaks spread and merged until nothing whatever was visible. He was not quite in darkness; sunlight penetrated the obscuring layer, but he could not see any details.

"Shan!" The cry contained almost a note of panic. "I can't see at all. Something's covering my helmet!" The cartographer straightened up from his camera and turned toward his friend.

"How come? You look all right from here. I can't see too clearly, though—"

Reflexes are wonderful. It took about five seconds to blind Shandara as thoroughly as Ridging. He couldn't even find his camera to close the shutter.

"You know," said Ridging thoughtfully after two or three minutes of heavy silence, "we should have been able to figure all this out without coming down here."

"Why?"

"Oh, it's plain as anything—"

"Nothing, and I mean *nothing*, is plain right now."

"I suppose a mapmaker would joke while he was surveying Gehenna. Look, Shan, we have reason to believe there's a magnetic storm going on, which strongly suggests charged particles from the Sun. We are standing, for practical purposes, on the Moon's south magnetic pole. Most level parts of the Moon are covered with dust—but we walked over bare rock from the foot of the rim to here. Don't those items add up to something?"

"Not to me."

"Well, then, add the fact that electrical attraction and repulsion are inverse square forces like gravity, but involve a vastly bigger proportionality constant."

"If you're talking about scale I know all about it, but you still don't paint me a picture."

"All right. There are, at a guess, protons coming from the sun. They are reaching the Moon's surface here—virtually all of them, since the Moon has a magnetic field but no atmosphere. The surface material is one of the lousiest imaginable electrical conductors, so the dust normally on the surface picks up *and keeps* a charge. And what, dear student, happens to particles carrying like electrical charges?"

"They are repelled from each other."

"Head of the class. And if a hundred-kilometer circle with a rim a couple of kilos high is charged all over, what happens to the dust lying on it?"

Shandara did not answer; the question was too obviously rhetorical. He thought for a moment or two, instead, then asked, "How about our faceplates?"

Ridging shrugged—a rather useless gesture, but the time for fighting bad habits had passed some minutes before.

"Bad luck. Whenever two materials rub against each other, electrons come loose. Remember your rubber-and-cat-fur demonstrations in grade school. Unless the materials are of identical electronic makeup, which for practical purposes means unless they are the same substance, one of them will hang onto the electrons a little—or a lot—better than the other, so one will have a negative net charge and the other a positive one. It's our misfortune that the difference between the plastic in our faceplates and that in the rest of the suits is the wrong way; when we rubbed the two, the faceplates picked up a charge opposite to that of the surrounding dust—probably negative, since I suppose the dust is positive and a transparent material should have a good grip on its electrons."

"Then the rest of our suits, and the gloves we wiped with in particular, ought to be clean."

"Ought to be. I'd like nothing better than a chance to check the point."

"Well, the old cat's fur didn't stay charged very long, as I remember. How long will it take this to leak off, do you think?"

"Why should it leak off at all?"

"What? Why, I should think—hm-m-m." Shandara was silent for a moment. "Water *is* pretty wonderful stuff, isn't it?"

"Yep. And air has its uses, too."

"Then we're . . . Ridge, we've got to *do* something. Our air will last indefinitely, but you still can't stay in a spacesuit too long."

"I agree that we should do something; I just haven't figured out what. Incidentally, just how sure are you that our air will last? The windows of the regenerators are made, as far as I know, of the same plastic our faceplates are. What'll you bet you're not using emergency oxygen right now?"

"I don't know—I haven't checked the gauges."

"I'll say you haven't. You won't, either; they're outside your helmet."

"But if we're on emergency now, we could hardly get back to the tractor starting this minute. We've got to get going."

"Which way?"

"Toward the rim!"

"Be specific, son. Just which way is that? And please don't point; it's rude, and I can't see you anyway."

"All right, don't rub it in. But Ridge, what *can* we do?"

"While this stuff is on our helmets, and possibly our air windows, nothing. We couldn't climb even if we knew which way the hills were. The only thing which will do us the least good is to get this dust off us; and that will do the trick. As my mathematical friends would say, it is necessary and sufficient."

"All right, I'll go along with that. We know that the material the suits are made of is worse than useless for wiping, but wiping and electrical discharge seem to be the only methods possible. What do we have which by any stretch of the imagination might do either job?"

"What is your camera case made of?" asked Ridging.

"As far as I know, same as the suits. It's a regular clip-on carrier, the sort that came with the suits—remember Tazewell's remarks about the dividends Air-Tight must have paid when they sold the suits to the Project? It reminded me of the old days when you had to buy a lot of accessories with your automobile whether you wanted them or not—"

"All right, you've made your point. The case is the same plastic. It would be a pretty poor wiper anyway; it's a box rather than a bag, as I remember. What else is there?"

The silence following this question was rather lengthy. The sad fact is that spacesuits don't have outside pockets for handkerchiefs. It did occur to Ridging after a time that he was carrying a set of geological specimen bags; but when he finally did think of these and took one out to use as a wiper, the unfortunate fact developed that it, too, left the wrong charge on the faceplate of his helmet. He could see the clear, smooth plastic of the bag as it passed across the plate, but the dust collected so fast behind it that he saw nothing of his surroundings. He reflected ruefully that the charge to be removed was now greater than ever. He also thought of using the map, until he remembered that he had put it on the ground and could never find it by touch.

"I never thought," Shandara remarked after another lengthy silence, "that I'd ever miss a damp rag so badly. Blast it, Ridge, there must be *something*."

"Why? We've both been thinking without any result that I can see. Don't tell me you're one of those fellows who think there's an answer to every problem."

"I am. It may not be the answer we want, but there is one. Come on, Ridge, you're the physicist; I'm just a high-priced picture-copier. Whatever answer there is, you're going to have to furnish it; all my ideas deal with maps, and we've done about all we can with those at the moment."

"Hm-m-m. The more I think, the more I remember that there isn't enough fuel on the Moon to get a rescue tractor out here, even if anyone knew we were in trouble and could make the trip in time. Still—wait a minute; you said something just then. What was it?"

"I said all my ideas dealt with maps, but—"

"No; before that."

"I don't recall, unless it was that crack about damp rags, which we don't have."

"That was it. That's it, Shan; we don't have any rags, but we do have *water.*"

"Yes—inside our spacesuits. Which of us opens up to save the other?"

"Neither one. Be sensible. You know as well as I do that the amount of water in a closed system containing a living person is constantly increasing; we produce it, oxidizing hydrogen in the food we eat. The suits have driers in the air cycler or we couldn't last two hours in them."

"That's right; but how do you get the water out? You can't open your air system."

"You can shut it off, and the check valve will keep air in your suit—remember, there's always the chance someone will have to change emergency tanks. It'll be a job, because we won't be able to see what we're doing, and working by touch through spacesuit gauntlets will be awkward as anything I've ever done. Still, I don't see anything else."

"That means you'll have to work on my suit, then, since I don't know what to do after the line is disconnected. How long can I last before you reconnect? And what do you do, anyway? You don't mean there's a reservoir of liquid water there, do you?"

"No, it's a calcium chloride drier; and it should be fairly moist by now—you've been in the suit for several hours. It's in several sections, and I can take out one and leave you the others, so you won't suffer from its lack. The air in your suit should do you for four or five minutes, and if I can't make the disconnection and disassembly in that time I can't do it at all. Still, it's your suit, and if I do make a mistake it's your life; do you want to take the chance?"

"What have I to lose? Besides, you always were a pretty good mechanic—or if you weren't, please don't tell me. Get to work."

"All right."

As it happened, the job was not started right away, for there was the minor problem of finding Shandara to be solved first. The two men had been perhaps five yards apart when their faceplates were first blanked out, but neither could now be sure that he hadn't moved in the meantime, or at least shifted around to face a new direction. After some discussion of the problem, it was agreed that Shandara should stand still, while Ridging walked in what he hoped was the right direction for what he hoped was five yards, and then start from wherever he found himself to quarter the area as well as he could by length of stride. He would have to guess at his turns, since even the sun no longer could penetrate the layer of dust on the helmets.

It took a full ten minutes to bump into his companion, and even then he felt undeservedly lucky.

Shandara lay down, so as to use the minimum of energy while the work was being done. Ridging felt over the connection several times until he was sure he had them right—they were, of course, designed to be handled by spacesuit gauntlets, though not by a blindfolded operator. Then he warned the cartographer, closed the main cutoffs at helmet and emergency tanks to isolate the renewer mechanism, and opened the latter. It was a simple device, designed in throwaway units like a piece of electronic gear, with each unit automatically sealing as it was removed—a fortunate fact if the alga culture on which Shandara's life for the next few hours depended was to survive the operation.

The calcium chloride cells were easy to locate; Ridging removed two of the half-dozen to be on the safe side, replaced and reassembled the renewer, tightened the connections, and reopened the valves.

Ridging now had two cans of calcium chloride. He could not tell whether it had yet absorbed enough water actually to go into solution, though he doubted it; but he took no chances. Holding one of the little containers carefully right side up, he opened its perforated top, took a specimen bag and pushed it into the contents. The plastic was not, of course, absorptive—it was not the first time in the past hour he had regretted the change from cloth bags—but the damp crystals should adhere, and the solution if there was any would wet it. He pulled out the material and applied it to his faceplate.

It was not until much later that he became sure whether there was any liquid. For the moment it worked, and he found that he could see; he asked no more. Hastily he repeated the process on Shandara's helmet, and the two set out rapidly for the rim. They did not stop to pick up camera or map.

Travel is fast on the Moon, but they made less than four hundred meters. Then the faceplates were covered again. With a feeling of annoyance they stopped, and Ridging repeated the treatment.

This time it didn't work.

"I supposed you emptied the can while you were jumping," Shandara remarked in an annoyed tone. "Try the other one."

"I didn't empty anything; but I'll try." The contents of the other container proved equally useless, and the cartographer's morale took another slump.

"What happened?" he asked. "And please don't tell me it's obvious, because you certainly didn't foresee it."

"I didn't, but it is. The chloride dried out again."

"I thought it held onto water."

"It does, under certain conditions. Unfortunately its equilibrium vapor pressure at this temperature is higher than the local barometer reading. I don't suppose that every last molecule of water has gone, but what's left isn't sufficient to make a conductor. Our faceplates are holding charge again—maybe better than before; there must be some calcium chloride dust on them now, though I don't know offhand what effect it would have."

"There are more chloride cartridges in the cyclers."

"You have four left, which would get us maybe two kilos at the present rate. We can't use mine, since you can't get them out; and if we use all yours you'd never get up the rim. Drying your air isn't just a matter of comfort, you know; that suit has no temperature controls—it depends on radiation balance and insulation. If your perspiration stops evaporating, your inner insulation is done; and in any case, the cartridges won't get us to the rim."

"In other words you think we're done—again."

"I certainly don't have any more ideas."

"Then I suppose I'll have to do some more pointless chattering. If it gave you the last idea, maybe it will work again."

"Go ahead. It won't bother me. I'm going to spend my last hours cursing the character who used a different plastic for the faceplate than he did for the rest of these suits."

"All right," Tazewell snapped as the geophysicist paused. "I'm supposed to ask you what you did then. You've just told me that that handkerchief of yours is a good windshield wiper; I'll admit I don't see how. I'll even admit I'm curious, if it'll make you happy."

"It's not a handkerchief, as I said. It's a specimen bag."

"I thought you tried those and found they didn't work—left a charge on your faceplate like the glove."

"It did. But a remark I made myself about different kinds of plastic in the suits gave me another idea. It occurred to me that if the dust was, say, positively charged—"

"Probably was. Protons from the sun."

"All right. Then my faceplate picked up a negative, and my suit glove a positive, so the dust was attracted to the plate.

"Then when we first tried the specimen bag, it also charged positively and left negative on the faceplate.

"Then it occurred to me that the specimen bag *rubbed by the suit* might go negative; and since it was fairly transparent, I could—"

"I get it! You could tie it over your faceplate and have a windshield you could see through which would repel the dust."

"That was the idea. Of course, I had nothing to tie it with; I had to hold it."

"Good enough. So you got a good idea out of an idle remark."

"Two of them. The moisture one came from Shan the same way."

"But yours worked." Ridging grinned.

"Sorry. It didn't. The specimen bag still came out negative when rubbed on the suit plastic—at least it didn't do the faceplate any good."

Tazewell stared blankly, then looked as though he were about to use violence.

"*All right!* Let's have it, once and for all."

"Oh, it was simple enough. I worked the specimen bag—I tore it open so it would cover more area—across my faceplate, pressing tight so there wouldn't be any dust under it."

"What good would that do? You must have collected more over it right away."

"Sure. Then I rubbed my faceplate, dust rag and all, against Shandara's. We couldn't lose; one of them was bound to go positive. I won, and led him up the rim until the ground charge dropped enough to let the dust stick to the surface instead of us. I'm glad no one was there to take pictures, though; I'd hate to have a photo around which could be interpreted as my kissing Shandara's ugly face—even through a space helmet."

AVRAM (JAMES) DAVIDSON (1923–1993)

While also a successful novelist, Avram Davidson, like Charles Beaumont, is most recognized as a Fantasy and Science Fiction short story writer. Like Marion Zimmer Bradley, Davidson was well versed in a range of Fantasy and Science Fiction subgenres, formulas, and themes He wrote Space Operas, stories of alternate universes, environmental allegories, tales of alien worlds, and tributes to folklore, history, and fairy tales. He also wrote humor and mysteries, and his work appeared in such varied magazines as Galaxy *and* The New Yorker.

Davidson's first story, "My Boy Friend's Name is Jello," appeared in The Magazine of Fantasy and Science Fiction *in 1954. He was the editor of that magazine and its related anthologies numbered 12, 13, and 14 from 1962 to 1964. As a Mystery Fiction writer, Avram Davidson wrote several novels under the "Ellery Queen" pseudonym from the 1960s to the 1990s. He was also a script writer for the television series* Alfred Hitchcock Presents.

"Or, All the Sea With Oysters" is not the Hard Science Fiction of Hal Clement, but it is a Science Fantasy about machines. It evokes memories of similar stories by H. G. Wells and Ray Bradbury.

Or, All the Sea With Oysters
(Galaxy, *May 1958*)

When the man came in to the F & O Bike Shop, Oscar greeted him with a hearty "Hi, there!" Then, as he looked closer at the middle-aged visitor with the eyeglasses and business suit, his forehead creased and he began to snap his thick fingers.

"Oh, say, I know you," he muttered. "Mr.—um—name's on the tip of my tongue, doggone it . . ." Oscar was a barrel-chested fellow. He had orange hair.

"Why, sure you do," the man said. There was a Lion's emblem in his lapel. "Remember, you sold me a girl's bicycle with gears, for my daughter? We got to talking about that red French racing bike your partner was working on—"

Oscar slapped his big hand down on the cash register. He raised his head and rolled his eyes up. "Mr. Whatney!" Mr. Whatney beamed. "Oh, *sure*. Gee, how could I forget? And we went across the street afterward and had a couple a beers. Well, how you *been*, Mr. Whatney? I guess the bike—it was an English model, wasn't it? Yeah. It must of given satisfaction or you would of been back, huh?"

Mr. Whatney said the bicycle was fine, just fine. Then he said, "I understand there's been a change, though. You're all by yourself now. Your partner . . ."

Oscar looked down, pushed his lower lip out, nodded. "You heard, huh? Ee-up. I'm all by myself now. Over three months now."

The partnership had come to an end three months ago, but it had been faltering long before then. Ferd liked books, long-playing records and high-level conversation, Oscar liked beer, bowling and women. Any women. Any time.

The shop was located near the park; it did a big trade in renting bicycles to picnickers. If a woman was barely old enough to be *called* a woman, and not quite old enough to be called an *old* woman, or if she was anywhere in between, and if she was alone, Oscar would ask, "How does that machine feel to you? All right?"

"Why . . . I guess so."

Taking another bicycle, Oscar would say, "Well, I'll just ride along a little bit with you, to make sure. Be right back, Ferd." Ferd always nodded gloomily. He knew that Oscar would not be right back. Later, Oscar would say, "Hope you made out in the shop as good as I did in the park."

"Leaving me all alone here all that time," Ferd grumbled.

And Oscar usually flared up. "Okay, then, next time *you* go and leave *me* stay here. See if I begrudge you a little fun." But he knew, of course, that Ferd—tall, thin, pop-eyed Ferd—would never go. "Do you good," Oscar said, slapping his sternum. "Put hair on your chest."

Ferd muttered that he had all the hair on his chest that he needed. He would glance down covertly at his lower arms; they were thick with long black hair, though his upper arms were slick and white. It was already like that when he was in high school, and some of the others would laugh at him—call him "Ferdie the Birdie." They knew it bothered him, but they did it anyway. How was it possible—he wondered then; he still did now—for people deliberately to hurt someone else who hadn't hurt them. How was it possible?

He worried over other things. All the time.

"The Communists—" He shook his head over the newspaper. Oscar offered advice about the Communists in two short words. Or it might be capital punishment. "Oh, what a terrible thing if an innocent man was to be executed," Ferd moaned. Oscar said that was the guy's tough luck.

"Hand me that tire-iron," Oscar said.

And Ferd worried even about other people's minor concerns. Like the time the couple came in with the tandem and the baby-basket on it. Free air was all they took; then the woman decided to change the diaper and one of the safety pins broke.

"Why are there never any safety pins?" the woman fretted, rummaging here and rummaging there. "There are *never* any safety pins."

Ferd made sympathetic noises, went to see if he had any; but, though he was sure there'd been some in the office, he couldn't find them. So they drove off with one side of the diaper tied in a clumsy knot.

At lunch, Ferd said it was too bad about the safety pins. Oscar dug his teeth into a sandwich, tugged, tore, chewed, swallowed. Ferd liked to experiment with sandwich spreads—the one he liked most was cream-cheese, olives, anchovy and avocado, mashed up with a little mayonnaise—but Oscar always had the same pink luncheon-meat.

"It must be difficult with a baby." Ferd nibbled. "Not just traveling, but raising it."

Oscar said, "Jeez, there's drugstores in every block, and if you can't read, you can at least reckernize them."

"Drugstores? Oh, to buy safety pins, you mean."

"Yeah. Safety pins."

"But . . . you know . . . it's true . . . there's never any safety pins when you look."

Oscar uncapped his beer, rinsed the first mouthful around. "Aha! Always plenny of clothes hangers, though. Throw 'em out every month, next month same closet's full of 'm again. Now whatcha wanna do in your spare time, you invent a device which it'll make safety pins outa clothes hangers."

Ferd nodded abstractedly. "But in my spare time I'm working on the French racer . . ." It was a beautiful machine, light, low-slung, swift, red and shining. You felt like a bird when you rode it. But, good as it was, Ferd knew he could make it better. He showed it to everybody who came in the place until his interest slackened.

Nature was his latest hobby, or, rather, reading about Nature. Some kids had wandered by from the park one day with tin cans in which they had put salamanders and toads, and they proudly showed them to Ferd. After that, the work on the red racer slowed down and he spent his spare time on natural history books.

"Mimicry!" he cried to Oscar. "A wonderful thing!"

Oscar looked up interestedly from the bowling scores in the paper. "I seen Edie Adams on TV the other night, doing her imitation of Marilyn Monroe. Boy, oh, boy."

Ferd was irritated, shook his head. "Not that kind of mimicry. I mean how insects and arachnids will mimic the shapes of leaves and twigs and so on, to escape being eaten by birds or other insects and arachnids."

A scowl of disbelief passed over Oscar's heavy face. "You mean they change their *shapes?* What you giving me?"

"Oh, it's true. Sometimes the mimicry is for aggressive purposes, though—like a South African turtle that looks like a rock and so the fish swim up to it and then it catches them: Or that spider in Sumatra. When it lies on its back, it looks like a bird dropping. Catches butterflies that way."

Oscar laughed, a disgusted and incredulous noise. It died away as he turned back to the bowling scores. One hand groped at his pocket, came away, scratched absently at the orange thicket under the shirt, then went patting his hip pocket.

"Where's that pencil?" he muttered, got up, stomped into the office, pulled open drawers. His loud cry of "Hey!" brought Ferd into the tiny room.

"What's the matter?" Ferd asked.

Oscar pointed to a drawer. "Remember that time you claimed there were no safety pins here? Look—whole gahdamn drawer is full of 'em."

Ferd stared, scratched his head, said feebly that he was certain he'd looked there before . . .

A contralto voice from outside asked, "Anybody here?"

Oscar at once forgot the desk and its contents, called, "Be right with you," and was gone. Ferd followed him slowly.

There was a young woman in the shop, a rather massively built young woman, with muscular calves and a deep chest. She was pointing out the seat of her bicycle to Oscar, who was saying "Uh-huh" and looking more at her than at anything else. "It's just a little too far forward ("Uh-huh"), as you can see. A wrench is all I need ("Uh-huh"). It was silly of me to forget my tools."

Oscar repeated, "Uh-huh" automatically, then snapped to. "Fix it in a jiffy," he said, and—despite her insistence that she could do it herself—he did fix it. Though not quite in a jiffy. He refused money. He prolonged the conversation as long as he could.

"Well, thank *you*," the young woman said. "And now I've got to go."

"That machine feel all right to you now?"

"Perfectly. Thanks—"

"Tell you what, I'll just ride along with you a little bit, just—"

Pear-shaped notes of laughter lifted the young woman's bosom. "Oh, you couldn't keep up with me! My machine is a *racer!*"

The moment he saw Oscar's eye flit to the corner, Ferd knew what he had in mind. He stepped forward. His cry of "No" was drowned out by his partner's loud, "Well, I guess this racer here can keep up with yours!"

The young woman giggled richly, said, well, they would see about that, and was off. Oscar, ignoring Ferd's outstretched hand, jumped on the French bike and was gone. Ferd stood in the doorway, watching the two figures, hunched over their handlebars, vanish down the road into the park. He went slowly back inside.

It was almost evening before Oscar returned, sweaty but smiling. Smiling broadly. "Hey, what a babe!" he cried. He wagged his head, he whistled, he made gestures, noises like escaping steam. "Boy, oh, boy, what an afternoon!"

"Give me the bike," Ferd demanded.

Oscar said, yeah, sure; turned it over to him and went to wash. Ferd looked at the machine. The red enamel was covered with dust; there was mud spattered and dirt and bits of dried grass. It seemed soiled—degraded. He had felt like a swift bird when he rode it . . .

Oscar came out wet and beaming. He gave a cry of dismay, ran over.

"Stand away," said Ferd, gesturing with the knife. He slashed the tires, the seat and seat cover, again and again.

"You crazy?" Oscar yelled. "You outa your mind? Ferd, no, don't, Ferd—"

Ferd cut the spokes, bent them, twisted them. He took the heaviest hammer and pounded the frame into shapelessness, and then he kept on pounding till his breath was gasping.

"You're not only crazy," Oscar said bitterly, "you're rotten jealous. You can go to hell." He stomped away.

Ferd, feeling sick and stiff, locked up, went slowly home. He had no taste for reading, turned out the light and fell into bed, where he lay awake for hours, listening to the rustling noises of the night and thinking hot, twisted thoughts.

They didn't speak to each other for days after that, except for the necessities of the work. The wreckage of the French racer lay behind the shop. For about two weeks, neither wanted to go out back where he'd have to see it.

One morning Ferd arrived to be greeted by his partner, who began to shake his head in astonishment even before he started speaking. "How did you *do* it, how did you *do* it, Ferd? Jeez, what a beautiful job—I gotta hand it to you—no more hard feelings, huh, Ferd?"

Ferd took his hand. "Sure, sure. But what are you talking about?"

Oscar led him out back. There was the red racer, all in one piece, not a mark or scratch on it, its enamel bright as ever. Ferd gaped. He squatted down and examined it. It *was* his machine. Every change, every improvement he had made, was there.

He straightened up slowly. "Regeneration . . ."

"Huh? What say?" Oscar asked. Then, "Hey, kiddo, you're all white. Whad you do, stay up all night and didn't get no sleep? Come on in and siddown. But I still don't see how you done it."

Inside, Ferd sat down. He wet his lips. He said, "Oscar—listen—"

"Yeah?"

"Oscar. You know what regeneration is? No? Listen. Some kinds of lizards, you grab them by the tail, the tail breaks off and they grow a new one. If a lobster loses a claw, it regenerates another one. Some kinds of worms—and hydras and starfish—you cut them into pieces, each piece will grow back the missing parts. Salamanders can regenerate lost hands, and frogs can grow legs back."

"No kidding, Ferd. But, uh, I mean: Nature. Very interesting. But to get back to the bike now—how'd you manage to fix it so good?"

"I never touched it. It regenerated. Like a newt. Or a lobster."

Oscar considered this. He lowered his head, looked up at Ferd from under his eyebrows. "Well, now, Ferd . . . Look . . . How come all broke bikes don't do that?"

"This isn't an ordinary bike. I mean it isn't a real bike." Catching Oscar's look, he shouted, "Well, it's *true!*"

The shout changed Oscar's attitude from bafflement to incredulity. He got up. "So for the sake of argument, let's say all that stuff about the bugs and the eels or whatever the hell you were talking about is true. But they're alive. A bike ain't." He looked down triumphantly.

Ferd shook his leg from side to side, looked at it. "A crystal isn't, either, but a broken crystal can regenerate itself if the conditions are right. Oscar, go see if the safety pins are still in the desk. Please, Oscar?"

He listened as Oscar, muttering, pulled the desk drawers out, rummaged in them, slammed them shut, tramped back.

"Naa," he said. "All gone. Like that lady said that time, and you said, there never are any safety pins when you want 'em. They disap—Ferd? What're—"

Ferd jerked open the closet door, jumped back as a shoal of clothes hangers clattered out.

"And like *you* say," Ferd said with a twist of his mouth, "on the other hand, there are always plenty of clothes hangers. There weren't any here before."

Oscar shrugged. "I don't see what you're getting at. But anybody could of got in here and took the pins and left the hangers. *I* could of—but I didn't. Or *you* could of. Maybe—" He narrowed his eyes. "Maybe you walked in your sleep and done it. You better see a doctor. Jeez, you look rotten."

Ferd went back and sat down, put his head in his hands. "I feel rotten. I'm scared, Oscar. Scared of what?" He breathed noisily. "I'll tell you. Like I explained before, about how things that live in the wild places, they mimic other things there. Twigs, leaves . . . toads that look like rocks. Well, suppose there are . . . things . . . that live in people places. Cities. Houses. These things could imitate—well, other kinds of things you find in people places—"

"*People* places, for crise sake!"

"Maybe they're a different kind of life-form. Maybe they get their nourishment out of the elements in the air. You know what safety pins *are*—these other kinds of them? Oscar, the safety pins are the pupa-forms and then they, like, *hatch*. Into the larval-forms. Which look just like coat hangers. They feel like them, even, but they're not. Oscar, they're not, not really, not really, not . . ."

He began to cry into his hands. Oscar looked at him. He shook his head.

After a minute, Ferd controlled himself somewhat. He snuffled. "All these bicycles the cops find, and they hold them waiting for owners to show up, and then we buy them at the sale because no owners show up because there aren't any, and the same with the ones the kids are always trying to sell us, and they say they just found them, and they really did because they were never made in a factory. They grew. They grow. You smash them and throw them away, they regenerate."

Oscar turned to someone who wasn't there and waggled his head. "Hoo, boy," he said. Then, to Ferd: "You mean one day there's a safety pin and the next day instead there's a coat hanger?"

Ferd said, "One day there's a cocoon; the next day there's a moth. One day there's an egg; the next day there's a chicken. But with . . . these it doesn't happen in the open daytime where you can see it. But at night, Oscar—at night you can *hear* it happening. All the little noises in the night-time, Oscar—"

Oscar said, "Then how come we ain't up to our belly-button in bikes? If I had a bike for every coat hanger—"

But Ferd had considered that, too. If every codfish egg, he explained, or every oyster spawn grew to maturity, a man could walk across the ocean on the backs of all the codfish or oysters there'd be. So many died, so many were eaten by predatory creatures, that Nature had to produce a maximum in order to allow a minimum to arrive at maturity. And Oscar's question was: then who, uh, eats the, uh, coat hangers?

Ferd's eyes focused through wall, buildings, park, more buildings, to the horizon. "You got to get the picture. I'm not talking about real pins or hangers. I got a name for the others—'false friends,' I call them. In high school French, we had to watch out for French words that looked like English words, but really were different. *'Faux amis,'* they call them. False friends. Pseudo-pins. Pseudo-hangers . . . Who eats them? I don't know for sure. Pseudo-vacuum cleaners, maybe?"

His partner, with a loud groan, slapped his hands against his thighs. He said, "Ferd, Ferd, for crise sake. You know what's the trouble with you? You talk about oysters, but you forgot what they're good for. You forgot there's two kinds of people in the world. Close up them books, them bug books and French books. Get out, mingle, meet people. Soak up some brew. You know what? The next time Norma—that's this broad's name with the racing bike—the next time she comes here, *you* take the red racer and *you* go out in the woods with her. I won't mind. And I don't think she will, either. Not *too* much."

But Ferd said no. "I never want to touch the red racer again. I'm afraid of it."

At this, Oscar pulled him to his feet, dragged him protestingly out to the back and forced him to get on the French machine. "Only way to conquer your fear of it!"

Ferd started off, white-faced, wobbling. And in a moment was on the ground, rolling and thrashing, screaming.

Oscar pulled him away from the machine.

"It threw me!" Ferd yelled. "It tried to kill me! Look—blood!"

His partner said it was a bump that threw him—it was his own fear. The blood? A broken spoke. Grazed his cheek. And he insisted Ferd get on the bicycle again, to conquer his fear.

But Ferd had grown hysterical. He shouted that no man was safe—that mankind had to be warned. It took Oscar a long time to pacify him and to get him to go home and into bed.

He didn't tell all this to Mr. Whatney, of course. He merely said that his partner had gotten fed up with the bicycle business.

"It don't pay to worry and try to change the world," he pointed out. "I always say take things the way they are. If you can't lick 'em, join 'em."

Mr. Whatney said that was his philosophy, exactly. He asked how things were, since.

"Well . . . not *too* bad. I'm engaged, you know. Name's Norma. Crazy about bicycles. Everything considered, things aren't bad at all. More work, yes, but I can do things all my own way, so. . . ."

Mr. Whatney nodded. He glanced around the shop. "I see they're still making drop-frame bikes," he said, "though, with so many women wearing slacks, I wonder they bother."

Oscar said, "Well, I dunno. I kinda like it that way. Ever stop to think that bicycles are like people? I mean, of all the machines in the world, only bikes come male and female."

Mr. Whatney gave a little giggle, said that was *right*, he had never thought of it like that before. Then Oscar asked if Mr. Whatney had anything in particular in mind—not that he wasn't always welcome.

"Well, I wanted to look over what you've got. My boy's birthday is coming up—"

Oscar nodded sagely. "Now here's a job," he said, "which you can't get it in any other place but here. Specialty of the house. Combines the best features of the French racer and the American standard, but it's made right here, and it comes in three models—Junior, Intermediate and Regular. Beautiful, ain't it?"

Mr. Whatney observed that, say, that might be just the ticket. "By the way," he asked, "what's become of the French racer, the red one, used to be here?"

Oscar's face twitched. Then it grew bland and innocent and he leaned over and nudged his customer. "Oh, *that* one. Old Frenchy? Why, I put *him* out to stud!"

And they laughed and they laughed, and after they told a few more stories they concluded the sale, and they had a few beers and they laughed some more. And then they said what a shame it was about Ferd, poor old Ferd, who had been found in his own closet with an unraveled coat hanger coiled tightly around his neck.

ROBERT SHECKLEY (1928–)

A New York–born Science Fiction writer like Alfred Bester and Avram Davidson, Robert Sheckley published his first story, "Final Examination," in Imagination *in 1952.*

Sheckley's grim worldview is reflective of the Cold War era in which he emerged as a writer. However, this mindset is not always or necessarily oppressive in his stories. Rather, it leads the reader to introspection and is often social satire. His worldview resembles that of Kurt Vonnegut, and like Vonnegut he irreverently exploits and ignores the conventions of Science Fiction.

Robert Sheckley's writing can generally be compared to that of Harlan Ellison and Barry N. Malzberg in that it transcends genre boundaries and is highly innovative. Like Ray Bradbury, Sheckley's specialty is the short story; and also like Bradbury his best novels are episodic—or connected short stories—in composition.

Sheckley's novel Immortality, Inc. *(1959) was made into the popular movie* Freejack *in 1992. The novel and movie both feature a story of greed, decadence, and horrific social decay.*

"The Store of the Worlds" is inventive and insightful. It is classic Robert Sheckley.

The Store of the Worlds

(Playboy, September 1959)

Mr. Wayne came to the end of the long, shoulder-high mound of gray rubble, and there was the Store of the Worlds. It was exactly as his friends had described: a small shack constructed of bits of lumber, parts of cars, a piece of galvanized iron, and a few rows of crumbling bricks, all daubed over with a watery blue paint.

He glanced back down the long lane of rubble to make sure he hadn't been followed. He tucked his parcel more firmly under his arm; then, with a little shiver at his own audacity, he opened the door and slipped inside.

"Good morning," the proprietor said.

He, too, was exactly as described: a tall, crafty-looking old fellow with narrow eyes and downcast mouth. His name was Tompkins. He sat in an old rocking chair, and perched on the back of it was a blue-and-green parrot. There was one other chair in the store, and a table. On the table was a rusted hypodermic.

"I've heard about your store from friends," Mr. Wayne said.

"Then you know my price," Tompkins said. "Have you brought it?"

"Yes," said Mr. Wayne, holding up his parcel. "All my worldly goods. But I want to ask first—"

"They always want to ask," Tompkins said to the parrot, who blinked. "Go ahead, ask."

"I want to know what really happens."

Tompkins sighed. "What happens is that: I give you an injection which knocks you out. Then, with the aid of certain gadgets which I have in the back of the store, I liberate your mind."

Tompkins smiled as he said that, and his silent parrot seemed to smile, too.

"What happens then?" Mr. Wayne asked.

"Your mind, liberated from its body, is able to choose from the countless probability worlds which the earth casts off in every second of its existence."

Grinning now, Tompkins sat up in his rocking chair and began to show signs of enthusiasm.

"Yes, my friend, though you might not have suspected it, from the moment this battered earth was born out of the sun's fiery womb, it cast off its alternate-probability worlds. Worlds without end, emanating from events large and small; every Alexander and every amoeba creating worlds, just as ripples will spread in a pond no matter how big or how small the stone you throw. Doesn't every object cast a shadow? Well, my friend, the earth itself is four-dimensional; therefore it casts three-dimensional shadows, solid reflections of itself, through every moment of its being. Millions, billions of earths! An infinity of earths! And your mind, liberated by me, will be able to select any of these worlds and live upon it for a while."

Mr. Wayne was uncomfortably aware that Tompkins sounded like a circus barker, proclaiming marvels that simply couldn't exist. But, Mr. Wayne reminded himself, things had happened within his own lifetime which he would never have believed possible. Never! So perhaps the wonders that Tompkins spoke of were possible, too.

Mr. Wayne said, "My friends also told me—"

"That I was an out-and-out fraud?" Tompkins asked.

"Some of them *implied* that," Mr. Wayne said cautiously. "But I try to keep an open mind. They also said—"

"I know what your dirty-minded friends said. They told you about the fulfillment of desire. Is that what you want to hear about?"

"Yes," said Mr. Wayne. "They told me that whatever I wished for—whatever I wanted—"

"Exactly," Tompkins said. "The thing could work in no other way. There are the infinite worlds to choose among. Your mind chooses and is guided only by desire. Your deepest desire is the only thing that counts. If you have been harboring a secret dream of murder—"

"Oh, hardly, hardly!" cried Mr. Wayne.

"—then you will go to a world where you *can* murder, where you can roll in blood, where you can outdo de Sade or Nero or whoever your idol may be. Suppose it's power you want? Then you'll choose a world where you are a god, literally and actually. A bloodthirsty Juggernaut, perhaps, or an all-wise Buddha."

"I doubt very much if I—"

"There are other desires, too," Tompkins said. "All heavens and all hells will be open to you. Unbridled sexuality. Gluttony, drunkenness, love, fame—anything you want."

"Amazing!" said Mr. Wayne.

"Yes," Tompkins agreed. "Of course, my little list doesn't exhaust all the possibilities, all the combinations and permutations of desire. For all I know, you might want a simple, placid, pastoral existence on a South Sea island among idealized natives."

"That sounds more like me," Mr. Wayne said with a shy laugh.

"But who knows?" Tompkins asked. "Even you might not know what your true desires are. They might involve your own death."

"Does that happen often?" Mr. Wayne asked anxiously.

"Occasionally."

"I wouldn't want to die," Mr. Wayne said.

"It hardly ever happens," Tompkins said, looking at the parcel in Mr. Wayne's hands.

"If you say so. . . . But how do I know all this is real? Your fee is extremely high; it'll take everything I own. And for all I know, you'll give me a drug and I'll just *dream*! Everything I own just for a—shot of heroin and a lot of fancy words!"

Tompkins smiled reassuringly. "The experience has no druglike quality about it. And no sensation of a dream, either."

"If it's *true*," Mr. Wayne said a little petulantly, "why can't I stay in the world of my desire for good?"

"I'm working on that," Tompkins said. "That's why I charge so high a fee—to get materials, to experiment. I'm trying to find a way of making the transition permanent. So far I haven't been able to loosen the cord that binds a man to his own earth—and pulls him back to it. Not even the great mystics could cut that cord, except with death. But I still have my hopes."

"It would be a great thing if you succeeded," Mr. Wayne said politely.

"Yes, it would!" Tompkins cried with a surprising burst of passion. "For then I'd turn my wretched shop into an escape hatch! My process would be free then, free for everyone! Everyone could go to the earth of his desires, the earth that really suited him and leave *this* damned place to the rats and worms—"

Tompkins cut himself off in midsentence and became icy calm. "But I fear my prejudices are showing. I can't offer a permanent escape from this world yet, not one that doesn't involve death. Perhaps I never will be able to. For now, all I can offer you is a vacation, a change, a taste of another world and a look at your own desires. You know my fee. I'll refund if the experience isn't satisfactory."

"That's good of you," Mr. Wayne said quite earnestly. "But there's that other matter my friends told me about. The ten years off my life."

"That can't be helped," Tompkins said, "and can't be refunded. My process is a tremendous strain on the nervous system, and life expectancy is shortened accordingly. That's one of the reasons why our so-called government has declared my process illegal."

"But they don't enforce the ban very firmly," Mr. Wayne said.

"No. Officially the process is banned as a harmful fraud. But officials are men, too. They'd like to leave this earth, just like everyone else."

"The cost," Mr. Wayne mused, gripping his parcel tightly. "And ten years off my life! For the fulfillment of my secret desires. . . . Really, I must give this some thought."

"Think away," Tompkins said indifferently.

All the way home Mr. Wayne thought about it. When his train reached Port Washington, Long Island, he was still thinking. And driving his car from the station to his house, he was still thinking about Tompkins's crafty old face, and worlds of probability, and the fulfillment of desire.

But when he stepped inside his home, those thoughts had to stop. Janet, his wife, wanted him to speak sharply to the maid, who had been drinking again. His son, Tommy, wanted help with the sloop, which was to be launched tomorrow. And his baby daughter wanted to tell about her day in kindergarten.

Mr. Wayne spoke pleasantly but firmly to the maid. He helped Tommy put the final coat of copper paint on the sloop's bottom, and he listened to Peggy tell her adventures in the playground.

Later, when the children were in bed and he and Janet were alone in their living room, she asked him if something was wrong.

"Wrong?"

"You seem to be worried about something," Janet said. "Did you have a bad day at the office?"

"Oh, just the usual sort of thing . . ."

He certainly was not going to tell Janet, or anyone else, that he had taken the day off and gone to see Tompkins in his crazy old Store of the Worlds. Nor was he going to speak about the right every man should have, once in his lifetime, to fulfill his most secret desires. Janet, with her good common sense, would never understand that.

The next days at the office were extremely hectic. All of Wall Street was in a mild panic over events in the Middle East and in Asia, and stocks were reacting accordingly. Mr. Wayne settled down to work. He tried not to think of the fulfillment of desire at the cost of everything he possessed, with ten years of his life thrown in for good measure. It was crazy! Old Tompkins must be insane!

On weekends he went sailing with Tommy. The old sloop was behaving very well, taking practically no water through her bottom seams. Tommy wanted a new suit of racing sails, but Mr. Wayne sternly rejected that. Perhaps next year, if the market looked better. For now, the old sails would have to do.

Sometimes at night, after the children were asleep, he and Janet would go sailing. Long Island Sound was quiet then and cool. Their boat glided past the blinking buoys, sailing toward the swollen yellow moon.

"I *know* something's on your mind," Janet said.

"Darling, please!"

"Is there something you're keeping from me?"

"Nothing!"

"Are you sure? Are you absolutely sure?"

"Absolutely sure."

"Then, put your arms around me. That's right . . ."

And the sloop sailed itself for a while.

Desire and fulfillment. . . . But autumn came and the sloop had to be hauled. The stock market regained some stability, but Peggy caught the measles. Tommy wanted to know the difference between ordinary bombs, atom bombs, hydrogen bombs, cobalt bombs and all the other kinds of bombs that were in the news. Mr. Wayne explained to the best of his ability. And the maid quit unexpectedly.

Secret desires were all very well. Perhaps he *did* want to kill someone or live on a South Sea island. But there were responsibilities to consider. He had two growing children and the best of wives.

Perhaps around Christmastime. . . .

But in midwinter there was a fire in the unoccupied guest room due to defective wiring. The firemen put out the blaze without much damage, and no one was hurt. But it put any thought of Tompkins out of his mind for a while. First the bedroom had to be repaired, for Mr. Wayne was very proud of his gracious old house.

Business was still frantic and uncertain due to the international situation. Those Russians, those Arabs, those Greeks, those Chinese. The intercontinental missiles, the atom bombs, the Sputniks. . . . Mr. Wayne spent long days at the office and sometimes evenings, too. Tommy caught the mumps. A part of the roof had to be reshingled. And then already it was time to consider the spring launching of the sloop.

A year had passed, and he'd had very little time to think of secret desires. But perhaps next year. In the meantime . . .

"Well?" said Tompkins. "Are you all right?"

"Yes, quite all right," Mr. Wayne said. He got up from the chair and rubbed his forehead.

"Do you want a refund?" Tompkins asked.

"No. The experience was quite satisfactory."

"They always are," Tompkins said, winking lewdly at the parrot. "Well, what was yours?"

"A world of the recent past," Mr. Wayne said.

"A lot of them are. Did you find out about your secret desire? Was it murder? Or a South Sea island?"

"I'd rather not discuss it," Mr. Wayne said pleasantly but firmly.

"A lot of people won't discuss it with me," Tompkins said sulkily. "I'll be damned if I know why."

"Because—well, I think the world of one's secret desire seems sacred, somehow. No offense. . . . Do you think you'll ever be able to make it permanent? The world of one's choice, I mean?"

The old man shrugged his shoulders. "I'm trying. If I succeed, you'll hear about it. Everyone will."

"Yes, I suppose so." Mr. Wayne undid his parcel and laid its contents on the table. The parcel contained a pair of army boots, a knife, two coils of copper wire, and three small cans of corned beef.

Tompkins's eyes glittered for a moment. "Quite satisfactory," he said. "Thank you."

"Good-bye," said Mr. Wayne. "And thank *you*."

Mr. Wayne left the shop and hurried down to the end of the lane of gray rubble. Beyond it, as far as he cold see, lay flat fields of rubble, brown and gray and black. Those fields, stretching to every horizon, were made of the twisted corpses of buildings, the shattered remnants of trees and the fine white ash that once was human flesh and bone.

"Well," Mr. Wayne said to himself, "at least we gave as good as we got."

His year in the past had cost him everything he owned and ten years of life thrown in for good measure. Had it been a dream? It was still worth it! But now he had to put away all thought of Janet and the children. That was finished, unless Tompkins perfected his process. Now he had to think about his own survival.

He picked his way carefully through the rubble, determined to get back to the shelter before dark, before the rats came out. If he didn't hurry, he'd miss the evening potato ration.

🕷 KURT VONNEGUT (JR.) (1922 *Spring* ~~2007~~)

One of the most critically recognized authors of the twentieth century, Indianapolis-born Kurt Vonnegut began as a Science Fiction writer and then soon expanded and transcended the genre. His first story, entitled "Report on the Barnhouse Effect," was published in Collier's *in 1950. His first novel was* Player Piano *(1952), a tale of humanity's surrender to increasingly powerful technology and machines.*

Humor, satire, and social criticism mark Vonnegut's writing. The author's experiences as a World War II prisoner of war and as a factory worker have supplied much subject matter for his fiction. The list of Vonnegut's landmark novels is impressive and includes The Sirens of Titan *(1959),* Mother Night *(1962),* Cat's Cradle *(1963),* God Bless You, Mr. Rosewater *(1965),* Slaughter House-Five, or The Children's Crusade: A Duty-Dance with Death *(1969),* Breakfast of Champions, or Goodbye, Blue Monday! *(1973),* Slapstick, or Lonesome No More *(1976),* Jailbird *(1979),* Dead-Eye Dick *(1982),* Galapagos *(1985),* Hocus Pocus, or What's the Hurry, Sam? *(1990), and* Timequake *(1997). His short story collections include* Welcome to the Monkey House *(1968) and* Bagombo Snuff Box *(1999).*

"Harrison Bergeron," collected in Welcome to the Monkey House, *is perhaps Kurt Vonnegut's most famous short story. It is a consummate tale of social criticism and the evils of censorship and too much government.*

Harrison Bergeron

(The Magazine of Fantasy and Science Fiction, *October 1961*)

The year was 2081, and everybody was finally equal. They weren't only equal before God and the law. They were equal every which way. Nobody was smarter than anybody else. Nobody was better looking than anybody else. Nobody was stronger or quicker than anybody else. All this equality was due to the 211th, 212th, and 213th Amendments to the Constitution, and to the unceasing vigilance of agents of the United States Handicapper General.

Some things about living still weren't quite right, though. April, for instance, still drove people crazy by not being springtime. And it was in that clammy month that the H-G men took George and Hazel Bergeron's fourteen-year-old son, Harrison, away.

It was tragic, all right, but George and Hazel couldn't think about it very hard. Hazel had a perfectly average intelligence, which meant she couldn't think about anything except in short bursts. And George, while his intelligence was way above normal, had a little mental handicap radio in his ear. He was required by law to wear it at all times. It was tuned to a government transmitter. Every twenty seconds or so, the transmitter would send out some sharp noise to keep people like George from taking unfair advantage of their brains.

George and Hazel were watching television. There were tears on Hazel's cheeks, but she'd forgotten for the moment what they were about.

On the television screen were ballerinas.

A buzzer sounded in George's head. His thoughts fled in panic, like bandits from a burglar alarm.

"That was a real pretty dance, that dance they just did," said Hazel.

"Huh?" said George.

"That dance—it was nice," said Hazel.

"Yup," said George. He tried to think a little about the ballerinas. They weren't really very good—no better than anybody else would have been, anyway. They were burdened with sashweights and bags of birdshot, and their faces were masked, so that no one, seeing a free and graceful gesture or a pretty face, would feel like something the cat drug in. George was toying with the vague notion that maybe dancers shouldn't be handicapped. But he didn't get very far with it before another noise in his ear radio scattered his thoughts.

George winced. So did two out of the eight ballerinas.

Hazel saw him wince. Having no mental handicap herself, she had to ask George what the latest sound had been.

"Sounded like somebody hitting a milk bottle with a ball peen hammer," said George.

"I'd think it would be real interesting, hearing all the different sounds," said Hazel, a little envious. "All the things they think up."

"Um," said George.

"Only, if I was Handicapper General, you know what I would do?" said Hazel. Hazel, as a matter of fact, bore a strong resemblance to the Handicapper General, a woman named Diana Moon Glampers. "If I was Diana Moon Glampers," said Hazel, "I'd have chimes on Sunday—just chimes. Kind of in honor of religion."

"I could think, if it was just chimes," said George.

"Well—maybe make 'em real loud," said Hazel. "I think I'd make a good Handicapper General."

"Good as anybody else," said George.

"Who knows better'n I do what normal is?" said Hazel.

"Right," said George. He began to think glimmeringly about his abnormal son who was now in jail, about Harrison, but a twenty-one-gun salute in his head stopped that.

"Boy!" said Hazel, "that was a doozy, wasn't it?"

It was such a doozy that George was white and trembling, and tears stood on the rims of his red eyes. Two of the eight ballerinas had collapsed to the studio floor, were holding their temples.

"All of a sudden you look so tired," said Hazel. "Why don't you stretch out on the sofa, so's you can rest your handicap bag on the pillows, honeybunch." She was referring to the forty-seven pounds of birdshot in a canvas bag, which was padlocked around George's neck. "Go on and rest the bag for a little while," she said. "I don't care if you're not equal to me for a while."

George weighed the bag with his hands. "I don't mind it," he said. "I don't notice it any more. It's just a part of me."

"You been so tired lately—kind of wore out," said Hazel. "If there was just some way we could make a little hole in the bottom of the bag, and just take out a few of them lead balls. Just a few."

"Two years in prison and two thousand dollars fine for every ball I took out," said George. "I don't call that a bargain."

"If you could just take a few out when you came home from work," said Hazel. "I mean—you don't compete with anybody around here. You just set around."

"If I tried to get away with it," said George, "then other people'd get away with it—and pretty soon we'd be right back to the dark ages again, with everybody competing against everybody else. You wouldn't like that, would you?"

"I'd hate it," said Hazel.

"There you are," said George. "The minute people start cheating on laws, what do you think happens to society?"

If Hazel hadn't been able to come up with an answer to this question, George couldn't have supplied one. A siren was going off in his head.

"Reckon it'd fall all apart," said Hazel.

"What would?" said George blankly.

"Society," said Hazel uncertainly. "Wasn't that what you just said?"

"Who knows?" said George.

The television program was suddenly interrupted for a news bulletin. It wasn't clear at first as to what the bulletin was about, since the announcer, like all announcers, had a serious speech impediment. For about half a minute, and in a state of high excitement, the announcer tried to say, "Ladies and gentlemen—"

He finally gave up, handed the bulletin to a ballerina to read.

"That's all right—" Hazel said of the announcer, "he tried. That's the big thing. He tried to do the best he could with what God gave him. He should get a nice raise for trying so hard."

"Ladies and gentlemen—" said the ballerina, reading the bulletin. She must have been extraordinarily beautiful, because the mask she wore was hideous. And it was easy to see that she was the strongest and most graceful of all the dancers, for her handicap bags were as big as those worn by two-hundred-pound men.

And she had to apologize at once for her voice, which was a very unfair voice for a woman to use. Her voice was a warm, luminous, timeless melody. "Excuse me—" she said, and she began again, making her voice absolutely uncompetitive.

"Harrison Bergeron, age fourteen," she said in a grackle squawk, "has just escaped from jail, where he was held on suspicion of plotting to overthrow the government. He is a genius and an athlete, is under-handicapped, and should be regarded as extremely dangerous."

A police photograph of Harrison Bergeron was flashed on the screen-upside down, then sideways, upside down again, then right side up. The picture showed the full length of Harrison against a background calibrated in feet and inches. He was exactly seven feet tall.

The rest of Harrison's appearance was Halloween and hardware. Nobody had ever borne heavier handicaps. He had outgrown hindrances faster than the H-G men could think them up. Instead of a little ear radio for a mental handicap, he wore a tremendous pair of earphones, and spectacles with thick wavy lenses. The spectacles were intended to make him not only half blind, but to give him whanging headaches besides.

Scrap metal was hung all over him. Ordinarily, there was a certain symmetry, a military neatness to the handicaps issued to strong people, but Harrison looked like a walking junkyard. In the race of life, Harrison carried three hundred pounds.

And to offset his good looks, the H-G men required that he wear at all times a red rubber ball for a nose, keep his eyebrows shaved off, and cover his even white teeth with black caps at snaggle-tooth random.

"If you see this boy," said the ballerina, "do not—I repeat, do not—try to reason with him."

There was the shriek of a door being torn from its hinges.

Screams and barking cries of consternation came from the television set. The photograph of Harrison Bergeron on the screen jumped again and again, as though dancing to the tune of an earthquake.

George Bergeron correctly identified the earthquake, and well he might have—for many was the time his own home had danced to the same crashing tune. "My God—" said George, "that must be Harrison!"

The realization was blasted from his mind instantly by the sound of an automobile collision in his head.

When George could open his eyes again, the photograph of Harrison was gone. A living, breathing Harrison filled the screen.

Clanking, clownish, and huge, Harrison stood in the center of the studio. The knob of the uprooted studio door was still in his hand. Ballerinas, technicians, musicians, and announcers cowered on their knees before him, expecting to die.

"I am the Emperor!" cried Harrison. "Do you hear? I am the Emperor! Everybody must do what I say at once!" He stamped his foot and the studio shook.

"Even as I stand here—" he bellowed, "crippled, hobbled, sickened—I am a greater ruler than any man who ever lived! Now watch me become what I *can* become!"

Harrison tore the straps of his handicap harness like wet tissue paper, tore straps guaranteed to support five thousand pounds.

Harrison's scrap-iron handicaps crashed to the floor.

Harrison thrust his thumbs under the bar of the padlock that secured his head harness. The bar snapped like celery. Harrison smashed his headphones and spectacles against the wall.

He flung away his rubber-ball nose, revealed a man that would have awed Thor, the god of thunder.

"I shall now select my Empress!" he said, looking down on the cowering people. "Let the first woman who dares rise to her feet claim her mate and her throne!"

A moment passed, and then a ballerina arose, swaying like a willow.

Harrison plucked the mental handicap from her ear, snapped off her physical handicaps with marvelous delicacy. Last of all, he removed her mask.

She was blindingly beautiful.

"Now—" said Harrison, taking her hand, "shall we show the people the meaning of the word dance? Music!" he commanded.

The musicians scrambled back into their chairs, and Harrison stripped them of their handicaps, too. "Play your best," he told them, "and I'll make you barons and dukes and earls."

The music began. It was normal at first—cheap, silly, false. But Harrison snatched two musicians from their chairs, waved them like batons as he sang the music as he wanted it played. He slammed them back into their chairs.

The music began again and was much improved.

Harrison and his Empress merely listened to the music for a while—listened gravely, as though synchronizing their heartbeats with it.

They shifted their weights to their toes.

Harrison placed his big hands on the girl's tiny waist, letting her sense the weightlessness that would soon be hers.

And then, in an explosion of joy and grace, into the air they sprang!

Not only were the laws of the land abandoned, but the law of gravity and the laws of motion as well.

They reeled, whirled, swiveled, flounced, capered, gamboled, and spun.

They leaped like deer on the moon.

The studio ceiling was thirty feet high, but each leap brought the dancers nearer to it.

It became their obvious intention to kiss the ceiling.

They kissed it.

And then, neutralizing gravity with love and pure will, they remained suspended in air inches below the ceiling, and they kissed each other for a long, long time.

It was then that Diana Moon Glampers, the Handicapper General, came into the studio with a double-barreled ten-gauge shotgun. She fired twice, and the Emperor and the Empress were dead before they hit the floor.

Diana Moon Glampers loaded the gun again. She aimed it at the musicians and told them they had ten seconds to get their handicaps back on.

It was then that the Bergerons' television tube burned out.

Hazel turned to comment about the blackout to George. But George had gone out into the kitchen for a can of beer.

George came back in with the beer, paused while a handicap signal shook him up. And then he sat down again. "You been crying?" he said to Hazel.

"Yup," she said.

"What about?" he said.

"I forget," she said. "Something real sad on television."

"What was it?" he said.

"It's all kind of mixed up in my mind," said Hazel.

"Forget sad things," said George.

"I always do," said Hazel.

"That's my girl," said George. He winced. There was the sound of a rivetting gun in his head.

"Gee—I could tell that one was a doozy," said Hazel.

"You can say that again," said George.

"Gee—" said Hazel, "I could tell that one was a doozy."

FRED(ERICK THOMAS) SABERHAGEN (1930–)

About fifty years after Hugo Gernsback (the founder of Amazing Stories *and other Science Fiction pulp magazines) came to the United States to market his batteries and related electrical equipment, Chicago-born Fred Saberhagen worked as an electronics technician. He did this between 1956 and 1962. Like both Gernsback and Kurt Vonnegut, Saberhagen was fascinated by the relationship of machines and technology to society. He began writing and publishing Science Fiction in 1961, and he continues to produce popular Science Fiction, Fantasy, and Mysteries to this day.*

In 1967, Saberhagen began work as a writer and editor for The Encyclopedia Britannica, *and he published the novel* Berserker *that same year. This was the first novel of the now-famous* Berserker *series. Saberhagen created other series of Fantasy and Science Fiction, including* The Empire of the East *and* Book of Lost Swords. *While these and other such sequences were highly popular, the* Berserker *series is probably Fred Saberhagen's most important contribution to Science Fiction.*

The Berserkers are a created group of machines that replicate and perpetuate themselves. These machines are linked by a common information processing network, and as they have grown stronger they have also gone increasingly amuck. Originally created to protect an old race, the Berserkers are now all-powerful and threatening.

In this series of stories, Fred Saberhagen investigates matters of humanity, technology, and human technology (a cross between the two). The stories, settings, and complications that the author imagines serve as effective instruments for a critique of society and technology.

Published just months before the novel Berserker, *the short story "Without a Thought (Fortress Ship)" is the very first installment of Fred Saberhagen's epic contribution to Science Fiction.*

Without a Thought

(Originally published as "Fortress Ship" in IF: Science Fiction, *January 1963)*

The machine was a vast fortress, containing no life, set by its long-dead masters to destroy anything that lived. It and a hundred like it were the inheritance of Earth from some war fought between unknown interstellar empires, in some time that could hardly be connected with any Earthly calendar.

One such machine could hang over a planet colonized by men and in two days pound the surface into a lifeless cloud of dust and steam, a hundred miles deep. This particular machine had already done just that.

It used no predictable tactics in its dedicated, unconscious war against life. The ancient, unknown gamesmen had built it as a random factor, to be loosed in the enemy's territory to do what damage it might. Men thought its plan of battle was chosen by the random disintegrations of atoms in a block of some long-lived isotope buried deep inside it, and so was not even in theory predictable by opposing brains, human or electronic.

Men called it a berserker.

Del Murray, sometime computer specialist, had called it other names than that; but right now he was too busy to waste breath, as he moved in staggering lunges around the little cabin of his one-man fighter, plugging in replacement units for equipment damaged by the last near-miss of a small berserker missile. An animal resembling a large dog with an ape's forelegs moved about the cabin too, carrying in its nearly human hands a supply of emergency sealing patches. The cabin air was full of haze. Wherever movement of the haze showed a leak to an unpressurized part of the hull, the dog-ape moved to skillfully apply a patch.

"Hello, Foxglove!" the man shouted, hoping his radio was again in working order.

"Hello, Murray, this is Foxglove," said a sudden loud voice in the cabin. "How far did you get?"

Del was too weary to show much relief that his communications were open again. "I'll let you know in a minute. At least it's stopped shooting at me for a while. Move, Newton." The alien animal, pet and ally, called an *aiyan*, moved away from the man's feet and kept single-mindedly looking for leaks.

After another minute's work Del could strap his body into the deep-cushioned command chair again, with something like an operational panel before him. That last near-miss had sprayed the whole cabin with fine, penetrating splinters. It was remarkable that man and *aiyan* had come through unwounded.

His radar working again, Del could say: "I'm about ninety miles out from it, Foxglove. On the opposite side from you." His present position was what he had been trying to achieve since the battle had begun.

The two Earth ships and the berserker were half a light year from the nearest sun. The berserker could not leap out of normal space, toward the defenseless colonies on the planets of that sun, while the two ships stayed close to it. There were only two men aboard Foxglove. Though they had more machinery working for them than did Del, both manned ships were mites compared to their opponent.

If a berserker machine like this one, not much smaller in cross-section than New Jersey, had drifted in a century earlier and found men crowded on one planet, there could have been no real struggle and no human survivors. Now, though the impersonal enemy swarmed through the galaxy, men could rise up in a cloud to meet them.

Del's radar showed him an ancient ruin of metal, spread out for a hundred miles before him. Men had blown holes in it the size of Manhattan Island, and melted puddles of slag as big as lakes upon its surface.

But the berserker's power was still enormous. So far no man had fought it and survived. Now, it could squash Del's little ship like a mosquito; it was wasting its unpredictable subtlety on him. Yet there was a special taste of terror in the very indifference of it. Men could never frighten this enemy, as it frightened them.

Earthmen's tactics, worked out from bitter experience against other berserkers, called for a simultaneous attack by three ships. Foxglove and Murray made two. A third was supposedly on the way, but still about eight hours distant, moving at c-plus velocity, outside of normal space and so out of communication with the others. Until it arrived, Foxglove and Murray must hold the berserker at bay, while it brooded unguessable schemes.

It might attack either ship at any moment, or it might seek to disengage. It might wait hours for them to make the first move—though it would certainly fight if the men attacked it. It had learned the language of Earth—it might try to talk with them. But always, ultimately, it would seek to destroy them and every other living thing it met. That was the basic command given it by the ancient warlords.

A thousand years ago, it would have easily swept ships of the type that now opposed it from its path, whether they carried fusion missiles or not. Now, it was no doubt in some electrical way conscious of its own weakening by accumulated damage. And perhaps in long centuries of fighting its way across the galaxy it had learned to be wary.

Now, quite suddenly, Del's detectors showed forcefields forming in behind his ship. Like the encircling arms of a great bear they blocked his path away from the enemy. He waited for some deadly blow, with his hand trembling over the red button that would salvo his atomic missiles at the berserker—but if he attacked alone, or even with Foxglove, the infernal machine would parry their missiles, crush their ships, and go on to destroy another helpless planet. Three ships were needed to attack. The red firing button was now only a last desperate resort.

Del was reporting the forcefields to Foxglove when he felt the first hint in his mind of another attack.

"Newton!" he called sharply, leaving the mike to Foxglove open. They would hear and understand what was going to happen.

The *aiyan* bounded instantly from its combat couch to stand before Del as if hypnotized, all attention riveted on the man. Del sometimes bragged: "Show Newton a drawing of different colored lights, convince him it represents a particular control panel, and he'll push buttons or whatever you tell him, until the real panel matches the drawing."

But no *aiyan* had the human ability to learn and to create on an abstract level; which was why Del was now going to put Newton in command of his ship.

He switched off the ship's computers—they were going to be as useless as his own brain, under the attack he felt gathering—and said to Newton: "Situation Zombie."

The animal responded instantly as it had been trained, seizing Del's hands with firm insistence, and dragging them one at a time down beside the command chair to where the fetters had been installed.

Hard experience had taught men something about the berserkers' mind weapon, although its principles of operation were still unknown. It was slow in its onslaught, and its effects could not be steadily maintained for more than about two hours, after which a berserker was evidently forced to turn it off for an equal time. But while in effect, it robbed any human or electronic brain of the ability to plan or to predict—and left it unconscious of its own incapacity.

It seemed to Del that all this had happened before, maybe more than once. Newton, that funny fellow, had gone too far with his pranks; he had abandoned the little boxes of colored beads that were his favorite toys, and was moving the controls around at the lighted panel. Unwilling to share the fun with Del, he had tied the man to his chair somehow. Such behavior was really intolerable, especially when there was supposed to be a battle in progress. Del tried to pull his hands free, and called to Newton.

Newton whined earnestly and stayed at the panel.

"Newt, you dog. Come, lemme loose. I know what I have to say: Four score and seven . . . hey, Newt, where're your toys? Lemme see your pretty beads." There were hundreds of tiny boxes of the varicolored beads, leftover trade goods that Newton loved to sort out and handle. Del peered around the cabin, chuckling a little at his own cleverness. He would get Newton distracted by the beads, and then . . . the vague idea faded into other crackbrained grotesqueries.

Newton whined now and then but stayed at the panel moving controls in the long sequence he had been taught, taking the ship through the feinting, evasive maneuvers that might fool a berserker into thinking that it was still competently manned. Newton never put a hand near the big red button. Only if he felt deadly pain himself, or found a dead man in Del's chair, would he reach for that.

"Ah, roger, Murray," said the radio from time to time, as if acknowledging a message. Sometimes Foxglove added a few words or numbers that might have meant something. Del wondered what the talking was about.

At last he understood that Foxglove was trying to help maintain the illusion that there was still a competent brain in charge of Del's ship. The fear-reaction came when he began to realize that he had once again lived through the effect of the mind-weapon. The brooding berserker, half genius, half idiot, had forborne to press the attack when success would have been certain. Perhaps deceived, perhaps following the strategy that avoided predictability at almost any cost.

"Newton." The animal turned, hearing a change in his voice. Now Del could say the words that would tell Newton it was safe to set his master free, a sequence too long for anyone under the mindweapon to recite.

"—shall not perish from the Earth," he finished. With a yelp of joy Newton pulled the fetters from Del's hands. Del turned instantly to the radio.

"Effect has evidently been turned off, Foxglove," said Del's voice through the speaker in the cabin of the larger ship.

The Commander let out a sigh. "He's back in control!"

The Second Officer—there was no Third—said: "That means we've got some kind of fighting chance, for the next two hours. I say let's attack now!"

The Commander shook his head, slowly but without hesitation. "With two ships, we don't have any real chance. Less than four hours until Gizmo gets here. We have to stall until then, if we want to win."

"It'll attack the next time it gets Del's mind scrambled! I don't think we fooled it for a minute . . . we're out of range of the mindbeam here, but Del can't withdraw now. And we can't expect that *aiyan* to fight his ship for him. We'll really have no chance, with Del gone."

The Commander's eyes moved ceaselessly over his panel. "We'll wait. We can't be sure it'll attack within—"

The berserker spoke suddenly, its radioed voice plain in the cabins of both ships: "I have a proposition for you, little ship." Its voice had a cracking, adolescent quality, because it strung together words and syllables recorded from the voices of human prisoners of both sexes and different ages, from whom it had learned the language. There was no reason to think they had been kept alive after that.

"Well?" Del's voice sounded tough and capable by comparison.

"I have invented a game which we will play," it said. "If you play well enough, I will not kill you right away."

"Now I've heard everything," murmured the Second Officer.

After three thoughtful seconds the Commander slammed a fist on the arm of his chair. "It means to test his learning ability, to run a continuous check on his brain while it turns up the power of the mindbeam and tries different modulations. If it can make sure the mindbeam is working, it'll attack instantly. I'll bet my life on it. That's the game it's playing this time."

"I will think over your proposition," said Del's voice coolly.

"Very well," answered the berserker.

The Commander said: "It's in no hurry to start. It won't be able to turn on the mindbeam again for almost two hours."

"But we need another two hours beyond that."

Del's voice said: "Describe the game you want to play."

"It is a simplified version of the human game called checkers."

The Commander and the Second looked at each other, neither able to imagine Newton able to play checkers. Nor could they doubt that Newton's failure would kill them within a few hours, and leave another planet open to destruction.

After a minute's silence, Del's voice asked: "What'll we use for a board?"

"We will radio our moves to one another," said the berserker equably. It went on to describe a checkers-like game, played on a smaller board with less than the normal number of pieces. There was nothing very profound about it; but of course playing would seem to require a functional brain, human or electronic, able to plan and to predict.

"If I agree to play," said Del slowly, "how'll we decide who gets to move first?"

"He's trying to stall," said the Commander, gnawing a thumbnail. "We won't be able to offer any advice with that thing listening. Oh, stay sharp, Del boy!"

"To simplify matters," said the berserker, "I will move first in every game."

Del could look forward to another hour free of the mindweapon when he finished rigging the checker board. When the pegged pieces were moved, appropriate signals would be radioed to the berserker; lighted squares on the board would show him where its pieces were moved. If it spoke to him while the mindweapon was on, Del's voice would answer from a tape, which he had stocked with vaguely aggressive phrases, such as: "Get on with the game," or "Do you want to give up now?"

He hadn't told the enemy how far along he was with his preparations because he was still busy with something the enemy must not know—the system that was going to enable Newton to play a game of simplified checkers.

Del gave a soundless little laugh as he worked, and glanced over to where Newton was lounging on his couch, clutching toys in his hands as if he drew some comfort from them. This scheme was going to push the *aiyan* near the limit of his ability, but Del saw no reason why it should fail.

Del had completely analyzed the miniature checker game, and diagrammed every position that Newton could possibly face—playing only even-numbered moves, thank the random berserker for that specification!—on small cards. Del had discarded some lines of play that would lead from poor early moves by Newton, further simplifying his job. Now, on a card showing each possible remaining position, Del indicated the best possible move with a drawn-in arrow. Now he could quickly teach Newton to play the game by looking at the appropriate card and making the move shown by the arrow. The system was not perfect, but—

"Oh, oh," said Del, as his hands stopped working and he stared into space. Newton whined at the tone in his voice.

Once Del had sat at one board in a simultaneous chess exhibition, one of sixty players opposing the world champion, Blankenship. Del had held his own into the middle game. Then, when the great man paused again opposite his board, Del had shoved a pawn forward, thinking he had reached an unassailable position and could begin a counterattack. Blankenship had moved a rook to an innocent-looking square and strolled on to the next board—and then Del had seen the checkmate coming at him, four moves away but one move too late for him to do anything about it.

The Commander suddenly said a foul phrase in a loud distinct voice. Such conduct was extremely rare, and the Second Officer looked around in surprise. "What?"

"I think we've had it." The Commander paused. "I hoped that Murray could set up some kind of system over there, so that Newton could play the game—or appear to be playing it. But it won't work. Whatever system Newton plays by rote will always have him thinking the same move in the same position. It may be a perfect system—but a man doesn't play any game that way, damn it. He makes mistakes, he changes strategy. Even in a game this simple there'll be room for that. Most of all, a man *learns* a game as he plays it. He gets better as he goes along. That's what'll give Newton away, and that's what our bandit wants. It's probably heard about *aiyans*. Now as soon as it can be sure it's facing a dumb animal over there, and not a man or computer, it'll attack."

After a little while the Second Officer said: "I'm getting signals of their moves. They've begun play. Maybe we should've rigged up a board so we could follow along with the game."

"We better just be ready to go at it when the time comes." The Commander looked hopelessly at his salvo button, and then at the clock that showed two hours must pass before Gizmo could reasonably be hoped for.

Soon the Second Officer said: "That seems to be the end of the first game; Del lost it, if I'm reading their scoreboard signal right." He paused. "Sir, here's that signal we picked up the last time it turned the mindbeam on. Del must be starting to get it again."

There was nothing for the Commander to say. The two men waited silently for the enemy's attack, hoping only that they could damage it in the seconds before it would overwhelm them and kill them.

"He's playing the second game," said the Second Officer, puzzled. "And I just heard him say 'Let's get on with it.' "

"His voice could be recorded. He must have made some plan of play for Newton to follow; but it won't fool the berserker for long. It can't."

Time crept unmeasurably past them.

The Second said: "He's lost the first four games. But he's *not* making the same moves every time. I wish we'd made a board. . . ."

"Shut up about the board! We'd be watching it instead of the panel. Now stay alert, Mister."

After what seemed a long time, the Second said: "Well, I'll be!"

"What?"

"Our side got a draw in that game."

"Then the beam can't be on him. Are you sure . . ."

"It is! Look, here, the same indication we got last time. It's been on him the better part of an hour now, and getting stronger."

The Commander stared in disbelief; but he knew and trusted his Second's ability. And the panel indications were convincing. He said: "Then someone—or something—with no functioning mind is learning how to play a game, over there. Ha, ha," he added, as if trying to remember how to laugh.

The berserker won another game. Another draw. Another win for the enemy. Then three drawn games in a row.

Once the Second Officer heard Del's voice ask coolly: "Do you want to give up now?" On the next move he lost another game. But the following game ended in another draw. Del was plainly taking more time than his opponent to move, but not enough to make the enemy impatient.

"It's trying different modulations on the mindweapon," said the Second. "And it's got the power turned way up."

"Yeah," said the Commander. Several times he had almost tried to radio Del, to say something that might keep the man's spirits up—and also to relieve his own feverish inactivity, and try to find out what could possibly be happening now. But he could not take the chance. Any interference might upset the miracle.

He could not believe the inexplicable success could last, even when the checker match turned gradually into an endless succession of drawn games between two perfect players. Hours ago the Commander had said goodbye to life and hope, and he still waited for the fatal moment.

And waited.

"—not perish from the Earth!" said Del Murray, and Newton's eager hands flew to loose his right arm from its shackle.

A game, unfinished on the little board before him, had been abandoned seconds earlier. The mindweapon had been turned off at the same time, when Gizmo had burst into normal space right in position and only five minutes late; and the berserker had been forced to turn all its energies to meet the immediate all-out attack of Gizmo and Foxglove.

Del saw his computers, recovering from the effect of the beam, lock his aiming screen onto the berserker's scarred and bulging midsection, as he shot his right arm forward, scattering pieces from the game board.

"Checkmate!" he roared out hoarsely, and brought his fist down on the big red button.

"I'm glad it didn't want to play chess," Del said later, talking to the Commander in Foxglove's cabin. "I could never have rigged that up."

The ports were cleared now, and the men could look out at the expanding cloud of gas, still faintly luminous, that had been a berserker; metal fire-purged of the legacy of ancient evil.

But the Commander was watching Del. "You got Newt to play by following diagrams, I see that. But how could he *learn* the game?"

Del grinned. "He couldn't. But his toys could. Now wait before you slug me." He called the *aiyan* to him and took a small box from the animal's hand. The box rattled faintly as he held it up. On the cover was pasted a diagram of one possible position in the simplified checker game, with a different-colored arrow indicating each possible move of Del's pieces.

"It took a couple hundred of these boxes," said Del. "This one was in the group that Newt examined for the fourth move. When he found a box with a diagram matching the position on the board, he picked the box up, pulled out one of these beads from inside, without looking—that was the hardest part to teach him in a hurry, by the way," said Del, demonstrating. "Ah, this one's blue. That means, make the move indicated on the corner by a blue arrow. Now the orange arrow leads to a poor position. See?" Del shook all the beads out of the box into his hand. "No orange beads left; there were six of each color when we started. But every time Newton drew a bead, he had orders to leave it out of the box until the game was over. Then, if the scoreboard indicated a loss for our side, he went back and threw away all the beads he had used. All the bad moves were gradually eliminated. In a few hours, Newt and his boxes learned to play the game perfectly."

"Well," said the Commander. He thought for a moment, then reached down to scratch Newton behind the ears. "I never would have come up with that idea."

"I should have thought of it sooner. The basic idea's a couple of centuries old. And computers are supposed to be my business."

"This could be a big thing," said the Commander. "I mean your basic idea might be useful to any task force that has to face a berserker's mindbeam."

"Yeah." Del grew reflective. "Also . . ."

"What?"

"I was thinking of a guy I met once. Named Blankenship. I wonder if I *could* rig something up. . . ."

✖✖ FREDERIK POHL (1919-)

Some sixty years after the first publication of his Science Fiction in the pages of pulp magazines, such as Astonishing Stories *and* Super Science Stories, *Frederik Pohl continues to write best-selling Science Fiction. He has written short stories and novels with equal dexterity. Throughout his professional career, Pohl has been an important Science Fiction writer, editor, anthologist, and publisher. (This was also the case with John W. Campbell Jr. and is true of Damon Knight.) Pohl began editing* Astonishing Stories *and* Super Science Stories *about the same time his first stories appeared there—1940. He edited* Galaxy *and* IF *between 1961 and 1969.*

In his early days, Pohl co-authored stories and novels with C. M. Kornbluth, Jack Williamson, Judith Merril, Isaac Asimov, and others. His work is often inventive and avante-garde; sometimes it is dark and sardonic. While Pohl has often utilized the conventions of Science Fiction in his stories, he has rarely been conventional. His autobiography, The Way the Future Was: A Memoir *(1978), is considered one of the cornerstones of Science Fiction history.*

"The Fiend" is an unsettling and provocative story. It explores definitions and limits of morality, and it asks the question, "What If?"

The Fiend

(Playboy, *April 1964*)

How beautiful she was, Dandish thought, and how helpless. The plastic identification ribbon around her neck stood out straight, and as she was just out of the transport capsule, she wore nothing else. "Are you awake?" he asked, but she did not stir.

Dandish felt excitement building up inside him; she was so passive and without defense. A man could come to her now and do anything at all to her, and she would not resist. Or, of course, respond. Without touching her, he knew that her body would be warm and dry. It was fully alive, and in a few minutes she would be conscious.

Dandish—who was the captain and sole crew member of the interstellar ship without a name carrying congealed colonists across the long, slow, empty space from the Earth to a planet that circled a star that had never had a name in astronomical charts, only a number, and was now called Eleanor—passed those minutes without looking again at the girl, whose name he knew to be Silvie but whom he had never met. When he looked again, she was awake, jackknifed against the safety straps of the crib, her hair standing out around her head and her face wearing an expression of anger. "All right. Where are you? I know what the score is," she said. "Do you know what they can do to you for this?"

Dandish was startled. He did not like being startled, for it frightened him. For nine years the ship had been whispering across space; he had had enough loneliness to satisfy him, and he had been frightened. There were 700 cans of colonists on the ship, but they lay brittle and changeless in their bath of liquid helium and were not very good company. Outside the ship the nearest human being was perhaps two light-years away, barring some chance-met ship heading in the other direction that was actually far more remote than either star, since the forces involved in stopping and matching course with a vessel bound home were twice as great as, and would take twice as much time as, those involved in the voyage itself. Everything about the trip was frightening. The loneliness was a terror. To stare down through an inch of crystal and see nothing but far stars led to panic. Dandish had decided to stop looking out five years before, but had not been able to keep to his decision, and so now and again peeped through the crystal and contemplated his horrifying visions of the seal breaking, the crystal popping out on a breath of air, himself in his metal prison tumbling, tumbling forever down to the heart of one of the ten million stars that lay below. In this ship a noise was an alarm. Since no one but himself was awake, to hear a scratch of metal or a thud of a moving object striking something else, however tiny, however remote, was a threat, and more than once Dandish had suffered through an itch of fear for hours or days until he tracked down the exploded light tube or unsecured door that had startled him. He dreamed uneasily of fire. This was preposterously unlikely in the steel-and-crystal ship, but what he was dreaming of was not the fire of a house but the monstrous fires in the stars beneath.

"Come out where I can see you," commanded the girl.

Dandish noted that she had not troubled to try to cover her nakedness. Bare she woke and bare she stayed. She had unhitched the restraining webbing and left the crib, and now she was prowling the room in which she had awakened, looking for him. "They warned us," she called. "'Watch the hook!' 'Look out for the space nuts!' 'You'll be sorry!' That's all we heard at the Reception Center, and now here you are, all right. Wherever you are. Where are you? For God's sake, come out so I can see you." She half stood and half floated at an angle to the floor, nibbling at imperceptible bits of dead skin on her lips and staring warily from side to side. She said, "What was the story you were going to tell me? A subspace meteorite destroyed the ship, all but you and me, and we were doomed to fly endlessly toward nowhere, so there was nothing for us to do but try to make a life for ourselves?"

Dandish watched her through the view eyes in the reviving room, but did not answer. He was a connoisseur of victims, Dandish was. He had spent a great deal of time planning this. Physically she was perfect, very young, slim, slight. He had picked her out on that basis from among the 352 female canned colonists, leafing through the microfile photographs that accompanied each colonist's dossier like a hi-fi hobbyist shopping through a catalogue. She had been the best of the lot. Dandish was not skilled enough to be able to read a personality profile and in any event considered psychologists to be phonies and their profiles trash, so he had had to go by the indices he knew. He had wanted his victim to be innocent and trusting. Silvie, 16 years old and a little below average in intelligence, had seemed very promising. It was disappointing that she did not react with more fear. "They'll give you fifty years for this!" she shouted, looking around to see where he could be hiding. "You know that, don't you?"

The revival crib, sensing that she was out of it, was quietly stowing and rearming itself, ready to be taken out and used again. Its plastic sheets slipped free of the corners, rolled up in a tight spiral, and slid into a disposal chute, revealing aseptic new sheets below. Its radio-warming generators tested themselves with a surge of high-voltage current, found no flaws, and shut themselves off. The crib sides folded down meekly. The instrument table hooded itself over. The girl paused to watch it, then shook her head and laughed. "Scared of me?" she called. "Come on, let's get this over with! Or else," she added, "admit you've made a boo-boo, get me some clothes, and let's talk this over sensibly."

Sorrowfully Dandish turned his gaze away. A timing device reminded him that it was time to make his routine half-hour check of the ship's systems and, as he had done more than 150,000 times already and would do 100,000 times again, he swiftly scanned the temperature readings in the can hold, metered the loss of liquid helium and balanced it against the withdrawals from the reserve, compared the ship's course with the flight plan, measured the fuel consumption and rate of flow, found all systems functioning smoothly, and returned to the girl. It had taken only a minute or so, but already she had found the comb and mirror he had put out for her and was working angrily at her hair. One fault in the techniques of freezing and revivification lay in what happened to such elaborated structures as fingernails and hair. At the temperature of liquid helium all organic matter was brittle as Prince Rupert's drops, and although the handling techniques were planned with that fact in mind, the body wrapped gently in elastic cocooning, every care exercised to keep it from contact with anything hard or sharp, nails and hair had a way of being snapped off. The Reception Center endlessly drummed into the colonists the importance of short nails and butch haircuts, but the colonists were not always convinced. Silvie now looked like a dummy on which a student wigmaker had failed a test. She solved her problem at last by winding what remained of her hair in a tiny bun and put down the comb, snapped-off strands of hair floating in the air all about her like a stretched-out sandstorm.

She patted the bun mournfully and said, "I guess you think this is pretty funny."

Dandish considered the question. He was not impelled to laugh. Twenty Years before, when Dandish was a teenager with the long permanented hair and the lacquered fingernails that were the fashion for kids that year, he had dreamed almost every night of just such a situation as this. To own a girl of his own—not to love her or to rape her or to marry her, but to possess her as a slave, with no one anywhere to stop him from whatever he chose to impose on her—had elaborated itself in a hundred variations nightly. He didn't tell anyone about his dream, not directly, but in the school period devoted to practical psychology he had mentioned it as something he had read in a book, and the instructor, staring right through him into his dreams, told him it was a repressed wish to play with dolls. "This fellow is role playing," he said, "acting out a wish to be a woman. These clear-cut cases of repressed homosexuality can take many forms . . .", and on and on, and although the dreams were as physically satisfying as ever, the young Dandish awoke from them both reproved and resentful.

But Silvie was neither a dream nor a doll. "I'm not a doll!" said Silvie, so sharply and patly that it was a shock. "Come on out and get it over with!"

She straightened up, holding to a free-fall grip, and although she looked angry and annoyed, she still did not seem afraid. "Unless you are really crazy," she said clearly, "which I doubt, although I have to admit it's a possibility, you aren't going to do anything I don't want you to do, you know. Because you can't get away with it, right? You can't kill me—you could never explain it, and besides, they don't let murderers run ships in the first place, and so when we land, all I have to do is yell cop and you're running a subway shuttle for the next ninety years." She giggled. "I know about that. My uncle got busted on income-tax evasion, and now he's a self-propelled dredge in the Amazon delta, and you should see the letters he writes. So come on out and let's see what I'm willing to let you get away with."

She grew impatient. "Kee-rist," she said, shaking her head. "I sure get the great ones. And, oh, by the way, as long as I'm up, I have to go to the little girls' room, and then I want breakfast."

Dandish took some small satisfaction in that these requirements, at least, he had foreseen. He opened the door to the washroom and turned on the warmer oven where emergency rations were waiting. By the time Silvie came back, biscuits, bacon, and hot coffee were set out for her.

"I don't suppose you have a cigarette?" she said. "Well, I'll live. How about some clothes? And how about coming out so I can get a look at you?" She stretched and yawned and then began to eat. Apparently she had showered, as was generally desirable on awakening from freeze-sleep to get rid of the exfoliated skin, and she had wrapped her ruined hair in a small towel. Dandish had left the one small towel in the washroom, reluctantly, but it had not occurred to him that his victim would wrap it around her head. Silvie sat thoughtfully staring at the remains of her breakfast and then after a while said, like a lecturer:

"As I understand it, starship sailors are always some kind of a nut, because who else would go off for twenty years at a time, even for money, even for any kind of money? All right, you're a nut. So if you wake me up and won't come out, won't talk to me, there's nothing I can do about it.

"Now, I can see that even if you weren't a little loopy to start with, this kind of life would tip you. Maybe you just want a little company? I can understand that. I might even cooperate and say no more about it.

"On the other hand, maybe you're trying to get your nerve up for something rough. Don't know if you can, because they naturally screened you down fine before they gave you the job. But supposing. What happens then?

"If you kill me, they catch you.

"If you don't kill me, then I tell them when we land, and they catch you.

"I told you about my uncle. Right now his body is in the deep freeze somewhere on the dark side of Mercury, and they've got his brain keeping the navigation channels clear off Belém. Maybe you think that's not so bad. Uncle Henry doesn't like it a bit. He doesn't have any company, bad as you that way, I guess, and he says his suction hoses are always sore. Of course he could always louse up on the job, but then they'd just put him some other place that wouldn't be quite as nice—so what he does is grit his teeth, or I guess you should say his grinders, and get along the best he can. Ninety years! He's only done six so far. I mean six when I left Earth, whatever that is now. You wouldn't like that. So why not come out and talk?"

Five or ten minutes later, after making faces and buttering another roll and flinging it furiously at the wall, where the disposal units sluiced it away, she said, "Damn you, then give me a book to read, anyway."

Dandish retreated from her and listened to the whisper of the ship for a few minutes, then activated the mechanisms of the revival crib. He had been a loser long enough to learn when to cut his losses. The girl sprang to her feet as the sides of the crib unfolded. Gentle tentacles reached out for her and deposited her in it, locking the webbing belt around her waist. "You damned fool!" she shouted, but Dandish did not answer. The anesthesia cone descended toward her struggling face, and she screamed, "Wait a minute! I never said I wouldn't—", but what she never said she wouldn't, she couldn't say, because the cone cut her off. In a moment she was asleep. A plastic sack stretched itself around her, molding to her face, her body, her legs, even to the strayed towel around her hair, and the revival crib rolled silently to the freezing room. Dandish did not watch further. He knew what would happen, and besides, the timer reminded him to make his check. Temperatures, normal; fuel consumption, normal; course, normal; freezer room showed one new capsule en route to storage, otherwise normal. Good-bye, Silvie, said Dandish to himself, you were a pretty bad mistake.

Conceivably later on, with another girl . . .

But it had taken nine years for Dandish to wake Silvie, and he did not think he could do it again. He thought of her Uncle Henry running a dredge along the South Atlantic littoral. It could have been him. He had leaped at the opportunity to spend his sentence piloting a starship instead.

He stared out at the ten million stars below with the optical receptors that were his eyes. He clawed helplessly at space with the radars that gave him touch. He wept a five-million-mile stream of ions behind him from his jets. He thought of the tons of helpless flesh in his hold, the bodies in which he could have delighted, if his own body had not been with Uncle Henry's on coldside Mercury, the fears on which he could have fed, if he had been able to inspire fear. He would have sobbed, if he had had a voice to sob with.

₰ P(HILIP) K(INDRED) DICK (1928–1982)

Philip K. Dick began his writing career with the publication of the short story "Beyond Lies the Wub" in 1952. Both a short story writer and novelist, Dick was most prolific from the 1950s through the 1970s.

While he published many enduring works of Science Fiction, the author's The Man in the High Castle *(1962) is probably his most critically regarded. This novel of Alternate History postulates what would have happened if the Axis powers had won World War II and Hitler had become ruler of what had been the free world.*

Another famous Philip K. Dick novel is Do Androids Dream of Electric Sheep? *(1968), which was the basis for Ridley Scott's movie* Blade Runner *(1982), one of the most important and profound Science Fiction movies ever made. Interestingly, Dick's 1968 novel (written in 1966) first appeared about the same time Robert Bloch's teleplay "What Are Little Girls Made Of?" debuted as an episode of the original* Star Trek *series on October 22, 1966. Both investigate the ethics and morality of cloning.*

A talented author of many variations of Science Fiction, including stories of alternate worlds, alien invasion, police states, and the environment, Philip K. Dick generally wrote stories about reality and unreality. His writing was often dark, paranoid, but also humorous. His style could resemble that of A. E. van Vogt and Frederik Pohl.

"We Can Remember It for You Wholesale" is the basis for the popular alternate reality movie Total Recall *(1990). As a story of alternate reality and technology gone wrong, "We Can Remember It for You Wholesale" foreshadows the recent movie* The Matrix *(1999).*

We Can Remember It for You Wholesale
(The Magazine of Fantasy and Science Fiction, *April 1966*)

He awoke—and wanted Mars. The valleys, he thought. What would it be like to trudge among them? Great and greater yet: the dream grew as he became fully conscious, the dream and the yearning. He could almost feel the enveloping presence of the other world, which only Government agents and high officials had seen. A clerk like himself? Not likely.

"Are you getting up or not?" his wife Kirsten asked drowsily, with her usual hint of fierce crossness. "If you are, push the hot coffee button on the darn stove."

"Okay," Douglas Quail said, and made his way barefoot from the bedroom of their conapt to the kitchen. There, having dutifully pressed the hot coffee button, he seated himself at the kitchen table, brought out a yellow, small tin of fine Dean Swift snuff. He inhaled briskly, and the Beau Nash mixture stung his nose, burned the roof of his mouth. But still he inhaled; it woke him up and allowed his dreams, his nocturnal desires and random wishes, to condense into a semblance of rationality.

I will go, he said to himself. *Before I die I'll see Mars.*

It was, of course, impossible, and he knew this even as he dreamed. But the daylight, the mundane noise of his wife now brushing her hair before the bedroom mirror—everything conspired to remind him of what he was. *A miserable little salaried employee,* he said to himself with bitterness. Kirsten reminded him of this at least once a day and he did not blame her; it was a wife's job to bring her husband down to Earth. *Down to Earth,* he thought, and laughed. The figure of speech in this was literally apt.

"What are you sniggering about?" his wife asked as she swept into the kitchen, her long busy-pink robe wagging after her. "A dream, I bet. You're always full of them."

"Yes," he said, and gazed out the kitchen window at the hover-cars and traffic runnels, and all the little energetic people hurrying to work. In a little while he would be among them. As always.

"I'll bet it had to do with some woman," Kirsten said witheringly.

"No," he said. "A god. The god of war. He has wonderful craters with every kind of plant-life growing deep down in them."

"Listen." Kirsten crouched down beside him and spoke earnestly, the harsh quality momentarily gone from her voice. "The bottom of the ocean—*our* ocean is much more, an infinity of times more beautiful. You know that; everyone knows that. Rent an artificial gill-outfit for both of us, take a week off from work, and we can descend and live down there at one of those year-round aquatic resorts. And in addition—" She broke off. "You're not listening. You should be. Here is something a lot better than that compulsion, that obsession you have about Mars, and you don't even listen!" Her voice rose piercingly. "God in heaven, you're doomed, Doug! What's going to become of you?"

"I'm going to work," he said, rising to his feet, his breakfast forgotten. "That's what's going to become of me."

She eyed him. "You're getting worse. More fanatical every day. Where's it going to lead?"

"To Mars," he said, and opened the door to the closet to get down a fresh shirt to wear to work.

Having descended from the taxi Douglas Quail slowly walked across three densely-populated foot runnels and to the modern, attractively inviting doorway. There he halted, impeding mid-morning traffic, and with caution read the shifting-color neon sign. He had, in the past, scrutinized this sign before . . . but never had he come so close. This was very different; what he did now was something else. Something which sooner or later had to happen.

REKAL, INCORPORATED

Was this the answer? After all, an illusion, no matter how convincing, remained nothing more than an illusion. At least objectively. But subjectively—quite the opposite entirely.

And anyhow he had an appointment. Within the next five minutes.

Taking a deep breath of mildly smog-infested Chicago air, he walked through the dazzling polychromatic shimmer of the doorway and up to the receptionist's counter.

The nicely-articulated blonde at the counter, bare-bosomed and tidy, said pleasantly, "Good morning, Mr. Quail."

"Yes," he said. "I'm here to see about a Rekal course. As I guess you know."

"Not 'rekal' but re*call*," the receptionist corrected him. She picked up the receiver of the vidphone by her smooth elbow and said into it, "Mr. Douglas Quail is here, Mr. McClane. May he come inside, now? Or is it too soon?"

"Giz wetwa wum-wum wamp," the phone mumbled.

"Yes, Mr. Quail," she said. "You may go in; Mr. McClane is expecting you." As he started off uncertainly she called after him, "Room D, Mr. Quail. To your right."

After a frustrating but brief moment of being lost he found the proper room. The door hung open and inside, at a big genuine walnut desk, sat a genial-looking man, middle-aged, wearing the latest Martian frog-pelt gray suit; his attire alone would have told Quail that he had come to the right person.

"Sit down, Douglas," McClane said, waving his plump hand toward a chair which faced the desk. "So you want to have gone to Mars. Very good."

Quail seated himself, feeling tense. "I'm not so sure this is worth the fee," he said. "It costs a lot and as far as I can see I really get nothing." *Costs almost as much as going*, he thought.

"You get tangible proof of your trip," McClane disagreed emphatically. "All the proof you'll need. Here; I'll show you." He dug within a drawer of his impressive desk. "Ticket stub." Reaching into a manila folder, he produced a small square of embossed cardboard. "It proves you went—and returned. Postcards." He laid out four franked picture 3-D full-color postcards in a nearly-arranged row on the desk for Quail to see. "Film. Shots you took of local sights on Mars with a rented moving camera." To Quail he displayed those, too. "Plus the names of people you met, two hundred poscreds worth of souvenirs, which will arrive—from Mars—within the following month. And passport, certificates listing the shots you received. And more." He glanced up keenly at Quail. "You'll know you went, all right," he said. "You won't remember us, won't remember me or ever having been here. It'll be a real trip in your mind; we guarantee that. A full two weeks of recall; every last piddling detail. Remember this: if at any time you doubt that you really took an extensive trip to Mars you can return here and get a full refund. You see?"

"But I didn't go," Quail said. "I won't have gone, no matter what proofs you provide me with." He took a deep, unsteady breath. "And I never was a secret agent with Interplan." It seemed impossible to him that Rekal, Incorporated's extra-factual memory implant would do its job—despite what he had heard people say.

"Mr. Quail," McClane said patiently. "As you explained in your letter to us, you have no chance, no possibility in the slightest, of ever actually getting to Mars; you can't afford it, and what is much more important, you could never qualify as an undercover agent for Interplan or anybody else. This is the only way you can achieve your, ahem, life-long dream; am I not correct, sir? You can't be this; you can't actually do this." He chuckled. "But you can *have been* and *have done*. We see to that. And our fee is reasonable; no hidden charges." He smiled encouragingly.

"Is an extra-factual memory that convincing?" Quail asked.

"More than the real thing, sir. Had you really gone to Mars as an Interplan agent, you would by now have forgotten a great deal; our analysis of true-mem systems—authentic recollections of major events in a person's life—shows that a variety of details are very quickly lost to the person. Forever. Part of the package we offer you is such deep implantation of recall that nothing is forgotten. The packet which is fed to you while you're comatose is the creation of trained experts, men who have spent years on Mars; in every case we verify details down to the last iota. And you've picked a rather easy extra-factual system; had you picked Pluto or wanted to be Emperor of the Inner Planet Alliance we'd have much more diffi- culty . . . and the charges would be considerably greater."

Reaching into his coat for his wallet, Quail said, "Okay. It's been my life-long ambition and so I see I'll never really do it. So I guess I'll have to settle for this."

"Don't think of it that way," McClane said severely. "You're not accepting second-best. The actual memory, with all its vagueness, omissions and ellipses, not to say distortions—that's second-best." He accepted the money and pressed a but- ton on his desk. "All right, Mr. Quail," he said, as the door of his office opened and two burly men swiftly entered. "You're on your way to Mars as a secret agent." He rose, came over to shake Quail's nervous, moist hand. "Or rather, you have been on your way. This afternoon at four-thirty you will, um, arrive back here on Terra; a cab will leave you off at your conapt and as I say you will never remember seeing me or coming here; you won't, in fact, even remember having heard of our existence."

His mouth dry with nervousness, Quail followed the two technicians from the office; what happened next depended on them.

Will I actually believe I've been on Mars? he wondered. *That I managed to fulfill my lifetime ambition?* He had a strange, lingering intuition that something would go wrong. But just what—he did not know.

He would have to wait and find out.

The intercom on McClane's desk, which connected him with the work area of the firm, buzzed and a voice said, "Mr. Quail is under sedation now, sir. Do you want to supervise this one, or shall we go ahead?"

"It's routine," McClane observed. "You may go ahead, Lowe; I don't think you'll run into any trouble." Programming an artificial memory of a trip to an- other planet—with or without the added fillip of being a secret agent—showed up on the firm's work-schedule with monotonous regularity. *In one month,* he cal- culated wryly, *we must do twenty of these . . . ersatz interplanetary travel has become our bread and butter.*

"Whatever you say, Mr. McClane," Lowe's voice came, and thereupon the in- tercom shut off.

Going to the vault section in the chamber behind his office, McClane searched about for a Three packet—trip to Mars—and a Sixty-two packet: secret Interplan spy. Finding the two packets, he returned with them to his desk, seated himself comfortably, poured out the contents—merchandise which would be planted in Quail's conapt while the lab technicians busied themselves installing false memory.

A one-poscred sneaky-pete side arm, McClane reflected; *that's the largest item. Sets us back financially the most.* Then a pellet-sized transmitter, which could be swal- lowed if the agent were caught. Code book that astonishingly resembled the real thing . . . the firm's models were highly accurate: based, whenever possible, on actual U.S. military issue. Odd bits which made no intrinsic sense but which would be woven into the warp and woof of Quail's imaginary trip, would coincide with his memory: half an ancient silver fifty cent piece, several quotations from John Donne's sermons written incorrectly, each on a separate piece of transparent tissue-thin paper, several match folders from bars on Mars, a stainless steel spoon engraved PROPERTY OF DOME-MARS NATIONAL KIBBUZIM, a wire tapping coil which—

The intercom buzzed. "Mr. McClane, I'm sorry to bother you but something rather ominous has come up. Maybe it would be better if you were in here after all. Quail is already under sedation; he reacted well to the narkidrine; he's completely unconscious and receptive. But—"

"I'll be in." Sensing trouble, McClane left his office; a moment later he emerged in the work area.

On a hygienic bed lay Douglas Quail, breathing slowly and regularly, his eyes virtually shut; he seemed dimly—but only dimly—aware of the two technicians and now McClane himself.

"There's no space to insert false memory-patterns?" McClane felt irritation. "Merely drop out two work weeks; he's employed as a clerk at the West Coast Emigration Bureau, which is a government agency, so he undoubtedly has or had two weeks' vacation within the last year. That ought to do it." Petty details annoyed him. And always would.

"Our problem," Lowe said sharply, "is something quite different." He bent over the bed, said to Quail, "Tell Mr. McClane what you told us." To McClane he said, "Listen closely."

The gray-green eyes of the man lying supine in the bed focussed on McClane's face. The eyes, he observed uneasily, had become hard; they had a polished, inorganic quality, like semi-precious tumbled stones. He was not sure that he liked what he saw; the brilliance was too cold. "What do you want now?" Quail said harshly. "You've broken my cover. Get out of here before I take you all apart." He studied McClane. "Especially you," he continued. "You're in charge of this counter-operation."

Lowe said, "How long were you on Mars?"

"One month," Quail said gratingly.

"And your purpose there?" Lowe demanded.

The meager lips twisted; Quail eyed him and did not speak. At last, drawling the words out so that they dripped with hostility, he said, "Agent for Interplan. As I already told you. Don't you record everything that's said? Play your vid-aud tape back for your boss and leave me alone." He shut his eyes, then; the hard brilliance ceased. McClane felt, instantly, a rushing splurge of relief.

Lowe said quietly, "This is a tough man, Mr. McClane."

"He won't be," McClane said, "after we arrange for him to lose his memory-chain again. He'll be as meek as before." To Quail he said, "So *this* is why you wanted to go to Mars so terribly bad."

Without opening his eyes Quail said, "I never wanted to go to Mars. I was assigned it—they handed it to me and there I was: stuck. Oh yeah, I admit I was curious about it; who wouldn't be?" Again he opened his eyes and surveyed the three of them, McClane in particular. "Quite a truth drug you've got here; it brought up things I had absolutely no memory of." He pondered. "I wonder about Kirsten," he said, half to himself. "Could she be in on it? An Interplan contact keeping an eye on me . . . to be certain I didn't regain my memory? No wonder she's been so derisive about my wanting to go there." Faintly, he smiled; the smile—one of understanding—disappeared almost at once.

McClane said, "Please believe me, Mr. Quail; we stumbled onto this entirely by accident. In the work we do—"

"I believe you," Quail said. He seemed tired, now; the drug was continuing to pull him under, deeper and deeper. "Where did I say I'd been?" he murmured.

"Mars? Hard to remember—I know I'd like to see it; so would everybody else. But me—" His voice trailed off. "Just a clerk, a nothing clerk."

Straightening up, Lowe said to his superior. "He wants a false memory implanted that corresponds to a trip he actually took. And a false reason which is the real reason. He's telling the truth; he's a long way down in the narkidrine. The trip is very vivid in his mind—at least under sedation. But apparently he doesn't recall it otherwise. Someone, probably at a government military-sciences lab, erased his conscious memories; all he knew was that going to Mars meant something special to him, and so did being a secret agent. They couldn't erase that; it's not a memory but a desire, undoubtedly the same one that motivated him to volunteer for the assignment in the first place."

The other technician, Keeler, said to McClane, "What do we do? Graft a false memory-pattern over the real memory? There's no telling what the results would be; he might remember some of the genuine trip, and the confusion might bring on a psychotic interlude. He'd have to hold two opposite premises in his mind simultaneously: that he went to Mars and that he didn't. That he's a genuine agent for Interplan and he's not, that it's spurious. I think we ought to revive him without any false memory implantation and send him out of here; this is hot."

"Agreed," McClane said. A thought came to him. "Can you predict what he'll remember when he comes out of sedation?"

"Impossible to tell," Lowe said. "He probably will have some dim, diffuse memory of his actual trip, now. And he'd probably be in grave doubt as to its validity; he'd probably decide our programming slipped a gear-tooth. And he'd remember coming here; that wouldn't be erased—unless you want it erased."

"The less we mess with this man," McClane said, "the better I like it. This is nothing for us to fool around with; we've been foolish enough to—or unlucky enough to—uncover a genuine Interplan spy who has a cover so perfect that up to now even he didn't know what he was—or rather is." The sooner they washed their hands of the man calling himself Douglas Quail the better.

"Are you going to plant packets Three and Sixty-two in his conapt?" Lowe said.

"No," McClane said. "And we're going to return half his fee."

"'Half'! Why half?"

McClane said lamely, "It seems to be a good compromise."

As the cab carried him back to his conapt at the residential end of Chicago, Douglas Quail said to himself, *It's sure good to be back on Terra.*

Already the month-long period on Mars had begun to waver in his memory; he had only an image of profound gaping craters, an ever-present ancient erosion of hills, of vitality, of motion itself. A world of dust where little happened, where a good part of the day was spent checking and rechecking one's portable oxygen source. And then the life forms, the unassuming and modest gray-brown cacti and maw-worms.

As a matter of fact he had brought back several moribund examples of Martian fauna; he had smuggled them through customs. After all, they posed no menace; they couldn't survive in Earth's heavy atmosphere.

Reaching into his coat pocket, he rummaged for the container of Martian maw-worms—

And found an envelope instead.

Lifting it out, he discovered, to his perplexity, that it contained five hundred and seventy poscreds, in 'cred bills of low denomination.

Where'd I get this? he asked himself. *Didn't I spend every 'cred I had on my trip?*

With the money came a slip of paper marked: *One-half fee ret'd. By McClane.* And then the date. Today's date.

"Recall," he said aloud.

"Recall what, sir or madam?" the robot driver of the cab inquired respectfully.

"Do you have a phone book?" Quail demanded.

"Certainly, sir or madam." A slot opened; from it slid a microtape phone book for Cook County.

"It's spelled oddly," Quail said as he leafed through the pages of the yellow section. He felt fear, then; abiding fear. "Here it is," he said. "Take me there, to Rekal, Incorporated. I've changed my mind; I don't want to go home."

"Yes, sir or madam, as the case may be," the driver said. A moment later the cab was zipping back in the opposite direction.

"May I make use of your phone?" he asked.

"Be my guest," the robot driver said. And presented a shiny new emperor 3-D color phone to him.

He dialed his own conapt. And after a pause found himself confronted by a miniature but chillingly realistic image of Kirsten on the small screen. "I've been to Mars," he said to her.

"You're drunk." Her lips writhed scornfully. "Or worse."

" 's God's truth."

"When?" she demanded.

"I don't know." He felt confused. "A simulated trip, I think. By means of one of those artificial or extra-factual or whatever it is memory places. It didn't take."

Kirsten said witheringly, "You *are* drunk." And broke the connection at her end. He hung up, then, feeling his face flush. *Always the same tone,* he said hotly to himself. *Always the retort, as if she knows everything and I know nothing. What a marriage. Keerist,* he thought dismally.

A moment later the cab stopped at the curb before a modern, very attractive little pink building, over which a shifting polychromatic neon sign read: REKAL, INCORPORATED.

The receptionist, chic and bare from the waist up, started in surprise, then gained masterful control of herself. "Oh, hello, Mr. Quail," she said nervously. "H-how are you? Did you forget something?"

"The rest of my fee back," he said.

More composed now, the receptionist said, "Fee? I think you are mistaken, Mr. Quail. You were here discussing the feasibility of an extra-factual trip for you, but—" She shrugged her smooth pale shoulders. "As I understand it, no trip was taken."

Quail said, "I remember everything, miss. My letter to Rekal, Incorporated, which started this whole business off. I remember my arrival here, my visit with Mr. McClane. Then the two lab technicians taking me in tow and administering a drug to put me out." No wonder the firm had returned half his fee. The false memory of his "trip to Mars" hadn't taken—at least not entirely, not as he had been assured.

"Mr. Quail," the girl said, "although you are a minor clerk you are a good-looking man and it spoils your features to become angry. If it would make you feel any better, I might, ahem, let you take me out . . ."

He felt furious, then. "I remember you," he said savagely. "For instance the fact that your breasts are sprayed blue; that stuck in my mind. And I remember Mr. McClane's promise that if I remembered my visit to Rekal, Incorporated I'd receive my money back in full. Where is Mr. McClane?"

After a delay—probably as long as they could manage—he found himself once more seated facing the imposing walnut desk, exactly as he had been an hour or so earlier in the day.

"Some technique you have," Quail said sardonically. His disappointment—and resentment—was enormous, by now. "My so-called 'memory' of a trip to Mars as an undercover agent for Interplan is hazy and vague and shot full of contradictions. And I clearly remember my dealings here with you people. I ought to take this to the Better Business Bureau." He was burning angry, at this point; his sense of being cheated had overwhelmed him, had destroyed his customary aversion to participating in a public squabble.

Looking morose, as well as cautious, McClane said, "We capitulate, Quail. We'll refund the balance of your fee. I fully concede the fact that we did absolutely nothing for you." His tone was resigned.

Quail said accusingly, "You didn't even provide me with the various artifacts that you claimed would 'prove' to me I had been on Mars. All that song-and-dance you went into—it hasn't materialized into a damn thing. Not even a ticket stub. Nor postcards. Nor passport. Nor proof of immunization shots. Nor—"

"Listen, Quail," McClane said. "Suppose I told you—" He broke off. "Let it go." He pressed a button on his intercom. "Shirley, will you disburse five hundred and seventy more 'creds in the form of a cashier's check made out to Douglas Quail? Thank you." He released the button, then glared at Quail.

Presently the check appeared; the receptionist placed it before McClane and once more vanished out of sight, leaving the two men alone, still facing each other across the surface of the massive walnut desk.

"Let me give you a word of advice," McClane said as he signed the check and passed it over. "Don't discuss your, ahem, recent trip to Mars with anyone."

"What trip?"

"Well, that's the thing." Doggedly, McClane said, "The trip you partially remember. Act as if you don't remember; pretend it never took place. Don't ask me why; just take my advice: it'll be better for all of us." He had begun to perspire. Freely. "Now, Mr. Quail, I have other business, other clients to see." He rose, showed Quail to the door.

Quail said, as he opened the door, "A firm that turns out such bad work shouldn't have any clients at all." He shut the door behind him.

On the way home in the cab Quail pondered the wording of his letter of complaint to the Better Business Bureau, Terra Division. As soon as he could get to his typewriter he'd get started; it was clearly his duty to warn other people away from Rekal, Incorporated.

When he got back to his conapt he seated himself before his Hermes Rocket portable, opened the drawers and rummaged for carbon paper—and noticed a small, familiar box. A box which he had carefully filled on Mars with Martian fauna and later smuggled through customs.

Opening the box he saw, to his disbelief, six dead maw-worms and several varieties of the unicellular life on which the Martian worms fed. The protozoa were dried-up, dusty, but he recognized them; it had taken him an entire day picking among the vast dark alien boulders to find them. A wonderful, illuminated journey of discovery.

But I didn't go to Mars, he realized.

Yet on the other hand—

Kirsten appeared at the doorway to the room, an armload of pale brown groceries gripped. "Why are you home in the middle of the day?" Her voice, in an eternity of sameness, was accusing.

"Did I go to Mars?" he asked her. "You would know."

"No, of course you didn't go to Mars; *you* would know that, I would think. Aren't you always bleating about going?"

He said, "By God, I think I went." After a pause he added, "And simultaneously I think I didn't go."

"Make up your mind."

"How can I?" He gestured. "I have both memory-tracks grafted inside my head; one is real and one isn't but I can't tell which is which. Why can't I rely on you? They haven't tinkered with you." She could do this much for him at least— even if she never did anything else.

Kirsten said in a level, controlled voice, "Doug, if you don't pull yourself together, we're through. I'm going to leave you."

"I'm in trouble." His voice came out husky and coarse. And shaking. "Probably I'm heading into a psychotic episode; I hope not, but—maybe that's it. It would explain everything, anyhow."

Setting down the bag of groceries, Kirsten stalked to the closet. "I was not kidding," she said to him quietly. She brought out a coat, got it on, walked back to the door of the conapt. "I'll phone you one of these days soon," she said tonelessly. "This is goodbye, Doug. I hope you pull out of this eventually; I really pray you do. For your sake."

"Wait," he said desperately. "Just tell me and make it absolute; I did go or I didn't—tell me which one." *But they may have altered your memory-track also,* he realized.

The door closed. His wife had left. Finally!

A voice behind him said, "Well, that's that. Now put up your hands, Quail. And also please turn around and face this way."

He turned, instinctively, without raising his hands.

The man who faced him wore the plum uniform of the Interplan Police Agency, and his gun appeared to be UN issue. And, for some odd reason, he seemed familiar to Quail; familiar in a blurred, distorted fashion which he could not pin down. So, jerkily, he raised his hands.

"You remember," the policeman said, "your trip to Mars. We know all your actions today and all your thoughts—in particular your very important thoughts on the trip home from Rekal, Incorporated." He explained, "We have a tele-transmitter wired within your skull; it keeps us constantly informed."

A telepathic transmitter, use of a living plasma that had been discovered on Luna. He shuddered with self-aversion. The thing lived inside him, within his own brain, feeding, listening, feeding. But the Interplan police used them; that had come out even in the homeopapes. So this was probably true, dismal as it was.

"Why me?" Quail said huskily. What had he done—or thought? And what did this have to do with Rekal, Incorporated?

"Fundamentally," the Interplan cop said, "this has nothing to do with Rekal; it's between you and us." He tapped his right ear. "I'm still picking up your mentational processes by way of your cephalic transmitter." In the man's ear Quail saw a small white-plastic plug. "So I have to warn you: anything you think may be held against you." He smiled. "Not that it matters now; you've already thought and spoken yourself into oblivion. What's annoying is the fact that under narkidrine at Rekal, Incorporated you told them, their technicians and the owner, Mr. McClane, about your trip—where you went, for whom, some of what you did. They're very frightened. They wish they had never laid eyes on you." He added reflectively, "They're right."

Quail said, "I never made any trip. It's a false memory-chain improperly planted in me by McClane's technicians." But then he thought of the box, in his desk drawer, containing the Martian life forms. And the trouble and hardship he had had gathering them. The memory seemed real. And the box of life forms; that certainly was real. Unless McClane had planted it. Perhaps this was one of the "proofs" which McClane had talked glibly about.

The memory of my trip to Mars, he thought, *doesn't convince me—but unfortunately it has convinced the Interplan Police Agency. They think I really went to Mars and they think I at least partially realize it.*

"We not only know you went to Mars," the Interplan cop agreed, in answer to his thoughts, "but we know that you now remember enough to be difficult for us. And there's no use expunging your conscious memory of all this, because if we do you'll simply show up at Rekal, Incorporated again and start over. And we can't do anything about McClane and his operation because we have no jurisdiction over anyone except our own people. Anyhow, McClane hasn't committed any crime." He eyed Quail, "Nor, technically, have you. You didn't go to Rekal, Incorporated with the idea of regaining your memory; you went, as we realize, for the usual reason people go there—a love by plain, dull people for adventure." He added, "Unfortunately you're not plain, not dull, and you've already had too much excitement; the last thing in the universe you needed was a course from Rekal, Incorporated. Nothing could have been more lethal for you or for us. And, for that matter, for McClane."

Quail said, "Why is it 'difficult' for you if I remember my trip—my alleged trip—and what I did there?"

"Because," the Interplan harness bull said, "what you did is not in accord with our great white all-protecting father public image. You did, for us, what we never do. As you'll presently remember—thanks to narkidrine. That box of dead worms and algae has been sitting in your desk drawer for six months, ever since you got back. And at no time have you shown the slightest curiosity about it. We didn't even know you had it until you remembered it on your way home from Rekal; then we came here on the double to look for it." He added, unnecessarily, "Without any luck; there wasn't enough time."

A second Interplan cop joined the first one; the two briefly conferred. Meanwhile, Quail thought rapidly. He did remember more, now; the cop had been right about narkidrine. They—Interplan—probably used it themselves. Probably? He knew darn well they did; he had seen them putting a prisoner on it. Where would *that* be? Somewhere on Terra? More likely on Luna, he decide, viewing the image rising from his highly defective—but rapidly less so—memory.

And he remembered something else. Their reason for sending him to Mars; the job he had done.

No wonder they had expunged his memory.

"Oh, God," the first of the two Interplan cops said, breaking off his conversation with his companion. Obviously, he had picked up Quail's thoughts. "Well, this is a far worse problem, now; as bad as it can get." He walked toward Quail, again covering him with his gun. "We've got to kill you," he said. "And right away."

Nervously, his fellow officer said, "Why right away? Can't we simply cart him off to Interplan New York and let them—"

"*He* knows why it has to be right away," the first cop said; he too looked nervous, now, but Quail realized that it was for an entirely different reason. His memory had been brought back almost entirely, now. And he fully understood the officer's tension.

"On Mars," Quail said hoarsely, "I killed a man. After getting past fifteen body-guards. Some armed with sneaky-pete guns, the way you are." He had been trained, by Interplan, over a five year period to be an assassin. A professional killer. He knew ways to take out armed adversaries . . . such as these two officers; and the one with the ear-receiver knew it, too.

If he moved swiftly enough—

The gun fired. But he had already moved to one side, and at the same time he chopped down the gun-carrying officer. In an instant he had possession of the gun and was covering the other, confused, officer.

"Picked my thoughts up," Quail said, panting for breath. "He knew what I was going to do, but I did it anyhow."

Half sitting up, the injured officer grated, "He won't use that gun on you, Sam; I pick that up, too. He knows he's finished, and he knows we know it, too. Come on, Quail." Laboriously, grunting with pain, he got shakily to his feet. He held out his hand. "The gun," he said to Quail. "You can't use it, and if you turn it over to me I'll guarantee not to kill you; you'll be given a hearing, and someone higher up in Interplan will decide, not me. Maybe they can erase your memory once more, I don't know. But you know the thing I was going to kill you for; I couldn't keep you from remembering it. So my reason for wanting to kill you is in a sense past."

Quail, clutching the gun, bolted from the conapt, sprinted for the elevator. *If you follow me*, he thought, *I'll kill you. So don't.* He jabbed at the elevator button and, a moment later, the doors slid back.

The police hadn't followed him. Obviously they had picked up his terse, tense thoughts and had decided not to take the chance.

With him inside the elevator descended. He had gotten away—for a time. But what next? Where could he go?

The elevator reached the ground floor; a moment later Quail had joined the mob of peds hurrying along the runnels. His head ached and he felt sick. But at least he had evaded death; they had come very close to shooting him on the spot, back in his own conapt.

And they probably will again, he decided. *When they find me. And with this transmitter inside me, that won't take too long.*

Ironically, he had gotten exactly what he had asked Rekal, Incorporated for. Adventure, peril, Interplan police at work, a secret and dangerous trip to Mars in which his life was at stake—everything he had wanted as a false memory.

The advantages of it being a memory—and nothing more—could now be appreciated.

On a park bench, alone, he sat dully watching a flock of perts: a semi-bird imported from Mars' two moons, capable of soaring flight, even against Earth's huge gravity.

Maybe I can find my way back to Mars, he pondered. But then what? It would be worse on Mars; the political organization whose leader he had assassinated would spot him the moment he stepped from the ship; he would have Interplan and *them* after him, there.

Can you hear me thinking? he wondered. Easy avenue to paranoia; sitting here alone he felt them tuning in on him, monitoring, recording, discussing . . . He shivered, rose to his feet, walked aimlessly, his hands deep in his pockets. *No matter where I go,* he realized, *you'll always be with me. As long as I have this device inside my head.*

I'll make a deal with you, he thought to himself—and to them. *Can you imprint a false-memory template on me again, as you did before, that I lived an average, routine life, never went to Mars? Never saw an Interplan uniform up close and never handled a gun?*

A voice inside his brain answered, "As has been carefully explained to you: that would not be enough."

Astonished, he halted.

"We formerly communicated with you in this manner," the voice continued. "When you were operating in the field, on Mars. It's been months since we've done it; we assumed, in fact, that we'd never have to do so again. Where are you?"

"Walking," Quail said, "to my death." *By your officers' guns,* he added as an afterthought. "How can you be sure it wouldn't be enough?" he demanded. "Don't the Rekal techniques work?"

"As we said. If you're given a set of standard, average memories you get—restless. You'd inevitably seek out Rekal or one of its competitors again. We can't go through this a second time."

"Suppose," Quail said, "once my authentic memories have been canceled, something more vital than standard memories are implanted. Something which would act to satisfy my craving," he said. "That's been proved; that's probably why you initially hired me. But you ought to be able to come up with something else— something equal. I was the richest man on Terra but I finally gave all my money to educational foundations. Or I was a famous deep-space explorer. Anything of that sort; wouldn't one of those do?"

Silence.

"Try it," he said desperately. "Get some of your top-notch military psychiatrists; explore my mind. Find out what my most expansive daydream is." He tried to think. "Women," he said. "Thousands of them, like Don Juan had. An interplanetary playboy—a mistress in every city on Earth, Luna and Mars. Only I gave that up, out of exhaustion. Please," he begged. "Try it."

"You'd voluntarily surrender, then?" the voice inside his head asked. "If we agreed, to arrange such a solution? *If* it's possible?"

After an interval of hesitation he said, "Yes." *I'll take the risk,* he said to himself, *that you don't simply kill me.*

"You make the first move," the voice said presently. "Turn yourself over to us. And we'll investigate that line of possibility. If we can't do it, however, if your authentic memories begin to crop up again as they've done at this time, then—" There was silence and then the voice finished, "We'll have to destroy you. As you must understand. Well, Quail, you still want to try?"

"Yes," he said. Because the alternative was death now—and for certain. At least this way he had a chance, slim as it was.

"You present yourself at our main barracks in New York," the voice of the Interplan cop resumed. "At 580 Fifth Avenue, floor twelve. Once you've surrendered yourself, we'll have our psychiatrists begin on you; we'll have personality-profile tests made. We'll attempt to determine your absolute, ultimate fantasy wish—then we'll bring you back to Rekal, Incorporated, here; get them in on it, fulfilling that wish in vicarious surrogate retrospection. And—good luck. We do owe you something; you acted as a capable instrument for us." The voice lacked malice; if anything, they—the organization—felt sympathy toward him.

"Thanks," Quail said. And began searching for a robot cab.

"Mr. Quail," the stern-faced, elderly Interplan psychiatrist said, "you possess a most interesting wish-fulfillment dream fantasy. Probably nothing such as you consciously entertain or suppose. This is commonly the way; I hope it won't upset you too much to hear about it."

The senior ranking Interplan officer present said briskly, "He better not be too much upset to hear about it, not if he expects not to get shot."

"Unlike the fantasy of wanting to be an Interplan undercover agent," the psychiatrist continued, "which, being relatively speaking a product of maturity, had a certain plausibility to it, this production is a grotesque dream of your childhood; it is no wonder you fail to recall it. Your fantasy is this: you are nine years old, walking alone down a rustic lane. An unfamiliar variety of space vessel from another star system lands directly in front of you. No one on Earth but you, Mr. Quail, sees it. The creatures within are very small and helpless, somewhat on the order of field mice, although they are attempting to invade Earth; tens of thousands of other ships will soon be on their way, when this advance party gives the go-ahead signal."

"And I suppose I stop them," Quail said, experiencing a mixture of amusement and disgust. "Single-handed I wipe them out. Probably by stepping on them with my foot."

"No," the psychiatrist said patiently. "You halt the invasion, but not by destroying them. Instead, you show them kindness and mercy, even though by telepathy—their mode of communication—you know why they have come. They have never seen such humane traits exhibited by any sentient organism, and to show their appreciation they make a covenant with you."

Quail said, "They won't invade Earth as long as I'm alive."

"Exactly." To the Interplan officer the psychiatrist said, "You can see it does fit his personality, despite his feigned scorn."

"So by merely existing," Quail said, feeling a growing pleasure, "by simply being alive, I keep Earth safe from alien rule. I'm in effect, then, the most important person on Terra. Without lifting a finger."

"Yes, indeed, sir," the psychiatrist said. "And this is bedrock in your psyche; this is a life-long childhood fantasy. Which, without depth and drug therapy, you never would have recalled. But it has always existed in you; it went underneath, but never ceased."

To McClane, who sat intently listening, the senior police official said, "Can you implant an extra-factual memory pattern that extreme in him?"

"We get handed every possible type of wish-fantasy there is," McClane said. "Frankly, I've heard a lot worse than this. Certainly we can handle it. Twenty-four hours from now he won't just *wish* he'd saved Earth; he'll devoutly believe it really happened."

The senior police official said, "You can start the job, then. In preparation we've already once again erased the memory in him of his trip to Mars."

Quail said, "What trip to Mars?"

No one answered him, so reluctantly, he shelved the question. And anyhow a police vehicle had now put in its appearance; he, McClane and the senior police officer crowded into it, and presently they were on their way to Chicago and Rekal, Incorporated.

"You had better make no errors this time," the police officer said to heavy-set, nervous-looking McClane.

"I can't see what could go wrong," McClane mumbled, perspiring. "This has nothing to do with Mars or Interplan. Single-handedly stopping an invasion of Earth from another star-system." He shook his head at that. "Wow, what a kid dreams up. And by pious virtue, too; not by force. It's sort of quaint." He dabbed at his forehead with a large linen pocket handkerchief.

Nobody said anything.

"In fact," McClane said, "it's touching."

"But arrogant," the police official said starkly. "Inasmuch as when he dies the invasion will resume. No wonder he doesn't recall it; it's the most grandiose fantasy I ever ran across." He eyed Quail with disapproval. "And to think we put this man on our payroll."

When they reached Rekal, Incorporated the receptionist, Shirley, met them breathlessly in the outer office. "Welcome back, Mr. Quail," she fluttered, her melon-shaped breasts—today painted an incandescent orange—bobbing with agitation. "I'm sorry everything worked out so badly before; I'm sure this time it'll go better."

Still repeatedly dabbing at his shiny forehead with his neatly folded Irish linen handkerchief, McClane said, "It better." Moving with rapidity he rounded up Lowe and Keeler, escorted them and Douglas Quail to the work area, and then, with Shirley and the senior police officer, returned to his familiar office. To wait.

"Do we have a packet made up for this, Mr. McClane?" Shirley asked, bumping against him in her agitation, then coloring modestly.

"I think we do." He tried to recall, then gave up and consulted the formal chart. "A combination," he decided aloud, "of packets Eighty-one, Twenty, and Six." From the vault section of the chamber behind his desk he fished out the appropriate packets, carried them to his desk for inspection. "From Eighty-one," he explained, "a magic healing rod given him—the client in question, this time Mr. Quail—by the race of beings from another system. A token of their gratitude."

"Does it work?" the police officer asked curiously.

"It did once," McClane explained. "But he, ahem, you see, used it up years ago, healing right and left. Now it's only a memento. But he remembers it working spectacularly." He chuckled, then opened packet Twenty. "Document from the UN Secretary General thanking him for saving Earth; this isn't precisely appropriate, because part of Quail's fantasy is that no one knows of the invasion except himself, but for the sake of verisimilitude we'll throw it in." He inspected packet Six, then. What came from this? He couldn't recall; frowning, he dug into the plastic bag as Shirley and the Interplan police officer watched intently.

"Writing," Shirley said. "In a funny language."

"This tells who they were," McClane said, "and where they came from. Including a detailed star map logging their flight here and the system of origin. Of course it's in *their* script, so he can't read it. But he remembers them reading it to him in his own tongue." He placed the three artifacts in the center of the desk. "These should be taken to Quail's conapt," he said to the police officer. "So that when he gets home he'll find them. And it'll confirm his fantasy. SOP—standard operating procedure." He chuckled apprehensively, wondering how matters were going with Lowe and Keeler.

The intercom buzzed. "Mr. McClane, I'm sorry to bother you." It was Lowe's voice; he froze as he recognized it, froze and became mute. "But something's come up. Maybe it would be better if you came in here and supervised. Like before, Quail reacted well to the narkidrine; he's unconscious, relaxed and receptive. But—"

McClane sprinted for the work area.

On a hygienic bed Douglas Quail lay breathing slowly and regularly, eyes half-shut, dimly conscious of those around him.

"We started interrogating him," Lowe said, white-faced. "To find out exactly when to place the fantasy-memory of him single-handedly having saved Earth. And strangely enough—"

"They told me not to tell," Douglas Quail mumbled in a dull drug-saturated voice. "That was the agreement. I wasn't even supposed to remember. But how could I forget an event like that?"

I guess it would be hard, McClane reflected. *But you did—until now.*

"They even gave me a scroll," Quail mumbled, "of gratitude. I have it hidden in my conapt; I'll show it to you."

To the Interplan officer who had followed after him, McClane said, "Well I offer the suggestion that you better not kill him. If you do they'll return."

"They also gave me a magic invisible destroying rod," Quail mumbled eyes totally shut now. "That's how I killed that man on Mars you sent me to take out. It's in my drawer along with the box of Martian maw-worms and dried-up plant life."

Wordlessly, the Interplan officer turned and stalked from the work area.

I might as well put those packets of proof-artifacts away, McClane said to himself resignedly. He walked, step by step, back to his office. *Including the citation from the UN Secretary General. After all—*

The real one probably would not be long in coming.

✺ SAMUEL R(AY) ("CHIP") DELANY (1942-)

Samuel "Chip" Delany has spent his professional life as both a writer and a university professor. A scholar of culture and literary history, and an accomplished editor and artist as well, he has always been progressive and innovative. He has intelligently and artistically written fiction and nonfiction about race, sex, and alternate lifestyles. Like Harlan Ellison, Delany has very successfully expanded the boundaries and definitions of Science Fiction, and he has earned several of the field's highest awards and citations.

Delany has done much to break down the barriers of Science Fiction, whether these be race related, lifestyle related, or legitimacy related. In the latter, the author, like H. G. Wells, has helped make Science Fiction worthy of scholarly and intellectual analysis. Delany's credibility in this regard is seen in his extensive inclusion and acclaim in American literature studies and anthologies.

As a seasoned academic, the author brings a perspective to Science Fiction that is consciously but not obnoxiously intellectual. A lifelong scholar of culture and anthropology, myth and linguistics, Samuel R. Delany debuted in Science Fiction in 1962 with his novel The Jewels of Aptor. *Theodore Sturgeon is his favorite author, and the influence of Sturgeon's writing on Delany is significant and noteworthy.*

As an author, Delany has used Science Fiction as a vehicle for social criticism. He consciously analyzes and responds to the social reality and paradigm. He is both writer and gentleman of the highest order.

The title for "Driftglass" nicely parallels and describes Delany's portrayal and allegory of the human experience set in a world not so very far away.

Driftglass
(IF: Science Fiction, June 1967)

Sometimes I go down to the port, splashing sand with my stiff foot at the end of my stiff leg locked in my stiff hip, with the useless arm a-swinging, to get wet all over again, drink in the dives with cronies ashore, feeling old, broken, sorry for myself, laughing louder and louder. The third of my face that was burned away in the accident was patched with skin-grafts from my chest, so what's left of my mouth distorts all loud sounds; sloppy sartorial reconstruction. Also I have a hairy chest. Chest hair does not look like beard hair, and it grows all up under my right eye. And: my beard is red, my chest hair brown, while the thatch curling down over neck and ears is sun-streaked to white here, darkened to bronze there, 'midst general blondness.

By reason of my being a walking (I suppose my gait could be called headlong limping) horror show, plus a general inclination to sulk, I spend most of the time up in the wood and glass and aluminum house on the surf-sloughed point that the Aquatic Corp ceded me along with my pension. Rugs from Turkey there, copper pots, my tenor recorder which I can no longer play, and my books.

But sometimes, when the gold fog blurs the morning, I go down to the beach and tromp barefoot in the wet edging of the sea, searching for driftglass.

It was foggy that morning, and the sun across the water moiled the mists like a brass ladle. I lurched to the top of the rocks, looked down through the tall grasses into the frothing inlet where she lay, and blinked.

She sat up, long gills closing down her neck and the secondary slits along her back just visible at their tips because of much hair, wet and curling copper, falling there. She saw me. "What are you doing here, huh?" She narrowed blue eyes.

"Looking for driftglass."

"What?"

"There's a piece." I pointed near her and came down the rocks like a crab with one stiff leg.

"Where?" She turned over, half in, half out of the water, the webs of her fingers cupping nodules of black stone.

While the water made cold overtures between my toes, I picked up the milky fragment by her elbow where she wasn't looking. She jumped, because she obviously had thought it was somewhere else.

"See?"

"What . . . what is it?" She raised her cool hand to mine. For a moment the light through the milky gem and the pale film of my own webs pearled the screen of her palms. (Details like that. Yes, they are the important things, the points from which we suspend later pain.) A moment later wet fingers closed to the back of mine.

"Driftglass," I said. "You know all the Coca-Cola bottles and cut-crystal punch bowls and industrial silicon slag that goes into the sea?"

"I know the Coca-Cola bottles."

"They break, and the tide pulls the pieces back and forth over the sandy bottom, wearing the edges, changing their shape. Sometimes chemicals in the glass react with chemicals in the ocean to change the color. Sometimes veins work their way through in patterns like snowflakes, regular and geometric; others, irregular and angled like coral. When the pieces dry, they're milky. Put them in water and they become transparent again."

"Ohhh!" she breathed as the beauty of the blunted triangular fragment in my palm assailed her like perfume. Then she looked at my face, blinking the third, aqueous-filled lid that we use as a correction lens for underwater vision.

She watched the ruin calmly.

Then her hand went to my foot where the webs had been torn back in the accident. She began to take in who I was. I looked for horror, but saw only a little sadness.

The insignia on her buckle—her stomach was making little jerks the way you always do during the first few minutes when you go from breathing water to air—told me she was a Biological Technician. (Back up at the house there was a similar uniform of simulated scales folded in the bottom drawer of the dresser and the belt insignia said Depth Gauger.) I was wearing some very frayed jeans and a red cotton shirt with no buttons.

She reached for my neck, pushed my collar back from my shoulders and touched the tender slits of my gills, outlining them with cool fingers. "Who are you?" Finally.

"Cal Svenson."

She slid back down in the water. "You're the one who had the terrible . . . but that was years ago! They still talk about it, down . . . ." She stopped.

As the sea softens the surface of a piece of glass, so it blurs the souls and sensibilities of the people who toil beneath her. And according to the last report of the Marine Reclamation Division there are to date seven hundred and fifty thousand who have been given gills and webs and sent under the foam where there are no storms, up and down the American coast.

"You live on shore? I mean around here? But so long ago . . . "

"How old are you?"

"Sixteen."

"I was two years older than you when the accident happened."

"You were eighteen?"

"I'm twice that now. Which means it happened almost twenty years ago. It is a long time."

"They still talk about it."

"I've almost forgotten," I said. "I really have. Say, do you play the recorder?"

"I used to."

"Good! Come up to my place and look at my tenor recorder. And I'll make some tea. Perhaps you can stay for lunch—"

"I have to report back to Marine Headquarters by three. Tork is going over the briefing to lay the cable for the big dive, with Jonni and the crew." She paused, smiled. "But I can catch the undertow and be there in half an hour if I leave by two thirty."

On the walk up I learned her name was Ariel. She thought the patio was charming, and the mosaic evoked, "Oh, look!" and "Did you do this yourself?" a half-dozen times. (I had done it, in the first lonely years.) She picked out the squid and the whale in battle, the wounded shark and the diver. She told me she didn't get time to read much, but she was impressed by all the books. She listened to me reminisce. She talked a lot to me about her work, husbanding the deep-down creatures they were scaring up. Then she sat on the kitchen stool, playing a Lukas Foss serenade on my recorder, while I put rock salt in the bottom of the broiler tray for two dozen Oysters Rockefeller, and the tea water whistled. I'm a comparatively lonely guy. I like being followed by beautiful young girls.

II

"Hey, Juao!" I bawled across the jetty.

He nodded to me from the center of his nets, sun glistening on polished shoulders, sun lost in rough hair. I walked across to where he sat, sewing like a spider. He pulled another section up over his horny toes, then grinned at me with his mosaic smile: gold, white, black gap below, crooked yellow; white, gold, white. Shoving my bad leg in front I squatted.

"I fished out over the coral where you told me." He filled his cheek with his tongue and nodded. "You come up to the house for a drink, eh?"

"Fine."

"Just—a moment more."

There's a certain sort of Brazilian you find along the shore in the fishing villages, old yet ageless. See one of their men and you think he could be fifty, he could be sixty—will probably look at the same when he's eighty-five. Such was Juao. We once figured it out. He's seven hours older than I am.

We became friends some time before the accident when I got tangled in his nets working high lines in the Vorea Current. A lot of guys would have taken their knife and hacked their way out of the situation, ruining fifty-five, sixty dollars worth of nets. That's an average fisherman's monthly income down here. But I surfaced and sat around in his boat while we untied me. Then we came in and got plastered. Since I cost him a day's fishing, I've been giving him hints on where to fish ever since. He buys me drinks when I come up with something.

This has been going on for twenty years. During that time my life has been smashed up and land-bound. In the same time Juao has married off his five sisters, got married himself and has two children. (Oh, those *bolitos* and *teneros asados* that Amalia of the oiled braid and laughing breasts would make for Sunday dinner/supper/Monday breakfast.) I rode with them in the ambulance 'copter all the way into Brasilia; in the hospital hall Juao and I stood together, both still barefoot, he tattered with fish scales in his hair, me just tattered, and I held him while he cried and I tried to explain to him how a world that could take a pubescent child and with a week of operations make an amphibious creature that can exist for a month on either side of the sea's foam-fraught surface could still be helpless before certain general endocrine cancers coupled with massive renal deterioration. Juao and I returned to the village alone, by bus, three days before our birthday—back when I was twenty-three and Juao was twenty-three and seven hours old.

"This morning," Juao said. (The shuttle danced in the web at the end of the orange line.) "I got a letter for you to read me. It's about the children. Come on, we go up and drink." The shuttle paused, backtracked twice, and he yanked the knot tight. We walked along the port toward the square. "Do you think the letter says that the children are accepted?"

"If it's from the Aquatic Corp. They just send postcards when they reject someone. The question is, how do *you* feel about it?"

"You are a good man. If they grow up like you, then it will be fine."

"But you're still worried." I'd been prodding Juao to get the kids into the International Aquatic Corp nigh on since I became their godfather. The operations had to be performed near puberty. It would mean much time away from the village during their training period—and they might eventually be stationed in any ocean in the world. But two motherless children had not been easy on Juao or his sisters. The Corp would mean education, travel, interesting work, the things that make up one kind of good life. They wouldn't look twice their age when they were thirty-five; and not too many amphimen look like me.

"Worry is part of life. But the work is dangerous. Did you know there is an amphiman going to try and lay cable down in the Slash?"

I frowned. "Again?"

"Yes. And that is what you tried to do when the sea broke you to pieces and burned the parts, eh?"

"Must you be so damned picturesque?" I asked. "Who's going to beard the lion this time?"

"A young amphiman named Tork. They speak of him down at the docks as a brave man."

"Why the hell are they still trying to lay the cable there? They've gotten by this long without a line through the Slash."

"Because of the fish," Juao said. "You told me why twenty years ago. The fish are still there, and we fishermen who cannot live below are still here. If the children go for the operations, then there will be less fishermen. But today . . ." He shrugged. "They must either lay the line across the fish paths or down in the Slash." Juao shook his head.

Funny things, the great power cables the Aquatic Corp has been strewing across the ocean floor to bring power to their undersea mines and farms, to run their oil wells—and how many flaming wells have I capped down there—for their herds of whale, and chemical distillation plants. They carry two-hundred-sixty-cycle current. Over certain sections of the ocean floor, or in sections of the water with certain mineral contents, this sets up inductance in the water itself which sometimes—and you will probably get a Nobel prize if you can detail exactly why it isn't always—drives the fish away over areas up to twenty-five and thirty miles, unless the lines are laid in the bottom of those canyons that delve into the ocean floor.

"This Tork thinks of the fishermen. He is a good man too."

I raised my eyebrows—the one that's left, anyway—and tried to remember what my little Undine had said about him that morning. And remembered not much.

"I wish him luck," I said.

"What do you feel about this young man going down into the coral-rimmed jaws to the Slash?"

I thought for a moment. "I think I hate him."

Juao looked up.

"He is an image in a mirror where I look and am forced to regard what I was," I went on. "I envy him the chance to succeed where I failed, and I can come on just as quaint as you can. I hope he makes it."

Juao twisted his shoulders in a complicated shrug (once I could do that) which is coastal Brazilian for, "I didn't know things had progressed to that point, but seeing that they have, there is little to be done."

"The sea is that sort of mirror," I said.

"Yes." Juao nodded.

Behind us I heard the slapping of sandals on concrete. I turned in time to catch my goddaughter in my good arm. My godson had grabbed hold of the bad one and was swinging on it.

"Tio Cal—?"

"Hey, Tio Cal, what did you bring us?"

"You will pull him over," Juao reprimanded them. "Let go."

And, bless them, they ignored their father.

"What did you bring us?"

"What did you bring us, Tio Cal?"

"If you let me, I'll show you." So they stepped back, dark-eyed and quivering. I watched Juao watching: brown pupils on ivory balls, and in the left eye a vein had broken in a jagged smear. He was loving his children, who would soon be as alien to him as the fish he netted. He was also looking at the terrible thing that was me and wondering what would come to his own spawn. And he was watching the world turn and grow older, clocked by the waves, reflected in that mirror.

It's impossible for me to see what the population explosion and the budding colonies on Luna and Mars and the flowering beneath the ocean really look like from the disrupted cultural melange of a coastal fishing town. But I come closer than many others, and I know what I don't understand.

I pushed around in my pocket and fetched out the milky fragment I had brought from the beach. "Here. Do you like this one?" And they bent above my webbed and alien fingers.

In the supermarket, which is the biggest building in the village, Juao bought a lot of cake mixes. "That moist, delicate texture," whispered the box when you lifted it from the shelf, "with that deep flavor, deeper than chocolate!"

I'd just read an article about the new vocal packaging in a U.S. magazine that had gotten down last week, so I was prepared and stayed in the fresh vegetable section to avoid temptation. Then we went up to Juao's house. The letter proved to be what I'd expected. The kids had to take the bus into Brasilia tomorrow. My godchildren were on their way to becoming fish.

We sat on the front steps and drank and watched the donkeys and the motor-bikes and the men in baggy trousers, the women in yellow scarves and bright skirts with wreaths of garlic and sacks of onions. As well, a few people glittered by in the green scales of amphimen uniforms.

Finally Juao got tired and went in to take a nap. Most of my life has been spent on the coast of countries accustomed to siestas, but those first formative ten were passed on a Danish collective farm and the idea never really took. So I stepped over my goddaughter, who had fallen asleep on her fists on the bottom step, and walked back through the town toward the beach.

III

At midnight Ariel came out of the sea, climbed the rocks, and clicked her nails against my glass wall so the droplets ran, pearled by the gibbous moon.

Earlier I had stretched in front of the fireplace on the sheepskin throw to read, then dozed off. The conscientious timer had asked me if there was anything I wanted, and getting no answer had turned off the Dvorak *Cello Concerto* that was on its second time around, extinguished the reading lamp, and stopped dropping logs onto the flame so that now, as I woke, the grate was carpeted with coals.

She clicked again, and I raised my head from the cushion. The green uniform, her amber hair—all color was lost under the silver light outside. I lurched across the rug, touched the button, and the glass slid into the floor. The breeze came to my face, as the barrier fell.

"What do you want?" I asked. "What time is it, anyway?"

"Tork is on the beach, waiting for you."

The night was warm but windy. Below the rocks silver flakes chased each other in to shore. The tide lay full.

I rubbed my face. "The new boss man? Why didn't you bring him up to the house? What does he want to see me about?"

She touched my arm. "Come. They are all down on the beach."

"Who all?"

"Tork and the others."

She led me across the patio and to the path that wound to the sand. The sea roared in the moonlight. Down the beach people stood around a driftwood fire that whipped the night. Ariel walked beside me.

Two of the fishermen from town were crowding each other on the bottom of an overturned washtub, playing guitars. The singing, raucous and rhythmic, jarred across the paled sand. Shark's teeth shook on the necklace of an old woman dancing. Others were sitting on an overturned dinghy, eating.

Over one part of the fire on a skillet two feet across, oil frothed through pink islands of shrimp. One woman ladled them in, another ladled them out.

"Tio Cal!"

"Look, Tio Cal is here!"

"Hey, what are you two doing up?" I asked. "Shouldn't you be home in bed?"

"Poppa Juao said we could come. He'll be here, too, soon."

I turned to Ariel. "Why are they all gathering?"

"Because of the laying of the cable tomorrow at dawn."

Someone was running up the beach, waving a bottle in each hand.

"They didn't want to tell you about the party. They thought that it might hurt your pride."

"My what. . . ?"

"If you knew they were making so big a thing of the job you had failed at—"

"But—"

"—and that had hurt you so in failure. They did not want you to be sad. But Tork wants to see you. I said you would not be sad. So I went to bring you down from the rocks."

"Thanks, I guess."

"Tio Cal?"

But the voice was bigger and deeper than a child's.

He sat on a log back from the fire, eating a sweet potato. The flame flickered on his dark cheekbones, in his hair, wet and black. He stood, came to me, held up his hand. I held up mine and we slapped palms. "Good." He was smiling. "Ariel told me you would come. I will lay the power line down through the Slash tomorrow." His uniform scales glittered down his arms. He was very strong. But standing still, he still moved. The light on the cloth told me that. "I . . ." He paused. I thought of a nervous, happy dancer. "I wanted to talk to you about the cable." I thought of an eagle, I thought of a shark. "And about the . . . accident. If you would."

"Sure," I said. "If there's anything I could tell you that would help."

"See, Tork," Ariel said. "I told you he would talk to you about it."

I could hear his breathing change. "It really doesn't bother you to talk about the accident?"

I shook my head and realized something about that voice. It was a boy's voice that could imitate a man's. Tork was not over nineteen.

"We're going fishing soon," Tork told me. "Will you come?"

"If I'm not in the way."

A bottle went from the woman at the shrimp crate to one of the guitarists, down to Ariel, to me, then to Tork. (The liquor, made in a cave seven miles inland, was almost rum. The too tight skin across the left side of my mouth makes the manful swig a little difficult to bring off. I got "rum" down my chin.)

He drank, wiped his mouth, passed the bottle on and put his hand on my shoulder. "Come down to the water."

We walked away from the fire. Some of the fishermen stared after us. A few of the amphimen glanced, and glanced away.

"Do all the young people of the village call you Tio Cal?"

"No. Only my godchildren. Their father and I have been friends since I was your age."

"Oh, I thought perhaps it was a nickname. That's why I called you that."

We reached wet sand where orange light cavorted at our feet. The broken shell of a lifeboat rocked in moonlight. Tork sat down on the shell's rim. I sat beside him. The water splashed to our knees.

"There's no other place to lay the power cable?" I asked "There is no other way to take it except through the Slash?"

"I was going to ask you what you thought of the whole business. But I guess I don't really have to." He shrugged and clapped his hands together a few times. "All the projects this side of the bay have grown huge and cry for power. The new operations tax the old lines unmercifully. There was a power failure last July in Cayine down the shelf below the twilight level. The whole village was without light for two days, and twelve amphimen died of overexposure to the cold currents coming up from the depths. If we laid the cables farther up, we chance disrupting our own fishing operations as well as those of the fishermen on shore."

I nodded.

"Cal, what happened to you in the Slash?"

Eager, scared Tork. I was remembering now, not the accident, but the midnight before, pacing the beach, guts clamped with fists of fear and anticipation. Some of the Indians back where they make the liquor still send messages by tying knots in palm fibers. One could have spread my entrails then, or Tork's tonight, to read our respective horospecs.

Juao's mother knew the knot language, but he and his sisters never bothered to learn because they wanted to be modern, and, as children, still confused with modernity the new ignorances, lacking modern knowledge.

"When I was a boy," Tork said, "we would dare each other to walk the boards along the edge of the ferry slip. The sun would be hot and the boards would rock in the water, and if the boats were in and you fell down between the boats and the piling, you could get killed." He shook his head. "The crazy things kids will do. That was back when I was eight or nine, before I became a waterbaby."

"Where was it?"

Tork looked up. "Oh. Manila. I'm Filipino."

The sea licked our knees, and the gunwale sagged under us.

"What happened in the Slash?"

"There's a volcanic flaw near the base of the Slash."

"I know."

"And the sea is as sensitive down there as a fifty-year-old woman with a new hairdo. We had an avalanche. The cable broke. The sparks were so hot and bright they made gouts of foam fifty feet high on the surface, so they tell me."

"What caused the avalanche?"

I shrugged. "It could have been just a God damned coincidence. There are rock falls down there all the time. It could have been the noise from the machines—though we masked them pretty well. It could have been something to do with the inductance from the smaller cables for the machines. Or maybe somebody just kicked out the wrong stone that was holding everything up."

One webbed hand became a fist, sank into the other, and hung.

Calling, "Cal!"

I looked up. Juao, pants rolled to his knees, shirt sailing in the sea wind, stood in the weave of white water. The wind lifted Tork's hair from his neck; and the fire roared on the beach.

Tork looked up too.

"They're getting ready to catch a big fish!" Juao called.

Men were already pushing their boats out. Tork clapped my shoulder. "Come, Cal. We fish now." We waded back to the shore.

Juao caught me as I reached dry sand. "You ride in my boat, Cal!"

Someone came with the acrid flares that hissed. The water slapped around the bottom of the boats as we wobbled into the swell.

Juao vaulted in and took up the oars. Around us green amphimen walked into the sea, struck forward, and were gone.

Juao pulled, leaned, pulled. The moonlight slid down his arms. The fire diminished on the beach.

Then among the boats, there was a splash, an explosion, and the red flare bloomed in the sky: the amphimen had sighted a big fish.

The flare hovered, pulsed once, twice, three times, four times (twenty, forty, sixty, eighty stone they estimated its weight to be), then fell.

Suddenly I shrugged out of my shirt, pulled at my belt buckle. "I'm going over the side, Juao!"

He leaned, he pulled, he leaned. "Take the rope."

"Yeah. Sure." It was tied to the back of the boat. I made a loop in the other end, slipped it around my shoulder. I swung my bad leg over the side, flung myself on the black water—

—mother-of-pearl shattered over me. That was the moon, blocked by the shadow of Juao's boat ten feet overhead. I turned below the rippling wounds Juao's oars made stroking the sea.

One hand and one foot with torn webs, I rolled over and looked down. The rope snaked to its end, and I felt Juao's strokes pulling me through the water.

They fanned below with underwater flares. Light undulated on their backs and heels. They circled, they closed, like those deep-sea fish who carry their own illumination. I saw the prey, glistening as it neared a flare.

You chase a fish with one spear among you. And that spear would be Tork's tonight. The rest have ropes to bind him that go up to the fishermen's boats.

There was a sudden confusion of lights below. The spear had been shot!

The fish, long as a tall and short man together, rose through the ropes. He turned out to sea, trailing his pursuers. But others waited there, tried to loop him. Once I had flung those ropes, treated with tar and lime to dissolve the slime of the fish's body and hold to the beast. The looped ropes caught, and by the movement of the flares, I saw them jerked from their paths. The fish turned, rose again, this time toward me.

He pulled around when one line ran out (and somewhere on the surface the prow of a boat doffed deep) but turned back and came on.

Of a sudden, amphimen were flicking about me as the fray's center drifted by. Tork, his spear dug deep, forward and left of the marlin's dorsal, had hauled himself astride the beast.

The fish tried to shake him, then dropped his tail and rose straight. Everybody started pulling toward the surface. I broke foam and grabbed Juao's gunwale.

Tork and the fish exploded up among the boats. They twisted in the air, in moonlight, in froth. The fish danced across the water on its tail, fell.

Juao stood up in the boat and shouted. The other fishermen shouted too, and somebody perched on the prow of a boat flung a rope and someone in the water caught it.

Then fish and Tork and me and a dozen amphimen all went underwater at once.

They dropped in a corona of bubbles. The fish struck the end of another line, and shook himself. Tork was thrown free, but he doubled back.

Then the lines began to haul the beast up again, quivering, whipping, quivering again.

Six lines from six boats had him. For one moment he was still in the submarine moonlight. I could see his wound tossing scarves of blood.

When he (and we) broke surface, he was thrashing again, near Juao's boat. I was holding onto the side when suddenly Tork, glistening, came out of the water beside me and went over into the dinghy.

"Here you go," he said, turning to kneel at the bobbing rim, and pulled me up while Juao leaned against the far side to keep balance.

Wet rope slopped on the prow. "Hey, Cal!" Tork laughed, grabbed it up, and began to haul.

The fish prised wave from white wave in the white water.

The boats came together. The amphimen had all climbed up. Ariel was across from us, holding a flare that drooled smoke down her arm. She peered by the hip of the fisherman who was standing in front of her.

Juao and Tork were hauling the rope. Behind them I was coiling it with one hand as it came back to me.

The fish came up and was flopped into Ariel's boat, tail out, head up, chewing air.

I had just finished pulling on my trousers when Tork fell down on the seat behind me and grabbed me around the shoulders with his wet arms. "Look at our fish, Tio Cal! Look!" He gasped air, laughing, his dark face diamonded beside the flares. "Look at our fish there, Cal!"

Juao, grinning white and gold, pulled us back into shore. The fire, the singing, hands beating hands—and my godson had put pebbles in the empty rum bottles and was shaking them to the music—the guitars spiraled around us as we carried the fish up the sand and the men brought the spit.

"Watch it!" Tork said, grasping the pointed end of the great stick that was thicker than his wrist.

We turned the fish over.

"Here, Cal?"

He prodded two fingers into the white flesh six inches back from the bony lip. "Fine."

Tork jammed the spit in.

We worked it through the body. By the time we carried it to the fire, they had brought more rum.

"Hey, Tork. Are you going to get some sleep before you go down in the morning?" I asked.

He shook his head "Slept all afternoon." He pointed toward the roasting fish with his elbow. "That's my breakfast."

But when the dancing grew violent a few hours later, just before the fish was to come off the fire, and the kids were pushing the last of the sweet potatoes from the ashes with sticks, I walked back to the lifeboat shell we had sat on earlier. It was three quarters flooded.

Curled below still water, Tork slept, fist loose before his mouth, the gills at the back of his neck pulsing rhythmically. Only his shoulder and hip made islands in the floated boat.

"Where's Tork?" Ariel asked me at the fire. They were swinging up the sizzling fish.

"Taking a nap."

"Oh, he wanted to cut the fish!"

"He's got a lot of work coming up. Sure you want to wake him up?"

"No, I'll let him sleep."

But Tork was coming up from the water, brushing his dripping hair back from his forehead.

He grinned at us, then went to carve. I remember him standing on the table, astraddle the meat, arm going up and down with the big knife (details, yes, those are the things you remember), stopping to hand down the portions, then hauling his arm back to cut again.

That night, with music and stomping on the sand and shouting back and forth over the fire, we made more noise than the sea.

IV

The eight-thirty bus was more or less on time.

"I don't think they want to go," Juao's sister said. She was accompanying the children to the Aquatic Corp Headquarters in Brasilia.

"They are just tired," Juao said. "They should not have stayed up so late last night. Get on the bus now. Say goodbye to Tio Cal."

"Good-bye."

"Good-bye."

Kids are never their most creative in that sort of situation. And I suspect that my godchildren may just have been suffering their first (or one of their first) hangovers. They had been very quiet all morning.

I bent down and gave them a clumsy hug. "When you come back on your first weekend off, I'll take you exploring down below at the point. You'll be able to gather your own coral now."

Juao's sister got teary, cuddled the children, cuddled me, Juao, then got on the bus.

Someone was shouting out the bus window for someone at the bus stop not to forget something. They trundled around the square and then toward the highway. We walked back across the street where the café owners were putting out canvas chairs.

"I will miss them," he said, like a long-considered admission.

"You and me both." At the docks near the hydrofoil wharf where the submarine launches went out to the undersea cities, we saw a crowd. "I wonder if they had any trouble laying the—"

A woman screamed in the crowd. She pushed from the others, dropping eggs and onions. She began to pull her hair and shriek. (Remember the skillet of shrimp? She had been the woman ladling them out.) A few people moved to help her.

A clutch of men broke off and ran into a side street. I grabbed a running amphiman, who whirled to face me.

"What in hell is going on?"

For a moment his mouth worked on his words for all the trite world like a bleached fish.

"From the explosion . . ." he began. "They just brought them back from the explosion at the Slash!"

I grabbed his other shoulder. "What happened!"

"About two hours ago. They were just a quarter of the way through, when the whole fault gave way. They had a god damn underwater volcano for half an hour. They're still getting seismic disturbances."

Juao was running toward the launch. I pushed the guy away and limped after him, struck the crowd and jostled through calico, canvas, and green scales.

They were carrying the corpses out of the hatch of the submarine and laying them on a canvas spread across the dock. They still return bodies to the countries of birth for the family to decide the method of burial. When the fault had given, the hot slag that had belched into the steaming sea was mostly molten silicon.

Three of the bodies were only slightly burned here and there; from their bloated faces (one still bled from the ear) I guessed they had died from sonic concussion. But several of the bodies were almost totally encased in dull, black glass.

"Tork—" I kept asking. "Is one of them Tork?"

It took me forty-five minutes, asking first the guys who were carrying the bodies, then going into the launch and asking some guy with a clipboard, and then going back on the dock and into the office to find out that one of the more unrecognizable bodies, yes, was Tork.

Juao brought me a glass of buttermilk in a café on the square. He sat still a long time, then finally rubbed away his white moustache, released the chair rung with his toes, put his hands on his knees.

"What are you thinking about?"

"That it's time to go fix nets. Tomorrow morning I will fish." He regarded me a moment. "Where should I fish tomorrow, Cal?"

"Are you wondering about . . . well, sending the kids off today?"

He shrugged. "Fishermen from this village have drowned. Still it is a village of fishermen. Where should I fish?"

I finished my buttermilk. "The mineral content over the Slash should be high as the devil. Lots of algae will gather tonight. Lots of small fish down deep. Big fish hovering over."

He nodded. "Good. I will take the boat out there tomorrow."

We got up.

"See you, Juao."

I limped back to the beach.

V

The fog had unsheathed the sand by ten. I walked around, poking clumps of weeds with a stick, banging the same stick on my numb leg. When I lurched up to the top of the rocks, I stopped in the still grass. "Ariel?"

She was keeling in the water, head down, red hair breaking over sealed gills. Her shoulders shook, stopped, shook again.

"Ariel?" I came down over the blistered stones.

She turned away to look at the ocean.

The attachments of children are so important and so brittle. "How long have you been sitting here?"

She looked at me now, the varied waters of her face stilled on drawn cheeks. And her face was exhausted. She shook her head.

Sixteen? Seventeen? Who was the psychologist, back in the seventies, who decided that "adolescents" were just physical and mental adults with no useful work? "You want to come up to the house?"

The head shaking got faster, then stopped.

After a while I said, "I guess they'll be sending Tork's body back to Manila."

"He didn't have a family," she explained. "He'll be buried here, at sea."

"Oh," I said.

And the rough volcanic glass, pulled across the ocean's sands, changing shape, dulling—

"You were—you liked Tork a lot, didn't you? You kids looked like you were pretty fond of each other."

"Yes. He was an awfully nice—" Then she caught my meaning and blinked. "No," she said. "Oh, no. I was—I was engaged to Jonni . . . the brown-haired boy from California? Did you meet him at the party last night? We're both from Los Angeles, but we only met down here. And now . . . they're sending his body back this evening." Her eyes got very wide, then closed.

"I'm sorry."

I'm a clumsy cripple, I step all over everybody's emotions. In that mirror I guess I'm too busy looking at what might have been.

"I'm sorry, Ariel."

She opened her eyes and began to look around her.

"Come on up to the house and have an avocado. I mean, they have avocados in now, not at the supermarket. But at the old town market on the other side. And they're better than any they grow in California."

She kept looking around.

"None of the amphimen get over there. It's a shame, because soon the market will probably close, and some of their fresh foods are really great. Oil and vinegar is all you need on them." I leaned back on the rocks. "Or a cup of tea?"

"Okay." She remembered to smile. I know the poor kid didn't feel like it. "Thank you. I won't be able to stay long, though."

We walked back up the rocks toward the house, the sea on our left. Just as we reached the patio, she turned and looked back. "Cal?"

"Yes? What is it?"

"Those clouds over there, across the water. Those are the only ones in the sky. Are they from the eruption in the Slash?"

I squinted. "I think so. Come on inside."

✾ LARRY NIVEN (PSD. FOR LAURENCE VAN COTT NIVEN) (1938–)

In 1964, IF magazine published the first Science Fiction by Larry Niven. The story, entitled "The Coldest Place," became the first installment of the author's Tales of Unknown Space series, which includes the Science Fiction classic novel Ringworld (1970). As did Robert Heinlein and Isaac Asimov, as well as Hal Clement, Greg Bear, David Brin, and Allen Steele, Larry Niven specializes in Hard Science Fiction. Like Samuel R. Delany, Niven is a prolific author who has produced some of Science Fiction's most enduring and celebrated novels and short stories.

Similar to Frederik Pohl, Niven has also successfully co-authored Science Fiction novels. Two of his collaborators are Jerry Pournelle and Steven Barnes. Effective novel collaborations are difficult to achieve, but Larry Niven has co-written several, including The Mote in God's Eye *(with Pournelle, 1974),* Dream Park *(with Barnes, 1981), and* Footfall *(with Pournelle, 1985).*

Niven is a self-proclaimed conservative who is pro-technology. He depicts technology in detail and speculates about its future roles. Such is the case with Ringworld *and other stories. One of the author's most enthralling sagas involves the tales of Gil Hamilton. In these Science Fiction suspense stories, Larry Niven takes the idea of futuristic organ transplants to an extreme.*

"The Jigsaw Man" was written for Harlan Ellison's now landmark anthology entitled Dangerous Visions. *It foreshadows Niven's stories of the "Organleggers" and Gil Hamilton that would shortly follow.*

The Jigsaw Man

(Dangerous Visions, *edited by Harlan Ellison, 1967*)

In A.D. 1900 Karl Landsteiner classified human blood into four types: A, B, AB, and O, according to incompatibilities. For the first time it became possible to give a shock patient a transfusion with some hope that it wouldn't kill him.

The movement to abolish the death penalty was barely getting started, and already it was doomed.

Vh83uOAGn7 was his telephone number and his driving license number and his social security number and the number of his draft card and his medical record. Two of these had been revoked, and the others had ceased to matter, except for his medical record. His name was Warren Lewis Knowles. He was going to die.

The trial was a day away, but the verdict was no less certain for that. Lew was guilty. If anyone had doubted it, the persecution had ironclad proof. By eighteen tomorrow Lew would be condemned to death. Broxton would appeal the case on some grounds or other. The appeal would be denied.

His cell was comfortable, small, and padded. This was no slur on the prisoner's sanity, though insanity was no longer an excuse for breaking the law. Three of the walls were mere bars. The fourth wall, the outside wall, was cement painted a restful shade of green. But the bars which separated him from the corridor, and from the morose old man on his left, and from the big, moronic-looking teenager on his right—the bars were four inches thick and eight inches apart, padded in silicone plastic. For the fourth time that day Lew took a clenched fistful of the plastic and tried to rip it away. It felt like a sponge rubber pillow, with a rigid core the thickness of a pencil, and it wouldn't rip. When he let go it snapped back to a perfect cylinder.

"It's not fair," he said.

The teenager didn't move. For all of the ten hours Lew had been in his cell, the kid had been sitting on the edge of his bunk with his lank black hair falling in his eyes and his five o'clock shadow getting gradually darker. He moved his long, hairy arms only at mealtimes, and the rest of him not at all.

The old man looked up at the sound of Lew's voice. He spoke with bitter sarcasm. "You framed?"

"No, I—"

"At least you're honest. What'd you do?"

Lew told him. He couldn't keep the hurt innocence out of his voice. The old man smiled derisively, nodding as if he'd expected just that.

"Stupidity. Stupidity's always been a capital crime. If you *had* to get yourself executed, why not for something important? See the kid on the other side of you?"

"Sure," Lew said without looking.

"He's an organlegger."

Lew felt the shock freezing in his face. He braced himself for another look into the next cell—and every nerve in his body jumped. The kid was looking at him. With his dull dark eyes barely visible under his mop of hair, he regarded Lew as a butcher might consider a badly aged side of beef.

Lew edged closer to the bars between his cell and the old man's. His voice was a hoarse whisper. "How many did he kill?"

"None."

"?"

"He was the snatch man. He'd find someone out alone at night, drug the prospect and take him home to the doc that ran the ring. It was the doc that did all the killing. If Bernie'd brought home a dead prospect, the doc would have skinned *him* down."

The old man sat with Lew almost directly behind him. He had twisted himself around to talk to Lew, but now he seemed to be losing interest. His hands, hidden from Lew by his bony back, were in constant nervous motion.

"How many did he snatch?"

"Four. Then he got caught. He's not very bright, Bernie."

"What did you do to get put here?"

The old man didn't answer. He ignored Lew completely, his shoulders twitching as he moved his hands. Lew shrugged and dropped back on his bunk.

It was nineteen o'clock of a Thursday night.

The ring had included three snatch men. Bernie had not yet been tried. Another was dead; he had escaped over the edge of a pedwalk when he felt the mercy bullet enter his arm. The third was being wheeled into the hospital next door to the courthouse.

Officially he was still alive. He had been sentenced; his appeal had been denied; but he was still alive as they moved him, drugged, into the operating room.

The interns lifted him from the table and inserted a mouthpiece so he could breathe when they dropped him into freezing liquid. They lowered him without a splash, and as his body temperature went down they dribbled something else into his veins. About half a pint of it. His temperature dropped toward freezing, his heartbeats were further and further apart. Finally his heart stopped. But it could have been started again. Men had been reprieved at this point. Officially the organlegger was still alive.

The doctor was a line of machines with a conveyor belt running through them. When the organlegger's body temperature reached a certain point, the belt started. The first machine made a series of incisions in his chest. Skillfully and mechanically, the doctor performed a cardiectomy.

The organlegger was officially dead. His heart went into storage immediately. His skin followed, most of it in one piece, all of it still living. The doctor took him apart with exquisite care, like disassembling a flexible, fragile, tremendously complex jigsaw puzzle. The brain was flashburned and the ashes saved for urn burial; but all the rest of the body, in slabs and small blobs and parchment-thin layers and lengths of tubing, went into storage in the hospital's organ banks. Any one of these units could be packed in a travel case at a moment's notice and flown to anywhere in the world in not much more than an hour. If the odds broke right, if the right people came down with the right diseases at the right time, the organlegger might save more lives than he had taken.

Which was the whole point.

Lying on his back, staring up at the ceiling television set, Lew suddenly began to shiver. He had not had the energy to put the sound plug in his ear, and the silent motion of the cartoon figures had suddenly become horrid. He turned the set off, and that didn't help either.

Bit by bit they would take him apart and store him away. He'd never seen an organ storage bank, but his uncle had owned a butchershop. . . .

"Hey!" he yelled.

The kid's eyes came up, the only living part of him. The old man twisted round to look over his shoulder. At the end of the hall the guard looked up once, then went back to reading.

The fear was in Lew's belly; it pounded in his throat. "How can you stand it?"

The kid's eyes dropped to the floor. The old man said, "Stand what?"

"Don't you know what they're going to *do* to us?"

"Not to me. They won't take me apart like a hog."

Instantly Lew was at the bars. "Why not?"

The old man's voice had become very low. "Because there's a bomb where my right thighbone used to be. I'm gonna blow myself up. What they find, they'll never use."

The hope the old man had raised washed away, leaving bitterness. "Nuts. How could you put a bomb in your leg?"

"Take the bone out, bore a hole in it, build the bomb in the hole, get all the organic material out of the bone so it won't rot, put the bone back in. 'Course your red corpuscle count goes down afterward. What I wanted to ask you. You want to join me?"

"Join you?"

"Hunch up against the bars. This thing'll take care of both of us."

Lew found himself backing away. "No. No, thanks."

"Your choice," said the old man. "I never told you what I was here for, did I? I was the doc. Bernie made his snatches for me."

Lew had backed up against the opposite set of bars. He felt them touch his shoulders and turned to find the kid looking dully into his eyes from two feet away. Organleggers! He was surrounded by professional killers!

"I know what it's like," the old man continued. "They won't do that to me. Well. If you're sure you don't want a clean death, go lie down behind your bunk. It's thick enough."

The bunk was a mattress and a set of springs mounted into a cement block which was an integral part of the cement floor. Lew curled himself into fetal position with his hands over his eyes.

He was sure he didn't want to die *now.*

Nothing happened.

After a while he opened his eyes, took his hands away and looked around.

The kid was looking at him. For the first time there was a sour grin plastered on his face. In the corridor the guard, who was always in a chair by the exit, was standing outside the bars looking down at him. He seemed concerned.

Lew felt the flush rising in his neck and nose and ears. The old man had been playing with him. He moved to get up . . .

And a hammer came down on the world.

The guard lay broken against the bars of the cell across the corridor. The lank-haired youngster was picking himself up from behind his bunk, shaking his head. Somebody groaned; and the groan rose to a scream. The air was full of cement dust.

Lew got up.

Blood lay like red oil on every surface that faced the explosion. Try as he might, and he didn't try very hard, Lew could find no other trace of the old man.

Except for the hole in the wall.

He must have been standing . . . right . . . there.

The hole would be big enough to crawl through, if Lew could reach it. But it was in the old man's cell. The silicone plastic sheathing on the bars between the cells had been ripped away, leaving only pencil-thick lengths of metal.

Lew tried to squeeze through.

The bars were humming, vibrating, though there was no sound. As Lew noticed the vibration he also found that he was becoming sleepy. He jammed his body between the bars, caught in a war between his rising panic and the sonic stunners which must have gone on automatically.

The bars wouldn't give. But his body did; and the bars were slippery with . . .

He was through. He poked his head through the hole in the wall and looked down.

Way down. Far enough to make him dizzy.

The Topeka County courthouse was a small skyscraper, and Lew's cell must have been near the top. He looked down a smooth concrete slab studded with windows set flush with the sides. There would be no way to reach those windows, no way to open them, no way to break them.

The stunner was sapping his will. He would have been unconscious by now if his head had been in the cell with the rest of him. He had to force himself to turn and look up.

He was *at* the top. The edge of the roof was only a few feet above his eyes. He couldn't reach that far, not without . . .

He began to crawl out of the hole.

Win or lose, they wouldn't get him for the organ banks. The vehicular traffic level would smash every useful part of him. He sat on the lip of the hole, with his legs straight out inside the cell for balance, pushing his chest flat against the wall. When he had his balance he stretched his arms toward the roof. No good.

So he got one leg under him, keeping the other stiffly out, and *lunged.*

His hands closed over the edge as he started to fall back. He yelped with surprise, but it was too late. The top of the courthouse was moving! It had dragged him out of the hole before he could let go. He hung on, swinging slowly back and forth over empty space as the motion carried him away.

The top of the courthouse was a pedwalk.

He couldn't climb up, not without purchase for his feet. He didn't have the strength. The pedwalk was moving toward another building, about the same height. He could reach it if he only hung on.

And the windows in that building were different. They weren't made to open, not in these days of smog and air conditioning, but there were ledges. Perhaps the glass would break.

Perhaps it wouldn't.

The pull on his arms was agony. It would be so easy to let go. . . . No. He had committed no crime worth dying for. He refused to die.

Over the decades of the twentieth century the movement continued to gain momentum. Loosely organized, international in scope, its members had only one goal: to replace execution with imprisonment and rehabilitation in every state and nation they could reach. They argued that killing a man for his crime teaches him nothing; that it serves as no deterrent to others who might commit the same crime; that death is irreversible, whereas an innocent man might be released from prison once his innocence is belatedly proven. Killing a man serves no good purpose, they said, unless for society's vengeance. Vengeance, they said, is unworthy of an enlightened society.

Perhaps they were right.

In 1940 Karl Landsteiner and Alexander S. Wiener made public their report on the Rh factor in human blood.

By mid-century most convicted killers were getting life imprisonment or less. Many were later returned to society, some "rehabilitated," others not. The death penalty had been passed for kidnapping in some states, but it was hard to persuade a jury to enforce it. Similarly with murder charges. A man wanted for burglary in Canada and murder in California fought extradition to Canada; he had less chance of being convicted in California. Many states had abolished the death penalty. France had none.

Rehabilitation of criminals was a major goal of the science/art of psychology.

But—

Blood banks were worldwide.

Already men and women with kidney diseases had been saved by a kidney transplanted from an identical twin. Not all kidney victims had identical twins. A doctor in Paris used transplants from close relatives, classifying up to a hundred points of incompatibility to judge in advance how successful the transplant would be.

Eye transplants were common. An eye donor could wait until he died before he saved another man's sight.

Human bone could *always* be transplanted, provided the bone was first cleaned of organic matter.

So matters stood at mid-century.

By 1990 it was possible to store any living human organ for any reasonable length of time. Transplants had become routine, helped along by the "scalpel of infinite thinness," the laser. The dying regularly willed their remains to the organ banks. The mortuary lobbies couldn't stop it. But such gifts from the dead were not always useful.

In 1993 Vermont passed the first of the organ bank laws. Vermont had always had the death penalty. Now a condemned man could know that his death would save lives. It was no longer true that an execution served no good purpose. Not in Vermont.

Nor, later, in California. Or Washington. Georgia. Pakistan, England, Switzerland, France, Rhodesia . . .

The pedwalk was moving at ten miles per hour. Below, unnoticed by pedestrians who had quit work late and night owls who were just beginning their rounds, Lewis Knowles hung from the moving strip and watched the ledge go by beneath his dangling feet. The ledge was no more than two feet wide, a good four feet beneath his stretching toes.

He dropped.

As his feet struck he caught the edge of a window casement. Momentum jerked at him, but he didn't fall. After a long moment he breathed again.

He couldn't know what building this was, but it was not deserted. At twenty-one hundred at night, all the windows were ablaze. He tried to stay back out of the light as he peered in.

This window was an office. Empty.

He'd need something to wrap around his hand to break that window. But all he was wearing was a pair of shoesocks and a prison jumper. Well, he couldn't be more conspicuous than he was now. He took off the jumper, wrapped part of it around his hand, and struck.

He almost broke his hand.

Well . . . they'd let him keep his jewelry, his wristwatch and diamond ring. He drew a circle on the glass with the ring, pushing down hard, and struck again with the other hand. It *had* to be glass; if it was plastic he was doomed. The glass popped out in a near-perfect circle.

He had to do it six times before the hole was big enough for him.

He smiled as he stepped inside, still holding his jumper. Now all he needed was an elevator. The cops would have picked him up in an instant if they'd caught him on the street in a prison jumper, but if he hid the jumper here he'd be safe. Who would suspect a licensed nudist?

Except that he didn't have a license. Or a nudist's shoulder pouch to put it in.

Or a shave.

That was very bad. Never had there been a nudist as hairy as this. Not just a five o'clock shadow, but a full beard all over, so to speak. Where could he get a razor?

He tried the desk drawers. Many businessmen kept spare razors. He stopped when he was halfway through. Not because he'd found a razor, but because he now knew where he was. The papers on his desk made it all too obvious.

A hospital.

He was still clutching the jumper. He dropped it in the wastebasket, covered it tidily with papers, and more or less collapsed into the chair behind the desk.

A hospital. He *would* pick a hospital. And *this* hospital, the one which had been built right next to the Topeka County courthouse, for good and sufficient reason.

But he hadn't picked it, not really. It had picked him. Had he ever in his life made a decision except on the prompting of others? No. Friends had borrowed his money for keeps, men had stolen his girls, he had avoided promotion by his knack for being ignored. Shirley had bullied him into marrying her, then left him four years later for a friend who wouldn't be bullied.

Even now, at the possible end of his life, it was the same. An aging body snatcher had given him his escape. An engineer had built the cell bars wide enough apart to let a small man squeeze between them. Another had put a ped-walk along two convenient roofs. And here he was.

The worst of it was that here he had no chance of masquerading as a nudist. Hospital gowns and masks would be the minimum. Even nudists had to wear clothing sometime.

The closet?

There was nothing in the closet but a spiffy green hat and a perfectly transparent rain poncho.

He could run for it. If he could find a razor he'd be safe once he reached the street. He bit at a knuckle, wishing he knew where the elevator was. Have to trust to luck. He began searching the drawers again.

He had his hand on a black leather razor case when the door opened. A beefy man in a hospital gown breezed in. The intern (there were no human doctors in hospitals) was halfway to the desk before he noticed Lew crouching over an open drawer. He stopped walking. His mouth fell open.

Lew closed it with the fist which still gripped the razor case. The man's teeth came together with a sharp click. His knees were buckling as Lew brushed past him and out the door.

The elevator was just down the hall, with the doors standing open. And nobody coming. Lew stepped in and punched O. He shaved as the elevator dropped. The razor cut fast and close, if a trifle noisily. He was working on his chest as the door opened.

A skinny technician stood directly in front of him, her mouth and eyes set in the utterly blank expression of those who wait for elevators. She brushed past him with a muttered apology, hardly noticing him. Lew stepped out fast. The doors were closing before he realized that he was on the wrong floor.

That damned tech! She'd stopped the elevator before it reached bottom.

He turned and stabbed the Down button. Then what he'd seen in that one cursory glance came back to him, and his head whipped around for another look.

The whole vast room was filled with glass tanks, ceiling height, arranged in a labyrinth like the bookcases in a library. In the tanks was a display more lewd than anything in Belsen. Why, those things had been *men!* and *women!* No, he wouldn't look. He refused to look at anything but the elevator door. *What was taking that elevator so long?*

He heard a siren.

The hard tile floor began to vibrate against his bare feet. He felt a numbness in his muscles, a lethargy in his soul.

The elevator arrived . . . too late. He blocked the doors open with a chair. Most buildings didn't have stairs; only alternate elevators. They'd have to use the alternate elevator to reach him now. Well, where was it? . . . He wouldn't have time to find it. He was beginning to feel really sleepy. They must have several sonic projectors focused on this one room. Where one beam passed the interns would feel mildly relaxed, a little clumsy. But where the beams intersected, *here*, there would be unconsciousness. But not yet.

He had something to do first.

By the time they broke in they'd have something to kill him for.

The tanks were faced in plastic, not glass: a very special kind of plastic. To avoid provoking defense reactions in all the myriads of body parts which might be stored touching it, the plastic had to have unique characteristics. No engineer could have been expected to make it shatterproof too!

It shattered very satisfactorily.

Later, Lew wondered how he managed to stay up as long as he did. The soothing hypersonic murmur of the stun beams kept pulling at him, pulling him down to a floor which seemed softer every moment. The chair he wielded became heavier and heavier. But as long as he could lift it, he smashed. He was knee deep in nutritive storage fluid, and there were dying things brushing against his ankles with every move; but his work was barely a third done when the silent siren song became too much for him.

He fell.

And after all that they never even mentioned the smashed organ banks!

Sitting in the courtroom, listening to the drone of courtroom ritual, Lew sought Mr. Broxton's ear to ask the question. Mr. Broxton smiled at him. "Why should they want to bring that up? They think they've got enough on you as it is. If you beat *this* rap, then they'll persecute you for wanton destruction of valuable medical sources. But they're sure you won't."

"And you?"

"I'm afraid they're right. But we'll try. Now, Hennessey's about to read the charges. Can you manage to look hurt and indignant?"

"Sure."

"Good."

The prosecution read the charges, his voice sounding like the voice of doom coming from under a thin blond mustache. Warren Lewis Knowles looked hurt and indignant. But he no longer felt that way. He had done something worth dying for.

The cause of it all was the organ banks. With good doctors and a sufficient flow of material in the organ banks, any taxpayer could hope to live indefinitely. What voter would vote against eternal life? The death penalty was his immortality, and he would vote the death penalty for any crime at all.

Lewis Knowles had struck back.

"The state will prove that the said Warren Lewis Knowles did, in the space of two years, willfully drive through a total of six red traffic lights. During that same period the same Warren Knowles exceeded local speed limits no less than ten times, once by as much as fifteen miles per hour. His record has never been good. We will produce records of his arrest in 2082 on a charge of drunk driving, a charge of which he was acquitted only through—"

"Objection!"

"Sustained. If he was acquitted, Counselor, the Court must assume him not guilty."

JAMES TIPTREE JR. (PSD. FOR ALICE HASTINGS BRADLEY SHELDON) (1915–1987)

Alice Sheldon (a.k.a. "James Tiptree Jr.) continued the contributions of Mary W. Shelley, Francis Stevens, Clare Winger Harris, C. L. Moore, Leigh Brackett, Katherine MacLean, and Marion Zimmer Bradley to Fantasy and Science Fiction. As did several of her female predecessors in the genres of Fantasy and Science Fiction, Sheldon proved that women writers were as talented as their male counterparts in these forms of storytelling.

Sheldon's male pseudonym remains the most famous in Science Fiction history. Using this moniker, the author was able to disguise her gender, but, more importantly, she was able to prove her abilities and talents based solely on the merits of her writing. Ultimately, Alice Sheldon earned many of Science Fiction's highest awards, including the Hugo and the Nebula (the former based on fan input, the latter based on peer—i.e., fellow writer— evaluation).

An accomplished psychologist and intellectual, Alice Sheldon earned her Ph.D. from George Washington University in 1967. Her background in psychology, anthropology, and related social sciences influenced her Science Fiction writing. Using her pseudonym, Sheldon was able to make significant observations about the human condition.

Tragically, like Robert E. Howard (archetypal writer of twentieth-century Heroic Fantasy and creator of Conan the Barbarian), Alice Sheldon took her own life in a period of deep depression.

"The Last Flight of Dr. Ain" is a grim, profound tale of environment and human evolution on the order of Harry Harrison's "Roommates" and Samuel R. Delany's "Driftglass."

The Last Flight of Dr. Ain

(Galaxy, *March 1969*)

Writing about your own story reminds me of those tremendous floats you see in small-town Labor Day parades. You have this moving island of flowers with people on it being Indian Braves or Green Bay Packers or Astronauts-Landing-on-the-Moon (Raising-the-Flag-at-Iwo-Jima has happily gone out of fashion) and great-looking girls being great-looking girls. That's the story. Under each float is an old truck chassis driven by a guy in sweaty jeans who is also working the tapedeck and passing cherry bombs to the Indians. That's the author. Now Harry wants me to crawl out and say hello. Well, I love saying hello. But my feeling is that the story is the game. Who really needs me and my carburetor troubles up there blowing kisses with Miss Harvest Home?

Still, Harry is one of those for whom I'd row quite a ways in a leaky boat, and you can always stop reading this and turn to the tale. So . . .

Remember way back in 1967 B.E.? Before Ecology, that was; we were worrying about The Bomb then. In those days I did my screaming to myself; it sounded pretty silly saying, I love Earth. Earth? Rocks, weeds, dirt? Oh, come on. A friend lectured me: People have to relate to people; *you can't relate to a planet.*

Sorry, you can. But you'd better not. Because—as we're all finding out—to love our Earth is to hurt forever. Earth was very beautiful with her sweet airs and clear waters, her intimacies and grandeurs and divine freakinesses and the mobile art works that were her creatures. She was just right for us. She made us human. And we are killing her.

Not because we're wicked, any more than a spirochete is wicked. (At this point maybe I'd better say that I do relate to some people, too.) Nor is modern Western technology the sole culprit. We're the current destructo champs, but man was always pretty good at eco-cide. Innocent goatherds turned north Africa into desert; did you know that people used to take pigs to be fattened on the acorns of the majestic oak forests where the Sahara blows now? War and fire finished off the flora of the Hebrides before gunpowder. And sheer numbers of people scratching a living devasted much of India and China into the lunar landscape it is today. It's just us, man collectively, doing what comes naturally. A runaway product of the planet Earth, we have become a disease of Earth.

And of course it's speeded up unbelievably. Virgin lakes I knew only ten years ago in Canada are shore-to-shore beer cans now. Here's a few of the things we've lost in the four decades I've been observing (I thought they'd last forever, see?): Learning to swim in the pure water of—gasp—Lake Michigan in front of Chicago . . . Ten thousand canvas-back ducks whistling down the wind of the peaks behind Santa Fé . . . The great bay of San Francisco before the bridges shackled it and the garbage poured in . . . Key West, a sleepy fishing village lush with tropical wildlife (and old John Dewey's doorknob head shining in the cantina) before the Navy and Disney heard of it . . . Timber wolves singing where shopping centers are now in Wisconsin . . . The magic trolley-ride to Glen Echo, in ten minutes from the heart of D.C. you were clicking along silently (and fumelessly) with flowers and songbirds coming in the window . . . A very nice life, only a few years back.

And it's the same all over, you know. I spent part of my childhood in Africa and it hurts to remember the beauty of the Ruwenzoris—the Mountains of the Moon—before the planes and the guns and the landrovers and Hemingway and the rest of the white man's crap rolled in. And even I can't believe I rode a pony in peaceful woodlands in a place now called Vietnam . . .

All gone. Gone under the concrete and plastic and bombs and oil and people and garbage unending, growing and spreading daily.

Can you stand one more?

I'm writing this in the moonlight on a coconut plantation on the "wild" shore of Yucatan. The jungle was homesteaded in 1936 and worked by a few Maya families. Miles of nothing but white coral beach, the Caribbean making slow music on the reef, shadows of palm-fronds wreathing over the sand. The moon is brighter than my lantern. A pelican crosses the moon, looking like a wooden bird from some mad giant's cuckoo clock. Paradise . . .

Ah oui.

The fish the pelican is hunting are tainted with chlorinated hydrocarbons now; her eggs are thin-shelled, may not hatch. The same for the flamingoes and roseate spoonbills and noble frigate-birds on the lagoon behind me. They are also scared up daily by Maya power-boats. On the shore, each wave as it breaks leaves myriad globules of tar from ships over the horizon, leaves also a dish-pan ring of plastic bottles, broken zoris, light bulbs and dis-membered dolls. (I wonder about those dolls. Do crazed tourists gather at midnight for strange rites at the rail?) The trash is not just ugly; each globule of tar smothers and poi-sons one more small sphere of the sea's life—and the oceans, we know now, are fragile and finite. The plastics too break down, releasing polychlorinated biphenyls to be absorbed by organisms. An average of 3,500 little bits of plastic per square kilometer was measured last year—in the Sargasso Sea. And we've all heard about the miles of floating human offal Heyerdahl met in mid-Atlantic. The refuse isn't all microscopic either; last month a forty-five-foot shrimp boat, apparently abandoned for insurance, broke up on the reef. The day of the marine junkyard is at hand.

But the point is that the human beings who are doing all this are not malicious or aberrant. They are doing what we have always done. It's right and natural in human terms to flush a toilet or an oilbilge, to throw away a broken light bulb or a broken boat, to zap an insect attacking your food or your child. Even the trawlers who are fishing with nets five miles long — killing everything in huge swathes of the Florida seas — are doing the human food-getting thing.

How can we stop? How can owe possibly change ourselves enough and in time?

I fear we can't — and there's where my real nightmare begins. Because if we do kill everything else on Earth, we probably won't die. At least, not right away. We will, I terribly fear . . . adapt.

You've seen the pictures of Calcutta and Bangladesh. Calcutta isn't a musical comedy; it's a symbol of a steady state humanity can reach, 'way down the entropic slide. I was there as a kid too. I remember stepping over and around the endless bodies, living and dead, inhabiting the pavement about one to a square yard as far as I could see to the horizon. Starving dwarf-children roving around racks of bones that were mothers trying to nurse more babies, toothless mouths and unbearable eyes turning on me from rag-heaps that were people — people — a million people born there and going to die there, unable to help themselves or even to protest, world without end forever. Surviving . . .

That's what we do, you know. We don't change our behaviour, we adapt to the results of it. Even to extremis where the human being is stripped down to a machine for keeping the genes alive, waiting for rescue. But if we pass the point of irreversible damage to our biosphere, our Earth, there will be no rescue. The beauty that is going is only another name for the health of Earth and her children, the condition of our humanity. As our Earth dies under us, what will we do? Change ourselves in time? Die?

Neither. When the last housefly and the last crabgrass plant have died in the world's last zoo, when the oceans are dead and the land is paved over, we'll go on. Our marvellous vitality will carry us down, shoulder-to-buttock, gasping our own poisons and scrabbling for algae soup as the conveyor belt creaks by. Don't worry: We'll survive.

Excuse me while I put out my garbage.

OK, Harry?

—*James Tiptree Jr.*

Dr. Ain was recognized on the Omaha-Chicago flight. A biologist colleague from Pasadena came out of the toilet and saw Ain in an aisle seat. Five years before, this man had been jealous of Ain's huge grants. Now he nodded coldly and was surprised at the intensity of Ain's response. He almost turned back to speak, but he felt too tired; like nearly everyone, he was fighting the flu.

The stewardess handing out coats after they landed remembered Ain too: A tall thin nondescript man with rusty hair. He held up the line staring at her; since he already had his raincoat with him she decided it was some kooky kind of pass and waved him on.

She saw Ain shamble off into the airport smog, apparently alone. Despite the big Civil Defense signs, O'Hare was late getting underground. No one noticed the woman.

The wounded, dying woman.

Ain was not identified en route to New York, but a 2:40 jet carried an "Ames" on the checklist, which was thought to be a misspelling of Ain. It was. The plane had circled for an hour while Ain watched the smoky seaboard monotonously tilt, straighten, and tilt again.

The woman was weaker now. She coughed, picking weakly at the scabs on her face half-hidden behind her long hair. Her hair, Ain saw, that mahogany mane which had been so splendid, was drabbed and thin. He looked to seaward, willing himself to think of cold, clean breakers. On the horizon he saw a vast black rug: somewhere a tanker had opened its vents. The woman coughed again. Ain closed his eyes. The smog closed in.

He was picked up next while checking in for the BOAC flight to Glasgow. Kennedy-Underground was a boiling stew of people, the air system unequal to the hot September afternoon. The check-in line swayed and sweated, staring dully at the newscast. SAVE THE LAST GREEN MANSIONS — a conservation group was protesting the defoliation and drainage of the Amazon basin. Several people recalled the beautifully colored shots of the new clean bomb. The line squeezed together to let a band of uniformed men go by. They were wearing buttons inscribed: WHO'S AFRAID?

That was when a woman noticed Ain. He was holding a news-sheet and she heard it rattling in his hand. Her family hadn't caught the flu, so she looked at him sharply. Sure enough, his forehead was sweaty. She herded her kids to the side away from Ain.

He was using *Instac* throat spray, she remembered. She didn't think much of *Instac*; her family used *Kleer*. While she was looking at him, Ain suddenly turned his head and stared into her face, with the spray still floating down. Such inconsiderateness! She turned her back. She didn't recall him talking to any woman, but she perked up her ears when the clerk read off Ain's destination. Moscow!

The clerk recalled that too, with disapproval. Ain checked in alone, he reported. No woman had been ticketed for Moscow, but it would have been easy enough to split up her tickets. (By that time they were sure she was with him.)

Ain's flight went via Iceland with an hour's delay at Kevlavik. Ain walked over to the airport park, gratefully breathing the sea-filled air. Every few breaths he shuddered. Under the whine of bull-dozers the sea could be heard running its huge paws up and down the keyboard of the land. The little park had a grove of yellowed birches and wheat ears foraged by the path. Next month they would be in North Africa, Ain thought. Two thousand miles of tiny wing-beats. He threw them some crumbs from a packet in his pocket.

The woman seemed stronger here. She was panting in the sea wind, her large eyes fixed on Ain. Above her the birches were as gold as those where he had first seen her, the day his life began . . . Squatting under a stump to watch a shrewmouse he had been, when he caught the falling ripple of green and recognized the shocking naked girl-flesh — creamy, pink-tipped — coming toward him among the golden bracken. Young Ain held his breath, his nose in the sweet moss and his heart going *crash!* — *crash!* And then he was staring at the outrageous fall of that hair down her narrow back, watching it dance around her heart-shaped buttocks, while the shrewmouse ran over his paralyzed hand. The lake was utterly still, dusty silver under the misty sky, and she made no more than a muskrat's ripple to rock the floating golden leaves . . . The silence closed back: the trees burning like torches where the naked girl had walked the wild wood, reflected in Ain's shining eyes . . . For a time he believed he had seen an Oread.

Ain was last on board for the Glasgow leg. The stewardess recalled dimly that he seemed restless. She could not identify the woman. There were a lot of women on board — and babies. Her passenger list had had several errors.

At Glasgow airport a waiter remembered that a man like Ain had called for Scottish oatmeal, and eaten two bowls, although of course it wasn't really oatmeal. A young mother with a pram saw him tossing crumbs to the birds.

When he checked in at the BOAC desk, he was hailed by a Glasgow professor who was going to the same conference at Moscow. This man had been one of Ain's teachers. (It was now known that Ain had done his postgraduate work in Europe.) They chatted all the way across the North Sea.

"I wondered about that," the professor said later. "Why have you come 'round about? I asked him. He told me the direct flights were booked up." (This was found to be untrue: Ain had apparently avoided the Moscow jet hoping to escape attention.)

The professor spoke with relish of Ain's work.

"Brilliant? Oh, aye. And stubborn, too, very very stubborn. It was as though a concept—often the simplest relation, mind you—would stop him in his tracks, and fascinate him. He would hunt all 'round it instead of going on to the next thing as a more docile mind would. Truthfully, I wondered at first if he could be just a bit thick. But you recall who it was said that the capacity for wonder at matters of common acceptance occurs in the superior mind? And, of course, so it proved when he shook us all up over that enzyme conversion business. A pity your government took him away from his line, there . . . No, he said nothing of this, I say it to you, young man. We spoke in fact largely of my work. I was surprised to find he'd kept up. He asked me what my *sentiments* about it were, which surprised me again. Now, understand, I'd not seen the man for five years, but he seemed—well, perhaps just tired, as who is not? I'm sure he was glad to have a change; he jumped out for a legstretch wherever we came down. At Oslo, even Bonn . . . Oh yes, he did feed the birds, but that was nothing new for Ain . . . His social life when I knew him? Radical causes? Young man, I've said what I've said because of who it was that introduced you, but I'll have you know it is an impertinence in you to think ill of Charles Ain, or that he could do a harmful deed. Good evening."

The professor said nothing of the woman in Ain's life.

Nor could he have, although Ain had been intimately with her in the university time. He had let no one see how he was obsessed with her, with the miracle, the wealth of her body, her inexhaustibility. They met at his every spare moment, sometimes in public, pretending to be casual strangers under his friends' noses, pointing out a pleasing view to each other, with grave formality. And later, in their privacies—what doubled intensity of love! He revelled in her, possessed her, allowed her no secrets. His dreams were of her sweet springs and shadowed places and her white rounded glory in the moonlight—finding always more, always new dimensions of his joy.

The danger of her frailty was far off then in the rush of birdsong and the springing leverets of the meadow. On dark days she might cough a bit, but so did he. In those years he had had no thought to the urgent study of the disease.

At the Moscow conference nearly everyone noticed Ain at some point or another, which was to be expected in view of his professional stature. It was a small high-calibre meeting. Ain was late in; a day's reports were over, and his was to be on the third and last.

Many people spoke with Ain, and several sat with him at meals. No one was surprised that he spoke little; he was a retiring man except on a few memorable occasions of hot argument. He did strike some of his friends as a bit tired and jerky.

An Indian molecular engineer who saw him with the throat spray kidded him about bringing over Asian flu. A Swedish colleague recalled that Ain had been called away to the transatlantic phone at lunch; and when he returned Ain volunteered the information that something had turned up missing in his home lab. There was another joke, and Ain said cheerfully, "Oh yes, quite active."

At that point one of the Chicom biologists swung into his daily propaganda chore about bacteriological warfare and accused Ain of manufacturing biotic weapons. Ain took the wind out of his sails by saying: "You're perfectly right." By tacit consent, there was very little talk about military applications, industrial dusting, or subjects of that type. And nobody recalled seeing Ain with any woman other than old Madame Vialche, who could scarcely have subverted anyone from her wheelchair.

Ain's own speech was bad, even for him. He always had a poor public voice, but his ideas were usually expressed with the lucidity so typical of the first-rate mind. This time he seemed muddled, with little new to say. His audience excused this as the muffling effects of security. Ain then got into a tangled point about the course of evolution in which he seemed to be trying to show that something was very wrong indeed. When he wound up with a reference to Hudson's bell bird "singing for a later race," several listeners wondered if he could be drunk.

The big security break came right at the end, when he suddenly began to describe the methods he had used to mutate and redesign a leukemia virus. He explained the procedure with admirable clarity in four sentences and paused. Then he said other sentences about the effects of the mutated strain. It was maximal only on the higher primates, he said; recovery rate among the lower mammals and other orders was close to 90 percent. As to vectors, he went on, any warm-blooded animal served. In addition, the virus retained viability in most environmental media and performed very well airborne. Contagion rate was extremely high. Almost off-hand, Ain added that no test primate or accidentally exposed human had survived beyond the twenty-second day.

These words fell into a silence broken only by the running feet of the Egyptian delegate making for the door. Then a gilt chair went over as an American bolted after him.

Ain seemed unaware that his audience was in a state of unbelieving paralysis. It had all come so fast: a man who had been blowing his nose was staring popeyed around his handkerchief. Another who had been lighting a pipe grunted as his fingers singed. Two men chatting by the door missed his words entirely and their laughter chimed into a dead silence in which echoed Ain's words: "—really no point in attempting."

Later they found he had been explaining that the virus utilized the body's own immunomechanisms, and so defense was by definition hopeless.

That was all. Ain looked around vaguely for questions and then started down the aisle. By the time he got to the door, people were swarming after him. He wheeled about and said rather crossly, "Yes, of course it is very wrong. I told you that. We are all wrong. Now it's over."

An hour later they found he had gone, having apparently reserved a Sinair flight to Karachi. The security men caught up with him at Hong Kong. By then he seemed really very ill, and went with them peacefully. They started back to the States via Hawaii.

His captors were civilized types; they saw he was gentle and treated him accordingly. He had no weapons or drugs on him. They took him out handcuffed for a stroll at Osaka . . . let him feed his crumbs to the birds, and they listened with interest to his account of the migration routes of the common brown sandpiper. He was very hoarse. At that point, he was wanted only for the security thing. There was no question of a woman at all.

He dozed most of the way to the islands, but when they came in sight he pressed to the window and began to mutter, the security man behind him got the first inkling that there was a woman in it and turned on his recorder.

". . . blue, blue and green until you see the wounds. Oh my girl! Oh beautiful, you won't die. I won't let you die. I tell you girl, it's over . . . Lustrous eyes, look at me, let me see you now alive! Oh great queen, my sweet body, my girl, have I saved you? . . . Oh terrible to know, and noble—Chaos' child green-robed in blue, and golden light . . . The thrown and spinning ball of life alone in space . . . Have I saved you?"

On the last leg, he was obviously feverish.

"She may have tricked me, you know," he said confidentially to the government man. "You have to be prepared for that, of course. I know her!" He chuckled confidentially. "She's no small thing. But wring your heart out—"

Coming over San Francisco, he was merry. "Don't you know the otters will go back in there? I'm certain of it. That fill won't last; there'll be a bay there again."

They got him on a stretcher at Hamilton Air Base, and he went unconscious shortly after takeoff. Before he collapsed, he'd insisted on throwing the last of his birdseed on the field.

"Birds are, of course, warmblooded," he confided to the agent who was handcuffing him to the stretcher. Then Ain smiled gently and lapsed into inertness. He stayed that way almost all the remaining ten days of his life. By then, of course, no one really cared. Both the government men had died quite early, after they finished analyzing the birdseed and throat-spray. The woman at Kennedy was only just then feeling sickish.

The tape-recorder they put by his bed functioned right on through, but if anybody had been around to replay it they would have found little but babbling. "Gaea Gloriatrix!" he crooned. At times he was grandiose and tormented. "Our life, your death!" he yelled. "Our death would have been your death too, no need for that, no need . . ."

At other times he was accusing. "What did you do about the dinosaurs?" he demanded. "How did you fix *them?* Did they annoy you? Cold. Queen, you're too cold! You came close to it this time, my girl," he raved. And then he wept and caressed the bedclothes and was maudlin.

Only at the end, lying in his filth and thirst, still chained where they had forgotten him, he was suddenly coherent. In the light clear voice of a lover planning a summer picnic he asked the recorder happily:

"Have you ever thought about *bears?* They have so much . . . funny they never came along further. By any chance were you saving them, girl?" And he chuckled in his ruined throat. And later, died.

ᴪ FRANK (PATRICK) HERBERT (1920–1986)

Frank Herbert began writing Science Fiction in the mid-1950s, and his early writing appeared into the 1960s in pages of Amazing Stories *and* Galaxy. *When he serialized* Dune *in the pages of* Analog *(formerly* Astounding*) in 1965 in five monthly installments from January through May of that year, Herbert made Science Fiction history.*

The initial novel Dune *stood by itself as epic Science Fiction. However, when* Chapterhouse: Dune *was published in hardcover form in 1985, Herbert completed a six-novel masterwork to be ranked with Isaac Asimov's* Foundation *Science Fiction series, J. R. R. Tolkien's* Lord of the Rings, *and C. S. Lewis's* Chronicles of Narnia *Fantasy series. Today, authors such as Robert Jordan and Terry Goodkind have tried to follow in the path of Frank Herbert's* Dune *series.*

Herbert wrote and published other significant stories beyond the Dune *chronicles. Most of his Science Fiction centers on elaborate fictional worlds and universes. It tends to be highly philosophical in nature and yet is also highly entertaining. Themes of artificial intelligence, genetics, and cybernetics were Herbert favorites.*

"Seed Stock" is a grim tale of adaptation, survival, primitive life, environment, and man versus nature. It is the kind of Science Fiction story that Jack London might have written had he been alive in 1970.

Seed Stock

(Analog: Science Fiction–Science Fact, *April 1970*)

When the sun had sunk almost to the edge of the purple ocean, hanging there like a giant orange ball—much larger than the sun of Mother Earth which he remembered with such nostalgia—Kroudar brought his fishermen back to the harbor.

A short man, Kroudar gave the impression of heaviness, but under his shipcloth motley he was as scrawny as any of the others, all bone and stringy muscle. It was the sickness of this planet, the doctors told him. They called it "body burdens," a subtle thing of differences in chemistry, gravity, diurnal periods and even the lack of a tidal moon.

Kroudar's yellow hair, his one good feature, was uncut and contained in a protective square of red cloth. Beneath this was a wide, low forehead, deeply sunken large eyes of a washed-out blue, a crooked nose that was splayed and pushed in, thick lips over large and unevenly spaced yellow teeth, and a melon chin receding into a short, ridged neck.

Dividing his attention between sails and shore, Kroudar steered with one bare foot on the tiller.

They had been all day out in the up-coast current netting the shrimp-like *trodi* which formed the colony's main source of edible protein. There were nine boats and the men in all of them were limp with fatigue, silent, eyes closed or open and staring at nothing.

The evening breeze rippled its dark lines across the harbor, moved the sweat-matted yellow hair on Kroudar's neck. It bellied the shipcloth sails and gave the heavily loaded boats that last necessary surge to carry them up into the strand.

Men moved then. Sails dropped with a slatting and rasping. Each thing was done with sparse motion in the weighted slowness of their fatigue.

Trodi had been thick in the current out there, and Kroudar pushed his people to their limit. It had not taken much push. They all understood the need. The swarmings and runnings of useful creatures on this planet had not been clocked with any reliable precision. Things here exhibited strange gaps and breaks in seeming regularity. The *trodi* might vanish at any moment into some unknown place—as they had been known to do before.

The colony had experienced hunger and children crying for food that must be rationed. Men seldom spoke of this any more, but they moved with the certain knowledge of it.

More than three years now, Kroudar thought, as he shouldered a dripping bag of *trodi* and pushed his weary feet through the sand, climbing the beach toward the storage huts and racks where the sea creatures were dried for processing. It hod been more than three years since their ship had come down from space.

The colony ship had been constructed as a multiple tool, filled with select human stock, their domestic animals and basic necessities, and it had been sent to plant humans in this far place. It had been designed to land once, then be broken down into useful things.

Somehow, the basic necessities had fallen short, and the colony had been forced to improvise its own tools. They had not really settled here yet, Kroudar realized. More than three years—and three years here were five years of Mother Earth—and they still lived on the edge of extinction. They were trapped here. Yes, that was true. The ship could never be reconstructed. And even if that miracle were accomplished, the fuel did not exist.

The colony was *here*.

And every member knew the predatory truth of their predicament: survival had not been assured. It was known in subtle things to Kroudar's unlettered mind, especially in a fact he observed without being able to explain.

Not one of their number had yet accepted a name for this planet. It was "here" or "this place."

Or even more bitter terms.

Kroudar dumped his sack of *trodi* onto a storage hut porch, mopped his forehead. The joints of his arms and legs ached. His back ached. He could feel the sickness of *this place* in his bowels. Again, he wiped perspiration from his forehead, removed the red cloth he wore to protect his head from that brutal sun.

Yellow hair fell down as he loosed the cloth, and he swung the hair back over his shoulders.

It would be dark very soon.

The red cloth was dirty, he saw. It would require another gentle washing. Kroudar thought it odd, this cloth: grown and woven on Mother Earth, it would end its days on *this place*.

Even as he and the others.

He stared at the cloth for a moment before placing it carefully in a pocket.

All around him, his fishermen were going through the familiar ritual. Brown sacks woven of coarse native roots were dumped dripping onto the storage hut porches. Some of his men leaned then against the porch uprights, some sprawled in the sand.

Kroudar lifted his gaze. Fires behind the bluff above them sent smoke spirals into the darkening sky. Kroudar was suddenly hungry. He thought of Technician Honida up there at the cook fire, their twin sons—two years old next week—nearby at the door of the shipmetal longhouse.

It stirred him to think of Honida. She had chosen *him*. With men from the Scientist class and the Technicians available to her, Honida had reached down into the Labor pool to tap the one they all called "Old Ugly." He wasn't old, Kroudar reminded himself. But he knew the source of the name. *This place* had worked its changes on him with more visible evidence than upon any of the others.

Kroudar held no illusions about why he had been brought on this human migration. It was his muscles and his minimal education. The reason was embodied in that label written down in the ship manifest—laborer. The planners back on Mother Earth had realized there were tasks which required human muscles not inhibited by too much thinking. The *kroudars* landed *here* were not numerous, but they knew each other and they knew themselves for what they were.

There'd even been talk among the higher echelons of not allowing Honida to choose him as mate. Kroudar knew this. He did not resent it particularly. It didn't even bother him that the vote among the biologists—they'd discussed his ugliness at greath length, so it was reported—favored Honida's choice on philosophical rather than physical grounds.

Kroudar knew he was ugly.

He knew also that his present hunger was a good sign. A strong desire to see his family grew in him, beginning to ignite his muscles for the climb from the beach. Particularly, he wanted to see his twins, the one yellow-haired like himself, and the other dark as Honida. The other women favored with children looked down upon his twins as stunted and sickly, Kroudar knew. The women fussed over diets and went running to the medics almost every day. But as long as Honida did not worry, Kroudar remained calm, Honida, after all, was a technician, a worker in the hydroponics gardens.

Kroudar moved his bare feet softly in the sand. Once more, he looked up at the bluff. Along the edge grew scattered native trees. Their thick trunks hugged the ground, gnarled and twisted, supports for bulbous, yellow-green leaves that exuded poisonous milky sap in the heat of the day. A few of the surviving Earth-falcons perched in the trees, silent, watchful.

The birds gave Kroudar an odd confidence in his own decisions. For what do the falcons watch, he wondered. It was a question the most exalted of the colony's thinkers had not been able to answer. Search 'copters had been sent out following the falcons. The birds flew offshore in the night, rested occasionally on barren islands, and returned at dawn. The colony command had been unwilling to risk its precious boats in the search, and the mystery of the falcons remained unsolved.

It was doubly a mystery because the other birds had perished or flown off to some unfound place. The doves, the quail—the gamebirds and songbirds—all had vanished. And the domestic chickens had all died, their eggs infertile. Kroudar knew this as a comment by *this place*, a warning for the life that came from Mother Earth.

A few scrawny cattle survived, and several calves had been born *here*. But they moved with a listless gait and there was distressed lowing in the pastures. Looking into their eyes was like looking into open wounds. A few pigs still lived, as listless and sickly as the cattle, and all the wild creatures had strayed off or died.

Except the falcons.

How odd it was, because the people who planned and conceived profound thoughts had held such hopes for *this place*. The survey reports had been exciting. This was a planet without native land animals. It was a planet whose native plants appeared not too different from those of Mother Earth—in some respects. And the sea creatures were primitive by sophisticated evolutionary standards.

Without being able to put it into those beautifully polished phrases which others admired, Kroudar knew where the mistake had been made. Sometimes, you had to search out a problem with your flesh and not with your mind.

He stared around now at the motley rags of his men. They were *his* men. He was the master fisherman, the one who had found the *trodi* and conceived these squat, ugly boats built within the limitations of native woods. The colony was alive now because of his skills with boat and net.

There would be more gaps in the *trodi* runs, though. Kroudar felt this as an awareness on the edges of his fatigue. There would be unpopular and dangerous things to do then, all necessary because *thinking* had failed. The salmon they had introduced, according to plan, had gone off into the ocean vastness. The flatfish in the colony's holding ponds suffered mysterious attrition. Insects flew away and were never seen again.

There's food here, the biologists argued. Why do they die?

The colony's maize was a sometime thing with strange ears. Wheat came up in scabrous patches. There were no familiar patterns of growth or migration. The colony lived on the thin edge of existence, maintained by protein bulk from the processed *trodi* and vitamins from vegetables grown hydroponically with arduous filtering and adjustment of their water. Breakdown of a single system in the chain could bring disaster.

The giant orange sun showed only a small arc above the sea horizon now, and Kroudar's men were stirring themselves, lifting their tired bodies off the sand, pushing away from the places where they had leaned.

"All right now," Kroudar ordered. "Let's get this food inside on the racks."

"Why?" someone asked from the dusk: "You think the falcons will eat it?"

They all knew the falcons would not eat the *trodi*. Kroudar recognized the objection: it was tiredness of the mind speaking. The shrimp creatures fed only humans—after careful processing to remove dangerous irritants. A falcon might take up a frond-legged *trodi*, but would drop it at the first taste.

What did they eat, those waiting birds?

Falcons knew a thing about *this place* that humans did not know. The birds knew it in their flesh in the way Kroudar sought the knowledge.

Darkness fell, and with a furious clatter, the falcons flew off toward the sea. One of Kroudar's men kindled a torch and, having rested, anxious now to climb the bluff and join their families, the fishermen pitched into the work that must be done. Boats were hauled up on rollers. *Trodi* were spread out in thin layers along racks within the storage huts. Nets were draped on racks to dry.

As he worked, Kroudar wondered about the scientists up there in the shining laboratories. He had the working man's awe of knowledge, a servility in the face of titles and things clearly superior, but he had also the simple man's sure awareness of when superior things failed.

Kroudar was not privy to the high-level conferences in the colony command, but he knew the physical substance of the ideas discussed there. His awareness of failure and hovering disaster had no sophisticated words or erudition to hold itself dancingly before men's minds, but his knowledge carried its own elegance. He drew on ancient knowledge adjusted subtly to the differences of *this place*. Kroudar had found the *trodi*. Kroudar had organized the methods of capturing them and preserving them. He had no refined labels to explain it, but Kroudar knew himself for what he could do and what he was.

He was the first sea peasant *here*.

Without wasting energy on talk, Kroudar's band finished the work, turned away from the storage huts and plodded up the cliff trail, their course marked by, here and there, men with flaming torches. There were fuzzy orange lights, heavy shadows, inching their way upward in a black world, and they gave heart to Kroudar.

Lingering to the last, he checked the doors of the huts, then followed, hurrying to catch up. The man directly ahead of him on the path carried a torch, native wood soaked in *trodi* oil. It flickered and smoked and gave off poisonous fumes. The light revealed a troglodyte figure, a human clad in patched shipcloth, body too thin, muscles moving on the edge of collapse.

Kroudar sighed.

It was not like this on Mother Earth, he knew. There, the women waited on the strand for their men to return from the sea. Children played among the pebbles. Eager hands helped with the work onshore, spreading the nets, carrying the catch, pulling the boats.

Not *here*.

And the perils *here* were not the perils of Home. Kroudar's boats never strayed out of sight of these cliffs. One boat always carried a technician with a radio for contact with shore. Before its final descent, the colony ship had seeded space with orbiting devices—watchers, guardians against surprises from the weather. The laboriously built fishing fleet always had ample warning of storms. No monster sea creatures had ever been seen in that ocean.

This *place* lacked the cruel savagery and variety of seas Kroudar had known, but it was nonetheless deadly. He *knew* this.

The women should wait for us on the shore, he thought.

But colony command said the women—and even some of the children—were needed for too many other tasks. Individual plants from home required personal attention. Single wheat stalks were nurtured with tender care. Each orchard tree existed with its own handmaiden, its guardian dryad.

Atop the cliff, the fishermen came in sight of the longhouses, shipmetal *quonsets* named for some far distant place and time in human affairs. Scattered electric lights ringed the town. Many of the unpaved streets wandered off unlit. There were mechanical sounds here and murmurous voices.

The men scattered to their own affairs now, no longer a band. Kroudar plodded down his street toward the open cook fires in the central plaza. The open fires were a necessity to conserve the more sophisticated energies of the colony. Some looked upon those flames as admission of defeat. Kroudar saw them as victory. It was *native* wood being burned.

Off in the hills beyond the town, he knew, stood the ruins of the wind machines they had built. The storm which had wreaked that destruction had achieved no surprise in its coming, but had left enormous surprise at its power.

For Kroudar, the *thinkers* had begun to diminish in stature then. When native chemistry and water life had wrecked the turbines in the river which emptied into the harbor, those men of knowledge had shrunk even more. Then it was that Kroudar had begun his own search for native foods.

Now, Kroudar heard, native plant life threatened the cooling systems for their atomic generators, defying radiation in a way no life should. Some among the technicians already were fashioning steam engines of materials not intended for such use. Soon, they would have native metals, though—materials to resist the wild etchings and rusts of *this place*.

They might succeed—provided the dragging sickness did not sap them further. If they survived.

Honida awaited him at the door to their quarters, smiling, graceful. Her dark hair was plaited and wound in rings around her forehead. The brown eyes were alive with welcome. Firelight from the plaza cast a familiar glow across her olive skin. The high cheekbones of her Amerind ancestry, the full lips and proudly hooked nose—all filled him with remembered excitement.

Kroudar wondered if the *planners* had known this thing about her which gave him such warmth—her strength and fecundity. She had chosen *him*, and now she carried more of their children—twins again.

"Ahhh, my fisherman is home," she said, embracing him in the doorway for anybody to see.

They went inside then, closed the door, and she held him with more ardor, stared up into his face which, reflected in her eyes, lost some of its ugliness.

"Honida," he said, unable to find other words.

Presently, he asked about the boys.

"They're asleep," she said, leading him to the crude trestle table he had built for their kitchen.

He nodded. Later, he would go in and stare at his sons. It did not bother him that they slept so much. He could feel the reasons for this somewhere within himself.

Honida had hot *trodi* soup waiting for him on the table. It was spiced with hydroponic tomatoes and peas and contained other things which he knew she gathered from the land without telling the scientists.

Whatever she put in front of him, Kroudar ate. There was bread tonight with an odd musty flavor which he found pleasant. In the light of the single lamp they were permitted for this room, he stared at a piece of the bread. It was almost purple—like the sea. He chewed it, swallowed.

Honida, watchfully eating across from him, finished her bread and soup, asked: "Do you like the bread?"

"I like it."

"I made it myself in the coals," she said.

He nodded, took another slice.

Honida refilled his soup bowl.

They were privileged, Kroudar realized, to have this privacy for their meals. Many of the others had opted for communal cooking and eating—even among the technicians and higher echelons who possessed more freedom of choice. Honida had seen something about *this place*, though, which required secrecy and going private ways.

Kroudar, hunger satisfied, stared across the table at her. He adored her with a devotion that went far deeper than the excitement of her flesh. He could not say the thing she was, but he knew it. If they were to have a future here, that future was in Honida and the things he might learn, form and construct of himself with his own flesh.

Under the pressure of his eyes, Honida arose, came around the table and began massaging the muscles of his back—the very muscles he used to haul the nets.

"You're tired," she said. "Was it difficult out there today?"

"Hard work," Kroudar said.

He admired the way she spoke. She had many words at her disposal. He had heard her use some of them during colony meetings and during the time of their application for mating choice. She had words for things he did not know, and she knew also when to speak with her body rather than with her mouth. She knew about the muscles of his back.

Kroudar felt such love for her then that he wondered if it went up through her fingers into her body.

"We filled the boats," he said.

"I was told today that we'll soon need more storage huts," she said. "They're worried about sparing the labor for the building."

"Ten more huts," he said.

She would pass that word along, he knew. Somehow, it would be done. The other technicians listened to Honida. Many among the scientists scoffed at her; it could be heard beneath the blandness of their voices. Perhaps it was because she had chosen Kroudar for mate. But technicians listened. The huts would be built.

And they would be filled before the *trodi* run stopped.

Kroudar realized then that he knew when the run would stop, not as a date, but almost as a physical thing which he could reach out and touch. He longed for the words to explain this to Honida.

She gave his back a final kneading, sat down beside him and leaned her dark head against his chest. "If you're not too tired," she said, "I have something to show you."

With a feeling of surprise, Kroudar became aware of unspoken excitement in Honida. Was it something about the hydroponic gardens where she worked? His thoughts went immediately to that place upon which the scientists pinned their hopes, the place where they chose the tall plants, the beautiful, engorged with richness from Mother Earth. Had they achieved something important at last? Was there, after all, a clear way to make *this place* arable?

Kroudar was a primitive then wanting his gods redeemed. He found himself full of peasant hopes for the land. Even a sea peasant knew the value of land.

He and Honida had responsibilities, though. He nodded questioningly toward the twins' bedroom.

"I arranged . . ." She gestured toward their neighbor's cubicle. "They will listen."

She had planned this, then, Kroudar stood up, held out his hand for her. "Show me."

They went out into the night. Their town was quieter now; he could hear the distant roistering of the river. For a moment, he thought he heard a cricket, but reason told him it could only be one of the huts cooling in the night. He longed wordlessly for a moon.

Honida had brought one of the rechargeable electric torches, the kind issued to technicians against emergency calls in the night. Seeing that torch, Kroudar sensed a deeper importance in this mysterious thing she wanted to show him. Honida had the peasant's hoarding instinct. She would not waste such a torch.

Instead of leading him toward the green lights and glass roofs of the hydroponic gardens, though, she guided their steps in the opposite direction toward the deep gorge where the river plunged into the harbor.

There were no guards along the footpath, only an occasional stone marker and grotesqueries of native growth. Swiftly, without speaking, she led him to the gorge and the narrow path which he knew went only down to a ledge which jutted into the damp air of the river's spray.

Kroudar found himself trembling with excitement as he followed Honida's shadowy figure, the firefly darting of her light. It was cold on the ledge and the alien outline of native trees revealed by the torch filled Kroudar with disquiet.

What had Honida discovered—or created?

Condensation dripped from the plants here. The river noise was loud. It was marsh air he breathed, dank and filled with bizarre odors.

Honida stopped, and Kroudar held his breath. He listened. There was only the river.

For a moment, he didn't realize that Honida was directing the orange light of the torch at her discovery. It looked like one of the native plants—a thing with a thick stem crouched low to the land, gnarled and twisted, bulbous yellow-green protrusions set with odd spacing along its length.

Slowly, realization came over him. He recognized a darker tone in the green, the way the leaf structures were joined to the stalk a bunching of brown-yellow silk drooping from the bulbous protrusions.

"Maize," he whispered.

In a low voice, pitching her explanation to Kroudar's vocabulary, Honida explained what she had done. He saw it in her words, understood why she had done this thing stealthily, here away from the scientists. He took the light from her, crouched, stared with rapt attention. This meant the death of those things the scientists held beautiful. It ended their plan for *this place*.

Kroudar could see his own descendants in this plant. They might develop bulbous heads, hairless, wide thick-lipped mouths. Their skins might become purple. They would be short statured; he knew that.

Honida had assured this—right here on the river-drenched ledge. Instead of selecting seed from the tallest, the straightest stalks, the ones with the longest and most perfect ears—the ones most like those from Mother Earth—she had tested her maize almost to destruction. She had chosen sickly, scrawny plants, ones barely able to produce seed. She had taken only those plants which *this place* influenced most deeply. From these, she had selected finally a strain which lived *here* as native plants lived.

This was native maize.

She broke off an ear, peeled back the husk.

There were gaps in the seed rows and, when she squeezed a kernel, the juice ran purple. He recognized the smell of the bread.

Here was the thing the scientists would not admit. They were trying to make *this place* into another Earth. But it was not and it could never be. The falcons had been the first among their creatures to discover this, he suspected.

The statement Honida made here was that she and Kroudar would be short-lived. Their children would be sickly by Mother Earth's standards. Their descendants would change in ways that defied the hopes of those who had planned this migration. The scientists would hate this and try to stop it.

The gnarled stalk of maize said the scientists would fail.

For a long while, Kroudar crouched there, staring into the future until the torch began to dim, losing its charge. He aroused himself then, led the way back out of the gorge.

At the top, with the lights of their dying civilization visible across the plain, he stopped, said: "The *trodi* run will stop . . . soon. I will take one boat and . . . friends. We will go out where the falcons go."

It was one of the longest speeches he had ever made.

She took the light from his hand, extinguished it, pressed herself against him. "What do you think the falcons have found?"

"The seed," he said.

He shook his head. He could not explain it, but the thing was there in his awareness. Everything here exuded poisonous vapors, or juices in which only its own seed could live. Why should the *trodi* or any other sea creature be different? And, with the falcons as evidence, the seed must be slightly less poisonous to the intruders from Mother Earth.

"The boats are slow," she said.

He agreed silently. A storm could trap them too far out for a run to safety. It would be dangerous. But he heard also in her voice that she was not trying to stop him or dissuade him.

"I will take good men," he said.

"How long will you be gone?" Honida asked.

He thought about this for a moment. The rhythms of *this place* were beginning to make themselves known to him. His awareness shaped the journey, the days out, the night search over the water where the falcons were known to sweep in their low guiding runs—then the return.

"Eight days," he said.

"You'll need fine mesh nets," she said. "I'll see to having them made. Perhaps a few technicians, too. I know some who will go with you."

"Eight days," he said, telling her to choose strong men.

"Yes," she said. "Eight days. I'll be waiting on the shore when you return."

He took her hand then and led the way back across the plain. As they walked, he said: "We must name *this place*."

"When you come back." she said.

HARRY HARRISON (1925-)

Born in America but now living in Ireland, Harry Harrison is one of the most important international Science Fiction and Fantasy writers of our day. His works have appeared in more than twenty languages. A prolific and often awarded writer, he continues to be an important editor, anthologist, and scholar of Science Fiction and Fantasy.

As an author, Harrison is known for several enduring series. These include his Deathworld *trilogy, his* Stainless Steel Rat *series, his* Eden *trilogy, and his* To the Stars *series. In addition, he has penned an array of popular novels and short stories, as well as juvenile fiction. Harrison's writing is intricately plotted, enthralling, cleanly written, intelligent and insightful, and socially significant.*

In 1970, talented Science Fiction author and editor Thomas Disch was preparing a new anthology of Science Fiction and Fantasy. He asked Harrison to provide an excerpt of Harrison's classic futuristic novel, Make Room, Make Room *(1966). [Harrison's novel had been made into the highly popular movie* Soylent Green *(1973). The movie featured Charlton Heston and the last film role of motion picture legend Edward G. Robinson.] Unable to find an appropriate excerpt from his novel for Disch's use, Harrison wrote "Roommates."*

While many insightful, important stories are reprinted in this volume, Harry Harrison's grim, disturbing short story "Roommates" may unfortunately be the most prophetic.

Roommates

(In Ruins of Earth: An Anthology of Stories of the Immediate Future, *ed. Thomas Disch, 1971*)

SUMMER

The August sun struck in through the open window and burned on Andrew Rusch's bare legs until discomfort dragged him awake from the depths of heavy sleep. Only slowly did he become aware of the heat and the damp and gritty sheet beneath his body. He rubbed at his gummed-shut eyelids, then lay there, staring up at the cracked and stained plaster of the ceiling, only half awake and experiencing a feeling of dislocation, not knowing in those first waking moments just where he was; although he had lived in this room for over seven years. He yawned and the odd sensation slipped away while he groped for the watch that he always put on the chair next to the bed, then he yawned again as he blinked at the hands mistily seen behind the scratched crystal. Seven . . . seven o'clock in the morning, and there was a little number 9 in the middle of the square window. Monday the ninth of August, 1999—and hot as a furnace already, with the city still imbedded in the heat wave that had baked and suffocated New York for the past ten days. Andy scratched at a trickle of perspiration on his side, then moved his legs out of the patch of sunlight and bunched the pillow up under his neck. From the other side of the thin partition that divided the room in half there came a clanking whir that quickly rose to a high-pitched drone.

"Morning . . ." he shouted over the sound, then began coughing. Still coughing he reluctantly stood and crossed the room to draw a glass of water from the wall tank; it came out in a thin, brownish trickle. He swallowed it, then rapped the dial on the tank with his knuckles and the needle bobbed up and down close to the *Empty* mark. It needed filling, he would have to see to that before he signed in at four o'clock at the precinct. The day had begun.

A full-length mirror with a crack running down it was fixed to the front of the hulking wardrobe and he poked his face close to it, rubbing at his bristly jaw. He would have to shave before he went in. No one should ever look at himself in the morning, naked and revealed, he decided with distaste, frowning at the dead white of his skin and the slight bow to his legs that was usually concealed by his pants. And how did he manage to have ribs that stuck out like those of a starved horse, as well as a growing potbelly—both at the same time? He kneaded the soft flesh and thought that it must be the starchy diet, that and sitting around on his chunk most of the time. But at least the fat wasn't showing on his face. His forehead was a little higher each year, but wasn't too obvious so long as his hair was cropped short. You have just turned 30, he thought to himself, and the wrinkles are already starting around your eyes. And your nose is too big—wasn't it Uncle Brian who always said that was because there was Welsh blood in the family? And your canine teeth are a little too obvious so when you smile you look a bit like a hyena. You're a handsome devil, Andy Rusch, and it's a wonder a girl like Shirl will even look at you, much less kiss you. He scowled at himself, then went to look for a handkerchief to blow his impressive Welsh nose.

There was just a single pair of clean undershorts in the drawer and he pulled them on; that was another thing he had to remember today, to get some washing done. The squealing whine was still coming from the other side of the partition as he pushed through the connecting door.

"You're going to give yourself a coronary, Sol," he told the gray-bearded man who was perched on the wheelless bicycle, pedaling so industriously that perspiration ran down his chest and soaked into the bath towel that he wore tied around his waist.

"Never a coronary," Solomon Kahn gasped out, pumping steadily. "I been doing this every day for so long that my ticker would miss it if I stopped. And no cholesterol in my arteries either since regular flushing with alcohol takes care of that. And no lung cancer since I couldn't afford to smoke even if I wanted to, which I don't. And at the age of 75 no prostatitis because. . . ."

"Sol, please—spare me the horrible details on an empty stomach. Do you have an ice cube to spare?"

"Take two—it's a hot day. And don't leave the door open too long."

Andy opened the small refrigerator that squatted against the wall and quickly took out the plastic container of margarine, then squeezed two ice cubes from the tray into a glass and slammed the door. He filled the glass with water from the wall tank and put it on the table next to the margarine. "Have you eaten yet?" he asked.

"I'll join you, these things should be charged by now."

Sol stopped pedaling and the whine died away to a moan, then vanished. He disconnected the wires from the electrical generator that was geared to the rear axle of the bike, and carefully coiled them up next to the four black automobile storage batteries that were racked on top of the refrigerator. Then, after wiping his hands on his soiled towel sarong, he pulled out one of the bucket seats, salvaged from an ancient 1975 Ford, and sat down across the table from Andy.

"I heard the six o'clock news," he said. "The Eldsters are organizing another protest march today on relief headquarters. *That's* where you'll see coronaries!"

"I won't, thank God, I'm not on until four and Union Square isn't in our precinct." He opened the breadbox and took out one of the six-inch-square red crackers, then pushed the box over to Sol. He spread margarine thinly on it and took a bite, wrinkling his nose as he chewed. "I think this margarine has turned."

"How can you tell?" Sol grunted, biting into one of the dry crackers. "Anything made from motor oil and whale blubber is turned to begin with."

"Now you begin to sound like a naturist," Andy said, washing his cracker down with cold water. "There's hardly any flavor at all to the fats made from petrochemicals and you know there aren't any whales left so they can't use blubber—it's just good chlorella oil."

"Whales, plankton, herring oil, it's all the same. Tastes fishy. I'll take mine dry so I don't grow no fins." There was a sudden staccato rapping on the door and he groaned. "Not yet eight o'clock and already they are after you."

"It could be anything," Andy said, starting for the door.

"It could be but it's not, that's the callboy's knock and you know it as well as I do and I bet you dollars to doughnuts that's just who it is. See?" He nodded with gloomy satisfaction when Andy unlocked the door and they saw the skinny, bare-legged messenger standing in the dark hall.

"What do you want, Woody?" Andy asked.

"I don' wan' no-fin," Woody lisped over his bare gums. Though he was in his early twenties he didn't have a tooth in his head. "Lieutenan' says bring, I bring." He handed Andy the message board with his name written on the outside.

Andy turned toward the light and opened it, reading the lieutenant's spiky scrawl on the slate, then took the chalk and scribbled his initials after it and returned it to the messenger. He closed the door behind him and went back to finish his breakfast, frowning in thought.

"Don't look at me that way," Sol said, "I didn't send the message. Am I wrong in guessing it's not the most pleasant of news?"

"It's the Eldsters, they're jamming the Square already and the precinct needs reinforcements."

"But why you? This sounds like a job for the harness bulls."

"Harness bulls! Where do you get that medieval slang? Of course they need patrolmen for the crowd, but there have to be detectives there to spot known agitators, pickpockets, purse-grabbers and the rest. It'll be murder in that park today. I have to check in by nine, so I have enough time to bring up some water first."

Andy dressed slowly in slacks and a loose sport shirt, then put a pan of water on the windowsill to warm in the sun. He took the two five-gallon plastic jerry cans, and when he went out Sol looked up from the TV set, glancing over the top of his old-fashioned glasses.

"When you bring back the water I'll fix you a drink—or do you think it is too early?"

"Not the way I feel today, it's not."

The hall was ink black once the door had closed behind him and he felt his way carefully along the wall to the stairs, cursing and almost falling when he stumbled over a heap of refuse someone had thrown there. Two flights down a window had been knocked through the wall and enough light came in to show him the way down the last two flights to the street. After the damp hallway the heat of Twenty-fifth Street hit him in a musty wave, a stifling miasma compounded of decay, dirt and unwashed humanity. He had to make his way through the women who already filled the steps of the building, walking carefully so that he didn't step on the children who were playing below. The sidewalk was still in shadow but so jammed with people that he walked in the street, well away from the curb to avoid the rubbish and litter banked high there. Days of heat had softened the tar so that it gave underfoot, then clutched at the soles of his shoes. There was the usual line leading to the columnar red water point on the corner of Seventh Avenue, but it broke up with angry shouts and some waved fists just as he reached it. Still muttering, the crowd dispersed and Andy saw that the duty patrolman was locking the steel door.

"What's going on?" Andy asked. "I thought this point was open until noon?"

The policeman turned, his hand automatically staying close to his gun until he recognized the detective from his own precinct. He tilted back his uniform cap and wiped the sweat from his forehead with the back of his hand.

"Just had the orders from the sergeant, all points closed for 24 hours. The reservoir level is low because of the drought, they gotta save water."

"That's a hell of a note," Andy said, looking at the key still in the lock. "I'm going on duty now and this means I'm not going to be drinking for a couple of days. . . ."

After a careful look around, the policeman unlocked the door and took one of the jerry cans from Andy. "One of these ought to hold you." He held it under the faucet while it filled, then lowered his voice. "Don't let it out, but the word is that there was another dynamiting job on the aqueduct upstate."

"Those farmers again?"

"It must be. I was on guard duty up there before I came to this precinct and it's rough, they just as soon blow you up with the aqueduct at the same time. Claim the city's stealing their water."

"They've got enough," Andy said, taking the full container. "More than they need. And there are 35 million people here in the city who get damn thirsty."

"Who's arguing?" the cop asked, slamming the door shut again and locking it tight.

Andy pushed his way back through the crowd around the steps and went through to the backyard first. All of the toilets were in use and he had to wait, and when he finally got into one of the cubicles he took the jerry cans with him; one of the kids playing in the pile of rubbish against the fence would be sure to steal them if he left them unguarded.

When he had climbed the dark flights once more and opened the door to the room he heard the clear sound of ice cubes rattling against glass.

"That's Beethoven's Fifth Symphony that you're playing," he said, dropping the containers and falling into a chair.

"It's my favorite tune," Sol said, taking two chilled glasses from the refrigerator and, with the solemnity of a religious ritual, dropped a tiny pearl onion into each. He passed one to Andy, who sipped carefully at the chilled liquid.

"It's when I taste one of these, Sol, that I almost believe you're not crazy after all. Why do they call them Gibsons?"

"A secret lost behind the mists of time. Why is a Stinger a Stinger or a Pink Lady a Pink Lady?"

"I don't know—why? I never tasted any of them."

"I don't know either, but that's the name. Like those green things they serve in the knockjoints, Panamas. Doesn't mean anything, just a name."

"Thanks," Andy said, draining his glass. "The day looks better already."

He went into his room and took his gun and holster from the drawer and clipped it inside the waistband of his pants. His shield was on his key ring where he always kept it and he slipped his notepad in on top of it, then hesitated a moment. It was going to be a long and rough day and anything might happen. He dug his nippers out from under his shirts, then the soft plastic tube filled with shot. It might be needed in the crowd, safer than a gun with all those old people milling about. Not only that, but with the new austerity regulations you had to have a damn good reason for using up any ammunition. He washed as well as he could with the pint of water that had been warming in the sun on the windowsill, then scrubbed his face with the small shard of gray and gritty soap until his whiskers softened a bit. His razor blade was beginning to show obvious nicks along both edges and, as he honed it against the inside of his drinking glass, he thought that it was time to think about getting a new one. Maybe in the fall.

Sol was watering his window box when Andy came out, carefully irrigating the rows of herbs and tiny onions. "Don't take any wooden nickels," he said without looking up from his work. Sol had a minion of them, all old. What in the world was a wooden nickel?

The sun was higher now and the heat was mounting in the sealed tar and concrete valley of the street. The band of shade was smaller and the steps were so packed with humanity that he couldn't leave the doorway. He carefully pushed by a tiny, runny-nosed girl dressed only in ragged gray underwear and descended a step. The gaunt women moved aside reluctantly, ignoring him, but the men stared at him with a cold look of hatred stamped across their features that gave them a strangely alike appearance, as though they were all members of the same angry family. Andy threaded his way through the last of them and when he reached the sidewalk he had to step over the outstretched leg of an old man who sprawled there. He looked dead, not asleep, and he might be for all that anyone cared. His foot was bare and filthy and a string tied about his ankle led to a naked baby that was sitting vacantly on the sidewalk chewing on a bent plastic dish. The baby was as dirty as the man and the string was tied about its chest under the pipestem arms because its stomach was swollen and heavy. Was the old man dead? Not that it mattered, the only work he had to do in the world was to act as an anchor for the baby and he could do that job just as well alive or dead.

Out of the room now, well away and unable to talk to Sol until he returned, he realized that once again he had not managed to mention Shirl. It would have been a simple enough thing to do, but he kept forgetting it, avoiding it. Sol was always talking about how horny he always was and how often he used to get laid when he was in the army. He would understand.

They were roommates, that was all. There was nothing else between them. Friends, sure. But bringing a girl in to live wouldn't change that.

So why hadn't he told him?

FALL

"Everybody says this is the coldest October ever, I never seen a colder one. And the rain too, never hard enough to fill the reservoir or anything, but just enough to make you wet so you feel colder. Ain't that right?"

Shirl nodded, hardly listening to the words, but aware by the rising intonation of the woman's voice that a question had been asked. The line moved forward and she shuffled a few steps behind the woman who had been speaking—a shapeless bundle of heavy clothing covered with a torn plastic raincoat, with a cord tied about her middle so that she resembled a lumpy sack. Not that I look much better, Shirl thought, tugging the fold of blanket farther over her head to keep out the persistent drizzle. It wouldn't be much longer now, there were only a few dozen people ahead, but it had taken a lot more time than she thought it would; it was almost dark. A light came on over the tank car, glinting off its black sides and lighting up the slowly falling curtain of rain. The line moved again and the woman ahead of Shirl waddled forward, pulling the child after her, a bundle as wrapped and shapeless as its mother, its face hidden by a knotted scarf, that produced an almost constant whimpering.

"Stop that," the woman said. She turned to Shirl, her puffy face a red lumpiness around the dark opening of her almost toothless mouth. "He's crying because he's been to see the doc, thinks he's sick but it's only the kwash." She held up the child's swollen, ballooning hand. "You can tell when they swell up and get the black spots on the knees. Had to sit two weeks in the Bellevue clinic to see a doc who told me what I knew already. But that's the only way you get him to sign the slip. Got a peanut-butter ration that way. My old man loves the stuff. You live on my block, don't you? I think I seen you there?"

"Twenty-sixth Street," Shirl said, taking the cap off the jerry can and putting it into her coat pocket. She felt chilled through and was sure she was catching a cold.

"That's right, I knew it was you. Stick around and wait for me, we'll walk back together. It's getting late and plenty of punks would like to grab the water, they can always sell it. Mrs. Ramirez in my building, she's a spic but she's all right, you know, her family been in the building since the World War Two, she got a black eye so swole up she can't see through it and two teeth knocked out. Some punk got her with a club and took her water away."

"Yes, I'll wait for you, that's a good idea," Shirl said, suddenly feeling very alone.

"Cards," the patrolman said and she handed him the three Welfare cards, hers, Andy's and Sol's. He held them to the light, then handed them back to her. "Six quarts," he called out to the valve man.

"That's not right," Shirl said.

"Reduced ration today, lady, keep moving, there's a lot of people waiting."

She held out the jerry can and the valve man slipped the end of a large funnel into it and ran in the water. "Next," he called out.

The jerry can gurgled when she walked and was tragically light. She went and stood near the policeman until the woman came up, pulling the child with one hand and in the other carrying a five-gallon kerosene can that seemed almost full. She must have a big family.

"Let's go," the woman said and the child trailed, mewling faintly, at the end of her arm.

As they left the Twelfth Avenue railroad siding it grew darker, the rain soaking up all the failing light. The buildings here were mostly old warehouses and factories with blank solid walls concealing the tenants hidden away inside, the sidewalks wet and empty. The nearest streetlight was a block away. "My husband will give me hell coming home this late," the woman said as they turned the corner. Two figures blocked the sidewalk in front of them.

"Let's have the water," the nearest one said, and the distant light reflected from the knife he held before him.

"No, don't! Please don't!" the woman begged and swung her can of water out behind her, away from them. Shirl huddled against the wall and saw, when they walked forward, that they were just young boys, teen-agers. But they still had a knife.

"The water!" the first one said, jabbing his knife at the woman.

"Take it," she screeched, swinging the can like a weight on the end of her arm. Before the boy could dodge it caught him full in the side of the head, knocking him howling to the ground, the knife flying from his fingers. "You want some too?" she shouted, advancing on the second boy. He was unarmed.

"No, I don't want no trouble," he begged, pulling at the first one's arm, then retreating when she approached. When she bent to pick up the fallen knife, he managed to drag the other boy to his feet and half carry him around the corner. It had only taken a few seconds and all the time Shirl had stood with her back to the wall, trembling with fear.

"They got some surprise," the woman crowed, holding the worn carving knife up to admire it. "I can use this better than they can. Just punks, kids." She was excited and happy. During the entire time she had never released her grip on the child's hand; it was sobbing louder.

There was no more trouble and the woman went with Shirl as far as her door. "Thank you very much," Shirl said. "I don't know what I would have done. . . ."

"That's no trouble," the woman beamed. "You saw what I did to him—and who got the knife now!" She stamped away, hauling the heavy can in one hand, the child in the other. Shirl went in.

"Where have you been?" Andy asked when she pushed open the door. "I was beginning to wonder what had happened to you." It was warm in the room, with a faint odor of fishy smoke, and he and Sol were sitting at the table with drinks in their hands.

"It was the water, the line must have been a block long. They only gave me six quarts, the ration has been cut again." She saw his black look and decided not to tell him about the trouble on the way back. He would be twice as angry then and she didn't want this meal to be spoiled.

"That's really wonderful," Andy said sarcastically. "The ration was already too small—so now they lower it even more. Better get out of those wet things, Shirl, and Sol will pour you a Gibson. His homemade vermouth has ripened and I bought some vodka."

"Drink up," Sol said, handing her the chilled glass. "I made some soup with that ener-G junk, it's the only way it's edible, and it should be just about ready. We'll have that for the first course, before—" He finished the sentence by jerking his head in the direction of the refrigerator.

"What's up?" Andy asked. "A secret?"

"No secret," Shirl said, opening the refrigerator, "just a surprise. I got these today in the market, one for each of us." She took out a plate with three small soylent burgers on it. "They're the new ones, they had them on TV, with the smoky-barbecue flavor."

"They must have cost a fortune," Andy said. "We won't eat for the rest of the month."

"They're not as expensive as all that. Anyway, it was my own money, not the budget money, I used."

"It doesn't make any difference, money is money. We could probably live for a week on what these things cost."

"Soup's on," Sol said, sliding the plates onto the table. Shirl had a lump in her throat so she couldn't say anything; she sat and looked at her plate and tried not to cry.

"I'm sorry," Andy said. "But you know how prices are going up—we have to look ahead. City income tax is higher, 80 percent now, because of the raised Welfare payment, so it's going to be rough going this winter. Don't think I don't appreciate it. . . ."

"If you do, so why don't you shut up right there and eat your soup?" Sol said.

"Keep out of this, Sol," Andy said.

"I'll keep out of it when you keep the fight out of my room. Now come on, a nice meal like this, it shouldn't be spoiled."

Andy started to answer him, then changed his mind. He reached over and took Shirl's hand. "It is going to be a good dinner," he said. "Let's all enjoy it."

"Not that good," Sol said, puckering his mouth over a spoonful of soup. "Wait until you try this stuff. But the burgers will take the taste out of our mouths."

There was silence after that while they spooned up the soup, until Sol started on one of his army stories about New Orleans and it was so impossible they had to laugh, and after that things were better. Sol shared out the rest of the Gibsons while Shirl served the burgers.

"If I was drunk enough this would almost taste like meat," Sol announced, chewing happily.

"They are good," Shirl said. Andy nodded agreement. She finished the burger quickly and soaked up the juice with a scrap of weedcracker, then sipped at her drink. The trouble on the way home with the water already seemed far distant. What was it the woman had said was wrong with the child?

"Do you know what 'kwash' is?" she asked.

Andy shrugged. "Some kind of disease, that's all I know. Why do you ask?"

"There was a woman next to me in line for the water, I was talking to her. She had a little boy with her who was sick with this kwash. I don't think she should have had him out in the rain, sick like that. And I was wondering if it was catching."

"That you can forget about," Sol said. "'Kwash' is short for 'kwashiorkor.' If, in the interest of good health, you watched the medical programs like I do, or opened a book, you would know all about it. You can't catch it because it's a deficiency disease like beriberi."

"I never heard of that either," Shirl said.

"There's not so much of that, but there's plenty of kwash. It comes from not eating enough protein. They used to have it only in Africa but now they got it right across the whole U.S. Isn't that great? There's no meat around, lentils and soybeans cost too much, so the mamas stuff the kids with weedcrackers and candy, whatever is cheap. . . ."

The light bulb flickered, then went out. Sol felt his way across the room and found a switch in the maze of wiring on top of the refrigerator. A dim bulb lit up, connected to his batteries. "Needs a charge," he said, "but it can wait until morning. You shouldn't exercise after eating, bad for the circulation and digestion."

"I'm sure glad you're here, Doctor," Andy said. "I need some medical advice. I've got this trouble. You see—everything I eat goes to my stomach. . . ."

"Very funny, Mr. Wiseguy. Shirl, I don't see how you put up with this joker."

They all felt better after the meal and they talked for a while, until Sol announced he was turning off the light to save the juice in the batteries. The small bricks of sea coal had burned to ash and the room was growing cold. They said good night and Andy went in first to get his flashlight; their room was even colder than the other.

"I'm going to bed," Shirl said. "I'm not really tired, but it's the only way to keep warm."

Andy flicked the overhead light switch uselessly. "The current is still off and there are some things I have to do. What is it—a week now since we had any electricity in the evening?"

"Let me get into bed and I'll work the flash for you—will that be all right?"

"It'll have to do."

He opened his notepad on top of the dresser, lay one of the reusable forms next to it, then began copying information into the report. With his left hand he kept a slow and regular squeezing on the flashlight that produced steady illumination. The city was quiet tonight with the people driven from the streets by the cold and the rain; the whir of the tiny generator and the occasional squeak of the stylo on plastic sounded unnaturally loud. There was enough light from the flash for Shirl to get undressed by. She shivered when she took off her outer clothes and quickly pulled on heavy winter pajamas, a much-darned pair of socks she used for sleeping in, then put her heavy sweater on top. The sheets were cold and damp, they hadn't been changed since the water shortage, though she did try to air them out as often as she could. Her cheeks were damp, as damp as the sheets were when she put her fingertips up to touch them, and she realized that she was crying. She tried not to sniffle and bother Andy. He was doing his best, wasn't he? Everything that it was possible to do. Yes, it had been a lot different before she came here, an easy life, good food and a warm room, and her own bodyguard, Tab, when she went out. And all she had to do was sleep with him a couple of times a week. She had hated it, even the touch of his hands, but at least it had been quick. Having Andy in bed was different and good and she wished that he were there right now. She shivered again and wished she could stop crying.

WINTER

New York City trembled on the brink of disaster. Every locked warehouse was a nucleus of dissent, surrounded by crowds who were hungry and afraid and searching for someone to blame. Their anger incited them to riot, and the food riots turned to water riots and then to looting, wherever this was possible. The police fought back, only the thinnest of barriers between angry protest and bloody chaos.

At first nightsticks and weighted clubs stopped the trouble, and when this failed gas dispersed the crowds. The tension grew, since the people who fled only reassembled again in a different place. The solid jets of water from the riot trucks stopped them easily when they tried to break into the Welfare stations, but there were not enough trucks, nor was there more water to be had once they had pumped dry their tanks. The Health Department had forbid the use of river water: it would have been like spraying poison. The little water that was available was badly needed for the fires that were springing up throughout the city. With the streets blocked in many places the fire-fighting equipment could not get through and the trucks were forced to make long detours. Some of the fires were spreading and by noon all of the equipment had been committed and was in use.

The first gun was fired a few minutes past 12 on the morning of December 21st, by a Welfare Department guard who killed a man who had broken open a window of the Tompkins Square food depot and had tried to climb in. This was the first but not the last shot fired—nor was it the last person to be killed.

Flying wire sealed off some of the trouble areas, but there was only a limited supply of it. When it ran out the copters fluttered helplessly over the surging streets and acted as aerial observation posts for the police, finding the places where reserves were sorely needed. It was a fruitless labor because there were no reserves, everyone was in the front line.

After the first conflict nothing else made a strong impression on Andy. For the rest of the day and most of the night, he along with every other policeman in the city was braving violence and giving violence to restore law and order to a city torn by battle. The only rest he had was after he had fallen victim to his own gas and had managed to make his way to the Department of Hospitals ambulance for treatment. An orderly washed out his eyes and gave him a tablet to counteract the gut-tearing nausea. He lay on one of the stretchers inside, clutching his helmet, bombs and club to his chest, while he recovered. The ambulance driver sat on another stretcher by the door, armed with a .30-caliber carbine, to discourage anyone from too great an interest in the ambulance or its valuable surgical contents. Andy would like to have lain there longer, but the cold mist was rolling in through the open doorway, and he began to shiver so hard that his teeth shook together. It was difficult to drag to his feet and climb to the ground; yet once he was moving he felt a little better—and warmer. The attack had been broken up and he moved slowly to join the nearest cluster of blue-coated figures, wrinkling his nose at the foul odor of his clothes.

From this point on, the fatigue never left him and he had memories only of shouting faces, running feet, the sound of shots, screams, the thud of gas grenades, of something unseen that had been thrown at him and hit the back of his hand and raised an immense bruise.

By nightfall it was raining, a cold downpour mixed with sleet, and it was this and exhaustion that drove the people from the streets, not the police. Yet when the crowds were gone the police found that their work was just beginning. Gaping windows and broken doorways had to be guarded until they could be repaired, the injured had to be found and brought in for treatment, while the Fire Department needed aid in halting the countless fires. This went on through the night and at dawn Andy found himself slumped on a bench in the precinct, hearing his name being called off from a list by Lieutenant Grassioli.

"And that's all that can be spared," the lieutenant added. "You men draw rations before you leave and turn in your riot equipment. I want you all back here at eighteen-hundred and I don't want excuses. Our troubles aren't over yet."

Sometime during the night the rain had stopped. The rising sun cast long shadows down the crosstown streets, putting a golden sheen on the wet, black pavement. A burned-out brownstone was still smoking and Andy picked his way through the charred wreckage that littered the street in front of it. On the corner of Seventh Avenue were the crushed wrecks of two pedicabs, already stripped of any usable parts, and a few feet farther on, the huddled body of a man. He might be asleep, but when Andy passed, the upturned face gave violent evidence that the man was dead. He walked on, ignoring it. The Department of Sanitation would be collecting only corpses today.

The first cavemen were coming out of the subway entrance, blinking at the light. During the summer everyone laughed at the cavemen—the people whom Welfare had assigned to living quarters in the stations of the now-silent subways—but as the cold weather approached, the laughter was replaced by envy. Perhaps it was filthy down there, dusty, dark, but there were always a few electric heaters turned on. They weren't living in luxury, but at least Welfare didn't let them freeze. Andy turned into his own block.

Going up the stairs in his building, he trod heavily on some of the sleepers but was too fatigued to care—or even notice. He had trouble fumbling his key into the lock and Sol heard him and came to open it.

"I just made some soup," Sol said. "You timed it perfectly."

Andy pulled the broken remains of some weedcrackers from his coat pocket and spilled them onto the table.

"Been stealing food?" Sol asked, picking up a piece and nibbling on it. "I thought no grub was being given out for two more days?"

"Police ration."

"Only fair. You can't beat up the citizenry on an empty stomach. I'll throw some of these into the soup, give it some body. I guess you didn't see TV yesterday so you wouldn't know about all the fun and games in Congress. Things are really jumping. . . ."

"Is Shirl awake yet?" Andy asked, shucking out of his coat and dropping heavily into a chair.

Sol was silent a moment, then he said slowly, "She's not here."

Andy yawned. "It's pretty early to go out. Why?"

"Not today, Andy." Sol stirred the soup with his back turned. "She went out yesterday, a couple of hours after you did. She's not back yet—"

"You mean she was out all the time during the riots—and last night too? What did you do?" He sat upright, his bone-weariness forgotten.

"What could I do? Go out and get myself trampled to death like the rest of the old fogies? I bet she's all right, she probably saw all the trouble and decided to stay with friends instead of coming back here."

"What friends? What are you talking about? I have to go find her."

"Sit!" Sol ordered. "What can you do out there? Have some soup and get some sleep, that's the best thing you can do. She'll be okay. I know it," he added reluctantly.

"What do you know, Sol?" Andy took him by the shoulders, half turning him from the stove.

"Don't handle the merchandise!" Sol shouted, pushing the hand away. Then, in a quieter voice: "All I know is she just didn't go out of here for nothing, she had a reason. She had her old coat on, but I could see what looked like a real nifty dress underneath. And nylon stockings. A fortune on her legs. And when she said so long I saw she had lots of makeup on."

"Sol—what are you trying to say?"

"I'm not trying—I'm saying. She was dressed for visiting, not for shopping, like she was on the way out to see someone. Her old man, maybe, she could be visiting him."

"Why should she want to see him?"

"You tell me. You two had a fight, didn't you? Maybe she went away for a while to cool off."

"A fight . . . I guess so." Andy dropped back into the chair, squeezing his forehead with his palms. Had it only been last night? No, the night before last. It seemed 100 years since they had had that stupid argument. But they were bickering so much these days. One more fight shouldn't make any difference. He looked up with sudden fear. "She didn't take her things—anything with her?" he asked.

"Just a little bag," Sol said, and put a steaming bowl on the table in front of Andy. "Eat up. I'll pour one for myself." Then, "She'll be back."

Andy was almost too tired to argue—and what could be said? He spooned the soup automatically, then realized as he tasted it that he was very hungry. He ate with his elbow on the table, his free hand supporting his head.

"You should have heard the speeches in the Senate yesterday," Sol said. "Funniest show on earth. They're trying to push this Emergency Bill through— some emergency, it's only been 100 years in the making—and you should hear them talking all around the little points and not mentioning the big ones." His voice settled into a rich Southern accent. "Faced by dire straits, we propose a survey of all the ee-mense riches of this the greatest ee-luvial basin, the delta, suh, of the mightiest of rivers, the Mississippi. Dikes and drains, suh, science, suh, and you will have here the richest farmlands in the Western World!" Sol blew on his soup angrily. "'Dikes' is right—another finger in the dike. They've been over this ground a thousand times before. But does anyone mention out loud the sole and only reason for the Emergency Bill? They do not. After all these years they're too chicken to come right out and tell the truth, so they got it hidden away in one of the little riders tacked onto the bottom."

"What are you talking about?" Andy asked, only half listening, still worrying about Shirl.

"Birth control, that's what. They are finally getting around to legalizing clinics that will be open to anyone—married or not—and making it a law that all mothers *must* be supplied with birth-control information. Boy, are we going to hear some howling when the blue-noses find out about that—and the Pope will really plotz!"

"Not now, Sol, I'm tired. Did Shirl say anything about when she would be back?"

"Just what I told you. . . ." He stopped and listened to the sound of footsteps coming down the hall. They stopped—and there was a light knocking on the door.

Andy was there first, twisting at the knob, tearing the door open.

"Shirl!" he said. "Are you all right?"

"Yes, sure—I'm fine."

He held her to him, tightly, almost cutting off her breath. "With the riots—I didn't know what to think," he said. "I just came in a little while ago myself. Where have you been? What happened?"

"I just wanted to get out for a while, that's all." She wrinkled her nose. "What's that funny smell?"

He stepped away from her, anger welling up through the fatigue. "I caught some of my own puke gas and heaved up. It's hard to get off. What do you mean that you wanted to get out for a while?"

"Let me get my coat off."

Andy followed her into the other room and closed the door behind them. She was taking a pair of high-heeled shoes out of the bag she carried and putting them into the closet. "Well?" he said.

"Just that, it's not complicated. I was feeling trapped in here, with the shortages and the cold and everything, and never seeing you, and I felt bad about the fight we had. Nothing seemed to be going right. So I thought if I dressed up and went to one of the restaurants where I used to go, just have a cup of koffee or something, I might feel better. A morale booster, you know." She looked up at his cold face, then glanced quickly away.

"Then what happened?" he asked.

"I'm not in the witness box, Andy. Why the accusing tone?"

He turned his back and looked out the window. "I'm not accusing you of anything, but—you were out all night. How do you expect me to feel?"

"Well, you know how bad it was yesterday, I was afraid to come back. I was up at Curley's—"

"The meateasy?"

"Yes, but if you don't eat anything it's not expensive. It's just the food that costs. I met some people I knew and we talked, they were going to a party and invited me and I went along. We were watching the news about the riots on TV and no one wanted to go out, so the party just went on and on." She paused. "That's all."

"All?" An angry question, a dark suspicion.

"That's all," she said, and her voice was now as cold as his.

She turned her back to him and began to pull off her dress, and their words lay like a cold barrier between them. Andy dropped onto the bed and turned his back on her as well so that they were like strangers, even in the tiny room.

SPRING

The funeral drew them together as nothing else had during the cold depths of the winter. It was a raw day, gusting wind and rain, but there was still a feeling that winter was on the way out. But it had been too long a winter for Sol and his cough had turned into a cold, the cold into pneumonia, and what can an old man do in a cold room without drugs in a winter that does not seem to end? Die, that was all, so he had died. They had forgotten their differences during his illness and Shirl had nursed him as best she could, but careful nursing does not cure pneumonia. The funeral had been as brief and cold as the day and in the early darkness they went back to the room. They had not been back half an hour before there was a quick rapping on the door. Shirl gasped.

"The callboy. They can't. You don't have to work today."

"Don't worry. Even Grassy wouldn't go back on his word about a thing like this. And besides, that's not the callboy's knock."

"Maybe a friend of Sol's who couldn't get to the funeral."

She went to unlock the door and had to blink into the darkness of the hall for a moment before she recognized the man standing there.

"Tab! It is you, isn't it? Come in, don't stand there. Andy, I told you about Tab my bodyguard. . . ."

"Afternoon, Miss Shirl," Tab said stolidly, staying in the hall. "I'm sorry, but this is no social call. I'm on the job now."

"What is it?" Andy asked, walking over next to Shirl.

"You have to realize I take the work that is offered to me," Tab said. He was unsmiling and gloomy. "I've been in the bodyguard pool since September, just the odd jobs, no regular assignment, we take whatever work we can get. A man turns down a job he goes right back to the end of the list. I have a family to feed. . . ."

"What are you trying to say?" Andy asked. He was aware that someone was standing in the darkness behind Tab and he could tell by the shuffle of feet that there were others out of sight down the hall.

"Don't take no stuff," the man in back of Tab said in an unpleasant nasal voice. He stayed behind the bodyguard where he could not be seen. "I got the law on my side. I paid you. Show him the order!"

"I think I understand now," Andy said. "Get away from the door, Shirl. Come inside, Tab, so we can talk to you."

Tab started forward and the man in the hall tried to follow him. "You don't go in there without me —" he shrilled. His voice was cut off as Andy slammed the door in his face.

"I wish you hadn't done that," Tab said. He was wearing his spike-studded iron knucks, his fist clenched tight around them.

"Relax," Andy said. "I just wanted to talk to you alone first, find out what was going on. He has a squat-order, doesn't he?"

Tab nodded, looking unhappily down at the floor.

"What on earth are you two talking about?" Shirl asked, worriedly glancing back and forth at their set expressions.

Andy didn't answer and Tab turned to her. "A squat-order is issued by the court to anyone who can prove they are really in need of a place to live. They only give so many out, and usually just to people with big families that have had to get out of some other place. With a squat-order you can look around and find a vacant apartment or room or anything like that, and the order is a sort of search warrant. There can be trouble, people don't want to have strangers walking in on them, that kind of thing, so anyone with a squat-order takes along a bodyguard. That's where I come in, the party out there in the hall, name of Belicher, hired me."

"But what are you doing here?" Shirl asked, still not understanding.

"Because Belicher is a ghoul, that's why," Andy said bitterly. "He hangs around the morgue looking for bodies."

"That's one way of saying it," Tab answered, holding on to his temper. "He's also a guy with a wife and kids and no place to live, that's another way of looking at it."

There was a sudden hammering on the door and Belicher's complaining voice could be heard outside. Shirl finally realized the significance of Tab's presence, and she gasped. "You're here because you're helping them," she said. "They found out that Sol is dead and they want this room."

Tab could only nod mutely.

"There's still a way out," Andy said. "If we had one of the men here from my precinct, living in here, then these people couldn't get in."

The knocking was louder and Tab took a half step backward toward the door. "If there was somebody here now, that would be okay, but Belicher could probably take the thing to the squat court and get occupancy anyway because he has a family. I'll do what I can to help you—but Belicher, he's still my employer."

"Don't open that door," Andy said sharply. "Not until we have this straightened out."

"I have to—what else can I do?" He straightened up and closed his fist with the knucks on it. "Don't try to stop me, Andy. You're a policeman, you know the law about this."

"Tab, must you?" Shirl asked in a low voice.

He turned to her, eyes filled with unhappiness. "We were good friends once, Shirl, and that's the way I'm going to remember it. But you're not going to think much of me after this because I have to do my job. I have to let them in."

"Go ahead—open the damn door," Andy said bitterly, turning his back and walking over to the window.

The Belichers swarmed in. Mr. Belicher was thin, with a strangely shaped head, almost no chin and just enough intelligence to sign his name to the Welfare application. Mrs. Belicher was the support of the family; from the flabby fat of her body came the children, all seven of them, to swell the Relief allotment on which they survived. Number eight was pushing an extra bulge out of the dough of her flesh; it was really number 11 since three of the younger Belichers had perished through indifference or accident. The largest girl, she must have been all of 12, was carrying the sore-covered infant, which stank abominably and cried continuously. The other children shouted at each other now, released from the silence and tension of the dark hall.

"Oh, looka the nice fridge," Mrs. Belicher said, waddling over and opening the door.

"Don't touch that," Andy said, and Belicher pulled him by the arm.

"I like this room—it's not big, you know, but nice. What's in here?" He started toward the open door in the partition.

"That's my room," Andy said, slamming it shut in his face. "Just keep out of there."

"No need to act like that," Belicher said, sidling away quickly like a dog that has been kicked too often. "I got my rights. The law says I can look wherever I want with a squat-order." He moved farther away as Andy took a step toward him. "Not that I'm doubting your word, mister, I believe you. This room here is fine, got a good table, chairs, bed. . . ."

"Those things belong to me. This is an empty room, and a small one at that. It's not big enough for you and all your family."

"It's big enough, all right. We lived in smaller. . . ."

"Andy—stop them! Look—" Shirl's unhappy cry spun Andy around and he saw that two of the boys had found the packets of herbs that Sol had grown so carefully in his window box, and were tearing them open, thinking that it was food of some kind.

"Put these things down," he shouted, but before he could reach them they had tasted the herbs, then spat them out.

"Burn my mouth!" the bigger boy screamed and sprayed the contents of the packet on the floor. The other boy bounced up and down with excitement and began to do the same thing with the rest of the herbs. They twisted away from Andy and before he could stop them the packets were empty.

As soon as Andy turned away, the younger boy, still excited, climbed on the table—his mud-stained foot wrappings leaving filthy smears—and turned up the TV. Blaring music crashed over the screams of the children and the ineffectual calls of their mother. Tab pulled Belicher away as he opened the wardrobe to see what was inside.

"Get these kids out of here," Andy said, white-faced with rage.

"I got a squat-order, I got rights," Belicher shouted, backing away and waving an imprinted square of plastic.

"I don't care what rights you have," Andy told him, opening the hall door. "We'll talk about that when these brats are outside."

Tab settled it by grabbing the nearest child by the scruff of the neck and pushing it out through the door. "Mr. Rusch is right," he said. "The kids can wait outside while we settle this."

Mrs. Belicher sat down heavily on the bed and closed her eyes, as though all this had nothing to do with her. Mr. Belicher retreated against the wall saying something that no one heard or bothered to listen to. There were some shrill cries and angry sobbing from the hall as the last child was expelled.

Andy looked around and realized that Shirl had gone into their room; he heard the key turn in the lock. "I suppose this is it?" he said, looking steadily at Tab.

The bodyguard shrugged helplessly. "I'm sorry, Andy, honest to God I am. What else can I do? It's the law, and if they want to stay here, you can't get them out."

"It's the law, it's the law," Belicher echoed tonelessly.

There was nothing Andy could do with his clenched fists and he had to force himself to open them. "Help me carry these things into the other room, will you, Tab?"

"Sure," Tab said, and took the other end of the table. "Try and explain to Shirl about my part in this, will you? I don't think she understands that it's just a job I have to do."

Their footsteps crackled on the dried herbs and seeds that littered the floor and Andy did not answer him.

♔ JOANNA RUSS (1937-)

Like Kurt Vonnegut, Joanna Russ has done much to give Science Fiction legitimacy in old canonical literary circles. She also has been a leader in expanding the genre, in making it progressive and far-reaching, and in providing a strong feminist voice for the genre. Her novel The Female Man *(1975) might be argued to be the most important work of feminist Science Fiction ever produced.*

Joanna Russ is a distinguished college and university lecturer and professor. She has authored a range of novels, short stories, nonfiction essays, and literary criticism for almost forty years. Her stories often feature strong female characters and address significant women's issues. Russ is invariably credible and insightful in her writing, and she effectively uses Science Fiction as a vehicle to express her informed worldview. She has an extensive knowledge of cultural and literary history and hard sciences, such as biology.

If we consider, for example, Joanna Russ's use of Science Fiction to discuss sexuality, then it is appropriate to place the author's contributions in this regard in the company of works by authors such as Philip José Farmer, Harlan Ellison, Marion Zimmer Bradley, Samuel R. Delany, and Alice Sheldon (a.k.a. James Tiptree Jr.). However, feminism and sexuality are not the only human and social issues Russ adeptly discusses. She also deals with such sensitive subjects as racism, religion, and politics.

"When It Changed" is a story that uses the idea of a female society to comment on the whole of humanity.

When It Changed

(Again, Dangerous Visions, *ed. Harlan Ellison, 1972*)

Katy drives like a maniac; we must have been doing over 120 kilometers per hour on those turns. She's good, though, extremely good, and I've seen her take the whole car apart and put it together again in a day. My birthplace on Whileaway was largely given to farm machinery and I refuse to wrestle with a five-gear shift at unholy speeds, not having been brought up to it, but even on those turns in the middle of the night, on a country road as bad as only our district can make them, Katy's driving didn't scare me. The funny thing about my wife, though: she will not handle guns. She has even gone hiking in the forests above the forty-eighth parallel without firearms, for days at a time. And that *does* scare me.

Katy and I have three children between us, one of hers and two of mine. Yuriko, my eldest, was asleep in the back seat, dreaming twelve-year-old dreams of love and war: running away to sea, hunting in the North, dreams of strangely beautiful people in strangely beautiful places, all the wonderful guff you think up when you're turning twelve and the glands start going. Some day soon, like all of them, she will disappear for weeks on end to come back grimy and proud, having knifed her first cougar or shot her first bear, dragging some abominably dangerous dead beastie behind her, which I will never forgive for what it might have done to my daughter. Yuriko says Katy's driving puts her to sleep.

For someone who has fought three duels, I am afraid of far, far too much. I'm getting old. I told this to my wife.

"You're thirty-four," she said. Laconic to the point of silence, that one. She flipped the lights on, on the dash—three kilometers to go and the road getting worse all the time. Far out in the country. Electric-green trees rushed into our headlights and around the car. I reached down next to me where we bolt the carrier panel to the door and eased my rifle into my lap. Yuriko stirred in the back. My height but Katy's eyes, Katy's face. The car engine is so quiet, Katy says, that you can hear breathing in the back seat. Yuki had been alone in the car when the message came, enthusiastically decoding her dot-dashes (silly to mount a wide-frequency transceiver near an I. C. engine, but most of Whileaway is on steam). She had thrown herself out of the car, my gangly and gaudy offspring, shouting at the top of her lungs, so of course she had had to come along. We've been intellectually prepared for this ever since the Colony was founded, ever since it was abandoned, but this is different. This is awful.

"Men!" Yuki had screamed, leaping over the car door. "They've come back! Real Earth men!"

We met them in the kitchen of the farmhouse near the place where they had landed; the windows were open, the night air very mild. We had passed all sorts of transportation when we parked outside—steam tractors, trucks, an I. C. flatbed, even a bicycle. Lydia, the district biologist, had come out of her Northern taciturnity long enough to take blood and urine samples and was sitting in a corner of the kitchen shaking her head in astonishment over the results; she even forced herself (very big, very fair, very shy, always painfully blushing) to dig up the old language manuals—though I can talk the old tongues in my sleep. And do. Lydia is uneasy with us; we're Southerners and too flamboyant. I counted twenty people in that kitchen, all the brains of North Continent. Phyllis Spet, I think, had come in by glider. Yuki was the only child there.

Then I saw the four of them.

They are bigger than we are. They are bigger and broader. Two were taller than I, and I am extremely tall, one meter eighty centimeters in my bare feet. They are obviously of our species but *off*, indescribably off, and as my eyes could not and still cannot quite comprehend the lines of those alien bodies, I could not, then, bring myself to touch them, though the one who spoke Russian—what voices they have—wanted to "shake hands," a custom from the past, I imagine. I can only say they were apes with human faces. He seemed to mean well, but I found myself shuddering back almost the length of the kitchen—and then I laughed apologetically—and then to set a good example (*interstellar amity*, I thought) did "shake hands" finally. A hard, hard hand. They are heavy as draft horses. Blurred, deep voices. Yuriko had sneaked in between the adults and was gazing at *the men* with her mouth open.

He turned *his* head—those words have not been in our language for six hundred years—and said, in bad Russian:

"Who's that?"

"My daughter," I said, and added (with that irrational attention to good manners we sometimes employ in moments of insanity), "My daughter, Yuriko Janetson. We use the patronymic. You would say matronymic."

He laughed, involuntarily. Yuki exclaimed, "I thought they would be *good-looking!*" greatly disappointed at this reception of herself. Phyllis Helgason Spet, whom someday I shall kill, gave me across the room a cold, level, venomous look, as if to say: *Watch what you say. You know what I can do.* It's true that I have little formal status, but Madam President will get herself in serious trouble with both me and her own staff if she continues to consider industrial espionage good clean fun. Wars and rumors of wars, as it says in one of our ancestors' books.

I translated Yuki's words into *the man's* dog-Russian, once our *lingua franca*, and *the man* laughed again.

"Where are all your people?" he said conversationally.

I translated again and watched the faces around the room; Lydia embarrassed (as usual), Spet narrowing her eyes with some damned scheme, Katy very pale.

"This is Whileaway," I said.

He continued to look unenlightened.

"Whileaway," I said. "Do you remember? Do you have records? There was a plague on Whileaway."

He looked moderately interested. Heads turned in the back of the room, and I caught a glimpse of the local professions-parliament delegate; by morning every town meeting, every district caucus, would be in full session.

"Plague?" he said. "That's most unfortunate."

"Yes," I said. "Most unfortunate. We lost half our population in one generation."

He looked properly impressed.

"Whileaway was lucky," I said. "We had a big initial gene pool, we had been chosen for extreme intelligence, we had a high technology and a large remaining population in which every adult was two-or-three experts in one. The soil is good. The climate is blessedly easy. There are thirty millions of us now. Things are beginning to snowball in industry—do you understand?—give us seventy years and we'll have more than one real city, more than a few industrial centers, full-time professions, full-time radio operators, full-time machinists, give us seventy years and not everyone will have to spend three-quarters of a lifetime on the farm." And I tried to explain how hard it is when artists can practice full-time only in old age, when there are so few, so very few who can be free, like Katy and myself. I tried also to outline our government, the two houses, the one by professions and the geographic one; I told him the district caucuses handled problems too big for the individual towns. And that population control was not a political issue, not yet, though give us time and it would be. This was a delicate point in our history; give us time. There was no need to sacrifice the quality of life for an insane rush into industrialization. Let us go our own pace. Give us time.

"Where are all the people?" said that monomaniac.

I realized then that he did not mean people, he meant *men*, and he was giving the word the meaning it had not had on Whileaway for six centuries.

"They died," I said. "Thirty generations ago."

I thought we had poleaxed him. He caught his breath. He made as if to get out of the chair he was sitting in; he put his hand to his chest; he looked around at us with the strangest blend of awe and sentimental tenderness. Then he said, solemnly and earnestly:

"A great tragedy."

I waited, not quite understanding.

"Yes," he said, catching his breath again with the queer smile, that adult-to-child smile that tells you something is being hidden and will be presently produced with cries of encouragement and joy, "a great tragedy. But it's over." And again he looked around at all of us with the strangest deference. As if we were invalids.

"You've adapted amazingly," he said.

"To what?" I said. He looked embarrassed. He looked inane. Finally he said, "Where I come from, the women don't dress so plainly."

"Like you?" I said. "Like a bride?" for the men were wearing silver from head to foot. I had never seen anything so gaudy. He made as if to answer and then apparently thought better of it; he laughed at me again. With an odd exhilaration—as if we were something childish and something wonderful, as if he were doing us an enormous favor—he took one shaky breath and said, "Well, we're here."

I looked at Spet, Spet looked at Lydia, Lydia looked at Amalia, who is the head of the local town meeting, Amalia looked at I don't know whom. My throat was raw. I cannot stand local beer, which the farmers swill as if their stomachs had iridium linings, but I took it anyway, from Amalia (it was her bicycle we had seen outside as we parked), and swallowed it all. This was going to take a long time. I said, "Yes, here you are," and smiled (feeling like a fool), and wondered seriously if male-Earth-people's minds worked so very differently from female-Earth-people's minds, but that couldn't be so or the race would have died out long ago. The radio network had got the news around planet by now and we had another Russian speaker, flown in from Varna; I decided to cut out when *the man* passed around pictures of his wife, who looked like the priestess of some arcane cult. He proposed to question Yuki, so I barreled her into a back room in spite of her furious protests, and went out on the front porch. As I left, Lydia was explaining the difference between parthenogenesis (which is so easy that anyone can practice it) and what we do, which is the merging of ova. That is why Katy's baby looks like me. Lydia went on to the Ansky Process and Katy Ansky, our one full-polymath genius and the great-great I don't know how many times great-grandmother of my own Katharina.

A dot-dash transmitter in one of the outbuildings chattered faintly to itself: operators flirting and passing jokes down the line.

There was a man on the porch. The other tall man. I watched him for a few minutes—I can move very quietly when I want to and when I allowed him to see me, he stopped talking into the little machine hung around his neck. Then he said calmly, in excellent Russian, "Did you know that sexual equality has been reestablished on Earth?"

"You're the real one," I said, "aren't you? The other one's for show." It was a great relief to get things cleared up. He nodded affably.

"As a people, we are not very bright," he said. "There's been too much genetic damage in the last few centuries. Radiation. Drugs. We can use Whileaway's genes, Janet." Strangers do not call strangers by the first name.

"You can have cells enough to drown in," I said. "Breed your own."

He smiled. "That's not the way we want to do it." Behind him I saw Katy come into the square of light that was the screened-in door. He went on, low and urbane, not mocking me, I think, but with the self-confidence of someone who has always had money and strength to spare, who doesn't know what it is to be second-class or provincial. Which is very odd, because the day before, I would have said that was an exact description of me.

"I'm talking to you, Janet," he said, "because I suspect you have more popular influence than anyone else here. You know as well as I do that parthenogenetic culture has all sorts of inherent defects, and we do not—if we can help it—mean to use you for anything of the sort. Pardon me; I should not have said 'use.' But surely you can see that this kind of society is unnatural."

"Humanity is unnatural," said Katy. She had my rifle under her left arm. The top of that silky head does not quite come up to my collarbone, but she is as tough as steel; he began to move, again with that queer smiling deference (which his fellow had showed to me but he had not), and the gun slid into Katy's grip as if she had shot with it all her life.

"I agree," said the man. "Humanity is unnatural. I should know. I have metal in my teeth and metal pins here." He touched his shoulder. "Seals are harem animals," he added, "and so are men; apes are promiscuous and so are men; doves are monogamous and so are men; there are even celibate men and homosexual men. There are homosexual cows, I believe. But Whileaway is still missing something." He gave a dry chuckle. I will give him the credit of believing that it had something to do with nerves.

"I miss nothing," said Katy, "except that life isn't endless."

"You are—?" said the man, nodding from me to her.

"Wives," said Katy. "We're married." Again the dry chuckle.

"A good economic arrangement," he said, "for working and taking care of the children. And as good an arrangement as any for randomizing heredity, if your reproduction is made to follow the same pattern. But think, Katharina Michaelason, if there isn't something better that you might secure for your daughters. I believe in instincts, even in Man, and I can't think that the two of you—a machinist, are you? and I gather you are some sort of chief of police—don't feel somehow what even you must miss. You know it intellectually, of course. There is only half a species here. Men must come back to Whileaway."

Katy said nothing.

"I should think, Katharina Michaelason," said the man gently, "that you, of all people, would benefit most from such a change," and he walked past Katy's rifle into the square of light coming from the door. I think it was then that he noticed my scar, which really does not show unless the light is from the side: a fine line that runs from temple to chin. Most people don't even know about it.

"Where did you get that?" he said, and I answered with an involuntary grin. "In my last duel." We stood there bristling at each other for several seconds (this is absurd but true) until he went inside and shut the screen door behind him. Katy said in a brittle voice, "You damned fool, don't you know when we've been insulted?" and swung up the rifle to shoot him through the screen, but I got to her before she could fire and knocked the rifle out of aim; it burned a hole through the porch floor. Katy was shaking. She kept whispering over and over, "That's why I never touched it, because I knew I'd kill someone. I knew I'd kill someone." The first man—the one I'd spoken with first—was still talking inside the house, something about the grand movement to recolonize and rediscover all the Earth had lost. He stressed the advantages to Whileaway: trade, exchange of ideas, education. He, too, said that sexual equality had been reestablished on Earth.

Katy was right, of course; we should have burned them down where they stood. Men are coming to Whileaway. When one culture has the big guns and the other has none, there is a certain predictability about the outcome. Maybe men would have come eventually in any case. I like to think that a hundred years from now my great-grandchildren could have stood them off or fought them to a standstill, but even that's no odds; I will remember all my life those four people I first met who were muscled like bulls and who made me—if only for a moment—feel small. A neurotic reaction, Katy says. I remember everything that happened that night; I remember Yuki's excitement in the car, I remember Katy's sobbing when we got home as if her heart would break, I remember her lovemaking, a little peremptory as always, but wonderfully soothing and comforting. I remember prowling restlessly around the house after Katy fell asleep with one bare arm hung into a patch of light from the hall. The muscles of her forearms are like metal bars from all that driving and testing of her machines. Sometimes I dream about Katy's arms. I remember wandering into the nursery and picking up my wife's baby, dozing for a while with the poignant, amazing warmth of an infant in my lap, and finally returning to the kitchen to find Yuriko fixing herself a late snack. My daughter eats like a Great Dane.

"Yuki," I said, "do you think you could fall in love with a man?" and she whooped derisively. "With a ten-foot toad!" said my tactful child.

But men are coming to Whileaway. Lately I sit up nights and worry about the men who will come to this planet, about my two daughters and Betta Katharinason, about what will happen to Katy, to me, to my life. Our ancestors' journals are one long cry of pain and I suppose I ought to be glad now, but one can't throw away six centuries, or even (as I have lately discovered) thirty-four years. Sometimes I laugh at the question those four men hedged about all evening and never quite dared to ask, looking at the lot of us, hicks in overalls, farmers in canvas pants and plain shirts: *Which of you plays the role of the man?* As if we had to produce a carbon copy of their mistakes! I doubt very much that sexual equality has been reestablished on Earth. I do not like to think of myself mocked, of Katy deferred to as if she were weak, of Yuki made to feel unimportant or silly, of my other children cheated of their full humanity or turned into strangers. And I'm afraid that my own achievements will dwindle from what they were—or what I thought they were—to the not-very-interesting curiosa of the *human* race, the oddities you read about in the back of the book, things to laugh at sometimes because they are so exotic, quaint but not impressive, charming but not useful. I find this more painful than I can say. You will agree that for a woman who has fought three duels, all of them kills, indulging in such fears is ludicrous. But what's around the corner now is a duel so big that I don't think I have the guts for it; in Faust's words: *Verweile doch, du bist so schoen!* Keep it as it is. Don't change.

Sometimes at night I remember the original name of this planet, changed by the first generation of our ancestors, those curious women for whom, I suppose, the real name was too painful a reminder after the men died. I find it amusing, in a grim way, to see it all so completely turned around. This, too, shall pass. All good things must come to an end.

Take my life but don't take away the meaning of my life.

For-A-While.

❦ DEAN R(AY) KOONTZ (1945–)

Today primarily a best-selling author of mainstream and suspense novels tinged with Dark Fantasy, Dean R. Koontz is a multitalented author who began writing Science Fiction in the 1960s. Through the years, the prolific Koontz has used an array of pseudonyms in addition to his own name. Like Ray Bradbury, Dean Koontz's strongest thematic element in his storytelling is autobiography.

Koontz's writing features strong, well-developed plotting. It incorporates multidimensional characters—many of whom are very realistically drawn and with whom readers

can relate. As much as Stephen King, his writing not only is popular culture, it also incor-
porates popular culture into its very fabric. A good deal of Dean Koontz's success as an au-
thor stems from his ability to tap into his readers' cultural heritage and personal experi-
ence. He utilizes the popular mythology that has molded and framed his own life and his
readers' lives in his storytelling. In other words, the author's ability to combine his autobi-
ography with the popular culture and mythology of his readers accounts for a great deal of
his best-selling status.

Dean R. Koontz's writing has been adapted for both film and television. Most notable
are the film versions of Demon Seed *(novel 1973, film 1977) and* Phantoms *(novel*
1983, film 1997).

"The Undercity" is vintage Dean R. Koontz Science Fiction. In many ways, it resem-
bles the writing of Harry Harrison of the same period.

The Undercity

(The Future City, *ed. Roger Elwood, 1973)*

Well, kid, it was a busy day. You might even say it was a harrowing day, and you
might be tempted to think that it was somehow out of the ordinary. But you must
understand, straight off, that it was perfectly normal as business days go, no better
and no worse than ten thousand days before it. And if I live so long, it won't be
appreciably different from any of ten thousand days to follow. Remember that. If
you want to enter the family business, kid, you have to be able to cope with long
strings of days like this one, calendars full of them.

Once, when the cities weren't a tenth as large as they are now, when a man
might travel and might have business contacts throughout the world, we were
called The Underworld, and we were envied and feared. We are still envied and
feared, but now we're called The Undercity, because that is the world to us, and
more than we can rightly handle anyway. I, for one, would be happy to roll things
back, to break down these hundred-story megalopolises and live in a time where
we could call ourselves a part of The Underworld, because things were a hell of a
lot easier then for our type. Just consider . . .

Nearly all forms of gambling were illegal back then. An enterprising young
man could step in, buck the law, and clean up a tidy sum with a minimal financial
outlay and with almost no personal risk at all. Cops and judges were on the take;
clandestine casinos, street games and storefront betting shops thrived. No longer.
They legalized it, and they gave us bank clerks for casino managers, CPA's instead
of bouncers. They made gambling respectable — and boring.

Drugs were illegal then, too. Grass, hash, skag, coke, speed . . . God, an enterprising young kid like yourself could make a fortune in a year. But now grass
and hash are traded on the open market, and all the harder drugs are available to
all the loonies who will sign a health waiver and buy them from the government.
Where's the thrill now? Gone. And where's the profit? Gone, too.

Sex. Oh, kid, the money to be made on sex, back then. It was *all* illegal: prosti-
tution, dirty movies, picture postcards, erotic dancing, adultery, you name it! Now
the government licenses the brothels, both male and female, and the wife or husband without a lover on the side is considered a throwback. Is this any way to
make a buck?

Hell, kid, even murder was illegal in those days, and a man could buy the big
trip for wiping someone off the slate. As you know, some folks never can seem to

learn the niceties of civilized life—their manners are atrocious, their business methods downright devious, their insults unnecessarily public and demeaning—and these people need to be eliminated from the social sphere. Now we have the code duello, through which a man can settle his grudges and satisfy his honor, all legally. The once-lucrative career as a hired assassin has gone the way of the five-dollar streetwalker.

Now, kid, you have got to hustle all day, every day, if you want to survive in this business. You've got to be resourceful, clever and forward-thinking if you expect to meet the competition. Let me tell you how the day went, because it was a day like all days . . .

I bolted down a breakfast of protein paste and cafa, then met Lew Boldoni on the fifth subbasement level in Wing-L, where only the repair robots go. Boldoni was waiting on the robotwalk beside the beltway, carrying his tool satchel, watching the cartons of perishables move past him.

"On time," he said.

I said, "As usual." Time is money; cliché but true.

We removed the access plate to the beltway workings, went down under the robotwalk. In less than five minutes, we were directly beneath the big belt, barely able to shout above the roar, buffeted by the wind of its continuous passage. Together, we opened one of the hydraulic lines and let the lubricant spew out over the traffic computer terminal, where it was sure to seep through and do some damage. Before a fire could start, we were out of there, up on the sidewalk again, putting the access plate back where it belonged. That done, just as the alarms were beginning to clang, we went in different directions.

We both had other business.

This bit of sabotage wouldn't pay off until much later in the day.

At 9:30 in the morning, right on time, I met a young couple—Gene and Miriam Potemkin—in a public hydroponics park on the eighty-third level, in that neighborhood they call Chelsea. She was twenty-one and a looker, bright and curious and unhappy. He was a year older than she was, but that was the only real difference between them. They sat on a bench by an artificial waterfall, both of them leaning forward as I approached, both with their hands folded in their laps, more like sister and brother than like wife and husband.

"Did you bring it?" he asked.

I removed a sealed envelope from my pocket, popped the seal and let them see the map inside, though I was careful not to let them handle it just then. I said, "And you?"

She lifted a small plastic satchel from the ground beside her and took another sealed envelope from it, reluctantly handed it over.

I opened it, counted the money, nodded, tucked the envelope into my pocket and gave them the map.

"Wait a minute, here!" Mr. Potemkin said. "According to this damn map, we'll be going out through the sewer! You know that's not possible. Sewage is pumped at pressure, and there's no way to survive in the system."

"True enough," I said. "But if you'll look closely at the map, you'll see that the sewage line is encased into a larger pipe, from which repairs can be made to the system. This larger pipe is everywhere twenty feet in diameter, sometimes as much as thirty, and is always enough larger than the sewage pipe itself to give you adequate crawl space."

"I don't know," he said. "It doesn't look easy . . ."

"No way out of the city is easy, for God's sake!" I told him. "Look, Potemkin, the city fathers say that the open land, beyond the cities, is unlivable. It's full of poisoned air, poisoned water, plague, and hostile plant and animal life. That's why the air freight exits are the only ones that are maintained, and that's why they're so carefully supervised. City law forbids anyone to leave the city for fear they'll return bearing one of the plagues from Outside. Now, considering all of this, could you reasonably expect me to provide you with an easy way out?"

"I suppose not."

"And that's damn straight."

Ms. Potemkin said, "It's really not like that Outside, is it? The stories of plagues, poisoned air and water, monsters—all of that's just so much bunk."

"I wouldn't know," I said.

"But you must know!"

"Oh?"

"You've shown us the way out," she said. "You must have seen what's beyond the city."

"I'm afraid not," I said. "I employ engineers, specialists, who work from diagrams and blueprints. None of my people would consider leaving the city; we've got too much going for us here."

"But," she insisted, "by sending us, you're showing your distrust of the old stories about the Outside."

"Not at all," I explained. "Once you've gone, my men will seal off this escape route so you can't come back that way, just in case you might bring a plague with you."

"And you won't sell it again?"

"No. We'll find other ways out. There are millions of them."

They looked at each other, unsure of themselves now.

I said, "Look, you haven't committed the map to memory. If you want, I can take it back and return half your money."

"No," he said.

She said, "We've made up our minds. We need open land, something more than layer on layer of enclosed streets and corridors."

"Suit yourself," I said. "And good luck."

I shook their hands and got the hell out of there; things to do, things to do . . .

Moving like a maintenance robot on an emergency call, I dropped down to the subbasements again, to the garbage monitoring decks, where I met with the day-shift manager, K. O. Wilson. We shook hands at precisely 10:20, five minutes behind schedule, and we went into the retrieval chamber, where he had the first two hours of discoveries laid out in neat, clean order.

Kid, I don't think I've ever talked about this angle of the family business before, because I'm not that proud of it. It's the cheapest form of scavenging, no matter how lucrative it is. And it *is* lucrative. You see, the main pipes of the garbage shuttle system are monitored electronically and filtered to remove any articles of value that might otherwise be funneled into the main sewage lines and pumped out of the city. I've got K. O. Wilson, of the first shift, and Marty Linnert, of the second shift, on my payroll. They see to it that I have time to look over the day's findings before they're catalogued and sent up to the city's lost-and-found bureau. Before you think too badly of your old man, consider that 20 per cent of the family's gross comes from the garbage operation.

"Six valuable rings, a dozen good watches, what appears to be one folder of a top-quality coin collection, a diamond tiara, and a mess of other junk," Wilson told me, pointing to the good items, which he had set aside for me.

I ignored the watches, took two of the rings, the tiara and the damp folder full of old coins. "Nothing else?"

"A corpse," he said. "That'll interest the cops. I put it on ice until you could get in and check over your stuff first."

"A murder?" I asked.

"Yeah."

Kid, the code duello hasn't solved everything. There are still those who are afraid to fight, who prefer to sneak about and repay their enemies illegally. And there are also those who aren't satisfied with taking economic and emotional revenge from those not eligible for the duels; they insist on blood, and they have it. Eventually, the law has them. We're not involved with people of this sort, but you should know the kind of scum that the city still supports.

I told Wilson, "I'll send a man around after noon to see what else you've got by then."

Ten minutes later, at 10:53, I walked into the offices of Boldoni and Gia Cybernetic Repairs, on the ninety-second floor, Wing-B, where I acted very shocked about the breakdown in the beltway system.

"City Engineer Willis left an urgent message for you," my secretary said. She handed it to me and said, "It's a beltway carrying perishables in the fifth subbasement."

"Is Mr. Boldoni there?" I asked.

"He accompanied the first repair team," she said.

"Call down and tell Willis I'm on my way."

I used the express drop and almost lost my protein paste and cafa—any inconvenience for a good customer, and the city is the best customer that Boldoni and Gia Cybernetic Repairs has on its list.

Willis was waiting for me by the beltway. He's a small man with very black hair and very dark eyes and a way of moving that makes you think of a maintenance robot with a short between his shoulder blades. He scuttled toward me and said, "What a mess!"

"Tell me," I said.

"The main hydraulic line broke over the traffic computer terminal and a fire started in the works."

"That doesn't sound so bad," I said.

He wiped his small face with one large hand and said, "It wouldn't have been if it had stopped there. We've got the fire out already. The only trouble is that the lubricant has run back the lines into the main traffic computer and the damn thing won't shut down. I've got perishables moving up out of the subterranean coolers, and no way to move them or stop them. They're piling up on me fast, Mr. Gia. I have to have this beltway moving inside the hour or the losses are going to be staggering."

"We'll do the job," I assured him.

"I went out on the limb, calling you before you could deliver a quick computerized estimate. But I knew you people were the fastest, and I needed someone who could be here immediately."

"Don't you worry about it," I told him. "Whatever the B & G computer estimates we'll shave by ten per cent to keep your bosses happy."

Willis was ecstatic, thanking me again and again. He didn't understand that the Boldoni and Gia house computer always estimated an additional and quite illegal 15 per cent surprofit, more than negating the 10 per cent discount I'd given him.

While he was still thanking me, Lew Boldoni came up from the access tunnel, smeared with lubricant, looking harried and nervous and exhausted. Lew is an excellent actor, and that is another qualification for success in this business.

"How is it down there?" I asked.

"Bad," Boldoni said.

Willis groaned.

Boldoni said, "But we're winning it."

"How long?" I asked.

"We'll have the beltway moving in an hour, with a jury-rigged system, and then we can take our time with the permanent repairs."

Willis groaned again, differently this time: in happiness.

I said, "Mr. Boldoni has everything in control, Mr. Willis. I'm sure that you'll be in business as usual shortly. Now, if you'll excuse me, I've got some other urgent business to attend to."

I went up in the express elevator, which was worse than coming down, since my stomach seemed to reach the fifty-ninth floor seconds before the rest of me.

I boarded a horizontal beltway and rode twelve miles east, the last six down Y-Wing. At 11:40, ten minutes behind schedule, I entered an office in the Chesterfield District where a nonexistent Mr. Lincoln Pliney supposedly did business. There, I locked the outer door, apologized for my tardiness to the two people waiting in the reception area, then led them into Lincoln Pliney's private office. I locked that door too, went to the desk, checked out my bug-detecting equipment, made sure the room hadn't been tapped, then sat down behind my desk, offered the customers a drink, poured, sat back and introduced myself under a false name.

My visitors were Arthur Coleman, a rather successful industrialist with offices on the hundredth level, and Eileen Romaine, a lovely girl, fifteen years Coleman's junior. We had all come together in order to negotiate a marriage between Coleman and Romaine, an illegal marriage.

"Tell me, Mr. Coleman," I said, "just why you wish to risk the fines and prison sentences involved with this violation of the Equal Rights Act?"

He squirmed a bit and said, "Do you have to put it that way?"

I said, "I believe a customer must know the consequences before he can be fairly expected to enter a deal like this."

"Okay," he said. "Well, I've been married four times under the standard city contract, and all four marriages have terminated in divorce at my instigation. I'm a very unhappy man, sir. I've got this . . . well, perversion that dominates the course of my private life. I need a wife who . . . who is not my equal, who is subservient, who plays a dated role as nothing more than my bedmate and my housekeeper. I want to dominate any marital situation that I enter."

I said, "Conscious male chauvinism is a punishable crime."

"As I'm aware."

"Have you seen a robopsych?" I asked. "Perhaps one of those could cure you of your malady."

"I'm sure it could," he said. "But you see, I don't really want to be cured. I *like* myself the way I am. I *like* the idea of a woman waiting on me and making her own life conditioned to mine."

"And you?" I asked Eileen.

She nodded, an odd light in her eyes, and she said, "I don't like the responsibility of the standard marriage. I want a man who will put me in my place, a man I can look up to, admire, depend on."

I tell you, kid, these antiquated lusts of theirs were distasteful to me. However, I believe in rebels, both good and bad, being a rebel myself, and I was ready to help them. Both had come to me by word-of-mouth referral within the past month. I'd researched the lives of both, built up two thick dossiers, matched them, and called them here for their first and final meeting under my auspices.

"You have both paid me a finder's fee," I told them. "Now, you will have sixty days to get to know each other. At the end of that time, you will either fail to contact me about a finalization of the contract, in which case I'll know you've found each other unsuitable, or you'll come back here and set up an appointment with my robosec. If you find you like each other, it will be a simple matter to arrange an illegal marriage, without the standard city contract."

Coleman wasn't satisfied with that. He said, "Just how will you pull this off, Mr. Pliney?"

"The first step, of course, is to have Eileen certified dead and disposed of. My people will falsify a death report and have it run through the city records. This may sound like an incredible feat to you; it is nevertheless possible. Once Eileen Romaine has ceased to exist, we will create a false persona in the name of Eileen Coleman. She will be identified as your sister; an entire series of life records will be planted in the computers to solidify her false identity. She can, naturally, then come to live with you, without the city records people realizing that there is anything sexual in your cohabitation."

"If you can do it," Coleman said, "you're a genius."

"No, just clever," I said. "And I will do it. In fact, on any date you pick, I'll have a man at your apartment to officiate at a clandestine wedding using the ancient, male chauvinist rituals."

"There will be no psycheprobes, as there are in other marriages?" she asked.

"Of course not," I said. "The city will have no reason to psycheprobe you under the Equal Rights Act because you won't, so far as the city is concerned, be married at all."

At that point, she burst into tears and said, "Mr. Pliney, you are the first person, outside of Arthur here, who's ever understood me."

I set her straight on that, kid, believe me. I said, "Lady, I don't understand you at all, but I sympathize with rebels. You're chucking out total equality and everything a normal human being should desire in return for a life-style that has long been shown to be inadequate. You're risking prison and fines for knowingly circumventing the Equal Rights Act. It's all crazy, but you've a right to be nuts."

"But if you don't understand us, not at all, why are you risking—"

"For the profit, Eileen," I said. "If this is pulled off, Mr. Coleman will owe me a tidy sum." I stood up. "Now, I must see you out. I've many, many things to do yet today."

When I was finally rid of the happy couple, I boarded an entertainment beltway into a restaurant district in Wing-P, and there I had my lunch: a fillet of reconstituted sea bass, a baked potato, strawberries from a hydroponic garden immersed in simulated cream. It was a rich lunch, but one that was easily digested.

A warning, kid: Stay away from greasy foods for lunch. In this business, your stomach can be the end of you; it curdles grease and plagues you with murderous heartburn.

By 1:30, I was back on the street. I phoned in to the offices of Boldoni and Gia and learned that the beltway on the fifth subbasement level was rolling again, though Boldoni now estimated permanent repairs as a two- or three-day job. It seemed that one of the B & G workmen had found a second potential break in the hydraulic line just before it was ready to go. He'll get a bonus for that, however he managed it.

At 1:45, I stopped around to see K. O. Wilson again, down at the garbage monitoring decks, picked up the best part of a set of pure silver dinnerware, an antique oil lantern, and a somewhat soiled set of twentieth-century pornographic photographs, which, while no longer titillating to the modern man, are well worth a thousand duo-creds as prime, comic nostalgia. Kid, the strangest damn stuff shows up in the garbage, sometimes so strange you won't believe it. Just remember that there are thirty million people in this damn hive, and that among them they own and accidentally throw out about anything a man could hope to find.

I delivered the dinnerware, lantern and pornography to Petrone, the family fence, and then got my ass on the move. I was twenty minutes behind the day's schedule.

At 2:15, I met a man named Talmadge at a sleazy little drug bar in one of the less pleasant entertainment districts on the forty-sixth level. He was sitting at a table in a dark corner, clasping his water pipe in both hands and staring down at the mouthpiece that appeared to have fallen from his lips to the tabletop.

"Sorry I'm late," I said.

He looked up, dreamy-eyed, smiled at me more than he had to, and said, "That's all right. I'm feeling fine, just fine."

"Good for you," I said. "But are you feeling too fine to go through with this?"

"No, no!" he said. "I've waited much too long already, months and months — even years!"

"Come on, then," I said.

I took him out of the drug bar and helped him board a public beltway that took us quickly away from the entertainment zone and deep into a residential area on the same level.

Leaning close to me, in a stage whisper, as if he enjoyed the role of a conspirator, Talmadge said, "Tell me again how big the apartment is."

I looked around, saw that no one was close to us, and, knowing that he would just grow louder and more boisterous if I refused to speak of it, I said, "Three times as large as regulations permit a single man like you. It has nine rooms and two baths."

"And I don't have to share the baths?"

"Of course not."

He was ecstatic.

Now, kid, this is the racket you'll be starting out in to get some experience in the business, and you should pay especially close attention. Even when your mother was alive, we had a bigger apartment than city regulations permit; now, with your mother gone, it's *much* bigger than allowed. How was this achieved, this lavish suite? Simple. We bought up the small apartments all around this, knocked out walls, refitted and redecorated. Then, through a falsification of land records in the city real estate office, we made it look as if the outsize apartment had always been here, was a fluke in the original designs. Now, although living space is at a premium, and though the city tries to force everyone into relatively similar accommodations, the government repair robots are far too busy to have the time to section up the large apartment, throw up new walls and so forth. Instead, because this sort of thing happens so seldom, the city allows the oversize apartment to exist and merely doubles or triples the tax assessment on whoever lives there. In a city of fifteen million apartments, you can pull a hustle like this at least twice a month, without drawing undue official concern, and you can clean up a very tidy sum from rich folks who need more than the legal living space.

At 2:38, Mr. Talmadge and I arrived at the entrance to his new home, keyed it and went inside. I took him on a grand tour of the place, waited while he checked the Tri-D fake-view in all the rooms, tested the beds, flushed the toilets in both johns, and finally paid me the money yet outstanding on our contract. In return, I gave him his ownership papers, copies of the falsified real estate claims, and his first tax assessment.

At 3:00, half an hour behind schedule, I got out of there.

On my way up to the offices of Boldoni and Gia, in the standard elevator, I had time to catch a news flash on the comscreen, and it was such bad news that it shattered the hell out of my schedule. You heard about it. Ms. and Mr. Potemkin, my first clients of the day, were apprehended in their attempt to sneak out of the city through the sewage service pipes. They accidentally ran into a crew of maintenance robots who gave pursuit. They'd only just then been brought to city police headquarters, but they wouldn't need long to fold up under a stiff interrogation.

I canceled my original destination on the elevator board, punched out the twenty-sixth level and dropped down in agonizingly slow motion, wishing to hell I'd used the express drop.

At 3:11, I rode by the offices of Cargill Marriage Counseling, which was the front I used for selling routes out of the city to people like the Potemkins. The place didn't seem to be under surveillance, so I came back on another beltway, opened up, went inside and set to work. I opened the safe, took out what creds I had bundled there, stuffed half a dozen different maps in my pockets, looked around to be sure I'd not left anything of value behind, then set fire to the place and beat it out of there. I had always used the name Cargill in that racket, and I'd always worn transparent plastic fingertip shields to keep from leaving prints; however, one can never be too careful, kid.

At 3:47, I rode back upstairs to the offices of Boldoni and Gia, checked on the beltway repair job with Lew, who had returned to the office. It was going well; the profit would keep Boldoni and Gia in the black; we're always in the black; we see to that.

I sent a man down to seek K. O. Wilson before shifts changed, then dialed the number for Mr. Lincoln Pliney (who is me, you recall), on the fifty-ninth floor in the Chesterfield District. The robosec answered on a cut-in, and I asked for messages.

In a metallic voice, the robosec said, "Mr. Arthur Coleman just stopped in and asked for an appointment, sir."

"Coleman? I just talked to him this morning."

"Yes, sir. But he left a number for you."

I took the number, hung up, dialed Coleman and said hello and identified myself to him.

He said, "Eileen and I want to go through with the deal."

"You've just met each other," I said.

"I know, but I think we're perfect for each other."

I said, "What does Eileen think?"

"The same as I do, of course."

"In one afternoon, you can't learn enough about each other—"

Coleman said, "It's true love."

I said, "Well, it's obviously true *something.*"

"We'd like to finalize things tonight."

"Impossible."

"Then we'll go somewhere else."

"To whom?"

"We'll find someone," he said.

I said, "You'll find some incompetent criminal hack who'll botch the falsification of Eileen's death certificate, and in the end you'll have to tell the police about me."

He didn't respond.

"Oh, hell!" I snapped. "Meet me in my Chesterfield District office in half an hour, with Eileen."

I hung up.

I'd intended to see a man who wanted to purchase a falsified Neutral Status Pass to keep him safe from duel challenges. See, kid, there are a lot of people who are healthy enough to have to go armed but who want to avoid having to accept challenges. The government has no sympathy with them and forces them to comply with the system. I'm always ready, however, to give them a paper disability to keep them whole and sane. I sympathize with rebels, like I said. And there's a profit in it, too. Anyway, I had to call the guy who wanted the Neutral Status Pass and postpone our appointment until tomorrow.

Then I ran off to tie the nuptial knots for Coleman and his lady.

You see, now, why I was late getting home. Scare you? I didn't think it would. Tomorrow, you can come along with me, watch me work, pick up some tips about the business. You're fifteen, plenty old enough to learn. I tell you, kid, you're going to be a natural for this business. I wish your mother could have lived to see what kind of daughter she brought into this world.

Well, kid, you better turn in. It's going to be a busy day.

ᛉ BARRY N(ORMAN) MALZBERG (1939–)

Barry N. Malzberg is an author of thought-provoking, complex, and unsettling stories. He has successfully written Crime and Suspense Fiction, Historical Romances, and Science Fiction and Fantasy. He has published novels and stories under various pseudonyms, as well as under his own byline. As a Science Fiction author, Malzberg's most prolific period was from about 1968 to 1977. He has contributed to Science Fiction and Fantasy magazines, such as Amazing Stories, Analog Science Fiction/Science Fact, Fantastic Stories, THE Magazine, Magazine of Fantasy and Science Fiction, *and* OMNI.

In the late 1960s, Malzberg was an editor for Amazing Stories *and* Fantastic Stories. *He is also the editor and co-editor of some exceptionally fine Science Fiction and Fantasy anthologies, and he works as an agent for writers.*

Malzberg uses Science Fiction as a vehicle for his social commentary and related philosophical and political statements. Often controversial and always interesting, he has used themes of alternate history and theology in some of his recent Science Fiction. As is the case with the most progressive Science Fiction authors, Malzberg seeks to expand the parameters of the genre. Because some of his Science Fiction writing is dark and depressing, it has been compared to that of Robert Sheckley.

"Opening Fire" is an inventive Science Fiction invasion story.

Opening Fire
(The New Mind, ed. Roger Elwood, 1973)

During the training sessions we were instructed that the aliens were kind and the aliens were benevolent and the aliens were a race of creatures whose motives were as sensible as our own and who must be approached in a spirit of mutual confidence. The aliens, who are known as the V'raquai, because that is as close as our language can reach the sounds of their own, were benign creatures and our contacts would be carried out in accord and harmony because they were no less spiritual and rational than we. We were taught all this about the V'raquai, the twenty of us in the training sessions, because it was very important, we were told, that we purge all xenophobia, bigotry and hatred from our systems *before* the contacts began.

Our instructors were reasonable, rational, benign, pleasant men with degrees in psychology and advanced rank in the services and it was impossible not to pay them honor. Nevertheless, I hate and fear the V'raquai and am revolted by them spiritually and physically to the depths of my being, and when I saw the films of their civilization brought into the Institute I wanted to attack the screen with my hands, so deep was the disgust.

I hate them and fear them and have ignored every lesson of the Institute and nevertheless hear that I am on the voyage, bound to meet the V'raquai on an edge of the spiral nebulae where the first discussions of our mutual self-interest will be held. And I have not concealed my hatred from any of them.

II

I am on the voyage despite my failure to respond to the training sessions because in the opinion of the senior staff I represent a valid point of view that is deserving and must be represented during these initial contacts. Xenophobia — the human instinct toward hatred of all forms of life different from its own — is part of the history of mankind and has enabled us at many stages of our development to survive; by force of sheer hatred or suspicion, forces that might destroy us. If man was not innately xenophobic he might not have developed the technology that enabled him to voyage among the stars where he first intercepted the ships of the V'raquai. Even though contacts with this alien race can prove mutually beneficial and all of our relations to date have been cordial, it is still the opinion of the senior staff that it might be better to have at least one dedicated xenophobe aboard in order to test the reactions of the crew and function as a standard against which the aliens' behavior may be measured. It is felt that the xenophobe will function as an early warning system in the event that the V'raquai make potentially menacing gestures, and it is also theorized that if the confidence of the xenophobe is won by the creatures, then the rest of the crew has nothing whatsoever to fear.

And that is why, despite the fact that I have failed the psychological profile, the Markson Index of toleration, the Zalo Charts of bigotry and various other measures of suitability, I am occupying quarters on this ship. "Bigotry has a long if dishonorable history in the race," our group head advised us on passage day, "and in view of its persistence it might be wise to give it a voice on this crew, if not precisely a position of honor."

III

I have a voice on this crew, if not precisely a position of honor. I am more aware than the others might think of how I am regarded, that mixture of pity and contempt with which all my activities are greeted, that bemused and sometimes concentrated hostility that attends most of my routine appearances. My presence, my role on this flight, is regarded by the remainder of the crew as somehow shameful—as if I were a filthy little secret that was being carried, helter-skelter at the speed of light, to the edges of the Crab Nebula—and at the same time, however, they are not completely able to repudiate me. How often, scurrying down these corridors, struggling over my papers, looking over the carefully assembled still-albums and tapes of the V'raquai statesmen, have I seen the eyes of a crew member passing over mine and then locking with a sudden acuity of perception as that light of hatred I emit at all times beams off something in the observer, and coughing, he must turn from me to speed forth on his duties.

IV

I take the words of the group head seriously and have never had any reason to doubt my feelings or, even, to re-evaluate them. Bigotry, hatred, xenophobia, hostility, the revulsion for all forms differing is built deep into our personalities. We are a suspicious race by natural selection; generations of predators have had their shot at us. If it were not for bigotry we would have all been eaten; the hatred of different life forms persists, in a milder and somewhat chastened form now as prejudice against other subgroups of mankind not analogous to one's own. It may be lamentable, but so was the use of saber-toothed tigers for stewing meat. Our hatred has taken us far; it is the price we must pay for our dominance. I know that the V'raquai, no less than any of the other races of the past, are antithetical to our own and if granted an equal opportunity would destroy us and this is why I hate them and my hatred is pure and cleansing and when I actually meet with them it will be reinforced and I will slowly parcel out my hatred to the members of the crew, converting them to my cause, and there will come a time, a natural, inevitable time when we will have to take the V'raquai by surprise and overpower and overthrow them and I will lead the revolt because of my natural force. They will know that I have always been right. They will acknowledge me as their leader.

V

In loose orbit at the nebulae, I catch my first actual glimpse of the V'raquai. One of their crewmen enters hurriedly in full gear for quick conference with our technical forces, something to do with atmospheric conditions in the conference room and the general schedule of the dialogue. The V'raquai is clad in full space armor since our atmosphere would kill them instantly. They subsist, we are told, in an ammonia and nitrogen environment. Under the dull, alien metal of the gear I can catch a hint of scales, ooze, corruption, odors and inconspicuous as I am trying to be in the rear of the room, checking through my tables (my official post on the expedition is as mathematician), I find myself seized by retching and must leave.

VI

Agreements are reached during the conferences which, of coarse, I do not attend. Only the captain, his political advisors and the senior sociologists are permitted to meet in the room with the four V'raquai who appear to comprise their own bargaining committee. The V'raquai will give us access to formulas, mysterious metals, cures for wasting diseases, a hint of the direction research must take for immortality. We will furnish them with grenades, incendiaries, bombs, leveling materials, the technological means for waging war, in short, against another race who is nameless but appears to be fighting them for dominance within their own solar system. This other race is implacably vicious and, the V'raquai assure our representatives, will have no dealings of any sort with civilized cultures. The talks go well. Tentative accords are reached for countersignature by the Premier and his advisors and plans for the next meeting are set. During these days I drift on the edges of the conference like most of the other crew members, getting occasional glimpses of the aliens as they make their strange and mysterious way to and from our ship. The environment on their own ship, they have explained, could not safely be adapted to humans. On the final day of the conference I am summoned to the quarters of the captain where I am greeted by him and one of the senior sociologists. A faint trail of the aliens' odor comes off them and their walls, causing my face to constrict with revulsion, but I try to conceal my feelings. Proximity to the V'raquai and the glimpses of them I have caught have not decreased my hatred. Sometimes I have felt myself seized by the dangerous urge to grab weaponry from the walls and kill them all. I could almost do this before the unthinking crew could stop me. But I have restrained myself. I am here, as I have been reminded by the Institute, merely as a checking device. I am not to perpetuate action.

"The talks have gone well," the captain says to me without preamble. "Now all is signed and we are finished."

"The talks have gone very well," the senior sociologist says. "They will change the course of future generations. We are highly satisfied and have so already advised headquarters." He seems uncomfortable as if he does not really want to be here or even question the uses of our discussion, but he holds himself in place nevertheless. It occurs to me that the senior sociologist, in his way, is as xenophobic as I, although in his case he thinks he had reasons. I have never sought explanations, which explains, I was told, my unique value.

"However," the captain says, "under the procedures we were handed, we must at this time call you in and ask. you: do you still hate the V'raquai as much as ever? Or have your feelings of hatred been reduced?"

"I hate them as much as ever," I say. "I do not trust them. They revolt me and they will destroy us. They are a cowardly, treacherous race and they have scales. No thing with scales may be trusted."

"This is pointless," says the senior sociologist, "pointless and embarrassing. How can you solicit . . ."

"It must be done," the captain says quite sharply, causing the sociologist to mumble. "Under the statutes."

"I still say . . ."

"Quiet! You still think they will destroy us," the captain says to me quietly, "and you do not trust them."

"I am repelled by them," I say quietly. "If I were not under the partial block of the drugs administered before the voyage, I would kill them myself. They breathe ammonia, have scales, speak treacherously, tell us nothing of themselves and I think they itch all the time, too. Dirty, poisonous creatures; how can any human sit with them?"

"I am sorry," the captain says awkwardly, after a pause, "I am truly sorry that you feel this way."

"No you're not, or you would listen . . ."

"Truly sorry," the captain says, and the cast of his face changes; it shudders, it pulses, it shows something alien of its own under the mask of the human features. "Nevertheless, it must be done."

He stands, goes to the door on the other side of the room, behind his desk, opens it. In the door stand two of the V'raquai in their garb, holding weaponry. "You heard," he says to them.

"We heard," one of them says.

"It wasn't my doing," the captain says, "you have to understand that we were instructed . . ."

"Of course," says the V'raquai. "Of course." He walks into the room determinedly, leading the other by a few spaces, pushes the senior sociologist from his path and closes the ground between us. I smell the rank odor coming from the creature, I feel my pain and its power. The senior sociologist gibbers in fury and then quiets as the captain steps to his side. He leans over, whispers, seems to be comforting. The two stand in frieze.

"You realize," says the treacherous V'raquai, lifting its weapon, "that you've given us no choice at all." I see the barrel of the weapon, see its opening then as the fire begins, "but really, there can be no progress between our races and no vanquishment of our terrible enemies until those like you are eliminated."

I feel the flame parting my back, tearing me open, vault ascension, then a feeling of departure as the filthy, evil bastard deposits its load of hatred upon me and then stalks from the room leading the others toward a new era of prosperity and interstellar accord. Dying at the hands of Others, then, as somehow I knew it must always be: and this then is why I hated them so.

ROGER (JOSEPH) ZELAZNY (1937–1995)

Multiple Hugo and Nebula award winner Roger Zelazny began his Science Fiction and Fantasy writing career early in the 1960s. As does Andre Norton, he had a substantial background in research that enhanced his writing. Zelazny served in the military, as did Robert A. Heinlein and Theodore Sturgeon.

Zelazny was equally adept at writing Fantasy and Science Fiction. His Amber *series is his most famous Fantasy work. This series is characterized by classic Fantasy conventions, such as the quest and epic struggles of Good and Evil. It also includes tributes to classic mythology and religion.*

Whether Fantasy or Science Fiction, Roger Zelazny's writing is characterized by detail, colorful prose, metaphor, and allegory. It contains complex plotting. In addition, his Science Fiction — short stories and novels — often features themes and portrayals of technology and related hard sciences.

"The Engine at Heartspring's Center" is not only representative of Roger Zelazny's larger body of work, it is prime Science Fiction allegory.

The Engine at Heartspring's Center
(Analog Science Fiction and Science Fact, *July 1974*)

Let me tell you of the creature called the Bork. It was born in the heart of a dying sun. It was cast forth upon this day from the river of past/future as a piece of time pollution. It was fashioned of mud and aluminum, plastic and some evolutionary distillate of seawater. It had spun dangling from the umbilical of circumstance till, severed by its will, it had fallen a lifetime or so later, coming to rest on the shoals of a world where things go to die. It was a piece of a man in a place by the sea near a resort grown less fashionable since it had become a euthanasia colony.

Choose any of the above and you may be right.

Upon this day, he walked beside the water, poking with his forked, metallic stick at the things the last night's storm had left: some shiny bit of detritus useful to the weird sisters in their crafts shop, worth a meal there or a dollop of polishing rouge for his smoother half; purple seaweed for a salty chowder he had come to favor; a buckle, a button, a shell; a white chip from the casino.

The surf foamed and the wind was high. The heavens were a blue-gray wall, unjointed, lacking the graffiti of birds or commerce. He left a jagged track and one footprint, humming and clicking as he passed over the pale sands. It was near to the point where the fork-tailed ice-birds paused for several days — a week at most — in their migrations. Gone now, portions of the beach were still dotted with their rust-colored droppings. There he saw the girl again, for the third time in as many days. She had tried before to speak with him, to detain him. He had ignored her for a number of reasons. This time, however, she was not alone.

She was regaining her feet, the signs in the sand indicating flight and collapse. She had on the same red dress, torn and stained now. Her black hair — short, with heavy bangs — lay in the only small disarrays of which it was capable. Perhaps thirty feet away was a young man from the Center, advancing toward her. Behind him drifted one of the seldom seen dispatch-machines — about half the size of a man and floating that same distance above the ground, it was shaped like a tenpin, and silver, its bulbous head-end faceted and illuminated, its three ballerina skirts tinfoil-thin and gleaming, rising and falling in rhythms independent of the wind.

Hearing him, or glimpsing him peripherally, she turned away from her pursuers, said, "Help me" and then she said a name.

He paused for a long while, although the interval was undetectable to her. Then he moved to her side and stopped again.

The man and the hovering machine halted also.

"What is the matter?" he asked, his voice smooth, deep, faintly musical.

"They want to take me," she said.

"Well?"

"I do not wish to go."

"Oh. You are not ready?"

"No, I am not ready."

"Then it is but a simple matter. A misunderstanding."

He turned toward the two.

"There has been a misunderstanding," he said. "She is not ready."

"This is not your affair, Bork," the man replied. "The Center has made its determination."

"Then it will have to reexamine it. She says that she is not ready."

"Go about your business, Bork."

The man advanced. The machine followed.

The Bork raised his hands, one of flesh, the others of other things.

"No," he said.

"Get out of the way," the man said. "You are interfering."

Slowly, the Bork moved toward them. The lights in the machine began to blink. Its skirts fell. With a sizzling sound it dropped to the sand and lay unmoving. The man halted, drew back a pace.

"I will have to report this—"

"Go away," said the Bork.

The man nodded, stooped, raised the machine. He turned and carried if off with him, heading up the beach, not looking back. The Bork lowered his arms.

"There," he said to the girl. "You have more time."

He moved away then, investigating shell-shucks and driftwood.

She followed him.

"They will be back," she said.

"Of course."

"What will I do then?"

"Perhaps by then you will be ready."

She shook her head. She laid her hand on his human part.

"No," she said. "I will not be ready."

"How can you tell, now?"

"I made a mistake," she said. "I should never have come here."

He halted and regarded her.

"That is unfortunate," he said. "The best thing that I can recommend is to go and speak with the therapists at the Center. They will find a way to persuade you that peace is preferable to distress."

"They were never able to persuade you," she said.

"I am different. The situation is not comparable."

"I do not wish to die."

"Then they cannot take you. The proper frame of mind is prerequisite. It is right there in the contract—Item Seven."

"They can make mistakes. Don't you think they ever make a mistake? They get cremated the same as the others."

"They are most conscientious. They have dealt fairly with me."

"Only because you are virtually immortal. The machines short out in your presence. No man could lay hands on you unless you willed it. And did they not try to dispatch you in a state of unreadiness?"

"That was the result of a misunderstanding."

"Like mine?"

"I doubt it."

He drew away from her, continuing on down the beach.

"Charles Eliot Borkman," she called.

That name again.

He halted once more, tracing lattices with his stick, poking out a design in the sand.

Then, "Why did you say that?" he asked.

"It is your name, isn't it?"

"No," he said. "That man died in deep space when a liner was jumped to the wrong coordinates, coming out too near a star gone nova."

"He was a hero. He gave half his body to the burning, preparing an escape boat for the others. And he survived."

"Perhaps a few pieces of him did. No more."

"It *was* an assassination attempt, wasn't it?"

"Who knows? Yesterday's politics are not worth the paper wasted on its promises, its threats."

"He wasn't just a politician. He was a statesman, a humanitarian. One of the very few to retire with more people loving him than hating him."

He made a chuckling noise.

"You are most gracious. But if that is the case, then the minority still had the final say. I personally think he was something of a thug. I am pleased, though, to hear that you have switched to the past tense."

"They patched you up so well that you could last forever. Because you deserved the best."

"Perhaps I already have. What do you want of me?"

"You came here to die and you changed your mind—"

"Not exactly. I've just never composed it in a fashion acceptable under the terms of Item Seven. To be at peace—"

"And neither have I. But I lack your ability to impress this fact on the Center."

"Perhaps if I went there with you and spoke to them . . ."

"No," she said. "They would only agree for so long as you were about. They call people like us life-malingerers and are much more casual about the disposition of our cases. I cannot trust them as you do without armor of my own."

"Then what would you have me do—girl?"

"Nora. Call me Nora. Protect me. That is what I want. You live near here. Let me come stay with you. Keep them away from me."

He poked at the pattern, began to scratch it out.

"You are certain that this is what you want?"

"Yes. Yes, I am."

"All right. You may come with me, then."

So Nora went to live with the Bork in his shack by the sea. During the weeks that followed, on each occasion when the representatives from the Center came about, the Bork bade them depart quickly, which they did. Finally, they stopped coming by.

Days, she would pace with him along the shores and help in the gathering of driftwood, for she liked a fire at night; and while heat and cold had long been things of indifference to him, he came in time and his fashion to enjoy the glow.

And on their walks he would poke into the dank trash heaps the sea had lofted and turn over stones to see what dwelled beneath.

"God! What do you hope to find in that?" she said, holding her breath and retreating.

"I don't know," he chuckled. "A stone? A leaf? A door? Something nice. Like that."

"Let's go watch the things in the tidepools. They're clean, at least."

"All right."

Though he ate from habit and taste rather than from necessity, her need for regular meals and her facility in preparing them led him to anticipate these occasions with something approaching a ritualistic pleasure. And it was later still after an evening's meal, that she came to polish him for the first time. Awkward, grotesque—perhaps it could have been. But as it occurred, it was neither of these. They sat before the fire, drying, warming, watching, silent. Absently, she picked up the rag he had let fall to the floor and brushed a fleck of ash from his flame-reflecting side. Later, she did it again. Much later, and this time with full attention, she wiped all the dust from the gleaming surface before going off to her bed.

One day she asked him, "Why did you buy the one-way ticket to this place and sign the contract, if you did not wish to die?"

"But I did wish it," he said.

"And something changed your mind after that? What?"

"I found here a pleasure greater than that desire."

"Would you tell me about it?"

"Surely I found this to be one of the few situations—perhaps the only—where I can be happy. It is in the nature of the place itself: departure, a peaceful conclusion, a joyous going. Its contemplation here pleases me, living at the end of entropy and seeing that it is good."

"But it doesn't please you enough to undertake the treatment yourself?"

"No. I find in this reason for living, not for dying. It may seem a warped satisfaction. But then, I am warped. What of yourself?"

"I just made a mistake. That's all."

"They screen you pretty carefully, as I recall. The only reason they made a mistake in my case was that they could not anticipate anyone finding in this place an inspiration to go on living. Could your situation have been similar?"

"I don't know. Perhaps . . ."

On days when the sky was clear they would rest in the yellow warmth of the sun, playing small games and sometimes talking of the birds that passed and of the swimming, drifting, branching, floating and flowering things in their pools. She never spoke of herself, saying whether it was love, hate, despair, weariness, or bitterness that had brought her to this place. Instead, she spoke of those neutral things they shared when the day was bright; and when the weather kept them indoors she watched the fire, slept, or polished his armor. It was only much later that she began to sing and to hum, small snatches of tunes recently popular or tunes quite old. At these times, if she felt his eyes upon her she stopped abruptly and turned to another thing.

One night then, when the fire had burned low, as she sat buffing his plates, slowly, quite slowly, she said in a soft voice, "I believe that I am falling in love with you."

He did not speak, nor did he move. He gave no sign of having heard.

After a long while, she said, "It is most strange, finding myself feeling this way—here—under these circumstances . . ."

"Yes," he said, after a time.

After a longer while, she put down the cloth and took hold of his hand—the human one—and felt his grip tighten upon her own.

"Can you?" she said, much later.

"Yes. But I would crush you, little girl."

She ran her hands over his plates, then back and forth from flesh to metal. She pressed her lips against his only cheek that yielded.

"We'll find a way," she said, and of course they did.

In the days that followed she sang more often, sang happier things and did not break off when he regarded her. And sometimes he would awaken from the light sleep that even he required, awaken and through the smallest aperture of his lens note that she lay there or sat watching him, smiling. He sighed occasionally for the pure pleasure of feeling the rushing air within and about him, and there was a peace and a pleasure come into him of the sort he had long since relegated to the realms of madness, dream, and vain desire. Occasionally, he even found himself whistling.

One day as they sat on a bank, the sun nearly vanished, the stars coming on, the deepening dark was melted about a tiny wick of falling fire and she let go of his hand and pointed.

"A ship," she said.

"Yes," he answered, retrieving her hand.

"Full of people."

"A few, I suppose."

"It is sad."

"It must be what they want, or what they want to want."

"It is still sad."

"Yes. Tonight. Tonight it is sad."

"And tomorrow?"

"Then too, I daresay."

"Where is your old delight in the graceful end, the peaceful winding-down?"

"It is not on my mind so much these days. Other things are there."

They watched the stars until the night was all black and light and filled with cold air. Then, "What is to become of us?" she said.

"Become?" he said. "If you are happy with things as they are, there is no need to change them. If you are not, then tell me what is wrong."

"Nothing," she said. "When you put it that way, nothing. It was just a small fear—a cat scratching at my heart, as they say."

"I'll scratch your heart myself," he said, raising her as if she were weightless.

Laughing, he carried her back to the shack.

It was out of a deep, drugged-seeming sleep that he dragged himself/was dragged much later, by the sound of her weeping. His time-sense felt distorted, for it seemed an abnormally long interval before her image registered, and her sobs seemed unnaturally drawn out and far apart.

"What—is—it?" he said, becoming at the moment aware of the faint, throbbing, pinprick aftereffect in his biceps.

"I did not—want you to—awaken," she said. "Please go back to sleep."

"You are from the Center, aren't you?"

She looked away.

"It does not matter," he said.

"Sleep. Please. Do not lose the—"

"—requirements of Item Seven," he finished. "You always honor a contract, don't you?"

"That is not all that it was—to me."

"You meant what you said, that night?"

"I came to."

"Of course you would say that now. Item Seven—"

"You bastard!" she said, and she slapped him.

He began to chuckle, but it stopped when he saw the hypodermic on the table at her side. Two spent ampules lay with it.

"You didn't give me two shots," he said, and she looked away. "Come on." He began to rise. "We've got to get you to the Center. Get the stuff neutralized. Get it out of you."

She shook her head.

"Too late—already. Hold me. If you want to do something for me, do that."

He wrapped all of his arms about her and they lay that way while the tides and the winds cut, blew and ebbed, grinding their edges to an ever more perfect fineness.

I think—

Let me tell you of the creature called the Bork. It was born in the heart of a dying star. It was a piece of a man and pieces of many other things. If the things went wrong, the man-piece shut them down and repaired them. If he went wrong, they shut him down and repaired him. It was so skillfully fashioned that it might have lasted forever. But if part of it should die the other pieces need not cease to function, for it could still contrive to carry on the motions the total creature had once performed. It is a thing in a place by the sea that walks beside the water, poking with its forked, metallic stick at the other things the waves have tossed. The human piece, or a piece of the human piece, is dead.

Choose any of the above.

𝕄 ORSON SCOTT CARD (1951-)

While many Science Fiction authors incorporate their personal philosophies and theologies into their stories, none more consciously incorporates his religious convictions into his work than Orson Scott Card. Popular Science Fiction writers represent all religions and belief systems, including Judaism, Christianity, Buddhism, Islam, agnosticism, and atheism. Orson Scott Card embraces the cultural heritage of Mormonism and uses this theology in much of his work. His popular and critically acclaimed Alternate History of the American frontier Hatrack River *series is a prime example. His extensive use of myth and epic storytelling is comparable to that of Roger Zelazny.*

Orson Scott Card has written hundreds of plays and audio scripts as well as prose. In recent years, he has maintained a substantial computer Web site on which he has interacted with his readers and on which he has shared installments of his latest, yet-to-be published writing.

"Ender's Game" is not only the first installment of Ender's Saga, *it is Orson Scott Card's first major Science Fiction sale. A fun and enthralling tale, it is the beginning of a Nathaniel Hawthorne–esque allegory replete with moral philosophy.*

Ender's Game

(Analog Science Fiction and Science Fact, *August 1977*)

"Whatever your gravity is when you get to the door, remember—the enemy's gate is *down*. If you step through your own door like you're out for a stroll, you're a big target and you deserve to get hit. With more than a flasher." Ender Wiggins paused and looked over the group. Most were just watching him nervously. A few understanding. A few sullen and resisting.

First day with this army, all fresh from the teacher squads, and Ender had forgotten how young new kids could be. He'd been in it for three years, they'd had six months—nobody over nine years old in the whole bunch. But they were his. At eleven, he was half a year early to be a commander. He'd had a toon of his own and knew a few tricks, but there were forty in his new army. Green. All marksmen with a flasher, all in top shape, or they wouldn't be here—but they were all just as likely as not to get wiped out first time into battle.

"Remember," he went on, "they can't see you till you get through that door. But the second you're out, they'll be on you. So hit that door the way you want to be when they shoot at you. Legs up under you, going straight *down*." He pointed at a sullen kid who looked like he was only seven, the smallest of them all. "Which way is down, greenoh!"

"Toward the enemy door." The answer was quick. It was also surly, as if to say, Yeah, yeah, now get on with the important stuff.

"Name, kid?"

"Bean."

"Get that for size or for brains?"

Bean didn't answer. The rest laughed a little. Ender had chosen right. This kid *was* younger than the rest, must have been advanced because he was sharp. The others didn't like him much, they were happy to see him taken down a little. Like Ender's first commander had taken him down.

"Well, Bean, you're right onto things. Now I tell you this, nobody's gonna get through that door without a good chance of getting hit. A lot of you are going to be turned into cement somewhere. Make sure it's your legs. Right? If only your legs get hit, then only your legs get frozen, and in nullo that's no sweat." Ender turned to one of the dazed ones. "What're legs for? Hmmm?"

Blank stare. Confusion. Stammer.

"Forget it. Guess I'll have to ask Bean here."

"Legs are for pushing off walls." Still bored.

"Thanks, Bean. Get that, everybody?" They all got it, and didn't like getting it from Bean. "Right. You can't *see* with legs, you can't *shoot* with legs, and most of the time they just get in the way. If they get frozen sticking straight out you've turned yourself into a blimp. No way to hide. So how do legs go?"

A few answered this time, to prove that Bean wasn't the only one who knew anything. "Under you. Tucked up under."

"Right. A shield. You're kneeling on a shield, and the shield is your own legs. And there's a trick to the suits. Even when your legs are flashed you can *still* kick off. I've never seen anybody do it but me—but you're all gonna learn it."

Ender Wiggins turned on his flasher. It glowed faintly green in his hand. Then he let himself rise in the weightless workout room, pulled his legs under him as though he were kneeling, and flashed both of them. Immediately his suit stiffened at the knees and ankles, so that he couldn't bend at all.

"Okay, I'm frozen, see?"

He was floating a meter above them. They all looked up at him, puzzled. He leaned back and caught one of the handholds on the wall behind him, and pulled himself flush against the wall.

"I'm stuck at a wall. If I had legs, I'd use legs, and string myself out like a string *bean*, right?"

They laughed.

"But I don't have legs, and that's *better*, got it? Because of this." Ender jackknifed at the waist, then straightened out violently. He was across the workout room in only a moment. From the other side he called to them. "Got that? I didn't use hands, so I still had use of my flasher. *And* I didn't have my legs floating five feet behind me. Now watch it again."

He repeated the jackknife, and caught a handhold on the wall near them. "Now, I don't just want you to do that when they've flashed your legs. I want you to do that when you've still got legs, because it's better. And because they'll never be expecting it. All right now, everybody up in the air and kneeling."

Most were up in a few seconds. Ender flashed the stragglers, and they dangled, helplessly frozen, while the others laughed. "When I give an order, you move. Got it? When we're at a door and they clear it, I'll be giving you orders in two seconds, as soon as I see the setup. And when I give the order you better be out there, because whoever's out there first is going to win, unless he's a fool. I'm not. And you better not be, or I'll have you back in the teacher squads." He saw more than a few of them gulp, and the frozen ones looked at him with fear. "You guys who are hanging there. You watch. You'll thaw out in about fifteen minutes, and let's see if you can catch up to the others."

For the next half hour Ender had them jackknifing off walls. He called a stop when he saw that they all had the basic idea. They were a good group, maybe. They'd get better.

"Now you're warmed up," he said to them, "we'll start working."

Ender was the last one out after practice, since he stayed to help some of the slower ones improve on technique. They'd had good teachers, but like all armies they were uneven, and some of them could be a real drawback in battle. Their first battle might be weeks away. It might be tomorrow. A schedule was never printed. The commander just woke up and found a note by his bunk, giving him the time of his battle and the name of his opponent. So for the first while he was going to drive his boys until they were in top shape—all of them. Ready for anything, at any time. Strategy was nice, but it was worth nothing if the soldiers couldn't hold up under the strain.

He turned the corner into the residence wing and found himself face to face with Bean, the seven-year-old he had picked on all through practice that day. Problems. Ender didn't want problems right now.

"Ho, Bean."

"Ho, Ender."

Pause.

"Sir," Ender said softly.

"We're not on duty."

"In my army, Bean, we're always on duty." Ender brushed past him.

Bean's high voice piped up behind him. "I know what you're doing, Ender, sir, and I'm warning you."

Ender turned slowly and looked at him. "Warning me?"

"I'm the best man you've got. But I'd better be treated like it."

"Or what?" Ender smiled menacingly.

"Or I'll be the worst man you've got. One or the other."

"And what do you want? Love and kisses?" Ender was getting angry now.

Bean was unworried. "I want a toon."

Ender walked back to him and stood looking down into his eyes. "I'll give a toon," he said, "to the boys who prove they're worth something. They've got to be good soldiers, they've got to know how to take orders, they've got to be able to think for themselves in a pinch, and they've got to be able to keep respect. That's how I got to be a commander. That's how you'll get to be a toon leader. Got it?"

Bean smiled. "That's fair. *If* you actually work that way, I'll be a toon leader in a month."

Ender reached down and grabbed the front of his uniform and shoved him into the wall. "When I say I work a certain way, Bean, then that's the way I work."

Bean just smiled. Ender let go of him and walked away, and didn't look back. He was sure, without looking, that Bean was still watching, still smiling, still just a little contemptuous. He might make a good toon leader at that. Ender would keep an eye on him.

Captain Graff, six foot two and a little chubby, stroked his belly as he leaned back in his chair. Across his desk sat Lieutenant Anderson, who was earnestly pointing out high points on a chart.

"Here it is, Captain," Anderson said. "Ender's already got them doing a tactic that's going to throw off everyone who meets it. Doubled their speed."

Graff nodded.

"And you know his test scores. He thinks well, too."

Graff smiled. "All true, all true, Anderson, he's a fine student, shows real promise."

They waited.

Graff sighed. "So what do you want me to do?"

"Ender's the one. He's got to be."

"He'll never be ready in time, Lieutenant. He's eleven, for heaven's sake, man, what do you want, a miracle?"

"I want him into battles, every day starting tomorrow. I want him to have a year's worth of battles in a month."

Graff shook his head. "That would have his army in the hospital."

"No, sir. He's getting them into form. And we need Ender."

"Correction, Lieutenant. We need somebody. You think it's Ender."

"All right, I think it's Ender. Which of the commanders if it isn't him?"

"I don't know, Lieutenant." Graff ran his hands over his slightly fuzzy bald head. "These are children, Anderson. Do you realize that? Ender's army is nine years old. Are we going to put them against the older kids? Are we going to put them through hell for a month like that?"

Lieutenant Anderson leaned even farther over Graff's desk.

"Ender's test scores, Captain!"

"I've seen his bloody test scores! I've watched him in battle, I've listened to tapes of his training sessions, I've watched his sleep patterns, I've heard tapes of his conversations in the corridors and in the bathrooms, I'm more aware of Ender Wiggins than you could possibly imagine! And against all the arguments, against his obvious qualities, I'm weighing one thing. I have this picture of Ender a year from now, if you have your way. I see him completely useless, worn down, a failure, because he was pushed farther than he or any living person could go. But it doesn't weigh enough, does it, Lieutenant, because there's a war on, and our best talent is gone, and the biggest battles are ahead. So give Ender a battle every day this week. And then bring me a report."

Anderson stood and saluted. "Thank you, sir."

He had almost reached the door when Graff called his name. He turned and faced the captain.

"Anderson," Captain Graff said. "Have you been outside, lately I mean?"

"Not since last leave, six months ago."

"I didn't think so. Not that it makes any difference. But have you ever been to Beaman Park, there in the city? Hmm? Beautiful park. Trees. Grass. No nullo, no battles, no worries. Do you know what else there is in Beaman Park?"

"What, sir?" Lieutenant Anderson asked.

"Children," Graff answered.

"Of course children," said Anderson.

"I mean children. I mean kids who get up in the morning when their mothers call them and they go to school and then in the afternoons they go to Beaman Park and play. They're happy, they smile a lot, they laugh, they have fun. Hmmm?"

"I'm sure they do, sir."

"Is that all you can say, Anderson?"

Anderson cleared his throat. "It's good for children to have fun, I think, sir. I know I did when I was a boy. But right now the world needs soldiers. And this is the way to get them."

Graff nodded and closed his eyes. "Oh, indeed, you're right, by statistical proof and by all the important theories, and dammit they work and the system is right but all the same Ender's older than I am. He's not a child. He's barely a person."

"If that's true, sir, then at least we all know that Ender is making it possible for the others of his age to be playing in the park."

"And Jesus died to save all men, of course." Graff sat up and looked at Anderson almost sadly. "But we're the ones," Graff said, "we're the ones who are driving in the nails."

Ender Wiggins lay on his bed staring at the ceiling. He never slept more than five hours a night—but the lights went off at 2200 and didn't come on again until 0600. So he stared at the ceiling and thought.

He'd had his army for three and a half weeks. Dragon Army. The name was assigned, and it wasn't a lucky one. Oh, the charts said that about nine years ago a Dragon Army had done fairly well. But for the next six years the name had been attached to inferior armies, and finally, because of the superstition that was beginning to play about the name, Dragon Army was retired. Until now. And now, Ender thought, smiling, Dragon Army was going to take them by surprise.

The door opened quietly. Ender did not turn his head. Someone stepped softly into his room, then left with the sound of the door shutting. When soft steps died away Ender rolled over and saw a white slip of paper lying on the floor. He reached down and picked it up.

"Dragon Army against Rabbit Army, Ender Wiggins and Carn Carby, 0700."

The first battle. Ender got out of bed and quickly dressed. He went rapidly to the rooms of each of his toon leaders and told them to rouse their boys. In five minutes they were all gathered in the corridor, sleepy and slow. Ender spoke softly.

"First battle, 0700 against Rabbit Army. I've fought them twice before but they've got a new commander. Never heard of him. They're an older group, though, and I know a few of their old tricks. Now wake up. Run, doublefast, warmup in workroom three."

For an hour and a half they worked out, with three mock battles and calisthenics in the corridor out of the nullo. Then for fifteen minutes they all lay up in the air, totally relaxing in the weightlessness. At 0650 Ender roused them and they hurried into the corridor. Ender led them down the corridor, running again, and occasionally leaping to touch a light panel on the ceiling. The boys all touched the same light panel. And at 0658 they reached their gate to the battleroom.

The members of toons C and D grabbed the first eight handholds in the ceiling of the corridor. Toons A, B, and E crouched on the floor. Ender hooked his feet into two handholds in the middle of the ceiling, so he was out of everyone's way.

"Which way is the enemy's door?" he hissed.

"Down!" they whispered back, and laughed.

"Flashers on." The boxes in their hands glowed green. They waited for a few seconds more, and then the grey wall in front of them disappeared and the battleroom was visible.

Ender sized it up immediately. The familiar open grid of most early games, like the monkey bars at the park, with seven or eight boxes scattered through the grid. They called the boxes *stars*. There were enough of them, and in forward enough positions, that they were worth going for. Ender decided this in a second, and he hissed, "Spread to near stars. E hold!"

The four groups in the corners plunged through the forcefield at the doorway and fell down into the battleroom. Before the enemy even appeared through the opposite gate Ender's army had spread from the door to the nearest stars.

Then the enemy soldiers came through the door. From their stance Ender knew they had been in a different gravity, and didn't know enough to disorient themselves from it. They came through standing up, their entire bodies spread and defenseless.

"Kill 'em, E!" Ender hissed, and threw himself out the door knees first, with his flasher between his legs and firing. While Ender's group flew across the room the rest of Dragon Army lay down a protecting fire, so that E group reached a forward position with only one boy frozen completely, though they had all lost the use of their legs—which didn't impair them in the least. There was a lull as Ender and his opponent, Carn Carby, assessed their positions. Aside from Rabbit Army's losses at the gate, there had been few casualties, and both armies were near full strength. But Carn had no originality—he was in a four-corner spread that any five-year-old in the teacher squads might have thought of. And Ender knew how to defeat it.

He called out, loudly, "E covers A, C down. B, D angle east wall." Under E toon's cover, B and D toons lunged away from their stars. While they were still exposed, A and C toons left their stars and drifted toward the near wall. They reached it together, and together jackknifed off the wall. At double the normal speed they appeared behind the enemy's stars, and opened fire. In a few seconds the battle was over, with the enemy almost entirely frozen, including the commander, and the rest scattered to the corners. For the next five minutes, in squads of four, Dragon Army cleaned out the dark corners of the battleroom and shepherded the enemy into the center, where their bodies, frozen at impossible angles, jostled each other. Then Ender took three of his boys to the enemy gate and went through the formality of reversing the one-way field by simultaneously touching a Dragon Army helmet at each corner. Then Ender assembled his army in vertical files near the knot of frozen Rabbit Army soldiers.

Only three of Dragon Army's soldiers were immobile. Their victory margin—38 to 0—was ridiculously high, and Ender began to laugh. Dragon Army joined him, laughing long and loud. They were still laughing when Lieutenant Anderson and Lieutenant Morris came in from the teachergate at the south end of the battleroom.

Lieutenant Anderson kept his face stiff and unsmiling, but Ender saw him wink as he held out his hand and offered the stiff, formal congratulations that were ritually given to the victor in the game.

Morris found Carn Carby and unfroze him, and the thirteen-year-old came and presented himself to Ender, who laughed without malice and held out his hand. Carn graciously took Ender's hand and bowed his head over it. It was that or be flashed again.

Lieutenant Anderson dismissed Dragon Army, and they silently left the battleroom through the enemy's door—again part of the ritual. A light was blinking on the north side of the square door, indicating where the gravity was in that corridor. Ender, leading his soldiers, changed his orientation and went through the forcefield and into gravity on his feet. His army followed him at a brisk run back to the workroom. When they got there they formed up into squads, and Ender hung in the air, watching them.

"Good first battle," he said, which was excuse enough for a cheer, which he quieted. "Dragon Army did all right against Rabbits. But the enemy isn't always going to be that bad. And if that had been a good army we would have been smashed. We still would have won, but we would have been smashed. Now let me see B and D toons out here. Your takeoff from the stars was way too slow. If Rabbit Army knew how to aim a flasher, you all would have been frozen solid before A and C even got to the wall."

They worked out for the rest of the day.

That night Ender went for the first time to the commanders' mess hall. No one was allowed there until he had won at least one battle, and Ender was the youngest commander ever to make it. There was no great stir when he came in. But when some of the other boys saw the Dragon on his breast pocket, they stared at him openly, and by the time he got his tray and sat at an empty table, the entire room was silent, with the other commanders watching him. Intensely self-conscious, Ender wondered how they all knew, and why they all looked so hostile.

Then he looked above the door he had just come through. There was a huge scoreboard across the entire wall. It showed the win/loss record for the commander of every army; that day's battles were lit in red. Only four of them. The other three winners had barely made it—the best of them had only two men whole and eleven mobile at the end of the game. Dragon Army's score of thirty-eight mobile was embarrassingly better.

Other new commanders had been admitted to the commanders' mess hall with cheers and congratulations. Other new commanders hadn't won thirty-eight to zero.

Ender looked for Rabbit Army on the scoreboard. He was surprised to find that Carn Carby's score to date was eight wins and three losses. Was he that good? Or had he only fought against inferior armies? Whichever, there was still a zero in Carn's mobile and whole columns, and Ender looked down from the scoreboard grinning. No one smiled back, and Ender knew that they were afraid of him, which meant that they would hate him, which meant that anyone who went into battle against Dragon Army would be scared and angry and less competent. Ender looked for Carn Carby in the crowd, and found him not too far away. He stared at Carby until one of the other boys nudged the Rabbit commander and pointed to Ender. Ender smiled again and waved slightly. Carby turned red, and Ender, satisfied, leaned over his dinner and began to eat.

At the end of the week Dragon Army had fought seven battles in seven days. The score stood 7 wins and 0 losses. Ender had never had more than five boys frozen in any game. It was no longer possible for the other commanders to ignore Ender. A few of them sat with him and quietly conversed about game strategies that Ender's opponents had used. Other much larger groups were talking with the commanders that Ender had defeated, trying to find out what Ender had done to beat them.

In the middle of the meal the teacher door opened and the groups fell silent as Lieutenant Anderson stepped in and looked over the group. When he located Ender he strode quickly across the room and whispered in Ender's ear. Ender nodded, finished his glass of water, and left with the lieutenant. On the way out, Anderson handed a slip of paper to one of the older boys. The room became very noisy with conversation as Anderson and Ender left.

Ender was escorted down corridors he had never seen before. They didn't have the blue glow of the soldier corridors. Most were wood paneled, and the floors were carpeted. The doors were wood, with nameplates on them, and they stopped at one that said "Captain Graff, supervisor." Anderson knocked softly, and a low voice said, "Come in."

They went in. Captain Graff was seated behind a desk, his hands folded across his pot belly. He nodded, and Anderson sat. Ender also sat down. Graff cleared his throat and spoke.

"Seven days since your first battle, Ender."

Ender did not reply.

"Won seven battles, one every day."

Ender nodded.

"Scores unusually high, too."

Ender blinked.

"Why?" Graff asked him.

Ender glanced at Anderson, and then spoke to the captain behind the desk. "Two new tactics, sir. Legs doubled up as a shield, so that a flash doesn't immobilize. Jackknife takeoffs from the walls. Superior strategy, as Lieutenant Anderson taught, think places, not spaces. Five toons of eight instead of four of ten. Incompetent opponents. Excellent toon leaders, good soldiers."

Graff looked at Ender without expression. Waiting for what, Ender wondered. Lieutenant Anderson spoke up.

"Ender, what's the condition of your army?"

Do they want me to ask for relief? Not a chance, he decided. "A little tired, in peak condition, morale high, learning fast. Anxious for the next battle."

Anderson looked at Graff. Graff shrugged slightly and turned to Ender.

"Is there anything you want to know?"

Ender held his hands loosely in his lap. "When are you going to put us up against a good army?"

Graff's laughter rang in the room, and when it stopped, Graff handed a piece of paper to Ender. "Now," the captain said, and Ender read the paper: "Dragon Army against Leopard Army, Ender Wiggins and Pol Slattery, 2000."

Ender looked up at Captain Graff. "That's ten minutes from now, sir."

Graff smiled. "Better hurry, then, boy."

As Ender left he realized Pol Slattery was the boy who had been handed his orders as Ender left the mess hall.

He got to his army five minutes later. Three toon leaders were already undressed and lying naked on their beds. He sent them all flying down the corridors to rouse their toons, and gathered up their suits himself. When all his boys were assembled in the corridor, most of them still getting dressed, Ender spoke to them.

"This one's hot and there's no time. We'll be late to the door, and the enemy'll be deployed right outside our gate. Ambush, and I've never heard of it happening before. So we'll take our time at the door. A and B toons, keep your belts loose, and give your flashers to the leaders and seconds of the other toons."

Puzzled, his soldiers complied. By then all were dressed, and Ender led them at a trot to the gate. When they reached it the forcefield was already on one-way, and some of his soldiers were panting. They had had one battle that day and a full workout. They were tired.

Ender stopped at the entrance and looked at the placement of the enemy soldiers. Some of them were grouped not more than twenty feet out from the gate. There was no grid, there were no stars. A big empty space. Where were most of the enemy soldiers? There should have been thirty more.

"They're flat against this wall," Ender said, "where we can't see them."

He took A and B toons and made them kneel, their hands on their hips. Then he flashed them, so that their bodies were frozen rigid.

"You're shields," Ender said, and then had boys from C and D kneel on their legs and hook both arms under the frozen boys' belts. Each boy was holding two flashers. Then Ender and the members of E toon picked up the duos, three at a time, and threw them out the door.

Of course, the enemy opened fire immediately. But they mainly hit the boys who were already flashed, and in a few moments pandemonium broke out in the battleroom. All the soldiers of Leopard Army were easy targets as they lay pressed flat against the wall or floated, unprotected, in the middle of the battleroom; and Ender's soldiers, armed with two flashers each, carved them up easily. Pol Slattery reacted quickly, ordering his men away from the wall, but not quickly enough — only a few were able to move, and they were flashed before they could get a quarter of the way across the battleroom.

When the battle was over Dragon Army had only twelve boys whole, the lowest score they had ever had. But Ender was satisfied. And during the ritual of surrender Pol Slattery broke form by shaking hands and asking, "Why did you wait so long getting out of the gate?"

Ender glanced at Anderson, who was floating nearby. "I was informed late," he said. "It was an ambush."

Slattery grinned, and gripped Ender's hand again. "Good game."

Ender didn't smile at Anderson this time. He knew that now the games would be arranged against him, to even up the odds. He didn't like it.

It was 2150, nearly time for lights out, when Ender knocked at the door of the room shared by Bean and three other soldiers. One of the others opened the door, then stepped back and held it wide. Ender stood for a moment, then asked if he could come in. They answered, of course, of course, come in, and he walked to the upper bunk, where Bean had set down his book and was leaning on one elbow to look at Ender.

"Bean, can you give me twenty minutes?"

"Near lights out," Bean answered.

"My room," Ender answered. "I'll cover for you."

Bean sat up and slid off his bed. Together he and Ender padded silently down the corridor to Ender's room. Bean entered first, and Ender closed the door behind them.

"Sit down," Ender said, and they both sat on the edge of the bed, looking at each other.

"Remember four weeks ago, Bean? When you told me to make you a toon leader?"

"Yeah."

"I've made five toon leaders since then, haven't I? And none of them was you." Bean looked at him calmly.

"Was I right?" Ender asked.

"Yes, sir," Bean answered.

Ender nodded. "How have you done in these battles?"

Bean cocked his head to one side. "I've never been immobilized, sir, and I've immobilized forty-three of the enemy. I've obeyed orders quickly, and I've commanded a squad in mop-up and never lost a soldier."

"Then you'll understand this." Ender paused, then decided to back up and say something else first.

"You know you're early, Bean, by a good half year. I was, too, and I've been made a commander six months early. Now they've put me into battles after only three weeks of training with my army. They've given me eight battles in seven days. I've already had more battles than boys who were made commander four months ago. I've won more battles than many who've been commanders for a year. And then tonight. You know what happened tonight."

Bean nodded. "They told you late."

"I don't know what the teachers are doing. But my army is getting tired, and I'm getting tired, and now they're changing the rules of the game. You see, Bean, I've looked in the old charts. No one has ever destroyed so many enemies and kept so many of his own soldiers whole in the history of the game. I'm unique — and I'm getting unique treatment."

Bean smiled. "You're the best, Ender."

Ender shook his head. "Maybe. But it was no accident that I got the soldiers I got. My worst soldier could be a toon leader in another army. I've got the best. They've loaded things my way — but now they're loading it all against me. I don't know why. But I know I have to be ready for it. I need your help."

"Why mine?"

"Because even though there are some better soldiers than you in Dragon Army — not many, but some — there's nobody who can think better and faster than you." Bean said nothing. They both knew it was true.

Ender continued, "I need to be ready, but I can't retrain the whole army. So I'm going to cut every toon down by one, including you. With four others you'll be a special squad under me. And you'll learn to do some new things. Most of the time you'll be in the regular toons just like you are now. But when I need you. See?"

Bean smiled and nodded. "That's right, that's good, can I pick them myself?"

"One from each toon except your own, and you can't take any toon leaders."

"What do you want us to do?"

"Bean, I don't know. I don't know what they'll throw at us. What would you do if suddenly our flashers didn't work, and the enemy's did? What would you do if we had to face two armies at once? The only thing I know is — there may be a game where we don't even try for score. Where we just go for the enemy's gate. That's when the battle is technically won — four helmets at the corners of the gate. I want you ready to do that any time I call for it. Got it? You take them for two hours a day during regular workout. Then you and I and your soldiers, we'll work at night after dinner."

"We'll get tired."

"I have a feeling we don't know what tired is." Ender reached out and took Bean's hand, and gripped it. "Even when it's rigged against us, Bean. We'll win."

Bean left in silence and padded down the corridor.

Dragon Army wasn't the only army working out after hours now. The other commanders had finally realized they had some catching up to do. From early morning to lights out soldiers all over Training and Command Center, none of them over fourteen years old, were learning to jackknife off walls and use each other as living shields.

But while other commanders mastered the techniques that Ender had used to defeat them, Ender and Bean worked on solutions to problems that had never come up.

There were still battles every day, but for a while they were normal, with grids and stars and sudden plunges through the gate. And after the battles, Ender and Bean and four other soldiers would leave the main group and practice strange maneuvers. Attacks without flashers, using feet to physically disarm or disorient an enemy. Using four frozen soldiers to reverse the enemy's gate in less than two seconds. And one day Bean came to workout with a 300-meter cord.

"What's that for?"

"I don't know yet." Absently Bean spun one end of the cord. It wasn't more than an eighth of an inch thick, but it could have lifted ten adults without breaking.

"Where did you get it?"

"Commissary. They asked what for. I said to practice tying knots."

Bean tied a loop in the end of the rope and slid it over his shoulders.

"Here, you two, hang on to the wall here. Now don't let go of the rope. Give me about fifty yards of slack." They complied, and Bean moved about ten feet from them along the wall. As soon as he was sure they were ready, he jackknifed off the wall and flew straight out, fifty yards. Then the rope snapped taut. It was so fine that it was virtually invisible, but it was strong enough to force Bean to veer off at almost a right angle. It happened so suddenly that he had inscribed a perfect arc and hit the wall hard before most of the other soldiers knew what had happened. Bean did a perfect rebound and drifted quickly back to where Ender and the others waited for him.

Many of the soldiers in the five regular squads hadn't noticed the rope, and were demanding to know how it was done. It was impossible to change direction that abruptly in nullo. Bean just laughed.

"Wait till the next game without a grid! They'll never know what hit them."

They never did. The next game was only two hours later, but Bean and two others had become pretty good at aiming and shooting while they flew at ridiculous speeds at the end of the rope. The slip of paper was delivered, and Dragon Army trotted off to the gate, to battle with Griffin Army. Bean coiled the rope all the way.

When the gate opened, all they could see was a large brown star only fifteen feet away, completely blocking their view of the enemy's gate.

Ender didn't pause. "Bean, give yourself fifty feet of rope and go around the star." Bean and his four soldiers dropped through the gate and in a moment Bean was launched sideways away from the star. The rope snapped taut, and Bean flew forward. As the rope was stopped by each edge of the star in turn, his arc became tighter and his speed greater, until when he hit the wall only a few feet away from the gate he was barely able to control his rebound to end up behind the star. But he immediately moved all his arms and legs so that those waiting inside the gate would know that the enemy hadn't flashed him anywhere.

Ender dropped through the gate, and Bean quickly told him how Griffin Army was situated. "They've got two squares of stars, all the way around the gate. All their soldiers are under cover, and there's no way to hit any of them until we're clear to the bottom wall. Even with shields, we'd get there at half strength and we wouldn't have a chance."

"They moving?" Ender asked.

"Do they need to?"

"I would." Ender thought for a moment. "This one's tough. We'll go for the gate, Bean."

Griffin Army began to call out to them.

"Hey, is anybody there!"

"Wake up, there's a war on!"

"We wanna join the picnic!"

They were still calling when Ender's army came out from behind their star with a shield of fourteen frozen soldiers. William Bee, Griffin Army's commander, waited patiently as the screen approached, his men waiting at the fringes of their stars for the moment when whatever was behind the screen became visible. About ten yards away the screen suddenly exploded as the soldiers behind it shoved the screen north. The momentum carried them south twice as fast, and at the same moment the rest of Dragon Army burst from behind their star at the opposite end of the room, firing rapidly.

William Bee's boys joined battle immediately, of course, but William Bee was far more interested in what had been left behind when the shield disappeared. A formation of four frozen Dragon Army soldiers was moving headfirst toward the Griffin Army gate, held together by another frozen soldier whose feet and hands were hooked through their belts. A sixth soldier hung to his waist and trailed like the tail of a kite. Griffin Army was winning the battle easily, and William Bee concentrated on the formation as it approached the gate. Suddenly the soldier trailing in back moved—he wasn't frozen at all! And even though William Bee flashed him immediately, the damage was done. The formation drifted to the Griffin Army gate, and their helmets touched all four corners simultaneously. A buzzer sounded, the gate reversed, and the frozen soldier in the middle was carried by momentum right through the gate. All the flashers stopped working, and the game was over.

The teachergate opened and Lieutenant Anderson came in. Anderson stopped himself with a slight movement of his hands when he reached the center of the battleroom. "Ender," he called, breaking protocol. One of the frozen Dragon soldiers near the south wall tried to call through jaws that were clamped shut by the suit. Anderson drifted to him and unfroze him.

Ender was smiling.

"I beat you again, sir," Ender said.

Anderson didn't smile. "That's nonsense, Ender," Anderson said softly. "Your battle was with William Bee of Griffin Army."

Ender raised an eyebrow.

"After that maneuver," Anderson said, "the rules are being revised to require that all of the enemy's soldiers must be immobilized before the gate can be reversed."

"That's all right," Ender said. "It could only work once, anyway." Anderson nodded, and was turning away when Ender added, "Is there going to be a new rule that armies be given equal positions to fight from?"

Anderson turned back around. "If you're in one of the positions, Ender, you can hardly call them equal, whatever they are."

William Bee counted carefully and wondered how in the world he had lost when not one of his soldiers had been flashed and only four of Ender's soldiers were even mobile.

And that night as Ender came into the commanders' mess hall, he was greeted with applause and cheers, and his table was crowded with respectful commanders, many of them two or three years older than he was. He was friendly, but while he ate he wondered what the teachers would do to him in his next battle. He didn't need to worry. His next two battles were easy victories, and after that he never saw the battleroom again.

It was 2100 and Ender was a little irritated to hear someone knock at his door. His army was exhausted, and he had ordered them all to be in bed after 2030. The last two days had been regular battles, and Ender was expecting the worst in the morning.

It was Bean. He came in sheepishly, and saluted.

Ender returned his salute and snapped, "Bean, I wanted everybody in bed."

Bean nodded but didn't leave. Ender considered ordering him out. But as he looked at Bean it occurred to him for the first time in weeks just how young Bean was. He had turned eight a week before, and he was still small and—no, Ender thought, he wasn't young. Nobody was young. Bean had been in battle, and with a whole army depending on him he had come through and won. And even though he was small, Ender could never think of him as young again.

Ender shrugged and Bean came over and sat on the edge of the bed. The younger boy looked at his hands for a while, and finally Ender grew impatient and asked, "Well, what is it?"

"I'm transferred. Got orders just a few minutes ago."

Ender closed his eyes for a moment. "I knew they'd pull something new. Now they're taking—where are you going?"

"Rabbit Army."

"How can they put you under an idiot like Carn Carby!"

"Carn was graduated. Support squads."

Ender looked up. "Well, who's commanding Rabbit then?"

Bean held his hands out helplessly.

"Me," he said.

Ender nodded, and then smiled. "Of course. After all, you're only four years younger than the regular age."

"It isn't funny," Bean said. "I don't know what's going on here. First all the changes in the game. And now this. I wasn't the only one transferred, either, Ender. Ren, Peder, Brian, Wins, Younger. All commanders now."

Ender stood up angrily and strode to the wall. "Every damn toon leader I've got!" he said, and whirled to face Bean. "If they're going to break up my army, Bean, why did they bother making me a commander at all?"

Bean shook his head. "I don't know. You're the best, Ender. Nobody's ever done what you've done. Nineteen battles in fifteen days, sir, and you won every one of them, no matter what they did to you."

"And now you and the others are commanders. You know every trick I've got, I trained you, and who am I supposed to replace you with? Are they going to stick me with six greenohs?"

"It stinks, Ender, but you know that if they gave you five crippled midgets and armed you with a roll of toilet paper you'd win."

They both laughed, and then they noticed that the door was open.

Lieutenant Anderson stepped in. He was followed by Captain Graff.

"Ender Wiggins," Graff said, holding his hands across his stomach.

"Yes sir," Ender answered.

"Orders."

Anderson extended a slip of paper. Ender read it quickly, then crumpled it, still looking at the air where the paper had been. After a few moments he asked, "Can I tell my army?"

"They'll find out," Graff answered. "It's better not to talk to them after orders. It makes it easier."

"For you or for me?" Ender asked. He didn't wait for an answer. He turned quickly to Bean, took his hand for a moment, and then headed for the door.

"Wait," Bean said. "Where are you going? Tactical or Support School?"

"Command School," Ender answered, and then he was gone and Anderson closed the door.

Command School, Bean thought. Nobody went to Command School until they had gone through three years of Tactical. But then, nobody went to Tactical until they had been through at least five years of Battle School. Ender had only had three.

The system was breaking up. No doubt about it, Bean thought. Either somebody at the top was going crazy, or something was going wrong with the war—the real war, the one they were training to fight in. Why else would they break down the training system, advance somebody—even somebody as good as Ender—straight to Command School? Why else would they ever have an eight-year-old greenoh like Bean command an army?

Bean wondered about it for a long time, and then he finally lay down on Ender's bed and realized that he'd never see Ender again, probably. For some reason that made him want to cry. But he didn't cry, of course. Training in the preschools had taught him how to force down emotions like that. He remembered how his first teacher, when he was three, would have been upset to see his lip quivering and his eyes full of tears.

Bean went through the relaxing routine until he didn't feel like crying anymore. Then he drifted off to sleep. His hand was near his mouth. It lay on his pillow hesitantly, as if Bean couldn't decide whether to bite his nails or suck on his fingertips. His forehead was creased and furrowed. His breathing was quick and light. He was a soldier, and if anyone had asked him what he wanted to be when he grew up, he wouldn't have known what they meant.

There's a war on, they said, and that was excuse enough for all the hurry in the world. They said it like a password and flashed a little card at every ticket counter and customs check and guard station. It got them to the head of every line.

Ender Wiggins was rushed from place to place so quickly he had no time to examine anything. But he did see trees for the first time. He saw men who were not in uniform. He saw women. He saw strange animals that didn't speak, but that followed docilely behind women and small children. He saw suitcases and conveyor

belts and signs that said words he had never heard of. He would have asked someone what the words meant, except that purpose and authority surrounded him in
the persons of four very high officers who never spoke to each other and never
spoke to him.

Ender Wiggins was a stranger to the world he was being trained to save. He
did not remember ever leaving Battle School before. His earliest memories were
of childish war games under the direction of a teacher, of meals with other boys in
the grey and green uniforms of the armed forces of his world. He did not know
that the grey represented the sky and the green represented the great forests of his
planet. All he knew of the world was from vague references to "outside."

And before he could make any sense of the strange world he was seeing for the
first time, they enclosed him again within the shell of the military, where nobody
had to say there's a war on anymore because no one within the shell of the military
forgot it for a single instant of a single day.

They put him in a spaceship and launched him to a large artificial satellite that
circled the world.

This space station was called Command School. It held the ansible.

On his first day Ender Wiggins was taught about the ansible and what it meant
to warfare. It meant that even though the starships of today's battles were
launched a hundred years ago, the commanders of the starships were men of today, who used the ansible to send messages to the computers and the few men on
each ship. The ansible sent words as they were spoken, orders as they were made.
Battleplans as they were fought. Light was a pedestrian.

For two months Ender Wiggins didn't meet a single person. They came to him
namelessly, taught him what they knew, and left him to other teachers. He had no
time to miss his friends at Battle School. He only had time to learn how to operate
the simulator, which flashed battle patterns around him as if he were in a starship
at the center of the battle. How to command mock ships in mock battles by manipulating the keys on the simulator and speaking words into the ansible. How to
recognize instantly every enemy ship and the weapons it carried by the pattern
that the simulator showed. How to transfer all that he learned in the nullo battles
at Battle School to the starship battles at Command School.

He had thought the game was taken seriously before. Here they hurried him
through every step, were angry and worried beyond reason every time he forgot
something or made a mistake. But he worked as he had always worked, and
learned as he had always learned. After a while he didn't make any more mistakes.
He used the simulator as if it were a part of himself. Then they stopped being
worried and gave him a teacher.

Maezr Rackham was sitting cross-legged on the floor when Ender awoke. He
said nothing as Ender got up and showered and dressed, and Ender did not bother
to ask him anything. He had long since learned that when something unusual was
going on, he would often find out more information faster by waiting than by
asking.

Maezr still hadn't spoken when Ender was ready and went to the door to leave
the room. The door didn't open. Ender turned to face the man sitting on the
floor. Maezr was at least forty, which made him the oldest man Ender had ever
seen close up. He had a day's growth of black and white whiskers that grizzled his
face only slightly less than his close-cut hair. His face sagged a little and his eyes
were surrounded by creases and lines. He looked at Ender without interest.

Ender turned back to the door and tried again to open it.

"All right," he said, giving up. "Why's the door locked?"

Maezr continued to look at him blankly.

Ender became impatient. "I'm going to be late. If I'm not supposed to be there until later, then tell me so I can go back to bed." No answer. "Is it a guessing game?" Ender asked. No answer. Ender decided that maybe the man was trying to make him angry, so he went through a relaxing exercise as he leaned on the door, and soon he was calm again. Maezr didn't take his eyes off Ender.

For the next two hours the silence endured, Maezr watching Ender constantly, Ender trying to pretend he didn't notice the old man. The boy became more and more nervous, and finally ended up walking from one end of the room to the other in a sporadic pattern.

He walked by Maezr as he had several times before, and Maezr's hand shot out and pushed Ender's left leg into his right in the middle of a step. Ender fell flat on the floor.

He leaped to his feet immediately, furious. He found Maezr sitting calmly, cross-legged, as if he had never moved. Ender stood poised to fight. But the other's immobility made it impossible for Ender to attack, and he found himself wondering if he had only imagined the old man's hand tripping him up.

The pacing continued for another hour, with Ender Wiggins trying the door every now and then. At last he gave up and took off his uniform and walked to his bed.

As he leaned over to pull the covers back, he felt a hand jab roughly between his thighs and another hand grab his hair. In a moment he had been turned upside down. His face and shoulders were being pressed into the floor by the old man's knee, while his back was excruciatingly bent and his legs were pinioned by Maezr's arm. Ender was helpless to use his arms, and he couldn't bend his back to gain slack so he could use his legs. In less than two seconds the old man had completely defeated Ender Wiggins.

"All right," Ender gasped. "You win."

Maezr's knee thrust painfully downward.

"Since when," Maezr asked in a soft, rasping voice, "do you have to tell the enemy when he has won?"

Ender remained silent.

"I surprised you once, Ender Wiggins. Why didn't you destroy me immediately afterward? Just because I looked peaceful? You turned your back on me. Stupid. You have learned nothing. You have never had a teacher."

Ender was angry now. "I've had too many damned teachers, how was I supposed to know you'd turn out to be a—" Ender hunted for a word. Maezr supplied one.

"An enemy, Ender Wiggins," Maezr whispered. "I am your enemy, the first one you've ever had who was smarter than you. There is no teacher but the enemy, Ender Wiggins. No one but the enemy will ever tell you what the enemy is going to do. No one but the enemy will ever teach you how to destroy and conquer. I am your enemy, from now on. From now on I am your teacher."

Then Maezr let Ender's legs fall to the floor. Because the old man still held Ender's head to the floor, the boy couldn't use his arms to compensate, and his legs hit the plastic surface with a loud crack and a sickening pain that made Ender wince. Then Maezr stood and let Ender rise.

Slowly the boy pulled his legs under him, with a faint groan of pain, and he knelt on all fours for a moment, recovering. Then his right arm flashed out.

Maezr quickly danced back and Ender's hand closed on air as his teacher's foot shot forward to catch Ender on the chin.

Ender's chin wasn't there. He was lying flat on his back, spinning on the floor, and during the moment that Maezr was off balance from his kick Ender's feet smashed into Maezr's other leg. The old man fell on the ground in a heap.

What seemed to be a heap was really a hornet's nest. Ender couldn't find an arm or a leg that held still long enough to be grabbed, and in the meantime blows were landing on his back and arms. Ender was smaller—he couldn't reach past the old man's flailing limbs.

So he leaped back out of the way and stood poised near the door.

The old man stopped thrashing about and sat up, cross-legged again, laughing. "Better, this time, boy. But slow. You will have to be better with a fleet than you are with your body or no one will be safe with you in command. Lesson learned?"

Ender nodded slowly.

Maezr smiled. "Good. Then we'll never have such a battle again. All the rest with the simulator. I will program your battles, I will devise the strategy of your enemy, and you will learn to be quick and discover what tricks the enemy has for you. Remember, boy. From now on the enemy is more clever than you. From now on the enemy is stronger than you. From now on you are always about to lose."

Then Maezr's face became serious again. "You will be about to lose, Ender, but you will win. You will learn to defeat the enemy. He will teach you how."

Maezr got up and walked toward the door. Ender stepped back out of the way. As the old man touched the handle of the door, Ender leaped into the air and kicked Maezr in the small of the back with both feet. He hit hard enough that he rebounded onto his feet, as Maezr cried out and collapsed on the floor.

Maezr got up slowly, holding on to the door handle, his face contorted with pain. He seemed disabled, but Ender didn't trust him. He waited warily. And yet in spite of his suspicion he was caught off guard by Maezr's speed. In a moment he found himself on the floor near the opposite wall, his nose and lip bleeding where his face had hit the bed. He was able to turn enough to see Maezr open the door and leave. The old man was limping and walking slowly.

Ender smiled in spite of the pain, then rolled over onto his back and laughed until his mouth filled with blood and he started to gag. Then he got up and painfully made his way to the bed. He lay down and in a few minutes a medic came and took care of his injuries.

As the drug had its effect and Ender drifted off to sleep he remembered the way Maezr limped out of his room and laughed again. He was still laughing softly as his mind went blank and the medic pulled the blanket over him and snapped off the light. He slept until pain woke him in the morning. He dreamed of defeating Maezr.

The next day Ender went to the simulator room with his nose bandaged and his lip still puffy. Maezr was not there. Instead, a captain who had worked with him before showed him an addition that had been made. The captain pointed to a tube with a loop at one end. "Radio. Primitive, I know, but it loops over your ear and we tuck the other end into your mouth like this."

"Watch it," Ender said as the captain pushed the end of the tube into his swollen lip.

"Sorry. Now you just talk."

"Good. Who to?"

The captain smiled. "Ask and see."

Ender shrugged and turned to the simulator. As he did a voice reverberated through his skull. It was too loud for him to understand, and he ripped the radio off his ear.

"What are you trying to do, make me deaf?"

The captain shook his head and turned a dial on a small box on a nearby table. Ender put the radio back on.

"Commander," the radio said in a familiar voice.

Ender answered, "Yes."

"Instructions, sir?"

The voice was definitely familiar. "Bean?" Ender asked.

"Yes, sir."

"Bean, this is Ender."

Silence. And then a burst of laughter from the other side. Then six or seven more voices laughing, and Ender waited for silence to return. When it did, he asked, "Who else?"

A few voices spoke at once, but Bean drowned them out. "Me, I'm Bean, and Peder, Wins, Younger, Lee, and Vlad."

Ender thought for a moment. Then he asked what the hell was going on. They laughed again.

"They can't break up the group," Bean said. "We were commanders for maybe two weeks, and here we are at Command School, training with the simulator, and all of a sudden they told us we were going to form a fleet with a new commander. And that's you."

Ender smiled. "Are you boys any good?"

"If we aren't, you'll let us know."

Ender chuckled a little. "Might work out. A fleet."

For the next ten days Ender trained his teen leaders until they could maneuver their ships like precision dancers. It was like being back in the battleroom again, except that now Ender could always see everything, and could speak to his toon leaders and change their orders at any time.

One day as Ender sat down at the control board and switched on the simulator, harsh green lights appeared in the space—the enemy.

"This is it," Ender said. "X, Y, bullet, C, D, reserve screen, E, south loop, Bean, angle north."

The enemy was grouped in a globe, and outnumbered Ender two to one. Half of Ender's force was grouped in a tight, bulletlike formation, with the rest in a flat circular screen—except for a tiny force under Bean that moved off the simulator, heading behind the enemy's formation. Ender quickly learned the enemy's strategy: whenever Ender's bullet formation came close, the enemy would give way, hoping to draw Ender inside the globe where he would be surrounded. So Ender obligingly fell into the trap, bringing his bullet to the center of the globe.

The enemy began to contract slowly, not wanting to come within range until all their weapons could be brought to bear at once. Then Ender began to work in earnest. His reserve screen approached the outside of the globe, and the enemy began to concentrate his forces there. Then Bean's force appeared on the opposite side, and the enemy again deployed ships on that side.

Which left most of the globe only thinly defended. Ender's bullet attacked, and since at the point of attack it outnumbered the enemy overwhelmingly, he tore a hole in the formation. The enemy reacted to try to plug the gap, but in the confusion the reserve force and Bean's small force attacked simultaneously, while the bullet moved to another part of the globe. In a few more minutes the formation was shattered, most of the enemy ships destroyed, and the few survivors rushing away as fast as they could go.

Ender switched the simulator off. All the lights faded. Maezr was standing beside Ender, his hands in his pockets, his body tense. Ender looked up at him.

"I thought you said the enemy would be smart," Ender said.

Maezr's face remained expressionless. "What did you learn?"

"I learned that a sphere only works if your enemy's a fool. He had his forces so spread out that I outnumbered him whenever I engaged him."

"And?"

"And," Ender said, "you can't stay committed to one pattern. It makes you too easy to predict."

"Is that all?" Maezr asked quietly.

Ender took off his radio. "The enemy could have defeated me by breaking the sphere earlier."

Maezr nodded. "You had an unfair advantage."

Ender looked up at him coldly. "I was outnumbered two to one."

Maezr shook his head. "You have the ansible. The enemy doesn't. We include that in the mock battles. Their messages travel at the speed of light."

Ender glanced toward the simulator. "Is there enough space to make a difference?"

"Don't you know?" Maezr asked. "None of the ships was ever closer than thirty thousand kilometers to any other."

Ender tried to figure the size of the enemy's sphere. Astronomy was beyond him. But now his curiosity was stirred.

"What kind of weapons are on those ships? To be able to strike so fast?"

Maezr shook his head. "The science is too much for you. You'd have to study many more years than you've lived to understand even the basics. All you need to know is that the weapons work."

"Why do we have to come so close to be in range?"

"The ships are all protected by forcefields. A certain distance away the weapons are weaker and can't get through. Closer in the weapons are stronger than the shields. But the computers take care of all that. They're constantly firing in any direction that won't hurt one of our ships. The computers pick targets, aim; they do all the detail work. You just tell them when and get them in a position to win. All right?"

"No." Ender twisted the tube of the radio around his fingers. "I have to know how the weapons work."

"I told you, it would take—"

"I can't command a fleet—not even on the simulator—unless I know." Ender waited a moment, then added, "Just the rough idea."

Maezr stood up and walked a few steps away. "All right, Ender. It won't make any sense, but I'll try. As simply as I can." He shoved his hands into his pockets. "It's this way, Ender. Everything is made up of atoms, little particles so small you can't see them with your eyes. These atoms, there are only a few different types, and they're all made up of even smaller particles that are pretty much the same. These atoms can be broken, so that they stop being atoms. So that this metal doesn't hold together anymore. Or the plastic floor. Or your body. Or even the air. They just seem to disappear, if you break the atoms. All that's left is the pieces.

And they fly around and break more atoms. The weapons on the ships set up an area where it's impossible for atoms of anything to stay together. They all break down. So things in that area—they disappear."

Ender nodded. "You're right, I don't understand it. Can it be blocked?"

"No. But it gets wider and weaker the farther it goes from the ship, so that after a while a forcefield will block it. OK? And to make it strong at all, it has to be focused, so that a ship can only fire effectively in maybe three or four directions at once."

Ender nodded again, but he didn't really understand, not well enough. "If the pieces of the broken atoms go breaking more atoms, why doesn't it just make everything disappear?"

"Space. Those thousands of kilometers between the ships, they're empty. Almost no atoms. The pieces don't hit anything, and when they finally do hit something, they're so spread out they can't do any harm." Maezr cocked his head quizzically. "Anything else you need to know?"

"Do the weapons on the ships—do they work against anything besides ships?"

Maezr moved in close to Ender and said firmly, "We only use them against ships. Never anything else. If we used them against anything else, the enemy would use them against us. Got it?"

Maezr walked away, and was nearly out the door when Ender called to him.

"I don't know your name yet," Ender said blandly.

"Maezr Rackham."

"Maezr Rackham," Ender said, "I defeated you."

Maezr laughed.

"Ender, you weren't fighting me today," he said. "You were fighting the stupidest computer in the Command School, set on a ten-year-old program. You don't think I'd use a sphere, do you?" He shook his head. "Ender, my dear little fellow, when you fight me you'll know it. Because you'll lose." And Maezr left the room.

Ender still practiced ten hours a day with his toon leaders. He never saw them, though, only heard their voices on the radio. Battles came every two or three days. The enemy had something new every time, something harder—but Ender coped with it. And won every time. And after every battle Maezr would point out mistakes and show Ender that he had really lost. Maezr only let Ender finish so that he would learn to handle the end of the game.

Until finally Maezr came in and solemnly shook Ender's hand and said, "That, boy, was a good battle."

Because the praise was so long in coming, it pleased Ender more than praise had ever pleased him before. And because it was so condescending, he resented it.

"So from now on," Maezr said, "we can give you hard ones."

From then on Ender's life was a slow nervous breakdown.

He began fighting two battles a day, with problems that steadily grew more difficult. He had been trained in nothing but the game all his life, but now the game began to consume him. He woke in the morning with new strategies for the simulator and went fitfully to sleep at night with the mistakes of the day preying on him. Sometimes he would wake up in the middle of the night crying for a reason he didn't remember. Sometimes he woke with his knuckles bloody from biting them. But every day he went impassively to the simulator and drilled his toon leaders until the battles, and drilled his toon leaders after the battles, and endured and studied the harsh criticism that Maezr Rackham piled on him. He noted that

Rackham perversely criticized him more after his hardest battles. He noted that every time he thought of a new strategy the enemy was using it within a few days. And he noted that while his fleet always stayed the same size, the enemy increased in numbers every day.

He asked his teacher.

"We are showing you what it will be like when you really command. The ratios of enemy to us."

"Why does the enemy always outnumber us?"

Maezr bowed his grey head for a moment, as if deciding whether to answer. Finally he looked up and reached out his hand and touched Ender on the shoulder. "I will tell you, even though the information is secret. You see, the enemy attacked us first. He had good reason to attack us, but that is a matter for politicians, and whether the fault was ours or his, we could not let him win. So when the enemy came to our worlds, we fought back, hard, and spent the finest of our young men in the fleets. But we won, and the enemy retreated."

Maezr smiled ruefully. "But the enemy was not through, boy. The enemy would never be through. They came again, with more numbers, and it was harder to beat them. And another generation of young men was spent. Only a few survived. So we came up with a plan—the big men came up with the plan. We knew that we had to destroy the enemy once and for all, totally, eliminate his ability to make war against us. To do that we had to go to his home worlds—his home world, really, since the enemy's empire is all tied to his capital world."

"And so?" Ender asked.

"And so we made a fleet. We made more ships than the enemy ever had. We made a hundred ships for every ship he had sent against us. And we launched them against his twenty-eight worlds. They started leaving a hundred years ago. And they carried on them the ansible, and only a few men. So that someday a commander could sit on a planet somewhere far from the battle and command the fleet. So that our best minds would not be destroyed by the enemy."

Ender's question had still not been answered. "Why do they outnumber us?"

Maezr laughed. "Because it took a hundred years for our ships to get there. They've had a hundred years to prepare for us. They'd be fools, don't you think, boy, if they waited in old tugboats to defend their harbors. They have new ships, great ships, hundreds of ships. All we have is the ansible, that and the fact that they have to put a commander with every fleet, and when they lose—and they will lose—they lose one of their best minds every time."

Ender started to ask another question.

"No more, Ender Wiggins. I've told you more than you ought to know as it is."

Ender stood angrily and turned away. "I have a right to know. Do you think this can go on forever, pushing me through one school and another and never telling me what my life is for? You use me and the others as a tool, someday we'll command your ships, someday maybe we'll save your lives, but I'm not a computer, and I have to *know!*"

"Ask me a question, then, boy," Maezr said, "and if I can answer, I will."

"If you use your best minds to command the fleets, and you never lose any, then what do you need me for? Who am I replacing, if they're all still there?"

Maezr shook his head. "I can't tell you the answer to that, Ender. Be content that we will need you, soon. It's late. Go to bed. You have a battle in the morning."

Ender walked out of the simulator room. But when Maezr left by the same door a few moments later, the boy was waiting in the hall.

"All right, boy," Maezr said impatiently, "what is it? I don't have all night and you need to sleep."

Ender wasn't sure what his question was, but Maezr waited. Finally Ender asked softly, "Do they live?"

"Does who live?"

"The other commanders. The ones now. And before me."

Maezr snorted. "Live. Of course they live. He wonders if they live." Still chuckling, the old man walked off down the hall. Ender stood in the corridor for a while, but at last he was tired and he went off to bed. They live, he thought. They live, but he can't tell me what happens to them.

That night Ender didn't wake up crying. But he did wake up with blood on his hands.

Months wore on with battles every day, until at last Ender settled into the routine of the destruction of himself. He slept less every night, dreamed more, and he began to have terrible pains in his stomach. They put him on a very bland diet, but soon he didn't even have an appetite for that. "Eat," Maezr said, and Ender would mechanically put food in his mouth. But if nobody told him to eat he didn't eat.

One day as he was drilling his toon leaders the room went black and he woke up on the floor with his face bloody where he had hit the controls.

They put him to bed then, and for three days he was very ill. He remembered seeing faces in his dreams, but they weren't real faces, and he knew it even while he thought he saw them. He thought he saw Bean sometimes, and sometimes he thought he saw Lieutenant Anderson and Captain Graff. And then he woke up and it was only his enemy, Maezr Rackham.

"I'm awake," he said to Maezr.

"So I see," Maezr answered. "Took you long enough. You have a battle today."

So Ender got up and fought the battle and he won it. But there was no second battle that day, and they let him go to bed earlier. His hands were shaking as he undressed.

During the night he thought he felt hands touching him gently, and he dreamed he heard voices saying, "How long can he go on?"

"Long enough."

"So soon?"

"In a few days, then he's through."

"How will he do?"

"Fine. Even today, he was better than ever."

Ender recognized the last voice as Maezr Rackham's. He resented Rackham's intruding even in his sleep.

He woke up and fought another battle and won.

Then he went to bed.

He woke up and won again.

And the next day was his last day in Command School, though he didn't know it. He got up and went to the simulator for the battle.

Maezr was waiting for him. Ender walked slowly into the simulator room. His step was slightly shuffling, and he seemed tired and dull. Maezr frowned.

"Are you awake, boy?" If Ender had been alert, he would have cared more about the concern in his teacher's voice. Instead, he simply went to the controls and sat down. Maezr spoke to him.

"Today's game needs a little explanation, Ender Wiggins. Please turn around and pay strict attention."

Ender turned around, and for the first time he noticed that there were people at the back of the room. He recognized Graff and Anderson from Battle School, and vaguely remembered a few of the men from Command School—teachers for a few hours at some time or another. But most of the people he didn't know at all.

"Who are they?"

Maezr shook his head and answered, "Observers. Every now and then we let observers come in to watch the battle. If you don't want them, we'll send them out."

Ender shrugged. Maezr began his explanation. "Today's game, boy, has a new element. We're staging this battle around a planet. This will complicate things in two ways. The planet isn't large, on the scale we're using, but the ansible can't detect anything on the other side of it—so there's a blind spot. Also, it's against the rules to use weapons against the planet itself. All right?"

"Why, don't the weapons work against planets?"

Maezr answered coldly, "There are rules of war, Ender, that apply even in training games."

Ender shook his head slowly. "Can the planet attack?"

Maezr looked nonplussed for a moment, then smiled. "I guess you'll have to find that one out, boy. And one more thing. Today, Ender, your opponent isn't the computer. I am your enemy today, and today I won't be letting you off so easily. Today is a battle to the end. And I'll use any means I can to defeat you."

Then Maezr was gone, and Ender expressionlessly led his toon leaders through maneuvers. Ender was doing well, of course, but several of the observers shook their heads, and Graff kept clasping and unclasping his hands, crossing and uncrossing his legs. Ender would be slow today, and today Ender couldn't afford to be slow.

A warning buzzer sounded, and Ender cleared the simulator board, waiting for today's game to appear. He felt muddled today, and wondered why people were there watching. Were they going to judge him today? Decide if he was good enough for something else? For another two years of grueling training, another two years of struggling to exceed his best? Ender was twelve. He felt very old. And as he waited for the game to appear, he wished he could simply lose it, lose the battle badly and completely so that they would remove him from the program, punish him however they wanted, he didn't care, just so he could sleep.

Then the enemy formation appeared, and Ender's weariness turned to desperation.

The enemy outnumbered him a thousand to one, the simulator glowed green with them, and Ender knew that he couldn't win.

And the enemy was not stupid. There was no formation that Ender could study and attack. Instead the vast swarms of ships were constantly moving, constantly shifting from one momentary formation to another, so that a space that for one moment was empty was immediately filled with a formidable enemy force. And even though Ender's fleet was the largest he had ever had, there was no place he could deploy it where he would outnumber the enemy long enough to accomplish anything.

And behind the enemy was the planet. The planet, which Maezr had warned him about. What difference did a planet make, when Ender couldn't hope to get near it? Ender waited, waited for the flash of insight that would tell him what to do, how to destroy the enemy. And as he waited, he heard the observers behind him begin to shift in their seats, wondering what Ender was doing, what plan he would follow. And finally it was obvious to everyone that Ender didn't know what to do, that there was nothing to do, and a few of the men at the back of the room made quiet little sounds in their throats.

Then Ender heard Bean's voice in his ear. Bean chuckled and said, "Remember, the enemy's gate is *down*." A few of the other toon leaders laughed, and Ender thought back to the simple games he had played and won in Battle School. They had put him against hopeless odds there, too. And he had beaten them. And he'd be damned if he'd let Maezr Rackham beat him with a cheap trick like outnumbering him a thousand to one. He had won a game in Battle School by going for something the enemy didn't expect, something against the rules—he had won by going against the enemy's gate.

And the enemy's gate was down.

Ender smiled, and realized that if he broke this rule they'd probably kick him out of school, and that way he'd win for sure: He would never have to play a game again.

He whispered into the microphone. His six commanders each took a part of the fleet and launched themselves against the enemy. They pursued erratic courses, darting off in one direction and then another. The enemy immediately stopped his aimless maneuvering and began to group around Ender's six fleets.

Ender took off his microphone, leaned back in his chair, and watched. The observers murmured out loud, now. Ender was doing nothing—he had thrown the game away.

But a pattern began to emerge from the quick confrontations with the enemy. Ender's six groups lost ships constantly as they brushed with each enemy force—but they never stopped for a fight, even when for a moment they could have won a small tactical victory. Instead they continued on their erratic course that led, eventually, down. Toward the enemy planet.

And because of their seemingly random course the enemy didn't realize it until the same time that the observers did. By then it was too late, just as it had been too late for William Bee to stop Ender's soldiers from activating the gate. More of Ender's ships could be hit and destroyed, so that of the six fleets only two were able to get to the planet, and those were decimated. But those tiny groups *did* get through, and they opened fire on the planet.

Ender leaned forward now, anxious to see if his guess would pay off. He half expected a buzzer to sound and the game to be stopped, because he had broken the rule. But he was betting on the accuracy of the simulator. If it could simulate a planet, it could simulate what would happen to a planet under attack.

It did.

The weapons that blew up little ships didn't blow up the entire planet at first. But they did cause terrible explosions. And on the planet there was no space to dissipate the chain reaction. On the planet the chain reaction found more and more fuel to feed it.

The planet's surface seemed to be moving back and forth, but soon the surface gave way in an immense explosion that sent light flashing in all directions. It swallowed up Ender's entire fleet. And then it reached the enemy ships.

The first simply vanished in the explosion. Then, as the explosion spread and became less bright, it was clear what happened to each ship. As the light reached them they flashed brightly for a moment and disappeared. They were all fuel for the fire of the planet.

It took more than three minutes for the explosion to reach the limits of the simulator, and by then it was much fainter. All the ships were gone, and if any had escaped before the explosion reached them, they were few and not worth worrying about. Where the planet had been there was nothing. The simulator was empty.

Ender had destroyed the enemy by sacrificing his entire fleet and breaking the rule against destroying the enemy planet. He wasn't sure whether to feel triumphant at his victory or defiant at the rebuke he was certain would come. So instead he felt nothing. He was tired. He wanted to go to bed and sleep.

He switched off the simulator, and finally heard the noise behind him.

There were no longer two rows of dignified military observers. Instead there was chaos. Some of them were slapping each other on the back; some of them were bowed, head in hands; others were openly weeping. Captain Graff detached himself from the group and came to Ender. Tears streamed down his face, but he was smiling. He reached out his arms, and to Ender's surprise he embraced the boy, held him tightly, and whispered, "Thank you, thank you, thank you, Ender."

Soon all the observers were gathered around the bewildered child, thanking him and cheering him and patting him on the shoulder and shaking his hand. Ender tried to make sense of what they were saying. Had he passed the test after all? Why did it matter so much to them?

Then the crowd parted and Maezr Rackham walked through. He came straight up to Ender Wiggins and held out his hand.

"You made the hard choice, boy. But heaven knows there was no other way you could have done it. Congratulations. You beat them, and it's all over."

All over. Beat them. "I beat *you*, Maezr Rackham."

Maezr laughed, a loud laugh that filled the room. "Ender Wiggins, you never played me. You never played a *game* since I was your teacher."

Ender didn't get the joke. He had played a great many games, at a terrible cost to himself. He began to get angry.

Maezr reached out and touched his shoulder. Ender shrugged him off. Maezr then grew serious and said, "Ender Wiggins, for the last months you have been the commander of our fleets. There were no games. The battles were real. Your only enemy was *the* enemy. You won every battle. And finally today you fought them at their home world, and you destroyed their world, their fleet, you destroyed them completely, and they'll never come against us again. You did it. You."

Real. Not a game. Ender's mind was too tired to cope with it all. He walked away from Maezr, walked silently through the crowd that still whispered thanks and congratulations to the boy, walked out of the simulator room and finally arrived in his bedroom and closed the door.

He was asleep when Graff and Maezr Rackham found him. They came in quietly and roused him. He awoke slowly, and when he recognized them he turned away to go back to sleep.

"Ender," Graff said. "We need to talk to you."

Ender rolled back to face them. He said nothing.

Graff smiled. "It was a shock to you yesterday, I know. But it must make you feel good to know you won the war."

Ender nodded slowly.

"Maezr Rackham here, he never played against you. He only analyzed your battles to find out your weak spots, to help you improve. It worked, didn't it?"

Ender closed his eyes tightly. They waited. He said, "Why didn't you tell me?"

Maezr smiled. "A hundred years ago, Ender, we found out some things. That when a commander's life is in danger he becomes afraid, and fear slows down his thinking. When a commander knows that he's killing people, he becomes cautious or insane, and neither of those help him do well. And when he's mature, when he has responsibilities and an understanding of the world, he becomes cautious and sluggish and can't do his job. So we trained children, who didn't know anything but the game, and never knew when it would become real. That was the theory, and you proved that the theory worked."

Graff reached out and touched Ender's shoulder. "We launched the ships so that they would all arrive at their destination during these few months. We knew that we'd probably have only one good commander, if we were lucky. In history it's been very rare to have more than one genius in a war. So we planned on having a genius. We were gambling. And you came along and we won."

Ender opened his eyes again and they realized that he was angry. "Yes, you won."

Graff and Maezr Rackham looked at each other. "He doesn't understand," Graff whispered.

"I understand," Ender said. "You needed a weapon, and you got it, and it was me."

"That's right," Maezr answered.

"So tell me," Ender went on, "how many people lived on that planet that I destroyed."

They didn't answer him. They waited awhile in silence, and then Graff spoke. "Weapons don't need to understand what they're pointed at, Ender. We did the pointing, and so we're responsible. You just did your job."

Maezr smiled. "Of course, Ender, you'll be taken care of. The government will never forget you. You served us all very well."

Ender rolled over and faced the wall, and even though they tried to talk to him, he didn't answer them. Finally they left.

Ender lay in his bed for a long time before anyone disturbed him again. The door opened softly. Ender didn't turn to see who it was. Then a hand touched him softly.

"Ender, it's me, Bean."

Ender turned over and looked at the little boy who was standing by his bed.

"Sit down," Ender said.

Bean sat. "That last battle, Ender. I didn't know how you'd get us out of it."

Ender smiled. "I didn't. I cheated. I thought they'd kick me out."

"Can you believe it! We won the war. The whole war's over, and we thought we'd have to wait till we grew up to fight in it, and it was us fighting it all the time. I mean, Ender, we're little kids. I'm a little kid, anyway." Bean laughed and Ender smiled. Then they were silent for a little while, Bean sitting on the edge of the bed, Ender watching him out of half-closed eyes.

Finally Bean thought of something else to say.

"What will we do now that the war's over?" he said.

Ender closed his eyes and said, "I need some sleep, Bean."

Bean got up and left and Ender slept.

Graff and Anderson walked through the gates into the park. There was a breeze, but the sun was hot on their shoulders.

"Abba Technics? In the capital?" Graff asked.

"No, in Biggock County. Training division," Anderson replied. "They think my work with children is good preparation. And you?"

Graff smiled and shook his head. "No plans. I'll be here for a few more months. Reports, winding down. I've had offers. Personnel development for

DCIA, executive vice-president for U and P, but I said no. Publisher wants me to do memoirs of the war. I don't know."

They sat on a bench and watched leaves shivering in the breeze. Children on the monkey bars were laughing and yelling, but the wind and the distance swallowed their words. "Look," Graff said, pointing. A little boy jumped from the bars and ran near the bench where the two men sat. Another boy followed him, and holding his hands like a gun he made an explosive sound. The child he was shooting at didn't stop. He fired again.

"I got you! Come back here!"

The other little boy ran on out of sight.

"Don't you know when you're dead?" The boy shoved his hands in his pockets and kicked a rock back to the monkey bars. Anderson smiled and shook his head. "Kids," he said. Then he and Graff stood up and walked on out of the park.

❦ SPIDER (PAUL) ROBINSON (1948-)

In the pages of The Magazine of Fantasy and Science Fiction, Fantastic Universe, *and* Weird Tales *in the 1950s, L. Sprague de Camp and Fletcher Pratt published a series of stories about Gavigan's Bar. The* Gavigan's Bar *stories were comedies that included a range of colorful and eccentric alien characters. These tales foreshadowed stories of the Mos Eisley Cantina in* Star Wars *and Spider Robinson's tales of Callahan's Crosstime Saloon. While Robinson's stories of Callahan and his cronies have been highly popular since their first installment in 1973, the author's talents go much further than these wry, sardonic vignettes.*

Born in New York and a resident of Canada since the early 1970s, Spider Robinson is a highly versatile author of Science Fiction whose writing has earned multiple Hugo and Nebula awards. Between 1975 and 1977, his criticism and reviews of Science Fiction in the pages of Galaxy *magazine earned him further acclaim. The high points of his career thus far have been the 1970s and 1980s, when he published novels such as the Hugo and Nebula award winning* Telempath *(1976),* Mindkiller *(1982), and* Time Pressure *(1987). These and other works have earned Spider Robinson favorable comparisons to Robert A. Heinlein.*

The comparison is valid when one considers Robinson's Heinleinesque portrayal of government and bureaucracy in "Melancholy Elephants." Replete with late twentieth-century popular culture history, the story features a philosophical discussion of the arts, copyrights and intellectual property rights, and, perhaps most important, racial memory—the basis for the story's title.

Melancholy Elephants
(Analog: Science Fiction–Science Fact, *June 1982*)

> *This story is dedicated to Virginia Heinlein.*

She sat zazen, concentrating on not concentrating, until it was time to prepare for the appointment. Sitting *seemed* to produce the usual serenity, put everything in perspective. Her hand did not tremble as she applied her make-up; tranquil features looked back at her from the mirror. She was mildly surprised, in fact, at just how calm she was, until she got out of the hotel elevator at the garage level and the mugger made his play: she killed him instead of disabling him. Which was obviously not a measured, balanced action—the offical fuss and paperwork could make her late. Annoyed at herself, she stuffed the corpse under a shiny new Westinghouse roadable whose owner she knew to be in Luna, and continued on to her own car. This would have to be squared later, and it would cost. No help for it—she fought to regain at least the semblance of tranquillity as her car emerged from the garage and turned north.

Nothing must interfere with this meeting, or with her role in it.

Dozens of man-years and God knows how many dollars, she thought; *funnelling down to perhaps a half hour of conversation. All the effort, all the hope. Insignificant on the scale of the Great Wheel, of course . . . but when you balance it all on a half hour of talk, it's like balancing a stereo cartridge on a needlepoint: It only takes a gram or so of weight to wear out a piece of diamond. I must be harder than diamond.*

Rather than clear a window and watch Washington, D.C. roll by beneath her car, she turned on the television. She absorbed and integrated the news, on the chance that there might be some late-breaking item she could turn to her advantage in the conversation to come; none developed. Shortly the car addressed her: "Grounding, ma'am. I.D. eyeball request." When the car landed she cleared and then opened her window, presented her pass and I.D. to a Marine in dress blues, and was cleared at once. At the Marine's direction she re-opaqued the window and surrendered control of her own car to the house computer, and when the car parked itself and powered down she got out without haste. A man she knew was waiting to meet her, smiling.

"Dorothy, it's good to see you again."

"Hello, Phillip. Good of you to meet me."

"You look lovely this evening."

"You're too kind."

She did not chafe at the meaningless pleasantries. She needed Phil's support, or she might. But she did reflect on how many, many sentences have been worn smooth with use, rendered meaningless by centuries of repetition. It was by no means a new thought.

"If you'll come with me, he'll see you at once."

"Thank you, Phillip." She wanted to ask what the old man's mood was, but knew it would put Phil in an impossible position.

"I rather think your luck is good; the old man seems to be in excellent spirits tonight."

She smiled her thanks, and decided that if and when Phil got around to making his pass she would accept him.

The corridors through which he led her then were broad and high and long; the building dated back to a time of cheap power. Even in Washington, few others would have dared to live in such an energy-wasteful environment. The extremely spare decor reinforced the impression created by the place's very dimensions: bare space from carpet to ceiling, broken approximately every forty metres by some exquisitely simple objet d'art of at least a megabuck's value, appropriately displayed. An unadorned, perfect, white porcelain bowl, over a thousand years old, on a rough cherrywood pedestal. An arresting colour photograph of a snow-covered country road, silkscreened onto stretched silver foil; the time of day changed as one walked past it. A crystal globe, a metre in diameter, within which danced a hologram of the immortal Shara Drummond; since she had ceased performing before the advent of holo technology, this had to be an expensive computer reconstruction. A small sealed glassite chamber containing the first vacuum-sculpture ever made, Nakagawa's legendary

Starstone. A visitor in no hurry could study an object at leisure, then walk quite a distance in undistracted contemplation before encountering another. A visitor in a hurry, like Dorothy, would not *quite* encounter peripherally astonishing stimuli often enough to get the trick of filtering them out. Each tugged at her attention, intruded on her thoughts; they were distracting both intrinsically and as a reminder of the measure of their owner's wealth. To approach this man in his own home, whether at leisure or in haste, was to be humbled. She knew the effect was intentional, and could not transcend it; this irritated her, which irritated her. She straggled for detachment.

At the end of the seemingly endless corridors was an elevator. Phillip handed her into it, punched a floor button, without giving her a chance to see which one, and stepped back into the doorway. "Good luck, Dorothy."

"Thank you, Phillip. Any topics to be sure and avoid?"

"Well . . . don't bring up hemorrhoids."

"I didn't know one could."

He smiled. "Are we still on for lunch Thursday?"

"Unless you'd rather make it dinner."

One eyebrow lifted. "And breakfast?"

She appeared to consider it. "Branch," she decided. He half-bowed and stepped back.

The elevator door closed and she forgot Phillip's existence.

Sentient beings are innumerable; I vow to save them all. The deluding passions are limitless; I vow to extinguish them all. The truth is limitless; I—

The elevator door opened again, truncating the Vow of the Boddhisatva. She had not felt the elevator stop—yet she knew that she must have descended at least a hundred metres. She left the elevator.

The room was larger than she had expected; nonetheless the big powered chair dominated it easily. The chair also seemed to dominate—at least visually—its occupant. A misleading impression, as he dominated all this massive home, everything in it and, to a great degree, the country in which it stood. But he did not look like much.

A scent symphony was in progress, the cinnamon passage of Bulachevski's "Childhood." It happened to be one of her personal favourites, and this encouraged her.

"Hello, Senator."

"Hello, Mrs. Martin. Welcome to my home. Forgive me for not rising."

"Of course. It was most gracious of you to receive me."

"It is my pleasure and privilege. A man my age appreciates a chance to spend time with a woman as beautiful and intelligent as yourself."

"Senator, how soon do we start talking to each other?"

He raised that part of his face which had once held an eyebrow.

"We haven't *said* anything yet that is true. You do not stand because you cannot. Your gracious reception cost me three carefully hoarded favours and a good deal of folding cash. More than the going rate; you are seeing me reluctantly. You have at least eight mistresses that I know of, each of whom makes me look like a dull matron. I concealed a warm corpse on the way here because I dared not be late; my time is short and my business urgent. Can we begin?"

She held her breath and prayed silently. Everything she had been able to learn about the Senator told her that this was the correct way to approach him. But was it?

The mummy-like face fissured in a broad grin. "Right away. Mrs. Martin, I like you and that's the truth. My time is short, too. What do you want of me?"

"Don't you know?"

"I can make an excellent guess. I hate guessing."

"I am heavily and publicly committed to the defeat of S. 4217896."

"Yes, but for all I know you might have come here to sell out."

"Oh." She tried not to show her surprise. "What makes you think that possible?"

"Your organization is large and well-financed and fairly efficient, Mrs. Martin, and there's something about it I don't understand."

"What is that?"

"Your objective. Your arguments are weak and implausible, and whenever this is pointed out to one of you, you simply keep on pushing. Many times I have seen people take a position without apparent logic to it—but I've always been able to see the logic if I kept on looking hard enough. But as I see it, S. '896 would work to the clear and lasting advantage of the group you claim to represent, the artists. There's too much intelligence in your organization to square with your goals. So I have to wonder what you *are* working for, and why. One possibility is that you're willing to roll over on this copyright thing in exchange for whatever it is that you *really* want. Follow me?"

"Senator, I *am* working on behalf of all artists—and in a broader sense—"

He looked pained, or rather, more pained. ". . . 'for all mankind,' oh my *God*, Mrs. Martin, really now."

"I *know* you have heard that countless times, and probably said it as often." He grinned evilly. "This is one of those rare times when it happens to be true. I believe that if S. '896 does pass, our species will suffer significant trauma."

He raised a skeletal hand, tugged at his lower lip. "Now that I have ascertained where you stand, I believe I can save you a good deal of money. By concluding this audience, and seeing that the squeeze you paid for half an hour of my time is refunded pro rata."

Her heart sank, but she kept her voice even. "Without even hearing the hidden logic behind our arguments?"

"It would be pointless and cruel to make you go into your spiel, ma'am. You see, I cannot help you."

She wanted to cry out, and savagely refused herself permission. *Control*, whispered a part of her mind, while another part shouted that a man such as this did not lightly use the words, "I cannot." But he *had* to be wrong. Perhaps the sentence was only a bargaining gambit. . . .

No sign of the internal conflict showed; her voice was calm and measured. "Sir, I have not come here to lobby. I simply wanted to inform you personally that our organization intends to make a no-strings campaign donation in the amount of—"

"Mrs. Martin, please! Before you commit yourself, I repeat, I cannot help you. Regardless of the sum offered."

"Sir, it is substantial."

"I'm sure. Nonetheless it is insufficient."

She knew she should not ask. "Senator, *why?*"

He frowned, a frightening sight.

"Look," she said, the desperation almost showing through now, "keep the pro rata if it buys me an answer! Until I'm convinced that my mission is utterly hopeless, I must not abandon it; answering me is the quickest way to get me out of your office. Your scanners have searched me quite thoroughly, you know that I'm not abscamming you."

Still frowning, he nodded. "Very well. I cannot accept your campaign donation because I have already accepted one from another source."

Her very worst secret fear was realized. He had already taken money from the other side. The one thing any politician must do, no matter how powerful, is stay bought. It was all over.

All her panic and tension vanished, to be replaced by a sadness so great and so pervasive that for a moment she thought it might literally stop her heart.

Too late! Oh my darling, I was too late!

She realized bleakly that there were too many people in her life, too many responsibilities and entanglements. It would be at least a month before she could honourably suicide.

"—you all right, Mrs. Martin?" the old man was saying, sharp concern in his voice.

She gathered discipline around her like a familiar cloak. "Yes, sir, thank you. Thank you for speaking plainly." She stood up and smoothed her skirt. "And for your—"

"Mrs. Martin."

"—gracious hos—Yes?"

"Will you tell me your arguments? Why shouldn't I support '896?"

She blinked sharply. "You just said it would be pointless and cruel."

"If I held out the slightest hope, yes, it would be. If you'd rather not waste your time, I will not compel you. But I am curious."

"Intellectual curiosity?"

He seemed to sit up a little straighter—surely an illusion, for a prosthetic spine is not motile. "Mrs. Martin, I happen to be committed to a course of action. That does not mean I don't care whether the action is good or bad."

"Oh." She thought for a moment. "If I convince you, you will not thank me."

"I know. I saw the look on your face a moment ago, and . . . it reminded me of a night many years ago. Night my mother died. If you've got a sadness that big, and I can take on a part of it, I should try. Sit down."

She sat.

"Now tell me: what's so damned awful about extending copyright to meet the realities of modern life? Customarily I try to listen to both sides before accepting the campaign donation—but this seemed so open and shut, so straightforward . . ."

"Senator, that bill is a short-term boon, to some artists—and a long-term disaster for all artists, on Earth and off."

" 'In the long run, Mr. President—' " he began, quoting Keynes.

"—we are some of us still alive," she finished softly and pointedly. "Aren't we? You've put your finger on part of the problem."

"What is this disaster you speak of?" he asked.

"The worst psychic trauma the race has yet suffered."

He studied her carefully and frowned again. "Such a possibility is not even hinted at in your literature or materials."

"To do so would precipitate the trauma. At present only a handful of people know, even in my organization. I'm telling *you* because you asked, and because I am certain that you are the only person recording this conversation. I'm betting that you will wipe the tape."

He blinked, and sucked at the memory of his teeth. "My, my," he said mildly. "Let me get comfortable." He had the chair recline sharply and massage his lower limbs; she saw that he could still watch her by overhead mirror if he chose. His eyes were closed. "All right, go ahead."

She needed no time to choose her words. "Do you know how old art is, Senator?"

"As old as man, I suppose. In fact, it may be part of the definition."

"Good answer," she said. "Remember that. But for all present-day intents and purposes, you might as well say that art is a little over 15,600 years old. That's the age of the oldest surviving artwork, the cave paintings at Lascaux. Doubtless the cave-painters sang, and danced, and even told stories—but these arts left no record more durable than the memory of a man. Perhaps it was the storytellers who next learned how to preserve their art. Countless more generations would pass before a workable method of musical notation was devised and standardized. Dancers only learned in the last few centuries how to leave even the most rudimentary record of their art.

"The racial memory of our species has been getting longer since Lascaux. The biggest single improvement came with the invention of writing: our memory-span went from a few generations to as many as the Bible has been around. But it took a massive effort to sustain a memory that long: it was difficult to hand-copy manu-scripts faster than barbarians, plagues, or other natural disasters could destroy them. The obvious solution was the printing press: to make and disseminate so many copies of a manuscript or artwork that *some* would survive any catastrophe.

"But with the printing press a new idea was born. Art was suddenly mass-marketable, and there was money in it. Writers decided that they should own the right to copy their work. The notion of copyright was waiting to be born.

"Then in the last hundred and fifty years came the largest quantum jumps in human racial memory. Recording technologies. Visual: photography, film, video, Xerox, holo. Audio: low-fi, hi-fi, stereo, and digital. Then computers, the ultimate in information storage. Each of these technologies generated new art forms, and new ways of preserving the ancient art forms. And each required a reassessment of the idea of copyright.

"You know the system we have now, unchanged since the mid-twentieth-century. Copyright ceases to exist fifty years after the death of the copyright holder. But the size of the human race has increased drastically since the 1900s— and so has the average human lifespan. Most people in developed nations now ex-pect to live to be a hundred and twenty, you yourself are considerably older. And so, naturally, S. '896 now seeks to extend copyright into perpetuity."

"Well," the senator interrupted, "what is *wrong* with that? Should a man's work cease to be his simply because he has neglected to keep on breathing? Mrs. Martin, you yourself will be wealthy all your life if that bill passes. Do you truly wish to give away your late husband's genius?"

She winced in spite of herself.

"Forgive my bluntness, but that is what I understand *least* about your position."

"Senator, if I try to hoard the fruits of my husband's genius, I may cripple my race. Don't you see what perpetual copyright implies? It is perpetual racial mem-ory! That bill will give the human race an elephant's memory. *Have you ever seen a cheerful elephant?*"

He was silent for a time. Then: "I'm still not sure I understand the problem."

"Don't feel bad, sir. The problem has been directly under the nose of all of us for at *least* eighty years, and hardly anyone has noticed."

"Why is that?"

"I think it comes down to a kind of innate failure of mathematical intuition, com-mon to most humans. We tend to confuse any sufficiently high number with infinity."

"Well, anything above ten to the eighty-fifth might as well be infinity."

"Beg pardon?"

"Sorry—I should not have interrupted. That is the current best-guess for the number of atoms in the Universe. Go on."

She struggled to get back on the rails. "Well, it takes a lot less than that to equal 'infinity' in most minds. For millions of years we looked at the ocean and said, 'That is infinite. It will accept our garbage and waste forever.' We looked at the sky and said, 'That is infinite: it will hold an infinite amount of smoke.' We *like* the idea of infinity. A problem with infinity in it is easily solved. How long can you pollute a planet infinitely large? Easy: forever. Stop thinking.

"Then one day there are so many of us that the planet no longer seems infinitely large.

"So we go elsewhere. There are infinite resources in the *rest* of the solar system, aren't there? I think you are one of the few people alive wise enough to realize that there are *not* infinite resources in the solar system, and sophisticated enough to have included that awareness in your plans."

The senator now looked troubled. He sipped something from a straw. "Relate all this to your problem."

"Do you remember a case from about eighty years ago, involving the song 'My Sweet Lord' by George Harrison?"

"Remember it? I did research on it. My firm won."

"Your firm convinced the court that Harrison had gotten the tune for that song from a song called 'He's So Fine,' written over ten years earlier. Shortly thereafter Yoko Ono was accused of stealing 'You're My Angel' from the classic 'Makin' Whoopee,' written more than thirty years earlier. Chuck Berry's estate eventually took John Lennon's estate to court over 'Come Together.' Then in the late '80s the great Plagiarism Plague *really* got started in the courts. From then on it was open season on popular composers, and still is. But it really hit the fan at the turn of the century, when Brindle's *Ringsong* was shown to be 'substantially similar' to one of Corelli's concertos.

"There are eighty-eight notes. One hundred and seventy-six, if your ear is good enough to pick out quarter tones. Add in rests and so forth, different time signatures. Pick a figure for maximum number of notes a melody can contain. I do not know the figure for the maximum possible number of melodies—too many variables—but I am sure it is quite high.

"*I am certain that is not infinity.*

"For one thing, a great many of those possible arrays of eighty-eight notes will not be perceived as music, as melody, by the human ear. Perhaps more than half. They will not be hummable, whistleable, listenable—some will be actively unpleasant to hear. Another large fraction will be so similar to each other as to be effectively identical: if you change three notes of the Moonlight Sonata, you have not created something new.

"I do not know the figure for the maximum number of discretely appreciable melodies, and again I'm certain it is quite high, and again I am certain that it is not infinity. There are sixteen billion of us alive, Senator, more than all the people that have ever lived. Thanks to our technology, better than half of us have no meaningful work to do; fifty-four percent of our population is entered on the tax rolls as artists. Because the synthesizer is so cheap and versatile, a majority of those artists are musicians, and a great many are composers. Do you know what it is like to be a composer these days, Senator?"

"I know a few composers."

"Who are still working?"

"Well . . . three of 'em."

"How often do they bring out a new piece?"

Pause. "I would say once every five years on the average. Hmmm. Never thought of it before, but—"

"Did you know that at present two out of every five copyright submissions to the Music Division are rejected on the first computer search?"

The old man's face had stopped registering surprise, other than for histrionic purposes, more than a century before; nonetheless, she knew she had rocked him. "No, I did not."

"Why would you know? Who would talk about it? But it is a fact nonetheless. Another fact is that, when the increase in number of working composers is taken into account, the *rate* of submissions to the Copyright Office is decreasing significantly. There are more composers than ever, but their individual productivity is declining. Who is the most popular composer alive?"

"Uh . . . I suppose that Vachandra fellow."

"Correct. He has been working for a little over fifty years. If you began now to play every note he ever wrote, in succession, you would be done in twelve hours. Wagner wrote well over sixty hours of music—the Ring alone runs twenty-one hours. The Beatles—essentially two composers—produced over twelve hours of original music in *less than ten years*. Why were the greats of yesteryear so much more prolific?

"There were more enjoyable permutations of eighty-eight notes for them to find."

"Oh my," the senator whispered.

"Now go back to the 1970s again. Remember the *Roots* plagiarism case? And the dozens like it that followed? Around the same time a writer named van Vogt sued the makers of a successful film called *Alien*, for plagiarism of a story forty years later. Two other writers named Bova and Ellison sued a television studio for stealing a series idea. All three collected.

"That ended the legal principle that one does not copyright *ideas* but *arrangements of words*. The number of word-arrangements is finite, but the number of *ideas* is *much* smaller. Certainly, they can be retold in endless ways—*West Side Story* is a brilliant reworking of *Romeo and Juliet*. But it was only possible because *Romeo and Juliet* was in the public domain. Remember too that of the finite number of stories that can be told, a certain number will be *bad stories*.

"As for visual artists—well, once a man demonstrated in the laboratory an ability to distinguish between eighty-one distinct shades of colour accurately. I think that's an upper limit. There is a maximum amount of information that the eye is capable of absorbing, and much of that will be the equivalent of noise—"

"But . . . but . . ." This man was reputed never to have hesitated in any way under any circumstances. "But there'll always be change . . . there'll always be new discoveries, new horizons, new social attitudes, to infuse art with new—"

"Not as fast as artists breed. Do you know about the great split in literature at the beginning of the twentieth century? The mainstream essentially abandoned the Novel of Ideas after Henry James, and turned its collective attention to the Novel of Character. They had sucked that dry by mid-century, and they're still chewing on the pulp today. Meanwhile a small group of writers, desperate for something new to write about, for a new story to tell, invented a new genre called science fiction. They mined the future for ideas. The infinite future—like the infinite coal and oil and copper they had then too. In less than a century they had mined it out; there hasn't been a genuinely original idea in science fiction in over thirty years. Fantasy has always been touted as the 'literature of infinite possibility'—but there is even a theoretical upper limit to the 'meaningfully impossible,' and we are fast reaching it."

"We can create new art forms," he said.

"People have been trying to create new art forms for a long time, sir. Almost all fell by the wayside. People just didn't like them."

"We'll *learn* to like them. Damn it, we'll have to."

"And they'll help, for a while. More new art forms have been born in the last two centuries than in the previous million years—though none in the last fifteen years. Scent-symphonies, tactile sculpture, kinetic sculpture, zero-gravity dance—they're all rich new fields, and they are generating mountains of new copyrights. Mountains of finite size. The ultimate bottleneck is this: that *we have only five senses with which to apprehend art, and that is a finite number.* Can I have some water, please?"

"Of course." The old man appeared to have regained his usual control, but the glass which emerged from the arm of her chair contained apple juice, She ignored this and continued.

"But that's not what I'm afraid of, Senator. The theoretical heat-death of artistic expression is something we may never really approach in fact. Long before that point, the game will collapse."

She paused to gather her thoughts, sipped her juice. A part of her mind noted that it harmonized with the recurrent cinnamon motif of Bulachevski's scent-symphony, which was still in progress.

"Artists have been deluding themselves for centuries with the notion that they create. In fact they do nothing of the sort. They discover. Inherent in the nature of reality are a number of combinations of musical tones that will be perceived as pleasing by a human central nervous system. For millennia we have been discovering them, implicit in the universe—and telling ourselves that we 'created' them. To create implies infinite possibility, to discover implies finite possibility. As a species I think we will react poorly to having our noses rubbed in the fact that we are discoverers and not creators."

She stopped speaking and sat very straight. Unaccountably her feet hurt. She closed her eyes, and continued speaking.

"My husband wrote a song for me, on the occasion of our fortieth wedding anniversary. It was our love in music, unique and special and intimate, the most beautiful melody I ever heard in my life. It made him so happy to have written it. Of his last ten compositions he had burned five for being derivative, and the others had all failed copyright clearance. But this was fresh, special—he joked that my love for him had inspired him. The next day he submitted it for clearance, and learned that it had been a popular air during his early childhood, and had already been unsuccessfully submitted fourteen times since its original registration. A week later he burned all his manuscripts and working tapes and killed himself."

She was silent for a long time, and the senator did not speak.

" 'Ars longa, vita brevis est,' " she said at last. "There's been comfort of a kind in that for thousands of years. But art is long, not infinite. 'The Magic goes away.' One day we will *use it up*—unless we can learn to recycle it like any other finite resource." Her voice gained strength. "Senator, that bill has to fail, if I have to take you on to do it. Perhaps I can't win—but I'm going to fight you! A copyright must not be allowed to last more than fifty years—after which it should be flushed from the memory banks of the Copyright Office. We need selective voluntary amnesia if Discoverers of Art are to continue to work without psychic damage. Facts should be remembered—but dreams?" She shivered. ". . . Dreams should be forgotten when we wake. Or one day we will find ourselves unable to sleep. Given eight billion artists with effective working lifetimes in excess of a century, we can no longer allow individuals to own their discoveries in perpetuity. We must do it the way the human race did it for a million years—by forgetting, and rediscovering. Because one day the infinite number of monkeys will have nothing else to write *except* the complete works of Shakespeare. And they would probably rather not *know* that when it happens."

Now she was finished, nothing more to say. So was the scent-symphony, whose last motif was fading slowly from the air. No clock ticked, no artifact hummed. The stillness was complete, for perhaps half a minute.

"If you live long enough," the senator said slowly at last, "there is nothing new under the sun." He shifted in his great chair. "If you're lucky, you die sooner than that. I haven't heard a new dirty joke in fifty years." He seemed to sit up straight in his chair. "I will kill S.4217896."

She stiffened in shock. After a time, she slumped slightly and resumed breathing. So many emotions fought for ascendancy that she barely had time to recognize them as they went by. She could not speak.

"Furthermore," he went on, "I will not tell anyone why I'm doing it. It will begin the end of my career in public life, which I did not ever plan to leave, but you have convinced me that I must. I am both . . . glad, and—" His face tightened with pain—"and *bitterly* sorry that you told me why I must."

"So am I, sir," she said softly, almost inaudibly.

He looked at her sharply. "Some kinds of fight, you can't feel good even if you win them. Only two kinds of people take on fights like that: fools, and remarkable people. I think you are a remarkable person, Mrs. Martin."

She stood, knocking over her juice. "I wish to God I were a fool," she cried, feeling her control begin to crack at last.

"Dorothy!" he thundered.

She flinched as if he had struck her. "Sir?" she said automatically.

"Do *not* go to pieces! That is an order. You're wound up too tight; the pieces might not go back together again."

"So what?" she asked bitterly.

He was using the full power of his voice now, the voice which had stopped at least one war. "So how many friends do you think a man my age has *got*, damn it? Do you think minds like yours are common? We *share* this business now, and that makes us friends. You are the first person to come out of that elevator and really surprise me in a quarter of a century. And soon, when the word gets around that I've broken faith, people will stop coming out of the elevator. You think like me, and I can't afford to lose you." He smiled, and the smile seemed to melt decades from his face. "Hang on, Dorothy," he said, "and we will comfort each other in our terrible knowledge. All right?"

For several moments she concentrated exclusively on her breathing, slowing and regularizing it. Then, tentatively, she probed at her emotions.

"Why," she said wonderingly, "it *is* better . . . shared."

"Anything is."

She looked at him then, and tried to smile and finally succeeded. "Thank you, Senator."

He returned her smile as he wiped all recordings of their conversation. "Call me Bob."

"Yes, Robert."

🎲 WILLIAM (FORD) GIBSON (1948–)

The origin of the popular subgenre of Science Fiction called Cyberpunk dates back to Fritz Lang's silent film Metropolis *(1926) and earlier works. In contemporary times, Cyberpunk has been defined in movies such as Ridley Scott's* Blade Runner *(1982) and the works of Science Fiction authors such as Rudy Rucker, Bruce Sterling, John Shirley, and Michael Swanwick. However, the author who has best defined this type of Science Fiction is William Gibson.*

Cyberpunk stories are characterized by tough characters in tough worlds, not unlike the 1920s and 1930s hard-boiled Detective Fiction of Erle Stanley Gardner, Dashiell Hammett, and Raymond Chandler. They include themes of high technology and virtual reality, and even elements of rock 'n' roll and punk cultures. Not too long ago, Cyberpunk Science Fiction was considered avante garde, sub- or even counterculture. Today, it is increasingly popular or mainstream culture. The 1999 movie The Matrix *is an example. [Gibson's Cyberpunk short story "Johnny Mnemonic" (1981) was made into a popular movie of the same title starring Keanu Reeves in 1995.]*

Influenced by the works of Philip K. Dick and J. G. Ballard and author of several Science Fiction short stories, William Gibson defined the subgenre with his 1984 novel Neuromancer. *His Cyberpunk short story "Burning Chrome" preceded* Neuromancer *and earned a Nebula award nomination. Today, William Gibson's Cyberpunk novels are consistently best-sellers.*

Burning Chrome

(Omni, *July 1982*)

It was hot, the night we burned Chrome. Out in the malls and plazas, moths were batting themselves to death against the neon, but in Bobby's loft the only light came from a monitor screen and the green and red LEDs on the face of the matrix simulator. I knew every chip in Bobby's simulator by heart; it looked like your workaday Ono-Sendai VII, the "Cyberspace Seven," but I'd rebuilt it so many times that you'd have had a hard time finding a square millimeter of factory circuitry in all that silicon.

We waited side by side in front of the simulator console, watching the time display in the screen's lower left corner.

"Go for it," I said, when it was time, but Bobby was already there, leaning forward to drive the Russian program into its slot with the heel of his hand. He did it with the tight grace of a kid slamming change into an arcade game, sure of winning and ready to pull down a string of free games.

A silver tide of phosphenes boiled across my field of vision as the matrix began to unfold in my head, a 3-D chessboard, infinite and perfectly transparent. The Russian program seemed to lurch as we entered the grid. If anyone else had been jacked into that part of the matrix, he might have seen a surf of flickering shadow roll out of the little yellow pyramid that represented our computer. The program was a mimetic weapon, designed to absorb local color and present itself as a crash-priority override in whatever context it encountered.

"Congratulations," I heard Bobby say. "We just became an Eastern Seaboard Fission Authority inspection probe. . . ." That meant we were clearing fiberoptic lines with the cybernetic equivalent of a fire siren, but in the simulation matrix we seemed to rush straight for Chrome's data base. I couldn't see it yet, but I already knew those walls were waiting. Walls of shadow, walls of ice.

Chrome: her pretty childface smooth as steel, with eyes that would have been at home on the bottom of some deep Atlantic trench, cold gray eyes that lived under terrible pressure. They said she cooked her own cancers for people who crossed her, rococo custom variations that took years to kill you. They said a lot of things about Chrome, none of them at all reassuring.

So I blotted her out with a picture of Rikki. Rikki kneeling in a shaft of dusty sunlight that slanted into the loft through a grid of steel and glass: her faded camouflage fatigues, her translucent rose sandals, the good line of her bare back as she rummaged through a nylon gear bag. She looks up, and a half-blond curl falls to tickle her nose. Smiling, buttoning an old shirt of Bobby's, frayed khaki cotton drawn across her breasts.

She smiles.

"Son of a bitch," said Bobby, "we just told Chrome we're an IRS audit and three Supreme Court subpoenas. . . . Hang on to your ass, Jack. . . ."

So long, Rikki. Maybe now I see you never.

And dark, so dark, in the halls of Chrome's ice.

Bobby was a cowboy, and ice was the nature of his game, *ice* from ICE, Intrusion Countermeasures Electronics. The matrix is an abstract representation of the relationships between data systems. Legitimate programmers jack into their employers' sector of the matrix and find themselves surrounded by bright geometries representing the corporate data.

Towers and fields of it ranged in the colorless nonspace of the simulation matrix, the electronic consensus-hallucination that facilitates the handling and exchange of massive quantities of data. Legitimate programmers never see the walls of ice they work behind, the walls of shadow that screen their operations from others, from industrial-espionage artists and hustlers like Bobby Quine.

Bobby was a cowboy. Bobby was a cracksman, a burglar, casing mankind's extended electronic nervous system, rustling data and credit in the crowded matrix, monochrome nonspace where the only stars are dense concentrations of information, and high above it all burn corporate galaxies and the cold spiral arms of military systems.

Bobby was another one of those young-old faces you see drinking in the Gentleman Loser, the chic bar for computer cowboys, rustlers, cybernetic second-story men. We were partners.

Bobby Quine and Automatic Jack. Bobby's the thin, pale dude with the dark glasses, and Jack's the mean-looking guy with the myoelectric arm. Bobby's software and Jack's hard; Bobby punches console and Jack runs down all the little things that can give you an edge. Or, anyway, that's what the scene watchers in the Gentleman Loser would've told you, before Bobby decided to burn Chrome. But they also might've told you that Bobby was losing his edge, slowing down. He was twenty-eight, Bobby, and that's old for a console cowboy.

Both of us were good at what we did, but somehow that one big score just wouldn't come down for us. I knew where to go for the right gear, and Bobby had all his licks down pat. He'd sit back with a white terry sweatband across his forehead and whip moves on those keyboards faster than you could follow, punching his way through some of the fanciest ice in the business, but that was when something happened that managed to get him totally wired, and that didn't happen often. Not highly motivated, Bobby, and I was the kind of guy who's happy to have the rent covered and a clean shirt to wear.

But Bobby had this thing for girls, like they were his private tarot or something, the way he'd get himself moving. We never talked about it, but when it started to look like he was losing his touch that summer, he started to spend more time in the Gentleman Loser. He'd sit at a table by the open doors and watch the crowd slide by, nights when the bugs were at the neon and the air smelled of perfume and fast food. You could see his sunglasses scanning those faces as they passed, and he must have decided that Rikki's was the one he was waiting for, the wild card and the luck changer. The new one.

I went to New York to check out the market, to see what was available in hot software.

The Finn's place has a defective hologram in the window, METRO HOLOGRAFIX, over a display of dead flies wearing fur coats of gray dust. The scrap's waist-high, inside, drifts of it rising to meet walls that are barely visible behind nameless junk, behind sagging pressboard shelves stacked with old skin magazines and yellow-spined years of *National Geographic.*

"You need a gun," said the Finn. He looks like a recombo DNA project aimed at tailoring people for high-speed burrowing. "You're in luck. I got the new Smith and Wesson, the four-oh-eight Tactical. Got this xenon projector slung under the barrel, see, batteries in the grip, throw you a twelve-inch high-noon circle in the pitch dark at fifty yards. The light source is so narrow, it's almost impossible to spot. It's just like voodoo in a nightfight."

I let my arm clunk down on the table and started the fingers drumming; the servos in the hand began whining like overworked mosquitoes. I knew that the Finn really hated the sound.

"You looking to pawn that?" He prodded the Duralumin wrist joint with the chewed shaft of a felt-tip pen. "Maybe get yourself something a little quieter?"

I kept it up. "I don't need any guns, Finn."

"Okay," he said, "okay," and I quit drumming. "I only got this one item, and I don't even know what it is." He looked unhappy. "I got it off these bridge-and-tunnel kids from Jersey last week."

"So when'd you ever buy anything you didn't know what it was, Finn?"

"Wise ass." And he passed me a transparent mailer with something in it that looked like an audio cassette through the bubble padding. "They had a passport," he said. "They had credit cards and a watch. And that."

"They had the contents of somebody's pockets, you mean."

He nodded. "The passport was Belgian. It was also bogus, looked to me, so I put it in the furnace. Put the cards in with it. The watch was okay, a Porsche, nice watch."

It was obviously some kind of plug-in military program. Out of the mailer, it looked like the magazine of a small assault rifle, coated with nonreflective black plastic. The edges and corners showed bright metal; it had been knocking around for a while.

"I'll give you a bargain on it, Jack. For old times' sake."

I had to smile at that. Getting a bargain from the Finn was like God repealing the law of gravity when you have to carry a heavy suitcase down ten blocks of airport corridor.

"Looks Russian to me," I said. "Probably the emergency sewage controls for some Leningrad suburb. Just what I need."

"You know," said the Finn. "I got a pair of shoes older than you are. Sometimes I think you got about as much class as those yahoos from Jersey. What do you want me to tell you, it's the keys to the Kremlin? You figure out what the goddamn thing is. Me, I just sell the stuff."

I bought it.

Bodiless, we swerve into Chrome's castle of ice. And we're fast, fast. It feels like we're surfing the crest of the invading program, hanging ten above the seething glitch systems as they mutate. We're sentient patches of oil swept along down corridors of shadow.

Somewhere we have bodies, very far away, in a crowded loft roofed with steel and glass. Somewhere we have microseconds, maybe time left to pull out.

We've crashed her gates disguised as an audit and three subpoenas, but her defenses are specifically geared to cope with that kind of official intrusion. Her most sophisticated ice is structured to fend off warrants, writs, subpoenas. When we breached the first gate, the bulk of her data vanished behind core-command ice, these walls we see as leagues of corridor, mazes of shadow. Five separate landlines spurted May Day signals to law firms, but the virus had already taken over the parameter ice. The glitch systems gobble the distress calls as our mimetic subprograms scan anything that hasn't been blanked by core command.

The Russian program lifts a Tokyo number from the unscreened data, choosing it for frequency of calls, average length of calls, the speed with which Chrome returned those calls.

"Okay," says Bobby, "we're an incoming scrambler call from a pal of hers in Japan. That should help."

Ride 'em, cowboy.

Bobby read his future in women; his girls were omens, changes in the weather, and he'd sit all night in the Gentleman Loser, waiting for the season to lay a new face down in front of him like a card.

I was working late in the loft one night, shaving down a chip, my arm off and the little waldo jacked straight into the stump.

Bobby came in with a girl I hadn't seen before, and usually I feel a little funny if a stranger sees me working that way, with those leads clipped to the hard carbon studs that stick out of my stump. She came right over and looked at the magnified image on the screen, then saw the waldo moving under its vacuum-sealed dust cover. She didn't say anything, just watched. Right away I had a good feeling about her; it's like that sometimes.

"Automatic Jack, Rikki. My associate."

He laughed, put his arm around her waist, something in his tone letting me know that I'd be spending the night in a dingy room in a hotel.

"Hi," she said. Tall, nineteen or maybe twenty, and she definitely had the goods. With just those few freckles across the bridge of her nose, and eyes somewhere between dark amber and French coffee. Tight black jeans rolled to midcalf and a narrow plastic belt that matched the rose-colored sandals.

But now when I see her sometimes when I'm trying to sleep, I see her somewhere out on the edge of all this sprawl of cities and smoke, and it's like she's a hologram stuck behind my eyes, in a bright dress she must've worn once, when I knew her, something that doesn't quite reach her knees. Bare legs long and straight. Brown hair, streaked with blond, hoods her face, blown in a wind from somewhere, and I see her wave goodbye.

Bobby was making a show of rooting through a stack of audio cassettes. "I'm on my way, cowboy," I said, unclipping the waldo. She watched attentively as I put my arm back on.

"Can you fix things?" she asked.

"Anything, anything you want, Automatic Jack'll fix it." I snapped my Duralumin fingers for her.

She took a little simstim deck from her belt and showed me the broken hinge on the cassette cover.

"Tomorrow," I said, "no problem."

And my oh my, I said to myself, sleep pulling me down the six flights to the street, *what'll Bobby's luck be like with a fortune cookie like that? If his system worked, we'd be striking it rich any night now.* In the street I grinned and yawned and waved for a cab.

Chrome's castle is dissolving, sheets of ice shadow flickering and fading, eaten by the glitch systems that spin out from the Russian program, tumbling away from our central logic thrust and infecting the fabric of the ice itself. The glitch systems are cybernetic virus analogs, self-replicating and voracious. They mutate constantly, in unison, subverting and absorbing Chrome's defenses.

Have we already paralyzed her, or is a bell ringing somewhere, a red light blinking? Does she know?

Rikki Wildside, Bobby called her, and for those first few weeks it must have seemed to her that she had it all, the whole teeming show spread out for her, sharp and bright under the neon. She was new to the scene, and she had all the miles of malls and plazas to prowl, all the shops and clubs, and Bobby to explain the wild side, the tricky wiring on the dark underside of things, all the players and their names and their games. He made her feel at home.

"What happened to your arm?" she asked me one night in the Gentleman Loser, the three of us drinking at a small table in a corner.

"Hang-gliding," I said, "accident."

"Hang-gliding over a wheatfield," said Bobby, "place called Kiev. Our Jack's just hanging there in the dark, under a Nightwing parafoil, with fifty kilos of radar jammed between his legs, and some Russian asshole accidentally burns his arm off with a laser."

I don't remember how I changed the subject, but I did.

I was still telling myself that it wasn't Rikki who was getting to me, but what Bobby was doing with her. I'd known him for a long time, since the end of the war, and I knew he used women as counters in a game, Bobby Quine versus fortune, versus time and the night of cities. And Rikki had turned up just when he needed something to get him going, something to aim for. So he'd set her up as a symbol for everything he wanted and couldn't have, everything he'd had and couldn't keep.

I didn't like having to listen to him tell me how much he loved her, and knowing he believed it only made it worse. He was a past master at the hard fall and the rapid recovery, and I'd seen it happen a dozen times before. He might as well have had NEXT printed across his sunglasses in green Day-Glo capitals, ready to flash out at the first interesting face that flowed past the tables in the Gentleman Loser.

I knew what he did to them. He turned them into emblems, sigils on the map of his hustler's life, navigation beacons he could follow through a sea of bars and neon. What else did he have to steer by? He didn't love money, in and of itself, not enough to follow its lights. He wouldn't work for power over other people; he hated the responsibility it brings. He had some basic pride in his skill, but that was never enough to keep him pushing.

So he made do with women.

When Rikki showed up, he needed one in the worst way. He was fading fast, and smart money was already whispering that the edge was off his game. He needed that one big score, and soon, because he didn't know any other kind of life, and all his clocks were set for hustler's time, calibrated in risk and adrenaline and that supernal dawn calm that comes when every move's proved right and a sweet lump of someone else's credit clicks into your own account.

It was time for him to make his bundle and get out; so Rikki got set up higher and farther away than any of the others ever had, even though—and I felt like screaming it at him—she was right there, alive, totally real, human, hungry, resilient, bored, beautiful, excited, all the things she was. . . .

Then he went out one afternoon, about a week before I made the trip to New York to see Finn. Went out and left us there in the loft, waiting for a thunderstorm. Half the skylight was shadowed by a dome they'd never finished, and the other half showed sky, black and blue with clouds. I was standing by the bench, looking up at that sky, stupid with the hot afternoon, the humidity, and she touched me, touched my shoulder, the half-inch border of taut pink scar that the arm doesn't cover. Anybody else ever touched me there, they went on to the shoulder, the neck. . . .

But she didn't do that. Her nails were lacquered black, not pointed, but tapered oblongs, the lacquer only a shade darker than the carbon-fiber laminate that sheathes my arm. And her hand went down the arm, black nails tracing a weld in the laminate, down to the black anodized elbow joint, out to the wrist, her hand soft-knuckled as a child's, fingers spreading to lock over mine, her palm against the perforated Duralumin.

Her other palm came up to brush across the feedback pads, and it rained all afternoon, raindrops drumming on the steel and soot-stained glass above Bobby's bed.

Ice walls flick away like supersonic butterflies made of shade. Beyond them, the matrix's illusion of infinite space. It's like watching a tape of a prefab building going up; only the tape's reversed and run at high speed, and these walls are torn wings.

Trying to remind myself that this place and the gulfs beyond are only representations, that we aren't "in" Chrome's computer, but interfaced with it, while the matrix simulator in Bobby's loft generates this illusion . . . The core data begin to emerge, exposed, vulnerable. . . . This is the far side of ice, the view of the matrix I've never seen before, the view that fifteen million legitimate console operators see daily and take for granted.

The core data tower around us like vertical freight trains, color-coded for access. Bright primaries, impossibly bright in that transparent void, linked by countless horizontals in nursery blues and pinks.

But ice still shadows something at the center of it all: the heart of all Chrome's expensive darkness, the very heart . . .

It was late afternoon when I got back from my shopping expedition to New York. Not much sun through the skylight, but an ice pattern glowed on Bobby's monitor screen, a 2-D graphic representation of someone's computer defenses, lines of neon woven like an Art Deco prayer rug. I turned the console off, and the screen went completely dark.

Rikki's things were spread across my workbench, nylon bags spilling clothes and makeup, a pair of bright red cowboy boots, audio cassettes, glossy Japanese magazines about simstim stars. I stacked it all under the bench and then took my arm off, forgetting that the program I'd brought from the Finn was in the right-hand pocket of my jacket, so that I had to fumble it out left-handed and then get it into the padded jaws of the jeweler's vise.

The waldo looks like an old audio turntable, the kind that played disc records, with the vise set up under a transparent dust cover. The arm itself is just over a centimeter long, swinging out on what would've been the tone arm on one of those turntables. But I don't look at that when I've clipped the leads to my stump; I look at the scope, because that's my arm there in black and white, magnification 40 x.

I ran a tool check and picked up the laser. It felt a little heavy; so I scaled my weight-sensor input down to a quarter-kilo per gram and got to work. At 40 x the side of the program looked like a trailer truck.

It took eight hours to crack: three hours with the waldo and the laser and four dozen taps, two hours on the phone to a contact in Colorado, and three hours to run down a lexicon disc that could translate eight-year-old technical Russian.

Then Cyrillic alphanumerics started reeling down the monitor, twisting themselves into English halfway down. There were a lot of gaps, where the lexicon ran up against specialized military acronyms in the readout I'd bought from my man in Colorado, but it did give me some idea of what I'd bought from the Finn.

I felt like a punk who'd gone out to buy a switchblade and come home with a small neutron bomb.

Screwed again, I thought. *What good's a neutron bomb in a streetfight?* The thing under the dust cover was right out of my league. I didn't even know where to unload it, where to look for a buyer. Someone had, but he was dead, someone with a Porsche watch and a fake Belgian passport, but I'd never tried to move in those circles. The Finn's muggers from the 'burbs had knocked over someone who had some highly arcane connections.

The program in the jeweler's vise was a Russian military icebreaker, a killer-virus program.

It was dawn when Bobby came in alone. I'd fallen asleep with a bag of takeout sandwiches in my lap.

"You want to eat?" I asked him, not really awake, holding out my sandwiches. I'd been dreaming of the program, of its waves of hungry glitch systems and mimetic subprograms; in the dream it was an animal of some kind, shapeless and flowing.

He brushed the bag aside on his way to the console, punched a function key. The screen lit with the intricate pattern I'd seen there that afternoon. I rubbed sleep from my eyes with my left hand, one thing I can't do with my right. I'd fallen asleep trying to decide whether to tell him about the program. Maybe I should try to sell it alone, keep the money, go somewhere new, ask Rikki to go with me.

"Whose is it?" I asked.

He stood there in a black cotton jump suit, an old leather jacket thrown over his shoulders like a cape. He hadn't shaved for a few days, and his face looked thinner than usual.

"It's Chrome's," he said.

My arm convulsed, started clicking, fear translated to the myoelectrics through the carbon studs. I spilled the sandwiches; limp sprouts, and bright yellow dairy-produce slices on the unswept wooden floor.

"You're stone crazy," I said.

"No," he said, "you think she rumbled it? No way. We'd be dead already. I locked on to her through a triple-blind rental system in Mombasa and an Algerian comsat. She knew somebody was having a look-see, but she couldn't trace it."

If Chrome had traced the pass Bobby had made at her ice, we were good as dead. But he was probably right, or she'd have had me blown away on my way back from New York. "Why her, Bobby? Just give me one reason. . . ."

Chrome: I'd seen her maybe half a dozen times in the Gentleman Loser. Maybe she was slumming, or checking out the human condition, a condition she didn't exactly aspire to. A sweet little heart-shaped face framing the nastiest pair of eyes you ever saw. She'd looked fourteen for as long as anyone could remember, hyped out of anything like a normal metabolism on some massive program of serums and hormones. She was as ugly a customer as the street ever produced, but she didn't belong to the street anymore. She was one of the Boys, Chrome, a member in good standing of the local Mob subsidiary. Word was, she'd gotten started as a dealer, back when synthetic pituitary hormones were still proscribed. But she hadn't had to move hormones for a long time. Now she owned the House of Blue Lights.

"You're flat-out crazy, Quine. You give me one sane reason for having that stuff on your screen. You ought to dump it, and I mean *now*. . . ."

"Talk in the Loser," he said, shrugging out of the leather jacket. "Black Myron and Crow Jane. Jane, she's up on all the sex lines, claims she knows where the money goes. So she's arguing with Myron that Chrome's the controlling interest in the Blue Lights, not just some figurehead for the Boys."

" 'The Boys,' Bobby," I said. "That's the operative word there. You still capable of seeing that? We don't mess with the Boys, remember? That's why we're still walking around."

"That's why we're still poor, partner." He settled back into the swivel chair in front of the console, unzipped his jump suit, and scratched his skinny white chest. "But maybe not for much longer."

"I think maybe this partnership just got itself permanently dissolved."

Then he grinned at me. The grin was truly crazy, feral and focused, and I knew that right then he really didn't give a shit about dying.

"Look," I said, "I've got some money left, you know? Why don't you take it and get the tube to Miami, catch a hopper to Montego Bay. You need a rest, man. You've got to get your act together."

"My act, Jack," he said, punching something on the keyboard, "never has been this together before." The neon prayer rug on the screen shivered and woke as an animation program cut in, ice lines weaving with hypnotic frequency, a living mandala. Bobby kept punching, and the movement slowed; the pattern resolved itself, grew slightly less complex, became an alternation between two distant configurations. A first-class piece of work, and I hadn't thought he was still that good. "Now," he said, "there, see it? Wait. There. There again. And there. Easy to miss.

That's it. Cuts in every hour and twenty minutes with a squirt transmission to their comsat. We could live for a year on what she pays them weekly in negative interest."

"Whose comsat?"

"Zürich. Her bankers. That's her bankbook, Jack. That's where the money goes. Crow Jane was right."

I stood there. My arm forgot to click.

"So how'd you do in New York, partner? You get anything that'll help me cut ice? We're going to need whatever we can get."

I kept my eyes on his, forced myself not to look in the direction of the waldo, the jeweler's vise. The Russian program was there, under the dust cover.

Wild cards, luck changers.

"Where's Rikki?" I asked him, crossing to the console, pretending to study the alternating patterns on the screen.

"Friends of hers," he shrugged, "kids, they're all into simstim." He smiled absently. "I'm going to do it for her, man."

"I'm going out to think about this, Bobby. You want me to come back, you keep your hands off the board."

"I'm doing it for her," he said as the door closed behind me. "You know I am."

And down now, down, the program a roller coaster through this fraying maze of shadow walls, gray cathedral spaces between the bright towers. Headlong speed.

Black ice. Dont think about it. Black ice.

Too many stories in the Gentleman Loser; black ice is a part of the mythology. Ice that kills. Illegal, but then aren't we all? Some kind of neural-feedback weapon, and you connect with it only once. Like Some hideous Word that eats the mind from the inside out. Like an epileptic spasm that goes on and on until there's nothing left at all . . .

And we're diving for the floor of Chrome's shadow castle.

Trying to brace myself for the sudden stopping of breath, a sickness and final slackening of the nerves. Fear of that cold Word waiting, down there in the dark.

I went out and looked for Rikki, found her in a café with a boy with Sendai eyes, half-healed suture lines radiating from his bruised sockets. She had a glossy brochure spread open on the table, Tally Isham smiling up from a dozen photographs, the Girl with the Zeiss Ikon Eyes.

Her little simstim deck was one of the things I'd stacked under my bench the night before, the one I'd fixed for her the day after I'd first seen her. She spent hours jacked into that unit, the contact band across her forehead like a gray plastic tiara. Tally Isham was her favorite, and with the contact band on, she was gone, off somewhere in the recorded sensorium of simstim's biggest star. Simulated stimuli: the world—all the interesting parts, anyway—as perceived by Tally Isham. Tally raced a black Fokker ground-effect plane across Arizona mesa tops. Tally dived the Truk Island preserves. Tally partied with the superrich on private Greek islands, heartbreaking purity of those tiny white seaports at dawn.

Actually she looked a lot like Tally, same coloring and cheekbones. I thought Rikki's mouth was stronger. More sass. She didn't want to *be* Tally Isham, but she coveted the job. That was her ambition, to be in simstim. Bobby just laughed it off. She talked to me about it, though. "How'd I look with a pair of these?" she'd ask, holding a full-page headshot, Tally Isham's blue Zeiss Ikons lined up with her own amber-brown. She'd had her corneas done twice, but she still wasn't 20-20; so she wanted Ikons. Brand of the stars. Very expensive.

"You still window-shopping for eyes?" I asked as I sat down.

"Tiger just got some," she said. She looked tired, I thought.

Tiger was so pleased with his Sendais that he couldn't help smiling, but I doubted whether he'd have smiled otherwise. He had the kind of uniform good looks you get after your seventh trip to the surgical boutique; he'd probably spend the rest of his life looking vaguely like each new season's media front-runner; not too obvious a copy, but nothing too original, either.

"Sendai, right?" I smiled back.

He nodded. I watched as he tried to take me in with his idea of a professional simstim glance. He was pretending that he was recording. I thought he spent too long on my arm. "They'll be great on peripherals when the muscles heal," he said, and I saw how carefully he reached for his double espresso. Sendai eyes are notorious for depth-perception defects and warranty hassles, among other things.

"Tiger's leaving for Hollywood tomorrow."

"Then maybe Chiba City, right?" I smiled at him. He didn't smile back. "Got an offer, Tiger? Know an agent?"

"Just checking it out," he said quietly. Then he got up and left. He said a quick goodbye to Rikki, but not to me.

"That kid's optic nerves may start to deteriorate inside six months. You know that, Rikki? Those Sendais are illegal in England, Denmark, lots of places. You can't replace nerves."

"Hey, Jack, no lectures." She stole one of my croissants and nibbled at the top of one of its horns.

"I thought I was your adviser, kid."

"Yeah. Well, Tiger's not too swift, but everybody knows about Sendais. They're all he can afford. So he's taking a chance. If he gets work, he can replace them."

"With these?" I tapped the Zeiss Ikon brochure. "Lot of money, Rikki. You know better than to take a gamble like that."

She nodded. "I want Ikons."

"If you're going up to Bobby's, tell him to sit tight until he hears from me."

"Sure. It's business?"

"Business," I said. But it was craziness.

I drank my coffee, and she ate both my croissants. Then I walked her down to Bobby's. I made fifteen calls, each one from a different pay phone.

Business. Bad craziness.

All in all, it took us six weeks to set the burn up, six weeks of Bobby telling me how much he loved her. I worked even harder, trying to get away from that.

Most of it was phone calls. My fifteen initial and very oblique inquiries each seemed to breed fifteen more. I was looking for a certain service Bobby and I both imagined as a requisite part of the world's clandestine economy, but which probably never had more than five customers at a time. It would be one that never advertised.

We were looking for the world's heaviest fence, for a non-aligned money laundry capable of dry-cleaning a megabuck online cash transfer and then forgetting about it.

All those calls were a waste, finally, because it was the Finn who put me on to what we needed. I'd gone up to New York to buy a new blackbox rig, because we were going broke paying for all those calls.

I put the problem to him as hypothetically as possible.

"Macao," he said.

"Macao?"

"The Long Hum family. Stockbrokers."

He even had the number. You want a fence, ask another fence.

The Long Hum people were so oblique that they made my idea of a subtle approach look like a tactical nuke-out. Bobby had to make two shuttle runs to Hong Kong to get the deal straight. We were running out of capital, and fast, I still don't know why I decided to go along with it in the first place; I was scared of Chrome, and I'd never been all that hot to get rich.

I tried telling myself that it was a good idea to burn the House of Blue Lights because the place was a creep joint, but I just couldn't buy it. I didn't like the Blue Lights, because I'd spent a supremely depressing evening there once, but that was no excuse for going after Chrome. Actually I halfway assumed we were going to die in the attempt. Even with that killer program, the odds weren't exactly in our favor.

Bobby was lost in writing the set of commands we were going to plug into the dead center of Chrome's computer. That was going to be my job, because Bobby was going to have his hands full trying to keep the Russian program from going straight for the kill. It was too complex for us to rewrite, and so he was going to try to hold it back for the two seconds I needed.

I made a deal with a streetfighter named Miles. He was going to follow Rikki the night of the burn, keep her in sight, and phone me at a certain time. If I wasn't there, or didn't answer in just a certain way, I'd told him to grab her and put her on the first tube out. I gave him an envelope to give her, money and a note.

Bobby really hadn't thought about that, much, how things would go for her if we blew it. He just kept telling me he loved her, where they were going to go together, how they'd spend the money.

"Buy her a pair of Ikons first, man. That's what she wants. She's serious about that simstim scene."

"Hey," he said, looking up from the keyboard, "she won't need to work. We're going to make it, Jack. She's my luck. She won't ever have to work again."

"Your luck," I said. I wasn't happy. I couldn't remember when I had been happy. "You seen your luck around lately?"

He hadn't, but neither had I. We'd both been too busy.

I missed her. Missing her reminded me of my one night in the House of Blue Lights, because I'd gone there out of missing someone else. I'd gotten drunk to begin with, then I'd started hitting Vasopressin inhalers. If your main squeeze has just decided to walk out on you, booze and Vasopressin are the ultimate in masochistic pharmacology; the juice makes you maudlin and the Vasopressin makes you remember, I mean really remember. Clinically they use the stuff to counter senile amnesia, but the street finds its own uses for things. So I'd bought myself an ultraintense replay of a bad affair; trouble is, you get the bad with the good. Go gunning for transports of animal ecstasy and you get what you said, too, and what she said to that, how she walked away and never looked back.

I don't remember deciding to go to the Blue Lights, or how I got there, hushed corridors and this really tacky decorative waterfall trickling somewhere, or maybe just a hologram of one. I had a lot of money that night; somebody had given Bobby a big roll for opening a three-second window in someone else's ice.

I don't think the crew on the door liked my looks, but I guess my money was okay.

I had more to drink there when I'd done what I went there for. Then I made some crack to the barman about closet necrophiliacs, and that didn't go down too well. Then this very large character insisted on calling me War Hero, which I didn't like. I think I showed him some tricks with the arm, before the lights went out, and I woke up two days later in a basic sleeping module somewhere else. A cheap place, not even room to hang yourself. And I sat there on that narrow foam slab and cried.

Some things are worse than being alone. But the thing they sell in the House of Blue Lights is so popular that it's almost legal.

At the heart of darkness, the still center, the glitch systems shred the dark with whirlwinds of light, translucent razors spinning away from us; we hang in the center of a silent slow-motion explosion, ice fragments falling away forever, and Bobby's voice comes in across light-years of electronic void illusion—

"Burn the bitch down. I can't hold the thing back—"

The Russian program, rising through towers of data, blotting out the playroom colors. And I plug Bobby's homemade command package into the center of Chrome's cold heart. The squirt transmission cuts in, a pulse of condensed information that shoots straight up, past the thickening tower of darkness, the Russian program, while Bobby struggles to control that crucial second. An unformed arm of shadow twitches from the towering dark, too late.

We've done it.

The matrix folds itself around me like an origami trick.

And the loft smells of sweat and burning circuitry.

I thought I heard Chrome scream, a raw metal sound, but I couldn't have.

Bobby was laughing, tears in his eyes. The elapsed-time figure in the corner of the monitor read 07:24:05. The burn had taken a little under eight minutes.

And I saw that the Russian program had melted in its slot.

We'd given the bulk of Chrome's Zürich account to a dozen world charities. There was too much there to move, and we knew we had to break her, burn her straight down, or she might come after us. We took less than ten percent for ourselves and shot it through the Long Hum setup in Macao. They took sixty percent of that for themselves and kicked what was left back to us through the most convoluted sector of the Hong Kong exchange. It took an hour before our money started to reach the two accounts we'd opened in Zürich.

I watched zeros pile up behind a meaningless figure on the monitor. I was rich.

Then the phone rang. It was Miles. I almost blew the code phrase.

"Hey, Jack, man, I dunno—what's it all about, with this girl of yours? Kinda funny thing here . . ."

"What? Tell me."

"I been on her, like you said, tight but out of sight. She goes to the Loser, hangs out, then she gets a tube. Goes to the House of Blue Lights—"

"She what?"

"Side door. *Employees* only. No way I could get past their security."

"Is she there now?"

"No, man, I just lost her. It's insane down here, like the Blue Lights just shut down, looks like for good, seven kinds of alarms going off, everybody running, the heat out in riot gear. . . . Now there's all this stuff going on, insurance guys, real-estate types, vans with municipal plates. . . ."

"Miles, where'd she go?"

"Lost her, Jack."

"Look, Miles, you keep the money in the envelope, right?"

"You serious? Hey, I'm real sorry. I—"

I hung up.

"Wait'll we tell her," Bobby was saying, rubbing a towel across his bare chest.

"You tell her yourself, cowboy, I'm going for a walk."

So I went out into the night and the neon and let the crowd pull me along, walking blind, willing myself to be just a segment of that mass organism, just one more drifting chip of consciousness under the geodesics. I didn't think, just put one foot in front of another, but after a while I did think, and it all made sense. She'd needed the money.

I thought about Chrome, too. That we'd killed her, murdered her, as surely as if we'd slit her throat. The night that carried me along through the malls and plazas would be hunting her now, and she had nowhere to go. How many enemies would she have in this crowd alone? How many would move, now they weren't held back by fear of her money? We'd taken her for everything she had. She was back on the street again. I doubted she'd live till dawn.

Finally I remembered the café, the one where I'd met Tiger.

Her sunglasses told the whole story, huge black shades with a telltale smudge of fleshtone paintstick in the corner of one lens. "Hi, Rikki," I said, and I was ready when she took them off.

Blue, Tally Isham blue. The clear trademark blue they're famous for, ZEISS IKON ringing each iris in tiny capitals, the letters suspended there like flecks of gold.

"They're beautiful," I said. Paintstick covered the bruising. No scars with work that good. "You made some money."

"Yeah, I did." Then she shivered. "But I won't make any more, not that way."

"I think that place is out of business."

"Oh." Nothing moved in her face then. The new blue eyes were still and very deep.

"It doesn't matter. Bobby's waiting for you. We just pulled down a big score."

"No. I've got to go. I guess he won't understand, but I've got to go."

I nodded, watching the arm swing up to take her hand; it didn't seem to be part of me at all, but she held on to it like it was.

"I've got a one-way ticket to Hollywood. Tiger knows some people I can stay with. Maybe I'll even get to Chiba City."

She was right about Bobby. I went back with her. He didn't understand. But she'd already served her purpose, for Bobby, and I wanted to tell her not to hurt for him, because I could see that she did. He wouldn't even come out into the hallway after she had packed her bags. I put the bags down and kissed her and messed up the paintstick, and something came up inside me the way the killer program had risen above Chrome's data. A sudden stopping of the breath, in a place where no word is. But she had a plane to catch.

Bobby was slumped in the swivel chair in front of his monitor, looking at his string of zeros. He had his shades on, and I knew he'd be in the Gentleman Loser by nightfall, checking out the weather, anxious for a sign, someone to tell him what his new life would be like. I couldn't see it being very different. More comfortable, but he'd always be waiting for that next card to fall.

I tried not to imagine her in the House of Blue Lights, working three-hour shifts in an approximation of REM sleep, while her body and a bundle of conditioned reflexes took care of business. The customers never got to complain that she was faking it, because those were real orgasms. But she felt them, if she felt them at all, as faint silver flares somewhere out on the edge of sleep. Yeah, it's so popular, it's almost legal. The customers are torn between needing someone and wanting to be alone at the same time, which has probably always been the name of that particular game, even before we had the neuroelectronics to enable them to have it both ways.

I picked up the phone and punched the number for her airline. I gave them her real name, her flight number. "She's changing that," I said, "to Chiba City. That's right. Japan." I thumbed my credit card into the slot and punched my ID code. "First class." Distant hum as they scanned my credit records. "Make that a return ticket."

But I guess she cashed the return fare, or else didn't need it, because she hasn't come back. And sometimes late at night I'll pass a window with posters of simstim stars, all those beautiful, identical eyes staring back at me out of faces that are nearly as identical, and sometimes the eyes are hers, but none of the faces are, none of them ever are, and I see her far out on the edge of all this sprawl of night and cities, and then she waves goodbye.

❧ GREG(ORY DALE) BEAR (1951–)

Greg Bear had his first story published in 1967, when he was sixteen years old. Between 1985 and 1990, he became one of the most important Hard Science Fiction writers of all time, ranking with Hal Clement, Arthur C. Clarke, David Brin, and Kim Stanley Robinson. Bear's major works from this time include Eon *(1985),* The Forge of God *(1987),* Eternity *(1988),* Tangents *(short stories, 1989), and* Queen of Angels *(1990). In 1993, in the wake of several new novel-length Science Fiction works about Mars by Ben Bova, Kim Stanley Robinson, and others, Bear published* Moving Mars.

He has also written Fantasy short stories and novels, and he has worked as both a journalist and an illustrator.

"Blood Music" earned both Hugo and Nebula awards for best novella. The timely topics of genetic engineering and DNA research are the joint focus of the story.

Blood Music

(Analog: Science Fiction–Science Fact, *June 1983)*

There is a principle in nature I don't think anyone has pointed out before. Each hour, a myriad of trillions of little live things—bacteria, microbes, "animalcules"—are born and die, not counting for much except in the bulk of their existence and the accumulation of their tiny effects. They do not perceive deeply. They do not suffer much. A hundred billion, dying, would not begin to have the same importance as a single human death.

Within the ranks of magnitude of all creatures, small as microbes or great as humans, there is an equality of "elan," just as the branches of a tall tree, gathered together, equal the bulk of the limbs below, and all the limbs equal the bulk of the trunk.

That, at least, is the principle. I believe Vergil Ulam was the first to violate it.

It had been two years since I'd last seen Vergil. My memory of him hardly matched the tan, smiling, well-dressed gentleman standing before me. We had made a lunch appointment over the phone the day before, and now faced each other in the wide double doors of the employees' cafeteria at the Mount Freedom Medical Center.

"Vergil?" I asked. "My God, Vergil!"

"Good to see you, Edward." He shook my hand firmly. He had lost ten or twelve kilos and what remained seemed tighter, better proportioned. At university, Vergil had been the pudgy, shock-haired, snaggle-toothed whiz kid who hot-wired doorknobs, gave us punch that turned our piss blue, and never got a date except with Eileen Termagent, who shared many of his physical characteristics.

"You look fantastic," I said. "Spend a summer in Cabo San Lucas?"

We stood in line at the counter and chose our food. "The tan," he said, picking out a carton of chocolate milk, "is from spending three months under a sunlamp. My teeth were straightened just after I last saw you. I'll explain the rest, but we need a place to talk where no one will listen close."

I steered him to the smoker's corner, where three diehard puffers were scattered among six tables.

"Listen, I mean it," I said as we unloaded our trays. "You've changed. You're looking good."

"I've changed more than you know." His tone was motion-picture ominous, and he delivered the line with a theatrical lift of his brows. "How's Gail?"

Gail was doing well, I told him, teaching nursery school. We'd married the year before. His gaze shifted down to his food—pineapple slice and cottage cheese, piece of banana cream pie—and he said, his voice almost cracking, "Notice something else?"

I squinted in concentration. "Uh."

"Look closer."

"I'm not sure. Well, yes, you're not wearing glasses. Contacts?"

"No. I don't need them anymore."

"And you're a snappy dresser. Who's dressing you now? I hope she's as sexy as she is tasteful."

"Candice isn't—wasn't responsible for the improvement in my clothes," he said. "I just got a better job, more money to throw around. My taste in clothes is better than my taste in food, as it happens." He grinned the old Vergil self-deprecating grin, but ended it with a peculiar leer. "At any rate, she's left me, I've been fired from my job, I'm living on savings."

"Hold it," I said. "That's a bit crowded. Why not do a linear breakdown? You got a job. Where?"

"Genetron Corp.," he said. "Sixteen months ago."

"I haven't heard of them."

"You will. They're putting out common stock in the next month. It'll shoot off the board. They've broken through with MABs. Medical—"

"I know what MABs are," I interrupted. "At least in theory. Medically Applicable Biochips."

"They have some that work."

"What?" It was my turn to lift my brows.

"Microscopic logic circuits. You inject them into the human body, they set up shop where they're told and troubleshoot. With Dr. Michael Bernard's approval."

That was quite impressive. Bernard's reputation was spotless. Not only was he associated with the genetic engineering biggies, but he had made news at least once a year in his practice as a neurosurgeon before retiring. Covers on *Time*, *Mega*, *Rolling Stone*.

"That's supposed to be secret—stock, breakthrough, Bernard, everything." He looked around and lowered his voice. "But you do whatever the hell you want. I'm through with the bastards."

I whistled. "Make me rich, huh?"

"If that's what you want. Or you can spend some time with me before rushing off to your broker."

"Of course." He hadn't touched the cottage cheese or pie. He had, however, eaten the pineapple slice and drunk the chocolate milk. "So tell me more."

"Well, in med school I was training for lab work. Biochemical research. I've always had a bent for computers, too. So I put myself through my last two years—"

"By selling software packages to Westinghouse," I said.

"It's good my friends remember. That's how I got involved with Genetron, just when they were starting out. They had big money backers, all the lab facilities I thought anyone would ever need. They hired me, and I advanced rapidly.

"Four months and I was doing my own work. I made some breakthroughs"— he tossed his hand nonchalantly—"then I went off on tangents they thought were premature. I persisted and they took away my lab, handed it over to a certifiable flatworm. I managed to save part of the experiment before they fired me. But I haven't exactly been cautious . . . or judicious. So now it's going on outside the lab."

I'd always regarded Vergil as ambitious, a trifle cracked, and not terribly sensitive. His relations with authority figures had never been smooth. Science, for him, was like the woman you couldn't possibly have, who suddenly opens her arms to you, long before you're ready for mature love—leaving you afraid you'll forever blow the chance, lose the prize. Apparently, he did. "Outside the lab? I don't get you."

"Edward, I want you to examine me. Give me a thorough physical. Maybe a cancer diagnostic. Then I'll explain more."

"You want a five-thousand-dollar exam?"

"Whatever you can do. Ultrasound, NMR, thermogram, everything."

"I don't know if I can get access to all that equipment. NMR full-scan has only been here a month or two. Hell, you couldn't pick a more expensive way—"

"Then ultrasound. That's all you'll need."

"Vergil, I'm an obstetrician, not a glamour-boy lab-tech. OB-GYN, butt of all jokes. If you're turning into a woman, maybe I can help you."

He leaned forward, almost putting his elbow into the pie, but swinging wide at the last instant by scant millimeters. The old Vergil would have hit it square. "Examine me closely and you'll . . ." He narrowed his eyes. "Just examine me."

"So I make an appointment for ultrasound. Who's going to pay?"

"I'm on Blue Shield." He smiled and held up a medical credit card. "I messed with the personnel files at Genetron. Anything up to a hundred thousand dollars medical, they'll never check, never suspect."

He wanted secrecy, so I made arrangements. I filled out his forms myself. As long as everything was billed properly, most of the examination could take place without official notice. I didn't charge for my services. After all, Vergil had turned my piss blue. We were friends.

He came in late at night. I wasn't normally on duty then, but I stayed late, waiting for him on the third floor of what the nurses called the Frankenstein wing. I sat on an orange plastic chair. He arrived, looking olive-colored under the fluorescent lights.

He stripped, and I arranged him on the table. I noticed, first off, that his ankles looked swollen. But they weren't puffy. I felt them several times. They seemed healthy but looked odd. "Hm," I said.

I ran the paddles over him, picking up areas difficult for the big unit to hit, and programmed the data into the imaging system. Then I swung the table around and inserted it into the enameled orifice of the ultrasound diagnostic unit, the hum-hole, so-called by the nurses.

I integrated the data from the hum-hole with that from the paddle sweeps and rolled Vergil out, then set up a video frame. The image took a second to integrate, then flowed into a pattern showing Vergil's skeleton. My jaw fell.

Three seconds of that and it switched to his thoracic organs, then his musculature, and, finally, vascular system and skin.

"How long since the accident?" I asked, trying to take the quiver out of my voice.

"I haven't been in an accident," he said. "It was deliberate."

"Jesus, they beat you to keep secrets?"

"You don't understand me, Edward. Look at the images again. I'm not damaged."

"Look, there's thickening here"—I indicated the ankles—"and your ribs— that crazy zigzag pattern of interlocks. Broken sometime, obviously. And—"

"Look at my spine," he said. I rotated the image in the video frame.

Buckminster Fuller, I thought. It was fantastic. A cage of triangular projections, all interlocking in ways I couldn't begin to follow, much less understand. I reached around and tried to feel his spine with my fingers. He lifted his arms and looked off at the ceiling.

"I can't find it," I said. "It's all smooth back there." I let go of him and looked at his chest, then prodded his ribs. They were sheathed in something tough and flexible. The harder I pressed, the tougher it became. Then I noticed another change.

"Hey," I said. "You don't have any nipples." There were tiny pigment patches, but no nipple formations at all.

"See?" Vergil asked, shrugging on the white robe, "I'm being rebuilt from the inside out."

In my reconstruction of those hours, I fancy myself saying, "So tell me about it." Perhaps mercifully, I don't remember what I actually said.

He explained with his characteristic circumlocutions. Listening was like trying to get to the meat of a newspaper article through a forest of sidebars and graphic embellishments.

I simplify and condense.

Genetron had assigned him to manufacturing prototype biochips, tiny circuits made out of protein molecules. Some were hooked up to silicon chips little more than a micrometer in size, then sent through rat arteries to chemically keyed locations, to make connections with the rat tissue and attempt to monitor and even control lab-induced pathologies.

"*That* was something," he said.

"We recovered the most complex microchip by sacrificing the rat, then debriefed it—hooked the silicon portion up to an imaging system. The computer gave us bar graphs, then a diagram of the chemical characteristics of about eleven centimeters of blood vessel . . . then put it all together to make a picture. We zoomed down eleven centimeters of rat artery. You never saw so many scientists jumping up and down, hugging each other, drinking buckets of bug juice." Bug juice was lab ethanol mixed with Dr. Pepper.

Eventually, the silicon elements were eliminated completely in favor of nucleo-proteins. He seemed reluctant to explain in detail, but I gathered they found ways to make huge molecules—as large as DNA, and even more complex—into elec-trochemical computers, using ribosome-like structures as "encoders" and "read-ers" and RNA as "tape." Vergil was able to mimic reproductive separation and re-assembly in his nucleoproteins, incorporating program changes at key points by switching nucleotide pairs. "Genetron wanted me to switch over to supergene en-gineering, since that was the coming thing everywhere else. Make all kinds of crit-ters, some out of our imagination. But I had different ideas." He twiddled his fin-ger around his ear and made theremin sounds. "Mad scientist time, right?" He laughed, then sobered. "I injected my best nucleoproteins into bacteria to make duplication and compounding easier. Then I started to leave them inside, so the circuits could interact with the cells. They were heuristically programmed; they taught themselves. The cells fed chemically coded information to the computers, the computers processed it and made decisions, the cells became smart. I mean, smart as planaria, for starters. Imagine an *E. coli* as smart as a planarian worm!"

I nodded. "I'm imagining."

"Then I really went off on my own. We had the equipment, the techniques; and I knew the molecular language. I could make really dense, really complicated biochips by compounding the nucleoproteins, making them into little brains. I did some research into how far I could go, theoretically. Sticking with bacteria, I could make a biochip with the computing capacity of a sparrow's brain. Imagine how jazzed I was! Then I saw a way to increase the complexity a thousandfold, by using something we regarded as a nuisance—quantum chit-chat between the fixed elements of the circuits. Down that small, even the slightest change could bomb a biochip. But I developed a program that actually predicted and took advantage of electron tunneling. Emphasized the heuristic aspects of the computer, used the chit-chat as a method of increasing complexity."

"You're losing me," I said.

"I took advantage of randomness. The circuits could repair themselves, com-pare memories, and correct faulty elements. I gave them basic instructions: Go forth and multiply. Improve. By God, you should have seen some of the cultures a week later! It was amazing. They were evolving all on their own, like little cities. I destroyed them all. I think one of the petri dishes would have grown legs and walked out of the incubator if I'd kept feeding it."

"You're kidding." I looked at him. "You're not kidding."

"Man, they *knew* what it was like to improve! They knew where they had to go, but they were just so limited, being in bacteria bodies, with so few resources."

"How smart were they?"

"I couldn't be sure. They were associating in clusters of a hundred to two hundred cells, each cluster behaving like an autonomous unit. Each cluster might have been as smart as a rhesus monkey. They exchanged information through their pili, passed on bits of memory, and compared notes. Their organization was obviously different from a group of monkeys. Their world was so much simpler, for one thing. With their abilities, they were masters of the petri dishes. I put phages in with them; the phages didn't have a chance. They used every option available to change and grow."

"How is that possible?"

"What?" He seemed surprised I wasn't accepting everything at face value.

"Cramming so much into so little. A rhesus monkey is not your simple little calculator, Vergil."

"I haven't made myself clear," he said, obviously irritated. "I was using nucleoprotein computers. They're like DNA, but all the information can interact. Do you know how many nucleotide pairs there are in the DNA of a single bacteria?"

It had been a long time since my last biochemistry lesson. I shook my head.

"About two million. Add in the modified ribosome structures—fifteen thousand of them, each with a molecular weight of about three million—and consider the combinations and permutations. The RNA is arranged like a continuous loop paper tape, surrounded by ribosomes ticking off instructions and manufacturing protein chains . . ." His eyes were bright and slightly moist. "Besides, I'm not saying every cell was a distinct entity. They cooperated."

"How many bacteria in the dishes you destroyed?"

"Billions. I don't know." He smirked. "You got it, Edward. Whole planetsful of *E. coli*."

"But Genetron didn't fire you then?"

"No. They didn't know what was going on, for one thing. I kept compounding the molecules, increasing their size and complexity. When bacteria were too limited, I took blood from myself, separated out white cells, and injected them with the new biochips. I watched them, put them through mazes and little chemical problems. They were whizzes. Time is a lot faster at that level—so little distance for the messages to cross, and the environment is much simpler. Then I forgot to store a file under my secret code in the lab computers. Some managers found it and guessed what I was up to. Everybody panicked. They thought we'd have every social watchdog in the country on our backs because of what I'd done. They started to destroy my work and wipe my programs. Ordered me to sterilize my white cells. Christ." He pulled the white robe off and started to get dressed. "I only had a day or two. I separated out the most complex cells—"

"How complex?"

"They were clustering in hundred-cell groups, like the bacteria. Each group as smart as a four-year-old kid, maybe." He studied my face for a moment. "Still doubting? Want me to run through how many nucleotide pairs there are in a mammalian cell? I tailored my computers to take advantage of the white cells' capacity. Four billion nucleotide pairs, Edward. And they don't have a huge body to worry about, taking up most of their thinking time."

"Okay," I said. "I'm convinced. What did you do?"

"I mixed the cells back into a cylinder of whole blood and injected myself with it." He buttoned the top of his shirt and smiled thinly at me. "I'd programmed them with every drive I could, talked as high a level as I could using just enzymes and such. After that, they were on their own."

"You programmed them to go forth and multiply, improve?" I repeated.

"I think they developed some characteristics picked up by the biochips in their *E. coli* phases. The white cells could talk to each other with extruded memories. They found ways to ingest other types of cells and alter them without killing them."

"You're crazy."

"You can see the screen! Edward, I haven't been sick since. I used to get colds all the time. I've never felt better."

"They're inside you, finding things, changing them."

"And by now, each cluster is as smart as you or I."

"You're absolutely nuts."

He shrugged. "Genetron fired me. They thought I was going to take revenge for what did to my work. They ordered me out of the labs, and I haven't had a real chance to see what's been going on inside me until now. Three months."

"So . . ." My mind was racing. "You lost weight because they improved your fat metabolism. Your bones are stronger, your spine has been completely rebuilt—"

"No more backaches even if I sleep on my old mattress."

"Your heart looks different."

"I didn't know about the heart," he said, examining the frame image more closely. "As for the fat—I was thinking about that. They could increase my brown cells, fix up the metabolism. I haven't been as hungry lately. I haven't changed my eating habits that much—I still want the same old junk—but somehow I get around to eating only what I need. I don't think they know what my brain is yet. Sure, they've got all the glandular stuff—but they don't have the *big* picture, if you see what I mean. They don't know *I'm* in here. But boy, they sure did figure out what my reproductive organs are."

I glanced at the image and shifted my eyes away.

"Oh, they look pretty normal," he said, hefting his scrotum obscenely. He snickered. "But how else do you think I'd land a real looker like Candice? She was just after a one-night stand with a techie. I looked okay then, no tan but trim, with good clothes. She'd never screwed a techie before. Joke time, right? But my little geniuses kept us up half the night. I think they made improvements each time. I felt like I had a goddamned fever."

His smile vanished. "But then one night my skin started to crawl. It really scared me. I thought things were getting out of hand. I wondered what they'd do when they crossed the blood-brain barrier and found out about *me*—about the brain's real function. So I began a campaign to keep them under control. I figured, the reason they wanted to get into the skin was the simplicity of running circuits across a surface. Much easier than trying to maintain chains of communication in and around muscles, organs, vessels. The skin was much more direct. So I bought a quartz lamp." He caught my puzzled expression. "In the lab, we'd break down the protein in biochip cells by exposing them to ultraviolet light. I alternated sun-lamp with quartz treatments. Keeps them out of my skin and gives me a nice tan."

"Give you skin cancer, too," I commented.

"They'll probably take care of that. Like police."

"Okay. I've examined you, you've told me a story I still find hard to believe . . . what do you want me to do?"

"I'm not as nonchalant as I act, Edward. I'm worried. I'd like to find some way to control them before they find out about my brain. I mean, think of it, they're in the trillions by now, each one smart. They're cooperating to some extent. I'm probably the smartest thing on the planet, and they haven't even begun to get their act together. I don't really want them to take over." He laughed unpleasantly. "Steal my soul, you know? So think of some treatment to block them. Maybe we can starve the little buggers. Just think on it." He buttoned his shirt. "Give me a call." He handed me a slip of paper with his address and phone number. Then he went to the keyboard and erased the image on the frame, dumping the memory of the examination. "Just you," he said. "Nobody else for now. And please . . . hurry."

It was three o'clock in the morning when Vergil walked out of the examination room. He'd allowed me to take blood samples, then shaken my hand—his palm was damp, nervous—and cautioned me against ingesting anything from the specimens.

Before I went home, I put the blood through a series of tests. The results were ready the next day.

I picked them up during my lunch break in the afternoon, then destroyed all of the samples. I did it like a robot. It took me five days and nearly sleepless nights to accept what I'd seen. His blood was normal enough, though the machines diag-nosed the patient as having an infection. High levels of leukocytes—white blood cells—and histamines. On the fifth day, I believed.

Gail came home before I did, but it was my turn to fix dinner. She slipped one of the school's disks into the home system and showed me video art her nursery kids had been creating. I watched quietly, ate with her in silence.

I had two dreams, part of my final acceptance. In the first, that evening, I wit-nessed the destruction of the planet Krypton, Superman's home world. Billions of superhuman geniuses went screaming off in walls of fire. I related the destruction to my sterilizing the samples of Vergil's blood.

The second dream was worse. I dreamed that New York City was raping a woman. By the end of the dream, she gave birth to little embryo cities, all wrapped up in translucent sacs, soaked with blood from the difficult labor.

I called him on the morning of the sixth day. He answered on the fourth ring. "I have some results," I said. "Nothing conclusive. But I want to talk with you. In person."

"Sure," he said. "I'm staying inside for the time being." His voice was strained; he sounded tired.

Vergil's apartment was in a fancy high-rise near the lake shore. I took the eleva-tor up, listening to little advertising jingles and watching dancing holograms dis-play products, empty apartments for rent, the building's hostess discussing social activities for the week.

Vergil opened the door and motioned me in. He wore a checked robe with long sleeves and carpet slippers. He clutched an unlit pipe in one hand, his fingers twisting it back and forth as he walked away from me and sat down, saying noth-ing.

"You have an infection," I said.

"Oh?"

"That's all the blood analyses tell me. I don't have access to the electron micro-scopes."

"I don't think it's really an infection," he said. "After all, they're my own cells. Probably something else . . . some sign of their presence, of the change. We can't expect to understand everything that's happening."

I removed my coat. "Listen," I said, "you really have me worried now." The ex-pression on his face stopped me: a kind of frantic beatitude. He squinted at the ceiling and pursed his lips.

"Are you stoned?" I asked.

He shook his head, then nodded once, very slowly. "Listening," he said.

"To what?"

"I don't know. Not sounds . . . exactly. Like music. The heart, all the blood vessels, friction of blood along the arteries, veins. Activity. Music in the blood." He looked at me plaintively. "Why aren't you at work?"

"My day off. Gail's working."

"Can you stay?"

I shrugged. "I suppose." I sounded suspicious. I glanced around the apartment, looking for ashtrays, packs of papers.

"I'm not stoned, Edward," he said. "I may be wrong, but I think something big is happening. I think they're finding out who I am."

I sat down across from Vergil, staring at him intently. He didn't seem to notice. Some inner process involved him. When I asked for a cup of coffee, he motioned to the kitchen. I boiled a pot of water and took a jar of instant from the cabinet. With cup in hand, I returned to my seat. He twisted his head back and forth, eyes open. "You always knew what you wanted to be, didn't you?" he asked.

"More or less."

"A gynecologist. Smart moves. Never false moves. I was different. I had goals, but no direction. Like a map without roads, just places to be. I didn't give a shit for anything, anyone but myself. Even science. Just a means. I'm surprised I got so far. I even hated my folks."

He gripped his chair arms.

"Something wrong?" I asked.

"They're talking to me," he said. He shut his eyes.

For an hour he seemed to be asleep. I checked his pulse, which was strong and steady, felt his forehead—slightly cool—and made myself more coffee. I was looking through a magazine, at a loss what to do, when he opened his eyes again. "Hard to figure exactly what time is like for them," he said. "It's taken them maybe three, four days to figure out language, key human concepts. Now they're on to it. On to me. Right now."

"How's that?"

He claimed there were thousands of researchers hooked up to his neurons. He couldn't give details. "They're damned efficient, you know," he said. "They haven't screwed me up yet."

"We should get you into the hospital now."

"What in hell could other doctors do? Did *you* figure out any way to control them? I mean, they're my own cells."

"I've been thinking. We could starve them. Find out what metabolic differences—"

"I'm not sure I want to be rid of them," Vergil said. "They're not doing any harm."

"How do you know?"

He shook his head and held up one finger. "Wait. They're trying to figure out what space is. That's tough for them: They break distances down into concentrations of chemicals. For them, space is like intensity of taste."

"Vergil—"

"Listen! Think, Edward!" His tone was excited but even. "Something big is happening inside me. They talk to each other across the fluid, through membranes. They tailor something—viruses?—to carry data stored in nucleic acid chains. I think they're saying 'RNA.' That makes sense. That's one way I programmed them. But plasmidlike structures, too. Maybe that's what your machines think is a sign of infection—all their chattering in my blood, packets of data. Tastes of other individuals. Peers. Superiors. Subordinates."

"Vergil, I still think you should be in a hospital."

"This is my show, Edward," he said. "I'm their universe. They're amazed by the new scale." He was quiet again for a time. I squatted by his chair and pulled up the sleeve to his robe. His arm was crisscrossed with white lines. I was about to go to the phone when he stood and stretched. "Do you realize," he said, "how many body cells we kill each time we move?"

"I'm going to call for an ambulance," I said.

"No, you aren't." His tone stopped me. "I told you, I'm not sick, this is my show. Do you know what they'd do to me in a hospital? They'd be like cavemen trying to fix a computer. It would be a farce."

"Then what the hell am I doing here?" I asked, getting angry. "I can't do anything. I'm one of those cavemen."

"You're a friend," Vergil said, fixing his eyes on me. I had the impression I was being watched by more than just Vergil. "I want you here to keep me company." He laughed. "But I'm not exactly alone."

He walked around the apartment for two hours, fingering things, looking out windows, slowly and methodically fixing himself lunch. "You know, they can actually feel their own thoughts," he said about noon. "I mean, the cytoplasm seems to have a will of its own, a kind of subconscious life counter to the rationality they've only recently acquired. They hear the chemical 'noise' of the molecules fitting and unfitting inside."

At two o'clock, I called Gail to tell her I would be late. I was almost sick with tension, but I tried to keep my voice level. "Remember Vergil Ulam? I'm talking with him right now."

"Everything okay?" she asked.

Was it? Decidedly not. "Fine," I said.

"Culture!" Vergil said, peering around the kitchen wall at me. I said good-bye and hung up the phone. "They're always swimming in that bath of information. Contributing to it. It's a kind of gestalt thing. The hierarchy is absolute. They send tailored phages after cells that don't interact properly. Viruses specified to individuals or groups. No escape. A rogue cell gets pierced by the virus, the cell blebs outward, it explodes and dissolves. But it's not just a dictatorship. I think they effectively have more freedom than in a democracy. I mean, they vary so differently from individual to individual. Does that make sense? They vary in different ways than we do."

"Hold it," I said, gripping his shoulders. "Vergil, you're pushing me to the edge. I can't take this much longer. I don't understand, I'm not sure I believe—"

"Not even now?"

"Okay, let's say you're giving me the right interpretation. Giving it to me straight. Have you bothered to figure out the consequences yet? What all this means, where it might lead?"

He walked into the kitchen and drew a glass of water from the tap then returned and stood next to me. His expression had changed from childish absorption to sober concern. "I've never been very good at that."

"Are you afraid?"

"I was. Now, I'm not sure." He fingered the tie of his robe. "Look, I don't want you to think I went around you, over your head or something. But I met with Michael Bernard yesterday. He put me through his private clinic, took specimens. Told me to quit the lamp treatments. He called this morning, just before you did. He says it all checks out. And he asked me not to tell anybody." He paused and his expression became dreamy again. "Cities of cells," he continued. "Edward, they push tubes through the tissues, spread information—"

"Stop it!" I shouted. "Checks out? What checks out?"

"As Bernard puts it, I have 'severely enlarged macrophages' throughout my system. And he concurs on the anatomical changes."

"What does he plan to do?"

"I don't know. I think he'll probably convince Genetron to reopen the lab."

"Is that what you want?"

"It's not just having the lab again. I want to show you. Since I stopped the lamp treatments, I'm still changing." He undid his robe and let it slide to the floor. All over his body, his skin was crisscrossed with white lines. Along his back, the lines were starting to form ridges.

"My God," I said.

"I'm not going to be much good anywhere else but the lab soon. I won't be able to go out in public. Hospitals wouldn't know what to do, as I said."

"You're . . . you can talk to them, tell them to slow down," I said, aware how ridiculous that sounded.

"Yes, indeed I can, but they don't necessarily listen."

"I thought you were their god or something."

"The ones hooked up to my neurons aren't the big wheels. They're researchers, or at least serve the same function. They know I'm here, what I am, but that doesn't mean they've convinced the upper levels of the hierarchy."

"They're disputing?"

"Something like that. It's not all that bad, anyway. If the lab is reopened, I have a home, a place to work." He glanced out the window, as if looking for someone. "I don't have anything left but them. They aren't afraid, Edward. I've never felt so close to anything before." The beatific smile again. "I'm responsible for them. Mother to them all."

"You have no way of knowing what they're going to do."

He shook his head.

"No, I mean it. You say they're like a civilization—"

"Like a thousand civilizations."

"Yes, and civilizations have been known to screw up. Warfare, the environment—"

I was grasping at straws, trying to restrain a growing panic. I wasn't competent to handle the enormity of what was happening. Neither was Vergil. He was the last person I would have called insightful and wise about large issues.

"But I'm the only one at risk."

"You don't know that. Jesus, Vergil, look what they're *doing* to you!"

"To me, all to me!" he said. "Nobody else."

I shook my head and held up my hands in a gesture of defeat. "Okay, so Bernard gets them to reopen the lab, you move in, become a guinea pig. What then?"

"They treat me right. I'm more than just good old Vergil Ulam now. I'm a god-damned galaxy, a super-mother."

"Super-host, you mean." He conceded the point with a shrug.

I couldn't take any more. I made my exit with a few flimsy excuses, then sat in the lobby of the apartment building, trying to calm down. Somebody had to talk some sense into him. Who would he listen to? He had gone to Bernard . . .

And it sounded as if Bernard was not only convinced, but very interested. People of Bernard's stature didn't coax the Vergil Ulams of the world along unless they felt it was to their advantage.

I had a hunch, and I decided to play it. I went to a pay phone, slipped in my credit card, and called Genetron.

"I'd like you to page Dr. Michael Bernard," I told the receptionist.

"Who's calling, please?"

"This is his answering service. We have an emergency call and his beeper doesn't seem to be working."

A few anxious minutes later, Bernard came on the line. "Who the hell is this?" he asked. "I don't have an answering service."

"My name is Edward Milligan. I'm a friend of Vergil Ulam's. I think we have some problems to discuss."

We made an appointment to talk the next morning.

I went home and tried to think of excuses to keep me off the next day's hospital shift. I couldn't concentrate on medicine, couldn't give my patients anywhere near the attention they deserved.

Guilty, angry, afraid.

That was how Gail found me. I slipped on a mask of calm and we fixed dinner together. After eating, holding onto each other, we watched the city lights come on in late twilight through the bayside window. Winter starlings pecked at the yellow lawn in the last few minutes of light, then flew away with a rising wind which made the windows rattle.

"Something's wrong," Gail said softly. "Are you going to tell me, or just act like everything's normal?"

"It's just me," I said. "Nervous. Work at the hospital."

"Oh, lord," she said, sitting up. "You're going to divorce me for that Baker woman." Mrs. Baker weighed three hundred and sixty pounds and hadn't known she was pregnant until her fifth month.

"No," I said, listless.

"Rapturous relief," Gail said, touching my forehead lightly. "You know this kind of introspection drives me crazy."

"Well, it's nothing I can talk about yet, so . . ." I patted her hand.

"That's disgustingly patronizing," she said, getting up. "I'm going to make some tea. Want some?" Now she was miffed, and I was tense with not telling.

Why not just reveal all? I asked myself. An old friend was turning himself into a galaxy.

I cleared away the table instead. That night, unable to sleep, I looked down on Gail in bed from my sitting position, pillow against the wall, and tried to determine what I knew was real, and what wasn't.

I'm a doctor, I told myself. A technical, scientific profession. I'm supposed to be immune to things like future shock.

Vergil Ulam was turning into a galaxy.

How would it feel to be topped off with a trillion Chinese? I grinned in the dark and almost cried at the same time. What Vergil had inside him was unimaginably stranger than Chinese, Stranger than anything I—or Vergil—could easily understand. Perhaps ever understand.

But I knew what was real. The bedroom, the city lights faint through gauze curtains. Gail sleeping. Very important. Gail in bed, sleeping.

The dream returned. This time the city came in through the window and attacked Gail. It was a great, spiky lighted-up prowler, and it growled in a language I couldn't understand, made up of auto horns, crowd noises, construction bedlam. I tried to fight it off, but it got to her—and turned into a drift of stars, sprinkling all over the bed, all over everything. I jerked awake and stayed up until dawn, dressed with Gail, kissed her, savored the reality of her human, unviolated lips.

I went to meet with Bernard. He had been loaned a suite in a big downtown hospital; I rode the elevator to the sixth floor, and saw what fame and fortune could mean.

The suite was tastefully furnished, fine serigraphs on wood-paneled walls, chrome and glass furniture, cream-colored carpet, Chinese brass, and wormwood-grain cabinets and tables.

He offered me a cup of coffee, and I accepted. He took a seat in the breakfast nook, and I sat across from him, cradling my cup in moist palms. He wore a dapper gray suit and had graying hair and a sharp profile. He was in his mid sixties and he looked quite a bit like Leonard Bernstein.

"About our mutual acquaintance," he said. "Mr. Ulam. Brilliant. And, I won't hesitate to say, courageous."

"He's my friend. I'm worried about him."

Bernard held up one finger. "Courageous—and a bloody damned fool. What's happening to him should never have been allowed. He may have done it under duress, but that's no excuse. Still, what's done is done. He's talked to you, I take it."

I nodded. "He wants to return to Genetron."

"Of course. That's where all his equipment is. Where his home probably will be while we sort this out."

"Sort it out—how? Why?" I wasn't thinking too clearly. I had a slight headache.

"I can think of a large number of uses for small, superdense computer elements with a biological base. Can't you? Genetron has already made breakthroughs, but this is something else again."

"What do you envision?"

Bernard smiled. "I'm not really at liberty to say. It'll be revolutionary. We'll have to get him in lab conditions. Animal experiments have to be conducted. We'll start from scratch, of course. Vergil's . . . um . . . colonies can't be transferred. They're based on his own white blood cells. So we have to develop colonies that won't trigger immune reactions in other animals."

"Like an infection?" I asked.

"I suppose there are comparisons. But Vergil is not infected."

"My tests indicate he is."

"That's probably the bits of data floating around in his blood, don't you think?"

"I don't know."

"Listen, I'd like you to come down to the lab after Vergil is settled in. Your expertise might be useful to us."

Us. He was working with Genetron hand in glove. Could he be objective? "How will you benefit from all this?"

"Edward, I have always been at the forefront of my profession. I see no reason why I shouldn't be helping here. With my knowledge of brain and nerve functions, and the research I've been conducting in neurophysiology—"

"You could help Genetron hold off an investigation by the government," I said.

"That's being very blunt. Too blunt, and unfair."

"Perhaps. Anyway, yes: I'd like to visit the lab when Vergil's settled in. If I'm still welcome, bluntness and all." He looked at me sharply. I wouldn't be playing on *his* team; for a moment, his thoughts were almost nakedly apparent.

"Of course," Bernard said, rising with me. He reached out to shake my hand. His palm was damp. He was as nervous as I was, even if he didn't look it.

I returned to my apartment and stayed there until noon, reading, trying to sort things out. Reach a decision. What was real, what I needed to protect.

There is only so much change anyone can stand: innovation, yes, but slow application. Don't force. Everyone has the right to stay the same until they decide otherwise.

The greatest thing in science since . . .

And Bernard would force it. Genetron would force it. I couldn't handle the thought. "Neo-Luddite," I said to myself. A filthy accusation.

When I pressed Vergil's number on the building security panel, Vergil answered almost immediately. "Yeah," he said. He sounded exhilarated. "Come on up. I'll be in the bathroom. Door's unlocked."

I entered his apartment and walked through the hallway to the bathroom. Vergil lay in the tub, up to his neck in pinkish water. He smiled vaguely and splashed his hands. "Looks like I slit my wrists, doesn't it?" he said softly. "Don't worry. Everything's fine now. Genetron's going to take me back. Bernard just called." He pointed to the bathroom phone and intercom.

I sat on the toilet and noticed the sunlamp fixture standing unplugged next to the linen cabinets. The bulbs sat in a row on the edge of the sink counter. "You're sure that's what you want," I said, my shoulders slumping.

"Yeah, I think so," he said. "They can take better care of me. I'm getting cleaned up, going over there this evening. Bernard's picking me up in his limo. Style. From here on in, everything's style."

The pinkish color in the water didn't look like soap. "Is that bubble bath?" I asked. Some of it came to me in a rush then and I felt a little weaker; what had occurred to me was just one more obvious and necessary insanity.

"No," Vergil said. I knew that already.

"No," he repeated, "it's coming from my skin. They're not telling me everything, but I think they're sending out scouts. Astronauts." He looked at me with an expression that didn't quite equal concern; more like curiosity as to how I'd take it.

The confirmation made my stomach muscles tighten as if waiting for a punch. I had never even considered the possibility until now, perhaps because I had been concentrating on other aspects. "Is this the first time?" I asked.

"Yeah," he said. He laughed. "I've half a mind to let the little buggers down the drain. Let them find out what the world's really about."

"They'd go everywhere," I said.

"Sure enough."

"How . . . how are you feeling?"

"I'm feeling pretty good now. Must be billions of them." More splashing with his hands. "What do you think? Should I let the buggers out?"

Quickly, hardly thinking, I knelt down beside the tub. My fingers went for the cord on the sunlamp and I plugged it in. He had hot-wired doorknobs, turned my piss blue, played a thousand dumb practical jokes and never grown up, never grown mature enough to understand that he was sufficiently brilliant to transform the world; he would never learn caution.

He reached for the drain knob. "You know, Edward, I—"

He never finished. I picked up the fixture and dropped it into the tub, jumping back at the flash of steam and sparks. Vergil screamed and thrashed and jerked and then everything was still, except for the low, steady sizzle and the smoke wafting from his hair.

I lifted the toilet lid and vomited. Then I clenched my nose and went into the living room. My legs went out from under me and I sat abruptly on the couch.

After an hour, I searched through Vergil's kitchen and found bleach, ammonia, and a bottle of Jack Daniel's. I returned to the bathroom, keeping the center of my gaze away from Vergil. I poured first the booze, then the bleach, then the ammonia into the water. Chlorine started bubbling up and I left, closing the door behind me.

The phone was ringing when I got home. I didn't answer. It could have been the hospital. It could have been Bernard. Or the police. I could envision having to explain everything to the police. Genetron would stonewall; Bernard would be unavailable.

I was exhausted, all my muscles knotted with tension and whatever name one can give to the feelings one has after—

Committing genocide?

That certainly didn't seem real. I could not believe I had just murdered a hundred trillion intelligent beings. Snuffed a galaxy. It was laughable. But I didn't laugh.

It was easy to believe that I had just killed one human being, a friend. The smoke, the melted lamp rods, the drooping electrical outlet and smoking cord.

Vergil.

I had dunked the lamp into the tub with Vergil.

I felt sick. Dreams, cities raping Gail (and what about his girlfriend, Candice?). Letting the water filled with them out. Galaxies sprinkling over us all. What horror. Then again, what potential beauty—a new kind of life, symbiosis and transformation.

Had I been thorough enough to kill them all? I had a moment of panic. Tomorrow, I thought, I will sterilize his apartment. Somehow, I didn't even think of Bernard.

When Gail came in the door, I was asleep on the couch. I came to, groggy, and she looked down at me.

"You feeling okay?" she asked, perching on the edge of the couch. I nodded.

"What are you planning for dinner?" My mouth didn't work properly. The words were mushy. She felt my forehead.

"Edward, you have a fever," she said. "A very high fever."

I stumbled into the bathroom and looked in the mirror. Gail was close behind me. "What is it?" she asked.

There were lines under my collar, around my neck. White lines, like freeways. They had already been in me a long time, days.

"Damp palms," I said. So obvious.

I think we nearly died. I struggled at first, but in minutes I was too weak to move. Gail was just as sick within an hour.

I lay on the carpet in the living room, drenched in sweat. Gail lay on the couch, her face the color of talcum, eyes closed, like a corpse in an embalming parlor. For a time I thought she was dead. Sick as I was, I raged—hated, felt tremendous guilt at my weakness, my slowness to understand all the possibilities. Then I no longer cared. I was too weak to blink, so I closed my eyes and waited.

There was a rhythm in my arms, my legs. With each pulse of blood, a kind of sound welled up within me, like an orchestra thousands strong, but not playing in unison; playing whole seasons of symphonies at once. Music in the blood. The sound became harsher, but more coordinated, wave-trains finally canceling into silence, then separating into harmonic beats.

The beats seemed to melt into me, into the sound of my own heart.

First, they subdued our immune responses. The war—and it was a war, on a scale never before known on Earth, with trillions of combatants—lasted perhaps two days.

By the time I regained enough strength to get to the kitchen faucet, I could feel them working on my brain, trying to crack the code and find the god within the protoplasm. I drank until I was sick, then drank more moderately and took a glass to Gail. She sipped at it. Her lips were cracked, her eyes bloodshot and ringed with yellowish crumbs. There was some color in her skin. Minutes later, we were eating feebly in the kitchen.

"What in hell is happening?" was the first thing she asked. I didn't have the strength to explain. I peeled an orange and shared it with her. "We should call a doctor," she said. But I knew we wouldn't. I was already receiving messages; it was becoming apparent that any sensation of freedom we experienced was illusory.

The messages were simple at first. Memories of commands, rather than the commands themselves, manifested themselves in my thoughts. We were not to leave the apartment—a concept which seemed quite abstract to those in control, even if undesirable—and we were not to have contact with others. We would be allowed to eat certain foods and drink tap water for the time being.

With the subsidence of the fevers, the transformations were quick and drastic. Almost simultaneously, Gail and I were immobilized. She was sitting at the table, I was kneeling on the floor. I was able barely to see her in the corner of my eye.

Her arm developed pronounced ridges.

They had learned inside Vergil; their tactics within the two of us were very different. I itched all over for about two hours—two hours in hell—before they made the breakthrough and found me. The effort of ages on their timescale paid off and they communicated smoothly and directly with this great, clumsy intelligence who had once controlled their universe.

They were not cruel. When the concept of discomfort and its undesirability was made clear, they worked to alleviate it. They worked too effectively. For another hour, I was in a sea of bliss, out of all contact with them.

With dawn the next day, they gave us freedom to move again; specifically, to go to the bathroom. There were certain waste products they could not deal with. I voided those—my urine was purple—and Gail followed suit. We looked at each other vacantly in the bathroom. Then she managed a slight smile. "Are they talking to you?" she asked. I nodded. "Then I'm not crazy."

For the next twelve hours, control seemed to loosen on some levels. I suspect there was another kind of war going on in me. Gail was capable of limited motion, but no more.

When full control resumed, we were instructed to hold each other. We did not hesitate.

"Eddie . . ." she whispered. My name was the last sound I ever heard from outside.

Standing, we grew together. In hours, our legs expanded and spread out. Then extensions grew to the windows to take in sunlight, and to the kitchen to take water from the sink. Filaments soon reached to all corners of the room, stripping paint and plaster from the walls, fabric and stuffing from the furniture.

By the next dawn, the transformation was complete.

I no longer have any clear view of what we look like. I suspect we resemble cells—large, flat, and filamented cells, draped purposefully across most of the apartment. The great shall mimic the small.

Our intelligence fluctuates daily as we are absorbed into the minds within. Each day, our individuality declines. We are, indeed, great clumsy dinosaurs. Our memories have been taken over by billions of them, and our personalities have been spread through the transformed blood.

Soon there will be no need for centralization.

Already the plumbing has been invaded. People throughout the building are undergoing transformation.

Within the old time frame of weeks, we will reach the lakes, rivers, and seas in force.

I can barely begin to guess the results. Every square inch of the planet will teem with thought. Years from now, perhaps much sooner, they will subdue their own individuality—what there is of it.

New creatures will come, then. The immensity of their capacity for thought will be inconceivable.

All my hatred and fear is gone now.

I leave them—us—with only one question.

How many times has this happened, elsewhere? Travelers never came through space to visit the Earth. They had no need.

They had found universes in grains of sand.

𝕄 OCTAVIA (ESTELLE) BUTLER (1947–)

Octavia Butler began her Science Fiction and Fantasy writing career when her story "Crossover" was published in the 1971 Clarion Workshop anthology. (The Clarion Workshop for aspiring writers of Science Fiction and Fantasy has been championed by Damon Knight, Kate Wilhelm, and others.) Butler made her first significant impact as a writer with her novel Patternmaster *(1976), the first in her* Patternist *series.*

An African American, Butler has built much of her Science Fiction and related social commentary around topics such as African American history and heritage, feminism, and sex. One of the author's more interesting books is Kindred *(1979), a Time Travel novel in which a black woman is transported back to the nineteenth-century American South and the horrors of slavery.*

In 1987, Octavia Butler published Dawn, *the first of her* Xenogenesis *series.*

Primarily a novel writer, Butler published "Bloodchild" between writing her two major Science Fiction series. As does the best of the author's writing, this tale features important social commentary and a compelling story line.

Bloodchild

(Isaac Asimov's Science Fiction Magazine, *June 1984*)

My last night of childhood began with a visit home. T'Gatoi's sisters had given us two sterile eggs. T'Gatoi gave one to my mother, brother, and sisters. She insisted that I eat the other one alone. It didn't matter. There was still enough to leave everyone feeling good. Almost everyone. My mother wouldn't take any. She sat, watching everyone drifting and dreaming without her. Most of the time she watched me.

I lay against T'Gatoi's long, velvet underside, sipping from my egg now and then, wondering why my mother denied herself such a harmless pleasure. Less of her hair would be gray if she indulged now and then. The eggs prolonged life, prolonged vigor. My father, who had never refused one in his life, had lived more than twice as long as he should have. And toward the end of his life, when he should have been slowing down, he had married my mother and fathered four children.

But my mother seemed content to age before she had to. I saw her turn away as several of T'Gatoi's limbs secured me closer. T'Gatoi liked our body heat, and took advantage of it whenever she could. When I was little and at home more, my mother used to try to tell me how to behave with T'Gatoi—how to be respectful and always obedient because T'Gatoi was the Tlic government official in charge of the Preserve, and thus the most important of her kind to deal directly with Terrans. It was an honor, my mother said, that such a person had chosen to come into the family. My mother was at her most formal and severe when she was lying.

I had no idea why she was lying, or even what she was lying about. It *was* an honor to have T'Gatoi in the family, but it was hardly a novelty. T'Gatoi and my mother had been friends all my mother's life, and T'Gatoi was not interested in being honored in the house she considered her second home. She simply came in, climbed onto one of her special couches, and called me over to keep her warm. It was impossible to be formal with her while lying against her and hearing her complain as usual that I was too skinny.

"You're better," she said this time, probing me with six or seven of her limbs. "You're gaining weight finally. Thinness is dangerous." The probing changed subtly, became a series of caresses.

"He's still too thin," my mother said sharply.

T'Gatoi lifted her head and perhaps a meter of her body off the couch as though she were sitting up. She looked at my mother and my mother, her face lined and old-looking, turned away.

"Lien, I would like you to have what's left of Gan's egg."

"The eggs are for the children," my mother said.

"They are for the family. Please take it."

Unwillingly obedient, my mother took it from me and put it to her mouth. There were only a few drops left in the now-shrunken, elastic shell, but she squeezed them out, swallowed them, and after a few moments some of the lines of tension began to smooth from her face.

"It's good," she whispered. "Sometimes I forget how good it is."

"You should take more," T'Gatoi said. "Why are you in such a hurry to be old?"

My mother said nothing.

"I like being able to come here," T'Gatoi said. "This place is a refuge because of you, yet you won't take care of yourself."

T'Gatoi was hounded on the outside. Her people wanted more of us made available. Only she and her political faction stood between us and the hordes who did not understand why there was a Preserve—why any Terran could not be courted, paid, drafted, in some way made available to them. Or they did understand, but in their desperation, they did not care. She parceled us out to the desperate and sold us to the rich and powerful for their political support. Thus, we were necessities, status symbols, and an independent people. She oversaw the joining of families, putting an end to the final remnants of the earlier system of breaking up Terran families to suit impatient Tlic. I had lived outside with her. I had seen the desperate eagerness in the way some people looked at me. It was a little frightening to know that only she stood between us and that desperation that could so easily swallow us. My mother would look at her sometimes and say to me, "Take care of her." And I would remember that she too had been outside, had seen.

Now T'Gatoi used four of her limbs to push me away from her onto the floor. "Go on, Gan," she said. "Sit down there with your sisters and enjoy not being sober. You had most of the egg. Lien, come warm me."

My mother hesitated for no reason that I could see. One of my earliest memories is of my mother stretched alongside T'Gatoi, talking about things I could not understand, picking me up from the floor and laughing as she sat me on one of T'Gatoi's segments. She ate her share of eggs then. I wondered when she had stopped, and why.

She lay down now against T'Gatoi, and the whole left row of T'Gatoi's limbs closed around her, holding her loosely, but securely. I had always found it comfortable to lie that way but, except for my older sister, no one else in the family liked it. They said it made them feel caged.

T'Gatoi meant to cage my mother. Once she had, she moved her tail slightly, then spoke. "Not enough egg, Lien. You should have taken it when it was passed to you. You need it badly now."

T'Gatoi's tail moved once more, its whip motion so swift I wouldn't have seen it if I hadn't been watching for it. Her sting drew only a single drop of blood from my mother's bare leg.

My mother cried out—probably in surprise. Being stung doesn't hurt. Then she sighed and I could see her body relax. She moved languidly into a more comfortable position within the cage of T'Gatoi's limbs. "Why did you do that?" she asked, sounding half asleep.

"I could not watch you sitting and suffering any longer."

My mother managed to move her shoulders in a small shrug. "Tomorrow," she said.

"Yes. Tomorrow you will resume your suffering—if you must. But for now, just for now, lie here and warm me and let me ease your way a little."

"He's still mine, you know," my mother said suddenly. "Nothing can buy him from me." Sober, she would not have permitted herself to refer to such things.

"Nothing," T'Gatoi agreed, humoring her.

"Did you think I would sell him for eggs? For long life? My son?"

"Not for anything," T'Gatoi said, stroking my mother's shoulders, toying with her long, graying hair.

I would like to have touched my mother, shared that moment with her. She would take my hand if I touched her now. Freed by the egg and the sting, she would smile and perhaps say things long held in. But tomorrow, she would remember all this as a humiliation. I did not want to be part of a remembered humiliation. Best just to be still and know she loved me under all the duty and pride and pain.

"Xuan Hoa, take off her shoes," T'Gatoi said. "In a little while I'll sting her again and she can sleep."

My older sister obeyed, swaying drunkenly as she stood up. When she had finished, she sat down beside me and took my hand. We had always been a unit, she and I.

My mother put the back of her head against T'Gatoi's underside and tried from that impossible angle to look up into the broad, round face. "You're going to sting me again?"

"Yes, Lien."

"I'll sleep until tomorrow noon."

"Good. You need it. When did you sleep last?"

My mother made a wordless sound of annoyance. "I should have stepped on you when you were small enough," she muttered.

It was an old joke between them. They had grown up together, sort of, though T'Gatoi had not, in my mother's lifetime, been small enough for any Terran to step on. She was nearly three times my mother's present age, yet would still be young when my mother died of age. But T'Gatoi and my mother had met as T'Gatoi was coming into a period of rapid development—a kind of Tlic adolescence. My mother was only a child, but for a while they developed at the same rate and had no better friends than each other.

T'Gatoi had even introduced my mother to the man who became my father. My parents, pleased with each other in spite of their very different ages, married as T'Gatoi was going into her family's business—politics. She and my mother saw each other less. But sometime before my older sister was born, my mother promised T'Gatoi one of her children. She would have to give one of us to someone, and she preferred T'Gatoi to some stranger.

Years passed. T'Gatoi traveled and increased her influence. The Preserve was hers by the time she came back to my mother to collect what she probably saw as her just reward for her hard work. My older sister took an instant liking to her and wanted to be chosen, but my mother was just coming to term with me and T'Gatoi liked the idea of choosing an infant and watching and taking part in all the phases of development. I'm told I was first caged within T'Gatoi's many limbs only three minutes after my birth. A few days later, I was given my first taste of egg. I tell Terrans that when they ask whether I was ever afraid of her. And I tell it to Tlic when T'Gatoi suggests a young Terran child for them and they, anxious and ignorant, demand an adolescent. Even my brother who had somehow grown up to fear and distrust the Tlic could probably have gone smoothly into one of their families if he had been adopted early enough. Sometimes, I think for his sake he should have been. I looked at him, stretched out on the floor across the room, his eyes open, but glazed as he dreamed his egg dream. No matter what he felt toward the Tlic, he always demanded his share of egg.

"Lien, can you stand up?" T'Gatoi asked suddenly.

"Stand?" my mother said. "I thought I was going to sleep."

"Later. Something sounds wrong outside." The cage was abruptly gone.

"What?"

"Up, Lien!"

My mother recognized her tone and got up just in time to avoid being dumped on the floor. T'Gatoi whipped her three meters of body off her couch, toward the door, and out at full speed. She had bones—ribs, a long spine, a skull, four sets of limb-bones per segment. But when she moved that way, twisting, hurling herself into controlled falls, landing running, she seemed not only boneless, but aquatic—something swimming through the air as though it were water. I loved watching her move.

I left my sister and started to follow her out the door, though I wasn't very steady on my own feet. It would have been better to sit and dream, better yet to find a girl and share a waking dream with her. Back when the Tlic saw us as not much more than convenient big warm-blooded animals, they would pen several of us together, male and female, and feed us only eggs. That way they could be sure of getting another generation of us no matter how we tried to hold out. We were lucky that didn't go on long. A few generations of it and we would have *been* little more than convenient big animals.

"Hold the door open, Gan," T'Gatoi said. "And tell the family to stay back."

"What is it?" I asked.

"N'Tlic."

I shrank back against the door. "Here? Alone?"

"He was trying to reach a call box, I suppose." She carried the man past me, unconscious, folded like a coat over some of her limbs. He looked young—my brother's age perhaps—and he was thinner than he should have been. What T'Gatoi would have called dangerously thin.

"Gan, go to the call box," she said. She put the man on the floor and began stripping off his clothing.

I did not move.

After a moment, she looked up at me, her sudden stillness a sign of deep impatience.

"Send Qui," I told her. "I'll stay here. Maybe I can help."

She let her limbs begin to move again, lifting the man and pulling his shirt over his head. "You don't want to see this," she said. "It will be hard. I can't help this man the way his Tlic could."

"I know. But send Qui. He won't want to be of any help here. I'm at least willing to try."

She looked at my brother—older, bigger, stronger, certainly more able to help her here. He was sitting up now, braced against the wall, staring at the man on the floor with undisguised fear and revulsion. Even she could see that he would be useless.

"Qui, go!" she said.

He didn't argue. He stood up, swayed briefly, then steadied, frightened sober.

"This man's name is Bram Lomas," she told him, reading from the man's armband. I fingered my own armband in sympathy. "He needs T'Khotgif Teh. Do you hear?"

"Bram Lomas, T'Khotgif Teh," my brother said. "I'm going." He edged around Lomas and ran out the door.

Lomas began to regain consciousness. He only moaned at first and clutched spasmodically at a pair of T'Gatoi's limbs. My younger sister, finally awake from her egg dream, came close to look at him, until my mother pulled her back.

T'Gatoi removed the man's shoes, then his pants, all the while leaving him two of her limbs to grip. Except for the final few, all her limbs were equally dexterous. "I want no argument from you this time, Gan," she said.

I straightened. "What shall I do?"

"Go out and slaughter an animal that is at least half your size."

"Slaughter? But I've never—"

She knocked me across the room. Her tail was an efficient weapon whether she exposed the sting or not.

I got up, feeling stupid for having ignored her warning, and went into the kitchen. Maybe I could kill something with a knife or an ax. My mother raised a few Terran animals for the table and several thousand local ones for their fur. T'Gatoi would probably prefer something local. An achti, perhaps. Some of those were the right size, though they had about three times as many teeth as I did and a real love of using them. My mother, Hoa, and Qui could kill them with knives. I had never killed one at all, had never slaughtered any animal. I had spent most of my time with T'Gatoi while my brother and sisters were learning the family business. T'Gatoi had been right. I should have been the one to go to the call box. At least I could do that.

I went to the corner cabinet where my mother kept her larger house and garden tools. At the back of the cabinet there was a pipe that carried off waste water from the kitchen—except that it didn't anymore. My father had rerouted the waste water before I was born. Now the pipe could be turned so that one half slid around the other and a rifle could be stored inside. This wasn't our only gun, but it was our most easily accessible one. I would have to use it to shoot one of the biggest of the achti. Then T'Gatoi would probably confiscate it. Firearms were illegal in the Preserve. There had been incidents right after the Preserve was established—Terrans shooting Tlic, shooting N'Tlic. This was before the joining of families began, before everyone had a personal stake in keeping the peace. No one had shot a Tlic in my lifetime or my mother's, but the law still stood—for our protection, we were told. There were stories of whole Terran families wiped out in reprisal back during the assassinations.

I went out to the cages and shot the biggest achti I could find. It was a handsome breeding male and my mother would not be pleased to see me bring it in. But it was the right size, and I was in a hurry.

I put the achti's long, warm body over my shoulder—glad that some of the weight I'd gained was muscle—and took it to the kitchen. There, I put the gun back in its hiding place. If T'Gatoi noticed the achti's wounds and demanded the gun, I would give it to her. Otherwise, let it stay where my father wanted it.

I turned to take the achti to her, then hesitated. For several seconds, I stood in front of the closed door wondering why I was suddenly afraid. I knew what was going to happen. I hadn't seen it before, but T'Gatoi had shown me diagrams and drawings. She had made sure I knew the truth as soon as I was old enough to understand it.

Yet I did not want to go into that room. I wasted a little time choosing a knife from the carved, wooden box in which my mother kept them. T'Gatoi might want one, I told myself, for the tough, heavily furred hide of the achti.

"Gan!" T'Gatoi called, her voice harsh with urgency.

I swallowed. I had not imagined a simple moving of the feet could be so difficult. I realized I was trembling and that shamed me. Shame impelled me through the door.

I put the achti down near T'Gatoi and saw that Lomas was unconscious again. She, Lomas, and I were alone in the room, my mother and sisters probably sent out so they would not have to watch. I envied them.

But my mother came back into the room as T'Gatoi seized the achti. Ignoring the knife I offered her, she extended claws from several of her limbs and slit the achti from throat to anus. She looked at me, her yellow eyes intent. "Hold this man's shoulders, Gan."

I stared at Lomas in panic, realizing that I did not want to touch him, let alone hold him. This would not be like shooting an animal. Not as quick, not as merciful, and, I hoped, not as final, but there was nothing I wanted less than to be part of it.

My mother came forward. "Gan, you hold his right side," she said. "I'll hold his left." And if he came to, he would throw her off without realizing he had done it. She was a tiny woman. She often wondered aloud how she had produced, as she said, such "huge" children.

"Never mind," I told her, taking the man's shoulders. "I'll do it."

She hovered nearby.

"Don't worry," I said. "I won't shame you. You don't have to stay and watch."

She looked at me uncertainly, then touched my face in a rare caress. Finally, she went back to her bedroom.

T'Gatoi lowered her head in relief. "Thank you, Gan," she said with courtesy more Terran than Tlic. "That one . . . she is always finding new ways for me to make her suffer."

Lomas began to groan and make choked sounds. I had hoped he would stay unconscious. T'Gatoi put her face near his so that he focused on her.

"I've stung you as much as I dare for now," she told him. "When this is over, I'll sting you to sleep and you won't hurt anymore."

"Please," the man begged. "Wait . . ."

"There's no more time, Bram. I'll sting you as soon as it's over. When T'Khotgif arrives she'll give you eggs to help you heal. It will be over soon."

"T'Khotgif!" the man shouted, straining against my hands.

"Soon, Bram." T'Gatoi glanced at me, then placed a claw against his abdomen slightly to the right of the middle, just below the last rib. There was movement on the right side—tiny, seemingly random pulsations moving his brown flesh, creating a concavity here, a convexity there, over and over until I could see the rhythm of it and knew where the next pulse would be.

Lomas's entire body stiffened under T'Gatoi's claw, though she merely rested it against him as she wound the rear section of her body around his legs. He might break my grip, but he would not break hers. He wept helplessly as she used his pants to tie his hands, then pushed his hands above his head so that I could kneel on the cloth between them and pin them in place. She rolled up his shirt and gave it to him to bite down on.

And she opened him.

His body convulsed with the first cut. He almost tore himself away from me. The sounds he made . . . I had never heard such sounds come from anything human. T'Gatoi seemed to pay no attention as she lengthened and deepened the cut, now and then pausing to lick away blood. His blood vessels contracted, reacting to the chemistry of her saliva, and the bleeding slowed.

I felt as though I were helping her torture him, helping her consume him. I knew I would vomit soon, didn't know why I hadn't already. I couldn't possibly last until she was finished.

She found the first grub. It was fat and deep red with his blood—both inside and out. It had already eaten its own egg case, but apparently had not yet begun to eat its host. At this stage, it would eat any flesh except its mother's. Let alone, it would have gone on excreting the poisons that had both sickened and alerted Lomas. Eventually it would have begun to eat. By the time it ate its way out of Lomas's flesh, Lomas would be dead or dying—and unable to take revenge on the thing that was killing him. There was always a grace period between the time the host sickened and the time the grubs began to eat him.

T'Gatoi picked up the writhing grub carefully and looked at it, somehow ignoring the terrible groans of the man.

Abruptly, the man lost consciousness.

"Good." T'Gatoi looked down at him. "I wish you Terrans could do that at will." She felt nothing. And the thing she held . . .

It was limbless and boneless at this stage, perhaps fifteen centimeters long and two thick, blind and slimy with blood. It was like a large worm. T'Gatoi put it into the belly of the achti, and it began at once to burrow. It would stay there and eat as long as there was anything to eat.

Probing through Lomas's flesh, she found two more, one of them smaller and more vigorous. "A male!" she said happily. He would be dead before I would. He would be through his metamorphosis and screwing everything that would hold still before his sisters even had limbs. He was the only one to make a serious effort to bite T'Gatoi as she placed him in the achti.

Paler worms oozed to visibility in Lomas's flesh. I closed my eyes. It was worse than finding something dead, rotting, and filled with tiny animal grubs. And it was far worse than any drawing or diagram.

"Ah, there are more," T'Gatoi said, plucking out two long, thick grubs. "You may have to kill another animal, Gan. Everything lives inside you Terrans."

I had been told all my life that this was a good and necessary thing Tlic and Terran did together—a kind of birth. I had believed it until now. I knew birth was painful and bloody, no matter what. But this was something else, something worse. And I wasn't ready to see it. Maybe I never would be. Yet I couldn't *not* see it. Closing my eyes didn't help.

T'Gatoi found a grub still eating its egg case. The remains of the case were still wired into a blood vessel by their own little tube or hook or whatever. That was the way the grubs were anchored and the way they fed. They took only blood until they were ready to emerge. Then they ate their stretched, elastic egg cases. Then they ate their hosts.

T'Gatoi bit away the egg case, licked away the blood. Did she like the taste? Did childhood habits die hard—or not die at all?

The whole procedure was wrong, alien. I wouldn't have thought anything about her could seem alien to me.

"One more, I think," she said. "Perhaps two. A good family. In a host animal these days, we would be happy to find one or two alive." She glanced at me. "Go outside, Gan, and empty your stomach. Go now while the man is unconscious."

I staggered out, barely made it. Beneath the tree just beyond the front door, I vomited until there was nothing left to bring up. Finally, I stood shaking, tears streaming down my face. I did not know why I was crying, but I could not stop. I went farther from the house to avoid being seen. Every time I closed my eyes I saw red worms crawling over redder human flesh.

There was a car coming toward the house. Since Terrans were forbidden motorized vehicles except for certain farm equipment, I knew this must be Lomas's Tlic with Qui and perhaps a Terran doctor. I wiped my face on my shirt, struggled for control.

"Gan," Qui called as the car stopped. "What happened?" He crawled out of the low, round, Tlic-convenient car door. Another Terran crawled out the other side and went into the house without speaking to me. The doctor. With his help and a few eggs, Lomas might make it.

"T'Khotgif Teh?" I said.

The Tlic driver surged out of her car, reared up half her length before me. She was paler and smaller than T'Gatoi—probably born from the body of an animal. Tlic from Terran bodies were always larger as well as more numerous.

"Six young," I told her. "Maybe seven, all alive. At least one male."

"Lomas?" she said harshly. I liked her for the question and the concern in her voice when she asked it. The last coherent thing he had said was her name.

"He's alive," I said.

She surged away to the house without another word.

"She's been sick," my brother said, watching her go. "When I called, I could hear people telling her she wasn't well enough to go out even for this."

I said nothing. I had extended courtesy to the Tlic. Now I didn't want to talk to anyone. I hoped he would go in—out of curiosity if nothing else.

"Finally found out more than you wanted to know, eh?"

I looked at him.

"Don't give me one of *her* looks," he said. "You're not her. You're just her property."

One of her looks. Had I picked up even an ability to imitate her expressions?

"What'd you do, puke?" He sniffed the air. "So now you know what you're in for."

I walked away from him. He and I had been close when we were kids. He would let me follow him around when I was home and sometimes T'Gatoi would let me bring him along when she took me into the city. But something had happened when he reached adolescence. I never knew what. He began keeping out of T'Gatoi's way. Then he began running away—until he realized there was no "away." Not in the Preserve. Certainly not outside. After that he concentrated on getting his share of every egg that came into the house and on looking out for me in a way that made me all but hate him—a way that clearly said, as long as I was all right, he was safe from the Tlic.

"How was it, really?" he demanded, following me.

"I killed an achti. The young ate it."

"You didn't run out of the house and puke because they ate an achti."

"I had . . . never seen a person cut open before." That was true, and enough for him to know. I couldn't talk about the other. Not with him.

"Oh," he said. He glanced at me as though he wanted to say more, but he kept quiet.

We walked, not really headed anywhere. Toward the back, toward the cages, toward the fields.

"Did he say anything?" Qui asked. "Lomas, I mean."

Who else would he mean? "He said 'T'Khotgif.' "

Qui shuddered. "If she had done that to me, she'd be the last person I'd call for."

"You'd call for her. Her sting would ease your pain without killing the grubs in you."

"You think I'd care if they died?"

No. Of course he wouldn't. Would I?

"Shit!" He drew a deep breath. "I've seen what they do. You think this thing with Lomas was bad? It was nothing."

I didn't argue. He didn't know what he was talking about.

"I saw them eat a man," he said.

I turned to face him. "You're lying!"

"*I saw them eat a man.*" He paused. "It was when I was little. I had been to the Hartmund house and I was on my way home. Halfway here, I saw a man and a Tlic and the man was N'Tlic. The ground was hilly. I was able to hide from them and watch. The Tlic wouldn't open the man because she had nothing to feed the grubs. The man couldn't go any farther and there were no houses around. He was in so much pain he told her to kill him. He begged her to kill him. Finally, she did. She cut his throat. One swipe of one claw. I saw the grubs eat their way out, then burrow in again, still eating."

His words made me see Lomas's flesh again, parasitized, crawling. "Why didn't you tell me that?" I whispered.

He looked startled, as though he'd forgotten I was listening. "I don't know."

"You started to run away not long after that, didn't you?"

"Yeah. Stupid. Running inside the Preserve. Running in a cage."

I shook my head, said what I should have said to him long ago. "She wouldn't take you, Qui. You don't have to worry."

"She would . . . if anything happened to you."

"No. She'd take Xuan Hoa. Hoa . . . wants it." She wouldn't if she had stayed to watch Lomas.

"They don't take women," he said with contempt.

"They do sometimes." I glanced at him. "Actually, they prefer women. You should be around them when they talk among themselves. They say women have more body fat to protect the grubs. But they usually take men to leave the women free to bear their own young."

"To provide the next generation of host animals," he said, switching from contempt to bitterness.

"It's more than that!" I countered. Was it?

"If it were going to happen to me, I'd want to believe it was more, too."

"It *is* more!" I felt like a kid. Stupid argument.

"Did you think so while T'Gatoi was picking worms out of that guy's guts?"

"It's not supposed to happen that way."

"Sure it is. You weren't supposed to see it, that's all. And his Tlic was supposed to do it. She could sting him unconscious and the operation wouldn't have been as painful. But she'd still open him, pick out the grubs, and if she missed even one, it would poison him and eat him from the inside out."

There was actually a time when my mother told me to show respect for Qui because he was my older brother. I walked away, hating him. In his way, he was gloating. He was safe and I wasn't. I could have hit him, but I didn't think I would be able to stand it when he refused to hit back, when he looked at me with contempt and pity.

He wouldn't let me get away. Longer-legged, he swung ahead of me and made me feel as though I were following him.

"I'm sorry," he said.

I strode on, sick and furious.

"Look, it probably won't be that bad with you. T'Gatoi likes you. She'll be careful."

I turned back toward the house, almost running from him.

"Has she done it to you yet?" he asked, keeping up easily. "I mean, you're about the right age for implantation. Has she—"

I hit him. I didn't know I was going to do it, but I think I meant to kill him. If he hadn't been bigger and stronger, I think I would have.

He tried to hold me off, but in the end, had to defend himself. He only hit me a couple of times. That was plenty. I don't remember going down, but when I came to, he was gone. It was worth the pain to be rid of him.

I got up and walked slowly toward the house. The back was dark. No one was in the kitchen. My mother and sisters were sleeping in their bedrooms—or pretending to.

Once I was in the kitchen, I could hear voices—Tlic and Terran from the next room. I couldn't make out what they were saying—didn't want to make it out.

I sat down at my mother's table, waiting for quiet. The table was smooth and worn, heavy and well-crafted. My father had made it for her just before he died. I remembered hanging around underfoot when he built it. He didn't mind. Now I sat leaning on it, missing him. I could have talked to him. He had done it three times in his long life. Three clutches of eggs, three times being opened and sewed up. How had he done it? How did anyone do it?

I got up, took the rifle from its hiding place, and sat down again with it. It needed cleaning, oiling.

All I did was load it.

"Gan?"

She made a lot of little clicking sounds when she walked on bare floor, each limb clicking in succession as it touched down. Waves of little clicks.

She came to the table, raised the front half of her body above it, and surged onto it. Sometimes she moved so smoothly she seemed to flow like water itself. She coiled herself into a small hill in the middle of the table and looked at me.

"That was bad," she said softly. "You should not have seen it. It need not be that way."

"I know."

"T'Khotgif—Ch'Khotgif now—she will die of her disease. She will not live to raise her children. But her sister will provide for them, and for Bram Lomas." Sterile sister. One fertile female in every lot. One to keep the family going. That sister owed Lomas more than she could ever repay.

"He'll live then?"

"Yes."

"I wonder if he would do it again."

"No one would ask him to do that again."

I looked into the yellow eyes, wondering how much I saw and understood there, and how much I only imagined. "No one ever asks us," I said. "You never asked me."

She moved her head slightly. "What's the matter with your face?"

"Nothing. Nothing important." Human eyes probably wouldn't have noticed the swelling in the darkness. The only light was from one of the moons, shining through a window across the room.

"Did you use the rifle to shoot the achti?"

"Yes."

"And do you mean to use it to shoot me?"

I stared at her, outlined in moonlight—coiled, graceful body. "What does Terran blood taste like to you?"

She said nothing.

"What are you?" I whispered. "What are we to you?"

She lay still, rested her head on her topmost coil. "You know me as no other does," she said softly. "You must decide."

"That's what happened to my face," I told her.

"What?"

"Qui goaded me into deciding to do something. It didn't turn out very well." I moved the gun slightly, brought the barrel up diagonally under my own chin. "At least it was a decision I made."

"As this will be."

"Ask me, Gatoi."

"For my children's lives?"

She would say something like that. She knew how to manipulate people, Terran and Tlic. But not this time.

"I don't want to be a host animal," I said. "Not even yours."

It took her a long time to answer. "We use almost no host animals these days," she said. "You know that."

"You use us."

"We do. We wait long years for you and teach you and join our families to yours." She moved restlessly. "You know you aren't animals to us."

I stared at her, saying nothing.

"The animals we once used began killing most of our eggs after implantation long before your ancestors arrived," she said softly. "You know these things, Gan. Because your people arrived, we are relearning what it means to be a healthy, thriving people. And your ancestors, fleeing from their homeworld, from their own kind who would have killed or enslaved them—they survived because of us. We saw them as people and gave them the Preserve when they still tried to kill us as worms."

At the word "worms" I jumped. I couldn't help it, and she couldn't help noticing it.

"I see," she said quietly. "Would you really rather die than bear my young, Gan?"

I didn't answer.

"Shall I go to Xuan Hoa?"

"Yes!" Hoa wanted it. Let her have it. She hadn't had to watch Lomas. She'd be proud. . . . Not terrified.

T'Gatoi flowed off the table onto the floor, startling me almost too much.

"I'll sleep in Hoa's room tonight," she said. "And sometime tonight or in the morning, I'll tell her."

This was going too fast. My sister. Hoa had had almost as much to do with raising me as my mother. I was still close to her—not like Qui. She could want T'Gatoi and still love me.

"Wait! Gatoi!"

She looked back, then raised nearly half her length off the floor and turned it to face me. "These are adult things, Gan. This is my life, my family!"

"But she's . . . my sister."

"I have done what you demanded. I have asked you!"

"But—"

"It will be easier for Hoa. She has always expected to carry other lives inside her."

Human lives. Human young who would someday drink at her breasts, not at her veins.

I shook my head. "Don't do it to her, Gatoi." I was not Qui. It seemed I could become him, though, with no effort at all. I could make Xuan Hoa my shield. Would it be easier to know that red worms were growing in her flesh instead of mine?

"Don't do it to Hoa," I repeated.

She stared at me, utterly still.

I looked away, then back at her. "Do it to me."

I lowered the gun from my throat and she leaned forward to take it.

"No," I told her.

"It's the law," she said.

"Leave it for the family. One of them might use it to save my life someday."

She grasped the rifle barrel, but I wouldn't let go. I was pulled into a standing position over her.

"Leave it here!" I repeated. "If we're not your animals, if these are adult things, accept the risk. There is risk, Gatoi, in dealing with a partner."

It was clearly hard for her to let go of the rifle. A shudder went through her and she made a hissing sound of distress. It occurred to me that she was afraid. She was old enough to have seen what guns could do to people. Now her young and this gun would be together in the same house. She did not know about our other guns. In this dispute, they did not matter.

"I will implant the first egg tonight," she said as I put the gun away. "Do you hear, Gan?"

Why else had I been given a whole egg to eat while the rest of the family was left to share one? Why else had my mother kept looking at me as though I were going away from her, going where she could not follow? Did T'Gatoi imagine I hadn't known?

"I hear."

"Now!" I let her push me out of the kitchen, then walked ahead of her toward my bedroom. The sudden urgency in her voice sounded real. "You would have done it to Hoa tonight!" I accused.

"I must do it to someone tonight."

I stopped in spite of her urgency and stood in her way. "Don't you care who?"

She flowed around me and into my bedroom. I found her waiting on the couch we shared. There was nothing in Hoa's room that she could have used. She would have done it to Hoa on the floor. The thought of her doing it to Hoa at all disturbed me in a different way now, and I was suddenly angry.

Yet I undressed and lay down beside her. I knew what to do, what to expect. I had been told all my life. I felt the familiar sting, narcotic, mildly pleasant. Then the blind probing of her ovipositor. The puncture was painless, easy. So easy going in. She undulated slowly against me, her muscles forcing the egg from her body into mine. I held on to a pair of her limbs until I remembered Lomas holding her that way. Then I let go, moved inadvertently, and hurt her. She gave a low cry of pain and I expected to be caged at once within her limbs. When I wasn't, I held on to her again, feeling oddly ashamed.

"I'm sorry," I whispered.

She rubbed my shoulders with four of her limbs.

"Do you care?" I asked. "Do you care that it's me?"

She did not answer for some time. Finally, "You were the one making choices tonight, Gan. I made mine long ago."

"Would you have gone to Hoa?"

"Yes. How could I put my children into the care of one who hates them?"

"It wasn't . . . hate."

"I know what it was."

"I was afraid."

Silence.

"I still am." I could admit it to her here, now.

"But you came to me . . . to save Hoa."

"Yes." I leaned my forehead against her. She was cool velvet, deceptively soft. "And to keep you for myself," I said. It was so. I didn't understand it, but it was so.

She made a soft hum of contentment. "I couldn't believe I had made such a mistake with you," she said. "I chose you. I believed you had grown to choose me."

"I had, but . . ."

"Lomas."

"Yes."

"I have never known a Terran to see a birth and take it well. Qui has seen one, hasn't he?"

"Yes."

"Terrans should be protected from seeing."

I didn't like the sound of that—and I doubted that it was possible. "Not protected," I said. "Shown. Shown when we're young kids, and shown more than once. Gatoi, no Terran ever sees a birth that goes right. All we see is N'Tlic—pain and terror and maybe death."

She looked down at me. "It is a private thing. It has always been a private thing."

Her tone kept me from insisting—that and the knowledge that if she changed her mind, I might be the first public example. But I had planted the thought in her mind. Chances were it would grow, and eventually she would experiment.

"You won't see it again," she said. "I don't want you thinking any more about shooting me."

The small amount of fluid that came into me with her egg relaxed me as completely as a sterile egg would have, so that I could remember the rifle in my hands and my feelings of fear and revulsion, anger and despair. I could remember the feelings without reviving them. I could talk about them.

"I wouldn't have shot you," I said. "Not you." She had been taken from my father's flesh when he was my age.

"You could have," she insisted.

"Not you." She stood between us and her own people, protecting, interweaving.

"Would you have destroyed yourself?"

I moved carefully, uncomfortably. "I could have done that. I nearly did. That's Qui's 'away.' I wonder if he knows."

"What?"

I did not answer.

"You will live now."

"Yes." *Take care of her,* my mother used to say. Yes.

"I'm healthy and young," she said. "I won't leave you as Lomas was left—alone, N'Tlic. I'll take care of you."

✹ GEORGE R(AYMOND) R(ICHARD) MARTIN
(1948–)

Today, George R. R. Martin is best known for his best-selling epic Fantasies A Game of Thrones *(1996),* A Clash of Kings *(1999), and* A Storm of Swords *(2000). For thirty years, however, he has been a master craftsman of Dark Fantasy and Science Fiction as well. He has had his stories adapted for television ("The Sand Kings," the first episode of the revived* Outer Limits *series); has written for television (the 1980s* Twilight Zone *series); and was heavily involved in the creation, production, and direction of the highly successful television series* The Beauty and the Beast.

Science Fiction and Dark Fantasy short stories comprised most of Martin's early writing career, and he continues to be a master of the form. Many of these works were originally published in Analog *and were later collected in* A Song for Lya *(1976),* Songs of Stars and Shadows *(1977),* Songs the Dead Men Sing *(1983),* Tuf Voyaging

(1986), and Portraits of His Children *(1987). The author's novels include* Dying of the Light *(1978),* Windhaven *(with Lisa Tuttle, 1981), and* The Armageddon Rag *(1983). He has also edited several anthologies and book series.*

"The Plague Star" is a classic installment from George R. R. Martin's Haviland Tuf *series. This novella embraces all the elements that have characterized the finest Science Fiction. A tribute to and extension of the 1930s Space Operas of Edmond Hamilton, E. E. "Doc" Smith, and Jack Williamson, "The Plague Star" features fast-paced action, varied character types, an ingenious plot, escapism, and quietly profound social commentary.*

The Plague Star

(Analog: Science Fiction–Science Fact, *January 1985 and February 1985*)

PROLOGUE

CATALOG SIX
ITEM NUMBER 37433-800912-5442894
SHANDELLOR CENTER FOR THE ADVANCEMENT
OF CULTURE AND KNOWLEDGE
XENOANTHROPOLOGY DIVISION

item description: crystal voice coding
item found: H'ro Brana (co/ords SQ19, V7715, I21)
tentative dating: recorded approx. 276 standard years ago
classify under:
    slave races, Hrangan
    legends & myths, Hruun
    medical,
    —disease, unidentified
    trade bases, abandoned

Hello? Hello?

Yes, I see it works. Good.

I am Rarik Hortvenzy, apprentice factor, speaking a warning to whomever finds my words.

Dusk comes now, for me the last. The sun has sunk beneath the western cliffs, staining the land with blood, and now the twilight eats its way toward me inexorably. The stars come out, one by one, but the only star that matters burns night and day, day and night. It is always with me, the brightest thing in the sky but for the sun. It is the plague star.

This day I buried Janeel. With my own hands I buried her, digging in the hard rocky ground from dawn through late afternoon, until my arms were afire with pain. When my ordeal was done, when the last spadeful of this wretched alien dirt had been thrown upon her head, when the last stone had been placed atop her cairn, then I stood over her and spat upon her grave.

It is all her fault. I told her so, not once but many times as she lay dying, and when the end was near she finally admitted her guilt. Her fault that we came here. Her fault that we did not leave when we might have. Her fault that she is dead— yes, no doubt of it—and her fault that I shall rot unburied when my own time comes, my flesh a feast for the beasts of the dark, and the flyers and night-hunters we once hoped to trade with.

The plague star twinkles but little, shines down upon the land with a clear bright light. This is wrong, I told Janeel once; a plague star ought to be red. It ought to glower, to drape itself with scarlet radiance, to whisper into the night hints of fire and of blood. This clear white purity, what has that to do with plague? That was in the first days, when our charter ship had just set us down to open our proud little trade complex, set us down and then moved on. In that time the plague star was but one of fifty first-magnitude stars in these alien skies, hard even to pick out. In that time we smiled at it, at the superstitions of these primitives, these backward brutes who thought sickness came from the sky.

Yet then the plague star began to wax. Night after night it burned more brightly, until it became visible even by day. Long before that time the pestilence had begun.

The flyers wheel against the darkening sky. Gliders, they are, and from afar they have a beauty. They call to my mind the shadowgulls of my homeplace, Budakhar upon the living sea, on the world Razyar. Yet here is no sea, only mountains and hills and dry desolation, and I know too that these flyers have small beauty when close at hand. Lean and terrible creatures they are, half as tall as a man, with skin like tanned leather pulled tight across their strange hollow bones. Their wings are dry and hard as a drumskin, their talons sharp like daggers, and beneath the great bony crest that sweeps back like a hooked blade from their narrow skulls, their eyes are a hideous red.

Janeel said to me they were sentient. They have a tongue, she said. I have heard their voices, thin keening screeching voices that scrape raw the nerves. I have never learned to speak this tongue, nor did Janeel. Sentient, she said. We would trade with them. Ho, they wanted no part of us or our trade. They knew enough to steal, yes, and that is where their sentience ended. Yet we and they have this much in common: death.

The flyers die. The night-hunters, with their massive twisted limbs and gnarly two-thumbed hands, with their eyes that burn in their bulging skulls like embers from a dying fire, ho, they die, too. They have a frightening strength, and those strange great eyes can see in the black when stormclouds cover even the plague star. In their caverns the hunters whisper of the great Minds, the masters they served once, the ones who will someday return and call on them to go forth to war once again. Yet the Minds do not come, and the night-hunters die—even as the flyers, even as those of the more furtive races whose bodies we find in the flint hills, even as the mindless beasts, even as the crops and trees, even as Janeel and I.

Janeel told me this would be a world of gold and gems for us; it is a world of death. H'ro Brana was the name in her ancient charts; I will not call it by that. She knew the names for all its peoples. I recall but one—*Hruun*. That is the true name of the night-hunters. A slave race, she said, of the Hrangans, the great enemy, gone now, defeated a thousand years past, their slaves abandoned in that long fall. It was a lost colony, she said, a handful of sentients eager for trade. She knew so much and I so little, but now I have buried her and spat upon her grave and I know the truth of it. If slaves they were, then bad slaves surely, for their masters set them upon a hell, beneath the cruel light of the plague star.

Our last supply ship came through half a year past. We might have gone. Already the plagues had begun. The flyers crawled upon the mountain summits, tumbled from the cliffs. I found them there, their skin inflamed and oozing fluid, great cracks in the leather of their wings. Night-hunters came to us covered with livid boils, and from us they bought umbrellas in great number, to keep them safe from the rays of the plague star. When the ship landed, we might have gone. Yet Janeel said stay. She had names for these sicknesses that killed the flyers and night-hunters. She had names for the drugs that would cure these ills. To name a thing is to understand, she thought. We might be healers, gain their brutal trust, and our fortunes would be made. She bought all the medicines that ship carried, and sent for others, and we began to treat these plagues that she had named.

When the next plague came, she named it, too. And the next, and the next, and the next. Yet there were plagues beyond counting. First she ran out of drugs, and soon out of names as well, and this dawn I dug her grave. She had been a slender, active female, but in dying she grew very stiff and her limbs puffed up to twice their size. I had to dig a large grave to fit her rigid, swollen corpse. I have named the thing that killed her: Janeel's Plague, I call it. I have no skill at names. My own plague is different from hers, and has no name. When I move, a living flame runs through my bones, and my skin has gone gray and brittle. Each dawn when I wake I find the bedclothes covered with bits of my flesh that have fallen away from my bones, and stained with blood from the wet raw places beneath.

The plague star is huge and bright above me, and now I understand why it is white. White is the color of purity, ho, and the plague star purifies this land. Yet its touch corrupts and decays. There is a fine irony in that, is there not?

We brought many weapons, sold few. The night-hunters and the flyers can use no weapons against this thing that slays them, and from the first have put more faith in umbrellas than in lasers. I have armed myself with a flamer from our storeroom, and poured myself a glass of dark wine.

I will sit here in the coolness and talk my thoughts to this crystal and I will drink my wine and watch the flyers, the few who still live, as they dance and soar against the night. Far off, they look so like shadowgulls above my living sea. I will drink my wine and remember how that sea sounded when I was but a Budakhar boy who dreamed of stars, and when the wine is gone I will use the flamer.

(long silence)

I can think of no more words to say. Janeel knew many words and many names, but I buried her this morning.

(long silence)

If my voice is ever found . . .

(short pause)

If this is found after the plague star has waned, as the night-hunters say it will, do not be deceived. This is no fair world, no world for life. Here is death, and plagues beyond numbering. The plague star will shine again.

(long silence)

My wine is gone.

(end of recording)

1

The Plague Star

"No," Kaj Nevis told the others firmly. "That's out. We'd be damned stupid to involve any of the big transcorps."

"Oh, stuff and nonsense," Celise Waan snapped back at him. "We have to get there, don't we? So we need a ship. I've chartered ships from Starslip before, and they're perfectly comfortable. The crews are polite and the cuisine is more than adequate."

Nevis gave her a withering look. He had a face made for it—sharp and angular, with hair swept back hard and a great scimitar of a nose, his small dark eyes half-hidden by heavy black eyebrows. "For what purpose did you charter these ships?"

"Why, for field trips, of course," Celise Waan replied. She plucked another cream ball from the plate in front of her, lifting it delicately between thumb and forefinger and popping it into her mouth. "I've supervised many important researches. The Center provided the funding."

"Let me point out the nose on your damn face," Nevis said. "This is not a field trip. We are not poking into the mating habits of primitives. We are not digging around for obscure knowledge that no sane person could possibly give a damn about, as you're accustomed to doing. This little conspiracy of ours is about to go after a treasure of almost unimaginable value. If we find it, we don't intend to turn it over to the proper authorities, either. You need me to see to its disposition through less-than-licit channels. And you trust me so little that you won't tell where the damn thing is until we're underway, and Lion here has hired a bodyguard. Fine, I don't give a damn. But understand this—I am not the only untrustworthy man on ShanDellor. Vast profit is involved here, and vast power. If you're going to continue to yammer at me about *cuisine*, then I'm leaving. I have better things to do than sit here counting your chins."

Celise Waan snorted disdainfully. She was a big, round, red-faced woman, with a loud, wet snort. "Starslip is a reputable firm," she said. "Besides, the salvage laws—"

"—are meaningless," said Nevis. "We have one set of laws here on ShanDellor, another on Kleronomas, a third on Maya, and none of them mean a damn thing. And if ShanDi law did apply, we'd get only one-quarter the value of the find—if we got anything at all. Assuming this plague star of yours is really what Lion thinks it is, and assuming that it's still in working order, whoever controls it will enjoy an overwhelming military superiority in this sector. Starslip and the other big transcorps are as greedy and ruthless as I am, I promise you. Furthermore, they are big enough and powerful enough so that the planetary governments watch them closely. In case it has escaped your notice, let me point out that there are only four of us. Five, if you count the hireling," he said, nodding toward Rica Dawnstar, who favored him with an icy grin. "A big liner has more than five pastry chefs. Even on a small courier, we'd be outnumbered by the crew. Once they saw what we had, do you imagine for even a second that we'd be allowed to keep it?"

"If they cheat us, we'll sue them," the fat anthropologist said, with a hint of petulance in her voice. She plucked up the last cream ball.

Kaj Nevis laughed at her. "In what courts? On what world? That's assuming we're allowed to live, which is unlikely on the face of it. You are a remarkably stupid and ugly woman."

Jefri Lion had been listening to the squabble with an uncomfortable expression on his face. "Here, here," he interrupted at last. "Let's have no name-calling,

Nevis. No call for it. We're all in this together, after all." A short, square block of a man, Lion wore a chameleon cloth jacket of military cut, decorated with rows of ribbons from some forgotten campaign. The fabric had turned a dusty gray in the dimness of the small restaurant, a gray that matched the color of Lion's bristling spade-shaped beard. There was a thin sheen of sweat on his broad, balding forehead. Kaj Nevis made him nervous; the man had a reputation, after all. Lion looked around to the others for support.

Celise Waan pouted and stared at the empty plate in front of her, as if her gaze could fill it with cream balls again. Rica Dawnstar—"the hireling," as Nevis called her—leaned back in her seat with a look of sardonic amusement in her bright green eyes. Beneath her drab jumpsuit and silvery mesh-steel vest, the long, hard body looked relaxed, almost indolent. No concern of hers if her employers wanted to argue all night and all day.

"Insults are useless," Anittas said. It was hard to tell what the cybertech was thinking; his face was as much polished metal and translucent plastic as flesh, and only minimally expressive. The shiny bluesteel fingers of his right hand interlocked with the mocha-colored fleshy digits of his left; he studied Nevis with two shining silvermetal eyes that moved smoothly in black plastic sockets. "Kaj Nevis has made some valid points. He is experienced in these areas, where we are not. What is the use of having brought him into this affair if we are unwilling to listen to his counsel?"

"Yes, that's so," Jefri Lion agreed. "What do you suggest then, Nevis? If we must avoid the transcorps, how will we reach the plague star?"

"We need a ship," Celise Waan said, loudly stating the obvious.

Kaj Nevis smiled. "The transcorps have no monopoly on ships. That's why I suggested we meet here today, rather than at Lion's office. This dump is close to the port. The man we want will be here, I'm sure."

Jefri Lion looked hesitant. "An independent? Some of them have rather, uh, unsavory reputations, don't they?"

"Like me," Nevis reminded him.

"Still. I've heard rumors of smuggling, even piracy. Do we want to take that kind of a chance, Nevis?"

"We don't want to take any chances at all," Kaj Nevis said. "And we won't. It's a matter of knowing the right people. I know lots of people. The right people. The wrong people." He made a small gesture with his head. "Now, way in the back there, that dark woman with all the black jewelry. That's Jessamyn Caige, mistress of the *Free Venture*. She'd hire out to us, no doubt. At a very reasonable rate."

Celise Waan craned around to look. "Is she the one, then? I hope this ship of hers has a gravity grid. Weightlessness makes me nauseous."

"When are you going to approach her?" Jefri Lion asked.

"I'm not," Kaj Nevis told them. "Oh, I've used Jessamyn to move a cargo or two for me, but I won't take the risk of actually riding with her, and I'd never dream of involving her in anything this big. The *Free Venture* has a crew of nine— more than enough to handle me and the hireling. No offense, Lion, but the rest of you don't count."

"I'll have you know I'm a soldier," Jefri Lion said, in a wounded tone. "I've seen combat."

"A hundred years ago," Nevis said. "As I said, the rest of you don't count. And Jessamyn would as soon kill all of us as spit." The small, dark eyes regarded each of them in turn. "That's why you need me. Without me, you are just naive enough to engage Jessamyn, or one of the transcorps."

"My niece serves with a very successful independent trader," Celise Waan said.

"And who might that be?" Kaj Nevis inquired.

"Noah Wackerfuss," she said, "of the *World of Bargains.*"

Nevis nodded. "Fat Noah," he said. "That would be a lot of fun, I'm damn sure. I might mention that *his* ship is kept constantly in weightlessness. Gravity would kill the old degenerate—not that it matters. Wackerfuss isn't especially blood-thirsty, that's so. Fifty-fifty chance he wouldn't kill us. He is, however, as greedy and as shrewd as they come. At the very least, he'd find a way to get a full share. At worst, he'd get it all. And his ship has a crew of twenty—all women. Have you ever asked your niece about the precise nature of her duties?"

Celise Waan flushed. "Do I have to listen to this man's innuendoes?" she asked Lion. "This was my discovery. I won't be insulted by this third-rate hoodlum, Jefri."

Lion frowned unhappily. "Really now, enough of this squabbling. Nevis, there's no need to flaunt your expertise. We brought you into this for good cause, I'm sure we all agree. You must have some idea of who we can engage to take us to the plague star, don't you?"

"Of course," Nevis agreed.

"Who?" prompted Anittas.

"The man is an independent trader, of sorts. Not a very successful one. And he's been stuck on ShanDellor, for want of a cargo, for half of a standard year now. He must be getting desperate—desperate enough, I'd think, so that he'll jump at this opportunity. He has a small, battered ship with a long, ridiculous name. It's not luxurious, but it will take us there, which is all that matters. There's no crew to worry about, only the man himself. And he—well, he's a little ridiculous, too. He'll give us no trouble. He's big, but soft, inside and out. He keeps cats, I hear. Doesn't much like people. Drinks a lot of beer, eats too much. I doubt that he even carries a weapon. Reports are that he barely scrapes by, flitting from world to world and selling absurd trinkets and useless little geegaws from this beat-up old ship of his. Wackerfuss thinks the man's a joke. But even if he's wrong, what can one man alone do? If he so much as threatens to report us, the hireling and I can dispose of him and feed him to his cats."

"Nevis, I'll have no talk like that!" Jefri Lion objected. "I won't have any killing on this venture."

"No?" Nevis said. He nodded toward Rica Dawnstar. "Then why did you hire her?" His smile was very nasty, somehow; her returning grin was pure mocking malice. "Just so," Nevis said, "I knew this was the place. Here's our man now."

None of them except Rica Dawnstar was much versed in the art of subtle conspiracy; the other three all turned to stare at the door, and the man who had just entered. He stood very tall, almost two-and-a-half meters, and his great soft gut swelled out above his thin metal belt. He had big hands, a long, curiously blank face, and a stiff, awkward posture; everywhere his skin was as white as bleached bone, and it appeared that he had not a hair on him anywhere. He wore shiny blue trousers and a deep maroon shirt whose balloon sleeves were frayed at the ends.

He must have felt their scrutiny, for he turned his head and stared back, his pale face expressionless. He kept on staring. Celise Waan looked away first, and then Jefri Lion, and finally Anittas. "Who is he?" the cyborg demanded of Kaj Nevis.

"Wackerfuss calls him Tuffy," Nevis said. "His real name, I'm told, is Haviland Tuf."

Haviland Tuf picked up the last of the green star-forts with a delicacy that belied his great size, then straightened to regard the gaming board with satisfaction. The entire cluster was red; cruisers and dreadnaughts and star-forts and all the colonies, red everywhere. "I must claim the victory," he said.

"Again," said Rica Dawnstar. She stretched, to untie the knots that hours bent over the game had put in her limbs. She had the deadly grace of a lioness, and beneath her silver mesh-steel vest her needler was snug in its shoulder holster.

"Perhaps I might be so bold as to suggest another contest," said Haviland Tuf.

Dawnstar laughed. "No thanks," she said. "You're too good at this. I was born a gambler, but with you it's no gamble. I'm tired of coming in second."

"I have been most fortunate in the games we have played thus far," Haviland Tuf said. "Undoubtedly, my luck will have run its course by now, and you will obliterate my poor forces on your next attempt."

"Oh, undoubtedly," Rica Dawnstar replied, grinning, "but forgive me if I postpone the attempt until the boredom becomes terminal. At least I'm better than Lion. Right, Jefri?"

Jefri Lion was seated in a corner of the ship's control room, perusing a stack of old military texts. His chameleon cloth jacket had turned the same brown as the synthawood panelling of the bulkhead behind him. "The game does not conform to authentic military principles," he said, with a hint of annoyance in his voice. "I employed the same tactics that Stephen Cobalt Northstar used when the 13th Human Fleet enveloped Hrakkean. Tuf's counterthrust was completely wrong under the circumstances. If the rules had been written properly, it ought to have been routed."

"Indeed," said Haviland Tuf. "You have the advantage of me, sir. You, after all, have the good fortune to be a military historian, and I am merely a humble trader. I lack your familiarity with the great campaigns of history. How fortunate for me that thus far, the deficiencies of the game itself, and my extraordinary fortune, have conspired to make up for my ignorance. Still, I would welcome the opportunity to strengthen my grasp of military principles. If you would care to assay the game once again, I will carefully study your subtle strategies so that I might in future incorporate a sounder, more authentic approach into my own poor play."

Jefri Lion, whose silver fleet had been the first eliminated in every game they had played during the past week, cleared his throat and looked uncomfortable. "Yes, uh, you see, Tuf," he began.

He was saved from embarrassment by a sudden shriek and stream of profanity that issued from the adjoining compartment. Haviland Tuf was on his feet at once; Rica Dawnstar was right behind him.

They emerged into the passageway just as Celise Waan staggered out of the living quarters, in pursuit of a small, fleet black-and-white form that went hurtling past them into the control room. "Catch it!" Celise Waan screamed at them. Her face was red and puffy and swollen, and she looked furious.

The door was small, Haviland Tuf large. "For what purpose, might I inquire?" he asked, blocking the way.

The anthropologist held out her left hand. There were three short, deep scratches across her palm, welling blood. "Look what it did to me!" she said.

"Indeed," said Haviland Tuf. "And what did you do to her?"

Kaj Nevis emerged from the living quarters with a thin, hard smile on his face. "She picked it up to toss it across the room," he said.

"It was on my bed!" said Celise Waan. "I wanted to take a little nap, and the damned creature was asleep on my bed!" She whirled to face Nevis. "And you, wipe that smirk off your face. It's bad enough we all have to be cooped up together in this shabby little ship. I simply refuse to share what little space there is with this impossible man's filthy little *animals*. And it's *your* fault, Nevis. You got us into this! Now do something. I demand that you make Tuf get rid of those vicious pests, do you hear me, I demand it!"

"Excuse me," Rica Dawnstar said from behind Tuf. He glanced back at her and moved aside. "Is this one of the vicious pests you had in mind?" Dawnstar asked, with a grin, as she stepped into the passageway. She was cradling a cat against her chest with her left hand, and petting it with her right. It was a huge tom with long, soft, gray hair and arrogant yellow eyes; it must have weighed twenty pounds, but Rica held it as easily as if it had been a kitten. "What do you propose Tuf do with old Mushroom here?" she asked as the cat began to purr.

"It was the other one that hurt me, the black-and-white one," Celise Waan said, "but that one's just as bad. Look at my face! Look at what they've done to me! I can scarcely breathe, and I'm breaking out all over, and whenever I try to get a little sleep I wake up with one of them on my chest. Yesterday I was having a little snack, and I put it down just for a moment, and when I came back the black-and-white one had knocked over my plate and was rolling my spice-puffs around in the dirt as if they were toys! Nothing is safe around these animals. I've lost two light pencils and my best pinky ring. And now *this*, this *attack!* Really, this is just intolerable. I must insist that these damned animals be put down in the cargo hold at once. *At once*, do you hear?"

"My hearing is quite adequate, thank you," said Haviland Tuf. "If your missing property has not turned up by the end of our voyage, I will be most pleased to reimburse you for its value. Your request in regard to Mushroom and Havoc, however, I must regretfully deny."

"I'm a passenger on this joke of a starship!" Celise Waan screamed at him.

"Must you insult my intelligence as well as my hearing?" Tuf replied. "Your status as a passenger here is obvious, madam; it is not necessary for you to point it out. Permit me to point out, however, that this small ship which you feel so free to insult is my home and my livelihood, such that it is. Furthermore, while you are undeniably a passenger here and therefore enjoy certain rights and perquisites, Mushroom and Havoc must logically have substantially greater rights, since this is their permanent abode, so to speak. It is not my custom to take passengers aboard my *Cornucopia of Excellent Goods at Low Prices*. As you have observed, the space available is scarcely adequate to my own needs. Regretfully, I have suffered various professional vicissitudes of late, and there is no gainsaying the fact that my supply of standards was veering toward inadequacy when Kaj Nevis approached me. I have bent all my efforts to accommodate you aboard this craft which you so malign, to the extent that I have given over my ship's living quarters to your collective needs and made my own poor bed in the control room. Despite my undeniable need, I am now coming to deeply regret the foolish and altruistic impulse that bid me take this charter, especially as the payment I have received was barely sufficient to refuel and provision for this voyage and pay the ShanDi landing tax. You have taken grievous advantage of my gullibility, I fear. Nonetheless, I am a man of my word and will do my best to convey you to this mysterious destination of yours. For the duration of the voyage, however, I must require you to tolerate Mushroom and Havoc, even as I tolerate you."

"Well, I never!" Celise Waan declared.

"I have no doubt," said Haviland Tuf.

"I'm not going to put up with this any longer," the anthropologist said. "There's no reason we all have to be crammed up inside one room like soldiers in a barracks. This ship was not nearly this small from outside." She pointed a pudgy arm. "Where does that door go?" she demanded.

"To the hold and cargo compartments," Haviland Tuf said evenly. "There are sixteen of them. Even the smallest, admittedly, has twice the space of my meager living quarters."

"Aha!" said Waan. "And are we carrying any cargo?"

"Compartment sixteen is packed with plastic reproductions of Cooglish orgy-masks, which I was unfortunately unable to sell on ShanDellor, a situation I lay entirely at the door of Noah Wackerfuss, who undercut my price and deprived me of my small hope of profit. In compartment twelve I store certain personal effects, miscellaneous equipment, collectibles, and bric-a-brac. The rest of the ship is quite empty, madam."

"Excellent!" said Celise Waan. "In that case, we will convert the smaller compartments into private rooms for each of us. It should be a simple matter to move our bedding."

"Quite simple," said Haviland Tuf.

"Then do it!" snapped Celise Waan.

"As you wish," said Tuf. "Will you be wanting to rent a pressure suit?"

"What?"

Rica Dawnstar was grinning. "The holds aren't part of the life-support system," she said. "No air. No heat. No pressure. No gravity, even."

"Ought to suit you just fine," Kaj Nevis put in.

"Indeed," said Haviland Tuf.

Day and night are meaningless aboard a starship, but the ancient rhythms of the human body still made their demands, and technology had to conform. Therefore the *Cornucopia*, like all but the huge triple-shift warships and transcorp liners, had its sleep cycle—a time of darkness and silence.

Rica Dawnstar rose from her cot and checked her needler, from long force of habit. Celise Waan was snoring loudly; Jefri Lion tossed and turned, winning battles in his head; Kaj Nevis was lost in dreams of wealth and power. The cybertech was sleeping too, though it was a deeper sort of sleep. To escape the boredom of the voyage, Anittas had parked on a cot, plugged into the ship's computer, and turned himself off. His cyberhalf monitored his biohalf. His breath was slow as a glacier and very regular, his body temperature down, his energy consumption cut to almost nothing, but the lidless silver-metal sensors that served him as eyes sometimes seemed to shift slightly, tracking some unseen vision.

Rica Dawnstar moved quietly from the room. Up in the control chamber, Haviland Tuf sat alone. His lap was full of gray tomcat; his huge pale hands moved over the computer keys. Havoc, the smaller black-and-white cat, was playing around his feet. She had gotten hold of a light pencil and was batting it to and fro on the floor. Tuf never heard Rica enter; no one heard Rica Dawnstar move unless she wanted them to hear.

"You're still up," she said from the door, leaning back against the jamb.

Tuf's seat swiveled around and he regarded her impassively. "A most remarkable deduction," he said. "Here I sit before you, active, busy, driven by the demands of my ship. From the scant evidence of your eyes and ears, you leap to the conclusion that I am not yet asleep. Your powers of reasoning are awesome."

Rica Dawnstar sauntered into the room and stretched out on Tuf's cot, still neatly made up from the previous sleep cycle. "I'm awake too," she said, smiling.

"I can scarcely believe it," said Haviland Tuf.

"Believe it," Rica said. "I don't sleep much, Tuf. Two or three hours a night. It's an asset in my profession."

"No doubt," said Tuf.

"On board ship, though, it's a bit of a liability. I'm bored, Tuf."

"A game, perhaps?"

She smiled. "Perhaps of a different sort."

"I am always eager to learn new games."

"Good. Let's play the conspiracy game."

"I am unfamiliar with its rules."

"Oh, they're simple enough."

"Indeed. Perhaps you would be good enough to elaborate." Tuf's long face was still and noncommittal.

"You would never have won that last game if Waan had thrown in with me when I asked her to," Rica said conversationally. "Alliances, Tuf, can be profitable to all parties concerned. You and I are the odd ones out here. We're the hirelings. If Lion is right about the plague star, the rest of them will divide wealth so vast it's incomprehensible, and you and I will receive our fees. Doesn't seem quite fair to me."

"Equity is often difficult to judge, and still more difficult to achieve," said Haviland Tuf. "I might wish my compensation were more generous, but no doubt many could make the same complaint. It is nonetheless the fee that I negotiated and accepted."

"Negotiations can be reopened," suggested Rica Dawnstar. "They need us. Both of us. It occurred to me that if we worked together, we might be able to . . . ah . . . insist upon better terms. Full shares. A six-way split. What do you think?"

"An intriguing notion, with much to recommend it," said Tuf. "Some might venture to suggest that it was unethical, true, but the true sophisticate retains a certain moral flexibility."

Rica Dawnstar studied the long, white, expressionless face for a moment, and grinned. "You don't buy it, do you, Tuf? Down deep, you're a stickler for rules."

"Rules are the essence of games, the very heart of them, if you will. They give structure and meaning to our small contests."

"Sometimes it's more fun just to kick over the board," Rica Dawnstar said. "More effective, too."

Tuf steepled his hands in front of his face. "Though I am not content with my niggardly fee, nonetheless I must fulfill my contract with Kaj Nevis. I would not have him speak poorly of me or the *Cornucopia of Excellent Goods at Low Prices.*"

Rica laughed. "Oh, I doubt that he'll speak poorly of you, Tuf. I doubt that he'll speak of you at all, once you've served your purpose and he's discarded you." She was pleased to see that her statement startled Tuf into blinking.

"Indeed," he said.

"Aren't you curious about all this? About where we're going, and why Waan and Lion kept the destination secret until we were aboard? About why Lion hired a bodyguard?"

Haviland Tuf stroked Mushroom's long gray fur, but his eyes never left Rica Dawnstar's face. "Curiosity is my great vice. I fear you have seen through to the heart of me, and now you seek to exploit my weakness."

"Curiosity killed the cat," said Rica Dawnstar.

"An unpleasant suggestion, but unlikely on the face of it," Tuf commented.

"But satisfaction brought him back," Rica finished. "Lion knows this is something huge. And hugely dangerous. To get what they want out of this, they needed Nevis, or somebody like Nevis. They have a nice four-way split set up, but Kaj has the kind of reputation that makes you wonder if he'll settle for a fourth. I'm here to see that he does." She shrugged, and patted her needler in its shoulder holster. "Besides, I'm insurance against any other complications that might arise."

"Might I point out that you yourself constitute an additional complication?"

She smiled icily. "Just don't point it out to Lion," she said, rising and stretching. "You think about it, Tuf. The way I see it, Nevis has underestimated you. Don't you go underestimating him. Or me. Never, never, *never* underestimate me. The time may come when you'll wish you had an ally. And it may come sooner than you'd like."

Three days shy of arrival, Celise Waan was complaining again over dinner. Tuf had served a spiced vegetable brouhaha in the manner of Halagreen; a piquant dish, but for the fact that this was the sixth such serving on the voyage. The anthropologist shoved the vegetables around on her plate, made a face, and said, "Why can't we have some real food?"

Tuf paused, speared a fat mushroom deftly with his fork, lifted it in front of his face. He regarded it in silence for a moment, shifted the angle of his head and regarded it from another angle, turned it around and regarded that aspect of it, and finally prodded it lightly with his finger. "I fail to grasp the nature of your complaint, madam," he said at last. "This mushroom, at least, seems real enough to my own poor senses. True, it is but a small sample of the whole. Perhaps the rest of the brouhaha is illusory. Yet I think not."

"You know what I meant," Celise Waan said in a shrill tone. "I want meat."

"Indeed," said Haviland Tuf. "I myself want wealth beyond measure. Such fantasies are easily dreamed, and less easily made real."

"I'm tired of all these puling vegetables!" Celise Waan screeched. "Are you telling me that there is not a bit of meat to be had on this entire puling ship?"

Tuf made a steeple of his fingers. "It was not my intent to convey such misinformation, certainly," he said. "I am not an eater of flesh myself, but there is some small poor quantity of meat aboard the *Cornucopia of Excellent Goods at Low Prices*, this I freely admit."

A look of furious satisfaction crossed Celise Waan's face. She glanced at each of the other diners in turn. Rica Dawnstar was trying to suppress a grin; Kaj Nevis was not even trying; Jefri Lion was looking fretful. "You see," she told them, "I told you he was keeping the good food for himself." With all deliberation, she picked up her plate and spun it across the room. It rang off a metal bulkhead and dumped its load of spiced brouhaha on Rica Dawnstar's unmade bed. Rica smiled sweetly. "We just swapped bunks, Waan," she said.

"I don't care," Celise Waan said. "I'm going to get a decent meal for once. I suppose the rest of you will be wanting to share now."

Rica smiled. "Oh no, dear. It's all yours." She finished up her brouhaha, cleaned her plate with a crust of onion bread. Lion looked uncomfortable, and Kaj Nevis said, "If you can get this meat out of Tuf, it's all yours."

"Excellent!" she proclaimed. "Tuf, bring me this meat!"

Haviland Tuf regarded her impassively. "True, the contract I made with Kaj Nevis requires me to feed you through the duration of this voyage. Nothing was said about the nature of the provender, however. Always I am put upon. Now I must cater to your culinary whims, it seems. Very well, such is my poor lot in life. And yet, now I find myself taken by a sudden whim of my own. If I must indulge your whim, would it not be equitable that you should similarly bend to mine?"

Waan frowned suspiciously. "What do you mean?"

Tuf spread his hands. "It is nothing, really. In return for the meat you crave, I ask only a moment's indulgence. I have grown most curious of late, and I would have that curiosity satisfied. Rica Dawnstar has warned me that, unsatisfied, curiosity will surely kill my cats."

"I'm for that," said the fat anthropologist.

"Indeed," said Tuf. "Nonetheless, I must insist. I offer you a trade—food, of the type you have requested so melodramatically, for a poor useless nugget of information, the surrender of which costs you nothing. We are shortly to arrive in the system of Hro B'rana, your chartered destination. I would know why we travel there, and the nature of what you expect to find on this plague star of which I have heard you speak."

Celise Waan turned to the others again. "We paid good standards for food," she said. "This is extortion. Jefri, put your foot down!"

"Um," said Jefri Lion. "There's really no harm, Celise. He'll find out anyway, when we arrive. Perhaps it is time he knew."

"Nevis," she said, "aren't you going to do anything?"

"Why?" he demanded. "It doesn't make a damn bit of difference. Tell him and get your meat. Or not. I don't care."

Waan glared at Kaj Nevis, and then even more fiercely at the cool pale face of Haviland Tuf, crossed her arms, and said, "All right, if that's the way it has to be, I'll sing for my supper."

"A normal speaking voice will be quite acceptable," said Tuf.

Celise Waan ignored him. "I'll make this short and sweet. The discovery of the plague star is my greatest triumph, the capstone of my career, but none of you have the wit or the courtesy to appreciate the work that went into it. I am an anthropologist with the ShanDellor Center for the Advancement of Culture and Knowledge. My academic specialty is the study of primitive cultures of a particular sort—cultures of colony worlds left to isolation and technological devolution in the wake of the Great War. Of course, many human worlds were so affected, and a number of these have been studied extensively. I worked in less well-known fields—the investigation of nonhuman cultures, especially those of former Hrangan slave worlds. One of the worlds I studied was Hro B'rana. Once it was a flourishing colony, a breeding ground for Hruun and dactyloids and lesser Hrangan slave races, but today it's a devastation. Such sentients that still live there live short, ugly, brutal lives, although like most such decayed cultures, they also have tales of a vanished golden age. But the most interesting thing about Hro B'rana is a legend, a legend unique to them—the plague star.

"Let me stress that the devastation on Hro B'rana is extreme, and the underpopulation severe, despite the fact that the environment is not especially harsh. Why? Well, the degenerate descendants of both Hruun and dactyloid colonists, whose cultures are otherwise utterly different and very hostile to each other, have a common answer to that: the plague star. Every third generation, just as they are climbing out of their misery, as populations are swelling once again, the plague star waxes larger and larger in their nighttime skies. And when this star becomes the brightest in the heavens, then the season of plagues begins. Pestilences sweep across Hro B'rana, each more terrible than the last. The healers are helpless. Crops wither, animals perish, and three-quarters of the sentient population dies. Those who survive are thrown back into the most brutal sort of existence. Then the plague star wanes, and with its waning the plagues pass from Hro B'rana for another three generations. That is the legend."

Haviland Tufs face had been expressionless as he listened to Celise Waan relate the tale. "Interesting," he said now. "I must surmise, however, that our present expedition has not been mounted simply to further your career by investigating this arresting folk tale."

"No," Celise Waan admitted. "That was once my intent, yes. The legend seemed an excellent topic for a monograph. I was trying to get funding from the Center for a field investigation, but they turned down my request. I was annoyed, and justly so. Those shortsighted fools. I mentioned my annoyance, and the cause, to my colleague, Jefri Lion."

Lion cleared his throat. "Yes," he said. "And my field, as you know, is military history. I was intrigued, of course. I buried myself in the Center databanks. Our files are not nearly as complete as those at Avalon and Newholme, but there wasn't time for a more thorough investigation. We had to act quickly. You see, my theory—well, it's more than theory, really—I believe, in fact I'm all but certain, that I know what this plague star is. It's no legend, Tuf! It's real. It must be a derelict, yes, abandoned but still operational, still carrying out its programs more than a millennium after the Collapse. Don't you see? Can't you guess?"

"I admit to failure," said Tuf, "lacking your familiarity with the subject at hand."

"It's a warship, Tuf, a warship in a long elliptical orbit around Hro B'rana. It's one of the most devastating weapons Old Earth ever put into the void against the Hrangans, in its own way as terrible as that mythical hellfleet they talk about from those last days before the Collapse. But it has vast potential for good as well as ill! It's the repository of the most advanced biogenetic science of the Federal Empire, a functioning artifact packed full of secrets lost to the rest of humanity."

"Indeed," said Tuf.

"It's a seedship," Jefri Lion finished, "a biowar seedship of the Ecological Engineering Corps."

"And it's *ours*," said Kaj Nevis, with a small grim smile.

Haviland Tuf studied Nevis briefly, nodded to himself, and rose. "My curiosity is satisfied," he announced. "Now I must fulfill my portion of the trade."

"Ahhh," said Celise Waan. "My meat."

"The supply is copious, though the variety is admittedly small," said Haviland Tuf. "I shall leave you the task of preparing the meat in a manner most pleasant to your palate." He went to a storage locker, punched in a code, and removed a small carton, which he carried back to the table under his arm. "This is the only meat aboard my vessel. I cannot vouch for its taste or quality. Yet I have not yet received a complaint on either count."

Rica Dawnstar burst into laughter and Kaj Nevis snickered. Haviland Tuf, neatly and methodically, removed a dozen cans of catfood from their carton, and stacked them in front of Celise Waan, Havoc leapt onto the table and began to purr.

"It's not as big as I expected," Celise Waan said, her tone as petulant as ever.

"Madam," said Haviland Tuf, "the eyes can often deceive. My main viewscreen is admittedly modest, a bare meter in diameter, and this must of course diminish the size of any object displayed thereon. The ship itself is of sizable dimensions."

Kaj Nevis came forward. "How sizable?"

Tuf folded his hands together atop the bulge of his stomach. "I cannot say with any precision. The *Cornucopia of Excellent Goods at Low Prices* is but a modest trading vessel, and its sensory instrumentation is not all that it might be."

"Approximately, then," Kaj Nevis snapped.

"Approximately," Tuf repeated. "Regarded at the angle at which my viewscreen is now displaying it, with the longest axis taken as 'length,' the ship we are approaching would seem to be, approximately, some thirty standard kilometers long, approximately some five kilometers in width, approximately some three kilometers in height, but for the domed section amidships, which rises slightly higher, and the forward tower which ascends, approximately, one additional kilometer above the deck from which it rises."

They had all gathered in the control room, even Anittas, who had been awakened from his computerregulated sleep when they emerged from drive. A hush fell over them; even Celise Waan seemed briefly at a loss for something to say. All of them stared at the viewscreen, at the long black twisted shape that floated against the stars, here and there shining with faint lights and pulsing with unseen energies.

"I was right," Jefri Lion muttered at last, to break the silence. "A seedship—an EEC seedship! Nothing else could possibly be so large!"

Kaj Nevis smiled. "Damn," he said.

"The system must be vast," Anittas said speculatively. "The Earth Imperials had a sophistication far beyond ours. It's probably an Artificial Intelligence."

"We're rich," burbled Celise Waan, her many and varied grievances forgotten for the moment. She grabbed hold of Jefri Lion's hands and waltzed him around in a circle, fairly bouncing. "We're rich, rich, we're rich and *famous*, we're all rich!"

"This is not entirely correct," said Haviland Tuf. "I do not doubt that you may indeed become wealthy in the near future; for the moment, however, your pockets contain no more standards than they did a moment ago. Nor do Rica Dawnstar and I share your prospects of economic advancement."

Nevis stared at him hard. "Are you complaining, Tuf?"

"Far be it from me to object," Tuf said in a flat voice. "I was merely correcting Celise Waan's misstatement."

Kaj Nevis nodded. "Good," he said. "Now, before any of us get any richer, we have to get aboard that thing and see what kind of shape it's in. Even a derelict ought to net us a nice salvage fee, but if that ship's in working order, there's no limit, no limit at all."

"It is obviously functional," Jefri Lion said. "It has been raining plagues on Hro B'rana every third generation for a thousand standard years."

"Yeah," said Nevis, "well, that's true, but it's not the whole story. It's dead in orbit now. What about the drive engines? The cell library? The computers? We've got a lot to check. How do we get aboard, Lion?"

"A docking might be possible," Jefri Lion replied. "Tuf, that dome, do you see it?" He pointed.

"My vision is unimpaired."

"Yes, well, I believe that's the landing deck under there. It's as big as a spacefield. If we can get the dome to open, you can take your ship right in."

"If," said Haviland Tuf. "A most difficult word. So short, and so often fraught with disappointment and frustration." As if to underline his words, a small red light came on beneath the main viewscreen. Tuf held up a long pale finger. "Take note!" he said.

"What is it?" asked Nevis.

"A communication," Tuf proclaimed. He leaned forward and touched a much worn button on his lasercom.

The plague star vanished from the screen. In its place appeared a weary-looking face—that of a man of middle years, sitting in a communications room. He had deep lines in his forehead and graven down his cheeks, a full head of thick black hair, and tired blue-gray eyes. He was wearing a uniform out of a history tape, and on his head was a green billed cap emblazoned with a golden theta. "This is *Ark*," he announced. "You have entered our defense sphere. Identify yourself or be fired upon. This is your first warning."

Haviland Tuf held down his SEND button. "This is the *Cornucopia of Excellent Goods at Low Prices*," he annunciated clearly, "Haviland Tuf commanding. We are harmless unarmed traders out of ShanDellor, *Ark*. Might we request permission to approach for docking?"

Celise Waan gaped. "It's manned," she said. "The crew is still alive!"

"A fascinating development," Jefri Lion said, tugging at his beard. "Perhaps this is a descendant of the original EEC crew. Or perhaps the chronowarp was employed! To warp the very weave of the fabric of time, to hurry it or hold it still, yes, they could do even that. The chronowarp! Think of it!"

Kaj Nevis made a snarling sound. "A thousand damn years and you tell me they're still alive? How the hell are we supposed to deal with that?"

The image on the viewscreen flickered briefly. Then the same tired man in the uniform of the Earth Imperials said, "This is *Ark*. Your ID is improperly coded. You are moving through our defense sphere. Identify yourself or be fired upon. This is your second warning."

"Sir," said Haviland Tuf, "I must protest! We are unarmed and unprotected. We mean you no harm. We are peaceful traders, scholars, fellow humans. Our intentions are not hostile, and moreover, we lack any means of doing harm to a ship as formidable as your *Ark*. Must we be met with belligerence?"

The screen flickered. "This is *Ark*. You have penetrated our defense sphere. Identify yourself immediately or be destroyed. This is your third and final warning."

"Recordings," said Kaj Nevis, with some enthusiasm. "That's it! No cold storage, no damned stasis field. There's no one there. Some computer is playing recordings at us."

"I fear you are correct," said Haviland Tuf. "The question must be asked: if the computer is programmed to play recorded messages at incoming ships, what else might it be programmed to do?"

Jefri Lion broke in. "The codes!" he said. "I have a whole set of Federal Empire codes and ID sequences on crystal chips in my files! I'll go get them."

"An excellent plan," said Haviland Tuf, "with but a single obvious deficiency, that being the time it will require to locate and utilize these encoded chips. Had we the leisure to accomplish this, I might applaud your suggestion. I fear we do not, alas. The *Ark* has just fired upon us."

Haviland Tuf reached forward. "I am taking us into drive," he announced. But as his long pale fingers brushed the keys, suddenly the *Cornucopia* shook violently. Celise Waan shrieked and went down; Jefri Lion stumbled into Anittas; even Rica Dawnstar had to grab the back of Tuf's chair to retain her footing. Then all the lights went out. Haviland Tuf's voice came out of the dark. "I fear I spoke too soon," he said, "or perhaps, more accurately, acted too tardily."

For a long moment, they were lost in silence and darkness and dread, waiting for the second hit that would spell an end to them.

And then the blackness ebbed a little; dim lights appeared on all the consoles around them, as the *Cornucopia*'s instrumentation woke to a flickering half-life. "We are not entirely disabled," Haviland Tuf proclaimed from the command chair where he sat stiffly. His big hands stretched out over the computer keys. "I will get a damage report. Perhaps we shall be able to retreat after all."

Celise Waan began to make a noise; a high, thin, hysterical wailing that went on and on. She was still sprawled on the deck. Kaj Nevis turned on her. "Shut up, you damned cow!" he snapped, and he kicked her. Her wail turned into blubbering. "We're dead meat sitting here like this," Nevis said loudly. "The next shot will blow us to pieces. Damn it, Tuf, move this thing!"

"Our motion is undiminished," Tuf replied. "The hit we took did not terminate our velocity, yet it did deflect us somewhat from our previous trajectory toward the *Ark*. Perhaps that is why we are not being fired upon now." He was studying wan green figures that uncoiled across one of the smaller telescreens. "I fear my ship has suffered some incapacitation. Shifting into drive now would be inadvisable; the stress would undoubtedly rend us to pieces. Our life support systems have also taken damage. The projections indicate that we will run out of oxygen in approximately nine standard hours."

Kaj Nevis cursed; Celise Waan began to beat her fists on the deck. "I can conserve oxygen by shutting down once more," Anittas offered. Everyone ignored him.

"We can kill the cats," Celise Waan suggested.

"Can we move?" Rica Dawnstar asked.

"The maneuvering engines are still operable," Tuf said, "but without the ability to shunt into stardrive, it will take us approximately two ShanDish years to reach even Hro B'rana. Four of us can take refuge in pressure suits. The viral airpacs will recycle oxygen indefinitely."

"I refuse to live in a pressure suit for two years," Celise Waan said forcefully.

"Excellent," said Tuf. "As I have only four suits, and we are six in number, this will be of help. Your noble self-sacrifice will be long remembered, madam. Before we put this plan into motion, however, I believe we might consider one other option."

"And what's that?" Nevis asked.

Tuf swiveled about in his command chair and looked at each of them in the dimness of the darkened control room. "We must hope that Jefri Lion's crystalline chip does indeed contain the proper approach code, so that we might effect a docking with the *Ark*, without being made the target of ancient weaponry."

"The chip!" Lion said. It was hard to see him. In the darkness, his chameleon cloth jacket had turned a deep black. "I'll go get it!" He went rushing back toward their living quarters.

Mushroom padded quietly across the room, and leapt up into Tuf's lap. Tuf settled a hand on him, and the big tom began to purr loudly. It was somehow a reassuring sound. Perhaps they would be all right after all.

But Jefri Lion was gone for too long a time.

When they finally heard him return, his footsteps were leaden, defeated.

"Well?" Nevis said. "Where is it?"

"Gone," Lion said. "I looked everywhere. It's gone. I could have sworn I had it with me. My files—Kaj, truly, I meant to bring it along. I couldn't bring everything, of course, but I duplicated most of the important records, the things I thought might prove useful—material on the war, on the EEC, some histories of this sector. My gray case, you know. It had my little computer, and more than thirty crystal chips. I was going over some of them last night, remember, in bed? I was reviewing the material about the seedships, what little we know, and you told me that I was keeping you awake. I had a chip full of old codes, I know I did, and I really meant to bring it along. But it's not there." He came closer. They saw he was carrying the hand computer, holding it out almost as an offering. "I went through the box four times, and searched all the chips I had out on my bed, on the table, everywhere. It's not here. I'm sorry. Unless one of you took it?" Jefri Lion glanced about the room. No one spoke. "I must have left the codes back on ShanDellor," he said. "We were in such haste to leave, I . . ."

"You senile old fool," said Kaj Nevis. "I ought to kill you right now, and save a little air for the rest of us."

"We're dead," wailed Celise Waan, "we're dead, dead, dead."

"Madam," said Haviland Tuf, petting Mushroom, "you continue to be premature. You are no more deceased now than you were wealthy a short time ago."

Nevis turned to face him. "Oh? You have an idea, Tuf?"

"Indeed," said Haviland Tuf.

"Well?" prompted Nevis.

"The *Ark* is our only salvation," Tuf said. "We must board her. Without Jefri Lion's code crystal, we cannot move the *Cornucopia of Excellent Goods at Low Prices* closer for a docking, for fear of being fired upon once again. This much is obvious. Yet an interesting concept has occurred to me." He raised a finger. "Perhaps the *Ark* might display less hostility toward a smaller target—a man in a pressure suit, say, propelled by air jets!"

Kaj Nevis looked thoughtful. "And when this man reaches the *Ark*, what then? Is he supposed to knock on the hull?"

"Impractical," admitted Haviland Tuf, "and yet I believe I have a method of dealing with this problem as well."

They waited. Tuf stroked Mushroom. "Go on," Kaj Nevis said impatiently.

Tuf blinked. "Go on? Indeed. I fear I must beg your indulgence. My mind is most distracted. My poor ship has suffered grievous harm. My modest livelihood lies ruined and devastated, and who will pay for the necessary repairs? Will Kaj Nevis, soon to enjoy such wealth, shower me with largesse? I fear not. Will Jefri Lion and Anittas buy for me a new ship? Unlikely. Will the esteemed Celise Waan grant me a bonus above and beyond my fee to compensate for my great loss? She has already promised to seek legal redress against me, to have my poor vessel confiscated and my landing license revoked. How then am I to cope? Who will succor me?"

"Never mind about that!" Kaj Nevis said. "How do we get inside the *Ark?* You said you had a way!"

"Did I?" said Haviland Tuf. "I believe you are correct, sir. Yet I fear the weight of my woes has driven the concept from my poor, distracted mind. I have forgotten it. I can think of nothing but my sorry economic plight."

Rica Dawnstar laughed, and clapped Tuf soundly across his broad back.

He looked up at her. "And now I am roughly pummeled and beaten as well, by the fierce Rica Dawnstar. Please do not touch me, madam."

"This is blackmail," screeched Celise Waan. "We'll have you put in prison for this!"

"And now my integrity is impugned, and I am showered with threats. Is it any wonder I cannot think, Mushroom?"

Kaj Nevis snarled. "All right, Tuf. You win." He looked around. "Do I hear any objections to making Tuffy here a full partner? A five-way split?"

Jefri Lion cleared his throat. "He deserves at least that, if his plan works."

Nevis nodded. "You're in, Tuf."

Haviland Tuf rose with immense, ponderous dignity, brushing Mushroom from his lap. "My memory returns to me!" he announced. "There are four pressure suits in the locker, yonder. If one of you would be so kind as to don one and render me your aid, together we shall go to procure a most useful piece of equipment from storage compartment twelve."

"What the hell," Rica Dawnstar exclaimed when they came back, carrying their booty between them. She laughed.

"What is it?" demanded Celise Waan.

Haviland Tuf, who loomed large in his silver-blue pressure suit, lowered the legs to the ground and helped Kaj Nevis get it upright. Then he removed his helmet and inspected their prize with satisfaction. "It is a spacesuit, madam," he said. "I would think that obvious."

It *was* a spacesuit, of sorts, but it was like no suit any of them had ever seen before, and clearly, whoever had constructed it had not had humans in mind. It towered over all of them, even Tuf; the ornate crest on the great beetling helmet was a good three meters off the deck, and almost brushed the top of the bulkhead. There were four thick double-jointed arms, the bottom two ending in gleaming, serrated pincers; the legs were broad enough to contain the trunks of small trees, and the footpads were great circular saucers. On the broad, hunched back were mounted four huge tanks; a radar antenna sprang from the right shoulder; and everywhere the rigid black metal of which it was constructed was filigreed in strange swirling patterns of red and gold. It stood among them like an armored giant of old.

Kaj Nevis jerked a thumb at the armor. "It's here," he said. "So what? How will this monstrosity help us?" He shook his head. "It looks like a piece of junk to me."

"Please," said Tuf. "This mechanism, which you so disparage, is an antique rich with history. I acquired this fascinating alien artifact, at no small cost to myself, on Unqi when I passed through that sector. This is a genuine Unquin battlesuit, sir, represented to be of the Hameriin dynasty, which fell some fifteen hundred years ago, long before humanity reached the Unquish stars. It has been fully restored."

"What does it *do*, Tuf?" asked Rica Dawnstar, always quick to come to the point.

Tuf blinked. "Its capabilities are many and varied. Two strike closest to home in regard to our present quandary. It has an augmented exoskeleton, and when fully charged will magnify the inherent strength of its occupant by a power of ten, approximately. Furthermore, its equipment includes a most excellent cutting laser, engineered to slice through duralloy of a thickness of one-half meter, or of plate steel of significantly greater thickness, when directly applied at zero range. In brief, this ancient battlesuit will be our means of entry into the ancient warship that looms as our only salvation."

"Splendid!" said Jefri Lion, clapping his hands together in approval.

"It might work at that," Kaj Nevis commented. "What's the drill?"

"I must admit to some deficiency of equipment for deep space maneuvering," Tuf replied. "Our resources include four standard pressure suits, but only two jetpacs. The Unquin battlesuit, I am pleased to report, has its own propulsion vents. I propose the following plan. I will don the battlesuit and make egress from the *Cornucopia of Excellent Goods at Low Prices*, accompanied by Rica Dawnstar and Anittas in pressure suits and jetpacs. We will proceed to the *Ark* with all due speed. If we make the journey safely, we will use the battlesuit's most excellent capabilities to gain entrance through an airlock. I am told that Anittas is expert in ancient cybernetic systems and obsolete computers. Very well, then. Once inside, he will no doubt have little trouble gaining control of the *Ark* and will supersede the hostile programming now in place. At that point, Kaj Nevis will be able to pilot my crippled ship in for a docking, and all of us will have attained safety."

Celise Waan turned a vivid shade of red. "You're leaving us to die?" she screeched. "Nevis, Lion, we must stop them! Once they're on the *Ark*, they'll blow us up! We can't trust them."

Haviland Tuf blinked. "Why must my morality be constantly assaulted by these accusations?" he asked. "I am a man of honor. The course of action you have suggested had never crossed my mind."

"It's a good plan," said Kaj Nevis. He smiled, and began to unseal his pressure suit. "Anittas, hireling, suit up."

"Are you going to let them abandon us here?" Celise Waan demanded of Jefri Lion.

"I'm sure they mean us no harm," Lion said, tugging on his beard, "and if they did, Celise, how do you propose I stop them?"

"Let us move the battlesuit down to the main airlock," Haviland Tuf said to Kaj Nevis while Dawnstar and the cybertech were suiting up. Nevis nodded, kicked his way free of his own pressure suit, and moved to help Tuf.

With some difficulty, they wrestled the huge Unquish suit down to the *Cornucopia*'s main lock. Tuf shed his pressure suit and unbolted the armored entry port, then pulled over a stepstool and began to climb laboriously inside. "Just a moment, Tuffy," Kaj Nevis said, grabbing him by the shoulder.

"Sir," said Haviland Tuf, "I do not like to be touched. Unhand me." He turned back and blinked in surprise. Kaj Nevis had produced a vibroknife. The slender, humming blade, which could slice through solid steel, was a blur of motion less than a centimeter from Tuf's nose.

"A good plan," Kaj Nevis said, "but let's make one little change. I'll wear the supersuit, and go with Anittas and little Rica. You stay here and die."

"I do not approve of this substitution," said Haviland Tuf. "I am chagrined that you too would truckle to unfounded suspicion of my motives. I assure you, as I have assured Celise Waan, that thought of treachery has never crossed my mind."

"Funny," said Kaj Nevis. "It crossed *my* mind. Seemed like a damn fine idea, too."

Haviland Tuf assumed a look of wounded dignity. "Your base plans are undone, sir," he announced. "Anittas and Rica Dawnstar have come up behind you. It is well known that Rica Dawnstar was hired to forestall just such behavior from you. I advise you to surrender now. It will go easier on you."

Kaj Nevis grinned.

Rica had her helmet cradled under her arm. She observed the tableau, shook her pretty head slightly, and sighed. "You should have taken my offer, Tuf. I told you the time would come when you'd be sorry you didn't have an ally." She donned the helmet, sealed it, scooped up an airjet. "Let's go, Nevis."

Comprehension finally dawned on the broad face of Celise Waan. To her credit, this time she did not succumb to hysteria. She looked about for a weapon, found nothing obvious, and finally grabbed Mushroom, who was standing nearby and watching events with curiosity. "You, you, YOU!" she shouted, heaving the cat across the room. Kaj Nevis ducked. Mushroom yowled mightily and bounced off Anittas.

"Kindly cease flinging about my cats," Haviland Tuf said.

Nevis, recovering quickly, brandished the vibroknife at Tuf in a most unpleasant fashion, and Tuf backed slowly away. Nevis paused long enough to scoop up Tuf's discarded pressure suit and slice it deftly into a dozen long silver-blue ribbons. Then, carefully, he climbed into the Unquin battlesuit. Rica Dawnstar sealed it up after him. It took Nevis some time to figure out the alien control systems, but after about five minutes, the bulging faceplate began to glow a baleful blood red, and the heavy upper limbs moved ponderously. He switched to the lower, pincered arms experimentally while Anittas opened the inner door of the lock. Kaj Nevis lumbered in, clacking his pincers, followed by the cybertech and, lastly, Rica Dawnstar. "Sorry, folks," she announced as the door was sliding shut. "It's nothing personal. Just arithmetic."

"Indeed," said Haviland Tuf. "Subtraction."

Haviland Tuf sat in his command chair, enthroned in darkness, watching the flickering instrumentation before him. Mushroom, his dignity much offended, had settled in Tufs lap, and was graciously allowing himself to be soothed. "The *Ark* is not firing on our erstwhile compatriots," he told Jefri Lion and Celise Waan.

"This is all my fault," Jefri Lion was saying.

"No," said Celise Waan. "It's *his* fault." She jerked a fat thumb toward Tuf.

"You are not the most appreciative of women," Haviland Tuf observed.

"Appreciative? What am I supposed to appreciate?" she said angrily.

Tuf made a steeple of his hands. "We are not without resources. To begin with, Kaj Nevis left us one functioning pressure suit," he pointed out.

"And no propulsion systems."

"Our air will last twice as long with our numbers diminished," Tuf said.

"But will still run out," snapped Celise Waan.

"Kaj Nevis and his cohorts did not use the Unquin battlesuit to destroy the *Cornucopia of Excellent Goods at Low Prices* after their exit, as well they might have."

"Nevis preferred to see us die a lingering death," the anthropologist replied.

"I think not. More likely, in point of fact, he wished to preserve this vessel as a last refuge should his plan to board the *Ark* somehow miscarry," Tuf mused. "In the nonce, we have shelter, provisions, and the possibility of maneuver, however limited."

"What we have is a crippled ship that is rapidly running out of air," said Celise Waan. She started to say something else, but just then Havoc came bounding into the control room, all energy and bounce, in hot pursuit of a bit of jewelry she'd sent rolling in before her. It landed by Celise Waan's feet; Havoc pounced on it, and sent it spinning with a tentative swipe. Celise Waan yelped. "My glowstone ring! I've been looking for that! Damn you, you filthy thief." She bent and snatched for the ring. Havoc closed with her, and she gave the cat a lusty blow with her fist. She missed. Havoc's claws were more accurate. Celise Waan shrieked.

Haviland Tuf was on his feet. He snatched up the cat and the ring, tucked Havoc safely under his arm, and handed the ring stiffly to its bleeding owner. "Your property," he said.

"Before I die, I swear I'm going to grab that creature by the tail and smash its brains on a bulkhead—if it has any brains."

"You do not sufficiently appreciate the virtues of the feline," said Tuf, retreating to his chair. He soothed Havoc's feelings as he had earlier soothed Mushroom. "Cats are most intelligent animals. In fact, it is well known that all cats have a touch of psi. The primitives of Old Earth were known to worship them."

"I've studied primitives who worship fecal matter," the anthropologist said testily. "That animal is a filthy beast!"

"The feline is fastidiously clean," Tuf said calmly. "Havoc herself is scarcely more than a kitten, and her playfulness and chaotic temperament remain undiminished," he said. "She is a most willful creature, and yet, that is but part of her charm. Curiously, she is also a creature of habit. Who could fail to be warmed by the joy she takes in play with small objects left lying about? Who could fail to be amused by the foolish frequency with which she loses her playthings beneath the consoles in this very room? Who indeed. Only the most sour and stony-hearted." Tuf blinked rapidly—once, twice, three times. On his long, still face, it was a thunderstorm of emotion. "Off, Havoc," he said, gently swatting the cat from his lap. He rose, then sank to his knees with a stiff dignity. On hands and knees, Haviland Tuf began to crawl about the room and feel beneath the control consoles.

"What are you doing?" demanded Celise Waan.

"I am searching for Havoc's lost toys," said Haviland Tuf.

"I'm bleeding and we're running out of air and you're looking for *cat toys!*" she said in exasperation.

"I believe I have just stated as much," Tuf said. He pulled a handful of small objects out from under the console, and then a second handful. After thrusting his arm all the way back and patting about systematically, he finally gave up, gathered his cache, dusted himself off, and began to sort the prizes from the dust. "Interesting," he said.

"What?" she demanded.

"These are yours," he said to Celise Waan. He handed her another ring and two light pencils. "These are mine," he said, shoving aside two more light pencils, three red cruisers, a yellow dreadnaught, and a silver star-fort. "And this, I believe, is yours." He held it out to Jefri Lion: a shaped crystal the size of a thumbnail.

Lion all but bounded to his feet. "The chip!"

"Indeed," said Haviland Tuf.

There was a moment of endless suspense after Tuf had lasered the docking request. A thin crack appeared in the middle of the great black dome, and then another, at cross angles to the first. Then a third, a fourth, more and still more. The dome split into a hundred narrow pie-shaped wedges, which receded into the hull of the *Ark*.

Jefri Lion let go of his breath. "It works," he said, in a voice full of awe and gratitude.

"I reached that conclusion some time ago," Tuf said, "when we successfully penetrated the defense sphere without being fired upon. This is merely a confirmation."

They watched the proceedings on the viewscreen. Beneath the dome appeared a landing deck fully as large as the ports of many a lesser planet. The deck was pockmarked with circular landing pads, several of which were occupied. As they waited, a ring of blue-white light flicked on around one vacant pad.

"Far be it from me to dictate your behavior," said Haviland Tuf, his eyes on his instruments, his hands in careful, methodical motion. "I would, however, advise that each of you strap in securely. I am extending the landing legs and programming us for a landing on the indicated pad, but I am uncertain how much damage the legs have sustained, uncertain even as to whether all three legs remain in place. Therefore I counsel caution."

The landing deck yawned blackly beneath them. They began a stately descent into its cavernous depths. The illuminated ring of the landing pad loomed larger and larger on one viewscreen; a second showed the wan blue light of the *Cornucopia*'s gravity engines flickering off distant metal walls and the silhouettes of other ships. In a third, they saw the dome reassembling itself, a dozen sharp teeth grinding together once more, as if they had just been swallowed by some vast spacefaring animal.

The impact was surprisingly gentle. They settled into place with a sigh and a whisper and only the smallest of bumps. Haviland Tuf killed their engines, and spent a moment studying the instruments and the scenes on his telescreens. Then he turned to face the others. "We are docked," he announced, "and the time has come to make our plans."

Celise Waan was busily unstrapping herself. "I want to get out of here," she said, "find Nevis and that bitch Rica, and give them both a good piece of my mind."

"A good piece of your mind might be considered an oxymoron," said Haviland Tuf. "I think your proposed course of action unwise in the extreme. Our former colleagues must now be considered our rivals. Having just abandoned us to death, they shall undoubtedly be nonplussed to discover us still alive, and might very well take steps to rectify this contradiction."

"Tuf is right," Jefri Lion said. He was moving from one screen to another, peering at them with fascination. The ancient seedship had rekindled his spirit and his imagination, and he was bristling with energy. "It's us against them, Celise. This is war. They'll kill us if they can, have no doubt of it. We must be similarly ruthless! This is a time for clever tactics."

"I bow to your martial expertise," Tuf said. "What strategies do you suggest?"

Jefri Lion tugged on his beard. "Well," he said, "well, let me think. What's the situation here? They have Anittas. The man's half-computer himself. Once he interfaces with the shipboard systems, he should be able to determine how much of the *Ark* is functional, yes, and perhaps to exercise some control over its functioning, too. That could be dangerous. He might be trying it right now. We know they got aboard first. They may or may not know we're aboard. We have the advantage of surprise, perhaps!"

"They have the advantage of having all the weaponry," said Haviland Tuf.

"No problem!" said Jefri Lion. He rubbed his hands together eagerly. "This is a warship, after all. The EEC specialized in biowar, true, but this was a military vessel and I'm sure the crew had personal sidearms, that sort of thing. There's got to be an armory. All we have to do is find it."

"Indeed," said Haviland Tuf.

Lion was rolling now. "Our advantage, well, not to be immodest about it, but our advantage is me. Aside from what Anittas can discover from the computers, they'll be blundering about in the dark. But I've studied the old Federal Empire ships. I know everything about them." He frowned. "Well, everything that wasn't lost or classified, anyway. At least I know a few things about the general plans of these seedships. We'll have to find the armory first, and it should be close. It was standard procedure to store weaponry near the landing deck, for ground parties

and such. After we're armed, we ought to look for—hmmmm, let me think—
well, yes, the cell library, that's crucial. The seedships had vast cell libraries,
cloning material from literally thousands of worlds preserved in a stasis field. We
must discover if the cells are still viable! If the stasis field has failed and the samples have decayed, all we have gained is a very large ship. But if the systems are
still operational, the *Ark* is literally priceless!"

"While I appreciate the importance of the cell library," Tuf said, "it strikes me
that a more immediate priority might be the location of the bridge. Making the
perhaps unwarranted but nonetheless attractive assumption that none of the original crew of the *Ark* is alive after the passage of a millennium, we are then alone on
this vessel with our enemies, and whichever party gains control of shipboard functions first will enjoy a rather formidable advantage."

"A good point, Tuf!" Lion exclaimed. "Well then, let's get to it."

"Right," said Celise Waan. "I want out of this cat trap."

Haviland Tuf raised a finger. "A moment, please. A problem presents itself. We
are three in number, and possess only a single pressure suit among us."

"We're inside a *ship*," Celise Waan said in a voice that dripped sarcasm. "What
do we need with suits?"

"Perhaps nothing," Tuf admitted. "It is true, as you imply, that the landing field
seems to function as a very large airlock; my instruments indicate that we are now
surrounded by an entirely breathable oxygen-nitrogen atmosphere, pumped in
when the closure of the dome was complete."

"So what's the problem, Tuf?"

"No doubt I am being overcautious," Haviland Tuf said. "I admit to some disquiet, however. This *Ark*, though perhaps abandoned and derelict, is nonetheless
dutiful. Witness the plagues it still regularly visits on Hro B'rana. Witness the efficiency with which it defended itself against our approach. We cannot know, as yet,
why this ship was abandoned, nor how the last of the crew met their end, but it
seems clear that it was their intent that the *Ark* live on. Perhaps the external defense sphere was only the first of several lines of automatic defense."

"An intriguing notion," said Jefri Lion. "Traps?"

"Of a particular kind. The atmosphere that awaits us may seethe with pestilence, plague, and biogenetic contagion. Dare we risk it? I would be more comfortable in a pressure suit, myself, though each of you is free to decide otherwise."

Celise Waan looked uncomfortable. "I should get the suit," she said. "We only
have one, and you owe it to me, after the beastly way I've been treated."

"We need not enter into that discussion again, madam," said Tuf. "We are on a
landing deck. Around us, I observe nine other spacecraft of varying design. One is
a Hruun fighter, one a Rhiannese merchant; two are of designs unfamiliar to me.
And five are plainly shuttlecraft of some sort, identical to each other, larger than
my own poor vessel here, undoubtedly part of the *Ark's* own original equipment.
It is my experience that spacecraft invariably are equipped with pressure suits. It is
my intention, therefore, to don our single remaining suit, exit, and search these
neighboring ships until I have found suits for each of you."

"I don't like it," Celise Waan snapped. "You get out, and we're still stuck here."

"Such are the vicissitudes of life," Tuf said, "that each of us must sometimes accept that which he does not like."

The airlock gave them a bit of trouble. It was a small emergency lock, with
manual controls. They had no difficulty opening the outer door, entering, and

sealing it behind them. The inner door was another and more difficult proposition.

Atmosphere came flooding back into the large chamber as soon as the outer door was closed, but the inner door was jammed somehow. Rica Dawnstar tried it first; the huge metal wheel refused to turn, the lever would not depress. "OUT OF MY WAY," Kaj Nevis said, his voice twisted into a rasping croak by the alien comm circuits built into the Unquin battlesuit, and boosted to deafening levels by external speakers. He trundled past her, the huge saucer feet ringing loudly on the deck, and the battlesuit's great upper arms seized the wheel and turned. The wheel resisted for a moment, then twisted and buckled, and finally came loose of the door entirely.

"Good work," Rica said over her suit speaker. She laughed.

Kaj Nevis growled something thunderously unintelligible. He seized the lever and tried to move it, and succeeded only in breaking it off.

Anittas moved closer to the stubborn inner lock mechanism. "A set of code buttons," he said, pointing. "The proper code sequence, if we knew it, would no doubt gain us entry automatically. There's a computer outlet, too. If I could interface, perhaps I could pull the correct code out of the system."

"WHAT'S STOPPING YOU?" Kaj Nevis demanded. His faceplate glowed balefully.

Anittas lifted his arms, turned his hands over helplessly. With the more obviously organic portions of his body covered by the silver-blue of his pressure suit, and his silver metallic eyes peering out through the plastic, he looked more like a robot than ever. Kaj Nevis, standing huge above him, looked like a much larger robot. "This suit," Anittas said, "is improperly designed. I cannot interface directly without removing it."

"REMOVE IT, THEN," Nevis said.

"Will that be safe?" asked Anittas. "I am unsure."

"There's air in here," Rica Dawnstar put in. She gestured toward the appropriate bank of indicators.

"Neither of you has removed your suit," Anittas pointed out. "Were I to make a mistake, and open the outer door instead of the inner one, I might die before I could seal up again."

"DON'T MAKE A MISTAKE," Kaj Nevis boomed.

Anittas crossed his arms. "The air might be unhealthy. This ship has been derelict for a thousand standard years, Kaj Nevis. Even the most sophisticated system goes down from time to time, experiences failures and glitches. I am unwilling to risk my person."

"OH?" Nevis thundered. There was a grinding sound. One of the lower arms came up slowly; the serrated metal pincer opened, seized Anittas about the middle, and pinned him against the nearest wall. The cybertech squawked protest. An upper arm came across, and a huge metal-gloved hand dug in under the collar of the pressure suit. It pulled. The helmet and the entire top of the suit came ripping off Anittas. His head almost came off, as well.

"I LIKE THIS SUIT," Kaj Nevis announced. He gave the cybertech a little squeeze with the pincer. Metal fabric tore and blood began oozing through. "YOU'RE BREATHING, AREN'T YOU?"

Anittas was almost hyperventilating, in fact. He nodded.

The battlesuit flung him to the floor. "THEN GET TO WORK," Nevis told him.

That was when Rica Dawnstar began to feel nervous. She backed away casually, leaned against the outer door as far from Nevis as she could get, and considered the situation while Anittas removed his gloves and the shards of his ruined suit and slid the bluesteel fingers of his right hand into the waiting computer plugs. She had strapped her shoulder holster on over her pressure suit, so her needler would be accessible, but suddenly its presence didn't seem entirely as reassuring as it usually did. She studied the thickness of the Unquin armor, and wondered if maybe she had been unwise in her choice of ally. A three-way split was much better than Jefri Lion's small fee, to be sure. But what if Nevis decided he didn't like a three-way split?

They heard a sharp, sudden *pop* and the inner door began to slide open. Beyond was a narrow corridor leading down into blackness. Kaj Nevis moved to the doorway and peered into the dark, his glowing red faceplate throwing scarlet reflections on the walls. Then he turned ponderously. "YOU, HIRELING!" he boomed at Rica Dawnstar, "GO SCOUT IT OUT."

She came to a decision. "Aye, aye, bossman," she said. She drew her needler, moved quickly to the door and down the corridor, followed it about ten meters to a cross-corridor. From there she looked back. Nevis, hugely armored, filled the airlock door. Anittas stood beside him. The cybertech, normally so silent, still, and efficient, was shaking. "Stay right there," Rica called back to them. "It's not safe!" Then she turned and picked a direction at random and began to run like hell.

It took Haviland Tuf much longer than he had anticipated to locate the suits. The nearest of the other spacecraft was the Hruun fighter, a chunky green machine bristling with weaponry. It was sealed up securely, however, and although Tuf circled it several times and studied the various instruments that seemed designed to command access, none of his tugging, prodding, pushing, or fiddling produced the desired result, and he was forced to give it up finally and proceed onward.

The second ship, one of the strange ones, was wide open, and he wandered through it with a certain amount of intellectual fascination. Its interior was a maze of narrow corridors whose walls were as irregular and pebbly as a cave, and soft to the touch. Its instruments were incomprehensible. Its pressure suits, when he located what looked to be pressure suits, might have been functional, but could never have been worn by anyone over a meter tall or bilaterally symmetrical.

The Rhiannese merchant, his third try, had been gutted; Tuf could locate nothing useful.

Finally, there was nothing to be done for it but to hike all the way to one of the five distant shuttlecraft that stood side by side, snug in custom launching berths. They were big ships, larger than the *Cornucopia of Excellent Goods at Low Prices*, with black pitted hulls and rakish wings, but they were clearly of human design and seemingly in good repair. Tuf finally puzzled his way into one of them, whose berth bore a metal plate with an engraved silhouette of some fanciful animal and a legend proclaiming it to be named *Griffin*. Pressure suits were located where they should have been located. They were in excellent shape, considering that they were a thousand years old, and quite striking as well: a deep green in color, with golden helmet, gloves, and boots, and a golden theta emblazoned upon the breast of each. Tuf selected two of them and carried them back across the echoing twilit plain of the landing deck, to where the scarred, crippled teardrop that was his *Cornucopia* squatted on its three splayed legs.

When he got to the base of the ramp that led up to the main lock, he almost stumbled over Mushroom.

The big tom was sitting on the deck. He got up and made a plaintive noise, rubbing himself against Tuf's booted leg.

Haviland Tuf stopped for an instant and stared down at the old gray tom. He bent awkwardly, gathered up the cat, and stroked him for a time. When he climbed the ramp to the airlock, Mushroom followed, and Tuf found it necessary to shoo him away. He cycled through with a pressure suit under each arm.

"It's about time," Celise Waan said when Tuf entered.

"I told you Tuf hadn't abandoned us," Jefri Lion said.

Haviland Tuf let the pressure suits fall to the deck, where they lay like a puddle of green and gold. "Mushroom is outside," Tuf said in a flat, passionless voice.

"Well, yes," Celise Waan said. She grabbed a suit and began squeezing into the green metallic fabric. It bound her tightly about the middle; the members of the Ecological Engineering Corps had seemingly been less fleshy than she. "Couldn't you have gotten me a larger size?" she complained. "Are you sure these suits still work?"

"The construction seems sound," Tuf said. "It will be necessary to infuse the airpacs with whatever living bacteria remain from the ship's cultures. How did Mushroom come to be outside?"

Jefri Lion cleared his throat uncomfortably. "Uh, yes," he said. "Celise was afraid you weren't coming back, Tuf. You were gone so long. She thought you'd left us here."

"A base and foundless suspicion," said Tuf.

"Uh, yes," said Lion. He looked away, reached for his own suit.

Celise Waan pulled on a golden boot, sealed it. "It's your fault," she said to Tuf. "If you hadn't been gone so long, I wouldn't have gotten restless."

"Indeed," said Tuf. "What, might I venture to ask, has your restlessness to do with Mushroom?"

"Well, I thought you weren't coming back, and we had to get out of here," the anthropologist said. She sealed up her second boot. "But you made me nervous, you know, with all your talk of plagues. So I cycled the cat through the airlock. I tried to get that damned black-and-white one, but it kept running away and hissing at me. The gray one just let me pick it up. I dumped it out and we've been watching it through the screens. I figured we could see whether or not it got sick. If it didn't show any symptoms, well, then probably it would be safe for us to risk coming out."

"I grasp the principle," said Haviland Tuf.

Havoc came bounding in the room, playing with something. She saw Tuf and headed toward him, walking with a pronounced kittenish swagger.

"Jefri Lion," said Tuf, "if you would, please apprehend Havoc, take her back to the living quarters, and confine her there."

"Uh, certainly," Lion said. He caught up Havoc as she went by him. "Why?"

"I would prefer henceforth to keep Havoc secure and separated from Celise Waan," Tuf said.

Celise Waan, helmet cradled under her arm, made a noise of derision. "Oh, stuff and nonsense. The gray one is fine."

"Permit me to mention a concept with which you are perhaps unfamiliar," said Haviland Tuf. "It is referred to as an incubation period."

"I'm going to kill that bitch," Kaj Nevis threatened as he and Anittas made their way down a dark hallway. *"Damn her. You can't get a decent mercenary anymore."* The

battlesuit's huge head turned to search for the cybertech, the faceplate glowing. *"Hurry up."*

"I cannot match your strides," Anittas said as he hurried up. His sides ached from the effort of keeping up with Nevis's pace; his cyberhalf was strong as metal and quick as electronic circuitry, but his biohalf was poor tired wounded flesh, and blood still oozed from the cuts Nevis had opened around his midsection. He was feeling dizzy and hot, as well. "It's not far now," he said. "Down this corridor and to the left, third door. It is a substantial substation. I felt it when I was plugged in. I will be able to meld with the main system." And rest, he thought. He was incredibly weary, and his biohalf ached and throbbed.

"I WANT THE DAMN LIGHTS ON," Nevis commanded. "AND THEN I WANT YOU TO FIND HER FOR ME. DO YOU UNDERSTAND?"

Anittas nodded, and pushed himself harder. Two small hot pinpoints of red burned on his cheeks, unseen by his silver-metal eyes, and for an instant his vision blurred and wavered, and he heard a loud buzzing in his ears. He stopped.

"WHAT'S WRONG NOW?" Nevis demanded.

"I am experiencing some loss of function," Anittas said. "I must reach the computer room and run a check on my systems." He started forward again, and staggered. Then his balance deserted him totally, and he fell.

Rica Dawnstar was positive that she had lost them. Kaj Nevis was pretty formidable in his giant metal monkey suit, no doubt of that, but he was anything but silent. Rica had eyes like one of Tuf's cats, another advantage in her profession. Where she could see, she ran; in the corridors that were totally black, she felt her way along, as quickly and quietly as she could. Down here the *Ark* was a maze of rooms and hallways. She threaded her way through the labyrinth, turning and twisting and turning once again, doubling back on herself, and listening carefully as Nevis's clanging tread grew steadily fainter and finally faded altogether.

Only then, when she knew she was safe, did Rica Dawnstar begin to explore the warren in which she found herself. There were light plates set in the walls. Some responded to the touch of her hand, others did not. She lit her way wherever she could. The first section she passed through was residential—small sleeping rooms off narrow corridors, each with a bed, desk, computer console, and telescreen. Some rooms were empty and sterile; in others she found beds unmade and clothing strewn across the floor. Everything was neat and clean. Either the residents had just moved out the night before, or the *Ark* had kept this whole portion of the ship sealed and inviolate and in repair, until their approach had somehow activated it.

The next section had not been so fortunate. Here the rooms were full of dust and debris, and in one she found an ancient skeleton, a woman, still asleep in a bed that had collapsed into shapeless decay centuries before. What a difference a little air can make, Rica thought.

The corridors led into other corridors, wider ones. She peered into storage rooms, into chambers full of equipment and others packed with empty cages, into spotless white laboratories in endless succession that lined the sides of a corridor as wide as the boulevards of Shandicity. That led her, eventually, to a junction with an even grander corridor. She hesitated, unsure for a moment, and drew her needler. This way to the control room, she thought to herself—or to something important, at any rate. She stepped out onto the main way, spotted something in the corner; dim shapes, hunched down into little niches in the wall. Cautiously, Rica moved toward them.

When she got close, she laughed and holstered her weapon. The dark shapes were a row of scooters of some kind—small three-wheeled vehicles, each with two seats and big soft balloon tires. They were set into charging-slots in the walls.

Rica pulled one out, swung herself lithely into the driver's seat, flicked on the power. The gauges registered a full charge. It even had a headlight, which cut through the dark and the shadows ahead quite nicely, thank you. Grinning, she rolled off down the broad corridor. She wasn't going very fast, but what the hell, at least she was getting there.

Jefri Lion led them to an armory. It was there that Haviland Tuf killed Mushroom.

Lion was flashing a hand torch over the room in swift, excited arcs, exclaiming at the stockpile of laser rifles, projectile weapons, screechguns, and light-grenades. Celise Waan was complaining that she had no familiarity with weapons, and didn't think she could kill anybody anyway. She was a scientist and not a soldier, after all, and she thought all this was barbaric.

Haviland Tuf held Mushroom cradled in his arms. The big tomcat had purred loudly when Tuf had reemerged from the *Cornucopia* and scooped him up, but no longer. Now he was making a pitiful sound, half mewing, half choking. When Tuf tried to stroke him, the long, soft gray fur came out in clumps. Mushroom screeched. Something was growing inside his mouth, Tuf saw; a web of fine black hairs crept from a black fungoid mass. Mushroom howled again, more loudly, and struggled to get free, wielding his claws uselessly against the metal of Tuf's suit. His big yellow eyes were covered with film.

The others had not noticed; their minds were on larger concerns than the cat that Tuf had voyaged with all his life. Jefri Lion and Celise Waan were arguing with each other. Tuf held Mushroom very still, despite the tom's struggles. He stroked him one last time and spoke soothingly to him. Then, in a single swift clean motion, he snapped the cat's neck.

"Nevis has already tried to kill us," Jefri Lion was saying to Celise Waan. "I don't care what your qualms are, really, you must do your part. You can't expect Tuf and me to carry the whole burden of our defense." Behind the thick plastic faceplate of his pressure suit, Lion frowned. "I wish I knew more about that battlesuit that Nevis is wearing," Lion said. "Tuf, will laser fire cut through that Unquin armor? Or would some kind of explosive projectile be more effective? A laser, I would think. Tuf?" He turned around, swinging the hand torch back and forth so shadows danced wildly against the chamber walls. "Tuf, where are you? Tuf?"

But Haviland Tuf was gone.

The door to the computer room refused to open. Kaj Nevis kicked it. The metal buckled inward in the center and the top of the door popped free of the frame. Nevis kicked it again, and again, his massive armored foot slamming with awful force against the thinner metal of the door. Then he shoved the crumpled remains of the barrier out of his way and entered, with Anittas cradled in his stiff lower arms. "I LIKE THIS DAMNED SUIT," he said. Anittas groaned.

The substation was filled with a thin subsonic humming, a buzz of anxiety. Tiny colored lights blinked on and off like fireflies.

"In the circuit," Anittas said. His hand flailed about weakly in what could have been either a gesture or a spasm. "Get me in the circuit," he repeated. The parts of him that were still organic looked terrible. His skin was covered with beads of black sweat; tiny drops of moisture as shiny as liquid ebony oozed from every fleshy pore. Mucus ran freely from his nose, and he was bleeding from his single organic ear. He couldn't stand or walk and his speech seemed to be deteriorating as well. The dull red glow from the battlesuit's helmet gave him a deep crimson caul that made him look even worse. "Hurry," he told Nevis. "The circuit, please, get me in the circuit."

"SHUT UP OR I'LL DUMP YOU HERE," Nevis answered. Anittas shuddered, as if the magnified volume of Nevis's voice was a physical assault. Nevis scanned the room until he found the interface station. He lugged the cybertech over there, and dropped him down in a white plastic chair that seemed to flow out of the console and deck. Anittas screamed. "SHUT UP!" Nevis repeated. He picked up the cybertech's arm clumsily, almost ripping it out of its socket. It was hard to gauge his strength in this damned suit, and fine manipulation was even harder, but he wasn't about to take it off—he *liked* this suit, yes he did. Anittas screamed again. Nevis ignored him, spread the tech's bluesteel fingers, jammed them into the interface. "THERE!" he said. He stepped back.

Anittas slumped forward, his head slamming against the metal and plastic of the console. His mouth gaped open. Blood dripped out, mingled with some thick black fluid, almost like oil. Nevis scowled. Had he gotten him there too late? Had the goddamned cybertech gone and croaked on him?

Then the lights blinked on, and the thin wild humming rose in pitch, and all the tiny little colored lights flashed on and off, on and off, on and off. Anittas was in the circuit.

Rica Dawnstar was rolling down the main way, feeling almost jaunty despite everything, when the blackness ahead of her became a blaze of light. Overhead, the ceiling panels stirred from long slumber, one after another, racing down the kilometers, turning the night into a day so bright it hurt her eyes for a moment.

Startled, she braked to a halt, and watched the wave of light recede into infinity. She glanced behind her. Back from where she'd come, the corridor was still filled with darkness.

She noticed something that hadn't been obvious before, in the dark. Set into the corridor floor were six thin parallel lines, translucent plastic guide-strips in red, blue, yellow, green, silver, purple. Each no doubt leading somewhere. Pity she didn't know which led where.

But as she watched, the silver tracery began to glow with an inner light. It stretched out in front of her, a thin, scintillating silvery ribbon. Simultaneously, the overhead panel just above her darkened. Rica frowned, and edged her scooter forward a couple of meters, out of the shadows and back into the light. But when she paused, that light went out as well. The silver ribbon in the floor throbbed insistently. "All right," Rica said, "we'll do it your way." She gunned her scooter and moved down the corridor, as the lights winked out behind her.

"He's come!" Celise Waan screeched when the corridor lit up. She seemed to jump a good meter in the air.

Jefri Lion stood his ground and scowled. He was holding a laser rifle in his hands. A high-explosive dart-pistol rode in a holster on one hip and a screechgun on the other. A huge two-man plasma cannon was strapped securely to his back. He wore a bandolier of mindbombs over his right shoulder, a bandolier of light-grenades over his left, and a large vibroknife sheathed on his thigh. Inside his golden helmet, Lion was smiling, his blood pounding. He was ready for anything. He hadn't felt this good in over a century, since the last time he saw action with Skaeglay's Volunteers against the Black Angels. To hell with all that dusty academic stuff. Jefri Lion was a man of action, and now he felt young again.

"Be quiet, Celise," he said. "No one's come. It's just us. The lights came on, that's all."

Celise Waan seemed unconvinced. She was armed, too, but she kept dragging the laser rifle along the deck because she said it was too heavy, and Jefri Lion was half afraid of what would happen if she tried to arm and throw one of her light-grenades. "Look," she pointed, "what's that?"

The floor had two bands of colored plastic inset into it, Jefri Lion saw. One was black, one orange. Now the orange one lit up. "It's some sort of computerized guideway," he pronounced. "Let's follow it."

"No," Celise Waan said.

Jefri Lion scowled. "Listen here, I'm the commander and you'll do what I say. We can handle anything we might meet. Now move along."

"No!" Celise Waan said stubbornly. "I'm tired. It's not safe. I'm staying right here."

"I'm giving you a direct order," said Jefri Lion impatiently.

"Oh, stuff and nonsense. You can't give me orders. I'm a full Wisdom and you're only an Associate Scholar."

"This isn't the Center," Lion said with irritation. "Are you coming?"

"No." She sat down in the middle of the corridor and crossed her arms.

"Very well, then. Good luck to you." Jefri Lion turned his back on her and began to follow the orange guide-light alone. Behind him, immobile, his army stubbornly and sullenly watched him depart.

Haviland Tuf had come to a strange place.

He had wandered down endless dark, narrow corridors, carrying Mushroom's limp body, hardly thinking, without plan or destination. Finally, he had emerged from one such corridor into what seemed to be a large cavern. The walls fell away on all sides of him. He was swallowed by empty darkness, and his bootsteps sent echoes ringing off distant walls. There were sounds in the dark—a low humming, at the threshold of hearing, and a louder sound, a liquid sound, like the ebb and flow of some endless underground ocean. But he was not underground, Haviland Tuf reminded himself. He was lost aboard an ancient starship called *Ark*, and surrounded by villains, and Mushroom was dead by his own hand.

He walked on. How long he could not say. His footsteps rang. The floor was level and bare and seemed to go on forever. Finally he walked right into something in the dark. He was moving slowly, so he was not hurt, but he dropped Mushroom in the collision. He groped ahead, tried to determine what sort of object had stopped him, but it was hard to tell through the fabric of his gloves. It was large and curved.

That was when the lights came on.

For Haviland Tuf, there was no explosion of light; what illumination existed in this place was dim, murky, subdued. As it shone down from above, it cast ominous black shadows everywhere, and gave the lighted areas a curious greenish cast, as if they were covered with some radiant moss.

Tuf gazed about. It was more a tunnel than a cavern, perhaps. He had walked all the way across it, a distance of at least a kilometer, he judged. But its breadth was nothing to its length; it must run the full length of the ship, along its major axis, for it seemed to vanish into dimness in both directions. The ceiling above was a shroud of green shadows; high, high overhead, echoes rang off its dimly seen curves. There were machines, a good many machines—computer substations built into the walls, strange devices the like of which Haviland Tuf had never seen, flat worktables with waldoes and microhands built into them. Yet the main feature of this huge, echoing shaft was the vats.

Everywhere there were vats. They lined both walls as far as the eye could see in either direction, and a few even bulged down from the ceiling. Some of the vats were immense, their swollen translucent walls large enough to contain the *Cornucopia*. Elsewhere they were cells the size of a man's hand, thousands of them, ascending from floor to ceiling like plastic honeycombs. The computers and work-stations dwindled into insignificance beside them, small details easily overlooked. And now Haviland Tuf discerned the source of the liquid sound he had heard. Most of the vats were empty, he saw through the greenish gloom, but a few—one here, one there, two farther on—seemed to be full of colored fluids, bubbling, or stirred by the feeble motions of half-seen shapes within.

Haviland Tuf regarded the vista before him for a long time, its scale making him feel very small. Yet finally he turned away, and bent to pick up Mushroom once again. As he knelt, he saw what he had walked into in the dark: a vat, a medium-large one, its transparent walls curving away from him. This vat was full of a thick, murky yellowish liquid, shot through with moving swirls of red. Tuf heard a faint gurgling, and felt a slight vibration, as if something were stirring inside. He leaned closer, peered in, and then craned his head up.

Within, floating, unborn and yet alive, the tyrannosaur stared down at him.

In the circuit there was no pain. In the circuit he had no body. In the circuit he was mind, pure sweet white mind, and he was part of something vast and powerful and infinitely greater than himself, greater than any of them. In the circuit he was more than human, more than cyborg, more than mere machine. In the circuit he was something like a god. Time was nothing in the circuit; he was as swift as thought, as swift as silicon circuitry opening and closing, as swift as the messages that raced along superconductive tendons, as swift as the flash of microlasers weaving their invisible webs in the central matrix. In the circuit, he had a thousand ears and a thousand eyes and a thousand hands to ball into fists and strike with; in the circuit he could be everywhere at once.

He was Anittas. He was *Ark*. He was cybertech. He was more than five hundred satellite stations and monitors, he was twenty Imperial 7400s ruling the twenty sectors of the ship from twenty scattered substations, he was Battlemaster, Codebreaker, Astrogator, Drive Doctor, Medcenter, Ship's Log, Librarian, Bio-Librarian, Microsurgeon, Clonetender, Maintenance and Repair, Communications, and Defense. He was all the hardware and all the software and all the back-up systems and all secondary and tertiary back-ups. He was twelve hundred years old and thirty kilometers long and the heart of him was the central matrix, barely two meters square and all but infinite in size. He touched here and there and everywhere and moved on, his consciousness racing down the circuits, branching, dancing, riding on the lasers. Knowledge raced through him in a torrent, like a great river running wild, with all the cool steady sweet white power of a high voltage cable. He was *Ark*. He was Anittas. And he was dying.

Down deep in his bowels, down in the ship's intestines, down at substation seventeen by airlock nine, Anittas let his silver-metal eyes track and focus on Kaj Nevis. He smiled. On his half-human face, it was a grotesque expression. His teeth were chrome steel. "You fool," he said to Nevis.

The battlesuit took one threatening step closer. A pincer raised itself with a grinding, metallic sound, opened and closed. "WATCH YOUR MOUTH."

"Fool I said and fool it is," Anittas told him. His laughter was a horrible sound; it was full of pain and metallic echoes, and his lips were bleeding freely, leaving wet red smears on those shining silver teeth. "You killed me, Nevis, and for nothing—for impatience. I could have given it all to you. It's empty, Nevis. The ship is empty, they're all dead. And the system is empty, too. I'm alone in here. No other mind in the circuit. It's an idiot, Kaj Nevis. The *Ark* is an idiot giant. They were afraid, those Earth Imperials. They'd achieved true Artificial Intelligence. Oh yes, they had their great AI warships, their robot fleets, but the AIs had minds of their own, and there were incidents. It's in the histories—there was Kandabaer and the action off Lear and the revolt of *Alecto* and *Golem*. The seedships were too powerful, they knew that as they built them. The *Ark* had duties for two hundred—strategists and scientists and eco-engineers and crew and officers—and she could carry more than a thousand soldiers, too, and feed all of them, and operate at full capacity, and lay waste to *worlds*, oh yes. And everything worked through the system, Nevis, but it's a safe system, a big system, a sophisticated system, a system that can repair itself and defend itself and do a thousand things at once—if you tell it to. The two hundred crewmen made it efficient, but you could run it with only one, Nevis. Not efficiently, no, not at anything near full capacity, but you could do it. It can't run itself—it's got no mind, no AI, it waits for orders—but one man can tell it what to do. One man! I could have done it easily. But Kaj Nevis got impatient and killed me."

Nevis moved still closer. "YOU DON'T SOUND DEAD TO ME," he said, opening and closing his pincer with a sudden menacing snap.

"But I am," said Anittas. "I am sucking power from the system, boosting my cyberhalf, giving myself back a speech capacity. But I'm dying all the while. Plagues, Nevis. The ship was horribly undermanned in its last days, only thirty-two left, and there was an attack, a Hruun attack. They broke the code, opened the dome, and landed. They stormed up the halls, more than a hundred of them. They were winning, threatening to take the ship. The defenders fought them every step of the way. They sealed off whole sectors of the *Ark*, evacuated all the air, turned off all the power. They got a few that way. They set up ambushes, fought them meter for meter. There are still places that are battle-scarred, dysfunctional, beyond the *Ark*'s repair capacities. They let loose plague and pestilence and parasite, and from their vats they summoned their pet nightmares, and they fought, and died, and won. In the end all the Hruun were dead. And you know what, Kaj Nevis? All but four of the defenders were dead as well. One of those was grievously wounded, two others sick, and the last was dead inside. Would you like to know their names? No, I thought not. You have no curiosity, Kaj Nevis. It is no matter. Tuf will want to know, as will the ancient Lion."

"TUF? LION? WHAT ARE YOU TALKING ABOUT? THEY'RE DEAD, BOTH OF THEM."

"Incorrect," Anittas said. "They are both aboard even now. Lion has found the armory. He's a walking arsenal, and he's coming for you. Tuf has found something even more important. Rica Dawnstar is following the silver trace to the main control room, the captain's chair. You see, Kaj Nevis, the gang's all here. I have awakened every part of the *Ark* that remains functional, and I am leading them all by the hand."

"STOP IT, THEN," Nevis commanded. He did not hesitate. The great metal pincer reached out and embraced Anittas about his biometal throat. Black sweat oozed down onto the pincer's serrated blade. "STOP THEM RIGHT NOW."

"I have not completed my story, Kaj Nevis," the cybertech said. His mouth was a smear of blood. "The last Imperials knew they could not go on. They shut down the ship, gave it up to vacuum and silence and the void. They made it go derelict. Yet not entirely, you see. They feared another attack, by the Hruun or perhaps, in time, others yet unknown. So they told the *Ark* to defend itself. They armed the plasma cannon and external lasers and kept the defense sphere functional, as we learned to our sorrow. And they programmed the ship to take a terrible vengeance for them, to return again and again and again to Hro B'rana, whence the Hruun had come, and to deliver its gift of plague and pestilence and death. To guard against the Hruun building up immunity, they subjected their plague tanks to constant radiation, to encourage endless mutation, and they established a program for automatic genetic manipulation to fashion ever newer and more deadly viruses."

"I DON'T GIVE A DAMN," Kaj Nevis said. "HAVE YOU STOPPED THE OTHERS? CAN YOU KILL THEM? I WARN YOU, DO IT NOW OR YOU'RE DEAD."

"I am dead anyway, Kaj Nevis," Anittas said, "I've told you that. The plagues. They left a secondary defense in place. Should the ship be breached once again, the *Ark* was programmed to wake itself, to fill the corridors with atmosphere, oh yes, but an atmosphere tainted by a dozen different disease vectors. The plague tanks have been churning and boiling for a thousand standard years, Kaj Nevis, mutating again and again. There is no name for what I have contracted. Some kind of spore, I think. There are antigens, medicines, vaccines—the *Ark* has been manufacturing those, as well—but it's too late for me, too late by far. I breathed it in, and it's eating my biohalf alive. My cyberhalf is inedible. I could have given us this ship, Kaj Nevis. Together we might have had the power of a god. Instead we die."

"*YOU* DIE," Nevis corrected. "AND THE SHIP IS MINE."

"I think not. I have kicked the idiot giant soundly, Kaj Nevis, and it is awake again. Still an idiot, oh yes, but awake, and ready for orders you have neither the knowledge nor the capacity to give. I am leading Jefri Lion straight here, and Rica Dawnstar is ascending toward central control even now. And more—"

"NO MORE," Nevis said curtly. The pincer crunched through metal and bone and took the cybertech's head clean off with a single swift snap. The head bounced off Anittas's chest, hit the floor, and rolled. Blood jetted from the neck, and a thick protruding cable gave a final futile hiss and threw off a blue-white spark before the body sagged against the computer console. Kaj Nevis drew back his arm and swung, smashing the console again and again, until it was a ruin and hundreds of shards of plastic and metal were scattered over the floor.

There was a high, thin whirring sound.

Kaj Nevis turned, faceplate glowing a bright bloody red, searching for the source.

On the floor, the head was looking at him. The eyes, the shiny silver eyes, tracked and focused. The mouth split into a wet grin. "And more, Kaj Nevis," the head said to him. "I have activated the final line of defense programmed by those last Imperials. The stasis field is down. The nightmares are waking up now. The guardians are about to come forth and destroy you."

"DAMN YOU!" Nevis shouted. He set a huge, flat foot atop the cybertech's head, and brought down all his weight. Steel and bone alike crunched under the impact, and Nevis worked his foot back and forth, back and forth, grinding away until there was nothing beneath his heel but a red-gray paste spotted by flakes of white and silver.

And then, at last, he had silence.

For a long ways, two kilometers or more, the six traces in the floor ran parallel, although only the silver was alive and glowing. The red broke away first, veering off to the right at a junction. The purple terminated a kilometer farther on, at a wide door that proved to be the entrance to a spotless automated kitchen-mess hall complex. Rica Dawnstar was tempted to pause and explore a bit more, but the silver trace was throbbing and the overhead lights were going out one by one, urging her onward, down the main way.

Finally she came to the end. The broad corridor she was following curved gradually to the left and met another corridor just as grand. Their terminus was a huge wheel from which a half dozen lesser hallways branched off like spokes. The ceiling was high above her. Looking up, Rica spotted at least three other levels, connected with catwalks, bridges, and great circling balconies. At the hub of the wheel was a single large shaft that ascended from floor to ceiling—an elevator, clearly.

The blue trace followed one spoke, the yellow a second, the green a third. The shining silver guideway led straight to the elevator doors. The doors opened at her approach. Rica drove her scooter right to the base of the shaft, stopped, dismounted, hesitated. The elevator beckoned. But it looked awfully enclosed in there.

She hesitated too long.

All the lights went out.

There was only the silver trace, a single thin line like a finger, pointing straight ahead. And the elevator itself, its lights still blazing.

Rica Dawnstar frowned, drew her needler, and stepped inside. "Up, please," she announced. The doors closed and the elevator began to ascend.

Jefri Lion walked with a spring in his step, despite the weight of the weapons he was carrying. He felt even better since leaving Celise Waan behind; that woman was nothing but a nuisance anyway, and he doubted that she'd be of much use in a skirmish. He had considered the possibility of stealth, and rejected it. He was not afraid of Kaj Nevis and his battlesuit. Oh, it was formidably armored, he had no doubt of that, but after all, it was of alien manufacture, and Lion was armed with the deadliest weaponry of the Earth Imperials, the height of the technological and military prowess of the Federal Empire of Old Earth as it had been before the Collapse. He'd never even heard of the Unquish, so what kind of armigers could they be? No doubt some obscure Hrangan slave race. He would deal with Nevis in short order if he found him, and with that treacherous Rica Dawnstar, too—her and that stupid needler. He'd like to see how a needler could possibly stand up against a plasma cannon. Yes, he'd like to see that.

Lion wondered what plans Nevis and his cohorts were making for the *Ark*. Something illegal and immoral, no doubt. Well, it made no matter, because he was going to take this ship—he, Jefri Lion, Associate Scholar in Military History at the ShanDellor Center, and one-time Second Tactical Analyst of the Third Wing of Skaeglay's Volunteers. He was going to capture an EEC seedship, perhaps with Tufs help if he could find him, but he would do it in any event. Afterwards, there would be no selling of this treasure for crass personal gain. No, he would take the ship all the way to Avalon, to the great Academy of Human Knowledge, and turn it over to them with the proviso that he remain in charge of its study. It was a project that would last him the rest of his life, and when it ended Jefri Lion, scholar and warrior, would be spoken of in the same breath as Kleronomas himself, who had made the Academy what it was.

Lion strode down the center of the corridor with his head thrown back, following the orange trace, and as he walked he began to whistle a jaunty marching tune that he had learned in Skaeglay's Volunteers a good forty years ago. He whistled and walked, walked and whistled.

Until the trace died out.

Celise Waan sat on the deck for a long time, her arms crossed tightly against her breasts, her face set in a petulant frown. She sat until the sound of Lion's footsteps had faded away entirely. She sat and brooded on all the insults and wrongs she had been forced to endure. They were all impossible, every one of them. She should have known better than to throw in her lot with such an unpromising and disrespectful crew. Anittas was more machine than man, Rica Dawnstar was an insolent little wretch, Kaj Nevis was no better than a common criminal, and Haviland Tuf was just unspeakable. Even Jefri Lion, her colleague, had proved unreliable in the end. The plague star was *her* discovery, and she had let them in on it, and what had it gotten her? Discomfort, rudeness, and finally abandonment. Well, Celise Waan didn't intend to stand for it anymore. She had decided not to share the ship with any of them. It was her find, and she would go back to Shandicity and claim it under the salvage laws of ShanDellor, as was her right, and if any of her wretched companions had any complaints, they would have to take her to litigation. Meanwhile, she didn't intend to talk to any of them, not ever again.

Her rear was getting sore and her legs had begun to fall asleep. She had been sitting in one position for a long time. Her back ached, too, and she was hungry. She wondered if there was any place she could get a decent meal aboard this derelict. Perhaps there was. The computers seemed to be working, and the defense systems, and even the lights, so perhaps the commissary was functioning as well. She got up and decided to go see.

It was obvious to Haviland Tuf that something was happening.

The noise level in the great shaft was rising, slowly but appreciably. He could make out a low humming sound quite distinctly, and those gurgling sounds were more noticeable as well. And in the tyrannosaur vat, the suspension fluid seemed to be thinning and changing colors. The red swirls had faded or been sucked away, and the yellow liquid grew more transparent with every passing moment. Tuf watched a waldo unfold from one side of the vat. It appeared as though it was giving the reptile an injection, though Tuf had difficulty observing the details, since the lighting was poor.

Haviland Tuf decided on a strategic retreat. He backed away from the dinosaur vat, and began to walk down the shaft. After he had come only a short way, he came upon one of the computer stations and work areas he had observed. Tuf paused.

He had experienced little difficulty discerning the nature and purpose of this chamber he had chanced upon. The *Ark* had at its heart a vast cell library, containing tissue samples from literally millions of different kinds of plant and animal and viral lifeforms from an uncounted number of worlds, or so Jefri Lion had informed him. These samples were cloned, as the ship's tacticians and eco-engineers deemed appropriate, and so the *Ark* and its lost sister ships could send forth disease to decimate a world's population, insects to devastate its crops, fast-breeding armies of small animals to wreak havoc on the ecology and food chain, or even terrible alien predators to strike fear into the heart of the enemy. Yet everything began with the cloning.

Tuf had found the cloning room. The work areas included equipment obviously intended for complex microsurgery, and the vats were undoubtedly where the cell samples were tended and grown to maturity. Lion had told him about the chronowarp as well, that vanished secret of the Earth Imperials, a field that could literally warp the fabric of time itself, albeit only in a small area, and at vast cost in energy. That way the clones could be brought to maturity in hours, or held, unchanging and alive, for millennia.

Haviland Tuf considered the work area, the computer station, and Mushroom, whose small body he still carried.

Cloning began with a single cell.

The techniques were no doubt stored in the computer. Perhaps there was even an instruction program. "Indeed," Haviland Tuf announced to himself. It seemed quite logical. He was no cybertech, to be sure, but he was an intelligent man who had operated various types of computer systems for virtually his entire lifespan.

Haviland Tuf stepped up to the work station, deposited Mushroom gently beneath the hood of the microscreen, and turned on the computer console. He could make no sense of the commands at first, yet he persisted.

After a few minutes he was intent on his labors—so intent that he did not notice the loud gurgling sound behind him when the thin yellow fluid in the dinosaur vat began to drain away.

Kaj Nevis smashed his way out of the system substation looking for something to kill.

He was angry—angry at himself for being impatient and unthinking. Anittas could have been useful; Nevis just hadn't considered the possibility of contagion in the ship's air. The damn cybertech would have had to have been killed eventually, of course, but that would not have been difficult. And now everything was falling apart. Nevis felt secure in the battlesuit, but still uneasy. He didn't like hearing that Tuf and the others had somehow gotten aboard. Tuf knew more about this damn suit than he did, after all; maybe he knew its weaknesses.

Kaj Nevis had already pinpointed one of those weaknesses himself—his air supply was running low. A modern pressure suit, like the one Tuf was wearing, included an airpac. The bacteria infused in its filters turned carbon dioxide into oxygen as fast as a human being could turn oxygen into carbon dioxide, so there was never any danger of running out of air, unless the damn bugs went and died on you. But this battlesuit was primitive; it carried a large but finite supply of air in those four huge tanks on its back. And the gauge in his helmet, if he was reading it correctly, indicated that one of those tanks was nearly empty. That still left three, which ought to give him more than enough time to get rid of the rest of them, if only he could find them. Still, it made Nevis uneasy. He was surrounded by perfectly breathable air, to be sure, but he was damned if he was going to crack his helmet after what had happened to the cybertech. The organic part of Anittas's body had decayed faster than Nevis would have believed, and the black goop that had eaten up the cybertech inside was as loathsome a sight as Kaj had ever seen, in a life that had featured lots of loathsome sights. He'd sooner suffocate, Kaj Nevis had decided.

But there was no danger of that. If the damned *Ark* could be contaminated, it could be cleansed, too. He'd find the control room and figure out how to do it. Even one clean sector would be enough. Of course, Anittas had said that Rica Dawnstar was already at the control room, but that did not faze him. In fact, he was kind of looking forward to that reunion.

He chose a direction at random and set off, his armored steps pounding against the deck. So let them hear him—what did he care. He *liked* this suit.

Rica Dawnstar sprawled in the captain's chair and surveyed the readouts she had projected on the main telescreen. Well-padded, large, covered with comfortable old plastic, the chair felt like a throne. It made a good place to rest. The trouble was, you really couldn't do anything *but* rest from there. The bridge had obviously been designed so that the captain sat in his throne and gave orders, and the other officers—there were nine other work stations on the upper bridge, twelve more in the lower-level control pit—did all the actual programming and punching of buttons. Lacking the foresight to have come aboard with nine flunkies, Rica was forced to move back and forth across the bridge, from one station to another, to try and get the *Ark* up and running again.

It took her a while—it was tedious work—and when she entered commands from the wrong substation, nothing happened. But slowly, step by step, she was figuring it all out. At least she felt as though she was making progress.

And she was secure. That had been her first objective, locking that elevator so that nobody else could come up and surprise her. As long as she was here and they were down there, Rica Dawnstar held the trump card. Every sector of the ship had its own substation, and every specialized function, from defense to cloning to propulsion to data storage, had its own sub-nexus and command post, but from up here she could oversee all of them, and countermand any command that anybody else might try and enter. If she noticed. And if she could figure out how. That was the problem. She could only man one station at a time, and she could only get things done when she figured out the proper sequence of commands. She was doing it, yes, by trial and error, but that was a lengthy and cumbersome progress.

She slumped back in her padded throne and watched the readouts, feeling proud of herself on several counts. She had managed to elicit a shipwide status check, it seemed. The *Ark* had already given her a full damage report on those sectors and systems that had been inoperative for a thousand years, waiting for repairs beyond the ship's capacities. Now it was telling her what programming was presently engaged.

The bio-defense listing was especially impressive, in a frightening sort of way. It went on and on. Rica had never heard of three-quarters of the diseases that had been unleashed to greet them, but they sounded unpleasant in the extreme. Anittas was no doubt one with the great program beyond the universe by now. Obviously, her next objective should be to try and seal off the bridge from the rest of the ship, irradiate and disinfect and try to see if she could get some uncontaminated air in here. Otherwise her suit was going to start getting pretty gamey in a day or two.

Up on the telescreen, it read:

BIO-DEFENSE PHASE ONE(MICRO)
REPORT COMPLETE
BIO-DEFENSE PHASE TWO (MACRO)
REPORT COMMENCING

Rica frowned. Macro? What the hell did that mean? Big plagues?

STAND-BY BIO-WEAPONS AT READY: 47

the screen told her, and it followed that cryptic bit of information with a lengthy list of species numbers. It was a boring list. Rica slumped back in the captain's throne again. When the list ended, more messages rolled across the screen.

ALL CLONING PROCEDURES COMPLETE
MALFUNCTIONS IN VATS: 671, 3312, 3379
MALFUNCTIONS ABORTED
STASIS FIELDS TERMINATED
RELEASE CYCLE COMMENCING

Rica Dawnstar wasn't sure she liked the sound of that. Release cycle, she thought. What was it releasing? On the one hand, Kaj Nevis was still out there; if this second-phase defense could discomfort, distract, or dispose of him, that was all to her benefit. On the other hand, she already faced the task of getting rid of all these plagues. She didn't need any more problems. The reports began to flash by more quickly.

SPECIES # 22-743-88639-04090
HOMEWORLD: VILKAKIS
COMMON NAME: HOODED DRACULA

it said. Rica sat up straight. She'd heard of Vilkakis and its hooded draculas. Nasty things. Some kind of flying nocturnal bloodsucker, she seemed to recall. Dim-witted, but incredibly sensitive to sound, and insanely aggressive. The message flicked out. In its place appeared a single line.

INITIATING RELEASE

the screen told her. It held a moment and was replaced by a shorter line, a single word that flashed once, twice, three times, and then was gone:

RELEASED

Now, could a hooded dracula possibly have Kaj Nevis for lunch? Unlikely, Rica thought—not so long as he wore that stupid armored suit. "Great," she said aloud. She didn't have a battlesuit, which meant that the *Ark* was creating problems for her, not for Nevis.

SPECIES # 13-612-71425-88812
HOMEWORLD: ABBATOIR
COMMON NAME: HELLKITTENS

Rica had no idea what a hellkitten was, but she didn't especially want to find out. She had heard of Abbatoir, of course—a quaint little world that had eaten three different colonizing parties; its lifeforms were supposed to be uniformly unpleasant. Unpleasant enough to chew through Nevis's battlesuit, though? That seemed doubtful.

INITIATING RELEASE

How many things was the ship going to belch forth? Forty-some-odd, she recalled. "Terrific," she said dourly. Fill up the ship with forty-plus hungry monsters, any one of them sufficient to lunch on her mother's favorite daughter. No, this wouldn't do, not at all. Rica stood up and surveyed the bridge. So where did she have to go to put an end to this nonsense?

RELEASED

Rica vaulted over the captain's chair, strode briskly back to the area she'd pegged as the defense command station, and told it to cancel its current programming.

SPECIES # 76-102-95994-12965
HOMEWORLD: JAYDEN TWO
COMMON NAME: WALKING-WEB

Lights flashed in front of her, and the small telescreen on the console told her that the *Ark*'s external defense sphere was down. But up on the main screen, the parade went on.

INITIATING RELEASE

Rica uncorked a string of curses. Her fingers moved swiftly over the console, trying to tell the system that it wasn't the external defenses she wanted dropped, it was bio-defense phase two. The machine didn't seem to understand her.

RELEASED

Finally she got a response from the board. It told her she was at the wrong console. She scowled and glanced around. Of course. This was external defense, weapons systems. There had to be some kind of bio-control station, too.

SPECIES # 54-749-37377-84921
HOMEWORLD: PSC92, TSC749, UNNAMED
COMMON NAME: ROLLERAM

Rica moved to the next station.

INITIATING RELEASE

The system responded to her cancel demand with a baffled query. No active program on this subsystem.

RELEASED

Four, Rica thought sourly. "That's enough," she said loudly. She stepped over to the next station, punched in a cancel, moved on without waiting to see if there was an effect, paused at another console to enter another cancel, moved on.

SPECIES # 67-001-00342-10078
HOMEWORLD: EARTH (EXTINCT)
COMMON NAME: TYRANNOSAURUS REX

She ran now. Run, cancel, run, cancel, run, cancel.

INITIATING RELEASE

She made a circuit of the entire bridge, as quickly as she could. By the time she was done, she wasn't even certain which command, at which station, had done the trick. But up on the screen, the message read:

RELEASE CYCLE TERMINATED
BIO-WEAPONS ABORTED: 3
BIO-WEAPONS RELEASED: 5
STAND-BY BIO-WEAPONS AT READY: 39

BIO-DEFENSE PHASE TWO (MACRO)
REPORT COMPLETE

Rica Dawnstar stood with her hands on her hips, frowning. Five loose. That wasn't too bad. She thought she'd managed to catch it after four, but she must have been a split-second too late. Oh, well. What the hell was a tyrannosaurus rex, anyway?

At least there was no one out there but Nevis.

Without the trace to guide him, Jefri Lion had wasted no time getting lost in the maze of interconnected corridors. Finally, he had adopted a simple policy; choose the wider corridors over the narrower, turn right where the passages were of the same size, go down whenever possible. It seemed to work. In no time at all, he heard a noise.

He flattened himself against a wall, although the attempt at concealment was somewhat compromised by the ungainly bulk of the plasma cannon on his back. He listened. Yes, definitely, a noise. Up ahead of him. Footsteps. *Loud* footsteps, though at some distance, but coming his way—Kaj Nevis in his battlesuit.

Smiling to himself with satisfaction, Jefri Lion unslung the plasma cannon and began to erect its tripod.

The tyrannosaur roared.

It was, thought Haviland Tuf, a thoroughly frightening sound. He pressed his lips firmly together in annoyance and squirmed back another half-meter into his

niche. He was decidedly uncomfortable. Tuf was a big man, and there was very little room down here. He sat with his legs jammed under each other awkwardly, his
back bent over in a painful manner, and his head bumping against the work station
above. Yet he was not ungrateful. It was a small niche, true, but it had given him a
place to seek shelter. Fortunately, he had been deft enough to attain that shelter.
He was fortunate, also, in that the work station, with its waldos and microscanner
and computer terminal, rested upon a heavy, thick, metal table that extruded itself
from floor and wall, and not simply a flimsy item of furniture to be easily brushed
aside.

Nonetheless, Haviland Tuf was not entirely pleased with himself. He felt foolish; his dignity had been decisively compromised. No doubt his ability to concentrate on the task at hand was, in its own way, commendable. Still, that degree of
concentration might be considered a liability when it allowed a seven-meter-tall
carnivorous reptile to sneak up on one.

The tyrannosaur roared again. Tuf could feel the work station vibrate overhead. The dinosaur's massive head appeared about two meters in front of his face,
as the beast leaned over, counterbalanced by its great tail, and tried to get in at
him. Fortunately, its head was too large and the niche too small. The reptile
pulled out and screamed its frustration; echoes rebounded all up and down the
central cloning chamber. Its tail lashed around and smashed into the work station;
the sheltering table shook to the impact, something shattered up above, and Tuf
winced.

"Go away," he said as firmly as he could. He rested his hands atop his paunch
and attempted to look stern.

The tyrannosaur paid him no heed.

"These vigorous efforts will avail you naught," Tuf pointed out. "You are too
large and the table too sturdily built, as would be readily apparent to you had you
a brain larger than a mushroom. Moreover, you are undoubtedly a clone produced
from the genetic record contained within a fossil. Therefore, it might be argued
that I have a superior claim to life, on the grounds that you are extinct and ought
properly to remain so. Begone!"

The tyrannosaur's reply was a furious squirming lunge and a wet bellow that
sprayed Tuf with fine droplets of dinosaur saliva. The tail came down once more.

When she first caught a flicker of movement out of the corner of her eye,
Celise Waan squeaked in panic.

She backpedaled and whirled to face—to face what? There was nothing there.
But she had been certain that she'd seen something, up near that open door.
What, though? Nervously, she unholstered her dart-pistol. She'd abandoned the
laser rifle quite a distance back. It was cumbersome and heavy, and the effort of
lugging it around had tired her out. Besides, she doubted that she'd be able to hit
anything with it. The pistol was much preferable, in her view. As Jefri Lion had
explained it, it threw explosive plastic darts, so she would not actually have to
score a *hit*, just come close.

Warily, she moved toward the open door. She paused to one side of it, raised
her pistol high, thumbed off the safety, and then peered quickly into the room.

Nothing.

It was some kind of storage room, she saw, full of plastisealed equipment piled
high on floater skids. She glanced around uneasily. Had she imagined it, then?
No. As she was about to turn away, she saw it once more, a tiny darting shape that

appeared on the periphery of her vision and vanished before she could quite get a clear look at it.

But this time she had seen where it had gone. She hurried after it, feeling bolder now; it had, after all, been quite small.

She had it cornered, she saw when she rounded the looming equipment skid. But what was it? Celise Waan moved closer, gun at the ready.

It was a cat.

It stared at her steadily, its tail flicking back and forth. It was kind of a funny cat. Very small—a kitten, really. It was pale white, with vivid scarlet stripes, an oversized head, and astonishing lambent crimson eyes.

Another cat, thought Celise Waan. That was all she needed: another cat.

It hissed at her.

She drew back, a little startled. Tuf's cats hissed at her from time to time, especially the nasty black-and-white one, but not like *that*. That hiss was almost, well, reptilian. Chilling, somehow. And its tongue . . . it seemed to have a very long, very peculiar tongue.

It hissed again.

"Here, kitty," she called. "Here, kitty."

It stared at her, unblinking, cold, haughty. Then it drew itself back and spat at her. The spittle struck her square in the center of her faceplate. It was thick greenish stuff, and it obscured her vision for a moment until she wiped it away with the back of her arm.

Celise Waan decided that she'd had enough of cats. "Nice kitty," she said, "come here, kitty. I've got a present for you."

It hissed again, drew back to spit.

Celise Waan grunted and blew it to hell.

The plasma cannon would dispose of Kaj Nevis handsomely; on that score Jefri Lion had no doubt. The strength of the armor on that alien battlesuit was an unknown factor. If it was at all comparable to the armored suits worn by the Federal Empire's own assault squads during the Thousand Years War, it might be able to deflect laser fire, to withstand small explosions, to ignore sonic attacks, but a plasma cannon could melt through five meters of solid duralloy plate. One good plasma ball would instantly turn any kind of personal armor into slag, and Nevis would be incinerated before he even understood what had hit him.

The difficulty was the size of the plasma cannon. It was unfortunately cumbersome, and the so-called portable version, with its small energy-pac, took almost a full standard minute after each shot to generate another plasma ball in its force chamber. Jefri Lion was acutely and uncomfortably aware that, were he to miss Kaj Nevis, he would be unlikely to get a second shot. Moreover, even on its tripod, the plasma cannon was unwieldy, and it had been many years since he had been in the field, and even then, his strong suits had been his mind and his tactical sense, not his reflexes. After so many decades at the ShanDellor Center, he had no great confidence in his eye-hand coordination.

So Jefri Lion concocted a plan.

Fortunately, plasma cannons had often been employed for automated perimeter defense, and this one had the standard minimind and autofire sequence. Jefri Lion erected the tripod in the middle of a broad corridor, approximately twenty meters down from a major intersection. He programmed in an extremely narrow field of fire, and calibrated the targeting cube with the utmost precision. Then he initiated the autofire sequence and stepped back with satisfaction. Inside the energy-pac he saw the plasma ball forming, burning brighter and brighter, and after a minute the ready light flashed on. Now the cannon was set, and its minimind was vastly quicker and more deadly accurate than Lion could ever hope to be firing manually. It was targeted on the center of the corridor intersection ahead, but it would fire only at objects whose dimensions exceeded certain preprogrammed limits.

So Jefri Lion could dash right through the cannon's target cube without fear, but Kaj Nevis, following in his absurdly huge battlesuit, would meet with a hot surprise. Now it only remained to lure Nevis into the appropriate position.

It was a stroke of tactical genius worthy of Napoleon or Chin Wu or Stephan Cobalt Northstar. Jefri Lion was infinitely pleased with himself.

The heavy footsteps had grown louder as Lion had worked with the plasma cannon, but in the last minute or so they had begun to fade; Nevis had obviously taken a wrong turn and would not be coming to the right position of his own accord. Very well then, Jefri Lion thought; he would bring him there.

He walked to the precise center of the fire zone with complete confidence in his own abilities, paused there briefly, smiled, and set off down the cross-corridor to attract the attention of his unwary prey.

Up on the great curved telescreen, the *Ark* revolved in three-dimensional cross-section.

Rica Dawnstar, having abandoned the captain's throne for a less comfortable but more efficient post at one of the bridge work stations, studied the display, and the data flashing by underneath it, with some annoyance. It seemed she had a lot more company than she had thought.

The system displayed intruding lifeforms as vivid red pinpoints of light. There were six pinpoints. One of them was on the bridge. Since Rica was quite alone, obviously that was her. But five others? Even if Anittas was still alive, there should have been only two additional dots. It didn't add up.

Maybe the *Ark* hadn't been derelict after all—maybe there was still someone aboard. Except the system claimed to depict authorized *Ark* personnel as green dots, and there was no green to be seen.

Other scavengers? Highly unlikely.

It had to mean that Tuf, Lion, and Waan had somehow docked after all. That made the most sense. And, indeed, the system claimed there was an intruding lifeform in a ship up on the landing deck.

All right. That added up. Six red dots equalled her and Nevis and Anittas (how had he lived through the damned plagues? the system insisted it was showing only *living* organisms) plus Tuf and Waan and Lion. One of the others was still up in the *Cornucopia*, and the rest . . .

It was simple to pick out Kaj Nevis. The system showed power sources as well, as tiny yellow starbursts, and only one of the red pinpoints was surrounded by a tiny yellow starburst. That had to be Nevis in his battlesuit.

But what was that second yellow dot flashing so brightly by itself in an empty corridor on deck six? A hellacious power source, but what? Rica didn't understand. There had been a second red dot quite near to it, but it had moved away, and now seemed to be trailing Nevis, edging steadily closer.

Meanwhile, there were the black dots: the *Ark*'s bio-weapons. The huge central axis that cored the asymmetric, tapered cylinder of the ship was positively livid with black pinpricks, but at least those were stationary. Other black dots, which had to be the beasties that had been released, were moving through the corridors. Only there were more than five. There was one clump of them—thirty or more discrete organisms, moving en masse like a shapeless black blotch upon the screen, throwing off strays from time to time. One of the strays had come up near a red light and had suddenly been extinguished.

There was a red dot in that central core area, too.

Rica asked for a display of that sector, and the screen gave her a much tighter cross-section. The red light was very close to a moving black dot down there—some sort of confrontation. She studied the readouts below the graphic. That particular black dot was species #67-001-00342-10078, the tyrannosaurus rex. It was massive, no doubt of that.

She noticed, with some interest, that a red light and one of the wandering blacks were both closing in on Kaj Nevis. That ought to be interesting. It looked like she was missing the party; all hell was breaking loose down there.

And she was up here, safe and secure and in control. Rica Dawnstar smiled.

Kaj Nevis was lumbering down a corridor, growing angrier and angrier, when a sudden explosive blow took him squarely in the back of his head. Inside his helmet, the sound was horrible. The force of the explosion knocked him forward and toppled him. He went smashing to the floor face first, too slow to break his fall with his arms.

But the suit absorbed most of the impact, and Nevis was unharmed. Lying there he made a quick check of his gauges, and smiled wolfishly; the battlesuit was undamaged, unbreached. He rolled over and rose ponderously to his feet.

Twenty meters away, at a corridor intersection, stood a man in a green-and-gold pressure suit, armed as if he had just looted a military museum, and holding a pistol in one gloved hand. "We meet again, blackguard!" the figure called out over external speakers.

"SO WE DO, LION" Nevis replied. "HOW GOOD TO SEE YOU, COME HERE AND SHAKE HANDS." He snapped his pincers. The right one was still stained with the cybertech's blood; he hoped Jefri Lion had noticed. A pity his cutting laser was so short-range, but no matter. He would simply catch Lion, take away his toys, and then play with him a while—pull off his legs, perhaps, and breach his suit, and let the damned air do the rest.

Kaj Nevis lumbered forward.

Jefri Lion stood his ground, raised his dart pistol, aimed it carefully with both hands, fired.

The dart struck Nevis in the chest. There was a loud explosion, but this time he had braced for it. His ears hurt, but he hardly even staggered. Some of the intricate filigree on the armor was blackened, but that was the extent of the damage. "YOU LOSE, OLD MAN," Nevis said. "I LIKE THIS SUIT."

Jefri Lion was silent and methodical. He holstered his dart pistol, unslung a laser rifle and raised it to his shoulder, took aim, fired.

The beam glanced off Nevis's shoulder, struck a wall, and burned a small black hole.

"Reflective microcoating," Jefri Lion said. He put away the laser rifle.

Nevis had eaten up more than three-quarters of the distance between them with his long, powered strides.

Finally Jefri Lion seemed to realize his danger. He threw down the laser rifle, turned, and darted around a corner, out of sight.

Kaj Nevis lengthened his strides and followed.

Haviland Tuf was nothing if not patient.

He sat calmly, with his hands folded atop his bulging stomach and his head aching from the repeated blows the tyrannosaur had inflicted on the sheltering table. He did his best to ignore the hammering that dented the metal above and made him even more uncomfortable, the blood-curdling bestial roars, the excessive and melodramatic displays of carnivore appetite that occasionally prompted the tyrannosaur to bend over and snap its numerous large teeth futilely at Tuf in his shelter. Instead Tuf thought about sweet Rodelyian popberries in honey-butter, tried to recall which particular planet had the strongest and most pungent variety of ale, and devised an excellent new strategy with which to overwhelm Jefri Lion should they ever game again.

Ultimately, his plan bore fruit.

The raging reptile, bored and frustrated, went away.

Haviland Tuf waited until it grew quite still and silent outside. He twisted himself around awkwardly, and lay for a moment on his stomach while the pins and needles in his legs flared and faded and vanished. Then he squirmed forward and cautiously stuck his head out.

Dim green light. Low humming, and distant gurgling sounds. No motion anywhere.

He emerged carefully.

The dinosaur had struck what remained of Mushroom's poor body numerous times with its massive tail. The sight filled Haviland Tuf with a vast and bitter sorrow. The equipment at this particular work station was in a shambles.

Yet there were other work stations, and he needed but a single cell.

Haviland Tuf gathered up a tissue sample and walked ponderously down to the next work station. This time he made it a point to listen for the sound of dinosaur footsteps behind him.

Celise Waan was pleased. She had handled herself quite adroitly, no doubt of it. That nasty little cat-thing wouldn't be bothering her again. Her faceplate was a bit smeared where the cat-spit had struck, but otherwise she had come off splendidly from the encounter. She holstered her pistol deftly, and stalked back out into the corridor.

The smear on her faceplate bothered her a little. It was up near her eyes, and it obscured her vision. She wiped at it with the back of her hand, but that only seemed to spread the smeariness around. Water, that was what she needed. Very well then. She had been looking for food anyway, and where you found food you always found water.

She walked briskly down the corridor, turned a corner, and stopped dead.

Not a meter away, another of those damned cat-things stood staring at her insolently.

This time Celise Waan acted decisively. She went for her pistol. She had some trouble getting it out, however, and her first shot missed the disgusting creature entirely and blew the door off a nearby room. The explosion was loud and startling. The cat hissed, drew back, spit just like the first one had, and then ran.

Celise Waan caught the spittle up near her left shoulder this time. She tried to get off a second shot, but the smeary condition of her helmet's faceplate made it difficult to see where she was aiming.

"Stuff and nonsense," she said loudly in exasperation. It was getting harder and harder to see. The plastic in front of her eyes seemed to be getting cloudy. The edges of the faceplate were still clear, but when she looked straight ahead everything was vague and distorted. She really had to get the helmet cleaned off.

She moved in the direction she thought the cat-thing had taken, going slowly so as not to trip. She tried to listen. She heard a soft scrabbling sound, as if the creature was nearby, but she couldn't be sure.

The faceplate was getting worse and worse. It was like looking through milk-glass. Everything was white and cloudy. This wouldn't do, Celise Waan thought. This wouldn't do at all. How could she hunt down that hideous cat-creature if she was half-blind? For that matter, how could she find where she was going? There was no help for it; she would have to take off this stupid helmet.

But the thought gave her pause; she remembered Tuf and his dire warnings about sickness in the ship's air. Well, yes, but Tuf was such a ridiculous man! Had she seen any proof of what he said? No, none at all. She'd put out that big gray cat of his, and it certainly hadn't seemed to suffer any for the experience. Tuf had been carrying it around the last time she'd seen him. Of course, he had done that big song and dance about incubation periods, but he was probably just trying to frighten her. He seemed to enjoy outraging her sensibilities, the way he had with his revolting catfood trick. No doubt he would find it perversely amusing if he frightened her into remaining in this tight, uncomfortable, smelly suit for weeks.

It occurred to her suddenly that Tuf was probably responsible for these cat-things that were harassing her. The very idea made Celise Waan furious. The man was a barbarous wretch!

She could hardly see a thing now. The milky center of her faceplate had grown almost opaque.

Resolute and angry, Celise Waan unsealed her helmet, took it off, and threw it down the corridor as far as she could.

She took a deep breath. The ship's air was slightly cold, with a faint astringency to it, but it was less musty than the recycled air from the suit's airpac. Why, it tasted good! She smiled. Nothing wrong with this air. She looked forward to finding Tuf and giving him a tongue-lashing.

Then she happened to glance down. She gasped.

Her glove . . . the back of her left hand, the hand she'd used to wipe away the cat-spit, why, a big hole had appeared in the center of the gold fabric, and even the metal weave beneath looked, well, *corroded*.

That cat! That damned cat! Why, if that spit had actually struck her bare skin, it would have . . . it could have . . . she remembered all of a sudden that she was no longer wearing a helmet.

Down the corridor, the cat-thing suddenly popped out of an open room.

Celise Waan shrieked at it, whipped up her pistol, and fired three times in rapid succession. But it was too fast. It ran away and vanished down around a corner.

She wouldn't feel safe until the pestilential thing was disposed of for good, she decided. If she let it get away, it might pounce on her at any unguarded moment, the way Tuf's obnoxious black-and-white pet was so wont to do. Celise Waan opened her pistol, fed in a fresh clip of explosive darts, and moved off warily in pursuit.

Jefri Lion's heart was pounding as it had not pounded in years; his legs ached and his breath was coming in hard, short little gasps. Adrenalin surged through his system. He pushed himself harder and harder. Just a little farther now, down this corridor and around the corner, and then maybe twenty meters on to the next intersection.

The deck underfoot shook every time Kaj Nevis landed on one of his heavy, armored saucer-feet, and once or twice Jefri Lion almost lost his footing, but the danger only seemed to add spice. He was running like he'd run as a youth, and even Nevis's huge augmented strides were not enough to catch him, though he could feel the other closing on him.

He had pulled out a light-grenade as he ran. When he heard one of Nevis's damnable pincers snap within a meter of the back of his head, Jefri Lion armed it and flipped it over his shoulder and pushed himself even harder, darting around the last corner.

He whirled as he made the turn, just in time to see a sudden soundless flash of blue-white brilliance blossom in the corridor he had evacuated. Even the reflected light that blazed off the walls left Jefri Lion momentarily dazzled. He backpedaled, watching the intersection. Seen directly, the light-grenade ought to have burned out Nevis's retinas, and the radiation ought to be enough to kill him within seconds.

The only sign of Nevis was a huge, utterly black shadow that loomed across the intersection.

Jefri Lion retreated, running backwards now, panting.

Kaj Nevis stepped out slowly into the intersection. His faceplate was so dark it looked almost black, but as Lion watched, the red glow returned, burning brighter and brighter. "DAMN YOU AND ALL YOUR STUPID TOYS," Nevis boomed.

Well, it didn't matter, thought Jefri Lion. The plasma cannon would do the job, there was no doubt of that, and he was only ten meters or so from the fire zone. "Are you giving up, Nevis?" he taunted, trotting backwards easily. "Is the old soldier too fast for you?"

But Kaj Nevis didn't move.

For a moment, Jefri Lion was baffled. Had the radiation gotten to him after all, even through the suit? No, that couldn't be it. Surely Nevis wouldn't give up the chase now, not after Lion had lured him so heartbreakingly close to the fire zone and his plasma-ball surprise.

Nevis laughed.

He was looking up over Lion's head.

Jefri Lion looked up, too, just in time to see something detach itself from the ceiling and come flapping down at him. It was all a sooty black, and it rode on wide dark batwings, and he had a brief vision of slitted yellow eyes with thin red pupils. Then the darkness folded over him like a cape, and leathery, wet flesh closed about him to muffle his sudden, startled scream.

It was all very interesting, Rica Dawnstar thought.

Once you mastered the system, once you got the commands down, you could find out all sorts of things. Like, for example, the approximate mass and body configuration of each of those little lights moving up on the screen. The computer would even work up a three-dimensional simulation for you, if you asked it nicely. Rica asked it nicely.

Now everything was falling into place.

Anittas was gone after all. The sixth intruder, back on the *Cornucopia*, was only one of Tuf's cats.

Kaj Nevis and his supersuit were chasing Jefri Lion around the ship. Except one of the black dots, the hooded dracula, had just gotten hold of Lion.

The red dot that was Celise Waan had stopped moving, although it hadn't winked out. The creeping black mass was coming toward her.

Haviland Tuf was alone in the central axis, putting something in a cloning vat and trying to ask the system to activate the chronowarp. Rica let the command go through.

All of the other bio-weapons were out in the corridors.

Rica decided to let things sort themselves out a little more down there before she took a hand.

Meanwhile, she'd rummaged up the program to cleanse the interior of the ship of plague. First she'd have to close all the emergency locks, seal off each sector individually. Then the process could begin. Atmosphere evacuation, filtration, irradiation, with massive redundancy built in for safety, and when the replacement atmosphere flowed back, it was infused with all the proper antigens. Complex and time-consuming—but effective.

And Rica was in no special hurry.

Her legs had collapsed first.

Celise Waan lay in the center of the corridor where she had fallen, her throat constricted with terror. It had all happened so suddenly. One moment she was rushing headlong down the hall in pursuit of the cat-thing. And then a wave of dizziness had swept over her, and suddenly she felt too weak to go on. She had decided to rest for a moment, had squatted down to catch her breath. But it didn't help. She only felt worse and worse, and when she tried to get up, her legs had buckled under her and she'd pitched forward onto her face.

After that her legs refused to move. Now she couldn't even feel them. She couldn't feel anything below her waist, in fact, and the paralysis was creeping up her body slowly. She could still move her arms, but it hurt when she did, and her motions were leaden and clumsy.

Her cheek was pressed against the hardness of the deck. She tried to raise her head, and failed. Her whole upper body shook with a sudden stabbing pain.

Two meters away, a cat-thing peered out from around a corner. It stood staring at her, its eyes huge and scary. Its mouth opened in a hiss.

Celise Waan tried to stifle a scream.

Her pistol was still in her hand. Slowly, jerkily, she dragged it forward to her face. Every motion was agony. She lined it up as best she could, squinting along the top of it, and fired.

The dart actually hit.

She was showered with pieces of cat-thing. One piece, raw and wet and disgusting, landed on her bare cheek.

It made her feel a little better. At least she'd killed the creature that had tormented her. At least she was safe from that. She was still sick and helpless, though. Maybe she should rest. A little nap, yes, she'd feel better after a little nap.

Another cat-thing bounded out into the corridor.

Celise Waan groaned, tried to move, gave up the effort. Her arms were growing heavier and heavier.

A second cat followed the first. Celise pushed her dart-gun to her cheek again, tried to aim. She was distracted when a third cat appeared. The dart went wide, exploded harmlessly way off down the corridor.

One of the cats spit at her. It struck her between the eyes.

The agony was unbelievable. If she could have moved, she would have torn her eyes from their sockets, rolled on the ground, pulled at her skin. But she couldn't move. She screamed.

Her vision distorted into a hideous blur of color and then was gone.

She heard . . . feet. Small, light, padding footsteps. Cat steps.

How many were there?

Celise felt a weight on her back. And then another, and another. Something nudged against her useless right leg; she could dimly sense it shifting.

There was a spitting sound, and agony flared on her cheek.

They were all around her, on top of her, crawling over her. She could feel the stiffness of their fur brushing against her hand. Something bit into the flesh of her neck. She screamed. The biting continued. It took hold, pulling, worrying at her with small sharp teeth.

Another one nipped at a finger. Somehow the pain gave her strength. She flailed at it, pulled back her hand. When she moved, there was a cacophony of hissing all around her as the cat-things protested. She felt them biting her face, her throat, her eyes. Something was trying to squirm down into her suit.

Her hand moved slowly, awkwardly. She brushed aside cat-things, was bitten, persisted. She fumbled at her belt, and at last she felt it, round and hard within her grip. She pulled it loose, brought it up toward her face, held it oh so tight.

Where was the stud that armed it? Her thumb searched. *There.* She twisted it a half-turn, pressed it in as Lion had told her to.

Five, she recited silently, four three two one.

In her last moment, Celise Waan saw the light.

Kaj Nevis had himself a good loud laugh as he watched the show.

He didn't know what the hell the damned thing was, but it was more than enough for Jefri Lion. Its wings folded over him when it hit, and for a few minutes he screamed and struggled, rolling around on the floor with the thing enveloping his head and shoulders. He looked like a man fighting an umbrella. It was downright comic.

After a while, Lion lay still, his legs kicking feebly. The screaming stopped. A sucking sound filled the corridor.

Nevis was amused and pleased, but he figured it was best not to leave any loose ends. The thing was intent on its feeding. Nevis walked up as quietly as he could manage, which wasn't very quietly, and grabbed it. It made a liquid popping sound when he pulled it off of what was left of Jefri Lion.

Damn, Nevis thought, it did one hell of a job. The whole front of Lion's helmet was staved in. The thing had a kind of bony sucker-beak, and it had punched right through Lion's faceplate and sucked off most of his face. Ugly. The flesh looked almost liquefied, and there was bone showing through.

The monster was flapping madly in his grip, and making a high, hideous noise, half shriek and half whine. Kaj Nevis held it at arm's length and let it flap while he studied it. It struck at his arm, again and again, to no effect. He liked those eyes; real mean, scary eyes. This thing could be handy, he thought. He pictured what it would be like to dump a couple hundred of these down into Shandicity some night. Oh, they'd meet his price. They'd give him any damn thing he asked for—money, women, power, the whole damn world if that was what he wanted. It was going to be fun owning this ship.

In the meantime, though, this particular creature might be a nuisance.

Kaj Nevis took hold of a wing with each hand, and ripped it in half. Then, smiling, he went back the way he had come.

Haviland Tuf checked the instrumentation again, adjusted the fluid flow slightly. Satisfied, he folded his hands atop his stomach and took up his position by the vat. Within, opaque red-black liquid swirled and churned. Tuf felt a certain sense of vertigo watching it; that was a side-effect of the chronowarp, he knew. In that tiny tank, so small he could almost encompass it with his two large hands, vast primal energies were at play, and time itself was hurrying at his command. It filled him with a singular sense of awe and reverence.

The nutrient bath was thinning gradually, becoming almost translucent. Within, Tuf fancied that he could almost see a dark shape taking form, growing, growing visibly, ontogeny taking place before his eyes. Four paws, yes, he could see them. And a tail. That was most definitely a tail, Tuf decided.

He moved back to the instrumentation. It would not do for his creation to be vulnerable to the contagions that had killed Mushroom. He recalled the inoculation the tyrannosaur had received shortly before its unexpected and inconvenient release. No doubt there was a way to administer the appropriate antigens and prophylactics before completing the birth process. Haviland Tuf commenced to do just that.

The *Ark* was almost clean. Rica had sealed the barriers throughout three-quarters of the ship, and the sterilization program was proceeding with its own inexorable, automated logic. The landing deck, engineering, drive room, control tower, bridge, and nine other sectors showed a clean pale blue now on the telescreen status display. Only the great central axis and the main corridors and laboratory areas in close proximity to it were still shaded with that corrosive reddish hue that signified an atmosphere laced through with disease and death in all those myriad forms.

That was the way Rica Dawnstar wanted it. In those interconnected central sectors, another kind of process was working itself out with similar remorseless logic. And the final equation, she had no doubt, would leave her in sole and complete control of the seedship and all its knowledge, power, and wealth.

Now that her environment was clean and safe, Rica had gratefully removed her helmet. She had ordered up some food as well—a thick white slab of protein from some creature called a meatbeast that *Ark* had held in a succulent stasis for a millennium, which she washed down with a tall chilled glass of sweetwater that tasted slightly of Milidian honey. She enjoyed the snack as she watched the reports flow by.

Things had simplified themselves considerably down there. Jefri Lion was gone. A pity, in a way; he'd been harmless enough, although unbelievably naive. Celise Waan was out of it too, and, surprisingly, she'd managed to take the hellkittens out with her. Kaj Nevis had disposed of the hooded dracula.

Nobody left but Nevis and Tuf . . . and her.

Rica grinned.

Tuf was no problem. He was busy making a cat. He could be taken care of easily, one way or the other. No, the only real obstacle now standing between Rica and the prize was Kaj Nevis and the Unquin battlesuit. Kaj was probably feeling real confident by this point. Good. Let him, she thought.

Rica Dawnstar finished her meal and licked the ends of her fingers. It was time for her zoology lesson, she figured. She called up reports on the three bio-weapons still out roaming the ship. If none of them would do, what the hey, she still had thirty-nine more in stasis just waiting for release. She could pick and choose her executioner.

A battlesuit? What she had was better than a hundred battlesuits.

When she had finished reading the zoological profiles, Rica Dawnstar was smiling broadly.

Forget the reserves. The only problem was making the right introductions. She checked out the geography up on the telescreen, and tried to consider just how devious a mind old Kaj Nevis had.

Not nearly devious enough, Rica suspected.

The damned corridors went on and on and never seemed to lead anywhere but to other corridors. His gauges showed that he had already begun drawing air from his third tank. Kaj Nevis knew he had to find the others quickly and get them out of the way so he could settle down to the problem of figuring out how this damned ship worked.

He was striding down one especially long, wide corridor when suddenly a kind of plastic stripe inset into the deck lit up under his feet.

Nevis paused, frowning.

The trace gleamed suggestively. It led straight ahead, and turned to the right at the next intersection.

Nevis took a single step. The section of the trace behind him winked out.

He was being pointed somewhere. Anittas had muttered something about leading people around the ship just before he'd had his little haircut. This was how he did it, then. Could the cybertech still be alive somehow, haunting the *Ark*'s computer? Nevis doubted it. Anittas had seemed pretty damned dead to him, and he had a lot of experience with making people dead. Who was this then? Dawnstar, of course. Had to be. The cybertech said he'd led her to the control room.

So where was she trying to lead him?

Kaj Nevis thought about it for an instant. In his suit, he felt nigh-on invulnerable. But why take chances? Besides, Dawnstar was a treacherous little bitch. She might very well just lead him around and around forever, until his air ran out.

He turned resolutely and stalked off, moving in the opposite direction from the seductive silver guideline.

At the next turn, a green trace blazed to life, pointing to his left.

Kaj Nevis turned right.

The passage dead-ended in twin spiral escalators. When Nevis paused, one of them began to corkscrew up. He grimaced and walked down the unmoving one.

He descended three decks. At the bottom, the passageway was narrow and dark, and led off in two directions. Before Nevis could make a choice, there was a metallic scraping sound, and a sliding panel came out of a wall and closed off the right-hand corridor.

The bitch was still at it, he thought furiously. He looked down to the left. The corridor seemed to widen somewhat as it went, but it also got darker, and here and there it was broken by the hulks of old machinery. Nevis didn't like the looks of it.

If Dawnstar thought she could herd him along into a trap by closing a few doors, she had another thought coming. Nevis turned back to the sealed right-hand passage, drew back his foot, and kicked. The noise was deafening. He kicked again, and again, and then began to use his armored fists. He brought all the augmented exoskeletal strength of the battlesuit to bear.

Grinning, he stepped over what remained of the sliding panel into the dim, narrow passage that Dawnstar had tried to forbid to him. Underneath his feet was bare metal; the walls almost brushed his shoulders. It was an accessway of some sort, Nevis figured, but maybe it led to someplace important. Hell, it had to lead to someplace important. Why else had Dawnstar tried to keep him out of it?

His saucer-feet rang on the floorplates. He walked. It grew darker, but Kaj Nevis was determined. At one point, the passage made a sharp right-hand bend, almost too narrow for him to get through in the battlesuit. He had to squeeze past that point with his arms retracted and his legs half-bent.

Around the turn, a small square of light appeared up ahead. Nevis moved toward it. Then, abruptly, he stopped. What was that?

There was a black blob of some sort, floating in the air ahead of him.

Kaj Nevis advanced cautiously.

The dark blob was small and round, barely the size of a man's fist. Nevis kept about a meter's distance from it, and studied it. Another creature—as damned ugly as the one that had dined on Jefri Lion, too, but weirder. It was brown and lumpy, and its hide looked like it was made of rocks. It looked almost like it *was* a rock, in fact; Nevis only knew it was alive because it had a mouth—a wet black hole in the rocky skin. Inside, the mouth was all moist and green and moving, and he could make out teeth, or what looked like teeth, except they looked metallic. He thought he saw a triple set of them, half-concealed by rubbery green flesh that pulsed slowly, steadily.

The weirdest thing was how incredibly still it was. At first, Nevis thought it was hovering in the air somehow. But then he came a little closer and saw that he'd been wrong. It was suspended in the center of an incredibly fine web, the strands so very thin they were all but invisible. In fact, the ends of them *were* invisible. Nevis could make out the thickest parts near the nexus where the creature sat pulsing, but the webbing seemed to get thinner and thinner as it spread, and you couldn't see where it attached to wall or floor or ceiling at all, no matter how hard you looked.

A spider, then. A weird one. The rocky appearance made him think it was some kind of silicon-based life. He'd heard of that, here and there. It was real goddamned rare. So he had some kind of silicon-spider here. Big deal.

Kaj Nevis moved closer. Damn, he thought. The web, or what he thought was the web . . . hell, the damned thing wasn't sitting on the web, it was *part* of the web. Those fine, thin, shiny web strands grew out of its body, he saw. He could barely make out the joinings. And there were more than he thought—*hundreds* of them, maybe thousands, most of them too thin to be seen from any kind of distance at all, but when you looked at them from the right angle, you could see the light gleaming off them, all silvery-faint.

Nevis edged back a step, uneasy despite the security of his armored suit, for no good reason that he could name. Behind the silicon-spider, light shone from the end of the accessway. There had to be something important there; that had to be why Rica Dawnstar had tried so hard to keep him away.

That was it, he thought to himself with grim satisfaction. That was probably the damned *control room* back there, and Rica was inside cowering, and this stupid spider was her last line of defense. It gave him the creeps, but what the hell else could it do to him?

Kaj Nevis shifted to his pincer arms and brought up the right pincer to snip the web.

The gleaming, bloodstained, serrated metal blades closed on the nearest visible strand, smoothly and easily. Gleaming, bloodstained, serrated shards of Unquish metal clattered down onto the floor plates.

The whole web began to vibrate.

Kaj Nevis stared at his lower right arm. Half of the pincer had been sheared off. Bile rose in his throat. He took a step backwards, another, a third, putting distance between him and the *thing* back there.

A thousand web strands, thinner than threads, became a thousand legs. They left a thousand holes in the metal walls when they moved, and they scored the floor with their lightest touch.

Nevis ran. He stayed ahead until he came to the narrow place where the passage turned.

He was still lowering the suit's massive arms and attempting to wedge himself through when the walking-web caught him. It bobbed as it moved toward him, suspended on countless invisible legs, its mouth pulsing. Nevis made terrified choking sounds. A thousand monomolecular silicon arms enveloped him.

Nevis brought up a huge powered hand to grab the head of the thing, to crush it to a pulp, but the arms were everywhere, waving, closing about him languidly. He pushed against them, and they cut through metal, flesh, bone. Blood came spurting from the stump of his wrist. He screamed, briefly.

Then the walking-web tightened its embrace.

A hairline crack appeared in the plastic of the empty vat. The kitten batted at it. The crack widened. Haviland Tuf reached in and caught up the kitten in one large hand, brought it close to his face. It was tiny, and a bit feeble yet: perhaps he had initiated birth too soon. He would be more careful on his next attempt, but this time the insecurity of his position and the need for constant vigilance lest wandering tyrannosaurs interrupt his work had resulted in a certain unseemly haste.

Nonetheless, he judged the trial a success. The kitten mewed. Haviland Tuf determined that it would be necessary to hand-feed it milk from a dropper, yet he had no doubt that he was equal to the task. The kitten's eyes were barely open, and its long gray fur was still wet from the fluids in which it had been so recently immersed. Had Mushroom ever truly been this small?

"I cannot name you Mushroom," he told his new companion solemnly. "Genetically you are one, it is true, yet Mushroom was Mushroom and you are you and I would not have you confused. I shall name you Chaos, a fitting companion to Havoc." The kitten moved in his palm and opened and closed one eye, as if it understood; but then, as Tuf knew, all cats have a touch of psi.

He looked about him. Nothing more remained to be done here. Perhaps it was time to search out his erstwhile and unworthy companions, and attempt to arrive at some sort of mutually beneficial accommodation. Cradling Chaos in his arm, he set off in search of them.

It was all over but the shouting, Rica Dawnstar decided when Nevis's red light vanished from the screen. Now it was down to her and Tuf, which meant that for all practical purposes, she was mistress of the *Ark*.

What the hell would she do with it, she wondered? Hard to say. Sell it to some arms consortium or the highest-bidding world? Doubtful. She didn't trust anyone with quite that much power. Power corrupts, after all. Maybe she should keep it, run it. She was corrupt enough already, she ought to be immune. But it would get awfully lonely living in this morgue alone. She could hire a crew, of course— bring aboard friends, lovers, flunkies. Only how could she trust them? Rica frowned. Well, it was a knotty problem, but she had a long, long time to get a handle on it. She'd think about it later.

Right now, she had a more immediate problem to consider. Tuf had just left the central cloning chamber and was wandering out into the corridors. What was she going to do about him?

She studied the display. The walking-web was still in its lair, snug and warm, probably still feeding. The rolleram, all four metric tons of it, was down in the main corridor of deck six, rolling back and forth like some kind of berserk living cannonball of enormous size, caroming off walls and searching in vain for something organic to roll over, crush, and digest.

The tyrannosaur was on the right level. What was it up to? Rica punched for more detail, and smiled. If her readouts could be believed, it was eating. Eating *what?* For a moment she drew a blank. Then it dawned on her. It had to be gulping down what remained of old Jefri Lion and the hooded dracula. The location seemed about right.

All things considered, it was pretty close to Tuf. Unfortunately, when it began to move again, it headed off in the wrong direction. Maybe she should arrange a meeting.

She couldn't underestimate Tuf, though. He had already escaped the reptile once; he might be able to do it again. And even if she maneuvered him onto the same level as the rolleram, the same problem presented itself. Tuf had a certain native cunning. She'd never be able to lead old Tuffy by the nose the way she had with Nevis. He was too subtle. She recalled the games they'd played aboard the *Cornucopia*. Tuf had won all of them.

Release a few more bio-weapons? Easily done.

Rica Dawnstar hesitated. Ah, hell, she thought, there was an easier way. It was time she took a hand directly.

Hooked over one arm of the captain's throne was a thin coronet of iridescent metal that Rica had earlier removed from a storage cabinet. She picked it up, ran it under a scanner briefly to check the circuitry, and slid it over her head at a rakish angle. Then she donned her helmet, sealed up her suit, and took out her needler. Once more into the breach.

Wandering about in corridors of the *Ark*, Haviland Tuf found a vehicle of sorts—a small, open, three-wheeled cart. He had been standing for some time, and before that had been hiding underneath a table. He was only too glad to be seated. He drove along at a smooth, steady, comfortable speed, sitting back against the cushion and looking straight ahead. Chaos rode in his lap.

Tuf drove through several kilometers of corridor. He was a cautious and methodical driver. At every intersection he stopped, looked right, looked left, and weighed his choices before proceeding. He turned twice, as dictated partly by stern logic and partly by sheerest whim, but stayed for the most part to the widest corridors. Once he stopped and dismounted to explore a set of doors that seemed interesting. He saw nothing, encountered no one. Now and again, Chaos moved about in his lap.

Then Rica Dawnstar appeared up ahead of him.

Haviland Tuf stopped his cart in the center of a great intersection. He looked right, and blinked several times. He looked left. Then he stared straight ahead, hands folded on top of his stomach, and watched as she came toward him slowly.

She stopped about five meters away, down the corridor. "Out for a drive?" she asked. In her right hand she carried her familiar needler. In her left hand was a tangle of straps that trailed down onto the deck.

"Indeed," said Haviland Tuf. "I have been occupied for some time. Where are the others?"

"Dead," Rica Dawnstar said. "Deceased. Gone. Eliminated from the game. We're the end of it, Tuf."

"A familiar situation," Tuf said flatly.

"This is the last game, Tuf," Rica Dawnstar said. "No rematch. And this time I win."

Tuf stroked Chaos and said nothing.

"Tuf," she said amiably, "you're the innocent in all this. I've got nothing against you. Take your ship and go."

"If you refer to the *Cornucopia of Excellent Goods at Low Prices*," said Haviland Tuf, "might I remind you that it suffered grave damage which has not yet been repaired?"

"Take some other ship, then."

"I think not," Tuf said. "My claim to the *Ark* is perhaps inferior to that of Celise Waan, Jefri Lion, Kaj Nevis, and Anittas, yet you tell me that all of them are deceased, and my claim is surely as good as your own."

"Not quite," said Rica Dawnstar. She raised her needler. "This gives my claim the edge."

Haviland Tuf looked down at the kitten in his lap. "Let this be your first lesson in the hard ways of the universe," he said loudly. "What matters fairness, when one party has a gun and one does not? Brute violence rules everywhere, and intelligence and good intent are trampled upon." He stared back at Rica Dawnstar. "Madam," he said, "I acknowledge your advantage. Yet I must protest. The deceased members of our group admitted me to a full share in this venture before we came aboard the *Ark*. To my knowledge, you were never similarly included. Therefore I enjoy a legal advantage over you." He raised a single finger. "Furthermore, I would advance the proposition that ownership is conferred by use, and the ability to use. The *Ark* should, optimally, be under the command of the person who has demonstrated the talent, intellect, and will to make the most effective use of its myriad capabilities. I submit that I am that person."

Rica Dawnstar laughed. "Oh, really?"

"Indeed," said Haviland Tuf. He cupped Chaos in his hand, and lifted the kitten for Rica Dawnstar to see. "Behold my proof. I have explored this ship, and mastered the cloning secrets of the vanished Earth Imperials. It was an awesome and intoxicating experience, and one I am anxious to replicate. In fact, I have decided to give up the crass calling of the merchant, for the nobler profession of ecological engineer. I would hope you would not attempt to stand in my way. Rest assured, I will furnish you with transport back to ShanDellor and see to it personally that you receive every fraction of the fee promised to you by Jefri Lion and the others."

Rica Dawnstar shook her head in disbelief. "You're priceless, Tuffy," she said. She stepped forward, spinning her needler around her finger. "So you think you ought to get the ship because you can use it, and I can't?"

"You have outlined the very heart of it," Tuf said approvingly.

Rica laughed again. "Here, I don't need this," she said lightly. She tossed her needler at him.

Tuf reached up and snatched it out of the air. "It would seem that my claim has been unexpectedly and decisively strengthened. Now I may threaten to shoot you."

"But you won't," Rica said. "Rules, Tuf. You play the game by the rules. I'm the kid who likes to kick over the board." She slung the tangled straps she had been dragging over her shoulder. "You know what I've been up to while you've been cloning yourself a kitten?"

"Obviously I do not," said Haviland Tuf.

"Obviously," Rica echoed sardonically. "I've been up on the bridge, Tuf, playing the computer and learning just about everything I need to know about the EEC and its *Ark*."

Tuf blinked. "Indeed."

"There's a swell telescreen up there," she said. "Think of it like a big gaming board, Tuf. I've been watching every move. The red pieces, that was you and the rest of them. Me, too. And the black pieces. The bioweapons, as the system likes to call them. I like the sound of *monsters* better myself. Shorter. Less formal."

"Fraught with strong connotations, however," Tuf put in.

"Oh, certainly. But to the point. We got through the defense sphere, we even handled the plague defense, but Anittas got himself killed and decided to get a little revenge, so he kicked loose the monster defense. And I sat up on top and watched the red and the black chase each other. But something was missing, Tuf. Know what?"

"I suspect this to be a rhetorical question," Tuf said.

"Indeed," mocked Rica Dawnstar, with laughter. "The *greens* were missing, Tuf! The system was programmed to show intruders in red, its own bio-weapons in black, and authorized *Ark* personnel in green. There were no greens, of course. Only that got me thinking, Tuf. The monster defense was obviously a last resort fallback position, sure. But was it intended for use *only* when the ship was derelict, abandoned?"

Tuf folded his hands. "I think not. The existence of the telescreen display capacity implies the existence of someone to watch said display. Moreover, if the system was coded to display ship's personnel, intruders, and monstrous defenders simultaneously and in variant colors, then the possibility of all three groupings being aboard and active at the same time must have been considered."

"Yes," said Rica Dawnstar. "Now, the key question."

In the corridor behind her, Haviland Tuf glimpsed motion. "Excuse me," he began.

Rica waved him quiet. "If they were prepared to turn loose these caged horrors of theirs to repel boarders in an emergency, *how did they prevent their own people from getting killed?*"

"An interesting quandary," Tuf admitted. "I eagerly anticipate learning the answer to this puzzle. I fear I will have to defer that pleasure, however." He cleared his throat. "Far be it from me to interrupt such a fascinating discourse. I feel obliged to point out, however . . ." The deck shook.

"Yes," Rica said, grinning.

"I feel obliged to point out," Tuf repeated, "that a rather large carnivorous dinosaur has appeared in the corridor behind you, and is presently attempting to sneak up on us. He is not doing a very good job of it."

The tyrannosaur roared.

Rica Dawnstar was undisturbed. "Really?" she said laughing. "Surely you don't expect me to fall for the old there's-a-dinosaur-behind-you gambit. I expected better of you, Tuf."

"I protest! I am completely sincere." Tuf turned on the motor of his cart. "Witness the speed with which I have activated my vehicle, in order to flee the creature's approach. How can you doubt me, Rica Dawnstar? Surely you hear the beast's thunderous approach, the sound of its roaring?"

"What roaring is that?" Rica asked. "No, seriously, Tuf, I was telling you something. The answer. We forgot one little piece of the puzzle."

"Indeed," said Tuf. The tyrannosaur was moving toward them at an alarming velocity. It was in a foul temper, and its roaring made it difficult to hear Rica Dawnstar.

"The Ecological Engineering Corps were more than cloners, Tuf. They were military scientists. They were *genetic engineers* of the first order. They could recreate the lifeforms of hundreds of worlds and bring them alive in their vats, but that was not *all* they could do. They could also tinker with the DNA itself, *change* those lifeforms, redesign them to suit their own purposes!"

"Of course," Tuf said. "Pardon me, but now I fear I must run away from the dinosaur." The tyrannosaur was ten meters behind Rica. It paused. Its lashing tail struck the wall, and Tuf's cart shook to the impact. Slaver was dripping from its fangs, and its stunted forelegs clawed the air with unseemly eagerness.

"That would be very rude," Rica said. "You see, Tuf, that's the answer. These bio-weapons, these monsters—they were held in stasis for a thousand years, likely for longer than that. But they weren't ordinary monsters. They were cloned for a special purpose, to defend the ship against intruders, and they had been genetically manipulated to just that end." The tyrannosaur took one step, two, three, and now it was directly behind her, its shadow casting her in darkness.

"How manipulated?" asked Haviland Tuf.

"I thought you'd never ask," said Rica Dawnstar. The tyrannosaur leaned forward, roared, opened its massive jaws, engulfed her head. "Psionics," she said from between its teeth.

"Indeed," said Haviland Tuf.

"A simple psionic capacity," Rica announced from inside the tyrannosaur's jaws. She reached up and picked something from between its teeth, with a *tsk*ing sound. "Some of the monsters were close to mindless, all instinct. They got a basic instinctual aversion. The more complex monsters were made psionically submissive. The instruments of control were psi-boosters. Pretty little things, like crowns. I'm wearing one now. It doesn't confer psi powers or anything dramatic like that. It just makes some of the monsters avoid me, and other ones obey me." She ducked out of the dinosaur's mouth, and slapped the side of his jaw soundly. "Down, boy," she said.

The tyrannosaur roared, and lowered its head. Rica Dawnstar untangled her harness and saddle and began to strap it into place. "I've been controlling him all the time we've been talking," she said conversationally. "I called him here. He's *hungry.* He ate Lion, but Lion was small, and dead, too, and he hasn't had anything else for a thousand years."

Haviland Tuf looked at the needler in his hand. It seemed worse than useless. He was a poor shot in any case. "I would be most glad to clone him a stegosaurus."

"No thanks," Rica said as she tightened the harness, "you can't get out of the game now. You wanted to play, Tuffy, and I'm afraid you lose all around. You should have gone away when I offered you the chance. Let's review your claim, shall we? Lion and Nevis and the others offered you a full share, yes, but of what? I'm afraid now you get a full share, whether you want one or not—a share of everything they got. So much for your legal argument. As for your moral claim on the basis of superior utility," she slapped the dinosaur again, and grinned, "I think I've demonstrated that I can put the *Ark* to more effective use than you can. Down a little more." The beast leaned over still further, and Rica Dawnstar vaulted into the saddle on its neck. "Up!" she barked. It stood.

"Therefore we put legality and morality aside, and again return to violence," Tuf said.

"I'm afraid so," Rica said from on top of her tyrant lizard. It came forward slowly, as if she were feeling her way. "Don't say I didn't play fair, Tuf. I've got the dinosaur, but you've got my needler. Maybe you'll get a lucky hit. So we're both armed." She laughed. "Only I'm armed to the teeth."

Haviland Tuf stood and tossed back her needler, overhand. It was a good throw. Rica leaned out to one side, caught it. "What's this?" she said. "Giving up?"

"Your scruples about fairness have impressed me," said Tuf. "I would take no advantage. You have a claim, I have a claim. You have an animal," He stroked his kitten. "I have an animal, too. Now you have a gun." He activated his cart and backed away from the intersection, rolling quickly down the corridor behind him, or at least as quickly as he could go in reverse.

"Have it your way," Rica Dawnstar said. She was done playing. She felt a little sad. Tuf was turning his cart about to flee headlong instead of backwards. The tyrannosaur opened its mouth wide, and slaver ran from half-meter-long teeth. It screamed a scream that was pure red primal hunger a million years old, and came roaring down on him.

It roared down the corridor and into the intersection.

Twenty meters away along the cross-corridor, the minimind of the plasma cannon took cognizance of the fact that something exceeding the programmed target dimensions had entered the fire zone. There was the faintest of clicks.

Haviland Tuf was turned away from the glare; he put his body between Chaos and the heat and awful noise. It lasted only an instant, fortunately, although the smell of burnt reptile would linger in that spot for years, and sections of the deck and walls would need to be replaced.

"I had a gun, too," said Haviland Tuf to his kitten.

Later, much later, when the *Ark* was clean and he and Havoc and Chaos were settled comfortably into the captain's suite, and he had moved all his personal effects and taken care of all the bodies and done what repairs he could and figured out how to placate the incredibly noisy creature that lived down on deck six, Haviland Tuf began to search the ship methodically. On the second day, he found a store of clothing, but the men and women of the EEC had been shorter than he, and more slender, so none of the uniforms fit.

He did, however, find a hat he took rather a liking to. It was a green duckbilled cap, and it fit snugly atop his bald, milk-white head. On the front of it, in gold, was the theta that had been the sigil of the corps.

"Haviland Tuf," he said to himself in the mirror, "ecological engineer."

It had a certain ring to it, he thought.

ᚠᚢ KIM STANLEY ROBINSON (1952–)

One of the most popular subgenres of contemporary Science Fiction is Alternate History. A host of authors, including Harry Turtledove, Harry Harrison, Barry N. Malzberg, and Philip K. Dick, have tried their hands at this story type with a great deal of success. It is one of the most popular themes for Science Fiction and Fantasy anthologies today. Kim Stanley Robinson's "Remaking History" is one of the classics of this type.

Robinson was a mildly successful Science Fiction writer between the appearance of his first stories in 1975 and his novel The Wild Shore, *the first of his* Orange County *trilogy, in 1984. His career took off from there. Like Jack Williamson, Robinson earned a Ph.D. and has written some very balanced, valuable, and well-researched scholarship on Science Fiction.*

To date, the author's contributions to Science Fiction are varied and important, but none is more important than his Mars *trilogy, which includes* Red Mars *(1993),* Green Mars *(1994), and* Blue Mars *(1996). A regular contributor to the instruction at the annual Clarion Workshop, Kim Stanley Robinson is recognized as one of the major talents writing Science Fiction today.*

Remaking History

(What Might Have Been, *ed. Gregory Benford and Martin H. Greenberg, 1989)*

"The point is *not* to make an exact replica of the Teheran embassy compound." Exasperated, Ivan Venutshenko grabbed his hair in one hand and pulled up, which gave him a faintly Oriental look. "It's the *spirit* of the place that we want to invoke here."

"This has the spirit of our storage warehouse, if you ask me."

"This *is* our storage warehouse, John. We make all our movies here."

"But I thought you said we were going to correct all the lies of the first movie," John Rand said to their director. "I thought you said *Escape From Teheran* was a dumb TV docudrama, only worth remembering because of De Niro's performance as Colonel Jackson. We're going to get the true story on film at last, you said."

Ivan sighed. "That's right, John. Admirable memory. But what you must understand is that when making a film, *true* doesn't mean an absolute fidelity to the real."

"I'll bet that's just what the director of the docudrama said."

Ivan hissed, which he did often while directing their films, to show that he was letting off steam, and avoiding an explosion. "Don't be obstructionist, John. We're not doing anything like that hackwork, and you know it. Lunar gravity alone makes it impossible for us to make a completely realist film. We are working in a world of dream, in a surrealist intensification of what really happened. Besides, we're doing these movies for our own entertainment up here! Remake bad historical films! Have a good time!"

"Sure, Ivan. Sure. Except the ones *you've* directed have been getting some great reviews downside. They're saying you're the new Eisenstein and these little remakes are the best thing to hit the screen since *Kane*. So now the pressure is on and it's not just a game anymore, right?"

"Wrong!" Ivan karate-chopped the air. "I refuse to believe that. When we stop having fun doing this"—nearly shouting—"I quit!"

"Sure, Sergei."

"Don't call me that!"

"Okay, Orson."

"JOHN!"

"But that's *my* name. If I call you that we'll all get confused."

Melina Gourtsianis, their female lead, came to Ivan's rescue. "Come on, John, you'll give him a heart attack, and besides it's late. Let's get on with it."

Ivan calmed down, ran his hands through his hair. He loved doing his maddened director routine, and John loved maddening him. As they disagreed about nearly everything, they made a perfect team. "Fine," Ivan said. "Okay. We've got the set ready, and it may not be an *exact* replica of the compound—" fierce glare at John—"but it's good enough.

"Now, let's go through it one more time. It's night in Teheran. This whole quarter of the city has been gassed with a paralyzing nerve gas, but there's no way of telling when the Revolutionary Guards might come barreling in from somewhere else with gas masks or whatever, and you can't be sure some of them haven't been protected from the gas in sealed rooms. Any moment they might jump out firing. Your helicopters are hovering just overhead, so it's tremendously noisy. There's a blackout in the compound, but searchlights from other parts of the city are beginning to pin the choppers. They've been breaking like cheap toys all the way in, so now there are only five left, and you have no assurances that they will continue to work, especially since twice that number have already broken. You're all wearing gas masks and moving through the rooms of the compound, trying to find and move all fifty-three of the hostages—it's dark and most of the hostages are knocked out like the guards, but some of the rooms were well-sealed, and naturally these hostages are shouting for help. For a while—and this is the effect I want to emphasize more than any other— for a while, things inside are absolutely chaotic. No one can find Colonel Jackson, no one knows how many of the hostages are recovered and how many are still in the embassy, it's dark, it's noisy, there are shots in the distance. I want an effect like the scene at the end of *The Lady from Shanghai*, when they're in the carnival's house of mirrors shooting at each other. Multiplied by ten. Total chaos."

"Now hold on just a second here," John said, exaggerating his Texas accent, which came and went according to his convenience. "I like the chaos bit, and the allusion to Welles, but let's get back to this issue of the facts. Colonel Jackson was the hero of this whole thing! He was the one that decided to go on with all them helicopters busting out in the desert, and he was the one that found Annette Bellows in the embassy to lead them around, and all in all he was on top of every minute of it. That's why they gave him all them medals!"

Ivan glared. "What part are you playing, John?"

"Why, Colonel Jackson." John drew himself up. "Natch."

"However." Ivan tapped the side of his head, to indicate thought. "You don't just want to do a bad imitation of the De Niro performance, do you? You want to do a new interpretation, don't you? Besides, it seems to me a foolish idea to try an imitation of De Niro."

"I like the idea, myself," John said. "Show him how."

Ivan waved him away. "You got all you know about this affair from that stupid TV movie, just like everyone else. I, however, have been reading the accounts of the hostages and the Marines on those helicopters, and the truth is that Colonel Jackson's best moment was out there in the desert, when he decided to go on with the mission even though only five helicopters were still functioning. That was his peak of glory, his moment of heroism. And you did a perfectly adequate job of conveying that when we filmed the scene. We could see every little gear in there, grinding away." He tapped his skull.

"De Niro would have been proud," Melina said.

John pursed his lips and nodded. "We need great men like that. Without them history would be dead. It'd be nothing but a bunch of broken-down helicopters out in a desert somewhere."

"A trenchant image of history," Ivan said. "Too bad Shelley got to it first. Meanwhile, the truth is that after making the decision to go on with the raid, Colonel Jackson appeared, in the words of his subordinates, somewhat stunned. When they landed on the embassy roof he led the first unit in, and when they got lost inside, the whole force was effectively without leadership for most of the crucial first half-hour. All the accounts of this period describe it as the utmost chaos, saved only when Sergeant Payton — *not* Colonel Jackson; the TV movie lied about that — when Payton found Ms. Bellows, and she led them to all the hostage rooms they hadn't found."

"All right, all right." John frowned. "So I'm supposed to be kind of spaced out in this scene."

"Don't go for too deep an analysis, John, you might strain something. But essentially you have it. Having committed the force to the raid, even though you're vastly undermanned because of the damned helicopters breaking down, you're a bit frozen by the risk of it. Got that?"

"Yeah. But I don't believe it. Jackson was a hero."

"Fine, a hero, lots of medals. Roomfuls of medals. If he pinned them on he'd look like the bride after the dollar dance. He'd collapse under their weight. But now let's try showing what really happened."

"All right." John drew himself up. "I'm ready."

The shooting of the scene was the part they all enjoyed the most; this was the heart of the activity, the reason they kept making movies to occupy their free hours at Luna Three. Ivan and John and Melina and Pierre-Paul, the theoreticians who traded directing chores from project to project, always blocked the scenes very loosely, allowing a lot of room for improvisation. Thus scenes like this one, which were supposed to be chaotic, were played out with a manic gusto. They were good at chaos.

And so for nearly a half-hour they rushed about the interior of their Teheran embassy compound — the base storage warehouse, with its immense rows of boxes arranged behind white panels of plywood to resemble the compound's buildings and their interiors. Their shouts were nearly drowned by the clatter of recorded helicopters, while intermittent lights flashed in the darkness. Cutouts representing the helicopters were pasted to the clear dome overhead, silhouetted against the unearthly brilliance of the stars — these last had become a trademark of Luna

Three Productions, as their frequent night scenes always had these unbelievably bright stars overhead, part of the films' dreamlike effect.

The actors playing Marines bounded about the compound in their gas masks, looking like aliens descended to ravage a planet; the actors playing hostages and Revolutionary Guards lay scattered on the floor, except for a few in protected rooms, who fought or cried for help. John and Pierre-Paul and the rest hunted the compound for Melina, playing Annette Bellows. For a while it looked as if John would get to her first, thus repeating the falsehood of the De Niro film. But eventually Pierre-Paul, playing Sergeant Payton, located her room, and he and his small unit rushed about after the clear-headed Bellows, who, as she wrote later, had spent most of her months in captivity planning what she should do if this moment ever came. They located the remaining comatose hostages and lugged them quickly to the plywood helicopter on the compound roof. The sound of shots punctuated the helicopters' roar. They leaped through the helicopter's door, shafts of white light stabbing the air like Islamic swords.

That was it; the flight away would be filmed in their little helicopter interior. Ivan turned off the helicopter noise, shouted "Cut!" into a megaphone. Then he shut down all the strategically placed minicams, which had been recording every minute of it.

"What bothers me about your movies, Ivan," John said, "is that you always take away the hero. Always!"

They were standing in the shallow end of the base pool, cooling off while they watched the day's rushes on a screen filling one wall of the natatorium. Many of the screens showed much the same result: darkness, flickering light, alien shapes moving in the elongated dancelike way that audiences on Earth found so surreal, so mesmerizing. There was little indication of the pulsing rhythms and wrenching suspense that Ivan's editing would create from this material. But the actors were happy, seeing arresting images of desperation, of risk, of heroism in the face of a numbingly loud confusion.

Ivan was not as pleased. "Shit!" he said. "We're going to have to do it again."

"Looks okay to me," John remarked. "Son of Film Noir Returns From the Grave. But really, Ivan, you've got to do something about this prejudice against heroes. I saw *Escape From Teheran* when I was a kid, and it was an inspiration to me. It was one of the big reasons I got into engineering."

Pierre-Paul objected. "John, just how did seeing a commando film get you interested in engineering?"

"Well," John replied, frowning, "I thought I'd design a better helicopter, I guess." He ignored his friends' laughter. "I was pretty shocked at how unreliable they were. But the way old De Niro continued on to Teheran! The way he extricated all the hostages and got them back safely, even with the choppers dropping like flies. It was great! We need heroes, and history tells the story of the few people who had what it takes to be one. But you're always downplaying them."

"The Great Man Theory of History," Pierre-Paul said scornfully.

"Sure!" John admitted. "Great Woman too, of course," nodding quickly at the frowning Melina. "It's the great leaders who make the difference. They're special people, and there aren't many of them. But if you believe Ivan's films, there aren't any at all."

With a snort of disgust, Ivan took his attention from the rushes. "Hell, we are going to have to do that scene again. As for my theory of history, John, you both have it and you don't. As far as I understand you." He cocked his head and looked at his friend attentively. On the set they both played their parts to the teeth: Ivan the tormented, temperamental director, gnashing his teeth and ordering people about; John the stubborn, temperamental star, questioning everything and insisting on his preeminence. Mostly this was role-playing, part of the game, part of what made their hobby entertaining to them. Off the set the roles largely disappeared, except to make a point, or have some fun. Ivan was the base's head of computer operations, while John was an engineer involved in the Mars voyage; they were good friends, and their arguments had done much to shape Ivan's ideas for his revisionist historical films, which were certainly the ones from their little troupe making the biggest splash downside—though John claimed this was because of the suspenseful plots and the weird low-gee imagery, not because of what they were saying about history. "*Do* I understand you?" Ivan asked curiously.

"Well," John said, "take the one you did last time, about the woman who saved John Lennon's life. Now that was a perfect example of heroic action, as the 1982 docudrama made clear. There she was, standing right next to a man who had pulled out a damn big gun, and quicker than he could pull the trigger she put a foot in his crotch and a fist in his ear. But in your remake, all we concentrated on was how she had just started the karate class that taught her the moves, and how her husband encouraged her to take the class, and how that cabbie stopped for her even though she was going the other direction, and how that other cabbie told her that Lennon had just walked into his apartment lobby, and all that. You made it seem like it was just a coincidence!"

Ivan took a mouthful of pool water and spurted it at the spangled dome, looking like a fountain statue. "It took a lot of coincidences to get Margaret Arvis into the Dakota lobby at the right time," he told John. "But some of them weren't coincidences—they were little acts of generosity or kindness or consideration, that put her where she could do what she did. I didn't take the heroism away. I just spread it around to all the places it belonged."

John grimaced, drew himself up into his star persona. "I suppose this is some damn Commie notion of mass social movements, sweeping history along in a consensus direction."

"No, no," Ivan said. "I always concentrate on individuals. What I'm saying is that all our individual actions add up to history, to the big visible acts of our so-called 'leaders.' You know what I mean; you hear people saying all the time that things are better now because John Lennon was such a moral force, traveling everywhere, Nobel Peace Prize, secular pope, the conscience of the world or whatnot."

"Well, he *was* the conscience of the world!"

"Sure, sure, he wrote great songs. And he got a lot of antagonists to talk. But without Margaret Arvis he would have been killed at age forty. And without Margaret Arvis's husband, and her karate instructor, and a couple cabbies in New York, and so on, she wouldn't have been there to save his life. So we all become part of it, see? The people who say it was all because of Lennon, or Carter, or Gorbachev—they're putting on a few people what we *all* did."

John shook his head, scattering water everywhere. "Very sophisticated, I'm sure! But in fact it was precisely Lennon and Carter and Gorbachev who made huge differences, all by themselves. Carter started the big swing toward human rights. Palestine, the new Latin America, the American Indian nations—none of those would have existed without him."

"In fact," Melina added, glancing mischievously at Pierre-Paul, "if I understand the Margaret Arvis movie correctly, if she hadn't been going to see Carter thank his New York campaign workers for the 1980 victory, she wouldn't have been in the neighborhood of the Dakota, and so she wouldn't have had the chance to save Lennon's life."

John rose up like a whale breaching. "So it's Carter we have to thank for that, too! As for Gorbachev, well, I don't have to tell you what all he did. That was a hundred-eighty degree turnaround for you Russkies, and no one can say it would have happened without him."

"Well—he was an important leader, I agree."

"Sure was! And Carter was just as crucial. Their years were the turning point, when the world started to crawl out from under the shadow of World War Two. And that was their doing. There just aren't many people who could've done it. Most of us don't have it in us."

Ivan shook his head. "Carter wouldn't have been able to do what he did unless Colonel Ernest Jackson had saved the rescue mission to Teheran, by deciding to go on."

"So Jackson is a hero too!"

"But then Jackson wouldn't have been a hero if the officer back in the Pentagon hadn't decided at the last minute to send sixteen helicopters instead of eight."

"And," Melina pointed out quickly, "if Annette Bellows hadn't spent most of a year daydreaming about what she would do in a rescue attempt, so that she knew blindfolded where every other hostage was being kept. They would have left about half the hostages behind without her, and Carter wouldn't have looked so good."

"Plus they needed Sergeant Payton to find Bellows," Ivan added.

"Well shit!" John yelled defensively, which was his retort in any tight spot. He changed tack. "I ain't so sure that Carter's reelection hinged on those hostages anyway. He was running against a flake, I can't remember the guy's name, but he was some kind of idiot."

"So?" Melina said. "Since when has that made any difference?"

With a roar John dove at her, making a big splash. She was much faster than he was, however, and she evaded him easily as he chased her around the pool; it looked like a whale chasing a dolphin. He was reduced to splashing at her from a distance, and the debate quickly degenerated into a big splash fight, as it often did.

"Oh well," John declared, giving up the attack and floating in the shallow end. "I love watching Melina swim the butterfly. In this gravity it becomes a godlike act. Those muscular arms, that sinuous dolphin motion . . ."

Pierre-Paul snorted. "You just like the way the butterfly puts her bottom above water so often."

"No way! Women are just more hydrodynamic than men, don't you think?"

"Not the way you like them."

"Godlike. Gods and goddesses."

"You look a bit godlike yourself," Melina told him. "Bacchus, for instance."

"Hey." John waved her off, jabbed a finger at the screens. "I note that all this mucho sophisticated European theorizing has been sunk. Took a bit of Texas logic, is all."

"Only Texas logic could do it," Pierre-Paul said.

"Right. You admit my point. In the end it's the great leaders who have to act, the rare ones, no matter if we ordinary folks help them into power."

"When you revise your proposition like that," Ivan said, "you turn it into mine. Leaders are important, but they are leaders because we made them leaders. They are a collective phenomenon. They are expressions of us."

"Now wait just a minute! You're going over the line again! You're talking like heroic leaders are a dime a dozen, but if that were true it wouldn't matter if Carter had lost in 1980, or if Lennon had been killed by that guy. But look at history, man! Look what happened when we did lose great leaders! Lincoln was shot; did they come up with another leader comparable to him? No way! Same with Gandhi, and the Kennedys, and King, and Sadat, and Olof Palme. When those folks were killed their countries suffered the lack of them, because they were special."

"They *were* special," Ivan agreed, "and obviously it was a bad thing they were killed. And no doubt there was a short-term change for the worse. But they're not irreplaceable, because they're human beings just like us. None of them, except maybe Lincoln or Gandhi, was any kind of genius or saint. It's only afterward we think of them that way, because we want heroes so much. But we're the heroes. All of us put them in place. And there are a lot of capable, brilliant people out there to replace the loss of them, so that in the long run we recover."

"The *real* long run," John said darkly. "A hundred years or more, for the South without Lincoln. They just aren't that common. The long run proves it."

"Speaking of the long run," Pierre-Paul said, "is anyone getting hungry?"

They all were. The rushes were over, and Ivan had dismissed them as unusable. They climbed out of the pool and walked toward the changing room, discussing restaurants. There were a considerable number of them in the station, and new ones were opening every week. "I just tried the new Hungarian restaurant," Melina said. "The food was good, but we had trouble, when the meal was over, finding someone to give us the check!"

"I thought you said it was a Hungarian restaurant," John said.

They threw him back in the pool.

The second time they ran through the rescue scene in the compound, Ivan had repositioned most of the minicams, and many of the lights; his instructions to the actors remained the same. But once inside the hallways of the set, John Rand couldn't help hurrying in the general direction of Annette Bellows's room.

All right, he thought. Maybe Colonel Jackson had been a bit hasty to rush into the compound in search of hostages, leaving the group without a commander. But his heart had been in the right place, and the truth was, he had found a lot of the hostages without any help from Bellows at all. It was easy; they were scattered in ones and twos on the floor of almost every room he and his commandos entered, and stretched out along with the guards in the rooms and in the halls, paralyzed by the nerve gas. Damn good idea, that nerve gas. Guards and hostages, tough parts to play, no doubt, as they were getting kicked pretty frequently by commandos running by. He hustled his crew into room after room, then sent them off with hostages draped over their shoulders, pretending to stagger down the halls, banging into walls—*really* tough part to play, hostage—and clutching at gas masks and such; great images for the minicams, no doubt about it.

When all his commandos had been sent back, he ran around a corner in what he believed to be the direction of Annette Bellows's room. Over the racket of the helicopters, and the occasional round of automatic fire, he thought he could make out Melina's voice, shouting hoarsely. So Pierre-Paul hadn't gotten to her yet. Good. Now he could find her and be the one to follow her around rescuing the more obscurely housed hostages, just as De Niro had in the docudrama. It would give Ivan fits, but they could argue it out afterward. No way of telling what had really happened in that compound twenty years before, after all; and it made a better *story* his way.

Their set was only one story tall, which was one of the things that John had objected to; the compound in Teheran had been four stories high, and getting up stairs had been part of the hassle. But Ivan was going to play with the images and shoot a few stair scenes later on, to achieve the effect of multiple floors. Fine, it meant he had only to struggle around a couple of narrow corners, jumping comatose Revolutionary Guards, looking fierce for the minicams wherever they were. It was really loud this time around; *really* loud.

Then one of the walls fell over on him, the plywood pinning him to the ground, the boxes behind it tumbling down and filling the hallway. "Hey!" he cried out, shocked. This wasn't the way it had happened. What was going on? The noise of the helicopters cut off abruptly, replaced by a series of crashes, a whooshing sound. That sound put a fine electric thrill down his spine; he had heard it before, in training routines. Air leaving the chamber. The dome must have been breached.

He heaved up against the plywood. Stuck. Flattening himself as much as possible he slithered forward, under the plywood and out into a small space among fallen boxes. Hard to tell where the hallway had been, and it was pitch-dark. There wouldn't be too much time left. He thought of his little gas mask, then cursed; it wasn't connected to a real oxygen supply. That's what comes from using fake props! he thought angrily. A gas mask with nothing attached to it. Open to the air, which was departing rapidly. Not much time.

He found room among the boxes to stand, and he was about to run over them to the door leading out of the warehouse—assuming the whole station hadn't been breached—when he remembered Melina. Stuck in her embassy room down the hall, wouldn't she still be there? Hell. He groped along in the dark, hearing shouts in the distance. He saw lights, too. Good. He was holding his breath, for what felt like minutes at a time, thought it was probably less than thirty seconds. Every time he sucked in a new breath he expected it to be the freezing vacuum, but the supply of rushing, cold—very cold—air continued to fill him. Emergency supply pouring out into the breach, actually a technique he had helped develop himself. Seemed to be working, at least for the moment.

He heard a muffled cry to one side, began to pull at the boxes before him. Squeak in the gloom, ah-ha, there she was. Not fully conscious. Legs wet, probably blood, uh-oh. He pulled hard at boxes, lifted her up. Adrenaline and lunar gravity made him feel like Superman with that part of things, but there didn't seem to be anywhere near as much air as before, and what was left was damned cold. Hurt to breathe. And harder than hell to balance as he hopped over objects with Melina in his arms. Feeling faint, he climbed over a row of boxes and staggered toward a distant light. A sheet of plywood smacked his shin and he cried out, then fell over. "Hey," he said. The air was gone.

When he came to he was lying in a bed in the station hospital. "Great," he muttered. "Whole station wasn't blown up."

His friends laughed, relieved to hear him speak. The whole film crew was in there, it seemed. Ivan, standing next to the bed, said, "It's okay."

"What the hell happened?"

"A small meteor, apparently. Hit out in our sector, in the shuttle landing chambers, ironically. But it wrecked our storage space as well, as you no doubt noticed."

John nodded painfully. "So it finally happened."

"Yes." This was one of the great uncontrollable dangers of the lunar stations; meteors small and large were still crashing down onto the moon's airless surface, by the thousands every year. Odds were poor that any one would hit something as small as the surface parts of their station, but coming down in such numbers. . . . In the long run they were reduced to a safety status somewhat equivalent to that of mountain climbers. Rockfall could always get you.

"Melina?" John said, jerking up in his bed.

"Over here," Melina called. She was a few beds down, and had one leg in a cast. "I'm fine, John." She got out of bed to prove it, and came over to kiss his cheek. "Thanks for the rescue!"

John snorted. "What rescue?"

They laughed again at him. Pierre-Paul pointed a forefinger at him. "There are heroes everywhere, even among the lowest of us. Now you have to admit Ivan's argument."

"The hell I do."

"You're a hero," Ivan said to him, grinning. "Just an ordinary man, so to speak. Not one of the great leaders at all. But by saving Melina, you've changed history."

"Not unless she becomes president," John said, and laughed. "Hey Melina! Go out and run for office! Or save some promising songwriter or something."

Ivan just shook his head. "Why are you so stubborn? It's not so bad if I'm right, John. Think about it. If I am right, then we aren't just sitting around waiting for leaders to guide us." A big grin lit his face. "We become the masters of our fate, we make our own decisions and act on them—we choose our leaders, and instruct them by consensus, so that we can take history any direction we please! Just as you did in the warehouse."

John lay back in his bed and was silent. Around him his friends grinned; one of them was bringing up a big papier-mâché medal, which vaguely resembled the one the Wizard of Oz pins to the Cowardly Lion. "Ah hell," John said.

"When the expedition reaches Mars, they'll have to name something after you," Melina said.

John thought about it for a while. He took the big medal, held it limply. His friends watched him, waiting for him to speak.

"Well, I still say it's bullshit," he told Ivan. "But if there is any truth to what you say, it's just the good old spirit of the Alamo you're talking about, anyway. We've been doing it like that in Texas for years."

They laughed at him.

He rose up from the bed again, swung the medal at them furiously. "I swear it's true! Besides, it's all Robert De Niro's fault, anyway! I was *imitating* the real heroes, don't you see? I was crawling around in there all dazed, and then I saw De Niro's face when he was playing Colonel Jackson in the Teheran embassy, and I said to myself, well hell, what would he have done in this here situation? And that's just what I did."

JACK WILLIAMSON (PSD. FOR JOHN STEWART WILLIAMSON) (1908-   )

The final story presented in The Prentice Hall Anthology of Science Fiction and Fantasy *is by one of the greatest living legends of Science Fiction. Jack Williamson published his first story in 1928 in the pages of Hugo Gernsback's* Amazing Stories. *Today, he continues to write cutting edge Science Fiction novels and short stories published by the world's biggest publishers.*

Like Edmond Hamilton, his friend and contemporary, Jack Williamson was impressed with the writings of Abraham Merritt, specifically "The People of the Pit." Also like Hamilton, Williamson's first Science Fiction was Space Opera. When he serialized his Legion of Space *novel in the pages of* Astounding Stories *in the early 1930s, he was already a respected and prolific author. [Read* The Legion of Space *and notice how closely this story line is imitated in the movie* Star Wars *(1977).] As Science Fiction evolved and matured in the twentieth century, so too did Jack Williamson evolve as a master Science Fiction writer. Although a good percentage of his writing has been well-crafted adventure and escapism, much has also been carefully crafted social commentary.*

As impressive as Williamson's more than seventy-year publishing history is, it does not match the significance of the author's contributions to Science Fiction, to literary history, and to academe, and his importance as a topnotch visionary and humanitarian. Once a full-time university professor, Dr. Williamson not only continues to be a university lecturer and to write first rate Science Fiction, he is busy building a Science Fiction library and archives in New Mexico.

The Purchase of Earth

(Science Fiction Age, *July 1998*)

"I'm here now," she said. "Getting my flyer secured."

I left the mower where it was and drove fast to the Canyon airport, memories of Talimena Whiteheart bubbling in my mind. She liked to brag of her Cherokee blood, though with her long dark eyes and thick black hair she looked more Spanish. My life had never been the same since we met. I was begging her to marry me the night she disappeared.

We'd been out to dance at La Loba, the hottest spot in Amarillo. She gave me a kiss that took my breath when we got to her apartment well past midnight, but wouldn't let me in. Next morning she was gone.

Her place was left locked and empty, with no sign of violence. She'd left no note, no hint of trouble, no word of any plans except to let me pick her up for work next morning because her red convertible was in the shop.

Nearly two years ago, and a dreadful time for me. Months of search turned up nothing. The cops gave me a rough interrogation. Her father suspected me of some foul play when he came from Oklahoma to clear out her apartment and take her car. I hadn't tried to find anybody else.

Recalling all her wild, happy, indomitable splendor, I had a ticket for speeding before I reached the airport. I saw her flyer from the parking lot. A queer craft, it was a mirror-bright silver bubble without wheels or wings. Yellow tape was stretched around it and a uniformed security officer was shouting to hold back a curious crowd.

She ran out to meet me, a total stranger till she spoke. Her garment was a sort of sari, a filmy fabric that looked like spun silver. She looked taller, her fine skin shining as if dusted with gold. Her hair clipped short, she wore a golden band around it with a huge, green-glowing gem on her forehead.

I was still staring, speechless, till her arms went around me. She kissed me on the mouth and her husky laugh at my befuddlement brought her old enchantment back. I caught her shoulders to see her better and asked again where she had been.

"Tomorrow." She laughed again. "You wouldn't believe it if I told you. What I want now is a rare beefsteak." Bare and bright under the sheer sari, her arms slid back to hold me close. I caught an odd, keenly sweet aroma. "I'm hungrier," she whispered, "for a night with you."

Her blunt candor astonished me again. We'd spent nights together, nights that kept me enslaved, but only when she was in the mood and drunk enough, and had time from her career. We'd been together on the Amarillo American, I on the city desk, she as fashion editor and producer of a TV fashion series. She refused to think of marriage; career came first.

I let her drive my car; she'd always loved to drive. Pulling out of the parking lot, we passed her shining flyer again and the gazing crowd around it.

"It actually flies?" I asked. "With no wings?"

"No wings." My wonder amused her. "And I've stranger things to show you." One hand on the wheel, she slid the other arm around me. "But not tonight."

"Your disappearance?" Curiosity gnawed me. "It baffled the cops and got me suspected of doing you in. Can't you tell me anything?"

"Simple enough." She made a willowy shrug and drew me closer. "They'd seen me on TV and mailed an offer. They phoned that night and sent a taxi to pick me up."

"They?"

"They." Her soft laugh mocked me. "You'll be meeting them tomorrow."

At La Loba she devoured a rare sirloin, and finished mine. The salted margaritas made her drunk enough. She let me drive us to the Pioneer, where she had phoned for her reservation. The sari came off as I shut the door, and that night with her was one I hope I don't forget.

Awake next morning before she was, I showered, dressed, and turned the TV on, volume low. Watching, I forgot everything. An unknown object had appeared in the sky northwest of Amarillo. Something bigger and blacker than a storm cloud, so a rancher reported. Panic had spread from its shadow. Church services were canceled. The state police had ordered the whole county evacuated. A military aircraft from the Cannon Air Base in New Mexico had lost power and gone down, though the pilot glided away and ejected safely. A better description had come from the pilot of a spy plane that flew high above it.

"Biggest damn thing I ever saw." He looked jittery. "God knows what keeps it up or what it is or where it came from."

What his photos showed was a thick disk rather than any saucer shape. "At least a mile across," he said. "Maybe five hundred feet tall." Flat on top, it had a tall dome in the middle and strange structures towering all around the rim.

"I might have landed on it," he said. "If I'd dared."

Talimena woke, enchantingly nude. She glanced at the screen, waved a kiss at me, and went on to the bathroom.

"That thing?" I called after her, "You know what it is?"

"You'll see it," she said. "But first things first."

I sat riveted to the news till she came back, still slick and dripping from the shower, to snap the TV off and help me strip. The gold dust had not washed off. Back in bed with her, I was impotent for half a minute, till her own electric wonder overwhelmed the wonder in the sky.

Afterward, again a dangerous stranger in the silver sari and that great jewel glowing on her forehead, she awed me into silence on the way down to breakfast. Service was slow, even with only a handful of people in the dining room.

"The cook went home to be with his family," a badly rattled waitress told us. "The manager's in the kitchen."

The other diners stared at Talimena till the waitress turned a TV on. A breathless announcer was stammering his story of that enormous object sinking slowly lower as he ran clips of men on horseback herding cattle out from under it. A calmer voice came on.

"People used to laugh at the SETI fanatics, keeping their radio dishes cocked for voices they never heard from outer space, but a White House spokesman has now confirmed that the incredible object now on the ground in the Texas panhandle, is in fact a gigantic spacecraft.

"The state department has issued a white paper documenting that radio and TV contact has been established. The aliens are not quite human, but they do display humanoid characteristics. They claim to have come from a distant base to welcome Earth into what they call their united galaxy.

"They have invited government officials to come aboard to meet their leaders. President McMillan has been with his cabinet since midnight, and the Congress is now in emergency session. Delegations from Washington and the Texas state government are on their way.

"Updates—"

"Turn the damn thing off!" Talimena shouted at the little group standing around the TV. "That's enough for now."

A fat man turned to scowl at her, his mouth yawning to protest.

"Sit down." Her voice rose commandingly. The jewel was flashing blue. "Let's get on with breakfast."

He sat down.

Our first waitress had disappeared, but a flustered girl replaced her. Talimena ordered ham and eggs, which she attacked with an eager appetite.

"They did feed me well," she spoke between bites, "but it's nice to be back to things I always loved."

I had orange juice and coffee, and forgot them.

"Don't take it so hard," she tried to cheer me. "They're absolutely wonderful. You'll love them when you get to know them. The changes may seem difficult at first, but they've come to save us from ourselves."

"Can't you tell me?"

She laughed at me and nodded.

"I guess I've teased you long enough. They're the Su'kyan. An expansive race. They've colonized five hundred planets in our galactic sector. We're in great good luck to be next on the list."

"Su'kyan?"

She laughed at my effort to say the name, with its gliding tones and an odd click in the middle. She said it again, correcting me.

"A lovely language! They have perfect pitch, and the tones change to turn every word into music. Not that you'll ever speak it well. Not without the surgery I had to correct the human anatomy. With practice, though, you can get by."

She stood up to stop my questions and had me drive her back to the airport. I stopped in the terminal drive to let her out.

"Park," she said. "Come aboard the station with me."

She tipped the security guard with a crisp new hundred-dollar bill. He took the yellow tape from around her silver teardrop. A door dilated in the side of it. She beckoned me in and nestled into the seat beside me. From inside, its shell was transparent as glass. I saw no controls, but the jewel shimmered on her forehead and the field fell silently away. I dared another question.

"Without wings, how does it fly?"

"Antigravity." A sinuous, carefree shrug. "Back at the base, I heard a lecture on antigravity propulsion and how it collapses space-time for interstellar jumps. Nothing I understood, but I've seen it work."

I asked about the syndicate base.

"Far off, toward Orion. I had the agent show me our sun from there. So dim I could barely make it out."

My head whirling, I found no nerve to ask for more about the syndicate. The teardrop carried us so high that the sky turned darkly purple, then down again toward the arid Texas prairie, where the station shone under the morning sun like an impossibly vast silver coin.

"Big, isn't it?" She pointed, marveling like a child. "The new capital of Earth!"

She landed us on it, near the central dome. I followed her out, blinking at titanic strange constructions all around us. The oval door in the little teardrop shrank shut, and it took itself silently away toward something like a hangar at the edge of the deck. I saw half a dozen helicopters lined up there, three with American military markings. Human figures were leaving the others, lugging tripods and cameras.

"Network people," she said. "Invited aboard to broadcast a historic event. We're lucky to be here."

Terrified into silence, I stood watching, trying to imagine what the aliens meant for us, till her jewel burned blue. An arched doorway was opening in the silvery dome. She led me up a ramp toward a platform below it. People were appearing there.

People? I squinted against the sun to see them.

"They look human." Dazed, I spoke to myself. "Almost."

"Of course." She nodded. "Though maybe not quite so human as they look. Galactic citizens differ a lot. The syndicate is a Su'kyan project. They try to pick worlds where the natives resemble them. It's pretty necessary, if we're going to live together."

I followed her up a ramp, but she stopped me at the top and went on to the aliens. Lean handsome beings, gold-dusted like she was, the full-busted women as tall as the men, all scantily clad in a rainbow of saris.

"Ty'roon!"

She called the leader's name and ran to meet him.

Smiling an almost human smile, he sang something that must have been a greeting, caught her in his gold-dusted arms, and thrust out a long scarlet tongue to lick her nose. She looked up to lick his, caught his arm and led him toward me.

I didn't get their words, but he smiled again and leaned to crush my hand in a double-thumbed grip.

The camera crews were climbing the ramp. A party of humans came behind, staring at everything around them. I recognized the governor of Texas, a raw-boned man in alligator boots and a high white hat, almost as tall as Ty'roon. Talimena introduced Ty'roon to a thin little bald man in a pin-stripe suit, the American Secretary of State.

The film crews bustled to arrange them in two groups, aliens facing humans, Ty'roon and Talimena standing between them. Ty'roon addressed the human leaders, his voice rising and falling in what really was a sort of eerie music, the huge gem on his forehead shimmering in time to it. Talimena translated.

"I speak to the people of Earth." Her jewel was blazing, and her pealing voice was strange with his alien accent. "You will soon know me well. I am Ty'roon Ak'narth, Agent of Earth. I inform you now that your planet has been purchased by the Ninth Sector Syndicate, which is duly chartered under the laws of the Galactic Union. As the agent of the syndicate, answering only to them, I am vested with full authority on all matters related to the planet Earth."

He spoke again, while Talimena listened. A man with a still camera crept warily forward, lights flashing. The statesmen were stricken dumb till the secretary grabbed for his muffled cell phone.

"You have no grounds for concern." Ty'roon had fallen silent, and Talimena translated again. "Instead, we bring you cause for great rejoicing. Our surveyors have found your planet utterly dysfunctional. You suffer from genocidal warfare. Terrorism unrestrained. Economic breakdowns. Famines and diseases. You've abandoned your religions and forgotten your ethics. You've lost faith even in your own primitive technologies. You've fallen close to race suicide."

Empty excuses, I thought. Propaganda designed to cover the invasion. The governor scowled at Ty'roon and muttered at the secretary.

"We bring your salvation," Talimena's accents echoed the invader's lilt. "We welcome you into galactic civilization. We bring you a new age of world harmony and peace, world security, liberation from your crippling barbarism."

Pale and quivering with panic, the secretary shrilled into his cell phone. The governor grew louder, red in the face and yelling at Ty'roon.

"You say you own us?" His clenched fist lifted. "What the hell does that mean?"

"The agent means exactly what he says." Talimena answered blandly. "Existing authorities may remain in place, at least for now, so long as they are faithful to the syndicate."

"How the blazing hell—"

The agent sang louder, his gem blazing red. Talimena spoke when he paused, smiling benignly at the apoplectic governor.

"He begs you to understand our landing as a rescue mission. The scouts reported fatal failings in your social system, especially your dependence on disease, war, and famine to control your alarming population overgrowth. Agent Ty'roon promises to end your suicidal warfare, to rid the planet of crime and terror, to control disease, to provide masses of your people with useful employment, adequate housing, nutrition, and sanitation. In short, to insure the survival of your race."

The secretary pushed his cell phone at an aide.

"Mr. Ty'roon—" The name came out as a squeaky stammer, and he tried again. "Ty—Ty'roon. I have conferred with our national leaders in Washington.

Our government regards your uninvited landing here as a violation of American territory. We demand the immediate removal of your craft and yourselves."

Talimena translated and sang the answer.

"Your words have been heard. Your insolence is forgiven, but your request is denied."

The secretary gabbled at his cell phone and shoved it back at the aide. He had to look up to the agent.

"President McMillan requires—" His voice became a husky squeak. He gulped and resumed, "requires your departure within twelve hours, Earth time, under pain of military action."

"Your words are heard," Talimena crooned again. "Agent Ty'roon advises that your primitive armaments offer us no credible threat. He begs you to avoid any reckless action that might result in destruction or loss of life to your own people."

"The hell he says!" the governor exploded. "Tell the bastard"

The agent was turning away.

"He has concluded the audience." Talimena raised a shining hand to silence the governor and turned to the secretary. "Your government will be informed when he has further orders."

Ty'roon and his party went back into the dome. The secretary and the governor huddled with their aides and led them back down the ramp. The camera crews gathered their equipment and followed. Trying to contain my own boiling emotion, I stood watching with Talimena till the helicopters had stuttered into the air.

"A great event, don't you think?" Elation lifted her voice. "A privilege to see."

"You—" I gulped back the words I wanted to use. "Traitor! You've sold us out. Sold your soul. Get me out of here."

"I'm sorry, Clint." The jewel had dimmed, and her regret seemed sincere. "Though I guess you've had no time to understand. If you left the station now, you'd be dead in a week."

"Huh?" Her solemn tone had chilled me. "Dead?"

"The Su'kyan carry malignant viruses and bacteria they've picked up on a hundred planets. Harmless to them, because they've developed immunities and vaccines. It's their nanoform vaccigenes that give us the golden tint.

"To you, however—"

"I don't care." I wanted to strike her. "I'll take my chances."

"Do you want to die?"

The question turned the cyclopean structures and machines that towered all around me into a nightmare jungle, the busy aliens to a swarm of malignant yellow insects, turned Talimena to the demon priestess who had conjured up the vision. For a moment it seemed too dreadful to be real, but it refused to go away. I took a long breath and said I didn't want to die.

"I hope you don't." I cringed from the arm she draped around me. "You'll have to stay aboard for your inoculations. They will take several days."

Helpless, I let her take me down into the station and on through lofty hallways floored with moving walks that glowed in varied colors to show where they led. The elevators were simply pits with zero gravity, where she took my hand and controlled our motion with the shimmer of her jewel. Her suite was huge, its furnishings so strange I felt afraid to touch anything.

She laughed at my dread.

"Don't mind the Su'kyan," she said. "You'll find them gentle and generous," she said. "Certainly to their friends."

She gave me a kind of chair that shaped itself to fit me and controlled my weight with a twisted knob. She got me a drink that came through a little window that opened in the wall. Something blood-red and tangily sweet. A bracer I needed.

"Why are they here?" I asked when my wits had begun to recover. "What are they going to do with us?"

"Ty'roon's a planner." Her own drink came out of the wall. "Here's to the future!" She clinked her glass against mine. "The new future of Earth!"

Uneasily, I asked what it would be.

"Ty'roon's an entrepreneur. He's making a place for Earth in the complex trading system of the sector. Its future will be agricultural. He has studied the climate and the soils and the native crops. His grand economic plan for the planet may surprise you."

She sipped her drink and let me wait.

"Marijuana," she said. "Cocaine. Morphine and heroin. Tobacco, of course. Even tea and coffee. In general, all the poisons that our plants have evolved to kill the insects that ate them."

She grinned at my dismay.

"The scouts learned to enjoy them," she said. "Even more than humans do. And with no ill effects, what with their different metabolisms."

Her jewel flickered at the wall and the slot opened again with a tray of small yellow cakes on the shelf.

"With no breakfast, you must be hungry." She handed one to me. "They won't hurt you," she said. "They make them for me. Their own grub made me sick. Nearly killed me. Their chemists have come up with stuff to fit the human metabolism."

Still too badly shaken to think of eating, I did try one of the cakes. The taste was flat and dry, slightly bitter.

"You see why I wanted a steak." She laughed when I put the cake back on the tray. "Drink up, anyhow. Alcohol is alcohol for everybody. And don't look so appalled. Ty'roon has a grand plan for Earth. His engineers are already at work on climatic modifications to reclaim the deserts and warm the tundras. He'll be able to employ several billion people."

"A drug farm!" I sipped my drink and looked away from the alluring contours under the sari, trying to get a grasp on the Su'kyan and the world ahead. "The whole planet?"

"Most of it. There must be food crops, of course, for the workers."

The chair reached a mechanical arm to take my drink when I moved to put it down.

"These diseases?" Trying to think, I watched her face. "Can you vaccinate everybody?"

"The workers will be well protected."

"Just the workers? What about everybody else?"

"Too bad for them." She shrugged regretfully. "Ty'roon had the engineers consider reservations on Greenland and Antarctica, but the climates wouldn't do, even with modification. They found no available space for the population overload."

"Your good friend Ty'roon" I recoiled from her golden smile. "He'll take care of his slaves and murder everybody else? Billions of innocent people!"

"Too bad if they die." She shrugged. "But you're unfair to him. He does have his duties to the syndicate, but he's kind and generous. He's been wonderful to me."

Her adoring tone was a needle through my heart.

"You love him?"

"I do." Her face had lit. "He's so splendid! So strong, so handsome, so tender. He knows everything. He'd do anything for me."

I sat blinking at her from the strange chair, aching with thoughts of all our nights together. She gazed away with an odd expression and turned back with a frown of regret.

"But sex—" She made a face. "We tried, but the experiment was unsatisfactory for him and painful for me." Smiling, she reached to touch my arm. "That's why I need you."

"I can't believe—" I shrank from her gold-nailed hand. "They've turned you to a monster!"

"To you, perhaps." She had flushed beneath the golden tan, but her voice stayed oddly quiet. "It all depends on who you are."

"So who are you?"

"A Cherokee." Her voice rose sharply. "My father used to brood about all you whites did to us. The diseases you brought us. The smallpox blankets you gave us. The treaties you broke. The hunting grounds you stole. The whole nations you exterminated."

She stabbed a golden finger at me. "Can you blame me?"

I swallowed hard and found no ready answer.

"You found my nation with a high stone-age culture. We had towns, built log cabins, wove blankets, made pottery, grew corn and beans and squash. We had our culture, our own religion.

"My father never forgot how you destroyed us. "Your traders cheated us. You tricked us into treaties that you never kept. You drove us off our lands in Georgia and the Carolinas.

"In spite of that, we tried to get along. We formed a government like yours. We learned your ways, adopted your religion. We invented a syllabary to write our language. We published our own newspaper.

"My father told me what happened when you found gold on our land. You passed the Indian Removal Act. Your great President Andrew Jackson ignored the courts when they tried to protect us. We were evicted. Your settlers plundered and burned the homes we left behind.

"Your great general Winfield Scott marched us west to Oklahoma in a dreadful winter, on foot and starving. He never let us stop to rest or let the sick recover. We were four months on the way. Four thousand died. We call that death march the "The Trail of Tears."

She shook her head, with a sad little smile.

"I think you will find Ty'roon and the Su'kyan kinder than you were."

SECTION FOUR

AN HISTORICAL PERSPECTIVE

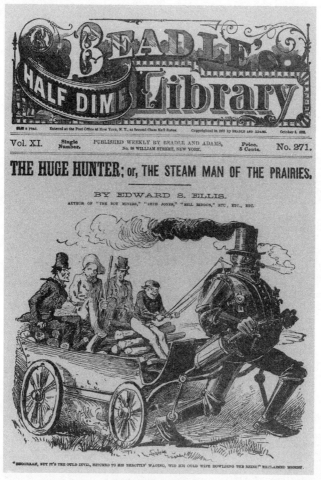

Taking their lead from Edward S. Ellis's *The Steam Man of the Prairies* (originally published in 1868 and reprinted on several occasions from 1869 to 1904), the dime novel serial adventures of Frank Reade (1876 to 1904) foreshadowed the Tom Swift novels begun in 1910.

HOW SCIENCE FICTION GOT ITS NAME

SAM MOSKOWITZ

N O MAN WITH ANY REAL KNOWLEDGE OF THE LITERARY WORLD and only a diminishing percentage of the general public any longer misunderstands the term "science fiction." As a field of literature, science fiction still lacks a satisfactory definition, but it does not suffer from the absence of a name.

Since no man has ever stepped forward to claim the origin of the term "science fiction," the logical thing to assume is that like Topsy, it just grew.

It grew all right, but considerable research made to ascertain the earliest date of its use as a separate term and how it developed reveals that it also had a gardener.

When Jules Verne started the first big wave of popularity for scientific speculative adventure with *Five Weeks in a Balloon*, published in France in 1863, the French publishers and the general press created a term for such stories: VOYAGES EXTRAORDINAIRES.

"Extraordinary voyages" became synonymous with the name Jules Verne, covering both what we consider his science fiction and his voyages.* His self-acknowledged imitators, cashing in on the popularity of such great tales as *Twenty Thousand Leagues Under the Sea* and *Voyage to the Center of the Earth*, were forced to call their works VOYAGES EXCENTRIQUES.

In England, Verne's stories were dubbed SCIENTIFIC ROMANCES, and the term became so entrenched that when C. A. Hinton wrote a series of semi-fictional scientific speculations as to the nature of the fourth dimension and other imaginative subjects in 1888, they were published under the title of *Scientific Romances*.

The rise of H. G. Wells with his *The Time Machine*, *The War of the Worlds*, and *When the Sleeper Wakes*, towards the end of the 19th century, found him inheriting that term along with the frequent use of SCIENTIFIC FANTASIES to describe some of his work that seemed too scientific to be fantasy and too borderline to be scientifically plausible. SCIENCE FANTASY is still commonly used today to describe work of that nature.

"Scientific romance," as a term, lingered to as recent a date as 1930, but it was already on the downgrade at the turn of the century as "romance" began to be thought of as love and kisses first and unusual adventure secondarily, if at all.

The need for some definite term to apply to scientific stories became increasingly acute as publications regularly featuring them became established in the United States. Frank Tousey's Frank Reade Library, begun in 1892, published stories which were referred to as THE JULES VERNE TYPE, written by Luis Senarens, a 16-year-old youngster disguised as "Noname." The inventions and adventures of Frank Reade ran for 192 weekly issues until the charge was brought against them that they were ruining the minds of the younger generation. As a sop to misguided fevers of the time, Frank Tousey discontinued the series.

---

*cf. Anthony Boucher, *Jules Verne: Voyagiste*, F&SF, September, 1956.

Frank Munsey then carried the ball for those who preferred their entertainment in the tradition of Jules Verne. When he changed the teen-age *Golden Argosy* into *Argosy* in 1896 and adopted a more adult formula, he began to use such stories with increasing frequency. As he launched other adventure magazines later, such as *Scrap Book*, *All-Story*, *Munsey* and *Cavalier*, fanciful tales of science became a regular part of the reading fare presented by each.

Since it was apparent that such fiction had a loyal following who swore by their literary choice as a devout man justifies his religion, it soon became imperative that some term be created to let those readers know their "poison" was on tap and thereby insure their patronage. At first such tales were referred to as OFF-TRAIL STORIES, but this was too all-inclusive and could also mean anything from a story told in the second person to a western yarn with a Christmas setting. To solve the problem, *Argosy* created the term DIFFERENT STORIES. For years, when the simple word "different" was carried in announcing a story, the connoisseurs knew what was coming.

Another term often found in the readers' departments of Munsey magazines was IMPOSSIBLE STORIES. That term received some use up until about 1920 when it all but disappeared.

Still, editors of Munsey publications found that "different" was not specific enough. It was awkward to state in every issue that "we will continue to present 'different stories.' " Therefore they evolved a new term that received widespread use throughout the publishing world, and in the early twenties was by far the most popular single reference to the genre, even though everything else under the sun kept popping up. The new term was PSEUDO-SCIENTIFIC STORIES, and they might still be using it today if it hadn't been for Hugo Gernsback.

Hugo Gernsback came to this country from Luxembourg as a very young man. He founded the first radio store in the United States, issued the first radio parts catalog, and built and sold the first home commercial (wireless) radio set. In 1908, when he was only 24 years old, he began publishing *Modern Electrics*, the world's first radio magazine. In 1909, he was first in America to use the word *television* in a technical article in that publication. Indeed, he was so impatient with the slow progress of science as compared to the powers of his imagination that he wrote a novel of the future which he serialized in his magazine, titled *Ralph 124C 41+*, in which he predicted everything from night baseball to space travel, and, most fabulous of all, though the year was only 1911, diagramed radar and described how it would work!

This love of scientific literature stayed with Gernsback, and as the title of his publication changed from *Modern Electrics* to *Electrical Experimenter* and finally to *Science and Invention*, he began using stories of that nature so frequently that by 1922 he was running two or more an issue.

There was, however, a real difference between the type of science story Gernsback ran and that run in *Argosy*. Gernsback *insisted* that the basic tenets of each story be scientifically accurate. Therefore the term popularly employed at the time, "pseudo-scientific," was abhorrent to him. He had to find a new term that would have a more dignified connotation.

The problem of devising a new term was brought to a head when it was decided to make up a cover for *Science and Invention* composed of a number of miniature make-believe magazine covers and logos, each showing a different department or regular feature of the magazine. Among the contrived cover logos were Popular Astronomy, Motor Hints, Wrinkles, Recipes and Formulas, etc. Since two science stories were used in every issue, this was too important a part of the magazine to be excluded. The result was SCIENTIFIC FICTION, probably the very first use of that particular term, and most certainly the first time it was used prominently.

The use of the term itself also presaged the creation of a publication of that type by crystallizing the name into a magazine cover design on the front cover of the December, 1922 issue of *Science and Invention*.

All science tales in Gernsback publications from that time on were referred to as "scientific fiction," with infrequent lapses into SCIENTIFIC STORIES. It is important to note that the use of the word "fiction" instead of the more commonly used "stories" is the element that gave "scientific fiction" as well as the later "science fiction" the distinction that won them popularity.

Since its metamorphosis as an adult magazine, a respectable portion of *Argosy*'s readership had been made up of followers of fantastic literature. There were many other good adventure magazines on the stands, such as *Blue Book, Popular, Top Notch, Adventure, Complete Stories*, and *Short Stories*, but *Argosy*, which featured the best and the most so-called "pseudo-scientific stories," enjoyed the top sales.

As a general fiction magazine, *Argosy* rarely ran more than one such story an issue, and occasionally it had a lapse and did not run any.

Gernsback's *Science and Invention* regularly ran two and sometimes more. In addition, its popular science features were so speculative in character as to virtually qualify as prophetic stories in non-fiction form. On top of this, its frequent references attesting to the accuracy of the science in the stories gave them such an air of respectability and prescience as to prove irresistible to devotees.

Undoubtedly *Argosy* was losing a portion of its fantastic story following to *Science and Invention*—all the more so since *Argosy* highlights "pseudo-scientific story" authors, such as George Allan England and Ray Cummings, were being featured in *Science and Invention*, in addition to its own crew of "scientific fiction" writers.

The importance Gernsback placed upon recruiting readership from itinerant science story lovers became vigorously apparent with the August, 1923 issue of *Science and Invention*. That issue contained six stories, and emblazoned on the cover in type 1½ inches high were the words: SCIENTIFIC FICTION NUMBER. The full-color cover, painted by Howard V. Brown, who later became a cover illustrator for Street and Smith's *Astounding Stories*, featured a space-suited figure from a scene in G. Peyton Wertenbaker's serial, *The Man From the Atom*.

That *Argosy* was well aware of the competition it was getting, particularly the appeal of the term "scientific fiction" with its promise of scientific accuracy, was soon evidenced. The scientific novel, *The Radio Man* by Ralph Milne Farley, which began in the June 28, 1924 issue of *Argosy-All Story* magazine, was prefaced by the equivalent of a full-page editorial stressing the fact that this story marked a departure in *Argosy*, since it was written by a scientist and all the science contained therein was scientifically accurate! On the cover this story was called A SCIENTIFIC ADVENTURE.

It is not precisely certain at what point *Argosy* first used Gernsback's term "scientific fiction," but by the September 14, 1929 issue, in a biography of Ray Cummings, popular fiction writer specializing in scientific adventures, the editor of *Argosy* used "scientific fiction" three times and other terms not at all!

Argosy and *Science and Invention* were not, however, the only magazines active on the "scientific fiction" scene at the time. *Weird Tales* magazine was founded in

March, 1923. Its editor, Edwin Baird, ran science stories along with tales of witches, goblins, ghouls, vampires and werewolves. In the First Anniversary Issue of that publication, dated May-June-July, 1924, Mr. Baird informed his readers that *Weird Tales* was dedicated to printing two primary classifications of fiction. One was the weird tale with all its ramifications of distorted psychology and horror. The other was the HIGHLY IMAGINATIVE STORY, which was Baird's term for what Gernsback called "scientific fiction."

Within a few months, however, *Weird Tales* had adopted *Argosy*'s term of "pseudo-scientific stories" on its contents page. It is of parenthetical interest to note that "pseudoscientific" was often used as a single word by *Argosy*.

Since the earliest days, a characteristic of the reader of this literature has been his enthusiasm for writing letters to the editor. He writes out of all proportion to his numbers. New publishers of science fiction magazines, accustomed to getting one or two letters a month for their other pulps, have been astonished to find their magazine getting from 50 to 200 an issue. Such letters to *Science and Invention* undoubtedly encouraged Gernsback to attempt an all "scientific fiction" magazine—as though he needed any particular encouragement.

In 1925, Hugo Gernsback mailed thousands of circulars to subscribers to *Science and Invention*, announcing that he was about to launch a new magazine dealing with the worlds of tomorrow, interplanetary travel and scientific invention in the tradition of Jules Verne and H. G. Wells. To create a name for the new magazine Hugo Gernsback contracted "scientific fiction" into SCIENTIFICTION and projected that as the title of the publication.

The response was slightly less than enthusiastic. Market research would have revealed what is generally known today, that followers of fantastic fiction of all types are in a large part collectors and dislike subscribing for fear their copy will be damaged in transit. Secondly, they cannot bear the thought of having to wait for a publication delayed in the mails when it is plainly visible on the newsstand. Present-day publishers, aware of these facts, often induce additional subscriptions by promising that copies will be mailed flat in sturdy envelopes so as to arrive *ahead* of newsstand date. Gernsback had no way of knowing this.

Feeling that perhaps the magazine name *Scientifiction* lacked general appeal, Gernsback waited a year and then, without asking anyone, set the title *Amazing Stories* down on the newsstands of the United States.

Though the magazine was *Amazing Stories*, the sub-title that ran on the editorial page read: "The Magazine of Scientifiction." The editorial of the first issue was devoted to telling readers just what "scientifiction" was. The editorial of the third issue called the readers "scientifiction fans." Shortly, the spine of the magazine carried a dual legend: *Amazing Stories: Scientifiction*. A contest was sponsored to find an artistic symbol for "scientifiction." The term "scientifiction" was used everywhere in the magazine and pushed by every promotional device at Gernsback's call (which included one of New York's earliest radio stations, WRNY) to popularize it as *the* term when referring to tales of spacesuits and rayguns.

The new publication was an immediate success. After a few issues it achieved a newsstand sale of 100,000. This figure, for a 25¢ publication of specialized appeal in the twenties, was considered quite a respectable one.

So fine a response indicated that a ready-made audience existed for "scientifiction." Where did it come from?

Some came from the ranks of *Science and Invention*. Most were recruited at the expense of *Argosy*, and a sizable number from *Weird Tales*.

The latter publication, now edited by Farnsworth Wright, who had purchased a controlling interest in the company, recognized the threat instantly.

Though afflicted with a form of cerebral palsy as an after-effect of sleeping sickness contracted during World War I—an illness which left him with an involuntary shake and shiver which could have made him the butt of grim humor, since he edited a magazine calculated to scare the daylights out of its readers—Wright brilliantly managed his publication through trying times. He discovered and encouraged dozens of authors who are today ranking names in the literary field and eventually became one of the most beloved and respected figures in pulp circles.

He recognized that Gernsback's *Amazing Stories* was directly competing with him, since it could easily siphon off readers that read *Weird Tales* primarily for its scientific stories. A still greater threat was the term "scientifiction" with its connotation of literary respectability that by implication wooed the reader with the thought: "If it isn't scientifiction it can't be scientifically accurate."

The first issue of *Amazing Stories* was dated April, 1926. The June, 1926 issue of *Weird Tales* carried a two-page editorial by Wright informing his readers that "pseudo-scientific stories" was a misnomer for the tales of science carried in his magazine. He stressed the point that there was a strong basis of science in all the science stories published in his magazine.

Wright knew he had to find a new term, and fast. The term had to have the word *science* in it, but it would not be prefaced by *pseudo*, which meant fake. Neither could the new term be "scientific fiction" or "science stories" alone, because his readership was divided into two factions. One wanted all "pseudo-science stories" eliminated and only weird material published. The other bemoaned the fact that too few stories of this type were being published. To make them both happy, Wright hit upon the combination WEIRD-SCIENTIFIC STORIES. This he used for the first time in the July, 1926 issue, announcing a forthcoming "weird-scientific story" by Marion Heidt Mimms, titled "The Chair." "Pseudo-scientific stories" was dropped for good. The implication was that while the magazine would continue to print bigger and better science stories, in which the science would be accurate, they be weird to boot!

This was the status of the field as far as the use of terms was concerned, up until the end of the decade. Gernsback used "scientifiction" in all of his publications, which included *Amazing Stories, Amazing Stories Quarterly, Science and Invention*, and *Radio News*. (It is worth noting that Gernsback took a flyer at the world's first television magazine, *Television News*, in 1927, which he published for two years.) *Argosy* gradually discarded "different stories" and "pseudo-scientific stories" and in serious discussion adopted Gernsback's earlier term of "scientific fiction." *Weird Tales* grimly held to its own term "weird-scientific."

Oddly enough, the last use of the term created by *Argosy*, "different stories," may not have been by *Argosy* at all, since *Mind Magic Magazine*, in its June, 1931 issue, announced a Ralph Milne Farley story scheduled for its next number as a "different" story.

In 1929, Hugo Gernsback lost control of the Experimenter Publishing Corp. and of *Amazing Stories*. Though the Editor-in-Chief position was nominally held by Arthur H. Lynch, editorial supervision of the publication passed into the hands of Dr. T. O'Connor Sloane, son-in-law of Thomas A. Edison, and a bearded octogenarian whose major claim to fame was the invention of the self-recording photometer, a device for recording the illuminating power of gas. His imagination also departed with the gas-lit era, for one of his favorite pastimes was to chide the childish notions of his readers that space travel would ever be possible!

Sloane had formerly been employed by Gernsback in the capacity of Associate Editor of *Amazing Stories*. In his first editorial in the May, 1929 issue, Sloane reverted to the use of the original Gernsback term "scientific fiction." The editorial page still bore the subtitle "The Magazine of Scientifiction" and the word "scientifiction" stayed on the backstrip of the magazine, but the spell was broken — for the first time a term other than "scientifiction" was used in an all-science-story magazine!

Between leaving his old company and organizing a new one, Gernsback left scarcely a thirty-day lapse. The initial publication of his new company was *Science Wonder Stories*, and the first issue of that magazine was dated June, 1929.

The real distinction that accrues to Science Wonder Stories, *however, was that it was the first publication in history to use the actual term* SCIENCE FICTION *in its pages.*

Technically, the term was first professionally used in Hugo Gernsback's editorial, "Science Wonder Stories," in the first issue, dated June but published in May, 1929. Actually, it is used as a matter of policy throughout the entire magazine, even down to letters in the readers' columns.

Though this marked the first use of "science fiction" in a publication, it did not denote the first use of the term in a chronological historical sense. That distinction also goes to Gernsback, who wrote a form letter over his signature in 1929, which was mailed to former subscribers of *Amazing Stories* and *Science and Invention*, announcing the new magazine and offering $50 for the best letter on the subject: "What Science Fiction Means To Me."

Among those receiving honorable mention for replying to that letter were today's famous science fiction authors Edward E. Smith, Ph.D. and Jack Williamson. They were certainly unaware of the fact that they were among the earliest human beings in history to use the term "science fiction" in any manner!

A careful searching of the six-point type of the readers' letters in all the issues of *Amazing Stories* before that date, and careful perusal of every other publication in any way connected with the publication of fantastic literature, fails to reveal the use of the words "science fiction" anywhere, even inadvertently, before the June, 1929 issue of *Science Wonder Stories*.

When this fact was brought home to him, Gernsback recalled that he had invented the new term to have something different from his former publication. "Scientifiction," through his own efforts, was inextricably associated with *Amazing Stories* (which he no longer published) and no other publication.

So the term "science fiction" came into existence, so quietly that its origin was hardly noted at the time and has been almost forgotten, even by the man who created it.

Since Gernsback did not beat the drums for the general adoption of the term "science fiction," how and under what conditions did it come to be universally accepted?

"Science fiction" (without the hyphen) was used throughout all of Gernsback's science fiction magazines as a matter of policy. At that time he had more such magazines than any other publisher, following *Science Wonder Stories* with *Air*

Wonder Stories, *Science Wonder Stories Quarterly*, and *Scientific Detective Monthly*, in addition to a group of booklets called *Science Fiction Series* and an attempt at paperbound books known as *Science Fiction Classics*.

In late 1929, another magazine entered the field of tales of space and time. This was *Astounding Stories of Super Science*, the first issue of which was dated January, 1930. Here was recorded the first major use of the term SUPER SCIENCE as a title for the genre. Would *Astounding* now attempt to popularize it?

The fourth (April, 1930) issue supplied the answer. In the first readers' column, titled "Reader's Corner," Harry Bates (*Astounding*'s initial editor and the man who later went on to write the story upon which the moving picture *The Day the Earth Stood Still* was based) handed Gernsback a quick decision. The words "science fiction" were used exclusively in his introductory notes.

Since Gernsback's departure, *Amazing Stories* had shown a tendency to swing away from "scientifiction," the term which Gernsback had made synonymous with the magazine, to "scientific fiction." This trend continued in a new book review column, "In the Realm of Books," handled by the science fiction collector C. A. Brandt, which carried the subtitle, "Mostly Scientific Fiction." This column, inaugurated in the September, 1929 issue of *Amazing Stories*, had the distinction of being the first book review column ever to appear in a science fiction magazine.

(Today's science fiction readers, aware of the fact that science fiction books have been published in quantity only for the past ten years, may wonder what Brandt found to review. The fact is that a minor boom in the publication of science fiction books took place in this period, partially as a result of the mushroom expansion of magazine science fiction during 1929. C. A. Brandt did not limit his selections to science fiction alone, but also would review good weird and fantasy material. In addition, he read many languages and reviewed new science fiction books that appeared in Germany, France and Italy, as well as the United States and Great Britain. The first two books reviewed were *The Greatest Adventure* by John Taine and *The Great Weird Stories*, edited by Arthur Neale. These were followed in quick succession by reviews of *The Light in the Sky* by Herbert Clock and Eric Boetzel, *Beware After Dark!* edited by T. Everett Harré, *Electropolis* by Otfrid von Hanstein, *The Earth Tube* by Gawain Edwards, *The Maracot Deep* by Arthur Conan Doyle, and *The Day of the Brown Horde* by Richard Tooker.)

In this column, as well as in his blurbs, sub-titles and cover listings, editor Sloane first employed the term "scientific fiction" and then, starting with his readers' columns, gradually and painstakingly adopted the uniform use of "science fiction" throughout the magazine. The process took three years.

Farnsworth Wright did not cotton to "science fiction" until 1934, when his ever-critical circulation problem forced him to let the public in on the fact that "science fiction" as well as "weird-scientific" stories could be found in his magazine. He still continued to use "weird-scientific" occasionally until he left the publication in 1939.

Though the term "science fiction" obtained general recognition in the field, no magazine carried it as the title or as part of the title of the publication.

The first publications to break the precedent were not professional journals, but semi-professional efforts published by the fans of science fiction themselves.

Among those fans were Jerry Siegel and Joe Shuster, who were to rise from their initial humble efforts to become the original creators of the comic strip character Superman. They published, out of Cleveland, a mimeographed fiction magazine titled purely and simply *Science Fiction*. The October, 1932 date of the first issue (the magazine lasted five numbers) lost them the distinction of being the first publication to use "science fiction" in the title by one month. That honor goes to the *Science Fiction Digest*, a printed monthly combination science fiction fan magazine and trade journal, whose first issue was dated September, 1932.

More than five years were to pass before the term was used in a professional title. Eventually, *Astounding Stories*, with John W. Campbell, Jr., in editorial control, changed its title to *Astounding Science-Fiction* with its March, 1938 number. The hyphen was kept in the title until November, 1946, when it was silently dropped.

One year later, Blue Ribbon Publications rang up another "first" by publishing the initial newsstand magazine to be called simply *Science Fiction*. The first issue was dated March, 1939.

Primary credit for the introduction and spread of "science fiction" as a proper name for the genre in non-fantasy markets belongs to the writers' magazines, such as *Author & Journalist*, *Writer's Digest*, *The Writer*, etc. Editors publishing in the tradition of Verne and Wells called their medium "science fiction" when sending editorial requirements to the writers' magazines. Such requirements were published as received. In that way, the entire publishing field came to refer to this new branch of magazine publishing as "the science fiction field."

Acceptance of the term, even publication of any significant quantity of science fiction material, was much slower in the book world. Pocket Books, Inc., broke the ice when they permitted Donald A. Wollheim, a former editor, writer and fan of science fiction, to talk them into publishing *The Pocket Book of Science-Fiction* in 1943.

A similar welcome in hardcover book-publishing had to wait until after World War II, when Crown issued, in 1946, *The Best in Science Fiction*, edited by Groff Conklin, a real estate expert who took to science fiction as an avocation.

The virility of the term "science fiction" is no better illustrated than in the manner in which it has taken hold in foreign nations. In England, Scotland, Canada and Australia, "science fiction" is quite frequently part of the title of science fiction magazines. The expression is equally popular in France where one publication was titled simply *Science Fiction Magazine* and where *Fiction* continues to spread the gospel by drawing for the main part from *The Magazine of Fantasy and Science Fiction* for its content.* The Dutch magazine *Planeet* ran the subtitle "science fiction" as does the Swedish periodical *Hapna!* The German usage of UTOPISCHE ROMANE (Utopian novels) to describe tales of space and time has bowed to "science fiction," largely due to the missionary work of the fan groups in that country.

The popular terms that preceded "science fiction" in this country died slowly. They died hard. But they died!

After purchasing *Wonder Stories* from Gernsback, Standard Magazines changed its title to *Thrilling Wonder Stories* and slanted it towards a younger group of readers. In time *Thrilling Wonder Stories* begat *Startling Stories*, which, in its first issue, dated January, 1939, ran on its spine the slogan: "The Best in Scientifiction." This it continued to do up until January, 1953, when trimming the pulp edges necessitated redesigning the publication, and the slogan was dropped.

That marked the end of the prominent usage of the word "scientifiction" except for a technicality. An abbreviation of "scientifiction" had been devised which

---

*By some inexplicable phenomenon of French linguistics, *la science* is feminine, as is *la fiction*; *le science fiction* is masculine. —A.B.

achieved widespread popularity. It was STF (pronounced *stef*), which has remained in common usage among science fiction lovers until today.

However, an abbreviation of "science fiction," SF, is beginning to make inroads and may eventually supplant it. England saw the publication in 1955 of a book edited by Edmund Crispin, titled *Best sf* (lower case, no periods). The author's use of the full term "science fiction" inside the book indicates that both he and the publishers felt the abbreviation was commonly accepted. Judith Merril, in a 1956 American anthology, also used the contraction, but hyphenated it in the title of her volume *S-F.*

Oddly enough, technical difficulties may have contributed to the demise of "scientifiction." Unindoctrinated printers and copyreaders insist upon changing it to "scientification"—as, for instance, the late Joseph Henry Jackson learned when, at the instance of Anthony Boucher, he attempted to popularize the term in the early 1940's in the book department of the San Francisco *Chronicle*. Regularly it appeared as "scientification," and the *Chronicle* shortly shifted to the use of "science fiction."*

The term "scientific fiction" merely faded away until today its use assumes an antiquarian aspect.

Similarly, when a 1949 cover of *The Writer's Monthly* featured a review of "pseudo science" publication requirements, many of the newer writers weren't quite sure what was being referred to, so anachronistic had the term become.

"Super science" as an appellation for the field was never a strong contender as "the" term. Despite the distinction of being a title twice, first for Popular's *Super Science Stories* and now for Crestwood's *Super Science Fiction*, its primary function is as a label for the more far-fetched forms of "space opera" dealing with movements of entire solar systems and disruptions on a galactic scale in the grand tradition of Edward E. Smith.

Williams and Wilkins attempted to establish FANTASCIENCE in 1934, when it published John Taine's novel *Before the Dawn*, but outside of being used in the title of Robert A. Madle's famous old fan magazine *Fantascience Digest* and at the head of a few fan columns, it never caught hold.**

If there is anything left to argue about, it is probably whether "science fiction" should be joined with a hyphen. When Hugo Gernsback reentered the science fiction field briefly with *Science-Fiction Plus* in 1953, the hyphen was deliberately inserted in "science-fiction" everywhere in the magazine to establish a different style. Production costs on this slick-paper experiment with five-color covers and no advertisements sank it after only seven issues, so it didn't last long enough to have any real influence. As recently as its May 12, 1956 number, however, *The Saturday Review* was still hyphenating "science-fiction."

For better or for worse, whether one likes it or not, accounts of high interplanetary adventure, jaunts into the future or past, visits to other dimensions or stories of the acquisition of superhuman physical and mental powers are tales of "science fiction." In the foreseeable future, no other term is likely to replace it.

---

*One more instance: The typist of Mr. Moskowitz' manuscript has almost invariably written "scientification" . . . and I wonder what F&SF's printers will have done.—A.B.

**The short-lived (1954–1955) Italian edition of F&SF was titled *Fantascienza*.—A.B.

SECTION FIVE
LISTS AND BIBLIOGRAPHIES

FANTASY AND SCIENCE FICTION FILM AND TELEVISION

For further information on Fantasy and Science Fiction movies, refer also to the bibliography of film studies books entitled "Studies of Nonprint F/SF." Books such as those from the Videohound series, the Overlook Encyclopedia of Film series, and Leonard Maltin provide important detailed information about Fantasy and Science Fiction motion pictures. Be warned, however, that even the best of such books have multiple errors. The very nature of the amount and extent of information they attempt to relate accurately, the number of contributors and editors involved, and the sheer amount of typesetting and proofreading necessary make it almost impossible for absolute accuracy throughout any one given film reference book.

Fantasy and Science Fiction have been part of television history since the medium achieved network status in late 1940s. Three good books on the subject of Fantasy and Science Fiction television are Alan Morton's *The Complete Directory to Science Fiction, Fantasy and Horror Television Series: A Comprehensive Guide to the First 50 Years, 1946 to 1996*, Roger Fulton and John Betancourt's *The SCI-FI Channel Encyclopedia of Science Fiction*, and Alex McNeil's *Total Television*, 4th ed. However, as is the case with similar reference works on motion pictures with extremely extensive information and detail, even these three volumes have incomplete information and minor errors.

What follows here is a brief list of significant film and television adaptations of stories found in this volume. This list also includes a few examples of film and television adaptations that are not directly taken from print Fantasy and Science Fiction, but are closely tied to these stories. This list is representative, not exhaustive.

DARK FANTASY

Mary W. Shelley, "The Mortal Immortal: A Tale" (1833)

Movie:	*Frankenstein* (1931) — 70 min.
	Bride of Frankenstein (1935) — 75 min.
	Son of Frankenstein (1939) — 99 min.
	Cocoon (1985) — 117 min.
Television:	*Frankenstein: The True Story* (1973) — 200 min.
	(made for TV movie)

Edgar Allan Poe, "The Fall of the House of Usher" (1839)

Movie:	*House of Usher* (1960) — 85 min.
Television:	*The Fall of the House of Usher* (1982) — 101 min.

Robert Louis Stevenson, "The Body Snatcher" (1884)

Movie:	*The Body Snatcher* (1945) — 77 min.

Bram Stoker, "Dracula's Guest" (1897)

Movie:	*Nosferatu* (1922) — 63 min.
	Dracula (1931) — 103 min.

Howard Phillips Lovecraft, "The Colour Out of Space" (1927)

Movie:	*The Thing (From Another World)* (1951) — 87 min.
	Invaders From Mars (1953) — 78 min.
	Invasion of the Body Snatchers (1956) — 80 min.

Shirley Jackson, "The Lottery" (1948)

Movie:	*The Lottery* (1969) — 28 min.

Damon Knight, "To Serve Man" (1950)

Television:	"To Serve Man," *The Twilight Zone* (3/2/62)

Charles Beaumont, "The Howling Man" (1959)

Television:	"The Howling Man," *The Twilight Zone* (11/4/60)

Richard Matheson, "Duel"

Television:	*Duel* (1971) — 90 min. (made for TV movie)

Robert R. McCammon, "Nightcrawlers" (1984)

Television:	"Nightcrawlers," *The Twilight Zone* (11/18/85)

FANTASY

Robert E. Howard, "The Tower of the Elephant" (1933)

Movie:	*Conan the Barbarian* (1982) — 129 min.
	Conan the Destroyer (1984) — 103 min.

J. R. R. Tolkien, "Riddles in the Dark" (1937)

Movie:	*The Hobbit* (1978) — 76 min.
	The Lord of the Rings (1978) — 128 min.

SCIENCE FICTION

Edward Page Mitchell, "The Clock That Went Backward" (1881)
Movie: *The Time Machine* (1960)—103 min.

H. G. Wells, "The Star" (1897)
Movie: *When Worlds Collide* (1951)—81 min.

Edgar Rice Burroughs, Under the Moons of Mars (1912)
Movie: *Star Wars* (1977)—121 min.

Curt Siodmak, "The Eggs of Lake Tanganyika" (1926)
Movie: *Them!* (1954)—94 min.
        Jurassic Park (1993)—126 min.

E. E. "Doc" Smith, "Robot Nemesis" (1934)
Movie: *Star Wars* (1977)—121 min.
        Terminator (1984)—108 min.
        Terminator 2: Judgment Day (1991)—136 min.

Eric Frank Russell, "Jay Score"
Television: *Star Trek* television series
Movie: *Star Trek* movie series

Fredric Brown, "Arena" (1944)
Television: "Fun and Games," *The Outer Limits* (3/30/64)
             "Arena," *Star Trek* (1/19/67)

Robert A. Heinlein, "The Long Watch" (1949)
Movie: *The Abyss* (1989)—145 min.

Ray Bradbury, "There Will Come Soft Rains" (1950)
Television: *The Martian Chronicles* (1979)—315 min.

Arthur C. Clarke, "The Sentinel" (1951)
Movie: *2001: A Space Odyssey* (1968)—139 min.

Katherine MacLean, "Pictures Don't Lie" (1951)
Television: "The Invaders," *The Twilight Zone* (1/27/61)

Philip K. Dick, "We Can Remember It for You Wholesale"
Movie: *Total Recall* (1990)—109 min.

Larry Niven, "The Jigsaw Man" (1967)
Movie: *Coma* (1978)—113 min.

Harry Harrison, "Roommates" (1971)
Movie: *Soylent Green* (1973)—100 min.

William Gibson, "Burning Chrome" (1982)
Movie: *The Matrix* (1999)—136 min.

Fantasy and Science Fiction story lines and themes have pervaded radio dramas and programs since the early days of radio broadcasting in the 1920s. The most famous (and infamous) Fantasy and Science Fiction radio event was Orson Welles and his Mercury Theater Players' October 30, 1938, adaptation of H. G. Wells's *War of the Worlds* for CBS's *The Mercury Theater on the Air*.

Beyond the Fantasy and Science Fiction radio series identified here, others were created, produced, and broadcast for smaller, more localized markets. Also, one-shot Fantasy and Science Fiction programs were provided for more generic drama series. This was the case with radio adaptations of *The War of the Worlds*, *The Day the Earth Stood Still*, and Jules Verne's *Twenty Thousand Leagues Under the Sea* (*The Day the Earth Stood Still* was broadcast as part of *Lux Radio Theater*, CBS, January 4, 1954; the Verne adaptation was broadcast as part of *Family Theater*, Mutual network, April 22, 1953). In addition, some radio series that were not strictly Fantasy and Science Fiction in subject matter often contained Fantasy and Science Fiction themes. Such was the case with radio's *Shadow*, *Little Orphan Annie*, and *Dick Tracy*.

Remember that in the early days of story radio, NBC had two services: the Red and the Blue Networks. The Blue Network became ABC in the 1940s.

Two excellent sources for information on Fantasy and Science Fiction radio are John Dunning's *On the Air: An Encyclopedia of Old-Time Radio* (an updated version of Dunning's *Tune in Yesterday*) and Jim and Meade Frierson III's *Science Fiction on Radio: A Revised Look at 1950–1975*.

Beyond Tomorrow	*NBC Short Story*
Buck Rogers in the 25th Century	*Og, Son of Fire*
CBS Mystery Theatre	*Out of This World*
Cinnamon Bear	*Quiet Please*
Dimension X	*The Sealed Book*
Escape	*The Shadow*
Exploring Tomorrow	*Starring Boris Karloff*
Flash Gordon	*Stay Tuned for Terror*
The Hall of Fantasy	*The Strange Dr. Weird*
The Haunting Hour	*Suspense*
The Hermit's Cave	*Tales of Tomorrow*
I Love A Mystery	*Tarzan*
Inner Sanctum Mysteries	*Theatre Five*
Jack Armstrong, All-American Boy	*2000 Plus*
Latitude Zero	*The Weird Circle*
Let's Pretend	*The Whistler*
Lights Out	*The Witch's Tales*
Mr. Keen, Tracer of Lost Persons	*X Minus One*
The Mysterious Traveler	

FANTASY AND SCIENCE FICTION COMIC STRIPS AND COMIC BOOKS

In the mid-1990s, we in the United States celebrated the 100th anniversary of the birth of the newspaper comic strip. Comic, political, and related illustrative art had existed worldwide for centuries by the 1890s, but newspaper comic strips first attained their unique form at the close of the nineteenth century. Originally, comic strips were conceived as sequential lineal drawings intended to elicit a chuckle or laugh—hence the term "comic" strip. Soon, however, newspapers and comic strip artists realized the medium could be used to relate not only humor, but humorous adventures, and just plain adventure stories. From these adventure stories came themes of Fantasy and Science Fiction in the newspaper strip.

By the 1920s, comic strips such as Roy Crane's *Wash Tubbs*, V. T. Hamlin's *Alley Oop*, Harold Gray's *Little Orphan Annie*, and others featured such themes. By the 1930s, the *Amazing Stories* pulp magazine stories of Philip Francis Nowlan's Buck Rogers were illustrated by Dick Calkins for hundreds of newspapers nationwide. In the 1930s also, Alex Raymond produced the beautifully illustrated Space Opera Romances of *Flash Gordon*. In the dark days of the Great Depression in the mid-1930s, the first comic books emerged and became popular. These first books were collections and adaptations of newspaper comic strips.

Although a number of very thorough and informative collections and books on the subjects of newspaper comic strips and comic books have been produced, four that are most pertinent to Fantasy and Science are Bill Blackbeard and Martin Williams's *The Smithsonian Collection of Newspaper Comics*, Bill Blackbeard and Dale Crain's *The Comic Strip Century*, Mike Benton's *The Illustrated History of Science Fiction Comics*, and Robert M. Overstreet's *The Overstreet Comic Book Price Guide* (issued annually). Strictly speaking, of course, almost all stories and art to appear in newspaper comic strips and comic books are forms of fantasy, if not Science Fiction.

Comic Strips	Comic Books
The Adventures of Tintin	*Action Comics*
Alley Oop	*Adam Strange*
Astérix	*Adventure Comics*
Barnaby	*Adventures into the Unknown*
B.C.	*Alien Encounters*
Beyond Mars	*Alien Legion*
Brick Bradford	*Alien Worlds*
Buck Rogers	*Aliens*
Dick Tracy	*All-American Comics*
Flash Gordon	*Amazing Adult Fantasy*
Hagar the Horrible	*Amazing Adventures*
Krazy Kat	*Amazing Mystery Funnies*
Little Nemo in Slumberland	*Astonishing*
Mandrake the Magician	*Atomic Knights*
The Phantom	*Battlestar Galactica*
Pogo	*The Beyond*
Prince Valiant	*Bizarre Adventures*
Superman	*Blue Bolt*
Tarzan	*Boris Karloff Tales of Mystery*
Thimble Theater (Popeye)	*Brick Bradford*
The Wizard of Id	*Buck Rogers*

Camelot 3000
Captain Comet
Captain Science
Captain Victory and the Galactic
  Rangers
Conan the Barbarian
DC Science Fiction Graphic Novel
Dick Tracy
Doctor Who
Famous Funnies
Fantastic Worlds
Flash Gordon
Forbidden Worlds
From Beyond the Unknown
The Funnies
Heavy Metal
House of Mystery
House of Secrets
Incredible Science Fiction
The Invaders
John Carter of Mars
Journey Into Mystery
Journey Into Unknown Worlds
Jumbo Comics
Kamandi, The Last Boy on Earth
Land of the Giants
Logan's Run
Lost in Space (Space Family Robinson)
Lost Worlds
Magnus, Robot Fighter
Marvel Classic Comics
Marvel Comics Super Special
Mighty Samson
Mysteries of Unexplored Worlds
Mystery in Space
The Outer Limits
Outer Space
The Outlanders
Out of this World
Planet Comics
Planet of the Apes
Rocket Comics
Rocket Kelly
Rocket to the Moon
Sandman (Neil Gaiman)
Sensation Comics
Shatter
Space Action
Space Adventures
Space Cabby
Space Detective
Space Hawk

Space Man
Spaceman, Speed Carter
Space Mysteries
Space: 1999
Space Ranger
Space Squadron
Space War
Space Western Comics
Star Rovers
Startling Comics
Starslayer
Star Trek
Star Wars
Strange Adventures
Strange Galaxies
Strange Planets
Strange Tales
Strange Worlds
Superman
Superworld Comics
Tales of Suspense
Tales of Terror
Tales of the Unexpected
Tales to Astonish
Target Comics
Tarzan
Tom Corbett, Space Cadet
Trekker
Twilight Zone
2001: A Space Opera
UFO Flying Saucers
Uncanny Tales
Unknown Worlds
Unknown Worlds of Science Fiction
Unusual Tales
Voyage to the Bottom of the Sea
Weird Wonder Tales
Weird Worlds
World of Fantasy
World of Wood
Worlds Unknown
Xenozoic Tales

and classics from William Gaines's
  E. C. Comics Publishers such as:
    The Haunt of Fear
    Tales from the Crypt
    Vault of Horror
    Weird Fantasy
    Weird Science
    Weird Science-Fantasy

FANTASY AND SCIENCE FICTION ON THE INTERNET

It is perhaps appropriate that authors, stories, media, and histories of Fantasy and Science Fiction are the subjects of hundreds of thousands of computer World Wide Web sites. One of the most important of contemporary technologies is preserving past visions of technologies to come. What would Shelley, Poe, Verne, Wells, and Gernsback have thought?

The Internet, a profound cultural and technological product, grows and changes by the moment. It is a rich source of information, and misinformation. Ray Bradbury will tell you this. Harlan Ellison would tell you that like television, the medium has not come close to realizing its potential. Certainly, as has been the case historically with all new and burgeoning mass media and communications forms, the Internet has its share of critics. And, it should. While book publications, for example, contain human errors, they have traditionally been much more effectively scrutinized than much of what has been quickly and emotionally hacked onto a Web page. So, as a general rule, Web sites found on the Internet, even more than most print media, need to be carefully considered and reviewed for legitimacy. Conversely, however, the Internet cannot and should not be ignored. It has great potential as a source of research, education, and entertainment.

Michael Wolff's *Your Guide to the Best SF on the Internet* is a useful book of information and lists regarding Fantasy and Science Fiction on the Internet. Computer search engines that are particularly helpful in locating Fantasy and Science Fiction topics include *www.Altavista.com* and *www.Yahoo.com*. Addresses for a few of the many specific viable Fantasy and Science Fiction Web sites currently in use follow.

> www.adventurehouse.com
> www.asfa-art.org
> www.best.com/~4forry/
> www.graphics-france.com/pulp
> www.ip.pt/pulp
> www.locusmag.com
> www.magicdragon.com/UltimateSF
> www.omnimag.com
> www.planetmag.com
> www.scifiarchive.com
> www.scifi.com
> www.sfcreators.com
> www.sfcrowsnest.com
> www.sf4m.org
> www.sfra.org
> www.sfrt.com
> www.sfsite.com
> www.sfwa.org
> www.thescifivine.com
> www.wands.demon.co.uk
> www.worldwide-top100.NU/scifi

What follows is a list of major themes, motifs, and/or settings of Fantasy and Science Fiction in the mass media. This list is by no means comprehensive; it is a place to begin. The examples provided are not necessarily archetypal, but they are probably easily recognized. The World Wide Web lists thousands of Fantasy and Science Fiction themes, motifs, and settings delineated in hundreds of thousands of Web sites. Through the years, many Fantasy and Science Fiction book-length studies and anthologies have provided partial and extensive lists of such story elements.

Abominations of Nature	*King Kong* (movie)
Admirable Monsters	Clive Barker's *Cabal* (print)
Aliens	
Good	*The Day the Earth Stood Still* (movie)
Bad	*Invasion of the Body Snatchers* (movie)
Antigravity	Hal Clement's *Mission of Gravity* (print)
Alternate Realities	*The Matrix* (movie)
Alternate Universes	*Sliders* (TV)
Apocalypse	Jack Vance's *The Dying Earth* (print)
Arthurian Legend	*Excalibur* (movie)
Bugs	*Them!* (movie)
Censorship	Ray Bradbury's *Fahrenheit 451* (print, movie)
Colonization	Ray Bradbury's *The Martian Chronicles* (print, TV)
Computers	*2001: A Space Odyssey* (movie)
Curses	Stephen King's *Thinner* (print)
Cyberpunk	William Gibson's *Neuromancer* (print)
Cyborgs	*The Six-Million Dollar Man* (TV)
Demonic Possession	William Peter Blatty's *The Exorcist* (print)
Devil Worship	Nathaniel Hawthorne's "Young Goodman Brown" (print)
Disease	Jack London's *The Scarlet Plague* (print)
Distant Future	*Buck Rogers* (multimedia)
Dragons	Anne McCaffrey's *Dragonflight* (print)
Dystopia	George Orwell's *1984* (print)
E(xtra) S(ensory) P(erception)	Stephen King's *The Dead Zone* (print)
Faustian Pacts	Robert Bloch's "That Hell-Bound Train" (print)
Feminism	Joanna Russ's *The Female Man* (print)
Genetic Engineering	Ira Levin's *The Boys from Brazil* (print)
Ghosts	Charles Dickens's *A Christmas Carol* (print)
Gothicism	Ann Radcliffe's *The Mysteries of Udolpho* (print)
Hard Science Fiction	John W. Campbell's *The Mightiest Machine* (print)
Heroic Fantasy	Robert E. Howard's Conan the Barbarian series (print)
Heroines	Catherine L. Moore's Jirel of Joiry series (print)
Human Organ Black Market	Larry Niven's *The Long Arm of Gil Hamilton* (print)
Imminent Death	Nevil Shute's *On the Beach* (print, movie)
Immortality	*Cocoon* (movie)
Intergalactic War	*Battlestar Galactica* (movie, TV)
Invasion	H. G. Wells's *The War of the Worlds* (print, radio drama)

Invisibility	Edward Page Mitchell's "The Crystal Man" (print)
Journeys Underground	Jules Verne's *Journey to the Centre of the Earth* (print)
Lost Worlds	Arthur Conan Doyle's *The Lost World* (print)
Mad Scientists	Sax Rohmer's Fu Manchu series (print)
Magic	*Willow* (movie)
Mars	Ray Bradbury's *The Martian Chronicles* (print)
Microscopic Worlds	Fitz-James O'Brien's "The Diamond Lens" (print)
The Moon	George Meiles's *A Trip to the Moon* (movie)
Mythology	H. P. Lovecraft's Cthulu Mythos (print)
Near Future	*Space: 1999* (TV)
Overpopulation	Harry Harrison's *Make Room, Make Room* (print)/ *Soylent Green* (movie adaptation)
Parody	Terry Pratchett's *The Colour of Magic* (print)
Plant Life	*The Day of the Triffids* (print/movie)
Politics	Jack London's *The Iron Heel* (print)
Post Apocalypse	William Hope Hodgson's *The Night Land* (print)
Prehistory	Edgar Rice Burroughs's *The Land That Time Forgot* series (print)
Psychic Detectives	Algernon Blackwood's John Silence stories (print)
Quests	J. R. R. Tolkien's *The Lord of the Rings* trilogy (print)
Race Relations	*Star Trek* (TV)
Reanimation	Mary Shelley's *Frankenstein*
Reincarnation	H. Rider Haggard's *She* (print, movie)
Revenge	*The Princess Bride* (movie)
Robots	Isaac Asimov's "Robbie" (print)
Science Fiction Fandom	Mack Reynold's *The Case of the Little Green Men* (print)
Science Fiction Publishing	Fredric Brown's *What Mad Universe* (print)
Sex	Philip Jose Farmer's *The Lovers* (print)
Space Opera	*Star Wars* (movie)
Spaceport Bars	Spider Robinson's *Callahan's Crosstime Saloon* stories
Steam Power	Edward S. Ellis's *The Huge Hunter* (print)
The Sun	David Brin's *Sundiver* (print)
Supermen	Philip Wylie's *Gladiator* (novel)
Superwomen	*The Bionic Woman* (TV)
The Supernatural	*The Omen* (movie)
Talking Animals	George Orwell's *Animal Farm* (print)
Technology	
Good	*Lost in Space* (TV)
Bad	Fred Saberhagen's Berserker stories (print)
Time Travel	H. G. Wells's *The Time Machine* (print)
Undersea Worlds	Jules Verne's *20,000 Leagues Under the Sea* (print)
Utopia	James Hilton's *Lost Horizon* (print)
Vampires	*Dracula* (print and movie)
Venus	Edgar Rice Burroughs' Carson of Venus series (print)
Virtual Reality	*VR5* (TV)
War	Robert A. Heinlein's *Starship Troopers* (print)
Werewolves	G. W. M. Reynolds's *Wagner the Wehr-Wolf* (print)
Zombies	*Night of the Living Dead* (movie)

CORNERSTONE STUDIES AND ANTHOLOGIES OF FANTASY AND SCIENCE FICTION IN PRINT MEDIA

The bibliography that follows is by no means complete, but it is a starting point for further fan and scholar investigation of print Fantasy and Science Fiction. The list is a selection of favorites from the author's personal library, and he would be happy to have other authors, editors, and anthology titles suggested to him for future inclusion. Studies and histories of Fantasy and Science Fiction have long helped to prove the legitimacy of these popular story genres as worthy of intellectual investigation. Anthologies (or collections that contain representative work from more than one author) enjoyed tremendous popularity in the first decades after the demise of pulp magazines and the beginning of paperback books. Numerous anthologies from the 1940s through the 1970s collected and reprinted Fantasy and Science Fiction stories from the golden days of the pulps. Fantasy and Science Fiction anthologies still exist, but they now concentrate on fiction written especially for the anthology rather than reprints. Also, while several viable and award-winning Fantasy and Science Fiction magazines remain, the number of titles of these periodicals has diminished. Subsequently, reprint source material is much more limited than it once was. A definite talent is required to effectively anthologize Fantasy and Science Fiction stories. This is why collections assembled by Groff Conklin, Ellen Datlow, August Derleth, James Gunn, Peter Haining, David G. Hartwell, Damon Knight, Leo Margulies, Sam Moskowitz, Terri Windling, and others are so very important to our appreciation of Fantasy and Science Fiction.

Three very useful bibliographic sources of print Fantasy and Science Fiction—available online or on CD—are Charles N. Brown and William G. Contento's *The Locus Index to Science Fiction (1984–1999)*, William G. Contento's *Index to Science Fiction Anthologies and Collections*, and Stephen T. Miller and William G. Contento's *Science Fiction, Fantasy, & Weird Fiction Magazine Index (1890–1999)*.

Ackerman, Forrest J, ed. *Ackermanthology!: 65 Astonishing, Rediscovered Sci-Fi Shorts.*
———. *Best Science Fiction for 1973.*
———. *The Collector's Guide to Monster Magazines.*
———. *Forrest J Ackerman's World of Science Fiction.*
———. *The Gernsback Awards 1926—Volume One.*
———. *Gosh! Wow! (Sense of Wonder) Science Fiction.*
Adams, Robert, ed. *Phantom Regiments.*
Adams, Robert, Martin H. Greenberg, and Pamela Crippen Adams, eds. *Barbarians* and 2.
———. *Hunger for Horror.*
———. *Robert Adam's Book of Soldiers.*
Adrian, Jack, ed. *Detective Stories from the Strand Magazine.*
———. *Strange Tales from the Strand Magazine.*
Aldiss, Brian W. *Trillion Year Spree: The History of Science Fiction.* "(An earlier version of this book is entitled *Billion Year Spree.* David Wingrove collaborated on *Trillion Year Spree.*)
———, ed. *All About Venus.*
———. *Evil Earths.*
———. *Galactic Empires.* Vols. 1 and 2.
———. *Penguin Science Fiction.*
———. *More Penguin Science Fiction.*
———. *Yet More Penguin Science Fiction.*
———. *Space Odysseys.*
———. *Space Opera.*
———, and Harry Harrison, eds. *Decade: The 1940s.*

————. *Decade: The 1950s.*
————. *Hell's Cartographers.*
Aldiss, Brian, and Sam J. Lundwall, eds. *The Penguin World Omnibus of Science Fiction.*
Alkon, Paul K. *Origins of Futuristic Fiction.*
Allen, L. David, ed. *Science Fiction: An Introduction.*
Amis, Kingsley. *New Maps of Hell: A Survey of Science Fiction.*
————, and Robert Conquest, eds. *Spectrum*, and *2–5.*
Anderson, Poul and Karen, eds. *The Night Fantastic.*
Anderson, Poul, Martin H. Greenberg, and Charles G. Waugh, eds. *Mercenaries of Tomorrow.*
————. *Terrorists of Tomorrow.*
Angelo, Michael. *Penny Dreadfuls and Other Victorian Horrors.*
Anthony, Piers, and Richard Gilliam, eds. *Tales of the Great Turtle: Fantasy in the Native American Tradition.*
————, Barry Malzberg, Martin H. Greenberg, and Charles G. Waugh, eds. *Uncollected Stars.*
Apostolou, John L., and Martin H. Greenberg, eds. *The Best of Japanese Science Fiction.*
Appel, Benjamin. *The Fantastic Mirror: Science Fiction Across the Ages.*
Armada Ghost Book, and *2–15.* (Christine Bernard, ed. 1–2; Mary Danby, ed. 3–15).
Arthur, Robert, ed. *Monster Mix: Thirteen Chilling Tales.*
Ash, Brian. *Faces of the Future: The Lessons of Science Fiction.*
————, ed. *Who's Who in Science Fiction.*
Ash, Constance, ed. *Not of Woman Born.*
Ashley, Michael. *The Complete Index to Astounding/Analog.*
————. *Gernsback Days.*
————, ed. *The History of the Science Fiction Magazine*, Vol. 1 (1926–1935), Vol. 2 (1936–1945), Vol. 3 (1946–1955), Vol. 4 (1956–1965).
————. *The Camelot Chronicles: Heroic Adventures from the Time of King Arthur.*
————. *The Illustrated Book of Science Fiction Lists.*
————. *Jewels of Wonder: An Anthology of Heroic Fantasies.*
————. *The Mammoth Book of Comic Fantasy* and *2.*
————. *The Mammoth Book of Fairy Tales.*
————. *The Mammoth Book of Short Horror Novels.*
————. *The Pendagron Chronicles: Heroic Fantasy from the Time of King Arthur.*
————, ed. *Phantom Perfumes and Other Shades: Memories of* Ghost Stories Magazine
————. *The Random House Book of Fantasy Stories.*
————. *The Random House Book of Science Fiction Stories.*
————. *Souls in Metal: An Anthology of Robot Futures.*
————. *Weird Legacies.*
————. *Who's Who in Horror and Fantasy Fiction.*
Asimov, Isaac, ed. *Before the Golden Age: A Science Fiction Anthology of the 1930's.*
————. *Great Science Fiction Stories by the World's Great Scientists.*
————. *The Hugo Winners*, Vol. 1 (1955–1961), Vol. 2 (1962–1970), Vol. 3 (1971–1975), Vol. 4 (1976-1979), Vol. 5 (1980–1982).
————. *More Soviet Science Fiction.*
————. *The New Hugo Winners*, Vol. 2 (1986–1988).
————. *Soviet Science Fiction.*
————. *The Super Hugos.*
————. *Where Do We Go From Here?*
————, Terry Carr, and Martin H. Greenberg, eds. *100 Great Fantasy Short Short Stories.*
————, and Groff Conklin, eds. *50 Short Science Fiction Tales.*
————, and Martin H. Greenberg, eds. *Amazing Stories: 60 Years of the Best Science Fiction.*
————. *Cosmic Critiques: How and Why Ten Science Fiction Stories Work.*
————. *Isaac Asimov Presents the Great SF Stories* 1 (1939), 2 (1940), 3 (1941), 4 (1942), 5 (1943), 6 (1944), 7 (1945), 8 (1946), 9 (1947), 10 (1948), 11 (1949), 12 (1950), 13 (1951), 14 (1952), 15 (1953), 16 (1954), 17 (1955), 18 (1956), 19 (1957), 20 (1958), 21 (1959), 22 (1960), 23 (1961), 24 (1962).
————. *The New Hugos: Award-Winning Science Fiction Stories.* (1983–1985).
————. *Visions of Fantasy: Tales From the Masters.*
————, Martin Greenberg, and Joseph D. Olander, eds. *The Future in Question.*
———— *100 Great Science Fiction Short Short Stories.*

————. *Space Mail.*

————, Martin H. Greenberg, and Charles G. Waugh, eds. *Catastrophes!*

————. *Caught in the Organ Draft: Biology in Science Fiction.*

————. *Isaac Asimov's Magical Worlds of Fantasy* 1 (Wizards), 2 (Witches), 3 (Cosmic Knights), 4 (Spells), 5 (Giants), 6 (Mythical Beasties), 7 (Magical Wishes), 8 (Devils), 9 (Atlantis), 10 (Ghosts), 11 (Curses).

————. *Isaac Asimov's Wonderful Worlds of Science Fiction* 1 (Intergalactic Empires), 2 (Science Fictional Olympics), 3 (Supermen), 4 (Comets), 5 (Tin Stars), 6 (Neanderthals), 7 (Space Shuttles), 8 (Monsters), 9 (Robots), 10 (Invasions).

————. *The Mammoth Book of Classic Science Fiction: Short Novels of the 1930s* (also entitled *Great Tales of Classic Science* Fiction). Thirteen Short Fantasy Novels.

————. *The Mammoth Book of Golden Age Science Fiction: Short Novels of the 1940s* (also entitled *Great Tales of Golden Age Science Fiction*).

————. *The Mammoth Book of Vintage Science Fiction: Short Novels of the 1950s.* (also entitled *Great Tales of Vintage Science Fiction.*)

————. *The Mammoth Book of New World Science Fiction: Great Short Novels of the 1960s.*

————. *Mutants.* (Originally published as *Young Mutants.*)

————. *The Science Fiction Solar System.*

————. *Tales of the Occult.*

————. *The 13 Crimes of Science Fiction.*

————, Charles G. Waugh, and Martin H. Greenberg, eds. *Great Tales of the Golden Age of Science Fiction.*

————. *Isaac Asimov Presents The Best Science Fiction of the 19th Century.*

————. *The Mammoth Book of Fantastic Science Fiction.*

————. *The Mammoth Book of Modern Science Fiction.*

————. *The Seven Deadly Sins and Cardinal Virtues of Science Fiction.* (Includes *The 7 Cardinal Virtues of Science Fiction* and *The 7 Deadly Sins of Science Fiction.*)

————. *The Twelve Frights of Christmas.*

————. *Astounding Stories: The 60th Anniversary Collection.* Three volume set.

Asquith, Cynthia, ed. *The First Ghost Book, The Second Ghost Book, The Third Ghost Book.*

Atheling, William A., Jr. (James Blish), ed. *The Issue at Hand: Studies in Contemporary Magazine Science Fiction.*

————. *More Issues at Hand.*

————. *The Tale That Wags the God.*

Bailey, J.O., ed. *Pilgrims Through Space and Time: Trends and Patterns in Scientific and Utopian Fiction.*

Baker, Mike, and Martin H. Greenberg, eds. *My Favorite Horror Story.*

Baldick, Chris, ed. *The Oxford Book of Gothic Tales.*

Barker, Martin. *A Haunt of Fears: The Strange History of the British Horror Comics Campaign.*

Barr, Marleen S. *Feminist Fabulation: Space/Postmodern Fiction.*

————, ed. *Future Females: A Critical Anthology.*

Bartter, Martha A. *The Way to Ground Zero: The Atomic Bomb in American Science Fiction.*

Bear, Greg, ed. *New Legends.*

Beaumont, Charles, ed. *The Fiend in You.*

Beck, Calvin, ed. *The Frankenstein Reader.*

Beck, Robert E., ed. *Literature of the Supernatural.*

Benedict, S.H., ed. *Tales of Terror and Suspense.*

Benford, Gregory, ed. *Far Futures: Five New Novellas of Hard SF by Five Modern Masters of the Form.*

————. *The New Hugo Winners,* vol. IV.

———— and Martin H. Greenberg, eds. *What Might Have Been,* Vol. 1-Alternate Empires; Vol. 2-Alternate Heroes.

———— and George Zebrowski, eds. *Skylife: Space Habitats in Story and Science.*

Bensen, D. R., ed. *The Unknown.*

————. *The Unknown Five.*

Benton, Mike. *Horror Comics: The Illustrated History.*

————. *Science Fiction Comics: The Illustrated History.*

Berglund, Edward P., ed. *The Disciples of Cthulu.*

Bernard, Christine, ed. *The Fontana Book of Great Horror Stories.*

The Best From Fantasy and Science Fiction. [Anthony Boucher and J. Francis McComas, eds., First (1952) through Third Series (1954); Anthony Boucher, ed., Fourth (1955) through Eighth (1959) Series; Robert P. Mills, ed. Ninth (1959), Tenth (1960), and Eleventh (1962) Series; Avram Davidson, ed., Twelfth (1963) through Fourteenth (1965) Series; Edward L. Ferman. ed. Fifteenth (1966) through Eighteenth (1969) and 19th (1971), 20th (1973), 22nd (1977), 23rd (1980), and 24th (1982) Series]

———. *Beyond the Stars: Tales of Adventures in Time and Space.*

Betancourt, John, ed. *The Best of Weird Tales.*

———. *New Masterpieces of Horror.*

———, and Robert Weinberg, eds. *Weird Tales: Seven Decades of Terror.*

Blackbeard, Bill, and Dale Crain, ed. *The Comic Strip Century: Celebrating 100 Years of an American Art Form.*

Blackbeard, Bill, and Martin Williams, eds. *The Smithsonian Collection of Newspaper Comics.*

Bleiler, Everett F. *Science-Fiction: The Early Years.*

———. *Five Victorian Ghost Stories.*

———. *Three Gothic Novels: The Castle of Otranto by Walpole, Vathek by Beckford, The Vampyre by Polidori.*

———. *Science-Fiction: The Gernsback Years.*

———, ed. *Eight Dime Novels.* (Reprints Edward S. Ellis's "The Huge Hunter; or, The Steam Man of the Prairies" one of at least six reprints, under various titles, of "The Steam Man of the Prairies" from No. 45 of *Irwin's American Novels, 1865.*)

——— and T .E. Ditky, eds. *The Best Science Fiction Stories,* 1949, 1950, 1951, 1952, 1953, and 1954.

———. *Frontiers in Space: Selections from The Best Science Fiction Stories—1951, 1952, and 1953.*

———. *Imagination Unlimited.*

———. *Men of Space and Time: Selections from Imagination Unlimited.*

———. *Science Fiction Omnibus (The Best Science Fiction Stories 1949 and 1950).*

———. *The Year's Best Science Fiction Novels,* 1952, 1953, 1954.

Bleiler, Richard. *The Annotated Index to the Thrill Book.*

Blish, James, ed. *New Dreams This Morning.*

Bloch, Robert. *The Eight Stage of Fandom.*

———, ed. *Monsters in Our Midst.*

———. *Out of My Head.*

———. *Psycho-Paths.*

———. *Robert Bloch's Psychos.*

Bloom, Harold, ed. *Writers of English: Lives and Works Series*

———. *Classic Fantasy Writers.*

———. *Classic Horror Writers.*

———. *Classic Science Fiction Writers.*

———. *Modern Fantasy Writers.*

———. *Modern Horror Writers.*

———. *Modern Science Fiction Writers.*

———. *Science Fiction of the Golden Age.*

Boardman, Tom, ed. *An ABC of Science Fiction.*

Borden, Bill, and Steve Posner, eds. *The Big Book of Big Little Books.*

Boucher, Anthony, ed. *A Treasury of Great Science Fiction.* Vols. 1 and 2.

Boyer, Robert H., and Kenneth J. Zahorski, eds. *Dark Imaginings: A Collection of Gothic Fantasy.*

———. *Fantasists on Fantasy.*

Bova, Ben, ed. *An Analog Yearbook.*

———. *The Best of Analog.*

———. *The Best of the Nebulas: Celebrating 25 Years of Nebula Awards.*

———. *The Many Worlds of Science Fiction.*

Boyer, Robert H., and Kenneth J. Zahorski, eds. *Dark Imaginings: A Collection of Gothic Fantasy.*

———. *Fantasists on Fantasy.*

———. *The Fantastic Imagination: An Anthology of High Fantasy,* and 2.

———. *The Phoenix Tree: An Anthology of Myth Fantasy.*

———. *Visions and Imaginings: Classic Fantasy Fiction.*

———. *Visions of Wonder: An Anthology of Christian Fantasy.*

Brackett, Leigh, ed. *The Best of Planet Stories #1.* (There were no further numbers in this series.)

Bradbury, Ray, ed. *Timeless Stories for Today and Tomorrow.*

Bradley, Marion Zimmer, ed. *Sword and Sorceress: An Anthology of Heroic Fantasy*, and 2–16.

Bretnor, Reginald, ed. *The Craft of Science Fiction*.

——. *Modern Science Fiction: Its Meaning and Its Future*.

——. *Science Fiction, Today and Tomorrow*.

Brians, Paul. *Nuclear Holocausts: Atomic War in Fiction 1895–1984*.

Broderick, Damien, ed. *Not the Only Planet: Science Fiction Travel Stories*.

Broderick, Damien. *Reading by Starlight: Postmodern Science Fiction*.

Brown, Bill, ed. *Reading the West: An Anthology of Dime Novels*. (Includes "Frank Reade, Inventor, Chasing the James Boys With His Steam Team," 1890.)

Brown, Fredric, and Mack Reynolds, eds. *Science Fiction Carnival*.

Budrys, Algis. *Benchmark: Galaxy Bookshelf*.

——, ed. *L. Ron Hubbard Presents the Best of Writers of the Future*.

Bukatman, Scott. *Terminal Identity: The Virtual Subject in Postmodern Science Fiction*.

Burnett, Whit and Hallie, eds. *19 Tales of Terror*.

Caidin, Martin, Jay Barbaree, and Susan Wright, eds. *Destination Mars: In Art, Myth, and Science*.

Calvino, Italo, ed. *Fantastic Tales: Visionary and Everyday*.

Campbell, John W., Jr., ed. *The Astounding Science Fiction Anthology*.

——. *Analog 1–3*.

——. *Astounding Tales of Space and Time*.

——. *Prologue to Analog*.

Campbell, Ramsey, ed. *Fine Frights: Stories that Scared Me*.

——. *New Tales of the Cthulu Mythos*.

——. *New Terrors*, and II.

Card, Orson Scott. *How To Write Science Fiction and Fantasy*.

——, ed. *Dragons of Dark*.

——, ed. *Dragons of Light*.

——. *Future on Ice*.

——, and Keith Ferrell, eds. *Black Mist and Other Japanese Futures*.

Carnell, John, ed. *The Best From New Worlds Science Fiction*.

——. *Lambda I and Other Stories*.

——. *New Writings in SF 1–8*.

Carr, Terry, ed. *The Best from Universe*.

——. *The Best Science Fiction Novellas of the Year* 1 (1980).

——. *The Best Science Fiction of the Year* 1 (1972)–16.

——. *Creatures From Beyond*.

——. *An Exaltation of Stars*.

——. *Fantasy Annual IV*.

——. *The Infinite Arena: Seven Science Fiction Stories About Sports*.

——. *New Worlds of Fantasy*, and 2–3.

——. *On Our Way to the Future*.

——. *The Others*.

——. *Science Fiction for People Who Hate Science Fiction*.

——. *This Side of Infinity*.

——. *Universe 1–17*.

——. *Year's Finest Fantasy*, and 2.

——, and Martin Harry Greenberg, eds. *A Treasury of Modern Fantasy*.

Carter, Lin, ed. *Adult Fantasy Series* (multi-volume series featuring a range of Dark and High Fantasy classic stories.)

——. *Flashing Swords 1–5*.

——. *The Magic of Atlantis*.

——. *Warriors and Wizards*.

——. *Weird Tales 1–4*.

Carter, M.L., ed. *The Curse of the Undead*.

Carter, Paul A. *The Creation of Tomorrow: Fifty Years of Magazine Science Fiction*.

Cawthorn, James, and Michael Moorcock. *Fantasy: The 100 Best Books*.

Cerf, Bennett, ed. *Famous Ghost Stories*.

———. *The Unexpected.*

Cerf, Christopher, ed. *The Vintage Anthology of Science Fantasy: Twenty Stories in the Modern Manner.*

Chalker, Jack L., and Mark Owings. *The Science-Fantasy Publishers: A Critical and Bibliographic History,* 3rd ed.

Chamber of Horrors.

Cheetham, Anthony, ed. *Bug-Eyed Monsters.*

———. *Science Against Man.*

Child, Lincoln, ed. *Tales of the Dark,* and 2–3.

———. *Tales of the Dark: Ten Masterpieces of Supernatural Terror.*

Chizmar, Robert, ed. *The Best of Cemetary Dance.*

Chizmar, Richard T., ed. *The Best From Cemetary Dance.*

———. *Legacies.*

Cholfin, Bryan, ed. *The Best of Crank!*

Clareson, Thomas D., ed. *Many Futures, Many Worlds: Theme and Form in Science Fiction.*

———. *SF: The Other Side of Realism.*

———. *Some Kind of Paradise: The Emergence of American Science Fiction.*

———. *Voices for the Future: Essays on Major Science Fiction Authors,* and Vols. 2–3.(Thomas L. Wymer co-edited vol. 3.)

Clarke, Arthur C., ed. *Project Solar Sail.*

———. *Time Probe: The Sciences in Science Fiction.*

Clarke, I. F. *The Pattern of Expectation: 1644–2001.*

———. *Voices Prophesying War: Future Wars, 1763–3749.*

Clear, Val, Patricia Warrick, Martin Harry Greenberg, and Joseph D. Olander, eds. *Marriage and the Family Through Science Fiction.*

Clem, Ralph, Martin H. Greenberg, Joseph D. Olander, eds. *The City 2000 A.D.*

Clute, John. *Science Fiction: The Illustrated Encyclopedia.*

———. *Look at the Evidence.*

———. *Strokes: Essays and Reviews, 1966–1986.*

———, and David Pringle, and Simon Ounsley, eds. *I Interzone Anthology,* and 2–3.

———, and John Grant, eds. *The Encyclopedia of Fantasy.*

———, and Peter Nicholls, eds. *The Encyclopedia of Science Fiction.*

Coffey, Frank, ed. *Modern Masterpieces of Horror.*

Collins, Charles M., ed. *A Feast of Blood.*

———. *Fright: Six Tales of the Uncanny and the Unknown.*

———. *Harvest of Fear.*

———. *A Walk With the Beast.*

Congdon, Don, ed. *Stories for the Dead of Night.*

———. *Tales of Love and Horror.*

Conklin, Groff, ed. *Best Science Fiction Stories.*

———. *Another Part of the Galaxy.*

———. *The Big Book of Science Fiction.*

———. *Br-r-r!: Ten Tales to Chill You to the Bone.*

———. *Dimension 4.*

———. *Elsewhere and Elsewhen.*

———. *4 for the Future.*

———. *Five-Odd.*

———. *Five Unearthly Visions.*

———. *The Graveyard Reader.*

———. *Great Science Fiction by Scientists.*

———. *Great Stories of Space Travel.*

———. *In the Grip of Terror.*

———. *Minds Unleashed.*

———. *The Omnibus of Science Fiction.*

———. *Possible Worlds of Science Fiction.*

———. *Science Fiction Adventures in Dimension.*

———. *Science Fiction Adventures in Mutation.*

———. *The Science Fiction Galaxy.*

————. *Science Fiction Oddities.*
————. *Science Fiction Omnibus.*
————. *Science Fiction Terror Tales.*
————. *Science Fiction Thinking Machines.*
————. *17 X Infinity.*
————. *Seven Trips Through Time and Space.*
————. *The Supernatural Reader.*
————. *13 Great Stories of Science Fiction.*
————. *A Treasury of Science Fiction.*
————. *12 Great Classics of Science Fiction.*
————. *Twisted: Weird Tales by Ray Bradbury, Theodore Sturgeon, Others.*
————. *Worlds of When.*

Cook, Fred. *Index to Argosy, 1930–1943.*
————. *Starmont Index to Character Pulps.*

Corn, Joseph J., and Brian Horrigan. *Yesterday's Tomorrows: Past Visions of the American Future.*

Cox, Michael, and R.A. Gilbert, eds. *The Oxford Book of English Ghost Stories.*
————. *Victorian Ghost Stories: An Oxford Anthology.*

Cramer, Kathryn, and David G. Hartwell, eds. *Christmas Ghosts.*
————. *Christmas Spirits.*
————, and Paul Pautz, eds. *The Architecture of Fear.*

Crispin, Edmund, ed. *Best SF: Science Fiction Stories.*

Cross, John Keir, ed. *Best Horror Stories.*

Crossen, Kendell Foster, ed. *Adventures in Tomorrow.*

Crowther, Peter, ed. *Moon Shots.*
———— and Edward E. Kramer, eds. *Dante's Disciples.*
————. *Tombs.*

Dalby, Richard, ed. *Chillers for Christmas.*
————. *Dracula's Blood: Vampire Classics.*
————. *Ghosts for Christmas.*
————. *Horror for Christmas.*
————. *The Mammoth Book of Ghost Stories, and 2.*
————. *The Mammoth Book of 20th Century Ghost Stories.*
————. *The Mammoth Book of Victorian and Edwardian Ghost Stories.*
————. *Mistletoe Mayhem: Horrific Tales for the Holidays*
————. *Shivers for Christmas.*
————. *Tales of Witchcraft.*
————. *Vampire Stories.*
————. *The Virago Book of Ghost Stories, and 2.*

Danby, Mary, ed. *Realms of Darkness.*
————. *65 Great Spine Chillers.*

Daniels, Les. *Living in Fear: A History of Horror in the Mass Media.*

Dann, Jack, ed. *Wandering Stars: An Anthology of Jewish Fantasy and Science Fiction.*
————. *More Wandering Stars.*

Dann, Jack, and Gardner Dozois, eds. *Aliens!*
————. *Angels!*
————. *Armageddons!*
————. *Bestiary!*
————. *Clones!*
————. *Demons!*
————. *Dinosaurs!*
————. *Dog Tales!*
————. *Dragons!*
————. *Future War!*
————. *Hackers!*
————. *Horses!*
————. *Invaders!*
————. *Little People!*

————. *Magic Cats!*
————. *Magic Cats II!*
————. *Mermaids!*
————. *Seaserpents!*
————. *Sorcerers!*
————. *Timegates!*
————. *Unicorns!*
————. *Unicorns II!*

Dann, Jack, and Janeen Webb, eds. *Dreaming Down Under.*
————, George Zebrowski, eds. *Faster Than Light.*

Datlow, Ellen, ed. *Off Limits: Tales of Alien Sex.*
————. *Omni: Best Science Fiction,* and 2–3.
————. *Omni Book of Science Fiction,* and 2–4.
————. *Omni: Visions,* and 2.

Datlow, Ellen, and Terri Windling, eds. *Black Swan, White Raven.*
————. *Black Thorn, White Rose.*
————. *Ruby Slippers, Golden Tears.*
————. *Silver Birch, Blood Moon.*
————. *Snow White, Blood Red.*
————. *The Year's Best Fantasy and Horror.* Annual Collections from First (1988) through Fourteenth (2001).

Davenport, Basil. *The Science Fiction Novel: Imagination and Social Criticism.*
————, ed. *Deals With the Devil.*
————. *Invisible Men.*

Davidson, Avram, ed. *Magic for Sale.*

Davin, Eric Leif, ed. *Pioneers of Wonder: Conversations with the Founders of Science Fiction.*

Day, A. Grove, and Bacil F. Kirtley, eds. *Horrors in Paradise: Grim and Uncanny Tales from Hawaii and the South Seas.*

The Day the Sun Stood Still.

de Camp, L. Sprague. *Literary Swordsmen and Sorcerers: The Makers of Heroic Fantasy.*
————, ed. *The Fantastic Swordsmen.*
————. *Science-Fiction Handbook.*
————. *The Spell of Seven.*
————. *Swords and Sorcery.*
————. *Warlocks and Warriors.*
————, and Catherine Crook de Camp. *Science Fiction Handbook, Revised: How to Write and Sell Imaginative Stories.*

Del Rey, Judy, ed. *Stellar Science-Fiction Stories 1–6*

Del Rey, Lester. *The World of Science Fiction 1926–1976: The History of a Subculture.*
————. *Best Science Fiction Stories of the Year* (1971), and 2 (1972)—4 (1974).
————. *Fantastic Science-Fiction Art (1926-1954).*
————, and Risa Kessler, eds. *Once Upon a Time: A Treasury of Modern Fairy Tales.*
————, Cecile Matschat, and Carl Carmer, eds. *The Year After Tomorrow.*

Derleth, August, ed. *Dark Mind, Dark Heart.*
————. *Dark Things.*
————. *New Horizons.*
————. *The Night Side.*
————. *Night's Yawning Peal: A Ghostly Company.*
————. *The Other Side of the Moon.*
————. *The Outer Reaches.*
————. *Over the Edge.*
————. *Portals of Tomorrow.*
————. *The Sleeping and the Dead.*
————. *Sleep No More.*
————. *Strange Ports of Call.*
————. *Time to Come.*
————. *Travellers by Night.*

———. *When Evil Awakes.*

———. *Worlds of Tomorrow.*

DeVore, Howard. *The Hugo, Nebula and World Fantasy Awards.*

Di Fate, Vincent, ed. *Infinite Worlds: The Fantastic Visions of Science Fiction Art.*

Dille, Robert C., ed. *The Collected Works of Buck Rogers in the 25th Century.*

Disch, Thomas M. *The Dreams Our Stuff Is Made Of: How Science Fiction Conquered the World.*

Ditky, T. E., ed. *The Best Science-Fiction Stories and Novels.* 1956.

Donawerth, Jane L., and Carol A. Kolmerten, eds. *Utopian and Science Fiction by Women: Worlds of Difference.*

Dozois, Gardner, ed. *The Best of Isaac Asimov's Science Fiction Magazine.*

———. *Another World.*

———. *A Day in the Life.*

———. *Beyond the Golden Age.*

———. *Explorers: SF Adventures to Far Horizons.*

———. *The Furthest Horizon: SF Adventures to the Far Future.*

———. *Isaac Asimov's Aliens.*

———. *Isaac Asimov's Mars.*

———. *Isaac Asimov's SF-Lite.*

———. *The Good Old Stuff: Adventure SF in the Grand Tradition.*

———. *The Good New Stuff: Adventure SF in the Grand Tradition.* (*The Good Old Stuff* and *The Good New Stuff* are combined in the one-volume SF Book Club edition, *The Good Stuff.*)

———. *Modern Classics of Fantasy.*

———. *Modern Classics of Science Fiction.*

———. *Modern Classic Short Novels of Science Fiction.*

———. *Roads Not Taken: Tales of Alternate History.*

———. *The Year's Best Science Fiction.* Annual collections from First (1984) through Sixth (1989); becomes *The Best Science Fiction Stories of the Year* from Seventh (1990) through Eighteenth (2001).

———, and Susan Casper, eds. *Ripper!*

———, and Sheila Williams, eds. *Isaac Asimov's Camelot.*

———. *Isaac Asimov's Cyberdreams.*

———. *Isaac Asimov's Earth.*

———. *Isaac Asimov's Ghosts.*

———. *Isaac Asimov's Moons.*

———. *Isaac Asimov's Robots.*

———. *Isaac Asimov's Skin Deep.*

———. *Isaac Asimov's System.*

———. *Isaac Asimov''s Vampires.*

———. *Isaac Asimov's Werewolves.*

Du Pont, Denise, ed. *Women of Vision: Essays by Women Writing Science Fiction.*

Durie, Alistair. *Weird Tales.*

Dziemianowicz, Stefan, Robert Weinberg, and Martin H. Greenberg, eds. *Famous Fantastic Mysteries: 30 Great Tales of Fantasy and Horror from the Classic Pulp Magazines Famous Fantastic Mysteries and Fantastic Novels.*

———. *Astounding Little Alien Stories.*

———. *Horrors! 365 Scary Stories.*

———. *100 Creepy Little Creature Stories.*

———. *100 Fiendish Little Frightmares.*

———. *100 Ghastly Little Ghost Stories.*

———. *100 Twisted Little Tales of Torment.*

———. *100 Vicious Little Vampire Stories.*

———. *100 Wicked Little Witch Stories.*

———. *100 Wild Little Weird Tales.*

———. *The Mists From Beyond.*

———. *Rivals of Dracula.*

———. *Rivals of Weird Tales.*

———. *Virtuous Vampires.*

———. *Weird Tales: 32 Unearthed Terrors.*

———. *Weird Vampire Tales.*

Earley, George W., ed. *Encounters With Aliens: UFOs and Alien Beings in Science Fiction.*

Elder, Joseph, ed. *Eros in Orbit.*

———. *The Farthest Reaches.*

Ellison, Harlan, ed. *Dangerous Visions* and *Again Dangerous Visions.*

Elrick, George S. *Science Fiction Handbook for Readers and Writers.*

Elrod, P.N., ed. *The Time of the Vampire.*

Elwood, Roger, ed.

———. *Alien Worlds.*

———. *Children of Infinity.*

———. *Continuum 1–4.*

———. *The Far Side of Time.*

———. *The 50-Meter Monsters and Other Horrors.*

———. *Future Kin.*

———. *Future Quest.*

———. *The Graduated Robot and Other Stories.*

———. *Invasion of the Robots.*

———. *The Other Side of Tomorrow.*

———. *Strange Gods.*

———. *Ten Tomorrows.*

———, and Vic Ghidalia, eds. *Horror Hunters.*

———. *Young Demons.*

———, and Virginia Kidd, eds. *Saving Worlds.* (Reprinted as *The Wounded Planet*)

———, and Sam Moskowitz, eds. *Alien Earth and Other Stories.*

———. *Strange Signposts: An Anthology of the Fantastic.*

———, and Robert Silverberg, eds. *Epoch.*

Emstev, Mikhail, and Eremei Parnov, eds. *World Soul: Best of Soviet SF.*

Enright, D. J., ed. *The Oxford Book of the Supernatural.*

Eshbach, Lloyd Arthur. *Over My Shoulder: Reflections on a Science Fiction Era.*

———, ed. *Of Worlds Beyond: The Science of Science Fiction Writing.*

Etchison, Dennis, ed. *Cutting Edge.*

———. *Masters of Darkness*, and II.

Evans, Hilary and Dik. *Beyond the Gaslight: Science in Popular Fiction.*

Evans, I.O., ed. *Science Fiction Through the Ages*, and 2.

Fabian, Stephen. *Stephen Fabian's Ladies and Legends.*

Fairfax, John, ed. *Frontier of Going: An Anthology of Space Poetry.*

Farrell, Edmund J., Thomas E. Gage, John Pfordresher, and Raymond J. Rodrigues, eds. *Fantasy: Shapes of Things Unknown.*

———. *Science Fact/Fiction.*

Fawcett, Bill, ed. *Cats in Space and Other Places.*

Fenner, Cathy, and Arnie Fenner, eds. *Spectrum: The Best in Contemporary Fantastic Art*, 1–8.

Ferman, Edward L., ed. *The Best Fantasy and Science Fiction from The Magazine of Fantasy and Science Fiction.*

———. *The Best Fantasy Stories From The Magazine of Fantasy and Science Fiction.*

———. *The Best from Fantasy & Science Fiction: A 40th Anniversary Anthology.*

———. *The Magazine of Fantasy and Science Fiction: A 30 Year Retrospective.*

———. *Oi, Robot: Competitions and Cartoons From The Magazine of Fantasy and Science Fiction.*

———. *Once and Future Tales From The Magazine of Fantasy and Science Fiction.*

———, and Barry N. Malzberg, eds. *Final Stage.*

———, and Robert P. Mills, eds. *Twenty Years of The Magazine of Fantasy and Science Fiction.*

———, and Kristine Kathryn Rusch, eds. *The Best from The Magazine of Fantasy and Science Fiction: A 45th Anniversary Anthology.*

Ferman, Edward L., and Anne Devereaux Jordan, eds. *The Best Horror Stories From The Magazine of Fantasy and Science Fiction.*

Ferman, Edward L. and Gordon Van Gelder, eds. *The Best from Fantasy and Science Fiction: The Fiftieth Anniversary Anthology.*

Fiedler, Leslie A., ed. *In Dreams Wake.*

The Fiend.

Filmer, Kath. *Skepticism and Hope in Twentieth-Century Fantasy Literature.*

Fischer, Marjorie, and Rolf Humphries, eds. *Pause to Wonder: Stories of the Marvelous, Mysterious and Strange.*

Fischer, William B. *The Empire Strikes Out: Kurt Lasswitz, Hans Dominik, and the Development of German Science Fiction.*

Fitz Gerald, Gregory, ed. *Neutron Stars.*
———— and John Dillon, eds. *The Late Great Future.*

Fles, Barthold, ed. *The Saturday Evening Post Fantasy Stories.*

The Fontana Book of Great Ghost Stories, and 2–12. (Robert Aickman, ed. 1–6; R. Chetwynd-Hayes, ed. 9, 12)

The Fontana Book of Great Horror Stories, and 2–9. (Christine Bernard, ed. 1–4; Mary Danby, ed. 5–9)

Foote, Bud. *The Connecticut Yankee in the Twentieth Century: Travel to the Past in Science Fiction.*

Frank, Janrae, Jean Stine, and Forrest J Ackerman, eds. *New Eves: Science Fiction About the Extraordinary Women of Today and Tomorrow.*

Frank Reade Library (E. F. Bleiler, ed.; ten volume set of facsimile reprints reprints of this dime novel series).

Franklin, H. Bruce. *Future Perfect: American Science Fiction of the Nineteenth Century.*
————. *War Stars: The Superwagon and the American Imagination.*

Franson, Donald. *History of the Hugo and Nebula Awards.*

Frenkel, James. ed. *Bangs and Whimpers: Stories About the End of the World.*

Frewin, Anthony. *One Hundred Years of Science Fiction Illustration.*

Friesner, Esther, ed. *The Chick is in the Mail.*
————. *Chicks in Chainmail.*
————. *Chicks 'N Chained Males.*
————. *Did You Say Chicks?!*

Frost, Brian J. *The Monster with a Thousand Faces: Guises of the Vampire in Myth and Literature.*

Full Spectrum, and 2–5. [Lou Aronica and Shawna McCarthy, eds. (1); Lou Aronica, Amy Stout, and Patrick LoBrutto, eds. (2); Lou Aronica, Amy Stout, and Betsy Miller, eds. (3 and 4); Jennifer Hershey, Tom DuPree, and Janna Silverstein, eds. (5)]

Galewitz, Herb, ed. *Great Comics Syndicated by the Daily News-Chicago Tribune.*

Gallagher Edward J. *The Annotated Guide to Fantastic Adventures: Starmont Reference Guide No. 2.*

Gammell, Leon. *The Annotated Guide to Startling Stories: Starmont Reference Guide No. 3.*

Garnett, David S., ed. *Zenith: The Best in New British Science Fiction.*

The Galaxy Reader, and 2–11. (H. L. Gold, ed. 1–6; Frederik Pohl, ed. 7–11)

Gelb, Jeff, ed. *Shock Rock.*

Gerrold, David. *Worlds of Wonder: How to Write Science Fiction and Fantasy.*

Ghidalia, Vic, ed. *The Devil's Generation.*
————. *Eight Strange Tales.*
————. *Feast of Fear.*
————. *Gooseflesh.*
————. *The Mummy Walks Among Us.*
————. *Nightmare Garden.*
————. *The Oddballs.*
————. *Satan's Pets.*
————. *Wizards and Warlocks.*
————, and Roger Elwood, eds. *Beware the Beast.*
————. *The Venus Factor: Agatha Christie's "The Last Seance" and Other Stories.*

Ghosts and Things.

Ginsburg, Mirra, ed. *Last Door to AIYA: A Selection of the Best New Science Fiction from the Soviet Union.*
————. *The Ultimate Threshold: A Collection of the Finest in Soviet Science Fiction.*

Gold, H.L., ed.
————. *Mind Partner and 8 Other Novelets from Galaxy.*
————. *The Weird Ones.*
————. *The World That Couldn't Be and 8 Other Novelets from Galaxy.*

Goldin, Stephen, ed. *The Alien Countdown.*

Gorman, Ed, and Martin H. Greenberg, eds. *Night Screams.*
———. *Predators.*
———. *Stalkers.*
Goulart, Ron. *The Encyclopedia of American Comics from 1897 to the Present.*
Grant, Charles L., ed. *After Midnight.*
———. *The Best of Shadows.*
———. *The Dodd Mead Gallery of Horror.* (Reprinted as *Gallery of Horror: 20 Chilling Tales by Modern Masters of Dread.*)
———. *Fears.*
———. *Horrors.*
———. *Midnight.*
———. *Nightmares.*
———. *Shadows,* and 2–10.
———. *Terrors.*
Great Tales of Fantasy and Science Fiction.
Greenberg, Martin H., ed. *Amazing Science Fiction Anthology: The Wonder Years 1926–1935.*
———. *All About the Future.*
———. *Amazing Science Fiction Anthology: The War Years 1936–1945.*
———. *Amazing Science Fiction Anthology: The Wild Years 1946–1955.*
———. *Amazing Stories: Visions of Other Worlds.*
———. *Coming Attractions.*
———. *Fantastic Lives: Autobiographical Essays by Notable Science Fiction Writers.*
———. *Frankenstein: The Monster Wakes.*
———. *Isaac's Universe.* (vol. 1-"The Diplomacy Guild"; vol. 2-"Phases in Chaos"; vol. 3-"Unnatural Diplomacy")
———. *Journey to Infinity.*
———. *Men Against the Stars.*
———. *Merlin.*
———. *My Favorite Fantasy Story.*
———. *My Favorite Science Fiction Story.*
———. *Nebula Award-Winning Novellas.*
———. *The Robot and the Man.*
———. *A Taste for Blood: 15 Great Vampire Novels.*
———. *Travelers of Space.*
———. *The Way It Wasn't: Great Science Fiction Stories of Alternate History.*
———. *Wizard Fantastic.*
———, and Willy Ley, ed. *Men Against the Stars.*
———, and A.R. Morlan, eds. *Zodiac Fantastic.*
———, and Joseph D. Olander, eds. *International Relations Through Science Fiction.*
———. *Science Fiction of the 50's.*
———. *Tomorrow, Inc.: Science Fiction Stories About Big Business.*
———, and Larry Segriff, eds. *Battle Magic.*
———, and Robert Silverberg, eds. *Dawn of Time: Prehistory Through Science Fiction.*
———. *First Contact.*
———. *Future Net.*
———, and Scott H. Urban, eds. *The Conspiracy Files.*
———, and Charles G. Waugh, eds. *Animal Brigade 3000.*
———. *Commando Brigade 3000.*
———. *Devil Worshippers.*
———. *House Shudders.*
———. *Monster Brigade 3000.*
———. *Vamps.*
———, and Frank D. Sherry, eds. *Red Jack.*
Greenberg, Rosalind M., Martin Harry Greenberg, and Charles G. Waugh, eds. *14 Vicious Valentines.*
Gunn, James. *Alternate Worlds: The Illustrated History of Science Fiction.*
———, ed. *The Road to Science Fiction—Volume 1: From Gilgamesh to Wells, Volume 2: From Wells to Heinlein, Volume 3: From Heinlein to Here, Volume 4: From Here to Forever, Volume 5: The British Way, Volume 6: Around the World.*
———. *The Science of Science-Fiction Writing.*
Haining, Peter, ed. *The Ancient Mysteries Reader: Eighteen Classic Tales Inspired by the Unknown.*
———. *Beyond the Curtain of Dark.*

———. *The Clans of Darkness: Scottish Stories of Fantasy and Horror.*
———. *The Classic Era of American Pulp Magazines.*
———. *Dead of Night: Thirteen Stories by the Masters of the Macabre.*
———. *Deadly Nightshade: Seventeen Strange Tales of the Dark.*
———. *The Dracula Scrapbook.*
———. *Dr. Caligari's Black Book: An Excursion into the Macabre in Thirteen Acts.*
———. *Everyman's Book of Classic Horror Stories.*
———. *The Evil People.*
———. *The Fantastic Pulps.*
———. *The Flying Sorcerers.*
———. *The Frankenstein Omnibus.*
———. *The Future Makers.*
———. *The Gentle Women of Evil.*
———. *Ghost Tour: An Armchair Journey Through the Supernatural.*
———. *The Ghouls.*
———. *Gothic Tales of Terror: Classic Horror Stories from Great Britain, Europe, and the United States, 1765–1840.*
———. *Great Irish Tales of Terror: A Treasury of Fear.*
———. *The Hollywood Nightmare: Tales of Fantasy & Horror from the Film World.*
———. *Irish Tales of Terror.*
———. *The Lucifer Society.*
———. *The Magic Valley Travellers: Welsh Stories of Fantasy and Horror.*
———, ed. *The Mammoth Book of 20th Century Ghost Stories.*
———. *The Midnight People.*
———. *The Monster Makers.*
———. *Nightfrights: Occult Stories for All Ages.*
———. *The Nightmare Reader.*
———. *The Satanists.*
———. *The Shilling Shockers: Stories of Terror From the Gothic Blue Books.*
———. *Stories of the Walking Dead.*
———. *Terror!: A History of Horror Illustrations from the Pulp Magazines.*
———. *Timescapes: Stories of Time Travel.* (Reprinted as *Time Travelers: Fiction in the Fourth Dimension.*)
———. *The Unspeakable People.*
———. *Vampires at Midnight* (formerly *The Midnight People*).
———. *The Vampire Hunters' Casebook: Fourteen Stories by Bram Stoker, Anne Rice, Robert Bloch, Joseph Sheridan LeFanu, and Others.*
———. *Vintage Science Fiction Stories that Inspired Landmark Films.*
———. *Weird Tales: A Selection, in facsimile, of the best from the world's most famous fantasy magazine.*
———. *Where Nightmares Are: An Anthology of the World's Great Horror Stories.*
———. *The Wild Night Company: Irish Stories of Fantasy and Horror.*
———. *The Witchcraft Reader.*
———. *Wizards of Odd.*
———, ed. *Knights of Madness.*
———. *The Mammoth Book of 20th Century Ghost Stories.*

Haldeman, Joe, ed. *Study War No More: A Selection of Alternatives.*
———, Charles G. Waugh, and Martin Harry Greenberg, eds. *Spacefighters.*

Hamlin, V.T. *Alley Oop.* (3 vol. set of comic strip reprints done by Kitchen Sink Press)

Harding, Lee, ed. *Beyond Tomorrow.*

Harrison, Harry, ed. *Astounding: John W. Campbell Memorial Anthology.*
———. *Astounding: John W. Campbell Memorial Anthology.*
———. *Backdrop of Stars: The Craft of Science Fiction.*
———. *Best Science Fiction 1967, 1968–1971.*
———. *Four for the Future.*
———. *The Light Fantastic: Science Fiction Classics from the Mainstream.*
———. *Nova 1, 2–4.*
———. *One Step From Earth: 9 Science Fiction Adventures in Matter Transmission.*
———. *The Outdated Man* (formerly *Nova 3*).
———. *SF: Author's Choice*, and 2–4.
———. *Thirteen Original Stories by the Greatest Wriers of Astounding.*
———. *War of the Robots.*

————. *The Year 2000.*
————, and Brian W. Aldiss, eds. *Best SF,* (1967), 2 (1968)—5 (1971).
————, and Bruce McAllister, eds. *There Won't Be War.*
————, and Carol Pugner, eds. *A Science Fiction Reader.*

Hartwell, David G. *Age of Wonders: Exploring the World of Science Fiction.* (Revised 1996.)
————. *Bodies of the Dead and Other Great A,erican Ghost Stories.*
————. *Christmas Forever.*
————. *Christmas Magic.*
————. *Christmas Stars.*
————. *The Screaming Skull and Other Great American Ghost Stories.*
————, ed. *The Ascent of Wonder: The Evolution of Hard SF.*
————. *Dark Descent: The Evolution of Horror* (later published in three parts: *The Color of Evil, Medusa in the Shield,* and *A Fabulous, Formless, Darkness*).
————. *Foundations of Fear* (later published in three parts: *Shadows of Fear, Worlds of Fear,* and *Visions of Fear*).
————. *Masterpieces of Fantasy and Enchantment.*
————. *Masterpieces of Fantasy and Wonder.*
————. *The Science Fiction Century.*
————. *The World Treasury of Science Fiction.*
————. *Year's Best SF* (1996), and 2 (1997) to 6 (2001)
————, and Damien Broderick, eds. *Centaurus: The Best of Australian Science Fiction.*
————, and Kathryn Cramer. *The Ascent of Wonder.*
————, and Glenn Grant, eds. *Northern Stars: The Anthology of Canadian Science Fiction Writers.*
————. *Northern Suns: The New Anthology of Canadian Science Fiction.*

Healy, Raymond J., ed. *New Tales of Space and Time.*
————, and J. Francis McComas, eds. *Adventures in Time and Space.*
————. *More Adventures in Time and Space.*

Hein, Rolland. *Christian Mythmakers.*

Heinlein, Robert A., ed. *Tomorrow, The Stars.*

Heintz, Bonnie L. et al., eds. *Tomorrow, and Tomorrow, and Tomorrow . . .*

Hillegas, Mark R. *The Future as Nightmare: H.G. Wells and the Anti-Utopians.*

Hipolito, Jane, and Willis E. McNelly, eds. *Mars, We Love You.*

Holdstock, Robert, ed. *The Encyclopedia of Science Fiction.*

Holmes, Robert, ed. *Macabre Railway Stories.*

Hoopes, Ned E., ed. *Speak of the Devil: 17 Diabolical Tales.*

Horn, Maurice, ed. *The World Encyclopedia of Comics.*

Horsting, Jessica, and James Van Hise, eds. *Midnight Graffiti.*

Hoskins, Robert, ed. *Against Tomorrow.*
————. *The Edge of Never.*
————. *First Step Outward.*
————. *The Future Now.*
————. *Infinity 1–5.*
————. *The Liberated Future: Voyages Into Tomorrow.*
————. *The Stars Around Us.*
————. *Strange Tomorrows.*
————. *Swords Against Tomorrow.*
————. *Wondermakers: An Anthology of Classic Science Fiction.*

Howard, Ivan, ed. *Novelets of Science Fiction.*

Huntington, John. *Rationalizing Genius: Ideological Strategies in the Classic American Science Fiction Short Story.*

Hutchison, Don. *The Great Pulp Heroes.*
————, ed. *Northern Frights,* and 2–4.

Ikin, Van, ed. *Australian Science Fiction.*

Jacobson, Karie, ed. *Simulations: 15 Tales of Virtual Reality.*

Jaffery, Sheldon. *The Arkham House Companion: Fifty Years of Arkham House.*
————. *The Collector's Index to Weird Tales.*

————. *Future and Fantastic Worlds: A Bibliographical Retrospective of DAW Books (1972–1987).*
————. *Horrors and Unpleasantries: A Bibliographical History and Collector's Price Guide to Arkham House.*
————, ed. *Sensuous Science Fiction from the Weird and Spicy Pulps.*
Jakubowski, Moaxim, and Edward James. *The Profession of Science Fiction: SF Writers on Their Craft and Ideas.*
James, Edward. *Science Fiction in the 20th Century.*
Janifer, Laurence M., ed. *18 Greatest Science Fiction Stories.*
————. *Masters' Choice.*
Jarvis, Sharon, ed. *Inside Outer Space: Science Fiction Professionals Look at Their Craft.*
Jones, Diana Wynne, ed. *Hidden Turnings: Stories Through Time and Space.*
Jones, Stephen, ed. *The Mammoth Book of Frankenstein.*
————. *The Mammoth Book of Dracula.*
————. *The Mammoth Book of Best New Horror,* and 2–12 (2001).
————. *The Mammoth Book of Terror.*
————. *The Mammoth Book of Vampires.*
————. *The Mammoth Book of Werewolves.*
————. *The Mammoth Book of Zombies.*
————, and Kim Newman, eds. *Horror: The 100 Best Books*
Joshi, S. T., ed. *Great Weird Tales.*
Justice, Keith L. *Science Fiction, Fantasy, and Horror References: An Annotated Bibliography of Works About Literature and Film.*
Kahn, Joan, ed. *The Edge of the Chair.*
————. *The Graveyard Shift: More Tales from the Edge of the Chair.*
————. *Some Things Dark and Dangerous.*
————. *Some Things Fierce and Fatal.*
————. *Some Things Strange and Sinister.*
————. *Some Things Weird and Wicked.*
Karloff, Boris, ed. *And the Darkness Falls.*
————. *Boris Karloff's Favorite Horror Stories.*
Karp, Marvin Allen, and Irving Settel, eds. *Suddenly: Great Stories of Suspense and the Unexpected.*
Kaye, Marvin, ed. *Devils & Demons: A Treasury of Fiendish Tales Old & New.*
————. *Don't Open This Book!*
————. *Fiends and Creatures.*
————. *Ghosts: A Treasury of Chilling Tales Old & New.*
————. *Haunted America.*
————. *Lovers and Other Monsters: Romantic Stories of Horror.*
————. *Masterpieces of Terror and the Unknown.*
————. *13 Plays of Ghosts and the Supernatural.*
————. *Weird Tales: The Magazine that Never Dies.*
————. *Witches and Warlocks.*
————, and John Gregory Betancourt, eds. *The Best of Weird Tales: 1923.*
Kessel, John, Mark L. Van Nane, and Richard Butner, eds. *Intersections: The Sycamore Hill Anthology.*
Ketterer, Dave. *New Worlds for Old: The Apocalyptic Imagination, Science Fiction, and American Literature.*
Keyes, Noel, ed, *Contact.*
Kidd, Virginia, ed. *Millenial Women.*
Kilian, Crawford. *Writing Science Fiction and Fantasy.*
King, Betty. *Women of the Future: The Female Main Character in Science Fiction.*
King, Stephen. *Danse Macabre.*
Knight, Damon. *In Search of Wonder: Essays on Modern Science Fiction.*
————, ed. *The Best from Orbit.*
————. *Beyond Tomorrow.*
————. *A Century of Great Short Science Fiction Novels.*
————. *Cities of Wonder.*
————. *The Clarion Awards.*
————. *The Dark Side.*
————. *Dimension X.*
————. *First Flight.*

————. *First Voyages.*

————. *The Futurians: The Story of the Great Science Fiction "Family" of the 30's that Produced Today's Top SF Writers and Editors.*

————, ed. *Happy Endings: 15 Stories by Masters of the Macabre.*

————. *The Metal Smile: 12 Battles of Wits Between Man and Machine.*

————. *Nebula Award Stories.*

————. *Now Begins Tomorrow: First Voyages of Today's Masters of Science Fiction.*

————. *One Hundred Years of Science Fiction.*

————. *Orbit 1–13.*

————. *A Science Fiction Argosy.*

————. *Science Fiction of the 30's.*

————. *Science Fiction of the 40's.*

————. *In Search of Wonder,* Revised and Enlarged 2nd ed.

————. *The Shape of Things.*

————. *A Shocking Thing.*

————. *13 French Science-Fiction Stories.*

————. *Tomorrow and Tomorrow: Ten Tales of the Future.*

————. *Worlds to Come.*

Kornbluth, Mary, ed. *Science Fiction Showcase.*

Kreuziger, Frederick A. *The Religion of Science Fiction.*

Kushner, Ellen, ed. *Basilisk.*

————, Delia Sherman, and Donald G. Keller, eds. *The Horns of Elfland.*

Kyle, David. *The Illustrated Book of Science Fiction Ideas & Dreams.*

————. *A Pictorial History of Science Fiction.*

Lackey, Mercedes, ed. *Sword of Ice and Other Tales of Valdemar.*

Lamb, Hugh, ed. *Terror by Gaslight: An Anthology of Rare Tales of Terror.*

————. *Cold Fear: New Tales of Terror.*

————. *Forgotten Tales of Horror.*

————. *Gaslit Nightmares,* and 2.

————. *The Man Wolf and Other Horrors.*

————. *New Tales of Terror.*

————. *Return from the Grave.*

————. *Star Book of Horror,* and 2.

————. *Tales from a Gaslit Graveyard.*

————. *The Taste of Fear.*

————. *The Thrill of Horror.*

————. *A Tide of Terror: An Anthology of Rare Horror Stories.*

————. *Victorian Nightmares.*

————. *Victorian Tales of Terror* and *More Victorian Tales of Terror.*

————. *A Wave of Fear.*

Last Train to Limbo.

Lawler, Donald L. ed. *Approaches to Science Fiction.*

Laumer, Keith, ed. *Dangerous Vegetables.*

Lee, Christopher, ed. *Christopher Lee's Treasury of Terror.*

————, and Michel Parry, eds. *From the Archives of Evil,* and 2.

Lefanu, Sarah. *In the Chinks of the World Machine: Feminism and Science Fiction* (also entitled *Feminism and Science Fiction*).

LeGuin, Ursula. *Dancing at the Edge of the World: Thoughts on Words, Women, Places.*

————. *The Language of the Night: Essays on Fantasy and Science Fiction.*

————, and Brian Attebery, eds. *The Norton Book of Science Fiction: North American Science Fiction 1960–1990.*

————, and Virginia Kidd, eds. *Edges: Thirteen New Tales from the Borderlands of Imagination.*

Lem, Stanislaw. *Microworlds: Writings on Science Fiction and Fantasy.*

Lesser, Robert. *Pulp Art.*

Lewis, Tony, ed., *The Best of Astounding.*

Licata, Tony, ed. *Great Science-Fiction.*

Lovecraft, Howard Phillips. *Supernatural Horror in Literature.*

Lowery, Lawrence F. *Lowery's The Collector's Guide to Big Little Books and Similar Books.*

Lundwall, Sam J. *Science Fiction: An Illustrated History.*

Lupoff, Richard, A., ed. *What If?*, and *2.*

Malmgren, Carl. *Worlds Apart: Narratology of Science Fiction.*

Malzberg, Barry. *The Engines of the Night: Science Fiction in the Eighties.*

Malzberg, Barry N., Martin Harry Greenberg, and Joseph D. Olander, eds. *Neglected Visions.*

Malzberg, Barry N., and Bill Pronzini, eds. *The End of Summer: Science Fiction of the Fifties.*

Manlove, Colin. Science Fiction: Ten Explorations.

Manson, Cynthia, and Charles Ardai, eds. *Future Crime: An Anthology of the Shape of Crime to Come.*
————, and Constance Scarborough, eds. *The Haunted Hour.*

Margolies, Joseph A., ed. *Strange and Fantastic Stories.*

Margulies, Leo, ed. *The Ghoul Keepers.*
————. *Get Out of My Sky.*
————. *3 From Out There.*
————. *3 in 1.*
————. *Three Times Infinity.*
————. *The Unexpected.*
————. *Weird Tales.*
————. *Worlds of Weird.*
————, and Oscar J. Friend, eds. *From Off This World.*
————. *My Best Science Fiction Story.*
————. *Race to the Stars.*

Marschall, Richard. *America's Great Comic Strip Artists.*

Martin, George R. R., ed. *New Voices: The John W. Campbell Award Nominees* 1 (1977) –4.
————. *Wild Cards.* I–XI. (*Wild Cards, Aces High, Joker's Wild, Aces Abroad, Down and Dirty, Ace in the Hole, Dead Man's Hand, One-Eyed Jacks, Jokertown Shuffle, Double Solitaire,* and *Dealer's Choice*).
————. *Wild Cards: A New Cycle.* I–II. (*Card Sharks* and *Marked Cards*).

Mason, Carol, Martin Harry Greenberg, and Patricia Warrick, eds. *Anthropology Through Science Fiction.*

Masters, Anthony, ed. *Cries of Terror.*

Masters of Science Fiction.

Mazzeo, Henry, ed. *Hauntings: Tales of the Supernatural.*

McCaffery, Anne, ed. *Alchemy and Academe.*
————. *Space Opera.*

McCaffrey, Larry. *Storming the Reality Studio: A Casebook of Cyberpunk and Postmodern Science Fiction.*
————, ed. *Across the Wounded Galaxies: Interviews with Contemporary Science Fiction Writers.*

McCammon, Robert, ed. *Under the Fang.*

McCarthy, Helen. *The Anime Movie Guide.*

McCarthy, Shawna, ed. *Isaac Asimov's Aliens and Outworlders.*
————. *Isaac Asimov's Fantasy!*
————. *Isaac Asimov's Space of Her Own.*

McCauley, Kirby, ed. *Beyond Midnight.*
————. *Dark Forces: New Stories of Suspense and Supernatural Horror.*
————. *Frights.*
————. *Night Chills.*

McComas, Annette Peltz, ed. *The Eureka Years: Boucher and McComas's Magazine of Fantasy & Science 1949–1954.*

McComas, J. Francis, ed. *Special Wonder* (later released in two vols.).

McCurdy, Howard E. *Space and the American Imagination.*

McKinley, Robin, ed. *Imaginary Lands.*

McSherry, Frank D. Jr., ed. The Fantastic Civil War.
————, Charles G. Waugh, and Martin H. Greenberg, eds. *Great American Ghost Stories.*
————. *A Treasury of American Horror Stories.*

Melvin, Kenneth B., Stanley L. Brodsky, and Raymond D. Fowler, Jr., eds. *Psy Fi One: An Anthology of Psychology in Science Fiction.*

Merril, Judith, ed. *SF: The Best of the Best.*
———. *Beyond Human Ken.*
———. *Beyond the Barriers of Space and Time.*
———. *Galaxy of Ghouls.* (Reprinted as *Off the Beaten Path.*)
———. *Judith Merril's England Swings SF.*
———. *SF: The Year's Greatest Science-Fiction and Fantasy* 1 (1957) through 12 (1968).

Meyers, Walter E. *Aliens and Linguists: Language Study and Science Fiction.*

Midnight Fright: A Collection of Ghost Stories.

Miller, Fred, D., Jr., and Nicholas D. Smith, eds. *Thought Probes.*

Mills, Robert P., ed. *A Decade of Fantasy and Science Fiction.*
———. *The Worlds of Science Fiction.*

Milstead, John W., Martin Harry Greenberg, Joseph D. Olander, and Patricia Warrick, eds. *Sociology Through Science Fiction.*

Mohan, Kim, ed. *Amazing Stories: The Anthology.*
———. *More Amazing Stories.*

Mohs, Mayo, ed. *Other Worlds, Other Gods.*

Moloney, Kathleen, and Shawna McCarthy, eds. *Isaac Asimov's Wonders of the World.*

Molson, Francis J., and Roger Schlobin. *Children's Fantasy* (Starmont Reader's Guide 14).

Moorcock, Michael, ed. *Wizardry and Wild Romance.*
———. *The Best Science Fiction from New Worlds,* and 2–6.
———. *New Worlds Quarterly,* and 2.

Morrison, Robert, and Chris Baldick, eds. *Tales of Terror From Blackwood's Magazine.*
———. *The Vampyre and Other Tales of the Macabre.*

Moskowitz, Sam. *Explorers of the Infinite: Shapers of Science Fiction.*
———. *Hugo Gernsback: Father of Science Fiction.*
———. *The Immortal Storm: A History of Science Fiction Fandom.*
———. *Science Fiction in Old San Francisco: Volume 1, History of the Movement, 1854–1890; Volume 2, "Into the Sun" and Other Stories, A Collection of Short Stories by Robert Duncan Milne.*
———. *Seekers of Tomorrow: Masters of Modern Science Fiction.*
———. *Strange Horizons: The Spectrum of Science Fiction.*
———, ed. *The Coming of the Robots.*
———. *Editor's Choice in Science Fiction.* (1954)
———. *Exploring Other Worlds: Eight Great Tales of Interplanetary Adventure.*
———. *Futures to Infinity.*
———. *Horrors Unknown.* (Byline misspells author's name as "Moscowitz.")
———. *The Human Zero and Other Science Fiction Masterpieces.*
———. *The Man Who Called Himself Poe.*
———. *Masterpieces of Science Fiction.*
———. *Microcosmic God.* (Byline misspells author's name as "Moscowitz.")
———. *Modern Masterpieces of Science Fiction.* (Reprinted, in part, as *Doorway Into Time* and *The Vortex Blasters.*)
———. *The Moon Era.*
———. *Other Worlds, Other Times.*
———. *Sense of Wonder.*
———. *Science Fiction by Gaslight: A History and Anthology of Science Fiction in the Popular Magazines, 1891–1911.*
———. *Three Stories.*
———. *Under the Moons of Mars: A History and Anthology of "The Scientific Romance" in the Munsey Magazines, 1912–1920.*
———. *When Women Rule.*
———, and Roger Elwood, eds. *Other Worlds, Other Times.*
———. *The Time Curve: Startling and Prophetic Tales by the World's Greatest Science Fiction Writers.*

Moylan, Tom. *Demand the Impossible: Science Fiction and the Utopian Imagination.*

Mullen, R.D., and Darko Suvin, eds. *Science-Fiction Studies: Selected Articles on Science Fiction, 1973–1975.*
———. *Science-Fiction Studies, Second Series: Selected Articles on Science Fiction, 1976–1977.*

Murray, Terry A. *Science Fiction Magazine Story Index.*

The Nebula Awards, and 2 to 33 (1999). [1 (1965)—Damon Knight, 2—Brian W. Aldiss and Harry Harrison, 3—Roger Zelazny, 4—Paul Anderson, 5—James Blish, 6—Clifford D. Simak, 7—Lloyd Biggle Jr., 8—Isaac Asimov, 9—Kate Wilhelm, 10—James Gunn, 11—Ursula K. LeGuin, 12—Gordon R. Dickson, 13—Samuel R. Delany, 14—Frederik Pohl, 15—Frank Herbert, 16—Jerry Parnelle, 17—Joe Haldeman, 18—Robert Silverberg, 19—Marta Randall, 20–22—George Zebrowski, 23–25—Michael Bishop, 26–28—James Morrow, 29–31—Pamela Sargent, 32—Jack Dann, 33—Connie Willis, *Nebula Awards Showcase 2000*—Gregory Benford.]

Nicholls, Peter (with David Langford and Brian Stableford). *The Science in Science Fiction.*

Night Visions. (This is a nine-volume set of Dark Fantasy anthologies edited by Alan Ryan, Charles L. Grant, George R.R. Martin, Clive Barker, Douglas E. Winter, Dean R. Koontz, Stanley Wiater, Robert R. McCammon, and F. Paul Wilson, respectively. The first six volumes were reprinted in mass market paperback as *In the Blood, Dead Image, The Hellbound Heart, Hardshell, The Skin Trade,* and *The Bone Yard.*)

Nolan, William F., ed. *The Pseudo-People: Androids in Science Fiction.*
——. *The Human Equation: Four Science Fiction Novels of Tomorrow.*
——. *3 to the Highest Power.*
——. *A Sea of Space.*
——. *Urban Horrors.*
——. *A Wilderness of Stars.*
——, and Martin H. Greenberg, eds. *Science Fiction Origins: The Original Stories on which Seven Classic Novels were Based.*
——, and William Schafer, eds. *California Sorcery.*

Nolane, Richard D. *Terra SF: The Year's Best European SF,* and 2.

Norton, Alden H., ed. *The Award Science Fiction Reader.*
——. *Horrors and Hauntings: Ten Grisly Tales.*
——. *Horror Times Ten.*
——. *Masters of Horror.*
——, and Sam Moskowitz, eds. *Ghostly by Gaslight.*
——. *Great Untold Stories of Fantasy and Horror.*
——. *Horrors in Hiding.*
——. *The Space Magicians.*

Norton, Andre, ed. *Grand Masters' Choice.*
——, and Martin H. Greenberg, eds. *Catfantastic,* and 2–4.

Nuetzel, Charles, ed. *If This Goes On.*

Notkin, Debbie, and the Secret Feminist Cabal, eds. *Flying Cups and Saucers: Gender Exploration in Science Fiction and Fantasy.*

Olander, Joseph D., and Martin H. Greenberg, eds. *Criminal Justice Through Science Fiction.*
——. *Time Passage: Science Fiction Stories About Death and Dying.*
——, and Patricia Warrick, eds. *American Government Through Science Fiction.*
——. *School and Society Through Science Fiction.*

Osborne, John, and David Paskow, eds. *Looking Back on Tomorrow: Worlds of Science Fiction.*

Overstreet, Robert M. *Overstreet's Comic Book Price Guide,* 30th ed. (2001).

Owen, Betty M., ed. *11 Great Horror Stories.*

Page, Gerald W., ed. *Nameless Places.*

The Pan Book of Horror Stories, 2–28. (Herbert van Thal, ed. 2–25, Clarence Paget, ed. 26–28)

Panshin, Alexei and Cory. *Science Fiction in Dimension: A Book of Explorations.*
——. *The World Beyond the Hill: Science Fiction and the Quest for Transcendence.*

Parnell, Frank H., and Mike Ashley, eds. *Monthly Terrors: An Index to the Weird Fantasy Magazines Published in the United States and Great Britain.*

Parrinder, Patrick. *Science Fiction: Its Criticism and Teaching.*

Parry, Michel, ed. *Beware of the Cat.*
——. *Book of Black Magic.*
——. *Countess Dracula.*
——. *The Devil's Children: Tales of Demons and Exorcists.*
——. *The Hounds of Hell: Stories of Canine Horror.*
——. *Mayflower Book of Black Magic,* and 2–4.
——. *The Reign of Terror.*

———. *The Rivals of Dracula.*
———. *The Rivals of Frankenstein.*
———. *The Roots of Evil: Weird Stories of Supernatural Plants.*
———. *Savage Heroes: Tales of Magical Fantasy.*
———. *Strange Ecstasies.*
———. *Superheroes.*
———. *The Supernatural Solution: Chilling Stories of Spooks & Sleuths.*
Path Into the Unknown: The Best of Soviet Science Fiction.
Pattrick, William (psd. for Peter Haining), ed. *Mysterious Air Stories.*
———. *Mysterious Railway Stories.*
———. *Mysterious Sea Stories.*
Pelan, John, ed. *Horror for the Next Millenium.*
Peyton, Richard, ed. *Journey Into Fear and Other Great Stories of Horror of the Railways.*
Phillips, Michael, ed. *Philosophy and Science Fiction.*
Phillips, Robert, ed. *Nightshade: 20th Century Ghost Stories.*
Philmus, Robert M. *Into the Unknown: The Evolution of Science Fiction From Francis Godwin to H. G. Wells.*
Pierce, John J. *Foundations of Science Fiction: A Study in Imagination and Evolutiuon* (4 vols.).
The Playboy Book of Horror and the Supernatural.
The Playboy Book of Science Fiction and Fantasy.
The Playboy Book of the Sinister and Strange.
Pohl, Carol and Frederik, eds. *Science Fiction: The Great Years,* and II.
———. *Science Fiction Discoveries.*
Pohl, Frederik. *The Way the Future Was: A Memoir.*
———, ed. *Assignment in Tomorrow.*
———. *The Expert Dreamers.*
———. *The IF Reader of Science Fiction* and *The Second IF Reader of Science Fiction.*
———. *Nightmare Age.*
———. *The Science Fiction Role of Honor.*
———. *The SFWA Grand Masters,* Vols. 1–3.
———. *The Seventh Galaxy Reader.*
———. *Shadows of Tomorrow.*
———. *Star of Stars: The Best Stories from the Famous STAR Collections.*
———. *Star Science Fiction,* and 2–6.
———. *Yesterday's Tomorrows.*
———, and Elizabeth Anne Hull, eds. *Tales From the Planet Earth.*
Pohl, Frederik, Martin H. Greenberg, and Joseph D. Olander, eds. *Galaxy,* and 2.
———. *Galaxy: Thirty Years of Innovative Science Fiction.*
———. *The Great Science Fiction Series.*
———. *Science Fiction of the 1940s.*
———. *Worlds of IF: A Retrospective Anthology.*
The Post Reader of Fantasy and Science Fiction.
Pournelle, Jerry, ed. *2020 Vision: Eight Fascinating Studies of Life in the Year 2020.*
Pratt, Fletcher, ed. *World of Wonder: An Introduction to Imaginative Fiction.*
Preiss, Byron, ed. *Weird Heroes,* 1–8.
———, and John Betancourt, eds. *The Ultimate Dragon.*
———. *The Ultimate Dracula.*
———. *The Ultimate Frankenstein.*
———. *The Ultimate Werewolf.*
———. *The Ultimate Witch.*
———. *The Ultimate Zombie.*
———, and Keith R.A. DeCandido, eds. *The Ultimate Alien.*
———, and Robert Silverberg, eds. *The Ultimate Dinosaur.*
Pringle, David. *Modern Fantasy: The 100 Best Novels.*
———. *Science Fiction: The 100 Best Novels—An English-Language Selection, 1949–1984.*
———, ed. *The Best of Interzone.*
———. *Imaginary People: A Who's Who of Fictional Characters from the Eighteenth Century to the Present Day.*

————. *The St. James Guide to Fantasy Writers.*

————. *The St. James Guide to Horror, Ghost, and Gothic Writers.*

————. *The Ultimate Encyclopedia of Fantasy.*

————. *The Ultimate Guide to Science Fiction: An A–Z of Science Fiction Books by Title,* 2nd ed.

Pronzini, Bill, ed. *Specter! A Chrestomathy of "Spookery".*

————, and Barry N. Malzberg, eds. *Bug-Eyed Monsters.*

————, and Martin H. Greenberg, eds. *The Arbor House Treasury of Horror and the Supernatural.*

Protter, Eric, ed. *A Harvest of Horrors.*

Purtill, Richard. *Lord of the Elves and Eldils: Fantasy and Philosophy in C.S. Lewis and J.R.R. Tolkien.*

Rabkin, Eric S. *The Fantastic in Literature.*

————, ed. *Fantastic Worlds: Myths, Tales, and Stories.*

————. *Science Fiction: An Historical Anthology.*

————, Martin H. Greenberg, and Joseph D. Olander, eds. *The End of the World.*

————. *No Place Else: Explorations in Utopian and Dystopian Fiction.*

Rathbone, Basil, ed. *Basil Rathbone Selects Strange Tales.*

Raymond, Alex. *Flash Gordon.* (six volume set of color comic strip reprints done by Kitchen Sink Press)

Resnick, Michael, ed. *Alternate Kennedys.*

————. *Alternate Outlaws.*

————. *Alternate Presidents.*

————. *Alternate Tyrants.*

————. *Alternate Warriors.*

————, and Martin H. Greenberg, eds. *By Any Other Fame: 23 Alternate Futures of the World's Most Famous and Infamous Celebrities.*

————. *Return of the Dinosaurs.*

————. *Sherlock Holmes in Orbit.*

Riley, Dick, ed. *Critical Encounters: Writers and Themes in Science Fiction.*

Robinson, Frank M. *Science Fiction of the 20th Century: An Illustrated History.*

————, and Lawrence Davidson. *Pulp Culture: The Art of Fiction Magazines.*

Roberson, Jennifer, ed. *Return to Avalon.*

Rock, James A. *Who Goes There? A Bibliographic Dictionary of Pseudonymous Literature in the Fields of Fantasy and Science Fiction.*

Rogers, Alva. *A Requiem for Astounding.*

Rose, Mark. *Alien Encounters: Anatomy of Science Fiction.*

Rosheim, David L. *Galaxy Magazine: The Dark and the Light Years.*

Rottensteiner, Franz. *The Fantasy Book: An Illustrated History from Dracula to Tolkein.*

————, ed. *View From Another Shore: From Poland's Stanislaw Lem to France's Gerald Klein, Europe's Most Exciting Explorers of Man's Outer Limits.*

Ruber, Peter, ed. *Arkham's Masters of Horror.*

Rucker, Rudy, Peter Lamborn Wilson, and Robert Anton Wilson, eds. *Semiotext[e] SF.*

Ruddick, Nicholas. *Ultimate Island: On the Nature of British Science Fiction.*

Russ, Joanna. *To Write Like a Woman: Essays in Feminism and Science Fiction.*

Ryan, Alan, ed. *Halloween Horrors.*

————. *Haunting Women.*

————. *The Penguin Book of Vampire Stories.*

————. *Perpetual Light.*

————. *Vampires: Two Centuries of Great Vampire Stories.*

Ryan, Charles C. *Starry Messenger: The Best of Galileo.*

Saberhagen, Fred, ed. *A Spadeful of Spacetime.*

Saberhagen, Fred, and Martin Harry Greenberg, eds. *Machines That Kill.*

————, and Joan Saberhagen, eds. *Pawn to Infinity: Science Fiction and the Game of Kings.*

Sadoul, Jacques. *2000 A.D.: Illustrations from the Golden Age of Science Fiction Pulps.*

St. James Guide to Science Fiction Writers, 4th ed.

Sallis, James, ed. *The Shores Beneath.*

Salmonson, Jessica Amanda, ed. *Amazons! and Amazons II.*

————. *The Haunted Wherry and Other Rare Ghost Stories.*

————. *Heroic Visions, and 2.*

————. *Tales by Moonlight.*

————. *What Did Miss Darrington See?: Am Anthology of Feminist Supernatural Fiction.*

Sammon, Paul M., ed. *Splatterpunks: Extreme Horror.*

Sampson, Robert. *Yesterday's Faces: A Study of Series Characters in the Early Pulp Magazines, Volume 1: Glory Figures; Volume 2: Strange Days; Volume 3: From the Dark Side; Volume 4: The Solvers; Volume 5: Dangerous Horizons; Volume 6: Violent Lives.*

Sandner, David, and Jacob Weisman, eds. *The Treasury of the Fantastic.*

Santesson, Hans Stefan, ed. *The Fantastic Universe Omnibus.*

————. *Crime Prevention in the 30th Century.*

————. *The Day After Tomorrow.*

————. *Gentle Invaders.*

————. *Gods for Tomorrow.*

————. *The Mighty Barbarians.*

————. *The Mighty Swordsmen.*

————. *Rulers of Men.*

Sargent, Pamela, ed. *Women of Wonder: The Classic Years.*

————. *Bio-Futures: Science Fiction Stories About Biology.*

————. *The Sudden Star.*

————. *Women of Wonder, More Women of Wonder, and New Women of Wonder.*

————. *Women of Wonder: The Contemporary Years.*

Sarrantonio, Al, ed. *999: New Stories of Horror and Suspense.*

Sauer, Rob, ed. *Voyages: Scenarios for a Ship Called Earth.*

Scarborough, Elizabeth, and Martin H. Greenberg, eds. *Warrior Princesses.*

Schiff, Stuart David, ed. *The Best of Whispers.*

————. *Death.*

————. *Mad Scientists: An Anthology of Fantasy and Horror.*

————. *Whispers, and II-VI.*

————, and Fritz Leiber, eds. *The World Fantasy Awards, and 2.*

Schlobin, Roger C. *Urania's Daughters: A Checklist of Women Science Fiction Writers (1692–1982).*

Schmidt, Stanley, ed. *Analog Readers' Choice.*

————. *Analog Writers' Choice.*

————. *Fifty Years of the Best of Science Fiction from Analog.*

————. *Unknown.*

————, and Martin H. Greenberg, eds. *Unknown Worlds: Tales from Beyond (A Collection of Classic Science Fiction and Fantasy Short Stories from the Annals of Unknown Worlds Magazine).*

Schwartz, Sheila, ed. *Earth in Transit.*

Science Fiction by the Rivals of H.G. Wells.

The Science Fiction Hall of Fame. (Vol. 1 — Robert Silverberg, ed.; Vols. 2A and 2B — Ben Bova, ed.; Vol. 3 — Clarke, Arthur C., and George W. Proctor, eds.)

The Science Fiction Novel: Imagination and Social Criticism.

Scithers, George, ed. *Black Holes and Bug-Eyed Monsters.*

————. *Asimov's Choice: Comets & Computers.*

————. *Isaac Asimov's Marvels of Science Fiction.*

————. *Isaac Asimov's Masters of Science Fiction.*

————. *Isaac Asimov's Worlds of Science Fiction.*

Scortia, Thomas N., ed. *Strange Bedfellows: Sex and Science Fiction.*

Searles, Baird, et al., eds. *A Reader's Guide to Fantasy.*

————. *A Reader's Guide to Science Fiction.*

Serling, Rod, ed. *Devils and Demons.*

————. *Rod Serling's Triple W: Witches, Warlocks and Werewolves.*

Shaw, Larry T., ed. *Great Science Fiction Adventures.*

————. *Terror!*

Sheppard, Leslie, ed. *Classic Vampire Stories.*

————. *The Dracula Book of Great Vampire Stories.*

Shippey, Tom, ed. *The Oxford Book of Fantasy Stories.*

————. *The Oxford Book of Science Fiction Stories.*

Shwartz, Susan, ed. *Moonsinger's Friends: An Anthology in Honor of Andre Norton.*
———. *Sisters in Fantasy, and II.*
Silverberg, Robert, ed. *Alpha*, and 2–9.
———. *Battlefields of Tomorrow: Science Fiction War Stories.*
———. *The Best of New Dimensions.*
———. *Dark Stars.*
———. *Deep Space.*
———. *Earthmen and Strangers.*
———. *The Ends of Time.*
———. *Explorers of Space.*
———. *The Fantasy Hall of Fame: Chosen by the Members of the Science Fiction & Fantasy Writers of America.* (1998).
———. *Far Horizons: All New Tales From the Greatest Worlds of Science Fiction.*
———. *Invaders from Space.*
———. *Legends: Short Novels by the Masters of Modern Fantasy.*
———. *The Mirror of Infinity: A Critics' Anthology of Science Fiction.*
———. *The New Atlantis and Other Novellas of Science Fiction.*
———. *New Dimensions* 1–11.
———. *Other Dimensions.*
———. *The Science Fiction Bestiary.*
———. *Science Fiction 101.* (Originally published as Robert Silverberg's Worlds of Wonder.)
———. *Strange Gifts: Eight Stories of Science Fiction.*
———. *Voyagers in Time.*
———. *Windows Into Tomorrow.*
———, Martin H. Greenberg, eds. *Time Travellers.*
———, and Joseph D. Olander, eds. *Car Sinister.*
Silverberg, Robert, and Martin H. Greenberg, eds. *The Arbor House Treasury of Great Science Fiction Short Novels.*
———. *The Arbor House Treasury of Great Science Fiction.*
———. *The Arbor House Treasury of Modern Science Fiction.*
———. *The Arbor House Treasury of Science Fiction Masterpieces.*
———. *The Fantasy Hall of Fame.* (1983).
———. *The Horror Hall of Fame.*
Singer, Kurt, ed. *Ghouls and Ghosts.*
———. *The Gothic Reader.*
———. *I Can't Sleep at Night.*
———. *The Plague of the Living Dead.*
———. *Tales from the Unknown.*
———. *Tales of the Uncanny.*
———. *Tales of Terror.*
———. *They are Possessed: Masters of Exorcism.*
———. *The Unearthly.*
The 6 Fingers of Time.
Skipp, John, and Craig Spector, eds. *The Book of the Dead.*
———. *Still Dead.*
Slung, Michelle, ed. *I Shudder at Your Touch: 22 Tales of Sex and Horror.*
———. *Shudder Again: 22 Tales of Sex and Horror.*
Slusser, George E., George R. Guffey, and Mark Rose, eds. *Bridges to Science Fiction.*
———, Erik S. Rabkin, and Robert Scholes, eds. *Coordinates: Placing Science Fiction and Fantasy.*
———, and Tom Shippey, eds. Fiction 2000: *Cyberpunk and the Future of Narrative.*
Snodgrass, Melinda M., ed. *A Very Large Array.*
Soviet Science Fiction.
Space Odyssey: An Anthology of Great Science Fiction Stories.
Spector, Robert Donald, ed. *Seven Masterpieces of Gothic Horror.*
Spinrad, Norman, ed. *Modern Science Fiction.*
———. *Science Fiction in the Real World.*
Stableford, Brian. *Scientific Romance in Britain, 1890–1950.*
———, ed. *The Dedalus Book of British Fantasy: The 19th Century.*
Sterling, Bruce, ed. *Mirrorshades: The Cyberpunk Anthology.*

Stern, Philip Van Doren, ed. *Great Tales of Fantasy and Imagination.*
———. *The Other Side of the Clock.*
———. *The Pocket Book of Ghost Stories.*
———. *Strange Beasts and Unnatural Monsters.*
———. *Travelers in Time.*
Strick, Philip, ed. *Antigrav.*
Stover, Leon E., and Harry Harrison, eds. *Apeman, Spaceman.*
Strating, J.J., ed. *European Tales of Terror.*
———. *Oriental Tales of Terror.*
———. *Sea Tales of Terror.*
Stugatsky, Boris & Arkady, eds. *Aliens, Travellers, and Other Strangers.*
Sturgis, Susanna J., ed. *Memories and Visions: Women's Fantasy & Science Fiction.*
———. *The Women Who Walk Through Fire: Women's Fantasy & Science Fiction, Volume 2.*
Sullivan, Jack, ed. *The Penguin Encyclopedia of Horror and the Supernatural.*
Sullivan, Tim, ed. *Tropical Chills.*
Survey of Science Fiction Literature.
Suvin, Darko. *Metamorphoses of Science Fiction: On the Poetics and History of a Literary Genre.*
———. *Positions and Presuppositions in Science Fiction.*
———. *Victorian Science Fiction in the UK: The Discourses of Knowledge and of Power.*
———, ed. *Other Worlds, Other Seas: Science Fiction Stories from Socialist Countries.*
———. *Russian Science Fiction Literature and Criticism, 1956–1974: A Bibliography.*
Swenson, William G. *Guide to Great Themes in Short Fiction.*
Tales from Beyond the Grave.
Tales from the Crypt. (paperback reprint of selected E.C. Comics)
Tales of the Incredible. (paperback reprint of selected comic book stories)
Tenn, William, ed. *Children of Wonder: 21 Remarkable and Fantastic Tales.*
Thomas, James Stuart. *The Big Little Book Price Guide.*
Thomsen, Brian, and Martin H. Greenberg, eds. *Mob Magic.*
Time Untamed.
Timmerman, John H. *Other Worlds: The Fantasy Genre.*
Todorov, Tzvetan. *The Fantastic: A Structuralist Approach to a Literary Genre.*
Torgeson, Roy, ed. *Chrysalis: The Best All-New Science Fiction Stories,* and 2–9.
Transit of Earth.
Turtledove, Harry, ed. *Alternate Generals.*
Tuck, Donald H. *The Encyclopedia of Science Fiction and Fantasy (Through 1968):* Vol. 1: *Who's Who and Works A–L;* Vol. 2: *Who's Who and Works M–Z;* Volume 3: *Paperbacks and Miscellaneous.*
Turner, Alice K., ed. *Playboy Stories: The Best of Forty Years of Short Fiction.*
———. *The Playboy Book of Science Fiction.*
Tymn, Marshall B., and Mike Ashley, eds. *Science Fiction, Fantasy, and Weird Fiction Magazines.*
———, Martin H. Greenberg, L. W. Currey, and Joseph D. Olander. *Index to Stories in Thematic Anthologies of Science Fiction.*
———, Robert J. Zahorski, and Robert H. Boyer, eds. *Fantasy Literature: A Core Collection and Reference Guide.*
Uslan, Muchael, ed. *Mysteries in Space: The Best of DC Science Fiction Comics.*
van Thal, Herbert, ed. *Striking Terror!: A Selection of Great Horror Stories.*
Varley, John, and Ricia Mainhardt, eds. *Superheroes.*
Virgil Finlay's Strange Science.
Virgil Finlay's Women of the Ages.
Wagar, W. Warren. *Terminal Visions: The Literature of Last Things.*
Wagner, Karl Edward, ed. *Echoes of Valor,* and II–III.
———. *HorrorStory,* and 2–5.
———. *Intensive Scare.*
Wagner, Patricia Cerf, and Herbert Wise, eds. *Great Tales of Terror and the Supernatural.*
Wake, Paul, Steve Andrews, and Ariel, eds. *Waterstone's Guide to Science Fiction, Fantasy & Horror.*

Ward, Don, ed. *Black Magic: 13 Chilling Tales.*
———. *The Dark of the Soul.*
Warner, Harry. *All Our Yesterdays: An Informal History of Science Fiction in the Forties.*
Warrick, Patricia S. *The Cybernetic Imagination in Science Fiction.*
———, Charles G. Waugh, and Martin H. Greenberg, eds. *Science Fiction: The Science Fiction Research Association Anthology.*
———, Martin H. Greenberg, and Joseph D. Olander, eds. *Science Fiction: Contemporary Mythology.*
Waugh, Carol-Lynn Rosel, Martin H. Greenberg, and Isaac Asimov, eds. *13 Horrors of Halloween.*
Waugh, Charles G., and Martin H. Greenberg, eds. *The Arbor House Celebrity Book of Horror Stories.*
———. *Love 3000.*
———. *Sci-Fi Private Eye.*
———. *Supernatural Sleuths.*
———, and Joseph D. Olander, eds. *Mysterious Visions: Great Science Fiction by Masters of Mystery.*
Webb, Wendy, Richard Gilliam, Edward E. Kramer, and Martin Greenberg, eds. *Phobias and More Phobias: Stories of Unparalleled Paranoia!*
Weinberg, Robert, ed. *The Weird Tales Story.*
———. *Far Below and Other Horrors.*
———. *Lost Fantasies.* Vols. 1–8.
———, Stefan Dziemianowicz, and Martin H. Greenberg, eds. *Between Time and Terror.*
———. *The Mists From Beyond.*
———. *100 Astounding Little Alien Stories.*
———. *100 Ghastly Little Ghost Stories.*
———. *100 Tiny Tales of Terror.*
———. *100 Wild Litle Weird Tales.*
———. *Rivals of Dracula.*
———. *Weird Vampire Stories.*
Weis, Margaret, ed. *The Art of Dungeons and Dragons.*
———. *A Dragon-Lover's Treasury of the Fantastic.*
———. *Fantastic Alice: New Stories from Wonderland.*
———. *A Magic-Lover's Treasury of the Fantastic.*
———, and Tracy Hickman, eds. *Treasure of Fantasy.*
Wells, Stuart W., III. *The Science Fiction Heroic Fantasy Author Index.*
Westfahl, Gary. *The Mechanics of Wonder: The Creation of the Idea of Science Fiction.*
Wilhelm, Kate, ed. *Clarion SF.*
Wilkins, Cary, ed. *A Treasury of Fantasy: Heroic Adventures in Imaginary Lands.*
Williams, A. Susan, ed. *The Lifted Veil: The Book of Fantastic Literature By Women.*
Williams, A. Susan, and Richard Glyn Jones, eds. *The Penguin Book of Modern Fantasy by Women.*
Williams, Sheila, and Cynthia Manson, eds. *Tales from Isaac Asimov's Science Fiction Magazine.*
Williamson, Jack, ed. *Teaching Science Fiction: Education for Tomorrow.*
Williamson, J. N., ed. *The Best from Masques.*
Willis, Connie, ed. *The New Hugo Winners*, Vol. 3. (1989–1991).
Wilson, Colin, ed. *The Mammoth Book of the Supernatural.*
Wilson, Robin, Scott, ed. *Clarion,* and 2–3.
———. *Paragons: Twelve Science Fiction Writers Ply Their Craft.*
———. *Those Who Can.*
Windling, Terri, ed. *Faery!*
Wingrove, David. *The Immortals of Science Fiction.*
Winter, Douglas E., ed. *Faces of Fear: Encounters with the Creators of Modern Horror.*
Wise, Herbert A., and Phyllis Fraser, eds. *Great Tales of Terror and the Supernatural.*
Wolfe, Gary. *The Known and the Unknown: The Iconography of Science Fiction.*
Wolf, Jack C., and Gregory Fitz Gerald, eds. *Past, Present, & Future Perfect.*
Wolf, Leonard K., ed. *The Essential Dracula.*
———. *Blood Thirst: 100 Years of Vampire Fiction.*
———. *The Essential Frankenstein.*
———. *Wolf's Complete Book of Terror.*

Wollheim, Donald A. *The Universe Makers: Science Fiction Today.*
————, ed., *The Annual World's Best SF* 1972–1990.
————. *Ace Science Fiction Reader.*
————. *Adventures in the Far Future.*
————. *Adventures on Other Planets and More Adventures on Other Planets.*
————. *The Avon Fantasy Reader.*
————. *The Best from the Rest of the World: European Science Fiction.*
————. *The DAW Science Fiction Reader.*
————. *Earth in Peril.*
————. *The End of the World.*
————. *Flight Into Space: Great Science Fiction Stories of Interplanetary Travel.*
————. *The Macabre Reader* and *More Macabre.*
————. *Men on the Moon.*
————. *The Pocket Book of Science Fiction.*
————. *Portable Novels of Science Fiction.*
————. *Prize Science Fiction.*
————. *Swordsmen in the Sky.*
————. *Tales of Outer Space.*
————. *Terror in the Modern Vein.*
————. *Ultimate Invader and Other Science Fiction.*
————. *The Viking Portable Library Novels of Science Fiction.*
————, and George Ernsberger, eds. *The Second Avon Fantasy Reader.*
————, and Terry Carr, eds. *World's Best Science* 1965–1971.

Wollmack, Jenny. *Aliens and Others: Science Fiction, Feminism, and Postmodernism.*

World Fantasy Awards. (1-Gahan Wilson, ed.; 2-Stuart David Schiff and Fritz Leiber, eds.)

Wuckel, Dieter, and Bruce Cassiday. *The Illustrated History of Science Fiction.*

Wu, Dingbo, and Patrick D. Murphy, eds. *Science Fiction from China.*

Wymer, Thomas L., et al., eds. *Intersections: The Elements of Fiction in Science Fiction.*

Wyndam, John, ed. *The Best From New Worlds.*

(The) Year's Best Fantasy Stories 1 (1975) through 14 (1988) (editors: Lin Carter, 1–6; Arthur W. Saha, 7–14). Vols. 1–6 are entitled *Lin Carter Presents the Year's Best Fantasy Stories.*

(The) Year's Best Horror Stories 1 (1971) through 19 (1991) (editors: Richard Davis, 1–3; Gerald W. Page, 4–7; Karl Edward Wagner, 8–19). Beginning with 19, volumes are entitled *Karl Edward Wagner Presents the Year's Best Horror Stories.*

Zebrowski, George, ed. *Synergy.*

CORNERSTONE STUDIES AND ANTHOLOGIES OF FANTASY AND SCIENCE FICTION IN NONPRINT MEDIA

As with the other bibliographies and lists found in this volume, this selection of studies of Fantasy and Science Fiction in nonprint media is representative, but by no means complete. It is designed as a starting point for further investigation. In this list, the reader will notice a distinct absence of books about Alfred Hitchcock's life and works, *Star Trek*, and *Star Wars*. To try to do these three major subjects justice in a relatively brief bibliography would be impossible. Perhaps if we take nothing more from this list than the observation that Fantasy and Science Fiction have dramatically pervaded the mass media of the twentieth century, then this list will have served its purpose.

MOTION PICTURES

Ackerman, Forrest J, ed. *Science-Fiction Classics: The Stories That Morphed Into Movies.*
———— and Jean Stine, eds. *Reel Futures: The Stories that Inspired Classic Science Fiction Movies.*
Annan, David. *Movie Fantastic: Beyond the Dream Machine.*
Benson, Michael. *Vintage Science Fiction Films, 1896–1949.*
Borst, Ronald V., Keith Burns, and Leith Adams, eds. *Graven Images: The Best of Horror, Fantasy, and Science-Fiction Film Art from the Collection of Ronald V. Borst.*
Brosch, Robert, photographer. *Horror, Science Fiction, and Fantasy: Movie Posters and Lobby Cards. (Color Collectors Guide, Volume II (1925–1970).*
Brosnan, John. *Future Tense: The Cinema of Science Fiction.*
————. *The Horror People.*
————. *Primal Screen: A History of Science Fiction Film.*
Brunas, Michael, John Brunas, and Tom Weaver. *Universal Horrors: The Studio's Classic Films, 1931–1946.*
Chizmar, Robert, ed. *Screamplays.*
Clemens, Carlos. *An Illustrated History of Horror and Science Fiction Films.*
Cline, William C. *In the Nick of Time: Motion Picture Sound Serials.*
Edelson, Edward. *Great Science Fiction from the Movies.*
Everman, Welch. *Cult Science Fiction Films.*
Golden, Christopher, ed. *CUT!: Horror Writers on Horror Film.*
Haining, Peter, ed. *The Ghouls: The Horror Films as an Integral Part of Cinema History.*
————. *The Hollywood Nightmare: Tales of Fantasy and Horror from the Film World.*
————. *Movie Monsters: Great Horror Film Stories.*
————. *Vintage Science Fiction Stories That Inspired Landmark Films.*
Hardy, Phil, ed. *The Overlook Film Encyclopedia: Horror.*
————. *The Overlook Film Encyclopedia: Science Fiction.*
Hershenson, Bruce. *Horror Movie Posters.*
Hunter, I. Q., ed. *British Science Fiction Cinema.*
Huss, Roy, and T. J. Ross, eds. *Focus on the Horror Film.*
Jancovich, Mark. *Rational Fears: American Horror in 1950s.*
Johnson, William, ed. *Focus on the Science Fiction Film.*
Kinnard, Roy. *Horror in Silent Films: A Filmography, 1896–1929.*
Luciano, Patrick. *Them or Us: Archetypal Interpretations of Fifties Alien Invasion Films.*

Maltin, Leonard, ed. *Leonard Maltin's Movie Encyclopedkia.*
———. *Leonard Maltin's 2000 Movie and Video Guide.*
Mayo, Mike. *Videohounds Horror Show: 999 Hair-Raising Hellish, Humorous Movies.*
Parrish, James Robert, and Michael R. Pitts. *The Great Science Fiction Pictures.*
Pickard, Roy. *Science Fiction in the Movies A–Z.*
Pohl, Frederik, and Frederik Pohl IV. *Science Fiction: Studies in Film.*
Skal, David J. *Hollywood Gothic: The Tangled Web of Dracula from Novel to Stage to Screen.*
———. *The Monster Show: A Cultural History of Horror.*
———. *Screams of Reason: Mad Science and Modern Culture.*
———. *V is for Vampire.*
Stanley, John. *Creature Features Movie Guide Strikes Again*, Fourth Revised Version. 1994.
Strickland, A.W., and Forrest Ackerman. *A Reference Guide to American Science Fiction Films.*
Thomsen, Brian, and Martin H. Greenberg, eds. *The Reel Stuff.*
Twitchell, James B. *Dreadful Pleasures: An Anatomy of Modern Horror.*
———. *The Living Dead: A Study of the Vampire in Romantic Literature.*
Warren, Bill. *Keep Watching the Skies! American Science Fiction Movies of the Fifties.*
Waugh, Charles G., Martin H. Greenberg, and Frank D. McSherry Jr., eds. *Cinemonsters: A Collection of Terrifying Tales that Spawned the Great Monsters of the Movies.*
Wolfe, Sebastian, ed. *Reel Terror: The Original Stories that Inspired the Great Horror Movies . . .*
Wright, Bruce Lanier. *Yesterday's Tomorrows: The Golden Age of Science Fiction Movie Posters.*
Wynorski, Jim, ed. *They Came From Outer Space: 12 Classic Science Fiction Tales that Became Major Motion Pictures.*

RADIO

Buxton, Frank, and Bill Owen. *The Big Broadcast (1920–1950): (A New, Revised, and Greatly Expanded Edition of Radio's Golden Age.*
Dunning, John. *On the Air: The Encyclopedia of Old-Time Radio.* (Revised edition of *Tune in Tomorrow,* 1976.)
Harmon, Jim. *The Great Radio Heroes.*
Higby, Mary Jane. *Tune in Tomorrow.*
Koch, Howard. *The Panic Broadcast: The Whole Story of the Night the Martians Landed: Orson Welles' Legendary Radio Show, Invasion from Mars.*
Lewis, Tom. *Empire of the Air: The Men Who Made Radio.*
McDonald, J. Fred. *Don't Touch That Dial!*
Maltin, Leonard. *The Great American Broadcast: A Celebration of Radio's Golden Age.*
Sabi, Bill. *Adventures in Time and Space on NBC Radio's "Dimension X" and "X Minus One."*

TELEVISION

Barnouw, Erik. *The Tube of Plenty: The Evolution of American Television.*
Barron, Neil. *Anatomy of Wonder: A Critical Guide to Science Fiction.*
Brooks, Tim, and Earle Marsh. *The Complete Directory of Prime Time Network Television Shows: 1946 to Present.*
Fulton, Roger, and John Betancourt. *The Sci-Fi Channel Encyclopedia of TV Science Fiction.*
Gerani, Gary, and Paul H. Schulman. *Fantastic Television.*
Glut, Donald F., and Jim Harmon. *The Great Television Heroes.*
Grossman, Gary H. *Saturday Morning TV.*

Haining, Peter, ed. *The Television Late Night Horror Omnibus: Great Tales from TV Anthology Series.*
Kaminsky, Stuart. *American Television Genres.*
Luciano, Patrick, and Gary Coville. *American Science Fiction Television Series of the 1950s.*
McDonald, J. Fred. *Television and the Red Menace.*
McNeil, Alex. *Total Television: A Comprehensive Guide to Programming from 1948 to the Present,* 5th ed.
Morton, Alan. *The Complete Directory to Science Fiction, Fantasy and Horror Television Series: A Comprehensive Guide to the First Fifty Years, 1946–1996.*
Settel, Irving, and William Laas. *A Pictorial History of Television.*

MULTIMEDIA

Barron, Neil. *Anatomy of Wonder: A Critical Guide to Science Fiction.*
Daniels, Les. *Living in Fear: A History of Horror in the Mass Media.*
Haining, Peter, ed. *Dead of Night: Horror Stories from Radio, Television, and Film.*
Naha, Ed. *The Science Fictionary: An A–Z Guide to the World of SF Authors, Film and Television Shows.*
Nesheim, Eric, and Leif Neisheim, eds. *Saucer Attack!: Pop Culture in the Golden Age of Flying Saucers.*
Nicholls, Peter. *The Encyclopedia of Science Fiction: An Illustrated A–Z.*
O'Brien, Daniel. *SF: UK—How British Science Fiction Changed the World.*
Pringle, David, ed. *The Ultimate Encyclopedia of Science Fiction.*
Schwartz, Julius, with Brian Thomsen. *Man of Two Worlds: My Life in Science Fiction and Comics.*
Twitchell, James B. *Preposterous Violence: Fables of Aggression in Modern Culture.*
Wolff, Michael, ed. *Net Sci-Fi: A Compendium of the Best Science Fiction on the Internet.*
Wright, Gene. *The Science Fiction Image: The Illustrated Encyclopedia of Science Fiction in Film, Television, Radio, and the Theater.*
———. *Who's Who & What's What in Science Fiction Film, Television, Radio & Theater: A Fact-Packed A–Z Encyclopedia.*

INDEX

CREDITS

Isaac Asimov, "Robbie" from *I, Robot*. Copyright 1950 by Isaac Asimov. Reprinted with the permission of Doubleday, a division of Random House, Inc.

J. G. Ballard, "The Drowned Giant" from *The Terminal Beach*. Originally published in *Playboy* (May 1965). Copyright © 1965 by J. G. Ballard. Reprinted with the permission of Farrar, Straus & Giroux, LLC.

Greg Bear, "Blood Music" from *Tangents* (New York: Warner Books, 1989). Originally published in *Analog* (June 1983). Copyright © 1983, 1989 by Greg Bear. Reprinted with the permission of Richard Curtis Associates.

Charles Beaumont, "The Howling Man" from *Charles Beaumont: Selected Stories*, edited by Roger Anker. Copyright © 1959 by Greenleaf Publishing Co., Inc., renewed © 1987 by Christopher Beaumont. Reprinted with the permission of Don Congdon Associates, Inc.

Alfred Bester, "Fondly Fahrenheit" from *Virtual Unrealities: The Short Fiction of Alfred Bester*. Copyright 1954 by Mercury Press, Inc. and Alfred Bester. Copyright © 1976 by Alfred Bester. Reprinted with the permission of Vintage Books, a division of Random House, Inc.

James P. Blaylock, "Thirteen Phantasms" from *Omni Online* (October 1996). Copyright © 1996 by James P. Blaylock. Reprinted with the permission of the author.

Robert Bloch, "Catnip" from *The Early Fears* (Minneapolis, Minn.: Fedogan & Bremer, 1994). Originally published in *Weird Tales* (March 1948). Copyright © 1976, 1994 by Robert Bloch. Reprinted with the permission of Ralph M. Vicinanza, Ltd.

Leigh Brackett, "The Enchantress of Venus" from *The Best of Leigh Brackett*, edited by Edmond Hamilton. Copyright 1949 by Love Romances Publishing Company, Inc. Copyright © 1977 by Leigh Brackett. Reprinted with the permission of Random House, Inc.

Ray Bradbury, "There Will Come Soft Rains" from *The Martian Chronicles*, originally in *Collier's* (May 6, 1950). Copyright 1950 and renewed © 1977 by Ray Bradbury. Reprinted with the permission of Don Congdon Associates, Inc.

Marion Zimmer Bradley, "Exiles of Tomorrow" from *Jamie and Other Stories: The Best of Marion Zimmer Bradley*. Originally published in *Fantastic Universe* (March 1955). Copyright © 1985, 1991 by Marion Zimmer Bradley. Reprinted with the permission of Academy Chicago Publishers.

Fredric Brown, "Arena" from *Astounding Science-Fiction* (July 1944). Copyright 1944 by Street and Smith Publications, renewed © 1972 by The Estate of Fredric Brown. Reprinted with the permission of the author's Estate and its agents, Scott Meredith Literary Agency, LP.

Octavia Butler, "BloodChild" from *BloodChild and Other Stories*. Copyright © 1995 by Octavia Butler. Reprinted by arrangement with Seven Stories Press, New York, NY.

Orson Scott Card, "Ender's Game" from *Unaccompanied Sonata and Other Stories* (New York: Dial Press, 1981). Originally published in *Analog* (August 1977). Copyright © 1977, 1978, 1979, 1980, 1981 by Orson Scott Card. Reprinted with the permission of Barbara Bova Literary Agency.

Arthur C. Clarke, "The Sentinel" from *10 Story Fantasy* (1950). Copyright 1950 by Arthur C. Clarke. Reprinted with the permission of the author and the author's agents, Scovil Chichak Galen Literary Agency, Inc.

Hal Clement, "Dust Rag" from *Astounding Science-Fiction* (September 1956). Copyright © 1956 by Street & Smith Publications, Inc. Reprinted with the permission of Ballantine Books, a division of Random House, Inc.

Mary Elizabeth Counselman, "The Three Marked Pennies" from *Weird Tales* (August 1934). Copyright 1934 by The Popular Fiction Publishing Company. Reprinted with the permission of Arkham House Publishers, Inc.

Avram Davidson, "Or All the Seas with Oysters" from *The Avram Davidson Treasury* (New York: Tom Doherty Associates, 1998). Originally published in *Galaxy* (May 1958). Copyright © 1958 by Galaxy Publishing Corp. Reprinted with the permission of the Avram Davidson Estate and Archive.

Samuel Delany, "Driftglass" from *Driftglass: Ten Tales of Speculative Fiction* (New York: New American Library, 1971). Originally published in *IF: Science Fiction* (June 1967). Copyright © 1967 by Galaxy Publishing Corp., renewed 1994 by Samuel Delany. Reprinted with the permission of the author and Henry Morrison, Inc., his agents.

Philip K. Dick, "We Can Remember It for You Wholesale" from *The Philip K. Dick Reader*. Copyright © 1987 by The Estate of Philip K. Dick. Reprinted with the permission of the author and the author's agents, Scovil Chichak Galen Literary Agency, Inc.

Lord Dunsany, "The Strange Drug of Dr. Caber" from *The Fourth Book of Jorkens*. Copyright 1948 by Lord Dunsany. Reprinted with the permission of Arkham House Publishers, Inc.

Philip José Farmer, "The Lovers" from *Startling Stories* (August 1952). Copyright 1952 by Better Publications, Inc. Reprinted with the permission of the author c/o Ralph M. Vicinanza, Ltd.

Jack Finney, "The Third Level" from *The Third Level*. Copyright 1948 by The Curtis Publishing Company. Copyright 1949, 1950, 1951, 1952, © 1955, 1956, 1957 by Jack Finney. Reprinted with the permission of Simon & Schuster, Inc.

Neil Gaiman, "Troll-Bridge" from *Angels Visitations: A Miscellany* (Minneapolis, Minn.: DreamHaven Books, 1993). Copyright © 1993 by Neil Gaiman. Reprinted with the permission of Writers House, Inc. As agent for the proprietor.

William Gibson, "Burning Chrome" from *Burning Chrome*. Copyright © 1981, 1982, 1983, 1985 by Omni Publications International Ltd. Copyright © 1986 by William Gibson. Reprinted with the permission of HarperCollins Publishers, Inc.

Edmond Hamilton, "The Harpers of Titan" from *Startling Stories* (September 1950). Copyright 1950 by Better Publications, Inc. Reprinted with the permission of the author's estate and their agents, the Scott Meredith Literary Agency.

Clare Winger Harris, "The Fate of the 'Poseidonia' " from *Amazing Stories* (June 1927). Reprinted with the permission of Forrest J Ackerman, 2495 Glendower Avenue, Hollywood, CA 90027-1110.

Harry Harrison, "Roommates" from *The Best of Harry Harrison*. Copyright © 1971 by Thomas M. Disch. Copyright © 1976 by Harry Harrison. Reprinted with the permission of Simon & Schuster, Inc.

Robert A. Heinlein, "The Long Watch" from *The Past Through Tomorrow: "Future History" Stories*. Copyright 1948 by The American Legion. Copyright © 1967 by Robert A. Heinlein. Reprinted with the permission of Penguin Putnam Inc.

Zenna Henderson, "The Anything Box" from *The Magazine of Fantasy and Science Fiction* (October 1956). Copyright © 1956 by Zenna Henderson. Reprinted with the permission of the author's Estate and the Estate's agents, Virginia Kidd Agency, Inc.

Frank Herbert, "Seed Stock" from *Eye*. Originally published in *Analog Science Fiction and Science Fact* (April 1970). Copyright © 1970 by Condé Nast Publications, Inc. Reprinted with the permission.

Shirley Jackson, "The Lottery" from *The Lottery and Other Stories* . Copyright 1948, 1949 by Shirley Jackson. Copyright renewed © 1976, 1977 by Laurence Hyman, Barry Hyman, Mrs. Sarah Webster and Mrs. Joanne Schnurer. Reprinted with the permission of Farrar, Straus & Giroux, LLC.

Stephen King, "The Raft" from *Skeleton Crew* (New York: Putnam, 1986). Originally published in *Gallery* (November 1982). Copyright © 1982, 1985 by Stephen King. Reprinted with the permission of Arthur B. Greene. All rights reserved.

Damon Knight, "To Serve Man" from *Far Out*. Originally published in *Galaxy Science Fiction* (November 1950). Copyright 1950 by Galaxy Publishing Corp. Copyright © 1961 by Damon Knight. Reprinted with the permission of Simon & Schuster, Inc.

Dean Koontz, "The Undercity" from *Future City*, edited by Roger Elwood. Copyright © 1973 by Roger Elwood. Reprinted with the permission of the William Morris Agency, Inc. on behalf of the author.

Tanith Lee, "Red As Blood" from *Red As Blood, or Tales from the Sisters Grimmer* (New York: Daw Books, 1983). Originally published in *The Magazine of Fantasy and Science Fiction* (1979). Copyright © 1979 by Mercury Press, Inc. Reprinted with the permission of Scovil Chichak Galen Literary Agency, Inc.

Fritz Leiber, "Smoke Ghost" from *Night's Black Agents*. Copyright © 1941 by Street & Smith Publishing Company. Copyright 1947, 1978 by Fritz Leiber, Jr. Reprinted with the permission of Richard Curtis Associates.

Frank Belknap Long, "Invasion" from *Startling Stories* (July 1950). Copyright 1950 by Better Publications, Inc. Reprinted with the permission of Scott Meredith Literary Agency, L.P.

H. P. Lovecraft, "The Colour Out of Space" from *Amazing Stories* (September 1927). Copyright 1927 by Experimenter Publishing Company. Reprinted with the permission of JABberwocky Literary Agency.

Katherine MacLean, "Pictures Don't Lie" from *The Diploids and 7 Other Stories*. First appeared in *Galaxy Science Fiction* (August 1951). Copyright 1951 by World Editions, Inc., renewed © 1979 by Katherine MacLean. Reprinted with the permission of the author and the author's agents, the Virginia Kidd Agency, Inc.

Barry Malzberg, "Opening Fire" from Roger Elwood, ed., *The New Mind* (New York: Collier Books,

1973) and reprinted in *The Best of Barry N. Malzberg* (New York: Pocket Books, 1976). Copyright © 1973 by Roger Elwood. Barry Malzberg. Reprinted with the permission of the author and his agents, Scott Meredith Literary Agency, Inc.

George R. R. Martin, "The Plague Star" from *Tuf Voyaging* (New York: Baen Publishing Enterprises, 1985). Originally published in *Analog* (January & February 1985). Copyright © 1985 by Davis Publications, Inc. Copyright © 1986 by George R. R. Martin. Reprinted with the permission of the author.

Richard Matheson, "Duel" from *Playboy* (April 1971). Copyright © 1971 by Playboy Enterprises, Inc., renewed 1999 by Richard Matheson. Reprinted with the permission of Don Congdon Associates, Inc.

Robert R. McCammon, "Nightcrawlers" from *Blue World* (New York: Pocket Books, 1990). Copyright © 1984 by Robert McCammon. Reprinted with the permission of the author.

Judith Merrill, "That Only a Mother" from *The Best of Judith Merrill*. Originally from *Astounding Science-Fiction* (October 1948). Copyright © 1976 by Judith Merrill. Reprinted with the permission of Warner Books.

C. L. Moore, "Shambleau" from *The Best of C.L. Moore*, edited by Lester Del Rey. Copyright 1933 by Popular Fiction Publishing Co.; renewed 1961 by C.L. Moore. Copyright © 1975 by C.L. Moore. Reprinted with permission.

Sam Moskowitz, "How Science Fiction Got Its Name" from *Explorers of the Infinite: Shapers of Science Fiction*, ed. Sam Moskowitz. Originally published in *The Magazine of Fantasy and Science Fiction* (February 1957). Copyright © 1957 by Sam Moskowitz. Reprinted with the permission of Gibson Press.

Larry Niven, "The Jigsaw Man" from *Three Books of Known Space*. Copyright © 1976 by Larry Niven. Reprinted with the permission of Ballantine Books, a division of Random House, Inc.

Andre Norton, "Mousetrap" from *The Book of Andre Norton* (New York: DAW Books, 1975). Originally published in *The Magazine of Fantasy and Science Fiction* (June 1954). Copyright 1954 by Mercury Press. Reprinted with the permission of the author.

Frederik Pohl, "The Fiend" from *Digits and Dastards* (New York: Ballantine Books, 1966). Originally published in *Playboy* (April 1964). Copyright © 1964 by HMH Publishing. Reprinted with the permission of the author.

Kim Stanley Robinson, "Remaking History" from *Remaking History and Other Stories* (New York: Tom Doherty Associates, 1994). Copyright © 1989 by Kim Stanley Robinson. Reprinted with the permission of the author, c/o Ralph M. Vicinanza Ltd.

Spider Robinson, "Melancholy Elephants" from *Melancholy Elephants* (New York: Tom Doherty Associates, 1985). Originally published in *Analog: Science Fiction, Science Fact* (June 1982). Copyright © 1982 by Spider Robinson. Reprinted with the permission of the author.

Joanna Russ, "When It Changed" from *The Zanzibar Cat* (Bronx: Baen Publishing Enterprises, 1984). Copyright © 1972 by Joanna Russ. Reprinted with the permission of the author.

Eric Frank Russell, "Jay Score" from *The Best of Eric Frank Russell*. Copyright 1941 by Street & Smith Publications, Inc. Copyright © 1978 by Eric Frank Russell. Reprinted with the permission of Ballantine Books, a division of Random House, Inc.

Fred Saberhagen, "Without a Thought (Fortress Ship)" from *Pawn to Infinity*, edited by Fred and Joan Saberhagen. Copyright © 1962 by Galaxy Pub. Corp., renewed 1990 by Fred Saberhagen. Reprinted with the permission of the author.

Robert Sheckley, "The Store of the Worlds" from *The Collected Short Stories of Robert Sheckley Book Four* (Eugene, Oregon: Pulphouse Publications, 1991). Originally published in *Playboy* (September 1959). Copyright © 1959, 1991 by Robert Sheckley. Reprinted with the permission of the author.

Curt Siodmak, "The Eggs from Lake Tanganyika" from *Amazing Stories* (July 1926). Reprinted with the permission of Forrest J Ackerman, 2495 Glendower Avenue, Hollywood, CA 90027-1110.

Clark Ashton Smith, "The City of the Singing Flame" from *Out of Space and Time*. Copyright 1931 by the Popular Fiction Publishing Company. Copyright 1942 by Clark Ashton Smith. Reprinted with the permission of Arkham House Publishers, Inc.

E. E. "Doc" Smith, "Robot Nemesis" from *The Best of E.E. "Doc" Smith* (New York: Jove Publications/Harcourt Brace Jovanovich, 1979). Originally published in *Fantasy Magazine* (1934). Reprinted by permission.

Leslie F. Stone, "The Conquest of Gola" from *Wonder Stories* (April 1931). Copyright © 1931 by Gernsback Publications, Inc. Reprinted with the permission of the Author's Estate and the Estate's Agent, Forrest J Ackerman, 2495 Glendower Avenue, Hollywood, CA 90027-1110.

Theodore Sturgeon, "Thunder and Roses" from *Thunder and Roses, Volume IV: The Complete Stories of Theodore Sturgeon* (Berkeley, Calif.: North Atlantic Books, 1997). Copyright 1947 by the Theodore Sturgeon Literary Trust. Reprinted with the permission of the author and the author's agents, Ralph M. Vicinanza, Ltd.

James Tiptree Jr., "The Last Flight of Dr. Ain" from *Galaxy* (March 1969). Copyright © 1969 by UPD

Publishing Corporation, renewed 1977 by the Estate of Alice B. Sheldon. Reprinted with the permission of the author's Estate and the Estate's agent, the Virginia Kidd Agency, Inc.

J. R. R. Tolkien, "Riddles in the Dark" from *The Hobbit*. Copyright 1938 and renewed 1966 by J. R. R. Tolkien. Reprinted with the permission of Houghton Mifflin Company and HarperCollins Publishers, Ltd.

A. E. van Vogt, "The Weapons Shop" from *Astounding Science-Fiction* (December 1942). Copyright 1942 by A. E. van Vogt. Reprinted with the permission of the Ashley Grayson Literary Agency.

Kurt Vonnegut, "Harrison Bergeron" from *Welcome to the Monkey House*. Copyright © 1961 by Kurt Vonnegut Jr. Reprinted with the permission of Delacourt Press/Seymour Lawrence, a division of Random House, Inc.

Stanley G. Weinbaum, "A Martian Odyssey" from *A Martian Odyssey and Other Science Fiction Tales*. Copyright 1949, 1952 by Fantasy Press. Reprinted with the permission of Forrest J Ackerman, 2495 Glendower Avenue, Hollywood, CA 90027-1110.

Jack Williamson, "The Purchase of Earth" from *Science Fiction Age* (July 1998). Copyright © 1998 by Jack Williamson. Reprinted with the permission of the author and the author's agent, Spectrum Literary Agency.

Jane Yolen, "The Malaysian Mer" from *Neptune Rising: Songs and Tales of the Undersea Folk*. Copyright © 1982 by Jane Yolen. Reprinted with the permission of Philomel Books, a division of Penguin Putnam Inc.

Roger Zelazny, "The Engine at Heartspring's Center" from *Analog: Science Fiction, Science Fact* (July 1974). Copyright © 1974 by Roger Zelazny. Reprinted with the permission of the agent for the author's Estate, Kirby McCauley, The Pimlico Agency, Inc.

PHOTOS

Section One (p. 5): NY A. C. Armstrong, "The Complete Works of Edgar Allan Poe 1884." Vol. 2, pg. 432–433, edited by Richard H. Stoddard. Illustration not attributed to but by Charles A. Platt.

Section Two (p. 29): Lail Finlay.

Section Three (p. 341): The Granger Collection.

Section Four (p. 1125): Courtesy of Department of Special Collections, Stanford University Libraries.

Color Plate One: Robert Weinberg. Copyright © 1935 by Popular Fiction Co. Reprinted by permission of Weird Tales Ltd.

Color Plate Two: Edd Cartier/Dean Cartier. "Unknown Worlds/From Unknown Worlds" copyright 1948 by Street & Smith Publications, Inc.; copyright renewed by The Condé Nast Publications, Inc. Illustration reprinted by permission of Edd Cartier/Cartier Studios.

Color Plate Three: Sue Cook.

Color Plate Four: The Granger Collection.